The Food
Chronology

THE FOOD CHRONOLOGY

A Food Lover's Compendium of
Events and Anecdotes,
from Prehistory to the Present

JAMES TRAGER

A Henry Holt Reference Book

HENRY HOLT AND COMPANY / NEW YORK

A Henry Holt Reference Book
Henry Holt and Company, Inc.
Publishers since 1866
115 West 18th Street
New York, New York 10011

Henry Holt® is a registered
trademark of Henry Holt and Company, Inc.

Published in Canada by Fitzhenry & Whiteside Ltd.,
195 Allstate Parkway, Markham, Ontario L3R 4T8.

Library of Congress Cataloging-in-Publication Data
Trager, James.
The food chronology: a food lover's compendium of events and
anecdotes from prehistory to the present/ James Trager.—1st ed.
        p.   cm.—(A Henry Holt reference book)
    1. Food—History—Chronology. 2. Chronology, Historical.
I. Title. II. Series.
TX355.T72   1995   95-6710
641'.09—dc20   CIP

ISBN 0-8050-3389-0

Henry Holt books are available for special promotions and
premiums. For details contact: Director, Special Markets.

First Edition—1995

Designed by Lucy Albanese and Betty Lew

Printed in the United States of America
All first editions are printed on acid-free paper.∞

1   3   5   7   9   10   8   6   4   2

Acknowledgments

The author is indebted to a number of people who contributed in their various ways to making this book possible. Among these are the restaurant impresario Joseph H. Baum; Leah Buuck and her son Arthur in New Orleans; Irena Chalmers; Harry Danforth, research microbiologist, U.S. Department of Agriculture; Rex E. T. Dull, agricultural economist, Foreign Agricultural Service, U.S. Department of Agriculture; Mary Goodbody; Barbara Haber of Radcliffe's Schlesinger Library; former Life Savers research director Charles Jacobson; my editor Paula Kakalecik of Henry Holt & Co.; Stanley Karnow; Ronald C. Lord, agricultural economist, Economic Research Service, U.S. Department of Agriculture; Luther Markwart of the U.S. Sugarbeet Growers Association; Cleveland H. Marsh, team leader for Import Quota Programs, U.S. Department of Agriculture; Gerald E. Maslon; Sheila Murphy and Simon Tanner-Tremaine of Aurum Press in London; my good wife, Chie Nishio; Harold P. Olmo of the University of California at Davis; Richard Rosskam, formerly of Good & Plenty; Alison Ryley of the New York Public Library; André Soltner of Lutèce; Elizabeth Sosland; Morton Sosland of *Milling & Baking News* in Kansas City; Joseph L. S. Terrell of the American Sugar Alliance; and Jeanne Voltz. None of these is responsible for any possible errors or omissions. Also helpful, intentionally or not, were the late James Beard, Adelle Davis, Euell Gibbons, Earle MacAusland, and Robert Rodale.

Quotations on pages 474–475 from George Orwell's *Down and Out in London and Paris* © 1933 used by permission of HarperCollins. Illustrations on pages 105, 115, 127, 140, 159, and 263 from the Rare Books and Manuscript Division of the New York Public Library: Astor, Lenox, and Tilden Foundations.

Preface

The history of food has always been notable more for fiction, legend, myth, apocrypha, and inaccuracies than for precise, verifiable truth. This book, done in the comprehensive style of the author's earlier Chronologies, attempts to bring order and reliability to the full, chaotic story of how the world has come through fat years and lean years to eat what it eats today.

French entomologist Jean-Henri Fabre (1823–1915) wrote, "History records the battlefields on which we lose our lives, but it disdains to tell us of the cultivated fields on which we live; it can tell us the names of the kings' bastards, but it cannot tell us the origin of wheat. Such is human folly." Fabre's wry comment suggests a dichotomy between battlefields and cornfields, when in fact wars have been fought, at least in part, over the rights to fertile acreage and waters rich in seafood. Political and economic history are often closely related to the history of what people can afford to eat.

The opportunity for error here is infinite; the chance of perfection is infinitesmal; and an understanding of this kind is therefore bound to be somewhat quixotic. *The Food Chronology* is based on diverse sources which often disagree, and, inevitably, it will contain mistakes, but the author does his best not to perpetuate misinformation, makes note of conflicting stories, attempts wherever possible to establish the facts, and leaves it for the reader to decide in some cases which story to believe.

Key to Symbols

- political events
- food availability
- human rights, social justice
- exploration, colonization
- economics, finance
- mergers and acquisitions
- grocery stores, supermarkets
- energy
- transportation
- food technology
- science
- medicine
- religion
- education
- communications

- literature, cookbooks
- art
- theater
- music
- everyday life
- environment
- seafood, marine resources
- animal husbandry
- agriculture
- nutrition
- consumer protection
- food brands
- beverages
- restaurants
- population

The Food
Chronology

Prehistory

Note:

Dates of entries in this section are based on archeological and paleontological findings that will continue into the foreseeable future; since new findings are forever raising questions about "facts" established earlier, the dates given are necessarily imprecise and sometimes conjectural.

1 million B.C.

Australopithecine ape-man becomes extinct as the human species becomes more developed. *Homo erectus erectus* is unique among primates in having a high proportion of meat relative to plant foods in his diet, but like other primates he is omnivorous, a scavenger who competes with hyenas and other scavengers while eluding carnivores such as leopards. Later generations will argue whether primitive man was a carnivore or vegetarian when in all likelihood he was omnivorous, using his superior brain to outwit other species while living on roots, berries, nuts, termites, and bone marrow.

400,000 to 360,000 B.C.

Homo erectus hominid of the Middle Pleistocene period (*Pithecanthropus pekinensis,* or Peking man) may use fire to cook venison, which supplements his diet of wild plants (such as hackberry), roots, nuts, acorns, legumes, and wild grains. By conserving his energies, he can track down swifter but less intelligent animals (but he still splits bones to get at the marrow because he does not use fire effectively to make the marrow easily available).

75,000 B.C.

Neanderthal man has become a skilled hunter, able to bring down large, hairy elephantlike mammals (*Mammonteus primigenius*), saber-toothed tigers, and other creatures that will become extinct. Like all other creatures on earth, he devotes virtually every waking hour to his quest for the food he needs to sustain life for himself and his family.

Neanderthal man cares for his sick and aged but engages in cannibalism when driven by necessity.

Humans require larger caloric intake than many of their fellow creatures to meet the demands of their larger brains. They cannot digest the long-chain carbohydrates, cellulose, lignins, and tannins in the plant tissues consumed by other species, their excessive protein needs are dictated in part by the fact that they cannot synthesize as many amino acids as some other mammals can, and—because of a metabolic defect (lack of the enzyme L-gulonalactone oxidase in the liver) shared with anthropoid apes, guinea pigs, a certain fruit-eating bat, some insect groups, and some birds that include the red-vented bulbul—they must have dietary sources of vitamin C (ascorbic acid), which most other animals, birds, and insects can synthesize. Without enough vitamin C (abundant not only in citrus fruits, peppers, and cabbage but also in animal organ meats), humans cannot synthesize collagen, the adhesive protein substance that holds cells to-

75,000 B.C.

gether, and without collagen their wounds do not heal, old scars may burst open, and they may exhibit symptoms of scurvy (*see* A.D. 80).

50,000 B.C.

⊕ Date palms flourish in parts of Africa and Asia, where they will become an important food source.

38,000 B.C.

⏚ *Homo sapiens* emerges from Neanderthal man. His control of fire, his development of new, lightweight bone and horn tools, weapons, and fishhooks, and his superior intelligence permit man to obtain food more easily and to preserve it longer. Hunters provide early tribes with meat from bison and tigers, while other tribespeople fish and collect honey, fruits, and nuts (as shown by cave paintings near Aurignac in southern France).

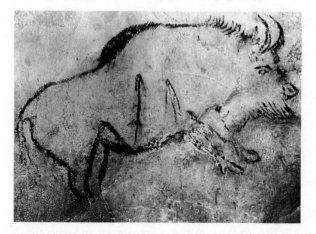

Prehistoric peoples hunted and scavenged, competing with other mammals to find sustenance. LASCAUX CAVES IN SOUTHERN FRANCE

🚹🚺 Increased availability of food in the next few thousand years will lead to an increase in human populations.

25,000 B.C.

⏚ *Homo sapiens* uses small pits lined with hot embers or pebbles preheated in fires to cook food that may

be covered with layers of leaves or wrapped in seaweed to prevent scorching.

🐟 Fishermen in Europe's Dordogne Valley have developed short baited toggles that become wedged at an angle in fishes' jaws when the line, made of plant fibers, is pulled taut.

12,000 B.C.

⏚ Halfan tribespeople on Egypt's lower Nile use grinding stones to produce a kind of flour from the seeds of wild cereal grasses. Limestone upper and lower grinding stones are used in Nubia, on the upper Nile, where flint-bladed reaping knives are employed to harvest wild cereals, which have begun to flourish since the end of the Ice Age has brought a warmer, moister climate.

Potters on the islands that will come to be known as Japan begin to make clay cooking pots and storage containers (*jōmonshikidoki*) (*see* 6000 B.C.; 200 B.C.). The people live by hunting, fishing, and gathering shellfish, some of which are dried, smoked, and stored along with nuts.

🐖 The dog, domesticated from the Asian wolf since about 14,000 B.C., is used in the Near East for tracking game (fossil remains found in a cave near Kirkuk in Iraq in the A.D. 1950s will be dated in the 1970s by fluorine analysis.)

11,000 B.C.

⊕ Vast fields of wild grain appear in parts of the Near East as the glaciers begin to retreat.

🍎 Human hunter-gatherers eat animal protein and some fish but live chiefly on roots, seeds, fruits, tender leaves, and shoots found most often on land that has recently been burned over or flooded and is growing back. Fire is used to clear land for wild food production.

10,000 B.C.

⊕ Climatic changes in Europe produce growths of birch, hazel, and oak forests on what once were bare steppes. Mammoths have disappeared, the reindeer move north, and wild cattle, red deer, and wild pigs begin to populate the continent.

 Goats are domesticated by Near Eastern hunter-gatherer tribespeople who have earlier domesticated the dog.

9000 B.C.

 Bows and arrows come into use for stalking animals in European forests, but spears remain the weapons most commonly used by hunters.

 Some modern observers will call this paleolithic period the "golden age" of nutrition, when man's cardiovascular system, taste buds, and food supply are all in harmony. Eating game meat each day, along with plenty of vegetables, fruits, nuts, berries, and some fish and shellfish but no dairy products and virtually no grain, hunter-gatherers get only about 20 percent of their caloric intake from fats, it will later be conjectured; they are two to six inches taller than their Bronze Age descendants will be, and they have almost no heart disease.

8500 B.C.

 Climatic changes in the Near East bring heavy rainfalls and warmer temperatures, leading to large encampments of hunter-gatherers who previously led more nomadic lives but now find perennial sources of wild grains (*see* agriculture, 8000 B.C.).

 Goat's milk becomes a food source in the Near East, where goats have been domesticated for the past 1,500 years.

8000 B.C.

 Temperatures in northern Europe become more temperate as glaciers recede, marking the end of the Ice Age; forests begin replacing tundra as these final postglacial climatic improvements begin, and while some humans have remained in the region, living on reindeer meat and milk, others now begin to move in with bows and arrows, fish traps, hooks, and other tools needed to obtain food from the

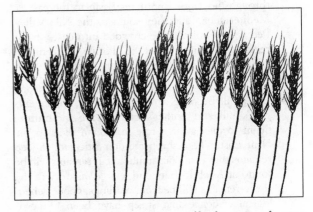

Agriculture permitted a given amount of land to support far more people than hunting and gathering.

land and waters, eating fish caught in nets of hair, thongs, and twisted fiber, along with shellfish, goose, and honey.

 Agriculture begins at the end of the Pleistocene era in the Near East. Women use digging sticks to plant and cultivate the seeds of wild grasses on small plots of cleared land (*see* 8500 B.C.). When the seeds are seen to produce crops of grain in the fall (or the following spring), and when it is observed that 25 acres are enough to support a family by farming instead of the hundreds or even thousands needed for each family that lives by hunting and gathering, more people will be encouraged to give up their nomadic life, live in one place, raise families, and start communities. Settled agricultural communities will be the basis of civilization, and agriculture will remain virtually the only culture for most of the world throughout the next 10 millennia (*see* 7000 B.C.; population, below).

 Earth's human population soars to 5.3 million, up from 3 million in 10,000 B.C., as agriculture provides a more reliable food source. Where it has taken 5,000 acres to support each member of a hunter-forager society, the same amount of land can feed 5,000 to 6,000 people in an agricultural society.

7700 B.C.

 Desert predominates over fertile lands in the arc extending from the head of the Persian Gulf

7700 B.C.

through the Tigris-Euphrates Basin to the eastern Mediterranean and then south to the Nile Valley. People and animals are crowded into oases in the region that will be called the "Fertile Crescent" by U.S. archeologist James Henry Breasted (A.D. 1865–1935).

Ewe's milk becomes a food source and supplements goat's milk and mother's milk as lamb and mutton begin to play a large role in human diets in the Near East, where sheep are domesticated. (Sheep remains that vastly outnumber goat remains will be found at Asiab in Iran, and a large majority of the sheep remains will be from yearlings, good archeological evidence that sheep have been domesticated.)

7300 B.C.

Dogs are domesticated by tribes in the British Isles (evidence from carbon 14 bone studies of fossil remains found at Star Carr in Yorkshire).

7200 B.C.

Sheep are domesticated in Greece (Argissa-Magula) (*see* 7700 B.C.). Because of the country's mountainous terrain, goat meat and goat's milk will be more widely consumed in much of Greece than lamb, mutton, or ewe's milk.

Domestication of swine has been delayed by the need of pigs for shade from the sun and by the fact

Swine were domesticated only after goats, sheep, cattle, and horses, which can all digest grass.

that they cannot be milked, cannot digest grass, leaves, or straw, and must therefore be given food that people themselves can eat—acorns, nuts, cooked grain, or meat scraps. But in some places pigs have been domesticated earlier than other animals.

Populations in the Middle East will increase in the next 2 millennia, and more permanent camps will be established by people who have lived until now in small groups that shifted camps every 3 or 4 months. Seed collecting will become more important to the food supply.

7000 B.C.

Glaciers begin to recede in the northern and southern continents of the Eastern and Western hemispheres, enabling hunters to pursue game in the new forests that have sprung up and permitting settlements in areas once too climatically forbidding for humans. The islands that will later be called Britain remain connected to the European continent, but configurations of land and sea throughout the world will change dramatically in the next 1,000 years as water floods into plains that have been dry in past millennia.

Greek fishermen catch fish at sea that are too large to be caught from shore, but most of the world lacks seaworthy ships.

Southeast Asia and Australasia will begin to have agriculture in the next 1,000 years as inhabitants deliberately cultivate crops in lands where they have lived since the end of the Ice Age (*see* 6500 B.C.).

Emmer wheat (*Triticum dicoccum*), domesticated from the wild *Triticum dicoccoides*, grows in the Kurdistan area lying between what will someday be southeastern Turkey and northwestern Iran. (Domestication involves a genetic change from wild-occurring plant populations.)

Barley (*Hordeum spolitalieum*), millet (*Panicum miliaceum*), and certain legumes, including lentils, are cultivated in Thessaly, where the Greeks may also have domesticated dogs and pigs (based on evidence found in excavations at Argissa-Magula).

6500 B.C.

The wheel will be invented sometime in the next 2 centuries by Sumerians in the Tigris-Euphrates Basin and will radically change transportation, making it easier to bring food to markets.

The aurochs, ancestor of domestic cattle, will be domesticated in the next 2 centuries if it has not been domesticated earlier. The fierce beast will be the last major food animal to be tamed for use as a source of milk, meat, power, and leather.

Chinese agriculture will begin in the next 500 years as farmers in the northern part of the country plant and harvest domesticated foxtail millet (*Setaria italica*) and panic millet while raising chickens, dogs, and pigs (*see* 7000 B.C.; Near East, 8000 B.C.; rice, 5000 B.C.).

6000 B.C.

Peoples of the Near East and Europe produce their first true pottery, permitting new forms of cookery (although food has earlier been boiled in gourds, shells, and skin-lined pits into which hot stones were dropped) (*see* Japan, 12,000 B.C.). Jōmon pottery has been made by the Chinese for at least 1,000 years, and there have also been potters in other parts of northern and southeast Asia.

Swiss lake dwellers make bread of crushed cereal grains and keep dried apples and legumes (including peas) in the houses they build on stilts (evidence from excavated remains of the houses and their contents). Bread represents an advance over the cakes of meal—cereal grains soaked and pressed into cakes that are dried in the sun or on hot stones—that humans have eaten for millennia.

Swiss lake dwellers (above) collect wild flax (*Linum usitatissimum*) or cultivate it and use its strong fibers to make lines and nets for fishing (and for animal traps and ropes and cords for building construction and navigational purposes).

Inhabitants of the Swiss lake regions (above) have domesticated dogs and plow oxen.

Village farmers begin to replace food-gathering tribespeople in much of Greece (*see* 7000 B.C.).

People living along the Euphrates will dig miles of canals in the next 2,000 years to harness the river's annual floodwaters and increase crop yields. They begin to use plows, drawn by oxen, to open up grasslands to crop cultivation (*see* 5000 B.C.).

5000 B.C.

Domesticated cattle are now common in the valleys of the Tigris and Euphrates Rivers, and Neolithic villagers often cooperate to build primitive irrigation canals and ditches (*see* 6000 B.C.).

Lands bordering the Nile River begin to dry out. The Egyptians build dikes and canals for irrigation and start to develop a civilization in North Africa.

Agricultural peoples inhabit the plains of southeastern Europe.

Rice cultivation begins in China's Yangzi River delta (*see* millet, 6500 B.C.). Rice (*Oryza sativa*) originally appeared as a weed in flooded patches used to grow taro root (*Colocasia esculenta*), a food plant of the arum family, which may have been the first crop ever cultivated; Chinese rice cultivation of both long-grain (indica) and short-grain (japonica) rice will be well established by 4000 B.C.

4350 B.C.

Domesticated horses provide parts of Europe with a new source of power for transportation and agriculture (evidence from Derivka in the Ukraine; *see* work collar, 10th century A.D.).

4000 B.C.

Asses, horses, buffalo, camels, and cattle are bred for meat in the Indus Valley and for use as draft animals.

Peoples of the Indus Valley (above) raise wheat, barley, peas, sesame seeds, mangoes, and date palms on irrigated fields, but the large fields of grain encourage a multiplication of insects, and the stores of dry grain bring an explosion in rodent populations. Bananas, lemons, limes, and oranges

4000 B.C.

are cultivated as are grapes for wine, which is also made from flowers (evidence from excavations at Mohenjo-Daro beginning in A.D. 1922 and at Harappa, 300 miles away, beginning in A.D. 1945).

 Chinese diets are rich in wild foods that supplement millet, barley, rice, vegetables, fish, and poultry. Foods are boiled, roasted, and—probably—steamed.

The world's population reaches roughly 85 million.

3600 B.C.

Bronze made by southwest Asian artisans is the first metal hard enough to hold an edge. Copper is alloyed with tin, which is even softer than copper, but the combination (5 to 20 percent tin) creates a metal with many more practical uses than copper has (see 5500 B.C.; iron, 2500 B.C.).

3500 B.C.

The Sumerian society, which marks the beginning of human civilization, develops in the valleys of the Tigris and Euphrates rivers, where annual floods deposit fresh layers of fertile silt. Agricultural tribespeople settle in communities and evolve an administrative system governed by priests.

The Sumerians (above) harness domestic animals to plows, drain marshlands, irrigate desert lands, and extend areas of permanent cultivation. By reducing slightly the number of people required to raise food, they permit a few people to become priests, artisans, scholars, and merchants.

The Sumerians (above) develop animal-drawn wheeled vehicles and oar-powered ships (see also 2500 B.C.; wheel, 6500 B.C.).

Bronze enables the Sumerians (above) to make objects that were impossible to make with softer, less fusible copper (see 3600 B.C.; iron, 2500 B.C.).

Antiquity

3000 B.C.

Gilgamesh in Sumerian cuneiform is the first known written legend and tells of a great flood in which man was saved by building an ark.

Sumerian foods mentioned in *Gilgamesh* (above) include caper buds, wild cucumbers, ripe figs, grapes, several edible leaves and stems, honey, meat seasoned with herbs, and bread—a kind of pancake made of barley flour mixed with sesame seed flour and onions.

The Sahara Desert has its beginnings in North Africa, where overworking of the soil and overgrazing are in some places exhausting the land in a region that is largely green with crops and trees (*see* Lhote, A.D. 1956).

Dolphins are killed in the Euxine (Black) Sea, but in some parts of the world the mammal is considered sacred and left unmolested.

Agriculture is now universal in easily cultivable parts of China, and large villages have grown up in agricultural communities.

Potatoes are cultivated in the Andes Mountains of the Western Hemisphere (*see* A.D. 1530).

The world's population reaches 100 million.

2980 B.C.

The Egyptian king Menes introduces water engineering to the Nile, making maximum use of the river's annual floods and bringing alluvial silt and fish to the delta (*see* 2600 B.C.).

2900 B.C.

Egypt's Fourth Dynasty is founded by Cheops (Khufu), who will reign for 23 years. (Dates for all early rulers are approximate and controversial.)

The Great Pyramid of Cheops at Giza will by some accounts be the work of 4,000 stonemasons and as many as 100,000 laborers, working under conditions of forced servitude and given rations consisting in large part of chickpeas (*Cicer arietinum*), onions, and garlic. Easily transported, chickpeas are a nourishing staple for the mass of Egyptian slaves and artisans.

2800 B.C.

The sickle, invented by Sumerian farmers of the Tigris and Euphrates valleys, is a curved instrument of wood or horn fitted with flint teeth. It will remain the predominant tool for harvesting grain until it is superseded by tools with tempered metal blades.

2700 B.C.

The legendary Chinese emperor Shen Nung orders government clerks to classify plants in terms of both food and medicinal value. The list that they submit to the "Divine Husbandman" includes barley, millet, rice, soybeans, and wheat as the five principal and sacred crops, and their herbal mentions cinnamon, which will be imported into Egypt before the end of the next millennium.

Barley and millet (above) are the chief grains in northern China, where rice cannot be planted extensively for lack of dependable water. Farmers are beginning to develop wheat and barley varieties that can flourish in areas where rainfall is sparse, such as far western China, but they are considered inferior to the millets that have been adapted to hot, rainy regions.

Corn (maize) and common beans grow under cultivation in the Western Hemisphere, with chilies and squash being grown in what later will be Mexico.

2600 B.C.

Oxen harnessed to plows in the Near East make it possible to plow deeper and to keep the soil productive longer.

The Egyptians preserve fish and poultry by sun drying.

Annual Nile floods permit the Egyptian peasant to produce enough barley and Emmer wheat to feed three, with the surplus going to the builders of flood control projects, public buildings, and pyramid tombs (*see* 2980 B.C.).

2500 B.C.

The Iron Age dawns in the Near East, where artisans produce a new metal much harder than the bronze used since 3600 B.C., but iron will not come into wide use for another 1,000 years.

Iron will revolutionize agriculture, permitting farmers to plow deeper with cast-iron implements than they ever could with wooden ones.

2475 B.C.

Maize is domesticated in primitive form in the isthmus that links the two continents of the Western Hemisphere, while potatoes and sweet potatoes are cultivated in the southern continent.

Olive trees are cultivated in Crete, which grows rich by exporting olive oil and timber.

2205 B.C.

Chinese farmers have domesticated dogs, goats, pigs, oxen, and sheep, whose meat supplements the fish in their diets.

Ancient Egyptians developed an agricultural society based on the Nile River's annual floods.

The Chinese have no large-scale irrigation projects but find ways to control the water needed to flood their rice fields.

2000 B.C.

The Hsia dynasty will rule much of north and north-central China until about 1700 B.C., but lack of records will make it impossible to determine details of the period with any accuracy.

Farmers in the Near East raise some cattle for meat, some for milk.

The Egyptians abandon efforts to domesticate antelope, gazelle, and oryx, devoting more effort instead to hunting, fowling, fishing, and gathering wild celery, papyrus stalks, lotus roots, and other plant foods to supplement the grain and vegetables they grow on their Nile floodplains.

Watermelon is cultivated in Africa, figs in Arabia, tea and bananas in India, apples in the Indus Valley; agriculture is well established in most of the central isthmus of the Western Hemisphere.

1801 B.C.

Egypt's Amenemhet III dies after a reign in which his engineers have developed a vast irrigation system.

1800 B.C.

Proscriptions against eating pork appear among some peoples of the Near East, possibly because they are sheepherding peoples and the pig is the domesticated animal of their farmer enemies (*see* 621 B.C.; Sharia, A.D. 629).

1750 B.C.

The great Indus Valley cities of Mohenjo-Daro and Harappa collapse as the soil of the region becomes too saline to support extensive crop growth after centuries of crude irrigation.

1700 B.C.

Babylonians employ windmills to pump water for irrigation.

Eastern Europeans cultivate rye (*Secale cereale*). It will soon become the major bread grain of the Slavs, Celts, and Teutons in northern areas where the growing season is too short for dependable wheat production (*see* ergotism, A.D. 857).

1680 B.C.

Leavened (raised) bread is invented in Egypt (time approximate). In the next few centuries the Egyptians will develop ovens in which several loaves may be baked at the same time. Bread for the rich will be made from wheat flour, that for the less affluent from barley, and that for the poor from sorghum.

1600 B.C.

The Shang dynasty, which begins in the next 100 years, will rule much of China until about 1200 or 1000 B.C.

Chinese hunters pursue deer, rabbits, elephants, and rhinoceri to provide food for their families and for the imperial Shan household. Fish and turtles are also prized as food, as are chestnuts, mulberries, apricots, and jujube (*Ziziphus jujuba* and *Z. spinosa*, which will be grown more widely than any other fruit in northern China).

Domestication of pigs, dogs, chickens, sheep, cattle, horses, species of water buffalo, and possibly deer will increase during the Shang dynasty (*see* 2205 B.C.; 1500 B.C.).

1520 B.C.

A volcanic eruption on the Greek island of Thera disrupts agriculture and fishing (*see* 1470 B.C.).

1500 B.C.

 Aryan nomads from the Eurasian steppes push into the Indian subcontinent, bringing with them flocks of sheep and herds of cattle (*see* ghee, below).

Horse-drawn vehicles are used by the Chinese (*see* Sumerians, 3500 B.C.).

Geometry helps the Egyptians survey boundaries of fields whose dividing lines are effaced by the annual floods of the Nile (*see* Euclid, 300 B.C.).

India's Aryan invaders (above) introduce a diet heavily dependent on dairy products, using ghee (clarified butter) rather than whole butter, which is too perishable for India's climate.

Water buffalo are domesticated, along with several species of fowl, by Chinese farmers of the Shang dynasty, whose monarch rules at Anyang on the Huanghe (Yellow) River (*see* 2,000 B.C.; poultry, 1400 B.C.).

All major food plants that will be used in the 20th century A.D., with the exception of sugar beets, are being cultivated somewhere in the world.

1470 B.C.

A volcanic eruption on the Greek island of Thera that is far more violent than the eruption of 1520 B.C. deposits ashes on Crete and emits poisonous vapors that destroy the Minoan civilization of 1600 B.C. Seismic waves 100 to 160 feet high, created by the eruption, rush in to fill the void created at Thera, temporarily dropping water levels on the eastern shores of the Mediterranean.

Egyptian croplands are engulfed by seawater from seismic waves (above), the land is made uncultivable, and famine ensues.

1400 B.C.

The Iron Age begins in Asia Minor as an economical method of smelting iron on an industrial scale is found.

The first domestic poultry is introduced into China from the Malayan Peninsula, where the jungle fowl *Gallus bankiva* has been domesticated.

1380 B.C.

A canal completed by slaves of Egypt's Amenhotep III connects the Nile with the Red Sea and will remain in use for centuries (*see* 609 B.C.).

1275 B.C.

A 40-year Israelite migration begins after 3 centuries of Egyptian oppression. The prophet Moses and his brother Aaron lead tribesmen and their flocks of sheep out of Egypt toward the Dead Sea in Canaan on a roundabout journey that will take them through the Sinai Peninsula, Kadesh, Aelana, and Petra.

The wandering Jews (above) will survive starvation at one point by eating "manna," possibly a white substance exuded by tamarisk trees when insects puncture their branches, or possibly a kind of mushroom.

1150 B.C.

 Egyptian aristocrats enjoy leavened bread and drink some wine (but mostly beer) as they dine at tables and sit on chairs that they have developed, but in the bread stalls of village streets, only flat breads are commonly available.

1028 B.C.

The Chou dynasty, which may have begun as early as 1122 B.C., will rule much of China from about now until 221 B.C. but will break down into warring states in about 480 B.C.

The Chinese will grow both winter and summer wheat crops, rotating winter wheat and barley with summer millets and buckwheat. Later historians will speculate that wheat and barley will gain importance only when tax levies force farmers to increase their agricultural yields and when population increases deplete supplies of wild game habitats and make more labor available for farm work.

Alcoholic beverages used by the Chinese are fermented chiefly from millet but sometimes from fruits and berries. They are consumed in quantity at every feast and on important ritual occasions.

1000 B.C.

 The Iron Age, which began 1,400 years ago in the Near East, moves to Europe in the Hallstatt region of what will become Austria. Iron tools, farm implements, and weapons begin to spread throughout Europe.

 The Chinese cut ice and store it for refrigeration; they preserve food chiefly by drying and pickling.

The Chinese cut down forests to create more farmland. The deforestation will lead to soil erosion, floods, and drought in millennia to come.

The soybean (*Glycine max*) is introduced into China (year approximate), probably from the Jung people to the northeast, but will not be popular for many years to come.

Land sown with grain in Egypt yields crops as bountiful as any the Egyptians will reap in the 20th century A.D.

950 B.C.

The household of Judea's King Solomon includes 700 wives and 300 concubines and consumes 10 oxen on an ordinary day, along with the meat of harts, gazelles, and hartebeests. The Book of Deuteronomy in 621 B.C. will say that the king had 12,000 horsemen scouring the countryside in search of "victual for all who came to Solomon's table," and that for feast days he sacrificed 22,000 oxen and any number of fattened fowl.

850 B.C.

"There is no part of man more like a dog than brazen Belly, crying to be remembered," writes the blind Greek poet Homer in his epic work the *Odyssey* about the wanderings of Odysseus (Ulysses) (date uncertain; may be as much as a century earlier).

Fish cultivation is discussed in a voluminous treatise by the Chinese author Fan-li (manuscript in British Museum, London) (*see* oyster cultivation, 110 B.C.).

801 B.C.

∞ Aryan religious epics, or Vedas, will lead in the next 200 years to a veneration of the cow in much of India and to a sanctification of dairy products.

800 B.C.

China's minister of agriculture teaches the peasants crop rotation. The emperor Kuan Chung's minister also teaches them to dig drainage ditches, rents them farm equipment, and stores grain surpluses to provide free food in time of famine.

Rice becomes an important part of Chinese diets (*see* 2300 B.C.). Southern Chinese rely on rice as their staple grain but vary their diets with dog, chicken, and wild game (deer, rabbit, antelope, badger, bear, fox, monkey, wild dog, wild boar, wild horse, panther, tiger, common rat, bamboo rat, goose, quail, partridge, pheasant, curlew, and finch). Food is roasted, broiled, boiled, steamed, simmered, and stewed; salt and plums are the chief seasoning agents. Rice will remain the staple of Chinese cuisine for millennia to come (*see* Japan, 200 B.C.).

Phoenician colonists plant chickpeas and olive trees on the Iberian Peninsula (*see* Egyptian use of chickpeas, 2900 B.C.; Octavian, 38 B.C.).

7th Century B.C.

700 B.C.

Aqueducts are built to carry water to the cities developing in the Near East.

Laws against animal slaughter are relaxed in India.

698 B.C.

Greek colonization of the Mediterranean in the next two centuries will be motivated primarily by a need to find new food sources as Greece's population expands.

650 B.C.

Greek hillsides are bare of trees, which have been cut down to provide wood for houses, for ships, and for the charcoal used by metalworkers. Loss of the trees leads in many areas to soil erosion and to a loss of fertile land (*see* Solon, 594 B.C.).

625 B.C.

Metal coins are introduced in Greece. Stamped with the likeness of an ear of wheat, the coins are a reminder that grain, usually barley, has previously served as a medium of exchange, but the new coins are lighter and easier to transport than grain and do not get moldy.

Greece's first coins provided a more practical medium of exchange than the sheaves of grain which they replaced.

621 B.C.

The Book of Deuteronomy, compiled by Israelite scribes, is among the five books of Moses containing what purports to be the dying testament of the prophet to his people (*see* 1275 B.C.).

The Law of Moses in Deuteronomy (above) imposes dietary restrictions:

"You shall not eat any abominable thing. These are the animals you may eat: the ox, the sheep, the goat, the hart, the gazelle, the roebuck, the wild goat, the ibex, the antelope, and the mountain-sheep. Every animal that parts the hoof and has the hoof cloven in two, and chews the cud, among the animals, you may eat. Yet of those that chew the cud or have the hoof cloven you shall not eat these: the camel, the hare, and the rock badger, because they chew the cud but do not part the hoof, are unclean for you. And the swine, because it parts the hoof but does not chew the cud, is unclean for you. Their flesh you shall not touch.

"Of all that are in the waters you may eat these: whatever has fins and scales you may eat. And whatever does not have fins and scales you shall not eat; it is unclean for you.

"You may eat all clean birds. But these are the ones which you shall not eat: the eagle, the vulture, the osprey, the buzzard, the kite, after their kinds; every raven after its kind; the ostrich, the night-hawk, the sea gull, the hawk, after their kinds; the little owl and the great owl, the water hen and the pelican, the carrion vulture and the cormorant, the stork, the heron, after their kinds; the hoopoe and the bat. And all the winged insects are unclean for you; they shall not be eaten. All clean winged things you may eat.

"You shall not eat anything that dies of itself; you may give it to the alien who is within your town, that he may eat it, or you may sell it to a foreigner. . . .

"You shall not boil a kid in its mother's milk" (*see* Sharia, A.D. 629; Maimonides, A.D. 1163).

Anthropologists will explain the Law of Moses (above) by saying that ancient Jews were shepherds who did not eat the meat that sustained their traditional enemies, who were pig-raising farmers, just as the Chinese, who were farmers and raised pigs, did not drink milk, which sustained their traditional Mongol enemies (*see* 1800 B.C.).

Rabbis will interpret the Law of Moses (above) to mean that pigeon, quail, duck, goose, and ordinary domestic chicken are acceptable birds; meat from cattle, sheep, goats, buffalo, chamois, yak, and all members of the deer family (antelope, caribou, eland, elk, hart, moose, stag) is acceptable, so long as it does not come from the animal's hindquarters. Meat from the camel, horse, pig, rabbit, and hare are forbidden, nor can kumyss, made from mare's milk, or chal, made from camel's milk, be consumed. Crab, lobster, oysters, and shrimp may not be eaten, either, nor can sturgeon or caviar derived from sturgeon. Insects, including bees, are forbidden, but not honey, which is not considered to be derived from an "unclean" creature since it contains no part of such a creature. Gelatin will be per-

mitted only if it is extracted from permitted animals which have undergone ritual slaughter, and isinglass only if it is derived from cod or other permitted fish and not from sturgeon or ling.

Jewish dietary laws will place no restrictions on consumption of cereals, fruits, or vegetables, but while Orthodox Jews will eat brisket of beef and prime ribs they will not eat meat from the hindquarters of animals—including lamb chops, sirloin steak, and the like—unless all the blood has been drained completely from the meat—difficult to do, since the hindquarters contain blood vessels that are hard to remove. Genesis 9:1–4 has said, "Only flesh with the life thereof, which is the blood thereof, shall ye not eat." The proscription against such meat will be based also on Genesis 32:33.

609 B.C.

A new canal to link the Nile with the Red Sea is begun by the Egyptian pharaoh Necho, but although the Greek historian Herodotus will write that Necho completed a channel "four days' journey in length and wide enough for two armies abreast," the canal will not be completed. More than 120,000 men will die in the effort to build it (*see* 1380 B.C.; 520 B.C.).

In the next 14 years Necho's ships will circumnavigate Africa, proceeding from east to west and taking 3 years (including a stop to plant and harvest a grain crop on the North African coast).

605 B.C.

Rome remains a small town but begins to experience food shortages. It will have occasional serious famines in this century.

Rome's Cloaca Maxima will be built in this century. The giant drainage system will drain the marshy area that will become the site of the Roman Forum.

Humped cattle from India become widespread in the Mediterranean countries.

6th Century B.C.

597 B.C.

⚡ Wheeled carts drawn by onagers (small Asiatic asses) bring food into Babylon, while riverboats powered by scores of oarsmen bring vegetable oils from fields north of the Tigris.

☿ Camel caravans bring occasional plagues to Babylon (above); flies and mosquitoes that breed in polluted irrigation canals carry malaria, dysentery, and eye diseases.

594 B.C.

⚔ The Athenian statesman Solon, 42, who has regained Salamis from the Megarians, establishes a timocracy (government by the richest) and begins constitutional reforms at Athens.

🌐 Solon (above) forbids export of any Athenian agricultural produce: his well-intentioned edict will lead to more planting of olive trees. Their roots soak up deep moisture but do not hold soil together, so while olive oil and silver mines will bring riches to Athens, Solon's edict will hasten the erosion of Greek hillsides (*see* Plato, 347 B.C.).

546 B.C.

⚔ Athens restores Peisistratus to power (he has obtained support from Thessaly and from Lygdamis of Naxos). He exiles his opponents, confiscates their lands, and uses them to benefit the poor, making the *hectemoroi* (sharecroppers) landowners and encouraging industry and trade.

538 B.C.

∞ The Old Testament Book of Leviticus contains dietary laws similar to those in Deuteronomy (*see* 621 B.C.).

528 B.C.

∞ Buddhism has its beginnings in India, where Siddhartha Gautama, 35, has found enlightenment after a long and severe penance at Buddh Gaya, near Benares. A prince who renounced the luxury of palace life 5 years ago, Siddhartha went into the wilderness wearing sackcloth, but he found the ascetic life futile. In the next 45 years he will travel up and down the Ganges River; he will be called the Buddha (Enlightened One) and will found monastic orders of a religion that will become dominant in China, Japan, and some other Asian countries (*see* 260 B.C.).

⏳ Vegetarianism will be an essential part of the Buddhist religion (above), although Siddhartha himself will abandon strict vegetarianism and die at age 84 after feasting on pork.

525 B.C.

☿ The Greek philosopher, sage, and mathematician Pythagoras dies, possibly at the hands of political enemies, at the Dorian colony of Crotona in southern Italy (year approximate). By some accounts he has been pursued to the edge of a bean field and allowed himself to be seized rather than run into

Fava beans were a dietary staple of Mediterranean peoples—the only bean known in Europe.

the field because he has a potentially fatal sensitivity to fava beans (*Vicia faba*), the only beans that will be available in Europe until the 16th century A.D. (Sensitive individuals, whose red blood cells lack the enzyme needed to break down the peptide glutathione in fava beans, may suffer hemolytic ane-

mia within a few minutes of exposure to the pollen of the fava plant or a few hours of eating the beans; symptoms may include jaundice and high fever, and in severe cases death may occur within 1 or 2 days.)

520 B.C.

The Persian emperor Darius digs a canal to connect the Nile with the Red Sea, continuing work begun nearly a century ago by the pharaoh Necho (*see* 609 B.C.; Suez, A.D. 1854).

Phoenicia continues to grow rich on trade in grain, cloth, wine, and the purple-black dye obtained from a gland of the rare purple sea snail, or murex. Long shallow-draft Phoenician galleys powered by oarsmen slaves and large square sails may long since have circumnavigated Africa (*see* Necho, 609 B.C.).

5th Century B.C.

500 B.C.

"In ancient times, people were few but wealthy and without strife," writes the Chinese philosopher Han Fei-tzu. "People at present think that five sons are not too many, and each son has five sons also and before the death of the grandfather there are already 25 descendants. Therefore people are more and wealth is less; they work hard and receive little. The life of a nation depends on having enough food, not upon the number of people."

490 B.C.

Persia's Darius I has a thousand animals slaughtered each day for the royal table at his capital of Persepolis (or so the historian Xenophon will record).

479 B.C.

The Chinese philosopher Confucius (K'ung Fu-tzu) dies at age 72, leaving behind writings that his followers will collect in the *Analects*, the *I Ching* (*Book of Changes*), and songs that include more than 300 traditional songs of the Chou dynasty; the songs give a picture of agriculture in Chou times, mentioning at least 44 food plants (the Old Testament mentions only 29), including bamboo shoots, cabbages, celery, chives, daylilies, gourds, kudzu, lotus, radishes, soybeans, hemp seeds, and various edible roots, shoots, and tubers (but not cockleburr, mallow, motherwort, mugwort, plantain, poke, or yarrow), and making hundreds of references to food (*see* Mencius, 289 B.C.). The Chinese also eat peaches (*Prunis persica*), plums (*Prunis salicina*), apricots, jujubes (*Ziziphus jujuba* and *Z. spinosa*, the most widespread fruit in north China), and chestnuts.

433 B.C.

The Athenian statesman Pericles, 57, concludes a defensive alliance with Corcyra (Corfu), the strong naval power in the Ionian Sea that is the bitter enemy of Corinth. Pericles also renews alliances with the Rhegium and Leontini in the west, threatening Sparta's food supply route from Sicily. Corinth appeals to Sparta to take arms against Athens, and the appeal is backed by Megara (which has been ruined by Pericles's economic sanctions) and by Aegina (which is heavily taxed by Pericles and has been refused home rule).

432 B.C.

The Peloponnesian Wars, which will occupy 20 of the next 27 years, begin in Greece following a revolt in the spring by the Potidaea in Chalcidice against their Athenian masters.

Spartan troops will lay waste the countryside around Athens in the Peloponnesian Wars (above), destroying not only grain fields but also olive trees, vineyards, and orchards, which will not recover for decades.

431 B.C.

✗ Sparta's Archidamus II gains support by calling for the liberation of the Hellenes from Athenian despotism, and he sets out to annihilate Athens. Pericles works to make Athens-Piraeus an impregnable fortress, planning to lay waste the Megarid each spring and autumn while the Spartans are occupied with sowing and reaping their own crops.

⚕ Pepper from India is fairly common in Greece, but *Piper nigrum* is used as medicine, not as a food seasoning.

400 B.C.

⏁ Sparta's king Agesilaus receives a gift of fat geese from Egypt for making what will be called *pâté de foie gras* (year approximate). The Greeks fatten geese (and also ducks) with wheat pounded in water (*see* A.D. 1779).

4th Century B.C.

350 B.C.

Cookbook: the Greek author Archestratus records a collection of recipes.

References to wheat first appear in Greek writings as wheat suitable for bread is introduced from Egypt.

347 B.C.

The academy founded by the Athenian philosopher Plato will continue for 876 years.

Plato urges temperance and bewails the changes in the Attic landscape since his youth. Green meadows, woods, and springs have given way to bare limestone partly because the planting of olive trees has led to the ruin of the land (*see* Solon, 594 B.C.).

335 B.C.

The philosopher Aristotle returns to Athens from Macedon and attempts to develop a deductive system as comprehensive as is possible with the scientific materials available. He concerns himself chiefly with the anatomical structures of animals, their reproduction, and their evolution, and he founds the study of comparative anatomy in an effort to categorize animal life into biological groups.

Aristotle describes various parts of the digestive canal in some detail, but in the absence of any chemical knowledge his ideas of physiology are primitive. Everything in life is subject to basic law, says Aristotle, but he believes that food is "cooked" in the intestinal tube and praises garlic for its medicinal qualities.

Aristotle (above) opens a lyceum in an elegant gymnasium dedicated to Apollo Lyceus, god of shepherds. The lyceum contains a museum of natural history, zoological gardens, and a library.

331 B.C.

Wheat is grown extensively in southeastern parts of the British Isles and is threshed under great barns, reports a traveler from the Greek colony at Marsilea, which will later be called Marseilles.

330 B.C.

The Persian king Darius III is murdered by his satrap Bessus after a 6-year reign. Alexander the Great sacks the Persian capital of Persepolis. It takes 20,000 mules and 5,000 camels to carry off the loot.

329 B.C.

Alexander the Great conquers Samarkand (Maracanda), capital of Sogdiana, in central Asia.

327 B.C.

Bananas (*Musa sapientum*) are found growing in the Indus Valley by Alexander the Great (*see* A.D. 1482).

Alexander the Great found bananas growing in the Indus Valley, where they had been eaten for centuries.

325 B.C.

The first known reference to sugarcane (*Saccharum officinarum*) appears in writings by Alexander the Great's admiral Nearchus, who writes of Indian reeds "that produce honey, although there are no bees." Cane sugar has been grown for many years in China, but the word "sugar" (adapted from the Arabic *sukhar*, which derives from the Sanskrit *sarkara*, meaning gravel or pebble) begins to appear frequently in Indian literature (*see* 300 B.C.).

Alexander (above) has brought the citron back from the Middle East to Greece, where it will be used with honey to make confections for the rich.

The poor of Athens exist mainly on fava beans, greens, beechnuts, turnips, wild pears, dried figs, barley paste, and occasional grasshoppers, with only sporadic welfare assistance. For the better off there are fish, olives, olive oil, and wine.

322 B.C.

Politics IV by Aristotle says, "When there are too many farmers the excess will be of the better kind; when there are too many mechanics and laborers, of the worst."

312 B.C.

Rome gets its first pure drinking water as engineers complete an aqueduct into the city.

301 B.C.

The Athenian philosopher Epicurus extols luxury and indulgence in eating and drinking. Pleasure is the only good and the end of all morality, says Epicurus, but a genuine life of pleasure must be a life of prudence, honor, and justice.

Indigenous Chinese regard the dairy products of nomadic tribes as unhygienic and many of their meat dishes as barbaric.

Chinese irrigation methods increased food production but often required intensive use of manpower.

History of Plants and *Theoretical Botany* by the Greek philosopher Theophrastus mention plant diseases such as rusts and mildews and describe "caprification" of figs (*see* A.D. 1885).

The Chinese build a vast irrigation system to reduce the flooding of Sichuan's Red Basin, which is becoming a rich area for rice cultivation even while millet remains the staple grain for most of the country. Farmers are developing practices that will enable them to feed one-quarter of the human race on a relatively small area of cultivable land, developing productive plant varieties, recycling nutrients, using water resources efficently, and building the peasant workforce of skilled workers essential to labor-intensive agriculture.

Among the many millet varieties grown by Chinese farmers are sticky varieties used especially for brewing alcoholic beverages, which are heavily consumed.

3rd Century B.C.

300 B.C.

Carthaginian planters own fertile lands in Libya; some have as many as 20,000 slaves.

Sugarcane from India is introduced to the Middle East, where it is planted in areas wet enough to support its growth (*see* 325 B.C.; A.D. 1099).

289 B.C.

 The Chinese Confucian philospher Mencius (Meng-tzu) dies (year approximate) at age 82 (approximate) (*see* Confucius, 479 B.C.). Like Confucius, he has held agriculture to be China's basic industry, with crafts, manufacturing, and trade less important, and he has made bold to criticize the policies of the Chou emperor whose court he graced: "If you do not interfere with the busy season in the fields, then there will be more grain and the people can eat; if you do not allow nets with too fine a mesh to be used in large ponds, then there will be more fish and turtles than they can eat. . . . Now when food meant for human beings is so plentiful as to be thrown to dogs and pigs, you fail to realize that it is time for garnering, and when men drop dead from starvation by the wayside, you fail to realize that it is time for distribution. When people die, you simply say, 'It is none of my doing. It is the fault of the harvest.' In what way is that different from killing a man by running him through, while saying all the time, 'It is none of my doing. It is the fault of the weapon.' Stop putting the blame on the harvest and the people of the whole empire will come to you."

221 B.C.

China's Qin (Ch'in) emperor Shihuang unites the country after 25 years of fighting and begins a dynasty that will continue only until 207 B.C. but will be the basis of the name "China."

Private land ownership with yeomen farmers has evolved in the later years of the Chou dynasty.

213 B.C.

China's Qin emperor suppresses books but specifically exempts writings on agriculture and medicine.

206 B.C.

The Han dynasty, which will rule China until A.D. 220, begins as the last Qin emperor dies and one of his minor officials assumes power. Private land ownership will gain official standing in the Han period.

 China's great Min River irrigation system has been completed by the Li family of engineers to improve Chinese agriculture.

 Staple foods during the Han dynasty will be grains—rice in the south, wheat, barley, and two kinds of millet in the north—plus soybeans, red lentils, and vegetables. Millet is considered superior to wheat or barley, which is generally boiled into porridge or steamed over stew but is tough, chewy, and has a somewhat bitter taste. Millet cooks into a soft, delicate porridge with a nutlike, almost sweet, taste or a fluffy mass of steamed grain. Grain is sometimes roasted or otherwise cooked and then dried to create instant rations for the military, which also uses dried beef jerky.

Garlic, leeks, and scallions will become common articles of diet in the Han period; the common people will eat taro root and yams.

Soybeans, boiled to make them palatable but generally scorned because they produce flatulence, will provide food only for the poor except in years when grain harvests are bad, when they will provide protection against famine. But many Chinese have perfected the technique of fermenting soybeans.

200 B.C.

Japanese potters now make pots and dishes with greater variety in simpler patterns designed for specific purposes (*see* 10,000 B.C.).

The Japanese begin producing salt from dried seaweed, which they boil to evaporate its water content. Salt is used for food preservation, and some soybeans are fermented to make what later will be refined into soy sauce and miso (soy) paste.

Rice cultivation begins by some accounts in Japan, where rice imported from Southeast Asia prospers under conditions of rich, alluvial soil, summer heat, and high humidity (*see* 800 B.C.; 8 B.C.). Consumption of meat and fish will decline as rice becomes more plentiful (*but see* A.D. 806).

The Japanese will use some of their rice to produce a wine called *sake*.

2nd Century B.C.

185 B.C.

Troops returning to Rome from the war with Syria's Antiochus III introduce eastern indulgence. Titus Livy will write nearly 200 years hence that "the Army of Asia introduced foreign luxury to Rome. It was then that meals began to demand more preparation and expense. . . . The cook, considered and employed until then as a slave at the lowest cost, became extremely expensive. What had been only a job became an art."

179 B.C.

Chinese imperial agricultural policy will take shape between now and 87 B.C. under Han emperors.

178 B.C.

The Han emperor Win restores plowing ceremonies to honor Chinese farmers. Agriculture, he says, is the basis of the empire. "Let the Field of Tribute be laid out and I, in person, shall lead the plow in order to provide offerings of millet for the ancestral temples."

170 B.C.

Rome's first professional cooks appear in the form of commercial bakers, but most Roman households continue to grind their own flour and bake their own bread.

167 B.C.

China's Han emperor Wen tries to abolish land taxes, but the effort will be short-lived (*see* 155 B.C.).

155 B.C.

China's Han emperor Qing, successor to Wen, reduces taxes from one-fifteenth to one-thirtieth of a farmer's crop (*see* 167 B.C.); tax collectors will take more than they are supposed to, but although taxes will soon be increased they will remain at about 10 percent through most of the Han period.

149 B.C.

The Roman statesman Marcus Porcius Cato the Elder dies at age 85, leaving as his legacy some commentaries on agriculture. *De Agriculture* (or *De Re Rustica*) urges farmers to plant grapes and olives, which draw moisture and nutrients from the subsoil, rather than grain, which is more subject to drought. Farming, Cato has written, has become more amusement than a source of income and pasturage far more profitable than tilling the soil.

141 B.C.

Jewish forces under Simon Maccabee liberate Jerusalem from the Seleucid emperor Demetrius II Nicator while he is occupied with conquering

Babylon. The Maccabee brothers and their followers have gained independence in Judea that will continue until 63 B.C.

 The Maccabee brothers (above) have improved agriculture in the region of Jerusalem.

140 B.C.

Rome's Gracchus brothers tried to reform land ownership and keep the poor from starving.

China's Han emperor Wu Di begins a 53-year reign during which he will extend the empire to the south, annex parts of Korea and Tonkin, and send his emissary Jang Qian halfway around the world to Bactria and Sogdiana in Central Asia to seek an east-west alliance against the Huns, or Hsiung Nu.

News of Jang Qian (above) and of Serica, "land of silk," will reach Rome, and caravans will begin to carry the first apricots and peaches (the "Chinese fruit") to Europe, while Jang Qian will be credited by some with introducing grapes, pomegranates, and walnuts to China (see 100 B.C.).

133 B.C.

Tiberius Sempronius Gracchus, 30, is elected Roman tribune on a platform of social reform. He proposes an agrarian law that would limit holdings of public land to 312 acres per person, with an additional 250 acres for each of two sons, but large landholders in Etruria and Campania block efforts to recover lands held in violation of the new law, and Gracchus is murdered. The great estates (*latifundia*) are not distributed among new settlers but grow at the expense of the small peasants and to some extent of Rome's urban proletariat.

123 B.C.

Gaius Sempronius Gracchus, 30, is elected Roman tribune on a platform similar to that of his late brother Tiberius. A more forceful man, Gaius puts through a far more extreme program, which includes a law obliging the government to provide grain to Rome's citizens at a price below the market average. The law protects the poor against famine and against speculators and establishes a precedent. State control of the grain supply will permit demagogues to gain popular support by distributing free grain.

110 B.C.

Romans cultivate oysters in the first Western efforts to domesticate marine wildlife. Cultured oyster beds are operated in the vicinity of Baia near the town that will become Naples, where local oysterman Sergius Orata makes a fortune selling his bivalves to the luxury trade (see 850 B.C.; A.D. 407).

103 B.C.

A second Servile War erupts in Sicily as slaves rebel under the leadership of Tryphon and Athenion. Slaves from lands conquered by Rome's legions provide much of the power for Roman agriculture, being able to follow verbal orders even though they are less powerful and less docile than horses, whose efficiency is limited also by a lack of metal horseshoes and proper harnesses.

101 B.C.

The Romans are the first people to apply waterpower to milling flour.

1st Century B.C.

100 B.C.

China receives alfalfa and grape seeds for the first time as Han envoy Jang Qian returns from Firghana (year approximate). Jang Qian will also be credited by some with introducing caraway seeds, coriander from Bactria, cucumbers, peas, pomegranates, and walnuts (see 140 B.C.).

Grape wine imported from western regions has been greatly prized by the Chinese and will continue to enjoy special status for the next 3 centuries.

85 B.C.

Chinese farmers begin using seed-drill plows with hoppers. The technology will not reach Europe until about 1700 (see Jethro Tull, A.D. 1701).

Chinese farmlands are mostly in the hands of tenants who rent property from landlords each of whom has several such tenants, each tenant, typically, tilling perhaps 7.7 acres of soil, which is enough to support a family of five. A few larger landlords hold vast properties and have, in addition to tenants, serfs and slaves—usually war captives and criminals—working their lands.

81 B.C.

The Japanese emperor Sujin begins a great ship-building effort in a move to provide his people with more of the seafood on which so many depend for sustenance.

80 B.C.

The Roman dictator Sulla halts public distribution of free grain (see 123 B.C.; 71 B.C.).

70 B.C.

Crassus and Pompey break with the Roman nobility and use their troops to gain the consulship. They restore the privileges of the tribunate, which were removed by Sulla.

Crassus and Pompey (above) resume distribution of free grain. Some 40,000 adult male citizens of Rome receive grain dispensations, and the number will rise rapidly (see 58 B.C.).

69 B.C.

The Roman general and epicure Lucius Licinius Lucullus defeats Armenia's Tigranes II, who has seized Syria, and begins a push into the mountains of Armenia and Parthia toward Pontus.

Cherries from the Black Sea kingdom of Pontus sent back to Rome by Lucullus (above) introduce a new fruit tree to Europe.

67 B.C.

Mediterranean pirates who have been interfering with Rome's grain imports from Egypt and North Africa are defeated by Quintus Caecilius Metellus.

66 B.C.

The Roman general Lucius Lucullus gave lavish banquets that included cherries, an exotic new fruit.

66 B.C.

⏱ Lucullus returns to Rome and begins entertaining on a lavish scale at feasts so extravagant that the word "Lucullan" will be used for millennia to denote flamboyant sumptuousness.

65 B.C.

✗ Rome's Asian and Syrian territories are reorganized by Pompey, who establishes four new Roman provinces. He leaves as client kingdoms Cappadocia, Eastern Pontus, Galatia, Judea, and Lycia.

🌾 Pompey introduces to Rome's orchards and cuisine apricots from Armenia, peaches from Persia, plums from Damascus, raspberries from Mount Ida

(southeast of the old city of Troy), and quinces from Sidon.

57 B.C.

👤 The Roman Senate gives Pompey power to supervise the city's grain supply as a grain shortage looms.

✒ Poetry: *De Rerum Natura* by the Roman poet-philosopher Titus Lucretius Caro, 39, is a six-volume didactic poem of Epicurean philosophy dealing with ethics, physics, psychology, and the materialistic atoms suggested by the Greek Democritus in 330 B.C. *"Quod ali cibus est aliis fiat acre venerum,"* says Lucretius ("What is food to one man may be a fierce poison to another").

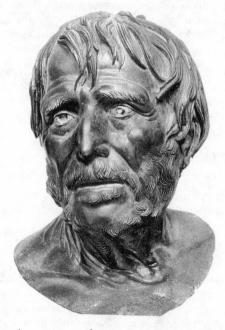

"One man's meat is another man's poison," said the Roman philosopher Lucretius.

54 B.C.

✗ Julius Caesar invades Britain. He fails to conquer the islands but does open them to Roman trade and influence (*see* A.D. 43).

Julius Caesar (above) finds the Britons making Cheshire cheese.

48 B.C.

Some 500 bargeloads of foodstuffs and other imports for Rome are pulled up the Tiber by oxen each month from the port of Ostia.

Julius Caesar introduces the Gallic art of making pork sausage into Rome.

44 B.C.

Julius Caesar is made dictator for life. He reduces the number of Romans receiving free grain from 320,000 to 150,000 and is assassinated at the Senate on March 15 by conspirators.

41 B.C.

Rome's triumvirate confiscates farmland in the Campania for distribution among returning legionnaires.

40 B.C.

Chinese engineers invent a winnowing machine with crank handle; it will not reach Europe until the late 18th century A.D.

Marc Antony's wife, Fulvia, at Rome receives dispatches describing the banquets enjoyed by her husband with Cleopatra of Egypt at Alexandria: "We have five or six courses of fish, oysters, mussels, sea-hogs with asparagus; then we have capons, pies, and patties of fish and venison, many kinds of sea fruits and lobsters and polypuses cooked in spicy sauces, and partridges, cutlets of deer and gazelles, pheasants inside sweet crusts, big game, piglets stuffed with becassins and quails, ducks and turkeys and peacocks roasted and served with all their wonderful feathers, woodcocks in all kinds of sauces, tunny fish of Calchedony, sturgeons of Rhodes, lampreys, and patisserie of many kinds that I had never tasted before, and wonderful fruit from the East" (the reference to "turkeys" will mislead future food historians; *see* A.D. 1523).

39 B.C.

Rome's triumvirate signs the Pact of Mycaenum recognizing the Mediterranean pirate Sextus Pompey as ruler of Sicily, Sardinia, Corsica, and the Peloponnese. Pompey's fleet can interrupt Rome's grain supply, and this puts him in a position to dictate terms.

38 B.C.

The Roman consul Octavian, 24, conquers Iberia. Roman legions will introduce chickpeas, originally brought to the Iberian Peninsula by Phoenicians in about 800 B.C., to the rest of Europe, where they will be widely cultivated and consumed.

30 B.C.

Poetry: *Georgics* by the Roman poet Virgil, completed after 7 years' work, is a didactic four-volume work ennobling the Italian land, its trees, grapevines, and olive groves, herds, flocks, and beehives.

27 B.C.

The Roman Empire, which will rule most of the Western world until A.D. 476, is founded January 23 by Octavian, who 1 week earlier received the name Augustus Caesar from the Senate in gratitude for his achievements. Helped by the rich Roman merchant Mycenas, Octavian makes himself emperor at age 35 with the title Imperator Caesar Octavianus, a title he will soon change to Augustus Caesar as he begins a 41-year reign.

The number of poor Romans receiving free grain is increased by Augustus from 150,000 to 200,000.

27 B.C.

The ordinary Roman diet consists chiefly of a gruel known as *puls*, made often from barley but sometimes of millet or wheat. It is made from oats only when no other grain is available.

"The Earth neither grows old, nor wears out, if it be dunged," writes Columella (above), who urges crop rotation that alternates grain with legumes.

Romans use blood and bones as fertilizer. They grow clover and will later grow alfalfa, but they disdain using human excrement for fertilizer.

24 B.C.

The emperor Augustus acts to reduce the exorbitant price of spices in Rome. He appoints the prefect of Egypt, Aeilius Gallus, to lead a campaign that incorporates the south Arabian spice kingdom into the Roman Empire, but the expedition will fail as a result of hunger, fatigue, disease, poor navigation, and bad roads.

Roman farmers struggled to produce a living from their lands, which yielded little grain.

4 B.C.

Poetry: *De Re Rustica* by Lucius Junius Moderatus Columella is a didactic poem that advises switching from grain to vines, ". . . for none in Italy can remember when seeds increased fourfold." The common yield for a bushel of seed is only two or three bushels of grain, and, while an acre of land may, at best, yield four to six bushels of wheat or barley, the more usual yield is two to three bushels, and most of Rome's grain comes from Egypt and North Africa (*see* A.D. 6).

Rice, imported from China, is by some accounts cultivated for the first time in Japan, at Kyoto (*see* 200 B.C.), but millet remains the cereal grain of most Japanese.

1st Century

2

The world's first official census counts 60 million Chinese, but the numbers are almost certainly exaggerated (*see* A.D. 280).

9

The Han emperor Wong Mong (Wang Mang) grants manumission to China's slaves and nationalizes the land, dividing the country's large estates and establishing state granaries.

The Han dynasty's chief legacy to Chinese cooking will be mien noodles, made from the finest wheat flour using techniques probably introduced from the West. Selling boiled noodles, swung noodles, and other noodle foods will hereafter be a significant business in China.

12

The Chinese repeal the radical land reforms made by the emperor Wong Mong 3 years ago in response to widespread protests.

14

Cookbook: *Of Culinary Matters* (*De Re Coquinaria*, or *De Re Culinaria*) by the Roman gastronome Marcus Gavius Apicius is the world's first known book of recipes. Apicius gives six recipes for roasting and braising crane. A nobleman, he prepares broiled broccoli, which is much enjoyed by the son of the new emperor Tiberius and prepares eggs with honey and pepper, a dish he calls *ovemele*, or egg honey (possibly the origin of the English word "omelette").

China's Han emperor Wong Mong orders his imperial attendant to prepare dried grain food and dried meat for a journey to inspect his troops.

Most Chinese eat from earthenware or wooden bowls; lacquerware, which has replaced ancient bronze bowls, is too expensive for any but rich aristocrats and merchants.

China's nobility enjoys exotic fruits such as long-an and lichee, which are brought to the Han court by fast horses from tropical southern border areas.

Apicius (above) instructs cooks to combine pounded asparagus tips with pepper, lovage, fresh coriander, savory, onion, wine, oil, eggs, and a fish-flavored sauce; after baking, he says, it should be sprinkled with more pepper.

16

The number of Romans receiving free grain rises to 320,000, up from 150,000 in 44 B.C. Close to one-third of the city is on the dole.

Rome imports some 14 million bushels of grain per year to supply the city alone—an amount requiring several hundred square miles of croplands to produce. One-third comes from Egypt and the rest mostly from North African territories west of Egypt.

Romans dote on asparagus, considering a dinner unimportant unless it features an asparagus dish as an appetizer.

Seven regional Chinese commissions are directed to establish annual high, low, and mean price levels for staples and to buy surplus goods at cost, but merchants and capitalists employed by the Han emperor Wong Mong as administrators will provoke revolts.

A horizontal waterwheel is described in Chinese writings, which discuss a mechanism in which the wheel employs a series of belts and pulleys to drive a bellows that works an iron furnace for the casting of agricultural implements.

The Jewish rabbi Jesus of Nazareth leaves Galilee after a brief ministry and travels to Jerusalem to observe Passover at a ritual Seder meal with his 12 apostles. He is betrayed by one of these disciples, condemned as a blasphemer, and crucified, probably April 3, and it will later be said that the superstition about it being unlucky to have 13 at a dinner table arose from this "Last Supper." But in Scandinavian mythology, which antedates Christianity, the god Loki intruded on a banquet in Valhalla, becoming the 13th guest, and another god, Balder, was slain. The source of the superstition about having 13 to dinner will remain a mystery.

A power shortage halts Rome's flour mills. The emperor Caligula commandeers all draft animals to keep the mills in operation.

Vomitoriums gain popularity in Rome. The emperor Claudius and others employ slaves to tickle their throats after they have eaten their fill that they can vomit, then return to the banquet tables and begin again. Most Romans live on bread, olives, wine, and some fish, but little meat.

Romans create the capon, gelding cocks to make them grow larger.

Vast quantities of grain are stored at Rome under the supervision of the *aediles*, who control the food supply. They introduce regulations to ensure the freshness of meat, fish, and produce sold in the city.

Roman armies under Titus Flavius Sabinus Vespasianus, 58, and his son Titus, 27, enter Galilee to put down a revolt of Jews who have massacred a body of Roman soldiers.

Roman interest in Palestine is based in part on Dead Sea salt deposits. Roman cheese is heavily salted, bread is salted to make it rise and keep better, and salt is added to wine and beer.

Pay received by Roman soldiers is called *salarium*, or salt money, basis of the English word "salary."

Panic strikes Rome as adverse winds delay grain shipments from Egypt and North Africa, producing a bread shortage. Ships laden with wheat from North Africa sail 300 miles to Rome's port of Ostia in 3 days given good winds, and the 1,000-mile voyage from Alexandria averages 13 days. The ships often carry 1,000 tons. Shipping adds little to the price (which may double if hauled overland); wheat is a cheap commodity, but the supply depends on favorable winds.

Nonfiction: *Historia Naturalis* by the Roman scholar Pliny the Elder (Gaius Plinius Secundus),

54, is a 37-volume encyclopedia of natural history that says of agriculture, "The farmer's eye is the best fertilizer."

The artichoke, says Pliny (above), is one of "the earth's monstrosities," but Roman gastronomes prize the bulbous vegetable.

Pliny (above) notes with disgust that pepper is purchased by weight as if it were gold or silver. He understands the Roman passion for spices such as cassia and ginger, whose fragrances have mysteriously Oriental overtones, but the only desirable quality of pepper, he says, is "a certain pungency; and yet it is for this we import it all the way from India." Romans use spices liberally in cooking; pepper is used largely to preserve meat.

80

Anthrax sweeps the Roman Empire in epidemic form, killing thousands of humans and animals (*see* below).

Anthrax (above) strikes the cattle and horses of tribespeople on the borders of China, where an extended drought withers the grasslands. The tribespeople begin moving westward to seek new pastures.

The tribespeople moving westward from Mongolia avoid scurvy by consuming large quantities of mare's milk. The milk contains four times as much of the accessory food factor ascorbic acid as does cow's milk (no milk is notably rich in ascorbic acid, but little is needed to avoid scurvy).

90

Roman ships break the Arab monopoly in the spice trade. The ships are large enough to sail without difficulty from Egyptian Red Sea ports to India, but

while spices become more plentiful, they drain Rome of her gold reserves.

Use of spices is one of the excesses that will bring about the fall of Rome, says the Christian prophet John of Ephesus in his *Revelations* (18:11–13). John writes metaphorically of Babylon, but he means Rome.

92

The Roman emperor Domitian decrees that no more land in Gaul shall be planted in vines since the country needs to boost wheat production (*see* Probus, A.D. 277).

95

A severe form of malaria appears in the farm districts outside Rome and will continue for the next 500 years, taking out of cultivation the fertile land of the Campania, whose market gardens supply the city with fresh produce. The fever drives small farmers into the crowded city, and they bring the malaria with them.

At least 10 aqueducts supply Rome with 250 million gallons of water per day, some 50 gallons per person, even after the public baths have used half the supply.

Iron plows with wheels help some of Rome's barbarian neighbors control the depth of plowing (and save the plowmen's energies). The barbarians use coulters to cut the soil and moldboards to turn it over. While Roman farmers practice cross-plowing, the barbarians plow deep, regular furrows that will lead to the cultivation of long strips of land rather than square blocks.

Malaria (above) lowers Rome's live-birth rate while rates elsewhere in the empire are rising.

2nd Century

110

Caravans make regular departures from Luoyang with Chinese ginger, cassia (a type of cinnamon), and silk to be bartered in Central Asia for gold, silver, grape wine, glassware, pottery, asbestos cloth, coral beads, and intaglio gems from Rome.

125

Plague sweeps North Africa in the wake of a locust invasion that destroys large areas of cropland. The plague kills as many as 500,000 in Numidia and possibly 150,000 on the coast before moving to Italy, where it takes so many lives that villages and towns are abandoned. Famine contributes to the death toll produced by the plague in North Africa and Italy.

"Bread and circuses (*panem et circensis*) keep the Roman citizenry pacified," writes Roman lawyer-satirist Decimus Junius Juvenalis (Juvenal), 65, in his *Satires*.

"Acorns were good enough until bread was invented," writes Juvenal in his *Satires XIV*. Roman bakeries produce bread in dozens of different varieties, and the Romans distribute free bread to the poor in times of need.

128

Roman agriculture declines as imports from Egypt and North Africa depress wheat prices, making it unprofitable to farm and forcing many farmers off the land.

166

Rome expropriates peasant lands and awards them to returning legionnaires, few of whom will make good farmers.

167

The first full-scale barbarian attack on Rome destroys aqueducts and irrigation conduits, but the emperor Marcus Aurelius repels the invaders.

189

The Roman mob blames a grain shortage on the mercenary freedman Cleander, who succeeded Perennis as prefect 4 years ago. Cleander is sacrificed to the mob.

Plague, possibly smallpox, kills as many as 2,000 per day in Rome. Dying farmers are unable to harvest their crops, dying carters are not able to deliver what grain there is, and food shortages bring riots in the city (above).

193

Rome's richest senator virtually buys the empire at auction for 300 million sesterces. Didius Julianus, 61, then professes himself appalled at the extravagance all about him and puts through a law forbidding the Romans to give or consume sumptuous feasts. Few people pay any attention, and Didius Julianus is put to death June 1 by the Pannonian legate Lucius Septimius Severus, 47, who has marched his men 800 miles from the Danube to Rome in 40 days.

194

China has famine in the vicinity of the eastern Han capital at Luoyang; grain prices skyrocket, and many go hungry.

195

"Scourges, pestilence, famine, earthquakes, and wars are to be regarded as blessings to crowded nations since they serve to prune away the luxuriant growth of the human race," writes the Carthaginian ecclesiast Tertullian (Quintus Septimius Florens Tertullianus), 35. He was converted to Christianity 5 years ago.

200

The average Roman breakfasts on bean meal mash and unleavened breadcakes cooked on cinders and dipped in milk or honey. Midday meals, often eaten standing up in a public place, consist generally of fruit, a sweetmeat, cheese, and watered wine (the *prandium*). The evening meal, or *convivium*, may include meat, fish, broccoli, cereals, and a porridge of breadcrumbs and onions fried in oil and seasoned with vinegar and chickpeas.

3rd Century

204

A trade recession in North Africa's Leptis Magna region is alleviated by the Roman emperor Septimius Severus, a native of Leptus, who buys up the country's olive oil for free distribution in Rome.

218

The new Roman emperor Varius Avitus Bassianus, 14 (a Syrian who calls himself Heliogabalus, or Elagabalus), has 600 ostriches killed to make ostrich-brain pies for one of his lavish banquets while his capable grandmother, Julia Maesa, runs the empire.

Heliogabalus maintains a fleet of fishing boats to catch eels, prized for their roe. Conger eels are kept in tubs and fattened on the flesh of Christian slaves killed in the Colosseum.

220

The Han dynasty, which has ruled China since 206 B.C., ends and the country enters a 45-year period that will be known as the Three Kingdoms.

Chinese politicians in the Han period (above) have taken economic measures and pushed technology to help the peasants, developing systematic price supports and an "ever-normal" granary, running government-sponsored controlled experiments in agronomy, issuing manuals, and standardizing weights and measures in order to increase farm production on a national basis and thereby increase their own power.

Chinese food technology, agriculture, and nutritional knowledge have taken giant strides in the Han period (above), and although most of the advances were made prior to 100 B.C. they have gained adherents through pressures of increased population and urbanization. New milling techniques have been applied to sesame and perilla seeds, introducing vegetable oil for use in woks (below).

Use of the wok—a curved-bottomed cooking pan ideal for stir frying and deep frying—has gained popularity in the Han period (above). A small quantity of oil goes a long way with the wok, forming a pool at the bottom; food can be moved up the wok's sides to drain for boiling; and the wok can be converted into a steamer by placing steamer racks in it and covering the whole with a lid.

222

Tea will be mentioned as a substitute for wine for the first time in Chinese writings of the next half century.

234

Ready-made bread rather than grain is issued to the poor of Rome by decree of the emperor Severus Alexander, now 26.

255

Thascius Caecilius Cyprianus, bishop of Carthage, says in *De Mortalitate*, "The world itself now bears witness to its failing powers." Writing to the Roman proconsul of Africa, Bishop Cyprian says, "There is not so much rain in the winter for fertilizing the seeds, nor in the summer is there so much warmth for ripening them. The springtime is no longer mild, nor the autumn so rich in fruit."

260

Runaway inflation makes the Roman denarius nearly worthless, paralyzing trade. The depression ruins craftsmen, tradesmen, and small farmers, who are reduced to bartering. Large landowners grow larger by buying up cheap land.

265

The Shin dynasty, which will rule China until 420, begins to unify the country.

China's small, independent landholders are her most productive farmers. Crops introduced by central Asian peoples in the north will gradually be adopted by farmers in western and southeastern China, and new land-tenure systems will be adopted as well.

269

Septimia Zenobia, queen of Palmyra, conquers Egypt and thereby gains control of Rome's grain supply.

272

The Roman emperor Aurelianus lays siege to Palmyra, his horsemen capture Zenobia and her young son Vaballathus on the banks of the Euphrates, she is forced to march in gold chains before the emperor's chariot in his triumphal procession, but Aurelianus spares her life.

273

The Roman emperor Aurelianus increases Rome's daily bread ration to nearly 1.5 pounds per capita and adds pork fat to the list of foods distributed free to the populace.

277

The Roman emperor Probus reintroduces wine grapes into Alsatia, which will be as famous for its wines as for its choucroute garnie and pâté de foie gras (*see* A.D. 92).

280

A Chinese census counts 16 million people, down from the 60 million reported in A.D. 2.

4th Century

305

Rich landowners dominate the Roman Empire and enjoy the title of senator, which makes them exempt from the crushing taxes imposed on the rest of the population. The Senate has lost all its power and the landowners almost never attend Senate sessions. Labor and property are evaluated in terms of a unit of wheat-producing land (*iugum*); members of municipal senates (*curiales* or *decuriones*) are charged with the responsibility of collecting taxes and paying arrears; smaller landowners are held responsible for providing recruits for the legions and with keeping wastelands under cultivation.

317

The earliest historically verified reference to tea is recorded, although the Chinese have been drinking the beverage for many years.

321

The Roman emperor Constantine assigns convicts to grind Rome's flour in a move to hold back the rising price of food in an empire whose population has shrunk as a result of plague. Barbarian peoples have used waterpower for years, and pressure mounts to use such power in Rome, where rulers have opposed it in the past lest it cause unemployment.

324

The empire will recover from the chaos of the 3rd century under Constantine. Jobs will become hereditary, even in the female line (if one marries a baker's daughter, one must become a baker).

360

Picts and Scots cross Hadrian's Wall and attack Roman forces in Britain. Roman authorities in Britain have encouraged production of wheat, which they export to supply the legions on the Rhine.

395

An estimated 330,000 acres of farmland lie abandoned in Rome's Campania, partly as a consequence of malaria from mosquitoes bred in swampy areas, but mostly because imprudent agriculture has ruined the land.

5th Century

406

✗ Hordes of Vandals cross the Rhine under their new king, Gunderic, who will reign until 428. Allied with the Alans and the Sciri, they follow the Moselle and the Aisne and proceed to sack Rheims, Amiens, Arras, and Tournai, and turn south into Aquitaine.

⏲ Butter, introduced by the invading Vandals, Alans, and Sciri (above), begins to replace olive oil.

🌾 Cultivation of rye, oats, hops, and spelt (a wheat used for livestock feed) is introduced into Europe by the invading Vandals, Alans, and Sciri (above), who also introduce a heavy wheeled plow that enables farmers to plow deeper, straighter furrows (*see* 90).

407

✗ Britain is evacuated by Roman legions who are needed closer to home. The British Isles return to Saxon rule after 360 years of Roman control.

🐟 The Romans (above) have introduced oyster cultivation into Britain (*see* 110 B.C.).

408

✗ Visigoths lay siege to Rome. The Visigoth king, Alaric, exacts a tribute from Rome that includes 3,000 pounds of pepper (5,000 pounds by some accounts). The spice is valued for alleged medicinal virtues and for disguising spoilage in meat that is past its prime.

409

✗ Vandals cross the Pyrenees into the Iberian Peninsula but find food supplies short as a Roman fleet blockades imports from the North African granary.

420

✗ The Shin dynasty that has ruled China since 265 ends and the country enters a 169-year period that will be known as the Six Dynasties.

423

💲 Visigoths settled south of the Danube by the Byzantine emperor Theodosius II organize a farmers' strike. Only payment of what amounts to a huge farm loan prevents them from occupying Rome.

439

✗ Carthage falls October 29 to the Vandals who have been led since 428 by Genseric (Gaiseric). He makes Carthage his capital.

🌾 The Vandals establish a North African granary that will enable them to enforce their will on other nations as they become dependent on North Africa for food staples.

444

⚡ The wheelbarrow is invented by the Chinese, who will make wide use of the one-wheeled vehicle in agriculture and commerce. (By some accounts the Chinese have used the wheelbarrow since 231; it will not reach Europe until about 1200.)

450

The Hawaiian Islands are discovered by Polynesian chief Hawaii-Loa, who has sailed across 2,400 miles of open water from the island of Raiatea, near Tahiti (date approximate). The Polynesians who land on the uninhabited islands have sustained themselves at sea by eating taro root and will cultivate the plant in Hawaii, cooking the tubers and pounding and kneading them to make a paste known as *poi*, which will often be allowed to ferment and eaten with fish, meat, and vegetables or with milk and honey. (Cultivation of taro root—which is also boiled, parboiled, and deep fried—has spread throughout Southeast Asia, the islands of the South Pacific, and as far west as Egypt.)

Metal horseshoes come into more common use in the Near East and in Europe, increasing the efficiency of horsepower in agriculture and transportation (*see* 770).

451

The Battle of Châlons ends in defeat for Attila's Huns at the hands of a Roman force under Flavius Aetius with help from the Visigoths. The Huns have triumphed over the Alans, Heruls, Ostrogoths, and Visigoths, ravaged much of the Italian countryside, and forced people to settle on marshy islands that will become the city of Venice (*see* 687).

452

Food shortages and plague reduce the numbers of Attila's surviving Huns in Europe. Attila will die next year, and his followers will be driven out of Italy by Roman troops with barbarian reinforcements.

455

Rome is sacked by the Vandals, whose pillage is so thorough that the name "Vandal" will become a generic word for a wanton destroyer.

Barter economy replaces organized trade as Romans and other city dwellers desert their towns for the countryside, where they will be less visible targets for barbarian attack (*see* 350).

460

A famine that will last for several years begins in the neo-Persian Empire.

6th Century

501

Famine, war, disease, and natural disasters will take a heavy toll of the decayed Roman Empire in this century.

536

A "dry fog" covers the Mediterranean region throughout the year, ushering in the most severe winter in memory. Volcanic dust, possibly from an eruption in the East Indies, is the cause.

541

The Great Plague of Justinian (bubonic plague) spreads from Egypt to Palestine and thence to Constantinople and throughout the Roman-Byzantine world, bringing agriculture to a standstill and causing widespread famine. As many as 5,000 to 10,000 die each day for a period in Constantinople, and the plague will continue with resulting famine for the next 60 to 70 years in Europe, the Near East, and Asia.

542

The Great Plague of Justinian, which came into Constantinople last year by way of rats imported from Egypt and Syria, fans out through Europe.

548

Nonfiction: *Topographia Christiana* by the Alexandrian explorer-monk Cosmas Indicopleustes describes the importance of the spice trade (especially in cloves and sweet aloes) in Ceylon and the harvesting of pepper in the hills of India (*see* 525).

554

Italian lands taken from the Ostrogoths are restored to their original owners by Justinian's Pragmatic Sanction, but the landowners have become serfs and the depopulated farmlands have reverted to wilderness.

Food production will begin to increase in northern and western Europe in the next 100 years as a result of agricultural technology introduced by the Slavs, who have made it possible to farm virgin lands whose heavy clay has discouraged agriculture. The Slavs employ a new, lightweight plow with a knife blade (coulter) that cuts vertically, deep into the soil, and a plowshare that cuts horizontally at grassroots level, together with a shaped board, or moldboard, that moves the cut soil or turf neatly to one side. The new plow will have the effect of changing the dimensions of farms: instead of being square, they will tend to take the form of long strips; and although far more efficient than the traditional scratch plow, it requires eight oxen to pull it, so farmers will form cooperative efforts to share plow oxen.

A population explosion will begin in northern and western Europe as the new agriculture (above) increases the availability of food.

589

The Sui dynasty, which will rule China until 618, begins to reunite the country after decades of internal wars, encouraging agriculture in an effort to restore food stocks after so many years of war and neglect.

The Sui emperor moves to establish a national granary that will serve to keep prices on an even keel and provide a reserve in case of shortages. The government will maintain prices in good crop years by buying up surpluses and hold prices down in years when harvests are poor by selling off stored surpluses.

The Sui emperor (above) imposes a kind of socialized agriculture on China, using ideas acquired from the Wei rulers of northern China. A male householder is to receive 80 mu (about five acres) of land to work during his active lifetime (the land reverts to the state when the man reaches age 60), with another 20 mu that can be planted with trees and passed on to his children. Men of high status receive more than the basic allotment, with noblemen getting from 40 to 10,000 mu of inheritable land (*see* 907).

7th Century

605 ─────────────────────────────

A Chinese Grand Canal is completed by a million laborers who link existing waterways to connect the new Chinese capital, established last year at Luoyang, to the Long River. The canal will be extended to Hangchow by 610.

610 ─────────────────────────────

The prophet Mohammed at Mecca begins secretly to preach a new religion, to be called Islam. Now 40, the onetime camel driver, who at 25 married the 40-year-old widow Khadija, his employer, has become a merchant. Having meditated for years on the ignorance and superstition of his fellow Arabs, he feels called upon to teach the new faith, which will grow to embrace a major part of mankind in the millennium ahead (*see* Sharia, 629).

618 ─────────────────────────────

The Tang dynasty, which will rule China until 907, begins under the leadership of Li Yuan and his son Li Shih-min, who will reign from capitals at Luoyang and Chang-an, retaining most of the institutions established in the previous Sui dynasty but reaching out to trade with other countries, notably those in western Asia.

Northern Chinese eat mutton and drink goat's milk, both of which are scorned in southern China. Their staple food is millet porridge.

Starch from sago palms, grown in southeast China, will rival milled grain for use in making cakes during the Tang period and in some areas will be second only to rice.

The Chinese import a special variety of honey from the mountains of Tibet. They also sweeten some foods with maltose—a kind of malt sugar derived from germinating greens—and in this century the technique of boiling down the juice of sugarcane to make a granular substance called sand sugar will be more widely disseminated (*see* 640).

Carp and bream constitute a major part of Chinese diet, with some carp ranging in size up to eight feet long, and eel is widely used; southern coastal inhabitants eat char, mullet, sculpin, whitebait, crabs, oysters, and shrimp.

Yams will gain importance as a food crop under China's Tang emperors. Heretofore scorned as suitable only in times of famine, and eaten along with the roots of water chestnuts when other crops fail, yams will supplement taro root, which is used along with meat to make a broth; but the mass of people eat little in the way of animal flesh, that little being mostly chicken, duck, goose, pork, and wild game such as rabbit. Songbirds are eaten all year round.

Peaches are China's most important fruit; bananas, cherries, kumquats (*Fortunella* spp.), loquats, lichee fruit, thorny limes, various oranges, quinces, melons, persimmons, plums, crab apples, and thorn apples are also widely used. Almonds from Turkestan, pine nuts from Korea and the mountains of Shansi, pistachios from Persia, and walnuts are popular among the rich.

Kumyss, a fermented beverage made from mare's milk, is popular with the Chinese, who often make themselves drunk with it at feasts but will later come to regard it as a barbarian drink. More commonly consumed is ale, made from fermented millet.

621 ───────────

The Chinese establish an imperial bureau for the manufacture of porcelain. Their technology will advance further under the Tang dynasty (*see* 1708).

629 ───────────

The prophet Mohammed returns to Mecca with a holy book, the Koran, in which he has established the monotheistic tenets of Islam that will be followed by millions of Muslims (*see* Sharia, below).

Muslims (Mohammedans) will recognize the authority of the Sharia, a complex legal system much like that of the Jewish Talmud. It forbids the eating of pork and thus follows the Mosaic law of Deuteronomy in 621 B.C. but permits camel meat.

The Sharia prohibits consumption of alcohol, but Mohammed's followers circumvent his prohibition against wine by boiling it down to a concentrate and sweetening it with honey and spices; Mohammed himself drinks nabidth, a mildly alcoholic ferment of raisins or dates mixed with water and aged for 2 days in earthenware jugs (but not longer lest it become too strong).

640 ───────────

A Welsh army defeats a Saxon army in the British Isles, where the Roman Church has lost power and where anarchy reigns. The Welsh victory is credited partly to the fact that each Welsh soldier has affixed a leek to his helmet so that Welshmen will not accidentally kill Welshmen, and the leek will become the national emblem of Wales.

A Chinese mission sent by the Tang emperor Tai Zong studies Indian techniques of sugar manufacturing at Behar in the Ganges Valley dating to 100

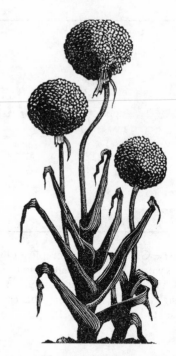

The leek became emblematic of Welsh nationalism after Welshmen wearing leeks defeated Saxons in battle.

B.C. (*see* 618). Extensive cultivation and manufacture of sugar in China will begin within a few years; a town at the junction of the Grand Canal and the Yangzi will become a center for sugar manufacturing (*see* 1280).

644 ───────────

Japan has a terrible famine, thousands die, and a new religion (*Tokoyonomushi*) springs up. Devotees worship a large worm, get drunk on sake, dance in the streets, and give away all their money.

645 ───────────

Japan begins a reformation of land laws. Roughly one-half acre of land is allotted to every male over age 6 (a female gets two-thirds that much, and a servant [*nuhi*] one-third), but the land must be cultivated in order to yield the wherewithal to pay taxes on it, taxes being paid in rice and other commodities (*see* 743).

(*see* 743)

675

∞ The Japanese emperor Tenchi imposes a Buddhist law that prohibits killing animals—cows, horses, wild pigs, and the like—for food, but few people observe the law (*see* 1123).

687

 The city of Venice elects its first doge and begins its rise as a major power in the Mediterranean. Built up from fishing villages settled by fugitives from the Huns, the city occupies some 60 marshy islands near the head of the Adriatic Sea, and its citizens have grown prosperous in the fish trade, in their salt monopoly, and by virtue of their central location.

8th Century

701

 Cold, dry weather in this century will contribute to famines in China, and the hunger will lead to revolts.

Arab and Persian mariners visit the Spice Islands (Moluccas) for the first time.

Arab merchants will introduce Oriental spices into Mediterranean markets in this century.

In this century the Arabs will lay waste the farmlands of Palestine, undoing the work of the Maccabees in the 2nd century B.C. and creating agricultural havoc that will not be repaired for 12 centuries.

702

Japan gets her first written law code. Among other things, it establishes regulations and gives instructions to aristocrats for production of dairy products, including cheese and yogurt, and preservation of foods, such as vinegar, which are used, along with rice, to pay taxes.

708

Tea drinking gains popularity among the Chinese, in part because a hot drink is far safer than water, which may be contaminated and may produce intestinal disease if not boiled. Tea (*cha* in Man-

Tea gained popularity in China partly because a hot drink was safer than cold water.

darin) is also valued for its alleged medicinal values (*see* 750; Japan, 805).

710

Sugar cane is planted in Egypt (*see* 300 B.C.; A.D. 711; 1279).

44

711

Some 12,000 Moors (Arabs and Berbers) from North Africa invade the Iberian Peninsula and defeat the Visigoth king Roderick, who dies fighting in July at the Battle of Wadi Bekka near Rio Barbate.

Moors invading the Iberian Peninsula (above) will introduce Asiatic methods of intensive irrigation in agriculture, the use of animals to fertilize fields with their droppings, improved plows, and technical improvements that will allow for alternating crops with more than one yield in good seasons.

The Arabs (above) will introduce rice, saffron, and sugar. They will also introduce barberry bushes (*Berberis vulgaris*), whose berries are used for a conserve and whose stems yield a juice valued for its alleged curative powers; but barberry bushes harbor black stem rust, which can be communicated to wheat crops under conditions of fog, dew, and warm rain.

716

The new king of Neustria, Chilperic II, authorizes delivery of a shipment of spices from Fos to the monastery of Corbie in Normandy. Included are one pound of cinnamon, two pounds of cloves, and 30 pounds of pepper.

729

Chinese eating sticks will be introduced in the next 20 years in Japan, where people heretofore have used one-piece pincers. Japanese *hashi* will be smaller than the Chinese sticks.

732

Pope Gregory II orders the Benedictine missionary Wynfrith Boniface, archbishop of Hesse, to forbid consumption of horseflesh by his Christian converts in order that they may be seen to differ from the surrounding Vandals, who eat horsemeat as part of their pagan rites.

743

Japan changes her laws to permit aristocrats and members of the clergy to cultivate land (*see* 645). The new farmland will be called *shoin*.

748

Ethelbert II of Kent sends a message to the Anglo-Saxon missionary Boniface in Germany requesting two well-trained goshawks "fit to hunt cranes," the goshawks of Kent being unsuited to the purpose. Boniface has earlier made a gift of two falcons and a goshawk to King Ethelbald of Mercia. Falconry is practiced not merely as a sport but also as a way to obtain food, and crane meat, although hard to digest unless allowed to decay for 2 or 3 days, is considered a delicacy.

750

Plague follows a famine in the Iberian Peninsula, taking a heavy toll.

The Chinese passion for tea drinking will reach its height in the next 50 years, being adopted even by Uighur tribesmen, who are gaining power and influence in the Middle Kingdom (*see* 708). Barge-loads of tea come up the Grand Canal to Luoyang from Chekiang. The cake tea and powdered tea is often flavored with ginger and tangerine peel.

754

The Chinese Buddhist priest Jian Zhen introduces sugar to Japan, but it is used only to mask the bad taste of foul-tasting medicinal herbs.

756

The Shosoin, built at Nara to house the belongings of the Japanese emperor Tenmu, will contain 10,000 items, including sun-dried fish, vegetables, fruit, roasted rice, and hoshii (rice that has been steamed and then dried to make it last). Jars containing dairy products will also be found in the Shosoin.

759

The Chinese general Kuo Tzu-i lays siege to the city of Yehching, creating such a shortage of food within its walls that rats sell at enormous prices.

761

A great Chinese famine in the Huai-Yangzi area late in the year drives men to cannibalism, according to some exaggerated accounts.

765

European writings make the first known mention of a three-field crop-rotation system, describing a northern system in which some spring plantings supplement the traditional winter plantings of the south. The system makes a given section of land productive 2 years out of 3, instead of every other year, as one field is sown with wheat or rye at the end of the year, a second is sown in the spring, and a third is left fallow. The second field is sown with barley, broad beans, chickpeas, lentils, oats, or peas—food with more protein value.

770

Horseshoes come into common use in Europe, making horses more efficient for pulling farm implements on stony ground (*see* 450).

780

The Frankish king Charles the Great (Charlemagne), 38, gives encouragement to the three-field system of crop rotation in his realms, which now include Lombardy, Venetia, Istria, Dalmatia, and Corsica (*see* 765).

795

Charlemagne bans the export of grain from his dominions in order to avoid food shortages.

800

An improved still is invented by the Arab scholar Jabir ibn Hayyan, but distillers are still able to do little more than separate liquids (like rosewater) from solids (*see* brandy, 1300).

9th Century

801

China will have fewer famines in this century as weather conditions improve, with fewer cold, dry summers but still not as many good crop years as in the Han period of 206 B.C. to A.D. 220.

Europe's famines will be less severe in this century than they have been in the past and will be in future, since almost everybody now lives on the land. Towns have practically disappeared, and since farm surpluses have no market, the farmers raise only enough for their own needs plus small quantities for barter.

Europe's peasantry is in effect enslaved to large landowners, who defend them in frequent wars, feed them in times of famine from stores held in reserve against such times, but generally exploit them.

Chinese aristocrats eat from translucent porcelain plates that Europe will not be able to duplicate for more than 900 years (*see* 621; 1708).

Chinese farmers in this century will begin using plows with concave-curved moldboards, but although such moldboards will not reach Europe until about 1700, Chinese agriculture will progress without the benefit of any modern technology until some mechanization is introduced early in the 20th century.

Agronomic science is now in a decline, despite the growing use of the three-field system (*see* 780), and while the Scandinavians will improve agriculture, which has been unprofitable since the 4th century, Europe will experience famines from now to the 12th century.

805

Tea (*ocha* in Japanese) is introduced to Japan as a medicine. The Buddhist bonze (priest) Saicho, 38, has spent 3 years visiting Chinese Buddhist temples on orders from the emperor, and he returns with tea, which has gained considerable prestige as a beverage in China during the Tang period but will play a much larger role in Japanese society (*see* 750; 1191).

806

Famine strikes Japan, where rice remains a staple food only for the rich (*see* 200 B.C.). It will not be consumed in any great quantity by the mass of Japanese for at least 800 years.

Southern Chinese in all walks of life rely on rice as their staple grain, but in the north of China, where rice cannot be grown, it is enjoyed only by the upper classes.

809

Famine sweeps the empire of Charlemagne as cold weather reduces harvests everywhere.

812

Charlemagne orders that anise, coriander, fennel, flax, fenugreek, sage, and other plants be planted on German imperial farms.

815

The bishop of Munich receives payment October 2 of overdue interest from one of his deacons, who delivers an oxcart containing a goose, a young wild boar, two chickens, some flour, and a good deal of beer. It is the first mention of beer at Munich, whose German name, *München*, comes from the word *Munichen*, meaning "at the monks."

827

Saracens from North Africa invade Sicily, beginning a 51-year war of conquest.

Spinach is introduced into Sicily by the Saracens, who found the plant originally in Persia.

833

A Chinese imperial order issued March 18 forbids drinking of wine on days of national mourning.

844

France's Charles the Bald, 21, decrees that a traveling bishop may requisition at each halt in his journey 50 loaves of bread, 50 eggs, 10 chickens, and 5 suckling pigs.

850

Coffee (*kahve*, or *kaffe*) is discovered, according to legend, by the Arab goatherd Kaidi in southern Ethiopia, who notices that his goats become frisky after chewing the berries from certain tall, tropical evergreen shrubs. The "berries" are beanlike seeds (*see* 1453).

857

The first recorded major outbreak of ergotism occurs in the Rhine Valley, where thousands die after eating bread made from rye infected with the ergot fungus parasite *Claviceps* (clubheaded) *purpura* (purple). The fungus contains several alkaloid drugs including ergotamine, which in baking is transformed into a hallucinogen (*see* 943 ff.).

869

Chinese rebels lay siege to Hao-chau, whose inhabitants grow so desperate for meat that by some exaggerated accounts they resort to slaughtering each other.

887

A prolonged siege of the Chinese city of Kuangling by Yang Hsing-mi creates such a shortage of food that the inhabitants eat cakes of mud flavored with whatever weeds can be found.

10th Century

Europe will suffer 20 severe famines in this century, some of them lasting for 3 to 4 years. An alimentary crisis will occur every few years for the next 3 centuries, in fact, and as populations grow and become more urbanized, the famines will strike more cruelly, although they may be fewer in number than in some earlier centuries.

The work collar, or broad-breast collar, for draft animals will come into general use in this century, allowing a horse to draw from its shoulders without pressing upon its windpipe and quadrupling a horse's efficiency as compared with horsepower derived from animals harnessed with neck yokes of the kind employed on oxen.

Horses will come into wider use in those parts of Europe where the three-field system produces grain surpluses for feed, but hay-fed oxen will be more economical, if less efficient, in terms of time and labor and will remain almost the sole source of animal power in southern Europe, where most farmers will continue to use the two-field system.

England receives her first shipments of East Indian spices, used chiefly for their alleged medical benefits.

China's Tang dynasty ends after nearly 300 years that many will recall as a golden age despite many famine years. More people have settled in southeastern parts of China, which have been Chinese territory off and on since the Shin dynasty of 265 to 420. The country enters a 53-year period in which rival warlords vie for control of the country (*see* 960).

Trade with China's neighbors in southern Asia has developed gradually during the Tang period, and black pepper has come into use among the rich, replacing the peppery seeds of plants called *fagara*. Coriander has been introduced from the Mediterranean, dill from Sumatra, saffron from Kashmir and other parts of India.

A Chinese government monopoly controls the salt trade. Salt is produced from seawater that is allowed to flood fields and evaporate, leaving crystals that are scraped off the soil and then boiled down to purify them. Ashes are spread on the fields before they are flooded.

New milling methods for wheat, introduced from the West during the Tang period, permit production of flour for dumplings, fried doughs, strips, noodles, pastries, and cakes. Horizontal millstones do the work, but the extraction rate is 80 percent or less, and flour spoils quickly, there being no way to remove the wheat germ, and wheat is still considered something of a luxury.

The Tang court has brought ice down from the high mountains in winter and early spring and kept it in pits for refrigeration of vegetables and fruits, especially melons; the practice has also been followed by aristocrats and rich merchants.

White mustard seeds, originally from the West, have been grown in northern China beginning in the Tang period. Cinnamon has come from the forests of southern Hunan and Lingnan, the best coming from the scrapings of young branches; sweet basil has come from southern Hunan.

Tofu (or toufu)—a curd made from various kinds of beans and peas—has come into use during the Tang period. Produced by adding sea salt to bean milk, originally to preserve it but then as a coagulant, it will become a Chinese dietary staple (*see* Japan, 1212). Other articles of diet include pickled deer, rabbit, goat, and sheep meat; pickled fish; rice cakes; fried and steamed breads, some containing sesame seeds, which have been introduced from the West and are sold on city street corners by Persian vendors.

The Tang emperors have followed the practice of the preceding Sui dynasty in allocating farmland to people according to their capacity to till it (*see* 581). A male head of household has theoretically received 100 mu (about six acres), of which 80 was to worked in his active lifetime, 20 was tree-crop land that could be passed on to his children, but the difficulty of finding honest administrators to enforce the system has enabled unscrupulous farmers to subvert the system with false registrations. The experiment in government land management has failed and will not be revived.

Farmland has been readily available during the Tang period in southern China, where slash-and-burn methods have been used to clear and cultivate.

Millet has been China's staple grain during the Tang period, with wheat production increasing in the north (often in rotation with millet) and rice popular in the rapidly growing southern region, where double-cropping has become common practice. Spinach, sugar beet, almonds, and figs have become more widely known.

The Chinese salt produced by flooding fields with seawater (above) contains copper, iodine, magnesium, manganese, potassium, and other minerals present in seawater and plant ash, helping people maintain proper sodium-potassium balance; salt produced from wells in western China is relatively poor in such trace minerals.

The Chinese ferment wine from millet and glutinous rice.

915

Famine strikes the Iberian Peninsula, possibly as a result of a wheat crop failure due to rust.

919

Famine returns to the Iberian Peninsula, which is ruled in the south by the Amayyad caliph Abd ar-Rahman III and in the Christian north by princes who are establishing the beginnings of León, Castile, and Navarre.

927

Famine devastates the Byzantine Empire. Constantinople's Constantine VII and his co-emperor father-in-law, Romanus Lecapenus, push through stringent laws to prevent great landed magnates from buying up the small holdings of poor farmers.

930

Nonfiction: The 50-volume *Engishiki*, translated from the Chinese after 22 years of work, is a Japanese book of ceremonial etiquette that includes, among other things, instructions in cooking and details on how to cook and preserve various foods. It specifies which district produces which specialties (e.g., pickles or preserved meat, used for paying tribute to the emperor).

943

Ergotism strikes Limoges in France, killing an estimated 40,000 people who have eaten bread made from rye infected with the *Claviceps* fungus (*see* 857). The victims suffer symptoms resembling madness and have no idea what is wrong (the word "ergot" will not be introduced until 1683) (*see* 1039).

945

Kyoto is invaded by several thousand farmers, who demonstrate against requisition of their rice and other crops by tax collectors.

960

The Sung dynasty, which will rule China until 1279 (it will be called the Northern Sung until 1117), begins as Sung Tai-zu begins to weaken the power of local landlords and restore unity to the country, which will be modernized in many ways during this dynasty, but loss of millet- and wheat-growing territories in the North will lead to increasing dependence on rice (*see* 1127).

Famines will be rare and localized events during China's Sung period and will usually be related to breakdowns in distribution systems, as new strains of rice, developed by selective breeding, and agricultural improvements enable farmers to produce food in greater amounts and varieties.

A centralized system of Chinese tax collection in the Sung period will rotate officials to minimize corruption and make provincial governors directly answerable to the state.

A Chinese cuisine unparalleled in the world will develop during the Sung period. Food in the Tang period was relatively simple, but regional specialties will gain prominence under the Sung as a middle class emerges, and items such as tea, once reserved for the few, will come into more general use.

961

Arabs on the Iberian Peninsula cultivate the autumn crocus (*Crocus sativa*) for the production of *za'faran* (saffron), using 75,000 blossoms (or 250,000 dried stigmas of blossoms) to make one pound of the valuable yellow spice that is used in recipes for the costliest dishes. The provinces of Alicante, Castellón de la Pana, and Valencia all produce saffron, much of it for export.

973

Cloves, ginger, pepper, and other Eastern spices are available for purchase in the marketplace at Mainz, reports the Moorish physician-merchant lbrahim ibn Yaacub, who has visited that city. The spices have been brought to Mainz by Jewish traveling merchants known as "Radanites" who have kept some international trade channels open in the three centuries of conflict between the Christian and Islamic worlds. In addition to spices, the Radanites have traded in numerous other commodities, transporting furs, woolen cloth, Frankish swords, eunuchs, and white female slaves to the Orient, while returning to Christian Europe with musk, pearls, precious stones, aloes, and spices that include cinnamon.

983

The Japanese poet-scholar Shitagou Minamoto dies at age 72, leaving his book *Wameiruishusho*, an encyclopedia whose listings include many food descriptions (24 kinds of grains, 35 kinds of fruits and nuts, 68 kinds of vegetables). Anyone who has eaten meat in Minamoto's lifetime has been barred entry to the Imperial Palace at Kyoto.

984

Nonfiction: *Ishinho* by the Japanese physician Yasuyori Tamba is a book about food and health giving advice about what foods to eat for good health and what foods should not be eaten together; he cites taboos against eating certain foods.

992

Venice is granted extensive trade privileges in the Byzantine Empire.

998

China's Sung emperor Chin Zong begins a 24-year reign in which he will concern himself deeply with agricultural affairs.

The imperial finances of Chin Zong (above) depend on taxes collected from rice farmers, so he will order distribution of new high-yielding rice varieties (*see* 1011).

Chinese farmers employ new knowledge of fertilizers (making more extensive use of river mud, manure, and lime) and new tools to cultivate their fields more effectively; irrigation networks and new seed strains enable them to resist droughts and increase their yields, sometimes with two crops per year.

1000

The Pillow-Book of Sei Shonagon will be compiled in the next 15 years by a lady-in-waiting to the late Japanese empress Sadako. Sei Shonagon, 37, will write of "chips of ice mixed with fruit juice and served in a new silver bowl."

The word "bannock" (initially spelled "bannuck") is mentioned for the first time to mean a thick oaten (or, sometimes, peasemeal) cake kneaded into water and formed into a flat round or oval shape, baked in the embers of a fire, and tossed over again on a griddle before eating.

"Grapes" found growing by Norseman Leif Ericsson in what will later be called either Newfoundland or Nova Scotia are either mountain cranberries, wild currants, or gooseberries, and his wild "wheat" is Lyme grass (*Elymus arenarius, var. villosus*), a tall wild grass with a wheatlike head whose seeds are used to make flour for bread in Iceland.

11th Century

1001

Food will become more abundant as a result of agricultural improvements in this century, but France will nevertheless have 26 famines and England will average one famine every 14 years.

Iron plows with wheels will replace wooden plows in much of northern Europe in this century.

1006

China's Sung emperor Chin Zong establishes granaries for emergency famine relief in every prefecture.

1011

China's Sung emperor Chin Zong imports rice varieties from Champa (Vietnam) that are highly resistant to drought, mature early (some Champa rice can be reaped in just 80 days, some in 120), can grow in higher elevations where other rice cannot be grown, make double-cropping feasible in some localities, and are cheap enough for the common people of China's cities. The new rice is distributed to peasants and will be widely planted by next year, but Yangzi Delta farmers prefer slow-maturing varieties with moderate gluten content, partly because of their better taste and keeping qualities, partly because they are more attractive to tax collectors, but they are too costly for any but rich families (who will scorn Champa rice as food for the poor and make polished white rice the standard of

good food). Intensively cultivated, rice will soon be growing in a vast number of varieties (more than any other grain)—early maturing, late maturing, drought resistant, flood resistant, hard, soft, yellow, pink, sticky (from the starch amylose), and nonsticky.

1022

China's Sung emperor Chin Zong dies after a 24-year reign in which he has imported not only drought-resistant Champa rice but also green lentils (a variety of mung bean) from India, which are well known for their heavy yields and large seeds.

1027

Southeastern China has famine following a drought that reduces the rice harvest in Fukien province despite planting of drought-resistant Champa varieties (see 1011).

1039

Ergotism breaks out in parts of France (see 943; 1089).

1040

Increased planting of oats in the three-crop system of the past 3 centuries has led to an expanded use of horses in Europe and thus to increased trade, larger towns, and more people who do not raise their own food.

 The Webenstepan brewery is founded at Freising, near Munich.

1060

West Africa is conquered from the kingdom of Ghana by Arabs, who are supported by Berbers greedy for the salt mines of Ankar. Founded in the 4th century, the kingdom of Ghana has ruled from near the Atlantic Coast almost to Timbuktu.

1061

A Chinese herbal describes hundreds of foods and sets new standards for botanical illustration.

1064

"Regulative granaries" established by China's Sung emperor Ying Zong buy up surplus grain in good harvests and release stocks in times of shortage (*see* 1069).

1066

The Battle of Hastings October 14 seals the Norman conquest of England by Norsemen under William, 39, duke of Normandy, who will be called William the Conqueror (*see The Domesday Book*, 1086).

English estates are distributed among William's allies—Norman barons, who receive 49 percent of the land; bishops and abbots, who receive 26 percent.

The French words *bœuf*, *mouton*, *veau*, *porc*, and *poularde*, introduced by the Normans (above), will be the basis of the English words "beef," "mutton," "veal," "pork," and "poultry."

1068

A new Chinese Sung emperor takes office, makes Wang An-shih, 47, his prime minister, and embarks on a series of reforms (*see* 1069).

1069

The Chinese prime minister Wang An-shih begins a radical program to reform Chinese agriculture after finding the nation's granaries stocked with emergency stocks of relief grain valued at 15 million strings of cash (*see* 1064). He offers peasant farmers loans at 2 percent interest per month in cash or grain to free them from usurers and monopolists who charge higher rates, and he revives the "ever-normal granary" system, giving his chief transport officer power to sell from state granaries when prices are high and buy when prices are low. But peasants will actually wind up paying up to 40 percent interest on loans (still far below rates available elsewhere in the countryside), land will be taxed according to its potential even in the absence of good data on such potential, and Wang An-shih's policies will alienate most Chinese.

Wang An-shih (above) will support land reclamation and water conservancy.

1070

Roquefort cheese is discovered in France by some accounts, although by others it is said to have been enjoyed more than 2 centuries ago by the emperor Charlemagne, who ate it in the company of the monks of Saint-Gall. He was told not to remove the green mold, liked the taste, and ordered that two cases of it be sent to him each year (he also enjoyed Brie).

1071

A two-pronged fork is introduced to Venice by a Greek princess who marries the doge. Rich Venetians adopt the new fashion, which has long been customary in the eastern Mediterranean and has come westward via Constantinople (*see* 1518; 1570).

1086

$ *The Domesday Book*, compiled on orders of England's William I, lists the properties and assets of landowners to provide a basis for taxation and administration (*see* 1066). Some 110,000 villeins and more than 25,000 serfs are listed, with the villeins holding 45 percent of the land, *liberi homines* (free men) 20 percent, *bordarii* (cottagers or small householders) 5 percent, and serfs no land at all although they constitute 10 percent of the population (villeins constitute 41 percent, *bordarii* 32 percent, *liberi homines* 14 percent). The royal commissioners oblige the landowners to give information under oath as to the size of every piece of land, its resources, and its ownership—past and present.

The *Domesday Book* (above) lists nearly 6,000 English water mills—one for every 400 inhabitants—grinding grain to produce flour for 3,000 communities south of the Severn and Trent rivers.

1089

Ergotism strikes a French village, whose inhabitants run through the streets in fits of madness (*see* 1039; 1581).

1099

Knights of the First Crusade plant fields of sugarcane in the Holy Land (*see* 300 B.C.; A.D. 1148).

12th Century

1104

Sugar serves as an emergency ration for soldiers of the First Crusade laying siege to Acre.

1110

Les Halles has its beginnings as France's 29-year-old Louis VI (who will be known as Louis the Fat) authorizes some peasant women to set up fish stalls outside his palace wall at Paris. The fish markets will thrive, other vendors will buy space from the Crown, and by 1137 Les Halles will have become the world's largest food market, sprawling over more than 21 acres (*see* 1866).

1117

Chinese rebels capture the Northern Sung emperor, whose dynasty has ruled since 960. The regime will reconstitute itself at Hangchow beginning in 1120, paying huge tributes to the new rulers in the North (*see* 1234).

1123

London's Smithfield meat market has its origin in a priory founded beside the "Smooth" field just outside the city's walls. The field will soon be the scene of St. Bartholomew's Fair, where drapers and clothiers will exchange goods and where a weekly horse market will be held (*see* 1639).

Japan's ex-emperor Shirakawa imposes a strict Buddhist law against killing any living thing (including fish, poultry, livestock, game, and game birds) (*see* 675). The Japanese have been more influenced by Buddhism than the Chinese, take its vegetarian principles more seriously, and have completely given up eating beef (*see* 1126).

1126

Japanese fishing nets are collected by order of the ex-emperor Shirakawa and burned in front of the imperial palace to ensure compliance with Buddhist law. Cormorants (used for fishing), hunting dogs, and falcons are ordered to be released (*see* 1123; 1129).

1128

Cistercian monks from Normandy settle in England and begin an extensive program of swamp reclamation, agricultural improvement, and stock breeding (*see* 1098). The Cistercians live austerely, depend for their income entirely on the land, and will have a salutary effect in improving English and European horse and cattle breeds and raising the standards of agriculture.

1129

A Japanese fisherman caught violating the Buddhist law of the ex-emperor Shirakawa is dragged before Shirakawa in punishment (*see* 1126). Shirakawa dies a few months later (July 7) at age 76 (*see* 1687).

1137

✘ France's Louis VI (the Fat) dies August 1 at age 56. He has established Les Halles (*see* 1110), which will be the central food market of Paris (and of France) until 1969.

1148

⏱ Knights and soldiers returning from the Second Crusade bring back sugar from the Middle East (*see* 1104). Still virtually unknown in Europe, even in the greatest castles, the sweetener will soon be prized above honey (*see* 1226).

1154

✘ England's king Stephen dies October 25 at age 54 and is succeeded by his adopted son Henry Plantagenet, who is crowned at age 21 and will reign until 1189 as Henry II, inaugurating a Plantagenet dynasty that will rule England until 1399.

🥛 England's domestic wine industry begins to decline as cheap French wines are introduced by Eleanor of Aquitaine, wife of the new king Henry II (above). The English call the red wine of Bordeaux "claret," a word that may stem from the Languedoc term *clairet*, meaning a very light red wine. Eleanor's native Bordeaux will be under English rule for the next 3 centuries (*see* 1453; Black Death, 1349).

1157

🍴 Ye Olde Bell opens at Hartley, outside London. The public house (pub) will survive for more than 800 years.

1163

∞ The Mosaic law of 621 against mixing meat and dairy products ("You shall not boil a kid in its

mother's milk") will be ascribed by the Spanish physician Moses ben Maimon (Maimonides), now 28, to an aversion by ancient Jews to a fertility ritual practiced by pagan cults in Canaan.

1176

🐖 English farmers introduce domestic rabbits from the Continent to provide a new source of protein (*see* cookbook, 1390). Some rabbits will, inevitably, escape captivity and run wild.

1182

⚡ England's port of Bristol sends wooden vessels "built shipshape and Bristol fashion" out to Spain (Jerez) for sherry, Portugal (Oporto) for port wine, Iceland for stockfish (dried cod), and Bordeaux and Bayonne in Gascony for woad from the plant *Isatis tinctoria* to make blue dye for Bristol's woolens.

1189

🍴 The Trip to Jerusalem is founded at Nottingham as a way station for Crusaders en route to the Holy Land. The English pub will survive for some 800 years.

1191

✘ England's Richard I (the Lion-hearted), 24, embarks on a Third Crusade, gains a brilliant victory over the Saracen leader Saladin at Arsuf, and leads the Christian host to within a few miles of Jerusalem. As a peace offering, Saladin presents his captor with charbet, made from snow obtained in the mountains of Lebanon; the fruit-flavored dish will make its way to Italy, where it will be known as *sorbetto*, and to France, where it will be called *sorbet*.

Zen Buddhism is introduced to Japan by the priest Aeisai, 50, who returns from a visit to China. His book *Kissayojoki*, which will be published in 1214, will make extravagant medicinal claims for tea, calling it a panacea (*see* 805; 1597; tea ceremony, 1449; 1591).

Zen Buddhists (above) have adopted strict vegetarianism, which will become popular in Japan with the spread of Zen Buddhism, especially in the *samurai* (warrior) class and, later, among the working classes.

The Chinese, although generally less observant than the Japanese of Buddhist dietary laws, do not eat beef without at least some sense of shame. They eat chicken and, sometimes, other poultry, but only on special occasions, and they consider raw fish a great luxury, prizing even salt fish above chicken and raising fish as an industry. Even the Mongols and other northern peoples eat relatively little meat, their horses being too valuable for transportation and power, their rams for breeding purposes, and their ewes as sources of dairy products, most of them soured or fermented—yogurt, sour cream cheese, and kumyss—which to southern Chinese are considered barbarian foods of the enemy. Except for marmots, birds, and other wild game, meat is consumed by the "barbarians" only on special occasions, or when herds are culled.

Aeisai (above) plants tea seeds in Japan, where tea bushes will be grown widely on the hillsides of Honshu.

1192

The Japanese daimyo Yoritomo Minamoto wins an imperial appointment as shōgun and establishes his seat of government at Kamakura as he continues his efforts to crush the Fujiwara clan in the north.

Minamoto's soldiers eat three times a day, and when hostilities end the Japanese will follow this practice, instead of eating only twice a day as in the past. The Kamakura court will follow traditional, ceremonial dietary codes based on rice, vegetables, and preserved fish, but the *samurai* (warrior) class will have a freer style of eating habits based more on game.

Hochoshi (cutting specialists) will arise during the Kamakura period; each group will have its own stylized secrets of cutting fish, meat, and vegetables, handed down by word of mouth from one generation to the next. Ceremonial cutting will become a spectacle for the nobility.

The Kamakura government (above) will encourage irrigation and cultivation of winter wheat to supplement rice and millet crops. Use of horses and oxen for cultivation will increase in the Kamakura period.

1194

Norsemen discover Spitzbergen, far to the north of the Arctic Circle. The island will later be an important fishery and whaling center (*see* 1557).

China's Huanghe (Yellow) River begins flowing southward from the Shandong massif after repeated alterations of its streambed. Taming the Huanghe will be the great engineering achievement of the Mongols, whose power is growing in northern China (*see* 1234). The river will retain its new course until 1853.

1200

Bock beer (or *bockbier*) is invented in the German town of Einbeck (year approximate). The dark beer is higher in extracts than other lager beer (*bock* is German for male goat).

13th Century

1202

England enacts her first laws to regulate the price of bread and limit the amount of profit a baker may earn (*see* 1266).

1203

Famine ravages England and Ireland as it will repeatedly throughout this century. Recurrent crop

Good crops brought joy to Europe's peasantry, for all too often there was famine.

failures will bring hardship to the British Isles, the German states, and Poland, but cheap grain from the Balkans will lower food prices in much of the Continent.

Livestock breeding and viniculture increase in parts of France and the Lowlands as cheap grain from the new granary in the Baltic Sea region makes it less profitable to grow wheat, rye, barley, and oats.

A large brewing industry develops at Hamburg and in the Lowlands as barley malt from the Baltic becomes more readily available at lower prices.

1204

Knights and soldiers returning from the Fourth Crusade plant Damson plum trees from Damascus in France and will hasten the spread to Europe of such Arabic food products as rice, sugar, and lemons.

1212

Tofu (soybean curd) is introduced to Japan from China, where it has been eaten for more than 2,000 years (*see* 907) and become popular with Buddhists as a substitute for meat and dairy products. The Chinese in the Sung period have also developed soy sauce, which adds flavor to the rice, oil, salt, vinegar, and tea that are dietary staples of the poor.

1216

Genghis Khan invades the Near East; his 60,000 Mongol horsemen ravage ancient centers of civilization, ruin irrigation works, and destroy every living thing in their path.

1217

✗ Vienna's bakers pay homage to Duke Leopold VI, who is about to leave on a Fifth Crusade against the Moors in Egypt and the Holy Land. They offer him rolls baked in the shape of crescents (*see* 340 B.C.; 1683).

1226

✴ Lübeck receives an imperial charter from the Holy Roman Emperor Frederick II, whereupon a caravan of wagons leaves town for France and the Rhineland to buy wine.

🜹 England's Henry III, now 19, asks the mayor of Winchester to obtain three pounds of sugar, a quantity considered enormous. Sugar is imported from the Middle East, processed in the form of cones called "loaves," and treated as a spice (*see* 1319).

🍷 Lübeck's city fathers have wine from France and the Rhineland (above) delivered to the deep cellars under the Rathaus. Czars and the Russian nobility will stock their cellars with wines from Lübeck, and French wines will come to be known as *Rotsbon*.

1227

✗ The Mongol leader Genghis Khan dies August 18 at age 65, leaving a vast empire that is divided among his three sons (*see* 1234).

1231

 Japan has a famine in the spring that will be followed by many similar famines in this century.

✊ The Japanese shōgun orders his people not to sell their children into slavery, but poor farmers will continue for centuries to sell daughters in order to avoid losing their farms and, with them, the means of keeping other members of the family alive.

1234

✗ Mongol forces capture a key town in northern China and next year will annex what remains of the Qin empire in that region. They exact large tributes from the Sung government at Hangchow (*see* 1117; 1271).

1235

♟ The Statute of Merton entitles an English lord to appropriate all of the commons as long as he leaves enough grazing for any freeholders who pasture their livestock there (*see* enclosure, 1351).

1237

🐟 An English ship founders off the French coast at a point near what will later be called Dinard. The captain reaches shore and supports himself by fishing and snaring the birds that fly low across the shore; in the evening, at low tide, he attaches his bird net to tall stakes set in the sand, and in the morning he finds that hundreds of young mussels, carried in by the sea, have attached themselves to his poles. The mussels grow to prodigious sizes and will be the basis of an industry.

1241

✗ The Hanseatic League begins in Germany.

1243

♟ Famine sweeps the German states, whose towns are infested, like most in Europe, by black rats that have come westward with the Mongols (*see* Black Death, 1333).

1250

✗ The Battle of Fariskur April 6 ends in victory for Egyptian forces, who rout the scurvy-ridden Seventh Crusaders of France's Louis IX and massacre most of them.

Cardamom, cinnamon, cloves, coriander, cumin, cubebs, ginger, mace, nutmeg, and saffron carried back by returning Crusaders are now to be found in rich English and European houses, are more widely used than pepper, but are in many cases valued more for supposed medicinal value than for culinary purposes.

Historian Jean, Sire de Joinville, 26, returns to France with Louis IX and will later write about the scurvy (above), "There came upon us the sickness of the host, which sickness was such that the flesh of our legs dried up, and the skin upon our legs became spotted; black and earth color like an old boot; and with us who had this sickness, the flesh of our gums putrefied; nor could anyone escape from this sickness but had to die. The sign of death was this, that when there was bleeding of the nose, then death was sure. . . . The sickness began to increase in the host in such sort and the dead flesh to grow upon the gums of our people, that the barber surgeons had to remove the dead flesh in order that the people might masticate their food and swallow it" (see da Gama, 1499; Magellan, 1522; Cartier, 1535; Hawkins, 1593; Lancaster, 1601; *Mayflower*, 1620; Anson, 1741, 1744; Lind, 1747).

1251

Shepherds and farmworkers in northern France abandon flocks and fields in a widespread insurrection. The rebels assemble at Amiens and then at Paris, they spread out to England, and the revolt spreads as far as Syria with bloody demonstrations and riots that meet with ruthless suppression.

1252

Sake (rice wine) production is halted by the Japanese shōgun to conserve rice.

1253

Franciscan friar Guillaume de Roubrock arrives at Karakorum on a mission from France's Louis IX and finds a silver fountain built for the Mongol prince Mangu Khan by Frankish goldsmith Guil-

laume Boucher. The fountain's four spouts dispense wine, mead, rice wine, and kumyss (mead and kumyss are alcoholic beverages made, respectively, from honey and mare's milk).

1258

Famine and disease follow crop failures in the German and Italian states.

1265

London's Covent Garden market has its beginnings in a fruit and vegetable stand set up on the north side of the highway between London and Westminster by monks of St. Peter's Abbey. They begin to sell surpluses from their garden that exceed the requirements of their Westminster Abbey (see 1552).

1266

England's Assize of Bread is an outgrowth of the 1202 laws and will remain in effect until 1815, although it will be difficult to enforce in small rural markets. Many bakers have been prosecuted for selling loaves that did not conform to the weights required by local laws, which they consider oppressive and unfair. The Assize relates the prices of a loaf of bread by royal order to the current price of

English lawmakers tried to regulate the prices that bakers could charge for their bread.

wheat and the grade of flour used, drastically limiting bakers' profits. If a penny loaf made from finely bolted white flour weighs two pounds, a "wheaten" loaf made from more coarsely bolted flour will be three pounds—half again as heavy, and a penny loaf of household bread made from unbolted flour "as it cometh from the mill" will be heavier still (*see* 1329). A baker buys his own wheat direct from a farmer, pays a miller to grind it, and bolts it himself, keeping the bran to sell for livestock or poultry feed. Bakers are ordered to mark each loaf of bread so that if a faulty one turns up "it will be knowne in whom the faulte lies." The bakers' marks will be among the first trademarks.

1271

✖ Kublai Khan, 55, a grandson of the late Genghis Khan, assumes the dynastic title that he will hold until his death in 1294 and founds the Mongol (Yuan) dynasty, which will rule China until 1368. The Sung emperors have lost control of northern and western China. Kublai had himself elected khan by his army in 1260 and will reign until his death in 1294.

Mutton will become a staple of China's imperial menu during the Yuan period (above), with four or five sheep slaughtered daily for the khan's table and huge vats for boiling whole sheep installed in the imperial kitchens. Cooking with lamb and kid will become more widespread among some people in all Chinese social classes, lamb's head and steamed kid being among the more popular dishes. Shops that specialize in selling roast lamb will proliferate in Chinese cities, but traditional Chinese will continue to scorn the meat of their "barbarian" invaders, who will not adopt Persian or Chinese delicacies, preferring their own simple, coarse fare of boiled mutton.

Leeks, wild onions, apples, melons, mulberries, and jujubes have become major components of the Chinese diet for those who can afford them.

1274

✖ China's Kublai Khan tries unsuccessfully to invade Japan. A typhoon November 20 sinks more than 200 Mongol ships, along with 13,000 men sleeping aboard, and the survivors flee back to the mainland in terror.

The Japanese continue their relatively peaceful lives, shopping at the markets of Edo, Kyoto, and Nara for kamaboko (a paste of small whitefish sometimes added to soups and other dishes), asuki sausage, aubergines, daikon (large radishes), kobo (burdock), persimmons in many varieties, mushrooms, lily bulbs, chestnuts and other nuts, fruits such as kumquats, bitter oranges, peaches, plums, pomegranates, and strawberries, and a sweet red bean paste served as a confection.

The Venetian traveler Marco Polo, 30, visits Yunnan and sees the "Tartars" eating raw beef, mutton, buffalo, poultry, and other flesh chopped and seasoned with garlic (which Buddhists avoid, along with onions and meat). Polo will enter the service of Kublai Khan next year and continue until 1292 (*see* 1280).

1279

✖ The Sung dynasty, which has ruled China since 960, ends with the destruction of a fleet carrying the last young Sung pretender. His predecessors, while losing control over vast territories in the north and west, have increased trade dramatically along the Yangzi and in coastal regions of the China Sea. The Mongol (Yuan) dynasty, founded in 1271, is left in full control of all China.

💲 The average Chinese family controls about 100 mu (now about seven acres) of land, but about 60 percent of the peasantry consists of small, independent freeholders, and most independent peasant families have only about 20 mu; large estates control much of the empire, especially in the most developed areas of the lower Yangzi delta, where the land is richest, markets closest, and land values highest. Large landlords find ways to avoid taxation (perhaps 70 percent of the land is tax exempt), obliging small landholders to shoulder most of the tax burden and driving them to become tenant farmers.

China's Mongol (Yuan) emperors will continue the policy begun in the Tang period of collecting taxes twice per year, keeping taxes relatively low, and retaining the government monopoly on salt.

The Chinese government has carefully controlled and supervised tea production during the Sung period and profited by controlling trade in that commodity.

Chinese during the Sung period have moved from sitting on the floor when they eat to sitting on chairs and eating from tables, but some people continue to sit on the floor at meals. The rich eat from porcelain dishes, with several being used for each diner. Spoons and eating sticks are the universal utensils.

Rice has become the staple food of China in the Sung period, accounting for 70 percent of the grain consumed versus 30 percent for wheat and millet (which are grown and consumed, along with sorghum, mostly in northern territories beyond Sung control). People in central and south China eat their rice steamed, boiled, or cooked in a gruel; those in the North eat wheat or millet flour made into noodles, steamed or baked breads, and whole-grain millet cooked into pastes or gruels. The very poor eat coarse grains, chaff, oilseed hulls, and beans of various kinds. Unlike Europeans, who eat cabbage and tubers, and store apples and pears in root cellars, the Chinese in all classes of society eat fresh fruits and vegetables in great variety, having found varieties that resist cold weather and perfected ways of growing fresh vegetables through the winter even in northern climes, protecting their intensive truck gardens from frost. Not even rich Europeans eat as well in this respect as the great mass of Chinese.

Pork is China's chief meat, but fish, lamb, and kid are also eaten by rich and poor alike (the same word is used for lamb, kid, and mutton); the rich enjoy better cuts, and their meat dishes also include horsemeat, beef, rabbit, venison (which may sometimes actually be donkey meat), chicken, duck, goose, pheasant, quail, and various other wild birds, sometimes owl and magpie. Camel hump is considered a delicacy, served only at the imperial table, but strict Buddhists avoid beef (which is losing popularity as Indian religious influence grows), and many Chinese find beef and mutton abhorrently malodorous.

Sushi, made with rice, vinegar, oil, and any meat or raw fish available, has become popular in China during the Sung period but will become better known as a Japanese specialty.

The inventory of the estate of a Genoese soldier lists a basket of macaronis (dried pasta; some historians will suggest that the word is derived from the Greek *makar*, meaning "blessed," as in sacramental food). While the Chinese have been eating noodles since at least 1100 B.C., lasagna (Marco Polo's term for noodles) has probably been used by the Italians only since the last century, mostly as an extender for soups and, sometimes, desserts; it is considered a luxury food and will remain so for more than a century (*see* 1400).

Chinese sugarcane has become an important cash crop in parts of Sichuan and Fukien during the Sung period, replacing staple grain crops.

1280

Marco Polo visits Hangchow and is awed by the countless ships bringing spices from the Indies and embarking with silks for the Levant. He will write that the city has 10 main open spaces plus many smaller ones (Chinese writings will say 414) where foodstuffs and other goods are sold. On the 3 or 4 days each week when a square is open for business, some 30,000 to 40,000 people will come to buy such foods as "roebuck, francolins [partridges], quails, fowls, capons, and so many ducks and geese that more could not be told; for they rear so many of them at [West] Lake (which borders the city), that for one Venetian groat may be had a pair of geese and two pair of ducks." He will also mention red deer, fallow deer, hares, and rabbits.

Marco Polo (above) will describe vegetables and fruits, including giant white pears "which weigh 10 pounds apiece." Oranges and mandarin oranges are sold in a special area behind the market street, and there are also apricots from Sichuan, grapes, and other fruit. The grain market is outside the north gate, there are two markets for pork, markets for vegetables, markets for meat other than pork (including beef, horse, donkey, venison, rabbit, and fowl), and markets for fish (fresh and preserved), and crabs.

Marco Polo traveled from Venice to the Chinese court of Kublai Khan, marveling at the cuisine.

Marco Polo (above) will describe the endless-chain foot-powered water pump used to irrigate Chinese farmland. This and other inventions are revolutionizing Chinese agriculture.

The Chinese at Hangchow (above) enjoy leafy and green vegetables and a great variety of buns—steamed, deep fried, and often filled—which are sold by street vendors and served at restaurants (below). Honeyed fruit and dried bananas are also sold.

Kublai Khan calls in Egyptian experts to improve Chinese techniques of refining sugar (*see* 440). A refined white sugar known as "sugar frost" has been made in Sichuan since late in the Tang dynasty, but the Egyptians have acquired a reputation for making exceptionally white sugar.

Peter the Great of Aragon, 44, declares that his court must always include an apothecary whose chief job will be to make candied fruits, nuts, and seeds called "comfits."

Marco Polo (above) will describe the enormous piles of fresh fish available in Hangchow's markets, saying, "There comes every day, brought from the Ocean sea up the river for the space of 25 miles, a great quantity of fish, and there is also a supply from that lake (where there are always fishermen who do nothing else), which is of different sorts according to the seasons of the year, and because of the impurities which come from the city it is fat and savory. . . . So great is the quantity of said fish one would never think it could be sold, and yet, in a few hours, it has all been taken away, so great is the multitude of inhabitants who are used to live delicately; for they eat both fish and flesh at the same meal." Conchs, crabs, scallops, sea snails, shark fins, and shrimp are all sold in the marketplace.

Hangchow (above) has restaurants that specialize in particular foods—blood soup, perhaps, or dishes made of heart, kidney, and lungs—and particular cooking styles. There are noodle shops (some serving noodles with vegetables or with meat), fish houses, restaurants serving vegetarian "temple" food prepared in the style of Buddhist temples, places specializing in iced foods. The restaurants have menus, and waiters carry orders in their heads, repeating them when they get to the kitchen and remembering who ordered what with absolute precision (mistakes are severely punished). Many restaurants have adjoining quarters for prostitutes, and patrons sometimes stay for 2 days. There are wine halls two and three stories high, and tea and wine kitchens that provide everything needed for a banquet, reserving the hall and arranging for the food, drink, dishes, utensils, napery, and guests' transportation, even giving the host advice on proper etiquette for his affair. Even inns and wayside teahouses now have large rectangular tables with benches on which patrons sit to eat. China has had restaurants since the 12th century, some of them selling deep-fried foods (also sold by street vendors, who appear at dawn and work until late at night, hawking food and drink of all kinds), but cooking is, with a few exceptions, considered an occupation suitable only for members of the lower classes (Confucius counseled his followers to avoid the kitchen).

1281

Kublai Khan employs imperial inspectors to examine the crops each year with a view to buying up surpluses for storage against possible famine.

1284

Ravioli is popular in Rome, where the people have been eating lagano cum caseo (fettucini) for years.

Rats are so prevalent in Europe that a story appears about a piper who leads children into a hollow because townspeople have refused to pay him for piping their rats into the river Weser. "Der Rattenfänger von Hameln" may also have reference to the Children's Crusade of 1212, but much distress is caused by rats, which consume grain stores, seeds, poultry, and eggs and which also bite infants and spread disease (*see* Black Death, 1340).

1290

A Chinese earthquake in Chihli (Hebei, or Beijrli) province September 27 kills an estimated 100,000, but while droughts, floods, and other natural disasters combine with brutal winters to produce famine virtually every year in parts of northern China, the country as a whole remains well fed.

Population in north China will reach 10 to 20 million (plus a few million in Mongol territory in central Asia) in this decade as compared with 50 million in the south.

1295

Famine strikes England with special severity despite the fact that more English land is tilled than ever has been before and ever will be again.

English grain exports supply the Continent with wheat from the South and barley and oats from the North. Collected in manorial barns and in market towns for carriage by wagon to the ports, the corn is carried in heavy wagons on well-maintained roads.

1296

 Marco Polo returns to Venice after having traveled from 1275 to 1292 in the service of the late Kublai Khan. Now 42, he brings home spices, oriental cooking ideas, descriptions of Brahma cattle, reports of cannibalism, and curious ideas of diet.

Costard mongers in English streets sell costard apples at 12 pennies per hundred; they are among the earliest cultivated varieties.

1300

The Hanseatic League, begun in 1241, is solidified by a network of agreements among towns on the Baltic and on north German rivers. Ships of the towns import salt from western Europe, wool and tin from England, and olives, wine, and other commodities from Lisbon, Oporto, Seville, and Cádiz, to which they carry dried and salted fish, hides, tallow, and other items of trade (*see* 1344).

The Baltic Sea has been rich in fish through most of this century and will remain so in the century to come. The Hanseatic fisheries have developed an efficient system for salting the herring, a fat fish, within 24 hours after catching it, and Europe holds the Hanse herring in higher esteem than fish salted at sea by Norfolk doggers or by English fishermen out of Yarmouth or Scarborough.

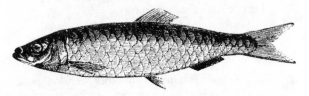

Herring from Baltic waters was the mainstay of diets for cities in the Hanseatic League.

The first brandy is distilled at the 92-year-old Montpellier medical school by French medical professor Arnaldus de Villa Nova (Arnaud de Villeneuve, or Arnoldus Villanovanus), 65 (*see* 800).

14th Century

1303

💲 The *carte mercatoria*, or merchant's charter, granted by England's Edward I, allows foreign merchants free entry with their goods and free departure with goods they have bought or have failed to sell (with the exception of wine, which is too much in demand to be allowed to leave the country). Edward's policy, with some modifications forced by English merchants and by certain towns, will endure for nearly 2 centuries.

1305

🌾 *Opus Ruralium Commodorum* by Bolognese agriculturist Pietro de Crescenzi (Petrus de Crescentiis), 75, is the first book on farming to appear in Europe since the 2nd century.

1312

💲 The Pepperers Guild and other London guilds receive permission to appoint a Weigher of the King's Beam—the *peso grosso*—which is used only for groceries sold by *averium ponderis*, or avoirdupois. The Pepperers, whose guild dates to before 1180, buy in gross (*see* 1328).

1313

🌾 The Chinese book *Nung shu* on agriculture by Wang Shen is a survey of farming since the agrarian revolution that began in the Sung dynasty.

1314

👤 Disastrous famines strike large parts of western Europe and will continue for the next 3 years.

💲 English wheat prices climb to 3 shillings, 3 pence per bushel as a short crop combines with export demand to inflate price levels.

1317

⚡ A fleet of Venetian great galleys makes the longest voyage undertaken by European trading vessels since ancient times. A quarrel between Venice and France has made land travel difficult. The galleys carry sugar, spices, currants, dates, wine, and other cargo.

1319

⚡ A cattle plague strikes England, forcing farmers in some places to use horses, which are immune to the disease, in place of oxen for plowing.

🕐 Sugar is imported for the first time into England by some accounts, having arrived in exchange for a shipment of wool (but *see* 1226). It will be used later in this century to preserve Chinese ginger, flavor cooked partridges, and candy orange peel (*see* 1456; Denmark, 1324).

1320

🖋 *Tsurezuregusa* (*Gleaning from My Leisure Hours*) (essays) by former Japanese *samurai* Kenko

Yoshida, 38, will be written in the next 11 years, illustrating the dominance of formality over taste in the Kamakura court. Yoshida will extol the carp as the only fish noble enough to be carved in front of the emperor; to pay tribute to the emperor with dried salmon is an insult, he will write.

1324

Sugar is imported for the first time into Denmark (*see* England, 1319; Sweden, 1390).

1328

Members of London's Pepperers Guild are officially registered as *grossariae* (*see* 1312; Grocers Company, 1429).

1329

Wheat sells in England for about 3 shillings per quarter (eight bushels), making the weight of a penny loaf of white bread 3 pounds, 13 ounces, of a penny wheaten loaf 5 pounds, 12 ounces, of a penny household loaf 7 pounds, 11 ounces, but since wheat prices vary from place to place the weights of penny loaves also vary. Bakers also sell farthing loaves and halfpenny loaves, so while weights are subject to change every 3 months, or whenever local magistrates set an assize, the bakers cannot generally make their loaves slightly heavier than required in order to avoid arrest for overcharging (*see* 1266; 1709).

1330

Principles of Correct Diet (*Yn-shan cheng-yao*) by Chinese imperial dietician Hoshoi (or Hu-ssu Hui) says that many diseases can be cured by diet alone.

1332

Trading in bitter oranges begins in the French Mediterranean town of Nice. No other kind of orange (a word derived from Hindi) is known in Europe, although a sour variety that will later be known as the Seville orange was introduced by the Arabs into the Mediterranean region during the 9th or 10th century (*see* 1529; 1635).

1333

Japan's Kamakura period ends after 148 years during which wheat cultivation has been introduced to supplement millet and rice crops. Japanese farmers have begun using more horses and oxen to help them in the fields.

Famine grips China following a severe drought.

The Black Death begins in China as starvation weakens much of the population and makes it vulnerable to a form of bubonic plague, but—perhaps because the Chinese are basically well nourished, with average daily caloric intake above 2,000—the plague will have relatively little effect on them, whereas it will take a fearsome toll in Western Europe (*see* 1343).

1335

English grain harvests amount to only 15 bushels of wheat, barley, and oats per capita after setting aside seed for the year to come. Part of the harvest goes to sustain work animals, livestock, and the mounts of knights and barons, while nearly one-third goes into making beer and ale.

1336

The duke of Burgundy gives a banquet at Dijon for France's Philippe de Valois; guests consume victuals that include a hogshead containing 300 quarts of mustard (Dijon mustard is famous throughout Europe).

1337

English merchants contribute 20,000 sacks of wool as a gift to pay the expenses of Edward III. The merchants depend on receipts from the sale of their wool at Bruges and Ghent to pay for the casks of wine that they import from Bordeaux.

1343

The Black Death, which began in China 10 years ago, strikes marauding Tatars, who attack some Genoese merchants returning from Cathay with silks and furs. Some die on the road home, while others carry the plague to Constantinople, Genoa, Venice, and other ports (see 1333; Cyprus, 1347).

1344

The term "Hanseatic League" is used for the first time to denote the confederation of Baltic traders now so prominent in fish export (see 1300; 1360).

Spanish olive oil, fruit, and fine manufactured goods are exported from the South, wool and hides from the North as Castile and Aragon increase their commerce.

1347

The Black Death reaches Cyprus, whence it will spread to Florence and find thousands of victims weakened and made vulnerable by famine (see 1348).

1348

The Black Death, which will devastate Europe, reaches Florence in April and spreads to France and England, where it arrives in July or August, although London is spared until November (see 1349).

England has her third cold, wet summer in a row, and this one is the worst. Rain falls steadily from midsummer to Christmas, crops are poor, food is short, and the hunger makes the country vulnerable to disease (see 1349).

The Black Death will extinguish nearly two-thirds of the population in some parts of Europe. At Locarno on Lake Maggiore the population will fall from 4,800 to 700.

1349

English landlords offer high wages to field hands as the Black Death kills from one-third to one-half the population. Reapers and mowers spared by the Black Death eat better than they ever have or ever will again.

The Black Death reaches Poland and moves on toward Russia, flourishing on poverty and malnutrition, especially in the larger cities.

English and Welsh vineyard owners will turn their arable lands over to pasturage (sheep raising requires far less labor than viniculture), as the Black Death (above) makes field hands much costlier than land. English and Welsh abbeys and monasteries continue to produce wines from their own vineyards (see 1536; Eleanor of Aquitaine, 1154).

1350

The Black Death reduces population pressure on food supplies, which has been growing in England and Europe in this century, and prices drop for lack of demand. Where a good horse brought 40 shillings in England 2 years ago, it now brings only 16, while a fat ox fetches only 4 shillings, a cow 1 shilling, and fat sheep sixpence, but wheat fetches 1 shilling per quarter (eight bushels), up from as little as 16 pence in good crop years, as the dearth of field hands reduces the crop and forces many landlords to turn farmland into pasturage (see 1349).

Salt production takes a sharp drop in northern Europe as a result of economic conditions and of the Hundred Years' War. Poor-quality salt from Brittany's Bourgneuf Bay begins to dominate the salt fish trade as good white salt becomes too costly. Great salt deposits will soon be opened in Poland, with a Genoese firm headquartered at Cracow receiving a monopoly in Polish salt production.

1351

An English Statute of Labourers fixes wages at their 1346 levels and attempts to compel able-bodied men to accept work when it is offered. The shortage of workers resulting from the Black Death has combined with prosperity produced by the Hundred Years' War to create an economic and social crisis in England.

The Statute of Labourers (above) helps keep wages within bounds as England adjusts to the fact that she no longer has a glut of labor, but while Parliament also orders victualers and other tradesmen to sell their goods at reasonable prices, the Statute of Labourers destroys the country's social unity without resolving its problems.

English landholders enclose common lands for sheep raising and begin to develop great fortunes while unrest spreads through the English yeomanry, which has emerged from its traditional passivity as it has shared in the plunder of war and in the higher wages paid to survivors of the Black Death (see 1450; Statute of Merton, 1235).

1356

The Battle of Poitiers September 19 is a triumph of English arms over France's John II, who is taken prisoner in the ongoing Hundred Years' War.

1358

French peasants and Parisians join in a violent rising of the Jacquerie in May against oppressive taxes imposed to ransom John II and other captives taken by the English at Poitiers in 1356 and to carry on the war. The rising is ruthlessly repressed in June with the aid of the English, who pause in their war with the French to join in the wholesale slaughter of rebellious serfs: 300 peasants trapped in a monastery are burned to death.

1359

England's Edward III begins a final expedition to France and penetrates the walls of Paris, but the south of France has been so devastated by war that the English have trouble provisioning their forces.

1360

English laborers who ask wages above the legal minimum established by the 1351 Statute of Labourers are ordered to be imprisoned with bail.

The Hanseatic League grows to include 52 towns that number among them Bremen, Cologne, Danzig, Dortmund, Gronigen, Hamburg, and Hanover. The number will be enlarged to 70 or 80.

1363

A leg of roast mutton sells in a London cookshop for as much as a farmworker earns in a day, and a whole roast pig sells for more than three times that amount to Londoners prospering by the war with France.

1364

Famine strikes France following a bad harvest, and plague in epidemic form follows on the heels of hunger.

Europeans commonly eat the main meal of the day at 9 o'clock in the morning.

1368

China's Ming dynasty, proclaimed January 20, will rule until 1644. Founded by the onetime Buddhist monk Qu Yuanzhang, 40, it will return the nation's diet and eating habits to their pre-Mongol status. Qu is a military deserter, drifter, and petty criminal who was illiterate until he reached maturity; 13 years ago he took advantage of a local rebellion to seize Chiang-ning (later to be called Nanjing), ending the state of anarchy that existed, and he now drives the Mongols out of Beijing, bringing to a conclusion the Mongol (Yuan) dynasty, which began in 1271, and beginning a reign that will continue until 1398 as the emperor Hung-wu, building a city within a city at Nanjing (which will be the Ming capital until 1420). The Ming dynasty will be marked by corrupt and incompetent administrators but no internal wars.

Chinese markets in the Ming period will sell live chickens, ducks, and geese. Produce more than a day old will be sold at sharply reduced prices.

Nonfiction: *Essential Knowledge for Eating and Drinking* (*Yn-shih hsü-chih*) by onetime Chinese bureaucrat Chia Ming, 99, who has been asked by the emperor for the secret of his long life (he will live to 106). "The essential is to be most conscious about what one drinks and eats," he has said. The scion of a rich family in northern Chekiang province, Chia stresses prevention in the absence of effective treatments.

Chinese in the Ming period will vary their basic diet of rice, wheat cakes, fish, pork, poultry, vegetables (notably cabbage, radishes, and turnips), oil (from amarinth seed, hempseed, perilla seed, rapeseed, and soybeans), and fruit with bear venison, wild boar, camel, deer venison, dogmeat, donkeymeat, fox, hare, horsemeat, mulemeat, tigermeat, wild goat, wolf, cormorant, magpie, owl, peacock, pheasant, quail, raven, squab, stork, swallow, mollusks, and shellfish of various kinds.

Chinese in the Ming dynasty will have fish farms on which they will grow carp and other freshwater fish, which they much prefer to saltwater fish and sell live in city markets.

Extremely cold winters and unreliable summer rains during much of the Ming period will inhibit China's agricultural development (*see* population, 1644).

Chinese population density has increased during the Mongol (Yuan) period, resources have diminished, and there has been an exacerbation of the gulf between poverty and wealth. Populations will grow further during the Ming period.

1375

The Hanseatic League opens up new lines of trade to supplement its commerce in herring, cod, salt, leather, hides, wool, grain, beer, amber, timber, pitch, tar, turpentine, iron, copper, horses, and falcon hawks.

Cookbook: *Le Viander de Taillevent* by Guillaume Tirel, 49, gives a detailed account of France's developing cuisine. Tirel began his career as a very young boy in Normandy, working as a helper in the kitchens of Louis, count of Evreux, assisting the bellows tenders (*souffleurs*) and spit turners (*hasteurs*), keeping their fires burning hot and steady, helping to render lard and clarify fat from dripping pans, working with the soup cooks (*potagiers*) by hacking, mincing, and mashing their ingredients, raising and lowering the chains that held the cauldrons of meat stock, pease porridge, and almond tea, plucking fowl, washing salt meat for the cooks (*queux*), helping to strain vinegar and crush sour grapes and crabapples for verjus. His nickname, Taillevent, meaning a flexible, quick-moving sail. He has served as cook to Philip VI of Valois and then to Charles V, and his book explains ragouts, galimafrees, mortreux, and hochepôts, describes sauce Robert and fameline, and recommends using plain and grilled bread as binders in making sauce (the use of flour as a binder is unknown). Tirel tells of having coaxed the king to eat his first cabbage.

England forbids transportation of seed oysters during the month of May. The English continue the oyster cultivation begun by the Romans in 110 B.C.

1376

English religious reformer John Wycliffe, 47, and his Reform party win control of London and oppose ownership of property by clergymen. England's Good Parliament appeals to Edward III to exclude foreigners from London's retail trade and asks the king to banish the Lombard bankers, enforce the 1351 Statute of Labourers, regulate fisheries, and ban export of English grain and yarn.

John Wycliffe (above) revises ordinances governing the sale of food and encounters opposition from London fishmongers and other victualers who depend on wines from France, spices from the Orient, and air-cured stockfish from Iceland (*see* Walworth, 1377).

1377

John Wycliffe's Reform party loses control of London to victualers headed by William Walworth. They raise food prices in the city.

The Hanseatic League retains its privileges in England and will keep them for nearly 2 centuries despite growing resentment against the League.

Population estimates based on an English poll tax suggest that the nation's population is little more than 2 million, down from at least 3.5 million and possibly 5 million before the Black Death (*see* 1546).

Serfs and small-scale landholders did the heavy work of farming in England as on the Continent.

1378

A London ordinance fixes the price to be charged by cooks and pastellers (pie bakers) for "the best capon baked in pastry" at 8 pence.

1381

Ghent comes under siege and food stocks dwindle away. Half starved by the time Lent comes, the people have no fish appropriate for Lenten meals.

Wat Tyler's rebellion creates anarchy in England as farm workers, artisans, and city proletarians stage an uprising against the 1351 Statute of Labourers and the 1377 poll tax. Mobs assemble in Essex, Kent, and Norfolk, sack palaces and castles at Norwich and Canterbury, take hostages, choose Wat (Walter) Tyler as their leader in June, and converge on London.

Richard II, now 14, is presented with a list of demands by Wat Tyler at Mile End June 14 and replies with empty promises to demands for abolition of serfdom, the poll tax, restrictions on labor and trade, and game laws, with a ceiling of 4 pence per acre on land rents and a ceiling on road tolls.

Fresh demands are made at Smithfield next day and Wat Tyler is betrayed and killed with a cutlass by William Walworth (*see* 1377), now lord mayor of London, during a conference with the young king.

Similar uprisings occur in Languedoc as France suffers economic distress and the Tuchins stage an uprising against the tax collectors.

1382

England repeals the reforms granted to Wat Tyler last year and reestablishes serfdom, but the people

have lost confidence in the Crown. The balladeered idolatry of the outlaw Robin Hood expresses their bitterness.

Florence has a revolution as wool combers led by Michele di Lando seize the palace, but the labor government fails when the bourgeoisie object to Michele's assignment to Salvestro de' Medici of rents from shops on the 37-year-old Ponte Vecchio. Rival merchants and industrialists exile Michele, they close their shops and factories, they persuade neighboring landowners to cut off the city's grain and food supply, and a half-century of oligarchy begins in Florence.

1383

Munich's Löwenbräu brewery has its beginnings in Bavaria (*see* 1552).

1384

Statutes of the Lega del Chianti, established in Tuscany, prohibit growers from picking grapes before September 29 "because prior to that date the wine would not be good."

1387

England's Richard II invites the country's rich barons to dine with him. The 200 cooks employed to feed his 2,000 guests have 1,400 oxen lying in salt, two freshly killed oxen, 120 sheep's heads, 13 calves, 12 boars, 110 marrow bones, 200 rabbits, 50 swans, 210 geese, 1,200 pigeons, 144 partridges, 720 hens, and 11,000 eggs. The cooks prepare mortrewes (a meat paste containing broth, ale, bread crumbs, egg yolks, salt, and spices). Minstrels and court musicians entertain the diners as they sit on backless benches called banquettes and eat gilded peacock, roasted boar, and venison off oak planks set on trestles, using half-loaves of bread as trenchers. Anise seed, borage, fennel, garlic, leek, mint, nutmeg, parsley, purslane, rosemary, rue, saffron, sage, and watercress are used to flavor and color the dishes, which include a pie of *smale briddes* (small birds), and for salad. Beverages include claret, Rhenish wine, malmsey, ale, mead, and fermented ciders made of apples, pears, and raspberries. Dessert is a marzipan castle four feet square and three feet high, surrounded by a moat with two drawbridges made of hardened dough.

1390

Sugar is imported for the first time into Sweden but remains a costly novelty, useful for covering up the taste of medical preparations made from herbs, entrails, and various odious ingredients but not much used otherwise (*see* Denmark, 1324).

Cookbook: *The Forme of Cury* is a manuscript containing recipes of dishes prepared for England's Richard II and his barons. Possibly prepared to guide the steward who superintends the king's illiterate cooks and to help him keep track of the costly spices used (notably saffron), the manuscript includes recipes for macaroni adopted from the Italians, and for hash, but many of the recipes are merely rude instructions, such as "Take chickens and ram them together, serve them broken . . ." "Take rabbits and smite them to pieces; seethe them in grease." To make "furmente with porpays," the work instructs cooks to "Take almaundes blanches. Bray hem and drawe hem up with faire water; make furmente as bifore and cast [th]e mylke [th]ereto & messe it with porpays." To make "salat," it says, "Take persel, sawge, grene garlec, chibolles [scallions], oynouns, leek, borage,

myntes, porrettes [young leeks], fenel, and toun cressis [garden cress], rew, rosemarye, purslarye; laue and waische hem clene. Pike hem. Pluk hem small wi[th] [th]yn honde, and myng hem wel with raw oile; lay on vyneger and salt, and serue it forth." It mentions "yfried spynoches," which is little known in France or England.

1392

Nearly 400 Hansa vessels embark for London from Danzig during the year with cargoes of grain, honey, salt, potash, furs, and beer.

1393

A German price table lists a pound of nutmeg as being worth seven fat oxen. In Europe, one pound of saffron is generally equal in value to a plowhorse, one pound of ginger will buy a sheep, and two pounds of mace will buy a cow.

1395

Guillaume Tirel, who has written under the pen name Taillevent, dies at age 69 (year and age approximate) (*see* 1375).

Philip the Bold (*le Hardi*), 53, duke of Burgundy, discourages planting of the high-yielding Gamay grape, insisting that growers plant the superior Pinot Noir wine grape.

1400

Italian shops produce pasta on a commercial basis (*see* 1279); durum wheat is used to mill a granular semolina flour, which, in turn, is used to make a straw-colored dough. Men tread barefoot on this dough for as much as a day to make it malleable, and a screw press powered by two men or a horse is then used to extrude the vermicelli under pressure through pierced dies. The shops employ night watchmen to protect the valuable pasta (*see* Naples, 1785).

👫 London's population reaches 50,000, but no other English city is as populous as Lübeck or Nuremberg, each of which has 20,000, much less as big as Cologne, which has 30,000. Most Britons and Europeans live on the land, as they will continue to do for the next 4 to 5 centuries.

Paris has 200,000 inhabitants: every house keeps poultry, and many have pigs despite laws forbidding it.

15th Century

1401

 The incidence of famine will decline in Europe in this century.

Paintings in The Very Rich Book of Hours *tried to beautify the hard work of supplying noblemen with food.*

Improvements in agricultural technology will have a powerful effect on conditions of European farm labor in this century. Labor will be emancipated in the economically advanced nations of Tuscany, Lombardy, and the Low Countries, further enslaved in the less advanced nations.

💲 The rise of capitalism in the first half of this century will begin a 3-century advance in Europe's agricultural technology.

The Hanseatic League will lose its trade to Dutch fishing interests in this century as copepod crops in the Baltic fail, diminishing fish populations that feed on these tiny crustaceans.

Inca terraces (*andanes*) in this century will turn steep slopes in the Andes of the Western Hemisphere into arable land. Soil and topsoil will be carried up from the valleys below.

1403

💲 The Hanseatic League gains complete control of Bergen, Norway, and enjoys a virtual monopoly in most of the commodities produced by northern Europe, including fish, the salt used for curing fish, whale oil, pitch and rosin employed in shipbuilding and maintenance, and eiderdown (*see* 1406).

1406

Hanseatic fishermen catch 96 English fishermen fishing off Bergen (*see* 1403). They bind the Englishmen hand and foot and throw them overboard to drown.

1407

The French government begins to protect producers of Roquefort cheese, which is aged for 6 months in caves to acquire the fungal growth that gives it its special character. Roquefort is made from the milk of sheep that graze on the stony soil of tableland that cannot be cultivated. No maker of blue-veined cheese will be allowed to use the name Roquefort unless he or she makes it from ewes' milk by approved methods in or about the village of Roquefort, south of Bordeaux (*see* 1971).

1416

The grand duke of Tuscany demarks Italy's Chianti Classico region.

1417

Merchants of the Hanseatic League agree not to buy wheat before it is grown, herring before it is caught, or cloth before it is woven. The League regulates city tariffs and prices to keep supplies of grain and meat cheap for townspeople even at the expense of peasants.

1418

Rouen falls to English forces led by Henry V, 30, who has laid siege to the place and in 2 months starved out a town twice the size of London.

Portuguese explorer lands in the Madeira Islands in the Atlantic off North Africa and plants sugarcane from Sicily in the islands (*see* 1425; 1456; grapes, 1420; Columbus, 1493).

1419

The mayor and aldermen of London issue a decree against blending wines, insisting that "each wine be sold whole in his degree and kin as he groweth" and that no one, citizen or foreigner, "mingle [any] manner of wine . . . but sell them as they grow." Merchants are forbidden to store prized Rhine wines in the same cellar as thin white wine, which is often used to stretch the superior wine, but Dutch wine merchants in the next 2 centuries will develop blending into an art that does not compromise the quality of good wine.

1420

Cookbook: *Du fait du cuisine* by Chiquart Amicco, longtime cook of Amadeus VIII, duke of Savoy (later to be Pope Felix V). He has written the work at the duke's request, gives the first recipe for entremets (specifically, a boar's head), and provides the recipe for a Parma pie into which the cook dumps four or more large pigs, 300 doves, 200 chickens, figs, dates, pine nuts, prunes, raisins, sage, parsley, hyssop, marjoram, creamy cheese, 600 eggs, white wine, white ginger, cream of paradise, saffron, cloves, and sugar, all of which are mixed and placed in earthenware baking dishes lined with lard and 30,000 sugared wafers. The meat alternates in layers with the fruit, herb, and spice mixture, another layer of wafers tops all of this, prevented from burning by a layer of spinach and beet leaves, the dishes are placed in a huge oven, and each dish, before it is served, is decorated with a checkerboard pattern in sugar. A small banner bearing the heraldic arms of each lord is inserted into the top of his individual pie. (The recipe for a fish version is given for meatless days.) Amicco also gives instructions for skinning and redressing swans and peacocks. Peacock meat, being tough, is boiled, larded, and roasted before being sliced up and often allowed to stand for a month or so after cooking, the accumulated mold being scraped from its surface before it is served. Chiquart suggests that the carcass of the peacock be discarded and its plumage used to cover a roast goose.

A mission from Herat (later Afghanistan) arrives at Beijing, the new Ming capital; the Ming emperor, according to the painter Ghiyath al Maqqash, sees to it that the emissaries are given "flour, a bowl of rice, two large bowls of sweets, a pot of honey, garlic, onion, vinegar, salt, a selection of vegetables, two jugs of beer, and a plate of desserts" for each day of their visit. Each group of 10 is provided with a sheep (the Ming court maintains flocks and herds

1420

to supply it with mutton, mutton tallow, and beef tallow) together with a goose and two fowl. The variety and low prices of food in the Chinese capital astonishes Western visitors.

China's Ming court at Beijing (above) has maintained an imperial herd of 70,000 beef cattle and milk cows to supply butterfat, table meat, and sacrificial offerings. While the number will soon be reduced to 30,000 head, the imperial dairy herd will produce butter for shortbread and pastries for more than 200 years to come.

Prince Henry the Navigator, 26, third son of Portugal's João I, has grapevines from Crete planted in the Madeira Islands, whose winemakers will turn their grapes into wine right after they are picked. Fortified Madeira wines will come to rival the sherries of Spain's Jerez region (*see* 1665; sugar, 1425).

1423

Carving forks are used in France, but individual diners will not use forks for centuries to come (*see* Coryate, 1611).

1425

Agents of Prince Henry the Navigator establish a Portuguese colony in Madeira and begin planting sugar (*see* 1418; 1432; wine, 1420).

1428

Japanese transport workers strike in protest against high prices as famine cripples the country. The strikers are joined by farmers who riot in the streets and wreck warehouses, temples, private houses, and sake production facilities.

1429

The Grocers' Company is formed in London to succeed the Pepperers Guild (*see* 1328). Henry VI

will grant the company a charter to sell wholesale—*vendre en gros*, source of the word "grocer"—and manage the trade in spices (now used widely in medicine), drugs, and dyestuffs. The Grocers' Company will remain active for more than 300 years (*see* 1493).

1430

The Spanish wine house Valdespine at Jerez de la Frontera begins producing sherry. It will survive as the oldest sherry bottler, winning a reputation for its manzanilla, fino, dry amontillado, medium amontillado, dry oloroso, medium oloroso, palo cortado, and sweet sherries.

1432

Madeira produces sugar cane that is refined there for the first time (*see* 1425). The industry employs more than 1,000 men—including convicts, debtors, and Jews who have refused to accept conversion to Christianity—brought from Portugal for the purpose (*see* 1456). By 1510 the islands will have about a dozen estates, using imported horses and workers.

1436

England passes her first Corn Laws, giving preferential treatment to trade with Scotland and Ireland (but subject to duty or bounty), permitting the export of wheat and barley from England and Wales without a state license when prices fall below certain levels because of surpluses and even offering bounties or subsidies to encourage exports, but imposing duties on imports to protect domestic prices (*see* 1463).

1443

John Stafford is installed as archbishop of Canterbury with a feast that includes pheasant, heron, swan, crane, curlew, partridge, plover, rails, quails, and three different venison dishes.

1444

Venetian efforts to find new spice routes are spurred by Niccolo de' Conti, a traveler who has returned to Venice after 25 years in Damascus, Baghdad, India, Sumatra, Java, Indochina, Burma, Mecca, and Egypt. Pope Eugenius IV orders de' Conti to relate the story of his travels to papal secretary Poggio Bracciolini as penance for his compulsory renunciation of Christianity.

1449

The Japanese shōgun Yoshimasa assumes power at age 14 to begin a 25-year rule in which the tea ceremony will gain popularity through his patronage among the *samurai* and noble classes. Yoshimasa will encourage painting and drama, his reign will otherwise be disastrous, but the tea ceremony, standardized by the priest Shuko, now 27, will for centuries remain a cherished part of Japanese culture (*see* Rikyu Sen, 1591).

The tea ceremony (above) has its origin in an 8th-century Chinese Tang dynasty book, *Classic of Tea*, by Lu Yü. A purist, Lu Yü called spiced tea and such no more than "the swill of gutters and ditches," but jasmine tea will become the most popular drink of northern China. The Japanese devotion to tea has gone far beyond anything in China, culminating in the hyperaesthetic tea ceremony.

1450

England's nobility encloses more lands to raise sheep at the expense of the peasantry. The landowning class is enriched by the rapidly developing wool trade and by the continuing war with France (*see* 1351; More, 1515).

1453

Constantinople falls to the Ottoman Turks, who end the Byzantine Empire, which has ruled since the fall of the Roman Empire in 476. The fall of Constantinople May 29 increases the need for sea routes to the Orient. Muslim rulers have imposed stiff tariffs on caravan shipments, with the highest duties being levied on spices, and the sultan of Egypt exacts a duty equal to one-third the value of every cargo entering his domain.

The Hundred Years' War, which has continued off and on since 1377, ends in France with the expulsion of English forces from every place except Calais. English rule of Bordeaux ends with the defeat (and death) of John Talbot, first earl of Shrewsbury, marshal of the king's armies, and constable of Aquitaine, who is shot in the throat with an arrow at the Battle of Castillon, five miles east of Bordeaux.

Danish and Dutch merchants have obtained exclusive rights to Portuguese salt during the Hundred Years' War (above), which has made export of Bourgneuf salt via the Strait of Dover difficult. The Portuguese salt, made at Setúbal, is of high quality and very cheap (*see* 1669).

Venice continues to import spices at higher prices and maintains her monopoly in the spice trade (*see* Lisbon, 1501).

France regains possession of the rich Bordeaux wine-growing areas following the success of French forces at Castillon (above) over the English, who may have been befuddled by drinking too much wine at Saint-Emilion (the English call it Semilione).

Coffee is introduced to Constantinople (above) by the Ottoman Turks (*see* 850). The beverage has been popular in the Middle East for the past century although many Muslim authorities disapprove of it, observing that Mohammed did not drink coffee (*see* 1475).

1454

Burgundy's Philippe le Bon takes the "vow of the pheasant" February 17, swearing to fight the Ottoman Turks.

Some 28 French musicians inside a huge pie perform at the Feast of the Pheasant for the duke of Burgundy Philippe le Bon (above). A Mother Goose rhyme about "four-and-twenty blackbirds baked in a pie" will commemorate the event.

1456

Sugar from Madeira reaches Bristol, giving many Englishmen their first taste of the sweetener (*see* 1432). The word "sweetmeat" comes into use to denote anything rich in sugar.

1461

Japan has plague and famine that bring an uprising against the Ashikaga shōgun Yoshimasa.

1463

English landowners gain a monopoly in the home grain market by a statute that prohibits imports of grain except when prices rise to levels at which the export of grain is prohibited. Food prices will rise in the next 2 centuries without compensating wage increases, but almost no grain will be imported (*see* 1436; 1773).

1467

The new archbishop of York is enthroned with feasts that required the purchase of 300 quarters of wheat, 300 tons of ale, 100 tons of wine, one pipe of hippocras, 105 oxens, six wild bulls, 1,000 sheep, 304 calves, 304 pigs, and 400 swans.

1468

The Spanish plant rice at Pisa on the Lombardy plain. It is the first European planting of rice outside Spain (*see* 711), and the Arborio variety, grown in the Po Valley, will be used to make risotto.

1473

Cyprus comes under the rule of Venice, which finds it valuable as a major sugar producer.

1475

Cookbook: *Concerning Honest Pleasure and Physical Well-Being (De Honeste Voluptate et Valetudine Vulgare)* by Vatican librarian Platina (Bartolomeo Sacchi), 54, is the world's first printed cookbook (or, perhaps more accurately, a philosophical treatise on the good life containing some recipes). Platina (whose pen name is a latinized version of his hometown, Piadena) is a onetime soldier, courtier, Greek tutor to the Medici family, and secretary to Cardinal Gonzaga, who now serves as librarian to Pope Sixtus IV. He gives recipes for larks' tongues, hummingbird livers, mirause Catalan style (capons or pigeons, cooked on a spit, then arranged in a casserole with almonds, ginger, cinnamon, and sugar—"a nourishing dish that warms the liver and kidneys and stirs the belly"), and pasta. He praises the peacock, saying that of all birds it deserves to be eaten first, that its aroma and taste are so good that it is suited only for the tables of kings, princes, and noblemen, and explains how to cook peacock "so that it should look alive."

Platina (above), whose book will be translated into Italian (in 1487), French, and German, notes that sugar is now being produced in Crete and Sicily as well as in India and Arabia: "The ancients used sugar only in medicines, and for this reason made no mention of sugar in their foods. They certainly missed out on a great delight, since nothing that is given to us to eat can be so tasty." Platina recommends various nuts and seeds that can be coated in sugar syrup and says that sugar may be eaten in marzipan, a paste of almond and sugar.

The world's first coffeehouse opens at Constantinople under the name Kiva Han (*see* 1453). Muslim fanatics will persecute coffee drinkers (*see* Venice, 1560).

1476

Paris *charcutiers* (pork butchers) band together by edict of France's Louis XI for the sale of cooked pork and raw pork fat only; they do not have the right to slaughter the pigs they need and will be dependent on general butchers until the next century. During Lent, they may sell salted herring and other seafish.

1482

Portuguese explorers on Africa's west coast find bananas being cultivated and adopt a version of the

local name for the fruit, *Musa sapientum* (*see* 327 B.C.; Berlanga, 1516).

💲 English wheat prices soar 74.7 percent following a bad harvest after years of plentiful food and stable prices.

1485

✒ Cookbook: *Mastery of the Kitchen* (*Küchenmeisterei*), published anonymously at Nuremberg, has sections devoted to meats, baked and fried foods, fast-day foods, sauces, and vinegar and wine. It recommends that fish and crayfish be cooked in wine rather than beer or vinegar, gives recipes for preparing turnips, spinach, peas, and sauerkraut, and will remain in print for 200 years.

1490

✊ The Portuguese plant sugar cane on the African island of São Tomé and bring in slaves from the kingdom of Benin and other African countries to work in the cane fields (*see* Cadbury, 1901).

1491

🌿 Spanish colonists plant sugar in the Canary Islands, where the cane flourishes.

1492

✳ Spanish navigator Christopher Columbus, 41, crosses the Atlantic with three ships, sights land October 12, and makes the first known European landing in the Western Hemisphere since early in the 11th century. He disembarks in the Bahamas on an island he names San Salvador under the impression that he has reached the East Indies.

Christopher Columbus (above) and his men will discover foods unknown in the Old World: turtle meat, sweet potatoes, capsicums (peppers), plantain (*Musa paradisiaca*), and allspice (*see* 1494).

🌿 Sweet potatoes, which originally came from the Western Hemisphere, have long been grown in the

Foods discovered by Christopher Columbus included maize, sweet potatoes, and peppers.

mid-Pacific and for a century or two have been cultivated as far west as the islands that will be called New Zealand, where Maori tribespeople have introduced the tuberous roots.

The capsicums (peppers) found by Columbus (above) are members of the Solanaceae family (*see* 1530). Chili peppers are mostly the fruit of *Capsicum annuum*.

Two members of the Columbus party (above) return from the interior of Cuba November 5 without gold but with "a sort of grain they call maiz [*Zea mays*], which was well tasted, bak'd, dry'd, and made into flour." Unknown to Columbus, at least 700 varieties of maize grow in the Western Hemisphere. He will bring maize seeds back to Spain, where they will be called "Indian corn" and grown in gardens as curiosities (*see* 1511; 1516).

"These fields are planted mostly with ajes [cassava]," Columbus writes in his log December 16. "The Indians sow little shoots, from which small roots grow that look like carrots. They serve this as bread, by grating and kneading it, then baking it in the fire." "The king [of Hispaniola] dined with me on the *Niña* and afterwards went ashore with me, where he paid me great honor," he writes December 26. "Later we had a meal with two or three kinds of ajes, served with shrimp, game and other foods they have, including their [cassava] bread, which they call cazabe."

1493

Christopher Columbus builds a fort on the island of Hispaniola using wreckage from his flagship, the *Santa María*. He sets sail for home January 4 in the *Niña*, arrives at Palos March 15, is sent back as governor with 1,500 men in a fleet of 17 ships that weighs anchor September 24, lands Sunday, November 3, on an island he calls Dominica, discovers Guadaloupe November 4, and sights Hispaniola November 22. He is accompanied by 20 agricultural experts, all of whom will succumb in the tropics.

Seville physician Diego Cheka lands on the islands with Columbus (above) in November and finds Hispaniola "filled with an astonishingly thick growth of wood; a variety of unknown trees, some bearing fruit, and some flowers . . . indeed every spot is covered with verdure." Dr. Cheka, who has some knowledge of botany, will write, "We found there a tree whose leaf has the finest smell of cloves that I have ever met with; it was like a laurel leaf but not so large; but I think it was a species of laurel." He describes allspice, but it is not in fruit and he does not know of his discovery and will err in saying, "We found other trees which I think bear nutmegs, because the bark tastes and smells like that spice, but at present there is no fruit on them. I have seen one root of ginger which an Indian wore hanging on his neck."

The Spaniards (above) eat ages (sweet potatoes), which are thought to be "a sort of turnip, very excellent for food," and Dr. Cheka notes that the natives make a kind of bread from it, seasoning it with hot pepper or with a spice known to the natives by various names that they also eat with fish and with "such birds as they can catch."

The horses and livestock landed by Columbus (above) at Santo Domingo (Hispaniola) are the first seen in the New World. Columbus left Palos with 34 stallions and mares, he has 20 remaining when he arrives, but his cattle weigh only 80 to 100 pounds when fully grown. (The horse originated in the Western Hemisphere and migrated to Asia before becoming extinct in its continent of origin at the close of the Ice Age.)

Sugarcane and cucumbers planted by Columbus at Santo Domingo have come from the Canary Islands. Columbus has a special interest in sugar: his first wife's mother owns canefields on an island near Madeira (*see* 1419; 1506).

Columbus lands a shore party on Guadeloupe November 4 under Diego Marqués, who gets lost in the island's rain forest. Five search parties try to locate them, and when Diego's men are found after 5 days they return to the ship with pineapples (*Ananas comosus* of the Bromeliaceae family, believed to have originated in Brazil), which the

Columbus found pineapples on Guadeloupe during his second voyage to the New World.

Caribs call *na-na*, meaning fragrance, or excellence. The seedless fruit can be propagated only by planting its crown or the sprouts that appear on its base, but it was cultivated for centuries—along with cherimoya, papaya, avocado, tomato, cacao, and soursop—from Paraguay to Panama before making its way to the West Indies. Columbus sends some of these *piñas de las Indias*, as he calls them, back to King Ferdinand in Spain, and, although most of them are dried out on arrival, one is in edible condition, giving Europe its first taste of the fruit. "In appearance, shape, and color, this scale-coated fruit resembles the pine cone; but in softness is the melon's equal; in flavor it surpasses all garden fruits. To it the king awards the palm," writes one of Ferdinand's courtiers." Pineapples will be growing in India by 1548, and by the end of the next century it will have been planted by missionaries and navigators in parts of Africa and China (*see* 1658).

London's Grocers' Company, created in 1429, receives permission to appoint a garbeller, whose function is to garbel (inspect) groceries, especially spices, and destroy adulterated products. A number of garbellers will be employed to fix seals of purity on spice cargoes before they can be weighed by the keeper of the King's Beam. A merchant whose goods are found to contain plugged peppercorns or nutmegs may have his goods seized; a dishonest merchant may be pilloried and have his adulterated spices burnt under his nose.

1494

Christopher Columbus discovers the island of Jamaica May 14 and names it San Iago (St. James). It will be a Spanish possession until 1655 (*see* below).

Genoese merchant Hieronomo de Santo Stefano visits Calicut on the Indian coast and observes trade in ginger and pepper (*see* Gama, 1498).

Cookbook: *De Partibus Aedium* by Italian author Francesco Mario Grapaldi, published at Parma, discusses the various foods and wines to be kept on hand in the perfect home.

Christopher Columbus (above) plants the first wheat seen in the New World, but efforts to culti-

vate wheat in the West Indies and elsewhere in Spanish America will be uniformly unsuccessful (*see* 1621).

Columbus's men find Jamaica (above) covered with 30-foot trees (*Pimenta dioica*) bearing spicy green berries that, when dried, turn brown, bear some resemblance to oversized black peppercorns, and have an aroma suggestive of a blend of cloves, cinnamon, and nutmeg. *Pimenta officinalis* will come to be known as allspice, *pimiento*, or *pimento* (Spaniards will call it *Pimienta Jamaica*, or Jamaica pepper).

Scotland's James IV orders his exchequer to give "eight bowles of malt to Friar John Cor wherewith to make *aquavitae*." It is the first recorded reference to Scotch whisky.

1495

Naples surrenders in February to France's Charles VIII, who is crowned king but loses the city following the Battle of Fornovo July 6 and escapes to France. He returns with the idea, learned in Italy, of growing oranges in sheltered gardens. The lean-to that he has built to protect orange trees from killing frosts will be expanded into elaborate buildings, called orangeries, in which the exotic trees will be grown in wheeled tubs. The French nobility will find it pleasant to dine and dance in orangeries at Versailles for centuries to come (orangeries, some of them large enough to hold hundreds of guests, will also be found at Dresden and other European capitals).

1496

Spanish forces take Tenerife in the Canary Islands and find bananas growing under intense cultivation (*see* 1482; 1516).

1497

Venetian merchant explorer John Cabot (Giovanni Caboto), 47, reaches Labrador June 24 after a 7-week voyage and notes vast codfish banks off the coast of Newfoundland. The fishing grounds have been visited in the past by Breton fishermen and will be called the Grand Banks (*see* 1504).

1498

Portuguese explorer Vasco da Gama's discovery of an all-water route to India and the Spice Islands (or Clove Islands) frees Europe from dependence on Venetian middlemen in the spice trade. He lands at Calicut, where Arab spice dealers, fearful of losing their monopoly, give him a rude reception, and he establishes a sea route that Portugal will control for nearly a century (*see* 1453; 1499).

The Portuguese found a sea route to the Spice Islands and brought down the price of pepper, cloves, and cinnamon.

Cookbook: *Apicius de re Coquinaria* is published at Milan.

1499

Vasco da Gama returns to Portugal from Mozambique with pepper, nutmeg, cinnamon, and cloves after having lost 100 of his 160 men to scurvy (*see* 1498; Crusaders, 1250). His success encourages others to attempt the sea voyage around Africa to India (*see* Cabral, 1500).

Oriental spices such as those brought back by Vasco da Gama (above) are widely used to preserve meat and to disguise the bad taste of spoiled meat, which constitutes the bulk of human diets in late winter and spring (although many relish the taste of such meat, calling it "well hung") (*see* capsicums, 1529).

1500

Portuguese explorer Pedro Álvares Cabral, 40, leaves the Cape Verde Islands with a fleet of 13 caravels bound for India, contrary winds drive him westward, he lands in Brazil on Good Friday, and takes possession in the name of King Manuel I Easter Monday. He then heads out across the South Atlantic for India, loses four ships in a storm off the Cape of Good Hope, but proceeds in the company of Bartolomeu Dias and Duarte Pereira. He will return loaded with spices to begin regular spice trade round the Cape of Good Hope.

Cookbook: *The Boke of Cokery* is the first such book published in English.

16th Century

1501

💲 Vasco da Gama wins control of the spice trade for Lisbon. He sets out with a fleet of 20 caravels to close the Red Sea and cuts off the trade route through Egypt to Alexandria, where Venetian merchants have been buying spices imported from the archipelago between Celebes on the west, New Guinea on the east, Timor on the south, and the open Pacific to the north (*see* 1499; 1504).

1502

✳ Christopher Columbus embarks May 11 on a fourth voyage to the New World, this time with 150 men in four caravels that take 8 months to make the Atlantic crossing, forcing the crews to eat wormy biscuit (dried bread), sharkmeat, and ships' rats in order to survive.

🥤 Columbus is given a drink of what the natives call *xocoatl* (pronounced *chocoatl*) aboard ship in the Gulf of Honduras. It is made from beans that have, according to native mythology, been grown by the gods in the Garden of Life. Quetzalcoatl, god of the air, is believed to have come to earth for a time and taught mortals how to cultivate various crops, including the cacao tree. While awaiting Quetzalcoatl's return, the people in the Western Hemisphere's midriff have for centuries kept his memory alive with religious rites that involve cocoa. Mixed with honey, spices, and vanilla, xocoatl is served cold and frosty. Columbus thinks little of it; he takes some of the beans home with him, but only as a curiosity (*see* Cortés, 1519).

1503

💲 Portuguese caravels return from the East Indies with 1,300 tons of pepper—a quantity six times the amount that Egypt's Mameluke regime has permitted to be shipped in any one year—and earn profits of as much as 6,000 percent. A 500-pound bag of cloves that costs 2 ducats in the Moluccas (a cluster of tiny, mountainous islands in the Malay archipelago) fetches 14 ducats when it arrives at Malacca on the western coast of the Malay Peninsula and 500 ducats when it reaches Calicut. By the time such a shipment reaches the port of London it is priced at 2,000 ducats, and dockworkers have their pockets stitched up to prevent pilferage (they are paid bonuses in peppercorns and cloves). A clove tree yields only about 7 pounds of the dried spice per year, so 500 pounds represents the annual yield of about 70 trees.

🕐 Cloves (above) are employed not only to preserve meat and disguise spoilage but also in preserves, syrups, sauces, sweetmeats, and clove tea (they are also used in orange pomanders to freshen the air and in wool closets to keep away moths).

1504

💲 Spices in the Lisbon market drop to 20 percent of Venetian prices, breaking Venice's monopoly in the spice trade and making her vulnerable to attack.

🎨 Venetian painter Jacopo de' Barbari produces the first still life—an oil painting of a partridge.

1504

Cod from Newfoundland's Grand Banks was dried for shipment home to the tables of Europe.

 Breton fishermen begin making annual visits to the Grand Banks off Newfoundland, which they have been visiting irregularly since before 1497. The cod they take is from the same family (*Gadidae*) as the hake.

1505

✕ Portuguese forces lay claim to Ceylon, which produces the world's most desirable cinnamon.

₴ An English worker can earn enough to buy eight bushels of wheat by working for 20 days, eight bushels of rye by working for 12 days, eight bushels of barley by working for 9 days (*see* 1599).

1509

✕ The Battle of Diu February 2 in the Indian Ocean brings victory to Portugal's Indian viceroy Francisco de Almeida, who destroys the Muslim fleet to establish Portuguese control over the spice trade.

₴ Portuguese navigator Ruy de Sequeira visits Malacca following defeat of the Muslim fleet in the Battle of Diu (above) and finds that its natives have been selling cloves to Arab merchants in exchange for copper, quicksilver, vermillion (a rosewood), cambay cloth, cumin, silver, porcelain, and metal bells (*see* 1511).

1510

🌾 Sunflowers from the Americas are introduced to Europe by the Spanish. In many countries they will be a major oilseed crop (*see* 1698).

1511

✕ Portuguese forces under Afonso de Albuquerque capture Malacca, center of the spice trade with the Arabs, to complete Portuguese control of Far Eastern spice sources (*see* 1509).

🌾 Italian scholar Peter Martyr Anglerius, 62, of the Spanish court gives the first description of corn (maize), which he has heard about from the late Christopher Columbus, who died 5 years ago (*see* 1492; Nonfiction, 1516).

1512

₴ Portuguese explorers find nutmeg trees to be indigenous to the island of Banda in the Moluccas. The Portuguese, who establish trading factories on islands such as Amboina, Ternate, and Tidore, will dominate the nutmeg and mace trade until 1602, but natives of Sumatra and Java will resist their efforts to take over the lucrative pepper trade.

🐟 The Newfoundland cod banks provide fish for English, French, Portuguese, and Dutch vessels, which use the island as a base, drying the catch there for shipment back to Europe.

1513

✊ Peasant and labor rebellions in Europe spread eastward from Switzerland. They will continue for the next four years.

✳ Puerto Rico's former colonial governor Juan Ponce de León, 53, sights land on Easter Sunday, calls it Florida after Pascua Florida (the Easter season), goes ashore at Ponte Vedra, near what later will be Jacksonville and St. Augustine (*see* 1565), where the natives are less hostile than those farther south, and finds the people living on venison, wild turkeys and other birds, fish, shellfish, and the corn and beans they cultivate. Ponce plants orange and lemon trees (*see* 1521).

🌾 Spaniards in this century will plant several varieties of peaches in Florida (above), and the trees will spread up the Atlantic Coast and westward to the Mississippi.

1514

Green peas come into use in England to a limited extent, but dried peas are more commonly used and are consumed as "pease porridge"—hot, cold, even 9 days old (*see* 1555).

1515

England's Henry VIII issues decrees designed to protect peasants from the results of land enclosure.

Fiction: *Utopia* by English envoy to Flanders Thomas More, 38, describes an imaginary island governed entirely by reason and offers solutions to the social ills that plague England in a time when landlords are driving the peasantry off farmlands in order to develop sheep pastures for the burgeoning wool industry.

1516

Nonfiction: *De Orbo Nove* by Peter Martyr Anglerius, now 67, uses Martyr's Latin word *maizium* for the "corn" discovered by Christopher Columbus's men in 1492 (they found tobacco on the same day) (*see* 1511). Most of the world will use variations such as "maize" for the grain that Americans will call corn.

The first sugar grown in the New World to reach Europe is presented to Spain's Carlos I by Hispaniola's inspector of gold mines who gives the king six loaves.

Spanish missionary Fra Tomás de Berlanga introduces wheat, oats, and bananas into the Santo Domingo colony on Hispaniola.

The Portuguese plant maize (above) in China, where foods from the Americas, including peanuts (first mentioned in 1538) and sweet potatoes, will be adopted more quickly, and more widely, than in Europe, Africa, or other parts of the world. Maize will be found to thrive in poor soils that cannot support wheat, barley, millet, rice, or other grains and to produce high yields. Peanuts will be found to help preserve soil fertility (only later will it be known that they have nitrogen-fixing nodules in

Maize from Central America came in many varieties and was soon widely planted throughout the world.

their roots). Sweet potatoes will be a staple food for the poor in China's southeastern coastal provinces by the early 18th century, and a staple of agriculture in Hunan, Sichuan, and other provinces by the late 19th century as migrants from the overcrowded Yangzi Delta take up lands in upland areas.

1518

Spanish colonists in Santo Domingo import more slave labor from Africa to perform the hard work of chopping cane in the colony's 28 sugar plantations. The island's native population has dwindled as a result of disease and exploitation.

Forks are observed at a ducal banquet in Venice where French silk merchant Jacques Le Saige notes that "these seigneurs, when they want to eat, take the meat up with a silver fork" (*see* 1071; cookbook, 1570).

1519

Spanish adventurer Hernando Cortés, 34, sails from Cuba to conquer New Spain. The Cortés expedition includes 500 Spaniards, nearly 300 Indians, and 16 horses—10 stallions, 5 mares, and a foal. It moves up from the coast at Veracruz. The Aztecs take Cortés to be the bearded white god Quetzelcoatl, whose return has been predicted by legend, and an allied army of Totonacs helps Cortés take advantage of the confusion to win an easy victory over Montezuma II. The conquistador enlists another army of Tlaxcalans, vanquishes the Cholulans, takes Montezuma prisoner, and by year's end is ruling the country through Montezuma.

Cortés (above) hears of bearded men in Mayan towns and pays a ransom to secure the release of one Gerónimo de Aguilar, who was shipwrecked off the coast of Yucatán in 1511 and who describes the foods he has eaten as a slave to a Mayan chief. The foods include *cacao* (chocolate), *cacahuates* (peanuts), *camotes* (sweet potatoes), and *uahs* (tortillas). Cortés also discovers turkeys, tomatoes, vanilla, papaya, and beans that the Mayans call *avacotl*, a word the Spanish will turn into *habichuela* and the French into *haricot* (*see* 1528).

The wild turkeys of the Yucatán (above) cannot be domesticated, but another variety, *Meleagris gallopavo*, from north of the Río Balsas, will be brought back to Europe and enjoy wide popularity (*see* 1523).

A Spaniard in Brazil finds the natives there eating sweet potatoes (*Ipomoea batatas*). The tuberous root, which is 4 to 10 percent sugar, will be considered an aphrodisiac when it is introduced to Europe.

Spaniards find that natives in the New World grow some foods that have long been familiar in Europe and the Middle East, among them certain berries and squashes, including pumpkins.

 An officer serving with Cortés (above) sees Montezuma drinking xocoatl (or tchocolatl)—fifty flagons of it a day. The Aztecs believe it cures diarrhea and dysentery. They sometimes make it with wine instead of water and season it with vanilla, pimiento, and pepper. Cortés tries the thick, bitter beverage and, never having tasted tea or coffee, believes that the Aztec drink, if sweetened with sugar, may have possibilities. He writes back to his patron, Carlos I, calling xocoatl a "drink that builds up resistance and fights fatigue." His Aztec hosts consider the beverage to have aphrodisiac powers and consume it at wedding ceremonies (*see* 1528).

1520

Cookbook: *De guisades manjares y potages* by Spanish cook Ruperto de Nola, who gives recipes for berenjenas (aubergine, or eggplant—called in German *Dollapfel*). Mentioned in the Ebers papyrus of 1552 B.C., the vegetable was known in the Andean valleys of South America as guinea squash before it appeared in Europe (*see* English introduction, 1587).

The Prospect of Whitby is mentioned for the first time in writing. The London pub will be the scene of cockfights, prize fights, and press-gang recruitment for the Royal Navy.

1521

Ponce de León lands in February near Charlotte Harbor on Florida's west coast, where he introduces cattle and (by some accounts) swine (*see* 1513; Soto, 1539). Now nearly 61, he is wounded by a native arrow, and although he is able to escape he dies of his wounds a few days later at Havana. Some of the livestock that he has left behind will run wild in the Florida swamps.

1522

Portuguese explorer Ferdinand Magellan (Fernão de Magalhães, or Hernando de Magallanes), 42, crosses the Pacific in 98 days, part of the time with nothing for the crew to drink but putrid water and nothing for the men to eat but pieces of leather so hard that they must first be soaked in seawater for 4 or 5 days (many crewmen have died of scurvy). He discovers islands March 15 that will be called the Philippines but is killed in a skirmish with the natives April 24. His lieutenant, Juan Sebastián de

Elcano (del Cano), returns to Seville aboard the *Vittoria* with 18 surviving sailors of the Magellan expedition and with a cargo of cloves that more than pays for the expedition that has accomplished the first circumnavigation of the world.

Italian scholar Antonio Pigafetta has accompanied the Magellan voyage (above) and gone ashore at several ports to study the clove and nutmeg trees. He has noted that ginger "in a green state . . . is eaten in the same manner as bread."

1523

Turkeys from New Spain are introduced in Old Spain (where they are called *gallopavo*, or peacock) and will soon appear in England, where they will get their name in a confusion with guinea fowl, originally from Africa, that has just been introduced from the eastern Mediterranean by "turkey merchants," meaning Turks (*see* Cortés, 1519). Some food historians will note that the Hebrew word for peacock is *tukki* and that Jewish traders may have taken the bird to England, where *tukki* became "turkey," but most authorities will reject this version, if only because the Jews were expelled from Spain in 1492 and those who converted to Christianity (or pretended to) and remained probably did not use Hebrew. Turkey will gradually replace peacock, swan, and other birds on English tables and by the end of the next century almost no one will still be eating peacock or swan, whose meat is, by comparison, tough and stringy (*see* 1555; France, 1538).

Conquistadors in Cuba recognize the possibilities of cultivating sugar there for the first time.

Maize grows in Crete and in the Philippines, where Magellan's men introduced the plant 2 years ago.

1524

Peru's 11th Inca king Huayana Capac dies at Quito and his empire is divided between his sons Huascar and Atahualpa. Without a written language, they rule a complex, orderly society of 12 million in which each head of family is allowed enough land for his own needs and must also help till common

lands that support the Inca court, the priesthood, and the engineers who build irrigation systems, stone roads, and fiber suspension bridges.

Spanish conquistador Pedro de Alvarado, 39, begins a 2-year campaign in which he will subdue Guatemala. Sent by Hernando Cortés at Mexico City, he introduces cows, pigs, goats, sheep, domesticated hens, wheat, rice, sugarcane, apples, peaches, pears, and citrus fruits to the Central American highlands.

Alvarado (above) finds the Aztecs eating foods that include a seed paste made from amaranth (*Amaranthus hypochondrachus*) which is used in tamales employed in worshipping the god Huitzilipochtli. The Spaniards will outlaw cultivation of amaranth in an effort to end human sacrifices to the god.

An English rhyme will say, "Turkeys, Carps, Hoppes, Piccarell, and Beer, Came Into England all in one year," but critics will question whether carp and pickerel, if not indigenous, were imported into England much earlier (*see* turkeys, 1523; hops, beer, 1551).

1525

Spanish conquistador Francisco Pizarro, 55, sails from Panama November 1 in two caravels with 112 men and a few natives to explore "Piru." He writes in his journal, "It is very flat country, they live by irrigation, it does not rain here. They raise many llamas, they raise many ducks and rabbits. The meat which they eat they do not roast or cook, and the fish they make into pieces and dry in the sun, and the same thing with the meat. They do not eat bread as we do, the maize they eat toasted and cooked, and that is their bread. They make wine in great quantity from this maize."

Chili (or chile) peppers and cayenne from the Americas are introduced by the Portuguese into India, where they will become the ingredients of the hottest curries. *Kari* is a Tamil word meaning "sauce." Curry (an English word) indicates the Indian way of preparing nearly all food, certain spices and herbs being used to accentuate, rather than smother, the flavor of the dish being cooked.

A conquistador who followed Francisco Pizarro into the Andes discovered the potato.

Curries, which are not always peppery (the traditional spice has been cardamom, the seed of a tropical East Indian plant), are served with rice or unleavened bread (*chapati* or *parata*).

1526

 Congolese king Mbemba Nzinga protests to Portugal's João III that his merchants are "taking every day our natives, sons of the land and sons of our noblemen and our vassals and our relatives" in exchange for goods from Europe and are selling his people as slaves to Brazilian sugar planters (*see* 1510).

✴ Francisco Pizarro encounters rough seas en route to Peru and makes a landing at what will be called

Port of Famine (*see* 1525). His freshwater barrels have breached, his food stores have spoiled, and 20 men die of hunger before the caravel he has sent back for fresh supplies arrives with flour and fresh meat.

💲 A history of the West Indies by the Spaniard Alveido notes that in Nicaragua "everything is bought with [cacao beans], however expensive or cheap, such as gold, slaves, clothing, things to eat, and everything else. . . . There are public women . . . who yield themselves to whomever they like for ten cacao beans . . . which is their money." (The beans will continue to be employed as currency for centuries.)

The Aztecs do not themselves harvest cocoa (the trees grow only at lower elevations where rainfall was more abundant); when they conquer rival tribes such as the Mayans, they exact tribute that often includes sacks of cacao beans, which the Mayans use in certain social and religious rituals. The beans are easy to count and handy to use as currency; eight of them buy a rabbit, ten a pig, 100 a slave. Tributes are paid in *cargas*, a *carga* being a load of 24,000 beans weighing 22½ to 27 kilograms.

1527

⏱ Conquistadors return to Spain with avocados, papayas, and tomatoes. They have found the natives of New Spain eating such foods in addition to beans, squash, algae, agave worms (maguey slugs), winged ants, tadpoles, water flies, larvae of various insects, white worms, iguana, and guinea pigs (*Cavia porcellis*), which they have domesticated. Two male guinea pigs and 20 females can provide a family with a *cuy* each day; the animal is eaten with its skin on, the hair having been removed as with a suckling pig (*see* 1528; tomato, 1543). The Aztecs also eat dog that as been fattened on avocados and other vegetables and never fed meat (*see* Banks, 1769), and they eat waterbugs, the eggs of waterbugs (said to taste like caviar), lake shrimp, frogs and tadpoles, large larval salamanders, edible algae, and tiny worms from Lake Tenochtitlán that are made into tortillas.

1528

Spanish explorer Álvar Núñez Cabeza de Vaca, 38, is wrecked on a Texas coastal island and held captive by the natives, who, he finds, travel up the river to lay in winter supplies of pecan nuts, produced by a variety of American hickory and used by the natives to season their hominy and corn cakes. They also concoct a beverage from the nut and extract from it an oil used to thicken venison broth (the word "pecan" comes from an Indian term meaning "bone shell," or "hard shell," although many pecan shells are soft).

Hernando Cortés is recalled to Spain and returns with foods never before seen in Europe (*see* below).

Spanish colonists introduce wheat into New Spain (*see* Mexico, 1941).

Sweet potatoes, haricot beans, turkeys, cacao beans, and vanilla are introduced to Spain by Hernando Cortés (above), who gives some of the haricot beans to Pope Clement VII (Giulio de' Medici). Fava beans have been the only beans known to Europe until now, and the new, kidney-shaped beans are called *fagioli*, an association with the traditional broad fava beans. The pope gives some of the large, kidney-shaped beans to Canon Piero Valeriano, who sows them in pots and finds that they flourish. Northern Italians will be quick to begin cultivation of fagioli (which will not be called haricot beans for more than a century; *see* 1640).

The Spaniards use the term *cacao* beans, a word derived from the Aztec *cacahuatl*, for the cocoa brought home by Cortés (above). The bright-leafed trees produce large pods that mature in all seasons throughout the year, he explains, and he describes how the pods are removed from the cacao tree; about 4 inches in diameter and 8 to 12 inches long, they are cut from the tree trunks with sharp knives and, when opened, reveal cacao beans embedded in a moist white pulp, all of which is scooped out onto banana leaves or coconut matting. One pod may yield 20 to 40 beans that in size, shape, and appearance resemble large shelled almonds. These are left to dry and ferment in the hot sun until much of the pulp has disappeared. Cleaned to eliminate any twigs and small stones, the beans are then roasted to permit easy removal of their thin outer shells. Finally, he reports, the dried, roasted beans are crushed in a stone trough between stone rollers into an aromatic paste that is mixed with water to make a beverage that is at least potable, if not especially palatable. Where the Aztecs have mixed cocoa paste with spices, Spanish nuns in their convent at Oaxaca have mixed it with sugar, which adds greatly to its acceptability. In Spain, it is mixed with orange or rose water, to which cinnamon, vanilla, almonds, pistachios, nutmeg, cloves, allspice, or aniseed may be added according to taste. Served cold, the exotic mixture—thick enough to hold up a spoon—is swizzled to a froth with a utensil adapted from the Aztecs, a wooden stick with several concentric loose disks around it.

Vanilla (above) is the word—a diminutive of *vaina*, or pod—used by the Spanish for what the Aztecs have called *tlilxochitl*, meaning "black flower" (the flower is not black, but the Aztecs confuse the flower with the pod). *Vanilla planifolia* is a member of the orchid family; its beanpod resembles that of a string bean but contains thousands of tiny seeds. Bernardo Díaz, a young lieutenant serving with Cortés, has reported that at one great banquet the late Montezuma II and his nobles quaffed more than 2,000 jugs of a frothy beverage made from cacao and vanilla. Montezuma's 371 tribute towns paid him tributes that included tlilxochitl, some of it from the Mazantla Valley (*see* 1532).

The Aztecs (above) also drink pulque, a wine that they make from the maguey plant.

1529

Isabella d'Este Gonzaga, 54, marquesa of Mantua, gives a banquet in the Great Hall of the castle at Farrara January 24 to celebrate the recent marriage of her nephew Ercole to Renée, daughter of France's Louis XII, which she has been instrumental in arranging (Ercole d'Este is the eldest son of the late Lucrezia Borgia). The 100 guests enjoy peacocks in full plumage, gilded wild boar, pigeons, oysters, sturgeons, caviar sprinkled with orange juice, risottos, tagliatelle (a puffed paste crust filled with layers of cheese), strawberries, candied Persian melons, figs, and almond cakes, all served on Isabella's 10-year-old Majolica dinner service.

Sweet oranges from the Orient are introduced into Europe by Portuguese caravels and will forever be called portugals in the Balkans, in parts of Italy, and in the Middle East (*see* 1332; Chinese orange, 1635).

The Turks plant capsicums from the New World at Buda and use them to make paprika (*see* Columbus, 1492). Peasants in the Mediterranean countries will find the peppers easy to grow and capable of giving spice to their dishes at little cost, whereas imported spices are far beyond their reach. Hungarians will develop capsicums in a vast variety of colors and degrees of pungency, and use of heavy spices will decline in the next few decades, even among the rich, partly because peppers have gained acceptance (*see* nutrition, 1928).

Vast fields of maize from America are grown in Turkey whence the grain will come to England as "turkey corn."

1530

Spain's Carlos I is crowned Charles V of the Holy Roman Empire and king of Italy February 23 by Pope Clement VII (Giulio de' Medici) at Bologna. Princes and prelates then feast on dainties in the palace while outside on the square, over a roaring fire, a whole ox is roasted for the people. The ox is stuffed with sheep, hares, geese, and galli d'India (a term used for exotic birds such as guinea fowl or turkeys).

Nonfiction: *On Civility in Children* (*De Civilitate Morum Puerilium*) by the Rotterdam philosopher Desiderius Erasmus, 64, who notes that the easiest way to learn table manners is to have them ingrained in childhood. "If you cannot swallow a piece of food," he says, "turn round discreetly and throw it somewhere." "Some people put their hands in the dishes the moment they have sat down. Wolves do that." "To lick greasy fingers or to wipe them on your coat is impolite; it is better to use the table cloth or the serviette."

The Italian painter-sculptor-architect Michelangelo, 55, leaves Florence hurriedly for Venice, taking with him all of his possessions, including napery, dinnerware, silverware, soup tureens, and menus he has illustrated for the guidance of servants.

The potato (*Solanum tuberosum*), discovered in the Andes by Spanish conquistador Gónzalo Jiménez de Quesada, 30, is a member of the Solanaceae family (which includes also capsicums, tomatoes, and tobacco). It will provide Europe with a cheap source of food in the centuries to come and thus spur population growth. Quesada finds the natives eating only the largest of the tubers (the swollen tips of an underground stem), which they call *papas*, and planting the smallest, thus steadily reducing the size of the tubers, which their ancestors domesticated sometime between 3700 and 3000 B.C. Since the tubers grow underground and are only about the size and shape of peanuts, the Spanish mistake them for a kind of truffle and call them *tartuffo*, which will persist with variations as the word for potato in parts of Europe (*see* 1539).

After the potato (above), the most important root crop for the Andean highlanders is the oca (*Oxalis tuberosa*). In addition, the Inca eat the leaves and seeds of lupine (*Lupinus mutabilis*), also called *tarwi* or *chocho*. Cultivated crops include quinoa (*Chenopodium quinoa*)—the Spaniards call it millet, or "small rice"—which thrives even in droughts that kill maize crops and is used in stews and soups, along with potatoes and chili, and, where maize is not grown, to make the fermented beverage that Europeans call *chicha*.

Seaweed is part of the Inca diet, eaten fresh on the seacoast and dried in sheets and blocks for trade in the Andean highlands, where it is known as *cochayuyo*.

Chicha (above) is a Taino word that the Spaniards learned in the Antilles; the beverage is known as *aka* or *asua* in Quechua and is important to religious ritual among the Inca as well as being a source of nourishment. Women and boys chew maize or quinoa (or, in some places, oca, yucca, other roots, or the fruit of the molle) and let the enzymes in their saliva work on what they chew to help ferment it before spitting it out. The Inca do not drink water unless there is no available alternative.

1531

Sugar becomes as important as gold in the Spanish and Portuguese colonial economies.

1532

✗ The Inca Atahualpa visits the Spanish camp of conquistador Francisco Pizarro, who has ascended the Andes (see 1526). Pizarro seizes the Inca November 16 and holds him for ransom, paralyzing the machinery of Inca government (see 1533).

☖ Franciscan friar Bernardino de Sahagún lands in New Spain and writes the first full description of vanilla (see 1528; 1571).

Count Cesare Frangipani in Rome invents the almond pastry that will bear his name.

🐖 Horses introduced into Peru by Francisco Pizarro (above) will be seen within 3 years running wild on the pampas of eastern South America. Within 70 years the horses will be running in herds of uncountable size and will be revolutionizing daily life.

1533

✗ Catherine (Caterina) de' Medici of Florence marries the French dauphin, Henri of Valois, 14, duc d'Orléans, who will become Henri II in 1547. Catherine is also 14, her family has grown rich in the spice trade and by supplying alum to the textile industry, and the cooks that accompany her to France are far more sophisticated and knowledgeable than French cooks (see below).

The Peruvian Empire ends August 29 with the strangulation of the last Inca, Atahualpa, who has professed himself a Christian and received baptism but is nevertheless assassinated (see famine, 1539).

☖ Cooks attending Catherine de' Medici (above) introduce to France such vegetables as broccoli, globe artichokes (Catherine is a devotee of artichokes, and the French nobility will soon savor fonds d'artichauts at festive banquets), savoy cabbage, and haricot beans—fagioli—given her by her brother Alessandro. The beans will be known in Provence as fayoun and will be the basis of cassoulet, the bean dish of Languedoc (see 1528; 1749).

The double boiler, called by Italians the bagno maria after a legendary medieval alchemist named Maria de Cleofa, reputed author of Tradtor della

Distillazone (about medicine, magic, and cookery), is introduced to the French court by the cooks of Catherine de' Medici (above). The French will call it a bain-marie.

Stuffed guinea hen is introduced by Catherine's cooks (above) and the dish will be known to the French as pintade à la Medicis. The Italians also introduce truffles and start the French digging enthusiastically for truffles of their own.

Pastries such as frangipani, macaroons, and Milan cakes, introduced only recently to Florence, will be introduced to France by Catherine's cooks (above) (see Frangipani, 1532).

A Florentine chef makes a different-flavored ice for each day of Catherine's wedding celebration, giving many Frenchmen their first taste of the dessert. By 1576, there will be 250 master ice makers in Paris.

1534

✹ French explorer Jacques Cartier, 43, sets out for the New World with two small ships and 36 men on orders from François I, who seeks a route to the spice islands that will free France from dependence on Spain and Portugal. Cartier sails into the Gulf of St. Lawrence, plants the cross at Gaspé Bay, and finds les sauvages growing beans.

∞ England's Henry VIII, now 43, breaks with the Church of Rome, which has voided the annulment of his marriage to Catherine of Aragon and excommunicated him. Henry will outlaw the nation's Catholic monasteries, upsetting the nation's land system; a merchant class will arise, more land will be enclosed, landlords will prevent peasants from grazing their cows and sheep on common land, the need for rural labor will decline, the enclosure system will lead to increased poverty and hunger, and the breakup of the monasteries will have other effects (see honey shortage and winemaking, 1536; More, 1515).

Pope Clement VII (Giulio de' Medici) dies September 25 after eating poisonous mushrooms. He has evaded Henry VIII's demand for nullification of the 1509 marriage to Catherine of Aragon and has refused to sanction Henry's marriage to

Anne Boleyn, who last year bore Henry's daughter Elizabeth.

✒ Fiction: *Gargantua* (*Les Grandes et inestimables chroniques du grand et énorme géant Gargantua*) by Lyons physician-novelist François Rabelais, 40, who describes an extraordinary feast for which are roasted 16 oxen, 3 heifers, 32 calves, 63 fat kids, 95 wethers (castrated young male sheep), 11 wild boars, 300 farrow pigs souced in sweet wine or musk, 18 fallow deer, 700 woodcocks, 400 capons, 6,000 pullets and as many pigeons, 600 crammed hens, 1,400 leverets or young hares and rabbits, 303 bustards, 220 partridges, 140 pheasants, and 1,700 cockerels "on top of the usual fare," which includes cream, curds, fresh cheese, coots, doves, river fowl, teals, plovers, storks, and sea-fowls. The birds consumed include turkeys (*see* 1523; 1530).

🐟 English fish consumption begins to decline as the king's break with Rome (above) relaxes church rules against eating meat on Fridays and during Lent. Some fast days will continue to be observed, particularly in the Lenten season, but Wednesdays will no longer be official fish days and even in Lent it will no longer be mandatory to serve fish. England will enact new fish laws to revive her coastal towns and to encourage the fishing industry, from which the English navy draws recruits (*see* 1554).

1535

🍎 Scurvy breaks out among the Huron and then among the French under Jacques Cartier.

"All our beverages froze in their casks," Cartier will write, "and on board our ships, below hatches as on deck, lay four fingers' breadth of ice."

🍳 The Lübeck tavern Haus der Schiffergesellschaft opens in Breite Strasse with tables built of ship planks at which sea captains, travelers, and merchants sit side by side in the great hall.

1536

✳ Jacques Cartier returns from New France with a Huron chief, the chief's two sons, three adult Huron, two little girls, and two little boys (all of

whom soon die). The Huron chief swears to François I that Saguenay is rich in cloves, nutmegs, and peppers and grows oranges and pomegranates.

⏳ England begins to suffer shortages of honey as monasteries that raised honey bees as a source of wax for votive candles are dissolved pursuant to the 1534 Act of Supremacy (*see* 1544).

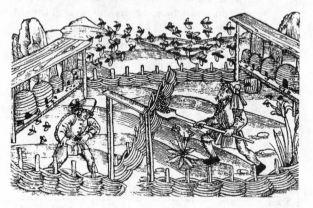

Honey remained the chief sweetener even after England's monastic apiaries disappeared.

🍎 Jacques Cartier (above) loses 25 men to scurvy in New France (*see* 1535). By mid-February, "out of the 110 men that we were, not ten were well enough to help the others, a thing pitiful to see." But although 50 Huron in the area also die of scurvy, a Huron chief shows Cartier how to grind the bark of the common arborvitae *Thuja occidentalis*, boil the ground bark in water, drink the infusion every other day, and apply the residue as a poultice to swollen, blackened legs. Cartier digs up arborvitae saplings and transplants them to the royal garden at Fountainebleau upon his return.

🥤 The breakup of English and Welsh monasteries (above) has virtually ended production of wine in the British Isles (*see* 1349; 1873).

1538

⏳ Poule d'Inde (chicken of the Indies, meaning turkey) is served in France (*see* 1523). The French will call hen turkey *dinde*, tom turkey *dindon*.

The first definite reference to Newfoundland fishing expeditions appears in Basque records, although Basque fishermen have been visiting the Grand Banks for some decades and possibly for a century (*see* 1497; 1504).

Peanuts are introduced into China by Spanish or Portuguese navigators, who will also introduce them into sub-Saharan Africa along with corn, potatoes, and capsicums (peppers) (*see* 1550). Tomatoes will also be introduced into China but will not be widely known there until the late 19th century.

1539

Famine strikes Cuzco as a result of Spanish mismanagement (*see* 1533). By September, people are dying of hunger and tens of thousands of Indians march in the streets with crosses, asking for food, which had been distributed in an orderly way by the Inca.

A fixed maximum on Spanish grain prices becomes a permanent facet of royal economic policy. Applied only sporadically until now, the *tasa del trigo* has the effect of favoring sheep raising over tillage, making Spain dependent on imports for her food, and making food prices so high that the Spanish worker can barely afford food, clothing, housing, and fuel.

Spanish conquistador Hernando de Soto, 39, lands in Florida May 25 with livestock that include 13 hogs—by some accounts the first hogs seen in North America (but *see* Ponce de Léon, 1521). De Soto joined Francisco Pizarro in Peru 8 years ago and has enriched himself with Inca gold.

Potatoes arrive in Spain with conquistadors returning from Quito (*see* 1530). Pedro de Cieza of the Pizarro expedition describes the tubers as something similar to chestnuts (*see* 1540).

Portugal's agrarian system declines as a result of dependence on slave labor introduced since 1441.

1540

Spanish explorer Francisco Vásquez Coronado, 30, arrives in the American Southwest and will say of the Zuñi that they "eat the best cakes that ever I saw. . . . They have the finest order and way to grind that we ever saw anyplace, and one Indian woman of this country will grind as much as four women of Mexico." Conquistador Gaspar Castaño de Sosa will come along in Coronado's wake and tell of seeing a Pueblo beehive oven (*horno*) on a roof at San Ildefonso. The Pueblo are famous for their bread, which they make by mixing cornmeal dough with lard and yeast, and their Hopi neighbors will make a paper bread called *piki*. Many tribespeople make a corn pudding (*pikami*) when blue corn is harvested.

Coronado (above) brings with him the first horses, mules, cattle, sheep, and hogs ever seen in the region. He finds that the Pueblo natives have only one domestic animal, the dog (their turkeys being only semidomesticated). Coronado will be credited with turning the Pueblo from dependence on wild game to raising domestic livestock for food, thus founding the American beef cattle, lamb, mutton, and pork industries.

A specimen potato from South America reaches Pope Paul III via Spain. The pope gives the tuber to a Frenchman, who introduces it into France as an ornamental plant (*see* 1539; 1740).

1541

Gonzalo Pizarro, a brother of the conquistador, sets out to find the cinnamon described in a letter of 28 July 1533 to Charles V by one Licenciado de la Gama. He leaves Quito with 6,000 pigs, 300 horses, 900 dogs, and many llamas and alpacas, most of which have been eaten, died, or run off by the time the starving expedition (some of whose members have deserted and made their way down the Amazon to the Atlantic) returns (*see* 1542).

Hernando de Soto discovers the Mississippi River May 8 (*see* 1539). A member of his party will tell later of coming upon a region where "the pecan nut, the mulberry, and two varieties of plums furnish the natives with articles of food."

England's archbishop Thomas Cranmer, 52, makes a rule that an archbishop must not have more than six flesh dishes or six fish dishes on fast days, followed by not more than four "second" dishes. A sliding scale is instituted for minor church dignitaries; minor orders must do with three flesh and two second dishes.

Duke Henrich von Braunschweig attends a meeting of the Reichstag, after which a banquet is served. The duke refers throughout the meal to a slip of paper and explains later that the chef has given him a list of the dishes to be served in order that he may choose only those which he wants. It is possibly the first written menu (but *see* Michelangelo, 1530).

1542

Gonzalo Pizarro writes to the emperor Charles V September 3 that there are very few trees of the kind described in 1533 and that they are far apart (*see* 1541). The buds and the leaves taste like cinnamon but the rest of the tree has no taste at all, and there is no profit to be had from the "cinnamon" trees of the eastern slope of the Andes.

Nonfiction: *A Compendyous Regyment, or a Dyetary of health* by English Carthusian monk, physician, and writer Andrew Boorde (or Borde), 52, includes recipes including one for a "Lord's dysshe, good for an Englisshe man, for it doth anymate hym to be as he is, whiche is, stronge and hearty . . . ; Beef is a good meate for an Englisshe man, so be it the beest be yonge, & that it be not cowe-fleshe; yf it be moderatly powdered [salted] that the groose bloude by salte be exhausted, gyd it doth make an Englisshe man stronge; Veal is good and easily digested; Brawn [boar's meat] is an usual meate in winter amonges the Englisshe men; Bacon is good for carters and plowmen, the whiche be ever labouring in the earth. . . . I do say that colloppes [slices of bacon] and egges is as holsome for them as a tallow candle is good for a blereyed mare. . . . Potage is not so moch used in alle Christendom as it is used in Englande. Potage is made of a lyquor the which fleshe is soden [boiled] in, with puttyingto chopped herbes and otemeal and salt. . . . Of all nacyons and countries, England is beste servyd of Fysshe, not onely of al maner of sea-fyssh, but also of fresshe-water fysshe, and al maner of sortes of salte-fysshe." Boorde describes water, "wyne," ale, "bere" ("a naturall drynke for a Dutche man"),

"cyder" ("the best is made of cleane peeres"), mead ("made of honey and water boyled both together"), and "metheglyn" ("made of hony and water, and herbes boyled and sodden together").

"Bread having too much bran in it is not laudable," Boorde (above) explains. "I do love manchet bread and great loaves the which be well moulded and thoroughly baked, the bran abstracted and thrown away, and that is good for all ages . . . Maslin bread is made half of wheat and half of rye. And there is also maslin made, half of rye and half of barley." But of bread rolls made for Roman patricians he says, "Many little loaves joined together, the which doth serve for great men, and it is saffroned: I praise it not."

1543

Chinese consumption of oils and fats is four to five times as high as in Japan, where diets are far leaner and less varied than what Chinese enjoy in the rich Yangzi Delta but not too different from what northern Chinese eat beyond the Great Wall.

Japan gets her first European visitors as some Portuguese from a Chinese ship land on the island of Taneko off Kyushu. The Namban, as they are called, introduce baked bread to the Japanese. They will also bring in tomatoes, maize, and other Western Hemisphere foods, but initially just as curiosities. Dutch visitors will introduce sweet cakes, which the Japanese will call *castella* (from Castile) and will continue to bake at Nagasaki for more than 4½ centuries.

Wheat, barley, broad beans, chickpeas, European vegetables, and cows are introduced into New Spain by a new viceroy sent out to replace Pedro de Alvarado, who died 2 years ago at age 46. The grains, vegetables, and livestock introduced into North America in the next few decades by English explorers will have come in many cases from Spaniards to the south.

1544

Northern Europe suffers a honey shortage as a result of the breakup of monasteries by the Reformation (*see* England, 1536). The decline in honey-bee colonies creates a growing need for cheap sugar, but sugar will remain a luxury for more than a century.

An epidemic of caracha kills an estimated two-thirds of the Peruvian llama flock. Under Inca rule, animals infected with the disease were slaughtered by state shepherds (there was a shepherd for every 500 llamas) and buried in out-of-the-way places, but this has not been done under the Spaniards. Meat and fish are generally eaten raw or dried, along with toasted maize; the poor eat mostly roots and greens, depending on where they live.

1545

Fishing grows poor in the Baltic Sea while becoming good in the North Sea, a development that will have important economic and political consequences.

1546

Nonfiction: *The Proverbs of John Heywood* by English epigrammatist John Heywood, 47, includes "When the sun shineth, make hay"; "A man may well bring a horse to the water, but he cannot make him drink"; "Butter would not melt in her mouth"; "The fat is in the fire"; "Half a loaf is better than none" (more precisely "Betters halfe a lofe than no bread"); "Out of the frying pan into the fire."

England's population tops 4 million, with many of the people desperately short of food after a series of bad harvests.

1548

The Edict of Châtellerault extends the gabelle (salt tax) to all of France's western provinces. The French have adopted the idea of taxing salt from the Normans, who learned it from the Arabs (the word "gabelle" comes from the Arabic *al quabala*). Civil war breaks out in Guienne, and royal troops are unable to handle the 40,000 peasants who gather at Cognac and Châteauneuf. The peasants rout the soldiers, seize Saintes, loot the town, and

lay waste the countryside beween Poitiers and Blaye. The Constable de Montmorency is sent to suppress the rebellion (*see* 1549).

1549

France's Henri II annuls last year's Edict of Châtellerault and rescinds the gabelle imposed on western provinces in exchange for an "indemnity" of 450,000 livres (*see* 1680).

Cookbook: *Banchetti, compositioni di vinande* by Italian author Christoforo di Messisbugo is published at Ferrara.

The city of Paris gives a dinner in June to honor Catherine de' Medici. The menu, which shows no sign of Italian influence, is made up chiefly of birds: 30 peacocks, 21 swans, 9 cranes, 33 young herons, 33 night herons, and 33 egrets. Many smaller birds are also served, along with young hares and rabbits.

1550

Spanish physician Blasus Villafranca at Rome makes public his experiments in artificial ice making (year approximate). He has filled a long-necked flask with a liquid, put it into a container of water, turned the bottle rapidly round, and gradually dropped saltpeter (potassium nitrate) into the water. When the flask is removed, the liquid inside is nearly frozen. By the end of the century, Italians will be mixing saltpeter in snow instead of dissolving it in water, and beginning in the next century confectioners will be icing apricots, grapes, peaches, and pears.

Corn (maize), sweet potatoes, and peanuts will be introduced in much of China in the next half-century (*see* 1538). All will produce large yields, spurring population growth by creating abundance with declining prices.

1551

Historiae Animalium by Swiss naturalist Konrad von Gesner, 35, is published in its first volume. Gesner has collected animals from the New World and the Old, and his work pioneers modern zoology.

∞ Spanish missionary Francis Xavier, 45, leaves Japan, where he has converted about 1,000 of the people to Christianity. He will die next year, but other Jesuits will take his place, and by 1582 the country will have an estimated 150,000 converts and 220 chapels, most of them in Kyushu.

Western missionaries and traders are not impressed by the bland Japanese diet, which consists mostly of millet, wheat noodles, rice (not yet a food for the common people), seafood and seaweed (for those living near the seacoast), and radishes. The Japanese, for their part, are appalled to see Westerners eating with their hands and wiping their mouths and hands on cloth napkins, which are then soiled with food stains but not discarded.

English and Welsh alehouses are licensed for the first time. The German method of "hopping" beer was introduced during the reign of the late Henry VIII, who died early in 1547, but many have criticized the use of hops, saying that beer is a "naturall drynke for a Dutche man but on no account for an Englyshe man." Laws have been passed fining brewers who put hops in their ale (*see* 1554).

1552

London's Covent Garden is granted to Sir John Russell, first earl of Bedford, whose family will retain the property until 1914 (*see* 1265). The land of the convent garden owned by the abbey of Westminster, now part of London, was confiscated along with other church properties in 1534 and will serve as London's produce and flower market beginning in 1661.

Parliament decrees September 3 that any English butcher who sells meat other than those fixed by the government is to be imprisoned.

Löwenbräu beer gets its name as a two-tailed heraldic lion is placed over the entrance to the brewery founded at Munich in 1383. The Bavarian brewery will become known as Löwenbräu, or Lion Brewery.

1553

The first written reference to the potato appears in *Chronica del Peru* by Pedro de León (Pedro Creca), which is published at Seville. The author calls the tuber a *battata* or *papa* (*see* 1540; 1563).

1554

Parliament reenacts the Corn Law of 1436 and enacts other statutes to encourage farming in England. The Corn Law regulates export and import of grain according to prices, other laws forbid the enlargement of farms and place restrictions on storing, buying, and selling grain, but none of the measures relieves England's food shortages or lowers food prices.

Nonfiction: *Cruydeboek* by Dutch botanist Dodonaeus (Rembert Dodoens), 37, makes the first mention of kohlrabi and Brussels sprouts, both varieties of cabbage (*see* Gerard, 1597).

Flemish artist Pieter Bruegel depicted the struggle between gluttony and austerity.

Parliament increases the number of England's fish days, partly to decrease demand for meat, partly to encourage shipbuilding and thus help build a source of manpower for the Royal Navy. Saturday becomes a fish day as well as Friday (*see* 1534; 1563).

The first identifiable description of the tomato appears in an Italian chronicle that calls the cherry-sized yellow fruit *pomo d'oro* (golden apple) (*see* 1519). By the end of the century, both red and yellow tomatoes will be found in European gardens but only as exotic ornamentals (*see* 1596).

Flemish hop growers emigrate to England and start growing hops in Kent for the English brewery trade (*see* 1551).

1555

Famine grips England; the peasantry discovers that peas taste good green as well as dried.

Turkeys can be had in English markets for as little as 4 shillings, whereas a swan or crane fetches 10.

Cookbook: *The Secrets of the Reverend Master Alexis of Piedmont* by Italian author Girolamo Rusceli, who serves as astrologer to the French queen mother Catherine de' Medici, now 36. Mostly a collection of remedies, it includes recipes for such things as confitures.

1557

Cookbook: *Libra Novo nel qual d'insegna a'far d'ogni sorte di uninando secondo la diuersita de i tempi, cosi de Carne come di Pesce* by Christoforo di Messisbugo expands on his 1549 work.

1558

Clear soy sauce will be brewed for the first time in the next 10 years in the Japanese village of Noda Shimofusa west of Edo. Soy sauce up to now has been a pastelike product (*see* Kikkoman, 1630).

Carrots, cabbages, cauliflower, parsnips, and turnips are introduced into England by Flemish weavers fleeing the persecution of Spain's Philip II (year approximate).

1559

English food prices soar to three times their 1501 levels, largely because the late Henry VIII had debased the coinage to raise quick money for his wars with Spain, France, and Scotland. The typical English wage is up only 69 percent above its 1501 level (*see* 1550).

Ice cream appears in Italy as ice and salt are discovered to make a freezing combination.

1560

A smallpox epidemic decimates Portugal's Brazilian colony and increases the need for African slaves to cut sugar cane.

Venice gets its first coffeehouse (*see* Vienna, 1475). The city is a major sugar-refining center, using raw sugar imported through Lisbon (whose spice trade has made it Europe's richest city), but Europe's chief sugar refiner is Antwerp, which also gets its raw materials from Lisbon but refines as much sugar in a fortnight as Venice does in a year (*see* coffee, 1582).

1561

English navigator John Hawkins, 30, hijacks a Portuguese ship carrying African slaves to Brazil, trades 300 slaves at Hispaniola for ginger, pearls, and sugar, and makes a huge profit. His enterprise marks the beginning of English participation in the slave trade (*see* 1563).

The English make no effort to break Portugal's monopoly in the spice trade, finding it easier and more profitable to seize Portuguese carracks than to bargain with the Moluccan natives for spices.

The city council of Vicenza votes 18 to 16 to exclude turkeys from banquets, calling them overly luxurious, but wild ducks are considered acceptable.

Marmalade is (according to one fanciful account) created by a physician to Mary, Queen of Scots, who returns from Calais August 19, landing at Leith because England has refused her passage. To keep her seasickness (*mal de mer*) at bay, he mixes orange and crushed sugar. It will be suggested that the word marmalade derives from the words "*Marie est malade*," but a far more likely derivation is from the Portuguese *marmelo* for quince, derived, in turn, from the Latin *melum* and the Greek words *mele* (honey) and *melon* (meaning apple) (*see* Keiller, 1797).

1562

Parliament acts to aid the employment of the poor as it did in 1551, but at the same time it raises the price level at which wheat, barley, and malt may be exported, thus making food and drink more costly at home and enriching the landed gentry at the expense of the lower classes.

1563

France has famine, which will be exacerbated in the next few years by the country's religious wars.

Japan has rice riots at Mikawa following requisition of crops by the Tokugawa family and imposition of heavy taxes. Buddhist temples of the Ikko sect are burned in retaliation by the daimyo Ieyasu.

Painting: A personification of Summer that includes an ear of maize is painted at Milan by German-born artist Giuseppe Arcimboldo, 36 (the "turkey corn" is familiar throughout much of the Mediterranean).

Portuguese missionary Luis Frois arrives in Japan and gives strongman Nobunaga Oda a velvet hat and sugar confections (*confeitos*) in a glass jar as a gesture of friendship. He will write home describing Japanese cuisine and eating habits, which do not yet include eating in company at common tables (each diner now has his own small table, a practice that will continue until the 18th century and—for ceremonial occasions—even to the final years of the 20th century).

Portuguese traveler Antonio Galvano writes about the island of Ternate in the Moluccas, where "from its highest place, flakes and streams like unto fire flow continually into the sea." Dense forests of clove trees and towering, evergreen nutmeg trees more than 80 feet high make the island a rich source of spices.

Guiseppe Arcimboldo's personification of autumn made heavy use of grapes and other fruit.

An official English document is published under the title "Arguments in favour of establishing Wednesday as an additional fish day," based on the need "for the restoring of the Navye for England to have more fish eaten and therefor one daye more in the weeke ordeyned to be a fysshe daye, and that to be Wednesdaye, rather than any other" (*see* 1554). Spurred on by Queen Elizabeth's desire to spur the nation's shipbuilding industry, develop a fishing fleet from which to draw naval recruits, and drive down the price of meat, Parliament enacts legislation giving England more meatless days (Fridays and Saturdays as well as Wednesdays) than any other country in Europe. Violations of the new law are punishable by 3 months' imprisonment or a £3 fine. Eating meat during Lent is also forbidden. A London woman is pilloried for having meat in her tavern during Lent (*see* 1595).

Sir John Hawkins brings the potato to England by some accounts, but the potato from Bogotá may be a sweet potato.

1564

The sweet potato reaches England aboard one of Sir John Hawkins's slave ships returning from New Castile. The tubers are planted to end England's reliance on imports for her sweet potato pies (*see* Hakluyt, 1584).

Boudewin Rousse de Ghent recommends lime juice as an antiscorbutic.

1565

Europe has poor harvests. Catherine de' Medici decrees that meals shall be limited to three courses.

St. Augustine, Florida, is founded by Spanish conquistador Pedro Menéndez de Avilés, whose forces have attacked Fort Carolina and slaughtered all its male inhabitants. He lands 600 colonists at St. Augustine, it is the first European colony in North America, and its residents introduce Spanish foods such as rice and wheat breads.

Sir John Hawkins finds carrots growing on Margarita Island off the coast of Venezuela, where they have evidently been planted by Spanish conquistadors.

Priests and nuns from St. Augustine (above) will trek across the Florida peninsula to what later will be Pensacola, bringing with them food and cooking ideas new to the natives.

1566

Theater: *Gammer Gurton's Needle* by clergyman-teacher William Stevenson, perhaps in collaboration, is performed at Christ's Church, Cambridge: "I cannot eat but little meat,/ My stomach is not good;/ But sure I think that I can drink/ With him that wears a hood./ That I go bare, take ye no care, I am nothing a-cold:/ I stuff my skin so full within/ Of jolly good ale and old./ Back and side go bare, go bare,/ Both foot and hand go cold;/ But belly, God send thee good ale enough,/ Whether it be new or old."

1567

Antwerp's sugar-refining industry moves to Amsterdam following the capture of Antwerp by the duke of Alva.

1568

English explorer David Ingram travels from the Gulf of Mexico north to Canada and finds "vines which beare grapes as big as a mans thumbs."

Spinach is grown for the first time in England and gains quick popularity because it appears in early spring when vegetables are scarce and Lenten dietary restrictions discourage consumption of other foods.

Cookbooks will advise rich families to keep silver saucepans for preparing spinach (above).

1569

Hunger and plague kill 500 people a day at Lisbon through much of the summer.

Large-scale traffic in black slaves begins between the African coast of Sierra Leone and the Brazilian bulge 1,807 miles away (*see* 1510; 1581).

Natives and colonists in Brazil (above) enjoy a diet based largely on feijoada completa, a kind of cassoulet or baked bean stew (*see* 1822).

London bans the sale of fresh fruit in the streets lest it spread disease. Fruit pies and tarts, especially apple tarts, are English favorites, but uncooked fruit is regarded with suspicion.

Slave ships returning from Brazil (above) bring maize, manioc (cassava), sweet potatoes, peanuts, and beans to supplement Africa's few subsistence crops. Manioc will prove highly resistant to locusts and to deterioration when left in the field, and it will serve as a reserve against famine.

1570

✗ France's Charles IX, 19, is married to Elizabeth of Hapsburg in rites celebrated with great banquets at which turkeys (*dindon* and *dinde*) are served.

⚱ Cookbook: *Cooking Secrets of Pope Pius V (Cuoco Secrete di Papa Pio Quinto)* by the late Bartolomeo de' Scappi is published at Venice with 28 pages of copperplate illustrations that include the first picture of a fork, a two-tined implement evidently of silver (*see* 1518; Coryate, 1611).

Bartolomeo de' Scappi's illustrated work revealed recipes from Rome's Vatican kitchens.

1571

☿ Spanish naturalist-physician Francisco Hernández calls vanilla *araco aromatico* and says that it is in high favor—for its alleged healing properties as well as for its taste and aroma—among grandees in New Spain, whence he has been sent by Philip II.

1572

$ The price of turkeys in London markets falls to 3 shillings, 4 pence, down from 6 shillings in 1555. A turkey hen costs more than a tom turkey.

1573

⚱ Poetry: *Five hundred good points of Husbandry* by Suffolk farmer Thomas Tusser uses rhymed proverbs to guide fellow farmers.

Cookbook: *The Treasurie of Commodious Conceits, and Hidden Secrets, Commonly Called The Good Huswives Closet of Provision, for the Health of Her Households* by English author John Partridge.

⏱ Tusser (above) says, "Fruit gathered too timely will taste of the wood,/ Will shrink and be bitter; and seldom prove good:/ So fruit that is shaken, and beat off a tree,/ with bruising and falling, soon faulty will be."

Tusser (above) describes the perfect cheese as being, among others things, "Not like Gehazi, dead white, like a leper; not like Lot's wife, all salt; not like Argus, full of eyes; not like Tom Piper, hoven and puffed like the cheeks of a piper; not like Crispin, leathery; not like Lazarus, poor; not like Esau, hairy; and not like Mary Magdelen, full of whey or maudlin."

Tusser (above) recommends September as the month to stock the stew-pond for Lent. "Thy ponds renew,/ Put eeles in stew,/ To leeve til Lent,/ And then be spent."

1574

✗ Leyden in the Lowlands comes under siege by Spanish forces under Luis de Requeséns y Zúñiga, who has succeeded the duke of Alva, gained a victory over Protestant rebels at Mookerheide in April, and advised Philip II in June to pardon the Protestants. William of Orange (the Silent), who has lost two brothers in the battle, cuts the dike in several places to flood the land, and his ships sail up to Leyden's city wall October 3 to relieve the siege.

Some 5,000 of Leyden's 15,000 people die of hunger in the 6-week siege by the Spanish (above), but burgomaster van der Werer cries defiance. He draws his sword and says, "You may eat me first; I will not surrender to the Spanish."

Ships bearing white bread and herring relieve Leyden's hunger. Together with Leyden hutspot (a stew of stale beef and root vegetables) they will be served October 3 each year after 1648 to celebrate the liberation of the Netherlands. A simmering stew (*cocido*) left behind by the departing Spaniards (according to some accounts), hutsput is discovered by Corenelis Joppensz, an orphan boy who has been given 6 guilders to venture through the lines to see if the city is still surrounded.

1575

Cookbook: *A Proper Newe Book of Cookery* contains recipes "To make a tarte of borage floures" and "To make a tarte of marigolds, prymroses, or cowslips."

The first European porcelain, created by Tuscany's Grand Duke Francesco Maria de' Medici, 34, is far inferior to the Chinese porcelain imported by Portuguese caravels. Almost all Europeans eat off earthenware plates or wooden trenchers (*see* d'Entrecolles, 1712).

1577

English explorer Sir Martin Frobisher, 42, explores the Atlantic coast of North America. His men receive one pound of biscuit and one gallon of beer each day, one pound of salt beef or pork on flesh days, and one dried codfish for every four men on fast days, with oatmeal and rice when the fish gives out. Each man also receives one-quarter pound of butter per day and a half-pound of cheese, with honey for sweetening and "sallet oyle" and vinegar, plus wild game, wild fowl, salmon, and fresh cod when it is available.

Nonfiction: *Description of England* by London-born topographer-clergyman William Harrison, 43, who says, "If the world last a while after this rate, the wheate and rie will be no graine for poor man to feed on." Barley is the common bread cereal in parts of Wales and the west of England; in the north of England and the Midlands, oats and rye, or a mixture of rye and wheat called maslin, or monk corn, are the staple cereal grains for rural people, but in bad harvest years even maslin is scarce and costly, forcing the poor to subsist on pease meal or ground beans.

Harrison (above) says that noblemen, gentry, and students generally dine at about 11 o'clock in the morning, merchants and husbandmen at noon, with a simple supper taken between 5 o'clock and 6 by the upper classes, an hour or so later by the yeomen. The poor eat whenever and whatever they can, living by the rule "When fish is scant, and fruit of trees, Supplie that want with butter and cheese." Breakfast for the poor is usually bread and cider; the midday meal may be bacon or a thick broth in addition to bread, cheese, and beer; supper is bread and milk or oatmeal porridge. Meat is a rare treat, and then it is pork or poached game. The working class eats breeves—rye or barley bread soaked in pot liquor, and the rye or barley in the bread may be stretched with peas, acorns, or beech mast. Each part of the country has its own puddings—Devonshire white cloud, Gloucestershire bag pudding, Hampshire hasty pudding, Worcestershire black pudding, and Yorkshire pudding. Pies—especially apple and mince—and tarts are prized for dessert.

1578

English navigator Francis Drake, 38, gets through the Strait of Magellan in a 16-day passage, reaches the coast of Chile in his 110-foot ship *Golden Hinde*, and tastes potatoes for the first time (*see* 1586).

1580

Spain and Portugal unite under one crown following the defeat of Portuguese troops by Spaniards August 25 at the Battle of Alcantara, near Lisbon. Spain's Philip II is proclaimed Philip I of Portugal. The Portuguese will not regain their independence until 1640.

1580

 Cocoa gains widespread use as a beverage in Spain (*see* 1527; 1615).

come to mean (*see* Boulanger, 1765; canard à presse, 1880; Terrail, 1913).

1581

Spain's Philip II unifies control of the oriental spice trade, eliminating the competition in sugar, spices, and slaves that existed before the Spanish takeover of Portugal last year.

Ergotism kills thousands in the German duchy of Luxembourg and in Spain where the disease is endemic (*see* 1039; 1587).

Nonfiction: *Il Trinciante* by Italian author Vincenzo Cervio is a book on carving that contains a large picture of a fork (*see* Scappi, 1570).

Cookbook: *Ein Neu Kockbuch* by Hungarian-born author Marx Rumpolt, published at Frankfurt-am-Main, gives the first potato recipes ever published in a German cookbook, but few Europeans eat potatoes even in the German states. Rumpolt is cuisinier de bouche to the queen of Denmark, and his book gives 20 recipes for turkey, only two for peacock. It also mentions goose liver.

1582

The Japanese Taira general Hideyoshi, 46, gains support from the Tokugawa daimyo Ieyasu, 39, at Edo and begins to eliminate the Nobunaga family in a great struggle for power. Japanese *samurai* warriors and army conscripts live, as they have for centuries, on rice (boiled, fried, or cooked in a pan), bonito (dried and scraped), other dried and salted fish, dried seaweed, dried vegetables, miso (soybean paste), and umeboshi (plums pickled in brine and dried).

Coffee (*kahveh*) is mentioned for the first time in print by Augsburg merchant Leonhard Rauwolf, who left Marseilles for Arabia in 1576, has returned, and begins publication of his *Travels* (*see* 850; 1601).

The Paris restaurant De La Tour d'Argent, overlooking the Seine, opens as an eating place for royalty, but it is not yet a restaurant as that word will

1583

England's minister to Constantinople William Harborne trades English woolens, tin, mercury, and amber for spices, cotton goods, silks, and dyes.

Spain dominates the world sugar trade and sells Brazilian sugar at high prices for use by European aristocrats and capitalists.

De Plantis by Italian physician-botanist Andrea Cesalpino contains the first modern classification of plants based on a comparative study of forms. Cesalpino's work will be acknowledged by Linnaeus in 1737.

An English manual says, "Picke not thy teeth with a forkette," but few people eat with forks (*see* Coryate, 1611; Washington, 1747).

1584

The Virginia colony planted on Roanoke Island by English navigator-courtier Walter Raleigh, 32, is named for England's virgin queen, who knights Raleigh for his services. Raleigh has secured the renewal of the patent on colonization granted in 1578 to his late half-brother Humphrey Gilbert, he has sent out an expedition in April under the command of captains Phillip Amadas and Arthur Barlow, both 34, they have sailed by way of the Canary Islands to Florida and thence up the coast in search of a suitable site for an English plantation in the New World, and have come to an inlet between Albemarle and Pamlico sounds (*see* 1587).

Nonfiction: *Discourse concerning Western Discoveries* by English geographer-cleric-historian Richard Hakluyt, 32, who describes the sweet potato as "the most delicate rootes that may be eaten, and doe farre exceed our passeneps or carets" (*see* 1564), but sweet potatoes will be slow to gain popularity.

Cookbook: *A Book of Cookrye Very Necessary for All Such as Delight Therein, Gathered by A.W.* by an English author who uses only his or her initials but gives instructions which include *How to boyle Piggs Petitoes* [feet] and *How to make a Pudding in a Turnep Root.* It also gives recipes for boiling "A Cony with a Pudding in his Belly," for a "Tarte of Brier hips," and for a "Hodgepodge."

 A pamphlet by Phillip Amadas and Arthur Barlow (above) describes the soil of the New World as "sweet smelling" and speaks of vines "bowed down with grapes, the woods abounded with game, the waters with fish" in "the goodliest land under the cope of heaven."

1585

Cookbook: *The Widowes Treasure* by John Partridge, who writes, "*To make fine Cakes* Take a quantity of fine wheate Flower, and put it in an earthen pot. Stop it close and set it in an Oven, and bake it as long as you would a Pasty of Venison, and when it is baked it will be full of clods. Then searce your flower through a fine sercer. Then take clouted Creame or sweet butter, but Creame is best: then take sugar, cloves, Mace, saffron and yolks of eggs, so much as wil seeme to season your flower. Then put these things into the Creame, temper all together. Then put thereto your flower. So make your cakes. The paste will be very short; therefore make them very little. Lay paper under them."

Jamaican ginger reaches Europe on a ship from the West Indies. It is the first Oriental spice to have been grown successfully in the New World.

Jesuit missionaries introduce deep-fried cookery (*tempura*) into Japan. The word *tempura* is derived from the Portuguese word *temporras,* meaning Friday, when deep-fried fish is eaten.

1586

Sir Francis Drake sets out to intercept and capture the annual Spanish treasure fleet off Cartagena in the Caribbean, misses it by a scant 12 hours, picks up potatoes as ship's stores somewhere in the Caribbean, and sails home to England via Virginia, carrying the potatoes as curiosities (*see* 1578).

1587

English colonist John White lands 150 new settlers, including 17 women, in the Virginia colony on orders from Sir Walter Raleigh, but the new arrivals land too late to plant crops for fall and winter, so White returns to England for supplies to see them through (*see* 1584; 1591).

Ergotism reaches endemic levels in the German states, bringing insanity and death to thousands who eat bread made from infected rye (*see* 1581, 1595). The disease remains endemic in Spain.

Cookbook: *The Good Husvvifes Iewell. VVherein is to be found most excellent and rare Deuises for Conseites in Cookerie, found out by the practice of Thomas Dawson . . .* by English author Dawson, who gives recipes for "sallets" and instructions *To make Fritters of Spinnedge.*

Pope Sixtus V writes that Rome is swarming with vagabonds in search of food as work goes forward to make the city a showplace of baroque palaces and cathedrals.

Eggplant is introduced into England (*see* cookbook, 1520). The variety is small, light brown in color, and egg shaped, but the English will generally use the French name *aubergine* for the vegetable (*see* 1806).

1588

A Spanish Armada sent against England by Philip II engages forces July 31 with a much smaller fleet of Royal Navy ships commanded by High Admiral William Howard, Sir Francis Drake, and Sir John Hawkins. A great storm blows up in the following week, the elements help the English defeat the armada by August 8, and the victory opens the world to English trade and colonization (*see* potatoes, below).

Nonfiction: *The Historie of the Great and Mightie Kingdome of China and the Situation Thereof; Togither with the Great Riches, Huge Citties, Politike, Governement, and Rare Inventions of the Same* by Spanish missionary Juan González de Mendoza appears in an English translation by one Richard

Parker, describing honey, pine nuts, artificial incubation, tree crops interplanted with maize, cormorant fishing, fish farming, and the practice of paying duck farmers to run their birds through rice fields near Guangzhou (Canton) in order to destroy snails as well as weeds (the work was originally published at Rome 3 years ago).

Cookbooks: *The Good Hous-wives Treasurie, Beeing a verye necessarie Booke instruction to the dressing of Meates*, published at London, gives a recipe for *Sauce for a Gooce* and instructions in *How To make Livering Puddinges* and *How To make Minst Pyes*, with recipes also for "A Lenton Pudding, A Haggas Pudding," and other pies and puddings; *The Good Huswives Handmaid for Cookerie* tells how *To seeth Fresh Salmon, To boyle a Capon with Orenges after Mistres Duffelds Way, To make Lumbardy Tarts, To make a Tarte of Apples and Orenge Pilles*, and *To make a Tart of Almonds*, and gives a recipe for "A tart to provoke courage either in man or woman."

Potatoes reach western Ireland by some accounts from the wreckage of ships in the Spanish Armada (above) that are washed up on Irish shores. The tubers are found to thrive in poor soils that will not support grain crops and can be planted and harvested with little equipment—even, if need be, with one's bare hands.

Potatoes are introduced into the Lowlands by Flemish botanist-physician Carolus Clusius (Charles de L'Écluse), 62, who may have received the tubers from English herbalist John Gerard. Once they are accepted, potatoes will take the place of asphodel, whose bulbs have been eaten since the days of ancient Greece (*see* 1597; 1601).

Virginia fields planted Indian fashion with maize, beans, squash, melons, and sunflowers yield "at the least two hundred London bushelles" per acre, whereas in England "fourtie bushelles of wheat [per acre]... is thought to be much," writes English mathematician Thomas Hariot, 28, about agriculture on Roanoke Island.

1589

The Bourbon dynasty, which will rule France until 1792, is founded by Henri of Navarre, 35, who will reign until 1610 as Henri IV.

Nicolas BruLart, chancellor to Henri IV (above), will open immense vineyards in Sillery-Champagne, north of the Marne. Grapes in the vineyards will be picked no later than 10 o'clock in the morning, and the juice will be separated from the black grapes to keep the wine as light as possible. Within a century it will be the palest bronze pink and subjected to slow fermentation as soon as spring temperatures activate the yeast in its unfermented sugar (*see* Dom Pérignon, 1698).

1590

France's Henri IV lays siege to Paris in mid-May after defeating the Catholic League in mid-March at the Battle of Ivry. The siege brings hunger and malnutrition that kill 13,000 in the city. Food supplies are inadequate for the 30,000 inhabitants and the 8,000-man garrison, by mid-June the Spanish ambassador has proposed grinding the bones of the dead to make flour, by July 9 the poor are chasing dogs and eating grass that grows in the streets, and a Fugger newsletter in August reports "great hunger in Paris; a pound of white bread costs half a crown. . . . Rumor has it that people are eating mice, cats, and dogs." By the end of August, "you could see the poor dying, eating dead dogs on the street; some ate garbage thrown into the river or rats or the flour made from the bones [though most who did died in agony]" and soon there is cannibalism as starving Parisians "began chasing children along the streets as well as dogs," but the duke of Parma Alessandro Farnese arrives with 14,000 men and lifts the seige.

The Natural and Moral History of the East and West Indies by the Jesuit missionary José de Acosta is published at Seville and will soon be translated into French, Italian, German, and Shakespearean English, finding a wide readership. Acosta, who will be called the American Pliny after the naturalist Pliny the Elder, who died in the eruption of Mount Vesuvius in A.D. 79, was in Peru from 1570 to 1585 and stopped on his way home for a few years in New Spain (Mexico). Acosta writes of the Andean highlands beyond Cuzco, "No trees grow there, and there is no firewood, but they replace bread by some roots which they call *papas*, which grow underground, and these are the food of the Indians, who by drying them and curing them make what they call

Missionary José de Acosta distinguished between cacao and coca, both unfamiliar to Europeans. NEW YORK PUBLIC LIBRARY

chuño, which is the bread and sustenance of the country. There are also roots and herbs which they eat. It is a healthy place, and the most populated of the Indies and the richest because of the abundance of cattle, which are easily raised there. . . . The native ones . . . are called *guanacos* and *pacos*." Acosta makes reference to two domesticated animals, the llama and the alpaca, and says, "There are also partridges to hunt to your heart's content."

Acosta (above) devotes one chapter of the book to both cacao and coca, the two presumably being subject to confusion among readers to whom these words are unfamiliar, and writes that *Chocholaté* is "loathsome to such as are not acquainted with it, having a scum or froth that is very unpleasant to taste. Yet it is a drink very much esteemed among the Indians, where with they feast noble men who pass through their country. The Spaniards, both men and women, that are accustomed to the country, are very greedy of this *Chocholaté*. They say they make diverse sorts of it, some hot, some cold, and some temperate, and put therein much of that 'chili'; yea, they make paste thereof, the which they say is good for the stomach and against the catarrh."

1591

French royalists besiege Rouen with help from Robert Devereux, 25, earl of Essex. The resulting starvation in Normandy's richest city resembles that seen in Paris last year at Paris (*see* 1592).

Plague and famine strike the Italian states. Nuremberg merchant Balthasar Paumgartner writes home to his wife Magdalene, "It is reckoned that in one year here, one-third of the folk in all Italy has died, and a highly necessary thing, too. For were it not for the pest, they must die anyway, as there would not be enough for so many to eat."

John White returns to Roanoke Island after having been delayed by England's war with Spain and finds that the colony there, including White's family, has vanished (*see* 1587; Hariot, 1588).

Japanese teamaster Rikyu Sen commits ritual suicide (*seppuku*) on orders from Toyotomi Hideyoshi. He has formalized the tea ceremony (*see* 1449), and the nine-volume book *Nanboroku* by his disciple Sokei Nanbo will record what Rikyu did and said with regard to the ceremony and the meal served afterward—*kaisakiryori*. It will become the Bible of tea-ceremony technique and of mainstream Japanese cookery, espousing the simplicity of Zen Buddhist vegetarianism combined with fish and game birds, with the emphasis always on aesthetic presentation.

1592

Rouen is relieved in April (*see* 1591), the duke of Parma receives a bullet in the arm soon thereafter, and he is dead by December.

A Russian census lists peasants under the names of landholders. The peasants will hereafter be considered the landlords' serfs (*see* 1597).

 Heineken beer has its beginnings in a Dutch brewery started under the name De Hooiberg (The Haystack) (*see* 1864).

Dutch (and English) households mostly brew their own beer and ale, preparing malt beverages at least once each month. Beer has become the general drink in England, consumed more commonly than the ale that was dominant a century ago; both are strong enough to merit such nicknames as angel's food, dragon's milke, go by the wall, lift leg, mad dog, stride wide, and whoresonnne. Hard cider is popular in England's West Country, as is perry, made from fermented pear juice, and the ancient drinks mead and metheglin, both made from fermented honey, continue to have their admirers.

1593

Nonfiction: *Wan-shu tsa-cha* by Shen Pang is rich in details relating to Chinese food supplies, table arrangements, the expenses entailed in giving an official banquet, and the like.

Potatoes are planted by Swiss botanist Gaspard Baubin, 33, who engages some farmers in the Vosges region to cultivate the tubers, which are now used as cattle food in several European countries (but *see* 1630).

English admiral Sir Richard Hawkins begins an abortive voyage round the world after reporting that 10,000 men have died of scurvy under his command in the Royal Navy. Sir Richard recommends orange and lemon juice as antiscorbutics (*see* 1564; Lind, 1747).

1594

The governor of China's Fukien province propagates sweet potatoes from Manila for famine relief. The tuber was introduced by the Spanish into the Philippines 30 years ago.

Lisbon closes her spice market to the English and Dutch, forcing creation of the Dutch East India Company to obtain spices directly from the Orient (*see* English East India Company, 1600).

Chinese farmers now grow maize and peanuts in addition to sweet potatoes (above) and in some cases grow such other New World crops as tomatoes, guava, and papaya, but will probably not grow chili peppers for another 40 or 50 years.

1595

The Dutch East India Company sends its first ships to the Orient, the Dutch make their first settlements on Africa's Guinea coast, Dutch ships arrive in the East Indies, and the Dutch begin colonization (*see* 1598).

England's wheat crop fails, and food prices rise sharply (*see* 1596).

Ergotism breaks out in epidemic form at Marbourg, France, and remains endemic in many of the German states (*see* 1592; 1597).

An English economist observes that adding a third fish day would save 13,500 cattle per year in London alone (*see* 1563), but not even the second fish day is strictly observed and will be dropped by the end of the century.

1596

Famine brings rural unrest to Austria, but food is plentiful—if costly—at Vienna. Food shortages due to crop failures raise grain prices, creating misery in much of Europe, in English cities, in Asia, in the Caribbean islands, and in Peru.

"Sundry New and Artificiall Remedies Against Famine" (pamphlet) by English author Sir Hugh Plat, 46, lists points in favor of macaroni and offers a number of suggestions for alleviating famine beyond the use of pasta. He has been trying to interest the Royal Navy in macaroni as a cheap and easily stored food for long sea voyages and will claim to have had some success in getting the Navy to adopt his ideas (*see* 1607; cookbook, 1602).

 Basque whaling captain François Sopite Zaburu devises the world's first factory ship. He builds a brick furnace on his deck and extracts whale oil from blubber which he has "tryed out" (boiled down) aboard ship, a procedure far more economical than dragging whale carcasses to shore factories.

 The tomato is introduced into England as an ornamental plant (*see 1534; 1752*).

1597

Akbar the Great orders that Indian peasants pay him one-third of the gross produce their fields are supposed to yield as determined by a detailed survey of the country's agricultural resources.

Ergotism is caused by eating spurred rye, concludes the faculty of medicine at Marbourg, France (rye infected with ergot fungus appears to have spurred grain heads) (*see 1595; 1674*).

Japanese strongman Toyotomi Hideyoshi orders his people not to eat meat in a move designed to crack down on Christian conversions and resist other Western influence (*see 1551*).

Cookbook: *A Booke of Cookerie. Otherwise called: The Good Huswives Handmaid for the Kitchen* by English author Edward Allde.

The Herball, or general histoire of plantes by English botanist John Gerard, 52, describes potatoes, which he has received directly from Virginia, mistakenly calling them "Batata virginian sive Virginianorum, et Pappus, Potatoes of Virginia." The only potato common in England, however, is the batata, or sweet potato.

Gerard (above) says about maize, "Turky wheate doth nourisheth far lesse than either Wheate, Rie, Barly or Otes. . . . The barbarous Indians, which know no better, are constrained to make a vertue of necessitie, and thinke it a good food; whereas we may easily judge that it nourisheth but little, and is of hard and euill digestion, a more convenient food for swine than for man."

Gerard (above) finds tomato plants to be "of a ranke and stinking savour" but admires the fruit as an ornamental.

Gerard (above) says of peppers (capsicums) that they are "well knowne in the shoppes at Billingsgate by the name of Gennie pepper."

Gerard (above) says that eggplant has "a mischievous qualitie" and warns about mushrooms, saying that "the earthie excrescences called mushrooms . . . fewe of them are good to be eaten and most of them do suffocate and strangle the eater." But eggplant will be cultivated in France in the next century, as will mushrooms, and the danger of eating them will decline.

Of parsnips, Gerard (above) writes, "There is a good, pleasant food or bread made of the roots of the parsnip, which I have myself not tried of, nor mean to." Of the carrot, he says, it was "found upon the mountains of Germanie . . . from whence it has been seen and conveyed by one friendly botanist unto another and in sundry regions" (*see* 1558; Hawkins, 1564).

Carrots (above) are a popular Lenten dish in France, partly because their color gives the illusion of forbidden meat.

The first English mention of tea appears in a translation of Dutch navigator Jan Huyghen van Linschoten's *Travels*. Linschoten calls the beverage *chaa* (*see* 1609; coffee, 1582, 1601).

1598

Some 14 Dutch ships leave early in the year on five well-equipped expeditions to India following Lisbon's closing of trade with Holland. The Dutch set out to trade directly with the East and commence a gradual conquest of Portuguese possessions. Cornelis de Houtman, 33, and Jacob van Neck, 34, establish cordial relations with the sultan of Bantam, who sees the Dutch as potential allies against the hated Portuguese, who enslave his people, and gives them a warm welcome (*see 1599*).

Nonfiction: *A Survay of London and Westminster* by English chronicler John Stow, 73, makes reference to the George Tavern, which is said to date to the 12th century and to have been frequented by Sir Richard Whittington, the merchant and philanthropist who became lord mayor of London in

1598

1397. The late John Skelton, who died in 1529, wrote a poem about the tavern.

French tillage and pasturage are "the true mines and treasures of Peru," says Maximilien de Bethune, 38, duc de Sully. One of Henri IV's highest officials, Sully calls *le labourage* et *le pastourage* the two breasts of France (*les deux mamelles de la France*) from which the nation takes her nourishment (*see* Boisguilbert, 1695).

English playwright William Shakespeare relates overweight and life expectancy in *Henry IV* (Part II). The kings warns a "surfeit-swell'd" Falstaff to "Leave gourmandizing; know the grave doth gape/ For thee thrice wider than for other men" (V, v). Twentieth-century statistics correlating obesity with shorter life expectancy will bear out the three-to-one ratio cited.

The blackness of Queen Elizabeth's teeth is noted by a German traveler visiting England. "Next came the Queen, in the Sixty-fifth year of her Age, as we were told," writes Paul Hentzner, "very majestic; her Face oblong, fair, but wrinkled; her Eyes small, yet black and pleasant; her Nose a little hooked; her Lips narrow; her Teeth black; (a defect the English seem subject to, from their too great use of sugar)." It is the first recorded association between sugar and tooth decay (*see* Hart, 1633).

1599

Plague and famine will decimate Andalusia and Castile in the next 2 years while other parts of the Iberian Peninsula will be relatively untouched. Spain has grown increasingly dependent on northern and eastern Europe for grain staples. Her standard of living has declined markedly as prices have risen above those seen elsewhere in Europe, and her small landowners (*hidalgos*) are being forced off the land, which is failing into the hands of large absentee landlords. American colonial demand for Spanish cloth, wine, olive oil, and flour has slackened with the development of agriculture in Peru and New Spain, and as a result Spanish workers are increasingly idle or unproductively employed.

Four Dutch vessels return from India with cargoes of pepper, cloves, cinnamon, and nutmeg to establish Holland's control of the Oriental spice trade. The first Dutch trading posts are set up at Banda, Amboina, and Ternate, the Dutch raise the price of pepper from 3 shillings per pound to 6 or 8, and 80 London merchants are motivated to form their own East India Company (*see* 1598; 1600).

Prices in western Europe are generally at least six times what they were a century ago. The nobility is impoverished and in many cases is forced to sell its land to the despised middle class.

An English worker must work 48 days to buy eight bushels of wheat, 32 days to buy eight bushels of rye, 29 days to buy eight bushels of barley (*see* 1506).

Gabrielle d'Estrées, marquise de Monceaux, duchesse de Beaufort, and mistress to France's Henri IV, dies suddenly at Paris. The king was about to divorce his wife to marry her (she has borne several of his children), and her name will survive on French menus to denote a dish of creamed truffles (it will also survive in the house of Vendôme). The king's name will be applied to grand marmite Henri IV, a big pot of boiled beef and chicken, beef marrow, and many vegetables.

"It is unseasonable and unwholesome in all months that have not an R in their names to eat an oyster," writes London author Henry Buttes in *Dyets Dry Dinner*. But while oysters spawn in such months in French and English waters, the concern of Buttes is not with any threat to their seeming inexhaustibility but rather with the difficulty of keeping oysters fresh in warm weather.

Sir Edward Kennel, commander in chief of the Royal Navy, offers his ships' companies a punch (possibly from the Hindu word *panch*, meaning five, to denote the five ingredients—spirits, sugar, citrus juice, water, and aromatic flavorings) made in this case from 80 casks of brandy, nine of water, 80 pints of lemon juice, 25,000 limes, 1,300 pounds of Lisbon sugar, five pounds of nutmegs, 300 biscuits, and a cask of Malaga, all brewed in a huge marble basin and served to 6,000 guests by ships' boys (who serve 15-minute shifts to avoid getting drunk from the fumes) sailing the punch in a rosewood boat. Punch is served in seaport taverns, usually in mazers (plain wooden or earthenware bowls), although middle-class Englishmen are now abandoning mazers in favor of glasses, pewter tankards, and two-handled cups. Punch will remain largely a drink of maritime towns until the 1620s or '30s (*see* Fish House Punch, 1732).

1600

$ The Honourable East India Company, the Governor and Merchants of London Trading into the East Indies is chartered December 31 to make annual voyages to the Indies via the Cape of Good Hope, challenging Dutch control of the spice trade (*see* 1599). Its initial capital is £70,000, its first governor Sir Thomas Smith (*see* 1601).

⚡ A new French canal links the Rhône and the Seine rivers (*see* 1603; 1765).

✒ Cookbook: *Cooking, or A Book about Different Foods to be Prepared in a Useful and Tasty Way* by Bohemian nobleman Rodovsky of Hustorany.

🌾 *Théâtre d'agriculture des champs* by French Huguenot squire Olivier de Serres, 61, seigneur de Pradel, is a revolutionary treatise on agriculture. The Languedoc landowner has imported maize from Italy and hops from England, he has introduced root crops for winter fodder, and he has sown grass on land normally left fallow. While the work impresses Henri IV who has parts of it read to him as he dines in public, only a few enthusiasts adopt the innovations of Serres, the peasants being too conservative and the nobles too preoccupied with other matters.

🥤 Smugglers break the Arabian monopoly in coffee growing. They take "seven seeds" of unroasted coffee beans from the Arabian port of Mocha to the western ghats of southern India (*see* Java, 1690).

17th Century

1601

The first English spice fleet sails out of Woolwich in January under the command of James Lancaster, a veteran of Francis Drake's 1588 battle with the Spanish Armada. Lancaster's 600-ton flagship *Red Dragon* is twice the size of the *Hector* or of any of the other three vessels outfitted by the East India Company (*see* 1600; 1602).

The East India Company's James Lancaster (above) doses his crew with lemon juice while at the Cape of Good Hope, then heaves to off Madagascar to take on more lemons and oranges. His 200 men are the only crew not decimated by scurvy.

The word "coffee" appears in an English account by William Parry of the Persian expedition of adventurer Anthony Sherley, who 2 years ago failed in an effort to make an alliance between Elizabeth and Persia's Shah Abbas. Sherley has also failed to make military alliances for the shah against the Turks, but he has introduced coffee to London, where it sells at £5 per ounce (*see* 1582; 1609).

Most Londoners drink beer, ale, wine, cider, and posset—a hot drink popular since the Renaissance that is made of milk curdled with ale, wines, or some other liquor and usually spiced with nutmeg. It will remain popular through this century and the next.

1602

English explorer Bartholomew Gosnold discovers a peninsula that will be called Cape Cod on the coast of what will be known as New England (*see* fish, below).

James Lancaster's English East India Company fleet arrives in June at Achin in northern Sumatra. Portuguese traders have antagonized the local ruler, and he is happy to meet the victors over Portugal's Spanish ally in 1588. Finding no ready market for his wrought iron and clothing stores, Lancaster engages a large Portuguese galleon, defeats her, and loots her cargo of jewels, plate, and merchandise, some of which he trades for pepper at the Dutch port of Bantam in Java.

The United East India Company chartered March 20 by the Staats-General combines various Dutch companies to eliminate cutthroat competition. It receives a 21-year monopoly and sweeping powers to wage defensive wars, make treaties, and build forts in the Indies. This new Dutch East India Company doubles and even triples European pepper prices.

Cookbooks: *Delightes for Ladies, To Adorn Their Persons, Tables, Closets and Distilatories: With Beuties, Banquets, Perfumes and Waters* by Sir Hugh Plat, now 50, contains recipes for candy and preserves. Plat will be credited with such improvements as the turnspit (*see* 1596). *A Closet for Ladies and Gentlemen, or, The Art of Preserving* is published at London.

Bartholomew Gosnold (above) anchors in the harbor of what will later be Provincetown and notes in his log that he "tooke there a great store of Cod Fysshes."

110

1603

A Russian famine kills tens of thousands. Czar Boris orders distribution to the neediest of grain from the palace granaries.

Philip III sends food to starving Portuguese colonists in drought-stricken northeastern Brazil.

Japan's Tokugawa shogunate begins to move the country from a rice economy to a money economy, and while Japan will have 125 crop failures in 265 years, with some degree of famine each time, her industry, commerce, and national wealth will increase. However, a rising living standard and a large population increase will produce economic troubles.

The English East India Company's James Lancaster returns home with 278 of his original 460 men and sells a cargo of more than 1 million pounds of pepper at a good profit to the company (see 1601; 1602). Lancaster is knighted and becomes a proprietor of the company (see Bantam, 1605).

France begins a canal project to link the Atlantic with the Mediterranean (see 1681).

1604

Cookbook: *Elinor Fettiplace's Receipt Book* contains 134 recipes. Lady Fettiplace (*née* Poole), 33, left her Gloucestershire home in 1589 to marry Richard Fettiplace at Appleton Manor, Berkshire.

1605

English ships of the East India Company reach Bantam and load up with pepper.

Nonfiction: *Description de l'île des hermaphrodites* satirizes the manners of the courtiers of France's Henri IV, saying that it is amusing "to watch them eat with their forks, because those who weren't as skillful as others let as much food fall on their plates and on the floor as they manage to put in their mouths" (see 1569; Coryate, 1611).

The recipe for a cordial that will come to be known as Chartreuse is given to the Chartreuse monastery at Paris by the marechal d'Estrées. Monks at the monastery are members of the Carthusian order founded in 1084 by Saint Bruno.

1606

France's Henri IV tells the king of Savoy that if he lives for another 10 years he wishes that "there would not be a peasant so poor in all my realm who would not have a chicken in his pot every Sunday" (*Je veux que le dimanche chaque paysan ait sa poule au pot*), but French peasants live mainly on bread and gruel and the king will be assassinated in 1610.

1607

English vagrants outside Northampton demonstrate in June against the enclosure of common lands and other abuses by the landed gentry; several are killed in "Captain Pouch's revolt" and three are hanged as an example.

Jamestown, Virginia, is founded May 14 by Capt. Christopher Newport of the London Company, who has sailed into the Chesapeake Bay April 26 with his ships the *Godspeed*, the *Sarah Constant*, and the *Discovery*. The colonists aboard his vessels have been supplied with horses, cattle, hogs, goats, sheep, and chickens; the hogs thrive on the roots, berries, and snakes they find in the forest and begin to multiply; the colonists find mussels and oysters lying "thicke as stones" and strawberries "four times bigger and better than ours in England" but lack the fishhooks and nets needed to catch the bass, flounder, herring, shad, sturgeon, and trout that abound in the streams and coastal waters of their new home. Newport sails for England June 22, leaving the colonists under the command of Capt. John Smith, 27. Coming for the most part from the gentry, the men are incompetent farmers, and most of the migratory birds, wild turkeys, grouse, eagles, hawks, and other fowl elude them. By autumn they are sick and starving, having buried at least 50. Capt. Smith goes up the Chickahominy River in December to trade for corn with the Algonquins and is captured but then released (see 1608).

A third English East India Company fleet sails in March for the Indies. The fleet includes the *Red Dragon* and the *Hector*, as in 1601, and will return with cloves and other cargo that will yield a profit of 234 percent (*see* 1621).

A broadside entitled "Certaine Philosophical Preparations of Foode and Beverage for Sea-men" is issued by Sir Hugh Plat, who will die next year at age 60 (*see* 1596). He lists 12 foods and medicines for use at sea, describing pasta as being "in the form of hollow pipes, or wafers," "called by the name of *macarone* amongst the Italians, and are not unlike (save only wantonely in forme) to the coscos of Barbary." Plat says, "There is sufficient matter to bee hadd al the yeare long, for the composition thereof." He recommends serving pasta "in stede of bread and meate" because it is "both pleasing and of good nourishment unto a hungry man."

Capt. John Smith (above) finds such an "abundance of fish, lying so thicke with their heads above the water, as for want of nets . . . we attempted to catch them with frying pans." Salmon, bigger than any caught in Europe, swim up 30 North American rivers.

Capt. John Smith tolerated no idlers in the "starving times" of the Virginia colony.

1608

Capt. Christopher Newport arrives at Jamestown in January with 110 new Virginia colony settlers (*see* 1607). He finds that disease and malnutrition have reduced the original contingent to a group of 40. Capt. John Smith is elected president of the Jamestown Council September 10 and tries to cope with the disease and famine that have ravaged the colony since late summer.

France exports so much grain that "it robbeth all Spain of their silver and gold that is brought thither out of their Indies," says English soldier George Carew, 53, Baron Carew of Clapton.

An Englishman reporting on his travels describes having seen Italians eating with forks, "not used in any other country that I saw on my travels, neither doe I thinke that any other nation in Christendome doth use it, but only Italy."

The Jamestown colonists (above) find the natives growing peanuts, a legume which the Powhatan tribesmen call "groundnuts" because they grow underground, whereas all other nuts grow on trees.

1609

Mare Liberum by Dutch jurist Hugo Grotius (Huigh de Groot), 26, urges freedom of the seas to all nations. Commissioned by the Dutch East India Company to support its claims against the Portuguese in an ongoing dispute over dominion of the oceans, his work is premised on the assumption that the sea's major known resource—fish—exists in inexhaustible supply.

The Virginia colony declines in population to 67 by January as food stocks run low despite the introduction of carrots, parsnips, and turnips (*see* 1608). The colonists discover that their stores of corn have rotted and been consumed by rats. In a period that will be called the "starving times" until crops can be harvested, Capt. John Smith disperses the survivors to various points depending on their aptitudes for fishing, gathering, and hunting. Some catch sturgeon, whose flesh is pounded and mixed with sorrel and other herbs to make "bread and good meat." Some gather cattail roots, marsh marigolds, Jerusalem artichokes, and other wild plants, but food remains scarce and summer brings hundreds of new arrivals to the colony. Capt. Smith orders idlers to work and arranges for the purchase of food from Indians but is obliged to return to England after sustaining a serious injury. Corn stocks soon disappear; the natives, no longer friendly, try to prevent the colonists from gathering wild foods; men, women, and children subsist on acorns, roots, walnuts, berries, mushrooms, and a little fish when they are lucky. Horses, dogs, cats, rats, and snakes are all consumed, and many colonists die of starvation (*see* 1610).

Spain's Philip III recognizes the independence of the Netherlands but does not seize the opportunity to reform Spanish society, which is rapidly decaying through the extravagance of the court and nobility. Shipments of silver from the Americas have diminished, sheep herding is replacing agriculture, and the country must import large quantities of food while exporting olive oil, wine, wool, and luxury goods, much of it to America.

Cookbook: *Libro del arte de cozina, en el qual se contiene el modo de guisar de comer en qual quier tiempo, assi de carne, come de pescado . . . assie de pasteles, tortas, y salsas . . .* by Spanish author Diego Granado Maldonado is published at Madrid.

Theater: *Coriolanus* by William Shakespeare, who relates hunger to political unrest: "They said they were an-hungry; sigh'd forth proverbs,/ That hunger broke stone walls, that dogs must eat,/ That meat was made for mouths, that the gods send not/ Corn for rich men only; with these shreds/ They vented their complainings" (I, i).

English traveler William Biddulph visits Constantinople and writes, "Their most common drink is coffa, which is a black kind of drink made of a kind of pulse, like pease, called coava; which being ground in a mill, and boiled in water, they drink it as hot as they can suffer; which they find to agree very well with them against their crudities and feeding on herbs and raw meats" (*see* 1601; 1650).

1610

France's Henri IV, now 56, is assassinated May 14 at Les Halles, the great Paris food market, when his carriage is stalled between two vendors' carts that have been overturned in a narrow lane and a fanatic seizes the opportunity.

English soldier Thomas West, Baron de la Warr, 32, is appointed first governor of the Virginia colony. His deputy, Sir Thomas Gates, arrives at the colony in late May with 175 new immigrants (*see* 1609). Gates finds Jamestown in ruins. Indians have killed or eaten all the livestock, the seines for fishing are gone, and only 60 survivors are left from the nearly 500 who were there in the fall of last year; only 150 of the 900 colonists landed in the last 3 years have survived, the others having succumbed to starvation and disease. The colonists are primarily English but include some French, German, Irish, and Polish artisans. Few want to remain in Virginia, and they set sail with Gates for Newfoundland, where the English have fishing rights, but en route downriver in June they meet the three ships of Baron de la Warr, who orders them to return. He sends his lieutenants to Bermuda for hogs and fish, the colonists resume cultivation of their cornfields and gardens, and they soon receive fresh supplies of cattle, hogs, sheep, and poultry (*see* 1611).

Community regulations posted at Cracow, Poland, make the first recorded mention of *beygls* (bagels)—round, chewy, hard glazed rolls of leavened dough that are dipped or poached in water that is close to the boiling point before they are baked. The regulations state that bagels will be given as gifts to any women in childbirth (*see* 1932; Lender's, 1927).

Holland receives her first shipment of tea from the Orient (date approximate). Europe gets its first taste of the beverage that has been popular for centuries in China and Japan.

1611

💲 The new governor of the Jamestown colony in Virginia introduces private enterprise (*see* 1610). The colony's agriculture has been a socialized venture until now, but Sir Thomas Cole assigns three acres to each man and gives him the right to keep or sell most of what he raises (*see* 1616).

🖋 Nonfiction: *Coryat's Crudities: Hastily gobled up in Five Moneth's Travels* by English country squire Thomas Coryate, 34, of Somersetshire, who traveled to the Continent 3 years ago and walked 1,975 miles through Europe, visiting Paris, Lyons, Cremona, Turin, Venice, Heidelberg, Zurich, and Strasbourg. "The Italian," he writes, "and also most strangers that are commorant in Italy, do always at their meales use forke when they cut their meat for while with their knife which they hold in one hand they cut the meate out of the dish, they fasten their forke, which they hold in their other hand, upon the same dish; so that whatsoever he be that sitting in the company of any others at meale, should unadvisedly touch the dish of meate with his fingers which all at the table doe cut, he will give occasion of offence unto his company, as having transgressed the lawes of good manners, insomuch that for his error he shall at least be brow beaten if not reprehended in wordes. This form of feeding I understand is generally used in all places of Italy; their forkes being for the most part of yron or steele, and some of silver, but those are used only by gentlemen. The reason of this their curiosity is, because the Italian cannot by any means indure to have his dish touched with fingers, seeing all men's fingers are not alike cleane." Coryate's neighbors back in Somersetshire ridicule his foppish affectation in using a fork at table (*see* Moryson, 1616).

🎭 Theater: *The Winter's Tale* by William Shakespeare: "Let me see; what am I to buy for our sheep-shearing feast? 'Three pound of sugar; five pound of currants; rice', what will this sister of mine do with rice? . . . I must have saffron, to color the warden pies; mace, dates, — that's out of my note; nutmegs seven; a race or two of ginger, — but that I may beg, — four pounds of prunes, and as many of raisins o' the sun" (IV, ii).

🐟 The Muscovy Company dispatches the first English ship to be fitted out for whaling (*see* 1557). The 150-ton *Mary Margaret* skippered by Steven Benet kills a small whale and 500 walrus in Spitzbergen's Thomas Smyth's Bay, but the ship is lost with all hands on her return voyage (*see* 1608; 1612).

1612

🐟 The Muscovy Company sends out four whaling ships, takes 17 whales, and pays its shareholders a 90 percent dividend. Its whaling ventures will have only occasional success in the next dozen years, however, and the English will virtually abandon whaling, not to resume for another 150 years.

1613

✳ An English ship arrives at Hirado, a small Japanese island off Nagasaki in Kyushu, and its captain presents the daimyo Chinshin Matsura with pepper-flavored beef, pork cooked with carrots, onions, and turnips, white bread, and wine.

💲 English merchant John Jourdain buys pepper in Sumatra and cloves at Amboina and Ceram in the Spice Islands.

👫 Spain's population falls as a consequence of wars and emigration to overseas colonies. The country becomes largely a wool-growing nation in a period of decadence and agricultural decline (*see* 1561).

1614

💲 England's Levant Company brings home pepper and other spices aboard its big Indiamen from Java and Sumatra for re-export to Constantinople.

1615

⚔ The Spanish infanta Anne of Austria, 14, marries France's Louis XIII, who has learned to cook his own food for fear of being poisoned (see chocolate, below).

🖋 Fiction: *Il ingenioso hidalgo don Quixote de la Mancha* by Spanish novelist Miguel de Cervantes Saavedra, 68, whose burlesque of romantic chivalry contains such aphorisms as "A finger in every pie"

(I, iii, 6); "Venture all his eggs in one basket" (I, iii, 9); and "The proof of the pudding is in the eating" (I, iv, 10).

Cookbooks: *The English Hus-wife, Contayning, The inward and outward vertues which ought to be in a compleat woman, As, her skill in Physicke, Cookery, Banquetingstuffe, Diftillation . . . Dayries, Brewing, Baking and all other things belonging to an Household* by author Gervase Markham, 47, who writes, "*How to bake Eeles* After you have drawn your Eeles, chop them into small pieces of three or four inches, and season them with Pepper, Salt and Ginger, and so put them into a Coffin with a good lump of butter, great Raisons, Onions small

Gervase Markham, an English contemporary of Cervantes, gave practical instructions in cookery. NEW YORK PUBLIC LIBRARY

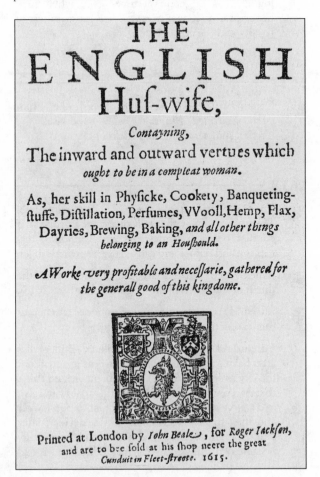

THE
ENGLISH
Huf-wife,
Contayning,
The inward and outward vertues which
ought to be in a compleat woman.

As, her skill in Physicke, Cookery, Banqueting-
ftuffe, Diftillation, Perfumes, VVooll, Hemp, Flax,
Dayries, Brewing, Baking, *and all other things
belonging to an Houfhould.*

*A Worke very profitable and neceffarie, gathered for
the generall good of this kingdome.*

Printed at London by *Iohn Beale*, for *Roger Iackfon*,
and are to bee fold at his fhop neere the great
Cunduit in Fleet-ftreete. 1615.

chopt, and so close it, bake it, and serve it up." He gives instructions, also, for preparing *A Herring Pye, Compound Sallet, To bake an Olive-Pye, To bake a Chickin Pie, Additions unto Sawces; To make any Quelquechose, To make finer Jumbals* (pastries), *Course Ginger Bread, A Warden Pie, A Spinnage Tart, To make a very good Banbury Cake, Rice Puddings,* and *To candy any Roots, Fruits, or Flowers. A New Booke of Cookerie* by English author John Murrell gives instructions in how, among other things, "To boyle a Capon larded with Lemmons," "To bake a Steake pye with a French pudding in the Pye," and "To make some Kick-Shaws [quelques choses] in paste." *Il Convito* by Italian author Ottavio Rabasco gives advice on how to plan banquets in private houses and for public occasions.

Gervase Markham (above) gives a recipe for mince pie: "Take a leg of mutton, and cut the best of the best flesh from the bone, and parboil it well: then put to it three pound of the best mutton suet, and shred it very small: then spread it abroad, and season it with pepper and salt, cloves and mace: then put in a good store of currants, great raisins and prune, clean washed and picked, a few dates sliced, and some orange-pills sliced: then being all well mixed together, put it into a coffin, or into divers coffins, and so to bake them: and when they are served up, open the lids, and strew store of sugar on the top of the meat, and upon the lid. And in this sort you may also bake beef or veal; only the beef would not be parboiled, and the veal will ask a double quantity of suet."

"Your cream being neatly and sweet kept," writes Markham (above), "you shall churn it [to make butter]. . . . Now for churning, take your cream and through a strong and clean cloth strain it into the churn; and then covering the churn close, and setting it in a place fit for the action in which you are employed (as in the summer in the coolest place in your dairy), and exceeding early in the morning or very late in the evening, and in the winter in the warmest place in your dairy, and in the most temperate hours, as about noon or a little before or after, and so churn it, with swift strokes, marking the noise of the same which will be solid, heavy and entire, until you hear it alter, and the sound is light, sharp and more spirity: and then you shall say that your butter breaks, which perceived both by this sound, the lightness of the churn-staff, and the sparks and drops which will appear yellow about the lip of the churn, and cleanse with your hand both the lid and inward sides of the churn, and having put all together you shall cover the churn again, and then with easy strokes round, and not to the bottom, gather the butter together into one entire lump and body, leaving no pieces thereof several or unjoined."

Anne of Austria brings along Spanish chocolate as a gift to her 14-year-old husband; it is served at their wedding feast, and use of chocolate will soon spread to the Lowlands and Italy, where drinking chocolate will become fashionable (*see* 1590; 1659).

1616

French explorer Samuel de Champlain, 49, returns from North America, where he has been lieutenant of Canada since 1612, and brings with him the Jerusalem artichoke, the tuber from a kind of sunflower which the French will initially call *artichaut de Canada* (Canadian artichoke), *poire de terre* (earth pear), or *topinambour* (after a tribe from Brazil); Italians will call it *girasole*, or turning to the sun).

Jamestown, Virginia, colonists each receive 100 acres of land after having worked until now for the London Company. Each colonist will soon be given an additional 50 acres for each new settler he brings to Virginia (*see* 1611; 1618).

Mitsui begins its rise toward becoming the world's largest business organization. Rebelling against his noble caste, Japanese *samurai* Mitsui Sokubei Takatoshi opens a sake and soy sauce establishment, and his wife, Shuho, finds that patrons will pawn their valuables for a drink of sake (*see* 1673).

An itinerary written by Fynes Moryson, Gent., is published at London and urges Englishmen to "lay aside the fork of Italy" (*see* Coryate, 1611; Jonson, below). Of his countrymen's diet he writes, "The English have an abundance of white meats, of all kinds of flesh, fowl, and fish of things good for food. In the seasons of the year they English eat fallow deer plentifully, as bucks in summer and odes in winter, which they bake in pasties, and this venison pasty is a dainty, rarely found in any other kingdom. England yea perhaps one County herefor, hath more

fallow deer than all Europe that I have seen. No kingdom in the world hath so many dove-houses. Likewise brawn [boiled and pickled pork] is a proper meat to the English, not known to others. English cooks, in comparison with other nations, are most commended for roasted meats" (*compare* Kalm, 1748).

Theater: *The Devil Is an Ass* by English playwright Ben Jonson, 44, who has one of his characters ask another what forks are, the reply being, "The laudable use of forks, brought into custom here, as they are in Italy, to the sparing of napkins" (*see* Morison, above). *The Queen of Corinth* by English playwright John Fletcher, 37, satirizes Thomas Coryate as "the fork-carving traveller." Anne of Austria, who last year married France's Louis XIII, will never use a fork, plunging her hands into the serving dish as in medieval times even when such behavior is no longer *comme il faut* for members of royalty and the aristocracy.

1617

Cookbook: *Arte de cocina* by Spanish chef Francisco Martínez Montiño, who supervises the kitchen staff serving Philip (Felipe) III, now 38.

1618

The Defenestration of Prague May 23 precipitates a Thirty Years' War that will devastate Europe in a conflict between Protestants and Catholics, disrupting agriculture and causing widespread hunger.

Jamestown produces a large enough crop to end the threat of starvation in the Virginia colony (*see* 1616).

Burgundy bans the planting of potatoes on charges that eating the tuber produces leprosy.

Eccentric London physician William Butler dies after having set up a number of taverns in and about the city to sell "Dr. Butler's Ale," a medicated drink that he concocted from sarsaparilla, caraway seed, and scurvy grass. Having studied first to be a lawyer and then to be a clergyman, Butler decided after graduation in 1572 to enter medicine and eventually became court physician to James I. Most of his taverns close or change their names following his death, but one will survive for centuries in Mason's Alley under the name Ye Olde Dr. Butler's Head.

 English gardeners are warned not to plant apricots or peaches in the cold climate of the British Isles.

1620

The 180-ton vessel *Mayflower* out of Southampton arrives off Cape Cod November 11 with 100 Pilgrims plus two more born at sea during the 66-day voyage in which those crowded aboard the poorly provisioned vessel have survived on "salt horse" (preserved beef), smoked bacon, smoked codfish, smoked herrings, dried fish, hardtack, brown and white biscuit, moldy cheese, root vegetables, grains, dried peas, and beer, the latter in ironbound casks guarded by cooper John Alden, 21. The English religious separatists observe ducks, geese, and partridges; they come across an Indian cache of maize and beans, find acorns, mussels, clams, lobsters, and herbs that include wild leeks and onions, but they are able to get through the winter largely through the help of the Pemaquid Samoset and the Wampanoags Hobomah and Massasoit, who have learned some English from earlier visitors and share tribal stores of maize, dried strawberries, and walnuts with the new colonists. Still, roughly half will die within 3 months of starvation, scurvy, and disease (*see* 1621).

Nonfiction: *Via Recta* by English author Tobias Venner, who writes, "Cream . . . is the very head and flower of milk; but it is somewhat of a gross nourishment, and by reason of the unctuosity of it quickly cloyeth the stomach, relaxeth and weakeneth the retentive faculty thereof, and is easily converted into phlegm, and vaporous fumes."

1621

Dutch forces complete their conquest of the three islands that constitute the Bandas from the Portuguese and vie with the English for control of the spice trade (*see* Amboina, 1623).

Another 35 colonists arrive at Plymouth, joining survivors of last year's *Mayflower* party. The Pil-

grims find beach plums and soft-shell crabs to help sustain them (*see* Thanksgiving, below).

The Dutch West India Company is chartered by Holland, whose vessels have been making inroads into Spain's overseas empire. The new company, which receives a monopoly in trade with Africa and the Americas, will annex much of Brazil and, later, Guiana; it will also annex Curaçao and other West Indian islands, defying the Spanish ban on foreign traders and, in some places, offering to finance cacao plantation owners and carry their products to market. Neither the French nor English will be able to match the service they offer, and the Dutch will for some years control the supply of cacao beans, which they will buy in bulk, process into chocolate, and export in small lots to foreign buyers.

The English East India Company completes its 12th voyage to the Indies, having earned an average profit of 138 percent on each voyage.

An Englishman calculates that 3,000 tons of spices bought in the Indies for £91,041 will fetch £789,168 at Aleppo, the trading center at the eastern end of the Mediterranean.

The Botanic Garden of Oxford opens with plants and trees selected for scientific study (*see* Chelsea Physic Garden, 1673).

New England's Pilgrims celebrate their first Thanksgiving Day (*see* 1863; dinner, below).

Potatoes are planted for the first time in the German states. Peasants resist any innovation, but potatoes and rice in the next century and a half will largely replace the dried peas, lentils, and chick-peas that have been the basic starches of European diets (*see* 1744).

Native Americans encountered by the English colonists boil or roast young ears of corn; use it in stews, which may also contain meat, roots, beans, wild peas, squashes, mulberries, and other foods; dry it to make a powder that is formed into cakes called pones, which are boiled and then baked on hot stones; boil coarser parts of the grain for hours to make pottages whose name is translated by the colonists as *hominy*; parch the kernels and eat them whole; use it to make corn flour for *no-cake*, which keeps well and is widely used by colonists as well as

Indians; and boil it with beans or other foods to make *succotash*. The colonists adopt the words hominy, no-cake, pone, samp, succotash, and suppawn from the Indians.

New England's Pilgrim colonists entertain 92 Indian guests, including Chief Massasoit, at a November Thanksgiving breakfast-dinner. The feast, which by some accounts continues for 3 days, includes roast duck, roast goose, venison from five deer shot by the Indian guests, clams, eels, leeks, watercress, wheat and corn breads, wild plums, homemade wine, and possibly wild turkeys shot by the colonists. Popcorn, which is introduced to the Pilgrims by the chief's brother, gives the colonists a novel treat, but their everyday fare runs to English puddings, made mostly from flour that is steamed in molds suspended over hearthfires in kettles. (Boston brown bread—produced from a mixture of rye and wholewheat flour, cornmeal, and molasses—will come from steamed pudding.)

Plymouth colonists (above) have difficulty growing wheat, barley, and peas in fields poorly cleared of stumps and rocks, but they are aided by a Wampanoag Indian who was kidnapped from Patuxet by slaver Thomas Hunt in 1615 and sold into slavery at Málaga, Spain. Tisquantum (or Squanto) has made his way back from Spain, presents himself at the Pilgrim settlement on Cape Cod Bay March 16, speaks some English, supplies the Pilgrims with game, and shows them how to catch eels, how to recognize wild foods, how to find groundnuts (peanuts), and how to plant maize and beans using alewives, shad, or menhaden as fertilizer, a European idea that he has learned either from French colonists in Maine and Canada or from English colonists in Newfoundland who have acquired the knowledge from the French. Tisquantum's people rely on gardening for at least half their food supply, obtaining the rest from deer and bear venison, nuts, berries, opossum, turtlemeat, shellfish, even skunk. Their maize is mostly low-growing flint corn with eight-rowed ears of white kernels. The Pilgrims, whose maize harvest is adequate in the fall but whose wheat, barley, and peas all fail, will soon plant hardier strains of wheat and—more extensively—rye.

Jamestown colonists build the first American grist mill to produce flour from their wheat. It is the first wheat grown successfully in the New World (*see* Columbus, 1494), but since the Virginia colonists lack farming tools and knowledge their wheat crops will be of only small significance for some time to come.

1622

The Plymouth Plantation receives 67 new arrivals, and earlier colonists are forced to go on short rations. The harvest is poor, and some settlers steal corn before it is harvested. Pumpkins—a squash variety known to them as "pompions"—help the Pilgrims survive (*see* 1623).

Virginia colonists who pick corn prematurely are subjected to public whipping. The population of the Virginia colony has quadrupled to some 1,400 in the last 5 years but is reduced this year by disease and Indian massacres.

1623

The Dutch, who monopolized Japan's European trade, were objects of curiosity to the Japanese.

The Massacre of Amboina by Dutch East India Company agents ends English East India Company efforts to trade with the Spice Islands, Japan, and Siam. The Dutch seize 10 rival English traders and torture them before executing them.

The Plymouth Plantation receives 60 new settlers, who are given lobster and a little fish along with spring water for lack of anything better to eat and drink (*see* 1622). The colony has six goats, 50 pigs, and many hens. Pilgrim fathers assign each family its own parcel of land, forsaking the communal Mayflower Compact. Given new incentive, women and children join with men to plant corn and increase production (*see* 1624).

 Brazil has 350 sugar plantations, up from just five in 1550 (*see* 1635).

1624

The Plymouth Plantation produces enough food for the first time to end the threat of starvation, but there is still no great abundance (*see* 1623); there are cows to provide milk and sometimes beef, but those colonists who cannot fend for themselves in obtaining venison, fowl, and fish continue to suffer from malnutrition and even outright hunger.

Theater: *Neptune's Triumph* by Ben Jonson contains the following exchange:

Cook: Were you ever a cook?

Poet: A Cook? no surely.

Cook: Then you can be no good poet: for a good poet differs nothing at all from a master-cook. Either's art is the wisdom of the mind.

1625

The Plymouth Plantation for the first time has "corn sufficient, and some to spare for others"; Governor William Bradford, writing home to England, credits part of the improvement to a revised plan of communal labor with equal rations, each family being assigned land according to its size: "This . . . made all hands very industrious." (*see* 1624).

Flemish painter Peter-Paul Rubens, 48, depicts a goiter in his portrait of France's queen mother Marie de' Medici, 52. The thyroid gland swelling is esteemed as a mark of beauty when only moderate in size (*see* Baumann, 1896).

1626

English philosopher-statesman Sir Francis Bacon experiments with the idea of freezing chickens by stuffing them with snow, publishes his work under the title "Touching the conservation and induration of bodies," but catches pneumonia (or bronchitis) and dies April 9 at age 65.

Dutch whalers establish the port of Smeerenberg in Spitzbergen to process right whales, so called by the English to distinguish them from "wrong" whales, which sink when dead. The whales are prized not as food but for their oil and whalebone, used respectively for illumination and lubrication and as stays.

1627

Barbados in the West Indies is colonized by some 80 English settlers, who arrive aboard the *William and John*, captained by John Powell but owned by a Dutch merchant in England. Capt. Powell captures a Portuguese ship bound for Lisbon with Brazilian sugar, he delivers her cargo to the *William and John*'s Dutch owner, the Dutchman sells the sugar for nearly £10,000, and he devotes the windfall to developing the new colony at Barbados, an island never seen by Christopher Columbus (*see* 1636).

The English East India Company will omit paying dividends to its stockholders in 16 of the next 50 years, but they will be the only dividendless years in the 180 years between 1602 and 1780 (*see* 1708).

Shad ascend the Hudson River March 11 with such regularity each year that Dutch colonists at Nieuw Amsterdam call the herring *elft* (the eleven fish). In other colonies it will be called the May Fish because

Shad swarmed up the Hudson River each March, providing Dutch colonists with plenty of food.

1627

it comes up the rivers to spawn in that month. Shad is considered the poor man's fish; most are dried and smoked for later use in stews.

Dutch colonists at Nieuw Amsterdam (above) will enrich the American cuisine in the next 37 years with cookies (*koekjes*), coleslaw, and waffles (*see* Irving, 1820).

Haig whisky is introduced by Scottish distiller John Haig, whose "dimple" bottle will be widely popular in centuries hence.

1628

De Alimentas by Italian professor of medicine Johannes Sala, who says, "Far the greater part of mankind live on bread alone, and of the rest of our race, who have other things, it is the settled practice to eat two or three times as much bread as anything else." Standards of living are generally measured by the amount of meat and fish consumed.

1629

Apple seeds are planted in the Massachusetts Bay Colony by Puritan Gov. John Endecott, 41, whose English trees mark the beginning of large-scale apple cultivation in North America (*see* Sullivan, 1779; "Johnny Appleseed," 1801).

"The aboundance of sea fish are almost beyond believing," writes Salem Puritan minister Francis Higginson, 42, of the Massachusetts Bay Colony. "And sure I would scarse have believed it, except I had seen it with my owne eys. I saw great store of whales and grampusse [grampus, or dolphins] and such aboundance of mackerils that it would astonish one to behold, likewise cod-fish in aboundance on the coast, and in their season are plentifully taken. There is a fish called a basse, a most sweet and wholesome fish as ever I did eat, it is altogether as good as our fresh sammon."

1630

Francis Higginson of the Massachusetts Bay Colony writes that the colony's offshore waters are so full of lobster that he is "soon cloyed with them, they were so great, and fat, and luscious." Lobster will for centuries be regarded as food for the poor.

Kikkoman soy sauce is originated at Noda, 25 miles upriver from Edo, by the Mogi and Takanashi families, who also develop miso (bean paste) to serve the growing community of Edo (*see* 1558). They adopt the name Kikko (tortoise shell) Man (10,000) because the tortoise is thought to live for 10,000 years and many have a hexagon pattern on their shells, which will be the Kikkoman trademark (*see* 1957).

Lemonade (*citron pressé*) is invented at Paris as sugar imported from the French West Indies drops in price (*see* artificial ice, 1550).

Lobsters were so plentiful on the New England coast that lobster meat was held in low esteem.

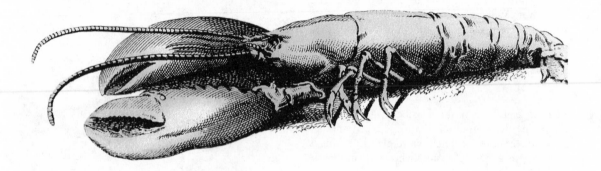

1631

Massachusetts colonists erect a grist mill at Watertown and in 2 years will set up another one at Dorchester and one at Boston (*see* 1621).

Potatoes are cultivated in so much of Europe, yield so much food per unit of land, and grow so well even in years when grain crops are at famine level that the tubers have encouraged the start of a population explosion in those parts of the continent where the new food is accepted and where the ravages of the Thirty Years' War have not totally disrupted society.

A ship comes into Boston harbor in January carrying lemon juice, which brings general relief from the scurvy that has affected so many colonists (*see* 1620; coffee advertisements, 1657).

1632

Nova Scotia is founded as the French colony of Acadia by settlers who will cut farms out of the region's dense forests.

Apple trees are planted by English colonists in territory that will become the New Jersey colony in 1665.

An act of Virginia colony's General Assembly orders all free adult men to plant grapevines, "the said vines [to] be weeded, tended, and well preserved," with fines for noncompliance. An earlier order by the House of Burgesses has compelled each man to plant 20 vines in an effort to develop a domestic wine industry that will free the colony of dependence on imported wines (*see* 1783).

1633

Speculation in tulip bulbs reaches new heights in the Netherlands, where one collector pays 1,000 pounds of cheese, four oxen, eight pigs, 12 sheep, a bed, and a suit of clothes for a single bulb of the Viceroy tulip. Tulip bulbs have been imported from Turkey since the last century, but the tulip's attribute of variation has been discovered only recently by a professor of botany at the 59-year-old University of Leyden, whose botanical garden is the first in the North (*see* 1636).

Klinike by English physician James Hart is one of the first medical treatises since ancient times to relate diet and health. The "immoderate use" of sugar, says Dr. Hart, "as also of sweet confections, and sugar-plums, heateth the blood, engendereth obstructions, cachexias, consumptions, rotteth the teeth, making them look black; and withal, causeth many times a loathsome, stinking breath . . . and ever this proverb (sweet meats hath often sour sauce) was verified, it holdeth in this particular" (*see* Hentzner, 1598). Not for another 2 centuries will it be known that certain kinds of streptococcus bacteria that thrive on sugar colonize the mouth and excrete acids that erode tooth enamel, but foods that do *not* contain sugar will also be found to cause tooth decay.

1634

Leonard Calvert, 27, brother of Cecilius (Cecil) Calvert, Lord Baltimore, 29, arrives in America late in March with between 200 and 300 people and establishes the Maryland colony on territory granted to his brother 2 years ago by England's Charles I. He has stopped in the Virginia colony to buy hogs, cows, bulls, and poultry, which will multiply quickly, and takes up residence in a former village of some friendly Indians, whose cleared lands are soon planted in crops. The Marylanders buy so much corn from the Indians that they ship 1,000 bushels of it to the Massachusetts colony, which has a shorter growing season, in exchange for salt fish and other goods. Women colonists go to the beaches at low tide each day to collect mussels and clams, and they gather wild greens and fruits; they milk the goats, and they barter with the Indians for venison and raccoon meat, but many find the lack of wheat, barley, and rye a "sore affliction."

Dijon, France, imposes regulations on mustard makers, requiring, among other things, that mustard be made only by workers wearing "clean and modest clothes." Later rules will require that *moutarde* be made only from brown or black mustard seeds and seasoned with wine or vinegar plus spices and herbs.

1635

Dutch forces invade and occupy northern Brazil, where Dutch planters will enter the lucrative sugar industry (*see* 1623; 1654).

Dutch forces capture Curaçao and St. Eustatius in the Caribbean, ending Spain's monopoly in cacao beans.

 The General Court of Massachusetts authorizes settlement of Concord and several families move inland to obtain more pasturage on the new frontier.

Massachusetts colonist Richard Mather writes of his voyage from England, "We had no want of good and wholesome beer and bread; and as our land stomachs grew weary of ship diet, of salt fish and salt beef, and the like . . . we used bacon and buttered peas, sometimes buttered bag-pudding, made with currants and raisins; sometimes drinked pottage of beer and oatmeal, and sometimes watered pottage well buttered." More affluent passengers on emigrant ships have their livestock and fowl aboard to be killed as the need arises, but most passengers must make do with spoiled meat and water that is often brackish, collecting rainwater from the deck and using it even though it tastes of tar.

The Chinese orange *Citrus sinensis* reaches Lisbon and is even sweeter than the "Portugals" introduced to Europe by the Portuguese in 1529.

Chocolate houses will by the middle of this century be in vogue in many of the German states as well as in France and the Italian peninsula. The high-priced cacao beans still come almost entirely from Spain, which imports them from her foreign possessions, but the Dutch West India Company has begun to challenge Spain in the cacao trade (*see* 1621).

1636

The conde-duque de Olivares invades northwestern France in a desperate gamble to defeat the French and restore Spanish power. His soldiers burn villages in Beauvaise and Picardy, plunder crops, and force peasants to flee with food, livestock, and belongings. Basque seaports are ravaged, but the French win a narrow victory at Corbie, forcing Spain into a war of attrition that will drain her for 23 years.

Springfield, Massachusetts, is founded by colonists who follow William Pynchon west to take advantage of the abundant pasturage in the area. Springfield will become an important meat-packing center.

A Dutch merchant serves a sailor a small breakfast of herring; while his back is turned, the sailor spies what he thinks is an onion, he eats it in a few quick gulps, and the merchant finds that he has lost a tulip bulb worth $25,000 to $50,000 in modern money (*see* 1634; 1637).

Painting: Dutch still-life painter Jan Davidsz de Heem, 30, moves to Antwerp because "there one could have rare fruits of all kinds, large plums, peaches, cherries, oranges, lemons, grapes and others, in fine condition and state of ripeness to draw from life."

A Dutch planter introduces sugarcane from Brazil into the West Indian island of Barbados, whose English settlers have been cultivating cotton, ginger, indigo, and tobacco for export while growing beans, plantains, and other food for their own consumption. Sugar will become the chief crop of Barbados and of all the Caribbean islands (*see* 1627).

1637

Dutch tulip prices collapse after years of speculation. Hundreds are ruined as the bottom falls out of the market (*see* 1634).

Gekkeikan Sake Co. is founded at Kyoto by a member of the Okura family, whose firm will grow to be the nation's largest sake producer.

1638

The Spanish ambassador to Rome gives a dinner at his residence on the Piazza di Spagna November 30. Don Manuel de Muera e Corte Real, marqués de Castel Rodrigo, wishes to honor the Holy Roman Emperor Ferdinand III's ambassador Fürst Johan Anton von Eckenberg, who arrived at Rome in June of last year. Hundreds of men sit down to tables lavishly decorated with ornaments of marzipan and sugar paste, napkins are intricately folded, and cold dishes are placed before the guests: meat pies baked in the shape of roses, poached and jellied capons, and larded turkey (still considered an exotic bird, called by the Italians *pollanche d'India*) with cannelloni. The various ambassadors are served individual dishes, including minestrone soup covered with artichokes and truffles; sweetbreads garnished with throstles, two for each guest, and sausages; plates of pistachios and sausages; and fried goats' heads. The second course, from the hot kitchen, consists of crusted veal with kidneys surrounded by grilled lemons and pomegranates; star-shaped pigeon pies stuffed with minced veal, artichokes, truffles, sweetbreads, and pistachio nuts; and leg of mutton roasted with juniper berries and served with little pies filled with pears in syrup and mashed prunes. The third course consists of larded and roasted partridges under crowns of paste with pastry ornaments filled with blancmange (a gelatinous sweet of Arab origin); capirostati (larded turkey stuffed with pigeons and brains with kidney sauce); and a pie of boned and roasted goats' heads served with bread. The fourth course consists of salami grassi (sausages filled with chicken meat, which has been fried and then covered with a spiced pastry); ogoia podidra (a Spanish soup containing such ingredients as sweetbreads, chopped cabbage, tripe, slices of beef, ham, and sausages, onions, and lentils); and young roasted turkeys, filled this time with little pastry shells containing capers, pomegranates, and quinces. Side dishes contain Spanish olives in beds of cedar leaves. The fifth course begins with pheasants on a buttered pastry bed and continues with minced sweetbreads mixed with truffles; ham and pine seeds served in the form of a huge raisin cake surrounded by little pies; and iced chocolate with whipped cream. The sixth and final course consists of cold dishes—ove missiche (egg yolks beaten with rose water, cooked in clarified sugar, and molded into shapes); a rich cake (*zuppa di Espagna*); and dishes containing spiced and candied sweetmeats. Dancers then serve the guests with jellied capons, which have been part of the table decorations, the napkins are changed, and fruit is served—grapes, quinces, and bergamot pears with parmesan cheese.

Honeybees will be introduced into the American colonies in the next few years, will soon escape from their domestic hives, and will establish wild colonies. Indians will call honeybees "the white man's fly," and as the bees move westward many pioneers will be led to believe that the bees are indigenous (*see* Irving, 1835).

1639

"Smithfield" hams shipped to England from the Virginia colony are sold at London's Smithfield Market, which is taken over by the city after 516 years and reorganized as a market for live cattle.

A new canal links France's Loire and Seine rivers (*see* 1603; 1681).

1640

Inflation in England reduces the value of money to one-third its value in 1540 and food prices outpace wage increases.

France enjoys power and prosperity under Louis XIII's chief minister, Armand-Jean de Plessix, cardinal de Richelieu, 54, but the mass of Frenchmen live on the edge of starvation.

Oudin's Dictionary introduces the word *haricot* for the fagioli beans brought to France by Catherine de' Medici in 1533. Oudin defines the bean as a variety of legume and uses a word derived from *héricoq*, used at least since the 14th century and probably derived from a Germanic word, *harigoté* or *aligoté*, meaning a stew or ragout of meat and vegetables, usually turnips.

Painting: *The Peasant Supper* by French painter Louis Le Nain, 52.

The Massachusetts Bay Colony sends 300,000 codfish to market and some colonists begin to grow rich in the cod fishery (*see* 1700).

The British West Indies have a population of 20,000, most of it employed in growing sugarcane.

1641

Malacca falls to Dutch forces, who gain control of the Strait of Malacca (*see* 1623; 1656).

Irish peasants begin a revolt against their landlords (who are mostly English), and the landlords respond with force, seizing livestock and standing crops in an effort to starve the peasantry (*see* 1649; potatoes, below).

💲 The first sugar factory in the English New World goes up in Barbados using equipment supplied on credit by Dutch investors against the value of the sugar to be produced. A Colonel Holdip shows the colonists "the manner of planting, the time of gathering, and the right placing of their coppers in their furnaces . . . and the true way of covering their rollers, with plates or bars of iron" (*see* 1636; 1685).

🌾 Irish peasants (above) plant potatoes in lazybeds—strips of between 500 and 800 yards in length—which provide enough potatoes for a typical family to survive if supplemented with a little pork, bacon, milk, butter, and cheese and which can be lengthened if other foods are lacking. (People in the Andes have used the same lazybed method for centuries.) Potatoes can be planted in almost any kind of ground, dug up as they are required, and popped straight into the pot (*see* 1649).

1642

✗ France's Cardinal Richelieu dies December 4 at age 57 after 18 years in which he has been the power behind the throne of Louis XIII. He leaves the Palais-Royal, which he has built for himself, to the king (*see* 1643).

🍎 Beriberi is observed in Java. Marked by debility, nervous disturbances, paralysis, heart weakness, swollen liver, weak and sore calf muscles, plugged hair follicles, and weight loss, the nutritional deficiency disease gets its name from the Sinhalese word *beri*, meaning "weakness."

1643

✗ France's Louis XIII dies May 14 at age 43. His widow, Anne of Austria, moves into the late Cardinal Richelieu's Palais-Royal with her 4-year-old son, Louis XIV, and finds it far more luxurious than the Louvre Palace (*see* restaurants, 1786).

France's nobility will rise in the next 5 years against Jules, Cardinal Mazarin, 41, in an armed struggle

that will disrupt transportation, raising the price of flour and bread.

🥤 Würzburger beer has its beginnings in a brewery started at Bavaria's Würzburg Castle.

1644

✗ The Ming dynasty, which has dominated China since 1368, ends in April with the suicide of the last Ming emperor, who hangs himself as Beijing falls to a 39-year-old bandit leader who has proclaimed himself emperor. A Ming general drives him into Hopeh (where he will be killed) and the Manchus begin the Qing (Ch'ing) dynasty, which will rule until 1912.

💲 Agrarian taxes in the Qing dynasty (above) will be the lowest in China's history, with tax collectors taking only 3 to 6 percent of the crop (although local officials will devise special imposts that will raise the levy in some places to as much as 60 percent). Tax dodging will be widespread; people will be able to survive, if only barely, and catastrophes such as wars of rebellion will drive them to the edge of starvation.

Scotland's Parliament imposes an excise tax, but Highlander distillers are outraged and the tax, which has been almost impossible to collect, will be allowed to lapse (*see* 1693).

🌐 Overuse of environmental resources under China's Qing dynasty (above) will produce occasional disasters, but famine relief will be rapid and well organized.

🌾 Food crops from the New World now grow even in remote parts of China, some communities being heavily dependent on potatoes and sweet potatoes. Food production has increased, despite the adverse climatic conditions of what later will be called the "Little Ice Age." The severe cold will soon begin to ameliorate, with warmer, wetter winters that will exacerbate problems of flooding, especially in areas that have suffered deforestation.

👫 China's population has by some accounts grown in the Ming period to an estimated 150 million, up from about 50 million in 1368, but the real population numbers are almost certainly much lower.

1648

Europe's Thirty Years' War ends October 24 in the Peace of Westphalia. Mercenary troops from Bohemia, Denmark, France, Spain, Sweden, and the German states have destroyed roughly 18,000 villages, 1,500 towns, and 2,000 castles, wreaking havoc on agricultural production.

Swedish Army officers back from the Thirty Years' War receive land grants from Queen Kristina, 21. Her grants will double the land held by the nobility as of 1611, and freehold peasants will face eviction as the expanding nobility applies German customs and attitudes toward the peasantry (*see* food crisis, 1650).

The Dutch ship *Haarlem* breaks up at Table Bay, South Africa. Ship officers Leendert Jansz and Nicholas Proot survive the wreck and are picked up 5 months later and returned to Holland, where they urge authorities to establish a settlement at Table Bay for provisioning East India fleets with fresh fruit, vegetables, and other stores (*see* Cape Town, 1652).

Flemish physician-chemist Jan-Baptista van Helmont, 69, writes that human digestion is the work of fermentation that converts food into living flesh. A different ferment causes each physiologic process, with central control vested in the solar plexus (*see* Sylvius, 1661).

Pilgrim colonists in the Massachusetts colony have poor crops and avoid starvation only by eating passenger pigeons, still abundant in the colony despite efforts to eradicate them (*see* Josselyn, 1672).

The population of the German states has fallen to 13.5 million (and possibly much less), down from an estimated 21 million at the outbreak of war in 1618. Much of the farmland in the northern states remains untilled, and food remains scarce.

1649

England's Charles I is beheaded January 30 at Whitehall, London, after 11 years of civil war in which some 100,000 have been killed; the country becomes a republic headed by Oliver Cromwell, 49, who will rule until his death in 1658. But Cromwell has no sympathy for radicals who oppose private ownership of land, and in the end it will be the gentry and nobility who profit from England's Civil War.

English troops under the command of Cromwell (above) storm Drogheda September 12, sack the town, massacre its garrison, do the same to the garrison at Wexford, and suppress an Irish uprising led by James Butler, 39, marquis of Ormond (*see* 1641). The English in the next 10 years will kill thousands of Irish by transporting them in leaky ships and destroying their livestock (their only wealth), taking their tools and lands, and leaving them with nothing but the potatoes that grow underground. With no means of growing cereal grains, the Irish will survive only by digging up potatoes from bogs and mountainsides and cooking them over peat fires (*see* 1641; 1670).

A new tax on Japanese farmers allows them barely enough for their basic needs and forces them to put their wives to work weaving cloth and to send surplus children to work in the city. The Tokugawa shōgun Iemitsu requisitions all rice, leaving the farmers with little to eat but millet.

Description of New Netherland by Dutch colonial governor Adriaen van der Donck says, "Fish of the finest qualities fill the rivers, the bays, and the sea, also, with life. Those in the fresh water were salmon, sturgeon, striped bass, drums, shad" The colonies' first lawyer, van der Donck remarks that although there are six-foot lobsters in the adjacent waters, "those a foot long are better for serving at table." Salmon swim up 30 Atlantic rivers from Connecticut to Canada on their spawning runs and are larger than any caught in Europe.

1650

Sweden suffers a food crisis after the worst harvest she will have in this century. By March the bakers of Stockholm are fighting at the town gates for flour, but while the nation's sociopolitical balance is jeopardized as the clergy and burghers side with the peasants, a threatened revolution does not materialize.

Maize is eaten for the first time in Italy, where "turkey corn" (*mais*) will be popular in polenta, in cornmeal mush, and hardened as a cake (date approximate; *see* pellagra, 1749).

 Dutch colonists at Nieuw Amsterdam receive their first shipment of tea (*see* 1610).

England's first coffeehouse opens at Oxford at the Angel Inn of Paris of St. Peter's (*see* 1609; London, 1652).

The London pub The Grapes opens in Narrow Street, Stepney, to serve local bargemen.

1651

The Japanese shōgun Iemitsu dies of beriberi at age 47 after a 28-year reign in which he has consumed a diet based heavily on white rice.

Nonfiction: *Jacula Prudentum* by the late English poet-clergyman George Herbert contains translations of proverbs that include "The eye is bigger than the belly" and "God's mill grinds slow, but sure." Herbert died in 1633 at age 40.

Cookbook: *Le Cuisinier François, enseignment la manière de bien apprester & assassonner toutes sortes de viands . . . legumes, & pâtisseries en perfection, &c.* by Paris chef F. P. (François Pierre) de La Varenne, France's first great cookery writer. La Varenne's book indicates a branching out of French cooking from medieval times, when recipes contained a superabundance of flavors and excessive use of sugar.

 "Rumbullion, alias Kill-Devill" is the "chiefe fudling they make in the Island" of Barbados, writes Richard Ligon. He calls rum (the word may come from the Latin *saccharum*, meaning "sugar") "a hott, hellish and terrible liquor" made of "suggar canes, distilled" (*see* 1641; 1655).

1652

Londoners get their first taste of coffee (below), tea, and cocoa; the growing popularity of these drinks will increase demand for sugar, and—since sugar is grown almost entirely with slave labor—their popularity will produce a rise in the slave trade.

West Indian sugar production and the African slave trade were inextricably linked.

Cape Town, South Africa, is founded by Dutch ship's surgeon Jan van Riebeeck, who goes ashore at Table Bay with 70 men carrying seeds, agricultural implements, and building materials (*see* 1648).

Massachusetts colonist Joseph Russell starts an off-shore whaling enterprise. Russell has founded New Bedford (*see* 1775; Nantucket, 1690).

London's first coffeehouse opens at the Sign of Pasqua Rosee's Head in St. Michael's Alley, Cornhill. One Daniel Edwards has obtained several bags of coffee from Constantinople and set his servant, Pasqua Rosee, up in business. Rosee distributes handbills stating that his coffee is "a very good help to digestion, quickens the spirits, and is good against sore eyes, dropsy, gout, King's-evil, &c." Within 10 years there will be 3,000 coffeehouses in London and neighboring cities. (The Sign of Pasqua Rosee's Head will become the Jamaica Wine House.)

1653

The Compleat Angler, or The Contemplative Man's Recreation by English biographer Izaak Walton, 60, is "a Discourse on Fish and Fishing, Not Unworth the Perusal of Most Anglers." A former ironmonger, Walton writes of trout, "if he is not eaten within four or five hours after he is taken [he] is worth nothing." "It is observed by the most learned physicians,"

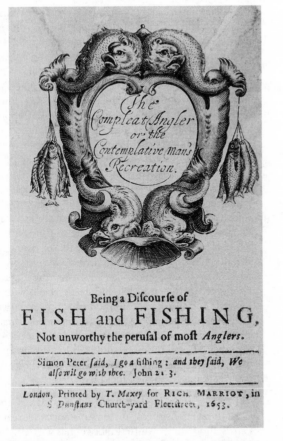

Izaak Walton knew all the angles of catching fish, which provided good food for English tables. NEW YORK PUBLIC LIBRARY

writes Walton, "that the casting off of Lent, and other fish days . . . hath doubtless been the chief cause of those many putrid, shaky, intermitting agues, unto which this nation of ours is now more subject, than those wiser countries that feed on herbs and salads and plenty of fish."

Spanish priest Bernabé Cobe describes three kinds of avocados—Mexican, West Indian, and Guatemalan. They come in hundreds of varieties, he writes, including round, tyriform, and "necked" (like a crooked-neck squash); in colors that include green, purple, maroon, and black; and in skin textures that may be barklike, scaly, or smooth (*see* Washington, 1751; Perrine, 1833).

1654 —————————————

Cookbook: *The Art of Cookery Refin'd and Augmented* by English gentleman-cook Joseph Cooper (or Copper, or Cowper), whose recipes include one for roasted capon in white wine with bacon, chestnuts, and pistachios. Cooper was brought in to serve Charles I in the 1640s.

Béchamelle (or Béchamel) cream sauce is devised by French financier Louis de Béchamel (or Béchamiel), marquis de Nointel, who serves Louis XIV in the honorary post of Lord Steward to the Royal Household. He has sunk a fortune into the Newfoundland fisheries, but Frenchmen cannot stomach the dried cod that he has had shipped from across the Atlantic, so he creates the white sauce to make the cod palatable. Two variants of the sauce, Soubise and Mornay, will commemorate the names of the commander of the French armies and of a Huguenot family, respectively.

Sugarcane is planted by the French in Martinique, which will become a major Caribbean sugar producer.

Asperge blanche (white asparagus) is widely cultivated in France and enjoys great popularity.

1655 —————————————

Royal Navy forces under the command of Vice Admiral William Penn, 34, capture the West Indian island of Jamaica from the Spaniards (who called it San Iago), freeing England from dependence on Spain for imports of sugar, molasses, and cacao beans from the island (*see* rum, below). The action precipitates a 3-year war with Spain.

Nonfiction: *Health's Improvement, or RULES Comprizing and Discovering the Nature, Method and Manner of Preparing all sorts of FOOD used in this NATION* by the late English physician Thomas Muffett says that beasts killed for food "eate much sweeter, kindlier and tenderer" if they are killed slowly and painfully. Muffett, who is believed to have written the work in 1595 but who died in June 1604 at age 51, was a student of spiders whose daughter Patience will be celebrated in a Mother Goose rhyme. He has written that meat is improved if an animal is destroyed "with fear dissolving his hardest parts and making his very heart become pulpy" rather than "if they be killed suddenly . . ." Dr. Christopher Bennett has enlarged on Muffett's work and written a brief preface, saying, " 'Tis a piece for my Palate not likely to disrelish any, where so much pleasure is interlarded with our profit. I may safely say upon this subject I know none that hath done better."

Cookbook: *Le Pâtissier François* by F. P. de La Varenne.

"Of the variety, excellency, making and true use of bread," Muffett (above) has written, "Concerning the Wheate: . . . the sorts of this Country are especially two, the one red called *Robus* . . . and the other very white and light called *Siligo*, whereof is made our purest manchet. Wheat nourisheth exceeding much and strongly: the hardest, thickest, heaviest, cleanest, brightest and growing in a fat soil, is ever to be chosen; for such wheat is most nourishing. . . . Chuse ever the yellowest without, the smoothest . . . white and full within, clean thrasht and winowed, then cleaned, washt and dryed, afterwards grossly grinded (for that makes the best flour) in a Mill wherein the grindstones are of French Marble, or some other close or hard stone. The *Meal* must neither be so finely grinded (as I said) least the bran mingle with it, nor too grossly, least you lose much flour, but moderately gross, that the bran may be easily separated, and the fine Flour not hardly Bolted. You must not presently mould up your meal after grinding, lest it prove too hot; or keep it too long lest it be fusty and create worms, or be otherwise tainted with long lie. Likewise, though the best manchet be made of the finest flour passed through a very fine boulter, yet that bread which is made of courser meale is of lighter digestion and of stronger nourishment. The *Water* must be pure, from a clear River, or Spring, not too hot . . . not too cold . . . but luke warm. The *Salt* must be very white, finely beaten, not too much, or too little, but to give an indifferent seasoning. The *Leaven* must be made of pure Wheate, it must not be too old least it prove too soure, nor too new least it work to no purpose . . . . When a just proportion is kept betwixt them both Leaven corrects the Meals and perfection, making altogether a well rellished mass called Bread which is justly called the staff of life. . . . Loaves made of pure Wheaten-meal require both more leaven and more labouring, and more baking, than either course cheate, or than Bread mingled of meal and grudgeons [the coarsest particles of husk and bran]. . . . *The Dough* of White Bread must be thoroughly wrought, and the *manner of moulding* must be first with strong kneading, then with rouling to and fro, and last of all with wheeling or turning it round about, that it may sit the closer; afterwards, cut it slightly in the midst round about, and give it a slit or two through from the top to the bottome with a small knife, to give a vent every way to the inward moisture whilst it is in baking. The Loaves should be neither too great nor too little: for as little loaves nourish least so if the loaves be too great the bread is scarce thoroughly baked in the midst. . . . It must not stay too long in the oven, least it prove crusty, dry and cholerique; not too little a while for fear it be clammy and of ill nourishment, fitter to cram Capons and Poultry, than to be given to sick or sound men. Bread being thus made strengtheneth the stomach and carries truly with it the staff of nourishment. In the Lords prayer we ask for all bodily nourishment in the name of Bread because Bread may be justly called the meat of meats. . . . Bread is never out of season, disagreeing with no sickness, age or complexion, and therefore truly called the companion of life."

"The milk of horned beasts (as Cows, Ewes and Goats) do consist of three substances, Cream, Curds and Whey," Muffett (above) has written, "so Butter is nothing but Cream twice Laboured. Pliny kneweth the true making of it, which I need not repeat, because it is nothing, or very little differeth from ours: Only I wonder with him, that *Africa*, and other Barbarous Countreys esteem it a Gentlemans dish, when here and in *Holland*, and in all the Northern Regions, it is the chief food of the poorer sort. For go from the elevation of 51 to 84 of the North pole, you shall every where find such store of good butter, as no where the like, no not in *Parma* nor *Placentia*, nor *Holland* itself, whence so much Butter and Cheese is dispersed throughout the whole world. In Iceland they make such a quantity, that having neither earthen Vessels nor Cask enough to keep it in, they make Chests of Firr, thirty or forty foot long, and five foot square, filling them yearly with salt butter, which they bury in the ground till they have occasion to use it."

French society uses a clean plate for each new dish but Englishmen continue to dine off trenchers—

wooden platters that give hearty eaters the name "trenchermen."

Rum from Jamaica (above) is introduced into the Royal Navy to replace beer, which goes sour after a few weeks at sea (*see* 1651; 1731).

1656

The Dutch in Ceylon make cinnamon a state monopoly but will not have complete control of the island's cinnamon until 1658. When prices fall too low, the Dutch will burn great quantities of the bark, and they will destroy groves of clove and nutmeg trees in the Moluccas, creating artificial scarcities that will force prices up, enriching the Dutch East India Company.

Cookbook: *The Perfect Cook being the Most Exact Directions for the Making of All Kind of Pastes, . . . Pies, Tarts . . . now Practiced by the Most Expert Cooks, Both French and English. As also The Perfect English Cook or right method of the whole art of cookery . . . To which Is added, The way of dressing all manner of flesh, fowl, and fish. The like never extant, with fifty-five way of dressing of eggs* by a Monsieur Marnetté is published at London.

London has 1,156 taverns (pubs), which serve as gathering places for the city's men.

1657

Coffee advertisements at London claim that the beverage is a panacea for scurvy, gout, and other ills.

Public sale of tea begins at London as the East India Company undercuts Dutch prices and advertises tea as a panacea for apoplexy, catarrh, colic, consumption, drowsiness, epilepsy, gallstones, lethargy, migraine, paralysis, and vertigo (*see* Garrway, below).

The first London chocolate shop opens to sell a drink known until now only to the nobility. The June 16 *London Public Advertiser* carries a notice reading, "In Bishopsgate, in the Queen's Head Alley, at a Frenchman's house is an excellent West India drink called chocolate—where you may have it ready at any time, and also unmade, at reasonable rates" (*see* 1656; 1659).

Tea is offered to Londoners at Thomas Garrway's coffee house in Exchange Alley between Cornhill and Lombard Street. Garrway advertises that tea "helpeth the Headache, giddiness, and heavyness thereof; it removeth the obstructions of the Spleen; it is good against Crudities, strengthening the weakness of the Ventricle or Stomack, causing good Appetite and Digestion, and particularly for Men of a corpulent Body, and such as are great eaters of Flesh, it vanquishes heavy dreams, easeth the Brain, and strengtheneth the Memory. It overcometh superfluous Sleep and prevents Sleepiness in general, a draught of the Infusion being taken so that without trouble whole nights may be spent at study without hurt to the Body, in that it moderately heateth and bindeth the mouth of the Stomack (it being prepared with Milk and Water), strengtheneth the inward parts, and prevents Consumptions, and powerfully assuages the pains of the Bowels, or griping of the Guts and Loosening."

Fire destroys much of Japan's capital city, Edo, and vendors who have heretofore sold prepared food from carts establish shops where patrons can sit down and eat rice, soup, broiled fish, and vegetables. The first one opens in front of Konryu Temple in the Asakusa district and gains quick popularity (*see* Paris, 1765).

1658

England's Lord Protector Oliver Cromwell dies September 3 at age 58, leaving the country still divided between royalists and republicans.

Nonfiction: *History of the Caribby Islands* by French chronicler Charles de Rochefort, who writes, "The Ananas, or pine-apple, is accounted the most delicious fruit, not only of these Islands, but of all America. It is so delightful to the eye and of so sweet a scent that Nature may be said to have been extremely prodigal of what was most rare and precious of her Treasury to this plant" (*see* 1493; 1790).

An English cookbook sanctions use of veal as food in defiance of an old Saxon tradition that had considered the killing of a veal calf a wanton act of the Norman invaders of 1066.

1658

The London periodical *Mercurious Politicus* carries an advertisement: "That excellent and by all Physitians approved China Drink called by the Chineans Tcha, by other nations Tay, alias Tea, is sold at the Sultaness Head, a cophee-house in Sweetings Rents, by the Royal Exchange, London."

1659

England's harvest comes up short, producing a dearth of food and higher prices that cause great suffering among the poor.

Paris police raid a monastery and send 12 monks to jail for eating meat and drinking wine during Lent.

Nonfiction: *Histoire générale des restaurants de France* (but France has no restaurants in the sense that the word will come to mean; *see* Boulanger, 1765).

Royal Navy official Samuel Pepys, 25, writes in his secret diary for January 24 that he has given a dinner at which was served "a dish of marrow bones, a leg of mutton, a loin of veal, a dish of fowl, three pullets, and two dozen of larks, all in a dish, a great tart, a neat's tongue, a dish of anchovies, a dish of prawns, and cheese."

1660

England's Charles II, son of the late Charles I, is proclaimed king May 8. Now 29, he returns from France May 26, arrives at Whitehall May 29, and will reign until 1685 as the monarchy is restored after 11 years of Commonwealth rule.

France's Louis XIV is married June 9 in the 13th-century Église Saint-Jean-Baptiste at Saint Jean de Luz to the Spanish infanta Marie-Thérèse (María Teresa), 22, daughter of Philip (Felipe) IV (*see* cocoa, below).

Charles II (above) strengthens England's 9-year-old Navigation Act October 1: certain "enumerated articles" from England's American colonies may be exported only to the British Isles. Included are tobacco, sugar, wool, indigo, and apples; the list will be amended to include rice, molasses, and other commodities (*see* 1663).

England's Charles II (above) builds the nation's first icehouse in St. James's Park, London.

Cookbook: *The Accomplisht Cook, or, The Art and Mystery of Cooking. Wherein the Whole Art is Revealed in a More Easie and More Perfect Method, Than Hath Been Publisht in Any Language* by English cook-gastronome Robert May, 72, who laments the fact that the custom of making dishes that startle and arouse the diner is fast disappearing. His book contains a cake recipe that calls for half a bushel of flour, three pounds of butter, 14 pounds of currants, two pounds of sugar, and three quarts of cream. He includes medieval recipes for dishes such as capilotado François: leg of mutton dressed with a pound of strained almond paste and a pound of sugar, garnished with chickens, pigeons, capons, cinnamon, and more sugar. Aside from artichokes, asparagus, primeurs, and spinach, the diet of the rich includes few vegetables, but truffles, mushrooms, and foie gras are much esteemed.

Painting: *Maidservant Pouring Milk* by Dutch painter Jan Vermeer, 27.

French planters start cultivation of cacao on Martinique; the first beans from the island will arrive at Paris in 1679.

Samuel Pepys at London notes in his secret diary that he has drunk a "cup of tee (a China drink) of which I never had drank before." His wife will not drink tea for another 7 years, and then only because "Mr. Pellingly, Potecary, recommended it." Tea sells for about 6 guineas per pound.

The Spanish infanta Marie-Thérèse (above) introduces the French court to cocoa, which will be endorsed by the Paris faculty of medicine and received with enthusiasm until it becomes surrounded with suspicion as an aphrodisiac in some circles and as a mysterious potion in others (*see* Mme. de Sévigné, 1671). Cocoa is generally drunk with cloves, sometimes with the addition of hazelnuts or almonds.

1661

London's Covent Garden becomes a market for fruit, vegetables, and flowers (*see* 1552; 1886).

Prussian-born medical professor Franz de Le Boë, 47, at Leyden (he calls himself Sylvius) echoes van Helmont's notion that human digestion is a process of chemical fermentation (*see* 1648; Borelli, 1680).

Cookbook: *The Ladies' Directory and Choice Experiments and Curiosities of Preserving and Candying Both Fruit and Flowers* by English author Hannah Woolley (or Wolley), 38.

Samuel Pepys gives a New Year's breakfast at which he provides his guests with a barrel of oysters, a dish of meat, some tongues, and a plate of anchovies.

Water ices are sold for the first time at Paris by Sicilian *limonadier* Francesco Procopio dei Coltelli from Palermo (*see* 1630). Fruit-flavored ices were originated by the Chinese, who taught the art to the Persians and Arabs (*see* Café Procope, 1670).

1662

England's Charles II marries the Portuguese princess Catherine da Braganza, 23, who introduces to the London court the Lisbon fashion of drinking tea.

Nonfiction: *History of the Worthies of Britain* by the late English clergyman-antiquary Thomas Fuller, who died last year at age 53. "He was a very valiant man who first adventured on eating of oysters," he has written, but the phrase has also been ascribed to the late James I.

Cookbook: *L'Arte de ben cucinare* by Bolognese-born cook Bartolomeo Stefani is published at Mantua, where Stefani is chief cook to the royal house of Gonzaga. The once powerful Gonzaga family eats frugally when alone but can still mount elaborate banquets for state occasions, as when Queen Kristina of Sweden visited in November 1655. Stefani's book contains recipes for unusual sauces and relishes employing fruit.

Samuel Pepys notes in his secret diary for January 11 that he has served his dinner guests "after oysters, at first course, a hash of rabbits, a lamb, and a rare chine of beef. Next a great dish of roasted fowl (cost me around 30 s.) and a tart and then fruit and cheese. My dinner was noble and enough." When Pepys hires a chef to prepare dinner for guests March 26, the menu includes a brace of stewed carp, six roasted chickens,

and a jowl of salmon for the first course; a tanzy (a pudding containing the herb tansy) and two neats' tongues and cheese for the second course. "And we were very merry all the afternoon talking and singing and piping on the flageolettes." Pepys often eats bread, butter, and cheese at bedtime in lieu of supper.

Catherine da Braganza (above) imports the Chinese orange to England (*see* 1635).

Catherine (above) is an inveterate tea drinker, and upper-class Englishmen will follow her example.

1663

Dutch forces hold the best pepper ports of India's Malabar coast, giving them a virtual stranglehold on the spice trade once controlled by Portugal.

Japan's Tokugawa government issues an order banning extravagant use of food and drink and demanding more restraint.

A Second Navigation Act passed by Parliament July 27 forbids English colonists to trade with other European countries. European goods bound for America must be unloaded at English ports and reshipped, even though English export duties and profits to middlemen may make prices prohibitive in America (*see* 1672).

Parliament reduces duties on English grain imports but also reduces subsidies on exports. The domestic price level at which exports may be halted is increased in a move that serves the interest of landowners but not that of townspeople (*see* 1673; 1689).

Samuel Pepys gives a special dinner at which he presents his guests with "a fricassee of rabbit and chickens, a leg of mutton boiled, three carps in a dish, a great dish of a side of lamb, a dish of roasted pigeons, a dish of four lobsters, three tarts, a lamprey pie, a most rare pie, a dish of anchovies, good wine of several sorts, and all things mighty noble, and to my great content."

England's Royal Society urges that potatoes be planted to provide food in case of famine.

Samuel Pepys (above) notes in his diary that he has enjoyed at a London tavern "a sort of French wine called Ho-Bryan which hath a good and most particular taste." Bordeaux landowner Arnaud de Pontac, who inherited the Château Haut-Brion and its vineyard in 1649 and will retain possession until his death in 1681, has introduced the practices of racking his wine from barrel to barrel on a regular basis, to separate young wine from early lees and allowing wine in casks to improve rather than spoil by "topping off" to compensate for evaporation.

1664

Nieuw Amsterdam becomes New York August 27 as 300 English soldiers take the town from the Dutch. It is renamed after James, duke of York, whose brother, Charles II, grants him the territory of New Netherlands.

Cookbook: *The Cook's Guide* by Hannah Woolley.

Samuel Pepys buys forks for his household, but most Englishmen continue to eat with their fingers and will continue to do so until early in the next century lest they be considered effete or, in the opinion of some clergymen, even sacrilegious. A man going out to dinner has for centuries brought his own spoon and knife, the spoon being folded into the pocket and the knife carried in a scabbard attached to the belt; more men now carry folding forks as well.

Friedrich Schwarze is founded by a German distiller at Oelde, near the Rhine southeast of Münster, where it will continue for more than 330 years to produce schnapps.

Pepys (above) makes an entry in his diary for November 24, 1664: "To a Coffee-house, to drink jocolatte, very good." Who picks up the tab he does not say; cocoa costs 10 to 15 shillings per pound, making it prohibitively dear for all but the very rich.

1665

Charles II decrees that England's American colonies may import European goods only through English ports and on English ships but, since he is married to the Portuguese infanta, Catherine da Braganza, he grants an exemption to Portugal's island "province" of Madeira, which is permitted to trade directly with the colonies and with England's Caribbean possessions (*see* Madeira wines, below).

London has its last major outbreak of the Black Death, which many relate to eating raw cherries, melon, or gooseberries, although fruit tarts and pies cause no concern (*see* 1569).

Potatoes are planted on a limited basis in Lorraine (*see* 1663; 1744; 1757; 1770; Parmentier, 1771).

England imports less than 88 tons of sugar, a figure that will grow to 10,000 tons by the end of the century as consumption of tea and chocolate (encouraged by cheap sugar) increases in popularity.

Madeira wine gains popularity in the American colonies as a result of the royal decree (above), which levies high taxes on all other wines (*see* 1420). Shipping the wine to the colonies by way of England's Caribbean islands, thus exposing it to heat for long periods of time, will prove to benefit Madeira (whereas it would ruin other wines), and English connoisseurs will actually come to prefer Madeira wine that has voyaged to America and been returned to England. In the next century, virtually all Madeira wine will be fortified to improve its keeping qualities, and although shippers will continue for more than 250 years to send Madeira round-trip to India in order that it may be "baked" twice, winemakers on the island will simply heat their product to obtain the same effect (*see* oidium mildew, 1852).

1666

Laws of gravity established by Cambridge University mathematics professor Isaac Newton, 23, state that the attraction exerted by gravity between any two bodies is directly proportional to their masses and inversely proportional to the square of the distance between them. Newton has returned to his native Woolsthorpe because bubonic plague at Cambridge has closed Trinity College, where he is a fellow; he has observed the fall of an apple in an orchard at Woolsthorpe and calculates that at a distance of one foot the attraction between two objects is 100 times stronger than at 10 feet.

The Newton pippin will be so named to commemorate the apple that inspired Newton's law of gravity (above).

Samuel Pepys notes in his diary that on Christmas Day he went to church alone, "my wife, desirous to sleep, having sat up til 4 this morning seeing her mayds make mince pies. I to church, then home, and dined well on some good ribbs of beef roasted and mince pies, and plenty of good wine of my owne" Pepys intensely dislikes Sir William Penn, the admiral whose son will found the Pennsylvania colony: "They sat down and eat a bit of their nasty victuals, and so parted, and we to bed." And, on another occasion, "We to Sir W. Pen's and supped with a little and bad, and nasty, supper, which makes me not love the family, they do all things so meanly, to make a little bad show upon their backs" (meaning that Penn puts his money into sartorial finery rather than good food). Pepys's diary will mention eating such vegetables as peas, both fresh and dried, asparagus, green corn, cabbage, onions, carrots, and colewort (kale).

The Great Fire of London that begins early in the morning of Sunday, September 2, in Pudding Lane continues for 4 days and nights, consuming four-fifths of the walled city plus 63 acres of property outside the city walls. It destroys some 13,200 homes plus many eating places but spares the wine merchant R. Christopher & Co. Ltd., which will grow in the next century to have cellars in the crypt beneath Bloomsbury Church (*see* 1667).

London's Cock Tavern (or Ale House), which dates to 1549, survives the Great Fire (above) (*see* Pepys, 1668). It will move in 1883 to make room for a branch of the Bank of England and reestablish itself at 22 Fleet Street.

1667

France's Louis XIV, now 28, takes as his mistress Françoise-Athénaïs Rochechouart de Mortemart, marquise de Montespan, 26. His longtime mistress Louise de La Vallière removes herself to a Carmelite nunnery. Both women will leave their marks on French menus, a cream-and-sorrel sauce being named for La Vallière, a sauce of white wine and mushrooms for Mme. de Montespan.

Cookbook: *Parfait Confiturieur* by French chef Jean Rédoux, who by some accounts is known for his crêpes Suzettes, possibly named for Suzette, Princesse de Carignan, who lives in the Château de Juvisy near Fontainebleau (but *see* Charpentier, 1895).

A Paris police force is created March 15 under the name La Lieutenance de Police; it will be reorgnized in 1800 as the Préfecture de Police, helping to keep the city's streets safe for citizens attending evening dinner parties.

Use of the fork will become firmly entrenched at court and among the aristocracy in the reign of Louis XIV (above), but Louis himself will rarely use one, preferring his fingers.

Samuel Pepys notes that he has bought "sparrow-grass in Fenchurch Street, 100 spears for 1 shilling sixpence." Tradesmen will continue for centuries to call asparagus "grass."

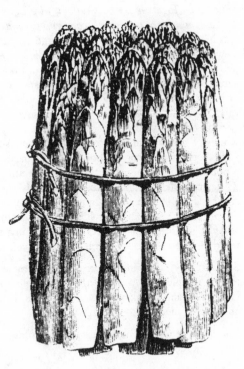

Asparagus—green or white—was known in England as "sparrowgrass" or simply "grass."

The first ice cream known to have been eaten in England is served at Windsor Castle.

1667

Ye Olde Cheshire Cheese reopens at 145 Lee Street, London, in a new building that replaces the one destroyed by last year's Great Fire.

1668

Italian physician-naturalist Francesco Redi, 42, disproves the notion of spontaneous generation. He shows that no maggots will develop in meat, no matter how putrified it may be, if it is covered with a thin cloth to protect it from flies that will lay eggs, but most people will continue for centuries to believe that maggots are products of spontaneous generation rather than of fly larvae (see Needham, 1748; Pasteur, 1859).

Cookbook: *The Closet of the eminently learned Sir Kenelm Digby, kt. opened: whereby is discovered several ways for making of metheglin, sider, cherry-wine, &c. Together with excellent directions for cookery; as also for perserving, conserving, candying, &c.* is published at London by George Hartman, steward to the late Sir Kenelm, who died 3 years ago at age 62. It includes a recipe for a pudding similar to plum pudding but made of stale bread crumbs "from two penny loaves" mixed with a quart of cream to which are added, in succession, two spoonfuls of flour, the yolks of four eggs, the whites of two, a quantity of ground nutmeg, sugar to taste, the marrow of two bones, three-quarters of a pound each of "raisins of the sun" and currants. These ingredients (some of them extremely expensive because English vessels must run the gantlet of Spanish and Venetian ships in the Mediterranean and also avoid Algerian pirates) are placed in a buttered dish and baked for 30 minutes.

Samuel Pepys notes in his diary, "Thence by water to the Temple, and there to the Cocke ale-house [*see* 1666] and drank and eat a lobster and sang, and mighty merry."

London's Ye Olde Watling has its beginnings in a tavern opened at 29 Bow Lane.

1669

Dutch colonists quit Brazil under pressure from the Portuguese, who pay them in Setubal salt to move to Guiana.

Famine in Bengal kills 3 million.

London's Yeomen of the Guard at the Tower of London get the name "Beefeaters" from the grand duke of Tuscany Cosimo de' Medici. Established in 1485 to guard the tower, the warders draw large daily rations of beef, says the grand duke.

England permits import of ready-processed chocolate, which greatly improves the quality of the beverage.

The Turkish ambassador at the court of Louis XIV popularizes coffee among the *haut monde* of Paris. Suleiman Aga offers it to all his visitors, but French aristocrat Marie, marquise de Sévigné (*née* de Rabutin-Chantal), 44, writes to her daughter Françoise-Marguerite, 24, comtesse de Grignan, in Provence, "There are two things Frenchmen will never swallow—the poetry of Racine and coffee" (*see* 1699).

The Cocoa-Tree Club opens in St. James's Street, London, and soon attracts prominent Tory patrons (Whigs and Tories will frequent different chocolate houses).

1670

An English visitor to Ireland reports, "What need they to work, whereof the labor of one man can feed forty?" The Irish find potatoes useful in their struggles against the English since their food supply, growing as it does beneath the ground, cannot readily be confiscated (*see* 1649).

English Puritan William Sayle arrives from the Bermudas at Albemarle Point on the Ashley River to found the Carolina colony on territory granted by Charles II in 1663 as a reward to eight courtiers who helped in his restoration 10 years ago. The daily ration for each colonist is one pint of peas, and lack of proper victuals will plague the settlers until the spring of 1673 (*see* rice, 1671; Charleston, 1672).

Nonfiction: *The Rules of Civility; or, Certain Ways of Deportment Observed in France among All Persons of Quality, upon Several Occasions* (*Nouveau Traité de la civilité qui se pratique en France parmi les honnestes gens* by French author Antoine de Courtin, 48, instructs the well-bred always to "wipe your spoon

Guests at a European family dinner ate with knives and spoons. Few people used forks. LIBRARY OF CONGRESS

before dipping it into a fresh dish, for there are people so fastidiously constituted that they object to eating what you have disarranged with a spoon which you have just taken out of your mouth."

Cookbook: *The Queen-like Closet* by Hannah Woolley contains recipes for preserving, cooking, and physicking plus directions for serving at table.

"Orange Girls" in English theaters sell Spanish Seville oranges, which are popular despite their sourness. One Orange Girl, Eleanor "Nell" Gwyn, 20, has become an actress—and mistress to Charles II.

English soldiers in the field ordinarily receive a daily ration consisting of two pounds of bread, one pound of meat or an equal amount of cheese, and one bottle of wine or two of beer.

The marquise de Sévigné writes April 15 to her daughter, the comtesse de Grignan, "Chocolate is not for me what it was. All those who spoke well of it, now revile it. One curses it; one accuses it of being the cause of all one's ills. It occasions dizziness and palpitations; it suits you for a while, and then it suddenly lights a running fever within you which leads to death." But on October 28 she writes, "The day before yesterday I took some [chocolate] to digest my dinner, in order to sup well, and yesterday I took some nourishment to hold me until the evening. It produced all the effects I wished. There you have what I find pleasant, it acts as it is supposed to." She will later write, "The marquise de C.

[Coetlogon] drank so much chocolate, being pregnant last year, that she was brought to bed of a little boy who was as black as the devil who died."

Café Procope opens in the rue des Fossés-Saint-Germain (later the rue de l'Ancienne Comédie) on the Left Bank at Paris. *Limonadier* Francesco Procopio dei Coltelli, who has gallicized his name, serves not only lemonade but also coffee, wines, "cremes glacées," fancy sherbets, and Italian pastries and sweetmeats (*see* 1630). By 1720, Paris will have some 300 cafés (*see* 1750).

1671

England's "Cavalier Parliament" forbids freeholders with incomes of less than £100 per year from killing game, even on their own property, and restricts use of shotguns to richer landholders, even though it is the smaller farmers who depend more on game to feed their families.

The Munich food store Dallmayr founded at Dienerstrasse (Footmen's Street) 14 and 15 will grow to be *Hoflieferant* (court purveyor) not only to the royal Bavarian court but also to the courts of 14 other European monarchs. It will stock fish in basins, a vast array of cheeses, rare teas and coffees, fine wines, and an endless assortment of made dishes that will be delivered to favored customers in carriages, each drawn by an impressive pair of *Rappen* (black horses). Dallmayr's box lunches will contain such dainties as cold baby quail stuffed with pâté and accompanied by a red currant tart; cold paillarde of lamb with crisp potatoes and a slice of cheese; open sandwiches of smoked salmon, sturgeon eggs filled with caviar, and mushrooms filled with a chicken-liver mixture; game or poultry with rémoulade, Cumberland, or some other sauce. Dallmayr's dessert selection will boggle the mind.

French police receive the right to search houses during Lent and give any forbidden items of food they may find to the hospitals.

Mme. de Sévigné writes in April to her daughter, the comtesse de Grignan, "Here is what I learned on coming home, which I cannot get out of my head, and which I hardly know how to tell you: it is that Vatel, the great Vatel, maître d'hôtel to M. Fouquet who was at present with M. le Prince [de Condé], this man of a nobility which distinguished him above all others, whose good head was capable of sustaining all the cares of a state—this man, whom I know, seeing at eight o'clock this morning the shipment of seafood [*la marée*] had not arrived was not able to bear the blow which he saw was going to fall on him, and, in a word, killed himself with his sword. You may imagine the horrible disorder which such a terrible misfortune caused to the fête. Imagine that the fish arrived, perhaps just as he died. I know nothing more at present; I think you will find this enough. I do not doubt but that the confusion must have been great. It is a grievous thing at a fête costing 50,000 écus."

Mme. de Sévigné (above) writes her daughter April 26: "This . . . is the account which Moreuil . . . has given me of what happened at Chantilly, regarding Vatel. . . . The king arrived Thursday evening, the hunt, the lanterns, the moonlight, the promenade, the collation in a place carpeted with jonquils, everything was as desired. They supped; there were some tables where the roast was lacking, because there were a number of diners who had been by no means expected. This dumbfounded Vatel; he said several times, 'I have lost my honor. This is a blow which I cannot bear.' He said to Gurville [his assistant and successor], 'My head is spinning; I haven't slept for a dozen nights; help me give the orders.' Gurville reassured him as best he could. The roasts which had been lacking, not at the king's table but at the twenty-fifth, kept haunting him. Gurville told M. le Prince. M. le Prince went right to his room and said to him, 'Vatel, everything is going well; nothing was so handsome as the king's supper.' He replied, 'Monseigneur, your goodness overwhelms me; I know that the roast was lacking at two tables.' 'Not at all,' said M. le Prince. 'Don't trouble yourself about it. Everything is going well.' The night passed: the fireworks did not succeed; they were obscured by a cloud; they had cost 16,000 francs. At four o'clock in the morning Vatel was roaming all over the place. He found everyone asleep. He met a little purveyor who brought him just two loads of seafood; he asked him, 'Is that all there is?' He answered him, 'Yes, sir.' He did not know that Vatel had sent to all the seaports. He waited awhile; the others did not come at all; his mind grew feverish; he believed that there would not be any more seafood at all. He found Gurville and said to him, 'Monsieur, I cannot survive this blow. I

have honor and reputation to lose.' Gurville laughed at him. Vatel went up to his room, set his sword against the door, and ran it into his heart. . . . At last he fell dead. The seafood, however, was arriving from all directions; they looked for Vatel to oversee its distribution; they went to his room; they knocked; they broke down the door; they found him drowned in his own blood; they ran to M. le Prince, who was in despair. . . . Nevertheless, Gurville tried to make up for the loss of Vatel. . . . They dined very well, they had a collation, they supped, they strolled, they gambled, they hunted; everything was perfumed with jonquils, everything was enchanted." Later chroniclers will speculate that heavy rains or floods might have made the roads impassable, thus delaying delivery of fish and oysters that Vatel (who was actually the comptroller, or officier de bouche, to the prince de Condé) had ordered for a reception for Le Grand Condé's cousin, Louis XIV (*see* Escoffier, 1935).

Rice is introduced into the Carolina colony by physician Henry Woodward (*see* 1670). The story that Dr. Woodward received some Madagascar rice seed from visiting sea captain James Thurber is one of several that will be told about the introduction of rice to the colony (another is that a planter perceived the land to be suitable for rice production and simply imported a barrel of seed; still another is that a ship from Madagascar was blown off course, put in to Charleston harbor [*see* 1672], colonist Landegrave T. Smith obtained rice seed from the ship's captain, and planted it in the governor's garden), but the grain will for years be merely a garden curiosity since nobody knows how to husk it and use it for food. Rice will not be cultivated seriously until about 1694 (*see* 1694).

Mme. de Sévigné (above) will credit a Mme. de Sablieu with the dubious distinction of having been the first to use milk in tea.

1672

Charleston is founded in the Carolina colony by Puritans from the Bermudas led by William Sayles (*see* 1670).

Cookbook: *The Ladies' Delight* by Hannah Woolley.

New-England's Rarities by English-American merchant John Josselyn calls a "pompion" (pumpkin) stew "an Ancient New-England dish," made by taking pumpkins "when ripe, cut them into Dice, and so fill a pot with them of two or three gallons, stew them upon a gentle fire a whole day, then as they sink they [housewives] fill again with fresh pompions not putting any liquor to them and when it is stirred enough it will look like baked Apples, this Dish putting Butter to it and Vinegar with some Spice as Ginger which makes it tart like an Apple, and so serve it up to be eaten with fish or flesh."

Josselyn (above) says of passenger pigeons, "of late they are much diminished, the English taking them with nets" (*see* 1648; 1800).

The first Paris coffeehouse opens at the Saint-Germain Fair. An Armenian known only as Pascal does well at the fair, but he fails in the coffeehouse he opens thereafter in the Quai de l'École and moves to London (*see* 1652; Vienna, 1683; Paris, 1754).

1673

French Jesuit missionary-explorer Jacques Marquette, 36, discovers the Mississippi River and writes of the rivers near its headwaters, "The way is so cut up by marshes and little lakes that it is easy to go astray, especially as the river is so covered with wild oats that one can hardly discover the channel." Père Marquette calls the grain a *fausse avoine*, or "false oat." French fur trader and explorer Pierre-Ésprit Radisson wrote in his journal of the "wild oats" about 15 years ago, saying, "We had there a kinde of rice, much like oats . . . and that is their food for the most part of the winter" (*see* 1750).

Parliament introduces export subsidies to help English landlords, who have suffered from falling grain prices (*see* 1689).

The first metal dental fillings are installed by English surgeons.

A French patent is granted for making porcelain at Rouen. A factory will begin production at St. Cloud in 1677, but the "porcelain" is soft paste (*pâte tendre*), which can be made into decorative objects but lacks the strength to resist wear (*see* 1712).

The Chelsea Physic Garden opens ("Physic" means pertaining to things natural as opposed to metaphysical; *see* Oxford, 1621). The Worshipful Society of

Apothecaries of London has acquired four acres in the heart of Chelsea, a riverside village on the Thames, to grow plants for the treatment of medical disorders (medicine and botany are closely related, with every disorder thought to have a potential remedy in some plant species) and for scientific research. The garden of officinal plants soon includes "nectarines of all sorts, peaches, apricocks, cherries, and plums." It will be closed to the public until 1983.

1674

Japan has a terrible famine. Food prices rise sharply, and there is great hunger among the masses of people.

Oxford physician Thomas Willis, 53, establishes the fact that the urine of diabetics is "wonderfully sweet as it were imbued with Honey or Sugar," but while he distinguishes late-onset diabetes from other forms of the disease, he suggests that it is a disease of the blood (*see* Cawley, 1783).

Ergotism strikes French peasants at Gatinais in a severe outbreak (*see* 1597; 1722).

1675

France applies the gabelle (salt tax) to Brittany, which has heretofore been exempt (*see* 1550; 1680).

England's Charles II issues a proclamation December 23 "for the suppression of Coffee Houses": "Whereas it is most apparent that the multitude of Coffee Houses of late years set up and kept within this kingdom . . . and through great resort of idle and disaffected persons to them, have produced very evil and dangerous effects; it is well for that many tradesmen and others, do herein misspend much of their time, which might and probably would be employed in and about their Lawful Calling and Affairs; but also for them in such houses . . . divers, false, malitious, and scandalous reports are devised and spread abroad to the Defamation of His Majesty's Government, and to the disturbance of the Peace and Quiet of the Realm; his majesty hath thought it fit and necessary, that the said Coffee Houses be (for the Future) put down and suppressed." Charles's intent is to suppress talk that might lead to the kind of rebellion that caused his father's execution in January 1649, but his proclamation prompts an outcry among merchants and other patrons of the coffeehouses (*see* 1676).

1676

England's Charles II revokes last year's order with regard to coffeehouses January 8. The establishments have become gathering places for men who may neglect their families to discuss business and politics over coffee but who will also in some cases launch great enterprises over coffee.

1677

Spain's territorial empire covers much of the known world, but her soil is barely cultivated, her food is costly, her population is dwindling, and she has become a third-rate power (*see* 1613).

France's Louis XIV sets aside a 20-acre field and commissions Jean de La Quintinie to create an orchard and vegetable garden to feed the court. The garden is to have walls, terraces, and greenhouses with espaliered apple and pear trees, and the greenhouses are expected to provide peas in winter, asparagus and strawberries in March.

French planters establish cacao plantations in Brazil to provide Parisian cocoa grinders with a good supply of the beans for the aristocracy's favorite beverage. Portuguese planters in the Amazon basin find labor scarce, there are severe shortages of river transport, and although the Brazilian port of Pará will be exporting 1,000 tons of cacao beans by the end of the next century, most of it will still be cacao collected from wild trees (*cacao bravo*).

1679

Franciscan missionary-explorer Louis Hennepin, 39, accompanies the expedition of René-Robert Cavelier, sieur de La Salle, 35, across the Great Lakes to the Mississippi River, where he finds peach trees growing along the riverbank.

1680

Surging demand for cocoa, tea, and coffee in England brings an increased demand for slaves to produce more sugar in British colonies (*see* 1652).

French controller-general Jean-Baptiste Colbert, 61, reorganizes the gabelle (salt tax) in May but does not suppress any of its abuses (*see* 1675). The *petite gabelle* sets up 17 boards with tribunals, procurators, and other functionaries. In some areas salt sells for 20 times its cost (*see* 1780).

De Motu Animalium by the late Italian mathematician-astronomer Giovanni Alfonso Borelli expresses the view that digestion is a mechanical process with blood pressure inducing gastric secretion (*see* Sylvius, 1661). Fevers, pains, and convulsions are the result of defective movements of the "nervous juices," says Borelli, who died last year at age 71 after having founded the iatrophysical school of medicine by applying mechanical principles for the first time to the study of human muscular movement (*see* Réaumur, 1752).

A French document refers to Camembert as "a very good cheese, well suited to aid digestion after a meal washed down with good wines" (*see* 1708).

Maryland colonists complain that "their supply of provisions becoming exhausted, it was necessary for them, in order to keep from starvation, to eat the oysters taken from along their shores."

1681

France's 50-mile-long Canal de Midi is completed in Languedoc to link the Gironde River at Toulouse with the port of Sète on the Mediterranean. The late engineer Pierre-Paul de Riquet planned the canal, which climbs to a height of more than 600 feet and employs swinging miter lock gates invented by Leonardo da Vinci in the 15th century. De Riquet spent most of his own personal fortune to pursue the project in the last 18 years but has died at age 76, 6 months too soon to see his work completed (*see* 1603).

The pressure cooker invented by French physicist Denys Papin employs a safety valve. Papin, who has taken refuge in England to escape religious persecution, issues a small pamphlet, "The New Digester, or

Engine for Softening Bones" in which he describes various experiments, including one in which he took an "old male and tame rabbet, which is ordinarily but a pitiful sort of meat," and cooking it in his machine so that it became as soft and savory as a young rabbit and turned its juice and bones into a good jelly. But Papin's cumbersome "digester" must be placed in a specially built furnace and is somewhat dangerous to use (*see* 1940; Evelyn, 1682).

French chefs prepare foods *en gelée*, using tasteless gelatin derived from animal bones by Denys Papin (above) (*see* 1816; Peter Cooper, 1845).

Cookbook: *The True Way of Preserving and Candying . . . Made publick for the benefit of all English ladies and gentlewomen; especially for my scholars* is published at London, presumably by the head of a cooking school.

France's Louis XIV restricts fishing for mussels but places no restraint on dragging for oysters, whose natural banks are called "inexhaustible" (*see* 1786).

1682

Methodus Plantarum Nova by English naturalist John Ray, 55, first demonstrates the nature of buds and divides flowering plants into dicotyledons and monocotyledons (*see* 1692; Linnaeus, 1737).

The Anatomy of Plants by English botanist Nehemiah Gray, 41, makes the first observations of sex in plants.

Food served at the French royal palace in Versailles is generally cold because the kitchens are so far from the dining rooms; the king, who eats with his fingers, is more interested in the quantity of his food than in its quality and pays little attention to the talents of his chefs.

English diarist John Evelyn, 62, notes April 12, "I went this afternoone with severall of the Royal Society to a supper which was all dress'd, both fish and flesh, in Monsieur Papin's Digestors, by which the hardest bones of beefe itself, and mutton, were made as soft as cheese without water or other liquor, and with lesse than 8 ounces of coales, producing an incredible quantity of gravy; and for close of a jelley made of bones of beefe, the best for clearness and good relish, and the most delicious

that I have ever seene or tasted. We eat pike and other fish bones, and all without impediment; but nothing exceeded the pigeons, which tasted just as if bak'd in a pie, all these being stew'd in their own juice without any addition of water save what swam about the Digester, as in *bal neo*; the natural juice of all these provisions acting on the grosser substances, reduc'd the hardest bones to tendernesse; but it is best descanted with more particulars for extracting tinctures, preserving and stewing fruite, and saving fuel, in Dr. Papin's booke, publish'd and dedicated to our society, of which he is a member . . . I sent a glass of the jelley to my wife, to the reproach of all that the ladies ever made of the best hartshorn" (*see* 1681).

The English nobility in this decade have begun storing ice for summer use. Charles II has had his own icehouse built in St. James's Park.

Philadelphia's Blue Anchor tavern opens. Sturgeon and sea turtle are the chief delicacies.

Mennonites begin leaving the German states to settle at Philadelphia and on fertile lands that will extend from Easton through Allentown, Reading, and Lebanon in the Cumberland Valley. They will introduce Pennsylvania "Dutch" (Deutsch) cooking and contribute dishes such as scrapple to the American cuisine.

1683

Ottoman troops lay siege to Vienna in July. A German-Polish army lifts the siege September 12 after 58 days (*see kipfel*, coffee, below).

France's Louis XIV hears cries of hungry beggars outside the palace at Versailles and sends an order to his aged controller of finance Jean-Baptiste Colbert: "The suffering troubles me greatly. We must do everything we can to relieve the people. I wish this to be done at once." But little in fact is done.

Vienna loses thousands to starvation in the 58-day siege by the Ottoman Turks (above). Survivors sustain themselves by eating cats, donkeys, and everything else edible.

The kipfel (or kipfl), a crescent-shaped roll, is created by Viennese bakers to celebrate the lifting of the city's siege (above). Most bakers have their bakeries in cellars beneath their shops. Working at night in order to have fresh bread for delivery in the morning, they have heard digging and hammering sounds, realized that the Turks were trying to tunnel beneath the city's walls, and have sounded the alarm. Some historians will say that the bakers produced the kipfel in anticipation of a Turkish victory, but in any case the roll that will become the French croissant may date to 1217 (*see* Buda, 1686; Marie-Antoinette, 1770).

The first coffeehouse in central Europe is opened at Vienna by Polish interpreter (and triple agent) Franz Georg Kolschitzky (or Franciszek Jerzy Kulczycki—his name can be spelled several different ways), who has been rewarded for smuggling the Holy Roman Emperor Leopold I's call for help to the duke of Lorraine. Kolschitzky has tasted coffee in his sallies among the 300,000-man Ottoman siege force and obtained several bags of the roasted beans after the Turks retreat. His establishment Haus zur Blauenflasche (the House at the Sign of the Blue Bottle) is near St. Stephan's Cathedral at 6 Dongasse but enjoys little success with the Turkish brew until Kolschitzky strains off the sandy sediment, adds milk, and sweetens the drink with honey (which soon will be replaced with sugar, and cinnamon will be added to create cappuccino). By some accounts it is Kolschitzky who persuades local baker Peter Wendler to turn his round rolls into crescents, or kipfeln, to celebrate the defeat of the Turks (*see* above), and he will be said to have obtained jelly doughnuts from a local street vendor (*see* 1700).

1684

England's Charles II roasts oxen and feeds the poor at his own expense as his country emerges from her coldest winter in memory. The Thames has frozen over, and even the sea has frozen for two miles from land.

England's East India Company gains Chinese permission to build a trading station at Guangzhou (Canton) after years of having to import Chinese silks, porcelain, and tea by way of Java.

Tea sells on the Continent for less than 1 shilling per pound, but an import duty of 5 shillings per pound makes tea too costly for most Englishmen and encourages widespread smuggling. The English con-

sume more smuggled tea than is brought in by orthodox routes (*see* 1784).

1685

England's Charles II dies February 6 at age 54 saying, "Let not poor Nelly starve," a reference to actress Nell Gwyn, now 34, who made her last stage appearance in 1682, has borne the king two sons, but will die in 2 years.

Cookbook: *The Manner of Making Coffee, Tea, and Chocolate* by French author Philippe Dufour is published at London. "The Ladies, also and Gentlemen of *Mexico*, make little delicate Cakes of *Chocolate*

Hannah Woolley's recipes for "Preparing, Candying, and Cookery" went through many editions. NEW YORK PUBLIC LIBRARY

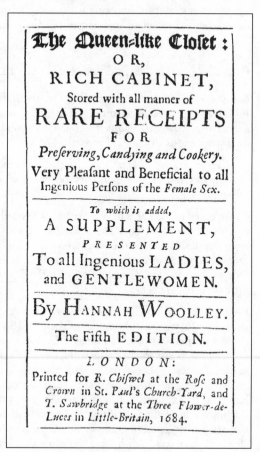

The Queen-like Closet:
OR,
RICH CABINET,
Stored with all manner of
RARE RECEIPTS
FOR
Preserving, Candying and Cookery.
Very Pleasant and Beneficial to all
Ingenious Persons of the *Female Sex*.

To which is added,
A SUPPLEMENT,
PRESENTED
To all Ingenious LADIES,
and GENTLEWOMEN.

By HANNAH WOOLLEY.
The Fifth EDITION.

LONDON:
Printed for R. *Chiswel* at the *Rose* and *Crown* in St. *Paul's Church-Yard*, and T. *Sawbridge* at the *Three Flower-de-Luces* in *Little-Britain*, 1684.

for daintiness, which are sold likewise in the Shops, to be eaten just as Sweet Meats," Dufour writes.

More London coffeehouses open following the death of King Charles (above), who tried to close such places down 10 years ago.

1686

Turkish troops lay siege to the Hungarian city of Buda, across the river from Pesth, and tunnel under Buda's walls, planning to take the city by surprise (*see* kipfel, 1683).

"Cordon Bleu" cookery has its origin in the Institut de Saint-Louis founded by Louis XIV's official mistress, Françoise d'Aubigné, 50, marquise de Maintenon, for 250 daughters of the impoverished nobility, especially of titled army officers. Cookery is among the subjects taught, and the school will become known for its cooking lessons and for the *cordon bleu* (blue ribbon) that girls wear beginning at age 17 to show that they are members of the senior class (*see* Distel, 1880). Mme. de Maintenon's name will make its mark on French menus, lamb à la Maintenon being a saddle of lamb stuffed with a mushroom purée.

Bakers working at night in Buda (above) hear the noise of Turks excavating tunnels under the city and sound a warning. The army is alerted, the city is saved, and the bakers are by some accounts commissioned to create a roll shaped like the half-moon on the Ottoman flag as a reminder (*see* Vienna, 1683).

The duc de Vendôme receives the Dauphin September 6 with a banquet at which 486 dishes are served, not including dessert (which alone consists of 876 dishes of fruits, salads, glasses of dried fruits and compotes, dishes of candied fruit).

"It is an unhappy thing that in later years a Kind of Drink called Rum has been common among us," writes Boston clergyman Increase Mather, 47, who has been president of Harvard College since last year. "They that are poor, and sicked, too, can for a penny or twopence make themselves drunk" (*see* 1655).

1687

A Japanese law imposed January 28 by the shōgun Tsunayoshi forbids the killing of animals (*see* 1129). Tsunayoshi's only son has died, he has become a devout Buddhist, and beginning February 27 he forbids his people to eat fish, shellfish, or birds (*see* Edo fire, 1689).

Cookbook: *The Accomplished Ladies Rich Closet of Rarities* by English author John Shirley.

1688

A "Glorious Revolution" ends nearly 4 years of Roman Catholic rule in England. Whig leaders send an invitation to James II's son-in-law William of Orange June 30, William issues a declaration to the English people September 21, lands at Tor Bay November 5, and moves to assume the throne as William III with his wife, Mary.

English navigator William Dampier, 36, finds breadfruit (*Artocarpus communis*) growing on the Pacific island of Guam (*see* 1697; Bligh, 1787).

English landowners will seize the opportunity of the Revolution (above) to enact a bounty on the export of grain, an act that will increase domestic prices of grain (and of food) for the next few years (*see* 1689).

England's William III (above) will discourage use of the nation's West Country cider in order to give Dutch distillers a market for their gin, which will become widely popular among people of the English working class.

1689

Parliament restores export subsidies for English grain after such subsidies have lapsed (*see* 1673; 1688).

Fire ravages the Japanese capital of Edo and is blamed on fires used to cook meat, despite Buddhist strictures against eating meat (*see* 1687). The Tokugawa government issues an edict forbidding consumption of any meat other than rabbit.

1690

💲 Commodity futures trading has its beginnings in Japan, where merchants trade rice receipts (*see* Chicago, 1865).

🐟 Nantucket colonists launch an offshore whaling industry. They have sent to the mainland for Cape Cod shipwright-whaler Ichabod Paddock, who has set up watchtowers and instructed the islanders (*see* 1659; 1712).

🌱 Dutch mariners smuggle coffee plants out of the Arab port of Mocha. They plant some in their Java colony and send others to the botanical gardens at Amsterdam (*see* 1690; 1713).

1691

🖋 Cookbook: *Nouvelle Instruction pour les confitures* by French author François Massialot.

🌱 German immigrant farmers in the Pennsylvania colony choose heavily wooded lands with clay loams in preference to the light, sandy uplands favored by the English. While the English girdle trees to kill them and then farm among the stumps, the Germans clear their land completely and plow deeply. Instead of planting tobacco, the Germans will stick to wheat, and instead of letting their stock roam freely they will build barns before building houses as they populate Maryland, Virginia, and other colonies.

1692

🧪 English naturalist John Ray tries to classify different animal species into groups largely according to their toes and teeth (*see* 1682; Linnaeus, 1737).

1693

💲 Scotland reimposes the tax on whisky first enacted in 1644 (*see* 1713).

🍳 White's Club is founded at London, which will grow to have more than 200 gentlemen's clubs. Jonathan Swift will call White's a "common ren-dezvous of infamous sharpers and noble cullies," but no London club in centuries to come will be more exclusive or have more royal members.

Philadelphia's State House Tavern opens.

1694

👤 "All France is nothing more than a vast poorhouse, desolate and without food," writes François de Salignac de La Mothe-Fénelon, 43, tutor to the grandson of Louis XIV, as the War of the League of Augsburg drains the French economy.

French government economic controls prevent the free flow of food into famine districts, and speculators corner grain supplies, adding artificial scarcity to the natural famine that grips the country.

💲 Parliament doubles the English salt tax to raise money for William III's 5-year-old war against France's Louis XIV.

🌱 Spaniards plant cacao in the Philippines, whence it will eventually make its way to Java, Ceylon, and India (year approximate).

English colonial administrator John Archdale is appointed governor of the Carolinas August 31. He will arrive in June of next year and encourage colonial planters to cultivate rice (*see* 1671), dividing among them a bag of the grain that he has obtained from the captain of a ship arrived from Madagascar. Archdale will return to England in 1696, but rice will be grown as a commercial crop in the Carolina colony's freshwater inland swamps, and by the end of the next century it will be widely cultivated by slaves in coastal South Carolina, particularly in the area of Georgetown, and will move into North Carolina and Georgia, with smaller crops harvested in Alabama, Mississippi, and Florida (*see* 1865).

1695

💲 A nation's wealth depends not on how much money she possesses but on what she produces and exchanges, writes French economist Pierre Le Pesant, 49, sieur de Boisguilbert, in *Le Détail de la France, la cause de la diminution de ses biens, et la facilité du remède* . . . Boisguilbert describes the ruin that the burdensome taxes of the late Jean-Baptiste Colbert have brought to all classes of society and says France could regain her prosperity by abandoning war and switching from a policy of mercantilist protection to one of free enterprise based on agriculture (*see* Sully, 1598).

The duc de Montaussier, the French dauphin's governor, invents the soup ladle but is ridiculed for suggsting that soup be thus served; guests at most French tables continue to dip into a common tureen with their own wooden or pewter spoons, an advance over the two-handled porringer passed around the table to be sipped from in turn. The French and English eat meat with their fingers, tearing it with their teeth. They dip into stews with their fingers or pieces of bread.

John de Kuyper & Son is founded in Holland, where it will become well known for its cordials (*see* 1933).

1696

Cookbook: *The Family-Dictionary; or, Household Companion; Containing, in Alphabetical Method, I. Directions for Cookery, in Dressing Flesh, Fowl, Fish . . . &c. II. Making All Sorts of Pastry Ware . . . &c. III. Making Conserves, Candies, Preserves, Pickles . . . &c. IV. The Making of All Kinds of Potable Liquors . . .* by English author William Salmon, 52.

Green peas create a sensation at the French court (*see* 1555). Françoise d'Aubine, Mme. de Maintenon, writes from Marly that "impatience to eat [peas], the pleasure of having eaten them, and the anticipation of eating them again are the three subjects I have heard very thoroughly dealt with. . . . Some women, having supped, and supped well at the King's table, have peas waiting for them in their rooms to eat before going to bed." Now 61, the king's former mistress has been secretly married to Louis since 1685, and she writes that it is proper to lick peas from their pods after they have been dipped in a simple sauce.

Grapefruit cultivation in America has its origin in seeds from the Polynesian pomelo tree (*Citrus grandis*) introduced into Barbados by an English sea captain named Shaddock. A sweeter and thinner

mutation of the fruit, or a botanist's development of the "shaddock," will be called grapefruit (*see* Lunan, 1814).

1697

The white Mission grape used to make sweet sacramental wine such as angelica is planted in southern California by Jesuit priest Juan Ugarte (*see* Serra, 1769). The grape is known in Spanish-speaking countries as the Criolla.

1698

Parliament opens the slave trade to British merchants, who will in some cases carry on a triangular trade from New England to Africa to the Caribbean Islands to New England. The merchant vessels will carry New England rum to African slavers, African slaves on "the middle passage" to the West Indies, and West Indian sugar and molasses back to England (or to New England for the rum distilleries). Molasses (the word comes from the Latin *melaceus*, meaning honeylike) is the brown syrup that remains after the sucrose in raw sugarcane has been crystallized in the manufacture of refined sugar, whose consumption has soared through the popularity of cocoa, coffee, and tea.

The steam engine, which is destined to play a major role in the world's agriculture, is pioneered by English engineer Thomas Savery, 48, who constructs a crude, steam-powered "miner's friend" designed to pump water out of coal mines (*see* Newcomen, 1705).

Nonfiction: *Aceteria: A Discourse of Sallets* by John Evelyn, now 79, who writes that lettuce is the supreme ingredient of salads: "By reason of its soporifous quality, lettuce ever was, and still continues, the principal foundation of the universal tribe of Sallets, which is to cool and refresh, besides its other properties" (which include a beneficial effect on "morals, temperance, and chastity"). "We have said how necessary it is that in the composure of a sallet, every plant should come in to bear its part, without being overpower'd by some herb of a stronger taste, so as to endanger the native sapor and virtue of the rest; but fall into their places, like the notes in music, in which there should be nothing harsh or grating; And though admitting some discords (to distinguish and illustrate the rest) striking in all the more sprightly, and sometimes gentler notes, reconcile all dissonancies, and melt them into an agreeable composition." *A Journey to Paris in the Year 1698* by Martin Lister, physician-in-ordinary to Princess Anne, sister-in-law of England's William III (she will become queen upon William's death in 1702): "The diet of the Parisians consists chiefly of *Bread* and *Herbs*; it is here, as with us, finer and coarser. But the common Bread, or *Pan de Gonesse*, which is brought twice a week into Paris from a Village so called, is purely white, and firm and light, and made altogether with Leaven; mostly in 3 Pound Loaves, and 3d a Pound. That which is Bak'd in *Paris* is coarser and much worse. As for the *fine Manchet*, or *French* Bread as we call it, I cannot much commend it; it is . . . often so bitter that it is not to be eaten, and we far exceed them now in this particular in *London*. In *Lent* the common People feed much on White *Kidney Beans*, and white or pale *Lentils*, of which there are great Provisions made in all the Markets, and to be had ready boiled. I was well pleased with this lentil; which is a pulse we have none of in *England*. There are two sorts of *White Lentils* sold here; one small one from *Burgundy*, by the Cut of *Briare*; and another bigger, as broad again from *Chartres*; A 3d also much larger is sometimes to be had from *Languedoc*. Those excepted, our *Seed Shops* far exceed theirs, and consequently our Gardens in the Pulp Kind for variety; both Pea and Bean."

Sunflowers introduced by the Russian czar Peter I, 26, on his return from the West will be the leading source of oilseeds in Russia and Eastern Europe (*see* 1510).

Sparkling champagne is pioneered at the French Abbey d'Hautvilliers by Benedictine cellar master Dom Pierre Pérignon, 60, who is not the inventor of sparkling wine (it has been evolving for years) but who properly identifies the dominant characteristics of wines from various sites in the valley (and in the hills of Champagne to the north and south), blends them to achieve consistent and well-balanced results, and uses corked bottles of strong English glass. Wine is bottled after its first fermentation; during the second year, there is a second "working" of the wine as the remaining yeast converts the sugar residue into alcohol. If air enters the bottle during fermentation, it will spoil the wine; to keep out the air, some cellarers have used a few drops of olive oil, which rises to the surface and forms a protective slick; others a stopper of oil-soaked rags; still others a tightly rolled grape leaf or the bark of a tree, jammed into the bottle's mouth. All these methods allow the gas from any continuing fermentation to escape: carbon dioxide created during the wine's second "working" easily breaks through the olive-oil film or bottle stopper and dissipates into the atmosphere. Cellar master since 1668, Dom Pérignon, after much experimentation with other woods, employs a cork bottle stopper and uses a risky method that involves starting a secondary fermentation in the tightly corked bottle, trapping the carbon dioxide in solution and hoping that its total volume will not explode the bottle. Having no other place to go, the carbon dioxide enters the wine, as Dom Pérignon discovers when he opens a bottle and the cork "pops." The novelty of a sparkling wine quickly captivates the court of Louis XIV, and Dom Pérignon will continue as cellarmaster until 1715 (*see* 1724; Moët and Chandon, 1743).

1699

English bread prices reach a level twice what they were in 1693 as poor crops continue to create shortages.

1700

Boston ships 50,000 quintals of dried codfish to market, the best of it to Bilbao, Lisbon, and Oporto (where it is traded for port wine). The refuse goes to the West Indies for sale to slaveowners.

Vienna has four coffeehouses and soon will have 10, each with its own loyal patronage of men who make the coffeehouse a home away from home (*see* 1683; 1842).

18th Century

1701

A seed-planting drill invented by Berkshire farmer Jethro Tull, 27, sows three parallel rows of seeds at once and will increase crop yields by reducing seed waste (*see* 1782; China, 85 B.C.; Swift, 1726).

1702

Traité des aliments (*Treatise of All Sorts of Foods*) by French scholar Louis Lémery, 25, says, "*Sparrowgrass* eaten to Excess sharpen the Humours and heat a little; and therefore Persons of a bilious Constitution ought to use them moderately; They cause a filthy and disagreeable Smell in the Urine, as every Body knows." (Anyone who eats asparagus excretes methylmercaptan, but not everyone can detect the odor.) About cucumbers, which were brought to France in the 9th century and to England in the 14th but are still considered an unhealthful vegetable, Lémery says that they are "hard on Digestion, because they continue long in the Stomach." He recommends them only for "young Persons of an hot and bilious Constitution." (His book will be published in English translation at London in 1704.)

Philadelphia's London Coffee House opens.

The Edo sushi shop Sasa Maki Kenukisushi opens, using tweezers to remove bones from the fish and serving sushi wrapped in bamboo leaves. It soon becomes popular with servants of the Tokugawa shōgun Tsunayoshi and will still be in business in 1995.

1703

St. Petersburg is founded May 27 by the Russian czar Peter the Great, who lays the cornerstone of the fortress of St. Peter and St. Paul on land recently gained from Sweden's Charles XII. Peter's "window on the west" will be Russia's capital until 1917.

The Methuen Treaty signed December 27 facilitates trade in English woolens and Portuguese wines, which come from vineyards in the Oporto area of northern Portugal, where 68,000 acres along the River Douro in the Alto Douro region are suitable for viniculture. English families own many of the vineyards, and England will admit the wine at duties one-third lower than those demanded of French wines in return for Portugal's agreement to import all her woolens from England. Heavy duties are levied on French spirits, and one result of the treaty will be to make port the national drink of England as the Portuguese learn to spike the pale white wines of the Douro with brandy. Portuguese vintners will complain that the English "want wine to feel like liquid fire in the stomach, burn like gunpowder, bear the tint of ink, and be like sugar of Brazil in sweetness, like the spices of India in aromatic flavor." Tawny port (its name is derived from its color, which comes, in turn, from long maturing in barrels) will be prized over ruby port, being much smoother because it has been aged in wood for 6 to 8 years (and sometimes longer).

The Salzburg café Tomaselli opens on the Alter Markt opposite the Saint Florian fountain.

1704

The "Cassette girls" arrive at Mobile on the Gulf Coast in quest of husbands. The 25 young French women carry small trunks (*cassettes*) filled with dowry gifts from Louis XIV. They will take roux (composed of browned fat and flour), use okra obtained from Congolese slaves, and borrow game, crawfish (swamp crayfish or crawdad), crabs, peppers, and powdered sassafras leaves (called *filé* powder and employed, like okra, as a thickening agent) from the Choctaw to develop a cuisine that will include gumbo (the word comes from Bantu), jambalaya (a mixture of meat, rice, tomatoes, peppers, and onions), and crawfish pie, expanding the local fare of maize products, beans, sweet potatoes, and local game and seafood (*see* 1784).

1705

Famine strikes France, causing widespread distress that will continue for years.

Factum de la France by the sieur de Boisguillebert proposes a single capitation tax—10 percent of the revenues on all property to be paid to the state (*see* 1695). Farmers oppose the idea of taxes, and it finds little support from anyone.

The Newcomen steam engine invented by English blacksmith Thomas Newcomen, 42, at Dartmouth will pave the way for an Industrial Revolution that will improve agricultural productivity. Helped by John Calley (or Cawley), Newcomen uses a jet of cold water to condense steam entering a cylinder. He thus creates atmospheric pressure that drives a piston to produce power that will be used beginning in 1712 to pump water out of coal mines (*see* Savery, 1698; Watt, 1765).

Augustus the Strong, elector of Saxony, orders his court alchemist Johann Friedrich Böttger to discover the secret of hard Chinese porcelain (*see* 1673; 1708).

1706

Crosse & Blackwell has its beginnings in a London firm founded to supply produce to the English colonies. It will ship its goods under the name Jackson (*see* 1830).

Tom's Coffee House, opened by London merchant Thomas Twining at 216 the Strand, will become a major importer of tea.

1707

The United Kingdom of Great Britain and Ireland created May 1 unites England and Scotland under the Union Jack with one Parliament. Its taxes will be imposed equally on the entire kingdom.

Projet d'une dixieme royale by the marshal of France Sébastien Le Prestre de Vauban is quickly seized by the police. Vauban says that salt is "a kind of manna with which God has blessed the human race, and upon which, consequently, it would seem that no taxes should have been imposed" (*see* 1680; 1790).

Fortnum & Mason's opens in Piccadilly, London. Started by William Fortnum, a former footman in Queen Anne's household, in partnership with grocer Hugh Mason, the shop will make its delicacies, wines, picnic hampers, game pies, and other culinary items a tradition in better English households for centuries (*see* clock, 1964).

1708

The United East India Company, created by a merger of Britain's two rival East India Companies, is the strongest European power on the coasts of India. The company ships Indian silks, cottons, indigo (for blue dye), coffee, and saltpeter (for gunpowder) as well as China tea, and it will pay regular dividends of 8 to 10 percent (*see* 1627).

Saxon alchemist Johann Friedrich Böttger at Meissen, 14 miles northwest of Dresden, discovers a formula for making hard-paste porcelain of the kind imported from China—brown stone made pliable with kaolin (*see* 1705; 1709).

A dictionary compiled by French scholar Thomas Corneille has an entry for the town of Vimoutiers and mentions its Monday market, with its excellent cheeses of Livarot and Camembert (*see* 1680; 1791).

1709

Famine ravages Europe as frost kills crops, fruit trees, and domestic fowl as far south as the Mediterranean coast. France has food riots. French officials set up grain depots in an effort to make food distribution more equitable, but they continue to export grain reserves. Restrictions on internal trade strangle shipments of food stores, keep food prices high, and contribute to the starvation.

"The fear of having no bread has agitated the people to the point of fury," writes French controller general of finances Nicolas Des Marets, 61, seigneur de Maillebois: "They have taken up arms for the purpose of seizing grain by force; there have been riots at Rouen, at Paris, and in nearly all the provinces; they are carrying on a kind of war that never ceases except when they are occupied with the harvest."

"The winter was terrible," writes the duc de Saint-Simon Louis de Rouvroy, 34, in his journal: "The memory of man could find no parallel to it. The frost came suddenly on Twelfth Night, and lasted nearly two months, beyond all recollection. In four days the Seine and all the other rivers were frozen, and what had never been seen before, the sea froze all along the coasts, so as to bear carts, even heavily laden, upon it [see England, 1684]. The violence of the cold was such that the strongest liquors broke their bottles in cupboards of rooms with fires in them. There were no walnut trees, no olive trees, no apple trees, no vines left. The other trees died in great numbers; the gardens perished, and all the grain in the earth. It is impossible to imagine the desolation of this general ruin."

Johann Friedrich Böttger at Meissen submits a paper to Saxony's August the Strong March 28 announcing his discovery of the formula for producing porcelain (see 1708). Ehrenfried Walther von Tschirnhausen will help Böttger open the Porzellän Manufaktur of Meissen next year to produce the red porcelain, using kaolin found near the Saxon town of Auenseiditz and at Elbogen in Bohemia. Employees will be threatened with severe punishment if they reveal Böttger's secret, and by 1715 the porcelain from Meissen will be known all over Europe. Böttger himself will be kept at Dresden and taken to Meissen only under guard (see Entrecolles, 1712).

The Fahrenheit alcohol thermometer introduced by German physicist Gabriel Daniel Fahrenheit, 23, has a scale on which 212° is the point at which water boils at standard atmospheric pressure (sea level). Fahrenheit will substitute mercury for alcohol in 1714, but ovens will not have thermometers for another 2 centuries, meat thermometers will not be available for even longer, and cooks in the meantime will have to rely on experience and guesswork to determine cooking times and temperatures.

Parliament enacts legislation giving British bakers two distinct systems of selling bread; they may continue as they have since 1266 to sell it by weight, with the weight based on the prevailing price of flour (Assize Bread), or they may bake it to standard weights with prices geared to weight (Priced Bread), but they must choose one system or the other and may not change once they have chosen. The quartern, or quarter-peck loaf, weighing 4 pounds, 5½ ounces, is the most commonly baked size (it is officially reckoned to be the yield from a quarter peck, or three and a half pounds, of flour). Bakers also produce peck loaves that weigh 17 pounds, 6 ounces and half-peck loaves weighing 8 pounds, 11 ounces. A 280-pound sack of low-protein flour is expected to yield 347 pounds of bread.

1710

A British copyright law established by Queen Anne will be the basis of all future copyright laws, but it has no effect on cookbooks, whose authors continue to plagiarize one another's work, repeating the same recipes over and over again and pirating new ones, often without changing a word.

Cookbook: *Royal Cookery* by English author Patrick Lamb.

Britain imports 60,000 pounds of tea, up from about 20,000 in 1700. By the end of the century, the figure will have topped 20 million pounds (not counting the considerable quantities smuggled in from France) as tea becomes a respectable alternative to beer and wine in a time when it is still unsafe to drink unboiled water (see 1797).

1711

The *Spectator* begins publication March 1 at London under the direction of playwright Richard Steele, 39, and essayist Joseph Addison, 38, who note in an early issue that good London households now serve tea in the morning and that dinner has been pushed forward to well past noon. Tea has come to edge out breakfast beer, and the English breakfast has begun to come into its own. Breakfast parties, given at noon, will become the custom later in the century.

1712

French missionary Père d'Entrecolles sends home the first accurate description of how the Chinese make porcelain using the white clay called kaolin, which has been found on a ridge near Beijing called *kao-ling* (the word means high ridge) (*see* 621; 1709; 1754).

French naval officer Amédée-François Frézier returns to Brest with wild strawberry plants from South America's Pacific coast. Only one of the Chilean pine or sand strawberry plants (*Fragaria chiloensis*) bears viable pollen, it produces large, pale yellow, insipid-tasting fruit, and Parisian botanist Bernard de Jussieu will plant it at the Jardin de Roi (later to be called the Jardin des Plantes) (*see* 1800).

1713

An extension of the British malt tax supersedes the Scottish tax on whisky enacted in 1693. Glaswegians riot, and there is general resistance to the new tax throughout Scotland. Edinburgh alone has an estimated 400 illicit stills, which pay no taxes, and there are even more on remote farms in the Highlands. Distillers who do pay the excise tax complain about those who do not and protest that tax-free whisky is being smuggled across the border into England (*see* 1784).

France's Louis XIV receives a coffee bush whose descendants will produce a vast industry in the Western Hemisphere. The five-foot bush from the Amsterdam greenhouses will be stolen and transported to Martinique (*see* 1690; 1723).

1714

Cookbook: *A Collection of Above Three Hundred Receipts in Cookery, Physick and Surgery* by English compiler Mary Kettilby.

Simpson's Fish Dinner House opens in Bird-in-Hand Court at 76 Cheapside, London, near the Bank of England, serving a 2-shilling "fish ordinary" that consists of a dozen Whitstable oysters, soup, roast partridge, three fish courses, haunch of mutton, and cheese, as it will continue to do, at ascending prices, for more than 250 years.

1715

France's gluttonous Louis XIV dies September 1 at age 76 after a 72-year reign. Philip II Bourbon, 41, serves as regent for the *roi de soleil*'s 5-year-old great-grandson, who will reign until 1774 as Louis XV.

French cuisine will come into full flower during the regency of Philip II Bourbon (above), which will continue until 1723. The regent will give intimate suppers at which fully set tables will be sent up from below stairs by means of pulleys. Aristocrats will try to outdo one another in having good chefs who will invent new dishes, garnishes, sauces, cutlets, and sausages that will be named after their masters.

French agriculture has declined during the long reign of Louis XIV (above), much of the peasantry has become impoverished, and great areas of land have gone out of cultivation (*see* Boisguillebert, 1695).

French distiller Jean Martell arrives at Cognac, 113 kilometers northeast of Bordeaux on the Charente River, and begins distilling brandy (burnt wine, known to Dutch immigrants as *brandewijn* and to Germans as *branndwein*) from the harsh local wine. By 1728, J. & F. Martell and others will have exported 17,000 barrels of cognac brandy. The best are made from grapes grown in open country known as the grand champagne, the second-best from those grown in the petite champagne. The French government will develop rules requiring that cognacs labeled V.S.O.P. (Very Superior Old Pale) or Réserve must be aged in wood for at least 4 years, and that those labeled V.V.O., V.V.S.O., V.V.S.O.P., X.O., Vielle Réserve, or Vieux must be aged in wood for at least 5 years. Most brands will have much older cognacs added to enhance their taste and bouquet (*see* Rémy Martin, 1724; Hennessy, 1765).

1716

✘ Japan's Tokugawa shōgun Ietsugu dies at age 7 after 4 years in power and is succeeded by Yoshimune, 39, who will rule until 1745. Yoshimune will build extensive irrigation projects to aid agriculture.

🍳 The Edo restaurant Yaozen opens in the Asakusa section. The proprietor, Zenshiro, is a former greengrocer and caterer who began as a farmer raising rice and vegetables for the daimyo's household. His great-great-grandson will turn the place into one of Tokyo's most expensive restaurants (*see* 1822).

China in this century will have restaurants at Yangchou that in some cases cook only lamb dishes, or are famous for frogs' legs, duck, pigs' trotters in vinegar, or other dishes, or simply for good food served in beautiful surroundings by beautiful young girls. Bars will stock wines from all over the country.

Some restaurants will have adjoining sheds where simple meals can be obtained and taken home, and the leftovers of rich patrons will be sold to the less affluent. Those who cannot afford restaurants will be able to buy food from itinerant street vendors.

Paris café proprietor Procope (Francesco Procopio dei Coltelli) dies and his son Alexandre takes over Café Procope, hiring Italian musicians to entertain patrons of the establishment, which remains strictly for men (*see* 1670). Some ladies have their coachmen stop in front of the place and bring them coffee, which they sip without alighting from their carriages.

1718

🖊 Cookbook: *Mrs. Mary Eales's Receipts* (later entitled *The Compleat Confectioner*) by English author Eales.

🌾 Potatoes arrive at Boston with some Irish Presbyterian immigrants (*see* 1719).

🍳 The Edo restaurant Momonjiya opens in Ryogoku, serving wild boar, venison, and badger meat. Origi-

Japanese cuisine—based largely on rice, millet, seaweed, and fish—was far less varied than that of the Chinese.

nally a drugstore that sold the meat of wild animals as medicine, it will still be operating in 1995.

1719

♠ Cookbook: *Neues Saltzburgisches Koch-buch, für Hochfürstliche und andere vornehmne Höfe, Kloster, Herrenhäuser Hof- und Haus-meister, Koch und Einkhäufer . . .* by German author Conrad Hagger.

✸ "Irish" potatoes are planted at Londonderry in the New Hampshire colony (*see* 1718) but will not gain wide acceptance in America for nearly a century.

1720

♟ A famine in Sicily weakens the population of Messina and thousands die in a typhus epidemic.

♟ Venice's Caffè Florian opens on the Piazza San Marco, where its immovable marble tables will attract visitors for more than 275 years. Proprietor Floriano Francesconi initially calls his coffeehouse the Caffè Venezia Triomphante, but patrons are soon saying, "Let's meet at Florian's" (the final "o" is dropped in the Venetian dialect), and Francesconi puts up a new sign that reads "Caffè Florian."

1721

⊕ Broccoli is introduced into England some 70 years after the "Italian asparagus" became popular in France (any dish *à parisienne* includes broccoli).

1722

✗ Russia's Peter the Great invades Persia from the north, saying he wants to rescue the shah from Afghan tyranny. He sends a flotilla down the Volga with 22,000 men to join at Dagestan with cavalry that has marched from Astrakhan. Defeating a force of Dagestanis, he occupies Derwent. He then prepares to sweep through the Caucasus, hoping to distract the Turks with his cavalry while his navy captures the Bosporus and the Dardanelles while the grand vizier at Constantinople is preoccupied with growing tulips (but *see* ergotism, below).

✳ French missionary-traveler Pierre-François-Xavier de Charlevoix, 40, descends the Mississippi to New Orleans. His *Histoire de nouvelle France* will describe the pecan nuts he has found growing along the river.

☿ Ergotism aborts Peter the Great's attack on the Ottoman Empire (above). He marshals his Cossacks on the Volga Delta at Astrakhan, but his horses eat hay containing infected rye, his troops eat bread made from infected rye grain, hundreds of horses and men go mad, many die, and Peter has to abandon his plans.

⊕ Durham mustard, produced at Durham, England, is the first commercial dry mustard. Mustard seeds have until now been brought to the table in their natural state and diners have crushed them with their knife handles on the sides of their plates, but by 1723 the *London Journal* will be carrying an advertisement reading "TO ALL FAMILIES ETC. — The Royal Flower of Mustard Seed is now used and esteemed by most of the Quality and Gentry. It will keep good in the Flower as long as in the seed, and one spoonful of the Mustard made of it will go as far as three of that sold at chandlers' shops, and is much wholesomer." The Ainsley family, flour millers since 1692, will take over after the death of the product's creator. As the *Gentleman's Magazine* of September 1807 will say, "It occurred to an old woman of the name of Clements, resident of Durham, to grind this [mustard] seed in a mill and pass the meal through the various processes which are resorted to in making flour from wheat. The secret she kept for many years to herself and [in] the period of her exclusive possession of it supplied the principal parts of the kingdom and particularly the metropolis with this article" (*see* Keen's, 1742).

Gruyère cheese is introduced into France, which will soon be its major producer. The most famous will be made at Jura in the Franche-Comté.

🍺 London brewer Ralph Harwood of the Bell Brewhouse at Shoreditch brews his first batch of porter, naming top-fermenting beer for the market porters and other manual workers who enjoy its body and low price. Also called "intire" or "entire butt" beer because it matures best in large containers where the fermentation utilizes the raw materials in their entirety, porter is a strong black beer whose cloudiness reflects its impurities (it is made from relatively cheap, coarse barley and from robust, less refined hops well suited to London's soft water). It will be brewed all over the British Isles by the middle of the century (*see* Whitbread, 1742).

1723

💲 British Prime Minister Sir Robert Walpole, 47, reduces duties on tea, which remains far less popular than coffee among Britons.

✳ France's first glassworks is established, at Bordeaux, but French vintners will continue for decades to import English, German, and Bohemian bottles.

⚱ Cookbook: *Court Cookery* by English author Robert Smith.

🌾 An American coffee industry that will eventually produce 90 percent of the world's crop has its beginnings in a seedling planted on the Caribbean island of Martinique by French naval officer Gabriel-Mathieu de Clieu, who has been helped by confederates to break into the French Jardin Royale at night and make off with the seedling (*see* 1713). Capt. de Clieu is obliged to share his water ration with the plant on the long voyage in order to keep it alive, but it will thrive on Martinique and become the ancestor of most coffee bushes in the Western Hemisphere (*see* Brazil, 1727).

🍳 The London inn The Three Compasses opens at 66 Cowcross Street near Smithfield Market and the 600-year-old Church of St. Bartholomew the Great.

1724

⚱ Nonfiction: *Tour Through England and Wales* by English novelist-essayist Daniel Defoe, 64, who writes, "Coming south from hence we passed Stilton, a town famous for its cheese, which is called our English parmesan and is brought to table with the mites or maggots round it so thick, that they bring a spoon with them to eat the mites with, as you do the cheese." Stilton is made with the help of the same fungus bacteria (*Penicillium glaucum* or *Penicillium roqueforte*) that gives France's Roquefort and Italy's (stracchino di) gorgonzola their blue-green veins and characteristic flavor; the fun-

gus grows on stone walls and is transferred naturally to cheese laid by in cool farm buildings.

🥤 French champagne growers appeal to the government for the right to ship their *vin gris* in bottles rather than barrels in order to control and ensure the foam *mousse* (*see* 1728; Dom Perignon, 1699).

E. Rémy Martin Cognac is introduced by a French distiller (*see* Martell, 1715; Hennessy, 1765).

1725

✗ Louis XV, now 15, is married in the cathedral at Strasbourg to Maria Leszczyńska, 22, daughter of Poland's former king, Stanisław Leszczyński.

👤 France has famine. Paris workers riot when a baker raises the price of bread by four sous.

🏷 The English chocolate firm Rowntree has its beginnings in a grocery store opened at Walmgate, York, by Quaker Mary Tuke under the name William Tuke & Sons. She will expand the business, specializing in tea, cocoa, and roasted coffee beans (*see* 1862).

🕐 King Stanisław (above) creates a craze at Paris for onion soup, tripe, and pig's feet; he has reportedly been so impressed with an onion soup that was served to him at an inn en route to Paris from Luneville that he visited the kitchen in his dressing gown and demanded that the chef show him how to make the soup (connoisseurs will come to prefer the onion soup of Brussels, made with beer, cream, and butter and served late at night in the rue des Bouchers).

Stanisław (above) will douse a kugelhupf with rum from the West Indies to create baba au rhum—a spongelike cake, sometimes containing raisins, that is soaked in a sauce of rum from the French West Indies and topped with whipped cream (its name comes either from the fictional Ali Baba or from the Polish word for good woman).

Stanisław (above) will be credited by some with having invented the madeleine, or with sending the recipe to his daughter, Maria, at Versailles; her consorts want to name it after her, but she, according to the story, chooses instead to name it for her father's cook (*see* 1814; fiction, 1913).

Petite bouchées à la reine—puff paste shells filled with a mixture of sweetbreads, chicken breasts, mushrooms, and truffles in a cream sauce—will be named after the new queen, Maria Leszczyńska, daughter of Stanisław (above), who will by some accounts sell the recipe to bakers in Lorraine.

The Madrid restaurant Casa Botín opens at 17 calle de Cuchilleros with a deep cellar that was originally the foundation of a house built about 1590. It will use evergreen oak to impart a special flavor to its Castilian specialties—roast suckling pig and baby lamb.

London has nearly 2,000 coffeehouses, up from just one in 1652.

1726

Fiction: *Travels into Several Remote Nations of the World* by "English sea-captain Lemuel Gulliver" (Jonathan Swift, 58) is a satire on cant and sham in Britain's courts, in her political parties, and among her statesmen. A character in *Gulliver's Travels* "gave it for his opinion that whoever could make two ears of corn, or two blades of grass, to grow upon a spot of ground where only one grew before, would deserve better of mankind, and do more essential service to his country, than the whole race of politicians put together."

Cookbook: *England's Newest Way in All Sorts of Cookery* by English author Henry Howard gives a recipe for a fricassee of mushrooms that calls for cream, white wine gravy, pepper, mace, nutmeg, anchovies, thyme, and shallots.

1727

Vegetable Staticks by English physiologist-parson Stephen Hales, 49, founds the science of plant physiology with its studies of the rate of plant growth (*see* 1733).

Nonfiction: *History of Japan and Siam* by the late German physician Engelbert Kämpfer, who visited Japan from 1692 to 1694 as a guest of the Dutch East India Company, died in 1716 at age 65.

Cookbook: *The Compleat Housewife, or, Accomplish'd Gentlewoman's Companion* by English cook Eliza (Elizabeth) Smith (*see* 1742).

Coffee bushes are planted for the first time in Brazil, which will become the world's largest coffee producer (*see* 1723).

Eliza Smith (above) gives a recipe for "katchup" that calls for 12 to 14 anchovies, 10 to 12 shallots, white wine vinegar, two types of white wine, spices (cloves, ginger, mace, whole nutmegs, whole peppercorns), and lemon peel (*see* tomato ketchup, 1812).

Engelbert Kämpfer (above) has written about the blowfish, "The Dutch call him Blazer, which signifys Blower, because he can blow and swell himself up into the form of a round Ball. He is rank'd among the Poisonous Fish, and eat whole, is said unavoidably to occasion death. . . . Many People die of it, for want, as they say, of thoroughly washing and cleaning it. . . . The Japanese won't deprive themselves of a dish so delicate in their opinion, for all they have so many Instances, of how fatal and dangerous a consequence it is to eat it" (*see* Cook, 1774).

1728

Virginia colonist William Byrd, 54, writes, "We had a haunch of venison for dinner, as fat and well tasted as if it had come out of Richmond park. . . . I believe the buck which gave us so good a dinner had eaten out his value in peas, which will make deer exceedingly fat."

French champagne producers win the right to ship their *vin gris* in bottles (*see* 1724). The Saint-Gobain glassworks will provide the enormous number of bottles required.

The round, flagon-style *bocksbutel* (or *boxbutel*) is introduced for the export of Franconia wines.

1729

Britain's death rate begins a sharp descent, producing population pressure on food supplies, but food remains more plentiful than in Ireland.

"A Modest Proposal" by Jonathan Swift is a tongue-in-cheek tract inspired by Irish population pressures: "I have been assured by a knowing American of my acquaintance that a young healthy child well nursed is at a year old a most delicious, nourishing and wholesome food, whether stewed, roasted, baked or boiled, and I make no doubt that it will equally serve in a fricasee or a ragout: I do therefore humbly offer it to public consideration that . . . 100,000 [infants] may, at a year old, be offered in sale to the persons of quality and fortune throughout the kingdom; always advising the mother to let them suck plentifully in the last month, so as to render them plump and fat for a good table."

1730

Cookbook: *The Complete Practical Cook; or A New System of the Whole Art and Mystery of Cooking* by English author Charles Carter.

New York sugar refiner William Bayard advertises his house "for Refining all Sorts of Sugar and Sugar Candy," saying that he has procured from Europe "an experienced Artist in the Mystery" and can supply "both double and single Refined Loaf Sugar, as also Powder and Shop-Sugars and Sugar Candies at Reasonable Rates." Most customers buy sugar in tall, conical loaves that weigh roughly a pound and can be sawed into cubes to make lump sugar or pounded into a powder and stored in a sugar castor, which resembles a giant salt shaker. New York refiners receive raw sugar, not cane (which will quickly spoil if not processed right after it is cut), from West Indies plantations (*see* 1820).

British politician Charles Townshend, Viscount Townshend of Raynham, 56, resigns from the Cabinet of Robert Walpole to devote himself to improving agriculture. Taking a cue from the Dutch, "Turnip Townshend" will find that he can keep livestock through the winter on his estates by feeding them turnips, thus eliminating the need to slaughter most of them each fall, making fresh meat available in all seasons, reducing the need to disguise the taste of spoiled meat with costly spices, and permitting the development of larger cattle (*see* 1732; Bakewell, 1755, 1760; Coke, 1772).

The Spanish wine-exporting firm Pedro Domecq has its beginnings in a company founded at Jerez de la Frontera. The Domecq family will acquire it in 1816, and it will grow to have more than 70 *bodegas* in the sherry-producing area, establishing a worldwide reputation for its very pale dry fino, fino amontillado, dry amontillado, medium amontillado, oloroso, palo cortado, and sweet sherries, sold under the brand name La Iña (and brandies sold under such names as Don Pedro, Fundador, and Presidente). Spanish wine merchants have fortified their wines in order to make them relatively stable (too many bottles and decanters of unfortified wine gather dust and go flat, whereas the fortified sherries retain their life) (*see* Allied-Lyons, 1994).

The Madrid tavern Los Gabrieles opens at 17 calle de Barbieri between the calle de las Infantas and the calle de Figueroa. The calle de Barbieri will grow to have more than 100 such *tascas*.

1731

Porcelain factories multiply in Europe as demand grows for china plates and cups (*see* 1708; 1768).

European teacups had no handles at first, being direct copies of Oriental cups.

Half a pint of rum in two equal tots becomes the official daily ration for all hands in the British Royal Navy (*see* 1655; Vernon, 1740).

1732

 Famine strikes western Japan as crops are ruined by an excess of rain and a plague of grasshoppers: 2.6 million go hungry, 12,400 die, more than 15,000 horses and work cattle starve to death in one of the worst of the 130 famines of the Tokugawa shogunate.

Scottish engineer-farmer Michael Menzies invents a crude threshing machine, but it does not gain any wide use (*see* Meikle, 1786).

Uppsala University botany student Carl von Linné (he will later call himself Carolus Linnaeus), 25, travels with another Swedish student, a Lapp interested in fish, through 4,600 miles of northern Sweden, studying plant life (*see* 1737).

Botanist Carolus Linnaeus traveled through Lapland to make first-hand observations of plant life.

Poor Richard's Almanack begins publication at Philadelphia. Primarily an agricultural handbook, it gives sunset and sunrise times, high and low tides, weather predictions, and optimum dates for planting and harvesting. Local printer Benjamin Franklin, 26, will publish new editions for 25 years, offering practical suggestions, recipes, and folksy urgings to be frugal, industrious, and orderly.

Cookbook: *Compleat City and Country Cook* by Charles Carter devotes 50 pages to meat dishes, 25 to poultry, 40 to fish, only 20 to vegetables, and a handful to pastries.

Painting: *Kitchen Table with Shoulder of Mutton* by French painter Jean-Baptiste-Siméon Chardin, 32.

Spargel (German white asparagus) (below) is generally served with a Hollandaise sauce.

The average bullocks sold at London's Smithfield cattle market weighs 550 pounds, up from 370 pounds in 1710 (*see* 1639; 1795).

London's beef, pork, lamb, and mutton for the next century and more will come largely from animals raised in Ireland, Scotland, and Wales, landed by ship at Holyhead, driven across the Isle of Anglesey, made to swim half a mile across the Menai Strait to the Welsh mainland, and then driven 200 miles to Barnet, a village on the outskirts of London, to be fattened for the Smithfield market. The meat will be generally tough and costly.

German asparagus growers in the region round Mannheim begin cultivating white asparagus, or spargel, with the top grade being called scangenspargel, the second grade spargelgemüse. Cultivation is a painstaking process involving much hand labor, and when labor costs rise in centuries to come the cultivation of spargel will almost cease.

The Philadelphia fishing club State and Schuylkill, established in May for gentlemen and their wives (membership is limited to 30), will be renamed the Fish House Club and become famous for its rum-based Fish House Punch (*see* 1599; 1741).

1733

A Molasses Act passed by Parliament to tax British colonists imposes heavy duties on the molasses, sugar, and rum imported from non-British West Indian islands.

Cookbook: *The House-Keeper's Pocket-book, and Compleat Family Cook* by English author Mrs. Sarah Harrison.

The Molasses Act (above) effectively raises the price of the rum that Americans consume at the rate of three imperial gallons (3.75 American gallons) per year for every man, woman, and child.

1734

Schwenkenfelders from Silesia emigrate to America and drop anchor near New Castle, Delaware, where they obtain the first fresh water they have had in months. They will settle in the Pennsylvania colony and introduce the autumn crocus (*Crocus sativa*), whose stamens yield the spice and dyestuff saffron.

Cookbook: *Five Hundred New Receipts in Cookery* by English author John Middleton.

An English seaman afflicted with scurvy is marooned on the coast of Greenland because the disease is thought to be contagious. The man cures himself by eating scurvy grass (*Cochlearia officinalis*) and is picked up by a passing ship. News of the incident will reach His Majesty's Hospital at Haslar, near Portsmouth (*see* 1747).

1735

Ergotism breaks out in Württemberg in a severe epidemic (*see* 1722; 1777).

Banshoko by Japanese Confucian scholar-magistrate Konyo Aoki gives instructions for growing and storing sweet potatoes, which are called *satsumoimo* (meaning potatoes from Kyushu). He distributes the book, along with seed potatoes, to farmers.

Pellagra is described for the first time by Don Gasper Casal, personal physician to Spain's Philip V (*see* Italy, 1749).

Botulism makes its first recorded appearance in one of the German states. An outbreak of the deadly food poisoning is traced to some sausage (*see* 1895).

A March 9 edict of France's Louis XV specifies the size and shape of the classic champagne bottle.

English distillers produce gin at a rate of 5.4 million gallons per year, nearly a gallon for every man, woman, and child (*see* 1736).

Governors of the Georgia colony pass a law forbidding import of rum and other spirituous liquors, but rum will continue to come in and the law will be repealed in 1742.

1736

Cookbook: *Mrs. McLintock's Receipts for Cookery and Pastry-Work* is published at Glasgow—the first Scottish cookbook.

Passenger pigeons sell at six for a penny in Boston (*see* 1672; 1800).

The Gin Act passed by Parliament forbids public sale of gin in London, but bootleggers spring up and sale of gin continues under such labels as "Colic and Gripe Waters" (*see* 1735). Gin is sold in drafts under such names as "Cuckold's Comfort," "Ladies' Delight," and "Make Shift" (*see* 1740). Parliament raises the tax on spirits, but this does little to reduce gin consumption, which is creating misery and even death among many Britons. The Gin Act will remain on the books until 1742 (*see* 1751).

1737

Genera Plantarum by Carolus Linnaeus inaugurates modern botany's binomial system of taxonomy (*see* 1732). Basing his system on stamens and pistils, Linnaeus divides all vegetation into Phanerogams (seed plants) and Cryptogams (spore plants such as ferns). Phanerogams are in turn divided into Angiosperms (concealed-seed plants such as flowering plants) and Gymnosperms (naked-seed plants such as conifers). Angiosperms are further divided into Monocotyledons (narrow-leaved plants with parallel veins) and Dicotyledons (broad-leaved plants with net veins). Each of these is divided into orders, families, genera, and species (*see* 1738; 1789).

Virginia colonist William Byrd, now 63, says of American deer, "They are . . . not quite as large as the European deer, but on the other hand [are of] much better flavor, and big and fat all the year long." The future city of Richmond is laid out this year on Byrd's land.

A group of men building a new meeting house at Northampton in the Massachusetts colony consumes 69 gallons of rum, 36 pounds of sugar, and several barrels of beer and cider in 1 week.

1738

More Frenchmen will die of hunger in the next 2 years than died in all the wars of Louis XIV, according to René-Louis de Voyer, 44, marquis d'Argenson, who will make the claim in later writings. Fragmentation of French landholdings to the point where a single fruit tree may constitute a "farm" has contributed to a decline in food production.

Classes Plantarum by Carolus Linnaeus expands the system of taxonomy he introduced last year (*see* 1789).

The Manufacture de Vincennes opens to begin French production of porcelain (*see* 1753; Entrecolles, 1712).

1739

English pastry master Edward Kidder dies April 23 at age 73 at his home in Holborn. He has taught more than 6,000 women the art of pastry making.

Potato crops fail in Ireland and will not revive until 1742. The effect is not calamitous since the tubers do not yet make up the bulk of most people's diets as they will a century hence, but Irish cotters (tenant farmers) are becoming increasingly dependent on potatoes for food while raising cereal grains and cattle for the export market, which provides them with rent money. Cotters select potatoes for high-yield varieties, thus inadvertently narrowing the genetic base of their plants, breeding potatoes with little or no resistance to the fungus disease *Phytophthora infestans* (*see* 1756).

Rome's Caffè Greco opens with seven narrow, high-ceilinged rooms at Via Condotti 86 near the Church of Trinità dei Monti Grinati Grandi. It will attract such patrons as Goethe, Rossini (who will compose some of his best music there), and Mendelssohn.

1740

Russia's extravagant czarina Anna Ivanovna collapses at the table during one of her great banquets October 17 and dies at age 47 after a 10-year reign. She has had the dining room of her winter palace at St. Petersburg lined with orange trees in bloom and offered her guests an endless array of delicacies.

Famine strikes Russia and France. French peasants are reduced to eating ferns and grass roots, but some survive by eating potatoes (*see* Parmentier, 1771).

The price of a four-pound loaf of bread rises to 20 sous at Paris, and 50 die in a prison riot protesting a cut in bread rations.

The London cheese shop Paxton & Whitfield has its beginnings in a store opened at 93 Jermyn Street that will grow to purvey such British cheeses as red, white, and blue Cheddars, blue Cheshire, English parmesans, double and single Gloucester, Ilchester blue, Leicester, Shropshire blue, Stilton, blue Vinney, Wensleydale, and Windsor red.

The unrestricted sale of gin and other cheap spirits reaches its peak in Britain. Some observers express fears that wholesale drunkenness is undermining the social fabric of the nation (*see* 1736; Hogarth, 1751).

Booth's distillery is founded at London. It will become famous for its House of Lords and High and Dry gin brands.

The Royal Navy's rum ration is diluted with water by Admiral Edward Vernon, nicknamed "Old Grog" because in foul weather he wears a cloak of grogram (later called grosgrain), a coarse fabric woven of silk and wool, stiffened with gum (*see* 1731). "Grog" will become a slang word for liquor, groggy for drunken dizziness.

The Paris restaurant Grand Véfour has its beginnings in the Café de Chartres opened in the Palais-Royal (*see* 1788; Boulanger, 1765).

1741

New York's journeymen bakers go out on strike for higher pay and better working conditions. Obliged to start before dawn and work in hot basements, they are among the most ill-used workers in the colonial food industry.

The *Boston Weekly News-Journal* for October 29 reports that a shipload of Irish immigrants has arrived "so reduc'd as to eat up their Tallow, Candles, etc. and for some Time had fed upon the Flesh of the humane Bodies deceas'd." Ships are often ill-provisioned for the ocean voyage because of owners' greed or mismanagement.

New England exports apples to the West Indies (see 1759).

Some 70 fishing vessels put out from Gloucester in the Massachusetts colony, 60 from Marblehead.

British admiral George Anson, 44, arrives on the southwest coast of South America after a 7-month voyage from England during which he has lost three of his six ships and two-thirds of his crew to scurvy. He resumes his voyage round the world (see 1744).

The *Salem Gazette*, published in the Massachusetts colony, carries an advertisement placed by J. Crosby, Lemon Trader, stating that he has fine orange juice "which some of the very best Punch Tasters prefer to Lemmon, at one dollar per gallon. Also very good Lime Juice and Shrub to put into Punch." Crosby imports the juices in demijohns and offers also lemons, limes, oranges, and pineapple to use as "sowrings." Punch is commonly made with rum, brandy, whiskey, cider, wine, or any combination of these spirits (see Fish House Punch, 1732). Also popular in the colonies is the West Indian drink known as *sangaree* (a corruption of the Spanish *sangria*), made generally with red wine, water, sugar, citrus fruit juices, and spices.

1742

Cookbook: Eliza Smith's *The Compleat Housewife, or, Accomplish'd Gentlewoman's Companion* of 1727 is published at Williamsburg in the Virginia colony and is probably the first cookbook published in Britain's American colonies.

Messrs. Keen & Sons set up a mustard business on Garlick Hill, London, to supply the city's taverns and chophouses with the condiment (see Durham mustard, 1722; Colman's, 1814).

London brewer Samuel Whitbread, 22, forms a partnership and goes into business in Whitecross Street, specializing in porter in competition with Ralph Harwood (see 1722). Whitbread, who was apprenticed at age 16 to John Wightman, Master of London's Brewer's Company, has seen the potential of

porter, which can be made in bulk and will not deteriorate if matured over long periods in wooden casks. He and his partner, Shewell, will move to nearby Chiswell Street in 1750 and by 1760 will have a porter tun room, "the unsupported roof span of which [a contemporary account will say] is exceeded in its majestic size only by that of Westminster Hall." Porter will have become the city's staple beverage, Whitbread's will produce 65,000 barrels of it per year by the late 1860s, it will be brewing ale as well by 1834, and the Chiswell Street brewery will continue operating until 1976 (see 1869).

The London restaurant Quaglino's has its beginnings by some accounts in a tavern opened in Bury Street. It will grow to become a small hotel.

The London restaurant Wilton's has its beginnings in a stall set up by fishmonger George William Wilton in Cockspur Street, near the Haymarket, to sell cockles, oysters, and shrimp. Wilton will retire in 1770, his son Francis Charles will take over the business, and his great-great-nephew Robert Thomas Wilton will apply for a license in the 1840s to sell wine and beer at Wilton's Shellfishmongers and Oyster Rooms, a restaurant that will move in the early 1980s to 55 Jermyn Street and will celebrate its 250th anniversary in 1992.

1743

The Amsterdam spice shop Jacob Hooy & Co. opens at Kloveniersburgwal 10–12. The Hooy family will run it for more than 200 years, selling the ingredients for rijsttafel—rice accompanied by at least half a dozen Indonesian side dishes that may include *sati babi manis* (pork on skewers), *ajam kunin* (yellow chicken), *ajam panggang* (broiled chicken), and *ran pang* (pork or beef with coconut), with a rijsttafel sauce such as *goreng sanbal* (vegetable oil, almonds, onion, garlic, and brown sugar), *buntjies* (hard-boiled eggs with *goreng sanbal*), *goreng udang* (cooked shrimp *sanbal*), *goreng hati* (cooked cubed liver), *lalap* (cucumber salad), *urapan* (mixed vegetable salad), *rudjak* (fruit salad), *pisang goreng* (fried bananas), and *surundeng* (grated coconut with peanuts).

Moët and Chandon has its beginnings in a Champagne business founded at Épernay by French entrepreneur Claude Moët, whose firm will become France's largest champagne producer, bottling the bubbly beverage in splits (or nips—6½ ounces), pints (13 ounces), bottles (or quarts, 26 ounces), magnums (2 quarts, 52 ounces), jeroboams (double magnums, 104 ounces), rheoboams (6 quarts, 156 ounces), methuselahs (8 quarts, 208 ounces, or 1.65 gallons), salmanazars (12 quarts, 312 ounces, or 2.44 gallons), balthazars (16 quarts, 416 ounces, or 3.3 gallons), and nebuchadnezzars (20 quarts, 520 ounces, or 4.07 gallons) (*see* Dom Pérignon, 1698; 1936).

1744

The first known record of ice cream in America is made by a William Blake, who visits the Maryland colony: "You saw a plain proof of the Great Plenty of the Country, a table set in the most splendent manner set out with Great Variety of Dishes, all serv'd up in the most elegant way, after which came a Dessert no less curious; among the Rareties of which it was Compos'ed was some fine Ice Cream which, with the Strawberries and Milk, eat most Deliciously."

Prussia's Frederick II, 32, distributes free seed potatoes to reluctant peasants, recognizing the potato as a cheap food source for his growing nation. Following a period of acute food scarcity, he sends a wagonload of potatoes to Kolberg, but citizens of the place send back a message saying, "The things have neither smell nor taste, not even dogs will eat them, so what use are they to us?" The king sends in Swabian troops and stations them in the fields to enforce his edict that the peasants plant potatoes or suffer their ears and noses to be cut off. He will eventually succeed in gaining acceptance for potatoes, partly by eating them himself (*see* 1757).

Lord Anson returns with the last Royal Navy ship of his original six after having lost more than four-fifths of his crew to scurvy (*see* 1741; Lind, 1747).

1745

Scotland has an uprising of Highland peasants who have been driven off the land by "lairds" who want to break up the clans and use the Highlands for sheep raising.

Philadelphia's Second Street Market opens to supply the city's homemakers with meat, poultry, fruit, and vegetables.

1746

British grain prices continue to fall, as they have been doing for 30 years and will continue to do for another 10. Death rates will fall, too, as more people are able to afford better diets (*see* Burke's Act, 1773).

White Horse Scotch whisky has its beginnings in the cellar of a tavern at Edinburgh.

1747

Prussian chemist Andreas Sigismund Marggraf, 38, discovers that beets and carrots contain small amounts of sugar (*see* Achard, 1793).

Cookbooks: *The Art of Cookery, Made Plain and Easy* by English author Mrs. Hannah Glasse, 39, whose book, published anonymously ("By a Lady") at her own expense, is the first modern manual of cookery in English, will go through 17 editions by 1803, and will appear in new and revised editions for more than a century as it becomes the Bible of British and colonial housewives. "I believe I have attempted a Branch of Cookery which Nobody has yet thought worth their while to write upon," the author says in a preface: "But as I have both seen, and found by Experience, that the Generality of Servants are greatly wanting in that Point, therefore I have taken it upon me to instruct them in the best Manner I am capable; and I daresay, that every Servant who can but read will be capable of making a tolerable good Cook, and those who have the least Notion of Cookery can't miss of being very good ones." A tradecard inserted in the third edition says that the author is Mrs. Glasse, which later becomes "H. Glasse," possibly a pen name. *Arte de Repostería* by Spanish author Juan de la Mata.

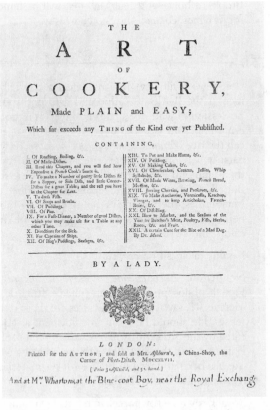

THE

ART

OF

COOKERY,

Made PLAIN and EASY;

Which far exceeds any THING of the Kind ever yet Published.

CONTAINING,

I. Of Roasting, Boiling, &c.
II. Of Made-Dishes.
III. Read this Chapter, and you will find how Expensive a *French* Cook's Sauce is.
IV. To make a Number of pretty little Dishes fit for a Supper, or Side Dish, and little Corner-Dishes for a great Table; and the rest you have in the Chapter for *Lent*.
V. To dress Fish.
VI. Of Soops and Broths.
VII. Of Puddings.
VIII. Of Pies.
IX. For a Fast-Dinner, a Number of good Dishes, which you may make use for a Table at any other Time.
X. Directions for the Sick.
XI. For Captains of Ships.
XII. Of Hog's Puddings, Sausages, &c.

XIII. To Pot and Make Hams, &c.
XIV. Of Pickling.
XV. Of Making Cakes, &c.
XVI. Of Cheesecakes, Creams, Jellies, Whip Syllabubs, &c.
XVII. Of Made Wines, Brewing, *French* Bread, Muffins, &c.
XVIII. Jarring Cherries, and Preserves, &c.
XIX. To Make Anchovies, Vermicella, Ketchup, Vinegar, and to keep Artichokes, French-Beans, &c.
XX. Of Distilling.
XXI. How to Market, and the Seasons of the Year for Butcher's Meat, Poultry, Fish, Herbs, Roots, &c. and Fruit.
XXII. A certain Cure for the Bite of a Mad Dog. By Dr. *Mead*.

BY A LADY.

LONDON:

Printed for the AUTHOR; and sold at Mrs. *Ashburn's*, a China-Shop, the Corner of *Fleet-Ditch*. MDCCXLVII.

[Price 3 s. *stitch'd*, and 5 s. *bound*.]

And at Mrs *Wharton's*, at the Blue-coat Boy, near the Royal Exchange.

Hannah Glasse's book, published anonymously, became the bible of British and colonial housewives. NEW YORK PUBLIC LIBRARY

Mrs. Glasse (above), who will be the most widely read cookbook writer in this century, does not say, "First, catch your hare," but does say, "Take your hare when it is cased." Her book of practical recipes is designed for housewives and their uneducated servants, who have no other way to acquire knowledge of cookery. Rivals will call it disorganized and say that the recipes are unoriginal (some are taken word for word from the 1727 book by Eliza Smith) and uneconomical, but 34 editions of this book will be published between now and 1842 at London, Dublin, and Edinburgh and in America, and later writers will copy many of Glasse's recipes.

Mrs. Glasse (above) gives four recipes for the preparation of Dover sole (*see* Kintner, 1877). She omits the meat gravy from fish dishes, substituting water, and she omits the extravagant French *cullis*

for thickening and flavoring sauces. She avoids deep frying.

Mrs. Glasse (above) uses calves' feet for her multi-hued "Ribband Jelly," obtaining red from cochineal, green from "spinach," yellow from "saffron," blue from "syrup of violets," and white from thick cream. She gives a recipe for a "Christmas Pye" that contains a bushel of flour, four pounds of butter, and at least seven different kinds of game and birds.

Mrs. Glasse (above) reflects the widespread English antipathy toward disguising the natural taste of meat, especially fowl and game birds, with highly-flavored foreign sauces, she improves the taste of many dishes by using butter instead of suet, she lightens the texture and flavor of others by substituting milk, or milk and eggs, for some or all of the cream, but she says, "I have heard of a cook that used six pounds of butter to fry twelve eggs, when everybody knows that understands cooking that half a pound is enough, or more than need be used; but then it would not be *French*. So much is the blind folly of this age that they would rather be imposed on by a *French* Booby than give encouragement to a good English cook."

Virginia schoolboy George Washington, 15, writes out a list of rules of behavior, copied from a French book of manners. One rule: "Cleanse not your teeth with the Table Cloth, Napkins, Fork, or Knife."

Scottish naval surgeon James Lind, 31, pioneers the conquest of scurvy. He conducts experiments with 12 scurvy victims aboard the Royal Navy's H.M.S. *Salisbury* and finds that cider, nutmeg, seawater, vinegar, elixir of vitriol (a sulfate), and a combination of garlic, mustard, myrrh, and balsam of Peru are all worthless as scurvy cures, but that two scurvy seamen given two oranges and a lemon each day recover in short order, an indication that citrus fruits contain an antiscorbutic element (*see* 1734; 1753).

1748

Observations upon the Generation, Composition, and Decomposition of Animal and Vegetable Substances by English naturalist John Tuberville Needham, 35, gives "proof" of spontaneous generation (*see* Redi, 1668). Needham says he has found flasks of broth teeming with "little animals" after having boiled them and sealed them, but his experimental techniques have been faulty (*see* Maupertuis, 1751).

Swedish botanist Peter Kalm, 33, describes English cooking (he has visited England en route to America): "Englishmen understand almost better than any other people the art of properly roasting a large cut of meat," he writes, but he adds that "the art of cooking as practiced by most Englishmen does not extend much beyond roast beef and plum pudding."

The London chocolate house John Batger's of Bishop's Gate opens to supply the growing demand for beverage chocolate.

1749

New England suffers a drought so severe that farmers whose powder-dry pastures catch fire must send to Pennsylvania and even to England for hay.

Haricot beans are planted extensively for the first time in France (*see* 1533; Oudin, 1640). The flageolets planted near Soissons will soon replace fava beans in the area.

Pellagra is described in Italy, where polenta made of cornmeal is a dietary staple in some areas (*see* 1735). Aztecs and Inca in the New World learned centuries ago to mix their maize with wood ashes, whose slaked lime (calcium hydroxide) altered the corn's protein potential, but whites have not followed their practice. The "corn sickness" will get its name in 1771 from the Italian words *pelle agra* (rough skin), its further symptoms being diarrhea, dementia, and—ultimately—death. By the end of the next century, Egypt and other African countries where peasants live mainly on cornmeal will be suffering pellagra epidemics (*see* 1907).

Justerini & Brooks has its origin in a London wine shop opened at 2, The Colonnade, by Italian wine merchant Giacomo Justerini, who enjoys immediate success in partnership with George Johnson. When Justerini returns to Italy in 1760, Johnson will take his own son Augustus into the partnership, the younger Johnson will be killed in 1785 when a runaway horse overturns his sedan chair in Piccadilly, and when *his* son Augustus Johnson II sells the firm in 1831 to Alfred Brooks it will become Justerini &

Brooks, a house at 2 Pall Mall that will be famous for its wines, cognac, and Scotch whisky.

1750

Chippewa (Ojibway) Indians defeat Sioux tribesmen at the Battle of Kathio and gain undisputed possession of wild rice stands in the lakes of northern Minnesota (*see* Marquette, 1673). Voyageurs call the rice (*Zizania aquatica*) *folle aveoine*, or wild oats; it was originally harvested in the waters of the Manomini River near what later will be Green Bay, Wisconsin, by another Algonquin tribe, the Manomines; the Chippewa call it *manomin* (good berry), and it supplies about 25 percent of their caloric intake (*see* 1862).

Famine ravages France.

Nonfiction: *Anti-Senèque, système d'Épicure* by French philosopher-physician Julien Offray de La Mettrie, 41, says the only pleasures are those of the senses, life should be spent in enjoyment as advocated by the 3rd century B.C. Athenian philosopher Epicurus, and the soul dies with the body. La Mettrie has been attacked in France for his materialist teachings and lives in Berlin.

Royal Crown Derby porcelain has its beginnings in a factory opened at Derby, England (year approximate). French Huguenot potter André Planché has been at Derby since 1740.

Coalport porcelain has its beginnings in Shropshire (year approximate). Landowner Edward Browne has had a chinaworks on his property, which contains both clay and coal. The works will be moved to Coalport in 1814, it will become famous for its "Indian-tree" patterned plates, and it will move in 1926 to Stoke-on-Trent (*see* Spode, 1800).

Ices and ice creams are sold year round in Paris by Buisson, successor to Procope, whose competitors follow suit after having sold *glace* only in summer (*see* 1670).

Britain raises the bounty on whales to 40 shillings per ton in a move that encourages Scotsmen to enter the whaling industry.

Massachusetts has 63 distilleries producing rum made from molasses—1,500 hogsheads of it per year—supplied in some cases by slave traders who sell it to the Puritan distillers for the capital needed to buy African natives who can be sold to West Indian sugar planters (*see* 1733).

1751

 The British government sharply increases the tax on gin and tightens regulations for the sale of gin in licensed premises (*see* 1736). A substantial rise in the price of grain also raises the price of spirits, forcing the poor to switch to beer, coffee, and tea. Porter (*see* 1722) will sell in London for 3 pence per quart until 1761, and the price will not reach 4 pence until 1799.

Système de la nature by Pierre de Maupertuis challenges the "proof" of spontaneous generation offered by John T. Needham in 1748 (*see* Spellanzini, 1768).

Painting: *Gin Lane* (engraving) by London painter-engraver William Hogarth, 53, who satirizes the excesses of drinking among the city's lower classes.

Artist William Hogarth lampooned London's excessive drinking in his engraving "Gin Lane." WEIDENFELD & NICOLSON ARCHIVES

England's Royal Worcester Porcelain Co. has its beginnings in a crockery firm founded June 4 by Dr. John Wall and potter William Davis to take over Benjamin Lund's Bristol factory, started 3 years ago. Dr. Wall will perfect soapstone porcelain, basing his work on the expertise of his workmen. His company's blue china teapots, cups, and saucers, with an underglaze chinoiserie design, are made from a paste containing soapstone (steatite), and by the 1760s the designs will be modeled on those of Meissen and Sèvres as well as those from China (*see* 1788; Cookworthy, 1754).

George Washington, now 19, visits Barbados with his brother Lawrence, who requires a warm climate to recover from an illness (*see* 1741). Young George samples such tropical fruits as "agovado" (avocado) pears, which he notes are abundant and the most popular local fruit, and shaddock (grapefruit; *see* 1696), but writes in his diary that "none pleases my taste as do's the pine [pineapple]."

Pennsylvania farmer-naturalist John Bartram, 52, describes Native American cookery in *Observations . . . made by John Bartram in his travels from Pensilvania to . . . Lake Ontario*, published at London. Bartram has farmed for 13 years at Kingessing, outside Philadelphia.

At least 60 New England vessels are engaged in whaling ventures (*see* 1712; 1775).

So vast is the Territory of North America that it will require many Ages to settle it fully," writes Benjamin Franklin, "and, till it is fully settled, Labour will never be cheap here, where no Man continues long a Labourer for others, but gets a Plantation of his own" (*see* 1755; Jefferson, 1782).

1752

France's Louis XV orders that grain surpluses be stored as a reserve against famine, but government grain buying drives up bread prices. Thousands of Frenchmen are reduced to starvation and suspicions arise that Louis is making millions of francs in profit from grain speculations (*see* 1768).

George Washington inherits his brother's Mount Vernon plantation in the Virginia colony and works to improve its agricultural practices. He builds a

1752

gristmill to produce flour, made from his own wheat, that will be shipped in barrels from his own cooperage. Washington will build two more mills, and his "superfine flour" will go to markets as far distant as the West Indies. He will be the largest flour producer in the colonies, giving him a large cash income that will enable him to buy good real estate and thus hedge against inflation as colonial currencies depreciate (*see* 1781).

French naturalist René-Antoine Ferchault de Réaumur, 69, proves that digestion is at least partially a chemical process (*see* Borelli, 1680). He places food inside tiny perforated metal cylinders and feeds these to hawks; when he recovers the cylinders and finds that the food inside is partially digested, he destroys the prevailing belief that the stomach digests food simply by grinding it physically (*see* Beaumont, 1822).

The Gardener's Dictionary by Philip Miller, 61, expresses doubts about eating tomatoes. Miller is "Gardener to the Worshipful Company of Apothecaries at their Botanick Garden in Chelsea."

The first Irish whiskey distillery is founded by distiller William Jameson.

France's Louis XV (above) allows the public to watch when he dines on Sunday afternoons, beginning his meals by bolting a boiled egg which he neatly decapitates with a single swipe of his fork. He is credited with having created and cooked the first asparagus-tip omelette.

The Japanese restaurant Tsubajin, opened by Jinbei at what later will be Kanazawa in Ishikawa Prefecture, northeast of Kyoto, will survive for more than 240 years (*see* Paris, 1765). Jinbei's specialty is *kaiseki*, the meal served after the tea ceremony.

1753

The Manufacture de Vincennes porcelain works founded in 1738 is declared the Manufacture Royale de Porcelaine de France (*see* Sèvres, 1756).

Treatise on the Scurvy by James Lind is an account of his citrus cure (*see* 1747; 1757).

Cookbook: *Everlasting Syllabubs* by Eliza Smith. Popular since the Renaissance, syllabub is a drink

made of hot, but not curdled, milk or cream mixed with brandy, table wine, port, sherry, hard cider, or beer and sugar, beaten to a froth with whipped cream floated on top.

1754

Money from sugar and other commodities grown in the New World with slave labor rivals money from East India Company ventures to create a growing leisure class in England. The Company has begun to export spices from India, challenging the Dutch (*see* 1780).

English porcelain production is pioneered by Quaker pharmacist William Cookworthy, 49, of Plymouth, who finds a deposit of kaolin in Cornwall (*see* Entrecolles, 1712; Royal Worcester, 1751). In 1756, Cookworthy will find a deposit of petuntse, the feldsparlike material that is mixed with kaolin to produce fine porcelain.

Paris has 56 coffeeshops, or cafés (*see* 1672).

1755

British forces take the French fort Beausejour commanding the neck of the Acadian (Nova Scotian) Peninsula June 16; Canada's new masters deport some 10,000 French-speaking Roman Catholics. About 1,500 regroup in the French territory of Louisiana south and west of New Orleans, bringing with them French recipes; some will spread as far west as the Texas border (*see* 1784).

"Experiments upon Magnesia, Quicklime, and other Alkaline Substances" by Scottish chemist-physician Joseph Black, 27, shows that magnesium is a distinct substance completely different from lime, with which it has been confused. Black last year laid the foundations of quantitative analysis with a doctoral thesis on causticization.

Nonfiction: *A Dictionary of the English Language* by lexicographer Samuel Johnson, 46, establishes the reputation of Doctor Johnson, who has not yet visited Scotland (*see* 1773) but who defines oats as "a cereal grass of the genus *avena* (*avoin* in France), the best-known species being Scots oats, a grain they fed to horses, fine live-stock and to men in Scotland." To which Doctor Johnson's Scottish biographer James Boswell will say, "Yes, and that is why in England you have such fine horses and in Scotland we have such fine people." Scottish oat cakes are thin, round cakes of oats combined with fat, baking soda, salt, and water and baked in a hot oven (*see* haggis, 1785).

Cookbooks: *Professed Cookery* by English author Ann Cook, who spends 66 pages criticizing Hannah Glasse's recipes in minute detail, saying, among other things, that they are too lavish and too generous with salt (*see* 1747); *Hjelpreda; hushaingen för nuga fruentibuler* by Swedish author Christina Warg, 52.

Fish and shellfish chowder is popular with the French at Acadia (above) and has gained favor among the British as well. Derived from the French word *chaudière*, meaning a large cauldron, it is prepared on ships throughout the Atlantic and has been introduced into Newfoundland and New England as well as to Nova Scotia.

Gorton's fish factory is founded at Gloucester in the Massachusetts colony (*see* 1623).

English stock breeder Robert Bakewell, 30, in Leicestershire develops a new breed of sheep that will be called Leicester.

Marie Brizard anisette is introduced by French entrepreneur Jean-Baptiste Roger, who has gone into business with an aunt to distill and sell the liqueur whose recipe she claims to have learned from a sailor in a dream. By 1761, Marie Brizard et Roger will be shipping the product to markets as far distant as the West Indies.

1756

French forces under the duc de Richelieu lay siege in May to the British fort of Mahón on the Balearic island of Minorca in the Seven Years' War, which has begun with Prussia's invasion of Saxony (*see* mayonnaise, below).

Ireland's potato crop fails as it did in the early 1740s and will do again next year—and again in 1765, 1766, and 1769—causing widespread distress each time (*see* 1784).

Scottish chemist Joseph Black shows that fixed air (carbon dioxide) is consistently distinguishable from normal air (*see* Priestley's carbonated water, 1767).

The Manufacture de Vincennes porcelain works moves to Sèvres—halfway between Paris and Versailles—on property donated by Louis XV's mistress, Jeanne-Antoinette Poisson, marquise de Pompadour, 34, and is renamed (*see* 1753). But Sèvres porcelain is soft-paste (*pa tendere*) porcelain of the kind produced by the Medicis in Florence since the end of the 16th century.

Mayonnaise is invented according to some accounts by the duc de Richelieu (above), whose invention, originally called Mahonnaise, takes its name from the fort that falls to the French in June. A bon vivant who sometimes invites his guests to dine in the nude, the duke has allegedly taken the yolks of two eggs, 200 grams of olive oil, half a lemon, and a little salt and pepper. (By other accounts, the word *mayonnaise* will be derived from the word *moyeu*, sometimes used for the yolk of an egg, and will not appear until the 19th century.)

Portugal's chief minister Sebastião José de Carvalho e Mello, marqués de Pombal, 57, defines his country's Douro region to protect the quality of port wine.

Pombal (above) reestablishes the Oporto Wine Company.

1757

An essay "On the Most Efficient Means of Preserving the Health of Seamen" by James Lind establishes principles of hygiene to guard against typhus and other diseases (*see* below).

Potato planting increases rapidly in northern Europe as the famine that accompanies the Seven Years' War gives impetus to potato culture (*see* Frederick, 1744).

James Lind describes his 1747 experiment with scurvy patients in a second edition of his 1753 *Treatise*. He reports that he divided 12 patients into pairs and experimented with six different diets, trying such things as vinegar, cider, and elixir vitriol (sulfuric acid, alcohol, and an extract of ginger and cinnamon). The best results were obtained, Lind reports, when diets were supplemented with oranges and lemons. He proposes novel ways to keep fruit juices and greens from deterioration on long voyages, suggesting that juices be put up in pint bottles and covered with a layer of olive oil before being tightly corked, and that leeks and other vegetables be cut into short lengths, sprinkled with a thin layer of bay salt, and then packed in salt, which will permit them to be prepared as fresh vegetables when the salt is washed away as much as 3 months later (*see* Cook, Pringle, 1775).

George Washington seeks election to the Virginia House of Burgesses from Fairfax County, campaigning for votes with 28 gallons of rum, 50 gallons of rum punch, 34 gallons of wine, 46 of beer, and 2 of cider royal. The county has 391 voters.

1758

Tableau Économique by French surgeon-general François Quesnay, 64, propounds a system under which the products of agriculture will be distributed without government restraint among the productive classes of the community (landowners and land cultivators) and the unproductive classes (manufacturers and merchants). Agriculture is the only true source of wealth, says Quesnay, and his disciple the marquis de Mirabeau will say that Quesnay's manifesto contributes as much to the stability of political societies as have the inventions of money and writing.

An advertisement appears September 18 in the *New York Gazette*: "Chocolate Made and Sold by Peter Swigart, Chocolate Makers, in Bayard-street, opposite Mr. John Livingston's Store-House; Choice Chocolate at the new current Price" (*see* 1769; Baker, 1764).

1759

Britain's grain crop fails, raising prices and provoking demands that the the government import grain (*see* alcohol, below).

The Virginia colony exports Albemarle pippins to England, which has no apples quite like them.

German anatomist Kaspar Friedrich Wolff, 26, observes the development of growing plants. Wolff will be a founder of modern embryology.

Cookbook: *A Complete System of Cookery* by William Verral, French chef to Britain's Lord Hackum, who states that his lordship's expensive kitchen contains not one clean pot or pan; *A New and Easy Method of Cookery, Treating I. Of gravies, soups, broths, &c., II. Of fish, and Their Sauces* . . . by Edinburgh cooking school teacher Elizabeth Cleland.

Porcelain teacups in Europe now generally have handles in a departure from Oriental design.

The British government changes its policy with regard to permitting free distillation of grain into alcohol in response to the failure of the grain crop (above). Upper-class Britons consume spirits—primarily rum and *arrack* (a Turkish spirit)—most often in the form of punch or toddy (hot, diluted with water, fruit juice, or tea)

Irish brewer Arthur Guinness establishes a Dublin brewery that will become the world's largest. By the end of the century it will be making only porter (*see* Whitbread, 1742), but Guinness's porter, even at 4 pence per quart, is expensive for a working man earning, at most, between 5 and 10 shillings per week, and only a small percentage of the population will drink beer before 1850. It is Guinness stout that will gain worldwide distribution, but most Irishmen now drink spirits or home-brewed beer (although private brewing will never exist to any great extent in Ireland).

1760

Large quantities of clove bark and nutmegs are burned at Amsterdam to maintain high price levels (*see* 1768).

Cookbook: *The Servants Directory or Housekeeper's Companion* by Hannah Glasse.

Robert Bakewell in Leicestershire begins experiments designed to improve beef cattle (*see* 1755; 1769).

English pigs are crossed for the first time with Chinese pigs (year approximate). The English pigs are slim and long-legged like their wild-boar ancestors, the Chinese pigs smaller, plump, and short-legged.

1761

Portugal abolishes slavery at home but continues to enslave Africans for work in her colonial African and Brazilian sugar plantations (*see* 1858; Madeira, 1775).

Britain takes £600,000 worth of exports from Guadeloupe, most of it in sugar, while Canada yields only £14,000 (*see* 1759; 1763).

England's Bridgewater Canal is opened after 3 years' work to link Liverpool with Leeds.

A French aristocrat, imprisoned briefly in the Bastille at Paris, discovers to his surprise that the four-course meal he was served on his first day was-intended for his servant; the meal prepared for his own consumption consisted of soup, filet of beef, chicken au jus, marinated artichokes, spinach au jus, a pear, a bunch of grapes, a bottle of old burgundy, and coffee.

France's first veterinary school opens at Lyons.

British grain prices will rise in this decade, and fewer Britons will grow their own food as public lands are enclosed and turned into pastures for sheep and more of the peasantry is driven off the land. A special act of Parliament must be obtained for each enclosure, a system that favors large landowners who need only to have the wherewithal for lawyers' and surveyors' fees and enough to pay for fences, hedges, roads, and drainage following passage of an enclosure act. Between 2 million and 3 million acres of open fields and waste lands will be enclosed between now and 1799, and by 1840 there will have been 3,500 enclosure acts, up from just 200 in the past 60 years. This will create distress among villagers who cannot afford the cost of enclosure and will thus be forced to sell out, often at cheap prices, or accept inferior land. Enclosure deprives peasants of land for pasturage and fields for their crops, but while it will make even poultry an expensive luxury it will make agriculture more efficient and lead to a great increase in food production.

1762

Dutch ironworkers at Mary Ann Furnaces in the Pennsylvania colony cast the first American iron cookstove.

Frenchmen discover a kaolin deposit that will lead to increased production of porcelain (*see* 1754; 1768).

English potter Josiah Wedgwood, 32, receives an appointment from George III, who names him "Potter to the Queen" (Charlotte). Wedgwood, who began his career by repairing Delft porcelain, has presented a set of his own pottery to the queen and will go on to create superior tableware (*see* 1763).

Fiction: *Émile* by French philosopher Jean-Jacques Rousseau, 50, who blames English "barbarism" on high meat consumption.

Cookbook: *The Complete Confectioner, or The Whole Art of Confectionery Made Plain and Easy* by Hannah Glasse; the book is far less successful than Glasse's 1747 *Art of Cookery* and will be incorporated into future editions of that work, which by 1800 will have grown into a much larger tome with nearly one-third of its pages devoted to useful household knowledge, including a discussion of the hothouse- and garden-grown fruits and vegetables available in the London markets at various seasons; the variety of meats, game, poultry, and fish; and detailed instructions for determining the freshness of such foods. "Always be careful your greens are nicely picked and washed. You should lay them in a clean pan for fear of dust. . . . Boil all your greens in a . . . saucepan by themselves. Boil no meat with them, for that discolors them. . . . Most people spoil garden things by overboiling them. All things that are green should have a little crispness, for if they are overboiled they neither have any sweetness or beauty." Glasse pours hot clarified butter, suet, or mutton fat on top of her potted meats and pickles; she covers her pots with a bladder or a piece of leather, tied down securely, to keep out dust. She urges her readers to wash pots and pans and never to leave victuals indefinitely in copper cooking vessels.

The sandwich is invented this year by some accounts at London's Beef Steak Club, above the Covent Garden Theatre, where John Montagu, 44, fourth earl of Sandwich, has spent 24 hours at the gaming tables without stopping to eat. He orders some beef or fowl and slices of bread, holds the meat between the slices, and eats as he goes on with his gambling (*see* Sandwich Islands, 1778).

Hannah Glasse (above) warns her readers to avoid artificial chemicals used to color pickles and certain desserts as these often contain harmful ingredients (*see* Smollett, 1771).

London's Boodles Club is founded with a membership that will soon include dandy Beau Brummel and philosopher Adam Smith.

Russia's population will increase in the next 34 years from 19 million to 29 million, partly because the potato has made food cheaper and more abundant, partly through acquisition of new territory.

1763

The Treaty of Paris signed February 10 ends Europe's Seven Years' War. France cedes to Britain her territories in Canada, Cape Breton Island, Grenada in the West Indies, and Senegal in Africa. France regains Gorée in Africa, Pondichéry and Chandernagor in India, and the sugar-rich islands of Guadeloupe and Martinique in the West Indies.

Spain cedes Florida to Britain in return for Havana. The Crown grants an Englishman several thousand acres of Florida land to create a working colony; he chooses a site south of St. Augustine and calls it New Smyrna after his wife's birthplace, will bring in some 1,500 Italians, Greeks, and Minorcans to work for 8 years as indentured servants on the promise of receiving 50 acres of land each, but a ship carrying African slaves to clear the land will be lost at sea, the project will fail, and the survivors—most of them Minorcans—will move to St. Augustine (*see* 1783).

Of 14,000 hogsheads of molasses brought into New England this year, only 2,500 from British sources; smugglers account for the remainder (*see* 1764; Molasses Act, 1733).

Josiah Wedgwood at Burslam perfects a vitrified "cream-color ware" that is not true porcelain but gives Britain a hard tableware far more durable than earthenware (*see* 1762). Queen Charlotte orders a complete dinner set of the new china and asks that it be named for her (it will be sold as Queensware beginning in 1765; *see* 1769).

"Some people have a foolish way of not minding, or pretending not to mind, what they eat," says Doctor Johnson, who for the first time meets Scotsman James Boswell, 23. "For my part, I mind my belly very studiously and very carefully, for I look upon it that he who does not mind his belly will hardly mind anything else."

Doctor Johnson cared about what he ate and drank. "Minding his belly," he called it.

New York's Fraunces Tavern has its beginnings in the Queen's Head Tavern named in honor of George III's wife, Charlotte. Jamaican-born entrepreneur Samuel Fraunces has taken over the house at the corner of Broad and Pearl streets, built in 1719 by colonist Stephen de Lancey, and turned it into a public house (*see* Washington, 1783).

1764

Mme. de Pompadour, *maîtresse-en-titre* to France's Louis XV, falls ill of bronchial pneumonia and dies April 15 at age 42. She has created *filet de volaille à la Bellevue*, and her name will be immortalized on French menus to denote a white wine and tomato sauce.

The Sugar Act passed by Parliament April 5 replaces the Molasses Act of 1733, but while it cuts in half the sixpence-per-gallon duty on molasses imported into British colonies from non-British islands in the West Indies, the British send customs officials to America and order colonial governors to enforce the new law and apprehend smugglers (*see* 1763).

Baccarat glass has its beginnings in a petition to France's Louis XV from the monseigneur de Montmorency-Laval, bishop of Metz, who asks permission to establish a glassware factory across the Meurthe River from Baccarat, a town of 600. A nearby salt factory that has used the bishop's vast woodlands as a fuel source has closed, the bishop's Compagnie des Cristalliers de Baccarat will be established next year, and by 1789 it will have 400 employees.

Prussia's Frederick the Great moves to improve his country's agriculture after studying the intensive farming methods employed in the Lowlands. Frederick institutes a modified rotation system that employs clover to enrich the soil, turnips whose green tops help smother weeds, wheat, and barley (the turnips and clover both make good animal fodder; *see* Townshend, 1730). Frederick also drains the marshes along the Oder, Werthe, and Netze Rivers.

Baker Chocolate has its beginnings in a business set up by Irish-American chocolate maker John Hannon with help from Massachusetts colony physician James Baker, who leases a small mill on the Neponset River at Dorchester, obtains millstones and kettles, and supplies Hannon, who is penniless, with the necessary capital (*see* 1777).

A new canal links France's Loire and Rhône Rivers (*see* 1600; 1603).

Colonial American shipping interests have 28,000 tons of shipping and employ some 4,000 seamen. Exports of tobacco are nearly double in value the exports of flour, with fish, rice, indigo, and wheat next in order of value.

Irish entrepreneur Richard Hennessy, 43, founds a firm for the purpose of exporting cognac brandy to his native County Cork, where it will find favor among the local gentry, who disdain the local whiskey (*see* Martel, 1715). According to some accounts, Hennessy came to France as an officer in the Irish Brigade and was wounded in 1745 at the Battle of Fontenoy, according to others he was exiled by British authorities for agitating against the Crown and settled in the Charente region. His son James will become a French citizen, enlarge Richard's business, and form James Hennessy & Cie.

France's first public restaurant, as opposed to an inn that serves food to overnight guests or a tavern that emphasizes drinking rather than eating, opens at Paris, where a tavernkeeper named Boulanger defies the monopoly of the caterers (*traiteurs*), whose guild members sell cooked whole joints of meat, poultry, and stews (ragouts) (but *see* China, 1280; Japan, 1657, 1716, 1718, 1752). At his Champ d'Oiseau tavern in the rue des Poulies (or rue Bailleul; accounts vary), Boulanger serves a "soup" made of mutton feet in a white sauce and calls it a *divin restorante* ("divine restorative"). The *traiteurs* sue, the case goes to the French parlement, Boulanger wins, and he gains the right to serve *restorantes* at his all-night place, whose menu he soon enlarges (*see* Beauvilliers, 1782).

1765

Scotsman James Watt, 29, invents a steam engine that produces power far more efficiently than the Newcomen engine of 1705. Mathematical instrument maker to the University of Glasgow, Watt employs a separate chamber, or condenser, to condense exhaust steam from the cylinder of his engine (*see* Boulton and Watt Foundry, 1769).

1766

Rust ruins the Italian wheat crop, food prices rise, and widespread hunger ensues.

France abolishes internal free trade in grain (*see* 1774).

English engineer James Brindley, 50, begins construction of a Grand Trunk Canal to connect the

Trent and Mersey rivers. It will open a water route from the Irish Sea to the North Sea.

Nonfiction: "Let them eat cake [if there is no bread]," writes Jean-Jacques Rousseau in his *Confessions*. He attributes the remark to "a great princess," but it will be widely ascribed in the 1780s and 1790s to Marie-Antoinette, the daughter of the Austrian empress Maria Theresa, who is now 11 and will become queen of France in 1774.

1767

An English writer complains that "as much superfluous money is expended on tea and sugar as would maintain four million more subjects on bread."

Cookbook: *The Complete English Cook; or, Prudent Housewife* by English author Ann Peckham.

French navigator Louis-Antoine de Bougainville, 38, explores Oceania in hopes of expanding French whaling operations into the Pacific.

A fleet of 50 American whalers makes a foray into the Antarctic, the first whaling venture into that region.

English clergyman-chemist Joseph Priestley, 34, pioneers carbonated water (*see* Black's carbon dioxide, 1756). "Sometimes in the space of two or three minutes [I have] made a glass of exceedingly pleasant sparkling water which could hardly be distinguished from very good Pyrmont," he writes. He will devise a more convenient way to make carbonated water (*see* carbonic acid, 1770).

1768

The price of bread at Paris reaches 4 sous per pound and a placard appears in the city: "Under Henri IV bread was sometimes expensive because of war and France had a king; under Louis XIV it sometimes went up because of war and sometimes because of famine and France had a king; now there is no war and no famine and the cost of bread still goes up and France has no king because the king is a grain merchant."

Government regulations discourage French farmers from increasing their grain acreage, critics say, and they demand free circulation of grain (*see* 1766; Turgot, 1774).

London has bread riots. Government grain stores are pillaged by the mob.

British customs officials at Boston seize the sloop *Liberty* June 10, the action precipitates riots, and Boston merchants adopt a nonimportation agreement August 1. Owner of the sloop is John Hancock, 31, whose late uncle has left him a fortune gained by profiteering in food supplied to the British troops and who has enhanced that fortune by smuggling wine into Boston.

The English wine-exporting firm Duff-Gordon is founded at Cádiz, Spain, by the local British consul, James Duff, and his nephew William Gordon (*see* Osborne, 1872).

Dutch colonial officials make a count of young and mature clove trees in the East Indies and find some 780,000; they set out to stop clove propagation until the number has been reduced to 550,000. Warehouses at Batavia are stocked with 3 million pounds of cloves, only 15 percent of which can be disposed of in any given year (*see* 1760). It is estimated that the Dutch alone have enough cloves to meet Europe's demand for the next 10 years.

Italian naturalist Lazzaro Spallanzani, 39, disproves the universally believed notion of spontaneous generation of organisms (in mutton broth) (*see* Needham, 1748; Maupertuis, 1751).

"The scrofulous are common in Switzerland, where the people support themselves above all on potatoes," writes Swiss physician Daniel Langhaus. "I am persuaded, myself, that the scrofulous troubles which prevail in our Cantons are entirely the result of this harmful dietary and the lack of exercise. The proof of which that they are extremely rare in countries where the potato is unknown" (*see* Parmentier, 1771).

A French apothecary named Darnet discovers kaolin at Saint-Yrieix-la-Perche in the Limousin, 25 miles south of Limoges. He noticed 3 years ago that his wife was digging up a white material beyond the village cemetery and using it to wash his linen clean. The increasing popularity of tea, coffee, and chocolate has boosted demand for graceful china cups and durable teapots, coffeepots, chocolate pots, bowls, and pitchers, which are now imported by the various Indies companies from China, whose artisans produce chinaware with European designs.

Benjamin Franklin, visiting London to plead the case of the colonies, writes to his daughter, begging her to send him the foods for which he is homesick: apples, cranberries, dried peaches, buckwheat flour, and cornmeal. He tries to show the Englishwomen in his kitchen how to make cornbread and corncakes.

The East India Company imports tea into Britain at the rate of 10 million pounds per year (*see* 1773).

1769

France's Louis XV, now 59, installs Jeanne Bécu, 23, comtesse du Barry, as his *maîtresse-en-titre* April 23. Her name will become associated on French menus with cauliflower, consommé du Barry being a combination of veal and oxtail soup with chouxfleur (the chef Auguste Escoffier will say in the 20th century that the quality of a consommé depends not only on the meat in the broth but also on the 16 vegetables, although in some countries only 6 are used).

The Great Famine of Bengal kills 10 million Indians, wiping out one-third of the population in the worst famine recorded thus far in world history. The maharajah of Mysore, Haidar Ali, forces the British to sign a treaty of mutual assistance, but the East India Company increases its demands on Bengal's remaining 20 million people to ensure "a reasonable profit."

Captain James Cook, 42, Royal Navy, sails the Pacific in H.M.S. *Endeavour*, conveying a scientific expedition bent on observing the transit of the planet Venus and bringing along naturalist Joseph Banks, 25, who writes in his diary of having eaten dog in Tahiti. "Few were there of the nicest of us but allowed as South Sea dog was next to an English lamb." But Banks notes that English dogs would not be as good since the Tahitian dogs have been fed only vegetables and never meat.

James Watt patents his 1765 steam engine with some improvements, grants two-thirds of the profits to ironworks owner John Roebuck, who has financed his experiments, and goes into partnership with engineer Matthew Boulton, 41, to found the Boulton & Watt Foundry at Birmingham (*see* Wilkinson, 1774).

Josiah Wedgwood opens a pottery works at Etruria, near Burslem (*see* 1763).

Cookbook: *The Experienced English House-Keeper, for the Use and Ease of Ladies, House-Keepers, Cooks, &c. Wrote Purely from Practice* by English writer Elizabeth Raffald (*née* Whittaker), 36, who went to work at age 15 as housekeeper for Lady Elizabeth Warburton at Arley Hall, Cheshire.

Robert Bakewell of 1755 Leicester sheep fame develops cattle with deeper, wider bodies, shorter and thicker necks, and more flesh over their hind quarters, ribs, loins, and backs. Bakewell works on his premise that "like produces like" and often inbreeds stock selected for bulky bodies set low on short legs.

The Bartlett pear has its beginnings in a pear originated by English schoolmaster John Stair of Reading Parish, whose fruit will be called in Britain the Stairs pear or the Williams (after a London nurseryman who may be unaware of its origin) (*see* 1798; Bartlett, 1817).

Spanish Franciscan missionary Junipero Serra, 56, plants the first wine grapes, oranges, figs, and olives to grow in California at the Mission of San Diego de Alcalá, which he has founded after reaching the site July 1 with several other friars and a company of soldiers (*see* Mission grape, 1697).

The *Weekly Post-Boy*, published at New York, carries a notice October 23 that "Peter Lowe, Living at the Upper end of Maiden-Lane, near the Broadway & opposite to Lavery's Street, Makes & sells Chocolate equal in Goodness to any made in this City, at the current Price." (*see* Swigart, 1758)

Gordon's gin is introduced by Scots-English distiller Alexander Gordon in the London suburb of

Finsbury, where he has taken a house near the Clerk's Well in Gosswell Street behind Charter House Square and the Islington Road. Gordon's product will become the world's largest-selling brand of gin.

1770

Austrian princess Marie-Antoinette, now 14, marries the French dauphin, 15, May 16 at Versailles (*see* kipfel, below).

Famine-stricken Prussians at Kolberg receive a wagon-load of potatoes sent by Frederick the Great but refuse to eat them (*see* 1744; Parmentier, 1771).

Captain Cook explores the eastern coast of New Holland (Australia) and reports that the "land naturly produces hardly anything fit for a man to eat and the Natives know Nothing of Cultivation." He makes a landing and takes possession of the island continent in the name of Britain's George III. The great variety of plants obtained by Cook's naturalists lead him to name his landfall Botany Bay (*see* 1788).

French colonial administrator Pierre Poivre, governor of Mauritius, breaks the Dutch monopoly in spices. He dispatches "messengers" on a clandestine trading voyage for the purpose of stealing nutmegs. The Dutch have regularly soaked nutmegs in milk of lime, which does not affect their taste but prevents them from germinating. Poivre's men carry off 400 nutmeg plants, 10,000 nutmeg seeds ready to germinate, 70 clove plants, and a chest of clove seeds, some of them already sprouting. The seeds and plants flourish on Mauritius, and plantings take root also on the Pacific islands of Réunion and Seychelles and in French Guiana on the northeastern coast of South America (*see* 1818; British, 1780).

English potter Josiah Spode, 37, opens a factory dedicated to perfecting earthenware. He uses the finer, whiter clays from Cornwall, will soon combine the clays with calcined animal bones to produce bone china, and in 1784 will pioneer in transfer printing and underglaze blue, taken from

hand-engraved copper plates, on earthenware, a technique known to the Chinese since the 14th century. He will be the first to add enamel decorations over the glaze on his wares but will die a pauper in 1797 (*see* 1800).

England grows enough potatoes for public sale of the tubers for the first time.

The kipfel roll, invented by Viennese bakers in 1683 or Budapest bakers in 1686, arrives at Paris with Marie-Antoinette (above). French bakers will add yeast to the puff pastry, and—by rolling the dough, cutting it into a triangle, shaping the triangle into a crescent, and adding extra layers—will turn the kipfel into the flaky croissant, which will become a traditional French breakfast treat.

The *New York Journal* reports April 26 that a remarkable quantity of shad has been taken at the Narrows: "one of the seines, as it was drawn toward the shore, was so filled with fish that the weight pressed it to the ground, whereby great numbers escaped. A second seine was then thrown around the fish, a third around the second, a fourth around the third, and all filled in a like manner. The number of shad taken by the first net was 3,000 pounds, that of the second net also totaled 3,000 pounds, the third net caught 4,000, and the fourth 1,500, or 11,500 pounds in all four seines." Planked shad is a colonial delicacy, first used with fish from the Delaware at the Schuylkill Club outside Philadelphia: the fish is nailed to a well-seasoned oak plank into which grooves have been carved to retain the juices of the cooking fish and then placed before the glowing embers of an open fire, a method now also used to prepare bluefish, cod, halibut, mackerel, pickerel, pike, and whitefish (*see* 1791).

Swedish chemist Tobern Olof Bergman, 35, discovers a way to make carbonic acid gas in commercial quantities for use in carbonated beverages (*see* 1794; Priestley, 1767; carbonated water, 1807).

1771

French agriculturist-botanist Antoine-Auguste Parmentier lists potatoes among vegetables that may be used in times of famine (he was taken pris-

Glasse, 1762; Accum, 1820). Smollett's poor health has obliged him to settle in Italy, and he dies September 17 at Livorno at age 50.

1772

🧪 Edinburgh physician Daniel Rutherford, 23, distinguishes nitrogen as a gas separate from carbon dioxide (*see* Davy, 1800; Wöhler, 1828).

✒ Cookbook: *The Frugal Housewife* by English author Susanna Carter is published at Boston.

🌾 English agriculturist Thomas William Coke, 20, begins a reform of agriculture and animal husbandry in northwest Norfolk. He will help persuade farmers there to switch from rye to wheat; he will breed Southdown sheep, Devon cattle, and improved Suffolk pigs, but farmers in Gloucestershire, Hertfordshire, and some other counties will not be persuaded to change their ways (*see* 1760; 1780).

Virginia colony lawyer Thomas Jefferson, 29, notes July 31 that he has eaten Irish potatoes from his garden.

🥛 Prussia's Frederick the Great issues a manifesto September 13: "It is disgusting to notice the increase in the quantity of coffee used by my subjects. . . . My people must drink beer. His Majesty was brought up on beer and so were his ancestors and his officers. Many battles have been fought and won by soldiers nourished on beer, and the King does not believe that coffee-drinking soldiers can be depended on to endure hardship or to beat his enemies in case of the occurrence of another war" (*see* 1775).

1773

💲 The Tea Act passed by Parliament May 10 lightens duties on tea imported into Britain to give relief to the East India Company, which has 7 years' supply in warehouses on the Thames and is being strained by storage charges. But the Act permits tea to be shipped at full duty of 3 pence per pound to the American colonies and to be sold directly to retail-

Auguste-Antoine Parmentier urged his fellow Frenchmen to eat potatoes as the Germans did.

oner five times by the Prussians during the Seven Years' War and obliged to survive on a diet of potatoes). In a thesis that is hailed by the Besançon Academy, he includes also acorns, horse chestnuts, and the roots of bryony vine, couch grass, gladiolus, and iris, but he campaigns for acceptance of the potato (*see* 1785).

☂ English physician-novelist Tobias Smollett describes adulteration of British foods in his novel *The Expedition of Humphry Clinker*. His hero Matthew Bramble writes to a friend that "the bread I eat in London is a deleterious paste, mixed up with chalk, alum, and bone-ashes, insipid to the taste, and destructive to the constitution. The good people are not ignorant of this adulteration; but they prefer it to wholesome bread, because it is whiter than the meal of corn: thus they sacrifice their taste and their health, and the lives of their tender infants, to a most absurd gratification of a mis-judging eye" (*see*

ers, eliminating colonial middlemen and undercutting their prices.

The Boston Tea Party December 16 demonstrates against the new English tea orders (above). Led by Lendall Pitts, scion of a Boston merchant family, a group of men, including silversmith Paul Revere, 38, disguise themselves as Mohawks, board the East India Company ships *Dartmouth*, *Beaver*, and *Bedford* at Griffen's Wharf, and throw 342 chests of tea from the London firm of Davison and Newman into Boston harbor (the tea is valued at more than £9,650). Agitator Samuel Adams, 51, has organized the action with support from John Hancock, whose smuggling of contraband tea has been made unprofitable by the new measures.

Tea is left to rot on the docks at Charleston. New York and Philadelphia send tea-laden ships back to England; Annapolis and Edenton, N. C., have their own "tea parties," but men of "sense and property" such as George Washington deplore the Boston Tea Party.

Parliament passes Burke's Act to permit the import of foreign wheat at a nominal duty when the home price reaches a certain level. The act will remain in effect long enough to establish regular imports of foreign grain, depending on the abundance of domestic harvests, and imports will for a short while exceed exports (*see* 1791).

Doctor Johnson sets out from Edinburgh August 18 to visit the western islands of Scotland in the company of James Boswell. At Aberdeen he stops at the New Inn and gets his first taste of Scottish cooking—Scotch broth with peas.

Virginia colony governor Lord Dunmore sends an order to a London firm for "12 large Cheshire Cheese, 2 Dozen Gloucester ditto, 2 Dozen bottles of Strong Beer, 15 ditto of Ale, 3 Hogsheads of Porter, 100 lb. Currants, 50 lb. Jar Raisins, 4 lb. Mace, 2 lb. Nutmegs, 1 lb. Cloves, 1 lb. Cinnemon, 24 lb. Black Pepper, 6 lb. Jamaica ditto, 100 lb. Split Peas, 50 lb. Maccaroni," etc.

Thomas Jefferson experiments with European foods with help from his Italian visitor Philippe (Filippo, or Filippi) Mazzei, 43, planting beans from Provence, Pisan broccoli and sorrel, cabbage from Savoy, Swedish chives, English gooseberries, Ger-

Thomas Jefferson experimented with agriculture on his Virginia estate and expanded his culinary horizons.

man kale, sour oranges from southern Europe, black pumpkin from Monaco, Alpine strawberries, and Neapolitan watermelon.

Jefferson (above) grafts a European chestnut onto a native species at his Monticello estate, noting in his diary March 23 that he planted them "in a row on piece." The European chestnut will not become an important orchard fruit in America until the early 1800s (*see* Washington, 1785).

Mazzei (above) plants 10,000 European vinifera cuttings on Thomas Jefferson's Monticello estate and elsewhere on land provided by Jefferson, who will try for much of his life to establish successful vineyards at Monticello.

1774

A meager harvest in France increases the hunger that has oppressed the country since last year's poor harvest. Controller-general Anne-Robert-Jacques Turgot, 47, reintroduces the free trade in grain abolished in 1766, but the rivers freeze, grain cannot be moved by barge, and the price of a four-pound loaf of bread rises in just a few months from 11 sous to 14 sous. A four-pound loaf has sold for as much as 16 sous in earlier years, but where in the past high prices were blamed on the weather, now the government is blamed.

France has "flour wars" as rioters throw grain merchants into ponds, loot mills and bakeries, seize grain from barges, march on Versailles, and force Louis XVI, 20, to promise bread at 2 sous per pound. Some 400 rioters are arrested, and two are hanged for breaking into bakeries. No conspiracy to raise prices is uncovered, but such a conspiracy is almost universally suspected (*see* 1768; 1776).

$ News of last year's Boston Tea Party reaches London in January via John Hancock's ship *Hayley*. Parliament passes coercive acts (below) to bring the colonists to heel.

George III gives assent March 31 to the Boston Port Bill, and Boston harbor is closed June 1 until the East India Company shall have been reimbursed for its tea and British authorities feel that trade can be resumed and duties collected (*see* 1773).

The American colonists thwart London's efforts to starve Boston into submission. Marblehead sends in codfish, Charleston sends rice, and Baltimore sends bread and rye whiskey. Col. Israel Putnam, 56, of Connecticut joins with citizens of Windham to drive a flock of 258 sheep to Boston.

The British ship *London* docks at New York April 22, and the Sons of Liberty prepare to follow the example set at Boston 4 months earlier, but while they are making themselves up as Mohawks an impatient crowd on the pier boards the vessel and heaves the tea on board into the Hudson. Colonists at York, Maine, and Annapolis, Maryland, conduct tea parties like the one at Boston.

English ironmaster John Wilkinson, 46, patents a precision cannon borer that will permit commercial development of the Watt steam engine of 1769. Wilkinson's borer permits accurate boring of cylinders (*see* steam flour mill, 1780).

Denmark's Royal Copenhagen Porcelain Manufactory is founded by Queen Juliane Marie, who goes into partnership with some Copenhagen merchants. The hand-painted Blue Fluted dinner service (Design No. 1) will be introduced in 1775, porcelain from the factory will be trademarked with three wavy blue lines, and the queen will acquire full ownership in 1779.

Joseph Priestley discovers oxygen, a gas he calls "dephlogisticated air." He heats red oxide of mercury in a glass tube and obtains a gas in which a candle burns more brightly than in the air. Air "spoilt" by mice is refreshed by the presence of green plants, says Priestley (*see* 1767; 1779).

Swedish chemist Karl Wilhelm Scheele, 32, discovers chlorine, which will be widely used to purify drinking water.

Thomas Jefferson tries with the help of Filippo Mazzei to grow olives at Monticello, but his cuttings will not take root (*see* 1772).

Captain Cook, Royal Navy, discovers New Caledonia in the Pacific but nearly dies of blowfish poisoning in September after dining with his two naturalists aboard H.M.S. *Resolution* (*see* Kämpfer, 1727). "Only the Liver and Roe was dressed of which the two Mr. Forsters and myself did but just taste. About 3 or 4 o'clock in the Morning we were seized with an extraordinary weakness in all our limbs attended with a numbness or Sensation like to that caused by exposeing ones hands or feet to a fire after having been pinched much by frost, I had almost lost the sence of feeling nor could I distinguish between light and heavy bodies, a quart pot full of Water and a feather was the same in my hand. We each of us took a Vomet and after that a sweat which gave great relief. In [the morning] one of the Pigs which had eat the entrails was found dead, the Dogs got the start of the Servants of what went from our table, so that they escaped, it soon made the dogs sick and they t[h]rew it all up again and not much affected." The tetrodotoxin in the blowfish—275 times more deadly than cyanide and not destroyed by cooking—is concentrated in the liver, roe, and ovaries (although smaller amounts may be found in the intestines, skin, and—in some species—muscle tissue and affects the central nervous system).

American colonists increase their consumption of coffee to protest British taxes on tea in the wake of last year's Boston Tea Party.

1775

✕ The American War of Independence begins April 19 at the Battles of Lexington and Concord. Silversmith Paul Revere, who has held meetings with his fellow patriots at Boston's Green Dragon tavern, stops at Buckman's Tavern to relay the message that British redcoats are marching on Lexington.

Britain has hired nearly 30,000 mercenaries from six small German despots, notably the landgrave of Hesse-Kassel, who has supplied 17,000 Hessians (see "Hessian fly," 1915).

The Royal Navy begins an 11-month siege of Boston.

✊ Portugal abolishes slavery in the Madeira Islands, whose sugar will hereafter be produced by free men (see 1761; sugar, 1432).

💲 American imports from Britain decline by 95 percent as a result of efforts by the association formed last year. English businessmen feel the loss of trade, support the colonists, and ask Parliament to repeal the so-called Intolerable Acts, but Prime Minister Frederick North, 43, Lord North, tells the House of Commons that Britons are paying 50 times more tax per capita than are the American colonists.

⏲ E. Lazenby & Sons is founded at London by local grocer's wife Elizabeth Lazenby, who has developed a sauce for meat dishes (see Crosse & Blackwell, 1919).

Aynsley bone china is manufactured for the first time in England.

🐟 The New Bedford, Mass., whaling fleet reaches 80 vessels. More than 280 whaling ships put out from American ports, 220 of them from Massachusetts (see 1751; 1845).

British mercantile interests re-enter the whaling industry largely abandoned by the English in 1612 as Dutch activity begins to wane (see 1789).

🍎 James Cook returns to England from the Pacific and the Royal Society awards him its Gold Copley Medal for having conquered scurvy. Sir John Pringle, chief medical officer of the British army and physician to George III, hails Captain Cook's achievement in bringing 118 men through all climates for 3 years and 18 days "with the loss of only one man by distemper," and while Cook has succeeded with sauerkraut and may "entertaine no great opinion of [the] antiscorbutic virtue" of concentrated citrus juices, Pringle suggests that, "as they had been reduced to a small proportion of their bulk by evaporation upon fire, it is probable, they were much weakened by that process, and that with their aqueous parts they had lost not a little of their aerial, on which so much of their antiseptic power depended. If, therefore, a further trial of these excellent fruits were to be made, it would seem more adviseable to send to sea the purified juices entire in casks; agreeably to a proposal I find

Captain Cook fed his crewmen sauerkraut to prevent scurvy and was honored by the Royal Society.

hath been made to the Admiralty some years ago by an ingenious and experienced surgeon of the navy" (*see* 1794; Lind, 1757).

Prussia's Frederick the Great moves to block the imports of green coffee, which are draining his country's gold; coffee has become nearly a match for beer as the national beverage (*see* 1772).

1776

The *London Gazeteer* for January 2 carries a letter from Benjamin Franklin, who writes, "Vindex Patriae, a writer in your paper, comforts himself, and the India Company, with the fancy, that the Americans, should they resolve to drink no more tea, can by no means keep that Resolution, their Indian corn not affording 'an agreeable, or easily digestible breakfast'" (*see* below).

The Declaration of Independence signed July 4 at Philadelphia follows military action in the American Revolution.

A good harvest in France reduces the price of bread, but the French again abolish internal free trade in grain (*see* 1774; 1787).

Inquiry into the Nature and Causes of the Wealth of Nations by Scottish philosopher Adam Smith, 53, of Kirkcaldy, Fifeshire, proposes a natural liberty of trade and commerce. Turnips, carrots, cabbages and such "things which were formerly never raised but by the spade . . . are now commonly raised by the plough," Smith writes.

Karl Wilhelm Scheele discovers uric acid in a kidney stone (*see* Garrod, 1859).

The Reinette d'Orléans apple is mentioned for the first time in print. It will be France's favorite eating apple.

Benjamin Franklin (above) continues, "Permit me, an American, to inform the gentleman, who seems ignorant of the matter, that Indian corn, taken for all and all, is one of the most agreeable grains in the world . . . and that johny or hoecake, hot from the fire, is better than a Yorkshire muffin. . . . Mr. Vindex's very civil letter will, I dare say, be printed in all our provincial news-papers . . . and together with

the other kind, polite and humane epistles of your correspondents Pacificus, Tom Hint, etc. etc. contribute not a little to strengthen us in every resolution of advantage to our . . . country, if not *yours*."

Cattle ranches begin to flourish on the Argentine pampas as Spain creates the Viceroyalty of La Plata with its capital at Buenos Aires.

The cocktail is invented by some accounts at an Elmsford, N.Y., tavern, where barmaid Betsy Flanagan decorates the bar she tends at Halls Corner with discarded tail feathers from poultry that has been roasted and served to patrons. An inebriated patron demands that she bring him "a glass of those cocktails," and Flanagan serves him a mixed drink garnished with a feather (but *see* 1795).

1777

George Washington leads his 11,000 ragged troops into Valley Forge, Pa., December 14 to spend the winter. At least 2,000 are barefoot, and food is scarce. Gen. William Howe, 58, has captured Washington's salt stocks, but German-American gingerbread baker Christopher Ludwick, 57, of Philadelphia has devised equipment to bake bread for the Continental Army and refuses any compensation for his services.

Ergotism kills 8,000 in France's Sologne district, where rye has become infected with the deadly fungus parasite *Claviceps purpura* (*see* 1720; 1816).

The Baldwin apple is discovered by Continental army officer Laomo Baldwin, 37, who has been invalided home to Wilmington, Massachusetts.

New York shopkeeper Philip Lindsay advertises that his place at 517 Hanover Square is equipped to supply ice cream "almost any day . . . for ready money only." British troops occupy the city (*see* Washington, 1789).

Gray Poupon mustard is introduced at Dijon, France, by Maurice Gray, whose secret formula will make his product popular for more than 2 centuries. He has obtained financial backing from a man named Poupon to set up shop and will invent automatic, steam-operated mustard-making machines.

An advertisement published at Boston promotes "Hannon's Best CHOCOLATE, Marked upon each Cake J. Hn. Warranted Pure, and ground exceeding fine. Where may be had any Quantity, from 50 wt. to a ton, for Cash or cocoa, at his Mills in Milton. N.B. If the Chocolate does not prove good the Money will be returned" (*see* 1764; 1779).

1778

The Sandwich Islands, discovered by Hawaii-Loa about 450 A.D., are rediscovered in January by Captain Cook of the Royal Navy. He lands on the island of Kauai and names the islands after John Montagu, earl of Sandwich, who is now 60 and first lord of the admiralty (*see* sandwich, 1762).

Philadelphia Pepper Pot soup (actually tripe soup seasoned with peppercorns) is invented by some accounts at Valley Forge, where a Philadelphia-born cook to Gen. Washington's Continental Army employs makeshift efforts to sustain the hungry troops wintering in Pennsylvania.

1779

Gen. John Sullivan, Continental Army, marches through western New York's Genessee Valley in a punitive expedition against the Tories and their Iroquois allies. He destroys Indian villages and goes on to defeat his foes in the Battle of Newtown near Elmira in the continuing War of Independence (*see* sweet corn, apples, below).

Experiments on Vegetables by Dutch plant pathologist Jan Ingenhousz, 49, establishes some of the principles of photosynthesis (which will get that name in 1898). Ingenhousz learned on a visit to England of Joseph Priestley's 1774 efforts to "improve" polluted air by introducing live plants, and he ascribes air purification to the action of sunlight on leaves to produce "dephlogisticated air" (to which French chemist Antoine Lavoisier will soon give the name "oxygen") (*see* 1784).

Richard Bagnal, an officer with Gen. Sullivan (above), finds sweet corn (*Zea mays saccharata*) along the Susquehanna River and makes the first written report of what has apparently been produced by a spontaneous natural mutation that keeps the sugar from turning to starch as readily as in ordinary varieties of maize. The Iroquois have been growing it for years, and Bagnal carries seeds back to his hometown of Plymouth, where he plants them. New England farmers begin raising sweet corn, but it will be little used by Americans for another 70 years and will remain largely unknown in the rest of the world for more than a century after that (*see* Jones, 1879).

Gen. Sullivan (above) finds apple-bearing trees being grown in the native settlements.

Jean-Joseph Clausse, 22, *chef de cuisine* to Louis-George Erasmé, duc de Contades, will create pâté de foie gras in the next 4 years (*see* 400 B.C.). The maréchal de Contades has been posted to Strasbourg as governor of Alsace since 1762 and will ask Clausse to prepare something special for important guests. Known to the ancient Egyptians and popular among rich and noble Romans, pâté is made from the enlarged livers of force-fed geese; Clausse will embed black Périgord truffles into the finely ground forcemeat. The people of Périgord will claim that local farmwives near Périgeux and Erac have truffled pâté earlier, and the French chef Doyen at Bordeaux will claim to have flavored a loaf of pâté with wine and planted truffles down its middle, but it is the Alsatian pâté of Jean-Joseph Clausse at Strasbourg that will win honors as maréchal de Estrades presents samples of it to officials throughout Europe (Louis XVI will acknowledge receipt of a few pâtés by giving the maréchal some property in Picardy and giving Clausse 20 pistols) (*see* 1784).

John Adams, 43, former U.S. minister to France, returns home in June and is immediately elected to the Massachusetts constitutional convention, despite criticism that he has abandoned democratic ways in setting his table with forks.

Benjamin Franklin, the new minister to France, celebrates the Fourth of July at Passy with a dinner that includes two Rouen ducks, two young turkeys, 24 chickens of various varieties, four hens, four young rabbits, six rock pigeons, six wood pigeons, 20 artichokes (to be eaten raw), 10 bunches of onions, 20 pounds each of red and white currants, two baskets each of strawberries and raspberries, plus pears, figs, and vine leaves. Franklin gives a

Sunday dinner each week to which he invites some 30 guests.

Massachusetts chocolate maker John Hannon disappears at sea after sailing for the West Indies to buy cacao beans (*see* 1777). Dr. James Baker takes over the company from Hannon's widow (*see* 1764; 1824).

Lazzaro Spallanzani proves that semen (carrying sperm) is necessary to fertilization (*see* 1780; 1856; Spallanzani, 1768).

1780

British forces in the Pacific go to war with the Dutch, who wind up losing some of their possessions in the East Indies and much of their power to control the spice trade. The Dutch have not been able to subjugate the sultan of Ternate and have concentrated their efforts upon growing clove trees at Amboina, some 300 miles to the south, while destroying as many wild clove trees as possible in the northern Moluccas in order to keep the sultan from flooding the market with low-priced cloves. The Dutch have stationed troops along the coast of Amboina and patrolled its waters with ships to prevent theft of the island's clove trees. The British have blockaded Dutch East Indian ports, and the Dutch East India Company's new inability to control prices of cloves, nutmegs, mace, and pepper is ruinous to it (*see* 1760; 1796).

The Continental Congress appeals to the states November 4 to contribute quotas of flour, hay, and pork to support the Continental armies.

French authorities make 3,700 seizures of contraband salt and arrest 2,300 men on the roads for trying to evade the gabelle (*see* 1680). Police also arrest 1,800 women and 6,000 children and confiscate 1,100 horses and 50 carts. Judges hand down 2,000 prison sentences, and 300 people are sent to the galleys for life.

James Watt designs a steam-operated flour mill (*see* 1769).

Delaware storekeeper Oliver Evans, 25, devises an automated flour mill. A cripple who has seen millers toil up long flights of stairs with heavy bags of grain to be dumped into chutes that flow into millstones, Evans invents a water-driven vertical conveyor belt that carries hoisting buckets, and he combines this with a horizontal conveyor that moves grain, meal, and flour from place to place on the ground (*see* 1787).

Lazzaro Spallanzani employs artificial insemination for the first time (with dogs) (*see* 1779).

Britain enjoys something of an agrarian revolution as better seed, more scientific crop rotation, more efficient tools, and improved livestock increase productivity (*see* Bakewell, 1769; Coke, 1772). But the yield of European agriculture remains little more than five or six times the original seed, on average, and agricultural methods on the Continent are still largely medieval. A third or more of the land is left fallow (partly because of a manure shortage), the land is communally cultivated, and most livestock is still killed every fall (*see* 1730).

British sugar consumption reaches 12 pounds per year per capita, up from 4 in 1700, as Britons increase coffee and tea consumption (*see* 1872).

The Dutch East India Company imports 450,000 tea sets, 40,000 chocolate sets, and 24,000 coffee sets, all from China.

Irish distiller John Jameson begins making a whiskey that will be popular for centuries.

1781

The American Revolution ends October 19 with the surrender of Gen. Charles Cornwallis, 42, at Yorktown, Va., but the British will not evacuate Savannah until July of next year and Charleston until December and will hold New York until November 1783.

The Lamb Tavern opens in London's Lytton Hall Market.

The Osaka sushi restaurant Sushiman opened by Mansuke will survive for more than 200 years.

1782

James Watt patents a double-acting rotary steam engine. He has improved on his engine of 1765 and employs the new engine to drive machinery of all kinds.

 Jethro Tull's seed-planting drill of 1701 is improved with gears for its distributing mechanism.

Edinburgh surgeon John Hunter tells medical students, "Some Physiologists will have it that the Stomach is a Mill; others that it is a fermenting Vat; others again that it is a Stew Pan; but in my view of the matter it is neither a Mill, a fermenting Vat, nor a Stew Pan—but a Stomach, gentlemen, a Stomach."

Nonfiction: *Letters from an American Farmer* by French-American farmer-author J. Hector St. John de Crèvecoeur (Michel-Guillaume-Jean de Crèvecoeur), 47, who settled in New York's Orange County 13 years ago.

Ice cream is served at a Philadelphia party given by the French envoy to honor the new American republic (*see* 1744; 1813).

"The indifferent state of agriculture among us does not proceed from a want of knowledge merely," writes Thomas Jefferson in *Notes on Virginia*, which he has written at the request of the French government. "It is from our having such quantities of land to waste as we please. In Europe the object is to make the most of their land, labor being abundant; here it is to make the most of our labor, land being abundant."

Jefferson (above) notes May 6 that a quart of currant juice makes "2 blue teacups of Jelly." In October he notes that "17 bushels of winter grapes (stems excluded) make 40 gallons of vinegar of the first running," but despite a great deal of effort (studying viniculture in France and Germany and purchasing hundreds of vines for shipment to Monticello) he will find it impossible to cultivate any grapes other than the native Virginia scuppernong.

La Grande Taverne de Londres, opened at 26 rue de Richelieu by Antoine de Beauvilliers, is the first true restaurant to be seen in Paris (*see* Boulanger, 1765). De Beauvilliers has been steward and chef (*officier de bouche*) to the comte de Provence, brother of Louis XVI, who will one day reign as Louis XVIII; he has well-attired waiters to serve the patrons in his elegant room, and his *cave* contains a fine assortment of good wines to complement his superior cuisine.

The Continental Congress proclaims victory in the American War of Independence April 19, but a mutiny of unpaid soldiers at Philadelphia has forced Congress to meet at Princeton, N.J. The Treaty of Paris September 3 recognizes the independence of the 13 colonies, Britain cedes vast territories to the Americans and grants them full rights to the Newfoundland fishery, but the last British troops do not leave New York until November 25.

Spain regains Florida from the British (*see* 1763). New Smyrna's settlers marry with Spanish residents of St. Augustine and introduce dishes such as pilau (a stew made with rice and chicken, pork, or seafood and datil peppers) and fromajardis (small cheesecakes) (*see* 1819).

Japan suffers her worst famine since 1732 following the eruption of Mount Asama (*see* 1784; 1833; riots, 1787).

Continental Army soldiers and officers are issued script certificates entitling them to tracts of land west of the Appalachians, the acreages varying according to rank and length of service. Many sell the certificates to those who want land (and to land speculators).

The phrase "not worth a Continental" is heard as inflation reduces the value of paper currency issued by the Continental Congress to finance the Revolution. Corn sells for $80 per bushel, shoes for $100 per pair, and George Washington, richest man in America, says he needs a wagonload of money to buy a wagonload of supplies.

English physician Thomas Cawley makes the first recorded diagnosis of late-onset diabetes. He notes the presence of sugar in a patient's urine (*see* 1788; Willis, 1674).

Cookbook: *Tofuhyakuchin* (*100 Tofu Recipes*) is published in Japan.

The Italian candy-making firm Confetti Mario Pelino has its beginnings in a shop opened at Sulmona by confectioner Bernardino Pelino, who specializes in sugar-coated nuts.

George Washington (above) bids farewell to his troops in a speech at New York's Fraunces Tavern (*see* 1763).

Famine continues in Japan; 300,000 die of starvation, and survivors are obliged in some cases to eat corpses in order to stay alive.

Ireland has famine, mostly in Ulster, as potato crops fail (*see* 1756; 1821).

Britain transports to Maine and Louisiana all Acadians who have remained in Nova Scotia and lower New Brunswick since the expulsion order of 1755. Another 1,600 Acadians arrive in Louisiana, where they will establish Cajun (a corruption of *Acadian*) cookery, combining their Canadian recipes with those of earlier arrivals (*see* 1704; New Orleans restaurant, 1953).

Parliament further lowers British import duties on tea (*see* 1773). The lower duties end the smuggling that has accounted for so much of the nation's tea imports and hurt the East India Company; the rewards of smuggling become too small to justify the risks.

Parliament imposes a new system of taxation on Scotch whisky after various commissions of inquiry (*see* 1713). The new system distinguishes between Highland and Lowland whiskies, with Highland distillers (located north of an imaginary line between Dundee and Greenock) required to pay taxes based on the capacity of their stills, rather than their output, while Lowland distilleries must pay on the basis of how much wash (fermented barley ale before distillation) they actually produce (*see* 1798).

English farmers show little interest in an iron plow developed by inventor James Small, continuing to use wooden plows (*see* Wood, 1819).

Karl Wilhelm Scheele discovers citric acid in certain plants.

Shaker leader Mother Ann Lee dies at Watervliet, N.Y., September 8 at age 48, disappointing zealous followers who had believed her to be immortal, but Shakerism will continue in America (*see* hogs, garden seeds, below).

Benjamin Frankin exhorts the French to set their clocks ahead 1 hour in spring and back 1 hour in fall to take advantage of daylight, but farmers resist the idea, insisting that cows cannot change their habits.

A French patent is granted February 28 to pastry cook Jean-Joseph Clausse for his pâté de foie gras aux truffes (*see* 1779). Clausse leaves the marshal's employ but remains in Strasbourg; he will marry Marie-Anne Maring, the pretty young widow of a local pâtissier, and go into business with her in 1789 to supply pâté to the gentry. He will continue until his death in 1827, making Strasbourg the goose-liver capital of the world, rivaled only by Périgord. Strasbourg will grow to have many pâté producers, the largest being Édouard Artzner and Louis Henry.

Who really invented foies gras aux truffes*? Claimants competed for the honor—and profits.*

Shaker gravies are made from water in which vegetables have been cooked, and the Shakers will be famed for their breads, pies, and doughnuts.

George Washington notes at Mount Vernon that he has spent £1 13s. 4p. for "a cream machine for Ice."

Franklin (above) receives from his daughter in America the medal of the new Society of the Cincinnati, formed to honor officers of the Continental Army. Franklin does not much care for the idea of an aristocratic idea and takes exception to displaying an eagle on the medal, saying that it "looks much like a turkey and . . . for my own part I wish the bald eagle had not been chosen as the representative of our country; he is a bird of bad moral character. . . . The turkey is a much more respectable bird, and withal a true original native of America. Eagles have been found in all countries, but the turkey was peculiar to ours. . . . He is besides (though a little vain and silly, it is true, but not the worse I hope for that) a bird of courage, and would not hesitate to attack a grenadier of the British guards, who should present to invade his farmyard with a *red* coat on."

Benjamin Franklin thought the turkey, not the bald eagle, should have been America's symbol.

The Massachusetts House of Representatives at Boston acts on a proposal by John Rowe that permission be granted to hang up "a representation of a Cod Fish" in the room where the House sits "as a memorial to the importance of the Cod Fishery to the welfare of this commonwealth." The 4-foot 11-inch model will be called the "Sacred Cod" (*see* 1795).

Shakers (above) will develop the Poland China hog by crossing backwoods hogs with white Big China hogs to produce the breed that will be the backbone of the U.S. pork industry for generations.

Shakers (above) will innovate the practice of retailing garden seeds in small, labeled paper packets (*see* Burpee, 1876).

Bushmill's distillery begins operations in the north of Ireland.

1785

French explorer Jean-François de Galaup, 44, comte de La Pérouse, looks for new whaling grounds in the Pacific. He embarks on an ill-fated voyage that will discover La Pérouse Strait between Sakhalin and Hokkaido.

American economic troubles worsen as states erect tariffs to keep out goods from abroad and from other states; farmers are unable to sell their surplus food crops because foreign markets have disappeared, and New Englanders can no longer find markets for the products of their shipyards (*see* 1786).

An American land ordinance provides for the sale of public lands at auction in tracts of 640 acres at a cash price of at least $1 per acre, but few would-be western settlers can put up $640 in cash (*see* 1800).

Poetry: "To a Haggis" by Scottish poet Robert Burns, 26, who calls haggis the "great chieftain o' the puddin' race." Made from the heart, liver, and lungs of a sheep, boiled in salt water, minced, and seasoned with salt, pepper, nutmeg, cayenne pepper, and chopped onion, to which is added a pound of chopped beef suet, grated liver, oatmeal, and a glassful of gravy, it is placed in a thoroughly cleaned sheep's stomach which has been turned inside out, boiled for 3 hours in a large pan, and served in a well-starched napkin accompanied by whisky. Haggis will be Scotland's national dish, served with great ceremony on Burns's birthday (January 25).

An English cleric, Parson Woodforde of Norfolk, notes, "We had for Dinner some Pyke and fryed Soals, a nice Piece of Boiled Beef, Ham, and a Couple of Fowls, Peas, and Beans, a Green Goose rosted, Gooseberry Pies, and Currant Tarts, the Charter (Charter pie [a chicken pie made from pastry, heavy cream, and onion]), hung Beef scraped &c."

Naples has 280 pasta shops, up from 60 in 1700; pasta hangs out to dry on balconies, on rooftops, and in the streets, and street vendors with charcoal-fired stoves sell cooked spaghetti with grated Romano cheese (*see* 1400; Jefferson, 1787; Agnese, 1824).

Antoine-Auguste Parmentier persuades Louis XVI to encourage cultivation of potatoes (*see* 1771). Louis lets him plant 100 useless acres outside Paris in potatoes; troops keep the field heavily guarded, arousing public curiosity, and when Parmentier allows the guards to go off duty one night, the local farmers, as he has hoped, steal into the field, confiscate the potatoes, and plant them on their own farms. The king, at Parmentier's suggestion, gives a banquet at which only potato dishes are served (Benjamin Franklin is one of the guests), and Parmentier persuades Marie-Antoinette to wear potato flowers in her hair. Courtiers will make potato eating fashionable, and provincials will follow suit (*see* 1789).

George Washington notes in his diary that he has put 2,000 of the "Common Chestnuts in a box with dry Sand—a layer of each—and two thousand of the Spanish Chestnut in like manner, to plant out in the next Spring" at his Mount Vernon plantation (*see* du Pont, 1805).

Punta Mes Vermouth is introduced by Benedetto Caparno in Turin's Piazza Castello—the first vermouth to be sold commercially. While another winery that will be famous for its vermouth has been established earlier by Francesco Cinzano, it is Carpano who is first to put his product on the market.

Montreal's Molson brewery is founded by English-born brewer John Molson, who emigrated from Lincolnshire 3 years ago and whose family will continue the enterprise for more than six generations.

A Dissertation on the Poor Laws by English writer Joseph Townsend suggests that hunger, "the stronger appetite," will provide a natural restraint on "the weaker" appetite and will thus "blunt the shafts of Cupid, or . . . quench the torch of Hymen" to maintain a food-population equilibrium (*see* 1791; 1798).

1786

Shays' Rebellion in Massachusetts aims to thwart further farm foreclosures in the continuing U.S. economic depression. State militia prevent seizure of the Springfield arsenal September 26 in a confrontation with 800 armed farmers led by Revolutionary War veteran Daniel Shays, 39, but the rebels succeed in having the state supreme court adjourn without returning indictments against them. Scattered fighting will continue through the winter (*see* 1787).

News of Shays' Rebellion (above) reaches a convention assembled at Annapolis to remedy the weaknesses of Articles of Confederation signed in 1781. Delegates will create a Congress with exclusive powers to coin money, forbidding states to levy tariffs or embargoes against each other that would restrict internal free trade (*see* 1785; Constitution, 1787).

Rhode Island farmers burn their grain, dump their milk, and leave their apples to rot in the orchards in a farm strike directed against Providence and Newport merchants who have refused to accept the paper money that has depreciated to the point of being virtually worthless. The strike has little effect, since 90 percent of Americans raise their own food, growing peas, beans, and corn in their gardens and letting their hogs forage in the woods for acorns.

French landowners, vintners, and manufacturers press for a measure of free trade that will give them a foreign market comparable to that of their envied British rivals. A commercial treaty signed with London provides for lower British tariffs on French wheat, wine, and luxury goods, French tariffs are lowered on British textiles, but British imports flood the French market, undercut domestic prices, and bring widespread unemployment, producing demands for renewal of tariff protection (*see* 1788).

1786

Demel's has its beginnings in a sugar bakery founded across from the stage door of Vienna's Burgtheater by Ludwig Dehne, a sugar baker's apprentice from Württemberg. After he dies in 1799, Dehne's widow, Antonia, will be appointed court caterer and the sugar bakery's name will be changed to Kaiser-und-Königliche Hofzuckerbäckerei (*see* 1857).

Scottish millwright and agricultural engineer Andrew Meikle, 67, develops the first successful threshing machine (*see* Menzies, 1732). It rubs the grain between a rotating drum and a concave metal sheet, employing a basic principle that will be used in future threshing machines (*see* Pitts, 1837).

Paris sends the Abbé Dicquemare to report on the state of oyster beds in the gulf at the mouth of the Seine. The naturalist reports that the oysters have diminished by half "in the last forty years. . . . The real causes of the deficit are the maneuvers of cupidity and the insufficiency of laws" (*see* 1681).

C. Shippam Ltd. is founded in England, where Shippam's meat and fish pastes and chicken spread will be popular for more than 200 years.

The Paris restaurant Aux Trois Frères Provençeaux opens at Arcades 96 through 98 of the Palais-Royal (*see* 1643), which is being developed into commercial shops and restaurants as a real estate speculation by Louis-Philippe-Joseph, duc d'Orléans. Proprietors Barthélemy, Maneille, and Simon of Aux Troix Frères Provençeaux are from Marseilles, not Provence, and are married to three sisters, making them all brothers-in-law but not "frères." They introduce Parisians to brandade de morue (salt cod purée). Other Palais-Royal tenants include Café Corazza (best known for its sorbets and maraschino ice cream) at Arcades 7 to 12; Café de Foy (Arcades 57 to 60); the Café de Caveaux (Arcades 89 through 92); Café des Aveugles (Arcade 103); Café Favrier (Arcade 113); Café Méchanique (Arcade 121), whose cook prepares dishes in the basement and sends them up through hollow table pedestals; Galérie de Valois (Arcades 142 to 144); Café de Valois (Arcade 173), where patrons play chess or dominoes as they sip coffee or lemonade; Badeleine (known for its fish dishes); the Véry Brothers (known for their truffled entrées); and Henneveu's (known not only for its food but also for the private rooms on its fourth floor), but none can match La Grande Taverne de Londres opened by Antoine de Beauvilliers in 1782 (*see* Véfour, 1788).

1787

A Constitutional Convention that has been meeting at Philadelphia draws up a Constitution for the new United States of America.

Rice riots at Osaka climax years of Japanese peasant unrest. Rice warehouses are broken open May 11, the riots spread throughout the city May 12, by May 18 they have spread to Edo and 30 other cities, and by May 20 nearly every large rice merchant has seen his house destroyed as the rioters break into 8,000 establishments that include not only rice warehouses but also pawnshops, sake breweries, and shops dealing in textiles, dyes, drugs, and oils.

China's rural masses remain richer, better educated, and better fed than French peasants, who are much better off than most other European peasants.

France's working class is ill paid, the typical working day is 14 to 16 hours, and workers are lucky to get 250 days of work per year. The basic food of the people is bread, which takes 60 percent of the average man's wages.

A French government edict intended to encourage agriculture removes the requirement that grain producers take their grain to market. The producers are permitted to sell directly to consumers or even to export their grain by land or sea with no restrictions whatever. French granaries are emptied in consequence, and the country is left unprepared for a bad harvest (*see* 1788).

An automated process for grinding grain and bolting (sifting) flour marks the beginning of automation in U.S. industry. Devised by Oliver Evans (*see* 1780), it requires some capital investment but can be operated by just two men, sharply lowers the cost of milling, and will make white bread widely available in America.

Cookbook: *Dissertation sur le cacao* by Jean-Pierre Buc'hoz gives recipes for chocolate biscuits, chocolate *draguées*, chocolate pastilles, chocolate mousse, chocolate marzipan, chocolate ice cream, chocolate olives (like chocolate truffles but baked in a slow oven), and chocolate diablotins (small, flat wafers).

British Royal Navy captain William Bligh, 33, sails for Tahiti on H.M.S. *Bounty* to obtain breadfruit plants for planting in the Caribbean islands as a new source of food for British colonists. As sailing master of Captain Cook's 1772–1775 voyage, Bligh developed an enthusiasm for breadfruit and has persuaded the admiralty that *Artocarpus communis* can be a boon to Caribbean agriculture (*see* 1789; Dampier, 1688).

U.S. Minister to France Thomas Jefferson travels alone by coach through southern France and northern Italy, taking extensive notes on the cultivation of olives, almonds, pistachios, walnuts, figs, pomegranates, and strawberries. He is interested in every phase of agriculture, and also in cheese making.

Jefferson (above) fails to persuade the Italians to import rice from the Carolinas, which he considers superior to the short-grain rice raised in northern Italy, but he procures some Italian rice for shipment to friends in South Carolina, and when he finds that Lombardy forbids export of unhulled rice on pain of death he bribes a muleteer "to smuggle a sack of rough rice for me to Genoa, where it can be spirited onto an American ship." Suspecting that the muleteer may not do as instructed, he fills his pocket with contraband grain and sends it to friends in Charleston with instructions for its cultivation.

Jefferson (above) returns to his post at Paris with a rice-husking machine, Tuscan wine, and a spaghetti die, which he uses to make pasta (*see* 1824; Agnesi, 1824; Buitoni, 1827).

Stockholm's Operakällaren opens as a backstage dive in the cellar of the new Swedish opera house. The rustic subterranean restaurant started by Georg Christian Förster and Petter Hellström will be world famous for its midday *brännvinsbord* (which will gradually become a *smörgåsbord* as salmon, game, pâté, and cheese are added to the original herring and aquavit) and be a popular meeting place for entertainers, artists, writers, and philosophers (*see* 1892).

1788

The United States Constitution becomes operative June 21 as New Hampshire ratifies the Constitution 57 to 47, the ninth state to ratify.

The Parliament at Paris presents Louis XVI with a list of grievances as the country suffers its worst economic chaos of the century.

French wheat prices soar as drought reduces the harvest. Grain reserves are depleted as a result of last year's edict permitting grain producers to sell without restriction, but Louis XVI's Swiss-born finance minister Jacques Necker, 55, suspends grain exports. He requires that all grain be sold in the open market once again to allay suspicions that the endless lines of heavy carts seen to be carrying grain and flour are bound for ports to be shipped abroad.

Most Frenchmen remain convinced that the king has an interest in the Malisset Company, which he has entrusted with victualing Paris, and that the king and the aristocracy are profiting at the people's expense. Hungry peasants and townspeople seize wagons in transit even when escorted in large convoys, farmers resist bringing their grain to market lest it be commandeered, and people starve.

Australia's Botany Bay becomes an English penal colony as the first shipload of convicts is landed January 18 (*see* Cook, 1770). The 736 prisoners and the new arrivals that follow are provisioned with oatmeal, cheese, salt meat, dried peas, vinegar (thought to prevent scurvy), salt, tea, and spirits.

Thomas Cawley in England notes abnormalities of the pancreas in the autopsy of a diabetic patient (*see* 1783). It is the first observation of any relationship between diabetes and the pancreas, but Cawley ignores it and persists in the belief that diabetes is a kidney disease (*see* Lancereaux, 1860).

Cookbook: *The English Art of Cookery* by English author Richard Briggs (*see* 1792).

Royal Worcester Porcelain Co. gets its name following a visit by Britain's George III and Queen Charlotte to the pottery founded in 1751.

The 48-year-old Café de Chartres at Paris is acquired by a restaurateur named Véfour, who began with a hut selling coffee in the garden of the Palais-Royal and now takes over Arcades 78 to 82 of the palace (*see* 1786). He will turn the café into a restaurant that will come to be called Le Grand Véfours, competing with the Véry brothers (*see* 1948).

1789

The French Revolution that begins with the tennis court oath June 20 follows widespread rioting triggered by rumors that the nobility and the clergy (the first and second estates) have plotted to collect all the nation's grain and ship it abroad. Jacques Necker has ordered requisitioning of all grain in April to assure fair distribution and convened the Estates General for the first time since 1614, but rumors abound that the first and second estates intend to disrupt the Estates General and starve the people.

Parisian women marched on Versailles, blaming the high cost of bread on a corrupt monarchy.

Journalist Camille Desmoulins, 29, jumps onto a table in the garden outside the Café de Foy in front of the Palais Royal at Paris July 13 and announces with a stutter that the revolution has begun. His fellow revolutionists—including Georges-Jacques Danton, 30; Jean-Paul Marat, 46; and (Maximilien-Marie-Isidore de) Robespierre, 31—will gather in the next few years at the Café de Chartres (*see* 1788). The apt phrase "Omelets are not made without breaking eggs" will be attributed to Robespierre, but he is probably just quoting a proverb.

The price of bread reaches 4.5 sous per pound at Paris in July, and in some places it is 6 sous per pound. Widespread unemployment has reduced the people's ability to avoid starvation, but the National Assembly permits duty-free grain imports to relieve the hunger.

France's nobility begins to emigrate as peasants rise against their feudal lords.

Elements of Chemistry (*Traité élémentaire de chime*) by French chemist Antoine-Laurent Lavoisier, 46, is the first modern chemical textbook. It lists 23 elements but includes as an inorganic element a substance that Lavoisier calls caloric (heat).

Genera Plantarum by French botanist Antoine-Laurent de Jussieu, 41, improves on the Linnaean system of 1737 and begins the modern classification of plants.

Traité sur la culture et les usages des pommes de terre by Antoine-Auguste Parmentier at Paris instructs readers on how to cultivate potatoes and cook them (*see* 1785; Tuileries gardens, 1793).

Thomas Jefferson returns from France, finds that he has been appointed secretary of state, and writes from Philadelphia to the U.S. chargé d'affaires at Paris, William Short, instructing him to send him "½ doz. plants of the Buré pear, as many Doyennois . . . plants of the Alpine strawberry . . . red and white . . . as many sky larks and red legged partridges as he can . . . [and] goats (these last can only be had of the king's stock)."

Sailors aboard H.M.S. *Bounty* bound for the West Indies with breadfruit plants mutiny April 28 in protest against being deprived of water, which is being lavished on the plants (*see* 1787). The mutineers cast Capt. Bligh adrift in a 22-foot open boat with 18 men near the island of Tofau, and he reaches Timor in the East Indies after a 45-day voyage across 3,600 miles of open sea in which he loses 7 of his 18 men (*see* 1791).

"I am so antiquated as still to dine at four," writes English author Horace Walpole, 72; most English people now dine at 5 or 6 o'clock.

Thomas Jefferson (above) asks the U.S. chargé d'affaires at Paris to have Adrien Betit, Jefferson's maître d'hôtel, send him "a stock of Maccaroni, Parmesan cheese, figs of Marseilles, Brugnolles, raisins, almonds, mustard, Vinaigre d'Estragon, other good vinegar, oil, and anchovies."

President George Washington, who takes office at New York's Federal Hall April 30, finds the summer heat unbearable and orders more than $200 worth of ice cream from a local confectioner (*see* 1777; Jefferson, 1802).

The first movable-frame beehive is constructed by Swiss naturalist François Huber, 39, who has discovered the aerial impregnation of the queen bee and the killing of males by worker bees. Huber is nearly blind, but his wife, his son, and a servant have helped him to study the life and habits of honeybees (*see* Langstroth, 1851).

Nine out of 10 Americans are engaged in farming and food production (*see* 1820).

Thomas Jefferson (above) asks that the Graves and other wines left behind in his Paris cellar be bottled before being shipped. He will teach his fellow Americans how to use wine in cookery and how to brew coffee in the French manner.

The first bourbon whiskey is distilled by Baptist minister Elijah Craig in the bluegrass country established as Kentucky County last year by the Virginia state assembly. The territory will become Bourbon County in the state of Kentucky, and although many others are making whiskey out of corn, Craig's corn whiskey (the word "bourbon" will not be used in print for whiskey until 1846) is so refined that it will become more popular than rum or brandy in America (*see* tax, 1791; Whiskey Rebellion, 1794).

1790

France abolishes the gabelle (salt tax) (*see* 1780); the courts of Louis XIV have convicted some 1,500, including dozens of children aged 12 to 15, of dealing in contraband salt (*see* 1804).

New York's Washington Market is established in lower Manhattan, taking its name from President Washington. The site will later be expanded through a gift of land from Trinity Church, whose purpose will be to move peddlers from the front of St. Mark's Church on lower Broadway (*see* Moore, 1822).

Congress votes April 10 to establish a patent office that will protect inventors and give them an incentive to develop new machines and methods. The first U.S. patent is awarded July 31 to Vermont inventor Samuel Hopkins for an improved method of "making Pot-ash and Pearl-ash," the first used in agriculture, the second in baking. Hopkins has devised a method of leaching the lye out of wood ashes, but most U.S. women are proud of their own yeast and continue to use that for baking rather than pearl ash (potassium carbonate) (*see* 1792).

Nonfiction: *Travels to Discover the Sources of the Nile* by Scottish explorer James Bruce, 60, who journeyed to Abyssinia (Ethiopia) in 1768 and describes cattle drivers who tripped up a cow and "cut off thicker, longer beefsteaks from the higher part of the buttock of the beast," used skewers to pin the flesh back into place, covered the wound with clay, forced the animal to rise, and drove it off with the others to provide a fuller meal in the evening, when they would meet their friends (*see* Charles Lamb dissertation, 1823).

England now eats off Wedgwood porcelain (*see* 1769), and the food eaten now includes cheddar cheese imported from the United States.

Chefs to the French aristocracy find employment in many cases with British families as the Revolution puts their former patrons to flight.

Pineapples are introduced into the Sandwich Islands (Hawaii) by Spanish adventurer Francisco de Paula Marín, who will become an interpreter and friend of Kamehameha I, with whom he will go fishing as he trades scissors for pearls and supports himself by making candles, trousers, and brandy (*see* 1778; first cannery, 1892).

The world's first carbonated beverage company is started at Geneva by Swiss entrepreneur Jacob Schweppe in partnership with Jacques and Nicholas Paul (*see* Priestley, 1767; Bergman, 1770). The partnership will dissolve within a few years, and Schweppe will move to London. He will open at 11 Margaret Street, Cavendish Square, to sell through chemists (pharmacists) his Schweppe's soda water in round-ended "drunken" bottles, so made in order to keep their corks damp and thus prevent the gas from escaping (*see* 1851).

The English house of Sandeman is established at Jerez de a Frontera, Spain, to export Spanish sherry and Portuguese port. It will grow to have 1,600 acres of vineyards producing grapes that will go into port wines and sherries—fino (crisply dry), dry amontillado, medium amontillado, oloroso (moderately sweet), medium oloroso, palo cordano, and sweet.

A tavern in Cumberland County, Maryland, lists its rates: "The best Dinner or Supper with a Pint of good Beer or Cyder, 1 shilling, 6 pence; Second-best or Family ditto with ditto 1 shilling, 2 pence; A good clean Bed with clean sheets for a single Person, 6 pence; Ditto with two persons in a Bed, each Person 4 pence."

1791

France's Louis XVI is arrested June 25 near the northwest frontier while attempting to flee; he is returned with his wife, Marie-Antoinette, and their children to Paris and imprisoned in the Temple, where a kitchen staff of 13 prepares and serves daily dinners and suppers of three potages, four entrées, three dishes of "roast or mixed grill," four entremets, bread, a plate of petits fours, three compotes, three plates of fruit, a bottle of champagne, a carafe each of Bordeaux, malvoisy (monembasia, known in Britain as malmsey), and Madeira, and coffee. Louis will remain thus imprisoned until he goes to the guillotine in January 1793 (Marie-Antoinette will meet the same fate nearly 9 months later).

France has famine, which the National Assembly has little power to relieve.

Free blacks and mulattoes at Saint-Domingue revolt to obtain the rights they have been granted by the French revolutionists at Paris, and within a few months some 2,000 whites have been killed along with 10,000 blacks and mulattoes. Sugar plantations are burned, but only after 70,000 tons of sugar have been produced (see 1792).

British landowners and farmers protest the low duty on grain imports, which are depressing their prices. Parliament responds by raising the domestic price level at which imports are permitted (see 1773; 1797).

Oliver Evans patents an "automated mill" in which power that turns the millstones also conveys wheat (grist) to the top of the mill (see 1787).

Cookbook: Nueva Arte de cocina by Spanish author Juan Altamiras.

Camembert cheese is according to some accounts reinvented by French farmer's wife Marie Harel (née Fontaine), 30, near Vimoutiers in the Orne Department (see 1708). By one account she has learned the secret of its manufacture from a priest, whom she has hidden on her farm to protect him from the revolutionists at Paris. Made from whole cows' milk (two quarts produce one round cheese weighing half a pound), the cheese has been known since the 12th century (gorgonzola has been made since the 9th century, parmesan and Pont l'Évèque since the 13th). Marie Harel, its alleged reinventor, will sometimes be confused with another Marie Harel, born in 1779 (see 1859).

The New York Journal reports April 26 that "a draught of shad was taken at the Narrows on Thursday last which consisted of 14,000 fish" (see 1770).

French colonist Étienne de Boré plants sugarcane in Louisiana, where efforts to cultivate the crop have been made since 1725 without much success. Boré brings in experts from Saint-Domingue to supervise the boiling kettles in which sugar is crystallized and will be elected mayor of New Orleans in recognition of his achievement.

Capt. William Bligh sails for Tahiti once again to obtain breadfruit (see 1789). Bligh has returned from the East Indies to England and voyages now on H.M.S. Providence to complete the mission he began in 1787 (see 1792; 1793).

President Washington prepares the first U.S. crop report in response to letters from Annals of Agriculture editor Arthur Young, 50, in England, who has written to ask what crops are produced on American farms, what the crops are worth, and so forth. Washington has conducted a personal survey by mail and compiled the results, giving all prices in English pounds but providing a conversion ratio (the dollar is worth 7 shillings, 6 pence).

Arthur Young (above) is an ardent advocate of up-to-date farming methods and of enclosure but he will admit that 19 out of 20 enclosure acts injure the poor, sometimes gravely. Driven off the land, peasant farmers are often obliged to work as laborers on land that they once owned themselves. Some will enlist in the army, go to work in factory towns, emigrate to America, or fall to drinking.

Congress imposes a 9¢-per-gallon tax on whiskey to discourage frontier farmers, blacksmiths, and store-keepers from diverting grain needed for food to use as distillery mash (and from competing with rum made in New England distilleries) (*see* Craig, 1789; Whiskey Rebellion, 1794).

"Increase the quantity of food, or where that is limited, prescribe bounds to population," writes Joseph Townsend in *A Journey Through Spain in the years 1786 and 1787* (*see* 1785). "In a fully peopled country, to say, that no one shall suffer want is absurd. Could you supply their wants, you would soon double their numbers, and advance your population *ad infinitum*. . . . It is indeed possible to banish hunger, and to supply that want at the expense of another; but then you must determine the proportion that shall marry, because you will have no other way to limit the number of your people. No human efforts will get rid of this dilemma; nor will men ever find a method, either more natural, or better in any respect, than to leave one appetite to regulate another" (*see* Malthus, 1798).

1792

A Parisian mob storms the Tuileries Palace August 10, Louis XVI is confined in the Temple, and French aristocrats emigrate to escape the gathering Reign of Terror. Chefs to great houses set up in business as *traiteurs* (caterers) to the public.

The Lancaster Road has its beginnings at the Philadelphia State House, where some 5,000 investors meet and subscribe $30 each to buy shares in the toll road that will be the first major publicly financed U.S. turnpike (*see* 1794; Cumberland Road, 1811).

Western Inland Lock Navigation Co. is incorporated through efforts by Continental Army veteran Gen. Philip J. Schuyler, 58, and Pittsfield, Mass., businessman Elkanah Watson, 34. The new company improves the channel of the Mohawk River, which will be the basis of a great inland waterway (*see* 1815).

The United States exports some 8,000 tons of pearl ash (potassium carbonate) to Britain and Europe for use in baking (*see* Hopkins, 1790).

Produced by burning wood, pearl ash releases the carbon dioxide in the dough baking in the oven, causes the bread to rise, and is revolutionizing the baking industry. (Potash-water is an aerated beverage much like soda water.)

Cookbooks: *The Universal Cook, and City and Country Housekeeper, Containing All the Various Branches of Cookery* by English authors Francis Collingwood and John Woollams; *The New Art of Cookery, According to the Present Practice; Being a Complete Guide to All Housekeepers, on a Plan Entirely New* by Richard Briggs, published at Philadelphia, is a new version of his 1788 book.

The first U.S. cracker bakery opens at Newburyport, Massachusetts, where baker Theodore Pearson specializes in making pilot's bread (ship's biscuit) (*see* Bent, 1801).

Capt. William Bligh loads Tahitian breadfruit aboard the decks of H.M.S. *Providence* for planting in the Caribbean islands (*see* 1791; 1793).

The Farmer's Almanac is founded by U.S. printer Robert B. Thomas, who establishes a format that will be continued for more than 200 years.

1793

The outbreak of war between Britain and France February 1 halts British imports of French grain. Since domestic output is barely sufficient to meet a growing demand, food shortages soon develop. Parliament establishes a Board of Agriculture to make "the principles of agriculture better known" and increase domestic food production.

French revolutionists turn the Tuileries gardens at Paris into a potato field. A French ordinance forbids consumption of more than one pound of meat per week on pain of death.

U.S. Secretary of State Thomas Jefferson signs a document September 15 offering his slave James Hastings, who followed him to Paris in 1785, his freedom if he will return to Monticello and teach "such person as I shall place under him to be a good cook." Hastings has received considerable training in the French culinary arts (*see* 1802).

Scots fur trader Alexander Mackenzie, 29, reaches the Pacific after the first crossing of the North American continent by a European. Mackenzie has sustained himself on his journey by eating pemmican (dried lean meat from a large game animal pounded to shreds and mixed thoroughly half and half with melted fat, bone marrow, and wild berries or cherries; the word *pemmican* comes from the Cree word for "fat").

U.S. farmers export grain and other foodstuffs to Britain and the Continent as the European war booms demand (*see* 1804; 1806).

Berlin chemist Franz Karl Achard, 40, reveals a process for obtaining sugar from beets (*see* 1799; Marggraf, 1747; Delessert, 1810).

A chinoiserie "Willow"-patterned blue-and-white porcelain tableware designed by Thomas Minton, 27, is introduced at Caughley, Shropshire. His son Herbert, born this year, will take over after Thomas's death in 1836, having successfully produced designs for other potteries, and will continue until his own death in 1858.

Capt. William Bligh sails into Jamaica's Port Royal Harbor with his ship H.M.S. *Providence* so loaded with breadfruit saplings that natives call it "the ship that have the bush" (*see* 1792). His men plant breadfruit in St. Vincent as well as in Jamaica, and they also plant seedlings of *Blighia sapida,* whose fruit (ackee) will become a West Indian food staple.

French chefs accompanying their aristocratic employers in their flight from the Revolution's Reign of Terror introduce the tall white toque to Britain along with French cooking, but master chefs continue to wear the short cap of black cloth originally worn to catch soot that fell from chimneys as they operated spits turning on hearth ovens (the short cap has also been useful when carrying platters down corridors to the dining room). Only the chief cook in a kitchen is entitled to wear the black cap.

1794

The Whiskey Rebellion begun by U.S. frontier farmers July 17 brings the first show of force by the new U.S. government. The farmers have converted their grain into whiskey in order to transport it more efficiently to market but have resisted a cash excise tax imposed on whiskey, which is itself a medium of exchange in western Pennsylvania. Federal militiamen put down the rebellion without bloodshed.

The French Legislative Assembly frees slaves in all French colonies. The action comes in the midst of the Reign of Terror and makes France the first nation to free her slaves. Some 500,000 Haitian slaves in the French colony of Saint-Domingue on Hispaniola rise against 40,000 white Frenchmen. The colony produces nearly two-thirds of the world's coffee, nearly half its sugar, and much of its cocoa, accounting for one-third of France's commerce.

Jay's Treaty signed November 19 settles outstanding disputes that remain between the United States and Britain. A modification of the treaty permits U.S. ships to carry cocoa, coffee, cotton, molasses, and sugar from the British West Indies to any part of the world.

The Lancaster Road opens to link the "bonnyclabber" Pennsylvania Dutch country and Lancaster with Philadelphia and the Delaware River (*see* 1792). Stockholders have subscribed $465,000 to finance it and will receive such handsome dividends—15 percent in some years—that their success will inspire similar toll road projects (*see* Cumberland Road, 1811).

French general of brigade Napoleon Bonaparte, 25, offers a prize of 12,000 francs to anyone who can invent a means of preserving food for long periods of time so that France's military and naval forces may be supplied on long campaigns (*see* Appert, 1795).

The founder of nutritional science and of modern chemistry Antoine Lavoisier goes to the guillotine May 8 at age 50 in retribution for his direction of *l'ancien régime's* tax organization, the Fermier Général: "La république n'a pas besoin de savants," says the vice president of the tribunal Coffinhall, but mathematician Joseph-Louis Lagrange says, "It required but a moment to sever that head, and perhaps a century will not be sufficient to produce another like it."

A British naval squadron tests the scurvy-prevention theories of James Lind, who dies July 13 at age 78 (*see* 1747; 1753). It sails for Madras with its hatches full of lemons and arrives 23 weeks later with only one seaman suffering from scurvy (*see* 1795).

Deinhard & Co. is founded May 1 by Koblenz wine merchant Johann Friedrich Deinhard, 22, whose Rieslings and Liebfraumilch, pressed from grapes on vineyards along the Rhine and Moselle rivers and aged in vast cellars beneath the town, will develop a worldwide reputation. By 1825, Deinhard will be the most important exporter of German wines. Americans consume absolute alcohol (in the form of whiskey, rum, applejack, other spirits, wine, beer, ale, and cider) at the rate of 7.1 gallons per person per year, a rate that will continue until 1830.

New York's Tontine Coffee House at the corner of Wall and Water streets opens fountains of Ballston soda and seltzer waters (*see* Priestley, 1767; carbonic gas, 1770). Within 15 years, wine and sugar will be added, and ginger ale will be introduced soon after (*see* carbonate water, 1807).

A Boston restorateur opens in a 17th-century house at the northwest corner of Milk and Congress streets under the management of French refugee Julien (Jean-Baptiste-Gilbert Payplat dis Julien), who introduces Bostonians to cheese fondue, truffles from Périgord, and a clear soup so delicious that news of it soon reaches another French refugee. Paris lawyer Jean-Anthelme Brillat-Savarin, 39, who was born at Belley in Ain, won election 5 years ago as a deputy to the Constituant Assembly and made president of the civil tribunal of Ain but fled the Terror in 1792 after being threatened with punishment as a traitor to the republic. He went to Switzerland and England before voyaging to America, and supports himself by giving language lessons and playing his violin in a New York theater orchestra. Brillat-Savarin journeys to Boston to sample consommé Julien and other examples of Julien's cuisine (Brillat-Savarin will return to France in 1796 to become a judge in the court of appeal at Paris and will later be secretary to the general staff of the Army of the Republic in Germany; *see* 1825).

Paris has 500 restaurants; many of its best chefs have long since fled the country, but only now do people other than royalty and aristocrats begin to enjoy the French cuisine that has developed since the arrival of Catherine de' Medici from Florence in 1533.

1795

Paris has bread riots April 1 (12 Germinal) as food prices soar, but reactionary sentiment sweeps the peasantry, which has grown rich supplying the black market and wants to maintain its position.

A poor British harvest drives up the price of bread, which now consists of 95 percent wheat flour.

British magistrates meeting at the Pelican Inn at Speenhamland, Berkshire, order a Poor Law giving bread to the nation's poor on a sliding scale based on the price of bread and the number of children in the family (*see* Malthus, 1798).

Parisian brewer-pickler-confectioner-chef Nicolas (François) Appert, 43, begins work on a method for preserving food in response to last year's offer by Napoleon Bonaparte of a reward for an effective process. Appert will move in the next year from Lombard Street to Ivry-sur-Seine to devote all his efforts to the project (*see* 1804).

Emigré U.S. physician Benjamin Thompson, 42, invents a stove that economizes on fuel. Having abandoned his wife and daughter at Concord, after the outbreak of the American Revolution and now known as Count Rumford (the elector of Bavaria gave him the Holy Roman Empire title in 1791), he shows that 1,200 of the poor of Munich can be fed on barley soup thickened with potatoes and bread and seasoned with vinegar at a cost of $3.44 per day, but the poor resist the idea of eating potatoes (*see* nutrition, below).

The German-language *Philadelphische Correspondenz* for September 15 carries an advertisement for a *kuchpowder* made by herb and spice dealer Friedrich Schinckel, Jr., of 2nd and Market streets, whose product becomes an overnight sensation and will be popular for years as family recipe books call for Schinckel powder and Schinckel Cook-Dust.

The Massachusetts House of Representatives moves into a new statehouse; the "Sacred Cod" is moved to hang in the House chamber opposite the speaker's desk (*see* 1784). Bostonians at their tables prefer young cod, known as "scrod."

 The average weight of cattle sold at London's Smithfield market is twice what it was in 1710 (*see* 1732; Bakewell, 1769; Coke, 1772).

Count Rumford (above) will be the first to apply the term "science of nutrition" to the study of human food and the first to apply science to the preparation of food.

The Royal Navy orders lime juice rations aboard all naval vessels after the fifth or sixth week at sea following confirmation last year of James Lind's theory that citrus juice is an antiscorbutic (*see* 1794). The juice (actually lemon juice as a rule) is usually combined with the rum ration (*see* 1740; 1805; 1884).

James B. Beam Distilling Co. has its beginnings in a Kentucky territory distillery started by farmer Jacob Beam. His sons and grandsons will carry on the operation at Clermont.

The cocktail gets its name by some accounts from the *coquetier*, or egg cup, used by New Orleans apothecary Antoine-Amadé Peychaud to make the first mixed drinks to be so called (but *see* 1776; *see also* 1806).

1796

British forces take Malacca and seize all Dutch property in the Far East except Java (*see* 1780; Dutch East India Company, 1799).

France suffers ruinous inflation as the *assignats* issued in 1790 decline in value. A bushel of flour sells for the equivalent of $5, up from 40¢ in 1790; a cartload of wood for $250, up from $4; a pound of soap for $8, up from 18¢; a dozen eggs for $5, up from 24¢ (*see* 1792; Bonaparte, 1800).

A Public Land Act passed by Congress May 18 authorizes the sale of U.S. government lands in minimum lots of 640 acres each at $2 per acre with payments to be made under a credit system (*see* 1800; Land Ordinance, 1785; farmers, 1820).

Poetry: "The Hasty Pudding" by Connecticut poet Joel Barlow, 42: "In *Haste* the boiling cauldron, o'er the blaze,/ Receives and cooks the ready-powder'd maize;/ In *Haste* 'tis served, and then in equal *Haste*,/ With cooling milk we make the sweet repast,/ No carving to be done, no knife to grate. The Tender ear, and wound the stony plate;/ But the smooth spoon, just fitted to the lip,/ and taught with art the yielding mass to dip,/ By frequent journeys to the bowl well stor'd/ performs the hasty eyes of the board." (Hasty pudding—also called loblolly, cornmeal porridge, and samp—is cornmeal mush cooked until thick; Indian pudding is made of cornmeal [from "Indian corn"] but contains also sugar, butter, salt, cinnamon, and baking powder.)

Cookbook: *American Cookery, or the Art of Dressing Viands, Fish, Poultry, and Vegetables, and the Best Modes of Making Pastes, Puffs, Pies, Tarts, Puddings, Custards, & Preserves, and All Kinds of Cakes, from the imperial Plumb to plain Cake adapted to This Country & All Grades of Life.* By Amelia Simmons, *An American Orphan* is the first cookbook to be published in America (at Hartford) by an American and the first to contain native American specialties. Simmons includes in her 47-page, vest-pocket-size compendium (which goes through four editions, with new material added to each) such dishes as Indian slapjack (pancakes), johnnycake, pickled watermelon rind, "cramberry" sauce, Jerusalem artichokes, spruce beer, Indian pudding, "pompkin" pie, a gingerbread that is much softer than the thin European variety, and six kinds of rice pudding (sample: "One quarter pound of rice, a stick of cinnamon, a quart of milk [stirred often to keep from burning] and boiled quick, cool and add half a nutmeg, four spoons rose-water, eight eggs; butter or puff paste a dish and pour the above composition into it, and bake one and half hour").

John Harvey & Sons, Ltd., of Bristol has its beginnings in a sherry-importing firm founded in Denmark Street by William Perry, who will be joined in 1816 by Thomas Urich, brother-in-law of Cornish sea captain Thomas Harvey. Urich will bring Harvey's son Thomas into the firm that will be famous for its "Bristol milk" and "Bristol cream" sherries from Jerez de la Frontera in Andalusia. (Sherry is fortified wine made generally from Palomino grapes, fermented with the aid of a special yeast known as a *flor*, or flower, aged in 132-gallon barrels, blended, and finished in a *solera*—a pile of barrels arranged in three tiers, with young wine going into the top tier while old wine for bottling is drawn out of the bottom tier. No more than half, and preferably no more than a third, of the wine in the bottom tier is ever drawn off at one time.)

The "Veuve Clicquot" (Widow Clicquot) begins improving French champagne. Nicole-Barbe Clicquot (*née* Ponsardin), 20, is the daughter of the mayor of Reims; her vintner husband, whom she married 3 years ago, has just died following the birth of their daughter, and she determines to carry on his business. She will pioneer the process of placing inverted champagne bottles into holes in a steeply sloping table top (*sur pointe*), gradually moving and turning them (*remuage*) over a period of several weeks, shaking them periodically until the sediment in the wine drops down to coat the cork, and then removing the cork's retaining wire for an instant to permit pressure to expel the sediment, whereupon the operator's thumb stops the flow, the lost wine is replaced, and a clean cork is quickly reinserted before the sparkle can be diminished. Veuve Clicquot will create pink champagne simply by pressing the grapes as soon as they are picked, and her brand will become a world leader (*see* 1820).

1797

George Washington at Mount Vernon receives a Polish visitor who reports that the former president's slaves are permitted to tend small vegetable gardens but not to keep chickens, ducks, geese, or pigs. Their rations are a peck of corn per week for each adult, half that amount for children. They are given 20 small salt herring per month and eat meat only at harvest time.

British sailors mutiny at Spithead April 15, demanding better treatment; the government meets their demands May 17, but a more serious mutiny breaks out at the Nore and is suppressed June 30 only by force. The mutinies bring conditions in the military to public notice and will lead to improved rations.

A poor wheat harvest forces Parliament to encourage imports, but grain prices shoot up as a result of the war with France, the breakdown in commerce,

and a halt in specie payments by the Bank of England (*see* 1795; 1801).

The United States enters the world spice trade. Salem, Mass., sea captain Jonathan Carnes returns to port with the first large cargo of Sumatra pepper (*see* 1805; 1818).

Cookbook: *The New and Complete Cook* by English author Anne Battam.

British tea consumption reaches an annual rate of two pounds per capita, a figure that will increase fivefold in the next century (*see* 1710). Working-class Britons spend on average £2 per year on tea out of an annual income of only £40 (*see* 1840).

Scottish grocer James Keiller at Dundee starts packing orange marmalade (*see* 1561). A Spanish brig has left a cargo of oranges on the dock at Tayside, Keiller sees the oranges being sold cheaply and brings home a cartload in a hired dray, the oranges turn out to be too bitter to eat, and Keiller's wife, Janet (*née* Pierson), a former kitchen maid, suggests that they turn the fruit into jam. The Scots have been using homemade marmalades of quince and other fruits for more than a century, but Keiller's is the first commercial marmalade. He sells his first batch in a matter of hours, goes back for more of the bitter oranges, and will soon be marketing Keiller's Marmalade in white stone pots (*see* 1868; Crosse & Blackwell, 1919).

1798

Britain has a poor crop year. Wheat prices climb to £12 per hundredweight, and there is widespread hunger (*see* typhus, Malthus, below).

A British commission investigating Scotch whisky hears evidence that distilling "spreads itself over the whole face of the country, and in every island from the Orkneys to Jura . . . under such circumstances that it is impossible to take account of its operations; it is literally to search for revenue in the woods and around the mountains" (*see* 1784; 1814).

Tableau Élémentaire de l'histoire naturelle des animaux by French naturalist George-Léopold-Chrétien-Frédéric Dagobert, 29, baron Cuvier, founds the science of comparative anatomy (*see* 1799).

A typhus epidemic kills thousands of Britons as starvation makes the country vulnerable to disease (*see* above).

The Stairs pear originated in 1770 is planted in a Massachusetts orchard but will be forgotten (*see* Bartlett, 1817).

A pasta factory opened by a Frenchman at Philadelphia finds a ready market, but upper-class Americans will continue to import pasta from Sicily (*see* Jefferson, 1789). The semolina flour needed for high-quality pasta is made from durum wheat, which will not be grown in America until the 20th century.

Rule's Restaurant opens in London's Maiden Lane, where it will serve jellied eel, jugged hare, mulligatawny stew, steak-and-kidney pie, and trifle as well as French and Italian dishes for the next 2 centuries. It will gain a reputation for fish grills, cold buffet, and sweets.

Essay on the Principles of Population by English parson Thomas Robert Malthus, 32, expounds the thesis that population increases in geometrical, or exponential, progression (1, 2, 4, 8, 16, 32, etc.), while food production ("subsistence") increases only in arithmetical progression (1, 2, 3, 4, 5, 6, etc.). Resting his case on the history of the American colonies in this century, Malthus poses the inevitability of a world food crisis and attacks proposals to reform Britain's Poor Law (*see* 1795). "A slight acquaintance with numbers will show the immensity of the first power in comparison with the second," says Malthus (*see* 1805; Townsend, 1785, 1791).

1799

The Dutch East India Company dissolves as its charter expires after 198 years in which stockholders have received annual dividends averaging 18 percent. Mincing Lane, London, becomes the spice-trading center of the world.

Baron Cuvier in France introduces the term *phylum* to denote a category more general than *class*; he takes the word from the Greek for "tribe" (*see* 1798).

Prussia's Friedrich Wilhelm III receives a loaf of beet sugar from Berlin chemist Franz Karl Achard and is persuaded to give Achard some land at Cunern in Silesia and finance his work with sugar beets (*see* 1793; 1802).

Cultivation of beets as a root vegetable gains importance in parts of Europe, but most farmers continue to cultivate the plant only for its greens.

George Washington dies at Mount Vernon December 14 at age 67. The news reaches Philadelphia December 18, and Oeller's Hotel in Chestnut Street, famous for its planked shad dinners, burns down that day. Washington was one of its best customers.

1800

Austrian troops starve Genoa into surrender June 4 but come under attack from Napoleon Bonaparte, who has advanced through the St. Bernard Pass with a French army of 40,000 in May and wins a narrow victory June 14 at the Battle of Marengo. Bonaparte is famished after the battle and demands that he be served a meal immediately; he is far from his provision wagons, but his *maître-queux*, Dunand, manages to scrape up a small chicken, six crayfish, four tomatoes, garlic, olive oil, and a bottle of cognac for a dish that will be called poulet (Chicken) Marengo.

Famine conditions in Britain force people to tighten their belts as they send off soldiers to fight the French.

Famine in China increases the importance of root crops such as sweet potatoes, which become the staple food for tens of millions in parts of the country. Maize has been planted in large areas of western China, and white potatoes, too, are widely grown, having been propagated by French missionaries in the past century for planting on land too poor for maize. The Qing court continues to eat well while peasants go hungry.

Napoleon Bonaparte acts to stop France's inflation and avert national bankruptcy (*see* 1796). He raises 5 million francs from French and Italian bankers and 9 million from a national lottery, introduces a new and tighter system of income tax collections, reduces the budgets of all his ministries, and restores confidence among the bourgeoisie.

Congress passes legislation to reduce the minimum amount of public land that may be sold at auction under the U.S. Land Ordinance of 1785. The bill, introduced by Congressman William Henry Harrison, 27, of the Northwest Territory, permits sale of 320-acre tracts at $2 per acre with a down payment of one-fourth and the balance to be paid in three annual installments (*see* 1796; 1804).

Spode bone china is introduced at Stoke-on-Trent by English potter Josiah Spode II, 46, who perfects a formula for combining hard feldspar paste with the ashes of calcined cattle bones (*see* 1770). Others have used bone ash in porcelain since 1749, but with less success. English bone china will replace hard-paste porcelain, and by 1833 there will be more than 5,000 patterns in the Spode line, a number that will be sharply reduced in later years as Spode's bone china, Lowestoft, and earthenware gain wide popularity (his firm will become part of Royal Worcester).

Passenger pigeons in America are estimated to number 5 billion and provide low-cost food in the Northwest Territory (*see* Josselyn, 1672; Wilson, 1810).

British planters have firmly established clove plantations at Penang on the Malayan Peninsula (*see* Zanzibar, 1818).

Sugar beets have a sugar content of roughly 6 percent; efforts begin to raise the figure by selective breeding (*see* Achard, 1793; Delessert, 1810).

French botanist Antoine-Nicolas Duchesne cross-breeds *Fragaria chiloensis* with *F. virginiana* in a market garden (date approximate) (*see* 1712). The result is a large-sized strawberry with good color and flavor (*see* 1819).

The duke of Beaufort's mother-in-law, Mrs. Edward Boscawn, writes April 22 that the duke "has been well employed in the county, as he always is. He has caused all the bakers' loaves in every parish to be suddenly weighed, and fined those that were short in weight, so now no one dares to defraud the poor, which was a practice gaining ground and wanted this unexpected prevention." Noting that the duke has instituted stricter regulations to prevent the waste of flour in his own large household, she writes, "It is amazing what a difference this established. . . . I tell you that because the famine is sore in the land." Sifting, or bolting, of ground grain has changed radically in the course of this century, accelerating demand for bread made from finer, whiter flour.

19th Century

1801

💲 Parliament passes a General Enclosure Act designed to simplify and facilitate the process of fencing in and consolidating British common lands, open fields, and wastelands to encourage efficient large-scale farming. Since 1760, it has passed 1,600 individual enclosure acts; the new law permits passage of such acts in batches. Small landholders in England, Scotland, and Wales will virtually disappear in the next few decades, and there will be a surge in the number of workers obliged to labor for low wages.

U.S. salt prices fall to a new low of $2.50 per bushel as additional sources come into production. Salt has been four times as costly as beef on the frontier but is essential to keep livestock (and people) healthy and meat from spoiling.

⚡ Completion of the trans-Pennine canal links England's Mersey and Humber rivers, permitting farmers to supply distant markets.

🕰 Cox's Orange Pippin, a new apple variety, is introduced by retired Buckinghamshire brewer, who has raised it in his garden near Slough (date approximate).

"Johnny Appleseed" arrives in the Ohio Valley with seeds from Philadelphia cider presses that will make the valley as rich a source of apples as Leominster, Mass., hometown of eccentric pioneer John (or Jonathan) Chapman, 26 (*see* 1806).

A bakery to produce ship's biscuit and hardtack opens six miles south of Boston at Milton, Mass. Retired ship's captain Josiah Dent will introduce the first biscuits to be called "crackers"—water biscuits made of unsweetened, unleavened dough rolled many times to have a fine grain that will make them crisper than previous biscuits and will cause them to make a cracking noise when eaten.

👨‍🍳 The Edo restaurant Komagata Dojo opens to serve roach, or mudfish, which is all it prepares. It will still be operating in 1995.

👫 The population of Edo, Japan's capital city, reaches 1 million and its main streets are lined with restaurants, many of them serving buckwheat noodles (*soba*), which gains popularity (*see* 1657). The city will flourish in the next 28 years, restaurants and caterers serving *tempura* will proliferate (*see* 1585), and fish shops will deliver prepared dishes to householders.

1802

💲 E. I. du Pont de Nemours has its beginnings in a gunpowder plant built on the Brandywine River near Wilmington, Del., by French-born entrepreneur Éleuthère Irénée du Pont, 31, whose enterprise will grow to play major roles in agriculture and food packaging (*see* chestnuts, 1805).

🧪 *Biologie oder Philosophie de lebenden Natur* by German naturalist Gottfried Reinhold Treviranus, 26, introduces the word "biology." The six-volume work will be completed in 1822.

The nitrogen potential of guano is studied by Prussian naturalist Friedrich Heinrich Alexander von

Humboldt, 32, who has crossed the Cordilleras to Quito, descended to Callao, and found great deposits of guano concentrated on islands off the west coast of South America. The guano represents droppings from seabirds over the course of thousands of years, nitrates from guano can be used both for fertilizer and explosives, and Peru will export guano to Europe in large quantities, primarily on the basis of Humboldt's reports (*see* 1809).

Cookbook: *Sushimeshi* (*Secret Sushi Recipes*) by Kyoto physician Sugino Gonbi includes 33 recipes.

An enormous cheese is delivered to the White House January 1. A Cheshire, Mass., farmer and Baptist preacher campaigned in the pulpit 2 years ago for Thomas Jefferson and, with his friend Darius Brown, has driven six horses across the snow from the Berkshires, a 3 weeks' journey, with the cheese, which is as large as a burr millstone and weighs 1,235 pounds (1,600 pounds by some accounts), loaded aboard his sleigh. Inscribed on one side as "the greatest cheese in America for the greatest man in America," it is served at a public New Year's Day reception in the East Room that afternoon, the Marine Band plays, and each guest slices off a wedge of Cheshire cheese; some of the cheese will still be left 3 years' hence and will be served at a White House reception with cake and hot punch.

A White House dinner given for President Jefferson and his guests February 2 includes rice soup, round of beef, turkey, mutton, ham, loin of veal, cutlets of veal, fried eggs, fried beef, and macaroni followed by ice cream (*see* Washington, 1789) and fruit, with good French wines where appropriate. Jefferson has returned from France with a taste for good food; critics complain that he has become Frenchified and "abjures his native victuals."

Jefferson (above) makes ice cream with a *sorbetière* (ice pail), using batches of ice and salt. A servant is instructed to turn a custard into the *sorbetière* (which he has probably acquired in France), surround the whole with salt and ice, let it stand, turn the *sorbetière* in the ice, loosen the ice, and stir from inside. When the cream is "well taken, put it in moulds, jostling it well down on the knee" (*see* Dolley Madison, 1813; portable freezer, 1846).

Soybeans are introduced into the United States via England but will not be widely grown in either country for more than a century (*see* 1920).

The world's first beet-sugar factory goes into production in Silesia but soon runs deep into debt (*see* 1799). A disciple of Franz Karl Achard is no more successful with a factory he sets up at Krayn, also in Silesia, but he does succeed in growing the white Silesian beet, which is higher in sugar content and will be the basis of all future sugar beet strains (*see* 1808).

The Paris *pâtisserie* Dalloyau opens at 101, rue du Faubourg Saint-Honoré, where its patrons throughout this century and the next will climb the spiral staircase at the rear to enjoy *thé*, petits-fours, and pastries. A second Dalloyau will open at 69, rue de la Convention.

1803

Danish subjects are forbidden to engage in the slave trade as of January 1, but planters in the Danish West Indies continue to use slave labor in their sugar fields.

Renewal of hostilities in Europe brings higher prices for American farm products and increases trade for U.S. shipping merchants such as Asa Clapp of Portland; George Cabot, Thomas Handasyd Perkins, and James Lloyd of Boston; and Cyrus Butler and Nicholas Brown of Providence.

Construction begins in Scotland on a 60.5-mile Caledonian Canal to connect the Atlantic with the North Sea across northern Scotland.

The Middlesex Canal opens December 21 to connect the Merrimack River with Boston Harbor.

A machine for paring apples, patented February 14 by Chester County, Pa., mechanic Moses Coates, is the first of many such devices that will receive patents over the years.

The first ice refrigerator (icebox) is patented by Maryland farmer Thomas Moore, who places one wooden box inside another, insulates the space in between with charcoal or ashes, and places a tin box

Iceboxes were a novelty; households relied on cool cellars or ice houses to keep foods from spoiling.

container at the top of the inner box. Moore's icebox will be in common use by 1838 (*see* Perkins, 1834).

Connecticut clockmaker Eli Terry, 31, introduces wooden-wheeled clocks much like those produced in the Black Forest since 1660 but will soon replace the wooden wheels with brass ones. To overcome sales resistance, he becomes the first U.S. merchant to offer merchandise on a free-trial, no-money-down basis, and when housewives discover the value of clocks for giving accurate time in cooking they are readily willing to pay for them rather than give them up.

💐 *A Treatise on Farming* by Loudon County, Va., farmer John Alexander Binns, 42, originates what will be called the "Loudon system" of soil treatment. Binns has experimented with crop rotation, deep plowing, and the use of gypsum as fertilizer.

👨‍🍳 *Almanach des gourmands* by Paris lawyer-gastronome Alexandre-Balthasar-Laurent (Grimod de La Reynière) is the world's first restaurant guide. Arrested at the behest of his family in 1786 for having committed so many indiscretions, the misshapen, clubfooted Grimod de la Reynière (who always

wears gloves; his webbed fingers were replaced with mechanical metal fingers by surgeons in his infancy) was sent to the Abbaye de Domèrvre near Toul, where he learned about cooking, and later inherited a fortune (plus a palace on the boulevard des Champs-Elysées). Spurned by a famous actress, he has turned his attention to the pleasures of the table and founded the Jury Dégustateur. His *Almanach* lists 500 restaurants and guides Parisians in the art of eating with pointers about shops, changing manners and customs, notes on menus, and information on seasonal specialties. It will be published annually for the next 8 years. The original marmite, or stockpot, of the restaurateur Déharme in the rue des Grands-Augustins has not been off the fire for 85 years, during which time it has cooked at least 300,000 capons, which are available at any hour of day or night.

1804

⚔️ Haiti is established with a black republican government in the western part of Hispaniola following defeat of a 5,000-man army sent out by the emperor Napoleon to subdue the rebels (*see* sugar production, below).

💲 Napoleon imposes a new tax on salt at the rate of 2 centimes per kilo, a duty that will be maintained until 1945 (*see* 1790). Frenchmen are forbidden to take even a single liter of seawater without permission from the Ministry of Finance. Pans and salt-works become subject to the general taxation laws.

Rust destroys part of Britain's wheat crop, bread prices rise, but Parliament imposes prohibitory duties that discourage imports of foreign grain. Customs and excise duties on food make up nearly half of Britain's total revenues (*see* Corn Law, 1815).

Congress permits 160-acre tracts of U.S. public lands to be sold at auction (*see* 1841).

⚡ Capt. John Chester's schooner *Reynard* lands the first shipment of bananas to arrive at New York. The fruit grows nowhere in the United States and must be imported by sailing ship from Caribbean or Central American ports, but only a handful of such imports will arrive in the next 50 years (*see* 1830; Baker, 1870).

The first steam locomotive to be tried on rails hauls five wagons containing 10 tons of iron and 70 men some 9.5 miles at nearly 5 miles per hour. English engineer Richard Trevithick, 33, has built the locomotive and will be the first to apply high-pressure steam power to agriculture (*see* 1811).

 Nicolas Appert opens the world's first vacuum-bottling factory, or cannery, at Massey (Seine-et-Oise) near Palaiseau and Paris (*see* 1795). He has subjected his vacuum-packed foods to public tests at Brest (*see* 1809).

Grimod de La Reynière's *Almanach des Gourmands* publicizes the products of Nicolas Appert (above) (*see* 1804; 1808).

Cookbooks: *The Very Newest Cookbook for Meat and Fast Days* by Maria Anna Busswald, *Former Cook of Her Excellency Rosalia, Countess von Attems, born Countess of Leslie, Written for the Benefit of the Female Sex and All Those Eager to Become Skilled in the Culinary Art.* Busswald gives recipes (in no particular order) for German sausages, gravy, Gesellschaftskraferln, doughnuts, and quince juice. *Culina Famulatrix Medicinae; or, Receipts in Modern Cookery* by English author Alexander Hunter.

Botanist William Bartram, now 65, declines an invitation from President Jefferson to join the Lewis and Clark expedition, which begins its ascent of the Missouri River May 14. Led by Capt. Meriwether Lewis, 29, and William Clark, 33, the expedition sights frequent herds of bison, estimated to number at least 10 million on the western plains and thought by some to number five or ten times that many.

Ohio farmer George Rennic drives a corn-fed herd of cattle across the mountains to Baltimore, losing less than 100 pounds per head and making a sound profit. Many western farmers will be inspired to follow his example, but there are still food surpluses west of the Alleghenies and shortages on the seaboard.

Haitian sugar production falls to 27,000 tons, down from 70,000 in 1791, as the revolution against France (above) disrupts agriculture (*see* 1825).

1805

A Royal Navy fleet commanded by Horatio Nelson defeats the French in the Battle of Trafalgar October 21 but Lord Nelson is killed by a French sharpshooter at age 47 (*see* scurvy, below).

Prussia abolishes internal customs duties to improve her domestic economy as she struggles to resist the French emperor Napoleon.

Salem, Mass., exports 7.5 million pounds of pepper which have come in from Sumatra and other East Indian sources.

Boston entrepreneur Frederic Tudor, 21, pioneers export of U.S. ice. He has declined to "waste his time" attending Harvard like his three brothers, has heard that lumber shipped from New England ports in winter will sometimes still have ice on its plank ends when unloaded weeks later at West Indian ports, and has engaged men to chop ice from nearby lakes and ponds to be stored in icehouses. Undaunted by a costly initial setback, Tudor will ship thicker ice in better-insulated ships, obtain a virtual monopoly in ice trade to Cuba, build icehouses at Caribbean and South American ports, and develop a large business (*see* 1833; Wyeth, 1825).

The Lewis and Clark expedition survives a bitter winter by eating wild roots which the men have been taught to find by Sacajawea, a Shoshone teenager whose French-Canadian husband serves as the expedition's guide and interpreter. Meriwether Lewis writes in his journal for September 20, "They now set before them . . . several kinds of fruits. Among these last is one which is round and much like an onion in appearance and sweet to the taste. It is called *quamash*, and is eaten either in its natural state or boiled in a kind of soup, or made into a cake, which is then called pashco. After the long abstinence this was a sumptuous treat" (he refers to *Camassia quamash*, a member of the lily family and a staple food of Pacific-area natives; other members of the expedition compare it to gingerbread, but *see* 1806). The expedition reaches the Pacific in November.

Tangerines (*Citrus reticulata*) reach Europe for the first time, coming directly from China. The loose-skinned mandarin species has been cultivated for years in China and Japan and by 1850 will be grown in many Mediterranean countries. (They may have come to southern Spain from Tangier, in Morocco, during or soon after the Middle Ages; *see* Florida, 1871.)

The first California orange grove of any size is planted at San Gabriel Mission near Los Angeles. California will rival Florida as an orange producer.

 Delaware powdermaker Éleuthère Irénée du Pont plants acres of European chestnuts on his estate (*see* Washington, 1785). The trees will be planted in orchards through parts of Delaware, Pennsylvania, and New Jersey (*see* blight, 1904).

Abolition of scurvy in the Royal Navy enables the British to win the Battle of Trafalgar (above; *see* 1794; 1884).

French entrepreneur Henri-Louis Pernod opens a distillery at Pontarlier, a few miles from the Swiss town of Couvet, where he will produce liqueurs (*see* U.S. ban on absinthe, 1912).

1806

London announces a blockade of the European coast from Brest to the Elbe May 6 but permits ships from neutral nations to pass if they are not carrying goods to or from enemy ports.

Congress authorizes construction of a road to connect Cumberland, Md., with the Ohio River (*see* 1811).

Congress authorizes construction of the Natchez Trace to follow the 500-mile Indian trail from Nashville to Natchez on the Mississippi River.

Cookbook: *A New System of Domestic Cookery, formed upon Principles of Economy and Adapted to the Use of Private Families* by English author Maria Eliza Rundell (*née* Ketellay), 61.

William Clark of the Lewis and Clark expedition records in his journal for June 11 that his Shoshone guide, Sacajawea, has prepared the edible bulbs of the camas plant (*Camassia quamash*) and says, "This root is palateable but disagrees with us in every shape we have used it. The natives are extremely fond of this root and present [it] to their visitors as a great treat. when we first arrived at the Chopunnish [Nez Percé] last fall at this place our men who were half starved made so free a use of this root it made them all sick for several days after" (*see* 1805; Douglas, 1826).

Eggplant (aubergine) is introduced to U.S. tables for the first time (*see* 1587).

Lt. Zebulon Pike, 27, notes in his journal that the flesh of the American buffalo (or bison) is "equal to any meat I ever saw." Bison number 200 million by some accounts and represent a major food source for the Plains Indians as well as providing them with blankets and clothing.

Ireland suffers a partial failure of her potato crop (*see* 1822).

The western high plains of America are "incapable of cultivation," writes Lt. Pike, (above), who leads an expedition to the Rocky Mountains (Pike's Peak) and compares the plains to the "sandy deserts of Africa" (*see* Long, 1820; buffalo meat, *above*).

"Johnny Appleseed" fills two long canoes with seeds, reaches the banks of the Muskingum River, runs out of seeds on White Woman Creek, but has left thousands of acres of cleared land seeded with trees that will become fruit-bearing orchards (*see* 1801; 1845).

The word "cocktail" appears in print for the first time in a Hudson, N.Y., newspaper, which calls it "a stimulating liquor, composed of spirits of any kind, sugar, water, and bitters" (*see* 1776; 1795; Angostura, 1818).

1807

A British Order in Council January 7 prohibits neutral nation ships from trading with France and her allies, but while the Royal Navy blockades Napoleon's ports, the French are agriculturally self-sufficient and suffer less than do the British.

Clearances begin on the Highland estates of the countess of Sutherlandshire, forcing peasants off the land to permit enclosure for sheep raising (*see* 1814).

The Milan Decree issued by Napoleon December 17 reiterates the paper blockade against British trade with the Continent.

An Embargo Act signed by President Jefferson December 22 prohibits all ships from leaving U.S. ports for foreign ports. The act is designed to force French and British withdrawal of restrictions on U.S.

trade, but its effect will be to make overseas sales of U.S. farm surpluses impossible. New England shippers protest the embargo and are joined by southern planters (*see* 1809).

Cookbook: *A New System of Domestic Cookery* by Mrs. Rundell is a U.S. reprinting of last year's English work.

The Institution for the Promotion of Science and Agriculture is incorporated March 20 at Cork City, Ireland.

The Bosc pear (originally the Beurré Bosc) is developed in the part of the Netherlands that will become Belgium in 1830. Related to the English Conference and Italian Abate Fetel varieties, it has firm, dry, yellowish-white flesh that retains its shape even when well cooked.

Water carbonated with carbonic gas is bottled and sold in the New York City area by Yale's first chemistry professor Benjamin Silliman, 28 (*see* Bergman, 1770; Durand, 1825; Matthews, 1833).

Napoleon encourages his troops to drink coffee as a stimulant rather than alcohol, but the British blockade (above) cuts off imports and obliges the French to extend their dwindling coffee supplies with chicory.

1808

Soaring Welsh food prices following a bad harvest produce a large-scale enclosure movement throughout Wales and parts of England (*see* 1801). Strip farming, heretofore widespread, will soon disappear as arable lands are consolidated in a few Anglo-Welsh hands.

Lectures on Animal Chemistry by Swedish chemist Jöns Jakob Berzelius, 29, explores the composition of blood, gall, milk, bone, fat, and other bodily substances. His studies will influence fundamental knowledge of life and bodily functions.

Nonfiction: *Manuel des amphitryons* by Grimod de La Reynière introduces Frenchmen to the elegant table and teaches them how to maintain one. The author considers it not unreasonable to spend 5 hours in the enjoyment of a good dinner.

Cookbook: *The New-England Cookery, or The Art of Dressing All Kinds of Flesh, Fish, and Vegetables, and the Best Modes of Making Pastes, Puffs, Pies, Tarts, Puddings, Custards, and Preserves, and All Kinds of Cakes, From the Imperial Plum to Plain Cake* by Montpelier, Vt., compiler Lucy Emerson (*née* Reed), 39, who, like Amelia Simmons in 1796, calls herself "an American Orphan" and borrows heavily from the Simmons book.

An article on beet sugar written by F. K. Achard at Berlin appears in the *Moniteur* and arouses French interest in domestic sugar production, as the British Orders in Council issued last year cut France off from sugar imports (*see* 1810; Achard, 1802).

The first Parisian restaurant of any substance with fixed prices opens in the Palais-Royal under the management of the restaurateur Véry.

1809

Nicolas Appert wins a prize of 12,000 francs (a great fortune) for his method of vacuum-packing food in jars (*see* 1804; Bonaparte, 1794). Appert's factory packs food for Napoleon's armies; his method of boiling meat and vegetables in jars, then sealing them with corks and tar, which has taken 14 years to perfect, will remain briefly a French military secret (*see* Durand, 1810).

Export of Chilean nitrates to Europe begins, but the nitrates are used less for fertilizer than for explosives (*see* Humboldt, 1802; War of the Pacific, 1879; Haber process, 1908).

Former President Thomas Jefferson writes a letter to Ithaman Bacon January 3 expressing the hope that Bacon will be able to able to fill his icehouse. "It would be a real calamity should we not have ice to do it, as it would require double the quantity of fresh meat in summer had we not ice to keep it" (*see* 1810).

The Alexander grape is discovered in New York's Finger Lakes region (year approximate), but viniculture in the area will not begin for another 20 years.

Edo sushi maker Yohei (only *samurai* and privileged citizens are permitted to use family names) invents nigirizushi—a small bowl containing vinegared rice covered with wasabi (grated horseradish) and topped with a slice of fish—which gains immediate popularity (nigirizushi will become a specialty at Edo).

France has a boom in mushroom cultivation. The common white mushroom grown on "farms" in quarry tunnels near Paris brings variety to the local cuisine.

The mint julep—brandy (bourbon will later be used) poured over crushed ice and garnished with mint leaves—is created by some accounts at White Sulphur Springs, a spa in western Virginia (but *see* 1858). It will be widely esteemed as protection against malaria. (The word "julep" derives from the Persian *gulab* and the Arabic *julab*, meaning rosewater—a scented liquid distilled from rose petals and used in North African and Middle Eastern cookery as well as perfumes.)

1810

Napoleonic general Jean-Baptiste-Jules Bernadotte, 47, is elected crown prince of Sweden; he will succeed to the throne in 1815, introducing French cuisine to supplement traditional Swedish cookery.

Prussia abolishes serfdom and gives ex-serfs the lands they have cultivated for their landlord masters, allowing them to sell the lands if they choose, but Prussian peasants will live for nearly a century under conditions not far removed from serfdom (*see* Russia, 1858).

Rural poverty worsens in Ireland. Authorities see consolidation of landholdings to create viable farms as the only solution, even though this means large-scale evictions. Some landlords encourage emigration to the United States or Canada.

Nicolas Appert announces his discovery of vacuum-packed food in *Le Livre de tous les ménages*, which is published in June with the subtitle *L'art de conserver, pendant plusieurs années, toutes les substances animales et végétales* (*see* 1809). Appert will revise his book for 1811, 1813, and 1831 editions, his nephew Prieur Appert and a collaborator will revise it thereafter, and it will remain the Bible of food preservation for most of the century.

French chemist Joseph-Louis Gay-Lussac, 32, studies Appert's conserves (above), finds no oxygen inside the jars, and states in December that "animal and vegetable substances, through their contact with air, promptly become disposed to putrefaction and fermentation, but in exposing them at boiling water temperatures, in well-closed vessels, the absorbed oxygen produces a new combination which no longer is likely to produce fermentation or putrefaction." Appert has stated that "the subject of heat has the essential quality in itself not only of changing the combination of the constituent parts of animal and vegetable products, but also that, if not destroying it, at least of arresting for many years the natural tendency of these same products to decomposition." The view of the eminent Gay-Lussac that the food in Appert's jars is preserved because oxygen has been removed will nevertheless prevail for more than half a century (*see* Pasteur, 1861).

The first British patent for a tin-plated steel container is issued to Peter Durand, whose tins will find greater use than the jars of Nicolas Appert (above).

A London cannery that will soon be shipping thousands of cases of tinned foods for use by the Royal Navy is opened under the name Donkin-Hall by Bryan Donkin, who has interests in an ironworks (*see* 1812).

French banker Benjamin Delessert, 37, sets up beet-sugar factories at Passy to supply France with sugar in the absence of imports blockaded by the Royal Navy. The factories will produce more than 4 million kilos of high-cost sugar in the next 2 years (*see* 1811; 1814).

English chemist William Hyde Wollaston, 44, discovers the amino acid cystine in bladder stones (*see* Braconnot, 1820).

French peasant Joseph Talon plants some acorns on a patch of stony, chalky earth; he will harvest truffles a few years hence at the roots of the new oaks and will embark on a career of buying up worthless lands in Périgord and sowing them with acorns, telling no one his secret.

Thomas Jefferson notes September 14 that "the ice in the ice house fails" (*see* 1809).

The Munich Oktoberfest has its beginnings in an extravagant party given by the Bavarian king Max Josef to celebrate the marriage of his son Ludwig (Louis), 24, to princess Theresia of Saxe-Hildburghausen, 18, who will bear him seven children (the site of the party will become known as Theresia's Meadow).

Old Overholt rye whiskey has its beginnings in a distillery opened by Pennsylvania farmer Abraham Overholt, 26.

1811

Construction begins on the Cumberland Road, which extends westward from Cumberland, Md., but states' rights political forces will block congressional appropriations to continue the first national undertaking to improve U.S. internal transportation (*see* 1806; 1817; Lancaster Road, 1792; Jackson, 1830).

French chemist Bernard Courtois, 34, isolates iodine while studying products obtained by leaching the ashes of burnt seaweed. Iodine will be used as an antiseptic and to purify drinking water (*see* nutrition, below).

The Russian ambassador to Paris Prince Aleksandr Borosovich Kurakin, 35, introduces the practice of serving meals in courses (*à la Russe*) instead of placing many dishes on the table at once (*see* 1852).

English poet George Gordon, 23, Lord Byron, returns to London after 2 years of travel in the Near East and visits Berry Brothers at 3 St. James's Street, where he weighs himself on the scale used to weigh coffee, tea, and other commodities (he weighs 13 stone, 12 pounds, up from the 9 stone, 11½ pounds he weighed at Cambridge). Byron will indulge in reckless eating and then struggle with rigorous dieting to maintain his weight, which will vary within a year between 14 stone, 6 pounds and 10 stone, 11½ pounds. (John Berry, son of a wine merchant from Exeter, took over a shop about a decade ago that had been in business since before 1699 and whose customers included Queen Anne. Its scales, suspended from a large beam attached to the ceiling, has recorded customers' weights in a ledger since 1765, including dates and details of what people

were wearing, and it has been fashionable to have oneself weighed on the great scales.)

Napoleon awards Benjamin Delessert the medal of the Légion d'Honneur for his success with beet sugar, orders the immediate allotment of 32,000 hectares to sugar beet cultivation, and tells the Paris Chamber of Commerce that "the English can throw into the Thames the sugar and indigo which they formerly sold on the Continent with high profit to themselves" (*see* 1810; 1813).

Iodine (above) will prove to be an essential nutrient in human diets (*see* Baumann, 1896).

Britain's blockade of French port cities works hardships on British wine lovers and French vintners. The comte de La Pallu, owner of Château Latour, receives a letter in April from the château's director noting that the inability to obtain Baltic oak barrel staves (from Polish, Latvian, and Lithuanian trees) has made good oak expensive in Bordeaux if, indeed, it can be found at all: "We shall soon have to renounce this quality of wood altogether and make do with what is here, even though the English don't like [the taste of red wine aged in French oak, which imparts more tannin and oak flavor to the wine]."

1812

Napoleon invades Russia in June but begins a retreat from Moscow October 19. Crippled by hunger, cold, and lack of irregulars, the invading force has dwindled from 500,000 to no more than 100,000 by mid-December, when the survivors finally straggle across the Niemen River.

The 30-month War of 1812, which begins June 18, will encourage U.S. manufacturing (it will otherwise gain nothing for either side) and U.S. agriculture will begin its long, slow yielding of supremacy to industry.

Russian colonists build Fort Ross (from *Rossiya*, meaning "Little Russia") above the mouth of California's Russian River as a base from which to hunt sea otters and grow food for Russian fur-trading colonies such as the one at Sitka, Alaska (*see* below).

British wheat prices soar to £30 per cwt, the highest level ever and one that will not be matched for another 160 years (*see* 1798; 1834).

Russian chemist Gottlieb Sigismund Iorchoff suggests the first understanding of catalytic processes. He shows that starch breaks down to the simple sugar glucose when boiled with dilute sulfuric acid.

An English canning factory at Bermondsey established by Bryan Donkin produces tinned foods for British naval and military forces, but such foods remain unavailable to the public, which is hard pressed by high food prices (*see* 1810; Donkin-Hall, 1814).

The first known recipe for tomato ketchup is published by émigré American cook James Mease, who supported the British in the American Revolution and has moved to Nova Scotia. He calls the condiment, which he made in New Jersey prior to 1782, "love apple or tomato catchup." Previous recipes for ketchup, or catsup (a term derived from the Malay Chinese dialect word *kechap*) have been for a spicy, soy-based fish sauce. Mease writes that "love apples" make a fine ketchup, which is used by the French in a variety of dishes, but he neglects to advise readers to strain the ketchup (*see* Kitchiner, 1816).

Creoles at New Orleans chop up tomatoes for gumbos and jambalayas, but elsewhere in America, and in Europe, the tomato remains almost almost entirely a garden ornamental (*see* 1820).

Russian colonists at Fort Ross in California (above) plant apple trees (including some that produce the slightly lopsided, round, red-flecked yellow Gravenstein variety) and other fruits (*see* grapes, 1817). Originally from northern Europe, Gravensteins will be harvested in August and September from vast orchards outside Sebastopol, north of Yerba Buena (San Francisco), and will be widely used in applesauce and apple juice as well as for eating.

1813

Former U.S. Secretary of State James Madison, 51, is inaugurated March 4 as fourth president of the United States; his wife, Dolley (*née* Payne), 40, serves ice cream at the inauguration party (*see* Jefferson, 1802).

The British East India Company loses its monopoly in the India trade but continues to monopolize the China trade (*see* 1833).

Continental Grain Company has its beginnings as French merchant Simon Fribourg, 31, moves with his wife from the Moselle Valley in Lorraine to the Belgian hill town of Arlon and begins trading in wheat and oats (*see* 1848).

Commercial salt production begins at Syracuse, N.Y., to compensate for the cutoff of salt shipments from Bermuda and Europe occasioned by the War of 1812 (*see* 1786; 1863).

English inventor Edward Howard devises a vacuum pan that will spur the growth of the canning industry; he will obtain a patent in 1835 (*see* 1849; Borden, 1853).

Théorie élémentaire de la Botanique by Swiss botanist Augustin-Pyrame de Candolle, 35, advances the sciences of plant morphology, taxonomy, and physiology beyond the levels established by Linnaeus in his *Philosophia Botanica* of 1750.

A flight of passenger pigeons seen by Haitian-born U.S. painter John James Audubon, 28, takes 3 days to pass overhead; Audubon describes it as a "torrent of life" (*see* 1803; 1830; Wilson, 1810).

France has 334 sugar plantations by year's end and has produced 35,000 tons of beet sugar (*see* 1814; Delessert, 1811).

"A Vindication of Natural Diet Based on a French Tract, The Return to Nature" (pamphlet) by English poet Percy Bysshe Shelley, 21, begins, "I hold that the depravity of the physical and moral nature of man originated in his unnatural habits of life." Shelley maintains that man was originally an herbivore and says, "There is no disease, bodily or mental, which adoption of a vegetable diet and pure water has not infallibly mitigated, wherever the experiment has been fairly tried."

Noilly Prat vermouth is introduced in France.

✖ Europe ends 22 years of war April 11 with Napoleon's unconditional abdication, and America's 3-year War of 1812 draws to a close with the Treaty of Ghent December 24.

French statesman Charles-Maurice de Talleyrand-Périgord, 60, is instrumental in restoring the French monarchy in the person of the 59-year-old comte de Provence, who will reign until 1824 as Louis XVIII. He names Talleyrand to the post of foreign minister and Talleyrand attends the Congress of Vienna, which convenes in September to work out a European peace settlement. Assisted by his niece, the comtesse de Dino, and chef Marie-Antoine (Antonin) Carême, 30, Talleyrand entertains four times each week at the French embassy in the Johannesgasse with dinners of 36 covers—four services, beginning with the relevées and entrées, followed by the roasts and salads, then the entremets, and, finally, the desserts. Talleyrand's guests are so impressed by Carême's ris de veau Florentine, spinach en branche, soufflés of ham with Madeira sauce, and eggs with crayfish tails, sherbets, compôtes, and cheeses that the foreign minister, who was originally excluded from all the committees, soon has them eating out of his hand and is presiding over the committees (*see* 1815).

✊ The duke of Sutherland George Granville Leveson-Gower, 56, destroys the homes of Highlanders on his Scottish estates to make way for sheep (*see* 1807). The duke is married to the countess of Sutherlandshire, and by 1822 he will have driven 8,000 to 10,000 people off her lands, which make up two-thirds of the county.

London banker Alexander Baring, 40, takes the position in a parliamentary debate that the working classes have no interest at stake in the question of British wheat exports and that it is "altogether ridiculous" to argue otherwise: "Whether wheat is 130s. or 80s., the labourer [can] only expect dry bread in the one case and dry bread in the other" (Parliament has allowed free export of wheat, and protests have come from manufacturing districts as food prices have risen) (*see* Corn Law, 1815).

💲 Parliament outlaws Scottish Highland stills with capacities below 500 gallons (*see* 1798). Its objec-

tive is to concentrate distilling in fewer hands, thus facilitating collection of taxes on Scotch whisky, but illicit stills continue to operate (*see* 1823).

French beet sugar production declines sharply as imports of cane sugar resume and undercut prices.

✒ Cookbooks: *L'Art du cuisinier* by Antoine de Beauvilliers of the Grand Taverne de Londres (*see* 1782), who closed his Paris restaurant during the Revolution but reopened it toward the end of the Directory. He extols such British dishes as "woiches rabettes," "plombpoutingue," and "machepotetesse." *The Universal Receipt Book, or Complete Family Directory* compiled by "A Society of Gentlemen in New York."

Hortus Jamaicensis by English botanist John Lunan uses the word "grapefruit" for the first time. The fact that the citrus fruit grows in grapelike clusters has evidently suggested the name (*see* Shaddock, 1696, 1751; Don Philippe, 1840).

England's Donkin-Hall factory introduces the first foods to be sold commercially in tins (*see* 1810; Dagett and Kensett, 1819).

The invention of the madeleine cake will be credited by some to Avice, pastry chef to Talleyrand (above) (but *see* 1725; Ranhofer, 1894).

A porter tun bursts at London's Horse Shoe brewery near Tottenham Court Road, killing eight people by "drowning, injury, Porter fumes, or drunkennes."

🥫 Colman's Mustard has its beginnings as English flour miller Jeremiah Colman of Norwich takes over a mustard and flour mill at Stoke Holy Cross, four miles south of the city (*see* Keen's, 1742). Colman, who bought a windmill at Magdalen Gate, Norwich, 10 years ago and started a flour business, decides to mill mustard in addition to flour, using fine brown and white mustard seed. He will establish himself in the mustard business in 1823, and by 1856 the concern will be so large that Colman will have to buy new premises just outside Norwich at Carrow on the Wensum River (Norwich will grow to envelop Carrow). Grocers throughout Britain will carry yellow-labeled red tins of Colman's Mustard, and it will be supplied to the Army and Royal Navy (*see* 1866).

1814

China was more concerned about a possible shortage of farm hands than having more mouths to feed.

China's population reaches nearly 375 million by some accounts, while India's has remained constant at about 150 million. Japan, which has a system of primogeniture that makes too many sons a problem, controls her population with infanticide, but in China, where infanticide has been used in the past and where methods of abortion are well known, there is less concern about having too many mouths to feed. China's high infant mortality rates keep the population from outgrowing the nation's food supply, and families are encouraged to have many sons.

1815

France's foreign minister Talleyrand-Périgord signs an alliance in January with Britain and Austria against Prussia, having won support for the French monarchy by means of gastronomy (*see* 1814).

Napoleon returns from exile but is defeated by Britain's 46-year-old Arthur Wellesley, duke of Wellington, with Prussian help at the Battle of Waterloo June 18. A Waterloo victory pie is created by English bakers, who use specially built ovens to make a meat pie that can feed hundreds of people. A dinner at the Louvre Palace celebrates the restoration of the French monarchy: chef Antonin Carême supervises preparations of the banquet for Louis XVIII and 1,200 guests.

Britain suffers economic depression as demand for military supplies abruptly ceases and Continental markets are unable to absorb backlogged inventories of English manufactured goods. Prices fall, thousands are thrown out of work, and 400,000 demobilized troops add to the problems of unemployment.

A Corn Law enacted by Parliament March 23 helps British landlords to maintain prices by restricting grain imports. The law permits wheat to enter the country duty-free only when the average domestic price exceeds a "famine" level of 80 shillings per bushel, but unemployment reduces demand, and the price of wheat falls to 9 shillings per bushel, down from a record 14 shillings, 6 pence in 1812 (*see* 1838).

Parliament repeals the 1266 Assize Laws with regard to the price of bread. The standard-size loaves of bread remain, but without price controls (*see* 1822).

Cookbook: *Le Pâtissier royal parisien* by Antonin Carême includes recipes for entremets as well as for pastries.

German and British gastronomes and gourmands help France's economy by flocking to enjoy Gallic cuisine.

Royal Doulton potteries is established in England.

The volcano Tambora on the island of Sumbawa in the East Indies erupts April 5, killing 20,000 and producing tidal waves and whirlwinds that raise enormous clouds of dust that will affect climatic conditions throughout the world (*see* agriculture, 1816).

Thomas Jefferson writes from Monticello March 21, "We have had a method of planting corn suggested by a Mr. Hall which dispenses with the plough entirely." Farmers have followed the Indian practice of planting their cornfields in "check-rows," dragging a four-runner sled over a field first in one direction and then in the other and cultivating between the rows thus created. Jefferson, now nearly 72, explains how Hall's patented process marks off the ground in squares, with a grain of corn and manure placed at each intersection, but is pleased that Hall "has given me the right to use it, for I certainly should not have thought the right worth 50.D. the price of a licence" (*see* corn planter, 1857).

Dutch chocolate and cocoa merchant Conrad J. van Houten establishes a chocolate factory that will begin the use of chocolate as a food in addition to its use as a beverage. Cocoa was considered an aristocratic drink before the French Revolution and its popularity has waned since 1789, partly because coffee is considered more Protestant and businesslike, partly because of cocoa's association with courtiers and clergymen (especially Jesuits, who have been accused of trying to monopolize the cacao trade). Van Houten has been in business since 1806 (*see* 1828; Cailler, 1819).

Russian soldiers bivouac in the Place de la Concorde and under the trees of the Tuileries and the Champs-Elysées at Paris following the Battle of Waterloo (above), and by some accounts they introduce the word "bistro" for café by ordering waiters to bring orders "*bystro, bystro*" (quickly, quickly). French café owners cover their counters with zinc to protect them from fist marks and wine stains (the word "zinc" will become a generic for café).

1816

Ireland's potato crop fails in August; excessive rain is blamed, and many go hungry in the resulting famine (*see* agriculture, below).

Cookbooks: *Apicius Redivivus; or, The Cook's Oracle: Wherein . . .* by London physician William Kitchiner, 46, gives exact recipes of ingredients and their order of use in recipes (*see* Apicius, 14 B.C.; Mrs. Beeton, 1861). Married in 1790 and divorced soon after, Dr. Kitchiner has hired the chef Henry Osborne to teach him the rudiments of cookery (his book includes some of Osborne's original recipes). At the bachelor residence he maintains at 43 Warren Street, Fitzroy Square, the abstemious Dr. Kitchiner gives luncheons and dinners consisting of but one course at a time when most formal dinners consist of three to five, each containing several dishes of the same sort of food (soups, fish, poultry, game, meat, vegetables, fruits, desserts, pastries, and savories), all placed on the table at the same time along with lavishly decanted wines, with guests given supper early in the morning. In his introduction, Kitchiner says, "The following Recipes are not a mere marrowless collection of shreds and patches, of cuttings and pastings—but a bonâfide register of practical facts—accumulated by a

perseverance, not to be subdued or evaporated by the igniferous Terrors of a Roasting Fire in the Dogdays;—in defiance of odoriferous and calefaceous repellents of Roasting, Boiling, Frying and Broiling; moreover, the author has submitted to a labour no preceding Cookery-Book-maker, perhaps, ever attempted to encounter,—having *eaten* each receipt before he set it down in his book. . . . *My receipts* are the results of experiments, carefully made and accurately and circumstantially related. *The time* requisite for dressing being stated. *The quantities* of the various articles contained in each composition being set down in *number, weight,* and *measure.*" Meat, says Kitchiner, should always be hung for "such a time . . . as will render it tender, which the finest meat cannot be, unless hung . . . till it had made some advance towards putrefaction." By the time he dies in 1823, Dr. Kitchiner's book will have gone through several editions and 15,000 copies will be in print. It will go through 13 English and six American editions (*see* ketchup, below).

French Trappist monks in northern Touraine invent Port au Salut cheese, using the milk of four cows to begin a major industry (*see* Port du Salut, 1878).

The Cook's Oracle (above) gives a recipe for gelatin, a portable soup whose preparation calls for boiling various bones. The resulting liquid, seasoned with salt and pepper, is boiled down to a syrup-like consistency and then poured into shallow pans to jell. The gelatin is then cut into small pieces and dried out for a week or so, after which it can be "preserved" for several years in "any climate." To make soup, the gelatin is simply dissolved in hot water: spices and vegetable extracts are then added.

The Cook's Oracle (above) gives a recipe for "tomata" ketchup containing anchovies and strained tomato pulp (*see* Mease, 1812; Randolph, 1824).

French chef Antonin Carême goes to work for the British prince regent, who has ruled since 1811. He has created beef Stroganov and Charlotte russe (ladyfingers with Bavarian cream) for the Russian czar Aleksandr I, from whose palace he has sent home secret information to the French foreign minister Talleyrand-Périgord (*see* 1815); paid an extraordinary salary of £1,000 per year by the prince regent (who also grants him the right to sell all uneaten pastries from the royal table), Carême continues to serve Talleyrand as he prepares food for the British.

Cold weather persists through summer in much of the world's temperate zones, apparently as a result of dust in the atmosphere following last year's volcanic eruption in the East Indies. Frost occurs from Canada to Virginia every night from June 6 to June 9, laundry laid out to dry on the grass at Plymouth, Conn., June 10 is found frozen stiff, heavy snows fall in the Northeast in June and July, and frost kills crops in what farmers will call "eighteen hundred and froze to death."

Cape Cod, Mass., cranberry production gets a boost from the discovery that cranberry vines grow more vigorously in places where the wind has blown sand over a mat of wild vines. The observation by Henry Hall at Dennis will lead to draining of swampy wastelands and development of commercial bogs growing a berry that is closely related to the European lingonberry.

Cinzano vermouth is introduced by an Italian vintner whose firm will become the world's largest vermouth bottler, exporting sweet vermouths from Italy and dry vermouths from France.

1817

Ireland has famine following the failure of last year's potato crop; thousands starve (*see* 1821; emigration, below).

U.S. farm prices fall as Europe's peace ends the foreign markets that have taken some of America's farm surpluses.

The Cumberland Road reaches west from Cumberland on the Potomac River to Wheeling, Va., on the Ohio. The road has a 30-foot wide gravel center on a stone base (*see* 1811; 1852).

Gov. De Witt Clinton, 48, of New York orders construction of a 363-mile Erie Canal, which will connect Buffalo on Lake Erie with Troy on the Hudson River. The state legislature authorizes state funds for the canal, and ground is broken July 4 (*see* 1819).

The Bartlett pear gets its name by some accounts from Massachusetts farmer Enoch Bartlett, 38, who buys the orchard in which Stairs pears, similar to the bon Chrétien grown in Europe, were planted in 1798 by Roxbury farmer-sea captain Thomas Brewer (*see* 1769; 1848).

"The hunter or savage state," writes President James Monroe, 59, "requires a greater extent of territory to sustain it than is compatible with progress and just claims of civilized life . . . and must yield to it."

Hereford cattle are imported into the United States for the first time and raised in Virginia. The English breed will become the dominant cattle breed on the western plains (*see* Corning, Sotham, 1840).

Russian colonists at Fort Ross plant the first grapevines seen in northern California (*see* 1814; Vallejo, 1841).

The German beer Bitburger Bräu is produced for the first time in the Eifel Hills of Bitburg, near the French border.

The Milan coffee shop Cova opens in the via Montenapoleone.

Irish emigration begins on a large scale as thousands die in the potato famine (above). Potatoes have provided a cheap source of food that has helped the country's population reach 6.5 million, up from just over 5 million in 1801.

1818

The Peul Diallo dynasty, which has ruled on Africa's Niger River since the 15th century, ends in a coup d'état by the Muslim usurper Marabout Cheikou Ahmadou. He will organize the movement of nomads in the region and establish patterns designed to conserve grass and water.

U.S. ships make 15 voyages to Sumatra for black pepper (*see* 1805; 1873).

London's Donkin, Hall & Gamble Preservatory in Blue Anchor Road, Bermondsey, turns out satisfactory canned soup, veal, mutton and vegetable stew, carrots, and beef (both boiled and corned, meaning salted), but tinned foods will not be available in food stores until 1830.

The tin can is introduced to America by Peter Durand (*see* 1810; 1847).

Slaughtering hogs and packing them in brine-filled barrels became a Cincinnati specialty. LIBRARY OF CONGRESS

Cincinnati begins packing pork in brine-filled barrels. Salt pork is a U.S. food staple, and Cincinnati will come to be called "Porkopolis."

Swiss chocolate maker Amédée Kohler founds a firm that will specialize in making confections (*see* Peter, 1904). French confectioners (the word *confection* originally meant a medicinal preparation made palatable with sugar, syrup, or honey) have been making chocolate almonds since 1670, and chocolate has long been used to flavor light cakes known as puffs (*see* Cailler, 1819; van Houten, 1828).

Clove trees are introduced into Zanzibar by the French, who have been growing cloves with great success on their Pacific islands (*see* 1778; Penang, 1800). The trees will by some accounts not be introduced into Zanzibar until the 1830s, when the new sultan, Sayyid Said, plants them in the gardens of his palace, but that island and the neighboring island of Pemba, 25 miles to the northeast, will grow to account for the major part of the world's production of cloves and clove oil, although Zanzibar cloves are less aromatic than those grown on Amboina (*see* hurricane, 1872).

 Angostura bitters are invented at Angostura, Venezuela, by German physician Johann Gottlieb Benja-

min Siegert, who served as a surgeon under Blücher 3 years ago at Waterloo and has emigrated to South America. Siegert brews his elixir from gentian root, rum, and other ingredients as a stomach tonic to overcome debility and loss of appetite in the tropics, but it will gain wider use as a cocktail ingredient used by British colonials to make "pink gin." Siegert's son will take the formula to Trinidad and produce Angostura bitters in an abandoned monastery at Port of Spain until long after Angostura has become Ciudad Bolívar (*see* 1878).

Cherry Heering is introduced at Copenhagen by local grocer Peter Heering, who uses Baltic cherries to make the distilled cordial that begins as a sideline but soon eclipses Heering's grocery business.

1819

Spain cedes eastern Florida to the United States February 22 along with all Spanish possessions east of the Mississippi.

Singapore is occupied by the East India Company on orders from colonial administrator Thomas Stamford Raffles, 38, lieutenant governor of Bengkulu in West Sumatra. Acting without authority, Raffles persuades the sultan and tenggong of Johore (who himself has no authority to do so) to cede the fishing village to Britain. Raffles, who aims to counter Dutch influence in the region, makes Singapore a crown colony, and it is soon a prosperous trading post, but Raffles holds his nose in July and runs the other way whenever he encounters the overpoweringly foul smell of the durian fruit (from the *Durio zibethinus* tree), whose sweet, custardy yellow flesh is prized by the locals above all other fruit but whose odor is detested by Europeans (*see* 1826; Raffles Hotel, 1886).

The first stretch of the Erie Canal opens after 2 years of construction to connect Utica and Rome, N.Y. (*see* 1818; 1825).

Automated flour-mill inventor Oliver Evans dies at New York April 21 at age 63.

An improved iron plow, patented by Cayuga County, N.Y., farmer Jethro Wood, 45, is constructed in several major pieces so that a farmer who breaks one part can replace it without having to buy a whole new plow. Other plow makers will infringe on Wood's patent, and many farmers will refuse to give up their old wooden plows, insisting that cast-iron plows poison the soil (*see* 1784; Deere, 1837).

Salmon, lobster meat, and oysters are packed in tin cans at New York by Ezra Daggett and Thomas Kensett (*see* Donkin-Hall, 1814; Kensett's patent, 1825).

Vermont inventor John Conant patents an iron cooking stove, but U.S. cooks and housewives spurn his stove, preferring the traditional practice of hearthside cooking (*see* 1795; 1850).

The world's first eating chocolate to be produced commercially is manufactured at Vevey, Switzerland by François-Louis Cailler, 23, who introduces the first chocolate to be prepared and sold in blocks made by machine. (Chocolate for beverage use has long been sold in cakes, made with a cornstarch binder and often containing sugar and spices.) Cailler starts a company that will specialize in fondants, but his chocolate is not candy (*see* Kohler, 1818; van Houten, 1828; Peter and Kohler, 1911).

U.S. diplomats in foreign posts receive instructions to send home any valuable new seeds and plants.

The first modern strawberries (called *Fragaria ananassa* because of their pineapple fragrance) are produced in England, where they are sold as Keen's seedlings (*see* 1800). Descended from plants that originated in Virginia and on South America's Pacific coast, the hybrids will be exported to the United States and give rise to an industry.

The Travellers' Club is founded at London, admitting to membership only men who have traveled at least 500 miles in a straight line from the city (foreign diplomats will be received as honorary visitors) (*see* Paris club, 1902).

1820

Congress enacts a land law April 24 allowing a farmer to purchase 80 acres of public land at $1.25 per acre in cash. A man can now buy a farm for $100 with no need for further payments, thousands of farmers are in debt to the government for public lands on which they have made down payments of only $80 each, and farmers who have paid in full are angry (*see* 1804).

The mechanical cultivator is introduced into agriculture, eliminating the need for hand power in weeding corn and giving farmers a tool superior to the crude plows they have used for the purpose (year approximate). The practical seed drill that will be introduced in the next decade or two along with the corn planter will increase the efficiency of farming (*see* harvester, 1831).

Sugar refining is New York City's second most important industry, surpassed only by ironworks and followed closely by brewing. Hogsheads of sugar, each containing 1,000 pounds, leave the city's refineries each day for shipment to inland cities and towns.

Fiction: *The Sketch Book* by Geoffrey Crayon (New York author Washington Irving, 37) contains "The Legend of Sleepy Hollow," which describes "the simple charms of a genuine Dutch country tea table": He describes "an enormous dish of balls of sweetened dough, fried in hog's fat, and called doughnuts, or oly koeks. . . . Such heaped-up platters of cakes of various and almost indescribable kinds known only to experienced Dutch housewives. There was the doughty doughnut, the tender oly koek, and the crisp and crumbling kruller" (*see* ring doughnut, 1847).

Neapolitan marine painter Michel Felice Corne plants tomatoes in his large garden at Newport, R.I. He had no success when he planted them 18 years ago at Salem, Mass., but he persuades his neighbors at Newport that tomatoes are good to eat and they are soon growing and eating tomatoes themselves.

Salem County, N.J., Horticultural Society president Col. Robert Gibbon Johnson eats a raw tomato in front of a skeptical crowd at the Salem courthouse in September, defying predictions that it will soon kill him. He has experimented with tomatoes in his garden and takes pleasure in eating them (*see* 1861).

Nebraska Territory is "a great American desert," says U.S. Army officer Stephen Harriman Long, 36, who commands an exploring expedition into the Rocky Mountains (*see* Pike, 1806; Deere, 1837; irrigation, 1848).

French chemist M. H. Braconnot isolates the amino acid glycine from gelatin and then proceeds to isolate leucine from muscle tissue. Amino acids will be found to combine in various ways to form protein, the basic substance of all living tissue (*see* 1816; Mulder, 1838).

A Treatise on Adulterations of Food and Culinary Poisons, exhibiting the fraudulent sophistications of bread, beer, wine, spirituous liquors, tea, coffee, cream, confectionery, vinegar, mustard, pepper, cheese, olive oil, pickles, and other articles employed in domestic economy and Methods for Detecting them by German-born English chemist Frederic Accum, 51, names names and enrages the vested interests, forcing Accum to flee to Berlin to avoid public trial. A professor at the Surrey Institution, Accum has shown that pepper is almost invariably adulterated with mustard husks, pea flour, juniper berries, and sweepings from storeroom floors; counterfeit China tea is made from dried thorn leaves colored with poisonous verdigris; pickles are treated with copper to look green (*see* 1850).

Johnnie Walker Scotch whisky has its beginnings in a grocery, wine, and spirit business opened at Kilmarnock, Scotland, by Ayrshireman John Walker, whose son Alexander will introduce the whisky that will become the world's largest-selling brand (*see* 1814 law). Like other such Scotch whiskies, Walker's

will be aged in oak casks that have previously been used to store sherry, which has soaked into the staves. The barrels give the new, white whisky a golden hue (*see* 1823).

Beefeater gin has its beginnings in a London distillery founded by James Burroughs.

Champagne producer Nicole-Barbe Clicquot (the "Veuve Clicquot") retires at age 43 to her château, where she will live until her death in 1866 (*see* 1796; Clicquot Club, 1901).

The Paris catering firm Potel & Chavot is founded by two French traiteurs. From 1829 to 1846 they will be *fournisseurs à la Court de France* (*see* Eiffel, 1889).

The U.S. population reaches 9.6 million, with some 83 percent of gainfully employed Americans engaged in agriculture.

1821

Ireland's potato crop fails again, as it did in 1816. The resulting famine, from Donegal to Youghal, will cause perhaps 50,000 deaths by the end of next year from starvation and allied diseases as an epidemic of fever in the western counties strikes a population weakened by hunger (*see* population, 1840).

Fire destroys part of New York, including a market at the end of Fulton Street that has been on the site since the middle of the last century. The land was donated to the city by the Beekman Estate in 1807 on condition that it remain a market (*see* 1822).

Game birds shot by market hunters are mainstays of the U.S. diet. A single market hunter kills 18,000 (48,000 by some accounts) migrating golden plover in March. Heath hen and prairie chicken are standard items on U.S. tables.

1822

Brazil's Portuguese regent, Dom Pedro, 24, proclaims independence from his father, João IV, who returned to Portugal last year after 13 years in exile, during which time feijoada—made of beans, two kinds of Portuguese sausages, pork, and garnishes— became established as the Brazilian national dish (*see* 1569; cacao, below).

Potato crops fail in the west of Ireland, as they will do again to some degree in 1831, 1835, 1836, and—most disastrously—in the mid-1840s (*see* 1739; 1816; 1821).

The first U.S. spice-grinding company is established at Boston by English immigrant William Underwood, who from 1812 to 1817 was apprentice to the London shop MacKey & Co., picklers and perservers. He opens a shop on Boston's Russia Wharf, where he produces a ground mustard from imported seed. By employing English-style labels on the bottles and tin canisters that contain his dry ground mustard and selling his product at a price 25 percent below that of imported English mustards, Underwood will drive the English out of the Charleston and New Orleans markets in the next 4 years (*see* fish, shellfish, 1846).

New York's Fulton Market reopens on the East River (*see* 1821). In addition to fresh catches from the fishing fleet, it receives produce from Long Island farms; new structures will be erected in 1831 and 1848, but the butchers' and greengrocers' stalls will move westward to the Hudson (North) River by the middle of the century, leaving the Fulton Market to fishmongers (*see* 1880).

U.S. Army physician William Beaumont, 37, begins pioneer observations on the action of human gastric juices (*see* Réaumur, 1752). Serving on Michilmacinac (Mackinac) Island in the strait between Lakes Michigan and Huron, Beaumont has saved the life of a young French-American voyageur employed by John Jacob Astor's American Fur Co., but the shotgun blast wound in St. Martin's left side has not completely healed and the remaining fistula permits Beaumont to make his studies (*see* 1833; hydrochloric acid, 1824).

The Japanese periodical *Ryoritsu* (*Culinary Connoisseur*) begins publication at Edo under the director of local restaurateur Zenshiro, who continues the restaurant Yaozen opened in 1716 by his eponymous great-grandfather. Famous artists such as Hokusai will contribute illustrations for it, and famous calligraphers and writers will also contribute. The periodical will continue for 70 years, and the restaurant will still be operating in 1995.

Poetry: New York lexicographer Clement Clark Moore, 44, goes by sleigh to Washington Market (*see* 1790) to buy a Christmas turkey on the evening of December 23 and gets the idea for a poem that will be published anonymously exactly 1 year hence under the title "A Visit from St. Nicholas." Since poultry spoils easily, householders try to purchase their holiday birds on December 23 or 24 (*see* Washington Market, 1940).

Vicomte François-René de Chateaubriand, 54, serves as French minister to the Court of St. James's at London, where his personal chef gives the name "chateaubriand" to the cut at the end of the beef tenderloin.

The Portuguese lose Brazil (above) but have planted cacao beans on their African islands of Principe and São Tomé to start an industry (the neighboring Spanish island of Fernando Po has cacao trees descended from seeds planted by Hernando Cortés in the 16th century).

Parliament enacts legislation outlawing the old standard British half-peck and quarter-peck loaves of bread: the only legal weights for loaves henceforth are to be the 16-ounce avoirdupois pound or fractions or multiples thereof. But the new law applies only to London and districts within 10 miles of the Royal Exchange (*see* 1836).

French vintner Charles Heidsick of Reims produces his first champagne.

The Café de Paris opens on the Boulevard des Italiens, Paris, where it will be a meeting place for the *haut monde* until 1894.

1823

A new British excise tax forces illegal Highland distilleries (there are an estimated 14,000 of them) to close down (*see* 1814). The government lowers the tax, on the premise that it will gain more revenue by collecting smaller taxes from many distillers than larger taxes, which are widely evaded, and agrees to license stills with capacities of as little as 40 gallons. Legal distilleries replace them, and the quality of Scotch whisky improves markedly after at least 2 centuries in which whisky making has been a major industry. With lower taxes, Lowland distillers will be encouraged to blend their product (Edinburgh distiller Andrew

Usher will introduce the first blended Scotch whisky) and mature it in used sherry casks for 3 or more years while Highlanders will continue making single-malt whiskies. Smugglers scoff at the idea of paying taxes, and distillers who comply with the new law are regarded as traitors (but *see* Glenlivet, 1824).

China's monopoly in the tea trade begins to fade as an indigenous tea bush is found growing in northern India's Upper Assam. Acting for the British government, Charles Bruce smuggles knowledgeable coolies out of China and puts them to work transplanting young tea bushes into nursery beds to begin tea plantations that will be more efficiently organized than Chinese plantations (*see* 1839).

English chemist-physicist Michael Faraday, 31, pioneers mechanical refrigeration with the discovery that certain gases, when kept under constant pressure, will condense until they cool (*see* Perkins, 1834; Gorrie, 1842).

Nonfiction: "A Dissertation upon Roast Pig" by English essayist Charles Lamb, 48, appears in the *London Magazine*: "Mankind, says a Chinese manuscript which my friend M. was obliging enough to read and explain to me, for the first seventy thousand ages ate their meat raw, clawing or biting it from the living animal, just as they do in Abyssinia to this day." The "manuscript" relates the tale of a Chinese boy, Bo-bo, who sets his house afire and accidentally discovers the virtue of "burnt," or cooked, pig. Bo-bo, says Lamb's "manuscript," called to his father, "The pig, the pig! Do come and taste how good the burnt pig eats"; his father, Ho-ti, was horrified at what his son had done, his ears "tingled with horror; he cursed his son, and he cursed himself that ever he should beget a son that should eat burnt pig. Bo-bo was strictly enjoined not to let the secret escape, for the neighbors would certainly have stoned them for a couple of abominable wretches, who could think of improving upon the good meat which God had sent them. Nevertheless, strange stories got about. It was observed that Ho-ti's small cottage was burnt down now more frequently than ever. . . . As often as the sow farrowed, so sure was the house of Ho-ti to be ablaze; and Ho-ti himself, which was the more remarkable, instead of chastising his son, seemed to grow more indulgent to him than ever. At length they were watched,

the terrible mystery discovered, and father and son summoned to take their trial at Pekin. . . . Evidence was given, the obnoxious food itself produced at court, and verdict about to be pronounced, when the foreman of the jury begged that some of the burnt pig, of which the culprits had been accused, might be handed into the jury box. He handled it, and they all handled it, and burning their fingers, as Bo-bo and his father had done before them, and Nature prompting to each of them the same remedy, against the face of all the facts, and the clearest charge which charge had ever given,—to the surprise of . . . all present, without leaving the box, or any manner of consultation whatever, they brought in a simultaneous verdict of Not Guilty. . . . Thus this custom of firing houses continued, till, in the process of time, says my manuscript, a sage arose, like our Locke, who made a discovery, that the flesh of swine, or indeed of any other animal, might be cooked (*burnt* as they call it) without the necessity of consuming a whole house to dress it. Then first began the rude form of the gridiron. Roasting by the string, or by the spit, came a century or two later, I forget in whose dynasty. Of all the delicacies in the whole *mundus edibilis* I will maintain it to be the most delicate. . . . There is no flavour comparable . . . to that of the crisp, tawny, well-matched, not over-roasted, *crackling*. . . . The very teeth are invited to their share of the pleasure at this banquet in overcoming the coy, brittle resistance—with the adhesive oleaginous—O call it not fat—but an indefinable sweetness growing up to it—the tender blossoming of fat—fat cropped in the bud—taken in the shoot—in the first innocence. . . . The lean, no lean, but a kind of animal manna—or rather, fat and lean . . . so blended and running into each other, that both together make but one ambrosian result." Lamb's essay is more than a tribute to pork and a tongue-in-cheek account of its incorporation into the Chinese diet.

Charles Lamb (above) receives a gift of Stilton cheese and describes it as "the best I've ever tasted. . . . The delicatest, rainbow-hued melting piece I have ever tasted."

Bourbon whiskey distilling increases in Kentucky (*see* Craig, 1789). Aging in charred oak barrels will not begin until 1860, and whiskey will not take on color until then (the color will generally derive more from added caramel than from wood char).

Old Crow bourbon whiskey has its beginnings in a sour mash produced according to scientific principles by Kentucky distiller James Crow.

Shakers build the first round barn at their Hancock, N.Y., community (*see* 1784). It has a silo at its center with stalls and stanchions radiating outward to save steps in feeding the livestock. In years to come the round barn will be widely adopted by midwestern dairy farmers.

The U.S. Army Corps of Engineers embarks on a career of building harbors, damming and channeling river, and generally developing waterways and other civil projects under terms of a bill signed by President Monroe May 24 to establish the corps, which had its real beginnings in 1775 when George Washington appointed Col. Richard Gridley chief engineer to the Continental Army just before the Battle of Bunker Hill. The corps will play a significant role in developing U.S. waterways and highways that will help farmers and ranchers get their products to market.

A Road Survey Act passed by Congress April 30 authorizes the Army Corps of Engineers (above) to survey possible road and canal routes.

London physician William Prout, 39, isolates hydrochloric acid from stomach juices and establishes that it is the chief agent of human digestion (*see* Beaumont, 1822; pepsin, 1835).

Cookbook: *The Virginia Housewife* by Mary Randolph, 72, is the first regional American cookbook. It contains recipes for such Southern specialties as Virginia ham, turtle soup, and gooseberry fool and has 13 recipes for tomatoes, including one for ketchup much like those found in British receipt books (*see* 1830).

Colby cheese has its beginnings in a Vermont factory started at Healdville by local dairyman Alfred Crowley, whose family will make the cheese for more than 170 years. A variation on cheddar, Colby is softer and more openly textured but less long-lasting than cheddar since it contains more moisture.

New York novelist James Fenimore Cooper, 34, starts the Bread and Cheese Society, inviting William Cullen Bryant, Washington Irving, Samuel F. B. Morse, and Daniel Webster to join.

Shakers introduced new ideas, but women's participation in farming was as old as the hills.

The Rhode Island red hen is produced at Little Compton, R.I., by a sea captain who has crossbred several domestic poultry breeds with an assortment of exotic fowl brought from the Orient. The Rhode Island red will be famous for its brown eggs, which New Englanders will prefer to white eggs, which may not come from local hens and may therefore not be fresh.

Italy's first commercial pasta factory is started at Imperia on the Italian Riviera by Paolo B. Agnese, whose family will continue the business for more than 150 years (*see* Naples, 1785).

Cadbury's Chocolate has its beginnings March 4 in a tea and coffee shop opened by Birmingham, England, Quaker John Cadbury, 23, who has served an apprenticeship at Leeds and for bonded teahouses in London. Given a sum of money by his father and told to sink or swim, Cadbury starts his business next door to his father's draper's shop and will install Birmingham's first plate glass window, employ a Chinese to preside over his tea counter, and experiment with grinding cocoa beans using a mortar and pestle. By 1841, Cadbury's product list will include 15 kinds of drinking and eating chocolate and 10 forms of cocoa, including Grenada, Spanish, Broma, and Trinidad (*see* Cadbury Brothers, 1847).

The name Baker Chocolate Co. is adopted by the 60-year-old Hannon Chocolate Co. now operated by Walter Baker, grandson of James, who advertises his products as far west as Ohio and Indiana (*see* 1779; Postum Co., 1927).

The Royal Navy reduces its daily rum ration from half a pint to a quarter pint, and tea becomes part of the daily ration (*see* 1740; 1850).

The Glenlivet started by Scottish entrepreneur George Smith, 32, is the first licensed Scotch whisky distillery (*see* 1823). Smith, whose heretofore illicit distillery on his farm at Upper Drumin is in the Highlands' most notorious smuggling district, has been encouraged by the duke of Gordon to apply for a distilling licence, and although Smith is initially regarded as a blackleg and must go about fully armed lest he be murdered, and although licensed distilleries established later in this decade will be burned by smugglers, smuggling will fade by the mid-1830s and Smith will continue producing his malt whisky until his death in 1871 (*see* Coffee's still, 1830).

London's Athenaeum Club is founded. It will be renowned for its library but not for its food.

1825

The Erie Canal brought cheap grain from the Great Lakes to New York for shipment to foreign markets.

The Erie Canal opens October 26 to link the Great Lakes with the Hudson River and the Atlantic. Gov. De Witt Clinton greets the first canal boat on the $8 million state-owned canal, which is 363 miles long, 40 feet wide, and 4 feet deep, with tow paths for the mules that pull barges up and down its length at 1½ miles per hour. The time required to move freight from the Midwest to the Atlantic falls to 8 or 10 days, down from 20 to 30, freight rates immediately drop from $100 per ton to $5, New York City becomes the Atlantic port for the Midwest, and the canal makes boom towns of Buffalo, Rochester, Cleveland, Columbus, Detroit, Chicago, and Syracuse (*see* 1819; 1836; 1917).

Buffalo, N.Y., becomes the meat-packing center of the United States as the Erie Canal (above) makes it a central shipping point.

The first U.S. patent for tin-plated cans is issued to Thomas Kensett (*see* 1819; 1847).

Nathaniel Jarvis Wyeth, an associate of Frederic Tudor, patents an improved ice-harvesting method (*see* 1805). Tudor will use sawdust to insulate blocks of ice at Wyeth's suggestion (*see* voyage to India, 1833).

Brillat-Savarin (below) says that without truffles there can be no truly gastronomic meal. Truffles have been used at least occasionally in France since the late 14th century but Périgord truffles have been popular only since the late 15th century, and they were almost unknown in England until the 17th century.

British colonists in Ceylon plant coffee bushes (but *see* 1861).

Avocados, discovered by the Spanish conquistadors in Central America, now grow in Africa, Polynesia, and the Sandwich Islands (Hawaii) (*see* Perrine, 1833).

Haitian sugar production falls to below one ton, down from 27,000 tons in 1804.

Nonfiction: *The Physiology of Taste (Physiologie du goût), or Meditations on Transcendental Gastronomy* by Jean-Anthelme Brillat-Savarin, now 70, is published at his own expense at Paris. "Tell me what you eat and I will tell you what you are," says

"Tell me what you eat and I will tell you what you are," said French gastronome Brillat-Savarin.

Brillat-Savarin (*see* payplat, 1794). "In compelling man to eat that he may live, Nature gives an appetite to invite him and pleasure to reward him."

Water, says Brillat-Savarin (above), is "the only liquid which truly appeases thirst."

Arthur Bell & Sons Ltd. is founded at Perth, Scotland. It will grow to own the Dufftown-Glenlivet, Blair-Athol, and Inchgower distilleries.

French-American pharmacist Elias Magloire Durand opens a Philadelphia apothecary shop that will become famous for its carbonated water, served at the first U.S. "soda fountain" (*see* Silliman, 1807; Matthews, 1833).

1826

Singapore's founder Sir Thomas Raffles dies of apoplexy in England July 5 at age 45, 7 years after establishing the British crown colony (*see* 1819; Raffles Hotel, 1886).

Herkimer, N.Y., dairyman Sylvanus Ferris and cheese buyer Robert Nesbit develop a profitable scheme. Nesbit serves as advance man, turning down cheese offered for sale by farmers, hinting at a bad market, and deprecating the cheese. Ferris comes along later and buys the cheese at low prices for resale at high prices in the New York market.

Boston's Quincy Market opens August 26 across the cobble-stoned square from Faneuil Hall. Josiah Quincy's handsome Greek revival building will soon be surrounded by pushcarts.

The first commercially practicable gas stove is designed by Northampton, England, gas company executive James Sharp and is installed in the kitchen of his home. Sharp will open a factory to produce the stoves in 1836 (*see* Reform Club, 1838).

The first workable reaper joins two triangular knives to two horizontal bars at the front of a machine that is pushed through a field of ripe grain by two horses. Scotsman Patrick Bell's lower bar is fixed, while the upper bar is geared to the ground wheels to give it a reciprocal motion; revolving sails hold the grain to the knives while a canvas drum lays aside the stalks in a neat swath, but horses cannot see ahead, they resist pushing Bell's reaper, it is difficult to turn, and it will achieve only moderate success (*see* McCormick, 1831).

Jean-Anthelme Brillat-Savarin dies February 2 at age 70.

Scottish botanist David Douglas, 28, travels through the American northwest as a collector for the Horticulture Society of London and records in his journal November 17, "On this day with a few hard nuts and roots of *Phalangiun Quamash* I made a good breakfast" (*see* Clark, 1806). He calls the plant *Scilla esculenta*, compares its taste to that of baked pears, but notes that it has a tendency to cause flatulence (*see* Whitman, 1836).

An English biscuit company that will become Huntley & Palmer's is established at Reading by Thomas Huntley (*see* 1851).

The first tea to be retailed in sealed packages under a proprietary name is introduced by English Quaker

John Horniman, whose sealed, lead-lined packages have been designed in part to protect his tea from adulteration (*see* Accum, 1820). Horniman's tea will acquire an enviable reputation and make his firm the largest in the business (*see* Tetley, 1837; Salada, 1886; Lipton, 1890; White Rose, 1901; Lyons & Co., 1917)).

Boston's Union Oyster House opens in a Union Street house used as a home during his exile by the duc d'Orléans Philippe-Égalité, who returned to France and was guillotined in 1793.

1827

Sandwich glass is introduced at Sandwich, Mass., on Cape Cod by Deming Jarves, 37, who has improved on a crude pressing machine recently invented by Cambridge, Mass., glassmaker Enoch Robinson. Jarves's Boston and Sandwich Glass Co. has a monopoly on glass compounded with red lead and will continue production until 1888.

The "congreve" (later to be called the "lucifer") invented by English chemist (pharmacist) John Walker, 28, of Stockton-on-Tees is the first friction match and will come into wide use for lighting kitchen fires and stoves. Its head is made of potash, sugar, and gum arabic, and it must be drawn swiftly through a piece of folded sandpaper to ignite (*see* 1836).

The coffee percolator, invented by a Frenchman, permits the brewing water to pass continually over the coffee grounds.

Nonfiction: *The House Servants' Directory, or A Monitor for Private Families* by African-American author Robert Roberts contains, along with recipes, advice on domestic economy, deportment, and cooking, e.g., "If vegetables are a minute or two too long over the fire, they lose all their beauty and flavor."

Britain's George IV establishes a uniform standard for an acre of land, setting the measurement for an imperial (or statute) acre at 43,560 square feet (1/640th of a square mile). The standard is to apply throughout the United Kingdom, but parts of Scotland and Ireland will continue to use somewhat dif-

ferent measures. Most of Europe will measure land in hectares (1 hectare = 2.47 acres).

The John Morrell meatpacking firm has its beginnings at Bradford, Yorkshire, where local woolcomber George Morrell sees a bargeload of oranges in the local canal, buys the fruit with an £80 bequest left to his wife by an uncle, and sells the oranges at a profit in the streets of Bradford. Morrell starts a business in produce, butter, eggs, cheese, bacon, and hams (*see* 1842).

Buitoni macaroni has its beginnings in the Italian hill town of San Sepolcro, where Giulia Buitoni opens a pasta factory. She pawned her gold jewelry a few years ago, rented a roadside stand for 1 lira per month, sold her homemade pasta, and started a family business to help provide for her many children. Her barber husband, Giovanbattista, helped out, but she was soon well aware that the pasta she made from soft-grain wheat was inferior to what she could make with semolina flour from durum wheat (*semolina di grano duro*). She organized a 40-mule caravan to bring back such wheat from Abruzzi in the south (*see* 1842).

Ballantine's Scotch is introduced at a distillery started at Dumbarton by Scotsman George Ballantine (*see* Allied-Lyons, 1986).

Delmonico's Restaurant has its beginnings in a café and pastry shop opened in lower Manhattan by Swiss wine merchant Giovanni Del-Monico and his older brother Pietro, who has run a pastry shop at Bern. Giovanni, who came to the West Indies on a trading ship, opened a small wine shop near the Battery 2 years ago, purchasing by the cask and selling by the bottle. Patrons of the new shop buy cakes, ices, and wine, which they either take home or consume on the premises, sitting at plain pine tables where they are impressed by the clean aprons and good manners of the brothers Del-Monico (*see* 1832).

1828

The "Tariff of Abominations" signed into law May 19 by President John Quincy Adams, 60, has raised duties on manufactured goods. Daniel Webster, 46, representing New England shippers and manufacturers, and Henry Clay, 51, representing western farmers, have championed the measure. Supporters of presidential candidate Andrew Jackson, 61, framed it to discredit President Adams and are astonished when it is passed and signed.

The Reciprocity Act passed by Congress May 24 allows for lower duties on imports from countries that reciprocate, but opponents of the Tariff of Abominations are not appeased.

A new British Corn Law introduced by the duke of Wellington gives consumers relief from the high food prices that have prevailed since the Corn Law of 1815. The new law imposes duties on a sliding scale based on domestic prices but prices remain too low to permit grain imports.

 Dutch chocolate maker Conrad J. van Houten patents an inexpensive method for pressing the fat from roasted cacao beans and produces the world's first chocolate candy. The defatted "mass" can be used to make a powder, and Van Houten has found that by adding the extra cocoa butter, as it will be called, to an experimental mixture of cocoa powder and sugar, the resulting sticky substance cools into a solid, moldable form (*see* beverage, below; Cadbury, 1847; Nestlé and Peter, 1875).

Cookbook: *Directions for Cookery* by U.S. author Eliza Leslie, published at Philadelphia, says, "Ham should always be accompanied by green vegetables such as asparagus, beans, spinach, cauliflower, brocoli, etc." It gives recipes for preparing artichokes, asparagus, beans (dried, green, lima, and string), beets, "brocoli," cabbage, carrots, cauliflower, celery, cucumbers, eggplant, mushrooms, "ochras," onions, parsnips, potatoes, pumpkin, radishes, rutabagas, salsify, spinach, squash, sweet corn, sweet potatoes, "tomatas" (baked, pickled, preserved, and "catchup"), and turnips.

Eliza Leslie (above) gives 29 recipes for preparing fish—blackfish, carp, catfish, cod, halibut, perch, rockfish, salmon, sea bass, shad, sturgeon, and trout, including a salmon dish with lobster sauce. She omits a recipe for "*real*" turtle soup, saying, "as when that very expensive, complicated, and difficult dish is prepared in the private family, it is advisable to hire a first-rate cook for the express

purpose. An easy way is to get it ready made, and in any quantity you please, from a turtle-soup house."

Eliza Leslie (above) writes that terrapins, "after being boiled by the cook, may be brought to table plain, with all the condiments separate, so that the company may dress them according to taste." Her recipes often call for allspice, black pepper, hot pepper, cassia, cayenne pepper, cinnamon, cloves, coriander, ginger, mace, mustard, nutmeg, or turmeric.

Chili (or chile) con carne is popular in Mexico's Texas territory, writes a U.S. visitor to San Antonio. "When they have to pay for their meat in the market, a very little is made to suffice a family; it is generally cut into a kind of hash with nearly as many peppers as there are pieces of meat—this is all stewed together" (*see* chili powder, 1835).

America's Shakers change their permissive attitude toward alcohol. They forbid the use of "beer, cider, wines, and all ardent liquors . . . on all occasions, at house-raisings, husking bees, harvestings, and all other gatherings."

Conrad van Houten (above) creates a pulverized cocoa powder that makes it possible to brew a cup of instant cocoa and will be the forerunner of other instant beverages.

1829

New Englanders sent a big cheese to the White House for President Jackson's inauguration.

President Andrew Jackson takes office March 4 and accepts the gift of a large wheel of cheese sent by New Englanders (*see* Jefferson, 1802). It stands in the hall of the White House for a week until it is gradually eaten away (*see* 1837).

The Welland Sea Canal opens to connect lakes Erie and Ontario via a tortuous waterway that has 25 locks to permit ships to circumnavigate Niagara Falls (*see* 1932).

German publisher Karl Baedeker, 28, issues a travel guide to Koblenz. His Baedeker handbooks in German, French, and English will describe the foods, accommodations, and sights to be found in cities of Europe and, later, North America and the Orient, awarding stars to indicate particularly interesting sights, even ranking the Old Masters in London museums (*see* Michelin, 1900).

London "bobbies" introduced September 29 by order of Home Secretary Robert Peel, 41, make the streets safer after dark for those invited to dinner parties. The city has one footpad, highwayman, or thief for every 22 inhabitants, and although such criminals thrive in the absence of good streetlighting they must now contend with the constables, headquartered at Scotland Yard, who constitute the first London police force.

Episcopal minister William Bostwick of Hammondsport, N.Y., plants grape vines in his rectory garden, using shoots obtained from Hudson Valley vineyards and beginning an industry that will flourish in the state's Finger Lakes region (*see* Alexander grape, 1809; Pleasant Valley Wine Co., 1860).

Catawba grapes, native to the Catawba River in North Carolina, are discovered in a Clarksburg, Md., garden by John Adlum, a Washington, D.C., grower. They will be the nation's most popular wine grape through most of this century, although Delaware, Moore's Diamond (possibly developed from the Iona), Concord, Dutchess, and Niagara grapes will also be widely planted in Finger Lakes vineyards, and the Elvira grape, originally from Missouri, will grow better in upstate New York than anywhere else (*see* Longworth, 1847).

Massachusetts Presbyterian clergyman Sylvester W. Graham, 35, attacks meats, fats, mustard, ketchup, pepper, and, most especially, white bread. He was called a "mad enthusiast" in his student days at Amherst College, was expelled on trumped-up charges, suffered a nervous breakdown, became a New Jersey minister, won appointment as general agent of the Pennsylvania State Society for Suppression of the Use of Ardent Spirits, met members of a vegetarian church in Philadelphia, and has become convinced that many Americans abuse their bodies with alcohol, bad food, and other excesses. Graham calls meats, condiments, and white bread injurious to the health or stimulating to carnal appetites (*see* 1839).

Pennsylvania's Yuengling brewery is founded at Pottsville, where it will mature its beers in caves dug into the side of a Delaware Valley hill. Yuengling will survive as the oldest U.S. brewing company.

1830

British voters turn out the Conservative party that has been in power for nearly half a century and install a Whig government headed by Charles Grey, 66. Earl Grey's name will be applied to various brands of tea and chutneys.

Paris revolutionists depose Charles X July 29 and make the duc d'Orléans king; he will reign until 1848 as Louis-Philippe.

Congress reduces U.S. duties on coffee, tea, salt, and molasses imports in response to pressure from consumers.

The Budapest pastry shop (*cukrászda*) Vilmos Ruszwurm opens in the heart of Buda near the Mátyás Church in a building that housed a Turkish biscuit maker in the 16th century. Its cakes, tortas, and rigó Jancsi will gain an international reputation.

Capt. John Pearsall's schooner *Harriet Smith* lands the first full cargo of bananas—1,500 stems—at New York (*see* Chester, 1804; Baker, 1870).

"In whatever proportion the cultivation of potatoes prevails . . . in that same proportion the working people are wretched," writes English political journalist William Cobbett, 67, in *Rural Rides*. The Industrial Revolution has turned England's peasantry into half-starved paupers and destroyed rural skills, says Cobbett.

Average U.S. per capita wheat consumption reaches 170 pounds; meat consumption is 178 pounds (*see* 1850).

The first known recipe for tomato ketchup appears in The *New England Farmer*, made by "a person regularly educated at the business in Europe" (*see* Randolph, 1824). The condiment is offered in bottles of various sizes priced from 33¢ to 50¢ (*see* 1837).

Domestic baking and brewing skills have been forgotten by the English peasantry, says William Cobbett (above). "Nowadays all is looked for at shops. To buy the thing ready made is the taste of the day: thousands who are housekeepers buy their dinners ready cooked." "The woman, high or low, ought to know how to make bread," Cobbett writes. "If she does not, she is unworthy of trust, and, indeed, a mere burden upon the community. . . . The servant that cannot make bread is not entitled to the same wages as one that can. . . . Anyone as well as she can take in a loaf from the baker or a barrel of beer from the brewer. Can she bake? is the question I always put. . . . Give me for a beautiful sight a neat and smart woman, heating her oven and setting her bread."

Tinned foods from London's Donkin, Hall & Gamble Preservatory reach English food shops for the first time.

French and Belgian bakers begin using minute quantities of highly toxic copper sulfate as well as the less toxic alum to whiten bread.

Crosse & Blackwell gets its name as London entrepreneurs Edmund Crosse and Thomas Blackwell, both about 25, pay £600 to acquire the 124-year-old firm that hired them as apprentices 11 years ago (*see* 1706; 1838).

Teacher's Highland Cream Scotch whisky has its beginnings in a distillery opened at Glasgow by William Teacher, 19.

The continuous still patented by the inspector general of Irish excise Aeneas Coffee speeds up distilling and makes for "cleaner" whiskey and gin. Coffee has used earlier models as the basis for his cheap, quick, continuous-process still: a small amount of wash (fermented malt made from any-thing containing starch or sugar), enough to provide the enzyme needed to convert corn starch into a fermentable sugar, is mixed with a mash of corn and water; allowed to ferment, the mixture is then piped into one end of Coffee's distilling system (two very tall, heated columns with a sequence of chambers), and high-proof alcohol comes out of the other end. The process eliminates most of the higher alcohols, esters, acids, and other "congeners," producing a more neutral, lighter-bodied "patent" whisky which Highland Scottish pot-still distillers scorn, claiming that their slower, more costly method retains more of the "impurities" that give aged whisky its characteristic flavor. Irish whiskey will continue to be made mostly in pot stills (*see* 1850).

1831

English rioters stormed warehouses and distributed bread to the hungry. ILLUSTRATED LONDON NEWS

British labor unrest culminates in the Bristol Riots of October 29 to 31, raising fears of a general revolution. City magistrates call in troops, a cavalry charge restores order, four rioters are arrested, 22 are transported, but discontent continues (*see* Reform Act, 1832).

The English biscuit firm Carr's of Carlisle is founded by baker Jonathan Dodgson Carr.

Boston's S. S. Pierce Co. has its beginnings in a shop opened to sell "choice teas and foreign fruits" by local merchant Samuel Stillman Pierce, who will ship wine from Madeira to New York to Buenos Aires and back to New York to satisfy an old Bostonian's taste for Madeira wines that have spent months at sea. His firm will put up buffalo tongue, terrapin stew, and Singapore pineapple in cans, and it will send a dogsled team to fetch Russian isinglass (a gelatin made from sturgeon bladders) for S. S. Pierce jellies (most New Englanders make their own gelatin by boiling down "a set of calves' feet").

English novelist Benjamin Disraeli, 27, writes to his sister from Cairo: "Oh the delicious fruits we have here and in Syria! Orange gardens miles in extent, citrons, limes, pomegranates; but the most delicious thing in the world is a banana, which is richer than a pineapple."

Gorham table silver is introduced by Gorham and Webster Co. of Providence, R.I., headed by local jeweler-silversmith Jabez Gorham, 39. Spoons, forks, and other items are hand forged and hand fabricated so that two men can produce only two dozen pieces per day.

The McCormick reaper, which enables one man to do the work of five, is demonstrated by Virginia farmer Cyrus Hall McCormick, 22, whose father

Cyrus McCormick's reaping machine permitted one man to harvest far more acreage than ever before.

tills some 1,200 acres near Lexington with nine slaves and 18 horses. Young McCormick's crude but effective horse-drawn reaper is so devised that the horse is hitched alongside it rather than behind as in the case of the 1826 Bell reaper. His reaper's knife vibrates in a line at right angles to the direction in which the machine is moving, a divider moves ahead to separate a swath from the field and turn the grain toward the blade, and a row of mechanical fingers ahead of the blade holds the straw straight to be cut. Severed stalks are deposited neatly on a platform, and the reaper permits horsepower to replace human power (*see* 1834; Hussey, 1833).

Growing and harvesting a bushel of U.S. wheat takes 3 man-hours of work, a figure that will begin to drop through use of the McCormick reaper (above).

The Garrick Club, founded at London, will attract a theatrical crowd and grow to have what many will say is the best dining room among London's many clubs.

1832

The (First) Reform Act, which passes the House of Lords June 4, enfranchises Britain's upper middle class; mill owners in the Midlands are enabled to agitate more effectively for removal of high tariffs on foodstuffs from abroad (*see* Wellington, 1828; Bristol Riots, 1831; Cobden, 1838; Second Reform Act, 1867).

South Carolina legislators hold a state convention November 19 to protest the 1828 Tariff of Abominations and a new tariff law, passed by Congress July 14, which reduces some of the duties in the 1828 Tariff of Abominations but retains the principle of protectionism.

The Austrian pastry shop Zauer in the Café Walther opens at the royal spa Isel, 4 days by coach from Vienna. It will be taken over by Viktor Zauer and grow to rival Demel's (*see* 1786), offering *zauerstollen*, *zauerkipfel*, *zauertorte*, and more conventional *schnitten*, *rouladen*, and *torten*, as well as *kugelhupf*, *schinkenkipfel* (baked croissant filled with chopped ham), *malakofftorte*, and *zwetschkenkuchen* (plum cake), including puff pastes filled with ground nuts and other delicacies containing hazelnuts, almonds, nougat, chocolate, sugar.

The enzyme diastase is separated from barley—the first enzyme to be isolated (*see* Payen and Persoz, 1833).

Nonfiction: *Domestic Manners of the Americans* by English novelist Frances Milton Trollope, 52, who came to America in 1827 after divorcing the father of her son Anthony and the boy's two older brothers. She has been impressed by the "excellence, abundance, and cheapness" of food in the markets of Cincinnati but suggests that the abundance has contributed to sloppy preparation. Deploring American eating habits, she reports that suppers are huge buffets that may include "tea, coffee, hot cake and custard, hoe cake, johnny cake, waffle cake, and dodger cake, pickled peaches, and preserved cucumbers, ham, turkey, hung beef, apple sauce and pickled oysters."

Painter John James Audubon writes of the blue-winged teal, saying, "So tender and savoury is its flesh that it would have quickly put the merit of the widely celebrated canvass-backed Duck in the shade. . . . I myself saw a friend of mine kill eighty-four by pulling the triggers of his double-barreled gun." He writes, also, "When a jug of sparkling Newark cider stands nigh, you, without knife or fork, quarter a Woodcock. Ah reader! —but alas! I am not in the Jerseys just now . . . I am . . . without any expectation of Woodcocks for my dinner, either to-day or to-morrow, or indeed for some months to come."

Gooderham & Worts distillery is founded at Toronto on land granted by the Crown.

The U.S. Army abolishes its daily liquor ration.

U.S. coffee imports reach 35 million pounds, up from nearly 12 million in 1821, despite high duties, as voices opposed to consumption of alcohol gain force (*see* 1844; tariff act, 1833).

A second Delmonico's Restaurant opens at 494 Pearl Street to augment the one at 23 and 25 William Street, New York (*see* 1827). John and Peter Delmonico, who have anglicized their names, bring over their nephew Lorenzo to help them in their enterprise (*see* 1837).

Madrid's Lhardy pâtisserie opens at 8 Carrera de San Jerónimo, a street that leads into the Porta del Sol. The city's population of 175,000 is about to expand dramatically, and Swiss confectioner Emile Lhardy will do so well that he will be able to expand his confectionery shop into a restaurant with white and Chinese salons on the second floor, facing the rear. Reserved rooms, or *separées*, on the floors above will be for use when ladies are invited (waiters will be trained to back into the white *separées*, coughing discreetly so as not to interrupt anything).

Viennese kitchen trainee Franz Sacher, 16, creates a sweet cake of chocolate, eggs, and marmalade for a dinner to honor Prince von Metternich. It will become famous as the Sachertorte.

An Enquiry into the Principles of Population by English scholar Thomas Rowe Edmonds, 29, says, "Amongst the great body of the people at the present moment, sexual intercourse is the only gratification, and thus, by a most unfortunate concurrence of adverse circumstances, population goes on augmenting at a period when it ought to be restrained. to better the conditions of the labouring classes, that is, to place more food and comforts before them, however paradoxical it may appear, is the wisest mode to check redundancy. . . . When [the Irish] are better fed they will have other enjoyments at command than sexual intercourse, and their numbers, therefore, will not increase in the same proportion as at present."

1833

A 3-year famine begins in Japan. The suffering will be even worse than in 1783.

A factory act voted by Parliament August 29 includes provisions that establish statutory minimums of time permitted British workers of whatever age to eat the food they have brought from home, but the new law applies only to textile factories and its safeguards are inadequate.

The Compromise Tariff Act submitted by Sen. Henry Clay (S.C.) and signed into law by President Jackson in March provides for gradual reduction of U.S. tariffs until July 1, 1842, when no rate is to be higher than 20 percent. Coffee is admitted duty free under the new law.

The Zollverein (customs union) formed at Berlin March 22 includes Prussia, Bavaria, Württemberg, Hesse-Darmstadt, but not Austria (*see* 1853).

The East India Company loses its prized monopoly in the China trade (most of it in tea) by an act of the British prime minister Charles Grey, now 69. The name Earl Grey will be used for a blend of Indian and Ceylonese tea flavored with oil of bergamot (a Chinese mandarin gave him the recipe) and as a generic name for scented teas such as jasmine.

The first cargo of U.S. ice for India leaves Boston to begin a voyage of 4 months and 7 days. Frederic Tudor, whose trade will bring a permanent change in eating habits, has loaded his ship *Tuscany* with 180 tons of ice—plus Baldwin apples, butter, and cheese—for Lord William Bentinck and the nabobs of the East India Company at Calcutta, two-thirds of the ice is still frozen upon arrival in May, and the voyage makes a profit (*see* 1805).

The Indians (above) have learned to make their own ice on a limited scale, sinking porous earthen pans filled with water into the Hooghly River near Calcutta on cold winter nights; the water, partially frozen, is taken out at sunrise and skimmed off into baskets, where it is stacked up to form a solid mass; the baskets are buried in a 14-foot pit lined and covered with straw (*see* 1846).

A Swiss millwright devises an alternative to the millstones that have been used to grind grain since ancient times; he replaces the stones with rollers and uses them to reduce the grain to flour more efficiently (*see* Sulzberger, 1839).

French chemists Anselme Payen and Jean-François Persoz extract the enzyme amylase from malt and observe that it converts starch into sugar (*see* diastase, 1832; Schwann, 1835; Kuhne, 1878).

Lockport, Ill., blacksmith John Lane creates a plow with a polished steel moldboard that scours furrows without clogging, but he is unable to market his moldboard plow (*see* Deere, 1837).

A reaper demonstrated near Carthage, Ohio, by Maine-born inventor Obed Hussey, 41, will rival the 1831 McCormick reaper and beat it to market.

Patented in December, Hussey's horse-drawn reaper features a sawtoothed cutting bar driven reciprocally by a crankshaft geared to the main wheels; the cut stalks fall onto a platform, from which they are raked by hand for binding. Production will begin next year, Hussey will open a large factory at Baltimore in 1838, and his reapers will be snapped up by grain farmers in New York, Pennsylvania, Maryland, and Illinois; McCormick's machine will not go into production until 1840 and will encounter resistance from farmers in hilly Virginia (but *see* 1847).

Experiments and Observations on the Gastric Juices and the Physiology of Digestion by William Beaumont will become a classic in clinical medicine (*see* 1822).

Antonin Carême dies at Paris January 12, age 48. The first great French chef, he has served royalty, Talleyrand, and London banker Baron (Nathan Meyer) de Rothschild, now 56 (for whom he reportedly invented the chocolate soufflé) in his brief but distinguished career.

Farmer's Register is published for the first time in Virginia with agriculturist Edmund Ruffin, 39, as editor. Ruffin has seen farmland eroded by tobacco growers and warns planters of the "growing loss and eventual ruin of your country, and the humiliation of its people, if the long-existing system of exhausting culture is not abandoned." "Choose, and choose quickly," says Ruffin, and he urges contour plowing, crop rotation, the use of furrows for careful drainage, and the use of lime and fertilizers to rejuvenate the soil.

The avocado (*Persea americana*) is introduced into southern Florida by horticulturist Henry Perrine, who plants Mexican varieties on his grant of land south of Miami, but although Mexicans use the fruit in avocado bread, in guacamole, and in other ways, the "alligator pear" will not be grown commercially until 1901 (*see* Cobe, 1653; Washington, 1751).

"Teetoteetoteetotal" abstinence from alcoholic beverages is advocated by English prohibitionist R. Turner in a stammering speech at Preston; by some accounts it is he who unwittingly introduces the word "teetotalism" into the language, but the term "T-Total" will be found in the records of the Laingsburg, Mich., Temperance Society in this decade. The society has two forms of pledges; the Old Pledge (O.P.) permits moderate drinking, while the T. pledge, whose adherents will be called "T-Totalers," requires total abstinence from "ardent spirits."

English-American entrepreneur John Matthews opens a shop at 33 Gold Street, begins manufacturing a compact apparatus for carbonation (by some accounts the first soda fountain), and introduces bottled carbonated water to New York merchants (*see* 1891; Silliman, 1807; Durand, 1825; ice cream soda, 1874).

1834

South Africa has a Kaffir War as Xhosa tribesmen (called Kaffir by the Dutch, who use it in the same sense that some Americans use the word "nigger") invade eastern regions in irritation at the steady encroachment of Dutch cattlemen and farmers. The Xhosa are driven back but only with difficulty (*see* 1877; Great Trek, 1835).

Some 35,000 slaves go free in South Africa August 1 as slavery is abolished throughout the British Empire amid complaints about the inadequacy of compensation to former slaveholders (*see* 1833; Great Trek, 1835).

A new British Poor Law enacted by Parliament August 14 limits the pay of charitable doles to sick and aged paupers, ending the system that has provided a dole to supplement low ages. The new law establishes oppressive workhouses where the sexes are segregated to discourage procreation and where able-bodied paupers are put to work (*see* Malthus, below).

British wheat prices fall to £10 per hundredweight, down from £30 in 1812.

Cyrus McCormick receives a patent for his reaper of 1831 and Obed Hussey begins manufacturing his reaper (*see* 1833; 1840).

Gas refrigeration has its beginnings in a compression machine invented in England by U.S. inventor Jacob Perkins, 58, who has lived abroad for years. He distills rubber to create a volatile liquid which is allowed to evaporate by absorbing heat from its surroundings; when the vapor is compressed, it turns back to liquid, giving off heat, and, by alternately compressing and expanding, heat is extracted from the region of expansion until Perkins has cooled water to the point that it freezes (*see* Faraday, 1823; Gorrie, 1842; Linde, 1873).

Cookbook: *The Newest or Great Universal Viennese Cookbook, a Guide to Cook for the Finest Tables in Ordinary Houses, Combining the Best of Taste and the Greatest Elegance, Taking Advantage of the Economic Possibilities to Make it Least Expense* by Anna Dorn, who writes in her introduction, "Every year the number of new cookbooks increases, but in spite of them the progress made in this most useful of the arts is not ever overpowering. On the contrary, we must regretfully admit that nowadays people no longer prepare the fine and nourishing dishes that our mothers used to make. We place dishes on the table that are either too heavily spiced or plain dull, that are neither good for people's health nor economical. What gastronomy gained in the last fifty years, our daily cooking has lost. . . . The author of this book, whose originality even some dreadful, envious people cannot dispute, spent her youthful years in the kitchen of one of the First Houses in Vienna. Later she became the housekeeper in the home of a well-to-do private man; and again, later, his wife. She realized that the principles of elegant cooking were no longer useful. Another twenty years as head of the house where seventeen people lived taught her to find a happy medium between elegant home making and a good life. . . . Yet this life she had to give up as an elderly widow, when the unhappy times, accidents, and the education of her children placed her in circumstances where she now has to live on very little." Dorn gives menus for every day in the year, almost every meal beginning with two soups and boiled beef, followed by vegetables (asparagus, spinach with baked liver, sauerkraut with ham, etc.), a meat dish (usually a roast or breast of lamb filled with mushrooms, larded veal schnitzel, chicken fricandeau), then a dish of game (fowl, venison, hare, or some small birds), salad, and a torte.

A Dictionary of Diet by English surgeon J. S. Forsyth speaks of the "delicious and wholesome drink" as well as sweetmeats that can be concocted from a cake of chocolate.

Sardines are canned for the first time in Europe (*see* first U.S. sardine cannery, 1876).

New Rochelle, N.Y., resident Lewis A. Seacor cultivates several blackberry bushes on a nearby farm; his neighbor, William Lawton, also begins growing blackberries, and the result will become known as "New Rochelle blackberries" (*see* 1853; Massachusetts, 1841).

Some 28 million acres of U.S. public lands will be offered for sale this year and next. As Americans move west of the Appalachians to take up the new lands, European immigrants will replace them.

English political economist Thomas R. Malthus dies at Haileybury December 23 at age 68, having had the satisfaction of seeing Parliament enact a new Poor Law (above), partly as a result of his *Essay on Population*, which has gone through many revised editions since 1798.

1835

Dutch (Boer) cattlemen in South Africa begin a Great Trek to the north and east of the Orange River in irritation at Britain's abolition of slavery last year.

London pathologist James Paget, 21, at St. Bartholomew's Hospital detects the parasite *Trichinella spiralis* for the first time. The parasite will later be associated with trichinosis, a disease produced by eating raw or undercooked pork products or meat from bears, polar bears, rats, foxes, or marine animals (*see* von Zenker, 1860; Paget's disease, 1877).

Berlin physiologist Theodor Schwann, 25, extracts the enzyme pepsin from the stomach wall and proclaims it the most effective element in the digestive juices (*see* 1824; Payen and Persoz, 1833; Kuhne, 1878).

Cookbook: *L'Art de la cuisine française au dix-neuvième siècle* (*The Art of French Cooking in the 19th Century*) by the late Antonin Carême, who died 2 years ago. His book contains hundreds of recipes along with detailed explanations of the techniques and hazards of classic cooking.

Sauce Béarnaise is created with butter and tarragon vinegar at the Pavilion Henri IV restaurant in Saint-Germain-en-Laye outside Paris (Henri IV was known as Le Grand Béarnais).

English settlers in Mexico's Texas Territory create chili powder by combining various ground peppers as a convenient way to make Mexican-style dishes (*see* 1828; Gebhardt, 1894).

Washington Irving describes honeybees in *A Tour of the Prairies*: "It is surprising in what countless swarms the bees have overspread the Far West within a moderate number of years. The Indians consider them the harbinger of the white man, as the buffalo is of the red man; and say that, in proportion as the bee advances, the Indian and the buffalo retire. . . . I am told that the wild bee is seldom to be met with at any great distance from the frontier."

Wild honeybees were domesticated to provide sweetening for settlers on the American frontier. LIBRARY OF CONGRESS

The *Maine Farmer* reports that tomatoes are being cultivated in many of the state's gardens (*see* 1820). The editor recommends the fruit as "a useful article of diet" that "should be found at every man's table." Coastal Maine housewives concoct ketchup from Spanish tomato-sauce recipes brought home by their seafaring husbands.

1835

Russia's bonded peasant population reaches close to 11 million, up from fewer than 10 million in 1816. The overabundance of serfs will create problems in years when crops are short.

1836

U.S. missionary Narcissa Whitman (*née* Prentiss), 28, accompanies her husband, Marcus, 34, to the Pacific Northwest, along with her friend Eliza Spalding (they are the first women to cross the Continent); she praises frontier food, writing, "I wish some of the feeble ones in the States could have a ride over the mountains; they would say like me, victuals even the plainest kind never relished so well before." "The Cammas grows here in abundance," she notes in her journal, "and is the principal resort of the Cayouse and many other tribes, to obtain it of which they are very fond. It resembles an onion in shape and color, when cooked is very sweet, tastes like figs [others will compare the taste to that of maple sugar, molasses, quince, or dates; *see* Douglas, 1826]. This is the chief food of many tribes during the winter." (Some settlers will be killed by eating the green-flowered poisonous white camas [genus *Zigadenus*], or death camas, which grows among the blue-flowered varieties. Native cooks keep the blue flowers attached until just before cooking in order to avoid accidents.)

James Fenimore Cooper, now 47, writes of New York's Fulton Market, "It is difficult to name fish or fowl, or beast, that is not . . . to be obtained in the markets of New York."

The Erie Canal, completed in 1825, is widened and deepened for the barge traffic that has repaid investors with toll receipts (*see* 1917).

Of 2.35 million tons of U.S. merchant shipping, some 60,000 tons are in steam.

A phosphorus match patented by Springfield, Mass., shoemaker Alonzo D. Phillips is the prototype of matches that will be used in future to light stoves and hearth fires (*see* 1827; safety match, 1853).

 French naturalist Charles Morren finds a way to cultivate vanilla commercially in places other than Mexico (*see* 1571). The orchidlike bloom of *Vanilla plenifolia*, he discovers, is double sexed and pollination of the flower depends on the bee *melipona*, native only to Mexican vanilla-growing districts, which has the habits and physical characteristics that make it uniquely suitable as a pollinator. Experiments will show that vanilla flowers can be pollinated by hand, with an expert able to pollinate about 200 flowers per day, and although Mexico will continue to produce the world's finest vanilla, French islands such as Madagascar and Réunion will become more prolific producers (*see* 1955).

Some 75 percent of gainfully employed Americans are engaged in agriculture, down from 83 percent in 1820 (*see* 1853).

The London Act of 1822 with regard to standard weights for bread loaves is applied for the first time throughout England and Wales, but the law does not take into account the amount of flour that has gone into a loaf. Traditional weights will continue to be used in Scotland (*see* 1878).

New York's Park Hotel, opened June 1 by fur merchant John Jacob Astor, 73, at the corner of Vesey and Barclay streets, has a dining room that will be a popular gathering spot for the city's merchants.

The first printed American menu is issued by New York's 5-year-old Delmonico's Restaurant at 494 Pearl Street and lists as one of its most expensive dishes "hamburger steak." The "bill of fare" offers a "regular dinner" at 12 cents and lists hamburger steak at 10 cents (the same price as roast chicken or ham and eggs; regular beefsteak is only 4 cents, as are pork chops, corn beef and cabbage, pig's head and cabbage, and fried fish. Roast beef or veal, roast mutton, veal cutlet, or chicken stew is 5 cents) (*see* 1837; hamburger, 1885).

London's Reform Club is founded by the Rt. Hon. Edward Ellice, MP, and Sir William Molesworth "to promote the social intercourse of the Reformers of England" (*see* gas ovens, 1838; Soyer, 1839).

1837

Britain's William IV dies June 20 at age 71 and is succeeded by his niece of 18, who will reign until

1901 as Queen Victoria. Her maître d'hotel and confectioner is Charles Elmé Fraccatelli, a pupil of the late Antonin Carême, whose dinners will generally include two soups, two fish dishes, two removes, six entrées, two roasts, two more removes, and eight entremets, headed by chocolate cream.

Famine strikes Japan, but the Tokugawa shōgun Ieyoshi refuses to open storehouses at Osaka to the starving people. A February riot led by the former police officer Heihachiro Oshio ends with 40 percent of Osaka in ashes, the riots spread throughout Japan, but the shōgun resists appeals to ease the tax burden on farmers, who have little or no cash crop (*see* 1833).

Economic depression begins in Britain.

Economic depression begins in the United States following the failure in March of a New Orleans cotton brokerage. Inflated land values, speculation, and wildcat banking have contributed to the crisis, 39,000 Americans go bankrupt, $741 million is lost, and the depression reduces thousands to starvation. One-third of all New Yorkers who subsist by manual labor are unemployed, and at least 10,000 are made dependent on almshouses, which are unable to prevent many from starving to death (*see* 1839).

Procter & Gamble is founded at Cincinnati by English-American candle maker William Procter, 35, and his Irish-American soap boiler brother-in-law James Gamble, 34, whose company will become a major player in the U.S. food industry.

A self-polishing steel plow fashioned by Vermont-born blacksmith John Deere, 32, at Grand Detour, Ill., can break the heavy sod of the Illinois and Iowa prairie (*see* Lane, 1833). Deere chisels the teeth off a discarded circular saw blade of Sheffield steel, creates a plow with the proper moldboard curve for breaking the sod, and saves farmers from having to pull their plows out of furrows for repeated cleaning with wooden paddles. The Deere plow will permit efficient farming in vast areas that have defied earlier efforts (*see* 1839).

The first steam-powered threshing machine, patented by Winthrop, Maine, inventors John A. Pitts and Hiram Abial Pitts, separates grain from its straw and chaff with far less effort than was heretofore required (*see* Meikle, 1786; Case, 1843).

Some 1,200 U.S. automated flour mills produce 2 million bushels of flour in the area west of the Alleghenies, with more millions being milled by millers on the eastern seaboard who have been licensed to use the 1790 Oliver Evans patent or who infringe on it.

French physiologist René-Joachim-Henri Dutrochet, 61, establishes the essential importance of chlorophyll to photosynthesis (*see* Ingenhousz, 1779).

Fiction: *The Posthumous Papers of the Pickwick Club* by English novelist Charles Dickens, 25, whose Mr. Pickwick goes to live at the George Tavern (*see* nonfiction, 1598) while fighting a breach-of-promise suit: "Mr. Pickwick and Sam [Weller] took up their present abode in very good Fashion with comfortable quarters, to wit the George and Vulture Tavern and Hotel, George Yard, Lombard Street." Dickens describes widespread hunger among Britain's urban poor in early installments of his novel *Oliver Twist*: "Please, sir, I want some more," says young Oliver, as the Industrial Revolution's dislocation of society creates problems in English agriculture.

Poetry: *History of the Dinner: A Survey of Eating in Our Time* by Russian gastronome Vladimir Sergeyevich Filimonov, 49, is approved for publication by the St. Petersburg censor. Governor of Archangel in 1831, Filimonov was sentenced to internal exile on charges (never proved) of conspiracy. His reminiscence, written in Estonia in 1832, is a reminiscence—part real, part fantasy—of an ideal feast enjoyed with his friends in the hills outside Moscow in the summer of 1815, when they celebrated the defeat of the French with dishes and ingredients from all over Europe: Welsh rabbit, fresh Parmesan, pilaf, Russian river fish including the sterleton, and pies. Filimonov does not mention Brillat-Savarin, is less witty and more personal, and makes no pretensions to science, but he borrows ideas from Brillat-Savarin's work and expresses pain at the lack of appreciation of good food and drink.

Outgoing President Andrew Jackson holds a public levee on Washington's Birthday, February 22, and serves a 1,400-pound cheese made from the milk of 50 cows. Four feet in diameter, it has been transported by canal from New England to New York and thence by ship to Washington, D.C., where it has stood for weeks in a hallway of the executive mansion (*see* Jackson, 1829). Visitors cram the White House's state dining room, and it will be said later that the room's floor was 12 inches deep in fragments of discarded cheese and rind; the odor will persist for weeks and even months.

Americans trying to sell tomato ketchup in Britain are advised to rename their product "tomato chutney" in order avoid confusion; ketchup in Britain still means a sauce based on anchovies or mushrooms, and British recipes for tomato chutney call for unstrained tomato pulp mixed with vinegar and spices (*see* 1830; Yerkes, 1872).

Society in America by English novelist-economist Harriet Martineau, 35, says of corn on the cob, "The greatest drawback is the way in which it is necessary to eat it. . . . It looks awkward enough: but what is to be done? Surrendering such a vegetable from considerations of grace is not to be thought of" (Martineau visited the United States from 1834 to 1836).

"The cookery in the United States is exactly what it is and must be everywhere else—in a ratio with the degree of refinement of the population," writes English novelist Frederick Marryat, 45, a retired Royal Navy captain. "In the principal cities you will meet with as good cookery in private homes as you will in London, or even Paris."

Sole Normande (fillet of sole with shellfish and mushrooms) is invented by Langlais, chef de cuisine at the restaurant Le Rocher de Cancale in the rue Montorgueil, Paris.

The shakeout of land speculators in the economic depression (above) makes more U.S. farmland available for real farmers.

Treatise on Bread and Breadmaking by Sylvester Graham inveighs against refined wheat flour. Graham societies spring up, and Graham hotels (many of them once temperance hotels) open in some U.S. cities as thousands of Americans follow vegetarian diets, eating day-old whole-grain bread, oatmeal gruel, beans and boiled rice prepared without salt (Graham says condiments may inflame a thirst for alcohol), and cold puddings (*see* 1829).

Scottish chemist Andrew Ure, 59, dismisses the idea that Britain's factory children may have rickets for lack of sunlight. Gaslight is more progressive and quite as healthy, says Ure (*see* Steenbock, 1923).

Tetley Tea is introduced at Huddersfield, England, where local merchants Joseph and Edward Tetley open a shop under the name Tetley Brothers—Dealers in Tea. The two have peddled their tea from a packhorse across the Yorkshire moors (*see* 1856).

Lea & Perrins Worcestershire Sauce is introduced by English chemists (pharmacists) John Wheeley Lea and William Perrins, who opened a shop at 68 Broad Street, Worcester, in 1823 and have sold groceries as well as pharmaceuticals. Their zesty sauce—containing vinegar, molasses, sugar, anchovies, onions, tamarinds, salt, garlic, cloves, chili peppers, asafoetida (a member of the fennel family used in the ancient world for its alleged contraceptive powers), and salt—has been mixed to a recipe obtained 2 years ago from a Lord Sandys, formerly governor of Bengal, and aged for 2 years until palatable (*see* BSN, 1988).

Delmonico's Restaurant reopens at the corner of William and Beaver Streets in New York (*see* 1836). A great fire destroyed the original William Street restaurant 2 years ago, and the new place—containing a three-story main dining room, private dining rooms, lounge, and ballroom—is far more splendid (it will be replaced in 1890 by an eight-story building whose dining and banquet rooms will be more splendid still). John and Peter's nephew Lorenzo Delmonico, now 24, goes to the market early each morning to select the freshest produce, freshest seafood, and best cuts of meat; he imports European cooks and recipes for the establishment, which will popularize green vegetables, salads, and ices (*see* 1845).

Columbia College student George Templeton Strong writes in his diary, "Evening . . . Went to Delmonico's [above] . . . and drank some of the only good chocolate I ever tasted, as much superior to the stuff that ordinarily goes under that name as champagne to small beer."

1838

Famine kills thousands in the north of Ireland as crops fail (*see* 1845; Poor Law, below).

Britain applies the Poor Law of 1834 to Ireland and adds to the hardship of the country's famine (above). Designed to discourage paupers from seeking relief, the Poor Law makes work inside the workhouse worse than the most unpleasant sort of work to be found on the outside, and it has the effect of stimulating emigration.

Lancashire calico printer Richard Cobden, 34, at Manchester founds an Anti–Corn Law League to oppose British protectionism (*see* 1839).

London's Reform Club installs gas ovens (*see* 1836; Sharp, 1826). Coal or wood is the common cooking fuel in most of the world, but Arab nomads use camel chips, American Indians buffalo chips, and Eskimos blubber oil (*see* Soyer, 1839).

French physician Charles Cagniard de La Tour, 61, shows that fermentation is dependent on yeast cells (*see* Pasteur, 1857).

Nonfiction: *The Young Lady's Friend* by U.S. author Mrs. John Farrar, who writes, "If you wish to imitate the French or English, you will put every mouthful into your mouth with a fork; but if you think as I do that Americans have as good a right to their own fashions as the inhabitants of any other country, you may choose the convenience of feeding yourself with your right hand, armed with a steel blade; and provided you do it neatly, and do not put in large mouthfuls, or close your lips tight over the blade, you are not to be considered but as eating them genteely."

Dutch chemist Gerard Johann Mulder, 36, coins the word "protein," adapting a Greek word meaning "of the first importance."

Iron in the blood is what enables blood to absorb so much oxygen, concludes Swedish chemist Jöns Jakob Berzelius, 59, at Uppsala, who pioneers an understanding of hemoglobin.

London's 132-year-old Crosse & Blackwell introduces a bottled chow mustard pickle (*see* 1830). The firm has shifted in the past 20 years from supplying produce to preserving fruit, vegetables, and meat for use aboard ships bound for distant outposts of the empire. It ships out jars and tins of truffled hare, pâté from the Périgord, truffled woodcock, and other delicacies to colonial officers.

French supply sergeant Gaetan Picon in Algeria invents an apéritif using oranges, gentian root, quinquina bark, and alcohol. He will name it the Amer Africaine when he gets out of the army, returns to his native Marseilles, and begins producing the liquor, but will change the name to Picon in 1862.

Schaefer beer has its beginnings as Prussian brewery worker Frederick Schaefer, 21, of Wetzlar arrives at New York and obtains a position with a brewery on Broadway between 18th and 19th streets. Schaefer and his younger brother Maximilian will purchase the brewery in 1842 and make F. and M. Schaefer one of the first U.S. breweries to produce lager beer.

Fresh menus are printed daily at New York's 2-year-old Astor House, writes Captain Frederick Marryat (*see* 1837; Delmonico's, 1836). Delmonico's menu, which does not change from day to day, runs to 12 pages and offers 371 dishes.

Former English butler William Claridge acquires a small London hotel-restaurant formerly run by the French chef Mivart at the corner of Brook Street and Davy Street. Mivart has established a reputation for his joints and steam puddings (*see* 1878).

1839

Britain's Anti–Corn Law League gains power by amalgamating opposition groups (*see* 1838). Richard Cobden's league attracts workers to its cause by promising that a removal of tariffs on foreign grain will reduce food prices, give Britons more money to buy clothing, and thus create more domestic demand and more jobs in the textile industry. Promoters of the league know that lowering food prices will enable them to lower wages (*see* 1841; 1846).

Congress appropriates $1,000 for the first free distribution of seeds to U.S. farmers.

John Deere produces 10 steel plows (*see* 1837; 1842).

Swiss engineer Jacob Sulzberger builds a flour mill at Budapest that employs rollers rather than millstones. The process will make white flour more affordable to consumers (*see* 1833; 1870).

A young Episcopalian minister attends a Christmas dinner on a South Carolina plantation between Charleston and Beaufort and describes a meal at which "about 20 sat down to a table groaning under a load of Beef, Venison, Ham, Geese, Ducks, Turkey, Chicken, Oyster Pie, hog hominy, rice, and sweet potatoes—wine—Brandy—Cordial—Gin—the Table Cloth was removed (except for the liquers) and a 2d. course came on. Plum pudding, mince, coconut, and various other descriptions of pies, whips, custards, jellies in a great variety—with other good things to match. After this came the 3d. course of viands—cake and various liquers, wine, and cordials." Slaves at such places are often permitted to visit other plantations at Christmas, and large feasts are prepared for them at which whole hogs, sheep, or steers are roasted and treats such as peach cobbler, apple dumplings, and plenty of liquor are served. Most New Englanders continue to ignore Christmas, as did their Puritan ancestors, but feast sumptuously at Thanksgiving.

Guests of wealthy plantation owners in America's Deep South enjoyed some memorable feasts.

The heath hen *Tympanuchus cupido cupido*, once common throughout New England and an important food source, is now found only on Martha's Vineyard, Mass. Market hunters have reduced the numbers of the game bird, which is closely related to the prairie chicken (*see* 1907).

Sugar production in Jamaica, British West Indies, will fall in the next two decades to between 20,000 and 25,000 tons per year, down from 70,000 tons in 1821, as a consequence of the end of slavery.

Lectures on the Science of Life by Sylvester Graham urges dietary measures for good health in two volumes. Graham blames American dyspepsia and sallow complexion on fried meat, alcohol, eating too fast, and the use of "unnatural," refined wheat flour (*see* Sulzberger, above). Espousing vegetarianism, he urges readers to eat fruits, vegetables, and unbolted (unsifted) whole wheat flour in bread that is slightly stale and is to be chewed thoroughly to promote good digestion, prevent alcoholism, and diminish the sex urge.

The white flour despised by Graham (above) has, indeed, been stripped of many nutrients, but most Americans get plenty of those nutrients from other dietary sources.

Some 95 chests of Assam tea arrive at London and are sold at auction (*see* 1823). As in China, harvesters in India and Ceylon pick only the four youngest, tiniest, tenderest leaves at the ends of branches (called *pe-ko*, or silver tip, in Chinese), but, unlike green China tea, the leaves from India are fermented, or cured ("fired"), and the original silver-tip, or pekoe, leaf turns brown, giving rise to the term "orange pekoe," which indicates the size of the leaf (the next larger size being pekoe and the largest souchong; the terms will be used only for the black teas of the East Indies; West India teas from Darjeeling, grown in the foothills of the Himalayas, have woodier, fruitier aftertastes). The new black tea, less astringent than green tea, begins to gain popularity (*see* duchess of Bedford, 1840).

London's Reform Club employs as its chef de cuisine French chef Alexis Soyer, 29, who was sent by his mother to the cathedral school at Meaux to study for the priesthood, was expelled at age 12, joined his brother Philippe, a cook at Paris, and was appreciated to the restaurant Chez Grignon. When Philippe moved to England in 1830 to flee the Revolution, Alexis went along and has worked for the duke of Sutherland, the marquis of Waterford, the marquis of Alisa, and others (it has been a mark of social status to employ a French cook for one's private kitchen). Soyer will remain at the Reform Club until 1852, and the press will call him "the great pacificator, who caused the Tory to dine in amity with the Whig" (*see* 1847).

1840

President Martin Van Buren, 57, loses his bid for reelection as the Whigs come to power with William Henry Harrison, now 68, whose supporters boast that their candidate eats raw beef without salt while the "elegant" Van Buren squanders the people's money raising raspberries, strawberries, celery, and cauliflower for the White House table.

Rep. John Ogle (Whig, Pa.) has delivered a speech April 14 heaping scorn on President Van Buren's extravagance (above). He has given the menu for a White House dinner: "*For the first course.*—Potage au tortue, Potage à la Julienne, et Potage aux pois. *Second course.*—Saumon, sauce d'anchois, Bass piqué à la Chambore [*sic*]. *Third course.*—Supreme de volaille en bordure à la galée, Filet de boeuf piqué au vin de Champagne, Paté chaud à la Toulouse. *Fourth course.*—Salade d'homard monté, Filets mignons de mouton en chevreuil, Cerveau de veau au supreme, Pigeons à la royal aux champignons. *Fifth course.*—Bécassines, Canard sauvages, Poulet de Guinée piquée. *Patisserie.*—Charlotte russe au citron, Biscuit à la vanille décoré, Coupe garnie de gelée d'orange en quartiers, Gelée au maraschin, Gelée au Champagne rose, Blanc mange, Sultane, Nougat, Petits gateaux variés. *Dessert.*—Fruits, et glace en pyramide, et en petits moules, Toste d'anchois, Café et liqueur. Followed by Sauterne, Hock, Champagne, Claret, Port, Burgundy, Sherry, and Madeira, 'choicest brands.' "

The Whig campaign song (above) is "Let Van from his coolers of silver drink wine/ And lounge on his cushioned settee,/ Our man on his buckeyed bench can recline/ Content with hard cider is he."

U.S. operating railways cover 2,816 miles, versus 1,331 in the United Kingdom, fewer than 300 miles in France. More than 300 U.S. railroad companies are in operation; tracks vary in gauge from 6 feet to 4 feet, 8.5 inches.

U.S. canals cover 3,300 miles.

Manufacture of the McCormick reaper begins with improvements added by Cyrus McCormick to his original 1831 machine (*see* 1834; 1847).

The Baltimore College of Dental Surgery, established in Maryland, is the first regular U.S. dental school. The American Society of Dental Surgeons is organized. The *American Journal of Dental Science* begins publication, but poor dental hygiene has destroyed the teeth of many Americans, limiting the kinds of food that they can take and thus compromising their nutritional health (*see* calcium, below).

Oyster canning begins at Baltimore using bivalves from Chesapeake Bay.

France sends a naval vessel into Arcachon Bay to guard its oysters from draggers and rakers (*see* 1759; Coste, 1853).

The first important U.S. breeding herd of quick-fattening Hereford cattle is established with stock imported from Britain by Erasmus Corning and William H. Sotham at Albany, N.Y. (*see* 1817).

Showman P. T. (Phineas Taylor) Barnum, 30, imports the first Dutch belted cows to be seen in the United States; he exhibits them as curiosities.

A U.S. farmer requires 233 man-hours to produce 100 bushels of wheat using primitive plow and harvesting cradle, down from 300 hours in 1831.

Grapefruit trees are introduced into Florida by Don Philippe, a Spanish nobleman (*see* Lunan, 1814; sweeter grapefruit, 1900).

Swiss chemist Charles J. Choss demonstrates the need of calcium for proper bone development (*see* Humphry Davy, 1808; vitamin D, 1922).

The first known wienerbrød is baked by the baker to the royal Danish court. The number of bakeries at Copenhagen is restricted by law to 50; when a baker dies, his son or (more rarely) his wife inherits the license, but no new bakeries will be permitted until the law is repealed in 1860, by which time the Viennese bakery will be familiar to every Dane. Danish pastry is at least 50 percent butter and often contains marzipan or almonds as well as sugar and cream.

London entrepreneur Thomas Wall inherits a Jermyn Street business that dates to the 18th century and will make it England's leading producer of sausage and meat pies (*see* 1965).

A Budapest factory established by Bohemian glue maker M. Leiner will grow to become Treforest Chemical Co., world's largest maker of bone gelatin.

San Francisco receives its first commercial shipment of wines and spirits from French-American vintner Jean Louis Vignes, 61, who came to California from Bordeaux some years ago, bought land around the settlement of Los Angeles, built up the vineyards of El Aliso, which will later be the site of Union Station, and brought in fine oak casks to replace the rough clay flasks and leather bottles used by Spanish-trained Indians. Vignes charges $2 per gallon for his best dry white table wine and $4 for his *aguardiente* (*see* Haraszthy, 1857).

Carling Brewing and Malting Co. is founded by London, Ont., brewer Thomas Carling (*see* Labatt, 1847).

A brewery started by Scots American Peter Ballantine on the Passaic River at Newark, N.J., will produce only ale until 1880 but by 1914 will be brewing half a million barrels of beer and ale per year.

Philadelphia brewer John Wagner begins producing lager beer in a small brewery behind his house in St. John Street, using a German method that begins with a yeast which ferments to the bottom of the vat rather than the top. His beer, which must be kept cool during fermentation and quite cold during storage, has a sparkling effervescence that marks a new departure for U.S. beer.

Afternoon tea is introduced by Anna, wife of the seventh duke of Bedford. Breakfasts are large, lunches sketchy, and dinner is not served until 8 o'clock, so people are hungry by late afternoon; the tea interval will become a lasting British tradition, but the English still drink more coffee than tea (*see* 1839; 1850; 1869).

Anna, duchess of Bedford, is credited with introducing the fashion of afternoon tea. PAINTING BY CATTERSON SMITH, BEDFORD ESTATE, WOBURN ABBEY

Durgin-Park's Market Dining Room opens upstairs over a warehouse in Boston's North Market Street, near the Faneuil and Quincy markets, where the restaurant will continue for more than 155 years (date approximate; Durgin-Park's will not be listed in the Boston Directory until 1874). Its surly waitresses serve chowder, broiled lobster, tripe, venison, bear steak, fried cod tongues, New England boiled dinner, Indian pudding, apple pandowdy, pies, and other specialities at communal tables that seat 10 or 15 patrons each (market men in white coats and straw hats sit side by side with the other patrons).

Antoine's restaurant has its beginnings in the Pension Alciatore founded by French-born chef

Antoine Alciatore, 27, in St. Louis Street in the French quarter of New Orleans. Alciatore, who worked in New York for 2 years before going to work in the kitchens of the St. Charles Hotel, quickly attracts a following, moves to larger quarters down the block, and sends to New York for Julie Freyss. She comes to New Orleans with her sister, marries Alciatore, and will bear him 18 children while helping to develop the restaurant at 50 St. Louis Street (*see* 1868).

Ireland's population reaches 9 million, up from 1.5 million in 1760—a 600 percent increase in 80 years made possible almost entirely by consumption of potatoes (production of bread grains would support at best only 5 million, partly because worldwide shortages of grain keep prices at levels which few Irishmen can afford) (*see* agriculture, 1641; 1842).

1841

Secretary of State Daniel Webster estimates U.S. lands west of Wisconsin not yet offered for sale to have 30,000 to 50,000 settlers. Congress gives each head of family the right, when the lands are opened for sale, to buy as much as 160 acres at a minimum price of $1.25 per acre, provided that a house has been built on the land he holds and the land is under cultivation (*see* 1804; Homestead Act, 1862).

Britain's new Peel ministry reduces import duties on raw materials and foodstuffs, thus encouraging grain imports, which lower food prices and reduce the national debt by increasing customs revenues (*see* Anti–Corn Law League, 1839).

Steam-powered machinery to produce biscuits (cookies) is employed for the first time at Reading, England.

Rail service between London and Brighton begins September 19, the 55-mile trip taking 4 hours instead of the 6 required by stagecoach. Food service is provided for passengers (see *Brighton Belle*, 1933).

Nonfiction: *A Treatise on Domestic Economy for the Use of Young Ladies at Home and at School* by Cincinnati clergyman's daughter Catherine Esther Beecher, 40, elevates the subject of woman's role in the kitchen to new heights and begins a movement toward serious education in the household arts. The *Treatise* will be reissued 15 times in the next 15 years.

Fiction: *Barnaby Rudge, a Tale of the Riots of 'Eighty* by Charles Dickens, whose character Dolly Varden will be the name of a U.S. trout species and of a spiced layer cake that will be a specialty of U.S. southern cookery.

Sir George Simpson of the Hudson's Bay Company visits the hacienda of Don Mariano Guadalupe Vallejo, 33, who 4 years ago laid out Sonoma, Calif., and partakes of his hospitality. Simpson, accompanied by a retinue of 50 men, has just opened a branch at Yerba Buena (later San Francisco), and his host, the richest man in the province, has headed the Spanish garrison charged with keeping an eye on the Russian colony at Fort Ross, 6 hours' ride to the north (*see* 1817). Vallejo has enlarged his original grant of 48,000 acres, enormous herds of cattle graze his lands along with elk and deer, and his adobe fort looks out over the myriad ducks and trumpeter swans on the marshes of San Pablo Bay. Acorn-fed pigs swarm about his hacienda. Simpson and his party remain for 2 days, eating at the barracks and out of doors. Everything, he notes, "had literally been seethed into chips, the beans, or *frijoles*, in particular having first been boiled, and lastly fried, with an intermediate stewing to break the suddenness of the transition, and every mouthful was poisoned with the everlasting compound of pepper and garlick; and the repast, be it observed, was quite an aristocratic specimen of the kind . . . all the cookery, as one may infer from the expenditure of so much labor, is the work of native drudges, unwashed and uncombed. When to the foregoing sketch are added bad tea, and worse wine [Vallejo's wine is pressed from Mission grapes, the only variety now grown in California], the reader has picked up a perfect idea of a California breakfast, California dinner, and California supper." Simpson describes eating baked bear paws, baked fish (probably dolphin from the bay), roast trumpeter swan stuffed with roasted nuts, and ragouts. He is also served East India sherry that has been imported from Acapulco on a 2 months' journey.

A New York State Fair at Syracuse begins the tradition of U.S. state fairs dedicated to the advancement of agriculture and the home arts.

A Dorchester, Mass., man exhibits the "Improved High Bush Blackberry" at a meeting of the Massachusetts Horticultural Society (*see* 1834); the name will be changed to Dorchester blackberry. Britons call the blackberry a *bramble*, Germans a *brombeere*; all successful blackberries have thorns (*see* 1853).

Irish agriculture falls into decay with 663,153 out of 690,114 land holdings having fewer than 15 acres. Tenant farmers raise grain and cattle to produce money for their rents while depending largely on potatoes for their own food. Whiskey is at times cheaper than bread, and the price discrepancy helps produce widespread drunkenness (*see* population, 1840; potato failure, 1845).

Irish cotters depended almost entirely on "praties" (potatoes) to sustain their families.

Londoner James Pimm invents Pimm's Cup, a bottled gin flavored with various herbs, spices, and sweeteners. This Pimm's No. 1 will be followed with five variations based on rum, whisky, and other liquors, but they will never account for more than a tiny percentage of the Pimm company business and will be dropped in 1974.

1842

The Webster-Ashburton Treaty signed August 9 by U.S. Secretary of State Daniel Webster and British foreign minister Alexander Baring, Baron Ashburton, 68, ends disputes over the border between Maine and Canada (the border between Oregon Territory and Canada remains in dispute). Webster has used gastronomy in negotiating the terms, courting Ashburton with Maine lobster, Chesapeake Bay crabmeat, Maryland terrapin, South Carolina rice, and canvasback duck.

New York gets its first shipment of milk by rail as the Erie Railroad line is completed to Goshen in Orange County. New Yorkers are unaccustomed to milk rich in butterfat and complain about the light yellow scum atop the milk (*see* 1884).

A live lobster from the Atlantic Coast arrives by rail at Cleveland, where it is boiled ceremoniously; it is then shipped to Chicago, where the *Daily American* pronounces it "as fresh as could be desired."

John Deere produces 100 plows and peddles them by wagon to farmers in the area of Grand Detour, Ill. (*see* 1837; 1847).

Mechanical refrigeration is pioneered by Florida physician John Gorrie, 39, who has set up a windmill to blow air through a stovepipe across a block of ice in his house at Appalachicola. He has been dependent on ice cut from New England lakes and ponds, stored in earth-insulated containers, and shipped out as disposable ballast on southbound sailing vessels; he has been willing to pay 1¢ per pound for the ice, but when an expected shipment fails to arrive he remembers his first-year physics lessons about the properties of compressing and expanding gas to generate freezing temperature; he sets a vessel of ammonia atop a stepladder, lets it drip, and thus invents an artificial ice-making machine whose basic principle will be employed in refrigeration (and air-conditioning). Gorrie, who has moved from South Carolina, will obtain a patent for his process in 1851, but, unable to obtain commercial backing, he will die in poverty 4 years later and it will be decades before Florida has a commercial ice plant (*see* Perkins, 1834; Carré, 1858; Linde, 1873).

New York industrialist-inventor Peter Cooper, 51, obtains a patent for a colored, "fruit-flavored" gelatin powder for desserts but does not develop the product (*see Cook's Oracle*, 1816; Jell-O, 1897).

German organic chemist Adolf Wilhelm Hermann Kolbe, 27, synthesizes acetic acid, found naturally in vinegar.

Starch is recovered from Indian corn for the first time at Jersey City, N.J., by English-American inventor Thomas Kingsford, 43, whose crude wet-milling process inaugurates an industry. Colgate & Co. employee Kingsford will set up his own cornstarch factory at Oswego, N.Y. Between 1865 and 1880, cornstarch-processing companies will spring up on the eastern seaboard and as far west as Nebraska, some making corn sugar, others cornstarch (*see* American Glucose, 1898).

France has nearly 60 sugar beet factories producing two pounds of sugar per capita annually (*see* 1810; 1878).

Animal Chemistry (*Die Thierchemie*) by German chemist Justus Freiherr von Liebig, 39, applies classic methodology to studying animal tissues, suggests that animal heat is produced by combustion, and founds the science of biochemistry. Liebig will call protein the muscle-building substance, absolutely essential to human strength (*see* nutrition, 1859).

English novelist Charles Dickens visits America and writes March 28 (his 30th birthday) while en route to Pittsburgh that for breakfast "there are upon the table tea and coffee, and bread and butter, and salmon, and shad, and liver, and steak, potatoes, and pickles."

John Morrell & Co. is established by the son of George Morrell, who takes over the 15-year-old company started by his father after saving it from a financial crisis. The firm has been curing its own hams and bacons (*see* 1827; 1868).

Hecker Flour has its beginnings in the Croton Flour Mill built at New York City by local millers John and George V. Hecker, who within 20 years will be operating mills with a total capacity of 4,000 hundredweight (*see* self-rising flour, 1852).

The Buitoni factory in Italy produces 3,600 pounds of pasta per day (*see* 1827; 1856).

Cadbury Brothers begins offering French eating chocolate to the English public (*see* 1824; 1847).

Philadelphia entrepreneur Stephen F. Whitman goes into business making candies in a little kitchen and selling them at a retail shop near the waterfront. Imported candies dominate the quality candy trade; most come from France, have exotic centers and fill-ings—nougat, caramel, fondant, French cream—and are elegantly designed and wrapped. Whitman, who sets out to compete with the foreign imports, will head his company for 44 years (*see* Whitman's Sampler, 1912).

Maine blacksmith's son Daniel Fobes finds work as a huckster at the sprawling market beneath Boston's Faneuil Hall, learns how to make candied popcorn balls using maple sugar, pours the sugar into molds for sale as a confection, and develops a business (*see* 1854).

Mott's Apple Cider and Mott's Vinegar are introduced by Bouckville, N.Y., entrepreneur Sam R. Mott, who crushes local apples with the power of horses hitched to a sweep that turns two large stone drums. He shovels the crushed apples into a crib with slatted slides, packs in straw, and has three men lean on a level that operates a jack screw to squeeze out the juice, which runs into a tank below and is soon ready for bottling. Waterpower and steam will soon replace the horses, Mott's son will help him, he will enlarge his cider mill, it will be the first U.S. mill to employ a scientifically controlled oxidation process instead of allowing conversion of cider to vinegar to occur in open tanks, the cider will soon be shipped beyond local upstate New York grocery stores to customers throughout New England and other states, and by the 1880s Mott's Champagne Cider will be going in 1,000-case lots along with casks of Mott's Vinegar by clipper ship to California (*see* Duffy-Mott, 1900).

Rochester, N.Y., entrepreneur W. B. Duffy enters the cider business, using methods similar to those of S. R. Mott (above) (*see* Duffy-Mott, 1900).

Vienna has 15,000 coffeehouses (*Kaffeehäuser*) (*see* 1700). The establishments are in most instances for men only, although some permit women if they are escorted by men. Many if not most have adopted the idea, originated in the last century by the Paris café Bucy, of offering patrons free newspapers from all over Europe (*see* 1925).

1843

Slavery is abolished in British India, where slaves have continued to produce sugar since the emancipation of slavery elsewhere in the British Empire 10 years ago.

English social reformer George Jacob Holyoake, 26, tells weavers at Rochdale, "Anybody can see that the little money you get is half-wasted, because you cannot spend it to advantage. The worst food comes to the poor, which their poverty makes them buy and their necessity makes them eat. Their stomachs are the waste-basket of the State. It is their lot to swallow all the adulterations on the market" (*see* cooperative society, 1844; Engels, 1845).

English social agitator Feargus O'Connor, 49, urges creation of a Chartist cooperative land association that will free working people from the tyranny of the factory and the Poor Law. Settling people on the land will take surplus labor off the market and force manufacturers to offer higher factory wages, he says (*see* below).

$ The price of pepper imported by New Englanders from Sumatra since 1805 drops to less than 3¢ per pound. (*see* 1873).

300 stems of Cuban red bananas are landed at New York and sold at 25¢ a "finger" wholesale by John Pearsall (*see* 1830). Now a New York commission merchant, Pearsall will go bankrupt within a few years, when a shipment of 3,000 stems arrives in too ripe a state to be sold (*see* Baker, 1870).

The J. I. Case threshing machine is introduced by former Oswego County, N.Y., farmer Jerome Increase Case, 24, who last year came West with six of the best threshing machines he could buy, sold five to prairie farmers, used the sixth to thresh wheat for farmers in Wisconsin, learned from experience the deficiencies of existing machines, and used money earned while learning to develop a superior machine. Case will build a factory at Racine, Wis., and develop a sales organization that will make J. I. Case the world's largest thresher producer and a major manufacturer of farm steam engines, tractors, and other farm equipment (*see* 1837; 1908).

 Fiction: *A Christmas Carol* by Charles Dickens, whose Ebenezer Scrooge shares roast goose with his clerk Bob Cratchit and the whole Cratchit family: "There never was such a goose! Bob said he didn't believe there ever was such a goose cooked. Its tenderness and flavour, size and cheapness, were the themes of universal admiration. Eked out by applesauce and mashed potatoes, it was a sufficient dinner for the whole family; indeed, as Mrs. Cratchit said with great delight (surveying one small atom of a bone upon the dish), they hadn't ate it all at last! Yet everyone had had enough, and the youngest Cratchits in particular, were steeped in sage and onion to the eyebrows! But now, the plates being changed by Miss Belinda, Mrs. Cratchit left the room alone—too nervous to bear witnesses—to take the pudding up and bring it in. . . . Hallo! A great deal of steam! The pudding was out of the copper. A smell like a washing-day! That was the cloth. A smell like an eating-house and a pastrycook's next door to each other, with a laundress's next door to that! That was the pudding! In half a minute, Mrs. Cratchit entered—flushed, but smiling proudly—with the pudding, like a speckled cannonball, so hard and firm, blazing in half of half-a-quartern of ignited brandy, and bedight with Christmas holly stuck into the top. Oh, a wonderful pudding!"

The Chartist Cooperative Land Association urged by Feargus O'Connor (above) will, he says, encourage intensive "spade husbandry" that will double the soil's productivity.

Copenhagen's Tivoli and Vauxhall Gardens open August 15 with amusements and restaurants that attract an initial crowd of 3,615 (3,165 by some accounts; more than 10,000 come the following Sunday, out of a total city population of 120,000, and the final count of visitors for the season is 174,608). Entrepreneur George Carstensen, 31, whose father was Danish consular secretary at Algiers when he was born, has persuaded Denmark's Christian VIII to grant him a concession of some 14 acres on a onetime battlefield beyond the city's west gate at a modest annual rent of 945 kroner and has been his own architect, contractor, and landscape gardener. Tivoli will grow to have a 2,000-seat concert hall, a variety theater, a pantomime-ballet theater, a dance hall, and 23 restaurants (Divan I and Divan II are the first; Belle Terrasse, Balkonen, and Perlen will come later) plus smaller eating establishments.

Paris has 3,000 cafés, up from 700 in 1789.

Japan's capital city of Edo has a population of 1.8 million and is second in size only to London (*see*

1801), but the nation's total population of nearly 30 million is controlled by infanticide (the Japanese call it *mabiki*, using an agricultural term that means "thinning out").

1844

A prizewinning essay on Britain's "National Distress" by English author Samuel Laing, 31, reveals the effects of machinery on the country's working class: "About one-third plunged in extreme misery, and hovering on the verge of actual starvation; another third, or more, earning an income something better than that of the common agricultural labourer, but under circumstances very prejudicial to health, morality, and domestic comfort—viz. by the labour of young children, girls, and mothers of families in crowded factories; and finally, a third earning high wages, amply sufficient to support them in respectability and comfort."

The Rochdale Society of Equitable Pioneers founded by 28 poor weavers at Rochdale, Lancashire, is the first modern cooperative society (*see* Holyoake, 1843). The society opens a store in Toad Lane, sells strictly for cash at local retail prices, and at year's end divides its profits among its members. Flour, oatmeal, butter, and sugar are its only initial wares, but the store soon adds tea and groceries and will later sell coal, clothing, and furniture.

Fruitlands is founded by Concord social reformer Amos Bronson Alcott, 44, whose utopian commune in northern Massachusetts does not succeed. He and his fellow communards at Fruitlands neglect practical necessities in their passion for talk and social reform activities, the failure of their crops reduces them to near-starvation, and they abandon the community within a few months.

Milk reaches Manchester by rail for the first time, and shipments soon begin to London (*see* 1863). Rail transport will lower British food prices and make fresh eggs, green vegetables, fresh fish, and country-killed meat available more quickly.

Nonfiction: English fiction writer William Makepeace Thackeray, 33, writes, "A man who brags regarding himself; that whatever he swallows is the same to him, and that his coarse palate recognizes no difference between venison and turtle, pudding or mutton-broth, brags about a personal defect—the wretch—and not about a virtue. It is like a man boasting that he has no ear for music, or no eye for colour, or that his nose cannot scent the difference between a rose and a cabbage—I say, as a general rule, set that man down as a conceited fellow who swaggers about not caring for his dinner."

Cookbook: *Praktisches Kochbuch* by German hausfrau Henriette Davidis-Holle is published for the first time. It will go through continuous revisions over the years and become a classic source for upper-middle-class German households.

French agricultural chemist Jean-Baptiste-Joseph-Dieudonné Boussingault, 42, publishes a listing of foods ranked according to their relative value as protein sources (*see* Mulder, 1838).

New England's Hood Dairy enteprise has its beginnings as Vermont farmer's son Harvey P. Hood, 23, moves to Boston with horses, harness, wagon, and sleigh. He starts work driving a bakery route in suburban Charlestown at $12 per month (*see* 1846).

U.S. coffee imports reach close to 150 million pounds, up from 35 in 1832, as coffee comes in free of duty and opposition to consumption of alcoholic beverages increases (*see* 1851).

1845

Potato crops fail throughout Europe, Britain, and Ireland as the fungus disease *Phytophthora infestans* rots potatoes in the ground and also those in storage (*see* 1784). Peculiar black spots appear on the leaves of the potato plants after a cold, wet summer. Irish potatoes are even less resistant than potatoes elsewhere, so up to half the crop is lost as fields turn black with devasted foliage. When dug up, the tubers appear sound, but within a month they go rotten, first with dry rot and then with wet rot. Since potatoes represent Ireland's most important food crop (most Irishmen live on a diet of potatoes supplemented by some vegetables and a little milk), millions go hungry.

Famine kills 2.5 million from Ireland to Moscow and is generally blamed on the wrath of God. The famine is especially severe in Ireland, where so many peasants depend on potatoes for food while exporting their grain and meat; British private charity and government relief do little to alleviate the suffering.

The English potato famine spurs free-trade supporters Richard Cobden and orator John Bright, 34, at Manchester to lead a wide-scale agitation against the Corn Laws that prevent free imports of grain. Whig leader John Russell, 53, is converted to free trade (*see* 1846).

Fernet-Branca Italian bitters are introduced at Milan by the Branca brothers, who name their compound of herbs, spices, and alcohol after a Swedish physician whose secret recipe they have perfected. Italy will have more than 300 such after-dinner *amari* (tonics designed to speed digestion), which will be sold at pharmacies and hawked by peddlers to relieve the heaviness experienced after consuming meals of pasta, bread, meat, potatoes, and dessert. Always taken before coffee (and sometimes, in winter, served steamed with a twist of orange), *amari* will for the next century be made mostly in monasteries or as homemade preparations whose recipes are passed on from one generation to the next (*see* Averna, 1868).

Cookbook: *Modern Cookery, in All Its Branches Reduced to a System of Easy Practice, for the Use of Private Families. And a Series of Receipts, Which Have Been Strictly Tested, and Are Given with the Most Minute Exactness* by English author Eliza Acton, 46, who includes recipes for oatmeal, polenta, Indian corn, hominy, pig's ears and feet, venison, wild pigeon, domestic pigeon, sturgeon, and conger eel.

"Johnny Appleseed" dies in March at age 70 in the home of a friend near Fort Wayne, Indiana (*see* 1806). A ragged, bearded man who appeared at cabin doors requesting bread, milk, and floor space on which to sleep, John Chapman had reached Indiana by 1828, has repaid his hosts with appleseeds, read to them from his Bible and a book by the Danish philosopher Søren Kierkegaard, and made himself a legend.

Chocolate Sprüngli AG has its beginnings in a Zurich factory opened in May by Swiss confectioner David Sprüngli and his son. An orphan who was apprenticed in his youth to a Zurich pastryshop owner, the elder Sprüngli will be the pioneer of chocolate in German-speaking Switzerland (*see* Lindt, 1875).

Temporary drinking shops spring up in Ireland (above) to sell spirits wherever public works schemes are established which pay the workers in cash.

Poland Spring Water is bottled for the first time at Poland Spring, Me., where an underground aquifer of fine sand and gravel produces water that is drawn off at an icy 45° to 48° F. Entrepreneur Hiram Ricker, whose family opened a small inn on the site in 1793, bottles the spring water (which is rich in calcium, iron, and magnesium) in order that it may be taken home by visitors, who have been coming to quaff ever since Ricker's father, Joseph, was allegedly cured of a fever by drinking it (*see* 1893).

The New York hotel-restaurant Sweet's opens at 2–4 Fulton Street (it will be a hotel until the 1930s). Proprietor Edward Sweet offers fish chowders and all manner of fresh fish and shellfish from the nearby Fulton Fish Market.

Fire destroys the Delmonico's Restaurant in Broad Street, New York (*see* 1832). Lorenzo Delmonico replaces it with a new establishment across from Bowling Green at which he will play host not only to New York society but also to visiting dignitaries and celebrities.

1846

The Mexican War, precipated by President James K. Polk, 50, begins January 13 and will end with the United States acquiring California and much of the Southwest (*see* 1848).

Famine sweeps Ireland as the potato crop fails again and food reserves are exhausted (*see* 1845). The entire crop has been planted with infected seed potatoes, and whatever grows is inedible. British Conservatives ascribe the famine to the divine hand of Providence and say it would paralyze trade to give away food to the Irish, Britons marshal private aid programs, Americans raise $1 million and send relief ships, but the aid programs are mismanaged, the Irish lack horses and carts for carrying imported grain to inland famine areas, they lack ovens and bakers for making bread, and close to a million die of starvation and hunger-related typhus.

$ Parliament finally repeals Britain's Corn Law June 28. Conservatives led by Benjamin Disraeli oppose Prime Minister Robert Peel's free-trade actions, denounce Peel for betraying his protectionist principles, but are unable to prevent repeal of the 1828 Corn Law, which is replaced by laws that reduce (and will soon virtually eliminate) duties on grain imports, reduce duties on wines, imported cheeses, butter, and other foods, and abolish duties on live animal imports.

Repeal of the Corn Law (above) removes the favored status that Ireland has enjoyed as a supplier to the British market. Large Irish landowners (most of them absentee landlords) switch from growing wheat to raising cattle. They throw cotters off the land so that it may be used for pasturage.

The United States moves closer to free trade July 30 with passage of the Walker Tariff Act, named for President Polk's Treasury Secretary Robert S. Walker of Alabama. The act taxes luxuries at a high rate but lowers import duties and enlarges the list of items admitted duty-free.

Britain and America will both benefit in the next 15 years by the lowering and suspension of tariffs. U.S. exports will double to $306 million in the first 10 years of the Walker Tariff Act while imports will triple to $361 million, customs revenues will more than double, and U.S. consumers will enjoy cheap manufactured products while Britons enjoy low food prices.

Of the United Kingdom's 3.2 million tons of merchant shipping, some 131,000 tons are steam-driven.

Some 175 U.S. ships leave port with 65,000 tons of ice for export as Boston's Tudor Ice Co. ships large tonnages to the Far East, where it is sold at high prices to buy silk, which is bought cheaply and sold at high prices in America (see 1833). Tudor's trade has stimulated the use of ice in the U.S. South and breathed new life into Boston's dwindling East Indian trade (see 1856).

Walden Pond yields 10,000 pounds of ice in 16 days, Concord, Mass., pencil maker Henry David Thoreau, 30, will write in his journal. "A hundred Irishmen with Yankee overseers" have come from Cambridge, Mass., to harvest the ice, the cakes are "sledded to the shore . . . rapidly hauled off onto an ice platform, and raised by grappling irons and block and tackle, worked by horses, onto a stack . . . and there placed side by side, and row upon row, as if they formed the solid based of an obelisk designed to pierce the clouds." The stack of ice, covered with hay and boards, measures "35 feet high on one side and six or seven rods square," but it will never get to market and will stay on the bank

Ice from New England lakes and ponds was shipped to the Southern states and even to India.

of the pond until September 1848, when it will almost have melted (*see* Thoreau, 1854).

 Philadelphia dairymaid Nancy Johnson devises a portable hand-cranked ice cream freezer (*see* 1849; Jefferson, 1802).

The word "osteoporosis" is introduced in medicine to delineate a condition, especially common in post-menopausal women (but also seen in men over age 60), marked by decrease in bone mass with concomitant increase in porosity and fragility. Caused by a disturbance of calcium metabolism (and perhaps insufficient calcium intake earlier in life), it can drain calcium deposits from the bone matrix until anywhere from 10 to 40 percent of the mineral is gone, creating fractures that are slow to heal, giving a woman "dowager's hump," and causing her to lose several inches in height (*see* 1868).

Cookbooks: *The Gastronomic Regenerator* by Alexis Soyer, who gives Reform Club recipes for 2,000 dishes ranging from elaborate roast peacock to simple roasts, chops, stews, and hashes. Written in just 10 months, during which time its author has supervised more than 60 servants and managed 39 important banquets, the book's initial printing of 2,000 copies sells out in 2 months at a guinea per copy, four editions will be printed in less than a year, and the book will become the acknowledged classic of haute cuisine, with sales of some 250,000 copies by 1890. The *Times of London* calls it "a pyramid which the remotest posterity will applaud." *The Jewish Manual*, "edited by a Lady" (probably Judith, Lady Montefiore) is the first Jewish cookbook in English. *The Indian Meal Book, Comprising the Best Receipts for the Preparation of That Article* is published in England. It does not use the word *maize*, which is considered food for cattle, but calls Indian corn the ideal solution to the widespread starvation (above). *The Young Housekeeper's Friend* by Mrs. [Mary] Cornelius of Boston. *Miss Beecher's Domestic Receipt Book* by Catherine E. Beecher.

"Yellow meal" (cornmeal) imported from the United States to relieve the Irish famine (above) will be consumed, reluctantly, as a porridge but will eventually be mixed with wheat flour to make sweet Irish soda cake.

Britons celebrate repeal of the Corn Law (above) by baking a meat pie containing 100 pounds of beef, five sheep, and one calf plus great quantities of hares, rabbits, pheasants, partridges, grouse, ducks, geese, turkeys, guinea fowls, common fowls, pigeons, and other small birds, all baked for 10 hours and drawn by 30 horses (the platform on which it is placed collapses, but the pie is unharmed).

William Underwood of Boston begins packing fish and shellfish in Maine (*see* 1822; deviled ham, 1867).

Prime Minister Peel (above) has been persuaded that reducing the cost of French wines by lowering import taxes on them will provide a cheap alternative to crude spirits in Britain and thus discourage drunkenness.

Dubonnet is introduced at Paris. The apéritif wine will gain worldwide popularity.

Harvey P. Hood uses his savings to start a milk route at Charlestown, Mass., but finds that the milk from nearby farmers is sometimes of dubious quality and that supplies are not always reliable (*see* 1844). He will buy a farm of his own at Derry, N.H., to produce milk whose quality he can control (*see* 1854).

The Homestead opens at Hot Springs, Va., where it will grow to become a popular spa with fine dining facilities.

Irish emigration to England, Canada, Australia, and America is spurred by the famine (above) and repeal of the Corn Law as cotters are thrown off the land and small farmers denied their favored status in the English market (*see* 1847).

1847

A relief expedition reaches the Donner Party in the Sierra Nevada February 19 and finds evidence of cannibalism. Trapped for 3 months by heavy snows in the worst winter ever, the wagon train of Oregon-bound emigrants has lost 12 members to starvation; 46 of the original 87 will ultimately survive (*see* Borden, 1848).

"The Communist Manifesto" (*Manifest des Kommunismus*) published late in the year calls for "1.

Abolition of property in land and application of all rents of land to public purposes. 2. A heavy progressive or graduated income tax. 3. Abolition of all right of inheritance. 4. Confiscation of the property of all emigrants and rebels. 5. Centralization of credit in the hands of the state, by means of a national bank with state capital and an exclusive monopoly. 6. Centralization of the means of communication and transport in hands of the state. 7. Extension of factories and instruments of production owned by the state; the bringing into cultivation of waste lands, and the improvement of the soil generally in accordance with a common plan. 8. Equal obligation of all to work. Establishment of industrial armies, especially for agriculture. 9. Combination of agriculture with manufacturing industries; gradual abolition of the distinction between town and country, by a more equable distribution of the population of the country," etc. German socialists Karl Marx, 29, and Friedrich Engels, 26, have written the pamphlet (*see* 1848).

Economic depression engulfs Britain, provincial banks fail, and even the 153-year-old Bank of England comes under pressure.

Cyrus McCormick forms a partnership with C. M. Gray and builds a three-story brick reaper factory on the north bank of the Chicago River near Lake Michigan (*see* 1834). McCormick has rejected sites at Cincinnati, Cleveland, Milwaukee, and St. Louis, deciding that Chicago may still be a swamp but is receiving great tonnages of grain via William Ogden's new Galena and Chicago Union Railroad and is clearly destined to become a grain transportation center (*see* 1848).

Obed Hussey introduces an improved version of his 1834 reaper, but he has moved his works to Baltimore and lacks the central geographical location (and capital) to compete successfully with McCormick (above) (*see* 1860).

John Deere builds a factory at Moline, Ill., to produce his self-polishing steel plows (*see* 1842; 1852).

Canada's Massey-Ferguson farm implement colossus has its beginnings in a machinery firm started by Ontario farmer Daniel Massey (*see* Massey-Harris, 1890).

A stamping process is developed to make tin cans cheap enough for wider sale (*see* 1830; Mason, 1858; Solomon, 1861; can opener, 1865).

Canned tomatoes are put up in small tin pails with soldered lids by the assistant steward of Lafayette College, established 21 years ago near Easton, Pa.

Boston confectioner Oliver Chase invents an automatic lozenge cutter—the world's first candy-making machine. He has been making his lozenges by clarifying brown sugar with eggs and pulverizing it in a mortar with a brass pestle, heating drops of peppermint oil, dropping the oil carefully into liquid gum arabic, kneading it to just the right consistency, then spreading out the mixture and cutting it into round shapes. His crude device looks like a clothes wringer with a series of holes cut in the rollers. The reel whirs, and a prepared sheet of candy paste fitted into one side of the machine emerges on the other side, enabling Chase to turn out quantities of lozenges, each perfectly shaped, with far less effort (*see* 1851; Necco, 1901).

Nonfiction: *Three Years' Wanderings in the Northern Provinces of China* by Scottish horticulturist Robert Fortune, 33, who writes, "In the knowledge and practice of agriculture, although the Chinese may be in advance of other Eastern nations they are not for a moment to be compared to the civilised nations of the West." But he admits that "for a few cash . . . a Chinese can dine in sumptuous manner upon his rice, fish, vegetables, and tea; and I fully believe, that in no country in the world is there less real misery and want than in China." Fortune has found beef and milk common fare in Foochow (*see* 1857).

Cookbooks: *Charitable Cookery, or the Poor Man's Regenerator* is published at London. Its author is Reform Club chef Alexis Soyer, who helps to establish a soup kitchen that serves 2,000 to 3,000 starving Londoners per day as the economic depression (above) creates widespread unemployment in the city. (He also helps to open a soup kitchen at Dublin.) Soyer's recipes use the ends, or peelings, of vegetables, which, he claims, have more flavor than the insides. *The Carolina Housewife* by "A Lady of Charleston."

The first ring doughnuts are introduced by Camden, Maine, baker's apprentice Hanson Crockett Gregory, 15, who knocks the soggy center out of a fried doughnut (by some accounts he is a schoolboy who complains to his mother that her deep-fried cakes are undercooked in the center and suggests that she poke a hole in the middle; the small cut-out centers will be fried separately and given to children) (*see* doughnut cutter, 1872).

Hawaii's Parker Ranch has its beginnings in a small parcel of land at the base of Mauna Kea volcano granted January 14 by Kamehameha III to Massachusetts-born *kamaaina* (longtime resident) John Palmer Parker, 57, who jumped ship to settle in the Sandwich Islands at age 19, married a granddaughter of Kamehameha 17 years later, and has served the royal family by providing hides and meat from wild cattle put ashore originally by George Vancouver from his ship *Discovery* in 1793. Parker has developed a ranching operation that will grow to embrace 227,000 acres with more than 50,000 head of Herefords—the largest privately owned ranch in the world.

South Australia's first wine grapes are planted near the German village of Tanunda by geologist Johann Menge (*see* Yalumba, 1849).

Ireland's potato crop is sound for the first time since 1844 but is small for lack of seed potatoes in the spring.

Ohio farmer Robert Reid moves west to Illinois and plants Gordon Hopkins Gourdseed corn, a reddish strain that he has brought with him and that has been grown successfully for years in Virginia. When he finds that it grows poorly in Illinois, he replants the patches where it has failed with Little Yellow Flint corn, an eight-rowed, hard-starch variety which the Indians of the Northeast have grown for centuries; the two varieties fertilize each other, and the accidental result is Reid's Yellow Dent. Its cobs are filled from tip to butt with plump, evenly spaced yellow kernels that will make it popular with farmers across the country, most of whom will give up other varieties in favor of Reid's Yellow Dent (*see* 1893).

U.S. farmers developed new strains of corn without benefit of scientific training. LIBRARY OF CONGRESS

Horticulturist Henderson Lewelling arrives in Oregon Territory after having traveled by covered wagon from Iowa. He begins an industry in the Willamette Valley by planting 700 grafted fruit trees—apples, sweet cherry, pear, plum, and quince, all less than four feet tall (*see* 1849; grapes, below).

Cadbury Brothers moves to larger premises in Birmingham as John Cadbury takes his brother Benjamin into partnership (*see* 1842). Cadbury has been roasting and grinding cocoa since 1831, he has been preparing sugar-sweetened chocolate powder and unsweetened cocoa powder, and for the past 5 years he has been offering French eating chocolate (*see* 1866; van Houten, 1828).

London, Ont., brewer John Labatt and a partner acquire a rebuilt 1832 plant and go into competition with Thomas Carling (*see* 1840).

Henderson Lewelling (above) introduces the Isabella variety of Lambrusca grape to Oregon's Willamette Valley, where a modest wine industry will develop, especially after Swiss immigrant Peter Britt plants European vinifera in the Rogue Valley and they make their way up to the Willamette.

New Jersey–born Cincinnati lawyer Nicholas Longworth, 66, produces the first American sparkling wine using Catawba grapes. Longworth first obtained Catawba cuttings from John Adlum (*see* 1829). His wine enjoys enormous success, but the warm, humid summers of the Ohio Valley will make vineyards vulnerable to mildew and rot; by the end of the next decade, Ohio's wine industry will be in decline.

New York's first Chinese immigrants arrive July 10 aboard the seagoing junk *Kee Ying*, 212 days under sail out of Guangzhou (Canton), with 35 passengers and crewmen (some of whom jump ship). Their arrival marks the beginning of the city's Chinatown, which will have 1,000 residents by 1887 (*see* general store, 1875).

More than 200,000 emigrants leave Ireland, up from 60,000 in 1842, and many go to America. The poor pay a fare of between £3 and £5 ($15 to $25) per head for passage aboard small sailing vessels, few of which are inspected and many of which are not seaworthy. Passengers provide their own food, which is often inadequate when poor winds make the passage a long one.

1848

The Treaty of Guadalupe Hidalgo February 2 ends the 2-year-old Mexican War. Mexico gives up 35 percent of her territory, including California and all lands north of the Rio Grande.

Famine strikes Europe with such severity that many countries, including Denmark and Belgium, permit free import of grain to relieve the hunger (*see* Fribourg, below).

Paris students and workers seize the city in response to last year's "Communist Manifesto" and proclaim a new French Republic; the revolution spreads to Berlin, Budapest, Milan, Prague, and Vienna and throughout much of Europe as the manifesto appears in virtually every European language.

Britain's Chartist movement of 1843 revives. Feargus O'Connor, now 54, was elected to Parliament from Nottingham last year and presents a Chartist petition that is claimed to have 6 million signatures, but a procession to support chartism that was scheduled for April 10 is called off when the government garrisons London on suspicion that a revolt will start that day. The government announces that the Chartist petition contains fewer than 2 million signatures.

Britain suspends the Habeas Corpus Act in Ireland in July as political seething follows in the wake of last year's famine and continuing high food prices despite improvement in the potato crop.

Belgian grain broker Michel Fribourg, 23, son of Simon (*see* 1813), journeys to Bessarabia with bags of gold, purchases quantities of grain to help relieve the famine (above), and returns with them to Arlon, traveling up the Danube and down the Rhine (*see* 1890).

The Chicago Board of Trade has its beginnings April 3 in a commodity exchange opened at 101 South Water Street by 82 local businessmen. Served by 400 vessels, 64 of them steamers, Chicago has become a major shipping point for grain and livestock from the Midwest bound for the Atlantic seaboard (*see* 1865).

Gold has been discovered January 24 on California's American River, news of it appears August 19 in the *New York Herald*, and by year's end some 6,000 men are working in the goldfields (*see* 1849).

The first U.S. patent for coating metal with a durable, heat-resistant enamel surface is issued to German-American inventor Charles Stümer, who says that his process can be "modified so as to render it in all the shades and colors in full variety." Cast-iron cooking pots have been enameled in Germany for at least 60 years.

News of last year's Donner Party experience reaches Galveston, Tex. Local surveyor–land agent Gail Borden, 47, determines to find ways to make foods that will be long-lasting and portable (*see* 1849).

U.S. inventor William G. Young obtains a patent for the Johnson Patent Ice-Cream Freezer invented by Nancy Johnson 2 years ago.

Chicago's Cyrus McCormick produces 500 reapers in time for the harvest (*see* 1847; 1849).

 Passenger pigeons appear to mate only occasionally in the eastern United States but remain plentiful in the new state of Wisconsin (*see* 1813; 1871).

Mormon farmers begin plowing the shores of Great Salt Lake and introduce irrigation to U.S. agriculture.

"Bartlett" pears are distributed by Dorchester, Mass., merchant Enoch Bartlett, now 69, who by some accounts has bought them from Roxbury farmer–sea captain Thomas Brewer (*see* 1817).

The American Pomological Society begins to standardize the names of apple varieties, hundreds of which are grown in U.S. orchards.

A Treatise on the Falsification of Foods and the Chemical Means Employed to Detect Them by English analytical chemist John Mitchell is published at London (*see* Accum, 1820; Hassall and Letheby, 1851).

U.S. commercial tomato ketchup products often contain boric acid, formalin, salicylic acid, benzoic acid, and coal tar, used to produce a bright red color. Packers cannot bottle an entire year's supply in the brief period from mid-August to mid-October when tomatoes are picked, so many concentrate tomato pulp during the season and preserve it for future use, often under unsanitary conditions.

The San Juan, Puerto Rico, restaurant La Mallorquina is founded, serving *criolla* foods such as asopao (a soupy rice dish made with chicken, crayfish, land crabs, shrimps, or squid), sopa de Gindules (green pigeon-pea soup), and carey encebollabo (sea-turtle steak with onions).

1849

U.S. commodity prices leap as a result of the California gold discoveries (*see* 1848). Workers strike for higher wages in order to live, but wage hikes do not keep pace with rises in the cost of living.

Britain reduces duties on food imports to nominal levels under the law passed in 1846.

Parliament abolishes Britain's Navigation Acts June 26, ending restrictions on foreign shipping. U.S. clipper ships are permitted to bring cargoes of China tea to British ports (*see* 1850).

Thousands of U.S. farmers buy $100 McCormick reapers after being deserted by workers gone to California. McCormick has stocked warehouses throughout the upper Mississippi Valley to meet the demand, he guarantees his reapers, lets farmers buy them on an installment plan geared to harvest conditions, never sues a farmer for payment, but pays his factory workers small wages for long hours of labor (*see* 1848; 1850).

Basque shepherds from Argentina and Uruguay flock to California in quest of gold. Many will later become sheepherders on the western range.

Food-canning technology improves with the invention of a machine that makes tops and bottoms, enabling two unskilled workers to produce 1,500 cans per day. It took two skilled tinsmiths to make just 120 per day without the machine (*see* 1870; vacuum pan, 1813).

Gail Borden invents a "meat biscuit" to provide a portable food for friends leaving in July for California (*see* 1848). Borden makes what he calls an "important discovery . . . an improved process of preserving the nutritious properties of meat, or animal flesh, of any kind, by obtaining the concentrated extract of it, and combining it with flour or vegetable meal, and drying or baking the mixture in an oven in the form of a biscuit or cracker." He will put 6 years and $60,000 into developing and promoting his "meat biscuit" (*see* 1852).

Cookbook: *The Modern Ménagère, Adapted to the Wants and Habits of the Middle Classes* by Alexis Soyer of London's Reform Club is in the form of an exchange of letters and recipes between friends. Soyer advocates increased consumption of vegetables, which are cheap but not much used by the middle and lower classes.

Henry David Thoreau laments what dam builders are doing to the shad, a fish "formerly abundant here and taken in weirs by the Indians, who taught this method to the whites by whom they were used as food and as manure" (*see* Tisquantum, 1621). The shad are disappearing, says Thoreau, as "the dam, and afterward the canal at Billerica and the factories at Lowell, put an end to their migrations hitherward" (*see* 1834; 1858).

Henderson Lewelling takes his first crop of Oregon apples to San Francisco and sells all 100 of them at $5 apiece to prospectors hungry for fresh fruit (*see* 1847; scurvy, below).

The comice pear (originally the Doyenne du comice) is introduced in France, where the new variety is grown initially in the palace gardens of Prince Louis-Napoleon Bonaparte, president of the republic. Its light green skin turns yellower with a rosy blush when ripe, and it will generally be acknowledged as the sweetest and juiciest of pears.

South Australia's Yalumba vineyard has its beginnings as émigré English brewer Samuel Smith plants wine grapes (*see* 1847; 1851).

Some 10,000 California gold seekers will die of scurvy in the next few years. More thousands will avoid scurvy by eating winter purslane (*Montia perfoliata*), an herb that will be called miner's lettuce.

The San Francisco restaurant Macao and Woosung, founded by Chinese immigrant Norman Asing, is the first recorded Chinese restaurant in America. Wearing a queue under his stovepipe hat, Asing speaks passable English and claims to have been baptized at Charleston, S.C., and naturalized as a U.S. citizen. His eating place will soon be followed by many more, all serving cheap, palatable dishes that cater to hungry prospectors.

The San Francisco saloon Poulet d'Or opens at 65 Post Street as the gold rush attracts dozens of French chefs to the Bay area, where newly rich miners demand haute cuisine along with other aspects of good living. The saloon quickly becomes known as the Poodle Dog and expands into a hotel-restaurant that will be an elegant French restaurant by the 1880s. Diners on the first floor will consume 20-course dinners while others will repair to upstairs salons or suites, reached by a private entrance, for dinners *à deux*. The Poulet d'Or will merge with two other French restaurants in 1906 but close in 1922 (*see* Ritz, 1932).

San Francisco's Tadich Grill has its beginnings in the New World Coffee Stand, a waterfront café opened by Dalmatian immigrant Nicholas Buja and two compatriots, who serve lunch to sailors who arrive with shiploads of goldseekers. The café will become a restaurant in 1882 and acquire the name Tadich Grill when Buja's nephew, John Tadich, takes over in 1887. It will move in 1912 to Leidesdorf and Clay Streets, Tadich will sell the business in 1928 to some Yugoslavs, who will keep Tadich's chef Louis Sokitch, and it will move in 1967 to 240 California Street, serving Dungeness crab, prawns, scallops, eastern oysters, Olympia oysters, Oregon razor clams, Coney Island clam chowder, oyster stew, grilled swordfish, sturgeon, petrale sole, rex sole, sand dab, cioppino, seafood casseroles, lobster thermidor, corned beef and cabbage, pot roast, beef tongue, skirt steak, sourdough bread (*see* 1850), cranshaw melon, and rice custard pudding.

1850

Britain enters a "Golden Age" of prosperity as she embraces free trade principles that remove tariffs on foodstuffs. Self-sufficient in food until now and generally even a food exporter, Britain becomes a net food importer, depending mostly on Russia for her grain, and depends on her manufacturing industry to provide the foreign exchange needed to feed her people. Food prices will rise far less swiftly than other prices, and British wage increases will more than keep pace with price increases.

Amsterdam merchant Charles Bunge moves his company's head office to Antwerp; after more than a century of trading in spices and other commodities from Dutch overseas possessions, Bunge will hereafter be a major grain trader (*see* 1876).

French farmer's son Léopold Louis-Dreyfus, 17, loads a cart with wheat grown at his native Sierentz and sells it at Basel, eight miles away across the Swiss border. The youngest of 13 sons, he sees little future in remaining at Sierentz (*see* 1852).

Cyrus McCormick buys out William Ogden for twice the $25,000 that Ogden invested in McCormick's Chicago reaper business (*see* 1847; 1851).

German-American entrepreneur Henry Miller begins buying up land in California (which is admitted to the Union as the 31st state September 9). The immigrant butcher has arrived at San Francisco with $6 in his pocket and instead of prospecting for gold has borrowed money to start buying property along rivers, cutting off backcountry homesteaders from the water and forcing them to sell out to him at distress prices. Learning of a new swamplands law that permits a settler to gain title to lands that are underwater and pay nothing if he agrees to drain the land, Miller loads a rowboat atop a wagon and has himself pulled across a large stretch of dry land, whereupon he files a map of the sections with a sworn statement that he has covered the land in a rowboat. By such means, and by purchasing land from speculators who have obtained rights while working as U.S. Government inspectors, Miller will one day own more than 14.5 million acres of the richest land in California and Oregon, a territory three times the size of New Jersey (*see* 1905; Haggin and Tevis, 1877).

The first U.S. clipper ship to be seen at London arrives from Hong Kong after a 97-day voyage. The *Oriental* carries a 1,600-ton cargo of China tea and her $48,000 cargo fee nearly covers the cost of her construction, but U.S. clipper ships soon abandon the China trade for the more profitable business of transporting gold seekers to California.

U.S. railroad trackage reaches 9,000 miles, up from little more than 3,000 in 1840. Canal mileage reaches 3,600, up from 3,000 in 1840.

Land grants to U.S. railroad companies in the next 21 years will cover more territory than France, England, Wales, and Scotland combined.

London inventor Thomas Masters creates the world's first oven thermometer (date approximate). His glass ring contains mercury and has an indicator guide telling what to put in the oven when the mercury reaches a particular point.

Reform Club chef Alexis Soyer at London supervises the first effort to roast an entire ox by gas. At the annual meeting of the Royal Agricultural Society at Exeter, he sets up a few unmortared bricks and some sheets of iron to enclose an outdoor space of about six by three feet with 216 gas jets. It takes 8 hours to roast a baron and saddleback of beef weighing 535 pounds, after which eight men carry the meat through the streets of the town in a triumphal march accompanied by a band playing "The Roast Beef of Old England."

Fiction: *Pendennis* by William Makepeace Thackeray, now 39, who introduces the Clavering family cook Alcide Mirobolant, formerly chef to the duc de Borodino and Cardinal Beccafico. Having become enamored of a certain Blanche, Mirobolant creates a meal in her honor, which he describes to Mme. Fribsby, an elderly milliner: "I declared myself to her in a manner which was as novel as I am charmed to think it was agreeable. . . . Cupid is the father of invention! —I inquired of the domestics what were the *plats* of which Mademoiselle partook with most pleasure; and built up my little battery accordingly. On a day when her parents had gone to dine in the world . . . , the charming Miss entertained some comrades of the pension; and I advised myself to send up a little repast suitable to so delicate young palates. Her lovely name is Blanche. The veil of the maiden is white; the wreath of roses which she wears is white. I determined that my dinner should be a spotless as the snow. At her accustomed hour, and instead of the rude *gigot a l'eau* which was ordinarily served at her too simple table, I sent her up a little *potage à la Reine*—*à la Reine Blanche* I called it,—as white as her own tint—and confectioned with the most fragrant cream and almonds. I then offered up at her shrine a *filet de merlan à l'Agnès*, and a delicate *plat*, which I have designated as *Eperlan à la Sainte Thérèse*, and of which my charming Miss partook with pleasure. I followed this by two little *entrées* of sweetbread and chicken; and the only brown thing which I permitted myself in the entertainment was a little roast of lamb, which I laid in a meadow of spinaches, surrounded with croustillons, representing sheep, and ornamented with daisies and other savage flowers. After this came my second service: a pudding *à la Reine Elisabeth* . . . ; a dish of opal-coloured plovers' eggs, which I called *Nid de tourtereaux à la Roucoule*; placing in the midst of them two of those tender volatiles, billing each other, and confectioned with butter; a basket containing little *gateaux* of apricots, which I know, all young ladies adore; and a jelly of maraquin, bland, insinuating, intoxicating as the glance of beauty. This I designated *Ambroise de Calypso à la Souveraine de mon Coeur*. And when the ice was brought in—an ice of *plombière* and cherries—how do you think I had shaped them, Madame Fribsbi? In the form of two hearts united with an arrow, on which I had laid, before it entered, a bridal veil in cut paper, surmounted by a wreath of virginal orange-flowers. I stood at the door to watch the effect of this entry." *The Personal History of David Copperfield* by Charles Dickens, who dines several times each week at Simpson's in the Strand, a restaurant whose origins date to 1528 (*see* restaurants, 1904).

Average U.S. per capita wheat flour consumption reaches 205 pounds, up from 170 pounds in 1830; Americans average 184 pounds of meat, up from 178, but they eat fewer than 50 pounds on average of any other food or food group and consume relatively little in the way of dairy products, vegetables, or fruit, mostly for lack of transportation and good methods of preservation.

The United States has 2,017 bakeries, according to Census figures (Washington, D.C., has 123 to serve a population of 40,000; Detroit only 12 for a population of 21,000), and they employ 6,727 workers, but more than 90 percent of U.S. bread is still baked at home.

California gold prospectors depend on sourdough bread and biscuits, using a fermented starter dough from the previous day's bread as a leaven to make a new batch each day. The action of the yeast is continuously transmitted through successive mounds of dough. Sourdough bakers proliferate in San Francisco, possibly using starter dough brought to the city by Basques from southern Europe or by gold seekers from Mexico.

Northerners supplement their staple diet of cured pork, white bread, other grain products, potatoes, corn, and apples with small quantities of fresh beef, fruits, and vegetables; southerners eat mostly bacon and salt pork, corn bread, and a few vegetables and fruits.

President Millard Fillmore, 50, and his wife, Abigail, install the first White House cooking stove; their cooks quit in protest, preferring to use the fireplace until an expert from the Patent Office spends a day showing them how to regulate the heat with dampers.

Nearly 15 percent of the world's sugar supply now comes from beets (*see* 1814; 1878).

Swiss immigrant Adam Blumer from Glarus introduces Emmenthaler cheese to America (year approximate). Produced since the 15th century in the canton of Bern's Emmenthal Valley, it will be produced in a dozen U.S. states; by 1950, Monroe, Wis., will have close to 300 factories producing the cheese that Americans will know simply as "Swiss" cheese.

Salmon is taken for the last time from England's Thames River, which is fast becoming heavily polluted. The fish will not reappear in the Thames for more than 120 years.

Jersey cows are introduced into the United States, where they will be an important dairy breed noted for the high butterfat content of their milk.

Open-ranging longhorn cattle herds on the western plains are estimated to number 50 million head, sharing the prairie with 20 million head of buffalo (*see* Herefords, 1840; Aberdeen Angus, 1873).

Milo maize (Kaffir corn) is introduced into the United States for use as livestock forage.

California (above) raises 15,000 bushels of wheat (*see* 1860).

The Elberta peach is imported into the United States from China by some accounts (but *see* 1870).

The Red Delicious apple is discovered as a chance seedling in Iowa. It will become the leading U.S. apple variety.

The chief gardener of the Société de Horticulture de Belge (Belgian Horticultural Society) at Brussels introduces what Frenchmen will call endive. When Belgium was gripped by famine 2 years ago, everything edible at the Brussels Botanical Gardens was brought out to relieve the hunger. Chicory is widely used as a substitute for coffee, and the gardener, looking for a better chicory root, had planted a variety in a dark basement. One root, inadvertently left behind, was discovered by an assistant several days later and found to have produced a cluster of pale leaves, or, in Flemish, *witloof*. Experimentation has shown that if earth is pressed around them, the chicory leaves will fold to form a hard white salad cone with a fresh, tart flavor. Farmers in the Brussels area are soon planting the roots in rows between their vegetables, taking them up before they flower, removing the eight-inch leaves for fodder, pruning away secondary shoots in September, placing the roots in trenches 16 to 18 inches deep underground in their cellars, covering them with light chaff or cornhusks to protect them from frost, and 6 weeks later harvesting *witloof* (white leaves). Belgium will retain a near monopoly on the production of endive (which Belgians will call chicory). Belgians and French will eat the leaves glazed, baked in casseroles, sautéed in butter, and stuffed with savory ground meat; Americans will eat them in salads.

French physiologist Claude Bernard, 37, demonstrates that the human liver can take the sugars broken down in digestion and build them into the complex sugar glycogen—the first evidence that the body can build up any substances of its own (*see* 1855).

The Lancet announces appointment of an analytical and sanitary commission to study the quality of British foods (*see* 1823; Hassall and Letheby, 1851, 1855).

The Royal Navy reduces its daily rum ration from one-quarter pint to one-eighth pint, to be dispensed before the midday meal (*see* 1731; 1824).

Scottish businessmen begin mixing pot-still whiskies from the Highlands with cheaper "patent" whiskies, producing blends, which will come to dominate the market (date approximate; *see* 1830; 1905).

U.S. distillers begin using charred white oak barrels to age their whiskey. The char helps to mellow the whiskey and give it color.

Stroh's brewery has its beginnings in the Lion brewery founded at Detroit by German-American brewer Bernard Stroh, 28, whose two oldest sons will take over after his death in 1882 and make Stroh's the largest brewery in Michigan. It will become one of the country's 10 largest.

San Francisco entrepreneur James A. Folger, 21, helps his employer supply coffee to the city's growing hordes of gold seekers. He came west with his two older brothers, Edward and Henry, from Nantucket but instead of prospecting for gold took a job helping William Bovee build a spice and coffee mill. He has stayed on as a clerk and salesman, learning the trade, and will become Bovee's partner in 1859 (*see* 1865).

Tea catches up with coffee in popularity among the British, with one pound of tea yielding 160 to 200 cups, making it more affordable than coffee. Chinese teas dominate the market. Keemun, or keemun conjou, is a black tea sometimes sold as English breakfast tea (which can also be a blend of several black teas). Some black teas from China, such as hu kwa, chung wa, and lapsang souchong, are smoked over woodfires, but green teas are also widely consumed, especially "gunpowder" tea— tightly curled little balls. Green teas are, like Indian teas, graded by leaf size—young hyson, hyson, and souchong (*see* 1840; 1869).

1851

The Castle & Cooke food empire has its beginnings in a Honolulu mercantile house started by former missionaries Samuel Northrup Castle, 43, and Amos Starr Cooke, 41, who arrived in the Sandwich Islands aboard the *Mary Frazier* in April of 1837. They sever their ties with the American Board of Commissioners for Foreign Missions of Boston (*see* 1964).

The London Great Exhibition that opens May 1 is the first world's fair and in 141 days attracts more than 6 million visitors. Held in a Crystal Palace built for the occasion, it is intended to show British industrial achievement and prosperity.

Cyrus McCormick exhibits his reaper at the London Great Exhibition (above), produces 6,000 reapers, and begins to enlarge foreign markets for his product (*see* 1849; 1854; 1879; self-rake device, 1852; Stanton, 1861).

Several tons of butter are shipped by rail from Ogdensburg, N.Y., to Boston in an ice-cooled wooden railcar insulated with sawdust.

J. M. Horton Ice Cream Co. is founded at New York, where it will become the leading supplier of ice cream to transatlantic ocean liners (*see* Borden, 1928).

 Candymaker Oliver Chase of Boston obtains a patent for a machine to produce powdered sugar (*see* 1847).

Scottish industrial chemist James Young, 40, patents a method for producing paraffin by dry distillation of coal. Paraffin will play a major role in sealing home preserves.

Nonfiction: *The Pantropheon, or The History of Cooking* by Alexis Soyer (possibly written by Adolphe Duhart-Fauvet, a teacher of French who lives in London). *Homes of the New World* (*Hemmen i den nya Världen*) by Swedish novelist Fredrika Bremer, 50, who has returned to her homeland after 2 years in America. Her book is a collection of letters written to her sister Agathe in which she has spoken, among other things, of enjoying a dinner at New Orleans, calling it "remarkably good, and gumbo is the crown of all the savory and remarkable soups in the world—a regular elixir of life of the substantial kind. He who has once eaten gumbo may look down disdainfully upon the most genuine turtle soup." But "Is there in this world any thing more wearisome, more dismal, more intolerable, more indigestible, more stupefying, more unbearable, any thing more calculated to kill both soul and body, than a great dinner at New York? People sit down to table at half-past five or six o'clock; they are sitting at table at nine o'clock, sitting and being served with one course after another, with one indigestible dish after another, eating and being silent. I have never heard such a silence as at these great dinners." (Novelist Charles Dickens has made similar comments.)

Fiction: *Moby-Dick* by U.S. novelist Herman Melville, 32, who refers to "old Amsterdam housewives' doughnuts or oly-cooks" (*see* Irving, 1809).

Cookbook: *Soyer's Shilling Cookery* by Alexis Soyer (*see* below).

Fredrika Bremer (above) says of corn on the cob, "Some people take the whole stem and gnaw [the kernels] out with their teeth: two gentleman do so who sit opposite . . . myself at table and whom we call 'the sharks,' because of their remarkable ability in gobbling up large and often double portions of everything which comes to table, and it really troubles me to see how their wide mouths . . . ravenously grind up the beautiful white, pearly maize ears." Arbiters of etiquette say that the kernels should be "scored with a knife, scraped off into the plate, and then eaten with a fork, especially by ladies."

The first wholesale ice cream business is founded by Baltimore milk dealer Jacob Fussell, who receives milk in steady supply from farmers in York County, Pa., who supply him with their entire output, but is faced with a problem of oversupply in the late spring and early summer months. Fussell uses up the excess by making ice cream, which he sells at less than half the price charged by others. His plant is so successful that he will open another one in 1856 at Washington, D.C., in 1862 at Boston, and in 1864 at New York (*see* Brazelton, 1858).

The first U.S. cheese factory opens on the Erie Canal outside Rome, N.Y., under the management of entrepreneur Jesse Williams, who will find that when curd is washed or soaked after milling it will produce an open and faster-curing cheese. His success with cheddar and washed-curd cheeses will lead British cheese maker Joseph Harding to systematize cheddar making in Somerset.

A 100-acre wheatfield remains the largest any one man can farm.

Ireland suffers widespread blindness as a result of the malnutrition experienced in the potato famine that began in 1846.

Diet evangelist Sylvester Graham dies at Northampton, Mass., September 11 at age 57 after several years of declining health (and popularity).

Articles exposing the adulteration of British foods will be published in the next 3 years by British chemist Arthur Hill Hassall and dietician Henry Letheby, who will document the whitening of bread with alum, the dilution of coffee with chicory, etc. (*see* 1850; 1855).

Huntley & Palmers biscuit works employs some 300 workers after 25 years in business.

The London Great Exhibition forbids sale of wine, spirits, beer, and other intoxicating beverages but permits tea, coffee, chocolate, cocoa, lemonade, ices, ginger beer, and soda water. The 61-year-old firm Messrs. Schweppe & Co., which received its first royal warrant 15 years ago, sells 177,737 dozen bottles, up from roughly 70,000 last year, and nearly 85,000 dozen of the total are sold at the Exhibition. White Rhine wine (hock) and soda is a popular British beverage, and Schweppe's soda water is a popular mixer (*see* 1858).

South Australia's Seppeltsfield vineyard is founded by Joseph Ernst Seppelt, who has emigrated from Silesia (*see* 1849). The valley near Adelaide—18 miles long, 5 miles wide—will come to be called Bibarossa after a Spanish wine-producing region and will produce most of the nation's best-known wines, such as Kaiserstuhl, Yolumba, Orlando, and Stonyflat, but most Australians will call wine "plonk" and stick to beer.

The first U.S. state Prohibition law is voted in Maine, where the mayor of Portland, Neal Dow, 47, has drafted the law, submitted it to the state legislature, and campaigned for its passage. An ardent temperance advocate, Dow will see his measure followed by other states (*see* 1852).

German-American brewer Valentin Blatz buys the 5-year-old City brewery at Milwaukee and begins increasing production of Blatz beer.

Average per capita U.S. coffee consumption reaches 6¼ pounds, up from 1¼ in 1821, partly as a result of growing Prohibitionist sentiment (above). Coffee is served at every meal in some households as well as between meals.

Better-class U.S. restaurants offer their patrons turtle soup, calf's-head soup, planked shad, boiled chicken with oyster sauce, boiled mutton with capers, and roast partridge. A bottle of Mumm's champagne in a silver bucket generally goes for $2, and $1 buys a bottle of imported Sauternes, while $2 buys a bottle of Hochheimer or 1811 Rudesheimer. One New York restaurant advertises strawberries in January and prices the berries, which have been shipped from southern Europe, at 50¢ each.

Chef Alexis Soyer of the Reform Club puts on a "gastronomic symposium of all nations" in connection with the London Great Exhibition (above). He takes a lease on Gore House, near the Crystal Palace, and turns it into an eating pavilion, saying in a prospectus that "Frenchmen will have *fricandeaux*, Turks pilaf, Persians sherbet, Spaniards *olla podidra*, Americans jonnycakes and canvasback ducks, Chinese stewed dog, Russians caviar, Cossacks train oil, Tartars mares' milk." The pavilion opens with a grand banquet dedicated to "the roast beef of old England" but is closed after threats to revoke Soyer's license because of a rowdy postbanquet party. Soyer assumes all debts and pays them

off within a month, leaving himself with scarcely £100, but will recoup his fortune with proceeds from the sale of his new cookbook *Soyer's Shilling Cookery* (above; *see* 1855).

Scott's restaurant has its beginnings as London fishmonger Tom Scott sets up in business at 18–20 Coventry Street, Piccadilly Circus, offering Whitstable, Colchester, and Portuguese oysters. He will expand by offering lobster dishes and other seafood delicacies.

China's population reaches 450 million, having exploded with help from such Western food crops as maize, sweet potatoes, white potatoes, and peanuts.

Brazil imports her last legal shipment of African slaves, but slaves continue to work the sugar plantations and illegal imports continue (*see* 1871).

Léopold Louis-Dreyfus, now 19, establishes his own grain business at Basel (*see* 1850). He is soon buying grain at Bern and will extend his operations throughout central Europe (*see* 1865).

German-American speculator Isaac Friedlander corners the San Francisco flour market, forces up bread prices, and makes his first fortune. He uses some of his profits to build the first West Coast flour mills, and although he will lose most of his money in further speculations he will be back on his feet by 1858, exporting wheat to Britain and Australia (*see* 1877).

The first through train from the East reaches Chicago February 20 by way of the Michigan Southern Railway. Railroads will make Chicago more than ever the grain and meat packing center of America.

Gail Borden returns from last year's London Great Exhibition with the Great Council Gold Medal for his meat biscuit (*see* 1849). He has promoted it as useful for naval expeditions and other voyages (some have gone with Elisha Kent Kane, 41, who is making his first Arctic expedition), for travelers "on long journeys, through destitute regions," for explorers "in making geological and minerological surveys of our newly acquired territories," and for all families, "especially in warm weather." Borden's ship encounters rough seas on the Atlantic, the two cows in the ship's hold become too seasick to be milked, an immigrant infant dies, and the hungry cries of the other infants determine Borden to find a way to produce a portable condensed milk that can keep without spoiling (*see* 1853).

The McCormick reaper invented in 1831 is improved by the addition of a self-rake device that sweeps the harvested grain from the reaper's platform to the ground, making it unnecessary for a man to clear the platform with a hand rake (*see* Marsh harvester, 1858).

The "bee-space" patented by former Andover, Mass., school principal Lorenzo Lorraine Langstroth, 42, makes possible the first practical movable-frame beehive (*see* Huber, 1789). Honeybees have immobilized the frames of previous hives by filling the space around the thin wooden frame, slipped vertically into the hive, with wax or even honeycombs. Langstroth has retired to Oxford, Ohio, and, after much experimentation, discovered that if he leaves a space of five-sixteenths of an inch in height around the frame, it will not get clogged and bees will be able to slip in and out without getting stuck. His hive will revolutionize the beekeeping industry, making possible economical honey production, but competitors will find it easy to infringe upon his patent and Langstroth will derive little financial benefit from it.

John Deere's plow factory at Moline, Ill., produces 4,000 plows (*see* 1847; 1855).

International Silver Co. has its beginnings in the Meriden Britannia Co. founded at Meriden, Conn., through a merger engineered by Horace C. Wilcox, 28, who has been acting with his younger brother Dennis as sales agent for the silverplate made at Hartford since 1847 by William, Asa, and Simeon Rogers. Rogers Bros. is included in the new company, which will become the leading U.S. tableware producer. Forks have for years been made of steel, but U.S. silversmiths now make coin-silver flatware and the well-appointed household must have silver forks, formerly used only by royalty and the very rich.

Service à la russe arrives in England but will not be common for another 20 or 30 years (*see* 1811). Instead of dishes being placed in turn on sideboards for waiters to serve to guests, a multitude of dishes will continue to be placed before English diners simultaneously in two or three great courses and several minor courses.

U.S. horticulturist Andrew Jackson Downing dies in a Hudson River steamboat explosion after having listed the names of apples indigenous to North America. They include the Grand Sachem, the Maiden Blush, the Vittles and Drink, the Sine Qua Non, the Jonathan, and the Mouse, the latter two being native to his native Hudson west bank.

The Holstein cow, which will be most significant to the development of the major U.S. dairy breed, arrives aboard a Dutch vessel (*see* 1625).

Hecker's Self-Rising Flour, introduced by the 10-year-old Croton Flour Mill of John and George Hecker, is the first product of its kind.

Heckers' added leavening to flour to produce the first self-rising flour.

Oidium mildew strikes vineyards in the Madeira Islands, dealing a heavy blow to winegrowers (*see* 1665; phylloxera, 1872).

California's Almadén Vineyard has its beginnings in vines planted south of San Jose by French-American vintner Étienne Thée. By the 1860s there will be half a dozen producers, most of them French, shipping wine by wagon to the port of Alviso (which will later be silted in) for transport by ship to San Francisco. Thée will bequeath the operation to his daughters and his son-in-law, Charles Lefranc (*see* Paul Masson, 1880).

Alcohol prohibition laws are adopted by Massachusetts, Vermont, and Louisiana (*see* 1855; Maine, 1851).

1853

The French emperor Napoleon III is married at Notre Dame Cathedral, Paris, January 30 to the Spanish beauty Eugénie, 26, whose name will be immortalized on French menus: a dish served with rice will be called *à l'Impéritrice*.

A U.S. Navy fleet commanded by Commodore Matthew C. Perry, 59, arrives in Japan July 8 with 1,600 men aboard seven black ships. Charged with requesting a trade treaty, Perry is served a meal at the Edo restaurant Momokawa. He will return in March of next year and obtain the treaty (*see* Townsend Harris, 1856).

Britain lowers her import duties on chocolate, which will hereafter be cheaper and more popular as both a beverage and a sweet.

Congress appropriate $150,000 March 3 for a survey of the most practicable transcontinental U.S. railroad routes to be made under the direction of the War Department (*see* Central Pacific, 1861; Union Pacific, 1862).

Swedish inventor J. E. Lundstrom patents a safety match that will supersede the "Lucifer" of 1827 and the phosphorus match of 1836 for lighting stoves and hearth fires.

Fiction: *Cranford* by English novelist Elizabeth Cleghorn Gaskell (*née* Stevenson), 43, who writes,

"When the ducks and green peas came, we looked at each other in dismay; we had only two-pronged black-handled forks. . . . What were we to do? Miss Matty picked up her peas, one by one, on the point of the prongs. . . . Miss Pole sighed over her delicate young peas as she left them on one side of her plate untasted; for they *would* drop between the prongs. I looked at my host; the peas were going wholesale into his capacious mouth, shovelled up by his large rounded knife. I saw, I tasted, I survived! My friends, in spite of my precedent, could not muster up courage enough to do an ungenteel thing." *Mr. Sponge's Sporting Tour* by Robert Smith Surtees, whose Lord Scamperdale finds "cakes, sweets, and jellies without end" plus "a round of beef, a ham, a tongue," and " 'Is that a goose or a turkey?' 'A turkey, my lord.' " After consuming "soup, game, tea, coffee, chocolate, eggs, honey, marmalade, crêpes, pines, melons, buns," cakes, and a few cases of champagne, the guests get into the table ornaments and eat the sugar ones—Temples, Pagodas, Rialtos.

Cookbook: *Home Cookery* by Boston author Mrs. J. Chadwick, who specializes in cake recipes but gives 13 for beef dishes (including beefsteak-and-oyster pie), 11 for lamb or mutton, seven for pork, seven for veal, one for gumbo soup, and one that runs two pages for turtle soup, beginning with instructions for killing the turtle. It contains four recipes for tomatoes, including one for tomato soup and one for tomato ketchup.

Potato chips are invented at Saratoga Springs, N.Y., where chef George Crum of Moon's Lake House gives a mocking response to a patron who has complained that his French fries are too thick. He shaves some potatoes paper thin and sends them out to the customers—who are delighted, order more, and encourage Crum to open a restaurant of his own across the lake. Crum's new restaurant will take no reservations, and millionaires including Jay Gould and Commodore Vanderbilt will stand in line along with everyone else (*see* Wise, 1921; Lay's, 1939).

Continued decline in French oyster production disturbs the government at Paris, which sends the embryologist-ichthyologist Jean-Jacques Coste, 46, to study the remains of ancient Roman oyster culture in Lake Fusaro (*see* 175 B.C.; 1375; 1840).

Oyster stalls have disappeared from the poorer sections of London; overfishing and pollution have made the bivalves a luxury available only to the rich.

The King Ranch has its origin as Texas steamboat captain Richard King, 29, begins acquiring land on Santa Gertrudis Creek between the Rio Grande and Neuces rivers. Acting on the advice of his friend Col. Robert E. Lee, 46, U.S. Army, King pays a Spanish family $300 for 15,500 acres—less than 2¢ per acre (see 1860).

Extreme drought parches the Southwest, lowering prices of land and cattle. Richard King (above) is able to buy longhorns at $5 per head.

Texas cattleman Samuel A. Maverick, 50, receives an anonymous note telling him to look after his strays on the Matagorda Peninsula or risk losing them. Maverick accepted 400 head of cattle in payment of a debt in 1845 and has never bothered to brand the animals on his 385,000-acre ranch, but he sends down a party of cowhands who round up about the same number that were turned loose on the peninsula 6 years ago, sells the cattle to Toutant Beauregard of New Orleans, and retires from ranching. The word "maverick" will become a generic for unbranded cattle and for political or intellectual independents who do not go along with their associates.

Fewer than half of Americans are actively engaged in agriculture, down from 83 percent in 1820, but most Americans still live on farms or in rural areas.

Concord, Mass., horticulturist Ephraim Wales Bull, 48, exhibits the first Concord grapes to the Massachusetts Horticulture Society. He produced the slip-skin Lambrusca variety from seed in September 1849 and begins selling cuttings from the parent vine at $5 each. Table grapes rather than wine grapes, Concords will be widely used to make port and within 10 years will be growing all across America (see Welch, 1869).

"New Rochelle blackberries" are exibited at a New York City farmers' club meeting (see 1834; 1841). William Lawton asks that the name "New Rochelle" be made official, but they will come to be known as Lawtons.

Blackberries (above) are widely used in syrups, pies, jellies, puddings, other desserts, and brandy.

Keebler biscuits are introduced at Philadelphia by baker Godfrey Keebler, whose Steam Cracker Bakery will become a leading U.S. producer of cookies (biscuits) and crackers.

Gail Borden, now 52, succeeds in his efforts to produce condensed milk (see 1852). He has lost between $60,000 and $100,000 in his meat biscuit venture, but now, using vacuum pans borrowed from Shakers at New Lebanon, N.Y., he develops a process for making a milk product that has no burnt taste or discoloration and lasts for nearly 3 days without souring. (He believes its keeping properties are due to the fact that it is condensed; only later will he learn that his heating process has destroyed microorganisms that cause milk to spoil; see Pasteur, 1857.) Borden travels to Washington to file a patent claim (see 1856).

Swedish coffee roaster Victor Theodor Engwall at Gävle founds a company that will become famous for its Gevalia Coffee.

The Paris tea shop Ladourée opens at 16, rue Royale. It will become a favorite meeting place for luncheons, pastries, and thé.

1854

The Crimean War, which begins March 28, will continue until 1856, bringing devastation to part of Russia's breadbasket. More British, French, and Russian troops will die of disease and malnutrition than from battle wounds (see Soyer, 1855).

The Kansas-Nebraska Act signed into law by President Franklin Pierce, 49, May 30 opens to white settlement western lands that have been reserved by sacred treaty for the Indians.

Quixiault, Lummi, Nisqualie, Puyallup, and other Puget Sound tribes that have ceded their lands in the Northwest receive treaty rights to fish for the salmon which climb the rivers of the region—rights guaranteed "in common with white men."

Railroads reach the Mississippi, but cattlemen continue to drive Texas cattle great distances overland as drought continues in the Southwest. The first Texas longhorns to reach New York arrive after a long trek that has made their meat tough and stringy.

The U.S. Supreme Court confirms Cyrus McCormick's reaper patents in the case of *Seymour v. McCormick*. Baltimore lawyer Reverdy Johnson, 60, and Washington lawyer Thaddeus Stevens, 62, defend the reaper inventor (*see* 1851; Stanton, 1861).

Massachusetts pencil maker Henry David Thoreau, now 37, describes ice harvesting on Walden Pond (*see* 1846), writing in his journal, "They told me that in a good day they could get out a thousand tons, which was the yield of about one acre. . . . They told me that they had some in the ice-houses at Fresh Pond five years old which was as good as ever." Knowing that the ice is destined for faraway ports, Thoreau writes, "Thus it appears that the sweltering inhabitants of Charleston and New Orleans, of Madras and Bombay and Calcutta, drink at my well" (*see* 1856; Tudor ice ships, 1846).

Boston candy maker Daniel Fobes pays a missionary $125 for the recipe of "Turkish Delight," made in Syria: Take 13 pounds and 13 ounces brown sugar and clarify it with an egg and rain water. Add 2 pounds clean starch, one dram pulverized alum, 5 grams cream of tartar, 3 drops oil of roses. Boil and stir. While hot, pour into squares to cool, and when cold cut with knife and roll pieces in finely pulverized sugar. This will give 18½ lbs. of "Turkish Delight." Fobes also makes pralines, invented in the 17th century by a cook of Marshal Praline, by boiling nuts in a syrup either of maple sugar or of brown sugar from New Orleans (*see* 1842; 1860).

Cookbook: *The New Family Book, or Ladies' Indispensable Companion* by an anonymous author is published at New York. It contains seven recipes for preparing beef, six for pork and ham, four for mutton, five for salmon, eight for cod.

Dairyman Harvey P. Hood gives up his retail dairy route at Charlestown, Mass., to concentrate on building a supply of quality milk for other Boston area routemen (*see* 1846). He collects milk each morning from farms near his own place at Derby, N.H., loads the cans into a freight car attached to the one daily train into Charlestown on the Concord Railroad, and sells the milk to peddlers, who deliver it throughout Boston (*see* 1890).

McSorley's Ale-House opens in New York's East 7th Street under the proprietorship of Irish-American publican John McSorley.

Some 16 million bushels of U.S. wheat are exported to Europe, up from 6 million in 1853 (*see* 1861).

John Deere hires his first salesman: George W. Vinton will travel across the country from the East Coast to the Pacific and from the Mexican border into Canada, establishing agencies for Deere "ploughs and agricultural implements" (*see* 1852; 1857).

Salesmanship persuaded farmers to let Mr. Deere's self-polishing steel plow break the plains.

The Sault St. Marie ("Soo") River Ship Canal opens to link Lake Huron and Lake Superior and to make the Great Lakes a huge inland waterway navigable by large ships.

Scottish-American mechanic James Oliver, 32, at South Bend, Ind., invents a steel plow whose working surface is remarkably smooth without being brittle. The surface of Oliver's plow is made from a steel casting that is chilled more quickly than its back-supporting sections (*see* 1869; Deere, 1837).

A £25 domestic gas oven introduced by the English firm of Smith and Phillips is one of the first such ovens to be put on the market in an age of coal and wood stoves (*see* Reform Club, 1838). Cooking fuel is so costly that hot meals are prepared only two or three times a week in most British homes, but gas ovens will not come into common use for another 20 years.

A military cookstove that can prepare food for a battalion with 47 pounds of wood instead of the usual 1,760 pounds is demonstrated August 27 by Alexis Soyer (above), whose invention will still be used in the British army in 1935. He has also invented a spirit stove so tiny that a newspaper has said it can be carried in one's hat (the British Admiralty has ordered the stoves for an Arctic expedition sent in search for explorer Sir John Franklin). Soyer's other inventions have included a cooking clock, a "magic" cooking pot, an egg-cooking machine, a vegetable drainer, and a tendon separator, and he has created new sauces for Crosse & Blackwell.

Cookbook: *A Shilling Cookery for the People* by former Reform Club chef Alexis Soyer contains recipes for sheep's head, boiled neck of mutton, and the like; it has sales of 248,000 copies (*see* 1851).

Scottish-American horticulturist William Saunders, 32, starts a movement that will lead to the establishment of the Patrons of Husbandry. He will write the preamble to its constitution, and it will spread throughout the country, playing an important role in bringing together the agricultural interests of the various states (*see* oranges, 1862).

South Carolina agronomist Robert Francis Withers Allston, 54, sends to the Paris Exposition samples of rice that he has grown and wins a silver medal. He will win a gold medal next year when the rice remains in perfect condition after a year and will be elected governor of the state. Beginning with 300 acres, he has increased his holdings to 1,500, of which 1,200 are planted in rice, and he has developed more scientific methods of cultivation and better varieties of seed.

Food and Its Adulterations: Comprising the Reports of the Analytical Sanitary Commission of 'The Lancet' is published at London (*see* 1850; 1851). A. H. Hassall scandalizes England with reports that all but the most costly beer, bread, butter, coffee, pepper, and tea contains trace amounts of arsenic, copper, lead, or mercury, but Crosse & Blackwell announces that it has stopped coppering pickles and fruits and will no longer use bole armenian to color sauces.

Alexis Soyer (above) has, with other Britons, read news dispatches from the Crimea describing in gruesome detail the poisonous food that British troops often throw away (*see* naval mutiny, 1797). He writes to the *Times* offering his services and goes off himself to assist nurse Florence Nightingale, 34, at Scutari. Dressed in his usual fancy pantaloons and waistcoats (he was always a fop and poseur), he improves the sanitation in hospital kitchens, brings order to the preparation of food, and gives the Army's soup so much better flavor that the commanding officer cannot believe it came from the same rations as earlier soup.

France's Napoleon III requests that the more celebrated *crus* (vineyards) of the Gironde (Médoc and Sauternes) be classified in terms of comparative quality for a new Paris Exposition. A commission of French wine dealers, courtiers, and experts is appointed at Bordeaux but will never grade the vineyards of St.-Emilion and Graves. Working hastily, it revises slightly the classifications made in 1641, 1647, 1698, and 1767 (the latter three of which took the previous classifications into account), selecting about 60 châteaux out of some 3,000 Bordeaux properties that produce red wine, and giving top honors among the Medocs to wines from Château Laffitte-Rothschild in Pauillac, Château Margeaux in Margeaux, and Château Latour in Pauillac. Wines from Château Haut-Brion (*see* Pepys, 1663) and Château d'Yquem also rank high, but the commission does not grade Château Mouton-Rothschild, acquired this year by the Rothschilds. The list will determine wine choices for the next 140 years, even after it becomes obsolete.

Miller's beer has its origin as Milwaukee brewer Frederick Miller buys the Best Brothers brewery, which sent the first shipment of Milwaukee beer to New York in 1852. The brewery will be rebuilt in 1888 and the company reorganized under the name Frederick Miller Brewing Co. (*see* 1856).

Prohibition laws are adopted by Delaware, Indiana, Iowa, Michigan, New Hampshire, New York, and the Nebraska Territory (*see* 1852; national party, 1869).

Boston's new Parker House hotel in School Street serves à la carte meals at all hours of the day instead of requiring that guests sit down at mealtimes to be served a meal dished out by the host. Its kitchen will become famous as the birthplace of the soft Parker House roll.

London has about 30 clubs, some of which serve excellent meals that cost no more than mediocre meals at a tavern. Most famous for their food are the Reform Club (above) and the Crockford Club, whose kitchen is under the direction of French chef Louis-Eustache Ude.

1856

The Treaty of Paris signed March 30 brings a formal end to the Crimean War (hostilities have ceased February 1). Russian diplomat Karl Robert Count Nesselrode, 75, who has worked since 1854 to re-establish peace, will be commemorated by gastronomes in Nesselrode puddings and Nesselrode pies, created by the count's head chef, one Mouy, and consisting of custard cream mixed with chestnut purée, candied fruits, currants, and white raisins or whipped cream.

Xhosa prophets in South Africa encourage tribesmen to believe that legendary heroes are about to return and drive out the whites with whom they have warred for years. The Xhosa slaughter their own cattle; two-thirds of them will starve to death in the next few years.

Boston exports more than 130,000 tons of "fine, clear" ice from Massachusetts lakes and ponds as 363 U.S. ships sail from various ports with a total of 146,000 tons of ice, up from 65,000 on 175 ships in 1846 (see 1880).

Mechanical ice making is pioneered by Australian inventor James Harrison, an emigrant printer from Scotland, who has settled at Geelong. He has by some accounts noticed that the ether he used to wash type had a cooling effect, and his ether compressor makes it possible to produce beer even in hot weather (see 1862; Perkins, 1834; Gorrie, 1851; Carré, 1858; Linde, 1873; Foster's beer, 1888).

The new Russian czar Aleksandr II, 37, places the first stone on a monument erected to the memory of a fisherman named Benkels of the town of Burgo, who, in the 14th century, invented the art of salting and packing herrings. He introduced the art

first into his native Flanders and then to Finland, whence it spread to the Baltic states.

The first calf to be butchered in Japan for years is slaughtered for U.S. envoy Townsend Harris, 52, at Shimoda, where he awaits recognition. A New York merchant dispatched by President Franklin Pierce to follow up Commodore Perry's opening of Japan and be the first U.S. consul general to that country, Harris has arrived at Shimoda in August. He also has a cow milked—the first cow's milk obtained for human consumption in Japan in many years (see 1866; 1872).

The German Mills American Oatmeal Factory, opened at Akron, Ohio, by German-American grocer Ferdinand Schumacher, 33, employs water-powered millstones to grind 3,600 pounds of oatmeal per day. U.S. farmers grow 150 million bushels of oats per year, and while most goes to feed horses, Schumacher will find a large market for his oatmeal among other German immigrants; his mills will become Akron's leading enterprise as he makes himself America's "Oatmeal King" (see 1875).

Baking powder is introduced commercially for the first time in the United States.

The Agen plum, which will be the basis of a large dried prune industry, is introduced into California's Santa Clara Valley by French immigrant Pierre Pellier, 39, who arrived in Chile early in 1849, heard about the gold discoveries in California, came north, and reportedly prospered in the diggings before the severe winter in the Sierra Nevadas sent him back to San Francisco and thence to San Jose. He has had cuttings of the famous French prune d'Agen stuck into raw potatoes and then packed in sawdust and placed in two leather trunks for the long voyage round Cape Horn to his brother Louis's orchard in San Jose, where he grafts the cions to rootstocks of wild plums. By 1870, some 650 acres will be under cultivation in the area, all producing the prune d'Agen, and by the turn of the century Americans, who have relied on Europe for prunes, will be enjoying prunes far superior to any grown in the old country (see Chinese plum, 1870).

The condensed milk patented by Gail Borden (below) is made from skim milk devoid of all fats and of certain necessary food factors. It will contribute to rickets in young working-class children (*see* Pekelharing, 1905).

A new Buitoni pasta factory opens at Città di Castello in Umbria under the direction of Giovanni Buitoni, son of Giovambattista and Giulia (*see* 1842). The new plant goes up near the old one at San Sepolcro where Buitoni has been making semolina flour from wheat brought in by the wagonload from the distant Puglia plateau (*see* 1884).

Gail Borden (above) is granted a patent for his condensed milk, which contains sugar to inhibit bacterial growth (*see* 1853; unsweetened condensed milk will not be canned satisfactorily until 1885). The milk gets a cold shoulder from New York customers accustomed to watered milk doctored with chalk to make it white and molasses to make it seem creamy (*see* 1841; 1855). Borden abandons the factory he has set up with two partners at Wolcottville, Conn., and sells a half share in his patent to one of his partners (but *see* 1857).

Joseph Tetley & Company, Wholesale Tea Dealers, opens in London's Mincing Lane (*see* 1837; 1888).

Schlitz beer has its origin at Milwaukee, where German-American bookkeeper Joseph Schlitz, 25, takes over the 7-year-old August Krug brewery following the death of his employer, Krug. Schlitz will marry Krug's widow, change the name of the brewery, and increase production (*see* 1874).

Swiss muleteer-stonemason Johannes Badrutt arrives at St. Moritz, is struck with its beauty, sees an opportunity, and leases the century-old, 30-room Pension Faller at 2,000 francs per year. He will buy it in 1858 for 58,500 francs, install flush toilets, and reopen it as the Engadiner Kulm (At the Summit of the Engadine)—the first hotel in St. Moritz Dorf (there are no other places to stay except boarding houses). Badrutt will make a wager in the early 1860s with some English guests who doubt that St. Moritz has sunny weather in winter, promising them free hotel space until spring and reimbursement of their return-trip travel expenses to London if there is as much as a single winter day without sunshine (he knows that their bar bills will be enough to compensate for any loss). As he expects, they will tell their friends

about St. Moritz, the town will become a winter resort, and business at the Kulm Hotel will boom as the English introduce the sports of skiing, curling, and, in 1880, bobsledding (the Kulm will expand to have 220 guest rooms in three buildings and an outstanding restaurant; *see* Palace Hotel, 1896).

Vienna's Café Central opens in the heart of the city, where it will flourish for decades as a literary gathering place.

1857

The Sepoy Mutiny, which begins May 10 at Meerut, ends control of India by the East India Company. The British army in India has introduced a new Enfield rifle which fires cartridges that are partially coated with grease and must be bitten open before being loaded. Sepoys (natives) make up 96 percent of the 300,000-man army, which controls a population of 210 million. Caste Hindus among them insist that the grease is beef fat from the sacred cow, Muslims insist that it is pork fat from flesh forbidden by Islamic law, and local chiefs encourage scattered revolts in hopes of regaining lost privileges.

Parliament eases British game laws after years of harsh penalties that made anyone caught poaching liable to transportation to Australia for 7 years. Poached game has been a dietary mainstay for many families.

Demand for Minneapolis flour begins on the Atlantic seaboard as a Minnesota Territory farmer ships a few barrels to New Hampshire in payment of a debt as economic depression makes specie payment difficult. The flour is made from winter wheat, which produces a whiter flour, and since Minnesota spring wheat yields a darker flour, the demand from the East will spur efforts to refine milling methods (*see* 1874; Washburn, Crosby, 1866).

Demel's in Vienna gets that name when founder Ludwig Dehne's grandson sells the Kaiser-und-Königliche Hofzuckerbäckerei, now famous for its *Kugelhupf*, to his first assistant, Christian Demel (*see* 1786). When the Burgtheater is torn down in 1887, Demel's Zuckerbäckerei will move to Kohlmarkt 14, where it will remain for well over a century, becoming the world's greatest patisserie as it delights *feinschmeckers* with its buffet lunch (consommé and warm dishes) and pastries— *demeltorte, havannatorte, dörytorte, salzgebäck torten*, petits fours, *nussbeugerln* and *mohnbeugerln* (crescents filled with poppy seeds or ground walnuts, honey, and cinnamon), *crème grenoble* (vanilla and chocolate with Curaçao plums), *crème délicieux* (chocolate with pineapple and raspberries), *crème schnitten* (regular or very thin), *jourgebäck, jubilaeumskrapfen* (biscuit dough filled with vanilla-raspberry cream and covered with raspberry gelée and ground almonds), *brioches-striezl, streuselkuchen* (strudel filled with cream and raisins), *potizen, nuss-schnitten, linzer-schnitten, butter-teigschnekerin* (puff paste filled with ground nuts and raisins), *bienenseich* (yeast cakes filled with vanilla cream and covered with sugared almonds), poppyseed strudel made with yeast, pineapple *bombes, zitronen törtzen* (sponge mix with a lemon icing), *kärtner reindling* (yeast cakes filled with raisins and nuts), *bavaroises* in different flavors every day, Belvedere strawberry ice, Metternich orange ice, and coffee (*see* 1961).

Cincinnati inventor Martin Robbins patents the first corn planter to drop seed automatically at intersections of check-rows (*see* Jefferson, 1815). His planter requires that a chain fitted with iron buttons at regular intervals be staked at each side of the cornfield (*see* 1864).

John Deere produces self-polishing steel plows at the rate of 10,000 per year (*see* 1852).

French chemist Louis Pasteur, 32, shows that a living organism causes the lactic fermentation that spoils milk (*see* 1859; Borden, 1853). Pasteur's analysis of fermentation also explains for the first time how the leavening process works in baking bread.

Claude Bernard pioneers modern physiology by applying the biochemical methods developed by Justus von Liebig in 1842 to the living animal, combining them with physiological methods. Bernard pursues his investigations of glycogen production by the human liver (*see* nutrition, 1859).

Michigan State College of Agriculture opens to offer the first state courses in scientific and practical agriculture.

Nonfiction: *A Residence Among the Chinese: Inland, on the Coast, and at Sea* by Robert Fortune, who says, "The food of these people is of the simplest kind—namely rice, vegetables, and a small portion of animal food, such as fish or pork, but the poorest classes in China seem to understand the art of preparing their food much better than the same classes at home. With the simple substances I have named, the Chinese labourer contrives to make a number of very savoury dishes, upon which he breakfasts or dines most sumptuously. In Scotland, in former days—and I suppose it is much the same now—the harvest labourer's breakfast consisted of porridge and milk, his dinner of bread and beer, and porridge and milk again for supper. The Chinaman would starve upon such food" (*see* 1847).

Fiction: *Madame Bovary* by French novelist Gustave Flaubert, 35: "At seven dinner was served. The men, who were in the majority, sat down at the first table in the vestibule; the ladies at the second in the dining room with the Marquis and Marchioness. Emma, on entering, felt herself wrapped round by the warm air, a blending of the perfume of flowers and of the fine linen, of the fumes of the viands, and the odor of the truffles. The silver dish covers reflected the lighted wax candles in the candelabra, the cut crystal covered with light steam reflected from one to the other pale rays; bouquets were placed in a row the whole length of the table; and in the large bordered plates each napkin, arranged after the fashion of a bishop's miter, held between its two gaping folds a small oval-shaped roll. The red claws of lobsters hung over the dishes; rich fruit in open baskets was piled up on moss; there were quails in their plumage; smoke was rising; and in silk stockings, knee breeches, white cravat, and frilled shirt, the steward, grave as a judge, offering ready carved dishes between the shoulders of the guests, with a touch of the spoon gave you the piece chosen. . . . Iced champagne was poured out. Emma shivered all over as she felt it cold in her mouth. She had never seen pomegranates nor tasted pineapples. The powdered sugar even seemed to her whiter and finer than elsewhere."

Cookbook: *Receipts for the Millions* by *Godey's Lady's Book* editor Sarah Josepha Hale (*née* Buell), 67, of Philadelphia, who writes, "To make good bread or to understand the process of making it is the duty of every woman; indeed an art that should never be neglected in the education of a lady. The lady derives her title from 'dividing or distributing bread'; the more perfect the bread, the more perfect the lady." More than 95 percent of the bread consumed in America is baked at home.

Weisswurst is invented by some accounts at Munich February 22 by the butcher-owner of the Ewige Lampe at Residenzstrasse 15, who finds himself with a shipment of wide sausage casings instead of the narrow ones he ordered. He fills them with a double portion of ground veal mixed with diced bacon, adds quantities of grated lemon rind, onion, parsley, salt, and white pepper, and is delighted to have his creation—eaten with a mustard made of green and yellow mustard flour, cloves, confectionary sugar, and wine vinegar—acclaimed by his patrons.

U.S. entrepreneur John West begins salting salmon at Westport, Ore. He will begin canning salmon in the 1870s (*see* 1963; Hume, 1864).

The California honey industry has its beginnings at San Diego, where hives of Italian honeybees are introduced. California will become the leading U.S. honey producer.

An English biscuit firm that will become Peak, Frean & Co. is founded at Dockhead by James Peak.

Brooklyn, N.Y., entrepreneur Eugene R. Durkee creates Durkee's Dressing in his kitchen. He will peddle the spiced mayonnaise-based combination salad dressing and meat sauce from door to door before selling it through retailers (*see* Glidden 1929).

The New York Condensed Milk Co. is founded May 11 by Gail Borden, who has obtained financial backing from New York grocery wholesaler Jeremiah Milbank, 39, whom he has met by chance on a train (*see* 1856). Commercial production of his condensed milk begins at Burrville, Conn. and Borden sets up a small office in Canal Street, peddles his product door to door, and now meets with more success. *Leslie's Illustrated Newspaper* helps Borden's sales by crusading against "swill milk" from Brooklyn cows fed on distillery mash (*see* 1861).

THE CITY MILK BUSINESS.
MARY, THE KITCHEN-MAID. "Why, John, what's the matter?"
MILKMAN. "Ah, Mary! if we don't have rain soon, I don't know what we'll do for Milk!"

Milk sold to New York households was often produced and delivered under dubious conditions. LIBRARY OF CONGRESS

Detroit grocer Hiram Walker, 41, builds a small steam-powered flour mill and distillery on the Ontario side of the Detroit River at a place that will be called Walkerville. A native of Massachusetts, he set up a Detroit grocery store in 1846, failed, but by 1849 was advertising 500 barrels of "good wheat whiskey at low prices for cash," entered the grain trade, and has become Detroit's largest commission merchant, with accounts all over the United States and Canada. He has analyzed the methods of his customers—millers as well as distillers—and decided to enter the distilling industry, but because state legislatures may be swayed by Prohibitionists he has acquired property in Canada to establish the business that his family will control until 1926 (*see* 1933). Walker's Club whiskey, which he will introduce in a few years, will develop a reputation for lightness and flavor (*see* "Canadian Club," 1891).

The California grape and wine industries have their true beginnings at Buena Vista in the Valley of the Moon near the Sonoma Mission, where Count Agoston Haraszthy de Mokcsa, 55, plants Tokay and Shiras grape varieties from his native Hungary on the estate of Salvador Vallejo, using no irrigation. The count, who arrived in America in the 1840s and founded Sauk City, Wis., came to California in 1849 and in 1852 planted the vines that produce Zinfandel, a wine unique to California; the vines he plants are the first varietal grape vines in America, and his Buena Vista winery will survive through the next century (*see* 1861; Vignes, 1840).

1858

The Japanese Tokugawa shōgun Iesada dies of beriberi at age 34, leaving no heir.

Portugal abolishes slavery in her colonial possessions, but emancipation is to take effect only after 20 years' "apprenticeship" (*see* 1761).

The first steam-driven tractors for field use are introduced; by 1888 some 38 U.S. companies will be listed as building tractors with steam traction engines, but their main purpose will be to generate power, delivered by belt pulleys, to drive threshing machines.

London's meat becomes fatter and juicier as the Smithfield market receives rail shipments of ready-dressed carcasses from Aberdeen, 515 miles away. Beef, mutton, pork, and veal arrive in perfect condition the night after the animals are slaughtered, and the meat is far less lean than if the animals had been driven to market as in the past.

The Marsh harvester patented August 17 by Canadian-born U.S. inventor Charles Wesley Marsh, 24, improves on the McCormick harvester. As the grain is cut, it falls onto a revolving apron carrier, which bears it in a continuous stream to the side, where an elevating apron delivers it to a receiver. From there it is taken to two men who ride the machine and bind the grain by hand, and the two men can bind more grain than four men working on the ground (*see* 1863; self-rake, 1852; self-binder, 1872).

St. Louis bag maker Judson Moss Bemis obtains his first order—for 200 cotton half-barrel flour sacks—on the promise that his machine-stitched bags will not tear. His little factory on the Mississippi levee, started with an $2,000 in personal savings, has six sewing machines, two small printing presses, and some wooden type contributed by a cousin. In 2 years it will be turning out 4,000 bags per day for flour and feed merchants, and by 1874 Bemis Bros. & Co. will have 200 employees manufacturing 20,000 cotton bags per day.

French inventor Ferdinand P. A. Carré devises the first mechanical refrigerator, employing liquid ammonia in the compression machine that he will demonstrate at the 1862 London Exhibition by using it to manufacture blocks of ice (*see* Harrison, 1856). Industrial concerns will make wide use of Carré's machine (*see* Lowe, 1865; Linde, 1873).

The Mason jar, patented November 30 by New York metalworker John Landis Mason, 26, is a glass container with a thread molded into its top and a zinc lid with a threaded ring sealer. "Be it known that I, JOHN L. MASON . . . have invented Improvements in the Necks of Bottles, Jars, &c., Especially such as are intended to air and water tight, such as are used for sweetmeats &c." The first Mason jar is produced at the glass shop of one Samuel Crowley at Batsto, N.J., and it soon goes into production at Whitney Glass Works in Glassboro, N.J. Mason's reusable screw-cap jar is far superior to earlier jars, which were sealed with corks and wax (*see* Appert, 1810). It will free farm families from having to rely on pickle barrels, root cellars, and smokehouses to get through the winter. Urban families, too, will use Mason jars to put up excess fruits and vegetables, especially tomatoes, sweet corn, berries, peaches, relish, and pickles, and the jars will soon be sealed with paraffin wax (*see* 1851). Mason's patent will run out before he can capitalize on it, and he will die in the poorhouse (*see* "Lightning" seal, 1882; Ball Brothers, 1887).

Le Gourmet begins publication at Paris, where local novelist-poet-gastronome Charles Monselet starts the gastronomic journal to teach the subtleties of culinary technique. It will enjoy considerable success until it is forced to stop in 1870.

Alexis Soyer dies in August at age 58. He has never recovered from the fever he contracted in the Crimea shortly after Florence Nightingale was stricken.

St. Louis entrepreneur Perry Brazelton opens an ice cream plant that he will follow with others in Chicago and Cincinnati (*see* Fussell, 1851).

Grenada in the Caribbean produces its first crop of nutmeg and mace to begin the island's career as the world's leading producer of those spices. An English sea captain bound home with spices from the East Indies presented seedlings to his hosts at the port of St. George's in 1843 (*see* 1955).

A hazelnut tree planted at a Hudson's Bay outpost at Scottsburgh in the Oregon Territory will lead to further plantings (*see* 1876). Hazelnut trees have been grown in China for thousands of years and were cultivated, also, in ancient Greece.

London's Express Country Milk Co. has its beginnings in a firm started by local retailer George Barham, 22, whose company will have the world's largest milk-bottling center (*see* Margarine Act, 1887).

Schweppe's Tonic Water has its beginnings in "an improved liquid known as quinine tonic water" patented at London. J. Schweppe & Co. Ltd. will make and sell the product beginning in 1880 (*see* 1851; 1953).

The mint julep created at Old White Springs in Virginia's Allegheny Mountains is made from brandy, cut loaf sugar, limestone water, crushed ice, and mountain mint, but the French brandy will generally be replaced by bourbon whiskey.

T. M. Harvey's Ladies' and Gentlemen's Oyster Saloon opens in a onetime Washington, D.C., blacksmith shop. Within 5 years, George Harvey's establishment will be so revered by gastronomes in both the North and South that his oyster boats will be allowed to penetrate Union and Confederate blockades to obtain shellfish. He will move in 1866 to larger premises at 11th Street and Pennsylvania Avenue and, later, to 1001 18th Street N.W., where he will serve diamondback terrapin stew and other delicacies as well as oysters.

business and go partners in buying China and Japanese tea directly from ships in New York harbor. Both originally from Maine, the two men buy whole clipper ship cargoes at one fell swoop, sell the tea at less than one-third the price charged by other merchants, identify their store with flaked gold letters on a Chinese vermilion background, and start a business that will grow into the first chain store operation (*see* 1863; A&P, 1869).

The vast A&P grocery chain began modestly as the Great American Tea Company. LIBRARY OF CONGRESS

1859

The A&P retail food chain has its beginnings in the Great American Tea Co. store opened at 31 Vesey Street, N.Y., by local merchant George Huntington Hartford, 26, who has persuaded his employer, George P. Gilman, to give up his hide and leather

The discovery of petroleum at Titusville, Pa., August 28 will lead to mechanization of U.S. agriculture and improved transport.

Louis Pasteur disproves the chemical theory of fermentation advanced by the German chemist Baron von Liebig. Pasteur also disproves the theory of spontaneous generation and shows that while some microorganisms exist in the air like yeast, and like yeast can transform whatever they touch, other microorganisms are anaerobic and cannot survive in the presence of air (*see* 1861; 1871; milk sterilization and "pasteurization," 1860).

Treatise on Gout and Rheumatic Gout by London physician Alfred Baring Garrod, 40, shows that Galen in the 2nd century was wrong in blaming gout on overindulgence. A staff doctor at University College hospital, Garrod says gout comes from an excess of uric acid in the blood (*see* Scheele, 1776) and can be controlled by avoiding foods high in purine and by using drugs such as colchicine.

Nonfiction: *Civilized America*, published at London, ridicules Americans for calling a cock a rooster and using similar euphemisms.

Cookbooks: *Domestic Cookery* by U.S. cook Elizabeth Lea gives recipes that include one for "Journey Cake" (*see* 1888); *The English Bread Book* by Eliza Acton gives recipes for making bread properly and describes the ways in which commercial bread is adulterated.

Paraffin wax, a by-product of kerosene produced from petroleum (above), will be used to seal Mason jars used for preserving foods (*see* Mason, 1858).

New York Tribune editor Horace Greeley, 48, visits Denver and finds that its residents subsist almost entirely on beans, bacons, and sourdough bread. The mining town's only hotel is a tent.

The yearbook of the Association Normande reports that in 1791 one Marie Harel, on her farm near Camembert, invented a cheese that took its name from the place of its manufacture, but others claim that it was Napoleon III who named the cheese after being presented with a gift of it by Marie Harel's daughter, Marie Harel Paynel, when he went to Vimoutiers for the inauguration of the Paris Grand Railroad; still others claim that the emperor did not pass through Vimoutiers but stopped, rather, at Surdon and received the cheese from Thomas Paynel, who married the second Marie Harel in 1813 (*see* cheesebox, 1890).

 Australian landowner Thomas Austin imports two dozen English rabbits to provide shooting sport. In 6 years Austin will have shot 200,000 on his own estate and killed scarcely half the rabbits on his property, and since five of the fast-multiplying animals consume more grass than one sheep, the rabbits will quickly become a major problem to sheep-raisers (*see* myxomatosis, 1951).

Physiologie der Nahrungsmittel: Ein grand Buch der Diätetik by German physician Jacob Moleschott, 37, concludes that a working man weighing 63.65 kilograms needs a total of 3,438 grams of food and water per day, including 2,800 grams of water, 404 grams of carbohydrate, 84 grams of fat, 130 grams of protein, and 30 grams of salt. He follows the theories of animal chemistry put forward by Liebig in 1842 and demonstrates that the analysis of food intake can provide a crude research tool (*see* Voit, 1881).

The Iona grape, discovered on Iona Island in the Hudson River near Peekskill, N.Y., by Dr. C. W. Grant will be widely used in wine making. It is a seedling of the Diana grape, which is a Catawba variety.

Powdery mildew (*Uncinula necator*) is recognized for the first time in California. The fungus disease, which affects vineyards, probably originated in Japan half a century ago and was introduced in 1845 into European vineyards, where it was called "oidium." The mildew reduces yield and quality, retards growth, and makes vines less resistant to winter damage.

The American Stranger's Guide to London and Liverpool at Table says, "The want of long standing still exists in London—and that is the difficulty of finding Restaurants where strangers of the gentler sex may be taken to dine. It is true that some have been opened where gentlemen may take their wives and daughters, but it has not yet become a recognized custom."

1860

British planters in Natal, South Africa, import workers from India to work their sugar plantations under 3-year indentures.

The Oneida Community in upstate New York grosses $100,000 from sales of the Newhouse trap, named for Community member Sewell Newhouse, who invented the device that is fast becoming the standard in North America and will eventually become so for most of the world. The major enterprise of the 12-year-old community is making traps, and men of the community have developed dishwashers and machines for paring apples and washing vegetables to spare themselves the tedium of kitchen chores.

Boston candy maker Daniel Fobes buys the business of competitor Albert Webster and becomes an all-round candy maker, manufacturing lozenges and other popular low-priced confections as well as his own specialties (*see* 1854; 1866).

An internal combustion engine patented at Paris by Belgian inventor Jean-Étienne Lenoir, 38, employs a carburetor that mixes liquid hydrocarbons to form a vapor. An electric spark explodes the vapor in a cylinder, but Lenoir's engine works on illuminating gas and has no compression (*see* Otto, 1866).

More than 1,000 steamboats ply the Mississippi, up from 400-odd in 1840.

Reaper inventor Obed Hussey falls under a train in New England and is killed August 4 at age 68 (*see* 1847). He sold his business 2 years ago and has been working on the invention of a steam plow.

The growth of railroad and steamship lines in the next four decades will encourage expansion of U.S. agriculture for export markets.

The clinical symptoms of acute trichinosis are noted for the first time by German pathologist Friedrich Albert von Zenker, 35, but the cause-effect relationship remains unknown (*see* 1835).

Diabetes is the result of a pancreatic disorder, says Paris physician Étienne Lancereaux, 31 (*see* Cawley, 1788; Langerhans, 1869).

The Seventh-Day Adventist Church, which will have an impact on the U.S. food industry, is founded at Battle Creek, Mich., by former followers of William Miller, whose 1836 prediction of the Second Coming in 1843 proved false but who continued to attract a wide following nevertheless (*see* sanitorium, 1866).

 The prince of Wales visits New York in October and is given a ball, reception, and supper at the Academy of Music in 14th Street. Climax of the elaborate dinner is a great beefsteak-and-kidney pie.

Texas cattleman Richard King, now 36, takes his old steamboat partner Mifflin Kenedy, 43, into partnership and the two pool their resources to import Durham cattle, which will improve their breeding stock (*see* 1853; 1868).

The U.S. wheat crop reaches 173 million bushels, more than double its 1840 level. Wheat from California goes mostly to Liverpool, carried in the holds of huge sailing ships that take 4 to 5 months for the voyage of 14,000 nautical miles around Cape Horn. So dependent are California growers on the English market that they use the British cental (100 pounds) rather than the bushel as a standard of measurement.

The U.S. corn crop reaches 839 million bushels, up from 377 million in 1840 (*see* 1870; 1885).

Mississippi agronomist Eugene Hilgard urges contour plowing and use of fertilizer: "Well might the Chickasaws and Choctaws question the moral right of the act by which their beautiful, park-like hunting grounds were turned over to another race. . . . Under their system these lands would have lasted forever; under ours, in less than a century the state will be reduced to the . . . desolation of the once fertile Roman Campagna" (*see* Ruffin, 1833).

The Fruit Manual by Scottish pomologist Robert Hogg discusses fruits grown in Britain, giving special emphasis to apple varieties such as the Blenheim, Carey Pippin, Cox's Orange Pippin, and Richmond Pippin. Hogg's pocket-sized book will grow in later editions to be weighty tomes.

Parliament passes the first British Adulteration of Foods Law after physician Edwin Lankester quotes recent cases in which three people have died after attending a public banquet at which green blancmange that was colored with arsenite of copper was served. Lankester has shown that sulfide of arsenic is used to color Bath buns yellow (*see* 1861).

Louis Pasteur sterilizes milk by heating it to 125° Centigrade at a pressure of 1.5° atmospheres (100° C. is equal to 212° F.). Pasteur will develop methods using lower heats to "pasteurize" milk, which changes the flavor slightly but has the benefit of preventing the spread of milk-borne diseases. The propagation of myths about pasteurization, especially in Britain, will delay introduction of pasteurized milk on a commercial basis for 50 years (*see* 1857; 1861; cattle tuberculosis test, 1892; Bang's disease, 1896).

Pasteurization (above) will also be used to prevent the spoilage of wine and beer.

Pleasant Valley Wine Co. is founded near Hammondsport, N.Y., by local clergyman William Bostwick, who uses Catawba grapes from his garden (*see* 1829; Great Western champagne, 1865).

New York Tribune writer Solon Robinson writes in his book *How to Live*, "Last Summer we got in the habit of taking the tea iced, and really thought it better than hot" (*see* 1871).

1861

Civil war begins in America April 12 as Confederate guns bombard Fort Sumter on an island in Charleston harbor.

"Without McCormick's invention, I feel the North could not win and that the Union would be dismembered," says Secretary of War Edwin M. Stanton, 46. The McCormick reaper sells for $150, up from $100 in 1849, but McCormick offers it at $30 down with the balance to be paid in 6 months if the harvest is good and over a longer term if the harvest is disappointing.

Slaves are emancipated in the Dutch West Indies, where sugar hereafter will be grown by free men.

Czar Aleksandr II completes the emancipation of Russian serfs begun in 1858. He allots land to the serfs for which they are to pay over a period of 49 years, but the land is given to village communes (*mir*s), not to individuals, and is to be redistributed every 10 or 12 years to assure equality. Since a peasant may buy only half the amount of land he cultivated as a serf and will often be unable to afford his annual "redemption" payments, he will be unable to gain economic independence, much less improve the land or his methods of cultivation (*see* agriculture, below).

U.S. tariffs rise as Congress passes the first of three Morrill Acts, which will boost tariffs to an average of 47 percent. Duties on tea, coffee, and sugar are increased as a war measure (*see* 1857; 1890).

Chicago ships 50 million bushels of U.S. wheat to drought-stricken Europe, up from 31 million in 1860, despite the outbreak of the Civil War (above) and the shortage of farm hands.

Philadelphia butcher Peter Arrell Brown Widener, 27, obtains a government contract to supply mutton to Union troops in and about Philadelphia. Widener will pocket a $50,000 profit, which he will invest in a chain of meat stores and in street railways, building a huge fortune.

Gail Borden licenses more factories to produce his condensed milk, which the Union Army purchases for use in field rations (*see* 1857). Borden's son John Gail fights for the Union, his son Lee with the Texas Cavalry for the Confederacy (*see* 1866).

The first U.S. butter factory is established at Walkill, N.Y., by entrepreneur Alanson Slaughter, beginning an industry, but most households continue to churn their own butter at home (*see* separator, 1877).

Henri Nestlé, 45, begins his rise to world prominence. The German-born Swiss businessman, who moved to the town of Vevey in 1843, has taken a financial interest in a local chemical firm operated by Christophe Guillaume Keppel, and he assumes ownership upon Keppel's retirement (*see* 1866).

Discovery of a cheap method of making ice makes it practicable to chill and freeze meat, but ways to refrigerate and ship bulk meat in good condition will not be found until 1880.

Roller mills come into use in Britain: refined wheat flour without wheat germ will become the dietary staple by the 1870s, and not just among the rich.

Baltimore canner Isaac Solomon reduces the average processing time for canned foods from 6 hours to 30 minutes by employing the late English chemist Humphry Davy's discovery that adding calcium chloride raises the temperature of boiling water to 240° F. and more (*see* 1874).

Louis Pasteur confutes theories that lack of oxygen is what keeps canned food from spoiling. He also notes that since milk is alkaline rather than acid, it requires more heat for sterilization, but heating milk to 110° C. will stop the growth of "vibrios" and preserve it indefinitely, he says (*see* 1895; fermentation, 1859; 1871).

Cookbook: *Book of Household Management* by English journalist Isabella Beeton (*née* Mayson), 25, gives recipes for Victorian dishes in a thick three-pound, 1,296-page volume with color plates whose contents appeared originally in her publisher husband Samuel Orchert Beeton's *Englishwoman's Domestic Magazine*. Mrs. Beeton, who has taken pastry-making lessons from an Epsom con-

Mrs. Beeton brought some precision to the recipes followed by English housewives. NEW YORK PUBLIC LIBRARY

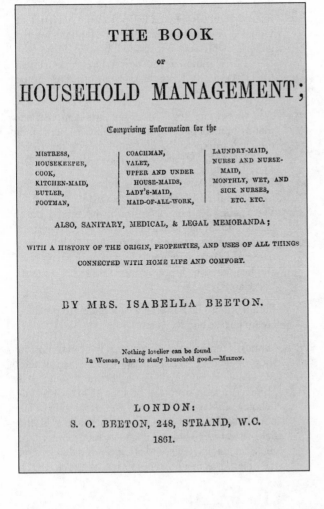

THE BOOK

OF

HOUSEHOLD MANAGEMENT;

Comprising Information for the

MISTRESS,	COACHMAN,	LAUNDRY-MAID,
HOUSEKEEPER,	VALET,	NURSE AND NURSE-
COOK,	UPPER AND UNDER	MAID,
KITCHEN-MAID,	HOUSE-MAIDS,	MONTHLY, WET, AND
BUTLER,	LADY'S-MAID,	SICK NURSES,
FOOTMAN,	MAID-OF-ALL-WORK,	ETC. ETC.

ALSO, SANITARY, MEDICAL, & LEGAL MEMORANDA;

WITH A HISTORY OF THE ORIGIN, PROPERTIES, AND USES OF ALL THINGS
CONNECTED WITH HOME LIFE AND COMFORT.

BY MRS. ISABELLA BEETON.

Nothing lovelier can be found
In Woman, than to study household good.—MILTON.

LONDON:
S. O. BEETON, 248, STRAND, W.C.
1861.

fectioner, gives costs and cooking times as well as ingredient quantities. "In order that the duties of the cook may be properly performed, and that he may be able to reproduce the steamed dishes with certainty, all terms of indecision should be banished from his art," she writes. "Accordingly, what is known only to him, will, in these pages, be made known to others. In them, all the indecisive terms expressed by a bit of this, some of that, a small piece of that, and a handful of the other, shall never be made use of, but all quantities be precisely and explicitly stated with a desire, also, that all ignorance of this most essential part of the culinary art should disappear, and that a uniform system of weights and measures should be adopted, we have an account of the weights which answer to certain measures" (but she herself often specifies a "pinch" of this or "two-penny's worth" of that). "What moved me, in the first instance, to attempt a work like this," she says in her preface, "was the discomfort and suffering brought upon men and women by household *mismanagement*. I have always thought that there is no more fruitful source of family discontent than a housewife's badly cooked dinners and untidy ways. Men are so well served out of doors—in their well ordered taverns and dining places, that in order to compete with the attraction of these places a mistress must be thoroughly acquainted with the theory and practice of cookery." Some 60,000 copies of Mrs. Beeton's book will be sold in its first year and it will continue to attract buyers for more than 50 years, selling over half a million copies by 1890.

America's first commercial pretzel bakery opens at Lititz, Pa., with local baker Julius Sturgis in charge.

Godey's Lady's Book calls the tomato a "delicious and wholesome vegetable" but warns its readers to cook tomatoes for at least 3 hours, since cooking them for less will result in "a sour porridge."

Mrs. Beeton (above) says of garlic, "The smell of this plant is generally considered offensive, and it is the most acrimonious in its taste of the whole of the alliaceous tribe. In 1548 it was introduced to England from the shores of the Mediterranean, where it is abundant, and in Sicily it grows naturally. It was in greater repute with our ancestors than it is with ourselves, although it is still used as a seasoning herb. On the Continent, especially in Italy, it is much used, and the French consider it an essential in many made dishes."

Mrs. Beeton (above) suggests sample menus, month by month, for large and small dinner parties of anywhere from 6 to 60 guests and daily menus for ordinary family dinners. An April dinner for six persons may begin with tapioca soup and boiled salmon with lobster sauce; the entrées are sweetbreads and oyster patties; the second course consists of haunch of mutton, boiled capon in white sauce, tongue, and vegetables; the third course is made up of soufflé of rice with lemon cream, charlotte à la parisienne, and rhubarb tart; dessert follows.

A middle-class hostess planning a picnic party for 40 is advised by Mrs. Beeton (above) to include a joint of cold roast beef, a joint of cold boiled beef, two ribs of lamb, two shoulders of lamb, four roast fowls, two roast ducks, one ham, one tongue, two veal-and-ham pies, two pigeon pies, six medium-sized lobsters, one piece of calf's head, 15 lettuces, six baskets of salad, six cucumbers, stewed fruit well sweetened and put into glass bottles well corked, three or four plain pastry biscuits to eat with the stewed fruit, two dozen fruit turnovers, four dozen cheesecakes, two cold cabinet puddings in molds, a few jam puffs, one large cold Christmas pudding ("this must be good"), a few baskets of fresh fruit, three dozen plain biscuits, a piece of cheese, six pounds of butter ("this, of course, includes the butter for tea"), four quartern loaves of household bread, three dozen rolls, six loaves of tinned bread ("for tea"), two plain plum cakes, two pound cakes, two sponge cakes, a tin of mixed biscuits, one-half pound of tea ("Coffee is not suitable for a picnic, being difficult to make"), a stick of horseradish, a bottle of good mint sauce well corked, a bottle of salad dressing, a bottle of vinegar, made mustard, pepper, salt, two dozen quart bottles of ale packed in hampers, ginger beer, soda water, lemonade (of each, two dozen bottles), six bottles of sherry, and six bottles of claret; champagne at discretion and any other light wine and brandy. Mrs. Beeton assumes that water can be obtained on the site. "Take three corkscrews," she reminds her reader.

Mrs. Beeton's recipes (above) include one for chocolate soufflé (see Carême, 1833).

Most Russian peasants can do no more than grow enough for their own families' needs with a small surplus in good years to sell for tax money (see emancipation, above). Most cultivate with wooden plows, harvest their crops with sickles or scythes, and thresh their grain with hand flails. One-third of the peasants have no horses, another third only one horse, and even in the richer parts of Russia the soil is drained by strip farming and a shortage of fertilizer (see Stolypin, 1906).

The California State Legislature commissions Count Agoston Haraszthy to bring select varieties of European wine grapes to the state (see 1857). Using $12,000 of his own money, Haraszthy will select 100,000 cuttings that represent 300 varieties from Europe's great vineyards, inaugurating the modern era of California wine production. Two of his sons will be married in 1863 at the hacienda of Gen. M. Guadalupe Vallejo to daughters of the general, who was imprisoned briefly during the Mexican War but has prospered since the gold rush (see 1841; 1920; Krug, below; report, 1862; grape phylloxera, 1868).

A lecture to the Royal Society of Arts demonstrates that 87 percent of London's bread and 74 percent of the city's milk is still adulterated despite the Adulteration of Foods Law enacted last year (see 1872).

Van Camp's Pork and Beans helps sustain Union troops in the field. Indianapolis grocer Gilbert C. Van Camp, 37, once a tinsmith, has mixed pork, beans, and tomato sauce in his Missouri Street store to create a new canned-food staple (it will become the world's largest-selling brand of pork and beans) and he secures an army contract (see 1882; Stokely–Van Camp, 1933).

Philadelphia's D. Bassett Co. is founded to produce cream cheese and ice cream.

Schrafft's candy has its beginnings in a small Boston shop opened at 85 Eliot Street by Bavarian-American confectioner William F. Schrafft, who has obtained a loan from the brother of his wife, Wilhelmina, at New Bedford. His gumdrops gain quick popularity (patrons send them to soldiers in the field), and he expands his line to include peppermint sticks, cinnamon balls, and other candies that Boston merchants buy in wholesale lots (see Shattuck, 1897).

Domingo Ghiardelli enters the confectionery business at San Francisco with capital acquired by setting up tents in the goldfields and selling goods to miners. Ghiardelli, who lived in Latin America before arriving in 1849, has seen cacao growing in Guatemala; he will build a chocolate factory, and by the turn of the century his firm will be specializing in the manufacture of chocolate bars.

California's Charles Krug winery is founded north of St. Helena in the Napa Valley by Prussian-American vintner (and freethinker) Krug, who builds two huge stone buildings, one to store his wines (which he has been making since 1858, originally with John Patchet at Napa), the other to house his horses, keeping both at a temperature of 59° F. (*see* Korbel, 1862). Krug will face stiff competition from Count Haraszthy (above), whose sparkling wine Eclipse will be the toast of San Francisco until his Buena Vista winery in Sonoma County fails.

The Hôtel Beau Rivage opens March 24 at Ouchy, a suburb of Lausanne on the northern shore of Lake Geneva, with 110 guest rooms and a table d'hôte dining room that will make it a worthy rival to the palatial hotels of nearby Vevey and Montreux, attracting English lords, Russian grand dukes, and some U.S. millionaires. A sister hotel, the Palace, will open in 1906.

The New York restaurant Doré's, opened in 14th Street by a man named Martinez, will for years be Delmonico's only serious rival.

1862

London decides not to recognize the Confederacy on which Britain has depended for cotton, in large part because the British are dependent on the North for grain exports.

U.S. troops drive the Chippewa (Ojibway) out of Minnesota. The bloody "Minnesota massacre" makes stands of wild rice available to white settlers.

 Union forces destroy Confederate saltworks on Chesapeake Bay, creating difficulties for salt pork producers in the South (*see* 1863).

British crops fail and hunger is widespread, especially in Lancashire, where thousands of mill hands have been thrown out of work by the cutoff of cotton from America. The Lancashire & Salford Provident Society issues tickets good for provisions as the Cotton Famine brings working-class people to the edge of starvation (*see* nutrition, below).

The Homestead Act voted by Congress May 20 declares that any U.S. citizen, or any alien intending to become a citizen, may have 160 acres of Western lands absolutely free (except for a $10 registration fee) provided he make certain improvements and live on the tract for 5 years. Enacted to redeem an 1860 Republican campaign promise after years of excessive land speculation, the law is to become effective January 1 (*see* below).

The Morrill Land-Grant Act voted by Congress July 2 gives the states 11 million acres of federal lands to sell, nearly twice the acreage of Vermont (home state of Sen. Justin Morrill, 52).

An Internal Revenue Act passed by Congress in July to finance the war effort taxes beer at $1 per barrel and imposes license fees on tavern owners.

The U.S. Produce Exchange is organized at New York (*see* Chicago Board of Trade, 1865).

English entrepreneur Henry Isaac Rowntree, 24, takes over the chocolate and cocoa manufacturing interests of William Tuke & Sons (*see* 1725). He will buy a foundry at York in 1864, convert it to cocoa manufacture, and go into business with his brother Joseph, now 26, in 1869, launching an enterprise that will compete with Cadbury's (*see* 1881).

The Illinois-Central Railroad facilitates Union troop movements with its north-south line. The company will sell off 800,000 acres of its land to settlers.

A patent for an "Improved Process of Preserving Green Corn" is issued to Maine inventor Isaac Winslow, who 19 years ago sold 12 tin cans of Maine sweet corn to Boston's S. S. Pierce.

Refrigerators manufactured by Daniel Siebe to the designs of Australian inventor James Harrison are exhibited at the International Exhibition and are the first mechanical refrigerators actually to be sold (*see* 1857; Linde, 1873).

Ergotism breaks out in Finland, where rye bread is major component of the peasants' diet.

The Morrill Land-Grant Act (above) provides funds to start U.S. land-grant colleges for the scientific education of farmers and mechanics (*see* below; 1890).

France's Napoleon III visits Paris banker James de Rothschild, 69, February 17 at Ferrières, the Rothschild estate, where he lunches on Sèvres porcelain painted by the late François Boucher, is entertained with music composed for the occasion by Rothschild's staff musician Gioacchino Rossini, now 69, and then joins Baron James in an afternoon hunting party on the Rothschild grounds. The hunters kill 1,231 head of game; upon their return, a choir from the Paris Opéra sings hunting songs while the boar is carved by master chefs and the pheasants are served *en plumage*.

Nearly 470,000 settlers will apply for homesteads in the next 18 years under terms of the Homestead Act (above). Roughly one-third of these will actually receive land, but while a farmer can make a living on 80 acres in the East, land in the West is generally so arid that even 160 acres will rarely permit economically viable agriculture (*see* 1909).

Congress creates an independent U.S. Department of Agriculture (*see* 1889).

The new Department of Agriculture (above) gives horticulturist William Saunders an appointment at Washington (*see* Patrons of Husbandry, 1855). He will import 12 seedless orange trees from Bahia, Brazil, in 1871 and all first growths of this variety in Florida and California will be propagated from these trees (*see* Hart, 1867; navel oranges, 1875).

The Northern Spy apple variety discovered by a farmer at West Bloomfield in western New York will become as popular as the Baldwin, Winesap, Rhode Island Greening, Seek-No-Further, Rome Beauty, and other New York favorites (year approximate).

British physician Edward Smith is asked by the government to investigate the health of unemployed Lancashire cotton workers (*see* Cotton Famine, above). He finds that while the poor consume more cheap foods such as bread and potatoes and less meat and milk, they still spend some money on small quantities of expensive foods rather than buying more of the cheap, filling foods, which they eat in large enough quantities to avoid feeling actively hungry. Dr. Smith notes that many mothers are not aware that milk is as necessary for their children after weaning as before and that many infants are fed chiefly on bread, warm water, and sugar, to which a little milk is sometimes added. Families average one pint of milk per week instead of the two to three per day recommended for infants (*see* 1875).

Iowa widow Annie Wittenmyer (*née* Turner), 35, works with the Sanitary Commission to devise a system for feeding Union soldiers in field hospitals as the Civil War continues. Women volunteers have scrounged milk, eggs, and vegetables for soldiers too sick to eat the regular pork-and-beans ration, but Wittenmyer's system ends confusion by establishing a diet kitchen in each hospital with "dietary nurses" who provide appropriate meals for each patient (*see* WCTU, 1874).

Gulden's Mustard is introduced by New York entrepreneur Charles Gulden, whose Elizabeth Street shop has easy access to sources of mustard seed, spices, and vinegar.

Crosse & Blackwell in England introduces canned soups (*see* Campbell and Anderson, 1869).

Confederate troops in America's ongoing Civil War (above) adopt peanuts as a cheap coffee substitute. Union troops, who call the peanut a "goober pea," carry it to the North, where it will become popular as a snack food.

Congress prohibits distillation of alcohol without a federal license, but "moonshiners" continue to make whiskey.

The U.S. Navy abolishes its rum ration September 1 through the influence of Rear Admiral Andrew Hull Foote, 56, an ardent temperance advocate who has made his ship the first in the Navy to stop issuing rum rations. The ration will later be revived.

Bacardí Co. is founded in Cuba by rum distiller Emilio Bacardí, whose Catalan father, Don Facundo Bacardí, emigrated from Spain in 1830 at age 14 and became a Cuban wine merchant (*see* 1919).

"Grape Culture, Wines, and Wine-Making with Notes upon Agriculture and Horticulture" by Agoston Haraszthy is published as a report to the California State Senate and Assembly (*see* 1861). Count

Haraszthy has traveled through Europe with his son Arpad and gives descriptions of what he saw in his investigations.

California wine making got its start with help from European enterprise and Chinese labor. LIBRARY OF CONGRESS

California's Korbel winery is founded near Santa Rosa in the Russian River Valley by three Czech brothers who log mature redwoods off some hillsides and plant vineyards from which Korbel will produce champagnelike sparkling wines (*see* 1954).

The martini cocktail is created according to one account by San Francisco bartender Jerry Thomas. When a traveler asks him for a cool and refreshing drink, Thomas mixes a dash of bitters, two dashes of maraschino, an ounce of Old Tom gin, a wineglass of vermouth, and two small lumps of ice, shakes the mixture thoroughly, strains it into a cocktail glass, and serves it with a quarter slice of lemon. When the traveler announces that he is about to leave for the town of Martinez, 40 miles distant, Thomas (who will also be credited with inventing the Tom and Jerry cocktail) decides to name his creation the "martini." (The claim that he originated it will be disputed, but the martini—made with varying amounts of gin and vermouth [or, sometimes, absinthe, cider, coffee liqueur, grenadine, or sake]—will become the most popular single gin cocktail, and it will be garnished variously with a twist of lemon, an olive [with or without pimento], artichoke hearts, pistachio nuts, red

caviar, tiny eggplants, maraschino cherries, crystallized violets, and watercress [with a pearl onion, it will be called a Gibson].)

Lorenzo Delmonico opens a third New York café-restaurant at Fifth Avenue and 14th Street, where he has acquired the Grinnell mansion to keep up with society's move uptown (*see* 1845). "To lunch, dine, or sup at Delmonico's is the crowning ambition of those who aspire at notoriety," Abram C. Dayton will write about the new eating place, "and no better studio for character does the city afford than that expensive resort at almost any hour of the day." Chef Charles Ranhofer will contribute to Delmonico's reputation as what Dayton will call "beyond all question the most palatial café or restaurant on this continent" (*see* 1868).

1863

Vicksburg, Miss., falls to Gen. Ulysses S. Grant, 41, July 4 after a short siege in which people have suffered for lack of food. Union forces gain control of the Mississippi, cutting off Confederate supplies of Texas beef.

Richmond has had bread riots in April and Mobile has riots in September as the Union starves the South.

Confederate President Jefferson Davis, 55, urges southerners to plant corn, peas, and beans. His April message gives priority to food crops over cotton and tobacco.

Union forces cut the South off from its salt deposits on the Louisiana Gulf Coast and destroy all its saltworks in Florida, North Carolina, and Virginia (*see* 1862).

Salt from wells in the area of Syracuse, N.Y., and Saginaw, Mich., keep the North well supplied.

Disruption of sugar plantations in the South sends U.S. sugar prices soaring and brings a vigorous increase in sugar planting in the Hawaiian Islands, dependent for years on the whaling industry, which is now in a decline as a result of the growing use of kerosene for lamp oil (*see* energy, 1859).

Bay Sugar Refining Co. is founded by German-American entrepreneur Claus Spreckels, 35, who has prospered as a San Francisco grocer and brewer since 1856 (*see* 1868).

Britain and France sign commercial treaties with Belgium to begin a period of free trade. The River Scheldt reopens to free navigation for the first time since 1648.

 The Great American Tea Co. founded in 1859 grows to have six stores and begins selling a line of groceries in addition to tea (*see* A&P, 1869).

The Marsh reaper patented in 1858 goes into production at Plano, Ill. Improvements have been made in the machine, and further refinements will bring it to perfection by 1878 (*see* Appleby binder, 1869; Deering, 1873).

Smithfield, R.I., inventor Timothy Earle is granted a patent for an egg beater with a rack-and-pinion movement (*see* 1870).

President Abraham Lincoln, 54, proclaims the first national Thanksgiving Day October 3 and sets aside the last Thursday of November to commemorate the feast given by the Pilgrims in 1621 for their Wampanoag benefactors. The president has acted partly in response to a plea from *Godey's Lady's Book* editor Sarah Josepha Hale, now 74, who has campaigned since 1846 for Thanksgiving Day observances and by 1852 had persuaded people to celebrate Thanksgiving on the same day in 30 of the 32 states, in U.S. consulates abroad, and on U.S. ships in foreign waters. (The date for observance will be changed in 1939 to the fourth Thursday in November.)

The University of Massachusetts has its beginnings in the Massachusetts Agricultural College founded at Amherst. It will be renamed in 1947.

Sutlers provide Union troops with canned meat, oysters, condensed milk (*see* Borden, 1861), pork and beans (*see* Van Camp, 1861), and vegetables, including green beans.

Confederate troops eat the meat-and-vegetable stew "burgoo" created by Lexington, Ky., chef Gus Jaubert, but there is widespread hunger in the South.

Granula is introduced by Dansville, N.Y., sanitarium operator James Caleb Jackson, 52, who has baked graham flour dough into oven-dried bread crumbs to create the first cold breakfast food (*see* Graham, 1837; Kellogg's Granula, 1877).

Wide-scale rustling (theft) begins on the Texas plains as cattle there are hit by the worst winter in years.

An epidemic of cattle disease in Britain over the next 4 years will boost meat prices and cause a boom in imports of tinned meats from Australia (*see* 1865).

The British epizootic (above) strikes hardest at Dutch cows, which have proved the sturdiest milkers for keeping in urban milk sheds but are the breeds most susceptible to disease. British dairymen are compelled to make wider and more efficient use of milk trains (*see* 1844), develop water coolers on farms and at milk depots, and use tinned-steel churns for transporting milk from the trains to urban markets.

La Villette opens at Paris. The central, hygienic slaughterhouse has been designed by Baron Georges-Eugène Haussmann, 54, prefect of the Seine since 1852.

The Field and Garden Vegetables of America by Hingham, Mass., market gardener Fearing Burr, Jr., 47, lists 52 lettuces and says of the tomato, or "love apple," "To a majority of tastes its flavor is not at first immediately agreeable." But he describes 24 tomato varieties.

English gardeners at Kew, outside London, record a blight of some kind which affects imported U.S. grapevines. French wine growers near Arles, in Provence, see leaves on their vines wither and drop; the new shoots have no vigor, the grapes do not ripen, and within 3 years most of the vines will be dead (*see* 1865).

Ovaltine has its beginnings at Bern, where Swiss scientist George Wander succeeds in producing a sweet-tasting malt extract which he will combine with whole milk, whole eggs, and cocoa to make a nourishing, easily digested, quickly absorbed emergency food for situations in which ordinary food may not be suitable. A German at the University of Bern has helped Wander set up a research laboratory to study the extraction of malt for use in combining infant mortality; Wander's Ovomaltine will be renamed Ovaltine when he applies for a British trademark, and his son Albert will develop the product further (*see* 1905).

Perrier water is introduced commercially by Source Perrier, which bottles the French spring water that bubbles up from a spring near Nîmes. The water contains calcium and sparkles because of its natural carbon dioxide content.

Toronto brewer Eugene O'Keefe resigns from his O'Keefe & Co. to start a new brewery. He will build a large plant in 1879 that will make his name familiar among beer drinkers.

Chase and Sanborn's coffee has its beginnings at Boston, where merchants Caleb Chase, 32, and James S. Sanborn begin selling coffee and tea (*see* 1878).

The New Orleans restaurant Begué's has its beginnings in a coffeehouse serving the city, which is occupied by Union troops. Open only for breakfast, it will soon serve snails, crawfish, tripe omelettes, tomatoes with parsley, beefsteak, cheese, apples, and brandy as well as coffee. Restaurants on Lake Ponchartrain serve only fish and game.

1864

Gen. Philip H. Sheridan, 33, takes command of the Army of the Shenandoah in August. Virginia's Shenandoah Valley is the breadbasket of the South; Sheridan has 50,000 troops and orders to "eat out Virginia clear and clean . . . so that crows flying over it for the balance of this season will have to carry their provender with them." He accomplishes his mission, and loss of the Shenandoah Valley as a food source forces the South to tighten its belt.

Gen. Grant's Army of the Potomac has laid siege to Petersburg, Va., near Richmond and in November orders that his troops be supplied with tons of cranberries in order that they may celebrate Thanksgiving in proper fashion. Gen. William Tecumseh Sherman, 44, takes Savannah December 25 as he continues a sweep across Georgia, looting or destroying plantation food stores.

U.S. wheat prices climb to $4 per bushel and food prices rise as European crops fail and the North ships wheat to hungry Europe.

Armour Packing Co. has its beginnings in a Milwaukee pork-packing firm started in partnership with John Plankinton by local commission merchant Philip Danforth Armour, 32, who has made nearly $2 million in 90 days selling short in the New York pork market. Armour went to California in his teens, dug sluiceways for gold miners at $5 to $10 per day, saved $8,000 in 5 years to give himself the wherewithal to start his business at Milwaukee, and has traveled to New York, where he found pork selling at $40 per barrel. Foreseeing a Union victory as Gen. Grant prepared to march on Richmond, Armour sold short at more than $33 per barrel, covered his sales at $18 per barrel, and has made a fortune (*see* 1868).

Kamehamea IV of the Sandwich Islands sells the Hawaiian island of Niihau to Mrs. Elizabeth Sinclair, an émigrée Scotswoman whose late husband acquired large holdings in New Zealand before being lost at sea. Feeling the property insufficient to keep her large family together, she has sold it, loaded her family, livestock, and movable possessions aboard her own clipper ship, and visited several places before deciding on Hawaii. The 12-mile-long, 46,000-acre island—plus the 65,000-acre Great Makaweli estate on Kaui—will remain in her family for more than a century after Mrs. Sinclair's death in 1890, being used to graze sheep and cattle.

Illinois inventors John Thompson and John Ramsay obtain a patent for the check-row corn planter, which will be used well into the next century (*see* Robbins, 1857). Instead of a chain fitted with iron buttons, Thompson and Ramsay use a knotted wire.

Cookbook: *The English and Australian Cookery Book, cooking for the many as well as the "upper ten thousand"* by Edward Abbott of Hobart is published at London and is the first Australian cookbook. Melbourne's Union Hotel had a Parisian chef as early as the 1850s, and Sydney got its first café with a French name in 1854.

Man and Nature by pioneer ecologist George Perkins Marsh, 63, of the U.S. foreign service warns that "the ravages committed by man subvert the relations and destroy the balance which nature had established . . . ; and she avenges herself upon the intruder by letting loose her destructive energies.

... When the forest is gone, the great reservoir of moisture stored up in its vegetable mould is evaporated. ... There are parts of Asia Minor, of Northern Africa, of Greece, and even of Alpine Europe, where the operation of causes set in action by man has brought the face of the earth to a desolation almost as complete as that of the moon. ... The earth is fast becoming an unfit home for its noblest inhabitants" (see agriculture, 1874).

The first U.S. salmon cannery opens on California's Sacramento River at Washington in Yolo County. Hapgood, Hume & Co., founded by Scotsmen William and George Hume in partnership with Hapgood, packs 2,000 cases, and although half spoil because the cans have not all been properly sealed, the cannery will soon be followed by others at San Francisco and at the mouth of every river north to Alaska (see 1866). William Hume will buy exclusive rights to use the name John West (see 1857) and will resell them to a Liverpool firm. His nephew Robert Deniston will become known as the "salmon king" of the Oregon River, selling his products through the British firm Pelling Stanley, which in 1888 will buy the rights to use the John West name (see 1878).

A grasshopper plague in the Great Plains shortens the U.S. wheat crop.

A farmer at Walla Walla in the Oregon Territory harvests 33 bushels of wheat per acre, other farmers move into the area, and wheat farms begin to proliferate in a breadbasket that will grow to embrace uplands from Pendleton, Oregon, to Idaho's Palouse prairie and eastern Washington.

France's lentil industry moves to Lorraine, where colder weather kills off the insect pests that have ruined lentil crops for years.

Britain's McDougall flour is introduced. It will become the nation's leading brand of household flour (see Hovis-McDougall, 1957).

Swiss confectioner Jean (né Johann Jakob) Tobler establishes himself in the chocolate business at Bern, making his confections by hand (see Suchard, 1970).

Heineken beer gets its name as Dutch brewer Gerard Adriaan Heineken acquires the 272-year-old De Hooiberg brewery at Amsterdam and develops a special yeast that will give his beer a distinctive taste. Heineken will open a second brewery, at Rotterdam, in 1874.

Pabst beer has its beginnings as German-American brewer Frederick Pabst, 28, and an associate succeed to control of Milwaukee's Empire brewery, which produces 4,895 barrels per year. Formerly a Great Lakes steamboat captain, Pabst was married 2 years ago to Marie Best, whose German-born grandfather, Jacob, started Milwaukee's Best brewery in 1844, and became a partner of Marie's father, Phillip, who has sold the enterprise to his sons-in-law Pabst and Emil Schandein. They will incorporate as Phillip Best Brewing Co. in 1873, and Schandein will die in 1888 (see 1889; Schlitz, 1856; Pabst Blue Ribbon, 1893).

The Paris brasserie Bofinger opened by Alsatians at 5 and 7, rue de la Bastille is the first café in the city to serve draft beer (see Brasserie Lipp, 1872).

The London fish-and-chips shop opened by Joseph Malines will be followed by many more in the next few years as steam trawlers are developed that can carry fish packed in ice. Taken from the North Sea, the fish will be kept chilled from the moment of catch until delivery to city retailers, who will deep-fry fish fingers and serve them in newspaper with deep-fried potatoes, all liberally doused with vinegar (see 1902).

Jack's opens at 615 Sacramento Street, San Francisco, as a hotel and restaurant. French-American entrepreneur Georges Voges names the place after jackrabbits, which will be on the restaurant menu along with English mutton chops and royal kidneys. Jack's will be taken over in 1884 by Jacques and Monique, the Redinger brothers Michel, Émile, and Paul will buy into it in 1902, they will rebuild it in 1907 after an earthquake and fire, and it will continue well after Paul's death in 1973, serving game, duck, sautéed rex sole, sand dabs, poached salmon, double lamb chops, New York–cut steak, chateaubriand, prime ribs, and tenderloin of beef, with meat that has been aged by the restaurant's supplier for 4 weeks.

European immigrants pour into the United States to take up free land under the 1862 Homestead Act and fill farm and factory jobs left vacant by Union Army draftees and Americans gone west both to avoid the draft and to claim free land.

✗ The American Civil War ends April 9 as Gen. Robert E. Lee surrenders to Gen. Grant at Appomatox Courthouse, Va. The retreating Confederate Army had 350,000 emergency rations stored at Richmond, and Lee ordered them shipped by rail to Amelia Courthouse April 2, but—owing to a failure in communications—he and his men find no provisions awaiting them there; the famished army of 30,000 to 35,000 has dwindled by April 9 to scarcely 25,000, all of them hungry, and Gen. Grant orders that they be issued immediate rations along with fodder for their horses.

President Lincoln is assassinated at Washington, D.C., April 14, and a 12-year Era of Reconstruction begins in the South with state legislatures run by "carpetbaggers" and "scalawags."

✊ The 13th Amendment to the Constitution is ratified by two-thirds of the states; beginning December 18, any denial of liberty, including slavery, is prohibited "without due process of law." Emancipation will have profound effects on southern agriculture— and on the nutrition of former slaves (see nutrition, below).

The Salvation Army has its beginnings in the Christian Mission founded in London's East End by English evangelist William Booth, 36, who will declare that "the submerged tenth" or "disinherited" live in a much lower standard of comfort "than the London cab horse, unable to buy as much food as [is] given to the worst criminals in our jails."

$ Wartime inflation has reduced the value of Confederate paper money to $1.70 per $100 by January and driven the gold value of the Union greenback to 46¢. A barrel of flour, when any was obtainable, has sold for $250 at Richmond in the closing months of the war, the Confederate money now becomes worthless, and the greenback will not regain its full value until the end of 1878.

Grain trader Léopold Louis-Dreyfus begins operations at Odessa, buying Russian wheat for sale to the West (see 1852; 1870).

Wisconsin farmer's son William Wallace "Will" Cargill, 21, buys a railroad ticket to the end of the line and acquires a small interest in a wooden grain elevator at Conover, Iowa. The second oldest of four sons of a onetime Scottish sea captain, young Cargill will build a network of elevators throughout the Midwest (see 1873).

Trading of wheat futures begins at Chicago after years of informal speculation in "to arrive" grains during the Crimean and Civil wars. Futures trading will enable the farmer to lock in a price for his crop before it is harvested and the miller to lock in the price of the wheat he needs for flour; speculators will buy (and sell) futures in hopes of higher (or lower) actual prices in weeks or months to come, but while the Chicago Board of Trade moves this year into the Chamber of Commerce Building at LaSalle and Washington streets and deals in futures, it will not be used for hedging until 1879 (see 1848; Liverpool, 1883). The New York and New Orleans markets continue to be "spot" markets dealing in actual grain (see 1872).

Chicago's Union Stock Yards open December 25 on a 345-acre tract of reclaimed swampland southwest of the city limits. With the Mississippi virtually shut down by the Civil War, Chicago has replaced Cincinnati, Louisville, and St. Louis as the nation's meat-packing center. The city doubled its packing capacity in a single year of the war with eight new large packing plants and many small ones to serve the nine railroads that converge on Chicago and that have spent $1.5 million to build the new Stock Yards, whose pens can hold 10,000 head of cattle and 100,000 hogs at any given time (see Armour, 1872; Swift, 1877).

San Francisco coffee roaster James A. Folger buys out his partner, William Bovee, and changes the name of the company (see 1850). Folger's coffee is roasted, ground, and packaged at a time when most coffee drinkers are obliged to buy green beans and do their own roasting and grinding. He obtains topquality Central American beans that have been shipped until now only to Europe, and J. A. Folger will become the nation's largest independent coffee company (see Kansas City, 1906; Procter & Gamble, 1963).

🏷$ Solari's opens in the New Orleans French Quarter to sell Creole delicacies, including jambalaya flavored with saffron, shrimp in a remoulade sauce, pecan pralines, and the like.

French-American milling engineer Edmund LeCroix revolutionizes flour milling with a small mill he builds for Alexander Faribault at Northfield, Minn., adapting a French machine to develop a middlings purifier that improves the yield of endosperm wheat particles free of bran. LeCroix simply takes the bolting cloth used for centuries to sift flour for finer granulation and combines it with fan-driven air currents used for years to clean wheat. His middlings purifier permits continuous improvement of the flour stream as it moves through the mill, blowing away the middlings (the bran and outer layers of the grain) to be used in animal feed and retaining the bran-free wheat grains.

"Patent" flour is introduced, using a newly patented process which involves raising the fixed bed stone for a second grinding that pulverizes any unprocessed wheat particles left after the first grinding. Edmund LeCroix (above) improves on the superior quality of this double-ground flour with his middlings purifier (*see* Washburn, Crosby, 1866; Smith, 1871).

Cans made of thinner steel come into general use, and the rim around the top of each can will lead to the invention of the can opener, which will permit cans to be opened more easily than with hammer and chisel (*see* 1870).

A compression machine built by U.S. inventor-balloonist Thaddeus Sobieski Coulincourt Lowe, 33, makes ice, pioneering artificial refrigeration. Lowe has been chief of the U.S. Army's aeronautics section since 1860 (*see* Linde, 1873).

Austrian botanist Gregor Johann Mendel, 43, elucidates natural laws of heredity in a paper read to the Brünn Society for the Study of Natural Science. Mendel entered an Augustinian order as a monk at age 21 and at 35 began studying the genetics of garden peas, using peas for his experiments because the stigma of the pea flower is usually pollinated by pollen from the same flower, which means that a new plant has in effect one parent and is thus assured of pure traits, e.g., yellow, green, smooth, wrinkled, dwarf, or tall. By preventing such self-pollination, and by pollinating hundreds of pea plants with pollen from other plants, Mendel has established that "in any given pair of contrasting traits, one trait is dominant and the other recessive."

Mendel's law (above), which will be basic to the development of new food-crop plant varieties, states that the first generation of progeny of mixed parents will all be hybrids, but in the second generation only half will be hybrids while one quarter will reflect the true trait of one parent and a second quarter the true trait of the second parent. Mendel's recognition that various dominant or recessive characteristics depend on certain basic units, later to be called genes, will be the basis of improved varieties of plant and animal life in the century to come, but established scientists will not begin to appreciate his work for nearly 40 years (*see* de Vries, 1900).

Nonfiction: *Cape Cod* by Henry David Thoreau, now 48, who has walked round the "great beach" and writes of Provincetown, with its salt fish stacked up on the wharves "looking like corded wood, maple and yellow birch with the bark left on." He has found fish drying everywhere, even in local backyards, and notes, "Where one man's fish ended another's began." Boston has become known as the "home of the bean and the cod."

Cookbook: *Mrs. Beeton's Everyday Cookery and Housekeeping Book* by Isabella Beeton (*see* 1861) gives a recipe for using leftover salt or fresh cod: binding it with béchamel sauce and baking it with a bread-crumb topping, it is called "cod à la béchamel."

"The people must live on canned fruits and vegetables," writes a visitor to Virginia Dale, Colo. (*see* Del Monte, below). "Corn, tomatoes, beans, pine apples, strawberry, cherry and peach, with oysters, and lobsters are the most common," writes Samuel Bowles. "They range from fifty cents to one dollar a can of about two quarts. Families buy them in cases of two dozen each at twelve to fifteen dollars a case; while away up in Montana, they are sold at only twenty-seven dollars a case."

Poor yeast is responsible for poor-quality U.S. bread, says Austrian stillmaster Charles Fleischmann, 31, who visits Cincinnati to attend his sister's wedding. Salt-rising bread is preferred in the North, baking soda hot bread is preferred in the South, and what little yeast bakers use is generally "slop" yeast from potato water or from the frothy "barm" at the top of ale vats, but Fleischmann will change that (*see* 1868).

Virginia agriculturist Edmund Ruffin, despondent over the defeat of the Confederate cause, dies by his own hand June 18 at age 71 at his plantation, Redmoor, in Amelia County (*see* 1833).

America's Civil War (above) has virtually ended rice cultivation in the Carolinas and Georgia, but rice growing has increased along the Mississippi River in Louisiana, Arkansas, and Texas (*see* 1671; California, 1908).

California's Sacramento Valley increases its wheat production. Hugh Glenn owns 50,000 acres in the valley (*see* 1851; 1868).

French wine growers near Tarascon, north of the Pyrenees, notice decay in vineyards where they may have experimented with cuttings of U.S. vines resistant to powdery mildew (*see* 1863; 1866).

Cattle disease in Britain raises prices, increasing demand for cheap, fatty American bacon and Australian canned meats (*see* 1864; 1866).

Emancipation of U.S. slaves under the 13th Amendment (above) will create a southern population of black sharecroppers, who will relocate too frequently to maintain vegetable gardens as they did under slavery. Their diets, as a result, will often be deficient in greens and vegetables. They may pick berries and gather greens in the summertime and may supplement their diets with the fish they catch and the squirrels and raccoons they shoot, but many will live almost exclusively on bacon, corn pone, corn bread spread with fat and molasses, and coffee sweetened with molasses, and this will have nutritional consequences. Corn and pork are also the staples of the settlers who live in sod houses and shanties on frontier farms out west, only the more prosperous being able to raise animals other than hogs for their own consumption.

Del Monte Corp. has its beginnings in a California food brokerage firm founded by James K. Armsby, whose company will become Oakland Preserving Co. in 1891, California Packing in 1916, and Del Monte in 1967—the leading U.S. packer of fruits and vegetables (*see* 1891).

Goodman's Matzohs (unleavened bread) have their beginnings in a Philadelphia bakeshop opened at the end of the war by German-American baker Augustus Gutkind, who has sailed for America, changed his name to Goodman, and taken a job as master baker for the Union Army. Gutkind's family has made matzohs for Passover in the province of Posen since 1766 (*see* 1883).

Royal Baking Powder has its beginnings at Fort Wayne, Ind., where a pharmacist mixes baking soda with cream of tartar to produce a powder (*see* Standard Brands, 1929). Bakers who have no baking powder are advised to beat cake ingredients by hand for at least an hour.

Anheuser-Busch has its beginnings at St. Louis, where German-American brewer Adolphus Busch, 26, goes into business with his father-in-law, Eberhard Anheuser (*see* 1873; Budweiser, 1876).

Hamm's beer is introduced at St. Paul, Minn., by German-American brewer Theodore Hamm, 40, who emigrated from Baden in 1854, has worked as a butcher and saloonkeeper, and now opens a brewery.

Great Western champagne is introduced by the Pleasant Valley Wine Co., of Hammondsport, N.Y. (*see* 1860). It is the state's first sparkling champagne.

Bookbinder's Restaurant opens near the Schuylkill River at Philadelphia, where it will be famous for its snapper soup.

London's Café Royal has its beginnings in the café-restaurant Daniel Nicols opened at 68 Regent Street, just off Piccadilly Circus, by former French wine merchant Nicols (originally D. N. Thévenon), 31, who arrived at Victoria station in the fall of 1863 with his wife, Célestine, having fled France to escape creditors. He had only £5 in his pocket when he came, but he has been able to borrow the wherewithal to start the eating place, which he will enlarge by acquiring a neighboring tailor's shop and rename Café Royal. A combination club, restaurant, and pub, it will attract artists, including the émigré U.S. painter-etcher James McNeill Whistler (who will sign his bills with butterflies), and writers, including Oscar Wilde, as it grows (*see* 1897).

Neapolitan restaurateur Giuseppe Ranieri acquires a Rome restaurant opened 12 years ago at via Mario de' Fiori 26 by a Frenchman named Renault. A one-time chef to Britain's Queen Victoria and to the emperor Maximilian in Mexico, Ranieri changes the restaurant's name and will make Ranieri's one of the city's foremost eating places, offering dishes such as ham-filled pancake, fontina del paese parmesan (with taleggio cheese), cannelloni à la casalinga, ravioli à la formarina, flattened chicken breasts, lamb chops, and mignonettes of veal Nantes.

Moscow's Tsentral'nya has its beginnings in the Filippov Café opened at what will be 10 Gorki Street.

1866

Japan's Tokugawa shōgun Iemochi dies of beriberi in August at age 20. White rice is the staple food of Edo, and beriberi is called the "Edo disease," but no one has yet discovered the connection between white rice and the disease (*see* nutrition, 1884). The shōgun has had his own dairy farm to produce milk for his family (*see* Townsend Harris, 1856).

Postwar economic depression begins in the United States as prices begin a rapid decline following the Civil War's inflation.

Les Halles is completed at Paris after 10 years' work to serve as the city's (and nation's) food market (*see* 1110; 1969).

Horses, mules, and oxen provide virtually all the power for agricultural production, but a crude internal combustion engine patented by Cologne engineer Nikolaus August Otto, 34, will sell by the thousands in the German states and in England in the next 10 years. Otto has read of the 1860 Lenoir engine, obtained backing from engineer-businessman Eugen Langen, 33, and shares patent rights with his brother William.

The Great Tea Race from Foochow to London pits 11 clipper ships that race to minimize spoilage of the China tea in their hot holds. The skippers crowd on sail, but the voyage still takes close to 3 months. More than 90 percent of Britain's tea still comes from China (*see* 1900).

British imports of tinned meat total 16,000 pounds as the continuing epizootic keeps domestic meat and dairy prices high (*see* 1865).

A U.S. patent is issued for a tin can with a key opener.

The Western Health Reform Institute is founded at Battle Creek, Mich., by Seventh-Day Adventist prophet Ellen Gould White (*née* Harmon), 38, whose sanitarium treatment combines vegetarian diet and hydrotherapy with some accepted medical methods. White, who espouses many of the ideas promoted by Sylvester Graham in the 1830s, puts patients with high blood pressure on a diet of grapes—and only grapes (10 to 14 pounds of grapes per day). Underweight is considered a mark of poor health, a belief that will persist for the next half century and more, so underweight patients are given 26 feedings per day, forbidden to engage in any physical activity (not even brushing their teeth), and obliged to lie motionless in bed with sandbags on their abdomens to aid the absorption of nutrients. White's "sanitorium," or "san," will incubate the infant U.S. breakfast food industry (*see* Kellogg, 1876; Post, 1893).

"As a people, we are the worst cooks and the most unwholesome feeders in the world," writes a contributor to *Harper's* magazine. "Hardly one in a hundred of our cooks can broil a steak or boil a potato, and not one in ten of our businessmen has a correct idea of feeding, bolting down hot rolls rendered chemically destructive of the stomach lining by preparations of soda, and swallowing hot coffee, either Mocha or rye as the case may be. It is not at all a good way of breakfasting. . . . We fry our food a good deal too much. Flour fried in fat is one of our delights. Dough-nuts, pancakes, fritters, are samples of what we do with good wheat flour. Fried ham, fried eggs, fried liver, fried steak, fried fish, fried oysters, fried potatoes, and last, not least, fried hash await us at morning, noon, and night."

"Conversation" candy enjoys a boom in America. It comes with little strips on which are printed sentiments that depend heavily on the slang of the day, e.g., "Why is a stylish girl like a thrifty housekeeper? Because she makes a big bustle about a little waist." "Why is love like a canal boat? Because it's an internal transport." "What does a girl do to show her dislike of a moustache? She sets her face against it." Oliver Chase of Boston and his crippled brother Daniel produce the Peerless Wafer (later to be called the Necco Wafer) (*see* 1851). Daniel devises a machine that employs a die to print words on the lozenge paste as it cuts the lozenges, and the brothers turn out candies that include wedding lozenges stamped with the words, "Married in Satin, Love Will Not Be Lasting," "Married in Pink, He Will Take to Drink," and "Married in White, You Have Chosen Right." Chase & Co. is the leading U.S. manufacturer of dry, or uncooked, confectionery (it also makes stick, or pipe, candy, including peppermint sticks); competitors include Fobes, Hayward & Co., formed last year when Daniel Fobes's partner Joseph Ball retired and Fobes admitted his brothers-in-law Daniel H. and Albert F. Hayward into the business.

A salmon cannery opens on the Columbia River; it will be followed by canneries at the mouth of almost every river north to Alaska (*see* 1878).

The first San Francisco salmon cannery opens (*see* 1864).

Cattlemen discover that livestock can survive the cold of the northern Great Plains and can eat the grasses there.

Cattle from Texas are driven north for the first time on the Chisholm Trail, named after the scout Jesse Chisholm. The cattle arrive at Abilene, Kans., for shipment by rail to points east (*see* 1867; 1871; 1885).

The first U.S. crop report is issued by the 4-year-old Department of Agriculture. Field-workers have conducted investigations to determine how much of various crops the nation's farmers produce.

Indian Corn: Its Value, Culture, and Uses by U.S. author Edward Enfield urges farmers to increase production. They grew nearly 840 million bushels per year—five times more than the total of wheat, other cereal grains, and major vegetables put combined—during the Civil War, but Enfield suggests that the national average of 20 to 30 bushels per acre can be raised to 50 bushels.

French vintners at Floirac in the Gironde district notice decay in their vines (*see* 1865; 1867).

German chemist H. Ritthausen isolates glutamic acid from wheat and introduces into protein chemistry the experimental method of acid hydrolysis and the subsequent precipitation of barium or calcium salts of certain amino acids by means of alcohol (*see* monosodium glutamate, 1908).

Henri Nestlé formulates a combination of farinaceous pap and milk for infants who cannot take mother's milk and starts a firm under his own name to produce the new infant formula (*see* 1861; 1875; Liebig, 1867).

Anglo-Swiss Condensed Milk Co. is founded at Cham, Switzerland, by U.S. entrepreneur George H. Page, 30, and his elder brother, Charles A., who is U.S. consul at Zurich. Their supervisor, John Baptist Meyenberg, now 18, will suggest the possibility of preserving evaporated milk in the same way as other canned foods, without sugar, but the Page brothers will enjoy such success with their sweetened condensed milk that they will reject Meyenberg's idea and he will emigrate to America (*see* baby food, 1877; Helvetia Milk Condensing Co., 1885; Nestlé, 1905).

Gail Borden adopts the trademark Eagle Brand to protect his condensed milk from competitors who have appropriated the name Borden (*see* 1861). Borden has made a fortune supplying his product to the Union Army; his plant at Elgin, Ill., produces condensed milk at a rate of 300,000 gallons per year (*see* 1875).

Breyer's ice cream is founded at Philadelphia (*see* National Dairy, 1926).

Washburn, Crosby County, erects its first flour mill on the Mississippi in Wisconsin. Former Maine timber baron Cadwallader C. Washburn, 48, served as a major general in the Union Army, has settled in Wisconsin, and becomes a miller. The hard-kernel winter wheat grown on the plains produces a flour that is darker than most consumers prefer (*see* 1857), but Washburn will find that the LeCroix middlings purifier, introduced last year, produces flour that is not only as white as any but has baking properties which are in some ways superior (*see* 1871).

Major Grey's chutney, made from cultivated Jamaica mangoes, is introduced by Crosse & Blackwell, which also introduces a marmalade. The identity of "Major Grey" will never be revealed, and later historians will come to the conclusion that the name was concocted.

Colman's Mustard receives a royal warrant from Queen Victoria (*see* 1814). So popular is the condiment that four trains are sometimes required to carry one day's output from the Norwich factory. Jeremiah Colman has his own trains with his bull emblem emblazoned on the sides of the cars, and he is so well known that the Post Office will deliver to his factory an envelope with a drawing of a large bull's head above the word "England."

Cadbury's Cocoa Essence, introduced by Richard Cadbury, 31, and his brother George, 27, is the first pure cocoa to be sold in Britain (*see* 1847). They have been running their father's Birmingham business and have come close to failing but are saved by the new product, which they advertise as "Absolutely Pure: Therefore Best." They have squeezed out excess cocoa butter to leave a pure, concentrated powder that need not be adulterated with the potato and sago flour used in all British cocoa powders until now to counteract the natural fats (*see* van Houten, 1828). The cocoa butter made available by the process enables Cadbury Brothers to increase production of chocolate candy (*see* slavery, 1901).

L. Rose Co. is established at London to supply lime juice to the Royal Navy.

Jack Daniel's Tennessee Sour Mash whiskey is introduced at Lynchburg by local distiller Jack Newton Daniel, 18, whose nephew Lemuel Motlow and his descendants will carry on the business, leaching the product of the stills through vats filled with 10 feet of charcoal (*see* Brown-Forman, 1956).

Dublin's Hotel Gresham opens in Upper O'Connell Street under the ownership of an Englishman, who competes with the Russell, facing St. Stephen's Green, and the Royal Hibernian in Dawson Street (it added the "Royal" after a visit from the late George IV).

1867

Alaska is ceded to the United States for $7.2 million March 30 by Russia's Czar Aleksandr II, now 48, under terms of a treaty arranged by Secretary of State William H. Seward, 65 (*see* Baked Alaska, below).

Britain's Second Reform Bill, passed August 15, opens county elections to owners of land that rents for at least £5 per year and to tenants who pay at least £12 per year.

U.S. wheat sells for $2.50 per bushel in late April, but the price falls to $1.45 by September and will soon drop much farther (*see* 1868).

The Grange, or the Patrons of Husbandry, is founded in the upper Mississippi Valley by former U.S. Department of Agriculture field investigator Oliver H. Kelley, 41. The organization's popular name derives from its lodges, which are designated by an archaic name for barn. Avowedly nonpolitical, the Grange's stated aims are educational and social, with emphasis on reading and discussion to increase farmers' knowledge, but the discussions will inevitably turn to freight rates, high taxes, and politics (*see* 1873).

French chemist Hippolyte Mège-Mouries, 50, begins development of a synthetic butter at the urging of the emperor Napoleon III, who may recall his uncle's encouragement of food canning and beet-sugar production (*see* 1794; 1811). Mège-Mouries works with suet, chopped cow's udders, and warm milk to begin a revolution in the butter industry (*see* margarine, 1869).

Sugar beets are introduced into the Utah Territory by Mormon leader Brigham Young, 66, who has machinery from Liverpool carted across the continent to Salt Lake City by ox-drawn wagon, but the beet-sugar factory he builds will be abandoned within 2 years (*see* 1880).

U.S. inventor Lucien Smith files a patent application for barbed wire, but no reliable machine exists to manufacture such wire in quantity (*see* 1873).

Nonfiction: *Seiyoeshokuju* (*Western Clothes, Food, and Living*) by Japanese educator Yukiji Fukuzawa, 43, includes instruction on table manners, table settings, and Western drinks including liqueurs.

Cookbook: *Die praktische israelitsche Köchin* by German author Rebekka Süsskind Hertz is published at Hamburg.

Chicago livestock dealer Joseph Geating McCoy, 29, buys 450 acres of land at $5 per acre in Abilene, Kans., builds pens and loading chutes with lumber he has brought from Hannibal, Mo., installs a pair of large Fairbanks scales, and promises Texas ranchers $40 per head for cattle the ranchers can sell at home for only $4 per head. Abilene is "a small, dead place of about one dozen log huts . . . four-fifths of which are covered with dirt for roofing," but it is the terminus of the Kansas Pacific Railway, which despite its name operates only between Chicago and Abilene. The railroad has promised McCoy one-eighth of the freight charge on each car of cattle he ships east, he sends out the first shipment (20 carloads) September 5, and by year's end some 35,000 head of longhorns have passed through Abilene, a figure that will more than double next year (*see* 1871; Chisholm Trail, 1866).

Iowa farmer William Louden, 25, modernizes dairy farming with a rope sling and wooden monorail hay carrier. Suspended beneath the peak of a barn, Louden's carrier enables a farmer to swing a load of hay without using a pitchfork, and the litter carrier hauls out manure, allowing a farmer to clean a stable or dairy barn in one-tenth the time it has taken until now. Louden's contributions will make possible large, efficient dairy herds.

The Illinois and Wisconsin Dairymen's Association is founded.

The town of Phoenix begins its growth in Arizona territory as the John Swirling Co. clears prehistoric canals, bringing water from the Salt River to the fertile lands of the valley (*see* Roosevelt Dam, 1911).

A meeting of France's Central Agricultural Society at Paris hears the report of a grower from the administrative department of the Gard, on the west bank of the Rhône, who tells of a mysterious malady that has been affecting vines in his region for the past 2 or 3 years (*see* 1863; 1868).

U.S. horticulturist Edmund Hart, 27, joins his brothers Walter and Ambrose in the wilderness of Federal Point, Fla., where they begin to grow citrus fruits. Edmund will soon have 150 varieties under culture and observation, and he will introduce the Hart Late, or Tardiff, orange, which will become known in California as the Valencia and will be the leading late orange variety in both that state and in Florida. He will be instrumental in establishing the best market varieties.

Arm & Hammer Baking Soda has its beginnings as Brooklyn, N.Y., spice dealer James A. Church

closes his factory to enter the baking soda business but retains the symbolic sign of the Roman god Vulcan that identified his Vulcan Spice Mill. Selling his product by the barrel with the help of a 7-foot, 4-inch giant known as Col. Powell, Church will soon adopt the name Arm & Hammer Saleratus, under which he will dominate the market.

C. F. Mueller Co. has its beginnings at Jersey City, N.J., where German-American baker Christian Frederick Mueller, 27, starts selling homemade egg noodles house to house from a pushcart. The city's large German population gives him a good reception, and by 1870 he will be buying flour by the barrel instead of by the bag; he will replace his pushcart with a horse and wagon, and his firm will grow to become the largest U.S. producer of macaroni, spaghetti, and egg noodles.

Liebig's Soluble Food for Babies, the first patent baby food, is introduced in Europe by Justus von Liebig, whose product, which is intended to be added to diluted milk, will be manufactured and sold in London next year by Liebig's Registered Concentrated Milk Co., introduced in America in 1869, and sold commercially for decades (*see* 1842; Nestlé, 1866; Gerber, 1927). Physicians say the product is superior to the milk of wet nurses.

Canned deviled ham is introduced by William Underwood & Co. of Boston (*see* 1822; red devil trademark, 1870).

Portland, Maine, entrepreneurs George Burnham, 36, and Charles S. Morrill, 31, put up some cans of sweet corn and establish a cannery on Casco Bay that will become famous for its canned bouillon, seafood, brown bread, and—most especially—oven-baked beans. They will found a company under the name Burnham & Morrill in 1870 (*see* 1875).

Boston confectioner Daniel Fobes of Boston advertises the discovery of "mocha," a combination of powdered coffee and powdered cocoa mixed in equal proportions with cocoa butter for use both as a beverage and in confectionery.

Ruppert's Brewery has its start as New York brewer Jacob Ruppert, 25, buys a tract of timberland on Third Avenue between 91st and 92nd streets to build his own plant after 4 years of managing his father's Turtle Bay Brewery. He clears the timber and erects a three-story building that will grow to become the world's largest lager brewery (*see* 1874).

Russia's Aleksandr II (above), his son of 22, Prussia's Wilhelm I, 70, and the Prussian statesman Otto von Bismarck, 42, come to Paris for a Universal Exposition and have a 16-course dinner together June 7 at the celebrated Café Anglais, where they are served Madeira; sherry; soufflés à la reine (soufflés with creamed chicken), fillet of sole à la vénétienne, sliced turbot au gratin, chicken à la portugaise, lobster à la parisienne, ducklings à la rouenaise, ortolans on toast; a Château d'Yquem, a Chambertin, a Château Margaux, a Château Latour, a Château Laffitte, and champagne.

Lobster à l'américaine is invented by some accounts at Peters' Restaurant in the passage des Princes, Paris, where three American visitors to the Universal Exposition arrive late in the evening and demand dinner. With most of his larder exhausted, Chef Fraisse, who has spent some time in the United States, improvises, taking a lobster that has already been cooked and poaching it in a highly seasoned sauce. His guests are delighted, and he names it in their honor. Conflicting claims will be advanced as to the authorship of the dish.

The Edo restaurant Nodaiwa opens, serving wild eel (*unagi*) (date approximate). Edo will become Tokyo next year, and Nodaiwa will later add cultivated eel to its menu, but wild eel will still constitute 30 to 40 percent of its dishes in 1995.

Sam's Grill opens in San Francisco under the name M. B. Moraghan and Sons. Sam Zenovich will buy the oyster saloon in 1932 and rename it after himself, his daughter will sell it in 1937 to Yugoslav entrepreneur Frank Seput, and it will move in 1946 to 374 Bush Street, where it will continue to serve plain food (rex sole, lamb chops, sirloin steak, veal porterhouse, lamb kidneys with bacon) in 13 private booths with red plaid pull curtains.

Delmonico's chef Charles Ranhofer at New York creates Baked Alaska—a brick of ice cream enclosed in a meringue and quickly baked in the oven—to celebrate the purchase of what many call "Seward's Folly" or "Seward's Icebox" (above).

German-American entrepreneur Charles Feltman employs a wheelwright named Donovan to build a burner in the back of the pie wagon he has been driving up and down the beach at Coney Island in Brooklyn, N.Y. His customers have asked for hot sandwiches, the burner enables him to keep warm sausages on hand, his frankfurters wrapped in a roll or bun (adapted from a Nuremberg custom) gain quick popularity, and by the turn of the century his huge Feltman's restaurant on the Coney Island boardwalk will have seven grills turning out 10¢ frankfurters and will employ 1,200 waiters (*see* "hot dog," 1906; Nathan Handwerker, 1916).

More than half of all U.S. working people are employed on farms.

1868

U.S. wheat prices fall to 90¢ a bushel in the fall and then to 67¢, down from a wartime high of $4 and a postwar peak of $2.50 (*see* 1867). The potato beetle has affected some farmers' crops, but so much grain comes out of warehouses that it depresses the price.

The Crimean War and Civil War have stimulated production of California wheat, which has a flinty character making it well suited to shipment overseas. California flour goes not only to the Rockies but also to China, Japan, Britain, and Europe.

The Peavey Co. has its beginnings at Sioux City, Iowa, where grocery-firm bookkeeper Frank Hutchinson Peavey, 18, persuades his employer and another local businessman that farming will be the backbone of the West and farmers will need implements and machinery. Peavey, whose uncle invented the peavey hook in Maine in 1857, organizes the firm Booge, Smith and Peavey to supply farmers with such items as McCormick reapers and Case threshing machines (*see* 1874).

A refrigerated railcar with metal tanks along its sides is patented by Detroit inventor William Davis, who dies at age 56. The tanks are filled from the top with cracked ice to transport fish, fresh meats, and fruits (*see* 1869).

A new mechanical cooler for English trains permits quick-cooled milk to be delivered by rail in new metal containers to cities such as London, Liverpool, Manchester, and Glasgow. The milk is far safer than milk from cows kept in town sheds (*see* 1863).

The first regularly scheduled U.S. dining car goes into service on the Chicago-Alton Railroad (*see* below). Menus on George M. Pullman's Palace Car Company dining cars will rival those at the best hotels of Boston and New York.

Claus Spreckels of San Francisco patents a sugar-refining method that takes just 8 hours instead of the usual 3 weeks (*see* 1863). Spreckels has gone back to Europe to study manufacturing methods. The California Sugar Refinery he opens will win him the title "Sugar King" (*see* 1883).

The Planet, Jr. seed planter patented by Moorestown, N.J., inventor Samuel Leeds Allen, 27, consists of two washbasins fastened together with a metal band containing drill holes (an attached handle permits the planter to be rolled over the ground). Allen will open a factory at Philadelphia in 1880 and expand his line to include a fertilizer driller, wheel hoes, potato diggers, and celery hillers.

Guys Hospital, London, physician Samuel Wilks, 44, gives the first clinical description of osteoporosis, or spongy hypertrophy of the bones, a kind of osteitis deformans (*see* 1846).

The Italian *amari* (digestive) Averna introduced at Caltanissetta, Sicily, has a milder flavor than Fernet-Branca (*see* 1845). Other *amari* brands will include Lucana, Montenegro, and Ramizati.

The 300,000-acre King-Kenedy ranch in Texas is divided between Richard King and Mifflin Kenedy (*see* 1860). King prospered through the Civil War by steamboat trade in cotton carried to British ships at Brownsville and will use his fortune to expand the King Ranch on the Neuces River (*see* Kleberg, 1886).

Montpellier stockbroker Gaston Bazille assembles scientists to discuss the blight affecting French grapevines at the château de Lagoy, a wine estate near Saint Rémy, 15 miles from Arles (*see* 1863; 1867). The men dig up healthy vines as well as those obviously affected and note the presence of a microscopic insect underground. The yellowish parasitic burrowing plant louse or aphid *Daktylosphaira vitifolia*, which eats away at the roots of grapevines, was identified by Asa Fitch in his 1856 book *The Noxious, Beneficial and Other Insects of the State of New York*. Bazille, who has invested heavily in vineyards, is told by Jules-Émile Blanchon, professor of pharmacy at Montpellier University, that the cause of the dead and dying vines is an aphid, *Phylloxera vastatrix* ("the devastator"), but its source is not immediately discerned. An official government commission, whose members include Blanchon, will start work next year to deal with the menace to France's wine grape production (*see* 1872).

Liverpool meatpacker John Morrell opens the first North American Morrell slaughterhouse at London, Ont., after having opened Irish plants in the 1850s and a New York buying office in 1864 to obtain American bacon (*see* 1842; Ottumwa, Iowa, 1877).

Chicago meatpacker P. D. Armour adds a second plant as business booms. Armour, who moved from Milwaukee last year, has with his partner John Plankinton invested $160,000 to take over a slaughterhouse on Archer Avenue and set up under the name Armour & Co. (*see* 1864; 1869).

Libby, McNeill and Libby is founded by Maine-born Chicago meatpacker Arthur A. Libby, 37, who has been working with his younger brother, Charles, for their Chicago meatpacker uncle, John C. Hancock. Deciding that there is no future in working for Hancock, Arthur establishes his own company to turn out corned beef in large packages and is soon joined by Charles and by Archibald McNeill (*see* 1875).

Tabasco sauce is formulated on Avery Island off Louisiana's Gulf Coast. Former New Orleans banker Edmund McIlhenny fled New Orleans with his wife, Mary (*née* Avery), when Union troops entered the city in 1862 and settled on his in-laws' 2,500-acre island, where the Avery family operated America's first salt mine (salt was essential for preserving the meat that fed Confederate troops). Union forces took over the island in 1863, the McIlhennys escaped to Texas, and when they returned in 1865 they found their plantation ruined and their mansion looted. Nothing much remained but a crop of red peppers (*Capsicum frutescens*). McIlhenny has crushed the peppers and mixed them with vinegar and salt to create a piquant sauce, aged the mixture for a few days in wooden barrels, siphoned off the liquid, and put up the sauce in empty cologne bottles. Encouraged by the response of friends, he produces 350 bottles for Southern merchants and next year will sell several thousand at $1 each, starting a business in Cajun Tabasco sauce, which will be popular for generations as a condiment to be served with seafood, especially shellfish. McIlhenny will soon open a London office to handle a growing European demand for his product.

Edmund McIlhenny mixed crushed red peppers, vinegar, and salt to start a worldwide business.

Commercial production of compressed yeast begins for the first time in America at Cincinnati. Charles Fleischmann has emigrated from Hungary and joined his brother Maximilian and Cincinnati yeast maker James F. Gaff to form Gaff, Fleischmann & Co. (*see* 1865). He sells to local housewives from a basket at first, then by horse and wagon (*see* 1870).

Scottish gardener George Baxter opens a shop in Spey Street, Fochabers, Morayshire, where he sells marmalade produced by his wife, Margaret, from a

recipe she has obtained from the duchess of Gordon. One of 50 gardeners serving the duke of Gordon, Baxter has seen no chance for advancement and left the duke's estate. Fortnum and Mason will buy the Baxters' "Castle Marmalade," which they will sell in competition with Keiller's (*see* 1797).

White Rock Spring Water has its origin at Waukesha, Wis., whose mineral springs have achieved some renown. New York railroad magnate Richard Dunbar visits Waukesha in quest of a cure for his diabetes, drinks from one spring, announces that he has been cured as if by magic, builds an elaborate pavilion over the spring, and spreads word of its miraculous powers. Another spring, much deeper than Dunbar's, will be purchased in 1871 by an H. M. Colver and promoted as White Rock Spring (*see* Welch, 1887).

George M. Pullman's dining car (above) is named the *Delmonico* for the New York restaurant, whose chef, Charles Ranhofer, has his pastry cooks create a "Temple de la Littérature," a monument to Washington, the Stars and Stripes, and other cakes for a dinner given to honor visiting novelist Charles Dickens (*see* 1876).

The Old Homestead Steak House opens in New York on the site of a trading post established in 1760 at what will be 56 Ninth Avenue. The restaurant, with its stained-glass skylight near the city's Gansevoort wholesale meat market, is patronized by the same butchers who supply it and will serve sirloin steaks and prime ribs for more than 125 years.

Boston restaurateur Jacob Wirth, newly arrived from Germany, opens for business at 60 Eliot Street (later renamed Stuart Street) to begin an enterprise that will prosper for a century. Wirth, who comes from a family of wine growers with vineyards at Kreuznach, near Bingen in Rhenish Prussia, imports Rhine wine for wholesale and retail sale as well as for use in the restaurant (he also acts as agent for Anheuser-Busch Co. Lagers of St. Louis). He will relocate across the street at 37–39 in 1878, with living quarters for his family upstairs, and in 1890 will acquire the ground floor of an adjoining house to double the size of his restaurant. Sawdust on the floor facilitates cleaning, guests sit at mahogany tables without cloths, and they are served by waiters wearing black coats and white aprons.

The New Orleans restaurant Antoine's, opened in 1840, moves to larger space in St. Louis Street. Antoine Alciatore closes his place promptly at 10:30 each evening, music is forbidden, there are no decorations, the color, pattern, and style of table setups will never change, and the specialties will include oysters en brochette and chicken Rochambeau (*see* 1871).

1869

A British Customs Duty Act abolishes even nominal duties on food imports (*see* 1850).

Sainsbury's has its beginnings in a dairy shop opened at 173 Drury Lane, London, by merchants John James and Mary Ann Sainsbury to sell butter, milk, and eggs. Walls, counter fronts, and floor are covered in easy-to-clean patterned tiles at a time when most food shops have wooden counters and sawdust-covered floors. Mary, who operates the business while her husband works out his notice with his previous employer, starts building a retail enterprise that will soon have branches in Queen's Crescent, Kentish Town, Chapel Street, and Islington, with more elaborate shops in the suburbs of Croydon, Balham, and Lewisham to sell not only dairy products but also its own Sainsbury's brands of cooked meats, smoked bacon and ham, and imported cheeses (*see* self-service store, 1950).

The A&P gets its name as the 10-year-old Great American Tea Co. is renamed the Great Atlantic and Pacific Tea Co. to capitalize on the national excitement about the new transcontinental rail link (below). Proprietors George Huntington Hartford and George F. Gilman attract customers by offering premiums to lucky winners, use cashier cages in the form of Chinese pagodas, offer band music on Saturdays, and employ other promotional efforts while broadening their line of grocery items to include coffee, spices, baking powder, condensed milk, and soap as well as tea (*see* 1871).

Bombay's Crawford Market opens with a design (iron girders and steeply pitched glass roofs) inspired by the Crystal Palace put up for London's Great Exposition of 1851. Flagstones have been imported from Caithness, Scotland.

The world grows smaller with the completion of the Suez Canal and a transcontinental U.S. rail link. Both facilitate shipping of grain and other farm products.

America's transcontinental railroad made it easier to ship California fruits and vegetables to the East.

The Central Pacific Railroad, which links up with the Union Pacific May 10 at Promontory Point in Utah Territory, has been built largely by Chinese workers, whose impressive stamina will be credited by many to the fact that they ate a balanced diet and drank only tea while their largely Irish counterparts, who built the Union Pacific, lived on beans, bully beef, and whiskey.

The transcontinental railway (above) will permit shipment of California grain, fruit, and vegetables to eastern markets in less than a week. Shipping 15,660 nautical miles via Cape Horn (13,436 miles via the Strait of Magellan) took up to 120 days, and although some shipping lines have used the Panama Railroad across the isthmus since 1855, many California shippers continue to send cargo around the tip of South America (*see* Tehuantepec National Railroad, 1906; Panama Canal, 1914).

The Central Pacific (above) will soon offer Silver Palace Hotel cars on extra deluxe runs, with passengers paying extra fares to enjoy oysters on the half shell, Maryland terrapin, antelope, quail, porterhouse steak, plover, pheasant en casserole, canvasback, fresh trout (in Colorado and Utah). Hock and champagne will be listed on menus as breakfast wines, the preferred champagne being Krug.

Boston gets its first shipment of fresh meat from Chicago by way of a refrigerated railcar developed last year by William Davis, but railroads resist losing their traffic in live animals bound for eastern markets (*see* Swift, 1877).

The clipper ship *Cutty Sark* launched in England sails for Shanghai to begin a 117-day voyage with 28 crewmen to handle the 10 miles of rigging that control her 32,000 square feet of canvas. Built for the tea trade, the ship has a figurehead wearing a short chemise, or "Cutty Sark."

The Suez Canal, which opens to traffic November 17, links the Mediterranean with the Gulf of Suez at the head of the Red Sea, bringing Oriental ports 5,000 miles closer to Europe, 3,600 miles closer to U.S. East Coast ports (*see* British wheat imports, 1873).

The first U.S. plow with a moldboard entirely of chilled steel is patented by James Oliver, who has established the Oliver Chilled Plow Works (*see* 1855).

The Appleby binder patented by U.S. inventor John Francis Appleby, 29, is based on an idea he had 12 years ago for an automatic mechanism that would knot the twine used to bind sheaves of harvested grain. Appleby invented a repeating rifle while serving in the Union Army, patented it in 1864, sold the patent for $500, and has used the money to finance development of his concept. His patented binder is the prototype of the Appleby knotter, which by the turn of the century will be used on nine-tenths of the world's machine-bound grain, but initially it employs wire rather than twine (*see* 1872).

Hippolyte Mège-Mouriès produces the first commercial margarine (*see* 1867). French chemist Michel Chevreul isolated a substance from animal fat in 1813 that formed pearly drops and thought it was a new fatty acid; he named it margaric acid, from the Greek for "pearl" (*margaron*), and although it later turned out that there was no such thing as margaric acid, Mège-Mouriès used an extract of animal fat that supposedly contained a large amount of this "acid," which inspired him to name his product *margarine*. It is patented in England under the name "butterine" (*see* Jurgens, 1871).

German medical student Paul Langerhans, 22, discovers tiny cells in the pancreas that produce glucagon and insulin, ductless gland secretions essential to normal human metabolism (they will be called hormones beginning in 1904, and the cells will be called the "islets of Langerhans") (*see* 1889; Lancereaux, 1860).

Nonfiction: *The American Woman's Home* by Catherine E. Beecher and her sister Harriet Beecher Stowe deplores the popularity of store-bought bread, which accounts for perhaps 2 percent of all bread eaten in America. Defenders of store-bought bread say that home-baked bread sits heavy on the stomach, but lightness is not the only criterion for judgment, say the Beecher sisters; commercially baked bread is "light indeed, so light that [its loaves] seem to have neither weight nor substance, but with no more sweetness or taste than so much cotton wool."

The transcontinental railroad (above) will increase demand for Fulton Market oysters; by 1892, the market will be shipping thousands of barrels of saddle rocks and bluepoints to Denver and other western cities each Christmas, and every steamer leaving New York after the first week in December will be carrying shipments of U.S. oysters for holiday tables abroad. The Fulton Market tempts retail buyers, some of whom come from Brooklyn by ferry, with displays of crayfish, lobsters (many of them bright red from the steaming pots), prawns, shrimp, salmon, and southern red snapper.

Daily weather bulletins are inaugurated by U.S. astronomer Abbe Cleveland, 30, the first U.S. Weather Bureau meteorologist. The reports help farmers.

U.S. wheat growers produce 290 million bushels, up from 70 million in 1866.

The coffee rust *Hamileia vastatrix* appears in Ceylon plantations and will spread throughout the Orient and the Pacific in the next two decades (*see* 1825). It will destroy the coffee-growing industry, and soaring coffee prices will lead to wide-scale tea cultivation (*see* 1884; tea consumption, 1898).

Armour & Co. adds beef to its line of pork products (*see* 1868). Armour will start handling lamb next year (*see* chill room, 1872).

Campbell Soup Co. has its beginnings in a cannery opened at Camden, N.J., by Philadelphia fruit wholesaler Joseph Campbell and tinsmith–icebox maker Abram Anderson, 35. They pack small peas and fancy asparagus (*see* 1894).

H. J. Heinz Co. has its beginnings at Sharpsburg, Pa., where local entrepreneur Henry John Heinz, 24, goes into business with partner L. C. Noble to pack processed horseradish in clear bottles, competing with horseradish packed in brown or amber bottles to disguise the fact that it often contains turnip fillers. Heinz has employed several local women for nearly a decade to help him supply Pittsburgh grocers with the surplus from his garden (*see* 1875).

Welch's Grape Juice has its beginnings at Vineland, N.J., where dentist Thomas Bramwell Welch develops a temperance substitute for the intoxicating wine used in his church's communion service. He picks 40 pounds of Concord grapes from his backyard, pasteurizes the juice in his wife's kitchen, bottles it, and begins selling "unfermented wine" to nearby churches (*see* 1896; Concord grapes, 1853).

A National Prohibition party is founded in September at Chicago (*see* WCTU, 1874).

California wineries produce 4 million gallons, up from about 58,000 in 1850. Within 20 years they will be producing more than 20 million gallons, despite infestations of grape phylloxera (*see* 1870).

Japan's Kirin brewery is founded at Yokohama under the name Spring Valley brewery by U.S. entrepreneur William Copeland.

The concept of bottled beer is introduced by English brewer Francis Manning-Needham, whose hygienic, reusable containers will quickly be adopted by Bass, Whitbread's, and other major brewers to supplement the kegs which they deliver by wagon to Britain's pubs, inns, hotels, and taverns.

1870

France declares war on Prussia July 19 and three German armies invade France. *Saucier* Georges-Auguste Escoffier, 23, of the fashionable Paris restaurant Le Petit Moulin Rouge is recruited as cook for the second section of the general staff of the French Army on the Rhine and given charge of provisions; he obtains a huge and superior-quality cut of beef for his horse-drawn supply wagon, spends the night roasting it, and serves it the morning of August 15 before the troops march on Gravelotte. Escoffier, who began his career at age 13 as an apprentice at his uncle's restaurant in Nice and moved 6 years later to Le Petit Moulin Rouge, serves the officers an evening meal of sautéed rabbit on a fondant of onion purée, and they proceed to gain the only French victory of the war (*see* restaurants, 1883).

Paris goes hungry as Prussian troops begin a 135-day siege September 19. Parisians eat many of the city's 50,000 horses plus cats, dogs, even animals from the zoo including the beloved elephants Castor and Pollux (*see* 1871).

Slavery is abolished in the Spanish colonies, including the sugar-rich islands of Cuba and Puerto Rico.

Léopold Louis-Dreyfus begins importing Russian wheat into Marseilles (*see* 1865). He has been buying grain at Odessa, investing the capital which he has earned in his trading operations and borrowing from Paris financiers to buy grain elevators, and using agents to buy grain on the spot throughout the Ukraine. Louis-Dreyfus will soon be marketing Russian and Romanian grain through his offices at Berlin, Bremen, Duisburg, Hamburg, Mannheim, and Paris (*see* 1904).

Large-scale banana traffic from the Caribbean to North American ports is pioneered by Wellfleet, Mass., fishing captain Lorenzo Dow Baker, 30, who is part owner of the 70-ton two-masted schooner *Telegraph of Wellfleet*. More and more banana cargoes from Honduras and Costa Rica have reached New Orleans, New York, and Boston since 1850, when men returning from the California gold mines developed a taste for the fruit. Baker buys 1,400 coconuts at 12 for a shilling and 608 bunches of bananas at a shilling each in Port Antonio, Jamaica, and puts in 11 days later at Jersey City, N.J., with the fruit beginning to turn yellow. An Italian merchant buys it at Baker's offering price of $2.25 per bunch while the coconuts sell at almost no profit (*see* 1871; Pearsall, 1843).

Mott's Cider and Mott's Vinegar voyage around Cape Horn to California by clipper ship in 1,000-case lots (*see* 1842; Duffy-Mott, 1900).

European flour millers develop porcelain rollers. Flour from rolling mills is whiter than flour from grinding mills since the dark wheat germ is flattened by the rollers into a tiny flake that is sifted off with the bran, but while the whiter flour is reduced in nutrients the loss is significant only in areas where bread remains the major part of human diets.

Porcelain rollers (above) are widely adopted in Austria and Hungary, where hard wheats predominate (*see* 1839; Glasgow, 1872; Minneapolis, 1879).

A can opener patented by U.S. inventor William W. Lyman is the first with a cutting wheel that rolls around a can's rim (*see* 1865).

The Dover rotary egg beater is patented May 31 (*see* 1863).

Springfield, Mass., inventor Margaret E. "Mattie" Knight, 32, obtains a patent for an attachment to bag-folding machines and produces the first square-bottomed paper bags, predecessors to the bags that will be used at virtually every U.S. grocery store (*see* 1872).

Cookbook: *The Young Wife's Cookbook. With Receipts of the Best Dishes for Breakfast, Dinner and Tea . . . With Miscellaneous Receipts and Invaluable Hints to Wives in Every Article of Household Use* by the late U.S. author Hannah Marie Peterson (*née* Bouvier), who has died at age 59.

"Go west, young man," says *New York Tribune* publisher Horace Greeley, who picks up the phrase first published in 1851 by John L. B. Soule in the *Terre Haute* (Indiana) *Express*. Greeley establishes the Union Colony in the Colorado Territory (it will later be called Greeley). He has been inspired by his agricultural editor Nathan C. Meeker, who digs the territory's first irrigation canal (*see* 1888).

Some 4 million buffalo roam the American plains south of the Platte River by some estimates. They will be virtually wiped out in the next 4 years, leaving perhaps half a million north of the Platte (*see* 1875).

Cattle drives up the Chisholm Trail from San Antonio, Tex., to Abilene, Kans., begin on a huge scale (*see* 1867). The overland treks will bring an estimated 10 million head up the trail in the next 20 years, and while J.G. McCoy at Abilene does not quite fulfill his promises to Texas cattle ranchers they do receive $20 at Abilene for a steer that is worth $11 in Texas and that sells at Chicago for $31.50 (*see* 1871).

The U.S. corn crop tops 1 million bushels for the first time (*see* 1885).

California wheat growers produce 16 million bushels, and the $20 million they receive is twice the value of all the gold mined in California for the year (*see* 1868). Great wheat farms in the Livermore and San Joaquin valleys average nearly 40 bushels per acre with some producing 60 per acre.

Grape phylloxerae reach California (date approximate), having traveled across the Rocky Mountains from the East Coast, but the aphids have a relatively mild effect compared to that in Europe, where vines are more densely planted (*see* 1868).

Grape phylloxerae reach Australia (date approximate). The aphids will be identified in 1875 at Geelong, just west of Melbourne, and in 1880 at Bendigo, central Victoria; the government will order eradication of all affected vineyards, and it will be nearly a century before wine grapes are grown again in these once-flourishing areas (*see* 1900).

The Chinese plum, which has been domesticated in Japan, is introduced into California, where it will be the basis of the modern plum industry (*see* Agen plum, 1856).

The U.S. Department of Agriculture imports 300 apple varieties from Russia. Included are the Duchess, Red Astrachan, and Yellow Transparent.

The McIntosh apple is propagated from a seedling found on his Matilda Township homestead by Ontario nurseryman Allan McIntosh. It will become the dominant variety in New England and eastern New York.

The Elberta peach is introduced according to some accounts by Marshalville, Ga., orchardman Samuel Rumph, who has developed the variety and has named it after his wife (but *see* 1850).

Florida horticulturist James Armstrong Harris, 23, purchases 525 acres on the shore of Orange Lake. The property is covered with wild orange trees which bear sour fruit, but Harris will convert them into trees bearing sweet oranges and pioneer commercial orange growing in the state (*see* Hart, 1867). He will transport his crops nine miles to the Ocklawaha River for shipment by steamer via Jacksonville to New York, going on to plant a large orange grove on Panasoffkee Lake in Sumter County and introducing the grapefruit to northern markets (*see* Darcy tangerine, 1871).

Italian toxicologist Francesco Selmi coins the word "ptomaine" to denote certain nitrogenous compounds easily detectible by smell and in some cases poisonous. It will be applied erroneously to food contaminants which are in many cases not detectible by smell.

The first U.S. food trademark (#82) registered by the U.S. Patent Office is a red devil. It is granted to Boston's 48-year-old William Underwood & Co. for the "deviled entremets" introduced in 1867.

The U.S. canning industry turns out 30 million cans of food, up from 5 million in 1860, despite the fact that it employs scarcely 600 people (*see* 1874).

Cincinnati's Gaff, Fleischmann markets compressed yeast wrapped in tinfoil that permits shipment anywhere; the yeast becomes popular even with ultraconservative bakers (*see* 1868; 1876).

Rokeach kosher foods have their beginnings in a kosher soap company started on Wythe Avenue in Brooklyn, N.Y., by entrepreneur Israel Rokeach, who will begin marketing gefilte fish, borscht, and kosher jams under the Rokeach label in the early 1900s (*see* 1937; Manischewitz, 1888).

An Oxford don spends his summer holiday in Scotland, where his hostess gives him breakfast that includes homemade marmalade (*see* 1868). He takes the recipe back to Oxford and gives it to the wife of his grocer. In the next few years, a young Paisley couple will produce a pale, clear jelly to which they will add finely shredded Seville orange peel, without pith, and market it as Golden Shred Marmalade. Within 50 years they will have expanded to mass-produce the product at three additional factories in England.

Canadian distiller Joseph Emm Seagram, 29, joins a 19-year-old firm of Waterloo, Ontario, millers and distillers that he will own by 1883. Joseph E. Sea-

gram and Sons will become a leading Canadian whisky maker (*see* Bronfman, 1928).

Brown-Forman Corp. has its beginnings in a Kentucky distillery founded by George Garvin Brown and his half brother. It will become Brown-Forman in 1890 (*see* Jack Daniel's, 1956).

The Hôtel du Cap opens February 25 at the tip of Cap d'Antibes on the French Riviera with a 16-course 2 o'clock luncheon that includes salmon with both hollandaise and genevoise sauces, filet de boeuf à la polonaise, suprême à la Régence, slabs of foie gras en belle vue, truffled pheasants with Périgord sauce, crayfish, asparagus, artichoke hearts, and four desserts. The 100-room hotel (25 have private baths) boasts central heating, will be renovated in 1911, and in 1928 will take over neighboring Eden Roc, originally a private estate.

1871

Paris capitulates to German troops January 28, ending the siege during which the local department store Au Bon Marché has distributed free food to the poor. The Germans withdraw on payment of 1,460 tons of gold, raised by issuing 6 percent government bonds, and the transfer of Alsace and Lorraine to a new, united German Empire. The French assembly meeting at Bordeaux (a Communist uprising has taken over Paris) deposes Napoleon III March 1 and accepts a peace treaty, but order is not restored at Paris until the end of May.

Brazil abolishes slavery, with emancipation to be effected by 1888 (*see* 1852; 1888).

Dodge City, Kans., has its beginnings in a sod house built on the Santa Fe Trail 5 miles west of Fort Dodge to serve buffalo hunters. Within a year the settlement will have grown into a town with a general store, three dance halls, and six saloons and will soon be shipping hundreds of thousands of buffalo tongues, buffalo hindquarters, and buffalo hides to market via the Santa Fe Railroad, which will reach Dodge City next year (*see* 1868).

Germany raises tariff barriers against food imports in a move to remain independent of France or any other country in food supply. German wheat prices will nevertheless fall 27 percent in the next 20 years and will fall 30 percent in Sweden, ruining many farmers and encouraging emigration to America.

A study undertaken to refute charges that British land ownership is excessively concentrated reveals that 710 landlords own one-quarter of all the land in England and Wales and fewer than 5,000 people own three-quarters of the land in the British Isles.

U.S. wheat and flour exports total 50 million bushels, while corn exports total 8 million.

The Illinois state legislature enacts a law giving the state powers to supervise grain elevators (*see* crime, 1872; Supreme Court decision, 1877).

C. A. Pillsbury & Co. is founded by Minneapolis miller Charles Alfred Pillsbury, 29, in partnership with his brother Fred, his father, George, 53, and his uncle John Sargent Pillsbury, 43, a hardware merchant who will serve as governor of Minnesota from 1875 to 1881. The New Hampshire–born founder came to Minneapolis 2 years ago, acquired part ownership in the Minneapolis Flouring Mill (daily capacity: 200 to 300 barrels), made it profitable, and has used its $6,000 profit to acquire the Alaska Mill (promptly renamed the Pillsbury Mill) at a foreclosure sale (*see* Pillsbury's Best XXXX, 1872).

Millwright George T. Smith, 30, has made improvements in the 1865 LeCroix middlings purifier, employing a traveling brush that keeps the cloth clean and thus permits better control of air currents. C. A. Pillsbury & Co. (above) persuades Smith to join it as chief miller.

George H. Christian retains Edmund LeCroix to install purifiers in the Minneapolis flour mill set up by C. C. Washburn in 1866, and it becomes the first large mill to be so equipped (*see* 1874).

Glasgow grocer Thomas Johnstone Lipton, 21, opens his first shop May 10 (his birthday) on the ground floor of a Stobcross Street tenement. Lipton sailed to America at age 17, worked in Carolina rice fields, learned about merchandising while employed in the grocery section of a New York department store, returned earlier in the year with an American rocking chair and barrel of flour for his mother, but could not persuade his Irish-born parents to back

him in a shop of his own. He has bought hams from a ship damaged by a storm, resold them at a profit of £18, and begins business, undercutting the competition by offering ham at 5 pence per pound. Wearing white overalls and an apron, he has profits of £2, 6d. the first day, works long hours, hangs a painted wooden ham over his door, attracts customers with cartoons in his windows, and then has two fat pigs driven through the streets of Glasgow, stopping traffic: painted on the pigs' scrubbed sides are the words, "I'm going to Lipton's, The Best Shop In Town for Irish Bacon." By year's end, Lipton has opened a second shop in High Street and will soon have shops in Edinburgh, Liverpool, London, and Manchester (*see* 1879; tea, 1890).

Huntington Hartford of A&P sends emergency rail shipments of tea and coffee to Chicago, most of whose grocery stores have burnt in a great October fire. When the city is rebuilt, Hartford will open A&P stores (*see* 1869; 1876).

The Texas Pacific Railroad, which will end the Chisholm Trail cattle drives, is chartered by Congress and is given a land grant, but while the road's 1,800 miles of main line will extend from New Orleans to El Paso via Shreveport, Texarkana, Dallas, and Fort Worth, it will never reach the Pacific (*see* 1885).

The first full shipload of bananas lands at Boston July 28 aboard Dow Baker's 85-ton schooner *Telegraph* 14 days out of Kingston, Jamaica. Seaverns & Co. sells the fruit on commission, and the firm's young buyer Andrew Preston assures Baker that a market exists for all the bananas he can obtain (*see* 1870; 1885).

Dutch margarine production begins in the spring at Oss in North Brabant as local butter merchants Jan and Anton Jurgens open the world's first fully operative margarine factory. British butter prices began rising in the 1860s, when an outbreak of cattle disease produced a severe shortage of domestic butter, the Jurgens and other Dutch firms have benefited from increased British imports, but only the richest Britons can afford butter at 2 shillings a pound, and the needs of working-class Britons have increased interest in a butter substitute. Jan and his brother Henri have visited Paris in the wake of the Franco-

Prussian War (above) and met with Hippolyte Mège-Mouries in his laboratory at Pantin (*see* 1869), and Mège-Mouries agreed to show them his process, knowing that sooner or later they would be able to develop a similar process themselves. The Jurgens brothers acquired rights from Mège-Mouries for 60,000 francs per year but found that his process was still primitive and have improved on it to create a product which they market under the name "butterine" (*see* United States, 1881; Jurgens, 1883).

Cookbook: *Jewish Cookery* by Philadelphia author Esther Levy (*née* Jacobs) is the first such book published in the United States and only the second in the English language (*see* 1846).

Passenger pigeons nesting in Wisconsin occupy 750 square miles and will continue such mass nestings until 1878 despite a great October fire, but fewer and fewer migratory birds return to their old habitats, possibly because market hunters have taken too large a toll, possibly because wetlands covering an area greater than New England are being drained and forests are being cleared for farms and for fuel (*see* 1878).

President Grant signs a congressional resolution "for the protection and preservation of the food fishes of the coasts of the United States" and names Spencer F. Baird to head a new U.S. Fish Commission.

The U.S. Fish Commission (above) engages fish culturist Seth Green to transport newly hatched Hudson River shad fry in eight large cans from Rochester, N.Y., across the continent to Tehama, Calif., where the fish (*Alosa sapidissima*) are released into the Sacramento River. Nearly two-thirds of the fry survive the 7-day trip, and within 9 years they will be spawning in Oregon's Umpqua and Coos rivers, spawning in the river at San Francisco in April just as they do in the Hudson (*see* 1885; salmon, 1875).

Texans drive 700,000 longhorns 700 miles from San Antonio north to the Abilene stockyards, moving at 12 miles per day through open, unsettled country that provides abundant grass and water for the livestock on the "Long Drive" up the Chisholm Trail (*see* 1870).

Herdsmen drove Texas longhorns all the way to New York before the railroads came through. HARPER'S WEEKLY

J. G. McCoy of Abilene has been unable to collect on his contract with the Kansas Pacific, whose officers say they never anticipated such volume, but McCoy has become mayor of Abilene and profited in real estate and other enterprises (*see* 1870).

Land planted to grain in Britain will decline by more than 25 percent in the next three decades as the railroads open up the western United States, making it unprofitable for British farmers to compete.

Florida orange grower Col. George L. Dancy pioneers commercial tangerine cultivation on his plantation at Buena Vista (*see* Harris, 1870). The Dancy tangerine will be the most popular U.S. variety for the next century and Florida will remain the largest producer of tangerines, although the fruit will also be grown in California, Arizona, Texas, and Louisiana.

California planter R. B. Ord makes the first commercially successful planting of avocados in the state, using Mexican trees at Santa Barbara (*see* 1913; Florida, 1901).

Mountain Valley Mineral Water is offered for sale at Hot Springs, Ark., by local pharmacist John Green, who has recently arrived from Tennessee and bought the Locket Spring 12 miles out of town. He and his brother will sell their cmpany in 1879 to St. Louis entrepreneur W. N. Benton, who will promote the mineral water with testimonial health claims as a cure for dyspepsia, dropsy, torpid liver, and Bright's disease.

The first U.S. trademark registration for a soft drink is awarded to Lemons' Superior Sparkling Ginger Ale (*see* Canada Dry, 1890).

New York's Fifth Avenue Hotel serves iced tea along with iced water and iced milk on hot summer days, and a New Orleans writers observes, "In these hot climates, cold tea lemonade, iced, is declared by the few who have tried it to be more fragrant and refreshing than the most liberal libations of soda-water or other effervescing liquids" (*see* 1860, 1878).

New Orleans restaurant owner Antoine Alciatore, now 61 and fatally ill, sails for Marseilles (he will die within a year), leaving Antoine's in the hands of his wife, Julie (*see* 1840; Oysters Rockefeller, 1899).

1872

Sweden's Charles IV dies at Malmö September 18 at age 46 after a 13-year reign. His brother, 43, will reign until 1907 as Oscar II, importing a French chef to bring refinement to the royal cuisine at Stockholm.

U.S. Grangers form cooperative ventures to purchase farm implements, machinery, feed, seed, clothing, and other necessities. Some local Granges adopt the English Rochedale plan of 1844, and in Iowa one-third of all grain elevators and warehouses are Granger-owned or -controlled (*see* 1867; 1873).

The Chicago Board of Trade moves into a building of its own at LaSalle and Washington (*see* 1865; 1930).

Illinois authorities investigate grain elevators under powers granted by the state legislature last year and discover that Chicago Board of Trade speculator Ira Y. Munn, a onetime president of the Board of Trade, controls most of the city's elevators. A bigtime speculator for much of the past decade, Munn may actually have been the first to undertake large-scale trading of futures (*see* 1879). So great is his power that he can compel railroads bringing grain into Chicago to deliver it to his houses regardless of who the consignees may be, and investigators establish that he has employed a systematic plan of short weights and false grades in his elevators. Expelled from the Board of Trade, Munn files suit, claiming that the state has no right to regulate warehouse operations (*see* Supreme Court decision, 1877).

Grand Union Tea Co. has its beginnings at Scranton, Pa., where entrepreneur Cyrus Jones, 20, opens a small shop selling tea, coffee, spices, baking powder, and flavoring extracts which he also peddles door to door. Jones's brother Frank, a trained bookkeeper, will soon join the enterprise, as will an experienced grocery clerk, and they will help young Cyrus rack up sales of $12,000 for the year, a figure that will grow to well over $1 billion within a century. Grand Union will establish headquarters at Brooklyn, N.Y., in 1897.

U.S. inventor Luther Childs Crowell, 61, patents a machine to make flat-bottomed paper bags. Springfield, Mass., inventor Margaret E. "Maggie" Knight, now 34, obtained a patent 2 years ago for an attachment to bag-folding machines and produced the first square-bottomed bags but sold the patent to her employers. Crowell's machine will be improved in 1883 by a machine that will make the automatic, or "flick," bag—a self-opening bag with a flat bottom and side pleats (*see* 1870; Union Bag, 1869).

Upstate New York weaver's daughter Amanda Theodosia Jones, 37, is awarded five patents (she will receive a sixth next year) for a vacuum process that she has developed for preserving food. She places the food in a container, drains air out through a series of valves, adds water heated to a temperature of between 100° and 120° F., and immediately seals the container (*see* 1890).

Production of the Appleby binder, patented 3 years ago, begins at Beloit, Wis., where a local firm produces the wire binding machine, but many farmers object to using metal wire lest it kill their stock and the enterprise fails (*see* Appleby reaper, 1874; knotting device, 1878).

Liverpool sugar refinery head Henry Tate, 53, obtains a patent for an invention that he has been shown which cuts sugar loaves into small pieces for household use. He will put the device into production (*see* 1878), and the fortune that he will soon make from Tate's Cubed Sugar will go in part to found the University Library at Liverpool and the Tate Gallery, Millbank, London, which will open in 1897 to house his extensive art collection.

Armour & Co. installs the world's largest chill room in a new plant at Chicago's Union Stock Yards (*see* 1865; 1869). Salt curing has been the chief way to keep perishable meats from spoiling, and meat processing has been a seasonal business, but Armour employs a new method that uses natural ice to maintain operations year round (*see* refrigerated railcars, 1869).

Porcelain rollers are installed in a new flour mill built at Glasgow, Scotland (*see* 1870; Minneapolis, 1874).

A doughnut cutter patented by Thomaston, Me., inventor John F. Blondell has a spring-propelled rod to push out the dough of a center tube, but most doughnuts continue to be made by hand (*see* 1847; Leavitt, 1920).

The Moorestown Canning Factory built 4 years ago by U.S. entrepreneur Jonas Yerkes produces 30,000 gallons of tomato ketchup in quart and pint bottles for sale throughout the United States (*see* 1837). Ketchup is a by-product of tomato canning: machines remove the skins from cored tomatoes, and where the skins were formerly discarded they are now mixed with sugar (which serves as a preservative and counteracts the sour taste of green tomatoes) to make tomato ketchup (*see* Heinz, 1876).

A French dairyman named Pommel near Grenet invents a new formula for a lightly salted cream cheese that will be marketed under the names Demi-Sel and Pommel (year approximate). Charles Gervais at Ferrières will market a similar product in silver foil.

Louis Pasteur publishes a classic paper on fermentation, showing that it is caused by microorganisms (*see* 1859; 1861). He has visited Whitbread's London brewery in Chiswell Street and carried out research into yeast that will spur Whitbread's to establish its own yeast laboratory (*see* 1876).

The *Western Stock Journal and Farmer* begins publication at Cedar Rapids, Iowa. Publisher Seaman Asahel Knapp, 39, will become a close friend of Henry C. Wallace, publisher of *Wallace's Farmer*, and of James C. Wilson, who will become secretary of agriculture (*see* agriculture, 1885; Hatch Act, 1887).

British sugar consumption reaches 47 pounds per capita, up from 12 pounds per year in 1780.

Japan's Meiji emperor Mutsuhito sets an example of "civilization and enlightenment" by eating beef, formerly taboo in Japan, and starts a fad for beef eating among his more affluent countrymen. Shops open to sell beef, which is pot boiled and flavored with miso paste or soy sauce, but most Japanese cannot bear the smell of people who have eaten animal fats (they are called *butakusai*) and few can afford beef (*see* restaurants, below; Townsend Harris, 1856).

A bumper U.S. corn crop leads to the start of a stock feeder cattle industry in the Midwest. The opening of new cattle lands in the West is beginning to have the effect of lowering beef prices.

The Wisconsin State Dairyman's Association and Northwestern Dairyman's Association are founded with help from Fort Atkinson, Wis., publisher and agriculturist William Dempster Hoard, 35. His paper, the *Jefferson County Union*, has campaigned vigorously for the general adoption of dairying in Wisconsin, that being better suited to the state's resources than any other agricultural pursuit. Hoard will lobby successfully next year to obtain advantageous rates from railroads for carrying refrigerator cars that will bring Wisconsin dairy products to eastern markets.

Grape phylloxerae attack vineyards in the Madeira Islands, which have been damaged since 1852 by oidium mildew but continue to find their largest export market in America (*see* Prohibition, 1920).

The Société d'Agriculture of the Gironde offers a prize of 20,000 francs for an effective method of halting the inroads of grape phylloxerae on vineyards (*see* 1868); the French government increases this to 300,000 francs (no one will ever receive the prize, despite some justified claims). Flooding a vineyard completely for a period of time will drown the aphids, but good vineyards are not flat; the aphids do not thrive in sand, and while beaches in Languedoc are soon planted in high-yielding Carignan and Aramon grapes, most vintners rely on chemical fumigation. Baron Paul Thénard, a chemist, finds that carbon bisulfide, made by passing sulfur vapor over red-hot charcoal, is extremely toxic to the aphid (as well as to most other insects); injected in the soil around the vines, it kills everything (including, at first, the vines themselves), and although the fumes of the highly flammable mixture make workers ill, fumigation will continue to be used for the next 70 years, richer growers employing sulfur carbonate of potassium (or sodium), which requires miles of pipes, nozzles, and pumps and tremendous quantities of water. By the end of this decade, most of the Bordeaux vineyards will nevertheless have been devastated, and eventually some two and a half million acres of vineyards will be laid waste.

Montpellier University professor Gaston Fouex observes that grape phylloxerae (above) must have come from abroad, arguing that if they were native to Europe they would long ago have wiped out European vines. The parasite must be native to a country where it can live without destroying its host, he says. Jules-Émile Planchon has already established that phylloxerae are native to America and exchanges visits with Charles Riley, a U.S. agronomist who is well known for his work on the Colorado potato beetle. Riley confirms that the aphids must have been carried across the Atlantic inadvertently from the U.S. East Coast on roots of native American vines (*Vitis labrusca*) intended for collectors and experimental use in Europe. Although the Catawba has no resistance, exposure over thousands of years has made most other U.S. vine roots immune to the phylloxerae (which cause leaf galls and weaken roots), but they do attack the European species *Vitis vinifera*. Count Haroszthy, who will die next year in Nicaragua (*see* 1861), Charles Krug, and other enterprising growers have brought diseased cuttings and rootstock of *Vitis vinifera* to California, and the aphid will take its toll in that state's vineyards, but the destruction wrought on Europe's vineyards will be far worse. Roots from New York State vineyards will be used to revive the European industry, and California's devastated vineyards will recover with help from European grape varieties grafted onto phylloxera-resistant American rootstocks (*see* 1876).

The Burbank potato developed by Massachusetts horticulturist Luther Burbank, 23, from a chance seedling is an improved variety that will come to be known as the Idaho potato (although it will also be widely grown in Washington State and Maine) and will eclipse such New England varieties as Green Mountain, Irish Cobbler, and Katahdin. It will provide Burbank with funds for developing not only new potato varieties but also new tomatoes, asparagus, sweet and field corn, peas, squash, apples, cherries, nectarines, peaches, quinces, ornamental flowers, and—most especially—plums, prunes, and berries (*see* 1875).

A tropical hurricane sweeps across Zanzibar, uprooting most of the island's full-grown clove trees (*see* 1818); fewer than 15 percent of the trees are undamaged. The island of Pemba is not touched and continues to export the spice, but Zanzibar's exports of cloves and clove oil will be minimal for the next decade (*see* 1955).

A strict Adulteration of Food, Drink and Drugs Act amends Britain's pure food laws of 1860, making sale of adulterated drugs punishable and making it an offense to sell a mixture containing ingredients added to increase weight or bulk without advising the consumer (chicory in coffee is a case in point) (*see* 1875).

Pillsbury's Best XXXX Flour is introduced by C. A. Pillsbury Co. at Minneapolis (*see* 1871; 1873).

The British wine-exporting house of Osborne is founded at Puerto de Santa María, Spain, by Thomas Osborne, who has been managing the Duff-Gordon firm (*see* 1768) for decades and absorbs that firm into his new enterprise.

Athen's Hôtel Grand Bretagne opens in a large private house built in the center of town for a Triestine Greek but never occupied. The house will be enlarged and new wings added to make it the city's leading hostelry, with a dining room that caters to international tastes.

Boston's Hotel Vendôme opens at the corner of Commonwealth Avenue and Dartmouth Street with a dining hall that seats 320. Its carved mahogany and cherrywood walls are set with large plate-glass mirrors and decorated with frescoes and a frieze.

Britain's Parliament passes a Licensing Act that sets strict limits on the number and kinds of places where alcoholic beverages may be sold and the hours such places may be open in an effort to curb excessive drunkenness. Riots occur in some areas, the Liberal party legislation rallies publicans and brewers to the Conservative party, and the unpopularity of the new law will help topple the Gladstone government in the general elections of 1874.

The Café de la Paix opens at Paris in the Hôtel Grand on the Boulevard des Capucines with carved pillars and landscaped ceilings.

Prunier's opens in the rue d'Antin at Paris, serving only oysters, snails, grills, and pieds de mouton poulettes (sheep's trotters with sauce poulette). Restaurateur-traiteur Alfred Prunier, whose sons make home deliveries with baskets of oysters on their heads, will move in 1875 to 9, rue Duphot near the Place de la Concorde and the Place de la Madeleine, attracting patrons with Belon oysters from Brittany, Marenne oysters from the Charente-Maritime, and portugaise oysters. Until the 1880s, no customer will be served unless he orders oysters, and they will always be raw oysters until the 1890s, when a Bostonian teaches Prunier how to make oyster pan stew, after which Alfred and his son Emil will also serve tournedos Boston, sea perch à l'angevine, and homard au champagne (*see* 1992; London, 1935).

The Paris restaurant Brasserie Lipp opens on the Boulevard Saint-Germain-de-Prés under the management of an Alsatian who names it after a famous eating place in Strasbourg. Refugees from Alsace and Lorraine have poured into Paris since the end of the Franco-Prussian War last year, and brasseries have proliferated (*see* 1864).

Tokyo's first Western-style restaurants open: Kayotei, Mikawaya, Nisshintei, and Seiyoken serve beef and other Western foods.

The Tokyo restaurant Toriyasu opens to serve duck dishes. Former *samurai* Daisuke Watanabe has crossbred wild and domestic ducks to create a new variety, and his friend, Kabuki actor Kikugoro Onoae, has advised him to open a restaurant.

Mennonite farmers in the Crimea send four young men on a scouting expedition to America after learning that Czar Aleksandr II plans to cancel their exemption from military service, freedom of worship, and right to have their own schools and speak their German language—rights granted by Cather-ine the Great in 1783. The young men are from well-to-do families in the Molotschna (Milk River) district and are led by Bernard Warkentin, Jr., 23, a miller's son from the village of Tjerpenije. He establishes a base at Summerfield, Ill., near East St. Louis, where some Mennonite families have settled earlier, and attends a local college for a year to improve his English. After traveling with his colleagues through Pennsylvania and west to Wyoming, and from Texas through the Dakotas into Manitoba, Warkentin will write letters home persuading many of his countrymen to resettle, and while most will go to Manitoba because of liberal laws regarding military service, many will settle in Kansas (*see* agriculture, 1874).

1873

Bengal suffers a famine as rice crops fail, creating shortages that bring starvation to much of India.

Britain's "golden age" comes to an end after 23 years as Germany and the United States challenge British industrial preeminence.

European investors withdraw capital from the United States, the Wall Street banking house Jay Cooke & Co., which has been financial agent for the Northern Pacific Railway, fails September 18, Black Friday on the stock exchange sends prices tumbling September 19, the exchange closes for 10 days, and by year's end some 5,000 business firms have failed, millions of working Americans are obliged to depend on soup kitchens and other charities, and tens of thousands come close to starvation (*see* 1874).

The Greenback party organized by Midwesterners claims that a shortage of money is the cause of hard times. If the government will issue greenbacks until as much money is in circulation as in the boom times of 1865 the country will again enjoy prosperity, say the Greenbackers. (They also demand control of the corporations, honesty in government, conservation of natural resources, and wide-scale reforms.)

The Grange (Patrons of Husbandry) reaches its membership peak of 750,000, but Rep. Ignatius Donnelly (R. Minn.) compares a nonpolitical farmers' organization to a gun that won't shoot (*see* 1867; 1876).

W. W. Cargill and his brother Sam take advantage of the economic depression (above) to buy out bankrupt grain elevator operators at distress prices (*see* 1865). They have been acquiring or building elevators along the route of the Southern Minnesota Railroad across southern Wisconsin and Minnesota with funds advanced by Milwaukee banks (*see* 1909).

Hard times helped Will Cargill add to his empire of Midwestern grain elevators.

Rep. Ignatius Donnelly (above) complains that it costs as much to ship wheat from Minneapolis to Milwaukee as to ship the same wheat from Milwaukee to Liverpool. U.S. railroads are making deals with elevator companies, commission agents, and others to control both shipping and marketing rates and forcing farmers to sell to the nearest elevator company, agent, or railroad at rates favorable to the buyer. Grain is often downgraded to No. 2 because it is said to be wet, frozen, or weedy and is then sold as No. 1 grade to millers, say the farmers.

A farmers' convention at Springfield, Ill., attacks monopolies, calling them "detrimental to the public prosperity, corrupt in their management, and dangerous to republican institutions."

The Northwest Farmers' Convention at Chicago urges federal regulation of transportation rates, government-built and government-owned railroads, an end to corporation subsidies and tariff protection for industry, a revision of the credit system, and the encouragement of decentralized manufacturing—demands that bankers, industrialists, and railroad operators call "un-American."

Good-quality Werner harvesters made by a Grange factory in Iowa sell for half the price of a McCormick harvester. When 22 plow manufacturers agree not to sell plows to Granges except at retail prices, some Granges set up factories to make their own machines and break the "machinery rings" (*see* 1872; 1875).

Deering harvesters are introduced by entrepreneur William Deering, 47, who has left the New York textile firm Deering Milliken and gone into partnership with a company at Plano, Ill. (*see* 1863; 1878; International Harvester, 1902).

Ralph's Grocery Co. opens at Los Angeles, which is still a dusty town of less than 10,000 people.

Rochester, N.Y., lawyer George Baldwin Selden, 27, experiments with internal combustion engines in an effort to develop a lightweight engine that will propel a road vehicle more efficiently than the "road locomotives" now used in some farm jobs (*see* 1876; Lenoir, 1860; Otto, 1866).

Britain receives her first wheat from India via the Suez Canal, completed in 1869. Impatient at having to rely on Russia, which has been the nation's chief source of supply, British entrepreneurs have worked to obtain a secure source of cheap wheat under British control and have pushed canals and railroads into the Indus and Ganges river valleys.

Piracy and native hostility end U.S. pepper trade with Sumatra after 937 voyages (*see* 1797. 1805).

DDT (dichlorodiphenyltrichloroethane) is prepared by German chemistry student Othmar Zeidler at Strasbourg. He reacts chloral hydrate (the "Mickey Finn" knockout drops of the underworld) and chlorobenzene in the presence of sulfuric acid and will describe DDT next year in the *Proceedings of the German Chemical Society* (*Berichte der chemischen Gesellschaft*), but he has no idea of the significance of his discovery (*see* 1939).

Swedish engineer Carl Linde introduces the first successful compression system using liquid ammonia as a refrigerant (*see* Perkins, 1834; Gorrie, 1842; Lowe, 1865; liquefied air, 1898).

Poultry, fish, and meat that has been frozen for 6 months is eaten at a public banquet in Australia (*see* 1856; 1925).

The thermos bottle has its beginnings in the Dewar vessel invented by Scottish chemist James Dewar, 31, who will invent the thermos flask in 1892.

Cookbook: *Le Grand Dictionnaire de Cuisine* by the late French novelist-playwright Alexandre Dumas (père), who died in December 1870 at age 68. Full of anecdotes and verse, the work, which includes the word "sandwichs," runs to 1,155 pages but will be republished in an 882-page version in 1882.

Retired London silk merchant George Grant brings four Aberdeen Angus bulls from Scotland to his farm at Victoria, Kans.—first of the breed to reach the United States. Foreign investment capital is pouring into the U.S. cattle-ranching industry (*see* 1881).

Barbed wire exhibited at the De Kalb, Ill., county fair by Henry Rose is studied by local farmer Joseph Farwell Glidden, 60, and his friend Jacob Haish, who independently develop machines for produc-

Barbed wire fenced in the western rangelands to protect farm crops from cattle.

ing coil barbed wire by the mile and obtain patents for two separate styles of the "devil's rope" that is destined to end the open range in the West; 80.5 million pounds of barbed wire will be manufactured in the next 74 years as the steel wire becomes important not only to farmers and ranchers but also to military operations (*see* 1867; Gates, 1875).

Nine Pekin ducks arrive at New York March 14 to begin an industry that will see duck farms established from Patchogue, Long Island, eastward to Moriches, Eastport, and Speonk, where tidewater creeks empty into Moriches Bay and the eastern end of Great South Bay. Stonington, Conn., sea captain James E. Palmer has obtained the white birds, a variety of mallard, from the imperial aviaries at Beijing (*see* 1874).

Louisiana's sugar crop falls to less than one-third its 1853 level as a result of the Civil War and emancipation; cane in many areas of the state has been replaced by rice, which demands less labor, and Louisiana sugar will never regain the world importance it enjoyed before the war.

Sugar production has shifted to Cuba, where U.S., British, and French capital have developed plantations that by 1900 will be exporting 10 times more sugar than Jamaica exported at the start of this century with only three times as much labor and with five times as much investment in machinery as in land.

Rice planting increases in Louisiana (above) as the industry shifts from South Carolina, which before the Civil War grew 60 percent of the nation's crop. With slave labor no longer available and South Carolina's swampland unable to support the weight of heavy equipment, cheap land in Louisiana has attracted German wheat farmers from the Midwest, who adapt their wheat-growing expertise to rice cultivation. In years to come, Louisiana, Arkansas, California, Mississippi, Texas, and Missouri will produce virtually all of the rice grown in the United States (*see* Wright, 1890).

The Paris Council of Hygiene rules that margarine may not be sold as butter (*see* 1869; New York, 1877).

Japan's Ministry of Justice issues an order making it an offense to sell spoiled or fraudulently labeled food. Government inspectors will begin checking food items next year to make sure that there are no violations (*see* 1880).

Henri Nestlé's Infant Milk Food is introduced in the United States (*see* 1866; 1875).

Coors Beer has its beginnings in the Golden Brewery started by German-American brewer Adolph Herman Joseph Coors, 26, and Jacob Schueler at Golden, Colorado Territory. Coors will buy out his partner in 1880.

St. Louis brewer Adolphus Busch becomes a full partner of his father-in-law and renames the Bavarian Brewery the E. Anheuser and Co.'s Brewing Association (*see* 1865; Budweiser, 1876).

British wine making resumes after a lapse of nearly 3½ centuries (*see* 1536). The young marquis of Bute, who has inherited the title along with a fortune and the remains of the medieval castle Coch in South Wales, begins planting vineyards which will continue production of wine until a lack of labor halts operations in 1915.

Vienna's Imperial Hotel opens April 28 on the Kärntner Ring with a dining room whose menu features the Imperial Torte, dedicated to the emperor Franz Joseph, which rivals the Sachertorte created in 1832.

Chicago's Grand Pacific Hotel opens at the corner of Clark Street and Jackson Boulevard. Hotelman John Burroughs Drake, 47, who has built the ornate, seven-story hostelry at a cost of $1.5 million, will give a game dinner for 500 guests every year for 30 years, serving roasts that include leg of black-tailed deer, loin of buffalo, leg of elk, saddle of antelope, raccoon, opossum, jack rabbit, grouse, golden plover, sandhill crane, Wilson's snipe, shoveler duck, gadwall duck, scalp duck, redhead duck, Grant quail, Carolina dove, spruce grouse, American coot, and pheasant. Ornamental dishes will include pyramid of game à la Bellevue, redwing starling au naturel, aspic of birds à la royale, boned quail in plumage, and boned snipe with truffles.

Delmonico's restaurant in New York is the scene of a $10,000 dinner given by one Henry Lukemeyer, for whom the restaurant has arranged a 30-foot oval pond as a centerpiece. Four swans, shanghaied out of Brooklyn's Prospect Park under heavy sedation, float on the pond, and when the drugs wear off the swans begin pecking furiously at one another, creating bedlam.

The Bologna restaurant Antico Brunetti has its beginnings in an eating place opened in a 12th-century tower off the Piazza Maggiore. In 100 years the Italian city will have 432 restaurants, 187 of them in the central area once surrounded by walls, and the oldest will be the Antico Brunetti, serving tortellini alla panna (squares of pasta filled with meat and covered with cream sauce), gramigna (small lengths of green spaghetti with a sausage meat sauce), lasagna verde al forno, tagliatelle, and veal dishes such as cotoletta alla bolognese (veal cutlet covered with slices of ham and cheese).

The U.S. economic depression that began last year continues, leaving tens of thousands of city dwellers without means of support. New York restaurateur Lorenzo Delmonico supervises the preparation of free meals for the hungry and reports that in one city ward alone 71,892 persons were fed between February 18 and April 7.

British farm wages fall, farmworkers strike in the east of England, and an agricultural depression begins that will lead to an exodus of farmworkers into the growing mill towns. Undercut by foreign producers of grain and meat, British agriculture begins a long decline.

The first Peavey grain elevator goes up at Sioux City, Iowa, where farm-equipment dealer Frank Peavey has heard customers complain of having no permanent market for their grain (*see* 1868). The 6,000-bushel "blind horse" elevator is powered literally by a sightless horse walking in an endless circle while towing a post attached to an axle at the center of a circle. The new elevator saves farmers from having to haul wagonloads of grain back to the farm because they could find no buyer in town, and it will be followed by warehouses that Peavey will build with partner J. S. Meckling along the Dakota Southern Railway between Sioux City and Yankton. S. D. Peavey will persuade Minneapolis flour mills that he can provide a steady supply of wheat, and he will pioneer in the mass buying and selling of grain (*see* 1884).

Sen. William Windom, 47, (R. Minn.) heads a committee that proposes a government-built, government-operated double-track freight line between the Mississippi Valley and the eastern seaboard that will prevent railroad companies from charging exorbitant freight rates (*see* 1877; farmers, 1873).

The Appleby harvester is introduced by George F. Appleby, who organizes the Appleby Reaper Works at Mazomanie, Wis., while continuing to work on developing an automatic binder (*see* binder, 1872; knotting device, 1878).

A Minneapolis flour mill employing fluted chilled steel rollers in addition to conventional millstones is opened by C. C. Washburn, who has made a fortune in Wisconsin land speculation and served as governor of Wisconsin (*see* 1866; 1879; Pillsbury, 1878; Gold Medal Flour, 1880).

New technology improves food canning—a drop press introduced by Allen Taylor and a pressure-cooking "retort" by either A. K. Shriver or Baltimore canner Isaac Solomon (*see* 1861). Live steam keeps the outside walls of the can under pressures comparable to those exerted by the heating contents of the can, thus speeding up the cooking of the contents without permitting the can to buckle or burst as it cools because of any buildup in pressure during the heating process. The retort gives canners accurate control of cooling temperatures and will lead to a large-scale expansion of the industry (*see* Howe floater, 1876).

The *Confectioners' Journal* begins publication at Philadelphia as U.S. candy makers proliferate.

Harper's magazine says, "Since the introduction of the four-tined silver fork, it has so entirely supplanted the knife that the usage of the latter in that way . . . is regarded as a vulgarism." (Right-handed Americans will hold their forks in their left hands when cutting meat and "genteely" transfer the fork from the left hand to the right when eating, whereas right-handed Europeans will spurn such mannerisms and eat with their forks in their left hands. Most of the world will continue for more than a cen-

tury to eat with sticks, as in China and Japan, or with its hands, as in India, Africa, and Latin America.)

Dutch farmers near Kalamazoo, Mich., tempt railroad travelers with the first large celery grown in the United States. Train butchers will soon be hawking it regularly on the Michigan Central.

Margarine is introduced into the United States (*see* 1881; Mège-Mouriès, 1869).

The first shipment of Montana cattle for the East arrives at the railhead at Ogden in the Utah Territory, to which cattleman James Forges has driven it from the Sun River range of Conrad Kohrs.

A decade of drought begins on part of the western U.S. cattle range while other parts enjoy plenty of rain (*see* 1886).

Turkey Red wheat—hard, drought-resistant, and high-yielding—is introduced into the United States by German-speaking Mennonites from Russia's Crimea (*see* population, 1872). The Santa Fe Railroad has brought the Mennonites to Kansas, where the road has been granted 3 million acres of land along its right-of-way and needs farmers who will occupy the land and produce crops that will generate freight revenue. Santa Fe official Carl R. Schmidt went to Russia last year and brought over a Mennonite delegation to see possible sites for settlement, has obtained passage of a law in the Kansas legislature giving exemption from military service to those who oppose war on religious grounds, has offered free passage to Kansas plus free transport of furniture, and has set up temporary living quarters, and the first Mennonites arrive August 16 at Hillsboro in Marion County. The 163 pioneers from 34 families pay in gold to buy 8,000 acres from the Santa Fe, they found the village of Gnadenau, a second group of 600 follows, then a third group of 1,100, and by fall the Mennonites are arriving by the thousands, each family bringing its Turkey Red seed wheat, originally obtained from Turkey and planted in the Crimea for years (*see* 1895).

George Perkins Marsh prepares a paper on the feasibility of irrigating western lands at the request of the U.S. Commissioner of Agriculture (*see* environment, 1864). Irrigation projects are possible, writes Marsh, if they are undertaken on a river-basin scale after thorough hydrological surveys "under Gov-

The April issue of *Poultry World* magazine carries an advertisement for "Imperial Pekin Ducks," offering a few pairs for sale at $20 per pair (*see* 1873). The July issue credits a "Mr. McGrath" of the firm of Fogg & Co., engaged in the Japan and China trade, with having discovered the duck last year (*see* 1875).

Condensed milk pioneer Gail Borden has returned to Texas and dies at Borden, Tex. (named for him), January 11 at age 72. He campaigned in recent years for sanitary dairying practices, and his son John Gail continues that effort, devoting his time to educating dairy farmers in how to produce better—and cleaner—milk (*see* 1866; 1875). Borden has selected a gravesite in New York's Woodlawn Cemetery, and his tombstone is engraved with the words "I tried and failed, I tried again and again and succeeded."

Several dozen milk companies open in Japan, and cow's milk begins to gain some popularity among the Japanese (*see* Townsend Harris, 1856).

Bovril has its beginnings in Johnston's Fluid Beef, produced commercially at Sherbrooke, Que., by Scottish entrepreneur John Lawson Johnston, who by some accounts has won a contract from the French government to supply canned meat for stocking forts against the kind of emergency that produced starvation 3 years ago in the Franco-Prussian War. His product gains quick popularity, and production will be moved to Montreal in 1880 (*see* Britain, 1886).

The ice cream soda is invented at the semicentennial celebration of Philadelphia's Franklin Institute. Robert N. Green demonstrates a soda fountain, possibly using the invention of James W. Tufts's Arctic Soda Water device, which spurts out seven varieties of beverages and 16 different kinds of syrups. When he runs out of cream after making $6 per day selling a mixture of syrup, sweet cream, and carbonated water, he substitutes vanilla ice cream and by the time the exhibition ends is averaging more than $600 per day.

Joseph Schlitz Brewing Co. is incorporated at Milwaukee with a capitalization of $200,000 (*see* 1856). Schlitz himself will drown next year at age 44 on a voyage to his native Germany, but his four nephews—Alfred, August, Henry, and Edward Uihlein—will keep management of the company in family hands for more than a century.

New York brewer Jacob Ruppert builds a new brewery with a capacity of 50,000 barrels and turns his old brewery into an icehouse (*see* 1867). His real estate investments will make Ruppert one of the city's leading financiers.

The first brut champagne is created by Mme. Pommery of the Pommery Champagne house at Reims.

The Women's Christian Temperance Union (WCTU) is founded at Cleveland, where 135 women meet November 18 at the Second Presbyterian Church and dedicate themselves to ending the traffic in liquor. Annie Turner Wittenmyer, now 47 and editor of the *Christian Woman*, is named president (*see* nutrition, 1862); Northwestern University dean Frances Caroline Elizabeth Willard, 35, is named corresponding secretary (*see* National Prohibition Party, 1869; Anti-Saloon League, 1895).

1875

Buffalo herds on the Western plains diminish drastically as market hunters kill them for their hides and decimate what has for thousands of years been the major source of food, fuel, and clothing for the Plains Indians. President Grant vetoes a bill that would protect the bison from extinction (*see* environment, 1870; 1879).

Comanche chief Quanah Parker, 30, ends his resistance to settlement of the Texas prairie by white ranchers, who join in the slaughter of bison (above) as a means of exterminating the Comanche.

U.S. Grangers fail in a scheme to produce farm equipment (*see* 1872). The Grange has bought up patents for cultivators, seeders, mowers, reapers, and many other machines and implements and has begun to manufacture them, but the effort falls victim to patent suits, lack of capital, defective machines, and lack of cooperation in a society of rural individualists.

David Sprüngli at Zurich pays Rodolphe Lindt (below) 1 million gold Swiss francs for the secret of his fondant chocolate, and the two firms merge their names. Lindt packaging more than a century hence will still bear the words "Lindt & Sprüngli AG Rod Lindt fils 1879 David Sprüngli 1845 Makers of exquisite Chocolate since 1845 Célèbres maîtres chocolateurs-confiseurs depuis 1845" (*see* Sprüngli, 1845; Lindt, 1879; lawsuit, 1927; Zurich shop, 1892).

New York's first Chinese general store opens at 8 Mott Street. Named for butcher-innkeeper James Mott, it sells groceries, herbs, and medicines to serve a Chinatown population that has grown as more and more Chinese have arrived in the city to escape mistreatment in the western states (*see* population, 1847). The area bounded by Baxter Street, the Bowery, Canal Street, and Chatham Square will become a Chinese enclave whose restaurants will include some of the best in the city (*see* Chinese Exclusion Act, 1882).

The orange crate, devised by U.S. inventor E. Bean, weighs 15 pounds, holds 90 pounds (about 200 pieces), and will lead to wide-scale marketing of the fruit (*see* Orange Growers Protective Union, 1885).

A machine is invented to strip the kernels from corncobs. It will lead to wide-scale canning of sweet corn (*see* Minnesota Valley Canning, 1903).

Producing tin cans for packing corned beef and other meats became big business. LIBRARY OF CONGRESS

Arthur A. Libby obtains patent rights to a tapered tin for compressed corned beef. His firm will export $2,500 worth of the product to London in two-pound tins next year (*see* 1868; 1878).

Ferdinand Schumacher introduces Steel Cut Oats, a new product whose flaky composition gives it a uniformly acceptable taste and consistency (*see* 1856). Schumacher uses a new machine invented largely by his employee Asmus J. Ehrrichsen, whose process is the first real innovation in milling oats, employing a series of horizontal knife blades to cut the hulled oats (groats) into a meal that has little or none of the floury residues that have made oatmeal pasty, lumpy, and glutenous. Another Schumacher employee, William Heston, improves on the Ehrrichsen-Schumacher process and obtains patents which he licenses Schumacher to use while reserving the right to use the new process himself (*see* Quaker, 1877).

Berlin chemist Ferdinand Tiemann, 27, patents a process for making synthetic vanillin, the key flavor ingredient in costly natural vanilla beans.

The first milk chocolate for eating is invented at Vevey (above) by the Nestlé shopman in collaboration with the foreman of Daniel Peter's chocolate factory (*see* Cadbury, 1847). They hit upon the idea of mixing sweetened condensed milk with chocolate and create a product that meets with immediate commercial success (*see* Peter and Kohler, 1904; Hershey, 1893).

Swiss confectioner Rodolphe Lindt at Bern (above) develops a technique for creating "fondant"— chocolate smoother than any heretofore known. He will tinker with his recipe (*see* 1879).

Cookbooks: *Cookery from Experience. A Practical Guide for Housekeepers in the Preparation of Every Day Meals . . . with Suggestions for Meals, Lists of Meats and Vegetables in Season, etc.* by U.S. author Sara T. Paul; *Breakfast, Luncheon and Tea* by Virginia novelist Marion Harland (Mary Virginia Terhune [*née* Hawes]), 44, who will have more success with her books on cookery and household management than with her novels.

British sugar consumption reaches 60 pounds per capita, up from 47 pounds in 1872 (*see* 1889).

The *New York Times* editorializes about Christmas turkey, saying, "If the lady of the household is ambitious, the bird is stuffed with oysters, and if she rules her husband she orders him to purchase the oysters and turkey himself. Almost all the good old gentlemen consider it part of the religion to go down to Fulton market, which is the aristocratic one." Christmas dinner generally begins with oyster soup and may include any of the many delicacies displayed at the Fulton and Washington markets: saddle of venison; hindquarters of bear meat; rice-fed Maryland turkey with black legs, wild turkey, woodcock, snipe, ruffed grouse, wild turkey; hare, rabbit, squirrel, raccoon; steak, joint of beef, chops; redhead, canvasback, or mallard duck; flounder, haddock, lobster, pickled salmon, smelts; vegetables of all kinds; imported and domestic cheeses; fruits such as cranberries, mandarin oranges from Louisiana, oranges from Florida and the West Indies, figs, Egyptian dates, and grapes; walnuts, hickory nuts, Italian chestnuts (preferred over American chestnuts for stuffing turkeys). Turkeys for sale in the outdoor market on Vesey Street may be cheaper but are not as likely to be fresh as those in the Washington Market, whose tradesmen are neatly dressed in starched white aprons and long blue gowns.

The U.S. Fish Commission plants Atlantic salmon in inland lakes. Land-locked salmon will be an important U.S. game fish and food fish (*see* shad, 1873; carp, 1879).

Illinois promoter John Warne Gates, 20, puts on a demonstration at San Antonio to show that barbed wire is safe and effective. He turns the main plaza of the town into a giant corral that can hold long-horned cattle (*see* Glidden, Haish, 1873). Barbed wire will begin the end of the open range in America and launch the career of "Bet-you-a-million" Gates (*see* 1877; 1898).

A Napa Valley, Calif., poultry dealer receives in July a consignment of six Pekin ducks—all that remain of a dozen secured for him in China by a brother-in-law (*see* 1874; 1882).

The first American state agricultural experiment station is established July 20 at Wesleyan University in Middletown, Conn.

Luther Burbank establishes a nursery at Santa Rosa, Calif., with money obtained from the sale of his 1872 Burbank potato. He will develop new forms of food and ornamental plant life by selection and cross-fertilization (*see* Shull, 1905).

Combines come into use on some U.S. wheat farms.

A Chinese orchardman in Oregon develops the Bing cherry.

Apples are grown for the first time in Washington's Yakima Valley.

Navel oranges are produced at Riverside, Calif., by Jonathan and Eliza C. Tibbetts, who 2 years ago obtained two trees from the USDA at Washington, D.C., which in 1871 received a dozen budded trees from Bahia, Brazil (*see* Saunders 1862). The seedless winter-ripening fruit are the first ever seen in the United States and will also be called Washington oranges (because the first trees came from Washington, D.C.) as they proliferate to dominate California groves (*see* Valencias, 1906).

A new British Sale of Food and Drugs Law tightens restrictions against adulteration, making any adulteration injurious to health punishable with a heavy fine and making a second offense punishable with imprisonment if the seller is proved to have guilty knowledge of the adulteration (*see* 1872). But adulteration continues (*see* pepper, 1891).

H. J. Heinz's firm Heinz & Noble is forced into bankruptcy after contracting to buy some crops that have come in more abundantly than expected, but Heinz pays off the firm's creditors with help from his wife (*see* 1869; ketchup, 1876).

English flour miller Joseph Rank begins a business at Hull that will grow to become the nation's largest milling enterprise. By 1914 it will own large mills in the docks of Hull, London, Barry, and Birkenhead (*see* Rank Hovis McDougall, 1962).

Barilla Alimentare Dolciaria S.p.A. has its beginnings in a retail shop opened at Parma by Italian baker Pietro Barilla, whose son Riccardo (born in 1880) will help him acquire a cast-iron press. By 1900, the firm will be producing two quintals (about 300 kilograms, or 441 pounds) of bread and pasta per day (*see* 1919).

Société Anonyme Lactée Henri Nestlé is founded at Vevey, Switzerland, in January by businessmen Jules Monnerat, 55, Samuel Roussy (Monnerat's nephew), Emil Louis Roussy, 33, and Gustave Marquis, who pay 1 million Swiss francs, outbidding Geneva bankers to acquire the operation which is selling hundreds of thousands of tins of baby food each year and is the town's foremost enterprise (*see* 1866). The bankers have offered nearly as much, but the Vevey businessmen offer more, providing

Nestlé and his wife with a splendid coach and a team of horses to sweeten their proposition, and they change the name March 8 to Farine Lactée Henri Nestlé (*see* 1890; milk chocolate, below).

Cadbury's opens a large factory outside Birmingham at a place it calls Bournville (to give it a French sound; the best chocolates still come from France).

B&M Baked Beans, produced for use by men in the fishing fleet of Burnham & Morill Co. at Portland, Maine, are the world's first canned baked beans (*see* 1867; 1927; Van Camp, 1862).

A British Trade Marks Act goes into effect; the first trademark registered is for Bass & Co. Pale Ale, made at Burton-on-Trent in Staffordshire since 1777.

The average British working-class family spends £15 to £20 per year on alcohol; some families spend a third or more of their income on drink.

French wine producers have their best vintage in history, despite encroachments in some areas by grape phylloxerae (*see* 1872; 1876).

U.S. tea imports reach 59 million pounds, up from 20 million in 1862, as import duties are removed.

Tea purchased by New York wholesalers had to pass muster with professional tasters. HARPER'S WEEKLY

Hires Rootbeer has its beginnings in a recipe for an herb tea discovered by Philadelphia pharmacist Charles Elmer Hires, 24, who takes his bride on a wedding trip to a New Jersey farm. The tea is made from 16 different wild roots and berries that include juniper, pipsissewa, spikenard, sarsaparilla, wintergreen, and hops. Hires takes the recipe back to Philadelphia and begins experimenting with improved formulas (*see* 1876).

New York Condensed Milk Co. begins selling fluid milk in addition to its condensed milk (*see* 1858; 1874; 1885).

A magnificent new Palmer House opens in Chicago to replace the hotel owned by merchant Potter Palmer that burned in the 1871 fire. The new hostelry has a lavish dining room with dishes that include broiled buffalo, antelope, bear, mountain sheep, boned quail in plumage, blackbirds, partridge, and other "ornamental dishes."

San Francisco's Palace Hotel opens October 2 with 755 20-by-20-foot rooms and a crystal roof over an inner court that includes a splendid dining room. Sen. William Sharon has completed the $5 million hotel begun by the late William Ralston, and it will long be the leading hotel on the West Coast, with meals prepared by chef Jules Harder, who has had 26 years' experience working at such leading kitchens as those of the Grand Union Hotel in Saratoga Springs, the Union Club in New York, and—for 10 years—Delmonico's.

Boston's Locke-Obers Restaurant, an outgrowth of Louis F. Ober's French Restaurant, opens at 3 and 4 Winter Place under the name Frank Locke's Winter Place Wine Rooms. The German silver domes (made by Reed & Barton) over the steam tables at the free-lunch bar have pulleys and counterweights that permit them to be raised with one hand while the other reaches for pigs' feet, poultry livers, and similar fare. Private rooms upstairs permit women to remove themselves from the alcohol and cigar smoke below; the downstairs rooms, with their leather-upholstered chairs, will be for men only until the 1970s, and the food served will be Boston's best for more than 80 years (*see* 1923).

1876

Famine will kill 9.6 million in northern China and 5 million in India in the next 3 years as drought withers wheat fields in China's Shansi province and on India's Deccan Plateau.

Antwerp grain merchant Ernest Bunge, son of Charles, emigrates to Buenos Aires and changes his name to Ernesto, leaving his brother Édouard to serve as broker and royal business associate to Léopold II, king of the Belgians (*see* 1850). Argentina's pampas are beginning to develop into a major wheat-producing area, and Ernesto, who has been accompanied by his brother-in-law Jorge (Georges) Born, aims to establish a trading monopoly in Argentine wheat, competing as Bunge y Born with the agents of Léopold Louis-Dreyfus (*see* 1870).

Argentina emerges as a grain-exporting nation (*see* meat, 1877).

A treaty negotiated by Hawaiian planter Henry Alpheus Pierce Carter, 39, places Hawaiian sugar on the free list for importation into the United States (*see* politics, 1891).

The Grange departs from its apolitical stance and begins to lobby for U.S. tax law revision, including an end to tax exemption for railroad properties (*see* 1873). The Grange also demands lower interest rates, better schools, cheap textbooks, and cheaper bread, coal, and clothing.

 Huntington Hartford's A&P grocery chain opens its 67th store (*see* 1871; 1880).

The first carload of California fruit reaches the Mississippi Valley, but the freight rate is too steep for most growers (*see* Columbian Exposition, 1893).

The *Train Bleu* makes its first run, connecting Calais and Rome by way of Nice three times per week with an all-sleeper train organized by Compagnie International des Wagons-Lits et des Grands Express Européens. Belgian engineer-founder Georges Nagelmakers, who crossed the United States in Pullman cars in 1871, ran some demonstration trains in 1873 between Paris and Vienna, Paris and Cologne, and Berlin and Ostend but must contend with the fact that most European railroads are operated by state monopolies and have customs tariffs at their borders. Nagelmakers has now signed up 21 nations and owns 58 sleeping cars, and his new company issues stock to the public to raise capital of 4 million Belgian francs. His *Train Bleu*, pulled by a boiler engine, its cars lighted by oil lamps and heated by briquettes, will connect Paris with the Riviera beginning in 1883, making the 700-mile run to Monte Carlo three times per week by way of

Dijon, Lyons, Marseilles, and Toulon, with passengers dressing for dinner and being served by footmen in blue satin knee breeches, white silk stockings, and elaborately braided tailcoats as they dine at tables provided with silver, bone china, and Belgian crystal. Nagelmakers demands the same standards from a restaurant-car chef as those that apply in fine hotel kitchens, and his cuisine (caviar, champagne, foie gras, saumon fumé, boeuf en gelée, sole Metternich, poulet en cocotte, dessert, cheese, and coffee) will match that of the best hotels in Paris (*see* Orient Express, 1883).

Canning becomes enormously more efficient with the introduction of the Howe "floater," which makes the tinsmith's soldering iron obsolete. A long line of cans, complete with tops and bottoms, floats slowly through the solder bath in the Howe machine, picking up enough melted solder to make tight joints and permitting two men and two helpers to turn out more than 1,000 cans per day, 100 times the number one man and a helper could make in the first half of the century. In another 10 years the same number of men will be able to produce 1,500 cans per day (*see* 1874; 1895; 1897).

Delaware canner A. B. Richardson applies for a patent on a new can shape and a new method for canning boneless hams but dies early in the year at age 50.

The first all-roller flour mill to be seen in America is displayed at the Philadelphia Centennial Exposition (International Exhibition of Arts, Manufactures and Products of the Soil and Mine) opened by President Grant at Fairmount Park but is dismantled after the fair (*see* Washburn, 1874; Pillsbury, 1878).

The Centennial Exposition at Philadelphia (above) has 20 exhibitors of candy-making machines. Rotary and revolving pans have replaced old copper cooking vessels and steam kettles, and candy making has become big business.

Seventh-Day Adventist surgeon John Harvey Kellogg, 24, assumes management of the Western Health Reform Institute founded at Battle Creek, Mich., in 1866. A champion of vegetarianism (which this year is embraced by Russian novelist Count Leo Tolstoy, 47), Kellogg will ask audiences, "How can you eat anything that looks out of eyes?" and he will develop vegetarian foods including a form of peanut butter and scores of dried cereals (*see* Granula, 1877).

 Bananas fetch 10¢ each at the Philadelphia fair. The foil-wrapped novelty gives most fairgoers their first taste of the tropical fruit (*see* Baker, 1871; Boston Fruit, 1885).

A colony of passenger pigeons in Michigan reportedly covers an area 28 miles long and three to four miles wide (*see* 1871; 1878).

The first successful U.S. sardine cannery is established by New York importer Julius Wolff, whose French sardine imports were interrupted by the Franco-Prussian War in 1871 (*see* 1834). Sardine canneries will soon open at Eastport, Lubec, and other points along the Maine coast.

Colorado cattleman Charles Goodnight, 40, settles one of the West's first sheepherder-cattlemen wars and heads back to Texas, where he discovers an enormous valley in the Palo Duro Canyon area where 10,000 bison are feeding near the Canadian River (*see* 1866). After having prospered as a Colorado Territory rancher, banker, and irrigation promoter, Goodnight was wiped out in the panic of 1873, but he has recovered with money made in cattle drives. He and his cowboys drive out the buffalo and establish the Old Home Ranch, the first in the Panhandle. Financed by Irish-American investor John G. Adair of Denver, Goodnight will develop the million-acre JA Ranch and the Goodnight-Adair partnership will net more than half a million dollars in 5 years.

Grape phylloxerae destroy more than half the standing vineyards in France's department of the Gard (*see* 1867) and begin to spread throughout the country with inadvertent help from the nation's growing network of railroad lines (*see* 1878).

California's vineyards begin to regain their former productivity thanks to efforts by Professor George Husmann—the first U.S. wine technician of any consequence—and Charles A. Whitmore, who have developed phylloxera-resistant roots on which not only all California wine grapes but also virtually all European wine grapes will now be grown (*see* 1868). Using cheap Chinese labor, California vintners clear land on steep slopes overlooking the

Napa, Sonoma, and Santa Clara valleys, plant vines, dig cellars back into the hills, and build big, cool, thick-walled stone wineries. By 1890 there will be 100 such vineyards within 60 miles of San Francisco Bay, but by 40 years later most of the vintner names will have disappeared.

Thompson Seedless grapes get their name from the Marysville, Calif., Horticultural Society, which is unaware of the variety's true origin and honors Yuba City, Calif., grower William Thompson. The grapes are actually an ancient Middle Eastern variety (Oval Kishmish, or Sultanina); Thompson purchased three cuttings in 1872 from the Rochester, N.Y., nursery firm Ellwanger and Barry, and he has exhibited fruit from his vines in the fall at the district fair in Marysville. The green table grapes will also be used for wine making and will be the most widely cultivated raisin variety (*see* Sun-Maid, 1912).

French immigrant David Garnot plants 50 hazelnut trees along a fence in Oregon (*see* 1858), but the nation will have no true hazelnut orchards until the turn of the century.

W. Atlee Burpee Co. is founded at Philadelphia by Canadian-American entrepreneur Washington Atlee Burpee, 18, who initially sells livestock by mail. He will enter the mail-order seed business in 1882 (*see* iceberg lettuce, 1894).

Philadelphia fairgoers (above) see bread and rolls raised with compressed yeast right before their eyes

Philadelphia fairgoers saw a Viennese baker demonstrate Fleischmann's Yeast.

at a model Viennese bakery set up by Gaff, Fleischmann and Co., which has invested all its resources in the display to spread the word about Fleischmann's Yeast (*see* 1870; 1919).

Heinz's Tomato Ketchup is introduced by Pittsburgh's H. J. Heinz, who has his first big success and joins with his brother and a cousin to establish F. and J. Heinz (*see* 1875). Heinz packs pickles and other foods as well as the ketchup, which is highly

It took Mr. Heinz years to decide whether he was making catsup or ketchup. PHOTO COURTESY HEINZ USA

sugared, and although other U.S. firms have been bottling tomato ketchup in small quantities commercially since the 1850s (*see* 1872), the Heinz brand, which is sold at the Philadelphia fair, will become far and away the industry leader (*see* vinegar, apple butter, 1880). Ketchup in Britain will continue to mean mushroom ketchup until well into the next century.

Lancaster, Pa., candy maker Milton Snaveley Hershey, 18, borrows $150 from a maternal aunt, trav-

els to Philadelphia, and opens a small shop in Spring Garden Street to sell the penny candy that he makes, but although he will remain there for 6 years his business will not prosper (*see* 1883).

Studies in Beer by Louis Pasteur is published (*see* 1871). The higher the temperature in drying of barley to produce malt, the darker the beer will be: the standard will be set at 170° F. for light beer, 190° F. for dark beer, and 250° F. for bock.

Budweiser beer wins top honors in a competition at the Philadelphia fair. The new beer has been developed by Adolphus Busch, whose E. Anheuser and Co. produces 15 other brands of beer, many of them pasteurized, and introduces refrigerated railcars for all its beers (*see* 1873; Michelob, 1896).

Budweiser would become the leading U.S. brand of beer and a big seller in Britain as well. PHOTO COURTESY ANHEUSER-BUSCH

Hires Rootbeer Household Extract is promoted at the fair with an exhibit displaying packages of dried roots, barks, and herbs (*see* 1875). Charles E. Hires has adopted the name "rootbeer" at the advice of his friend Russell Conwell, 33, who says hard-drinking Pennsylvania coal miners will be more attracted to "rootbeer" than to "herb tea" (*see* 1886).

The Beringer/Los Hermanos Winery is founded at St. Helena in California's Napa Valley by German-American vintners Jacob Bell and Frederick Beringer, who have acquired 600 acres to grow vines and employ Chinese workers to dig their cellars and German master carvers to produce the heads of their oak casks (*see* Nestlé, 1971).

The first Fred Harvey restaurant opens in the Santa Fe Railroad depot at Topeka, Kans. English-American restaurateur Frederick Henry Harvey, 41, who has been in the United States since 1850 and has worked as a freight solicitor for J. F. Joy's Chicago, Burlington & Quincy Railroad, has suffered from dyspepsia from eating at railroad lunchrooms. Joy has turned down his proposal that clean, well-run restaurants would attract passengers, but Harvey has approached Charles F. Morse, general manager of the Atchison, Topeka, and Santa Fe, who has been receptive to the idea. Topeka's Harvey House restaurant, opened with Morse's blessings, is soon followed by a more splendid establishment at Florence, Kans., which employs the chef from Chicago's Palmer House Hotel at $5,000 per year (he pays $1.50 per dozen for prairie hens, 75¢ per dozen for quail, 10¢ a pound for fresh creamery butter). More Harvey Houses will open along the Santa Fe line and at other major rail depots and junctions, Harvey will also operate hotels and a fleet of Santa Fe dining cars. By the time of his death in early 1901 there will be 47 Fred Harvey restaurants, all serving good food on Irish linen, with Sheffield silverware, served by well-trained "Harvey Girls," plus 30 Fred Harvey dining cars (*see* 1888) and 15 Fred Harvey hotels.

Lorenzo Delmonico sells his Fifth Avenue restaurant at 14th Street and moves farther uptown (*see* 1868). His new establishment, facing Madison Square at 26th Street, is even more elegant than any previous Delmonico's, but Lorenzo will die of a stroke in 1881. Ben Wenberg, 41, a local business-man who imports fruit from Cuba, comes into Delmonico's after a cruise and shows the proprietor a new way to cook terrapin or seafood, with sweet cream and butter, egg yolks, cognac, sherry, and cayenne pepper; this delights Lorenzo so much that he insists on calling the new dish seafood à la Wenberg, but either because Wenberg and Delmonico have a quarrel or because Wenberg objects to hearing his name used by so many people (accounts vary), the dish will be removed from the menu until it is reinstated (by popular demand) under the name Lobster Newberg (it will later be mistakenly called Lobster Newburg), and in the 1880s it will be the most popular lobster specialty at Coney Island's resort hotels, which will buy as much as 3,500 pounds of lobster per day (*see* Ranhofer, 1894; Delmonico's, 1897)

Cavanaugh's Restaurant opens as an oyster house at 258 West 23rd Street, New York. William Cavanaugh's establishment will develop a reputation for lobster, crabmeat, roast beef, filet mignon, and green-turtle steak.

The Sacher Hotel opens at Vienna with a restaurant that serves the Sachertorte invented in 1832.

The Tokyo restaurant Chikoyotei has its beginnings in a sake shop. It will later specialize in eel (*unagi*) dishes and will still be operating in 1995.

The Tokyo restaurant Ueno Saiyoken opens serving French cuisine. Proprietor Shigetake Kitamura worked for a government minister after the Meiji Restoration 9 years ago, saw the need for a hotel and restaurant catering to Western visitors, and opened such a place 4 years ago at Tsukiji. Ueno Saiyoken will become a gathering place for aristocrats, and the emperor's family will use it to entertain guests from foreign countries.

1877

Republican Rutherford Birchard Hayes, 54, of Ohio is sworn in as president of the United States March 4 following congressional resolution of last year's disputed election returns. Hayes's pious wife, Lucy (*née* Webb), the first college-educated First Lady, refuses to permit intoxicating beverages to be served at the White House table (critics ridicule her as "Lemonade Lucy"), but stewards at the executive mansion will find ways to avoid complying with her rules.

 Famine kills 4 million in Bengal (*see* 1873). British colonial authorities are unable to relieve the continuing starvation.

$ British butter prices fall to as little as 2 pence a pound, depressing demand for margarine (*see* 1871).

Swiss watch assembler's son Georges André, 21, comes down from his native mountain village of Sainte-Croix and starts a grain business at Nyon. Using funds advanced by his father, he buys Russian durum wheat, has it unloaded at Marseilles, ships it by rail to Switzerland, and undersells bread wheat produced by Swiss farmers (*see* Garnac, 1935).

Government regulation of U.S. business gains legal support from the Supreme Court March 1 in the case of *Munn v. Illinois*. The Court rejects Ira Munn's claim (*see* crime, 1872), and its landmark decision sustains the 1871 Illinois state law supervising grain elevators.

San Francisco "grain king" Isaac Friedlander files for bankruptcy (*see* 1852). Calling him "the money king as well as the grain king," the Grange has attacked Friedlander in its fight for regulation of railroads and grain warehouses. He has "used his power with such a merciless hand that farmers would receive no more for a large crop than for a small one," the Grange will claim after his death next year. "He had the wheat growers so completely under his control that even with larger crops, farmers were growing poorer, year by year." Backed by San Francisco bankers, Friedlander has developed a network of agents and intelligence sources to estimate the size of the California wheat crop, thus enabling him to charter the appropriate number of ships to transport it, but this year he has overchartered.

California land speculators James Ben Ali Haggin, 49, and Lloyd Tevis, 53, use political influence to have Congress pass a Desert Land Act offering land at 25¢ per acre to settlers who will agree to irrigate and cultivate the land for 3 years. Haggin and Tevis have acquired hundreds of thousands of acres by buying up old Spanish land grants, often of dubious value, and they acquire 96,000 acres in the San Joaquin Valley by hiring scores of vagabonds to enter false claims which they then transfer to themselves, ousting settlers who have not yet perfected their titles under old laws and have not heard about the new law. The Haggin-Tevis lands will become the basis of Kern County Land Co. (*see* 1890; Tenneco, 1961).

John Morrell & Co. takes over a slaughterhouse at Ottumwa, Iowa (*see* 1868). Morrell will build its own plant at Ottumwa next year and begin to challenge the big Chicago meatpackers (*see* AMK, 1967).

Barbed-wire prices drop from 18¢ a pound to 8¢ as the Bessemer steelmaking process of 1856 is applied to barbed-wire production. All barbed-wire patents were acquired last year by Washburn & Moen Co. of Worcester, Mass., and sales of barbed wire leap from last year's 840,000 pounds to 12.86 million pounds. A ton of barbed wire represents two miles of three-strand "devil's rope," and sales will climb to 26.7 million pounds next year, 50.3 million in 1879, 80.5 million in 1880, and 120 million in 1881 (*see* Gates, 1875, 1898).

Distillers Company Ltd. is created by a consolidation of six Scottish distilleries which begin a great whisky cartel. The syndicate will be joined in 1919 by John Haig, in 1924 by Robert Burnett, and in 1925 by Buchanan-Dewar's (Black & White, Dewar's White Label) and John Walker (Johnnie Walker Red Label and Black Label).

The Quaker Mill Co. begins operations at Ravenna, Ohio, making oatmeal with a process patented by William Heston (*see* Schumacher, 1875). Heston and his partner Henry D. Seymour register as a trademark the "figure of a man in Quaker garb," but their venture suffers for lack of business acumen and will soon be acquired by distiller Warren Corning, who will use the Quaker symbol on a brand of whiskey (*see* Quaker Oats, 1884, 1888).

New England Glass Works is founded by William Libbey and his son Edward, who take over a 59-year-old Boston firm for which they have been Chicago representatives. Edward Drummond Libbey will have labor troubles when his father dies in 1883, move to Toledo, and start Libbey Glass Co., concentrating on cheap blown tumblers (*see* Owens, 1895).

The Supreme Court upholds state power to fix freight rates for intrastate traffic and for interstate traffic originating within a state's borders March 1 in the case of *Peik v. Chicago and Northwestern Railroad Co.* But a later decision will limit state regulation to intrastate shipments, exempt the much larger volume of freight that crosses state lines, and weaken the farmers' victory in the *Peik* decision (*see* 1886; Interstate Commerce Act, 1887).

The first shipment of Chicago-dressed beef to reach Boston arrives in a railcar designed to prevent spoilage by meat packer Gustavus Franklin Swift, 38, who is determined to save the cost of transporting whole live animals. Swift's partner James Hathaway has sold his interest in the firm anticipating failure, but Swift, who moved from Boston to Chicago 2 years ago, has refused to be thwarted by the railroads that demand exorbitant rates to make up for lost tonnage. He uses a railroad that has not carried livestock shipments and steals a march on such Boston competitors as Reardon & Sons, Nelson Morris & Co., Hammond & Co., and John Cudahy (*see* 1881).

Argentina challenges Australia as a source of meat for Europe by sending its first refrigerator ship to France with a cargo of meat. The S.S. *Paraguay* employs an ammonia compression system devised by French engineer Charles Albert Abel Tellier, 49, but it is not entirely successful (*see* 1880; Linde, 1873).

Lard and beef fat from the fast-growing U.S. meat-packing industry begins arriving in the Netherlands, where it will be used to make margarine. Thousands of pounds are soon arriving each week (*see* Jurgens, 1871).

A centrifugal cream separator invented by Swedish engineer Carl Gustaf Patrik de Laval, 32, allows cream to rise to the surface of a bowl or pan, eliminating the need of space-consuming shallow pans and the labor of skimming the cream that rises to the top. It will prove a boon to dairy farmers and their wives, and, by reducing the cost of producing butter, the Laval separator will lead to a vast expansion of the Danish, Dutch, and Wisconsin butter industries (*see* hand separator, 1887).

Dodge County, Wis., farmer John Jossi invents brick cheese—a more elastic, slightly milder version of Limburger (*see* Liederkranz, 1892).

German country doctor Robert Koch, 33, of Wollstein demonstrates a technique for fixing and straining bacteria. Koch, who last year obtained a pure culture of the anthrax bacillus by using the eye of an ox as a sterile medium, will confirm Louis Pasteur's suggestion that every disease produced by microorganisms is produced by a specific bacillus (*see* anthrax vaccines, 1881; 1883).

English researchers A. Downes and T. P. Blunt discover the germicidal qualities of ultraviolet rays. Their findings will lead to new techniques for sterilization.

The Oneida Community introduces tableware that will be called Community Plate silver. Its Wallingford, Conn., branch has developed the silverware.

"Sole is certainly the most useful of all the fish to visit us in London," writes London chef-restaurateur August Kintner. "He is boiled, baked, and fried, but seldom stewed; and there is yet another mode of making his acquaintance—namely on the gridiron, which is almost peculiar to England. . . . The boiled sole of England is worthy of no less fame than the beef-steak and the mutton-chop."

The Halifax Fisheries Commission created by the Treaty of Washington in 1871 awards Britain $4.5 million for U.S. fishing rights in the North Atlantic November 23.

Congress establishes a U.S. Entomological Commission to control grasshoppers, which have been devastating western farms and rangelands.

New York State outlaws the representation of margarine as "butter," but the law will be widely ignored.

Granula is introduced at Battle Creek, Mich., by John Harvey Kellogg, who has created the cold cereal breakfast food by mixing wheat, oatmeal, and cornmeal and baking half-inch-thick biscuits, which he grinds up and sells at 12¢ per pound in one-, two-, and five-pound packages (*see* 1876; Jackson, 1863; Granola, 1881).

Anglo-Swiss Condensed Milk Co. enters the infant-cereal business, competing with Nestlé (*see* 1866).

Nestlé responds by producing its own condensed milk (*see* 1882).

1878

✗ Chile and Bolivia verge on war over the control of nitrate deposits, essential to world production of explosives and fertilizer. Bolivia boosts the export tax on nitrates being mined by Chilean Nitrate Co. in Antofagasta, the company appeals to the Chilean government, and Bolivia temporarily rescinds Chilean Nitrate's contract (*see* 1879).

The worst famine thus far in history kills at least 10 million Chinese and possibly twice that number (*see* Bengal, 1877); drought continues in much of Asia as it has since 1876.

The Bland-Allison Act passed by Congress February 28 makes the silver dollar legal tender and requires that the Treasury buy $2 million to $4 million worth of silver each month. Silver was discoved at Oro City (renamed Leadville this year) in Colorado 4 years ago, active prospecting began in the spring of last year (*see* restaurants, below).

Congress votes May 31 to reduce circulation of greenbacks; $346.7 million worth are in circulation, and by December 17 they have regained their face value for the first time since 1862.

Nearly 10,500 U.S. business firms fail as the economic depression that began in 1873 continues.

Venezuelan merchant George Wupperman, 26, takes over the U.S. agency for Angostura Bitters (*see* Siegert, 1818). Wupperman has married the daughter of a Hudson River steamboat fleet operator and emigrated to New York; when he dies in 1915, leaving eight grown children, his widow, Josephine, will assume management of the business.

Salt wells go into production in New York's Wyoming County as a high tariff encourages production.

A knotting device patented July 8 by George F. Appleby will be essential to perfecting the twine binder (*see* 1872). The firm of Gammon & Deering begins large-scale production 6 months later of Marsh harvesters equipped with the new twine binder (*see* 1879).

The first commercial milking machines are produced at Auburn, N.Y., by Albert Durant, who introduces a machine invented by L. O. Colvin.

Charles A. Pillsbury at Minneapolis installs steel rollers to replace millstones and thus multiplies the output of his flour mills (*see* 1871; Washburn, 1874; A Mill, 1880).

The 4-year-old Washburn Mill at Minneapolis explodes, killing 18 men, wrecking six mills, and destroying a roundhouse, a machine shop, and a factory (*see* 1871; Washburn, 1874). Cadwallader C. Washburn rushes to the scene, calls in his advisers, paces off the diminsions of a new mill, and announces that it will be the most modern flour mill ever built in America (*see* A mill, 1880).

Western Cold Storage Co. opens an ice-cooled cold store at Chicago (*see* 1887).

Libby, McNeill & Libby adopts the Morgan machine, which compresses beef into tins neatly and efficiently (*see* 1875). Libby has been been packing corned beef in tapered tins by hand (*see* 1890).

Beet sugar extraction mills are demonstrated at the Paris World Exhibition. Most European countries will be encouraged by the Paris exhibit to plant sugar beets and build factories (*see* 1811; 1880).

The Silvertown Refinery owned by London sugar magnate Henry Tate, now 59, introduces the world's first sugar cubes (*see* 1872).

The Hutchinson Bottle Stopper, patented by U.S. inventor Charles G. Hutchinson, is made of wire with a rubber washer, seals in the carbonation of effervescent drinks when pulled up tight, and when pushed in permits a beverage to be poured or swallowed from the bottle, but the rubber imparts a taste to the beverage (*see* Painter, 1892).

German physiologist Wilhelm Kuhne, 41, introduces the word "enzyme" to denote a complex organic substance whose catalytic action produces such chemical changes as digestion (*see* Payen and Persoz, 1833; Schwann, 1835; coenzymes, 1911).

Cookbook: *The Dinner Year-Book* by Marion Harland.

Opera: *H.M.S. Pinafore* 5/25 at London's Opera Comique, with music by Arthur S. Sullivan, 36, and lyrics by William S. Gilbert, 41, that include "Things are seldom what they seem./ Skim milk masquerades as cream."

 The last mass nesting of passenger pigeons is seen at Petoskey, Mich. (*see* 1871; 1914).

Alaska gets its first salmon cannery (*see* 1866; 1890; 1930).

The Matador Ranch is established in the southern Texas Panhandle by Chicago promoter Henry H. Campbell, who will be backed by Scottish financiers and will spread his holdings over most of the Panhandle and up into the Montana Territory (*see* Prairie Cattle Co., 1881).

Report on the Lands of the Arid Region of the United States by U.S. geologist John Wesley Powell, 44, points out that land west of the 96th meridian is arid, only a few areas of the Pacific Coast and the mountains receive as much as 20 inches of rain per year, an economy based on traditional patterns of farming is not possible under these circumstances, dry-land farming depends on irrigation, water rights in the West are more valuable than land titles and should be tied by law to each tract of land, only a small fraction of the land is irrigable, the Homestead Act of 1862 must be revised if it is to apply to western lands, western land policies must be geared to the region's climatic conditions, optimum irrigation will depend on large dams and canals financed and built under federal government leadership, and the best reservoir sites should be identified and reserved at the outset (*see* 1869).

English-born upstate New York agronomist Albert Norman Jones, 35, develops a hybrid stringless wax bean that will be known as the Jones Ivory Pod. It will be the parent of many stringless varieties (*see* sweet corn, 1879).

France's Parliament enacts legislation barring entry of foreign plants, roots, and leaves. U.S. plants are smuggled in, not only for grafting but also for planting in place of original grapevines, but grafting vines onto phylloxera-resistant U.S. rootstocks on a large scale becomes prohibitively expensive, and the new law (which will not be repealed until 1891) will lead to overproduction of low-quality wines in the Midi.

Grape phylloxerae are reported for the first time in Spain (they have already reached Italy earlier) and Burgundy (at Meursault) (*see* 1872). The phylloxerae will sharply reduce production of Palo Cortado grapes, and 85 percent of sherries will come to be made from Palomino grapes, which experts consider slightly inferior. Growers of Pinot Noir grapes can afford to fumigate and therefore resist grafting onto U.S. rootstocks, lest they compromise the flavor that has characterized their grapes, but growers of Gamay and other varieties graft without qualms (*see* 1901).

Downy mildew, brought in on U.S. vine wood, reduces the French wine-grape crop and weakens the wine produced.

A Weights and Measures Act passed by Parliament institutes new standards for the weight of a loaf of bread (*see* 1836; 1916).

Henry Maillard's "Celebrated Vanilla Chocolates and Breakfast Cocoa" are advertised in New York as being "sold by grocers everywhere." Maillard operates a "chocolate school" which gives free lessons to those who wish to know the correct way to make chocolate or cocoa.

The first roasted coffee to be packed in sealed cans is packed by Boston's 15-year-old Chase and Sanborn.

Hills Brothers Coffee has its beginnings at San Francisco as Maine-born merchants Austin H. and Reuben W. Hills start a coffee business in the public market. They will open a retail shop in 1882 under the name Arabian Coffee & Spice Mills but will quit the retail trade 2 years later to sell through other grocers (*see* 1900).

Travelers on the Rock Island Railroad find iced tea for sale (*see* 1871). Cookbooks begin offering recipes for iced tea (*see* 1904).

Baedeker's London and Its Environs lists Claridge's as the city's "first" hotel (*see* 1838). It has grown to encompass six houses, and William Claridge will sell it for £60,000 in 1881 (*see* 1894).

Denver has half a dozen restaurants offering *haute cuisine* to the town's new silver millionaires (*see* above); one restaurant, Carpiot's, is known as the

Delmonico's of the West. Georgetown, Colo., Tombstone, Ariz., and Virginia City, Nev., all have fine French restaurants.

1879

The War of the Pacific begins February 14 as Chilean troops occupy Antofagasta (*see* 1878). Bolivia proclaims a state of war, Peru refuses to guarantee neutrality, the United States is unsuccessful in its attempts at mediation, and Chilean forces proceed to occupy the entire Bolivian coast, whose nitrate deposits make it valuable (*see* 1884).

The Irish Land League is founded by nationalist Michael Davitt, 33, to campaign for independence from Britain.

Britain has her worst harvest of the century, crops fail throughout Europe, demand for U.S. wheat raises prices, and the high prices bring prosperity to U.S. farmers, who increase their wheat acreage as railroads build new lines to give farmers easier access to markets.

Ireland's potato crop fails again as in 1846 and the widespread hunger produces agrarian unrest (*see* Irish Land League, above).

India has a poor crop and much of the harvest is consumed by rats, which will plague many districts in the next 2 years and will always consume a significant portion of the nation's grain stores. Famine continues in China.

Germany's policy of free trade ends July 13 with a new protective tariff law. German industry has been depressed since the financial crisis of 1873 with its ensuing depression, and imports from foreign producers have hurt German agriculture.

Hedging of wheat stocks by trading in futures begins on the Chicago Board of Trade, which was established in 1865 (*see* Munn, 1872; Hutchinson, 1888; Norris, 1903).

Thomas Lipton's British grocery store chain makes him a millionaire at age 29 (*see* 1871). By the end of the century he will have more than 60 shops in London alone (*see* tea, 1890).

The perfected twine binder patented by George F. Appleby February 18 answers the objections of farmers to self-binders that use metal wire (*see* 1872; knotting device, 1878). Further refinements will produce a twine binder that will be used with various reapers through most of the 20th century.

McCormick's reaper sells for $1,500 in the United States, up from $150 in 1861, and there are complaints that the reaper is costlier at home than in Europe (*see* 1875; Northwest Alliance, 1880).

Hungarian engineers invited to America by C. C. Washburn of Washburn, Crosby County, install steel rollers in a new Minneapolis flour mill (*see* 1866; 1878; Gold Medal, 1880).

Saccharin (benzosulfamide) is discovered accidentally at Baltimore's new Johns Hopkins University by chemist Ira Remsen, 33, and his German student Constantin Fahlberg, who are investigating the reactions of a class of coal tar derivatives (toluene sulfamides). They will publish a scientific description of the new compound in February 1880 calling special attention to its sweetness. Fahlberg will file a patent claim without mentioning Remsen's contribution, return to Germany, obtain financial backing, and organize a company to produce his sugar substitute "saccharine"—at least 300 times sweeter than sugar and a boon to diabetics (*see* Wiley, 1907; sodium cyclamate, 1937).

Chocolate maker Rodolphe Lindt at Bern finds that by adding just the right amount of cocoa butter he can produce a rich chocolate that remains solid until it melted on the tongue (*see* 1875). He will continue to experiment with his manufacturing process until he discovers that the more he kneads and mixes his chocolate mass the smoother it becomes, and the smoother the mass the smoother the texture of the chocolate. Lindt will develop a process that will come to be called "conching," from the Spanish word *concha*, or shell, because that will be the shape of the earliest troughs used for the process. Lindt's smoother chocolate will give as much impetus to the consumption of eating chocolate as has the development of milk chocolate (*see* 1875), whose sales will come to dwarf those of stronger-tasting dark chocolate, especially in America (*see* 1899).

Russian pathologist Ivan Petrovich Pavlov, 30, shows with studies on dogs that the stomach produces gastric juices even without the introduction of food. Pavlov will proceed to develop the concept of acquired, or conditioned, reflex.

Cookbook: *The Cooking Manual* by Juliet Corson, head of the New York Cooking School, who says, "In no other land is there such a profusion of food, and certainly in none is so much wasted from sheer ignorance, and spoiled by bad cooking."

Buffalo hunters kill the last of the southern bison herd at Buffalo Springs, Tex., opening the area to beef cattle ranching.

The U.S. Fish Commission places carp in Wisconsin lakes (*see* shad, 1873; salmon, 1875). The common carp (*Cyprinus carpio*) lives up to 25 years in the wild (up to 40 in captivity), can survive in waters above 90° F., and can even withstand freezing for short periods, powers that will help it proliferate in U.S. inland waters, growing to weights of roughly 30 pounds and providing a new food source.

Agronomist Albert N. Jones develops a new variety of sweet corn that will be known as Amber Cream (*see* 1779; beans, 1878; wheat, 1886).

Wheatena whole-wheat cooked cereal is introduced by a small bakery owner in New York's Mulberry Street who grinds the wheat, sells it in labeled packages, and advertises it in newspapers to compete with oatmeal (*see* Quaker, 1877). The bakery and its Wheatena will be acquired in 1885 by an Akron, Ohio, physician named Fuller who operates a firm he calls Health Foods.

The first milk bottles appear at Brooklyn, N.Y., where the Echo Farms Dairy delivers milk in glass bottles instead of measuring it into the pitchers of housewives and serving maids from barrels carried in milk wagons. Some competitors will soon follow suit (*see* Borden, 1885) but Boston's Hood Dairy will not use bottles until 1897.

The Inglenook winery near Rutherford in California's Napa Valley is founded by Finnish seacaptain Gustave Niebaum (originally Nybom), who has made a fortune in the seal trade. He has studied viniculture and will produce varietal wines that include Chardonnay, White Pinot (Chenin Blanc), Traminer, Semillon, Cabernet Sauvignon, Pinot Noir, and Charbono—an Italian type. The economic depression that began in 1873 has driven bulk wine prices down to 10¢/gal. but Napa has continued to produce more wine than any other California county. By 1883, Niebaum will have cool, vaulted cellars built into the side of a hill with storage casks made from oak imported from Germany's Black Forest (*see* 1964).

Gage & Tollner's opens at Brooklyn, N.Y. The seafood house of restaurateurs Charles M. Gage and Eugene Tollner, which will move in 1892 to 374 Fulton Street, opposite Borough Hall, attracts New York notables, who cross the East River by ferry to enjoy oysters, clams, lobster bisque, crabmeat Virginia, scallops, lobster, terrapin, and other aquatic dishes. "Our Cooking Strictly to Order," the restaurant's menus will proclaim for more than a century.

The Chicago restaurant Schlogl's opens. It will become a gathering place for the city's literati.

The Rome restaurant Dassetto opens at via Zanardelli 14 near the Piazza Navona. It will gain a reputation for being the city's finest eating place, featuring Parma ham served with figs, lobster, quail, pheasant, tournedos Rossini, duck with oranges; and griglia al cartoccio (mullet rushed from the coast, cooked in a paper bag, and served with a sauce of capers, mushrooms, and ham) (from May to September).

1880

The Northwest Alliance has its beginnings in a local founded by Chicago editor Milton George, whose organization will become a leading political activist group among farmers (*see* Farmers' Alliance, 1882).

The word "boycott" enters the English language through an incident in Ireland's County Mayo. Tenant farmers organized by the Irish Land League refuse to harvest crops on estates managed by Charles Cunningham Boycott, 48, a retired British army captain. The Land League wages a campaign of economic and social ostracism against absentee landlords (*see* Parnell, 1881).

Tenant farmers work one-fourth of U.S. farms (which number just over 4 million).

 More than 95 A&P grocery stores are scattered across America from Boston to Milwaukee; the Great Atlantic & Pacific Tea Co. will not have a store on the West Coast for another 50 years (*see* 1869; 1876; 1912).

New York's Fulton Market is torn down and replaced (*see* 1822; 1907).

The first totally successful shipment of frozen beef and mutton from Australia to England arrives in early February as the S.S. *Strathleven* docks with 400 carcasses. The meat sells in London at 5½ pence/lb. and is soon followed by the first cargo of frozen mutton and lamb from New Zealand (*see* 1877). Imported products account for 17 percent of British meat consumption (the figure includes livestock and preserved meat, most of it salted, along with dried "Hamburg" beef and tinned, boiled mutton and beef from Australia, eaten in quantity despite its poor quality because it is half the price of fresh meat).

U.S. export of wheat and flour combined reach 175 million bushels, up from 50 million in 1871.

U.S. ice shipments to tropical ports reach a high of 890,364 tons carried by 1,735 ships, up from 146,000 tons aboard 363 ships in 1856. On long voyages 40 percent of the cargo may melt, but the remaining ice sells for as much as $56 per ton.

New England's ice crop fails due to an unseasonably warm winter, ice prices soar, and the high prices spur development of ice-making machines (*see* 1889).

A "history of the trade in tin" notes that Baltimore now produces 45 million one-pound cans of food per year.

Robert Koch discovers a vaccine against anthrax through the accident of an assistant (*see* 1881).

L'École de Cordon Bleu is founded at the Palais-Royal, Paris, by cooking teacher Marthe Distel, who takes a name derived from the blue ribbon worn by seniors at the school opened by Mme. de Maintenon in 1686 and undertakes to teach daughters of the bourgeoisie. The Grand Diplôme awarded by the new school to its best pupils will be the highest credential that a cook can have (*see* 1895).

Nonfiction: *A Tramp Abroad* by U.S. humorist Mark Twain (Samuel L. Clemens), 44, lists American dishes that the author has yearned for while in Europe: buckwheat cakes with maple syrup, squash, fried chicken, Sierra Nevada brook trout, Mississippi black bass, terrapin, coon, possum, soft-shelled crabs, wild turkey, canvasback duck, succotash, Boston baked beans, chitterlings, hominy, sliced tomatoes with sugar and vinegar, sweet corn, eight kinds of hot bread, fruit pies and cobblers, and porterhouse steak for breakfast.

Cookbooks: *First Principles of Household Management and Cookery; a Textbook for Schools and Families*, *The Appledore Cook Book; Containing Practical Receipts for Plain and Rich Cooking*, and *Miss Parloa's New Cook Book and Marketing Guide* by Boston cooking school director Maria Parloa, 37, whose latter book lists 93 "essential" utensils for the kitchen, including an apple corer, darning needle, melon mold, jagging iron, whip churn, squash strainer, and 44 different pots and pans. Parloa, who writes for an affluent readership, says that a dinner for 12 need cost no more than $25— this at a time when a semiskilled worker is lucky to earn $10 per week and unskilled workers make about $1 per day. Her menus for dinner guests almost never list pork or ham, which are generally disdained as meat for the poorer classes.

 Painting: *5 o'Clock Tea* by émigrée U.S. painter Mary Cassatt, 36.

Nearly one out of every four urban American households employs at least one domestic servant, but only upper-class families can afford cooks skilled in French cuisine. The cookery in middle- and lower-middle-class homes follows traditional Anglo-Saxon American or ethnic recipes, with wide use of scalloped dishes and gravies.

 Cattle drives up the Chisholm Trail reach their peak (*see* 1871; railroad, 1885).

U.S. wheat production reaches 500 million bushels, up 221 percent over 1866 figures. Eighty percent of the wheat is cut by machine, but wheat prices have dropped 27 percent since 1866.

Sacramento Valley, Calif., wheat grower Hugh Glenn harvests 1 million bushels (*see* 1865). He has 1,000 men working for him, and they use enormous steam-powered combines to harvest 100 acres per day for as little as 25¢/acre.

Steam plows and combines helped a relative handful of Californians farm thousands of acres each. LIBRARY OF CONGRESS

U.S. corn production reaches 1.5 billion bushels, up 98 percent over 1866 figures, and corn exports total 116 million bushels, but corn prices have dropped 15 percent since 1866. While many in Europe go hungry, Midwestern farmers burn corn for fuel; prices are too low to warrant shipping the crop to market.

Sugar beets are raised on a commercial scale for the first time in the United States (*see* Paris World Exhibition, 1878), domestic cane and beet production meets only 10 percent of U.S. sugar needs, and less than 0.05 percent of this will come from beets until the end of the 1880s. Another 19 percent will come from the territories of Hawaii, Puerto Rico, and the Philippines, but sugar imported from Cuba, Germany, and Java accounts for 71 percent of U.S. sugar consumption (*see* Spreckels, 1883; Havemeyer, 1887).

The Japanese government establishes a law making it a criminal offense to sell food or drink that is hazardous to health (*see* 1873).

The Pillsbury A mill goes up at Minneapolis and will be the largest flour mill in the world (*see* 1878; 1889).

Washburn, Crosby Co. of Minneapolis prepares to market Gold Medal Flour after winning a gold, a silver, and a bronze medal for flour samples it has entered in the Miller's International Exhibition. It stencils the words "Gold Medal" on the heads of the 196-pound barrels that serve as flour dispensers in grocery stores (*see* 1879; 1905).

Washburn, Crosby's Gold Medal Flour went into home-baked bread, biscuits, and cakes everywhere.

Thomas's English Muffins are introduced in New York by English-American baker Samuel Bath Thomas, who opens a retail bakery in 20th Street between 9th and 10th avenues and delivers to hotels and restaurants by pushcart.

"Philadelphia" brand cream cheese is introduced by a New York distributor named Reynolds, who has it made for him by Empire Cheese Co. of South Edmeston, N.Y. (*see* Pommel, 1872). William E. Lawrence and Son of Chester, N.Y., in Orange County originated the concept of a packaged, rectangular cream cheese, and by 1906 they will be producing Neufchâtel cream cheese in large volume (*see* Philadelphia brand, 1900).

R. T. French Co. has its beginnings as New York entrepreneur Robert Timothy French goes into partnership with his eldest son, George J., to operate Jackson Spice Co., grinders and packers of spices. The Frenches will merge in 1883 with a Fairport, N.Y., baking powder firm and relocate their operations to Fairport before moving in 1885 to Rochester, N.Y. (*see* mustard, 1904).

Heinz's White Vinegar, Apple Cider Vinegar, Apple Butter, and mincemeat preserve and jelly are introduced by Pittsburgh's F. and J. Heinz (*see* 1876; 1886).

Pistachio nuts become available for the first time in the United States (date approximate) but the nuts, a relative of cashews, will not become widely popular until they are sold in vending machines in the 1930s.

The Paul Masson winery is founded on a hill outside Saratoga in California's Santa Clara Valley by vintner Masson, a son-in-law of Charles Lefranc (*see* 1852). Masson will have made California wines for 58 years before retiring in 1901.

California's Del Monte Hotel on the Monterey Peninsula is opened by Central Pacific Railroad boss Charles Crocker, 58, whose $325,000 structure accommodates 750 and will rival the finest resort hotels in the East. Guests enjoy melons, vegetables, fruits, and grapes grown in the hotel's gardens or brought down from San Francisco, and fresh flounder, pompano, rock cod, salmon, and sole from the Bay is served daily (*see* Oakland Preserving Co.'s "Del Monte" label, 1891).

The New Orleans restaurant Commander Palace opens in what has been a private house at 1403 Washington Avenue, corner of Coliseum Street, part of what once was the J. F. E. Livaudais Plantation in what is now the city's Garden District. By the turn of the century, Emile Commander's establishment will rival that of the late Antoine Alciatore in gastronomic appeal (*see* 1974; Antoine's, 1871).

Delmonico's at New York has a dinner for 30 in honor of Civil War hero Gen. Winfield Scott Hancock, who will soon be the Democratic party's presidential candidate. Guests begin with raw oysters, have their choice of two soups, and, after hors d'oeuvres, enjoy a fish course, relèves, entrées that includes saddle of lamb, filet of beef, chicken wings with green peas, lamb chops garnished with beans and mushroom-stuffed artichokes, terrapin en casserole à la Maryland, sorbet, roast (meaning canvasback ducks and quails), and desserts that

include timbale Madison, banana mousse, ice creams, whipped creams, jelly dishes, pastry, fruit, petits fours, coffee, and liqueurs. Everything but the canvasback duck has been prepared in the French fashion and thus labeled.

Delmonico's chef Charles Ranhofer follows the dinner for Gen. Hancock (above) 3 months later with a much larger one to honor Suez Canal builder Ferdinand de Lesseps, now 74. He covers his pâté de foie gras with truffles and puts truffles into his timbales, his entrées are all French dishes, and his desserts include exotic fruit dishes.

P. J. Clarke's opens in New York at the northeast corner of Third Avenue and 55th Street, where the saloon will continue for well over a century (*see* 1945 film *The Lost Weekend*).

The Paris restaurant Drouant opens in the Place Gaillon, near the Opéra, where it will establish a reputation for its pâté of woodcock en croute, roasted turbot with sorrel and other fish, gratin of lobster Joinville, oursins, shrimps, cockles, clams, mussels, lobster, oysters, gigot de sept heures (leg of lamb that takes 7 hours to prepare), chicken in a pie crust stuffed with peaches, paupiette of chicken with morels and cream, and civet of baby boar with chestnut purée, all served on white Limoges porcelain, often in *salons particuliers*. Beginning in 1905, the 10 members of the Académie Goncourt will meet at a round table under crystal chandeliers in Salon 15 on the third floor for lunch on the first Tuesday of each month to discuss the merits of new books, and at its December lunch (November beginning in 1959) will award the coveted Goncourt prize for the year's best novel.

The Paris restaurant De La Tour d'Argent begins serving canard à presse, or caneton au sang, perfected by Frédéric Belair (*see* 1582). Its thighs are severed from the body of a roast duck to be grilled and flambéed while the carved breast and wings are set on an alcohol burner and the rest of the carcass put under a giant silver press, which squeezes its inherent juices into a rich sauce (*see* 1890).

The Tokyo restaurant Imaasa opens in Shinbashi serving sukiyaki and shabu-shabu, always made with Matsuzaka beef from 3-year-old cows, to businessmen in the district. It will still be operating in 1995.

A Chinese Exclusion Treaty signed at Beijing November 17 gives Washington power to "regulate, limit, or suspend" entry of Chinese laborers into the United States. The treaty will be ratified by the U.S. Senate and will take effect in 1882 (*see* seafood, 1882).

1881

Irish Nationalist leader Charles Stewart Parnell, 35, agitates for home rule and is imprisoned on charges of obstructing operation of a new land policy. From prison Parnell directs tenant farmers to pay no rent, thus enhancing his power (*see* Boycott, 1880).

Chicago meat packer Gustavus F. Swift perfects a refrigerator car to take Chicago-dressed meat to eastern butchers (*see* 1877). Sides of meat hang from overhead rails inside the car, and when the car reaches its destination the rails are hooked up with rails inside the customer's cold storage building, making it easy to slide the meat from railcar to cold store without loss of time or change of temperature. The efficiency of Swift's system, beginning with a disassembly line from the moment of slaughter to the butchering of carcasses into primal sections, will lower the price of meat in New York, New England, and down the Atlantic seaboard.

The first U.S.-made margarine is produced in a West 48th Street, New York, factory by Community Manufacturing Co., a subsidiary of the U.S. Dairy Co. (*see* 1874; 1886).

The first British cold store opens at London, which soon begins to receive shipments of chilled beef from America. When it is discovered that meat kept at 30° F. maintains its quality better than meat preserved with early freezing methods, U.S. meat will begin a domination of British markets that will continue for more than 25 years (*see* 1877).

Louis Pasteur finds a vaccine to prevent anthrax in sheep and hogs (*see* 1861; Koch, 1883).

Nonfiction: *Culture and Cooking* by Catherine Owen, who writes, "Talleyrand said England was a country with twenty-four religions and only one sauce. He might have said two sauces and he would have been literally right as regards both England and America. Everything is served with brown sauce or white sauce. And how often the white sauce is like bookbinder's paste, the brown a bitter, tasteless brown mess."

A report shows that the average Briton's expenditure for meat is higher than for bread, with average per capita meat consumption estimated at 1.75 pound per week, but Irish music and drama critic George Bernard Shaw, 25, embraces vegetarianism. "A man of my spiritual intensity does not eat corpses," he will later say, and he will claim to be "seldom less than ten times as well as an ordinary carcass eater."

Britons spend more on "luxuries" such as sugar, tea, and butter than on potatoes.

William Underwood & Co. of Boston puts up a sardine factory at West Jonesport, Maine. Underwood has been packing lobster, clams, mackerel, and chowders since 1846 at plants in West Jonesport and Southwest Harbor (*see* red devil, 1870). It will fry the sardines in oil and pack them under French names (*see* Wolff, 1876; Rogers, 1903).

Cattle ranges in the U.S. Southwest wither in a severe drought, but cattle raising remains profitable.

The Prairie Cattle Co. of Edinburgh, Scotland, declares a 28 percent dividend. The company buys out Texas Panhandle rancher George W. Littlefield, 39, whose LIT squatter ranch claims no land rights but who receives more than $125,000 (*see* 1882).

The Texas state capitol burns down at Austin; legislators demand the biggest capitol building in the country, with a dome at least one foot higher than the one in Washington. They arrange with a group of Chicago contractors and financiers to build the new capitol, and they trade 3 million acres of Panhandle prairie to the Chicago syndicate. Chicago dry goods merchant John Villiers Farwell, 56, and his brother Charles Benjamin, 58 (a U.S. congressman), form the Capitol Freehold Land and Investment Co., wind 800 miles of barbed wire around their holdings, and the XIT Ranch they establish is the largest in the Panhandle. It will soon be driving 12,000 head per year from its 200-mile Texas range 1,200 miles up the Montana Trail to the leased XIT range in the Montana Territory, the last great cattle drives from Texas.

1881

An International Phylloxera Conference at Bordeaux hears heated debates between "sulfurists," who favor fumigation of vineyard soil, and "Americanist" grafters, who favor reviving vineyards with phylloxera-resistant U.S. rootstocks (*see* 1878), but laborious breeding programs will be needed for scientists to develop rootstocks compatible with different soils, and where the old vines bore fruit for 70 to 80 years, the new, grafted vines will rarely last even 40 (*see* Munson, Bordeaux mixture, 1882; champagne, 1901).

California imposes quarantine regulations to keep out insect pests and plant diseases.

The loganberry, introduced by Santa Cruz, Calif., judge James Harvey Logan, is a cross of the red raspberry with a California wild blackberry. The University of California will make loganberry seeds available to the public in 1883 (*see* Boysen, 1920).

German physician Karl von Voit at Munich suggests that a man requires 118 grams of protein per day, 500 grams of carbohydrate, and 56 grams of fat for a total of what will later be reckoned as 3,055 kilocalories (*see* Moleschott, 1859; Atwater, 1902).

The first U.S. pure food laws are passed by New York, New Jersey, Michigan, and Illinois (*see* 1904).

Jumbo Rolled Oats, introduced by Akron, Ohio, oatmeal king Ferdinand Schumacher, save him money, give him an advantage over competitors who have copied his steel-cut method, and permit a housewife using a double boiler to prepare breakfast in 1 hour—less than half the time needed for steel-cut oats and at less expense (*see* 1875; 1886).

J. H. Kellogg adopts Granola as a new name for his cold breakfast food (*see* 1877). He has been sued for using the name Granula by the Dansville, N.Y., originators of that name (*see* peanut butter, 1890; Granose, 1895).

Rowntree & Co. at York begins production of fruit-flavored crystallized gumdrops and boxed chocolates (heretofore a French specialty), supplementing its line of Superior Rock Cocoa and Homeopathic Cocoa to satisfy the growing British taste for sweets (*see* 1862). Henry Rowntree will die in 1883 at age 45, and his brother Joseph will sell control of the business (*see* Elect Cocoa, 1887).

William H. Luden is incorporated at Reading, Pa., to make confectionery and amber-colored cough drops (*see* Fifth Avenue candy bar, 1936).

California's Italian Swiss Colony winery begins production at Asti in the Russian River Valley, where Andrea Sbarbaro has founded a communal refuge for San Francisco's unemployed and needy Italian Swiss. The commune will not prosper, but Sbarbaro will turn it into a private company.

New York restaurateur Lorenzo Delmonico dies at Sharon Springs, N.Y., September 3 at age 68.

1882

Charles Stewart Parnell and his associates are released from Ireland's Kilmainham Prison May 2 after agreeing to stop boycotting landowners, cooperate with the Liberal party, and stop inciting Irishmen to intimidate tenant farmers from cooperating with landlords (*see* 1880; 1881).

Crop failures in southern Japan bring widespread starvation. Recruiting agents sent by planters persuade peasants to emigrate to Hawaii's sugar fields; 100,000 Japanese workers and their families will move in the next 30 years.

Germany will assume leadership of European industry in the next two decades, but the Germans will attempt to maintain self-sufficiency in food production where the British have not. Germany will plant another 2 million acres to food crops and use high tariffs to protect her farmers from foreign competition even though such a policy means keeping domestic food prices high.

Electricity illuminates parts of London beginning January 12; incandescent bulbs go on in at least 30 buildings between Holborn Circus and the Old Bailey. Electricity illuminates parts of New York beginning September 4 as inventor Thomas Alva Edison, 35, throws a switch in the offices of financier J. P. (John Pierpont) Morgan, 45. Electric streetlights will encourage patronage of restaurants and greatly expand urban night life throughout the world.

The wire "Lightning" seal patented by a U.S. inventor clamps down a glass lid (*see* Mason, 1858; Ball Brothers, 1887).

A botanist in Jamaica divides cacao trees into two basic classes, Criollo and Forastero (Trinitario, a cross between the two, and other hybrids will dominate production in some countries). Criollo trees, the same kind that grew in Aztec times, produce cocoa that is generally regarded as superior in flavor, but Criollos are susceptible to disease and a century hence will account for only a negligible part of the world crop. Forastero trees, cultivated in Brazil and Ecuador since the 18th century, are hardier; they yield beans that have a higher fat content and a stronger flavor but must be fermented for several days before they can be used.

German bacteriologist Friedrich August Johannes Löffler, 30, at Berlin's Friedrich Wilhelm Institute discovers the bacilli that produce swine fever (hog cholera), swine erysipelas, and glanders (another livestock disease).

Japan's first Western-style cooking school opens at Tokyo for the instruction of women, who learn how to handle frying pans, measuring cups, and other Western kitchen tools.

Tokyo has 116 bakeries, producing French- and English-style loaves as well as sweet buns, but bread is regarded very much like cake; rice remains the staple.

The loss of cheap Chinese labor spurs development of machinery to clean and bone fish in California's salmon canneries as the 1880 Chinese Exclusion Act takes effect, barring entry of Chinese laborers for a period of 10 years (*see* 1866; 1895; Smith, 1903).

Pekin duck breeders are advertised at $5 per pair in Kansas, Indiana, and Ohio in October (*see* 1875). Duck farms spring up across the country, but Long Island remains the center of the industry (*see* 1888).

Drought continues on western U.S. ranch lands.

Edinburgh's Prairie Cattle Co. pays $350,000 to acquire the Quarter Circle T Ranch of Texas Panhandle rancher Thomas Bugbee, who 6 years ago drove a small herd from Kansas to the Canadian River and established the ranch (*see* 1881; 1884).

The Farmers' Alliance claims 100,000 members in eight state alliances and 200 local alliances. The Alliance is now headed by Milton George (*see* 1880; 1889).

The hybrid Müller-Thurgau grape variety developed by Swiss ampelographer Hermann Müller, 32, from Thurgau will come to be the most widely planted grape in German vineyards (it will also be known as the *Rivaner*).

U.S. hybridizer Thomas Volney Munson, 38, helps the French reestablish their vineyards in the wake of the grape phylloxera disaster (*see* 1881). He will be awarded the Légion d'Honneur in 1888.

Bordeaux mixture, invented by French botanist Pierre M. Alexis Millardet, 46, is a solution of copper sulfate, lime, and water which stains everything it touches a brilliant blue but effectively combats the fungus diseases attacking French vineyards and will prove effective against potato blight (*see* 1847). It will help revive the French wine industry (*see* consumer protection, below).

Fraudulent "French" wines, made from raisins imported chiefly from Greece and Turkey, will flood the French, British, and U.S. markets in this decade as grape phylloxera continues to ruin vineyards; French wine production will fall by almost half, and wines previously considered suitable only for vinegar or distillation will find ready buyers (France's raisin imports, mostly through Marseilles and Sète, will rise in this decade to 1 million tons per year, up from a few thousand before the grape phylloxera disaster; *see* 1890). Some of the wines will have bogus Bordeaux or Burgundy labels and will even be labeled "first growth."

"The evidence regarding the adulteration of food indicates that they are largely of the nature of frauds upon the consumer . . . and injure both the health and morals of the people," reports a U.S. congressional committee. The practice of fraudulent substitution "has become universal," the committee says, and it issues a list of people who have died from eating foods and using drugs adulterated with poisonous substances (*see* 1889).

Van Camp Packing Co. is incorporated and packs 6 million cans of pork and beans per year for shipment to Europe as well as to many U.S. markets (*see* 1861; 1894).

Nashville, Tenn., wholesale grocer Joel Cheek quits his firm to devote full time to developing a coffee blend (*see* Maxwell House, 1886).

Red Star Yeast has its beginnings in the Meadow Springs Distillery, founded at Milwaukee in December by three German-American businessmen. By 1886 they will be producing yeast at the rate of 203,130 pounds per year and selling it under various brand names, all of which will soon be of secondary importance to the Red Star brand (*see* 1919).

Toronto baker George Weston establishes an enterprise that will grow to become an international food-processing and -retailing empire.

Anglo-Swiss Condensed Milk Co. boss George Page decides to buy a plant at Middletown, N.Y., from the Orange County Milk Association and begin operations in America (*see* 1877; Nestlé merger, 1905).

Lüchow's restaurant opens at 110 East 14th Street, New York. German restaurateur August Lüchow has obtained help from piano maker William Steinway, 47, to buy a small beer hall that he will expand by acquiring a livery stable, a museum, and other adjacent structures. Songwriter Harry von Tilzer will write "Down Where the Würzburger Flows" at one of his tables, he will pay Victor Herbert to conduct a Viennese string ensemble on the premises for nearly 4 years, and when Lüchow dies a bachelor in 1926 he will leave the gigantic eating place (accommodating nearly 1,000 diners) to the Eckstein family, whose staff will continue serving such delicacies as smoked freshwater eel, *pfifferling* (wild Black Forest mushrooms), homemade head cheese vinaigrette, *bauernwurst*, knackwurst, bratwurst, *leberwurst*, *blutwurst*, *schwarzwälder pfifferlinge* (Black Forest mushrooms), *huhn und topf* (boiled chicken served in its own broth with carrots, celery, onions, turnips, noodles, and marrow balls), *gespickter hasenrücken* (larded saddle of Canadian hare with sour cream sauce, red cabbage, and *spätzle*), and *preiselbeeren pfannkuchen* (a giant pancake prepared at the table with cinnamon and sugar, sprinkled with lemon juice, and spread with a thick layer of Swedish lingonberries) (*see* 1933).

Chinese restaurants are now to be found in virtually all major U.S. cities and many smaller cities, often being the best places in town to eat; the Chinese Exclusion Act of 1880, which takes effect this year, will have little effect on these restaurants (the new law excludes laborers but permits entry of merchants, students, teachers, and temporary visitors; *see* California agriculture, 1884).

The Treaty of Ancon October 20 ends the war among Chile, Peru, and Bolivia over the nitrate-rich Atacama Desert. Chile gains territory at Peru's expense (*see* 1879; 1884).

The Liverpool Corn Trade Association authorizes trading of grain futures, permitting purchase and sale of contracts for grain to be delivered months later (*see* Chicago, 1865). Grain traders can reduce their risks through arbitrage—selling grain at a profit for future delivery at the same time that they buy it from farmers.

Claus Spreckels of San Francisco gains a monopoly on West Coast sugar refining and marketing (*see* 1868; 1880). He has obtained a large concession of land in the Sandwich (Hawaiian) Islands to keep his big refinery supplied with cane and also uses some sugar beets, having established sugar beet farms near Salinas (*see* politics, 1891).

B. H. Kroger Co. has its beginnings in a Cincinnati grocery store opened by local grocery salesman Bernard H. Kroger, 23, whose 17-foot-front store is called the Great Western Tea Company. He has put up $372 in capital, a partner has put up $350, and Kroger buys out the partner by year's end for $1,550. He will have four stores by mid-1885, and his company will grow to have more than 1,250 stores in 20 states.

The *Express d'Orient* (Orient Express), which leaves for Constantinople October 4 from the Gare de l'Est, Paris, is Europe's first transcontinental train (*see Train Bleu*, 1876). Designed for Georges Nagelmakers and his Compagnie Internationale des Wagons-Lits et des Grands Express Européens, it has two sleeping cars, an elaborate restaurant car (which serves specialties of the countries through which the train passes), and a baggage car containing a lavish kitchen. By the turn of the century, the company will be operating wagons-lits on the *Flèche d'Or* (Golden Arrow) between London and Paris, the *Rome Express*, *Simplon Express*, *Nord Express*, an express between Paris and St. Petersburg, the

Lombardy Express, Italy and Riviera Express, Arlberg Express, Iberia Express (between Paris and Madrid), and *Lusitania Express* (between Madrid and Lisbon). It will also be running wagon-lit trains between Douala and Yaoundé in the Cameroons, between Casablanca and Ouijda, and between Oran and Algiers in North Africa, between Abidjan and Ouagadougou in West Africa, between Pointe-Noire and Brazzaville in French Equatorial Africa, and between Elisabethville and Gilolo in the Congo, most of them with restaurant cars serving the finest cuisine in the grand manner.

An Owasco, N.Y., cannery installs the first successful pea-podder machine, replacing 600 workers (*see* pea viner, 1889).

English-American inventor William Horlick, 37, produces the first "malted milk" (he will coin the term in 1886) at Racine, Wis. He has combined dried whole milk with extract of wheat and malted barley in powder and tablet form, and his "diastoid" is the first dried whole milk that will keep (*see* evaporated milk, 1885).

Robert Koch develops a preventive inoculation against anthrax (*see* Pasteur, 1881).

Cookbook: *The Cottage Kitchen: A Collection of Practical and Inexpensive Receipts* by Marion Harland.

Some 40,000 tons of Jurgens Dutch margarine are shipped to Britain, which imports most of her margarine and butter. Such imports increase to about 120,000 tons, up from 60,000 to 70,000 in 1873, with the margarine going mostly to poor, working-class Britons, who cannot begin to afford the price of butter (*see* 1871; van den Bergh, 1895).

"No other country on earth offers more of everything needed to make a good meal, or offers it more cheaply, than Australia," writes French journalist Edmond-Marin La Avislée, but, he adds, "there is no other country, either, where the cuisine is more elementary, not to say abominable." Australian factories since the 1870s have been making Rosella tomato sauce, Arnott's biscuits, Ixol jams, and MacRobertson's chocolates.

Drought strikes the northern plains states. Railroad builder James J. Hill, 44, who is pushing his Great Northern track across the plains, urges diversified farming. He buys 600 purebred bulls, distributes them among the farmers in the region, and offers prizes for the best cattle produced.

Buffalo-born widow Harriet W. R. Strong, 39, inherits 20 acres of semiarid land in southern California after the suicide of her husband, who has lost the family fortune in a silver-mining venture. She studies crops that have done well, plants walnut trees, and when drought threatens to ruin her first harvest she will design and patent a system of flood control/storage dams to regulate water flow and ensure safety in case of a break. Engineers from as far away as Central America will adopt her ideas, she will pioneer in winter irrigation, her walnut orchard will become the largest in the world, extending for 25 miles, and she will grow citrus fruits and pomegranates as well.

Purdue University chemistry professor Harvey Washington Wiley, 39, gains appointment as chief of the Division of Chemistry in the U.S. Department of Agriculture (*see* "Poison Squad," 1902).

ConAgra, Inc., has its beginnings at Grand Island, Nebr., where German-born miller Henry Glade, 39, buys the State Central Flouring Mill built in 1867 by Germans Henry Koenig and Frederick Wiebe. Glade, who learned the trade at Dubuque, Iowa, and was managing a mill by age 14, promptly razes the mill and replaces it with a new steam-powered steel roller mill employing six men and having a daily capacity of 100 barrels, each containing 196 pounds of flour (*see* 1910).

White Lily Foods Co. has its beginnings in a document signed at Knoxville, Tenn., July 16 by local feed and seed broker J. Allen Smith, 33, originally from Georgia, who agrees to take over the Knoxville City Mills, headed by Jasper Lillie. Its 85-horsepower, four-millstone, steam-driven mill shut down 3 years ago, leaving the area without its chief source of baking flour, but Smith restarts the mill, produces a flour with a finer particle size that makes it ideal for the beaten biscuits eaten by southern families at every meal, and in 1885 will complete a new, large-capacity roller mill which carries the wheat and bran through seven sets of steel roller presses (*see* 1904).

The A. Goodman bakery established at Philadelphia in 1865 moves to Manhattan, where Goodman and his sons will manufacture matzohs, noodles, spaghetti, and dehydrated soups until 1946, when operations will be moved to larger premises in Long Island City.

Oscar Mayer wieners have their beginnings in a Chicago retail shop opened to sell fresh and cured meats. German-American butcher Oscar F. Mayer, 23, who has been in America since 1873 and in Chicago since 1876, operates the North Side shop in Sedgewick Street in partnership with his brother Gottfried, who has apprenticed in the art of sausage making and ham curing in Bavaria, and his brother Max. (Ham and sausage are preserved and given their reddish color by soaking them in a brine containing saltpeter—potassium nitrate or sodium nitrate.) Young Oscar will put his name on his meats, and by 1904 will have eight salesmen selling his sausages to grocers throughout Chicago and elsewhere in northern Illinois and southern Wisconsin (*see* 1929).

Candy maker Milton S. Hershey, now 25, comes to New York, works for another candy maker, and then opens a small caramel factory on Sixth Avenue between 42nd and 43rd streets. He has learned a new technique for caramel making (*see* 1876; 1886).

Copenhagen's Carlsberg brewery introduces the first absolutely pure brewers' yeast culture. Carl Jacobsen, Carlsberg's owner, has backed Danish biochemist Emil Christian Hansen, 41, in his experiments to free yeast from bacteria. Yeast propagated from a single selected cell will eliminate brewing failures, a fact recognized by Schlitz brewery head William J. Uihlein at Milwaukee (*see* 1874). He obtains a pure yeast culture from Copenhagen.

California's Concannon Vineyard is founded in the Livermore Valley of Alameda County by printer and rubber-stamp maker James Concannon at the suggestion of Joseph S. Alemany, archbishop of San Francisco, who needs more wine for sacramental uses. The vineyard will grow to produce mostly white wines, including Moselle, Sauvignon Blanc, Semillon, Johannisberg Riesling, and Château Concannon.

New York's Hoffman House hotel hires the head chef of the Café des Anglais in Paris, formerly private chef to the Rothschilds, and pays him a staggering $300 per month at a time when the city has scores of "15¢ houses"—restaurants where 15 cents will buy a meal consisting of a hot joint of meat with bread, butter, potatoes, and pickles.

Monte Carlo's Grand Hotel engages Swiss manager César Ritz, 33, and he, in turn, hires as chef Jean Giroix, whose hors d'oeuvres, sauces, game preparations, and petits fours have won him a reputation at Le Petit Moulin Rouge at Paris. When the nearby Hôtel de Paris at Monte Carlo hires Giroix away, Ritz hires Georges-Auguste Escoffier, now 37, who has worked with Giroix at Le Petit Moulin Rouge in Paris (*see* politics, 1870; Savoy, 1889).

1884

The War of the Pacific, which began in 1879 between Chile and Peru, ends April 4 with the Treaty of Valparaiso, which deprives Bolivia of access to the sea (*see* 1883). Victorious Chile gained the Peruvian province of Tarapaca last year in the Treaty of Ancona and now gains nitrate-rich Bolivian territories (*see* Haber process, 1908; Grace, 1890).

Reaper magnate Cyrus McCormick dies March 13 at age 75, leaving a fortune of $200 million to his widow, four sons, and three daughters. Nancy "Nettie" Fowler McCormick, 50, who has served as his private secretary and business counsel, takes over management of her late husband's McCormick Harvesting Machine Co. His son Cyrus, Jr., 25, assumes the presidency, but it is Mrs. McCormick who will run the enterprise for the next 18 years (*see* International Harvester, 1902).

Frank Peavey moves his headquarters to Minneapolis, where electric lights were introduced last year (*see* 1874). The Minneapolis Millers Association has long been his biggest customer, and within a year the city will be the largest U.S. wheat-receiving market, taking in 33 million bushels annually (*see* 1886).

A congressional committee reports that a number of individuals, many of them "foreigners of large means," have acquired ownership of land tracts in Texas, some of them embracing more than 250,000 acres: "Certain of these foreigners are titled noblemen. Some of them have brought over from

Europe, in considerable numbers, herdsmen and other employees who sustain to them a dependent relationship characteristic of the peasantry on the large landed estates of Europe." Two British syndicates hold 7.5 million acres of land (*see* 1888; Prairie Cattle Co., 1882).

Texas rancher John Simpson Chisum dies at Eureka Springs, Ark., December 23 at age 60. His herds have been estimated to total as many as 100,000 head, making him at one time the largest cattle owner in the country and probably in the world.

The Dairylea milk producers' cooperative has its beginnings in an association of Orange County, N.Y., farmers who pool their efforts to market their milk effectively in competition with Harlem River Valley farmers, who ship milk into New York City at a rate of 50,000 quarts per day. The 40-quart milk can introduced in 1876 is now standard for shipment on night trains to the city (*see* 1842; 1907).

The Milan *salumeria* Peck opened at Via Spadari 9 by Czech immigrant Franz Peck from Prague will grow to have five different shops—including the Casa del Formaggio, the Bottega del Maiale (pork shop), the Bottega del Vino, and the Rosticceria Peck, all owned by the Stoppani brothers—where generations of Milanese will buy pâtés, freshly made pastas, porcini, sausage, meats, and fruits. Peck will continue for more than a century to offer roasts, loins, saddles, and breasts of white veal, sausages, parmigiano and reggiano cheeses, pâtés, head cheese, mussels, scampi, cold lobster, smoked salmon, smoked trout, smoked eel, sturgeon, herring of various types, smoked herring eggs, caviar, pasta dishes, and Italian wines.

Cookbooks: *Mrs. Lincoln's Boston Cook Book* by Boston Cooking School director Mary Johnson Lincoln (*née* Bailey), 40, who writes, "Nothing in the whole range of domestic life more affects the health and happiness of the family than the quality of its daily bread." Mrs. Lincoln warns readers that brown sugar is inferior to white sugar and prone to infestation by "a minute insect," reflecting efforts by sugar refiners to denigrate brown sugar. *Practical Cookery, with Demonstrations* by Maria Parloa, who founded the Boston Original Cooking School. *Cookery for Beginners: A Series of Familiar Lessons for Young Housekeepers* by Marion Harland.

The soft-shell clam *Mya arenaria*, also called the long-neck or steamer clam, is introduced to the U.S. Pacific Coast (*see* shad, 1871, 1885).

Ceylon's coffee output falls to 150,000 bags, down from 700,000 in 1870, when the rust disease caused by *Hamileia vastatrix* began making deep inroads (*see* 1869). The last shipment of coffee beans will leave the island in 1899.

Chinese farmworkers account for half of California's agricultural labor force, up from 10 percent in 1870. The Chinese have raised dikes at the mouths of the San Joaquin and Sacramento rivers and are reclaiming millions of acres of rich farmlands (*see* Chin Lung, 1898).

Beriberi plagues the Japanese Navy, affecting one man in three (*see* politics, 1866), but the director of the Naval Medical Bureau Baron Kanehiro Takaki sends two ships on a 287-day voyage during which the men on one ship are served a diet of meat, cooked fish, and vegetables, while the men on the other ship get the usual Japanese diet of polished white rice and raw fish. Some 160 men out of 360 come down with beriberi on the second ship and 75 die, while on the first ship nobody dies, and the 16 cases of beriberi are found to occur only among men who refused to accept the prescribed diet. Takaki orders Western-style rations to be served aboard all Japanese naval vessels (*see* 1642; 1887; naval victory, 1905).

Scurvy reappears in Britain's Royal Navy; the Admiralty orders a daily lemon ration aboard all warships where the old 1795 order has lapsed.

Swiss miller Julius Michael Johannes Maggi, 38, introduces powdered pea and beet soups under the name Maggi & Companie. He will begin large-scale manufacture of powdered pea and bean soups in January of next year at Kempettal and by 1889 will be offering a wide variety of powdered soups (*see* Arome, 1889).

Quaker Oats becomes one of the first food commodities to be sold in packages. Put up in cardboard canisters, the cereal will be widely and aggressively advertised throughout the United States and Britain (*see* 1877).

Buitoni's high-gluten pasta is introduced commercially (*see* 1856; 1887).

Black and White Scotch whisky is introduced by Glasgow distiller James Buchanan.

London's first A.B.C. tea shop opens near Bridge Station but is generally ridiculed. Londoners prefer the old coffee shops with their high-backed benches (*see* Lyons, 1894).

1885

Memoirs of a Revolutionist (*Paroles d'un Révolté*) by Russian philosopher Prince Petr Alekseevich Kropotkin, 43, declares that the "Golden Age of the small farmer is over. . . . He is in debt to the cattle dealer, the land speculator, the usurer. Mortgages ruin whole communities, even more than taxes" (*see* 1861; 1905).

United Fruit Co. has its beginnings in the Boston Fruit Co. established by Andrew Preston and nine partners who have been persuaded to set up an independent agency to import bananas by Dow Baker (*see* 1871). Now a prosperous shipper and a partner in Standard Steam Navigation, Baker has built the *Jesse H. Freeman* schooner with auxiliary steam engines that permit him to send 10,000 stem cargoes north to Boston in 10 to 12 days from his new base in Jamaica, and the new company prospers as banana harvests increase (*see* 1899).

The Missouri, Kansas, and Texas Railroad reaches the heart of the Texas cow country and ends the need to drive cattle long distances to railheads (*see* 1871).

Salmonella bacteria get their name from a paper by U.S. veterinarian Daniel Elmer Salmon, 35, who describes the microorganisms that produce gastroenteritis with fever when ingested in infected food. Chief of the year-old Bureau of Animal Husbandry in the Department of Agriculture, Salmon has based his paper on work done by researcher Theobald Smith, 26, but the bacteria he describes will be called salmonellae.

Cookbooks: *Creole Cookbook* by Greek-born New Orleans *Times-Democrat* writer (Patricio) Lafcadio (Tessima Carlos) Hearn, 35, who will open an eating place under the name "5-Cent Restaurant" and pass out handbills advertising it as "the cheapest eating house in the South. It is neat, orderly, and

respectable as any other in New Orleans. You can get a good meal for a couple of nickels. All dishes 5¢." Hearn will change its name to Hard Times and it will fail, partly because many New Orleans saloons will, on any given day, lay out crab gumbo, oyster jambalaya, roast beef, baked beans, shallots, salads, fried tripe, fried hominy, and succotash (the list will change daily), all available free to a customer who pays 15 cents for a glass of wine (the average spent on drinks is, of course, much higher).

The hamburger sandwich is invented by some accounts at Seymour, Wis., where Outagamie County Fair concessionaire Charles Nagreen, 15, finds that his customers want his butter-fried ground beef but do not want to stand about eating when they could be strolling about the fairgrounds. He places the beef between bread slices and calls it a "hamburger" (but *see* also Delmonico's, 1836; Menches, 1892; Louis Lassen, 1900).

The North American lobster catch reaches an all-time high of 130 million pounds, but oil refineries have been fouling the ocean off New Jersey and lobsters have been disappearing from the New Jersey shore. They will soon begin to decline along the coasts of Massachusetts and Maine as well.

The Maryland oyster catch reaches nearly 15 million bushels.

Another 910,000 shad fry from the East Coast will be planted in the Columbia River this year and next (*see* 1871); the fish will be popular on the West Coast only for its roe (a spawning female typically contains 30,000 pinhead-sized eggs and may have as many as 156,000), but it will grow so prolifically that in years when catches in Atlantic coastal streams are low, some shad will be shipped across the United States from west to east to supply demand.

Congress prohibits barbed wire fencing of public lands in the U.S. West on February 25, and President Grover Cleveland, 48, issues a proclamation August 7 ordering removal of all unlawful enclosures (*see* 1877).

Texas rancher's wife Henrietta Maria Morse King (*née* Chamberlain), 53, and her daughter, Alice Gertrudis King, inherit the 600,000-acre King Ranch upon the death of its co-founder Richard King April 14 at age 59. Mrs. King will be instrumental in adding to her late husband's vast holdings, inducing a railroad to build through her property, solving the problem of water by importing a new kind of well-drilling rig that taps an artesian reservoir, and helping to develop a new breed of cattle—the Santa Gertrudis strain (a cross between a shorthorn and a Brahman). King's lawyer, Robert Justus Kleberg, now 30, will marry Alice next year and assume management of the ranch, which now employs 1,000 hands and grazes 100,000 head (he will also assume a $500,000 debt left by King, who borrowed money to buy more land).

The U.S. corn crop tops 2 billion bushels for the first time in history, double the 1870 crop (*see* 1906). Most goes into hog and cattle feed, but U.S. cattle are still fattened largely on grass.

Iowa State College of Agriculture and Mechanical Arts professor Seaman Knapp resigns his position to take charge of a colonization plan being developed at Lake Charles, La., by Jabez Bunting Watkins, who wants to settle people on 1.5 million acres of land with rice farms, mills, banks, schools, and the like (*see* periodical, 1872; Hatch Act, 1887).

Commercial production of calimyrna (California + Smyrna) figs begins in California, but immature figs drop off the trees until growers employ caprification, following the advice of the 3rd century B.C. Greek botanist Theophrastus. The growers plant one wild (or capri) fig tree to every 100 cultivated trees, and Blastophoga wasps that live in the capri trees "set" the fruit so that it will mature on the cultivated trees (*see* 1900).

The Orange Growers Protective Union of Southern California is organized as the Santa Fe Railroad extends its service in the Los Angeles area (*see* 1881; 1887; California Fruit Growers Exchange, 1895).

Jacob's Cream Crackers are introduced at Dublin using a triple-fermentation bread process used in America to produce soda crackers. Irish baker William Jacob began business at Waterford in 1850, moved soon after into a converted coach factory at Dublin, and equipped it with a biscuit-cutting machine, two ovens, and a five-horsepower engine. His family has built a modern factory to replace the bakery destroyed by fire 5 years ago, and George Jacob, a member of the family, has

returned from a visit to America with samples of U.S. soda crackers. The cream cracker, made on cutters used earlier to manufacture ship's biscuit, contains no cream but is the product of a mixing process, known as "creaming," which blends two materials together and gives the cracker a flaky texture. An instant success, the cracker will be made at Aintree, near Liverpool, beginning in 1914 and its basic recipe will be adapted to modern mixing and baking techniques.

Morton's salt is introduced by the new Joy Morton Co. firm, which will be the only nationwide U.S. marketer of salt. Morton, 30, has spent 6 years with E. L. Wheeler & Co., a firm that grew out of the Alonzo Richards firm started as agents for Onandaga Salt at Chicago in 1848 to market salt from Syracuse that arrived via the Erie Canal and Great Lakes (*see* 1912).

Fresh milk in bottles is added to the line of the New York Condensed Milk Co., now headed by John Gail Borden. The modern milk bottle was invented last year by Hervey D. Thatcher of Potsdam, N.Y., and Borden is quick to take advantage of it (*see* 1861; 1879; automatic filler and capper, 1886; evaporated milk, 1892).

Evaporated milk is produced commercially for the first time at Highland, Ill. John B. Meyenberg, now 37, has established the Helvetia Milk Condensing Co. with help from local Swiss Americans (*see* Anglo-Swiss, 1866). When fire devastates Galveston, Tex., in November and fresh milk is hard to obtain, Helvetia Milk donates 10 cases of its product (*see* Carnation milk, 1899).

Keen's English Chop House is founded at New York. It will move in 1903 to 72 West 36th Street, where it will remain for more than 90 years, serving loin mutton chops under ceilings hung with clay churchwarden pipes.

New York's Exchange Buffet opens September 4 across from the Stock Exchange at 7 New Street; it is the world's first self-service restaurant (*see* Horn & Hardart, 1902).

The Tokyo tempura shop Tenmo opens in Nihonbashi. The proprietor, Mosaburo, had to give up his popular tempura stand when construction of streetcar lines began and has started a place that will still be thriving in 1995.

Fauchon opens on the Place de la Madeleine in Paris as an épicerie (grocery store) extraordinaire. Located on the northeast corner of the square, it will grow to occupy three adjoining houses and have outlets in more than 500 cities, including Hong Kong, selling fruits, vegetables, épicerie (canned goods), conserves, confections, wines and spirits, and more pâté de fois gras at retail than any competitor.

The Rome candy shop Moriondo e Gariglio opens at Via del Corso 416 with sweets made in its own kitchen—bonbons, fruit drops, and cat's tongues (long slivers of chocolate), to name a few.

A minister to Britain's Queen Victoria says, "The time cannot be far distant when some fresh arrangements will have to be made to enable the people of London to buy their fruit and vegetables without the loss of time and the inconvenience that at present exists." But the market now at Covent Garden will not be relocated until the mid-1970s (see 1661; 1970).

More than half of Britain's 7.36 million tons of merchant shipping is in steam, up from less than 9 percent in 1856.

The Supreme Court reverses its decision in the 1877 Peik case and forbids individual states to fix rates on rail shipments passing beyond their borders. The ruling handed down October 25 in Wabash, St. Louis & Pacific Railway v. Illinois says that only the federal government may regulate interstate railway rates, and the decision affects 75 percent of the volume on U.S. railroads (see Interstate Commerce Act, 1887).

The first trainload of California oranges leaves Los Angeles for the East (see Columbian Exposition, 1893).

Plow and cultivator manufacturer John Deere dies at Moline, Ill., May 17 at age 81. His son Charles has gone into partnership with Alvah Mansur and produces rotary-drop corn planters as well as plows and cultivators (see tractor, 1892).

Oberlin College chemistry student Charles Martin Hall, 22, and French metallurgist Paul Louis Toussain Heroult, 23, pioneer commercial aluminum production, paving the way for aluminum pots, pans, and beverage cans.

An automatic bottle filler and capper is patented for use with milk bottles (see bottled milk, 1885; 1897).

French chemist Henri Moissan, 34, isolates fluorine, which occurs naturally in drinking water in many locales (see Motley, 1916).

Fiction: The Mayor of Casterbridge by English novelist Thomas Hardy, 46, who writes of a man who attends a country fair with his wife and daughter, orders frumenty (a "mixture of corn in the grain, flour, milk, raisins, currants and what-not" composing an "antiquated slop") for his family, arranges to have his own portion heavily laced with rum, and, having overimbibed, auctions off his wife.

Cookbook: Mrs. Rorer's Philadelphia Cookbook; A Manual of Home Economics by U.S. author Mrs. S. T. Rorer (Sarah Tyson Rorer [née Heston]), 37.

A decade of intermittent drought begins on the U.S. Great Plains after 8 years of extraordinary rainfall. Close to 60 percent of U.S. range livestock die in blizzards and from lack of grass on overgrazed lands.

North Dakota rancher Theodore Roosevelt, 28, sustains heavy losses, gives up, and returns to his native New York to enter politics (see blizzards, 1887).

Agronomist Albert Jones develops his first hybrid variety of winter wheat—Golden Cross (see corn, 1879). He has had no scientific or agricultural training but has perfected his own methods and will develop 25 other winter wheat varieties, all of considerable economic value, and will be the foremost U.S. propagator of winter wheat, with hybrids suitable to almost every climate and soil in the United States or Canada (see 1919).

Manitoba farmer Angus MacKay, 45, demonstrates the Canadian prairie's ability to produce good wheat crops; he plants Red Fife wheat on a field that he left fallow last year and reaps 35 bushels of hard wheat per acre.

Dutch researcher Christian Eijkman, 28, is sent to Java to study beriberi, which has become a major problem in the East Indies (see 1896; Takaki, 1884).

Congress passes an Oleomargarine Act to tax and regulate the manufacture and sale of margarine (*see* 1881; 1890).

English grocer's son William Hasketh Lever, 35, and his brother James Darcy Lever introduce Sunlight Soap, manufactured from vegetable oils instead of tallow. They leased a financially failing soap factory 2 years ago to begin Lever Brothers, an enterprise that will grow to rival Procter & Gamble (*see* 1837) as a manufacturer and marketer not only of soap but also of food products (*see* Mac Fisheries, 1920).

Diamond Crystal Salt Co. has its beginnings in the St. Clair Rock Salt Co. founded by St. Clair, Mich., investors, including Charles F. Moore, who back Buffalo, N.Y., inventor J. L. Alberger and employ his new process for producing salt economically from brine deposits. The company name will be changed when chemical analysis shows the salt to be the purest yet found (*see* General Foods, 1929).

A fire destroys oatmeal king Ferdinand Schumacher's new Jumbo mill at Akron along with his Empire mill and other properties, consuming 100,000 bushels of oats plus quantities of other grains (*see* 1881). He has no insurance to cover his losses in the disastrous May fire but recovers in part by absorbing a small local competitor and entering the Consolidated Oatmeal Co. pool, whose members control half the nation's oatmeal trade.

H. J. Heinz of Pittsburgh calls on London's 179-year-old Fortnum and Mason while on holiday in England and receives orders for all the products he takes out of his Gladstone bag (*see* 1880; 1888).

New York grocery wholesaler Joseph Seeman, 26, and his brother Sigel pool their savings of $4,500, borrow another $4,000 from an older brother, buy out their uncle David and his partner, David Lewi, and adopt White Rose as their brand name, using it to sell first oats, then canned corn, then canned tomatoes, cocoa, canned peas, and canned salmon (*see* White Rose Tea, 1901).

Candy maker Milton S. Hershey returns to Lancaster after having gone bankrupt at New York (*see* 1883) and starts a new caramel business. Assisted by his Aunt Mattie and, later, by his mother, he

soon has a prosperous enterprise in tissue-wrapped caramels, but it is undercapitalized (*see* 1891).

Maxwell House coffee gets its name (*see* 1882). The 17-year-old hotel at Nashville, Tenn., serves its guests coffee made from the blend perfected by Joel Cheek, who is persuaded by the praise of the guests to market his blend under the name Maxwell House (*see* Postum, 1928).

Salada Tea has its beginnings in the Golden Tea-Pot Blend of the Salada Ceylon Tea Co. introduced by Canadian wholesale grocery salesman Peter C. Larkin, who is convinced that Ceylon teas will replace China teas in America as they have in England (China still supplies most of the world's market for tea, including blacks and oolongs as well as greens, and will continue to do so until the 1890s, when mechanized equipment for firing and packing, standardized grading, trade names, and worldwide advertising will give India and Ceylon teas dominance). He packs Ceylon teas in a lead foil container sealed with a glue-on wraparound label, and while "Salada" is the name of a small Indian tea garden and has no significance, Larkin finds that people ask for "that Salada tea," so beginning in 1892 he will label his product "Salada" in large letters, run small newspaper advertisements, and persuade grocers to let him glue white-enamel-letter Salada Tea signs in their windows (*see* 1902).

Coca-Cola goes on sale May 8 at Jacob's Pharmacy in Atlanta, where local pharmacist John Styth Pemberton has formulated a headache and hangover remedy whose syrup ingredients include dried leaves from the South American coca shrub, from which cocaine is made, and an extract of kola nuts from Africa plus fruit syrup. He has had no success with his "Globe of Flower Cough Syrup," "Triplex Liver Pills," and other concoctions, but has been advertising his Coca-Cola "esteemed Brain Tonic and Intellectual Beverage" since March 29. His bookkeeper Frank M. Robinson has named the product and written the name Coca-Cola in a flowing script. Pemberton has persuaded fountain man Willis E. Venable at Jacob's to sell the beverage on a trial basis, Venable adds carbonated water, and by year's end Pemberton has sold 25 gallons of syrup at $1 per gallon, but he has spent $73.96 in advertising and will sell two-thirds of his sole ownership in the product next year for $1,200 (*see* Candler, 1891).

Moxie is introduced under the name Moxie Nerve Food by Lowell, Mass., physician Augustin Thompson, who has been introduced by a Lt. Moxie to the properties of gentian root, which is the beverage's chief ingredient other than sparkling water.

Dr. Pepper is introduced as "The King of Beverages, Free from Caffeine" by Waco, Tex., chemist Robert S. Lazenby, who has experimented with a soft drink formula developed by Charles Alderton, a fountain man at the town's Old Corner Drug Store. The fountain man has called his drink, which contains an artificial black-cherry flavor, Dr. Pepper's Phos-Ferrates. (By another account, the new soda pop is the creation of Wade Morrison, who owns the Waco pharmacy. Morrison, who will market the drink in partnership with Lazenby, allegedly used a combination of 23 ingredients—including mountain herbs, roots, and seltzer—learned as an assistant to former Confederate Army surgeon Charles T. Pepper at the Rural Retreat, Va., pharmacy opened by Pepper in 1872 but has come to Texas after being fired from his Virginia job for courting Pepper's daughter.) (*see* 1904)

Hires Rootbeer is introduced in bottles, but advertising emphasizes the advantages of brewing the drink at home from Hires extract (*see* 1876).

Charles Hires improved his root beer, but a new cola drink from Atlanta would eclipse it.

HIRES' IMPROVED ROOT BEER

Package 25 Cents

Bovril is introduced at London with invitations to free tastings at the Colonial and Continental Exhibition in South Kensington (*see* 1874). John Lawson Johnston's sold out his Montreal business in 1884 following a disastrous fire and has resumed production at 10 Trinity Square, London (*see* 1887).

Singapore's Raffles Hotel opens November 18 at the corner of Brasbasah and Beach roads (*see* Raffles, 1826). It began a few years ago as a "tiffin" house—a modest place made over from a house that had belonged to a Captain Dare and his wife—for British colonials to have lunch and tea beneath ceiling fans, but an extension will be built in 1896 to meet the demands of the growing port city (*see* Singapore Sling, 1915).

1887

China's Huanghe (Yellow) River floods its banks. The resulting crop failures and famine kill 900,000.

New York sugar refiner Henry Osborne Havemeyer, 40, founds Sugar Refineries Co. His 17 refineries account for 78 percent of U.S. refining capacity (*see* American Sugar Refining, 1891).

Wesson Oil and Snowdrift Co. has its beginnings in the Southern Cotton Oil Co. founded at Philadelphia. Its cottonseed-cru shing mills in the Carolinas, Georgia, Arkansas, Tennessee, Louisiana, and Texas will make Southern the largest prime producer of cottonseed oil and the first U.S. manufacturer of vegetable shortening (*see* Wesson, 1899).

Italian pasta maker Francesco Buitoni, whose grandmother started the family business, opens a second factory, this one in Perugia (*see* 1884; 1941; Perugina, 1907).

The Interstate Commerce Act approved by Congress February 1 orders U.S. railroads to keep their rates fair and reasonable (*see* Hadley, 1885; ICC, 1888; Elkins Act, 1903).

The hand separator comes into use on U.S. dairy farms, enabling farmers to separate their cream by machine in their own creameries (*see* 1877). Dairy farming has grown by leaps and bounds in the Midwest in this decade, enabling more Americans to enjoy milk, butter, and cheese the year round.

Geman chemist Emil Fischer, 35, isolates the isomeric hexose sugar mannose and works with an associate to synthesize the fruit sugar fructose. Other sugars have already been isolated, including glucose, galactose, and sorbose.

Ball-Mason jars are introduced by Ball Brothers Glass Manufacturing Co. of Muncie, Ind. (*see* Mason, 1858). William Charles Ball, 35, and his brothers Lucius Lorenzo, Frank C., Edmund Burke, and George Alexander began making tin oil cans at Buffalo, N.Y., 10 years ago, switched to glass oil and fruit jars in 1884, and have moved to Muncie, where natural gas has been discovered and which has offered free gas and a generous land site. Green, aqua, and clear glass Mason jars bearing the mark "Patented Nov. 30, 1858" will continue to be marketed well into the next century (*see* Kerr, 1903; *Ball Blue Book*, 1905).

Western Cold Storage Co. in Chicago installs ice-making machines, but cold stores in most places continue to be cooled by harvested ice cut from lakes and hauled ashore by teams of horses (*see* 1878). Hundreds of icehouses dot the banks of the Hudson River north of New York, Maine's Kennebec River, ponds in the Midwest, and small lakes in Massachusetts (Wenham Lake is so well known as a source of ice that Norwegian harvesters label ice from Lake Koepegaard "Wenham") (*see* 1889).

English physician David Bruce, 32, identifies the source of "Malta fever" or "Mediterranean fever," which has caused illness and even death among British troops. He finds that milk from local goats contains a bacterium that later will be found in cow's milk and that causes undulant fever, or brucellosis (*see* Bang, 1896).

Cookbook: *Miss Parloa's Kitchen Companion; a Guide for All Who Would Be Good Housekeepers* by Maria Parloa.

The Doboś (or Dobosch) torte created by Budapest baker József C. Doboś , 40, is a round cake of eight to 12 layers made of egg yolks and whites, sugar, lemon juice, flour, and salt covered with a caramel glaze. Doboś will find a way to package it for shipment to other countries, it will have many imitators, and Doboś will not publish the authentic recipe until 1906, when he will donate it to the Budapest Pastry and Honey Bread Makers' Guild. He will open a specialty food shop which will carry more than 60 cheeses and 22 kinds of champagne.

Blizzards continue in the northern Great Plains (*see* 1886). The worst storm of the hard winter rages for 72 hours at the end of January, and millions of head of open-range cattle are killed in Montana, Kansas, Wyoming, and the Dakotas. Whole families are found frozen to death in tar-paper cabins and in dugouts, the big ranching syndicates go bankrupt, and the homesteaders that move in to start farms include former cowboys. Friction will soon develop between the farmers and the surviving ranchers.

The Hatch Act voted by Congress March 2 authorizes the establishment of agricultural experiment stations in all states having land-grant colleges. The legislation is based on a bill drafted 5 years ago by Seaman Knapp when he was professor of agriculture at Iowa State College of Agriculture and Mechanical Arts professor at Ames (*see* 1885).

U.S. wheat prices fall to 67¢/bushel, the lowest since 1868, as the harvest reaches new heights. Britons and other importers of American wheat enjoy lower food prices.

Beriberi can be prevented by proper diet, says Baron Takaki in a report of his 1884 Japanese Navy study published in the British medical journal *Lancet* (*see* Eijkman and Grijns, 1896).

Britain's Margarine Act establishes statutory standards for margarine, but dairy magnate George Barham fails in his demand that if any coloring be allowed in margarine it should be pink, green, or—preferably—black (*see* United States, 1950).

Hovis bread has its beginnings in Smith's Patent Germ Flour, registered October 6 by English flour miller Richard "Stoney" Smith, 51, of Stone, Staffordshire, and Macclesfield miller Thomas Fitton of the firm S. Fitton & Sons. A firm believer in the nutritive virtues of wheat germ, the heart of the wheat kernel, Smith has devised a process for separating the germ from the flour, cooking it lightly in steam, adding a little salt, and returning it to the flour, which is used to produce a good-tasting brown loaf with a longer shelf life than ordinary brown bread. Analytical chemist William Jago stated last year that the "prepared germ meal and flour yield a bread far superior in nutritive value, flavour and texture" to conventionally made breads (*see* 1887).

Log Cabin Syrup is introduced by St. Paul, Minn., grocer P. J. Towle, who blends maple syrup (45 percent) and cane-sugar syrup to produce a product much lower in price than pure maple syrup. He markets it in a tin container shaped and decorated to look like the boyhood home of his boyhood hero Abraham Lincoln (*see* Postum Co., 1927).

The Log Cabin Syrup tin was distinctive, and the product contained some real maple syrup.

White Rock Mineral Springs Co. is founded in Wisconsin by Charles Welch with an initial capitalization of $100,000 (*see* 1868). Welch has bought the spring outside Waukesha and will promote "White Rock Lithia Water" throughout the country (*see* Psyche, 1893).

France imports 12 million hectoliters of wine and exports only 2 million as grape phylloxerae continue to devastate vineyards (*see* 1882; 1890).

Hundreds of ruined French wine-grape growers emigrate to Algeria, as they have done each year in this decade. Grape phylloxerae reached Algeria 2 years ago, but Algerian vineyards continue to multiply as French imports of Algerian wine increase to compensate for the shortfall in French wines.

Bovril creator John Lawson Johnston demonstrates his "fluid beef" product at another Colonial and Continental Exhibition, publicizing it with frosted-glass simulations of the ice palaces built at Montreal winter carnivals, and enjoys such phenomenal success that he contracts with the Midland Railway to supply "twenty best and ten comon urns" for dispensing Bovril at railway stations (*see* 1886). Johnston tells an interviewer that the name Bovril "came to me over a cigar" (it is a combination of the Latin *bos*, meaning "ox," and *Vrilys*, a name used in the 1871 Bulwer-Lytton novel *The Coming Race* to denote the "life force"). When the first advertisements for the product appear in 1889, they will describe it as "Johnston's Fluid Beef (brand Bovril)," but the word Bovril will thereafter be used on its own (*see* Benson, 1893).

Rowntree & Co. introduces Elect Cocoa, a powdered dark chocolate (*see* 1881). Joseph Rowntree's son John Wilhelm has been working with his father in the business since 1885, and John's brother (Benjamin) Seebohm, now 16, will soon join it (*see* 1897).

German-born restaurateur Peter Luger, 22, opens a Brooklyn, N.Y., steakhouse at 178 Broadway, near Bedford Avenue at the end of the Williamsburg Bridge, where it will attract patrons for more than a century with prime steaks, lamb chops, German fried potatoes, creamed spinach, apple strudel, and beer.

1888

Brazil's slaves go free May 13 after 370 years of backbreaking labor without compensation in the canefields (*see* 1871). Sugar planters and other slaveowners receive no compensation.

Drought in the Midwest causes a major crop disaster, European wheat crops are also short, and although wheat prices on the Chicago Board of Trade rise moderately after a government crop report in May predicts a wheat shortage, the price rises from $1 per bushel to $2 in the week beginning September 22. Speculator B. P. "Old Hutch" Hutchinson has begun buying September futures in August, he has soon cornered a major part of all the wheat sold in Chicago or deliverable to the

Board of Trade, and his wheat "corner" yields him profits of up to $1 per bushel on the wheat he sells to millers or to speculators who have sold short (*see* 1879; Leiter, 1897).

U.S. cattlemen go bankrupt and foreign investors liquidate their American holdings after a drastic decline in cattle herds following the 1886–1887 drought on the western plains (*see* 1884).

Prospectors boring for natural gas in central Kansas discover a new salt field (*see* 1892).

The American Cereal Co. is created by a merger of all seven major U.S. oatmeal producers. More than 50 percent of the stock goes to Ferdinand Schumacher, whose holding is worth $2.5 million (*see* 1886); 12 percent to Henry Parsons Crowell for the Quaker Oats brand and the Ravenna mill, which he now owns (*see* 1877); and another 12 percent to Chicago–Cedar Rapids oatmeal producer Robert Stuart (*see* 1893; Quaker Oats, 1891).

The Fred Harvey dining car menu of a westbound Santa Fe express train includes 12 entrées of fish, meat, and poultry, eight vegetables, and a wide assortment of desserts, all for 75¢ with second helpings on request. Dining cars are heavily decorated with marquetry, rare inlaid woods, ormolu, Turkish carpets, beveled-edged French mirrors, and looped and fringed portières.

Dining cars on U.S. railroads tried to offer cuisine as good as any to be found in a fine restaurant. LIBRARY OF CONGRESS

The Relation of Alimentation and Disease by U.S. physician James Henry Salisbury, 64, proclaims the discovery that most bodily disorders are caused by starchy foods. "By structure, man is about two-thirds carniverous and one third herbivorous" and our teeth are "meat teeth," Dr. Salisbury writes. "Our stomach is designed to digest lean meat." "Only the small intestine works on plant foods." "Health alimentation would consist of a diet of about one part vegetables, fats, fruits, to about two parts of lean meat." Since only a small part of the intestine works on starch, undigested starch "ferments" in the stomach and intestines, says Dr. Salisbury, producing acid, vinegar, alcohol, and yeast, which "poison and paralyze the tissues" and can cause heart disease, tumors, mental derangement, and—especially—tuberculosis (*see* Hay, 1929; Salisbury steak, below).

Nonfiction: *Life on the Mississippi* by Mark Twain, now 52, reports a conversation between two businessmen aboard a Cincinnati riverboat: "Why, we are turning out oleomargarine *now*, by the thousands of tons. And we can sell it so dirt-cheap that that whole country has *got* to take it—can't get around it, you see. Butter don't stand any chance—there ain't any chance for competition." But butter will continue to outsell margarine in the United States until 1957.

Cookbooks: *Virginia Cookery-Book* by U.S. author Mary Stuart Smith gives a recipe for Johnny-Cake (*see* 1859); *Hot-Weather Dishes* by Mrs. S. T. Rorer.

Salisbury steak, named for Dr. James H. Salisbury (above), will make its way onto U.S. menus, where the chopped lean beef, pressed into cakes and broiled, will continue to appear for more than a century. "This [muscle pulp] should be as free as possible from connective, or glue, tissue, fat, and cartilage," Dr. Salisbury writes. "The pulp should not be pressed too firmly together before broiling, or it will taste livery. Simply press it sufficiently to hold it together, make the cakes half an inch to a inch thick, broil slowly and moderately well over a fire free from blaze and smoke. When cooked, put it on a hot plate and season to taste with butter, pepper, and salt; also use either Worcestershire or Halford sauce, mustard, horse radish, or lemon juice on the meat if desired."

Two Massachusetts truck farmers at Wrentham buy an incubator, two Pekin drakes, and 10 ducks for $175; the Weber brothers will sell 600 ducklings at $1.20 each in 1890 and their success will inspire others to go into duck raising (*see* 1882).

Congress enacts emergency legislation and places Major John Wesley Powell in charge of an irrigation survey to select reservoir sites, determine irrigation product areas, and carry out part of his 1878 plan (*see* 1889).

H. J. Heinz reorganizes a food packing firm under his own name (*see* 1886; "57 Varieties," 1892).

A small New York dairy store opens at 135 Madison Street on the Lower East Side under the direction of Lithuanian-born merchant Isaac Breakstone, 24, and his brother Joseph. Isaac, who has been in the ice cream business after several years of peddling, arrived in New York 6 years ago and was greeted at the pier by Joseph, who had arrived 6 months earlier; their Madison Street shop will continue until 1895, and in 1896 they will start a wholesale butter business under the name Breakstone Brothers at 29 Jay Street, Brooklyn (*see* 1899).

B. Manischewitz Co. has its beginnings in a Cincinnati plant opened by Russian-American baker Behr Manischewitz. His company will establish a Jersey City, N.J., plant in 1931 to manufacture products for Passover while continuing to make other products at Cincinnati, and in later years it will build a plant at Vineland, N.J., to become a major producer of borscht, chicken soups, vegetable soups, gefilte fish, and other kosher foods as it grows to become the world's largest baker of matzoh and matzoh products (*see* Rokeach, 1870; Monarch wine, 1934).

An advertisement for Smith's Patent Process Germ Flour in the October 1 issue of *British Baker, Confectioner & Purveyor* consists largely of a testimonial by William Jago for the process used to make what later will be called Hovis bread (*see* 1887). The advertisement has been placed by S. Fitton & Son, Flour Mills, Macclesfield (*see* Hovis, 1890).

Tetley Tea is introduced into U.S. markets by agents Wright and Graham, who merchandise Tetley's Indian and Ceylon teas through department stores such as New York's R. H. Macy Co., a radical innovation at a time when most Americans consume far more green and Formosan (Taiwanese) tea than black tea (*see* 1856; J. Lyons, 1973).

Widmer's winery begins production in New York's Finger Lakes district at Naples, where it will produce wines and vermouths, using grapes that include the Dutchess, the Iona, the Niagara, the Noah, the Ontario, and the Elvira, a green grape originated shortly after the Civil War in a Missouri nursery.

The Ramos Gin Fizz created by New Orleans saloonkeeper Henry C. Ramos of the Imperial Cabernet Saloon at the corner of Carondelet and Gravier streets is a frothy mixture of gin, lemon juice, orange flower water, egg whites, a little cream, and sometimes a drop or two of vanilla extract.

Foster's Beer is introduced in Australia by Americans using refrigeration, pasteurization, bottom fermentation, and bottling to create a product that will help make beer the national beverage (*see* Harrison, 1856).

The Genoa restaurant Manuvlina opens at Via Roma 300 in Recco with Ligurian cooking: eggs in parsley sauce, celeriac tartlets, zucchini, potato dumplings, lasagna with funghi, spinach-filled pasta, and grigliata shortbread.

Madrid's Grand Café de Gijón opens at 21 Paseo de Calvosotelo. Proprietor Manuel Ronzález soon attracts a daily crowd of writers, painters, and politicians. A barber will buy the café in 1913, and, after his death in 1922, his widow will take over with her two sons. She will die in 1970 at age 103, and the sons will continue to operate the place.

The Hotel Del Coronado opens across the bay from San Diego, Calif., with 399 rooms and a main dining room measuring 156 feet by 61 feet whose arched ceiling is made of natural sugar pine fitted together entirely by wooden pegs. Inventor Thomas A. Edison personally supervises installation of the lighting system. Built by Indiana railroad magnate Elisha Babcock, the first Pacific coast resort hotel is located on an island, purchased by Babcock with help from Evansville, Ind., flour miller John Levi Igleheart, 25, for $110,000, and is reached via a 10-minute ferry ride from downtown. Babcock will be wiped out in a financial panic, and the hotel will be acquired by sugar kings J. D. and Adolph Spreckels,

Terrapin bisque was always on the menu in the dining room of San Diego's Hotel Coronado. LIBRARY OF CONGRESS

sons of Claus, who will always make sure that terrapin bisque is on the hotel's menu.

The Boston restaurant Dunn's advertises that it serves a 10-course dinner for 25 cents—20 cents for ladies.

The first Childs restaurant opens at New York and is soon followed by four others. Samuel Shannon Childs, 25, and his brother William, Jr., invest $1,600 to start the chain that will have 40 units by 1913 and grow to have 107 restaurants in 29 U.S. cities by the time Samuel S. dies in 1925—the largest restaurant chain of its kind, serving nearly 1 million patrons each week. They use all-white furnishings and equipment, dress their young waitresses in white uniforms, obtain the best food available, insist on absolute cleanliness in the preparation of that food, and maintain the lowest prices for their buttercakes and other Childs favorites.

1889

✗ Austria's Archduke Rudolf, 31, is found dead January 30 with his mistress, Baroness Marie Vetsera, 17, at the hunting lodge Mayerling, which he has had built for her in an old castle outside Vienna. Rudolf's valet, Johann Loschek, has built great fires to warm the rooms, produced two bottles of Tokay

wine that had been buried in the snow, and prepared pheasant with freshly cut mushrooms, leeks, and potatoes baked over charcoal and sprinkled with coarse salt. The couple retired for the night; sometime before dawn, Rudolf shot the beautiful Marie and turned the pistol on himself, leaving the Hapsburg emperor, Franz Joseph, without an heir.

✴ Oklahoma Territory lands formerly reserved for Native Americans are opened to white homesteaders by President Benjamin Harrison, 55, at high noon April 22, and a race begins to stake land claims. "Sooners," who have entered the territory prematurely, claim prior rights in many areas, bitter fights break out, but by sundown there are booming tent towns at Guthrie and at Oklahoma City, formerly a small water and coaling station for the Santa Fe Railroad but suddenly a city of 10,000 (*see* 1891).

💲 Kansas and Nebraska farmers pay 18 to 24 percent interest rates on loans, with rates sometimes going as high as 40 percent. Local brokers and then local loan companies secure funds from eastern investors and take healthy cuts for themselves.

🤝 An English syndicate acquires C. A. Pillsbury & Co. and merges it with the Washburn Mill Co. of Minnesota state senator W. D. Washburn to create Pillsbury-Washburn Flour Mills. Pillsbury's three principal mills produce 10,000 barrels of flour per day to make it the world's largest flour miller, and this first major milling merger will lead to further mergers (*see* 1880; 1909; Northwestern Consolidated Milling, 1891).

✿ A U.S. ice shortage caused by an extraordinarily mild winter gives impetus to the development of ice-making plants (*see* 1880; Western Cold Storage, 1887). The failure of the ice crop will lead to serious food spoilage next year with a consequent rise in epidemics. By year's end the country will have more than 200 ice plants, up from 35 in 1879.

The slow-cooking Aladdin Oven invented recently by self-made Boston businessman Edward Williams Atkinson, 29, saves fuel but takes 90 minutes to reach a temperature above 200° F., never rises above 350°, cools quickly if its door is opened, and takes a long time to regain its highest heat. The iron and steel used in standard kitchen ranges conduct heat rather than containing it and thus dissipate a lot of energy; Atkinson, who has gained a knowledge of heat resistance from his fire insurance business, lines a box of wood or fiber with tin, cuts a hole in the bottom, and inserts the top of a kerosene lamp in the hole, but his oven, although ideal for slow-cooked stews, takes 5 hours to cook most meat dishes and 12 hours to bring broth to the boiling point (*see* nutrition, below).

The pea viner introduced to expedite pea canning takes the whole pea vine and separates peas from pods in a continuous operation (*see* 1883).

British dairymen get their first milking machines. William Murchland at Kilmarnock, Scotland, manufactures the machines (*see* Colvin, 1878).

 The first large-scale English margarine plant begins production in a converted hat factory at Godley in Cheshire. Danish entrepreneur Otto Mønsted competes with U.S. and Dutch firms that are producing margarine in volume (*see* 1876; 1880; 1890).

 German physiologists J. von Mering and O. Minkowski remove the pancreas of a dog and observe that although the animal survives, it urinates more frequently, and the urine attracts flies and wasps (*see* Langerhans, 1869). When they analyze the urine, they find that the dog has a canine equivalent of diabetes, which ultimately causes it to go into a coma and die (*see* Sharpey-Schafer, 1916).

Japanese bacteriologist Shibasaburo Kitazato, 37, at Berlin isolates the bacilli of tetanus and symptomatic anthrax (*see* Koch, 1883).

U.S. Army Medical Corps assistant surgeon Bailey K. Ashford, 25, finds hookworm infestation in hospitalized Puerto Ricans following an August 8 hurricane that has killed 2,100 and left thousands homeless. A parasite identified by German physicians in the 1780s but introduced into the Americas from Africa 2 centuries earlier, hookworm causes debilitating anemia and pains. Victims in the United States from South Carolina to Mississippi often try to relieve the pain by swallowing clay and resin (*see* 1902).

Nonfiction: *House and Home; a Complete Housewife's Guide* by Marion Harland.

Lenox china is introduced by Trenton, N.J., ceramist Walter Scott Lenox, 30, who has established the Ceramic Art Co. His porcelain will be ranked in quality with that of Wedgwood and Spode (*see* 1918).

The Eiffel Tower designed by French engineer Alexandre-Gustave Eiffel, 57, is completed at Paris for the Universal Exhibition that opens May 6. Eiffel gives a banquet for the press, hiring the catering firm Potel & Chavot for the occasion (*see* 1820; 1900).

British sugar consumption rises to 76 pounds per capita, up from 60 pounds in 1875, to make Britain the heaviest sugar user in the world by far.

The Maine salmon catch reaches 150,000 pounds.

The Hudson River shad catch reaches an all-time high of 4.33 million pounds. The catch begins to decline, and although it will climb back up to 4.25 million pounds in 1942, it will then fall off drastically, and water pollution will spoil its taste.

The constitutional conventions of the new states of North Dakota and Montana hear Major John Wesley Powell urge delegates to measure land values by the acre-foot—the area that can be covered with 12 inches of water from irrigation or natural sources (*see* 1888). County lines should follow drainage divides, says Powell, with each river valley a political unit whose inhabitants can work cooperatively, but the politicians pay little heed.

Rust finishes off Ceylon's coffee industry (*see* 1869). Demand increases for Latin American coffee.

Discontented U.S. farmers south of the Mason-Dixon line merge their farm organizations into the Southern Alliance (*see* 1882).

Congress votes to give the 27-year-old U.S. Department of Agriculture Cabinet rank; President Cleveland appoints Jerimiah McLain Rusk, 59, the first secretary of agriculture.

MIT chemist Ellen Richards (*née* Swallow), 47, joins with Baltimore scientist Mary Abel (*née* Hinman) and Boston businessman Edward W. Atkinson (above) to advance the ideas of Wesleyan University agricultural chemist Wilbur Olin Atwater, 35, who has studied in Germany and established an Office of Experiment Stations in the Department of Agriculture. Atkinson has read surveys indicating that U.S. and European families spend 40 to 50 percent of their budgets on food—far more than was necessary for proper nutrition. Richards is convinced that more research is needed not only to eliminate adulterated food but also to get more people to eat more nutritious food. Abel, who learned of German nutritional research while her husband studied pharmacology in Germany, was impressed by Berlin's *Volksküchen* (people's kitchens) and wrote a prize-winning essay last year explaining the nature and function of food components and urging U.S. housewives to do as European women did, substituting cheese, beans, and cheaper cuts of meat for tenderloin and porterhouse steaks (*see* 1890).

Wilbur Atwater (above) is convinced that nutritionally inadequate diets produce not only physical but also moral degradation, and he agrees with Edward Atkinson's idea that wage rates are dependent in large part on the nutritive "efficiency" of the food consumed: diets high in protein and energy (meaning fat) mean that more work can be done and higher wages paid; American workers are more productive than their German counterparts because their diets are higher in protein and fats (*see* 1895).

A pure food law is proposed in Congress but meets with ridicule (*see* 1882; 1891).

A New York margarine factory employee tells a state investigator that his work has made "his hands so sore . . . his nails came off, his hair dropped out and he had to be confined to Bellevue Hospital for general debility," but the "bogus butter" made from hog fat and bleaches is widely sold as "pure creamery butter" and is no worse than "butter" made from casein and water or from calcium, gypsum, gelatin fat, and mashed potatoes (*see* 1890).

The flavor-enhancing agent Arome, introduced by Maggi & Cie., will find wide popularity in Europe (*see* 1884; MSG, 1908; Fabrique de Produits Maggi, 1890).

Aunt Jemima Pancake Flour, invented at St. Joseph, Mo., is the first self-rising flour for pancakes and the first ready-mix food ever to be introduced commercially. Editorial writer Chris L. Rutt of the *St. Joseph Gazette* and his friend Charles G. Underwood used their life savings last year to buy an old flour mill on Blacksnake Creek, but a falloff in westward migration by wagon train has decreased demand for mill products. Faced with disaster, Rutt and Underwood have experimented for a year and come up with a formula combining hard wheat flour, corn flour, phosphate of lime, soda, and a pinch of salt, which they package in one-pound paper sacks and sell as Self-Rising Pancake Flour, a name Rutt changes to Aunt Jemima after attending a minstrel show at which two black-faced comedians do a New Orleans–style cakewalk to a tune called "Aunt Jemima" (*see* 1893).

Calumet Baking Powder has its beginnings at Chicago, where local food salesman William M. Wright, 39, turns his bedroom into a laboratory and develops a baking powder which he produces at night and sells during the day. Wright will make a fortune, much of which he will invest in Calumet Farm, whose 550 Kentucky-bred trotters will win major races, including the Hambletonian, and whose thoroughbreds will win eight Kentucky Derby races and, after his death, two Triple Crowns—Whirlaway in 1941 and Citation in 1948.

McCormick Spices have their beginnings at Baltimore, where local entrepreneur Willoughby McCormick, 25, employs two girls and a boy in a one-room factory with cellar and backyard. He goes into business selling flavoring extracts, fruit syrups, juices, and nonfood items such as glue and liniment (*see* 1902).

Milwaukee's Pabst Brewing Co. takes that name and produces 585,300 barrels for the year (*see* Pabst, 1864). Pabst now rivals Anheuser-Busch as the nation's largest brewer (*see* 1904; blue ribbon, 1893).

California's Cresta Blanca winery is founded at Livermore by Charles Wetmore, who will produce table wines, sparkling wines, and vermouth. Livermore Valley vineyards, which produce mostly white wines, are planted not on hillsides but on a rocky plain; roots extend as deep as 30 feet in search of moisture and sustenance. Wetmore's operation will wind up at Fresno.

London's Savoy Hotel opens August 6. Gilbert & Sullivan opera impressario (Richard) D'Oyly Carte, 45, has had the seven-story hotel (it will be enlarged to have 15) built of reinforced concrete on a steel frame (timber is used only for floors and window frames), it has its own artesian well, its elevators run all night, a single room goes for 7½ pence per night (double with bath, 12 pence), and D'Oyly Carte engages César Ritz of Monte Carlo's Grand Hotel as manager. Ritz brings along as *maître chef de cuisine* Auguste Escoffier, who starts after-theater suppers in the hotel restaurant (he will regularly prepare cuisse de nymphes à l'aurore (frogs' legs served cold in a jelly of cream and white wine flavored with paprika) for the prince of Wales (*see* pêche Melba, 1894).

1890

✗ Kansas farmers should "raise less corn and more hell," Populist party leader Mary Elizabeth Lease (*née* Cylens), 36, tells them. She began speaking in behalf of Irish home rule in 1885 and makes 161 speeches as she stumps the state. Told by "the Kansas Python" that Kansas suffers "from two great robbers, the Santa Fe Railroad and the loan companies," the farmers vote against the Republicans and elect independent-party candidates to Congress.

💲 From 75 to 90 percent of all Kansas farms are mortgaged at interest rates averaging 9 percent. Banks have foreclosed on roughly one-third of all farm mortgages in the state in the past decade, as drought prevented farmers from producing enough to keep up interest payments on loans taken out to buy farm machinery and seed.

Third-party platforms begin to call for federal warehouses in which farmers may store their crops and receive in return certificates redeemable in currency for 80 percent of the market price, permitting them to hold crops off the market until prices improve.

The Supreme Court virtually overrules its 1877 decision upholding state regulation of business March 24. The court's decision in *Chicago, Milwaukee, St. Paul Railroad v. Minnesota* denies Minnesota's right to control railroad rates and in effect reverses the court's ruling in *Munn v. Illinois*.

The Sherman Anti-Trust Act passed by Congress July 2 curtails the powers of U.S. business monopolies. "Every contract, combination in the form of trust or otherwise, or conspiracy in restraint of trade or commerce among the several States, or with foreign nations, is hereby declared to be ille-

gal." But the new law will have little initial effect; legally or illegally, sugar refiners, meatpackers, margarine makers, distillers, and others will—like railroads, petroleum refiners, and the like—continue to make price-fixing agreements and block efforts by newcomers to enter their industries (*see* 1895; Clayton Act, 1914).

Kern County Land Co. is founded by speculators Lloyd Tevis and James Ben Ali Haggin, who have battled Henry Miller and Charles Lux for Kern River water rights in California, have won 75 percent of the rights, and have seen their 400,000 acres in the lower San Joaquin Valley grow (*see* 1850; 1877). Company lands will continue to grow until they cover 2,800 square miles, an area more than twice the size of Rhode Island.

🤝 Massey-Harris Co. is created by a merger of the Massey Manufacturing Co. with its chief competitor, A. Harris and Son, to become the largest producer of farm equipment in the British Empire (*see* 1847). H. A. Massey retired to Cleveland in 1871, his son Charles moved the company to Toronto in 1878 and acquired the Toronto Light Binder before dying prematurely in 1884, and Massey is again headed by H. A. Massey, now 67, who effects the merger. Massey-Harris will produce the first self-propelled combine (*see* Ferguson, 1953).

Belgian grain trader Arthur Fribourg, 41, son of Michel, establishes a firm under his own name at Antwerp (*see* 1848; 1904).

American Biscuit & Manufacturing Co. is created by a merger of western bakeries under the leadership of Chicago lawyer Adolphus Williamson Green, 47, whose new company controls some 40 bakeries in 13 states (*see* National Biscuit, 1898).

New York Biscuit Co. is created by a merger of some 23 bakeries in 10 states, including Newburyport's 98-year-old John Pearson & Son and Boston's 89-year-old Bent & Co. Boston's 85-year-old Kennedy Biscuit Works has become the largest U.S. bakery and joins New York Biscuit in May as Chicago lawyer-financier W. H. (William Henry) Moore, 41, his brother James, 38, and two associates contribute financing and aggressive leadership in a bid to give New York Biscuit control of the entire industry (*see* Nabisco, 1898).

American Biscuit (above) is headed by St. Joseph, Mo., cracker baker F. L. Sommer, whose Premium Saltines are famous for their parrot trademark and their "Polly wants a cracker" slogan. A. W. Green dispatches Sommer to open a bakery at New York that will challenge New York Biscuit in its own territory, and a price war begins that will continue until 1898.

Thomas Lipton enters the tea business to assure supplies of tea at low cost for his 300 grocery shops (*see* 1879). He offers "The Finest the World Can Produce" at 1 s., 7 d./lb. when the going price is roughly a shilling higher (*see* 1893).

The United States has 125,000 miles of railroad in operation, Britain 20,073 miles, and Russia 19,000.

Cudahy Packing Co. is founded by Irish-American meatpacker Michael Cudahy, 38, who was brought into the business 3 years ago by P. D. Armour, has gone into partnership with Armour in South Omaha, and now takes over Armour's interest in Armour-Cudahy Packing. Cudahy will introduce methods for curing meats under refrigeration and develop improved railroad cars, making it possible to cure meat all year round and transport it to distant cities (*see* 1910).

The U.S. Women's Pure Food Vacuum Preserving Co. founded by Amanda Jones uses her methods to preserve rice, tapioca pudding, and a line of luncheon meats (*see* 1872). Jones will sell her interest to a meatpacking company, and her concern will remain in business until 1923.

The Babcock Tester invented by Wisconsin agricultural chemist Stephen Moulton Babcock, 47, accurately measures the butterfat content of milk by dissolving the milk's casein in sulfuric acid. This liberates the butterfat, which is raised by centrifugal force into a glass tube for easy measurement. Butterfat content is used as a basis for paying dairy farmers.

Margarine will be improved in the next few years by the addition of vegetable oils such as palm oil and arachis oil from peanuts (*see* 1889). Manufacturers will be able to keep prices down through use of such oils, consumers will in many cases prefer the taste of margarine made from nuts and milk to that of margarine made from animal fat, and the improvement in flavor and quality will do much to break down prejudice against the product. Jurgens, van den Bergh, Lever Brothers, and other major producers will use large-scale advertising campaigns to attract buyers, and big stores will use giveaways of cheap sugar, coffee, tea, and crockery to push margarine sales.

Peanut butter is invented according to some accounts by a St. Louis physician, who has developed the butter as a health food, but the name of the physician will never surface and the product is more likely the invention of John Harvey Kellogg at Battle Creek, Mich. (*see* 1904; Granola, 1881; hydrogenation, 1901).

A light, rounded wooden box invented by a M. Ridel will permit the fragile cheese known as Camembert to be shipped abroad and achieve worldwide fame (*see* 1859; 1910).

Libby, McNeill & Libby develops a key opening device for rectangular meat cans (*see* 1878). The company has been selling its corned beef and other products in cans since 1885 and pioneers in making cans easier to open (*see* 1891).

The first aluminum saucepan is produced at Cleveland by Henry W. Avery, whose wife will use the pan until 1933 (*see* 1888).

Nonfiction: *Delicate Feasting* by U.S. gastronome Arthur Child, who writes, "In modern Paris, formerly the mecca of gourmands, it is becoming most difficult to dine, and everywhere, even in the best restaurants—we will say no more about private houses—we see the disastrous consequences of the absence of criticism. . . . The hurry and unrest of contemporary life do not conduce to the appreciation of fine cooking, nor is fine cooking possible where it is necessary to produce food in very large quantities," but Child allows that only in Paris can one still hope to find "in all most satisfactory conditions the best of the cook's art."

Cookbook: *Dainty Dishes for All the Year Round* by Mrs. S. T. Rorer.

Commercial bakeries now produce 20 percent of U.S. bread, up from less than 10 percent in 1850 (*see* 1900).

Alaska has 38 salmon canneries, up from one or two in 1878, and 4,000 men sail north from San

Francisco each summer to catch and can the fish, returning at the end of the 6-week season. Chinese from San Francisco's Chinatown work from 6 in the morning until 8 at night to cut, clean, and can the red salmon, chinooks, silversides, and dog salmon caught largely by Italians and Scandinavians (*see* Smith, 1903).

The New York–New Jersey shad catch totals 13.5 million pounds.

Cattlemen and sheepherders engage in open conflict as the once "inexhaustible" range of 17 western states and territories becomes fully stocked with 26 million head of cattle and 20 million head of sheep competing for grass on the prairie.

A second Morrill act passed by Congress August 30 supplements the 1862 law, establishing experiment stations, extension services, and agricultural research programs to aid U.S. farmers.

It now takes 37 man-hours to plant, cultivate, and harvest an acre of wheat in America, down from 148 hours in 1837.

Former Oregon wheat farmer Salmon Lusk Wright, 38, acquires the 320-acre Crystal rice plantation near Crowley in Acadia Parish, La. Since rice is the sole crop thereabouts, planters cannot use crop rotation to renew their soil, but Wright, the son of an Indiana flour miller and meat packer who shipped products by flatboat to New Orleans, will use his knowledge of soil building and maintenance to make Crystal the South's most famous rice property, despite the fact that he has had no previous experience in rice farming. Only two varieties of rice—Honduras and Japan—are now grown in Louisiana; Wright will find that either these are not fully adapted to local conditions or the seeds have deteriorated (*see* 1903).

Ellen Swallow Richards and Mary Hinman Abel open the New England Kitchen January 1 at 142 Pleasant Street, Boston, to sell cheap, nourishing food—beef broth, vegetable soup, pea soup, tomato soup, fish chowder, cornmeal mush, boiled hominy, oatmeal mush, pressed beef, beef stew, Indian pudding, rice pudding, and oatmeal cakes—based on weight or measure (*see* 1889). Their motive is to change the eating habits of working-class Americans, and they have developed precise recipes for soups, chowders, and stews, but the response is tepid (one woman says, "I don't want

eat what's good for me. I'd ruther eat what I'd ruther") and after 6 months Abel returns to Baltimore (*see* 1891).

Milk is pasteurized by law in many U.S. communities despite opposition by some dairy interests and people who call pasteurization "unnatural" (*see* 1860; Evans, 1917).

Hovis bread flour is introduced under that name by S. Fitton & Son, which has conducted a contest to rename Smith's Patent Germ Flour (*see* 1888). London student Herbert Grime has suggested the name, which is derived from the Latin *hominis vis,* meaning "the strength of man" (*see* 1896).

Henri Nestlé dies at Montreux, Switzerland, July 7 at age 74 after 15 years in retirement (*see* 1875). The company that bears his name opens a plant at Payerne to supplement those at Vevey and Berzhar (*see* 1898).

Fabrique de Produits Maggi, S.A., is founded by Julius Maggi (*see* Arome, 1889; bouillon concentrate, 1892).

Knox's Gelatine is introduced at Johnstown, N.Y., by local entrepreneur Charles B. Knox and his wife Rose (*née* Rosetta Markward), 33, who have invested their savings of $5,000 to buy a company and initiate packaging of unflavored granulated gelatin in premeasured portions. Consumers and manufacturers have used Irish moss (a red alga), Iceland moss (a lichen), agar-agar (a seaweed), fruits rich in pectin, and isinglass (a gelatin made from fish), mostly to clarify beer, wines, and other liquids, but Knox's Gelatine is easier to use (*see* Jell-O, 1897). Rose will take over the business after her husband's death in 1908 and continue to run it until she is 88 (*see* cookbook, 1896).

John Mackintosh & Sons has its beginnings in a Halifax, England, pastry shop opened by Mackintosh and his wife, Violet. They introduce sweets under the name Mackintosh's All-Celebrated Toffee, will incorporate in 1899 under the name John Mackintosh Ltd., and by 1903 will be exporting to Italy, Spain, and China (*see* 1904).

French production of raisin wine reaches 4.3 million liters, up from 2 million in 1881 (*see* 1882).

New England dairyman H. P. Hood begins retail distribution but will not pasteurize his milk until

1896 (*see* 1854). Now 69, Hood has been joined by his sons George and Gilbert, who will help him consolidate some of the nearly 2,000 competing milk routes in greater Boston, establish new ones, and set up new receiving stations for milk in various parts of New England (*see* 1897).

Unsweetened condensed milk is introduced commercially by the 5-year-old Helvetia Milk Condensing Co. at Highland, Ill. (*see* Borden, 1855; Meyenberg, 1885; Our Pet, 1894).

Canada Dry Ginger Ale has its beginnings in a small Toronto plant opened by local pharmacist John J. McLaughlin to manufacture carbonated water for sale in siphons to corner drugstores as a mixer for fruit juices and flavored extracts. McLaughlin will soon start making his own extracts and will develop a beverage that he will call McLaughlin Belfast Style Ginger Ale (*see* 1907; Lemon's, 1871).

New York's Imperial Hotel opens at the southeast corner of Broadway and 32nd Street with a Palm Room in green marble, a luxurious lobby, and a dining room that attracts the city's parvenus.

The New York restaurant Sherry's, opened at Fifth Avenue and 37th Street by Louis Sherry, is elegant enough to rival Delmonico's.

The St. Louis restaurant Busch's Grove opens at 9160 Clayton Road, serving dishes that include a garlicky "Bellevue" salad and prime ribs with cottage fries.

England and Wales have 103,000 public houses (pubs), one for every 300 people. Major brewers such as Bass, Whitbread, and Worthington compete for the pub trade by signing pubs to exclusive contracts (*see* 1989).

Christiana's (Oslo's) Frognerseteren Hoved-Restaurant opens with a menu that includes kokt laks med agurksalaten (boiled salmon with cucumber salad), multer med krem, and raspberry cake.

The Paris restaurant De La Tour d'Argent inaugurates the practice of presenting each guest who orders pressed duck with a card bearing the duck's number (*see* 1880). The prince of Wales receives number 328, the practice of numbering its ducks will continue for more than a century, the restaurant will have its own duck farms, and although it will offer more than a dozen other duck or duckling dishes, most of them much tastier than the rather dry canard à presse, it is pressed duck that will be the choice of most visitors (*see* 1913).

1891

Hawaii's king David Kalakaua dies January 20 at age 54 after a 16-year reign and is succeeded by his sister, 52, who will reign until 1893 as Queen Lydia Liliuokalani. The white elite, which owns 80 percent of arable lands in the islands, has united in the Hawaiian League to oppose Kalakaua, who has favored the interests of sugar magnate Claus Spreckels, and the sugar planters form an Annexation Club in a plot to overthrow the queen (*see* Spreckels, 1883; abdication, 1893).

Russian crops fail, reducing millions to starvation; the rural peasantry raids towns in search of food. President Harrison responds to an appeal by Cassius Marcellus Clay, 81, who was Abraham Lincoln's minister to Russia, and orders that U.S. flour be shipped to the hungry Russians (*see* 1892).

Oklahoma Territory lands ceded to the United States by the Sac, Fox, and Potawatomie become available to white settlement September 18 under terms of a presidential proclamation that opens 900,000 acres (*see* 1889; 1893).

Tight money conditions bankrupt Kansas farmers; some 18,000 prairie schooners (covered wagons) cross the Mississippi, headed back east (*see* 1889; 1890; 1894).

Britain's food industry employs nearly 600,000 workers; the number of jam makers has increased 80 percent since 1881, the number of greengrocers has increased by 40 percent, and there have been corresponding increases in the numbers of grocers, fishmongers, and other traders in food.

Candy maker Milton S. Hershey verges on bankruptcy until a cousin, William L. Blair, agrees to invest some of his inheritance in Hershey's caramel company, which will soon employ 2,000 workers at Lancaster and another 400 at Chicago (*see* 1886; 1892).

American Sugar Refining is incorporated in New Jersey by H. O. Havemeyer, whose 4-year-old Sugar

Refineries Co. is dissolved by the New York courts. The new company begins taking over the entire U.S. sugar industry in one colossal trust (*see* 1892).

Ceresota Flour is introduced by Northwestern Consolidated Milling Co., a new firm created by a merger of six Minneapolis millers who have been disturbed by the 1889 Pillsbury-Washburn merger.

Quaker Oats Co. is created by seven independent millers who form what critics will call the "oatmeal trust." They hire five stout men to dress as Quakers, ride atop the engines and cars of a train running between Cedar Rapids, Iowa, and Portland, Ore., and jump down at each stop to distribute free sample boxes of Quaker Oats (*see* 1893; 1901).

Atlanta pharmacist Asa G. Candler, 40, acquires ownership of Coca-Cola for $2,300. He buys up stock in the firm but will achieve great success only when he changes Coca-Cola advertising to end claims such as "Wonderful Nerve and Brain Tonic and Remarkable Therapeutic Agent" and "Its beneficial effects upon diseases of the vocal chords are wonderful." Candler will make Coca-Cola syrup the basis of a popular 5¢ soft drink (*see* 1886; 1892).

New York's Gristede Brothers grocery chain begins with a carriage-trade store opened by Diedrich and Charles Gristede at 42nd Street and Second Avenue.

The first electric oven for commercial sale is introduced at St. Paul, Minn., by Carpenter Electric Heating Manufacturing Co. (*see* 1893).

The four-masted ship *Shenandoah* sets sail from San Francisco with a record 5,200 tons of wheat, but although California wheat has remained competitive through reduced freight rates as larger and larger vessels have entered the trade, the state's wheat exports now begin to fall precipitously.

A Libby, McNeill & Libby employee invents the first machine to solder rectangular tins automatically (*see* 1890). The new machine supplements one invented earlier by Libby employee James Brown, whose machine solders round tins, and it will save Libby $50,000 its first year (*see* sauerkraut, 1904).

Nonfiction: *Common Sense in the Household: A Manual of Practical Housewifery* by Marion Harland, now 60, who writes, "It is an idea which should have been exploded long ago that plain roast, boiled, and fried, on Monday, Tuesday, Wednesday, and Thursday, cod-fish on Friday, with pork-and-beans every Saturday, are means of grace, because economical."

Cookbook: *La Scienza in cucina e l'arte di mangiar bene* by Italian author Pellegrino Artusi, a native of Lugo di Romagna, will be the best-known cooking guide of its kind for generations.

U.S. Department of Agriculture scientists in this decade will begin planting date palms in the California's Coachella Valley; by 1915, the date palms will be firmly rooted and receiving irrigation with Colorado River water delivered by the All-American Canal.

Boston's New England Kitchen opens an annex across the street in November to bake and sell bread (*see* 1890). Businessman Edward Atkinson has arranged financing for the shop, which uses a recipe for "health bread" from Atkinson's treatise on nutrition (*see* 1892).

A New York version of the New England Kitchen opens in December at 341 Hudson Street. Columbia University metallurgist Thomas Egleston has obtained a $5,000 contribution from sugar baron Thomas Havemeyer to finance the project, but dietary restrictions of immigrant Jews and taste preferences of Italian immigrants frustrate nutrition reformers and the experiment will be short lived.

Julia C. Lathrop, 33, an MIT student of Ellen Swallow Richards, accepts a position at Chicago's Hull House, opened 2 years ago in the South Halsted Street slums by Jane Addams, 31, and Ellen Gates Starr, 32. Mary Hinman Abel has trained Lathrop, who sets up a people's kitchen modeled on the ones in Boston in New York. The operation will continue for 32 years, by which time the Boston and New York experiments (plus one in Philadelphia) will long since have been abandoned.

British butchers convicted of selling meat unfit for human consumption may be required on a second offense to put up signs on their shops stating their record (*see* 1875). A Public Health Act passed by Parliament provides for the public exposure of wrongdoing.

U.S. merchants continue with impunity to misrepresent their food products, selling "deviled ham" that is really minced tripe dyed red. North Dakota alone consumes 10 times as much "Vermont" maple syrup as the state of Vermont produces. Congress enacts a law requiring the country of origin to appear prominently on product labels following revelations that Maine herring is being labeled "imported French sardines" and sold in fancy boxes with labels in French (*see* Canadian Club, below).

British consumers are so accustomed to having their pepper adulterated that a store selling pure ground pepper may have it returned because the color is "too dark" and the flavor "too strong." On the Continent, Europeans prefer white pepper, which has only one-quarter the strength of black pepper (most of the pungency of black pepper comes from volatile oils and other properties found near the outer husks). Despite the Pure Food law of 1875, ground pepper is so commonly adulterated that knowledgeable consumers in Britain buy only whole peppercorns, but shops are obliged by public taste to sell ground pepper mixed with pepper dust (composed of dried, powdered autumn leaves), hot pepper dust (made from the ground hulls of black mustard), or white pepper dust (ground from rice) (*see* 1900).

Rath Packing Co. is founded at Waterloo, Iowa, by E. F. and J. W. Rath, whose firm will grow to become a worldwide supplier of canned and smoked hams, bacon, sausage, and luncheon meats.

Beech-Nut Packing Co. has its beginnings in the Imperial Packing Co. founded at Canojoharie, N.Y., by local farmer Walter Lipe, his brother Raymond, Bartlett Arkell, and John Zieley. Their smokehouse cures ham and bacon to be shipped down the Mohawk River to New York for sale alongside the company's fancy pail lard (*see* 1899).

The "Del Monte" label, which will become the leading label for U.S. canned fruits and vegetables, is used for the first time. Oakland Preserving Co. executives at Oakland, Calif., have been inspired by Charles Crocker's 11-year-old Hotel Del Monte at Monterey and appropriate its name to identify their premium quality fruit ("extras") (*see* 1865; 1895).

Britons in this decade will switch from cognac and soda to whisky and soda as good brandies grow prohibitively expensive due to the devastation of France's Cognac region by grape phylloxerae. The newly blended Scotch whiskies are more palatable to many than the old single-grain malt whiskies and have more character than the grain whiskies produced in the patent still of 1830 (*see* 1850; lawsuit, 1905).

Hiram Walker's Club whiskey becomes "Canadian Club" following passage of U.S. legislation (above; *see* 1857). Imitations marketed by Kentucky distillers have also played a role in making the company decide to rename its brand (*see* Allied-Lyons, 1986).

New York City has more soda fountains than saloons. *Harper's Weekly* reports that marble chips from the construction of St. Patrick's Cathedral on Fifth Avenue are being used to make sulfuric acid for the production of 25 million gallons of soda water.

New York's $1.2 million Holland House opens on Fifth Avenue, a few blocks north of Madison Square, with a dining room which challenges that of the Imperial Hotel opened last year. The luxurious hotels encourage lavish wining and dining: 15-course dinners invariably begin with oysters, followed by soup, clear and thick. Hors d'oeuvres (timbales, palmettes, mousselines, crustades, bouchets) ensue, then a fish course, then an entrée of oysters, crabs, lobsters, shrimp, or frog's legs. A roast (saddle of lamb, mutton, venison, antelope, turkey, goose, or capon) is served with one or two vegetables, then a punch or sherbet (an adaptation of the Norman custom of serving Calvados *trow*), then a game course (venison, bear, five different kinds of wild duck, geese, grouse, prairie hen, English or American hare, partridge, pheasant, pigeons, wild turkey, or woodcock), then a cold dish consisting of an aspic of goose, oysters, partridge, prawns, or whatever the chef may have in his icebox), then a sweet dish, or perhaps two sweet dishes, one cold (jellies, creams, blancmange, charlottes, and the like) and one hot (fritters, a pudding, pancakes, omelette, or soufflé). Dessert consists of cheese, fresh fruit, preserved fruits, dried fruits, candied fruits, mottoes, bonbons, ices, ice cream (fancy and cakes), followed by Turkish or French coffee. Sauternes or hock are served with the oysters, sherry with the soup, Rhine wine with the fish, claret with the entrée, champagne with the roast, more champagne with the cold dishes and the hot or cold sweet dishes, port with the dessert, and liqueur with the coffee.

1892

 The Populist party polls more than a million votes in the U.S. presidential election as farmers register their protest against the railroads and against farm-machine makers.

Famine continues to cripple Russia, but by late January some 3 million barrels of U.S. flour are en route to relieve the starvation that is killing millions (*see* 1891).

London children in Bethnal Green live almost entirely on bread; 83 percent of them have no other solid food for 17 out of 21 meals each week. Black treacle (molasses) and cheap jam make the bread palatable (*see* 1894).

Cheap grain from America and Russia depresses French farm prices. Only one French farm holding in 15 has a horse-drawn cultivator, one in 150 has a mechanical reaper, and French farmers demand higher import duties to protect them from more efficient overseas competitors.

American Sugar Refining controls 98 percent of the U.S. sugar industry (*see* 1891); H. O. Havemeyer's Sugar Trust uses political influence to suppress foreign competition with tariff walls, and the company saves itself millions of dollars per year in duties by having its raw-sugar imports shortweighted (*see* 1895; Spreckels, 1897).

New York's 14-story Rhinelander Sugar House near City Hall is torn down after decades of dominating the city skyline.

Asa Candler organizes the Coca-Cola Co. at Atlanta (*see* 1891; 1895).

The first Hawaiian pineapple cannery opens (*see* 1790). A Baltimore cannery in this decade will pack pineapples from the Bahamas, using handmade containers, but it will have little success. English-born horticulturist Capt. John Kidwell, who arrived at Honolulu in 1880, has built the cannery after a decade of patient, scientific efforts to develop qual-

ity pineapple and grow it commercially in the Manoa Valley of Honolulu, where previously the plants have been torn up as an agricultural nuisance. After failing in an effort to grow the Kona variety, Capt. Kidwell has imported the smooth Cayenne variety with a view to supplying the market for fresh fruit in San Francisco but has found, like others before him, that pineapples do not travel well. He processes the fruit of 1,000 plants in partnership with John Emmeleuth but finds the high U.S. tariffs on canned fruits an impossible obstacle and will ship only a few thousand cases before finally giving up (*see* Dole, 1902).

George A. Hormel Co. is founded by Austin, Minn., butcher-meatpacker George Albert Hormel, 31 (who pronounces his name with emphasis on the first syllable). He converted an abandoned creamery on the Cedar River into an abbatoir last year, slaughters 610 hogs by year's end, and will personally split 100,000 carcasses before letting anyone else do the job as he builds a business in ham, bacon, sausage, and fresh pork (*see* 1926).

The first successful U.S. gasoline tractor is produced by Waterloo, Iowa, farmer John Froelich, who will organize Waterloo Gasoline Traction Engine Co. early next year. John Deere Plow Co. will acquire the firm (*see* 1902).

Baltimore machine shop foreman William Painter, 54, patents a clamp-on tin-plated steel bottle cap with an inner seal disk of natural cork and a flanged edge; he also patents a capping machine for beer and soft drink bottles. The new bottle cap will replace the unsanitary Miller Plunger patented in 1874 and the 1878 Hutchinson Bottle Stopper, both widely used. Painter will design an automatic filler and capper with a capacity of 60 to 100 bottles per minute and establish Crown Cork and Seal at Baltimore to market his bottle caps and machines (*see* New Process Cork, 1913).

The Dewar vessel invented by Scottish chemist Sir James Dewar, now 50, at Cambridge University is a vacuum flask that will lead to advances in food preservation (*see* 1873; Thermos bottle, 1904).

Homogenized milk has its beginnings in patents granted to French inventor Paul Marix for the manufacture of margarine. Marix has forced a liquid mixture through a small hole to obtain an emulsion. His third patent, granted April 4, is for a complex system in which emulsification is obtained by centrifugally forcing a liquid mixture to against a fixed surface by means of a turbine (*see* Gaulin, 1899).

The hamburger sandwich is invented by some accounts at Akron, Ohio, by Akron County Fair concessionaire Frank Menches, 27, who has nearly run out of sausage. He grinds up the meat he has left and serves it as a meat patty (but *see* also Nagreen, 1885; Louis Lassen, 1900).

Liederkranz cheese, invented by Monroe, N.Y., delicatessen man Emile Frey, 23, is a milder version of Limburger. Frey's employer has asked him to copy the Limburger-like Bismarck Schlosskäse, which his choral society has been ordering from Germany but which falls to pieces en route to America. The choral society, which calls itself Liederkranz and has its own Liederkranz Hall in New York's East 58th Street, approves the taste and confers its name on the new cheese, which will be produced initially by the Monroe Cheese Co. (*see* 1926; Jossi, 1877; Borden, 1929).

Canadian druggist William Saunders, 56, crosses Red Fife wheat with an early ripening variety obtained from India and produces the hardy Markham wheat strain on a farm in British Columbia. Saunders has been named head of the Dominion Experimental Farms and his Markham variety will expand Canadian wheat production (*see* MacKay, 1886).

Boston's New England Kitchen delivers hot lunches in the spring to a local high school, charging 15¢ each, and is rewarded with a contract to supply all of the city's high schools with hot lunches beginning in 1894—the first such program anywhere in the United States (*see* 1891). The Kitchen will open a branch in the city's West End and another at Olneyville, R.I., a manufacturing suburb of Providence (*see* Columbian Exposition, 1893).

Danish veterinarian Bernhard Laurits Frederik Bang, 44, develops a method for eradicating tuberculosis from dairy herds (*see* Bang's disease, 1896).

The first U.S. cattle tuberculosis test is made March 3 on a herd at Villa Nova, Pa., with tuberculin brought from Europe by the dean of the University of Pennsylvania veterinary department.

R. H. Macy partner Nathan Straus, 44, launches a campaign for pasteurized milk; he will establish milk stations in New York and other large cities.

Congress is petitioned to hold pure food law hearings (*see* 1891; Wiley, 1902).

The *Ladies' Home Journal* announces that it will accept no more patent medicine advertisements. The *Journal* has been edited since 1889 by Dutch-American editor Edward William Bok, 29 (*see* 1883; 1904).

H. J. Heinz adopts "57 Varieties" as an advertising slogan (the firm produces well over that number of products). Henry J. Heinz has seen a car card advertising 21 shoe styles while riding on a New York elevated train and adapts the idea (*see* 1888; 1900).

Fabrique de Produits Maggi introduces bouillon concentrate in granulated form (*see* 1890). The concentrate will be marketed in bouillon cubes beginning in 1906 (*see* 1912; Nestlé merger, 1947).

Fig Newtons are introduced by the 87-year-old Kennedy Biscuit Works of the 2-year-old New York Biscuit Co. Kennedy bakery manager James Hazen has been persuaded to try out a new machine to make preserve-filled cookies invented by James Henry Mitchell of Philadelphia; he calls the cookies "Newtons," having named a series of earlier cookies "Beacon Hill," "Brighton," and "Melrose" (like Newton, all are names of Boston suburbs). Since fig is the preserve most often used to fill the cookies, those made by other New York Biscuit bakeries to fill a rising demand will be Fig Newtons (*see* National Biscuit Co., 1898).

Swiss chocolate maker David Sprüngli buys a retail shop in Zurich's Bahnhofstrasse (*see* 1875). It will grow to have more than 30 ovens and 30 bakers (six of them apprentices) turning out cherry tarts, schwarzwälder, and other pastries that will be served in a large upstairs restaurant and sold downstairs along with chocolates in a great variety of shapes and sizes made in pewter molds, chocolate truffles (balls of chocolate and fresh cream rolled in cocoa powder), 30 varieties of hand-dipped chocolates (including squares with fillings of orange, lemon, strawberry, mint, and nougat), other candies, and small sandwiches, along with vanilla, chocolate, strawberry, apricot, hazelnut, lemon, and mocha ice cream.

San Francisco *confiseur* Simon Blum begins making candy, delivering his confections to the mansions of the Budds, Crockers, Fairs, Spreckels (*see* 1937).

Caramel maker Milton S. Hershey visits England and finds that his biggest customer there is cutting up slabs of imported Hershey caramel into bite-sized pieces and dipping them in chocolate (*see* 1891). The "Caramel King," as he will soon be called, suspects that caramels may be a passing fad, whereas chocolate is *food*. He uses chocolate to flavor some of his caramels and becomes interested in the manufacture of chocolate (*see* 1893).

New York Condensed Milk Co. adds evaporated milk to its Borden product line and begins selling fresh milk in Chicago—its first significant geographic expansion (*see* 1885; Meyenberg, 1885; Elgin, 1894).

Heublein Club cocktails are introduced at Hartford, Conn., by the 17-year-old firm G. F. Heublein & Bro. started by restaurateur's sons Gilbert and Louis Heublein. The Connecticut governor's Foot Guards have ordered a gallon each of martinis and Manhattans prepared in advance for an outing, which has been rained out two weekends in a row, and the prepared cocktails are about to be dumped, but they turn out when tasted to be better than when freshly made and the Heublein brothers are inspired to bring out the world's first bottled cocktails (*see* A-1 Sauce, 1906).

Campari apéritif is introduced by Italian entrepreneur Davide Campari, whose father, Gaspare, opened a café at Milan in 1867. The younger Campari acquires a factory at Sesto Giovanni to produce the apéritif after having studied the distilling art in France.

Denver's Brown Palace Hotel opens in August, located in what had been the pasture of Colorado pioneer Henry Cordis Brown, now 70. It has a ship's tavern whose head captain is dressed in nautical garb with four stripes on his sleeve; its breakfast menu includes creamed chipped beef, chicken hash and cream, broiled Rocky Mountain trout, liver and bacon, and double-thick lamb chops.

Montreal's seafood restaurant Des Jardins opens at 1175 Mackay Street. Its specialties will include Omble Arctic (arctic char), Malpeque oysters from Prince Edward Island, and sole au vermouth.

Stockholm's 105-year-old opera house is demolished along with its famous Operakällaren restaurant, but a new opera house will open in 1895 with a formal street-level restaurant boasting crystal chandeliers, oak paneling, red velour upholstery, lush carpeting, and windows overlooking the harbor and royal palace.

1893

"The Significance of the Frontier in American History" by University of Wisconsin historian Frederick Jackson Turner, 31, observes that the frontier has been the source of the individualism, self-reliance, inventiveness, and restless energy so characteristic of Americans but that it is now ending. He delivers his paper at a meeting of the American Historical Association held at Chicago during the World's Columbian Exposition, which opens to show the world what progress Chicago has made since the fire of 1871.

A vast section of northern Oklahoma Territory opens to land-hungry settlers September 16. Thousands of "Boomers" jump at a signal from federal marshals and rush in by foot, on horseback, in buggies and wagons, and on bicycles to stake and claim quarter-section farms, but as in 1889 they find that "Sooners" have sneaked across the line earlier by cover of night and started building houses on the 165- by 58-mile Cherokee Strip— 6 million acres purchased from the Cherokees in 1891 for $8.5 million.

Economic depression continues in America as European investors withdraw funds.

American Cereal Co. pays $7,500 to acquire American Health Food Co., a minor competitor in the breakfast food industry. It takes advantage of the spring financial panic to acquire Pettijohn's California Breakfast Food, which has promoted its wheat flakes with advertisements attacking oatmeal (*see* Johnson, Boswell, 1755). "My *horse* eats oats," one Pettijohn ad has said, and it has gone on to quote a college president to the effect that while horses and Scottish Highlanders may be able to digest oats without difficulty, in most people oatmeal can produce colic, flatulence, biliousness, rash, "eruptions," and other troubles. American Cereal pays $12,340 for Pettijohn and its emblem—a brown bear bearing on its flank the words, "Bear in Mind Our Trade Mark"; it spends another $50,000 to improve the Pettijohn plant and promote the cereal in ways that do not disparage oatmeal (*see* Quaker Oats, 1901).

The Swiss *épicerie* Confiserie Hanselmann opens at St. Moritz in the Grisons. Baker Fritz Hanselmann of the Hotel Kulm, who came to work 3 years ago, receives backing from hotel owner Kaspar Badrutt on condition that he supply all the hotels of the village with his breads and rolls (the Palace Hotel, which opens in 1896, will always have its own baker, but every other hotel, auberge, inn, and restaurant will buy Hanselmann's flaky croissants, milk rolls, French bread, English toast bread, rye bread, graham bread, fruit bread, Stollen, Butschella (a fat raisin bun), macaroons, lebkuchen, napoléons, éclairs, chocolate cream cakes, apple squares, walnut tortes, lemon rolls, plum tarts, strawberry frappés, and purple frappés (made from the myrtle, a wild huckleberry). Hanselmann will serve open sandwiches (smoked salmon, ham, ham and melted cheese, scrambled egg, sardines, and caviar), bundnerfleisch, entrecôte, wiener schnitzel, and green salads for lunch, and St. Moritz schoolchildren will grow up eating Hanselmann's pasta ruttli—crumbly bits of pastry that have broken off the edges of pies and tarts and are distributed free to the children. His daughter, Clara, will be born next year and succeed her parents as owner of the shop, which she will still be running at age 75.

Philadelphia's Reading Terminal Market opens to give the city the world's largest indoor market. Built by the Philadelphia & Reading Railway Co., it is modeled after the great roofed-gallery markets of Europe with refrigeration controlled by a basement installation.

The Columbian Exposition at Chicago (above) features an entire electric kitchen (*see* electric oven, 1891). Each saucepan, broiler, etc., has its own electrical outlet, but the electrical appliances burn out easily, repairmen are hard to find, and such appliances will not come into wide use for another 30 years.

The École de la Société Suisse des Hôtelières opened October 15 at Lausanne's Hôtel Angleterre will move in 1903 to the Association Figuiers on the Avenue de Cour and expand as its enrollment grows (*see* 1943).

U.S. Rural Free Delivery begins with five test postal routes in hilly West Virginia.

Rural U.S. telephone companies begin to proliferate as patents granted to Alexander Graham Bell in 1876 expire.

Nonfiction: *Children of the Poor* by Danish-born New York journalist Jacob August Riis, 44, who writes, "Half the drunkenness that makes so many homes miserable is at least encouraged, if not directly caused, by mismanagement and bad cooking at home." He encourages establishment of home economics classes for tenement girls and their families.

The National Household Economic Association is founded with goals that include securing "skilled labor in every major department in our homes," elevating domestic service to a more skilled level by organizing schools of household science and service, and establishing employment bureaus for servants. Women's clubs in Chicago, New York, and Philadelphia organize employment bureaus and plan training schools for domestic help, but servants cannot afford the tuition of such schools, and employers are reluctant to pay for the training of servants who may soon quit to work elsewhere.

Reid's Yellow Dent corn wins a prize at the the World's Columbian Exposition in Chicago (*see* 1847). Farmer James Reid, whose father created the strain, has perfected and improved it, and it has become the basic commercial variety of America's Corn Belt (*see* hybrid corn, 1921).

Seabrook Farms has its beginnings in a 78-acre property purchased by New Jersey farmer Arthur Seabrook, who will raise vegetables with his wife and, later, his son Charles (*see* 1920).

Reformers set up a model workmen's cottage in the Massachusetts pavilion at the World's Columbian

Exposition in Chicago and demonstrate how a worker can eat well on $500 per year. The cottage serves 30¢ meals, cooked in an Aladdin-equipped kitchen (*see* 1889), to thousands of fairgoers, whose menus indicate the nutritional value of each item listed.

Quaker's dietetic pastry flour wins a "highest" award at the Chicago fair (above). Produced by a division of American Cereal Co., the flour is an advance over self-rising flour.

Aunt Jemima Pancake Mix is promoted at the Chicago fair (above) by St. Joseph, Mo., miller R. T. Davis, who has acquired Chris Rutt's mix of 1889 and improved it by adding rice flour, corn sugar, and powdered milk so that it can be prepared by adding only water. Davis sets up a 24-foot-high flour barrel, arranges displays inside the barrel, and engages former Kentucky slave Nancy Green, 59, to demonstrate the Aunt Jemima mix at a griddle outside the barrel (*see* 1910).

Shredded Wheat is pioneered by Nebraska lawyer Henry Drushel Perky, 50, who finds that boiled wheat helps his digestion. Having enlisted the help of Watertown, N.Y., designer Harry Ford to create a machine that will shred wheat, he travels to Denver, persuades his brother John to manufacture the patented machine, goes into business with John under the name Cereal Machine Co. to produce hand machines that people can use to make their own wheat biscuits, and opens a Denver restaurant in which all foods served contain Shredded Wheat (*see* 1894).

Cream of Wheat is introduced at Grand Forks, N.D., where Thomson S. Amidon, chief miller at the Diamond Mill, has persuaded the mill's owners George Ball, Emory Mapes, and George Clifford to produce a cereal made of "purified" wheat middlings (*see* LeCroix, 1865). It takes 15 minutes to cook (30 minutes for infants), and when New York flour brokers Lamont, Corliss & Co. receive 10 cases they wire back within 3 hours for another 50. Some 550 cases are sold the first year, and although Cream of Wheat will not show a profit until 1900, the cereal will be so popular by 1897 that its makers will move their operations to Minneapolis (*see* 1902).

C. W. (Charles William) Post, 38, develops Postum—a nutritious beverage of wheat berries, molasses, and wheat bran designed to replace coffee. A Texas inventor, real estate developer, and farm machinery salesman whose health and financial fortunes have declined, Post is an ulcer patient at the Western Health Reform Institute, operated since 1876 by John Harvey Kellogg, and has followed Kellogg's regimen of hot baths, exercise, and foods that include a Caramel Coffee made of bran, molasses, and burnt bread crusts (such imitation coffee drinks have been available for decades). After more than 10 months without apparent improvement, he has asked Kellogg to let him market the Caramel Coffee in lieu of paying his bill, but Kellogg has refused (*see* 1895).

Caramel maker Milton S. Hershey, now 36, visits the Chicago fair (above) and sees chocolate-making machinery exhibited by J. M. Lehman Co., a Dresden firm. He buys the equipment, has it shipped to his Lancaster, Pa., plant along with additional equipment from Germany, and begins experiments with it (*see* 1891; 1894).

Milwaukee's Pabst beer wins a blue ribbon at the World's Columbian Exposition and will hereafter be sold as Pabst Blue Ribbon (*see* 1889).

Mott's Apple Cider and Vinegar win top honors for quality at the World's Columbian Exposition (above) (*see* 1842; Duffy-Mott, 1900).

Poland Spring water wins the Medal of Excellence at the World's Columbian Exposition (*see* 1845; 1904).

White Rock soda water is promoted at the Chicago fair by Charles Welch, who has had the pavilion over his spring at Waukesha, Wis., dismantled and moved to Chicago, where it has been reassembled to serve as a refreshment stand (*see* 1887). White Rock executives at the fair purchase rights to the painting *Psyche at Nature's Mirror* by British artist Paul Thumann and will make his scantily clad Psyche the White Rock Girl trademark (*see* 1895).

Thomas Lipton registers a new trademark for the tea he has been selling since 1890 and which is sold only in packages, never in bulk. Over the facsimile signature "Thomas J. Lipton, Tea Planter, Ceylon," Lipton prints the words "Nongenuine without this signature" (*see* Victoria's Jubilee, 1897).

Bovril employee S. R. Benson quits to go into business as an "advertiser's agent" with Bovril as his first client (*see* 1887). He will create a sustained and coordinated advertising effort, featuring testimonials to the product's alleged health-promoting virtues, and its use by famous explorers and military heroes, that will make Bovril a household name in Britain by the end of the century (*see* Colman's mustard, 1926).

New York's new Waldorf Hotel engages Swiss chef Oscar Tschirky, 26, formerly in charge of private dining rooms at Delmonico's, as maître d'hôtel. Oscar of the Waldorf will be credited with creating the Waldorf salad, made from bits of apple, lettuce, and mayonnaise (*see* 1931; cookbook, 1896). Respectable New York women can now eat in the public rooms of restaurants without causing gossip, but the only proper way for a gentleman to entertain a lady is to take her to dinner, to theater, and, afterward, to supper, and the only way for a man to make a splash is to spend money on food. Escorts are judged by the quantity and quality of food that they supply.

Maxim's opens May 21 at 3, rue Royale, Paris, where Reynolds Bar waiter Maxime Gaillard has taken over a location operated until 3 years ago as an ice cream parlor by an Italian named Imoda, who for some reason hung out a German flag on Bastille Day, causing such a furor that an outraged mob tore the building down. Gaillard, who has dropped the "e" at the end of his first name to make it more English, has borrowed the money to buy the place from a neighborhood butcher and wine dealer. He attracts only fiacre and hansom-cab drivers and coachmen at first, and he will be nearly bankrupt by next year (*see* 1894).

1894

U.S. wheat sells at 49¢ per bushel, down from $1.05 in 1870. Prairie schooners headed back east have canvas covers painted with the words "In God we trusted, in Kansas we busted."

Ralston Purina has its beginnings in the Robinson-Danforth Commission Co. founded by St. Louis feed merchants George Robinson, 32, and William H. Danforth, 24. They have mixed corn and oats to produce a feed that will not give horses and mules colic as corn alone may do (*see* Purina, 1897).

England's 36-mile Manchester Ship Canal opens to link Manchester with the Mersey River.

U.S. ice-making plants produce 1.5 million tons of machine-made ice (*see* 1889; 1926).

The death of his aunt Mattie Snavely at age 62 in April comes as a blow to caramel maker Milton S. Hershey, but his business, which has owed so much to Aunt Mattie's faith and financial encouragement, is now on a sound footing; with exports going to China, Japan, and Australia as well as to Europe, it is grossing about $1 million per year (*see* 1893). Hershey & Blair is reincorporated under the name Lancaster Caramel Company, and Hershey also incorporates Hershey Chocolate Co. He moves his Chicago production lines to Bloomington, Ill., so as to be close to the dairy farms that provide fresh milk for his Crystal A caramels, opens factories at Mt. Joy and Reading, Pa., and spends the summer in Europe. The people at J. M. Lehmann help get him into Swiss factories that make milk chocolate, and while he does not learn their recipes he experiments on his own, using fresh milk, not powder. Fresh milk gives chocolate better flavor, but it has to be condensed to eliminate excess moisture and keep from spoiling, so Hershey learns how to condense it. Ordinary milk shortens the product's shelf life substantially, and shelf life will always be a paramount consideration in the formulation of any commercial food product. Hershey learns the correct proportions of milk, how to add the sugar, what kind of cacao beans to use, how to roast them, how long to conch in order to reduce the moisture content of a milk-and-chocolate paste and give it a smoother texture. Impressed with German technology, he favors J. M. Lehmann & Co. with an order for additional machinery, including conching equipment. Hershey's first chocolate is used as coating for his caramels (*see* 1900).

The New York Condensed Milk Co. acquires Elgin Condensed Milk Co. of West Elgin, Ill., which the late Gail Borden helped found in the early 1850s (*see* 1892; 1899).

Fiction: "A Woman's Kingdom" by Russian playwright–story writer Anton Pavlovich Chekhov, 34: "In addition to the family dinner, consisting of cabbage soup, suckling pig, goose with apples, and so on, a so-called 'French' or 'chef's' dinner used to be prepared in the kitchen on great holidays, in case any visitor in the upper storey wanted a meal. When they heard the clatter of crockery in the dining room, Lysevich began to betray a noticeable excitement; he rubbed his hands, shrugged his shoulders, screwed up his eyes and described with feeling what dinners her father and uncle used to give at one time, and a marvelous *matelote* of turbots the cook here could make; it was not a *matelote*, but a veritable revelation! He was already gloating over the dinner, already eating it in imagination and enjoying it. When Anna Akimovna took his arm and led him to the dining-room, he tossed off a glass of vodka and put a piece of salmon in his mouth; he positively purred with pleasure. He munched loudly, disgustingly, emitting sounds from his nose, while his eyes grew oily and rapacious. The *hors d'oeuvres* were superb; among other things, there were fresh white mushrooms stewed in cream, and *sauce provençale* made of fried oysters and crayfish, strongly flavoured with some bitter pickles. The dinner, consisting of elaborate holiday dishes, was excellent, and so were the wines."

Cookbooks: *The Epicurean; The Complete Treatise of Analytical and Practical Studies on the Culinary Art, Including Table and Wine Service, How to Prepare and Cook Dishes . . . etc. and a Selection of Interesting Bills of Fare of Delmonico's, from 1862 to 1894, Making a Franco-American Culinary Encyclopedia* by New York chef Charles Ranhofer of Delmonico's, who gives a recipe for Petites Madeleines (*see* 1814):

1⅛ cups melted butter	2 tablespoons brandy
2 cups sugar	2 pinches salt
4½ cups sifted cake flour	grated lemon peel or ¼ teaspoon lemon extract
5 whole eggs	1 teaspoon baking soda
4 egg yolks	

Melt the butter in a saucepan. Beat well together the remaining ingredients, then add the melted butter. Mix and fill buttered madeleine molds two-thirds full. Bake in a 350° oven for 20 minutes, until light brown. Makes five dozen petites madeleines (*see* Fiction, 1913).

Lobster Thermidor is created January 24 at the Paris restaurant Maire to honor the opening of Vic-

torien Sardou's play *Thermidor* at the Comédie-Française (the play is condemned for demeaning the French Revolution and will not be given another performance for 30 years).

Chef Charles Ranhofer (above) gives his own recipe for Lobster Newberg (*see* 1876), replacing the cognac and sherry with Madeira and adding egg yolks to thicken the sauce.

The Saratoga Club at Saratoga Springs, N.Y., is acquired by sportsman Richard Canfield, 29, who will turn it into a casino. The club sandwich, created by some accounts in the club's kitchens, will consist of a freshly toasted slice of white bread spread lightly with homemade mayonnaise, a layer of iceberg lettuce (*see* above), thin slices of freshly cooked chicken or turkey breast, another slice of toast with mayonnaise, slices of bacon, slices of tomato, and another slice of toast with mayonnaise. (The club sandwich will by other accounts be created in the club car of a U.S. passenger train.)

The Carey Act passed by Congress August 18 grants 1 million acres of federally owned desert lands to certain states on condition that they irrigate the land, reclaim it, and dispose of it in small tracts to settlers. Sen. Joseph M. Carey, 49, (R. Wyo.) has sponsored the legislation.

California's Irvine Co. ranch is incorporated by James Irvine, Jr., 27, whose late father came from Ireland to seek his fortune in the gold fields, made money as a wholesale merchant in San Francisco, joined with three other men to buy up sheep rangeland from Spanish settlers who had fallen into debt to Anglo-American merchants in Los Angeles, and bought out his partners in 1876. The younger Irvine will develop a vast ranching and farming empire, including a 100,000-acre ranch in Montana.

Iceberg lettuce is introduced commercially by the 18-year-old W. Atlee Burpee Co., whose crisp, cool, crunchy, bland-tasting head lettuce will be scorned by gastronomes in favor of Bibb (or limestone), Boston (or butter), Cos (or Romaine), leaf, and other, more flavorful lettuces but will be widely popular in France as well as in the United States (*see* club sandwich, below).

A study of children in London's Bethnal Green district shows that 83 percent receive no solid food besides bread at 17 out of 21 meals per week (*see* 1892). Scurvy, rickets, and tuberculosis are widespread in such districts, as they are in many British and European industrial centers.

Minute Tapioca has its beginnings in Tapioca Superlative, introduced by Whitman Grocery Co. of Boston, which soon renames its product in honor of the minutemen who fought the British at Lexington and Concord in 1775. Local housewife Susan Stavers has obtained South American manioc (cassava) roots, imported duty free since 1883, and used to produce starch; she has run them through her coffee grinder to produce translucent tapioca granules that make a smooth pudding. Local publisher John Whitman has bought rights to her process, organized a company, and sells boxes of the tapioca, which Stavers has sold in paper bags (*see* 1926).

Shredded Wheat maker H. D. Perky receives a visit at Denver from John Harvey Kellogg, who returns to Battle Creek determined to invent a better breakfast food (*see* 1881; Granose, 1895).

H. D. Perky (above) moves his Natural Food Co. to Boston and opens a Roxbury plant with 11 machines to produce shredded wheat on a commercial basis (*see* 1893; 1895).

Our Pet Evaporated Cream is introduced in a 5¢ miniature can by Helvetia Milk Condensing Co., whose new product will gain wide popularity (*see* 1890; Pet Milk, 1923).

German-American café owner William Gebhardt at New Braunfels, Tex., runs pepper (capsicum) bits through a small home meat grinder three times and dries the ground pepper into a powder—the first commercial chili (or chile) powder (*see* 1835). Gebhardt will open the first chili powder factory next year, making five cases per week and selling the product from the back of a wagon while he develops improved machinery to increase production.

Van Camp Packing Co. becomes the first company to take out a full-page advertisement in a national magazine to promote a food product (*see* 1882); the ad contains a coupon offering a full-sized can of Van Camp's Pork and Beans for 6¢ (*see* tuna, 1914).

Joseph Campbell Preserve Co. gets a new president as Arthur Dorrance, 45, succeeds Campbell, with whom he formed a new partnership in 1876 and who will die in 1900 (*see* 1869; "condensed" soup, 1897).

The Paris restaurant Maxim's, opened last year, escapes bankruptcy with help from vaudeville star Irma de Montigny, who has been refused a table at Weber's in the rue Royale, walks across the street to Maxim's, and helps Maxim Gaillard gain backing from her rich admirer Bernard de Contades. Gaillard will die early next year, leaving the debt-ridden establishment to his maître d'hôtel, Eugene Cornuché, who will attract the city's most elegant courtesans as Maxim's gains a reputation for elegance and fine cuisine, prepared by its talented chef, Chauveau (*see* 1900).

Savoy Hotel owner Richard D'Oyly Carte buys Claridge's, which he will rebuild in 1898 into a nine-story building with electric lights, lifts, 209 apartments, each with private bath, and 57 suites (*see* 1878). A staff of more than 500 will serve Claridge's guests, and by 1908 it will be fashionable for unaccompanied ladies to have lunch at the restaurant at Claridge's or to take tea beneath the palms in the hotel's foyer, where they will be served by liveried footmen while they listen to music played by a Hungarian band.

Chef Auguste Escoffier creates pêche Melba at London's 5-year-old Savoy Hotel to honor the Australian *grande cantrice* Madame Nellie Melba (Helen Porter Mitchell), 33, who is singing in Richard Wagner's 1850 opera *Lohengrin* at Covent Garden. Escoffier, who has never heard Melba sing in *Lohengrin* or any other opera but knows that she is partial to peaches and ice cream, tops a scoop of vanilla ice cream onto a peeled and poached peach half (using peaches obtained from the Paris suburb Montréal) and will later enhance the dish by covering it with sauce cardinale—a purée of raspberries flavored with old kirsch—and almond slivers. He gives the name "Melba toast" to the thin-sliced toast he has created (originally to satisfy the wife of hotelman César Ritz) by grilling a slice, splitting it down the middle, and grilling it a second time. Escoffier will create poularde Tosca to celebrate Melba's title role in the 1900 Puccini opera, soufflé Tetrazzini for diva Luisa Tetrazzini, and poularde Belle Hélène for actress Sarah Bernhardt, now 49. (To honor other female patrons at a time when respectable women are only beginning to be seen in public restaurants, Escoffier will also create potage Miss Betsy, filets mareille Olga, fondant du volaille Louisette, fraises Sarah Bernhardt, salade Irma, salade Noémi, oeufs Magda, soufflé Hilda, and bombe Miss Helyette.)

London's first J. Lyons & Co. tea shop, opened in September at 213 Piccadilly, is an outgrowth of a catering company started 7 years ago by Joseph Lyons in partnership with Montague Gluckstein, Montague's older brother, Isidore, and the Gluck-steins' brother-in-law Barnett Salmon, of the Salmon & Gluckstein tobacco business (who is much older and will die in 1897; the tobacco company will be sold in 1902 to Imperial Tobacco). J. Lyons & Co. began operations April 10 in a basement office beneath the Olympic Exhibition Centre, West Kensington, with one telephone and one typewriter, it moved in August to the former Cadby Hall piano factory on the Hammersmith Road (the site will later be expanded to cover 10 acres), and it soon caters a dinner given by the prince and princess of Wales. Joseph Lyons, who is distantly related by marriage to the Glucksteins, operates the white-fronted shop with gold letters. Its bright decor, smartly dressed waitresses, and quality food at low prices make it an immediate success, and by year's end there are eight more such Lyons establishments, all in London, to launch an empire of Lyons tea shops that will sell Welsh rabbit, meat pies, canned spaghetti on toast, fried potatoes, and assorted biscuits, buns, and cakes. There will be 96 Lyons tea shops by 1904, all with the same menu and charging the same prices (*see* 1933; Trocadero, 1896).

1895

💲 The Supreme Court emasculates the 1890 Sherman Anti-Trust Act January 21 in the case of *U.S. v. E. C. Knight Co.* The court upholds H. O. Havemeyer's 3-year-old Sugar Trust, dismissing an antitrust case on the ground that control of the manufacturing process affects interstate commerce only incidentally and indirectly (*see* Clayton Act, 1914).

The world wheat price falls to £5/cwt. as North American producers make large initial offerings, but the price rises when it turns out that the Kansas wheat crop totals only 18 million bushels—less than half a million metric tons (*see* Carleton, below).

British butter prices touch bottom as quantities of it pour in from Ireland, Australia, and New Zealand (*see* 1877). The lower butter prices have a severe impact on the "butterine" trade (*see* van den Bergh, below; Jurgens, 1897).

Van den Bergh is incorporated at Rotterdam by six Dutch margarine makers—including Jacob van den Bergh, 47; Henry, 45; Isaac, 42; Arnold, 38; and Zadok, 36—whose father, Simon, now 76, started the family butter business. Britons have been importing butter from the Lowlands since the Middle Ages, and the van den Berghs have prospered in that trade. Like the Jurgens family (*see* 1871), they have come from the town of Oss in North Brabant and heretofore have financed their operations without help. Now they obtain from public investors the money they need for expansion (*see* 1908; Margarine Union, 1920).

Beatrice Foods has its beginnings in the Beatrice Creamery Co. started at Beatrice, Neb., by local entrepreneur George Everett Haskell, 30, whose firm will grow to become the largest U.S. marketer of processed foods and the third largest U.S. dairy company. Haskell 3 years ago acquired the bankrupt Fremont Butter and Egg Co., for which he had worked at $10 per week, he will arrange with the De Laval Separator Co. to finance the purchase of separators by Nebraska farmers, and there will be 30,000 De Laval separators on Nebraska farms by 1905 (*see* de Laval, 1877; Beatrice, 1905).

Rickert Rice Mill is founded at New Orleans by Frank Rickert, whose father came to the United States in 1841 from Schleswig-Holstein. He takes over a business founded in 1875 and will run the rice mill until 1915, when his sons Frederick William, now 17, Frank, and Marion become partners. They will introduce the use of pearling cones in place of hullers and will market rice under the Rickert name and also supply the A&P, B. F. Kroger, Safeway, First National Stores, Kellogg, and other major buyers with rice to be sold under their own names.

The California Fruit Growers Exchange cooperative is organized to market the produce of California growers in the face of discriminatory freight rates (*see* 1885; Sunkist, 1919).

Baker's Coconut Co. has its beginnings at Philadelpia, where local miller Franklin Baker, 47, accepts a cargo of fresh coconuts in lieu of cash for a consignment of flour that he has shipped to a merchant at Havana. Political unrest in Cuba has made it impossible for the merchant to raise cash. When Baker finds that he cannot sell the coconuts in Philadelphia markets, he buys machinery and develops a method for producing shredded coconut meat of uniform quality, a product which he promotes to local housewives. The coconut business will prove so successful that Baker will sell his flour mill in 2 years and establish the Franklin Baker Co., dealing in coconut meat (*see* 1927).

Cleveland's Arcade opens in a structure designed by architects Charles Hubbell and W. Dominick Benes to provide an open-air market for city housewives. Guests at an inaugural banquet, held in the long, skylighted court, dine on bouillon, boned turkey in aspic, tenderloin of beef, boiled ham and tongue, chicken and potato salads, relishes, rolls, butter, ice cream and strawberries, salted almonds, assorted cakes, fruits, and confections (but no wines out of respect to the many members of temperance societies in attendance). The market will soon be crowded with vendors and purveyors from France, Germany, Italy, Scotland, Finland, Poland, Serbia, Romania, and Hungary (*see* West Side Market, 1912).

The New Orleans specialty food shop T. Pittari's opens to sell live Maine lobsters, Black Angus beef, and game meats, including bear and buffalo. It will continue for more than 70 years to offer foods unobtainable elsewhere in the area.

Budapest's Central Market (Nagyvásárcsarnok) opens on Tolbuhin Boulevard in downtown Pest. Designed by Budapest Institute of Technology architecture professor Samu Pecz, the glass-covered cast-iron structure has a tunnel leading up from the Danube so that barges from the provinces can be unloaded easily and their cargoes brought into the market. The washable concrete floors can hold the weight of heavy horse-drawn wagons laden with foodstuffs, there are 12 large fish tanks to hold white *fogas* (pike-perch) from Lake Balaton, 80 cooling chambers, 27 booths for wholesale merchants, and 97 for retail vendors.

The "diesel" engine invented by German engineer Rudolf Diesel, 37, operates on a petroleum fuel less highly refined and less costly than gasoline; it has no electrical ignition system and is simpler than a gasoline engine and more trouble free. Diesel will work with Friedrich Krupp of Essen and the Augsburg-Nuremberg machine factory to build a successful engine.

Germany's 53.2-mile Kiel (Nord-Ostsee) Ship Canal opens to connect the North Sea with the Rhine.

The Ohio Valley Improvement Association organized October 8 at Cincinnati works to make the Ohio a navigable channel for commerce. The U.S Army Corps of Engineers will build 49 locks and movable dams on 980 miles of river between Pittsburgh and Cairo, Ill.

Ohio glassmaker Michael Joseph Owens, 36, patents an automatic bottle-blowing machine. Owens is manager of Edward Drummond Libbey's Toledo glass factory (*see* 1877; 1903).

A patent for a corkscrew is awarded to U.S. inventor Samuel Henshell.

L'École de Cordon Bleu, opened by Marthe Distel at the Palais-Royal, Paris, in 1880, moves to larger quarters at 29, rue de Faubourg Saint-Honoré (*see* 1934).

Cookbook: *The Star Cook Book; A Monitor for the American Housewife in the Dining Room and Kitchen, Containing the Choicest Original and Selected Recipes for Economical and Practical Housekeeping* by U.S. author Mrs. Grace Townsend.

The elaborate "Chantilly" silver pattern, introduced by Gorham, will be the most popular U.S. flatware pattern for more than 80 years. Eating with the knife has been considered a sign of ill breeding since the 1880s, but many Americans will continue to eat with their knives until well into the next century, even though forks now have three or four tines and are much easier to use than the two-tine forks that were once common.

The Breakers is completed at Newport, R.I., for railroad heir Cornelius Vanderbilt II, 52, and his wife, whose 70-room "cottage" on Ochre Point Road has 33 servants' rooms (chambermaids never enter the kitchen, kitchen maids never see the bedroom suites) and a chef whose staff can prepare dinner for 200 and who does not need help from caterers unless Mrs. Vanderbilt's guest list exceeds 100. Her main dining room is 58 feet long and 42 feet wide, and she often uses her Sèvres porcelain dinner service and Dresden teacups as servants wearing the Vanderbilt livery (to keep them from being confused with the guests) serve from a two-tiered butler's pantry which opens into the kitchen.

The Po' Boy sandwich of New Orleans is created according to some accounts by a Mme. Bégué, owner of a coffee stall in the city's old French market, who takes a long, thin loaf of French bread, slits it in half lengthwise, butters it generously, slices it in thirds or fourths, not cutting through the bottom crust, and puts a different filling into each section (year approximate; *see* also 1929). Its name will be said to derive from the pleas of hungry black youths who beg, "Please give a sandwich to a po' boy." Fried oysters almost invariably go into one section of the sandwich; other fillings may include tomato with a strip of broiled bacon, French sausage, chicken salad, fried eggs with hot chili sauce or chopped green pepper and onion, or any other appetizing tidbit at hand.

Massachusetts fishermen using a line trawl catch a record 211.5-pound cod measuring more than six feet in length.

Columbia River salmon canning reaches its peak of 634,000 cases (*see* 1866; CRPA, 1899).

Canned salmon from the Columbia River was shipped to grocery stores all over the world.

The U.S. Department of Agriculture sends agronomist Mark Alfred Carleton, 29, out to Kansas to investigate the wheat crop shortfall (above). Car-

leton reports that the only good drought-resistant wheat grown in Kansas is the Turkey Red introduced by Russian Mennonites in 1874; his report creates a clamor for the "miracle" wheat that will soon replace spring wheat completely in Kansas and be the dominant variety grown in mid-America until the late 1930s (*see* 1896).

Wallace's Farmer begins publication at Des Moines, Iowa, under the rubric "Good Farming—Clear Thinking—Right Living." Former Presbyterian minister Henry Wallace, who moved to Iowa after his health failed some years ago to become a farmer, is editor in chief; his son Henry Cantwell Wallace, 29, is associate editor; and his son John P. is advertising manager. Henry C. took over a 320-acre Iowa farm when he turned 21, saw corn sell for as little as 15¢ per bushel, sold his farm machinery, entered the Iowa State College of Agriculture, received his B.S.A. degree 3 years ago, became assistant professor of agriculture in charge of dairying, and will campaign in the family journal for progressive agricultural practices (*see* 1921; Pioneer Hi-Bred, 1926).

Florida ships 30 million pieces of fruit, down from 1 billion last year. All the state's lemon trees have been killed by a freeze, which has ruined the Marion County nursery of horticulturist Myron Eugene Gillett, 36, who has organized the Florida Fruit and Vegetable Association. Gillett will increase his holdings to have extensive groves on Lake Lucerne and on Temple Terraces on the Hillsborough River and will do extensive scientific research on the cultivation and marketing of citrus fruits.

The word "calorie" is applied to food for the first time by W. O. Atwater (*see* 1889), who takes the kilocalorie, or large calorie (the amount of heat needed to raise the temperature of a kilogram of water 1° Celsius—from 15° C. to 16° C. at a pressure of 1 atmosphere—or 4 pints of water 1° F.), and he uses this calorie as a measure of the energy contained in foods for a guide to economical food buying based solely on calories per dollar. Atwater urges Americans to eat more white flour and fewer potatoes, since flour is a cheaper source of carbohydrate, and discards wheat bran and potato skins as refuse. The only milk he favors is condensed milk laced with sugar. Tomatoes are used only sparingly as a flavoring and are overcooked to make them more digestible.

Canned foods are shown to keep from spoiling not because air has been driven out of the container but because bacteria have been killed or inhibited in their growth (*see* Appert, 1810; Pasteur, 1861). S. C. Prescott at MIT and William Lyman Underwood conduct studies that will lead to safer canning methods by producing charts that give optimum processing times and temperatures.

Belgian bacteriologist Emilie Pierre-Marie van Ermengem, 44, isolates the botulism bacterium *Clostridium botulinum*. The anaerobic bacterium, whose toxin is twice as deadly as tetanus toxin and 12 times deadlier than rattlesnake venom, has been associated in Europe with sausages whose cases provide an airless environment, but botulism in the United States stems largely from nonacidic foods that have been improperly bottled or canned (*see* 1920).

Granose, introduced in February, is the world's first flaked breakfast cereal. John Harvey Kellogg has run boiled wheat through his wife's machine for rolling out dough, baked the thin film in an oven, and been persuaded by his brother Will Keith, 35, not to grind the flakes into granules but to sell them instead as flakes. Since a 10-ounce package sells for 15¢, Kellogg and his brother sell 60¢/bushel wheat at $12/bushel retail (*see* 1894; Sanitas Corn Flakes, 1898).

Shredded Wheat biscuits develop a market (*see* 1894). H. D. Perky acquires a large bakery at Worcester, Mass., to satisfy the growing demand (*see* 1898).

Del Monte canned goods are introduced by California's Oakland Preserving Co., which also markets an ordinary line but identifies its premium grade with the name Del Monte and a label picture of Charles Crocker's hotel on Monterey Bay, which has been rebuilt since the 1887 fire that destroyed the original structure (*see* 1891; 1916).

Swans Down Cake Flour is introduced by Evansville, Ind., miller Addison Weeks Igleheart, whose family has been making flour at Evansville since 1856 and selling Swans Down family flour since 1876 (*see* Coronado Beach Hotel, 1885). He has developed a low-gluten cake flour from winter wheat, which he has ground, sifted through silk screens, and ground again. Igleheart sells some to a cake pan salesman who needs flour to demonstrate his pans, and the salesman is so impressed that he quits selling pans to sell the new cake flour. Swans Down will be advertised in the *Ladies' Home Journal* beginning in 1898—the first national advertising for any packaged cake flour (*see* 1904).

"Coca-Cola is now sold in every state of the Union," boasts Asa Candler of Atlanta, but the beverage has yet to be bottled (*see* 1892; 1899).

White Rock Mineral Water and Ginger Ale are promoted as mixers for alcoholic beverages by New York White Rock representative Frank T. Huntoon, who decides that promoting mineral waters only with health claims shuts them out of a larger market. He sells ginger ale (first produced in 1809), sarsaparilla, and root beer under the label White Rock, which will soon be a generic for carbonated water (*see* 1893; Cliquot Club, 1901; Canada Dry, 1907).

The Anti-Saloon League of America is organized at Washington, D.C. (*see* WCTU, 1874; Carry Nation, 1900).

Postum is introduced as a coffee substitute at Battle Creek, Mich., by C. W. Post, who has quit "the san" uncured and discouraged but has taken up residence with a Christian Science family, embraced their religion, and begun almost immediately to feel better (*see* 1893). He has opened his own sanitarium, La Vita Inn, purchased a secondhand gasoline stove for $46.85, acquired a hand-operated peanut roaster and coffee grinder, spent $21.91 for ingredients, and produces his first commercial batch in a horse barn on his property January 1. Post sells his Postum in paper bags from handcarts, persuades local newspapers to give him advertising space on credit, writes most of his own advertising, and frightens readers by attributing "lost eyesight," "coffee neuralgia," grouchiness, and poor school grades on caffeine: "Does [the coffee habit] reduce your working force, kill your energy, push you into the big crowd of mongrels, deaden what thoroughbred blood you may have and neutralize all your efforts to make money and fame?" (*see* 1901; Grape Nuts, 1897).

The Palace Hotel opens July 29 at St. Moritz, Switzerland. Johannes Badrutt's luxurious hostelry (his son Kaspar is managing director) will attract international celebrities for the next century, providing them with sumptuous cuisine winter and summer, with New Year's Eve guests consuming 176 pounds of caviar and endless bottles of champagne (*see* 1856; Hanselmann, 1893; Sevruta House, 1912).

Crêpes Suzettes are invented at Monte Carlo's Café de Paris by assistant waiter (*commis de rang*) Henri Charpentier, not quite 16, who has apprenticed under Auguste Escoffier. He prepares the dish of thin pancakes with liqueur sauce at a luncheon given by the visiting prince of Wales, whose party includes one Suzette, the young daughter of one of the prince's guests. The invention will be ascribed to others (*see* cookbook, 1667), but Charpentier will insist until his death early in 1962 that he was the originator and that the flaming sauce caught fire quite by accident.

The prince of Wales (above) always has roast beef and Yorkshire pudding at luncheon on Sundays as a change from richer foods, but his dinners seldom have fewer than 12 courses, mostly elaborate dishes such as ortolans cooked in brandy, *côtelettes bécassines à la Souvarov* (snipe boned and halved, stuffed with foie gras and forcemeat, shaped into small cutlets, and grilled in a pig's caul, served on silver dishes with small slices of truffle and Madeira sauce), and partridge or pheasant stuffed with snipe or woodcock, the smaller birds being stuffed with truffles, and the whole garnished with a rich sauce. He often has grilled oysters as a supper dish, followed by cold quails à la grecque. For luncheons at Ascot he has kitchen pie, and deer pudding is served no fewer than four times per week when he is at Balmoral Castle.

The first U.S. pizzeria opens in New York at 53½ Spring Street.

The Tokyo restaurant Rengatei opens in the Ginza. The proprietor, Motojiro, begins serving French-style cuisine to foreigners and Japanese businessmen, but will soon adapt his dishes to Japanese tastes by eliminating butter and spices, serving omurice and hayashirice instead of bread, substituting *hashi* for cutlery, and introducing such dishes as breaded pork cutlet and deep-fried shrimp (*see* 1904).

1896

Failure of India's wheat crop raises world prices, but increased world competition keeps a lid on them. The decline in the U.S. wheat crop last year has encouraged Australia, Canada, and Russia to enter the export market and compete actively for European sales (*see* 1895; Kubanka, 1899).

Staffordshire flour miller Thomas Fitton acquires Imperial Mills on the Embankment at London to produce Hovis flour, which has gained such popularity that S. Fitton & Son needs to cut the cost of freight on the huge quantities it ships to England's southern counties (*see* 1890). Richard "Stoney" Smith has taken samples of the flour to London and found an enthusiastic reception from bakers and storekeepers (*see* Hovis Bread-Flour Co., 1898).

Advertisements used health claims to sell Britons on brown bread and biscuits made with Hovis Flour.

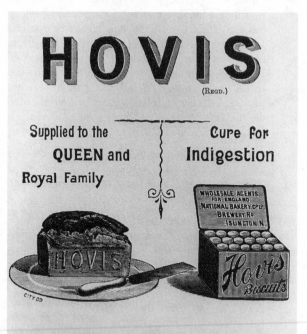

National Tea Co. has its beginnings in a small tea store opened on Chicago's North Side. It will grow into a chain of stores that in some states will rival the A&P.

S&H Green Stamps are issued for the first time by Sperry & Hutchinson Co., a Jackson, Mich., company founded by local entrepreneurs Thomas A. Sperry and Shelly B. Hutchinson. Participating stores issue one S&H stamp for every 10¢ a customer spends, books filled with S&H stamps are exchangeable for merchandise at "premium parlors" set up for the purpose, the A&P will soon be a major user of the stamps, and other companies will spring up to compete with S&H. By 1914, trading stamps will be given out with 6 percent of all U.S. retail purchases, primarily at grocery stores (*see* 1951).

Bernhard L. F. Bang in Denmark discovers the bacterium of infectious abortion in cows (*see* 1892). Since it is one of several bacteria that cause undulant fever, or brucellosis, in humans, it will be called *Brucella abortus* (*see* Bruce, 1887), but the condition it produces in cattle will be called Bang's disease (*see* 1900; Evans, 1917).

Cookbooks: *Fannie Farmer's Boston Cooking School Cookbook* by Fannie Merritt Farmer, 39, who has been director of the school since 1891. A paralytic stroke forced her to drop out of high school, but she recovered enough to help with household duties, developed an aptitude for cooking, and was enrolled by her parents in the Boston Cooking School, from which she was graduated 7 years ago. She uses a precise system of standardized measurements (she introduces the concept of *level spoonfuls*) that will make her work an enduring best-seller in America (but not in Europe). "The time is not far distant," Farmer says, "when knowledge of the principles of diet will be an essential part of one's education. Then mankind will eat to live, will be able to do better mental and physical work, and disease will be less frequent." She gives recipes for everyday and classic dishes, most of her menus being for family dinners and luncheons of soup, meat or fish, potatoes or sweet potatoes, two vegetables, dessert, cheese, and coffee. The book will go through more than 20 revised editions before Farmer's death early in 1915. *The Cook Book* by "Oscar" (Tschirky) of the Waldorf, who has

Fannie Farmer gave precise measurements in the recipes of her famous cookbook.

never himself cooked anything more difficult than scrambled eggs (*see* restaurants, 1893). *Mrs. Lincoln's Cook Book: What to Do and What Not to Do in Cooking* by Mary Johnson Lincoln. *The Art of Cooking by Gas* and *The National Cookbook* by Marion Harland. "Dainty Desserts" by Rose Knox, now 39, is a booklet containing recipes which she has developed using the Knox Gelatine that she and her husband, Charles, produce at Johnstown, N.Y. (*see* 1890).

"To be fashionable nowadays, we must 'brunch,'" says the 55-year-old London weekly magazine *Punch*.

U.S. women's magazines generally advise readers to serve two-course meals at both lunch and dinner: meat or fish plus rice or potatoes with a vegetable and dessert. Recommended everyday dishes include "scalloped" fish; oysters; chicken; boiled, mashed, or baked potatoes; boiled vegetables; and rolls. Dishes for Sunday dinner may include mutton stew, boiled potatoes, and turnips, followed by jellied wafers and cheese. Breakfast continues to feature steak and pork chops.

British bakers create a giant meat pie to celebrate the jubilee of the repeal of the Corn Laws in 1846.

Chop suey is invented by some accounts at New York by one of the cooks serving Chinese goodwill emissary Li Hong Zhang, who has grown tired of American fare at banquets. Other accounts will credit the invention to a San Francisco cook, who has served a mixture of leftover meat and vegetables late at night to a group of drunken miners, but at least one authority will trace the origin of tsap seui to Toisan, a rural country near Guangzhou. More authentically *American*-invented "Chinese" dishes will include chow mein, egg foo yong, and fortune cookies (*see* 1916).

Farmers plant Turkey Red wheat throughout much of Kansas, Nebraska, Oklahoma, and Texas, where it will soon be the predominant winter wheat variety, and in Montana, Minnesota, and the Dakotas, where it is planted in spring for fall harvesting.

U.S. botanist George Washington Carver, 32, joins Alabama's Tuskegee Institute as director of its Department of Agriculture (*see* peanuts, 1914, 1921).

Dutch physicians Christiaan Eijkman and Gerrit Grijns in Java find that chickens fed polished rice suffer from a disease resembling beriberi (*see* Takaki, 1887). They decide that the rice must contain a toxin which is neutralized by something in rice hulls (*see* 1906; Eijkman, 1886).

German biochemist E. Baumann finds iodine in the human thyroid gland. The mineral is absent from all other human body tissues (*see* Marine, 1905).

The U.S. Department of Agriculture issues a bulletin entitled "Chemical Composition of American Food Materials" based on work by W. O. Atwater and others, who have compiled data on the protein, fat, carbohydrate, ash, water, and refuse content of foods (*see* 1895). The bulletin will be revised in 1899 and 1906 (*see* 1950).

A committee of the American Public Health Association blames drunkenness on "bad cooking, unpalatable meals, and the extravagant use of ice." It urges the establishment of people's kitchens modeled on Boston's New England Kitchen of 1890 to teach economical cooking in the slums.

Congressional hearings on the whiskey trade reveal that U.S. distillers and rectifiers sell 105 million gallons of "Old Bourbon" whiskey per year but only 2 million are genuine, the remainder being "blends" which may contain anything from ethyl alcohol to prune juice (*see* Bottled in Bond Act, 1897).

S&W canned foods have their beginnings in a San Francisco wholesale grocery firm started at the corner of Market and Fremont streets by local entrepreneurs Samuel Sussman and his cousins Gustav and Samuel I. Wormser (*see* Dole, 1902).

Tootsie Rolls are introduced at New York by Austrian-American confectioner Leo Hirschfield, 29, whose penny candy is the first to be wrapped in paper. Hirschfield names the chewy, chocolatey confection after his 6-year-old daughter, Clara, whom he calls "Tootsie."

Cracker Jack—a molasses-covered popcorn candy—is introduced at Chicago by German-American confectioner F. W. Rueckheim and his brother Louis. F. W. Rueckheim came to Chicago shortly after the fire of 1871 (he arrived with just $200 to help clean up the debris), started operating a one-popper popcorn stand in partnership with William Brinkmeyer, and in 1872 opened an establishment at 113 Fourth Avenue (later Federal Street) to manufacture "Popcorn Specialities." Louis arrived in 1873 and bought Brinkmeyer's interest, the Rueckheim brothers added marshmallows and other confections to their line in 1875, and after moving five times they settled in a three-story brick building at 266 South Clinton Street. Their new product will get its name in 1896, when an enthusiastic salesman exclaims, "That's a crackerjack!" Packaging expert Henry Eckstein will join the Rueckheims in 1899 and develop a box lined with sealed wax paper to retain crispness, Rueckheim Bros. & Eckstein will adopt the slogan "The More You Eat, the More You Want," and the 1908 song "Take Me Out to the Ball Game" will help their sales. They will sell Cracker Jack in boxes containing coupons redeemable for prizes beginning in 1910 (the first redeemable prize will be a tan or gray flannelette baseball uniform), pack prizes (magnifying glasses, strings of beads, metal whistles, metal trains, spinning tops, and similar novelties) with the Cracker Jack beginning in 1912 (F. W. Rueckheim's idea). They will use Jack and his dog Bingo in advertising beginning in 1916 and show them on the box beginning in 1918 (*see* Borden Co., 1964).

Michelob beer is introduced by Adolphus Busch of 1876 Budweiser fame, whose St. Louis brewery Anheuser-Busch is the largest in the country. Michelob will be sold only on draft until 1961 (*see* corn syrup, 1923).

The Olympia Brewing Co., founded at Olympia, Wash., by German-American brewer Leopold F. Schmidt will grow to have the largest brewery on the West Coast.

Welch's Grape Juice production moves to Watkins Glen, N.Y., close to a vast grape-growing region (*see* 1869). Charles Welch has been running his father's Unfermented Wine business since 1872 (*see* 1897).

The London restaurant Trocadero, opened October 1 off Piccadilly by J. Lyons & Co., will double in size when its owners acquire an adjoining property in 1902, giving it a frontage onto Shaftesbury Avenue. J. Lyons, which has opened 18 teashops since 1894, will make the Trocadero restaurant, grillroom, bar, ballroom, and banquet suites (holding from 40 to 400 guests) famous for its food and wine, and the Troc will continue until 1965 (*see* Throgmorton, 1900).

New York playboy Herbert Barnum Seeley, grandson of the late circus impresario P. T. Barnum, gives a December dinner for 20 at Louis Sherry's. To entertain his guests, Seeley has the exotic dancer "Little Egypt," star of the World's Columbian Exposition at Chicago 3 years ago, dance on the table in the private dining room wearing only black lace stockings and high-heeled slippers.

1897

Britain's Queen Victoria celebrates her Diamond Jubilee. Chef Auguste Escoffier of London's Carleton House creates cherries Jubilee à la reine to celebrate the occasion, and tea magnate Thomas Lipton contributes £25,000 ($125,000) to feed 300,000 impoverished Londoners during Jubilee week (*see* Lipton, 1893; 1898).

The United States annexes the Hawaiian Islands under terms of a June 16 treaty that is ratified by the Hawaiian Senate September 9 (*see* 1882). Sugar planters, who proclaimed the Republic of Hawaii in 1894, have pushed for annexation (*see* 1898).

American Sugar Refining makes a deal with Claus Spreckels in San Francisco to eliminate competition (*see* 1891; 1895; 1899).

The Dingley Tariff Act passed by Congress July 24 raises U.S. living costs by increasing duties to an average of 57 percent. It hikes rates on sugar, salt, tin cans, glassware, and other items, but an influx of gold from the Klondike helps end the 4-year economic depression and begin a decade of prosperity.

Europe's wheat crop falls short of its needs, and wheat futures are bid up on the Chicago Board of Trade as speculator Joseph Leiter, 28, makes a spectacular effort to corner the market (*see* Hutchinson, 1888). Son of the onetime Marshall Field partner Levi Leiter, the young Harvard graduate has been given $1 million by his father to start a real estate business but instead, after having sailed his yacht round the world, has started to buy wheat futures at 65¢ per bushel and made a neat profit which he invests in more futures, continuing to buy until he has acquired 12 million bushels for December delivery, 9 million of them from meat packer P. D. Armour. Leiter refuses to take his profit of several million dollars in hopes of still higher profits, but Armour discovers that grain elevators at Duluth are bulging with wheat, charters 25 lake vessels and tugs that can crash through the ice to Duluth, and sends them north to get wheat that will break Leiter's corner in the market (*see* 1898).

The Berlin Exchange bans trading in futures after seeing what has gone on in Chicago; German grain traders, merchants, and speculators shift their operations to Amsterdam and Liverpool.

U.S. farmers reap profits of millions of dollars as wheat prices rise to $1.09 per bushel, highest since 1891, partly as a result of Joseph Leiter's buying of futures (above).

Dutch margarine maker Gerard Jurgens, son of Johannes, is sent to Britain to open the company's first provincial sales offices as margarine prices rise from their 1895 lows. Beginning at Manchester, Jurgens opens offices at Bristol, Leith, and Dundee;

the company will open offices next year at Glasgow, Leeds, Liverpool, Aberdeen, and Inverness, at Newcastle in 1900, and at Birmingham in 1901 to supply the needs of retail grocers and cooperatives without having to go through middlemen (*see* 1883; Margarine Union, 1920).

Rowntree & Co. Ltd. is incorporated with Joseph Rowntree as chairman (*see* 1887). The company built a new factory outside York in 1890 (*see* Kit Kat, 1935).

J. M. Smucker Co. has its beginnings at Orrville, Ohio, south of Cleveland, where local farmer Jerome M. Smucker, 39, makes apple butter in a copper kettle over a wood fire, puts it up in stoneware crocks, and has his wife peddle it to Wayne County housewives from the tailgate of a wagon. His descendants will acquire other firms, building an enterprise that will be the largest U.S. producer of jams, jellies, and preserves.

U.S. railroads are subject to the 1890 Sherman Anti-Trust Act, says the Supreme Court March 22 in a 5-to-4 decision handed down in the *Trans-Missouri Freight* case, but the court nullifies the "long and short haul" clause of the 1887 Interstate Commerce Act November 8 in *Interstate Commerce Commission v. Alabama Midland Railway*.

Japan gets her first railroad dining car. For first-class passengers only, it has a Western-style menu. Economy-class dining cars will open within a year or two, offering only Japanese foods (which have been available for years from vendors walking through the cars selling wooden boxes, called *bento*, containing rice with seafood, vegetables, fruit, and the like).

Hobart Electric Manufacturing Co. is incorporated in Ohio July 21 (it will be reincorporated as Hobart Manufacturing in 1903) with Herbert Lincoln Johnston, 28, as inventor, designer, pattern maker, and test engineer. In 2 years he will invent the world's first electric coffee mill for store use, and he will invent an electric meat chopper in 1911 (*see* mixing machine, 1918).

Joseph Campbell Preserve Co. chemist John T. Dorrance, 24, develops his idea of a double-strength "condensed" soup that will give Campbell's Soup dominance in the industry (*see* 1894). A nephew of company president Arthur Dorrance, John is an MIT graduate with a doctorate from the University of Göttingen, has worked at some famous Paris restaurants to study the proper flavoring of soup, has passed up faculty positions at Göttingen, Columbia, Cornell, and Bryn Mawr, and persuades his uncle to hire him as a research chemist. He is paid $7.50 per week and within the year has succeeded in producing condensed soup in four varieties: Beefsteak Tomato, Consommé, Chicken, and Oxtail (*see* 1898).

The introduction of double seams and improved crimping of body and ends makes tin cans more reliable (*see* 1876; 1895; aluminum, 1960).

Cookbook: *One Hundred Ways to Use Liebig's Extract of Beef; A Guide for American Housewives* by Maria Parloa, who has closely associated herself with Ellen Swallow Richards and Mary Hinman Abel and has been an enthusiastic supporter of the New England Kitchen (*see* 1890).

The first known published recipe for brownies appears in the Sears, Roebuck catalogue. Probably created when a careless cook failed to add baking powder to a chocolate-cake batter, the dense, fudgy squares have been made for some time by housewives who received the recipe by word of mouth: two squares unsweetened chocolate or six tablespoons cocoa melted with two tablespoons butter, two eggs beaten light with one cup sugar, these ingredients to be mixed, beaten thoroughly, and then combined with one teaspoon baking powder, one cup flour, ½ cup chopped walnuts, one teaspoon vanilla, and ¼ teaspoon salt, baked in a greased eight-inch square pan in a moderate oven (350° F.) for 35 minutes, then cut into squares before being removed from the pan.

Britons begin to eat lunch, dooming the classic British breakfast, which still often includes kippers (smoked herring, split open and fried in butter), finnan haddie (smoked haddock, often from the Scottish fishing port of Findhorn), kedgeree (rice mixed with fish, usually salmon, and hard-boiled egg—a dish introduced from colonial India), roast beef, kidneys, bacon, sausages, porridge, snipe (Scotland), scones (Scotland), cold toast, butter, marmalade, treacle, eggs, and tea with milk.

More than 1.2 million pounds of sturgeon are landed in New York and New Jersey, but although fish weighing as much as 200 pounds are still caught far up the river, pollution begins to reduce the Hudson's "Albany beef" industry.

Forty-nine million pounds of shad are landed on the U.S. East Coast.

The drought that began on the U.S. western plains in 1886 finally comes to an end.

The Bottled-in-Bond Act signed into law by President William McKinley, 54, requires that whiskey be aged for at least 4 years in government-bonded rack warehouses and bottled at 100 proof (50 percent alcohol) under government supervision to prevent the kinds of abuses revealed in last year's congressional hearings (*see* definition of bourbon, 1964).

Grape Nuts is introduced as a health food by C. W. Post of 1895 Postum fame, who will claim that his ready-to-eat cold cereal (a mixture of whole wheat, malted barley flour, salt and yeast, baked in the form of bread sticks, shredded, baked again very slowly, and then ground up) prevents appendicitis, helps cure tuberculosis and malaria, and makes loose teeth tighter. Post believes that grape sugar (dextrose) is formed during the repetitive baking process, recommends that his cereal be sprinkled on salad at dinner as well as being consumed at breakfast and lunch (he also recommends deep breathing, exercise, and drinking lots of water), and includes a copy of his pamphlet "The Road to Wellville" with each brown-and-tan box (*see* Post Toasties, 1904).

Purina breakfast cereal is introduced by the 3-year-old St. Louis livestock food company Robinson-Danforth, which names its product Purina to signify purity (*see* Ralston, 1902).

Jell-O is introduced by LeRoy, N.Y., cough medicine manufacturer Pearl B. Wait, whose wife, Mary, gives the product its name. Wait's gelatin dessert is made from a recipe adapted from one developed by Peter Cooper in 1845. The powder is 88 percent sugar (*see* 1899).

U.S. confectioners Albert J. Bonomo and his son Victor start a company that will become famous for Bonomo's Turkish Taffy, a variation on "Turkish Delight" (*see* 1854).

H. P. Hood in Boston begins distributing milk in glass bottles instead of ladling it from large cans into customers' pitchers (*see* 1890; Brooklyn, 1879; Borden, 1885). Hood stables more than 1,200 horses, his routemen must harness their horses and load their wagons before driving to the often distant points at which their rounds begin, and they must start work shortly after midnight in order to commence deliveries at 4 o'clock in the morning.

Welch's Grape Juice production moves to Westfield, N.Y. (*see* 1896). Charles Welch processes 300 tons of grapes at Westfield, a stronghold of the Women's Christian Temperance Union in the heart of the 90-mile Chautauqua and Erie grape belt along the southeastern shore of Lake Erie (*see* 1945).

France's Midi (the departments of Gard, Hérault, Aude, and Pyrénées-Orientales) produce nearly half the nation's wine, up from 10 percent before the grape phylloxera infestation that began in the 1860s.

Hamburg's Hotel zu den Vier Jahreszeiten (Four Seasons) is purchased at auction February 24 by Friedrich Haerlin, 40, whose restaurant Haerlin will for years be Hamburg's finest. Haerlin left his home in Stuttgart with 50 marks and a ticket for Geneva and, helped by his wife, Thekla, has done well enough to purchase the hotel.

Naples hails the opening of the Grand Hotel Excelsior-Victoria amid lush gardens and groves of lemon and orange trees with a dining room that serves homemade cannelloni, veal piccata, and Muscat grapes.

London's Connaught Hotel has its beginnings in the Coburg Hotel, opened in May on Grosvenor Square with a dining room that seats 75 (named for the late Prince Albert of Saxe-Coburg, the hotel will become the Connaught in 1915) (*see* 1935).

London restaurateur Daniel Nicols dies at age 64 (*see* 1865). His Café Royal's high-ceilinged restaurant, grillroom, and brasserie (the "domino room") with their gilded walls and enormous mirrors attract such notables as Aubrey Beardsley, Max Beerbohm, and Augustus John. Nicols, who in his later years called himself "Daniel de Nicols," has not only paid off his French creditors with interest but also acquired a country house with deer park. His widow, Célestine, will survive for another 20 years, continuing the operation with the help of capable managers, and the Café Royal will be enlarged in the 1920s to occupy an entire building given over to dining facilities, with everything from small private suites for four diners to huge ballrooms for wedding receptions, debutante cotillions, and similar functions (see 1951).

The Brussels restaurant La Villa Lorraine has its beginnings in an inn opened at the edge of the Bois de Cambre (year approximate). It initially serves only enormous sandwiches, tartines de fromage blanc, and beer but will grow to become the city's most prestigious eating place.

The Tokyo restaurant Botan (Button) opens in the Kanda district, serving poultry dishes. Proprietor Yashiro Sakurai has worked in the button department of a company handling Western-style clothes.

New York's Waldorf-Astoria Hotel opens a block east of Herald Square with a Palm Garden restaurant whose waiters speak French and German as well as English. Guests must wear formal attire; the chef earns $10,000 per year (see 1931).

William F. Schrafft Co. of Boston engages confectionery salesman Frank G. Shattuck, who disposes of the factory's output for the balance of the year within 3 months and proceeds to open a retail candy shop in New York's Herald Square (see 1861). The shop will begin serving lunch next year, becoming the first Schrafft's restaurant (see 1906).

A new Delmonico's restaurant that will survive until 1923 opens November 15 at the northeast corner of Fifth Avenue and 44th Street in New York (see 1876). Charles Crist Delmonico (he has received permission from the state legislature to add his great-uncle's name) plays host to more than 1,000 patrons, who dine in the Ladies' Restaurant, the Palm Garden, the Gentlemen's Elizabethan Café, the private dining and banquet rooms, the ballroom, and the Roof Conservatory. Delmonico's best customer is Col. William D'Alton Mann, publisher of the gossip sheet *Town Topics* and a notorious blackmailer. His editorial rooms are a block or two away, and he frequently breakfasts at Delmonico's, starting with two or three double Manhattan cocktails, which he follows with four double Southdown mutton chops coiled around grilled lamb's kidneys and wreathed in country-style

sausages served with southern yams and accompanied by Louis Roderer champagne. Mann's corner table gives him a full view of the entire room, enabling him to pick up bits of gossip which he suppresses for fees that are seldom less than $1,500 and are often much higher (his victims, according to sworn court testimony, will include Col. John Jacob Astor, Anthony Cassatt, Chauncey DePew, Clarence Mackay, J. P. Morgan, Henry Plant, Reginald Vanderbilt, and William C. Whitney).

"Diners" make their first appearance as Boston, New York, and Phildelphia replace their horse-drawn trolleys with electric cars; obtained by enterprising promoters for $20 each, the discarded trolleys are fitted with stoves and dishes and resold as lunch wagons (see 1919).

1898

✕ Sir William Crookes, 66, president of the British Association for the Advancement of Science, says, "We eagerly spend millions to protect our coasts and commerce; and millions more on ships, explosives, guns, and men; but we omit to take necessary precautions to supply ourselves with the very first and supremely important munition of war—food."

The Spanish-American War begins April 22. A joint resolution proposing annexation of the Hawaiian Islands is introduced in the House May 4, President McKinley signs the measure July 7, and Hawaiian sugar planters gain free access to U.S. markets (see 1897). A peace protocol signed August 12 ends the conflict between Spain and the United States; the Treaty of Paris December 10 brings hostilities to a formal end, Spain withdraws from Cuba, and she cedes Puerto Rico, Guam, and the Philippines to the United States, which pays $20 million for the sugar-rich Philippines (see agriculture, "embalmed beef" scandal, below).

China has serious famine as the northern provinces suffer drought, while in Shandong province the Huanghe (Yellow) River overflows its banks to create disastrous floods (see Chin Lung, below).

$ U.S. wheat futures reach $1.85 per bushel as the outbreak of the Spanish-American War booms demand. Joseph Leiter has paper profits of $7 million (see 1897), but he holds contracts for 35 million bushels, and when wheat pours into Chicago in June, Leiter's corner on the market is broken. He not only loses his profit but winds up with a debt of $10 million, which is paid by his father, Levi, whose daughter Mary arrives at Bombay December 30 to serve as vicereine of India.

The United States exports $200 million worth of wheat and flour, up from $60 million worth in 1870.

Hovis Bread-Flour Company Ltd. is founded by Thomas Fitton, Richard Smith, and two London partners (*see* 1896). Smith will die in late August 1900 at age 64, but only after seeing the new firm post a first-year profit of £26,000 and declare a dividend of 7 percent. Fitton will survive until 1928 (*see* 1899).

Tea magnate Thomas Lipton, now 48 and worth an estimated £10 million ($50 million), converts all his holdings into a huge limited liability company and turns his attention to yachting (he will finance the America's Cup challenger *Shamrock* next year and four more *Shamrocks* between 1901 and 1930, none of them successful) (*see* 1909).

Sugar prices soar following the outbreak of the Spanish-American War (above). Sugar broker George Edward Keiser started buying stock in Cuban-American Sugar at $5 per share and continues to buy as the price soars to $300, buying so much that he winds up controlling the company.

Nestlé acquires the Norwegian Milk Condensing Co. plant at Kap (*see* 1890; 1900).

American Glucose Refining Co. is created by New York financier Jules Semon Bache, 36, in a $40 million consolidation of companies that include H. O. Havemeyer's 7-year-old American Sugar Refining Co. (*see* cornstarch, 1842; U.S. Glucose, 1902).

National Biscuit Co. is created by a consolidation of New York Biscuit, American Biscuit and Manufacturing, United States Baking, and United States Biscuit (*see* 1890). Chicago lawyer-financier William H. Moore and his associates at New York Biscuit have forced a price war against their sole remaining competitor—American Biscuit and Manufacturing—to bring about the merger, which has a virtual monopoly in the U.S. biscuit and cracker industry. Adolphus W. Green heads the new company, whose 114 bakeries account for 90 percent of all

National Biscuit Company held a virtual monopoly in U.S. cracker and cookie manufacture. LIBRARY OF CONGRESS

major U.S. commercial bakeries (*see* Uneeda Biscuit, below).

The Supreme Court establishes the right of the courts to decide the reasonableness of U.S. railroad rates—and the doctrine of judicial review—in the case of *Smyth v. Ames* March 7.

Standard Fruit and Steamship Co. has its beginnings in the Vaccaro Brothers Co. started at New Orleans by Italian-American banana importers Joseph, Felix, and Lucca Vaccaro, whose brother-in-law Salvador D'Antoni helps them acquire the two-masted schooner *Frances* (*see* 1926).

Mechanical refrigeration gets a boost from Swedish inventor Carl von Linde, who perfects a machine that liquefies air (*see* 1873; Freon 12, 1931).

The word "photosynthesis" is introduced to denote the process by which plants synthesize carbohydrates from carbon dioxide, water, and inorganic salts, using sunlight for energy and chlorophyll as a catalyst (*see* Ingenhousz, 1779; von Sachs, 1862).

Cookbooks: *Good Cooking* and *Left Overs: How to Transform Them into Palatable and Wholesome*

Dishes with Many New and Valuable Recipes by Sarah Tyson Rorer, who last year became food editor of the *Ladies' Home Journal* and who travels the country demonstrating tableside cookery. She has become an admirer of breakfast food pioneer John Harvey Kellogg and promotes his ideas in her magazine.

U.S. Secretary of Agriculture James Wilson sends Seaman Knapp to China, Japan, and the Philippines (above) to investigate rice varieties, production, and milling (*see* Knapp, 1885). Knapp's findings will lead to a marked expansion U.S. rice growing (*see* 4-H Club, 1910).

Chinese-born California farmer Chin Lung, 34, leases 200 acres on a sharecropping basis from Ernest A. Denicke, who receives 45 percent of the vegetables that Chin plants between Denicke's asparagus rows and 25 percent of vegetables he plants on another 40 acres. Chin will do well enough by this arrangement to move in 1900 to San Joaquin County and lease 1,125 acres on the Sargent and Barnhart Reclamation Tract near Stockton, where Chinese tenant farmers have grown potatoes and sweet potatoes for more than 30 years (*see* Shima, 1899). Paying $7,000 per year, Chin will extend the lease over the next 3 years, paying more each year, and employ some 500 workers, recruited from Stockton's Chinatown, to help cultivate, harvest, and sack the asparagus, beans, onions, and potatoes that he grows in the rich Delta land (*see* Alien Land Act, 1913).

U.S. Department of Agriculture botanist Walter Tennyson Swingle, 27, is promoted to the position of agricultural explorer. He has worked on Florida citrus diseases and discovered treatments for some of them. In his new job he will find many new citrus rootstocks, some of them disease resistant, and in attempting to rejuvenate old citrus varieties he will discover what will come to be called neophyosis, a kind of parthenogenesis peculiar to citrus trees that permits raising of a new generation without cross-pollination and thus rejuvenating a citrus variety without vegetative propagation, which diminishes a plant's reproductive capacity. Swingle will be credited with creating the tangelo—a cross between the tangerine and grapefruit.

U.S. troops sent to fight in the Spanish-American War (above) fall ill from eating what critics call "embalmed" beef, and many die (contaminated meat kills more men than die of battle wounds). The deaths raise a public outcry for reform of the meat-packing industry (*see* 1905; Armour, 1901) and increase demands for pure food laws that would regulate meatpackers (*see* St. Louis Exposition, 1904).

Joseph Campbell Preserve Co. adds Vegetable to its line of condensed soups (*see* 1897). Campbell's Soups appear for the first time in cans with red-and-white labels whose colors have been suggested by Cornell football uniforms (*see* 1904).

J. T. Dorrance's Campbell's Soup cans sported the colors of Cornell's football players.

Tennessee widow Anna Stokely (*née* Rorex) and her four sons set up shop on the French Broad River with initial capital of $3,900 to pack produce from the family's large farms. They install an old steam engine to heat water in the three-sided shed which they use as a factory, cook tomatoes in a few metal tubs, pack them in a few hundred tin cans, and send them out in homemade wooden boxes for sale, initially to customers in eastern Tennessee, then to residents of Knoxville and Chattanooga. William B. Stokely, who was 17 when his father, John, died (he had seven younger siblings), has taken charge of the farms and runs the cannery with his mother. When he goes off to college next year his brother James R. will take over, and when James goes to college the next brother, John, will succeed him. By the time the youngest brother, George, is ready for college, William and James will have finished and will be back running the business, shipping product to markets in Memphis, Nashville, Atlanta, New Orleans, Charlotte, Louisville, Birmingham, and other major southern cities (*see* 1917).

Sanitas Corn Flakes are introduced by Sanitas Nut Food Co., set up at Battle Creek, Mich., by J. H.

Kellogg's Sanitas Corn Flakes helped launch a vast industry of cold breakfast foods. PHOTO COURTESY KELLOGG CO.

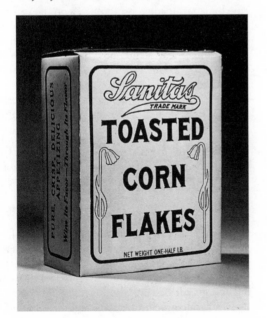

Kellogg with his brother Will Keith (*see* Granose, 1895). The world's first cornflakes, sold by mail order, quickly turn rancid and have little acceptance in a market oriented toward wheat cereals, but the Kelloggs persevere. They will call their company the Sanitas Food Co. beginning in 1900 (*see* 1902).

Henry D. Perky promotes Shredded Wheat as "the perfect food" and embarks on a lecture tour (*see* 1895). "From the most abject physical wreck, I have succeeded, by the use of naturally organized food, in reorganizing my body into perfectly healthy condition," says Perky (who will die in 1906 at age 66). "I will use no other bread or cereal food product other than shredded whole wheat biscuit, and dishes made from these biscuit. I am 55 years of age and feel younger than 20 years ago." In a message to mothers, Perky's company says, "Do you know that children crave natural food until you pervert their tastes by the use of unnatural food? Unnatural food develops unnatural and therefore strong propensities and desires in children. Like begets like—pure food, pure minds" (*see* 1900).

Uneeda Biscuits are created by National Biscuit's A. W. Green (above), who seeks to establish a brand name that will surmount the anonymity of the cracker barrel seen in every grocery shop. Green decides to concentrate the company's efforts behind a flaky soda cracker, retains N. W. Ayer & Son as his advertising agency, and is advised by Ayer's Henry N. McKinney that a manufacturer must "insure his future sales by adopting a trade name and trade dress which will belong exclusively to him by trademark and trade right." McKinney suggests the name Uneeda Cracker, Green changes it to Uneeda Biscuit, and the name is registered December 27 with the U.S. Patent Office (*see* 1900).

Entenmann's baked goods are introduced by Brooklyn, N.Y., entrepreneur William Entenmann, who starts a home-delivery bakery service (*see* 1982).

U.S. troops awaiting transport to Cuba in the Spanish-American War (above) enjoy Cuba Libres (made of rum and Coca-Cola by a bartender at the Tampa Bay Hotel in Tampa); workers in Cuba's Daiquiri iron mines will soon enjoy a cocktail called the Daiquiri (made of rum, lime juice, and sugar).

Pepsi-Cola is introduced by New Bern, N.C., pharmacist Caleb Bradham, who has been mixing fountain drinks since 1893 and has developed a cola drink formula (*see* 1902).

Martinson's Coffee is founded near the docks at New York by Latvian-born entrepreneur Joseph Martinson, 18, who specializes in supplying hotels and restaurants. When vacuum packing of coffee is introduced in 1900, Martinson will be one of the first to market his coffee in the new way (*see* Hill Bros., 1900).

Annual British tea consumption averages 10 pounds per capita, up from 2 pounds in 1797 (*see* 1869). Black tea from India and Ceylon has long since gained dominance over Chinese green teas, but many connoisseurs still prefer China's green teas, especially gunpowder and hysson, and Chinese black teas, notably keemun or congou from North China (also called English Breakfast tea).

The Paris Ritz opens June 5 in a 17th-century townhouse in the Place Vendôme with chef Auguste Escoffier as *maître chef de cuisine*. César Ritz has found that the duc de Lauzun's property was for sale, he has suggested the name "Grand Marnier" to London liqueur maker Marnier La Postolle for La Postolle's orange-flavored cordial, La Postolle has given him funds to buy the townhouse, and Ritz opens the new hotel with 170 guest rooms. (Richard D'Oyly Carte buys the Berkeley Hotel in Piccadilly in order to obtain the services of George Reeve-Smith, who replaces Ritz as managing director of London's Savoy.) Escoffier has 80 chefs and sous chefs in his kitchen, which is one-fifth the size of the Place Vendôme, and continues his practice, developed at the Savoy, of dividing his staff into specialists—one squad for sauces, another for fish, a third for entremets, a fourth for soups, and so forth—in order to increase efficiency and shorten patrons' waiting time (*see* Carlton, 1899; London Ritz, 1902).

Louis Sherry's opens on New York's Fifth Avenue at 44th Street, opposite Delmonico's (*see* 1897). French-American caterer Sherry has operated a four-story establishment since 1881 to serve the city's carriage trade, and his new restaurant will be among the city's finest for 21 years.

1899

English chocolate manufacturer-philanthropist Seebohm Rowntree, now 28, of York estimates that between one quarter and one third of the British population lives in "poverty" with "earnings insufficient to obtain the minimum necessaries for the maintenance of mere physical efficiency."

United Fruit Company is incorporated by banana exporter Minor C. Keith and the Boston Fruit Co., which has been distributing Keith's fruit since the failure of his New Orleans distributor (which cost Keith $1.5 million) (*see* 1871; 1885). Andrew Preston is president of the new firm, Keith first vice president. United Fruit controls 112 miles of railroad with 212,494 acres of land, more than 61,000 acres of it in production (*see* 1929).

Russian-born Alabama banana dealer Samuel Zemurray, 21, expands his operations to New Orleans after several years of selling fruit to grocers. Taken to America in steerage from his native Bessarabia by an aunt 7 years ago, "Sam the Banana Man" (as grocers call him) worked for $1 per week helping an aged peddler, earned enough to buy $750 worth of bananas at Mobile and ship them inland by rail express, telegraphed grocers in towns along the route to come to the railroad sidings for ripe bananas, made a profit of $35 on the venture, and reinvested it in more ambitious ventures. He brought the rest of his family to Alabama in 1896, settled them near Selma, now has $100,000 in the bank, tries earnestly to learn Spanish, and will borrow heavily to acquire part ownership of two tramp steamers and buy 5,000 acres of banana properties in Honduras, naming his enterprise Cuyamel Fruit Co. (*see* politics, 1911).

American Beet Sugar Co. is organized as the first Colorado beet-sugar refinery opens at Grand Junction.

C. A. Swanson & Sons has its beginnings in the Jerpe Commission Co., started at Omaha by Swedish-American grocer Carl A. Swanson, 21, with local entrepreneurs Frank D. Ellison and John P. Jerpe. Swanson arrived from Sweden 4 years ago speaking no English, has lived with two sisters at Omaha, and has gone to night school while working as a grocer's clerk. Begun with $456 in capital, the wholesale grocery firm will be incorporated in

1905 with a capitalization of $10,000 and will prosper in poultry, eggs, and butter (*see* 1945).

Beech-Nut Packing Corp. is adopted as the new name for the 8-year-old Imperial Packing Co. of Canojoharie, N.Y., to suggest the beechwood fires whose smoke is used in the smokehouse that cures the company's ham and bacon. Beech-Nut has specialized also in fancy pail lard, acquired U.S. rights to a German vacuum jar, and perfected a superior flint glass jar for its bacon, but co-founder Walter Lipe, who has named his daughters Virginia Ham and Roseanne Bacon, will bring in outside investors in order to expand into peanut-butter making, they will wrest control of the company, and he will commit suicide (*see* coffee, 1924).

New York Condensed Milk Co. becomes Borden's Condensed Milk Co. It will be renamed Borden Co. in 1919 and Borden, Inc. in 1968 (*see* Elgin, 1894; Liederkranz cheese, 1929).

New York's Breakstone Brothers relocates to 300 Greenwich Street, where it specializes in sweet and sour cream (*see* 1888). The business prospers, it will soon move to larger quarters at 344 Greenwich Street as it expands to become a wholesaler of butter, soft cheeses, and sour cream, and by 1912 it will have manufacturing plants in upstate New York (*see* 1918).

Flour-milling pioneer Charles A. Pillsbury dies at Minneapolis September 17 at age 56 (*see* 1889).

The California Fruit Canners Association is created by a consolidation of 11 old-line companies representing nearly half the state's packers, including Dawson & Cutting, the first commercial fruit packers in the West, and Italian-American packer John Mark Fontana (*see* 1916).

The American Sugar Refining trust has almost a 100 percent monopoly in the U.S. industry (*see* 1897; 1907).

Bachelor Swiss candy maker Rodolphe Lindt sells his business to David Sprüngli (*see* 1875; 1879).

Jell-O is acquired for $450 from Pearl Wait by his LeRoy, N.Y., neighbor Orator Francis Woodward, who has just started a company to produce a cereal which he calls Grain-O (*see* 1897; 1906).

Jewel Tea Co. has its beginnings in a door-to-door peddling operation that will grow to become Jewel Companies, a major U.S. grocery store chain.

The first U.S. concrete grain elevator goes up at the western edge of Minneapolis. Frank C. Peavey, who has expanded with new elevators throughout the Northwest and has been paying huge insurance premiums on the wooden elevators and their contents, has sent his son-in-law, Frank T. Heffelfinger, and Minneapolis banker C. F. Haglin to Europe in search of the best method for storing grain (*see* 1886). They have returned with praise for a Romanian concrete elevator, and Peavey has defied the conventional wisdow that only wood has the necessary "give" for storing grain. Skeptics call his 80-foot-tall concrete tank "Peavey's Folly" and predict that it will explode when grain is drawn out of its bottom, but the concrete structure proves its critics wrong and will lead to a general replacement of wooden elevators throughout the country (*see* 1900).

Wesson Oil is developed by Southern Oil Co. chemist David Wesson, 38, who introduces a new method for deodorizing cottonseed oil. His vacuum and high-temperature process will revolutionize the cooking oil industry and largely overcome the prejudice against cottonseed oil, which until now has been deodorized only by heating it with a steam coil and blowing live steam through it at atmospheric pressure (*see* 1900; Wesson Oil and Snowdrift, 1925).

A patent for "composition milk" (*procédé et appareil pour fixer la composition des liquides*) is granted December 26 to French inventor Auguste Gaulin, owner of the Gaulin Dairy Machinery Equipment Co. at Paris (*see* 1900; Marix, 1892).

Britain's Hovis Bread-Flour Co. hires John Figgins Morton, 17, to develop its sales department, which has only two "travellers" and two commission agents to sell the company's patent germ flour (*see* 1898). Morton will inaugurate Hovis bread-baking competitions next year, and by 1905 there will be 30 salesmen as Morton distributes Hovis Cycle Road Maps and Guides, indicating cafeterias where cyclists may find Hovis Bread. The power of advertising will make Hovis a household name, suggestive of health and wholesome quality (*see* 1918).

Nonfiction: *The Theory of the Leisure Class* by University of Chicago social scientist Thorstein Bunde Veblen, 42, says that society adopts decorum (or etiquette) and refined tastes as evidence of gentility because they can be acquired only with leisure. Veblen has little to say about food or eating habits, but he notes that certain foods and beverages are esteemed as evidence of conspicuous consumption, as is drunkenness. Having a large belly tells the world that the man with the protruding abdomen is a person of substance (Veblen does not realize that it is also an indication that the typical American male finds it difficult to adjust his diet to his increasingly sedentary life).

Chopped beefsteak is called Hamburg steak in America, says a new French-German-English dictionary of foods published under the title *Blueher's Rechtschreibung* (*see* 1836; Louis Lassen, 1900).

Wisconsin's last wild passenger pigeon is shot (*see* 1878; 1911).

The Columbia River Packers Association is created by seven chinook salmon canneries at the mouth of the river, one of which packs its fish under the name Bumble Bee. CRPA will acquire several sailing vessels in 1901, load them with lumber, coal, building and canning materials, and build a cannery on the Nushagak River at Bristol Bay in northwestern Alaska that will be followed by many more CRPA Alaskan canneries (*see* 1938).

The Russian grain harvest is 65 million tons, double the harvest of 30 years ago, as 200 million acres are planted to grain.

U.S. cerealist Mark Carleton introduces Kubanka durum wheat from southeastern Russia into North Dakota, which will be the leading U.S. producer of the wheat most suitable for macaroni and spaghetti (*see* 1895; Kharkov, 1900).

Japanese-born California farmer George Shima, 35, begins experimenting with potato growing in the Sacramento and San Joaquin river deltas (*see* Chin Lung, 1898). Shima changed his name from Kinji Ushijima when he arrived from his native Kyushu 10 years ago, worked initially as a farmworker, became a labor contractor, saw that low-lying swamp and waste lands could be acquired for $5, $3, and even less per acre at a time when prime farmland went for $150, and joined with some former student friends to start a 15-acre farm near Woodbridge, using labor-intensive, high-yield methods learned in Japan, where land is scarce. He begins to obtain outside backing for a massive dike construction program, using dredges and heavy machinery to deepen natural channels, lower the water table, and drain fertile land for cultivation. Shima will have leased holdings of about 1,000 acres by next year, plus 2,000 in joint tenantship, growing cash crops that include onions, potatoes, fruits, and berries; he will eventually reclaim more than 28,800 acres of mosquito-ridden wastelands, obtain seeds and advice from agricultural experts at Stanford University and the University of California, Berkeley, and produce 40 to 50 bushels of potatoes per acre on land that yields far less when planted to rice or other grain crops. By 1909, Shima will be known as the "Potato King" (*see* Alien Land Act, 1913).

San Francisco businessman Horace Fletcher celebrates his 50th birthday August 10 by bicycling 200 miles. The 5-foot, 6-inch importer of oriental goods has used strict diet to reduce his weight from 217 pounds to 152 and thus regained good health. He withdrew from business 4 years ago so broken in health that no insurance company would write a policy on his life, but he has built himself up on a diet of milk, breakfast food, and maple sugar, averaging 11¢ per day on food (*see* 1901).

Armenian-American confectioner-peddler Peter Paul Halajian at Naugatuck, Conn., advertises "Good candies at low prices. See our mixed candy at 10¢ a pound, three pounds for 25¢ . . . Fruits and nuts of all kinds. Peter Paul" (*see* 1919).

Coca-Cola is bottled for the first time by Chattanooga, Tenn., lawyers Benjamin F. Thomas and Joseph B. Whitehead, who have traveled to Atlanta and persuaded Asa Candler to let them try bottling his beverage under contract (*see* 1895). Coca-Cola Company will give seven parent bottlers contracts to establish local bottling companies and supply them with syrup, it will acquire these bottlers over the years (the last one in 1974), but most Coca-Cola continues to be dispensed by soda jerks from syrup mixed with carbonated water (*see* 1916; Britain, 1900; 1909).

Coca-Cola dropped its health claims and was promoted as a drink for young sophisticates. LIBRARY OF CONGRESS

Carnation evaporated milk is supplied in 16-ounce cans to Klondike-bound gold seekers by Elbridge Amos Stuart, who has set up a small plant at Kent, Wash., near Seattle with help from John Meyenberg of Helvetia Condensed Milk in Highland Park, Ill. (*see* Our Pet, 1894).

An Indiana Quaker who became a grocer at El Paso, Tex., Stuart has come to suspect that bad milk is the cause of so many children dying of "summer complaint" and has invested his savings in a new process to manufacture canned, sterilized, evaporated milk. Production begins September 6 with an output of 55 cases (*see* 1906).

The breakfast menu at Singapore's Raffles Hotel for June 2 includes 10 courses: porridge, fried fish, mutton chops, deviled cold beef and salad, boiled eggs, cheese, toast, jam, and tea or coffee. A glass of Benedictine is suggested to follow (*see* 1886; 1900).

London's new Carlton Hotel, opened by César Ritz, has a restaurant kitchen with 60 cooks headed by chef Auguste Escoffier, formerly of the Paris Ritz, who has set up a small factory with his brother Robert to bottle some of his concoctions and has a prosperous business selling his bottled Sauce Robert, Sauce Diable, Cumberland Sauce, etc., to the German kaiser, the Russian czar, the British royal family, the House of Lords, major shipping companies, and top hotels. To serve as many as 500 guests per meal, Escoffier buys sole, Scotch salmon, salmon-trout, and turbot in London but brings over lamb, poultry, foie gras, early vegetables, and fruit from Les Halles in Paris (*see* 1901).

Oysters Rockefeller (or Oysters à la Rockefeller) is created by Jules Alciatore, 39, at the 59-year-old New Orleans restaurant Antoine's, founded by his late father. Jules apprenticed under the eye of his mother for 6 years, and was then sent to France where he worked in the kitchens of Paris, Strasbourg, and Marseilles, became chef of the Pickwick Club in 1887, and has returned to his native New Orleans. The dish, which he names after the head of the Standard Oil Co. trust (because it is so rich), begins with raw, washed, and sponged spinach, which is put through a food chopper twice with equal amounts of parsley and green onion tops; four or five drops of Tabasco sauce are sprinkled over this mixture with salt and pepper plus about one-third cup brown bread crumbs, finely ground. A third of a cup of butter is rolled in and kneaded thoroughly to create the sauce, to which a little absinthe may sometimes be added. Three dozen oysters on the half shell are placed in a baking pan filled nearly to the top with rock salt and baked in a 450° F. oven for 5 minutes until the edges of the oysters begin to curl; one tablespoon of the green butter sauce is then placed on each oyster and the pan is returned to the hot oven, where it is allowed to bake for 5 minutes more, but not long enough to brown the oysters (they should be only semicooked).

Rector's Lobster Palace opens one block north of Shanley Brothers on the west side of Broadway between 43rd and 44th streets in New York. Restaurateur Charles Rector, whose father, George, runs Rector's Oyster Palace in Chicago, will attract some of New York's more notable trenchermen (*see* Brady, 1902).

1900

💲 U.S. wheat fetches 70¢/bushel as 34 percent of the crop goes abroad, and corn brings 33¢/bushel as 10 percent of the crop is exported. Texas steers bring $4.25/hundredweight, but the price index for U.S. farm products will rise by a spectacular 52 percent in the next decade as more efficient transport enables Britain and Europe to import North American grain at low rates.

Meat consumption among British working-class families has more than doubled since 1880, and consumption of butter and milk also shows a marked increase. The wages of Lancashire factory workers allow them a breakfast of coffee or tea, bread, bacon, and eggs (except when egg prices are too high), a dinner of potatoes and beef, an evening meal of tea, bread and butter, cheap vegetables and fish, and a light supper.

Typical U.S. food prices: sugar 4¢/lb., eggs 14¢/doz., butter 24¢ to 25¢/lb. Boardinghouses offer turkey dinner at 20¢ and supper or breakfast at 15¢, but a male stenographer earns $10 per week and an unskilled girl $2.50.

The first full-size concrete grain elevator in North America goes up at Duluth, Minn., where "elevator king" Frank C. Peavey's 3.3-million-bushel elevator reduces insurance rates on stored grain by 83 percent and more (*see* 1899). The Peavey elevator makes wood obsolete for building large elevators.

Battle Creek, Mich., has 42 breakfast cereal plants (*see* Kellogg; 1898; Post, 1897).

National Sugar Manufacturing Co. is incorporated in New Jersey (*see* Jack Frost trademark, 1913).

National Starch Manufacturing Co. is founded (*see* 1842; 1906).

🤝 Milton S. Hershey sells his Lancaster Caramel Co. for $1 million in cash (*see* 1894). American Caramel Co. has offered him $500,000 outright for his business, his lawyer has demanded twice that amount,

he has got his price, and as part of the sales agreement Hershey retains that part of his old factory which contains chocolate-making equipment so that he may continue production of chocolate (*see* Hershey bars, below).

Duffy-Mott Co. is created by a merger of W. B. Duffy Cider Co. of Rochester, N.Y., with the S. R. Mott Co. (*see* 1842). The new concern will be incorporated in 1914 (*see* applesauce, 1930).

⚡ Steam tractors appear on wheatfields of the U.S. Pacific Northwest, but their main use is to draw portable threshing machines, many of which are still pulled by 40 horses driven abreast.

Some 2.5 horsepower is available to each man working on a U.S. farm, up from 1.5 in 1850 (*see* 1930).

U.S. railroads charge a freight rate that averages 75¢/ton-mile, down from $1.22 in 1883. The Great Northern charges only $35 for a railcar traveling 500 miles between St. Paul, Minn., and Minot, N.D.; the Chicago and Northwestern $40 for a railcar traveling the 750 miles between Chicago and Pierre, S.D.

Only 25 percent of the U.S. commercial shipping fleet remains in sail, down from 56 percent in 1870. More than 60 percent of world shipping is in steamships, up from 16 percent in 1870.

Genetic laws revealed by Gregor Mendel in 1865 become generally known for the first time as Dutch botanist Hugo de Vries, 52, at the University of Amsterdam, German botanist Karl Erich Correns, 35, and Austrian botanist Erich Tschermak von Seysenegg, 29, working independently, discover Mendel's published work and make public his Mendelian laws (*see* Bateson, 1902).

Cookbooks: *La Grande Cuisine Illustrée* by French chef Prosper Salles, who has succeeded Jean Giroix at Monte Carlo's Hôtel de Paris, and his assistant, Prosper Montagné, 35 (the book contains only recipes executed by them or under their supervision); *Home Helps, with Illustrations. A Practical and Useful Book of Recipes with Much Valuable Information on Cooking and Serving Breakfasts, Luncheons, Dinners and Teas* edited by Sarah Tyson Rorer.

The French government gives a dinner in the Tuileries gardens at Paris in July for 23,000 people to honor all the mayors of France. The 80-year-old catering firm Potel & Chavot arranges to have five miles of tablecloth, 250,000 plates, 2,430 roast pheasants, and countless bottles of champagne.

The average French adult consumes an estimated 1 pound, 5 ounces of bread per day (children are taught to eat with a fork in one hand and pusher of bread in the other); the figure will decline in the next 65 years to less than 10 ounces.

Commercial bakeries now produce 25 percent of U.S. bread, up from 20 percent in 1890, mostly because the urban population is eight and a half times what it was in 1850, whereas the rural population has merely doubled, and industry employs more women (they now account for 17 percent of the workforce). Population concentrations have made possible the mass distribution of perishable bakery products. There are seven times more commercial bakers than in 1850, and the value of their products has increased thirteenfold.

Per capita U.S. wheat flour consumption averages 224 pounds, up from 205 pounds in 1850 (see 1920).

The hamburger sandwich is invented by some accounts at New Haven, Conn., where Louis Lassen grinds 7¢/lb. lean beef, broils it, and serves it between two slices of toast (no catsup or relish) to customers at his 5-year-old three-seat Louis Lunch (but see also Nagreen, 1885; Menches, 1892).

Grape phylloxerae take firm hold in northeastern Victoria (see 1870). Grafting is used rather than eradication, and the aphids will never reach South Australia, thanks to stringent quarantine precautions. Cyprus, parts of Hungary, the French Midi, Portugal's Collares vineyards, and Chile will also be spared the ravages of phylloxerae.

German vineyards remain largely free of grape phylloxerae (see 1882); only 1.5 percent of the vines have been attacked.

Mark Carleton makes another trip to Russia and returns with hard red Kharkov wheat, a winter variety that withstands winterkill and gives high yields (see 1899; 1914).

The average U.S. farmworker produces enough food and fiber for seven people, up from 4.5 in 1860.

The world has 100 million acres of irrigated cropland, up from 20 million in 1880.

The first sluice gate on the Colorado River brings irrigation water from Arizona to California's Imperial Valley (see Salton Sea, 1905).

Artichokes are grown on 500 acres of California farmland between San Francisco and Half Moon Bay. Growers will move south until they reach Castroville, a coastal town that will come to produce 75 percent of the U.S. crop (but only a small percentage of the world crop, almost all of which will continue to come from Mediterranean countries, primarily Italy). California artichoke acreage will reach 12,000 by 1926 but will decline 9,000 by the early 1990s as growers plant more plants per acre for higher yields.

California harvests its first commercial crop of figs, 130 years after the introduction of figs by Franciscan missionaries (see 1885).

Honeydew melons are introduced into the United States (year approximate).

Grapefruit becomes an important food in the United States as botanical development makes the fruit sweeter. U.S. citrus growers will account for 90 percent of world grapefruit production.

English biochemists Frederick Gowland Hopkins, 39, and S. W. Cole isolate the amino acid tryptophan (see niacin; 1945; Hopkins, 1906). Thirteen amino acids have now been isolated; eight will be found essential to adult human nutrition (see Rose, 1949).

Milk bottles are introduced in England but only for pasteurized milk (see Borden, 1885; Hood, 1897). Most British milk remains unpasteurized, and bottles will not be widely used for another two decades (see 1901; 1942).

Regulations limiting bacteria in U.S. milk to 1 million per cubic centimeter prove difficult to enforce despite growing use of pasteurization (see 1890). Contaminated milk remains a major source of food-borne disease (see Evans, 1917).

The best-quality ground pepper offered to Londoners contains equal parts of black peppercorns, hot pepper dust, and white pepper dust (see 1891). Most of the ground pepper in the shops contains very little real pepper and may be composed largely of ground olive pits.

Four Britons die December 1 and 2,000 fall ill from drinking beer treated with arsenic.

Uneeda Biscuits have sales of more than 10 million packages per month, while all other packaged crackers sell scarcely 40,000 per month (*see* 1898). N. W. Ayer advertising copywriter Joseph Geisinger poses his 5-year-old nephew Gordon Stile in boots, oil hat, and slicker holding a box of Uneeda Biscuits, and a photographer takes a picture that will become a famous trademark designed to suggest that the crackers remain crisp even in damp weather (*see* Animal Crackers, 1902).

Per capita U.S. sugar consumption averages 65.2 pounds per year (*see* 1923).

World beet-sugar production reaches 5.6 million tons, a figure that will more than quadruple in the next 64 years.

H. J. Heinz erects an electric sign six stories high with 1,200 lights to tell New Yorkers about the "57 Good Things for the Table" that include Heinz tomato soup, tomato ketchup, sweet pickles, India relish, and peach butter (*see* 1892; 1905).

Wesson Oil is put on the market by Southern Oil Co. (*see* 1899). David Wesson has made the pure cottonseed oil palatable and will work from 1901 to 1911 on a process for hydrogenating it (*see* 1925; Normann, 1901).

Milton Hershey (above) introduces the first Hershey chocolate bars (plain and with almonds), which will have sales next year of $622,000 (*see* 1903).

Mead Johnson Co. is founded at Evansville, Ind., to produce the infant cereal Pablum, which will be sold for more than half a century only through physicians' recommendations. Founder Mead Johnson is a brother of New Jersey pharmaceutical-supply maker Robert Wood Johnson of Johnson & Johnson.

A model Shredded Wheat factory goes up at Niagara Falls, N.Y. A picture of H. D. Perky's "Palace of Light" factory will appear on every package of Shredded Wheat, and the new factory will also produce Shredded Wheat crackers called Triscuits (*see* 1898; National Biscuit Co., 1928).

The Empire cheese plant, which has made Philadelphia brand cream cheese since 1880, burns down at South Edmeston, N.Y. A new company, whose name is unintentionally misspelled Phenix Cheese by its farmer founders, resumes production (*see* Kraft, 1909).

Nestlé builds a factory at Fulton, N.Y., and begins U.S. production of baby food (*see* 1898; 1901).

Homogenized milk (*lait homogénéisé*) produced by Auguste Gaulin's process is exhibited at the Paris International Exposition but is thought to be of scientific value only (*see* 1899). The ability of the milk's constituents to remain fixed is considered remarkable, and Gaulin's process will for some time be called "fixation." He is the first to use the term "homogenized," but he recognizes the imperfections in his process and undertakes a scientific study of milk in order to improve it. The largest fat globules, he observes under a microscope, are 500 to 600 times smaller than the diameter of the hairlike tubes through which they pass, and further reduction can be ascribed only to the friction caused by forcing the milk through the tubes (*see* 1902).

Coca-Cola goes on sale in Britain for the first time August 31 (*see* 1899; 1909).

Hills Bros. in San Francisco begins packing roast ground coffee in vacuum tins to begin a new era in coffee marketing. It is the beginning of the end for the coffee roasting shops common now in every town and the coffee mill seen in almost every U.S. kitchen (*see* Chase and Sanborn, 1878).

California's Beaulieu Vineyard is founded at Rutherford in the Napa Valley by French-American vintner Georges de Latour, whose table wines must compete with spirits that retail at 50¢ per bottle. Latour's widow will carry on the 600-acre business that her daughter and granddaughter will sell to Heublein in 1969.

Kansas prohibitionist Carry Nation (*née* Moore), 54, declares that since the saloon is illegal in Kansas, any citizen has the right to destroy liquor, furniture, and fixtures in any public place selling intoxicants. Nation, who stands six feet tall, weighs 170 pounds; her second husband, David Nation, is an elderly widower who served in the Civil War and became a newspaper editor. She made her first foray last year at Medicine Bow, when she and another WCTU member walked into Strong's saloon singing hymns. Thrown out, the two women marched over to a drugstore that sold whiskey, rolled its keg into the street, and destroyed it. She now loads a buggy with rocks and bits of brick, sets out for neighboring Kiowa, Kans., and goes into Dobson's saloon singing, "Who Hath sorrow? Who Hath woe?" She breaks glasses and bottles behind the bar. At the Hotel Carey in Wichita she is arrested for destroying a huge mirror, smashing bottles, decanters, and gilded signs, and throwing a brick through a canvas depicting Cleopatra at her bath (complete with pubic hair). The exploit gains her national publicity as she continues a campaign of hatchet wielding through Kansas cities and towns, and although she will be arrested, fined, imprisoned, clubbed, and shot at, she will persevere (*see* Anti-Saloon League, 1895; 18th Amendment and Volstead Act, 1919).

New York publisher Bernarr Macfadden, 32, opens a restaurant at 487 Pearl Street with prices that undercut the competition to help promote *Physical Culture*, the magazine that he has published since 1898. Most items on the menu are priced at 1¢ at a time when other restaurants charge 15¢ for a full meal (saloon-bars offer "free" lunches for a nickel or less).

Singapore's Raffles Hotel serves a Criterion Dinner August 18 (*see* 1899). Despite the warm weather, men in starched collars and shirt fronts sit down with women in high-stayed corsets to consume canapés of pâté de foie gras, printanière d'Orleans soup, boucher des dames à la Du Barry, paupiettes de rouget à la Joinville, ortolans à la financière, filet de bœuf à la Richelieu, suprême de chapon à la Toulouse, roast turkey with cranberry sauce, lettuce with mayonnaise, brussels sprouts, asparagus, green beans, petits fours amandine, cheeses, fruits, black coffee, and appropriate wines.

The London restaurant Throgmorton, opened by J. Lyons & Co. across from the Stock Exchange in Throgmorton Street, contains three separate restaurants and bars, all below street level, and quickly becomes a popular luncheon spot for Exchange members and staff workers (*see* Trocadero, 1896; tea, 1903).

Visitors to the Paris International Exposition (above) find that the hunting pavilion built in 1853 for the late Napoleon III at the Carrefour de Longchamps in the Bois de Boulogne (beside a 40-foot-high waterfall created in 1854) has been turned into an elegant restaurant, Les Grandes Cascades.

Maxim's gets a new decor that helps it attract patrons from the crowds that have come to see the Paris International Exposition (above) and come to Maxim's as much to see the attractive music hall stars and former ballet beauties (*les grandes horizontales*, such as Liane de Pougy, Améliane d'Élisande, and Caroline Otéro) who come to the place after midnight, as for Maxim's food (*see* 1894). Maxim's is soon playing host to international celebrities, including the prince of Wales and actress Lily Langtry, who cannot be seen together in London (*see* 1907).

The Paris restaurant Lucas Carton opens at the corner of the Rue Royale and the Boulevarde Malsherbes (year approximate). Old families will have Sunday lunch at the establishment, which will be favored by the government as a semiofficial dining spot.

The *Guide Michelin* published at Paris is the first systematic evaluation of European restaurants. Financed by tire producers André and Édouard Michelin, the *Guide* rates restaurants using a system of three stars (worth a special journey), two stars (worth a detour), or one star and will be updated periodically (the star awards were originated by Karl Baedeker) (*see* 1829; Michelin, 1911).

Half of all U.S. working women are farmhands or domestic servants (*see* 1960). Some 45.8 million Americans are rural residents, 30.2 million urban.

20th Century

1901

✕ Queen Victoria dies January 22 at age 81 after a reign of nearly 64 years. J. Lyons & Co. undertakes the job of catering to all the troops who are drafted into London for the queen's funeral (*see* Trocadero restaurant, 1896; tea, 1903).

✊ British chocolate heir William Cadbury visits Trinidad and is told that cacao workers in Portugal's African islands of São Tomé and Principe are, for all practical purposes, treated as slaves (*see* 1902).

💲 Chicago meatpacker P. D. Armour dies at Pasadena, Calif., January 29 at age 68, never having recovered from the shock brought on by charges that his company, along with other meatpackers, sold the U.S. Army chemically treated "embalmed beef" during the Spanish-American War of 1898. Armour leaves a fortune estimated at $50 million; his son, J. Ogden Armour, succeeds as president of the company and will hold that position until he retires in 1923, by which time Armour will be the world's largest meatpacker.

Margarine prices soar worldwide following a bad U.S. corn crop, which has led to a reduction in livestock populations and consequent lower supplies of lard and beef fat. U.S. meatpackers form a price-fixing cartel, which is blamed by European margarine makers and consumers for the higher prices (*see* 1902).

Nestlé acquires a small English cream-sterilizing plant at Tudbury and enlarges it (*see* 1900; 1903).

New York Glucose Co. is founded by Standard Oil director Edward Thomas Bedford, 52, who began his career selling vegetables to housewives in Bridgeport, Conn., at age 17 became a flour salesman for Boyd & Thompson in New York, and wound up as a lieutenant of oil baron John D. Rockefeller. New York Glucose manufactures products from cornstarch (*see* Corn Products Refining Co., 1906).

The Quaker Oats Co. is incorporated by Henry P. Crowell and Robert Stuart, who will sell all their brands under the Quaker label (*see* 1891; 1893). They have failed in an effort to consolidate 21 other millers with the American Cereal Co. and thus control more than 95 percent of U.S. oat-milling capacity, but they will drop nonstandard packages, and their holding company will be roughly twice the size of their major competitor, Great Western Cereal, maker of Mother's Oats (*see* 1911).

One-fourth of U.S. agricultural produce is exported, according to testimony given at hearings of the U.S. Industrial Commission.

C. W. Post has profits of $385,000 from his Postum and Grape Nuts and plows half of it back into advertising (*see* 1897; 1904).

🤝 American Can Co. is created by a merger of 175 U.S. can makers engineered by W. H. Moore (*see* National Biscuit, 1898) and Indiana banker Daniel Reid. The Can Trust turns out 90 percent of U.S. tin-plated steel cans (*see* Continental Can, 1904).

New England Confectionery Co. (NECCO) is created at Boston by a merger of three companies, including one founded by Oliver Chase in 1847 (*see* 1927).

The U.S. Industrial Commission (above) hears a government witness testify that a steam sheller can shell a bushel of corn in 1.5 minutes versus 100 minutes for370 the same job done by hand, and that a wheat combine can do in 4 minutes what it would take a man 160 minutes to reap, bind, and thresh by hand.

Tarrytown, N.Y., inventor Thomas Holt is granted a patent for an egg beater with perforated blades.

A hydrogenation process invented by English chemist William Normann saturates unsaturated and polyunsaturated fatty acids to keep them from turning rancid. The process will find wide application in the production of edible fats and foods containing oils (*see* below).

Cookbook: *The Settlement Cookbook* by Milwaukee settlement house worker Lizzie Black (Mrs. Simon Kander) is published with funds raised by volunteer women through advertisements after the settlement house directors have refused a request for $18 to print a book that would save students in a class for immigrants from having to copy recipes off the blackboard. The book will earn enough money in 8 years to pay for a new settlement house building and be a perennial best-seller, with sales of half a million copies in the next 75 years. On the cover of every copy are the words "The way to a man's heart," taken from the phrase "The way to a man's heart is through his stomach" from the novel *Fern Leaves* by the late Sara Payson Willis Parton, who wrote under the name Fanny Fern before her death in 1872 at age 61. *Ausführliches Kochbuch für die einfache u. feine jüdische Küche . . . in 3759 Rezepten* by German author Marie Elasser is published at Frankfurt-am-Main.

Reichardt Duck Farm is founded at Petaluma, Calif., to raise fresh Pekin ducks for San Francisco's Chinatown restaurants and other customers. A dairy and poultry town, Petaluma is becoming "the egg basket of the world," using an incubator invented in 1879.

Grape phylloxerae attack vines in France's Champagne district, which heretofore has not been affected (*see* Burgundy 1878). The aphids appear along the Marne, and a massive grafting program is undertaken. The first 20 years of this century will be worse for French vintners than any experienced thus far as mildew attacks newly planted grafted vines in humid weather, forcing growers to spray at great expense.

Commercial avocado production begins in Florida (*see* Perrine, 1833). Several avocado groves flourish outside Miami, and two trees growing in a Miami dooryard are selected, given the names Trapp and Pollock, and propagated for breeding by budding. Within 65 years, Florida will have 6,800 acres planted to avocados, nearly all of them in Dade County (*see* California, 1913).

The hydrogenation process invented by William Normann (above) turns polyunsaturated fats into saturated fats that will be linked to heart disease when it is found that the human liver can synthesize serum cholesterol from saturated fats (*see* 1913; heart disease, 1921).

Profits from Lizzie Black's cookbook enabled her Milwaukee settlement house to expand.

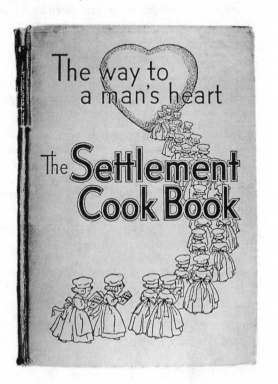

Obesity and heart disease are observed for the first time to have a strong correlation.

Horace Fletcher, now 51, gains international scientific attention when his personal physician, Ernest Van Someren, 30, reads a paper to the British Medical Association claiming that Fletcher, by thoroughly masticating his food, has reduced his intake of protein and "significantly and objectively increased his well-being" (*see* 1899). The late British prime minister William E. Gladstone, who died 3 years ago at age 88, said toward the end of his life, "I have made it a rule to give every tooth of mine a chance, and when I eat, to chew every bite 32 times. To this rule I owe much of my success in life." Fletcher has taken the rule to heart, and Van Someren claims that it has cured him of "gout, incapacitating headaches, frequent colds, boils on the neck and face, chronic eczema of the toes . . . , frequent massive dyspepsia," and, even worse, "loss of interest" in life and in his work (*see* 1902).

Horace Fletcher preached the gospel of mastication—chewing each bite thirty-two times. LIBRARY OF CONGRESS

Beriberi kills thousands in the Philippines following introduction of polished white rice by U.S. occupation authorities (*see* 1898; Grijns, 1906).

Britain establishes statutory standards for milk to protect consumers, but pasteurization is not required. British milk remains a source of diseases that include undulant fever and tuberculosis of the bone (*see* Evans, 1917).

The hydrogenation process invented by William Normann (above) extends the shelf life of foods containing fats.

The first soluble "instant" coffee is invented by Japanese-American chemist Satori Kato of Chicago, who sells the product at the Pan American Exposition at Buffalo (*see* G. Washington, 1909).

White Rose Ceylon tea is introduced by New York's Seeman Brothers (*see* 1886). There are now five brothers in the firm, but its president is Sylvan L. Stix, who makes tea the company's lead item, backing it with car cards on the city's elevated trains and streetcars (*see* Redi-Tea, 1953).

Clicquot Club Ginger Ale is introduced by Boston entrepreneur H. Earle Kimball, whose beverage will be the first nationally advertised ginger ale. Kimball has started a company with an investment of less than $25,000, named his product after the French champagne introduced in 1796, and will soon spend $1 million per year in advertising (*see* White Rock, 1895; Canada Dry, 1907).

Britons increase their consumption of whisky and mineral water as good French wines become harder to obtain because of grape phylloxera infestation (above; *see* 1891). Despite lower duties on French wine, it will be half a century before wine regains its prestige and profitability.

Russia's Kristall vodka monopoly has its beginnings in the State Wine Store established under the direct control of the Finance Ministry. It will close from 1914 to 1921 but will then continue without interruption until 1994, producing Stolichnaya vodka and 70 other brands of liquor.

Restaurateur Fred Harvey dies at Leavenworth, Kans., February 9 at age 65, leaving an enterprise that includes 47 restaurants, 30 dining cars, and 15 hotels (*see* 1876).

Oddenino's opens in London's Regent Street under the direction of Italian restaurateur Cavaliere Auguste Oddenino.

London has some 200 men's clubs, some of them with good kitchens that prepare excellent meals. The number will dwindle in this century to about 40, most of which admit wives for luncheon or dinner.

César Ritz suffers a nervous breakdown at age 51, leaving his chef Auguste Escoffier in charge of the kitchen at London's Carlton Hotel (*see* 1899). Escoffier will not retire until 1919, when he is 73 (*see* cookbook, 1902).

The Paris restaurant Buffet de la Gare de Lyon (its name will be changed in 1968 to Le Train Bleu) opens with ceremonies attended by President Émile Loubet. More than two dozen painters have been engaged to paint scenes of destinations reached by train from the station, including the arena at Arles, the grape harvest in Burgundy, and the Battle of Flowers at Nice. The suite of salons, their ceilings hung with enormous chandeliers and their walls decorated with nymphs and cherubs, covered with gold leaf, overlooks arriving and departing trains. *Becs fins* enjoy roast beef served from silver-plated trolleys set in mahogany bases, clafoutis of apricots, and other delicacies.

1902

The Treaty of Vereeniging signed May 31 ends the Boer War in South Africa (*see* nutrition, below).

William Cadbury sees an advertisement for the sale of a São Tomé cacao plantation. Workers are listed as assets at so much per head—a strong suggestion of slavery (*see* 1901; 1903).

$ European imports of U.S. margarine, lard, and beef tallow drop again as high U.S. corn prices continue to discourage ranchers and pig farmers from raising livestock (*see* 1901). Domestic U.S. prices of meat, dairy products, and margarine skyrocket.

"Prices That Stagger Humanity" headlines Joseph Pulitzer's *New York World* in a campaign against the "beef trust" (24¢/lb. for sirloin steak, 18¢ for lamb chops, pork chops, or ham).

Hawaiian Pineapple Co., Ltd., is founded by James Drummond Dole, 24, whose Massachusetts Unitarian clergyman father is a first cousin of Hawaii's territorial governor Sanford B. Dole (*see* cannery, 1892). Young Dole, whose great-uncle Daniel Dole was one of the early missionaries, visited the islands during his years at Harvard, gave up his original plan of starting a coffee plantation there, and last year used his nest egg of $1,200 to stake out a 12-acre homestead 23 miles northwest of Honolulu at Wahiawa, where the fertile plain—located between the watersheds of the Kolau and Waianae rivers and cut by deep gulches—looks promising. He set out 75,000 pineapple plants and has financed the new company initially by selling stock to local friends and associates (who subscribed to 772 shares at $20 each, producing $15,440). But pineapples are notoriously perishable, and the North American mainland is 2,300 miles away. A Honolulu newspaper has editorialized that "if pineapple paid, the vacant lands near town would be covered with them.... Export on any great or profitable scale is out of the question." Dole returned to Boston in December of last year, gave a local printer a $20 share for printing up a prospectus, told prospective investors that he intended to "extend the market for Hawaiian pineapples into every grocery store in the United States," and raised an additional $14,000. On his way back to Honolulu he has stopped at San Francisco and discussed his project with Samuel Sussman and Jacob Blumlein, partners in Sussman Wormser & Co. (later S&W Fine Foods), who showed interest but did not commit themselves (*see* 1903).

International Harvester is founded by Cyrus McCormick, Jr., who persuades financier J. P. Morgan to underwrite a trust that merges the four top U.S. harvesting-machine makers. Charles Deering of William Deering & Co. is chairman of the board, McCormick president, and the company controls 85 percent of all U.S. reaper production (*see* 1884; 1912).

Sheffield Farms is created by a merger of New York milk dealers whose businesses go back in some cases to 1841. Sheffield's president is Loton Horton, nephew of a prominent ice-cream maker (*see* 1925).

Corn Products Co. is created by a merger of United States Glucose with National Starch (*see* 1900). The new starch trust, capitalized at $80 million, controls 84 percent of U.S. cornstarch output, introduces Karo corn syrup, and will for several years be engaged in a trade war with New York Glucose (*see* 1901; Corn Products Refining Co., 1906).

The *Twentieth Century Limited* goes into service for the New York Central Railroad June 15 to begin a 65-year career on the New York–Chicago route. The New York Central's new all-Pullman luxury express has two buffet, smoking, and library cars featuring a $1.50 dinner at a time when other roads charge a standard $1. Butter aboard the *Limited* is from the Lake Champlain farm of Dr. William Seward Webb, president of the Wagner Palace Car Co. and a son-in-law of William H. Vanderbilt, who raises Jersey and Holstein cattle (the *Limited*'s commissary orders enough for one pound per passenger for the two meals eaten en route). Specialties of the *Limited* include Lobster Newberg on toasted cornbread and watermelon-rind pickles. A Boston section, which will be discontinued in the 1930s, serves fresh Maine lobster, Cotuit oysters, and Boston scrod.

The *Broadway Limited* goes into service June 16 for the Pennsylvania Railroad to begin a career of more than 75 years on the New York–Chicago route. Like the Central's luxury express, it makes the run in 20 hours and offers fine cuisine in its dining car.

Homogenized milk pioneer Auguste Gaulin is awarded a patent July 16 for an improved system that will be the basis for all future homogenizers (*see* 1900). Homogenized milk must first be pasteurized to destroy the enzyme lipase, which would catalyze the splitting of milk-fat molecules and produce a rancid flavor.

Gaulin has built an apparatus consisting of a concave agate valve, fitted perfectly to and held elastically by a spring against a perforated die through which milk—heated to 185° F.—is passed under a pressure of 3,750 to 4,500 pounds per square inch. (Later processors will use pressures of about 2,500 pounds per square inch at a temperature of 140° to 175° F. [60° to 80° C.].) This reduces milk-fat globules to such small diameters (one to two microns) that they are nearly unaffected by gravity and will not rise to the surface of milk (*see* 1904).

Mendel's Principles of Heredity—A Defence by English biologist William Bateson, 41, supports the work by Hugo de Vries and others published 2 years ago. Bateson has explored the fauna of salt lakes in western Central Asia and in northern Europe and will introduce the term "genetics" (*see* 1926).

The Carnegie Institution of Washington, established with a $10 million gift from Scottish-American steel magnate Andrew Carnegie, 66, will devote its efforts to scientific research (*see* agriculture, 1905).

English physiologists William Maddock Bayliss, 42, and Ernest Henry Starling, 36, discover the hormone secretin manufactured by glands on the wall of the small intestine (they will introduce the word "hormone" in 1904). Working at London's University College, they find that secretin acts on the liver to increase the flow of pancreatic juice when the acid contents of the stomach enter the duodenum.

Hookworm disease is endemic in the U.S. South, reports Charles Wendell Stiles, 35, chief of the Division of Zoology of the U.S. Public Health Service (*see* 1899). Standard Oil Co. head John D. Rockefeller, 63, establishes the General Education Board, which will help to conquer hookworm disease in the South (*see* 1909).

Cookbooks: *Le Guide culinaire, cuisinier des petits ménage, contenant les véritables principes d'une cuisine économique, succulente & variée avec 1,000 recettes* by Auguste Escoffier of London's Carlton Hotel is a manual for professional chefs that refines and simplifies earlier standards. It will become a classic. Escoffier says a sauce must fit the roast—or the fish—as closely as a tightly fitting skirt fits a woman. Coffee, he says, should never be served except at the end of a meal. Fruit is the only proper thing to serve after pastries. *The Home Science Cookbook* by Mary Johnson Lincoln, now 58.

Britain imports £50 million worth of meat and £4.1 million worth of fish. The average Englishman consumes more than 56 pounds of cheap imported meat per year as U.S. pork, Argentine beef, and New Zealand lamb flood the market.

An English writer is told by an old Hampshire woman, "Nothing's good enough now unless you buys it in a public house or shop. It wasn't so when I was a girl. We did everything for ourselves, and it were better, I tell 'e. We kep' a pig then—so did everyone; and the pork and brawn it were good, not like what we buy now. We put it mostly in brine, and let it be for months; and when we took it out and boiled it, it were red as a cherry and white as milk, and it melted just like butter in your mouth. . . . And we didn't drink no tea then. . . . We had beer for breakfast then, and it did us good. Better than all these nasty cocoa stuffs we drink now. . . . And we had a brick oven then and could put a pie in and a loaf and whatever we wanted and it were proper victuals."

The U.S. Bureau of Fisheries begins studying the life history of the terrapin to find means for its artificial cultivation as harvest of wild terrapin decline to the point that only the very rich can afford the dish (since the 1890s, terrapin stew, terrapin à la Maryland, terrapin à la Baltimore, and terrapin Newberg at elegant cafés has fetched $4 per plate). By 1909, Bureau scientists will have shown that diamondback terrapin can be grown in confinement almost as easily as poultry; modern methods will make it possible for terrapin farm owners to produce the turtles for as little as $1/lb. of solid meat, which now brings $5 to $6/lb.

The National Reclamation Act (Newlands Act) passed by Congress June 17 authorizes the federal government to build great irrigation dams throughout the West. The act encourages family farms by limiting to 160 acres the size of individual holdings entitled to federal water and by specifying that such water is to go only to owners who are bona fide residents, but small farmers in years to come will charge that the legislation's chief beneficiaries are large farmers. A 1926 amendment will let larger landowners have water provided that they sign contracts agreeing to sell acreage exceeding the 160-acre limit within 10 years at a government-approved price that does not include the value added by the federal water.

Hart-Parr Co. of Charles City, Iowa, markets the first gasoline tractors (*see* 1892). Some are 11-ton monsters that are so hard to start that farmers leave them running all night.

W. O. Atwater recommends a diet containing 150 grams of protein per day for workingmen but will later reduce the number to 60 (*see* 1895). Karl von

Voit at Munich raises his 118-gram estimate of 1881 to 145 grams (but *see* Chittenden, 1904).

San Francisco diet reformer Horace Fletcher visits Washington, D.C., in December, climbs the 854 steps of the 14-year-old Washington Monument, and climbs down again without resting (*see* 1901; 1903).

Two out of five Britons who applied for enlistment during the Boer War (above) were rejected as "medically unfit," and the proportion was even higher among men from industrial areas, where poverty contributes to poor nutrition among working-class people.

A survey in the English city of Leeds shows that in the poorest sections half the children are marked by rickets and 60 percent have bad teeth (*see* School Meals Act, 1906).

A survey of British milk consumption shows that in middle-class families the average person drinks 6 pints per week, while in the lower middle class the average is 3.8 pints, among artisans 1.8 pints, and among laborers 0.8 pints. Britain is Europe's biggest meat eater and smallest milk drinker.

Fish-and-chips shops (below) will make a significant contribution to raising protein levels of urban British diets.

A "Poison Squad" of young volunteers tests the safety of U.S. foods for Harvey W. Wiley of the Department of Agriculture (*see* 1883; 1907).

Congress limits substitution of margarine for butter. Britain establishes statutory limits for butter.

Barnum's Animal Crackers are introduced by the National Biscuit Co., which controls 70 percent of U.S. cracker and cookie output (*see* 1898). The new animal-shaped crackers appear just before Christmas in a box topped with a white string so that it may be hung from Christmas trees, and it joins the line of Nabisco products that includes Uneeda Biscuits, Premium Saltines, Social Tea Biscuits, Ginger Snaps, Nabisco Sugar Wafers, Jinjer Wafers, Zuzus, Lemon Snaps, Vanilla Wafers, Saltinas, Crown Pilot Crackers, and other brands including Fig Newtons, many in In-er-Seal cartons (*see* Fig Newtons, 1892; Lorna Doone, Oreo, 1912; Loose-Wiles, 1903).

Ralston Purina gets its name as officials of the 8-year-old Robinson-Danforth Commission Co. at St. Louis make an arrangement with officials of the Ralston Health Club, a worldwide organization established by Washington, D.C., university professor Albert Webster Edgerly, 50. He is sometimes called "Dr. Ralston," and his book *Complete Life Building* propounds simple rules and facts about common foods and promotes good nutrition, urging readers to avoid heavy use of preservatives and artificial sweeteners. Ralston Purina promotes its 3-year-old Purina breakfast food and introduces Ralston cereals that will compete with those of Quaker Oats, Post, and Kellogg (*see* 1932; Purina, 1899).

Ralston Purina introduced breakfast foods that competed with Kellogg, Post, and the others.

Kellogg's makes its Sanitas Corn Flakes lighter and crisper and gives them a malt flavoring to help them compete with their many imitators (*see* 1898; 1906).

Force Wheat Flakes are introduced in Britain in June, giving Britons their first taste of a dried breakfast food. The cereal is made by the Force Food Co. of Canada, which advertises Force in the United States with widely read verses about "Sunny Jim" (*see* H-O Oats, 1924).

Cream of Wheat maker Emory Mapes hires a Chicago restaurant waiter to pose for photographs at $5 per hour and creates a trademark that will make the cereal famous (*see* 1893). The J. Walter Thompson advertising agency places the first national advertising for Cream of Wheat in the *Ladies' Home Journal* with copy written by Emory Mapes (*see* 1939).

Presto brand self-rising cake flour, made from a formula which incorporates leavening, is introduced by the H-O (Hornby's Oatmeal) Co. of New York, which will register the trademark in 1906.

Drake Bakeries, founded by New York baker Newman E. Drake, will produce mostly packaged sweet goods with names such as Devil Dogs, Yankee Doodles, Ring Dings, and Yodels.

Willoughby McCormick adopts the trade name Banquet Brand for his spices (*see* 1890).

McClure's magazine carries an advertisement for Hershey's chocolate: the illustration shows a box of Hershey's powdered milk chocolate for drinking, but the headline says, "Hershey's Milk Chocolate— A Sweet to Eat" (*see* 1900). Readers are invited to sample Hershey's "two combinations of rich sterilized milk and pure chocolate for eating and drinking. If not at dealers, send 50 cents for ½-pound can for drinking and 6 cakes for eating." The address given is 1020 Chestnut St., Phila., Pa. (*see* 1903).

Salada Tea is introduced in New York (*see* 1886). The company will build a modern plant at Boston, move its headquarters to that city, and in 20 years make its tea the largest-selling brand in Canada, second-largest in North America.

Pepsi-Cola Co. is founded in North Carolina (*see* 1898). Caleb Bradham gives up his pharmacy to devote full time to Pepsi-Cola (*see* 1903).

Philadelphia's Broad Street Pharmacy installs a soda fountain with space behind it for "soda jerks" to concoct malted milks, milk shakes (called "frappes" in New England), phosphates, sodas, and sundaes (date approximate). Soda fountains heretofore have been flush with the wall, but other pharmacies will adopt the new style and soda jerks will soon be making banana splits (*see* 1904).

Horn & Hardart Baking Co.'s Automat—the first coin-operated automatic restaurant—opens at 818 Chestnut Street, Philadelphia. Joseph B. Horn and Frank Hardart met in 1888 and soon thereafter opened a small basement lunch counter at Philadelphia. Hardart toured Europe 2 years ago, saw an automatic restaurant in Berlin, and has paid a German importer $30,000 for the mechanism that permits patrons to drop nickels into slots to open glass doors and obtain food from compartments that are refilled by employees behind the scenes. The company's engineer, John Fritsche, has made improvements in the mechanism, and the Automat becomes so popular that Philadelphia will soon have scores of them (*see* Exchange Buffet, 1885; New York Automat, 1912).

French-American hotel manager Raymond Orteig takes over New York's Martin Hotel-Restaurant and turns it into the Lafayette (*see* 1912). Martin's onetime restaurant manager Louis Bustanoby opens the Café des Beaux Arts, which rivals Martin's, Rector's (*see* 1899), Sherry's (*see* 1890), and Delmonico's among gastronomes such as railroad equipment salesman and financial manipulator James Buchanan "Diamond Jim" Brady, 46, who has amassed a fortune of nearly $12 million.

The flamboyant Broadway sport "Diamond Jim" Brady (above) has a legendary appetite that has endeared him to restaurant proprietors (Charles Rector calls him "the best 25 customers I have"). For breakfast, Brady customarily consumes a gallon of freshly squeezed orange juice, hominy, eggs, corn bread, muffins, flapjacks, chops, fried potatoes, and a beefsteak. At 11:30 in the morning he enjoys a snack consisting of two or three dozen clams and oysters. Lunch, at 12:30, is made up of more oysters and clams, two or three deviled crabs, a brace of broiled lobsters, a joint of beef, salad, and several kinds of pie, plus more orange juice. Afternoon tea for Brady consists of a platter heaped with seafood and washed down with a few bottles of lemon soda (he drinks no alcohol and avoids coffee and tea).

Frequently accompanied by singer-actress Lillian Russell, 40, with whom he shares a passion for corn on the cob (Oscar of the Waldorf will claim that she outeats her escort), Brady typically begins dinner with two or three dozen Lynnhaven oysters, each six inches from tip to tail, shipped up from Baltimore in barrels marked with his name. He goes on to eat half a dozen crabs, claws and all, at least two bowls of soup (usually green turtle), six or seven lobsters, two portions of terrapin, two whole canvasback ducks, a sirloin steak (or a saddle of mutton plus perhaps half a dozen venison chops or roast chicken with caper sauce), vegetables, and dessert (commonly a 12-egg soufflé). Brady sometimes puts away three or even four helpings of all the main dishes, washing everything down with a few beakers of fresh orange juice, and he finishes up by eating most of a box of chocolates. After theater, where they may have consumed another box of candy, Brady and Russell commonly down a supper of gamebirds, shorebirds, or wild fowl, along with more orange juice or lemon soda.

Charles Rector (above) has sent his son George to Paris, where, under an assumed name, he has begun work, initially washing pots, at the Café Marguéry. George will return to New York in 2 years with the knowledge, demanded by Jim Brady, of how to prepare Sole Marguéry. Brady has threatened to take his business elsewhere unless Rector's could obtain the secret recipe and will meet George's ship at the pier, shouting, "Did you get the sauce?" George prepares the sauce by taking the bones and trimmings of two soles to make a white wine fumet flavored with two or three shallots, a sprig of thyme, some bay leaf, a little parsley, salt, and white pepper, simmering it for 15 minutes, straining the cooking liquor, and adding a quart of mussels. He will take seasoned, flattened fillets, place them on a buttered baking dish with several tablespoons of the fumet around them, cover them with a buttered, greaseproof paper, poach them gently, let them drain, place them in an oval dish, surround them with a double row of mussels and shrimp (kept hot and covered while making the sauce), strain the fumet, add the cooking liquor boiled down to one-third of the quantity (removed from the heat, and allowed to cool slightly), add six egg yolks, whisk the sauce over a low heat, incorporate a quarter pound of slightly melted butter, cover the filets with this sauce, and place them in a hot oven..Brady will eat nine portions of sole that night.

The New York restaurant Angelo's opens at 46 Mulberry Street in "Little Italy" to serve the city's Italian population with Florentine, Milanese, and Livornese dishes, including baked mussels, *antipasto di mare*, stuffed artichoke, *perciattli a filetto di pomodoro*, pasta, *linguine gra'mare chiara, polipi affogati* (octopus in a marinara sauce), whiting in broth garnished with clams and mussels in their shells, *osso buco, risotto Milanese, animelle à la cacciatore* (sweetbreads hunter style, sweetbreads being the thymus glands of a calf, located below the neck and near the heart), and *zuppa Pavese* (with fried bread, whole egg, and Parmesan cheese).

London caterer Rosa Lewis (*née* Ovenden), 35, and her husband, Excelsior, a butler, acquire the lease on the Cavendish Hotel in Jermyn Street. Having cooked over the years for the former prince of Wales (now Edward VII), the German kaiser Wilhelm II, Lord and Lady Asquith, Lord and Lady Randolph Churchill, and other members of the nobility, she has imported Virginia hams and sold them to Jackson's of Piccadilly while building up a clientele (it has become fashionable to have Rosa Lewis on hand for dinner parties, balls, and end-of-the-week country house parties). She and her staff of pretty young cooks take over the hotel's kitchen, continuing to cook for hostesses who entertain the king while her husband tries to run the hotel but spends much of his time drinking. She will soon divorce Excelsior, paying his debts in full, and will acquire adjoining houses in Duke Street as she makes the Cavendish resemble a country house, with a discreet side entrance and sitting rooms where the king can give private supper parties (*see* 1909).

More fish-and-chips shops open to serve London's working class (*see* 1864). Fast deep-sea trawlers extend British fishing operations to Iceland and the White Sea, packing the skate, cod, hake, and plaice in ice, and shipping it by rail the day it is landed, and the London shops serve it in newspaper with fried potatoes and vinegar (*see* consumer protection, 1968).

Fouquet's opens to give Paris a new restaurant of *haute cuisine*.

The Travellers Club opens at Paris in a private house (*hôtel particulier*) at 25, avenue des Champs-Elysées that was turned into a luxurious restaurant for the Paris International Exposition 2 years ago (*see* London club, 1819). The club offers fine dining to its 1,400 members—most of them English, French, and American.

1903

Russia's harvest fails again as it did in 1891. Since millions live at the edge of starvation even in the best of years, the crop failure produces famine that kills millions.

A manifesto issued by czar Nicholas II, 31, March 12 concedes reforms, including religious freedom, but resentment against the czar mounts as famine takes a heavy toll (above) and Russian industrial wages fall beginning in October while food prices rise (*see* 1905).

William Cadbury visits Lisbon to investigate the question of alleged slavery in the Portuguese African cacao islands São Tomé and Principe (*see* 1902). Portuguese authorities tell Cadbury that his suspicions are unfounded and invite him to see for himself (*see* 1905).

Milton Hershey breaks ground in March at Derry Church, 13 miles east of Harrisburg, Pa., for a chocolate factory whose products will dominate the chocolate candy and beverage industry by taking milk chocolate out of the luxury class. Hershey lays out Chocolate Avenue and Cocoa Avenue, builds new houses for his workers to rent or buy, and constructs a street railway to connect his cornfield at Derry Church (it will be renamed Hershey in 1906) with five neighboring towns in the area which he has selected for milk production, water supply, and rail links to U.S. ports and consumer markets. By year's end, he has a series of one-story buildings with a total of six acres of floor space, and by the time he begins making chocolate in 1905 he will have several hundred workers (*see* 1900; 1911).

Nestlé builds a new factory at Hegge, Germany, and forms a new company, Nestlé Kindermehl

GmbH, with head offices at Berlin (*see* 1901). An increase in German customs duties on infant cereal has motivated the move (*see* chocolate, 1904).

James D. Dole's Hawaiian Pineapple Co. packs 1,893 cases of fruit (*see* 1902). Dole has received a visit in March from J. H. Hunt, founder of the San Francisco firm Hunt Brothers, who inspects Dole's property and announces that he and the S&W partners are prepared to support him, with Hunt Brothers acting as selling agents for the wholesale trade. Hunt, Sussman, Blumlein, and A. G. Baumgartner each invests $10,000 and are soon joined by two well-known food brokers, L. R. Bowles and Harry Cartan. Dole's cannery, measuring only 44 by 88 feet, employs the crudest hand-operated equipment and uses handmade cans; he and his 15 employees insert small pieces of broken pineapple through a small opening in the top of each can, which is then soldered shut (*see* 1904).

Chicago meatpacker G. F. Swift dies at Chicago March 29 at age 63, having increased Swift & Co.'s capital worth 80-fold to some $25 million; his five sons retain control and management of the company.

Sunshine Biscuit Co. has its beginnings in the Loose-Wiles Biscuit Co. started by Kansas City bakers Jacob Leander Loose, 53, James S. Loose, and John H. Wiles, who break away from the 5-year-old National Biscuit Co. trust. Loose-Wiles will build a bakery at Boston in 1908 and in 1912 will erect a "thousand window bakery" at Long Island City, N.Y., to make Sunshine Biscuits that will be promoted on the premise that they are more wholesome than biscuits made in traditional basement bakeries (*see* 1946; Hydrox, 1910).

Best Foods, Inc., has its beginnings in the Simon Levi Co. founded by New York food wholesaler Levi with 10,000 square feet of warehouse space and a horse-drawn delivery wagon (*see* Hellmann's, 1932; Corn Products Refining Co., 1958).

Minnesota Valley Canning Co. is founded to pack sweet corn at La Seur, Minn., where promoter Silver Smith has persuaded 67 local merchants to put up $100 each for construction of a cannery (*see* peas, 1907; Green Giant, 1925).

Caloric Stove Corp. has its beginnings in the Caloric Gas Stove Works founded at Philadelphia by German-American stove maker Samuel Klein, 47.

The Elkins Act passed by Congress February 19 strengthens the Interstate Commerce Act of 1887. The new law forbids railroads to deviate from published rate schedules and holds railroad officials personally liable in cases of rebating (*see* Hepburn Act, 1906).

The Trans-Siberian Railway is completed with the exception of a 100-mile stretch along the mountainous shores of Lake Baikal. Built in 12 years, the new rail line will bring hundreds of thousands of settlers into the black-soil wheat-growing areas of central Asia (*see* 1904).

William Normann receives a patent for his 1901 process of hydrogenating fats and oils.

The first commercial U.S. flour-bleaching process, perfected at Jackson, Mo., by James N. Alsop of the Cape County Milling Co., uses nitrogen peroxide gas from an airstream passing over electric arcs. Alsop encounters patent conflicts with a similar process developed in Scotland, but owners of the Alsop system will acquire U.S. rights to the Andrews system (*see* benzoyl peroxide, 1917; Agene, 1919).

The Owens Bottle Machine Co. is founded by Michael J. Owens, who has improved his 1895 machine to create a completely automatic mechanism containing more than 9,000 parts. Hand-blown bottles and jars have been produced mostly by the blow-over process in which excess glass above the lip is cracked off and the sharp mouth ground smooth. Using the new machine, two men can produce 2,500 bottles or jars (or electric lightbulbs) per hour.

Portland, Ore., inventor Alexander Hewitt Kerr introduces a lacquered metal lid for jars with an attached rubber-compound gasket held in place by a screw-type ring top (*see* Ball Brothers, 1887). Kerr will move his company to Oklahoma in 1915.

A machine devised by U.S. inventor A. K. Smith cuts off a salmon's head and tail, splits the fish open, cleans it, and drops it into hot water all in one continuous operation. The Smith machine adjusts itself automatically to the size of the fish and will be called the "Iron Chink" because it replaces Chinese hand labor in West Coast canneries, which have been hurt by the Chinese Exclusion acts of 1882 and 1902.

Arthur R. Rogers of the William Underwood sardine cannery at Jonesport, Maine, filed a patent application last year for a machine similar to Smith's (above; *see* 1881). A patent will be granted in 1905 for the Rogers machine, which, according to the inventor's application, will "separate the fish according to sizes and feed them to my improved apparatus for severing their heads and cleaning them."

A San Pedro, Calif., packer puts white albacore tunafish into cans and launches a major industry. Canned tunafish—used in salads, sandwiches, and casseroles—will become a staple in many U.S. household cupboards (*see* Van Camp, 1914).

Scottish entrepreneur Angus Watson sets up a canned fish business at Newcastle (*see* Lever, 1922).

The Philippine Islands are self-sufficient in rice. They will be net importers of rice from 1904 to 1968.

Louisiana rice planter Salmon L. Wright begins experiments with improving seed and cultivation (*see* 1890). He will develop new varieties, some of which will eventually replace the Honduras and Japan varieties now grown in Louisiana (*see* 1912).

The A.B.-Z. of Our Own Nutrition by Horace Fletcher launches a fad by urging readers to chew their food not only carefully but excessively (32 times) and never to eat when angry or worried (*see* 1902). Fletcher's theory is that most people eat too much and that the longer one chews the less one eats. "Nature will castigate those who don't masticate," says Fletcher, his book is translated into Italian, and it will soon be published in French, German, and Spanish translations as well. Physical culturist-publisher Bernarr Macfadden, Harvard philosophy professor William James, 61, and Yale economics professor Irving Fisher, 37, will be among the thousands of "Fletcherites" persuaded to adopt Fletcher's mastication method (*see* 1919; Chittenden, 1904).

Caleb Bradham trademarks the name Pepsi-Cola and sells 7,968 gallons of his syrup as compared with 881,423 for Coca-Cola syrup (*see* 1902; 1907).

Sanka Coffee is introduced by German coffee importer Ludwig Roselius, who has received a shipload of beans that were soaked with seawater by a storm and has turned the beans over to researchers. They have perfected a process to remove caffeine from coffee beans without affecting the delicate flavor of the beans, and Roselius has named the product Sanka, using a contraction of the French *sans caffeine* (*see* 1923).

J. Lyons & Co. introduces Maharajah Tea, packaged in Cadby Hall. Lyons, which has bought in bulk to supply its teashops, has for years been displaying the tea near its cash registers and now begins selling it through grocers (*see* 1917; Victoria's funeral, 1901; Popular Café, 1904).

Millionaire Chicago horseman Cornelius Kingsley Garrison Billings, 42, celebrates the opening of his $200,000 stable by giving a March 29 dinner in the grand ballroom of Louis Sherry's at New York. The room has been transformed into a woodland scene for the occasion, saddle horses have been hired from local riding academies and taken to the ballroom in freight elevators, miniature tables have been attached to the pommels of the saddles, and waiters dressed as grooms at a hunting party serve Billings and his 36 guests. Oat-filled feeding troughs are then set before the mounts, whose hooves are padded to spare the sodded floor.

1904

Japanese naval forces attack Port Arthur in southern Manchuria February 8, beginning a 19-month war with Russia.

Some 520,000 people in England and Wales are on poor relief—the largest number since 1888, according to a report issued November 29. Another 250,000 are in workhouses, up 11 percent over last year. One-third of the English population lives at or below the poverty line, one-sixth the population of London, half the population of Scotland.

Belgian grain trader Arthur Fribourg at Antwerp retires from business, having built a flour mill at Arlon with his brother Paul and their father,

Michel (*see* 1890). The Fribourgs have also put up a mill in the Grand Duchy of Luxembourg and purchased a Belgian mill at Auverlais. Arthur's sons Jules, 27, and René, 25, inherit the firm and change its name to Fribourg Frères, competing with international firms such as Louis Dreyfus & Cie. and Bunge (*see* 1921).

White Lily Flour and other brands of the J. Allen Smith Co. at Knoxville, Tenn., have become so popular that the firm builds a new mill building and power plant with steel elevators that can hold 200,000 bushels of wheat (*see* 1883). Its big wooden barrels have become familiar to grocery clerks from southern Virginia to northern Florida, and children in much of the South now wear dresses, shirts, and other garments sewn from White Lily flour and cornmeal sacks. Made exclusively from soft winter wheat, whose protein content is lower than that of other flours, White Lily is ideal for baking biscuits, piecrusts, and cakes. Smith, now 54, wrote legislation, enacted last year by the Tennessee state legislature, which outlaws adulteration of flour and contamination of feed grains (*see* 1972; St. Louis exposition, below).

James D. Dole enlarges his Hawaiian Pineapple Co. cannery (*see* 1903). He increases production to 8,810 cases and will raise that figure next year to 25,022 (*see* 1906).

Anderson, Clayton & Co. is founded at Oklahoma City by local stenographer William Lockhart Clayton, 24, with his brothers-in-law Monroe D. and Frank E. Anderson. The partnership will move to Houston in 1916 and become the world's largest firm of cotton merchants before entering the food industry (*see* Chiffon margarine, Seven Seas salad dressings, 1964).

C. W. Post has a personal fortune estimated at $10 million (*see* 1901). His Postum Co., which last year netted $1.3 million, is the world's largest single user of molasses. Post has introduced a second cereal drink called Monk's Brew, which is exactly the same as Postum but sells for about one-fifth of Postum's price, and has thereby put most of his competitors out of business (unsold packages of Monk's Brew are returned to the factory and repackaged as Postum) (*see* 1906; Elijah's Manna, below).

Italian-American merchant Giuseppi Di Giorgio, 30, founds the Baltimore Fruit Exchange. He has been in the fruit business since age 14, will buy Earl Fruit Co. of California in 1911, and will enter the transcontinental fruit shipping and commission business (*see* 1919).

Continental Can Co. is organized to compete with American Can and break the "can trust" (*see* 1901). Entrepreneur Edwin Norton of Norton Brothers, who helped to create American Can 3 years ago, joins with some other can makers to start a consortium that will supply such companies as Campbell (below) and William Underwood (*see* Campbell, 1936).

The Swift Beef Trust acquires Derby Foods. Incorporated in Illinois in 1888, Derby is a producer of pickled meat products (*see* peanut butter, 1928).

Swiss General Chocolate Co., Peter and Kohler, Amalgamated is created by a merger of Jean-Jacques Kohler Chocolate of Lausanne and Daniel Peter Chocolate of Vevey (*see* 1818; 1866). The new firm signs a 99-year agreement giving Nestlé the rights to market Peter and Kohler milk chocolate under the Nestlé trademark (*see* 1905; 1911).

A new rail line reaches the lower Rio Grande Valley of Texas and opens up the region for citrus fruits and vegetables on lands irrigated with river water.

The Tropical Fruit Steamship Company, Ltd., is founded by the United Fruit Co., which has contracted with shipyards to build three new refrigerator ships (*see* 1899). The company will operate its new S.S. *San José*, S.S. *Limón*, and S.S. *Esparta* under British colors. It installs commercial radio equipment on its ships (the first to do so) and depends on radio communications to determine when and where bananas are available for loading (*see* 1910).

Léopold Louis-Dreyfus launches his first Black Sea grain vessel, naming it after his friend Carol I of Romania (who names him Romanian consul at Paris) (*see* 1870; 1915).

The Thermos bottle, introduced by German entrepreneur Reinhold Burger, will find wide use in lunch boxes, picnic hampers, and such. Burger has recognized a commercial potential for the Dewar vacuum flask of 1892 and offered a prize for the best name to be used. King-Seeley Thermos Co. will obtain U.S. rights to the words *Thermos bottle* but will lose exclusive rights in 1962 after surveys show that 68 percent of Americans think the term generic for any vacuum-insulated bottle.

The April 16 issue of *Scientific American* carries the first U.S. article on milk homogenization (*see* Gaulin, 1902): "The only apparent change in the milk was in the fat globules, the other constituents, including the proteins, being found to be unchanged, and there was no decrease in digestibility as shown by experiments in artificial digestion. The treated milk kept perfectly sweet for over six weeks, and remained sweet for several days after opening. It showed no tendency to cream, but was perfectly homogeneous when the bottles were opened. The process is thought to be especially applicable in putting up milk to be kept a long time, or partly condensed milk to which no sugar has been added." Manufacturers of evaporated milk will be using the homogenization process by 1912, but dairies will be slow to adopt it (*see* 1919).

Fiction: *Reginald* (stories) by English author Saki (H. H. [Hector Hugh] Munro), 34, who writes, "She was a good cook, as cooks go, and as cooks go, she went."

Cookbooks: *The Frugal Gourmet's Culinary Handbook* by Australian-born chef and restaurateur Charles Fellows, 38, whose work, containing 4,000 recipes (more than 70 for consommé), is aimed at professional cooks. Fellows and a Pittsburgh colleague invented a mechanical dishwasher in 1897. *What to Have for Luncheon* by Mary Johnson Lincoln.

The hamburger sandwich gains popularity at the St. Louis exposition, where the chopped beef specialty is fried and sold by German immigrants living in South St. Louis (*see* Lassen, 1900).

The ice cream cone is introduced at the St. Louis exposition by Syrian immigrant pastry maker Ernest A. Hamwi, who sells waferlike Zalabia pastry at a fairground concession, serving them with sugar and other sweets. When a neighboring ice cream stand runs out of dishes, Hamwi rolls some of the ice cream in his wafers, lets them cool, calls them "cornucopias," and sells them to the ice cream concessionaire. But an ice cream cone mold patent has been issued earlier in the year to Italian immigrant Italo Marchiony, who claims that he has been making ice cream cones since 1896; other claimants challenge Hamwi's right to call himself the ice cream cone originator.

The banana split is created by Latrobe, Pa., pharmacy apprentice David Strickler, 23, who has returned from a visit to Atlantic City, where he was inspired by watching a soda jerk. He places three scoops of ice cream on a split banana, tops it with chocolate syrup, marshmallow, nuts, whipped cream, and a cherry, sells it for a dime, and is soon imitated by other soda jerks, who will generally use three different ice cream flavors—chocolate, strawberry, and vanilla—topped with chocolate, strawberry, and pineapple, nuts, whipped cream, a cherry, but no marshmallow. Strickler will eventually take over the pharmacy and will continue making banana splits until he sells the place in 1965.

Tokyo restaurateur Motojiro of Rengatei in the Ginza (*see* 1895) finds it difficult to obtain vegetables because of the Russo-Japanese War (above) and uses thinly sliced raw cabbage doused with Worcestershire sauce. He serves it with rice and pork cutlets, creating a dish that will remain one of Japan's most popular dishes for more than 90 years.

A New York Zoological Park forester observes that the park's native chestnut trees, *Castanea dentata*, are dying of a strange fungus disease which will later be identified as *Endothia parasitica*, a bark blight. A Japanese exhibit has introduced the blight, which begins to wipe out the trees, whose nuts have been an important food source. European trees have developed a resistance to the disease through thousands of years of exposure, but by the late 1930s, almost the entire range of the native chestnut—9 million acres of forests—will have been destroyed, although several hundred trees in Michigan, Wisconsin, and the southern Appalachians will survive, possibly because they have developed an immunity. Loss of the native chestnuts will require the United States to import millions of pounds of chestnuts each year from Europe, most of them from Italy.

An *entente cordiale* settles Anglo-French disputes in the Newfoundland fishery.

Hawaiian growers in this decade will use machines to cover fields with thick black mulch paper in long rows, workers will punch holes in the paper to plant slips, suckers, or crowns, and the paper will discourage growth of weeds that would otherwise strangle the plants, making it impossible to grow pineapples on a commercial scale (it takes about 20 months to produce a harvestable, five-pound pineapple). James D. Dole will also find ways to overcome the nematodes, insect pests, and lack of iron in the red soil of Hawaiian pineapple fields.

Most English farmers have turned from raising grain and meat animals, which cannot compete with imports, to dairy farming, market gardening, poultry raising, and fruit growing. They are unable to meet the demand for butter, cheese, and lard, much of which is imported—along with Dutch margarine—from Denmark and North America. Most English fruit goes into jams, whose manufacture is being improved.

Britain's Interdepartmental Committee on Physical Deterioration publishes a report demonstrating the alarming extent of poverty and ill health in British slums. One out of four infants dies in its first 12 months in some areas, the committee reports, and it deplores the rapid decline in breast-feeding, due in part to the employment of married women in industry, but due mostly to the chronic ill health that makes women incapable of producing milk. One third of the children surveyed actually go hungry (see School Meals Act, 1906).

Xerophthalmia is reported among Japanese infants whose diets are devoid of fats (see Denmark, 1917).

A man can work hard and remain healthy on less than 50 grams of protein per day, says physiological chemist Russell Henry Chittenden, 48, head of Yale University's Sheffield School of Science. In his book *Physiological Economy in Nutrition* he disputes Atwater and Voit (see 1902), gives evidence to support his contention, claims that he personally feels better on a low-protein diet, and urges such diets for older people. Chittenden, who has been won over to the cause of Horace Fletcher (see 1903), emphasizes good health rather than economy, says "the taking of an excess of food is just as harmful as insufficient nourishment, involving as it does not only wasteful expenditure, but, what is of even greater moment,

an expenditure of energy on the part of the body which may in the long run prove disastrous. . . . If our standards are unnecessarily high, then surely we are not only practicing an uneconomical method of sustaining life, but we are subjecting ourselves to conditions the reverse of physiological, and which must of necessity be inimical to our well being." He rejects vegetarianism, saying that meats have "certain stimulating qualities which distinguish them from grosser vegetable foods." Along with tea and coffee, they stimulate the brain and nerves, he says, and he agrees with Sir William Roberts, who said that in the struggle for human existence, "which is almost exclusively a brain struggle," it is the meat eaters who prevail. Chittenden invites Fletcher to his laboratory, concludes that Fletcher is able to survive on far less food intake than either Voit or Atwater recommended and still maintain his weight at 165 pounds, but although he gains the support of *Ladies' Home Journal* food editor Sarah Tyson Rorer (who has come to believe that the energy required to digest protein may cause nervous prostration and headaches), he will have difficulty persuading many other people that adult protein intake can safely and beneficially be reduced by two-thirds.

Peanut butter is introduced at the St. Louis exposition as a health food for the elderly (see 1890; hydrogenation, 1901; Peter Pan, 1928; Skippy, 1932).

Pure Food Law advocates take space at the St. Louis exposition to dramatize the fact that U.S. foods are being colored with potentially harmful dyes. North Dakota Food Commissioner Edwin F. Ladd reports that "more than 90 percent of the local meat markets in the state were using chemical preservatives, and in nearly every butcher shop could be found a bottle of 'Freezem,' 'Preservaline,' or 'Iceine.' . . . In the dried beef, in the smoked meats, in the canned bacon, in the canned chipped beef, boracic acid or borates is a common ingredient. . . . Of cocoas and chocolates examined about 70 percent have been found adulterated. . . . Ninety percent of the so-called French peas we have taken up . . . were found to contain copper salts. Of all the canned mushrooms, 85 percent were found bleached by sulphites. There was but one brand of catsup which was pure. Many catsups were made from the waste products from canners—pulp, skins, ripe tomatoes, green tomatoes, starch paste, coal-tar colors, chemical preservatives, usually benzoate of soda or salicylic acid. . . . While potted chicken and potted turkey are common products, I have never found a can in the state which really contained determinable quantities of either chicken or turkey."

Swans Down Cake Flour wins the grand prize at the St. Louis exposition (*see* 1895; 1926).

Puffed rice is introduced as a popcornlike snack at the St. Louis exposition. Minnesota-born food scientist Alexander P. Anderson at Columbia University 3 years ago filled test tubes with cereal starch, sealed them, heated them, and found that when the tubes shattered a puffy, porous mass of starch popped out. He repeated the experiment, using whole grains, and has persuaded Quaker Oats Co. in Chicago to develop the first steam-injected puffing "guns." Quaker will develop the puffed grain into a breakfast cereal next year (*see* 1913).

Postum Co. (above) introduces Elijah's Manna, the name arouses the wrath of clergymen, Britain denies C. W. Post a trademark for his new corn flakes, and he quickly renames them Post Toasties (*see* 1904; 1906).

Post Toasties began life as Elijah's Manna; opposition from clergymen forced C. W. Post to rename it.

John Mackintosh Ltd. begins manufacturing in the United States (*see* 1890). The company will market its first chocolate beginning in 1912 (*see* Hailey, 1932).

Campbell's Pork and Beans is introduced by the Joseph Campbell Preserve Co. (*see* 1900).

The Campbell Kid cartoon characters, created by Philadelphia artist Grace Wiederseim (*née* Gebbie), will be used to advertise Campbell's products for decades (*see* Joseph Campbell Co., 1905).

The Campbell Kids would frolic through magazine advertisements for decades. COURTESY CAMPBELL SOUP CO.

French's Cream Salad Mustard, developed by George F. French, is introduced by R. T. French Co. of Rochester, N.Y. (*see* 1880). Milder than other brands and suitable mostly for use in salad dressing, it will claim to be the world's largest-selling prepared mustard, outselling all others combined in the U.S. market. By 1915, sales of the product will top $1 million (*see* Colman's, 1926; Worcestershire sauce, 1930).

Libby, McNeill & Libby begins marketing canned sauerkraut (*see* 1891). It will begin packing pickles and seasonings next year (*see* 1906).

Brewer Frederick Pabst dies of a pulmonary embolism at Milwaukee January 1 at age 67 (*see* blue ribbon, 1893). He leaves an estate valued at $12 million, and his brewery continues to rival that of Anheuser-Busch in St. Louis.

Poland Spring water wins top honors as "the best spring water in the country" at the St. Louis exposition (above) (*see* 1893; 1980).

Dr. Pepper is introduced at the St. Louis exposition (above) but will remain a southwestern soda pop brand until the mid-1920s (*see* 1886).

Iced tea is created by some accounts at the St. Louis exposition (above). English tea concessionaire Richard Blechynden, who has been sent to the United States to promote Indian and Sinhalese black teas, has tried to attract fairgoers with a troupe of colorfully dressed Sinhalese who serve hot tea in a special pavilion in Muslim style. Frustrated when sweltering fairgoers pass him by, he pours his tea over ice and serves it cold, but, as in the case of the ice cream cone (above), evidence will be produced of prior invention (*see* 1860; 1878).

Green and Formosan teas continue to outsell black tea 5 to 1 in the United States. Iced tea (above), made mostly from black tea, will grow to account for nearly 90 percent of U.S. tea sales.

The London restaurant Simpson's-in-the-Strand reopens (*see* Dickens, 1850). Simpson died in 1862, leaving the business to a man named Cathie, who kept the name Simpson's. The old building was razed 4 years ago to permit widening of the Strand, and the reopened restaurant will be famous for a soup made of stock containing bits of chicken, bound with egg, and thickened with cream (served originally to the late Queen Victoria at Balmoral Castle); beef roasts; saddles of mutton; lamb-and-raisin pie; roast potatoes; cabbage; and onion sauce. Simpson's will give free second helpings until 1939.

The London restaurant L'Etoile opens in Charlotte Street, Soho, under the direction of a restaurateur named Rossi, who has been a captain at the Café de Paris in Paris.

London's Popular Café, opened by J. Lyons & Co. in Piccadilly, seats 2,000 on three floors and will continue until 1939 (*see* tea, 1903; Corner Houses, 1909).

1905

Russian forces at Port Arthur surrender to Japanese infantry January 2 as St. Petersburg verges on revolution (below). The Battle of Tsushima Strait May 27 between Kyushu and Korea ends in victory for Admiral Heichiro Togo, 58, a triumph which is

credited to the elimination of beriberi from the Japanese Imperial Navy (*see* nutrition, 1884).

A Russian revolution begins as news of the loss of Port Arthur (above) and of "Bloody Sunday" incites the nation. Revolutionary terrorists at Moscow murder the Grand Duke Serge, uncle of the czar, February 4, and peasants seize their landlords' land, crops, and livestock.

A New York law limiting hours of work in the baking industry to 60 per week is unconstitutional, the Supreme Court rules April 17 in the case of *Lochner v. New York.* The owner of a Utica bakery has been convicted of violating the law, but the court rules that Lochner's right of contract is guaranteed under the 14th Amendment and "the limitation of the hours of labor does not come within the police power." A dissenting opinion by Justice Oliver Wendell Holmes, 64, says the word " 'liberty' is perverted" when used to prevent the state from limiting hours of work as "a proper measure on the score of health," and "a constitution is not intended to embody a particular economic theory, whether of paternalism . . . or of laissez-faire."

English Quaker Joseph Burtt spends 6 months at cacao plantations on the African islands of São Tomé and Principe at the suggestion of cocoa magnate William Cadbury and observes that nearly half of the newly arrived laborers at one plantation died within a year. Working conditions are tantamount to slavery, Burtt reports (*see* 1903; 1909).

Holly Sugar Corp. has its beginnings in a beet-sugar refinery opened at Holly, Colo. Holly will grow to become the largest U.S. independent processor of sugar beets, with nine factories scattered through Colorado, Wyoming, Montana, Texas, and California.

Joseph Campbell Preserve Co. renames itself the Joseph Campbell Co. and advertises in *Good Housekeeping* magazine: "21 Kinds of Campbell's Soups—16 million cans sold in 1904" (*see* 1904; Franco-American, 1915).

Anchor Hocking Glass Co. has its beginnings in the Hocking Glass Co. founded by former Ohio Flint Glass Co. decorator Isaac Jacob Collins, 30, who will merge with Anchor Cap Co. in 1937 to create Anchor Hocking.

1905

The Supreme Court orders dissolution of the Beef Trust January 20 in *Swift v. United States*, but the court order will merely change the form of the trust.

Nebraska's 10-year-old Beatrice Creamery Co. acquires large companies at Topeka, St. Louis, and Denver. Continental Creamery at Topeka has rights to the name Meadow Gold Butter and exclusive creamery rights to National Biscuit Co.'s In-er-Seal package developed by Peters Machinery Co. (*see* 1928).

Nestlé merges with its major competitor, Anglo-Swiss Condensed Milk Co. (*see* 1875; 1918; Anglo-Swiss, 1882; Swiss General, 1904).

"The Railroads on Trial" by journalist Ray Stannard Baker, 35, appears in *McClure's* magazine. The series will be instrumental in the fight for U.S. railroad regulation (*see* Hepburn Act, 1906).

The New York State Board of Regents gives college credit for agricultural courses taught at secondary schools at the persuasion of Liberty Hyde Bailey, 47, director of the New York State College of Agriculture at Cornell University (he serves Cornell also as dean of its faculty and professor of rural economy).

Articles on the Beef Trust by Charles E. Russell appear in *Everybody's* magazine.

Nonfiction: *The Jungle* by U.S. novelist Upton Beall Sinclair, 27, who has been given a $500 advance by the Socialist periodical *The Appeal to Reason*. He has lived for 7 weeks among the stockyard workers of Chicago, and his Lithuanian hero Jurgis is lured by steamship company posters to emigrate and takes a job in the stockyards of "Packingtown," where he encounters a variety of capitalistic evils (*see* meatpacking, below).

Cookbooks: *Mrs. Rorer's Menu Book* by Sarah Tyson Rorer, who recommends meals that are notably lighter than those suggested in the 1890s. *The Ball Blue Book: The Guide to Home Canning* has its beginnings in *The Correct Method for Preserving Fruit*, issued by Ball Brothers of Muncie, Ind. (*see* 1887). Later editions will give recipes for chow-chow relish, crystal pickles, green-tomato relish, watermelon-rind pickles, and the like for rural U.S. families who preserve their garden produce each summer.

Opera: *The Merry Widow* (*Die lustige Witwe*) 12/28 at Vienna's Theater-an-der-Wien, with music by Hungarian composer Franz Lehar, 35, who has placed an entire act in the Paris restaurant Maxim's (although he has never been there).

Some 41 million cases of canned foods are packed in the United States. The figure will rise in the next 25 years to 200 million (*see* 1935).

U.S. millers begin selling flour in small, consumer-sized bags rather than in barrels; Washburn, Crosby markets its Gold Medal Flour in the new bags (*see* 1880; Betty Crocker, 1921).

New York society queen Caroline Astor (*née* Schermerhorn), now 74, whose annual ball has usually been held on the third Monday in January, gives her last great formal dinner November 17 at her home at 840 Fifth Avenue (she will die in October 1908 at age 77). Her late adviser Ward McAllister died early in 1895 at age 67, and Mrs. Astor has carried on without him, following his principles that one soup—a clear turtle soup—rather than two should be served at dinner, that one white sauce, or brown sauce, should never follow another, that truffles should never be served twice, that Nesselrode pudding rather than a hot French pudding should be the final course, and that only the truly elegant could appreciate the superior sophistication of French cuisine (he sneered at American cooking and non-French European cooking). Victor Herbert's orchestra plays muted dinner music in the background while guests, who include Prince Louis Alexander of Battenberg, nephew of Britain's Edward VII, enjoy a meal, served by waiters dressed in the Astor blue livery, which opens with hors d'oeuvres (perhaps mousse de jambon), followed by tortue claire, terrapin, and filet de bœuf à là moelle or à la jardiniere (with truffles in a black sauce). The dinner, like most formal dinners of the time, includes 14 covers with one or two hot entrées, one cold entrée (perhaps pâté de foie gras en Bellevue), artichokes with sauce barigoule or sauce Italienne, or asparagus with hollandaise sauce. After a sorbet or punch à la Toscane flavored with maraschino or bitter almonds, dinner continues with roast canvasback duck, woodcocks, snipe, or truffled capons, with salad, followed by Camembert with crackers, served with Johannisberg or Tokay wine. Champagne has been served with the terrapin and roast, vin ordinaire and claret through the dinner. After the women have had fruit and left the table, the men enjoy Madeira.

 Water from the Colorado River has been diverted to California by sluice gates built since 1900 and is creating the Salton Sea (*see* Laguna Dam, 1909).

U.S. botanist George Harrison Shull, 31, journeys to Santa Rosa, Calif., on a grant from the Carnegie Institution established 3 years ago and studies plant hybridization methods pioneered by Luther Burbank in 1875 (*see* 1921).

Just 100 men own more than 17 million acres of California's vast Sacramento Valley, while in the arid San Joaquin Valley many individuals own tracts of 100,000 acres and more.

Roughly 12 acres of farmland are cultivated for every American. The number will fall rapidly as the population increases and as land is made more productive.

Vitamin research is pioneered at the University of Utrecht; Dutch nutritionist C. A. Pekelharing finds that mice die on a seemingly ample diet but survive when their diet includes a few drops of milk. Pekelharing concludes that "unrecognized substances" must exist in food (*see* 1906; Funk, 1911).

Iodine compounds prove useful in treating goiter. Cleveland physician David Marine, 25, has moved west from Baltimore and been struck by the fact that every dog in town—and many of the people—has goiters. He begins a campaign for the iodization of table salt (*see* Baumann, 1896; Kendall, 1915).

Upton Sinclair exposes U.S. meatpacking conditions in *The Jungle* (above). The 308-page bestseller has eight pages devoted to such matters as casual meat inspection, lamb and mutton that is really goatmeat, deviled ham that is really red-dyed minced tripe, sausage that contains rats killed by poisoned bread, and lard that sometimes contains the remains of employees who have fallen into the boiling vats. Many readers turn vegetarian, sales of meat products fall off, and Congress is aroused (*see* Meat Inspection Act, 1906).

THE JUNGLE

BY

UPTON SINCLAIR

NEW YORK
Doubleday, Page & Company
1906

Indignation aroused by a young novelist led to the first U.S. meat inspection and pure food laws.

France passes the first important legislation designed to protect quality wines. Destruction of French vineyards by grape phylloxerae has led to importation of inferior North African wines that have been blended with French wines, compromising their quality.

The London borough of Islington brings a test case in November against a barkeeper for selling whisky "not of the nature, substance, and quality demanded." The borough contends that a blend containing a patent-still spirit is not whisky; a decision based on the Food and Drug Act is rendered in favor of the borough, an appeal fails, and a royal commission is convened to study the production of Scotch whisky (*see* 1850; 1908).

Production of edible coconut fat, suitable for cooking, begins at Ringelshain, Bohemia, and the fat is marketed under the trade name Ceres. Johann Schicht, 50, whose family has been making soap at Ringelshain since 1848, has gained a reputation throughout the Austro-Hungarian Empire for his Swan soap; he will die prematurely in 1907, but his sons Heinrich, 25, and Georg, 21, will soon become major players in the margarine trade, competing with cheap lard imported from the United States (until the government imposes a 40 percent tariff on imported lard to placate Hungarian hog farmers, who have demanded protection against Serbian competition) and coconut fat sold by a Viennese firm. Sales of Ceres grow quickly, and Schicht introduces a kosher brand, which gains favor among Galician and Hungarian Jews, whose dietary laws prevent them from using lard (*see* Margarine Union, 1920).

Heinz Baked Beans are test-marketed in the north of England by Pittsburgh's H. J. Heinz Co. Adver-

Heinz's Baked Beans won over British housewives with their easy preparation.

tising advises British working-class wives that baked beans make a nourishing meal for men returning from work (Heinz beans will be canned at Harlesden beginning in 1928, and Britons will consume baked beans at twice the U.S. per capita rate).

Hebrew National Foods has its beginnings at New York, where Isadore Pinkowitz starts producing kosher frankfurters. His son Leonard Pines will take over the business after Pinkowitz's death in 1936, and the enterprise will grow to have a line that includes salami, sauerkraut, mustard, and other kosher products (*see* ConAgra, 1993).

Royal Crown Cola has its beginnings at Columbus, Ga., where local grocery wholesaler Claude A. Hatcher starts bottling soft drinks under the name Royal Crown. Hatcher Grocery will soon organize the Union Bottling Works (*see* 1912).

Ovomaltine is introduced by Swiss entrepreneur Albert Wander, whose product will be called Ovaltine in the English-speaking countries (*see* 1863). Made of malt extract, evaporated milk, powdered eggs, and cocoa powder, the beverage powder will be prescribed by physicians for convalescent patients or those suffering from wasting disease. Wander Co. of North America will erect an Ovaltine Food Products plant at Villa Park, Ill., in 1917.

The first Rotary Club is organized at Chicago, beginning a rise in men's luncheon clubs which will meet at hotels and public restaurants (*see* Kiwanis, 1915).

The New York dairy restaurant Ratner's opens in April in Pitt Street serving soup, gefilte fish, whitefish, and a few other kosher dishes under sanitary conditions for the city's large and growing Jewish population, which is concentrated on Manhattan's Lower East Side. Jacob Harmatz, 21, and Morris Ratner, 22, have flipped a coin to decide whose name would be on the front, and Harmatz has lost (*see* 1918).

The New Orleans restaurant Galatoire's, opened by Jean Galatoire at 209 Bourbon Street, accepts no reservations, requires that men wear jackets and ties, and will remain in the same family for four generations, serving shrimp rémoulade, shrimp à la créole, oysters en brochette, pompano meunière sautéed with almonds, trout Marguéry, and softshell crab in season.

Mary, baroness Curzon, former vicereine of India, dies of a heart attack at Carlton House Terrace, London, July 18, at age 36—7 months after returning to England. Daughter of the late Chicago merchant prince Levi Leiter, she went out to India with her husband in 1899 and will be commemorated in Europe (but not in Britain) with Lady Curzon Soup—a clear turtle soup with curry powder and heavy cream (or an egg yolk), served in demitasse cups with warm cream over each serving.

The Kiel Regatta brings Britain's Edward VII face to face with his cousin, Germany's Wilhelm II, who meets the chef Auguste Escoffier for the first time and will engage his services (see 1913).

China has famine as crops fail in much of the country. Russia, too, has crop failures (see 1907).

Battle Creek Toasted Corn Flake Co. is incorporated February 19 by W. K. (Will Keith) Kellogg, now 46, and St. Louis insurance man Charles D. Bolin. Bolin puts up $35,000 to start the company, whose stock is owned largely by Kellogg's brother J. H. even though the younger Kellogg has his signature printed on each package. W. K. has bought commercial rights to the cereal from his brother, added malt, sugar, and salt to improve its taste, and wraps the box in waxed paper to keep the flakes fresh. He runs the company and devotes two-thirds of his budget to advertising (see 1902; Post Toasties, below).

Corn Products Refining Co. is created by E. T. Bedford (see New York Glucose, 1901), who absorbs Corn Products Co. and several other large concerns. The corn-processing industry has been stagnating under the leadership of the "gluten trust," but Bedford's new company, which controls 90 percent of U.S. corn-refining capacity, will revitalize it. Its Karo syrup, introduced in 1902, will soon be a household name (see 1913; 1916; Mazola oil, 1911).

A. E. Staley Co. is founded U.S. entrepreneur Augustus Eugene Staley, who buys cornstarch in bulk canvas bags at 2¢/lb., repackages it in one-pound boxes under the name Cream Corn Starch, and sells it at 7¢/lb. He will soon build a huge corn-milling complex at Decatur, Ill., to manufacture his own starch and will be the second largest U.S. corn processor after Corn Products Refining Co.

(above). Staley will also be a major processor of soybeans and an important factor in the chemical industry (see soybean refinery, 1922).

James D. Dole's Hawaiian Pineapple Co. announces August 1 that it has made a net profit of $30,489 (see 1904). The Oahu Railway and Land Co. extends its narrow-gauge line from Waipahu to Wahiawa so that pineapples can move to town by rail, and Dole is instrumental in persuading the American Can Co. to establish a can-manufacturing plant in Honolulu. He takes an option on five acres of O.R.&L. land in the Iwilei district and makes plans to move his cannery to Honolulu (see 1908).

Sales of Jell-O reach nearly $1 million. Francis Woodward, who once offered to sell the brand for $35, now stops making Grain-O to devote all his efforts to Jell-O (see 1899; Postum Co., 1925).

Planters Nut and Chocolate Co. is founded at Wilkes-Barre, Pa., by Italian-American entrepreneur Amedeo Obici, 19, who arrived in America 7 years ago without money or English but with the knowledge that he had an uncle somewhere in Pennsylvania. He found the uncle, worked at his fruit stand in exchange for room and board, eventually bought a $4.50 peanut roaster, improved it by adding pulleys that turn the nuts automatically and prevent them from burning, and has expanded his peanut stand into a store and restaurant. In partnership with his future brother-in-law Mario Peruzzi, he starts a firm that by 1912 will be using so many raw peanuts that Obici will open his own shelling plant and buy directly from farmers to avoid being squeezed by middlemen (see Mr. Peanut, 1916).

Rafetto Corp. is founded in New York at 144 West Houston Street to make fresh white and green pasta—cannelloni, cappelletti, cappetelli, fettucine, lasagna, manicotti, ravioli, stewed tomatoes, tomato purée, and other specialties for the city's growing number of Italian restaurants and householders.

Loma Linda Foods has its beginnings in a California bakery started by the General Conference of Seventh-Day Adventists to produce whole-wheat breads and health cookies for the patients and staff of what will become Loma Linda University Medical Center (see Adventists, 1860). By the 1930s it will be producing soy-based meat substitutes in a plant near Riverside (see Worthington Foods, 1939; 1990).

The Hepburn Act passed by Congress June 29 extends jurisdiction of the Interstate Commerce Commission established in 1887 and gives the ICC powers to fix railroad rates (*see* Elkins Act, 1903).

Mexican engineers complete the $50 million, 190-mile Tehuantepec National Railroad across the Isthmus of Tehuantepec between Salina Cruz and Puerto Mexico, reducing the distance from California to East Coast markets by 4,330 miles and delivery time to 30 days (*see* transcontinental railroad, 1869; Panama Canal, 1914).

Nonfiction: *The Devil's Dictionary* by U.S. journalist Ambrose Gwinnett Bierce, 64, who defines "edible" as: "good to eat, and wholesome to digest, as a worm to a toad, a toad to a snake, a snake to a pig, a pig to a man, and a man to a worm."

The "hot dog" gets its name from a cartoon by Chicago cartoonist Thomas Aloysius "Tad" Dorgan, 29, who shows a dachshund inside a frankfurter bun (*see* Feltman, 1867). English-born caterer Harry Magely Stevens has been selling frankfurters in buns with mustard and sauerkraut at New York's Polo Grounds since the turn of the century (*see* Nathan's, 1916). Britons continue to call sausages "bangers."

The San Francisco earthquake April 18 and an ensuing 3-day fire destroy 28,188 buildings—an estimated $500 million property damage. One man and his girlfriend are dancing in a small hotel off Market Street when the quake strikes at 5:13 A.M., having been up all night. They have persuaded the chef to open his kitchen, their dinner has just been served, and one of them will later say, "We were thrown about like rowboats in a storm; an oak beam came crashing down inches from our table, and I remember thinking how extraordinary it seemed to be eating sweetbreads and drinking champagne at that moment."

The King Ranch of Texas grows by acquisition to cover nearly a million acres with 75,000 head of cattle and nearly 10,000 horses (*see* 1886; 1940).

Agrarian reforms to end the communal (*mir*) system of landholding established in Russia in 1861 are introduced by the country's new prime minister, Pyotr Arkadevich Stolypin. Peasants are permitted to withdraw from a commune, to receive their shares of the land, and to own and operate the land privately.

The U.S. corn crop exceeds 3 billion bushels, up from 2 billion in 1885 (*see* 1963).

Florida's citrus groves are frozen by an ice storm.

California orange growers begin to set out Valencia orange seedlings to raise fruit that will mature in the summer and will make the state a year-round source of oranges, but most California oranges continue to be the Washington navels introduced in 1875.

Commercial kiwifruit cultivation begins in New Zealand. The berry of a woody vine (*Actinidia sinensis*) native to China's Yangzi Valley, it is grown from plants collected by a British botanist and brought to the West at the turn of the century.

Cambridge University biochemists Frederick Gowland Hopkins, now 45, and H. G. Willcock find that mice fed "zein" from corn plus the amino acid tryptophan (which Hopkins has isolated with S. W. Cole) will live twice as long as mice fed "zein" alone.

A British School Meals Act passed by the Liberal government under pressure from the emerging Labour party provides free meals for children (*see* 1904; Leeds survey, 1902). Many have been unable to profit from their education because they have come to school without breakfast, and the new measure permits local authorities to add up to a halfpenny per pound to taxes in order to fund a school meals program.

Gerrit Grijns suggests a new explanation for beriberi (*see* 1896). It may be caused not by a toxin in rice hulls, he says, but rather by the absence of some essential nutrient in polished rice (*see* Suzuki et al., 1912).

A Pure Food and Drug Bill introduced by Sen. Weldon B. Heyburn (D. Idaho) encounters Republican opposition. Sen. Nelson W. Aldrich (R. R.I.) asks, "Is there anything in the existing condition that makes it the duty of Congress to put the liberty of the United States in jeopardy? . . . Are we going to take up the question as to what a man shall eat and what a man shall drink, and put him under severe penalties if he is eating or drinking something different from what the chemists of the Agricultural Department think desirable?"

But the Heyburn bill (above) regulates producers and sellers, not consumers, and its prohibitions are only against selling diseased meat, decomposed foods, or dangerously adulterated food, and it requires only that labels give truthful descriptions of contents (*see* Wiley, 1902; Sinclair, 1905).

The Senate approves the Heyburn bill (above) February 21 by a 63-to-4 vote following pressure by the 59-year-old American Medical Association on Sen. Aldrich, the House approves it 240 to 17 June 23, and President Theodore Roosevelt signs it into law (*see* 1911).

A meat inspection amendment to the Agricultural Appropriation Bill, introduced by Sen. Albert J. Beveridge (R. Ind.), passes without dissent, but the measure does not provide for federal funding of meat inspection.

The Neill-Reynolds report made public by President Roosevelt June 24 inspires Rep. James W. Wadsworth (R. N.Y.) to introduce a meat inspection amendment that provides for federal funding of meat inspection. Settlement house workers Charles P. Neill and James Bronson Reynolds prepared the report; the Wadsworth measure passes both houses of Congress and is signed into law.

Germany imposes a limit of 0.125 percent of sulfurous acids in foods, including dried cut fruits. The dried fruit industry has exposed freshly cut fruits to the fumes of burning sulfur for years to promote rapid drying, kill yeasts and molds, kill enzymes in the fruit which cause quick browning and deterioration, repel insects, and enable the cured fruit to be stored for months with minimum loss in nutritive values and eating qualities (*see* 1907).

C. W. Post perfects his Post Toasties corn flakes, which compete for sales with Kellogg's Corn Flakes (above; *see* 1904; 1914).

A-1 Sauce is introduced to the United States from England by G. F. Heublein & Bro. of Hartford, Conn. (*see* cocktails, 1892). A chef to George IV created the sauce in the 1820s (*see* Smirnoff, 1939).

Libby, McNeill & Libby adds ketchup, bulk pickles, and bottled pickles to its line of canned meats (*see* 1904).

Libby (above) buys a milk condensery at Morrison, Ill., and begins packing canned milk (*see* 1908).

E. A. Stuart's Carnation Milk adopts the slogan "The milk from contented cows" (*see* 1899). A Chicago advertising man has created the slogan (*see* nonfat dry milk, 1954).

The Bronx Cocktail created at New York's Waldorf-Astoria Hotel by bartender Johnny Solon is a mixture of gin, sweet and dry vermouth, and orange juice.

Frank G. Shattuck Co. is founded by Schrafft Candy salesman Shattuck to operate retail stores (*see* 1897). Backed by George Frederick Schrafft and his brother William Frederick, Shattuck has opened a restaurant in his New York store at Herald Square and will open more; by 1928 there will be 29 Schrafft's restaurants in New York, four in Boston, and one in Syracuse, each with uniformed waitresses—many of them Irish immigrants—serving luncheon and dinner at reasonable prices (*see* Pet Inc., 1968).

The Washington, D.C., restaurant Occidental Grill opens at 1475 Pennsylvania Avenue NE, close to the Willard Hotel, where it will serve politicians and celebrities for at least 89 years.

1907

China's famine continues (*see* 1906). Foreign missionaries begin relief operations in January, the American Red Cross appeals for funds to relieve the hunger and sends 5,000 bushels of wheat for spring planting, it is reported in February that 500,000 Chinese are expected to die from starvation and many succumb to smallpox, Chinese officials block distribution of famine relief supplies, the government fears a general uprising as conditions worsen, the U.S. State Department reports in April that 400,000 Chinese are receiving foreign relief, but reports later in the month say that 5,000 are dying each day. The Famine Relief Commission sends potatoes to Shanghai, the Red Cross announces in late May that the famine is over and contributions are no longer needed, but a U.S. military attaché at Beijing says in mid-June that the famine continues and that relief will not reach victims in time. A letter published in July says that 15 million Chinese along the Yangzi River are slowly starving to death.

Russia's famine continues despite a $15 million government appropriation in early January (*see* 1906). A former member of the Duma arrives in the United States in February to raise money for famine relief and says 1 million peasants face starvation within 3 months if aid is not forthcoming. The United States sends 600,000 tons of wheat in May to relieve the famine-stricken areas, but by September an estimated 30 million peasants are reportedly short of food (*see* scurvy, below). Czar Nicholas II signs a $3 million famine appropriation bill in May, Western reporters are informed in early June that no further aid is needed, but the Duma is obliged in December to pass a $7.5 million famine appropriation bill (*see* 1911).

Famine in Armenia and eastern Turkey force emigration of many people to the United States.

Japan has August floods which destroy rice crops and leave thousands starving.

Romanian peasants revolt in Moldavia beginning in March to protest their inability to buy land; they also protest their exploitation by the Crown and by grain merchants such as Léopold Louis-Dreyfus. Some 10,000 will die before Carol I can regain control of the country in April.

A U.S. economic crisis looms as a result of drains on the money supply by the Russo-Japanese War of 1904–1905, the demands imposed by the rebuilding of San Francisco following last year's earthquake and fire, several large railroad expansion programs, and the fact that a late season has tied up farmers' cash. New York Stock Exchange prices suddenly collapse March 13.

The American Sugar Refining trust is found to have defrauded the government out of import duties (*see* 1899). The courts convict several company officials and recover more than $4 million (*see* Domino Sugar, 1911).

Britain and Ireland have 23,100 miles of operating railway, Canada 22,400, Austria-Hungary 25,800, France 29,700, Germany 36,000, Russia 44,600, India 29,800, the United States 237,000.

The S.S. *Lusitania* launched by Britain's Cunard Line makes her maiden transatlantic voyage in September. The 31,550-ton luxury liner can carry 2,000 passengers with a crew of 600 and is the first ship equipped and staffed to serve deluxe cuisine. Shipping magnates will hereafter use good food, good wines, and good service as well as posh accommodations and decor to compete for business on the transatlantic route.

The American Cyanamid Co. founded July 22 by U.S. entrepreneur Frank Sherman Washburn, 46, builds a plant on the Canadian side of Niagara Falls to produce calcium cyanamid for nitrogen fertilizer using the European Frank-Caro process for fixation of atmospheric nitrogen. German chemists Adolf Frank, now 73, and Nicodem Caro, now 36, developed the process in the late 1890s and it requires vast amounts of power, but by the end of 1909 Cyanamid will have an annual production capacity of 5,000 tons (*see* Haber process, 1908).

Work by Philadelphia chemist Mary Engel Pennington, 34, attracts the attention of U.S. Department of Agriculture chemist Harvey W. Wiley, who makes her first chief of the U.S. Food Laboratory. She has been operating her own laboratory, specializing in bacteriological analysis, and Wiley assigns her to work on the problem of keeping refrigerated food fresh. Like outside air, the air within a refrigerated locker loses its ability to hold moisture as it approaches the freezing point. Food in the locker dries out, and adding humidity just makes it moldy. Pennington's solution to the problem of humidity control in refrigeration will be widely adopted in industry.

Yale zoologist Ross Granville Harrison, 37, perfects a method of culturing animal tissues in a liquid medium, making it possible to study tissues without the variables and mechanical difficulties of in vivo examinations. The method will permit Harrison to make discoveries about embryonic development and facilitate research in embryology.

Broadway musical: *The Follies of 1907* 7/18 at the Jardin de Paris on the roof of the New York Theater, with 50 "Anna Held Girls" in an extravaganza staged by showman Florenz Ziegfeld, 38, who has chosen his *Follies* girls with an eye to slenderness of figure, creating a new ideal to replace the ample figure now in vogue (but *see* nutrition, below).

New York's Fulton Fish Market moves into a new building on the East River (*see* 1880; 1939).

The first canned tunafish is packed at San Pedro, Calif., by A. P. Halfhill (*see* Van Camp, 1914).

An increase in scurvy is reported in famine-stricken areas of Russia (above), with several thousand cases reported in March.

Pellagra is observed for the first time in Mississippi, where processed cornmeal is a dietary staple (*see* 1749; 1913).

Researches on the Chemistry of Proteins by German chemist Emil Fischer, 55, is based on the Nobel laureate's work in synthesizing simple sugars, purine derivatives, and peptides.

A slim figure is still considered a mark of ill health, despite the *Ziegfeld Follies* ideal (above), and this belief will persist for another decade, with patent medicines which promise a remedy for underweight outnumbering those which promise weight loss before overweight loses its reputation as a mark of robust well-being. The slim figure, meanwhile, will become an impossible dream for millions of women whose genetic predisposition makes such a body unrealistic no matter what weight-loss diet they try.

The Nutrition of Man by Russell E. Chittenden expands on his ideas that adult Americans eat too much protein (*see* 1904).

W. O. Atwater dies of cancer at age 53 (*see* 1901). His obituaries hail him as the founder of the home economics profession, whose research played a vital role in changing U.S. eating habits.

The Prolongation of Life by Russian-born French bacteriologist Elie (originallly Ilya) Ilich Metchnikoff (originally Mechnikov), 62, suggests that "friendly bacteria" in yogurt will crowd out "poisonous bacteria" that shorten human life. Mechnikov, who will win the Nobel Prize next year for his discovery of phagocytes—white blood cells that devour infectious organisms—has become obsessed with the idea that aging and most degenerative diseases are exacerbated by putrefaction caused by the hundreds of millions of bacteria which inhabit the intestinal tract, especially the colon. These bacteria can gradually be starved out, he says, by reducing intake of the protein they feed on. Having read that rural Bulgarians often live into their 90s and 100s, he has journeyed to Bulgaria, found that people there eat enormous quantities of yogurt, concluded that something in yogurt extends the lifespan, probably by accelerating the extermination of their intestinal bacteria, and given the name *Bacillus bulgaricus* to the lactic acid bacterium which he has identified (he has also identified the *Streptococcus lactis* bacterium, which ferments milk to make yogurt). Metchnikoff will eat quantities of yogurt himself in the conviction that lactic acid bacteria are hostile to the human bacteria which produce intestinal "intoxication" (but *see* 1916).

Harvey W. Wiley, head of the U.S. Department of Agriculture's Bureau of Chemistry, issues an order (Food Inspection Decision No. 76) July 13 limiting the sulfur content of foods to 350 parts per million (*see* Germany, 1906). The action is aimed at French wines containing high concentrations of sulfur dioxide, the French government retaliates by imposing a limit of 1,000 parts per million on sulfur dioxide in the dried cut fruits which France has been importing in quantity from California, U.S.

Chemist Harvey W. Wiley led the fight to clean up America's food industry. LIBRARY OF CONGRESS

congressmen from that state urge the Bureau of Chemistry to defer enforcement of the order, but the State of Pennsylvania moves in September to bar sale of cured fruits containing any sulfurous acid (*see* 1908).

Saccharin and other benzoic acid derivatives should be banned from use in food, says Harvey W. Wiley (above). Rep. James S. Sherman (R. N.Y.) says saccharin saves his canning firm thousands of dollars per year, Wiley interrupts him at a White House conference to say, "Yes, Mr. President, and everyone who eats these products is deceived, believing he is eating sugar, and moreover his health is threatened by this drug!" President Roosevelt replies angrily, "Anybody who says saccharin is injurious is an idiot! Dr. Rixey [his personal physican] gives it to me every day." Wiley has developed important refining techniques for the sugar industry, Ira Remsen heads the scientific board named by the president to review the data on saccharin, and the board's final report in 1910 will conclude that a continuous daily consumption of 300 milligrams of saccharin presents no hazard (*see* 1879; sodium cyclamate, 1937).

Minnesota Valley Canning Co. at Le Seur begins packing peas in addition to sweet corn (*see* 1903; giant symbol, 1925).

The Kellogg brothers adopt "the Sweetheart of the Corn" as an advertising symbol for Kellogg's Corn Flakes (*see* 1906). Kellogg stenographer Fanny Bryant is photographed with her arms full of cornstalks, and the Kelloggs are excommunicated from the Seventh-Day Adventist Church (which moved its headquarters 4 years ago from Battle Creek to a suburb of Washington, D.C.) (*see* 1911; 40% Bran Flakes, 1915).

Perugina has its beginnings in a small confectionery founded at Perugia in central Italy with help from pasta maker Francesco Buitoni (*see* 1887). Its initial products are wedding cakes, Baci ("the chocolate kiss with a message"), and confetti—sugar-coated almonds given traditionally in Italy and France (where they are called *dragées*) at christenings and weddings. By 1951, the firm will have 42 stores on the Continent, including some in Rome (*see* Nestlé, 1988).

Hershey milk chocolate Kisses are introduced by Hershey Chocolate Co. to compete with Buds, sold by a Lititz, Pa., candy maker since 1893. Each chocolate titbit comes individually wrapped in silver foil, and by the time blue-and-white paper streamers are added in 1921 Hershey will be turning out millions of Kisses per day (*see* Hugs, 1993).

Canada Dry Pale Dry Ginger Ale is registered in January as a trademark by John J. McLaughlin, who 3 years ago found a way to eliminate the dark brown color of his Belfast Style Ginger Ale and has also eliminated the sharpness found in other ginger ales (*see* 1890). McLaughlin calls his product "the Champagne of Ginger Ales," and demand for the beverage will soon oblige him to bottle it at Montreal and Edmonton (*see* New York, 1922).

John McLaughlin promoted his Canada Dry Ginger Ale as the "champagne of ginger ales."

The Coca-Cola Company buys out its Atlanta advertising agency (whose proprietors start a Dallas retail company under the name Neiman-Marcus) (*see* 1899; Britain, 1909; distinctive bottle, 1916).

Pepsi-Cola sales increase to 104,000 gallons, up from 7,968 gallons in 1903, as Caleb Bradham establishes a network of 40 bottling plants (*see* 1920).

Mackeson Milk Stout is introduced by the Hythe, Kent brewery acquired by the Mackeson family in 1801 (*see* Whitbread, 1929).

New York's Plaza Hotel opens October 1 on the Grand Central Plaza south of Central Park. The 1,000-room hotel has a large kitchen, a bakery, and dining rooms that will remain popular for more than 88 years. Most of the city's luxury apartment houses have their own dining rooms.

Metropole hotels open at Brussels and Moscow (year approximate), providing new levels of luxury dining and accommodations.

Paris restaurant owner Eugene Cornuché sells Maxim's to a British company, which rids it of *les grandes cocottes* and welcomes more "respectable" female patrons such as actress Sarah Bernhardt and operatic diva Dame Nellie Melba (*see* 1900; 1931).

An executive order issued by President Theodore Roosevelt in mid-March bars Japanese laborers from entering the continental United States by way of Canada, Hawaii, or Mexico, a move whose impact is mostly on California farm labor (*see* Chinese Exclusion Treaty, 1880; "gentlemen's agreement," 1908).

1908

Sugar magnate Claus Spreckels dies at San Francisco January 10 at age 79. Two of his four sons wrested control of his vast Hawaiian sugar plantations in 1899, but a family reconciliation has left his son Rudolph in charge of the Spreckels enterprises.

The U.S. recession that began with last year's financial panic depresses demands for luxury food items, including canned pineapple. Hawaii's eight packers produce 400,000 cases (Dole's Hawaiian Pineapple Co. alone packs 242,822 cases) and have orders for only 120,000 cases. Pineapples pile up on the wharves of Honolulu.

Hawaiian Pineapple Co.'s James D. Dole summons his competitors to a meeting as the glut of pineapple production (above) depresses prices (*see* 1904). The packers agree to subscribe to a fund of $50,000 and undertake a joint program of national advertising to win acceptance for canned Hawaiian pineapple, regardless of brand, in the big eastern U.S. markets, the first advertising campaign for a commodity by any growers' association (*see* Sunkist, 1919). "Don't Ask for Pineapple Alone," say the ads; "Insist on *Hawaiian* Pineapple." Consumption of Hawaiian pineapple will quadruple in the next 18 months (*see* 1911; Libby, 1909).

Libby, McNeill & Libby builds a plant at Sunnyvale, Calif., that will be the world's largest fruit-canning and -freezing facility (*see* 1906; 1909).

J. A. Folger and Co. moves its headquarters to Kansas City, Mo., but the coffee firm retains an office at San Francisco (*see* 1865; Procter & Gamble, 1963).

Mrs. Baird's Bakeries has its beginnings at Fort Worth, Texas, where Ninnie Lilla Baird (*née* Harrison), 39, starts selling the bread she has baked each Monday for her neighbors, friends, and eight children since 1905, still using her small, wood-fired kitchen oven but expanding operations to a shed behind her house. By 1910 she will have purchased a commercial oven from a hotel, burning artificial "Pintsch" gas and baking 40 loaves at a time. Her husband, William, will die in 1911, by which time the family bakery will be a thriving concern, with customers lining up in their automobiles as early as 5 o'clock in the morning to buy fresh bread right out of the oven. Mrs. Baird will "retire" in 1920 but will continue as active head of the business until her death in 1961, making her company one of the nation's largest family-owned wholesale bakers, with 11 highly automated Texas bread and cake bakeries.

Dutch margarine makers Van den Bergh and Jurgens sign a pooling agreement under which Van den Bergh agrees to give Jurgens its quality manufacturing secrets (*see* 1895). Jurgens proceeds to produce quality margarine at its Dordrecht factory, and by 1913 it will be making 480 tons per week, up from 150 in 1906 (Van den Bergh will be making 680 tons, up from 480, and Britain's Maypole Co. will be making 1,000 tons per week, up from 330) (*see* 1919).

The Brussels pâtisserie Wittamer opens at 12, place du Grand-Sablon under the direction of Henri Wittamer, a *pâtissier* of Austrian descent, and his wife, Marie, who will expand from baking brioches, wedding cakes, birthday cakes, lingot d'or (puff pastry, fruit, and meringue), boussolet (sponge cake, peaches, and apricots macerated in Cointreau and served in a meringue), and friandises (fondant cookies) into handmade chocolates and food catering. They will become famous also for their homemade conserves (strawberry, rhubarb, and myrtille); melon, myrtille, citron, and cassis ices; pear filled with pear sherbet; and sorbet d'orange sanguine (made with blood oranges).

Nearly 90 percent of the horsepower used on English and Welsh farms comes from horses (*see* 1939).

J. I. Case Co. turns to selling gasoline tractors after 66 years of producing farm equipment that have made it the leading U.S. maker of farm steam engines (*see* 1902; Froelich, 1892).

General Electric Co. introduces the first commercially successful electric toaster, pricing it at about $1.45. Its wire body, resting on a porcelain base, holds a slice of bread close to bare electric coils, but only about 10 percent of U.S. homes are wired for electricity (*see* 1918).

The Model T Ford introduced August 12 will soon outsell all other motorcars and be adapted as a pickup truck for farmers. Ford's $850.50 "flivver" has a wooden body on a steel frame that makes it "stronger than a horse and easier to maintain." It comes only in black. Less than 2 percent of all U.S. farm families own motorcars, but there are 200,000 cars on the road, up from 8,000 in 1900.

The Haber process for synthesizing ammonia invented by German chemist Fritz Haber, 40, and his colleague W. H. Nernst will free the world from its dependence on Chilean nitrates for making nitrogen fertilizers (and explosives). Using far less energy and at much lower cost than the Frank-Caro process (*see* American Cyanamid, 1907), the Haber process combines nitrogen and hydrogen directly, using as a catalyst iron (plus some aluminum, potassium, and calcium) and employing high temperatures. Since ammonia is one part nitrogen to three parts hydrogen, it can easily be reduced to sulfate of ammonia or sodium nitrate for fertilizers (or nitric acid for munitions).

German industrial chemist Karl Bosch, 34, will adapt the Haber process (above) and Badische-Anilin-und-Sodafabrik will employ it to produce sulfate of ammonia and sodium nitrate but mostly to make nitric acid (*see* war, 1914).

Swiss-born French chemist Jacques-Edwin Brandenburger, 35, patents a transparent wrapping material called "cellophane" that will find wide use in the food industry (*see* 1912).

Tokyo University chemist Kikunae Ikeda isolates from seaweed the flavor enhancer monosodium glutamate (MSG), which gives a meaty flavor to vegetable diets. He calls the white salt ajinimoto, meaning "the essence of taste" (*see* Arome, 1889).

The Ajinimoto company will become the world's leading MSG producer, and the name Ajinimoto will become a generic for MSG in Japan (in China, where it will be said by some to add a harsh, heavy, metallic taste to food, it will be called Wei-ch'in or Ve-tsin) (*see* 1934; 5´-inosinic acid, 1913).

Fewer than 60 heath hens remain on Martha's Vineyard. They constitute the world's last colony of the birds once plentiful in New England (*see* 1839; 1929).

Half of all Americans live on farms or in towns of less than 2,500, and the country has 6 million farms.

California rice cultivation begins on an experimental basis in an area where sufficient water exists (*see* 1865). The state will grow to rival Louisiana, Texas, and Arkansas as a rice producer but only with the benefit of vast irrigation projects.

The American Home Economics Association is founded with Ellen Swallow Richards, now 66, as president (*see* 1890). Richards has promoted the fledgling science of nutrition, writing some of the U.S. Department of Agriculture's first bulletins on the subject. She has set up demonstration kitchens and pioneer school lunch programs, testing food products for adulterants and encouraging other women to raise the status of homemaking. Through the efforts of her association (and those of other home economists), U.S. women will boost consumption of oranges and otherwise improve the nutrition of their families.

President Roosevelt intervenes in the controversy over sulfur dioxide in dried fruits in February (*see* 1907). He suspends enforcement of Dr. Wiley's order limiting sulfur content to 350 parts per million, appoints five scientists to a board to study the question, and directs them to investigate the fruit-curing process and determine what dangers, if any, are presented to human health by sulfurous acid in foods. Selected groups of men are fed large amounts of dried cut fruit (one man, a police officer, consumes 28 pounds of dried cut fruits in 30 days), the men are then tested and examined, and no negative findings are made. Future tests by competent researchers will consistently confirm the safety of sulfur dioxide as routinely used in the dried fruit industry, but some people will suffer severe allergic reactions to sulfites and laws will be passed requiring that any food product containing more than 10 parts per million state that fact on its label (*see* 1942).

Chicago imposes the first U.S. law making pasteurization of milk compulsory (unless it comes from tuberculin-tested cows).

The 31-year-old British wine-exporting firm Williams and Humbert of Jerez de la Frontera, Spain, introduces Dry Sack sherry, a name derived from a 16th-century English term for dry Spanish wine.

A commission appointed by the British Crown investigates disputes between distillers of single-malt Scotch whiskies and blenders who market brands consisting almost entirely of "patent" whisky (*see* 1905; 1909).

Iceland bans the sale of intoxicating beverages, a prohibition that will continue until 1934.

Tea bags are pioneered by New York tea and coffee wholesaler Thomas Sullivan, who operates a small retail shop in the city's spice district. He sends samples of his various tea blends to customers in small hand-sewn muslin (or China silk) bags instead of in the small metal cans generally used. Finding that they can brew tea simply by pouring boiling water over a tea bag in a cup, the customers place hundreds of orders for Sullivan's tea bags, which will soon be packed by a machine designed specifically for the purpose.

New England entrepreneur Hugh Moore develops a vending machine that sells drinking water at a penny per cup and individual cups that will be improved and sold as Dixie Cups (*see* 1909).

The downtown Los Angeles cafeteria Philippe's opens under the management of Philippe Mathieu, originally from Aix-en-Provence. (The term "cafeteria" was by some accounts first used in Chicago in the 1890s by a Spanish restaurateur who opened a smorgasbord restaurant.) Mathieu came to L.A. at the turn of the century, bought a delicatessen, and sold French bread, cooked meats, pickled vegetables, and olives from open barrels. Patrons began buying loaves of bread, slitting them open, and filling them with meat and pickles, which has led Mathieu to go into sandwich making. Philippe's

French-dip sandwich will be invented in 1918, either when a customer orders a roast meat sandwich in a French roll and asks Mathieu to dip one end of it into the roasting pan's meat juices, or when Mathieu himself accidently drops a roll in the gravy. He will sell the business in 1927, but it will continue for decades to attract patrons, who plant their feet on the sawdust-covered floor, eat at long communal tables lined with stools, check the time on neon wall clocks, and stop at the candy counter as they leave.

Chef Auguste Escoffier makes his second visit to the United States, goes into ecstasies over chicken à la Maryland at Martin's, and expresses admiration for soft-shell crabs. Canvasback duck and terrapin also win his approval.

A "gentlemen's agreement" concluded February 18 binds Japan to issue no further passports to workers for emigration directly to the United States; the Japanese acquiesce to last year's presidential order barring indirect Japanese immigration (*see* 1924).

1909

A court at Birmingham, England, orders an inquiry after allegations by suffragist Laura Ainsworth that she was repeatedly force-fed. Imprisoned for obstructing the police as part of a campaign to obtain voting rights for women, she has followed the lead of other imprisoned suffragists and gone on a hunger strike. Recovering in a nursing home from her treatment, she has filed an affidavit claiming that after 3 days she was pinioned by a wardress while a prison doctor tried to force a cup through her teeth and a tube up her nostrils. Other British suffragists who refuse food will be similarly treated.

Cadbury Brothers announces in November that it will no longer buy Portuguese cacao (*see* 1905). William Cadbury has visited both Principe and São Tomé, and he persuades two other Quaker cocoa and chocolate firms (Fry and Rowntree) to join in a boycott of cacao from the Portuguese African islands, but while working conditions in São Tomé improve, the system of cacao slavery remains (*see* 1910).

Nearly two decades of Hawaiian plantation disturbances begin with a strike by exploited Japanese workers. It is the first major Hawaiian strike (*see* 1882).

💲 Libby, McNeill & Libby buys its first pineapple lands on the Hawaiian island of Oahu. Libby will pack 29,000 cases of pineapple next year (*see* 1908; Alaskan salmon, 1912).

Chicago speculator James A. Patten corners the wheat market, driving up the world price (*see* Leiter, 1898). When he closes out his contracts for 35 million bushels at prices in the neighborhood of $1.34 per bushel, he has made a profit of at least $2 million, plus another $2 million for his partners, but he scoffs at suggestions that he has "manipulated" the market, and when bakers blame high bread prices on the high price of flour, Patten asks how often they have lowered their prices when the price of flour went down.

W. W. Cargill travels to Montana to participate in the dedication of an irrigation project his company has financed, discovers that money has been borrowed in his name all over the West, returns home, catches pneumonia, and dies October 17 at age 64 (*see* 1873). His creditors demand payment, and a struggle begins for control of the nearly bankrupt company (*see* 1916).

J. L. Kraft Bros. & Co. is founded at Chicago by Ontario-born entrepreneur James Lewis Kraft, 35, in partnership with his accountant, Oliver Blackburn, and his brothers Herbert, Fred, Norman, and John with an initial investment of $15,000. Kraft came to the United States 5 years ago, invested some of his small savings in a horse and wagon, and started a cheese delivery service with working capital of $65. Cheese is not a popular food (average annual U.S. consumption is less than one pound), and Kraft lost $3,000 plus his horse in his first year, but he marries Pauline Elizabeth Platt, goes into competition with Phenix Cheese Corp., and will prosper by introducing pasteurizing processes and packaged cheese (*see* 1900; 1915; Kraft-Phenix, 1928).

The Tillamook Cheese Co-Operative Creameries Association is founded on the northern Oregon coast for the purpose of making and marketing high-quality Cheddar cheese. Swiss dairy farmers in the area have found that their milk spoiled en route to Portland, transport being slow and unreliable, so have turned to cheese making.

C. A. Pillsbury & Co. is leased from its British owners and then brought back under U.S. ownership and control (*see* 1889; Bake-Offs, 1949).

✳ Belgian-American chemist Leo Baekeland, 46, develops Bakelite—the world's first polymer. A synthetic shellac plastic material made from formaldehyde and phenol, it does not transmit heat and will come into wide use for the handles of kitchen pots and cooking appliances.

The Melitta drip coffeemaker invented by Dresden *hausfrau* Melitta Bentz is introduced at the Leipzig Fair and begins a movement away from percolators. Bentz began experimenting with coffee filters 2 years ago, first cutting a circle out of a sheet of blotting paper from her son's schoolbook and sticking into the bottom of a brass pot that she had poked full of holes. By putting coffee grounds on top of the filter and pouring boiling water over it, she has obtained better-tasting coffee in less time and without the bother of wrapping loose grounds in a cloth bag and boiling water around it. Her husband, Hugo, hired a tinsmith last year to make pots based on her idea, and they sell more than 1,200 drip coffeemakers at the fair. By 1912 her company will be making a line of coffee filters that will soon be replaced by cone-shaped filters, and the metal pots will be replaced by porcelain and plastic models as her drip-coffee method gains worldwide popularity.

G. Washington soluble coffee powder is introduced by Brooklyn, N.Y., kerosene-lamp maker George Constant Louis Washington, 38. Born in Belgium, Washington settled in Guatemala 2 years ago after making a small fortune in kerosene lamps, and when he noticed a fine powder on the spout of a silver coffee carafe he began experiments that led to the development of the powder for making instant coffee (*see* Kato, 1901; Nescafé, 1938).

⚕ The Rockefeller Sanitary Commission (it will become the Rockefeller Foundation in 1913) begins a campaign to eradicate hookworm disease in the South (*see* Stiles, 1902).

⬥ The Hershey Industrial School for Orphan Boys is chartered at Hershey, Pa., and will enroll its first four boys next year. Chocolate king Milton S. Hershey, now 52, did not marry until 1898, and his wife, who will die in 6 years, has been prevented by ill health from having children (*see* 1918).

Theater: *Liliom* by Hungarian playwright Ferenc Molnár, 31, 12/7 at Budapest's Vígszínház. Molnár has written the play at a marble-topped table in Budapest's Café New York.

U.S. ice cream sales reach 30 million gallons, up from 5 million in 1899. Philadelphia has 49 ice cream manufacturing plants and 52 ice cream "saloons."

Soil is indestructible, says a report issued by the U.S. Bureau of Soils, which has made the first National Soil Survey (*see* 1933; 1934).

A river and harbors bill enacted by Congress empowers the U.S. Army Corps of Engineers to construct locks and dams on U.S. waterways.

Smelt are planted in the Great Lakes where they will become an important food fish species.

Laguna Dam is completed on the Colorado River north of Yuma, Ariz., to irrigate more desert land.

Colorado is the most irrigated state in the nation with more than 3 million acres under irrigation.

Congress doubles the acreage allotted under the Homestead Act of 1862 following the failure of tens of thousands of homesteaders in regions of the West for lack of enough land. But it takes at least four sections of land (2,560 acres) to support a family raising livestock in the West, so the new act is inadequate (*see* 1916; Powell, 1878).

The first kibbutz is started at the Jordan Valley village of Degania Aleph in Palestine, which is part of the Ottoman Empire.

Strawberries are frozen for market in the Pacific Northwest (*see* Birdseye, 1914).

Britain's Royal Commission report on Scotch whisky makes reference to the wide variation in quality among whiskies from different Scottish distilleries and among whiskies made in different years from the same distilleries (*see* 1908), but the authors say that they have received "no evidence to show that the form of the still has any necessary relation to the wholesomeness of the spirit produced." The report concludes by defining Scotch whisky as a spirit obtained by distillation in Scotland from a mash of cereal grains saccharified by the diastase of malt, with or without the addition of unmalted barley grains. Makers of single-malt whiskies, made on pot stills, express outrage at the ruling that "patent" whisky, made on the continuous still, can be called whisky.

Coca-Cola is exported to Britain for the first time (*see* 1900; 1907; distinctive bottle, 1916).

Sir Thomas Lipton (he was knighted in 1901 and made a baronet in 1902) begins blending and packaging his tea at New York. His U.S. business will be incorporated in 1915. (*see* 1893; 1914).

The first J. Lyons & Co. Corner House opens in London's Coventry Street with 600 seats (*see* Popular Café, 1904). It will be enlarged to seat 4,500, and it will be followed by other West End Corner Houses, each containing up to nine restaurants on four or five floors and each having its own menu, its own band or musical ensemble, and shops offering confectionery, cakes, fruit, teas, and coffees (plus flowers and theater tickets) (*see* 1915).

Rosa Lewis of the Cavendish Hotel prepares a banquet for the British Foreign Office (*see* 1902; 1912).

The New Orleans German restaurant Kolb's gets its name as German-American restaurateur Conrad Kolb renames the Valentine Merz saloon on St. Charles Avenue, which he took over 10 years ago. He will make it into the city's largest and most elaborate German restaurant, and it will remain in business until August 1994.

1910

A Mexican social revolution begins as Francisco Indalécio Madero, 37, leads opposition to President Porfirio Díaz, who has controlled the country since 1876 and allowed white landowners to take over the lands of its 6 million Indians and 8 million *mestizos*. The exploited peons start breaking up the large landholdings and distributing farmland among the *campesinos*.

China abolishes slavery March 10.

Labour in Portuguese West Africa by William Cadbury exposes the abuses of slavery on cacao plantations (*see* 1909). Stollwerck Bros. of Cologne joins with Cadbury, Fry, and Rowntree in their boycott of Portuguese cacao, but U.S. companies resist it (*see* below).

German peasants still work 18-hour days and are treated little better than serfs.

 Cudahy Packing Co. moves to Chicago after 20 years at Omaha and will remain at Chicago for more than 40 years (*see* 1890; 1950).

Nebraska flour miller Henry Glade dies in December at age 66 (*see* 1883). His Grand Island mill will be reorganized next year as the Henry Glade Milling Co. with his son Fred as president (*see* 1919).

 The world's first glass-lined milk car goes into service on the Boston & Maine Railroad for Boston's Whiting Milk Co.

The first refrigerated tank car for wine (originally designed for milk) brings California wine to the east, but most California wine is shipped by steamer or sailing vessel around Cape Horn in oak or redwood barrels at a cost of 3¢/gal. plus the cost of the barrels (versus an almost prohibitive 7¢/gal. by rail in tank cars) (*see* 1915).

The United States has 1,000 miles of concrete road, up from 144 in 1900 (*see* surfaced roads, 1921).

Tularemia afflicts ground squirrels of Tulare County, Calif. Physician George Walter McCoy, 34, and his colleague Charles Willard Chapin recognize the disease and will name the responsible organism *Bacterium tularensis*. An epizootic of wild rabbits and other animals that is communicable to humans, tularemia is the first distinctly American disease and will remain a threat to people preparing wild rabbits for cooking without taking proper precautions.

Nonfiction: *Home Life in Tokyo* by Japanese writer-philologist Jukichi Inouye describes meals and ingredients, detailing new foods and preparation techniques introduced by the Portuguese in the 16th century and by other Westerners in the 19th. Rice, he explains, is not only the nation's principal foodstuff but is also the grain from which the national drink, sake, is made. He writes about the popularity of daikon (large radishes), the rhizome of lotus plants, tender bamboo shoots, and the bulb of the tiger lily. "But in point of utility, the soybean comes next to rice. . . . Soy sauce, which enters into almost all dishes, is made from the bean, wheat, and salt." "Miso-[soup] with soybean paste contains strips of garden radish, edible seaweed . . . , bean curd, eggplant, or other vegetable according to the season."

Pickled vegetables are an invariable accompaniment to Japanese meals, Inouye writes. "The commonest of these is the garden radish, which has been pickled in a paste of powdered rice-bran and salt until it assumes a rich golden hue. . . . Most foreigners consider their smell nauseous; but to the Japanese a meal, however rich or dainty, would appear incomplete without these vegetables, pickled or salted." "Seaweeds are also in great demand. Of these, principal are the the konbu and the laver, which is obtained in thin sheets and taken . . . with soy alone or with rice rolled in it. . . . Japan is especially rich in fish. . . . It may be boiled, roasted, salted, or taken raw." Inouye describes sushi as a "lump of rice which has been pressed into a roundish form with a slight mixture of vinegar and covered . . . with a slice of fish or lobster . . . or rolled in . . . laver." "There is no 'dessert' at a Japanese meal. Fruits are eaten at odd hours, especially by children."

Cookbook: *Home Helps: A Pure Food Cook Book* by Mary Johnson Lincoln.

A U.S. Government survey reveals that Americans on average eat 17.5 pounds of canned fruits and vegetables per year.

70 percent of U.S. bread is baked at home, down from 80 percent in 1890 (*see* 1924).

A French chemist named Roger adds *Penicillium candidum* to Camembert cheese (*see* 1890). The bacterium gives it a coating of white dust (*see* 1928).

Wyoming's Shoshone Dam is completed by the Bureau of Reclamation. The arch of rubble on the North Platte River rises 328 feet high.

Africa's cacao industry begins shifting to Britain's Gold Coast (later Ghana), using seeds from trees on the Portugese islands of Principe and São Tomé.

Florida orange shipments finally regain their 1894 levels, but Florida's northern groves have been abandoned and population in the Orlando area has suffered a huge decline.

A blueberry developed by New Jersey botanist Frederick Covine is plump and almost seedless and will revolutionize blueberry cultivation, creating the basis of a multimillion-dollar industry.

The National 4-H Clubs have their beginnings in a three-leaf clover pin awarded by Iowa schoolteacher Jessie (*née* Celestia Josephine) Field Shambaugh, 29, who in 1901 formed a Boys Corn Club and a Girls Home Club to foster feelings of pride and self-worth in her students. She began 4 years ago to establish such clubs in each of the 130 Page County schools, where she has taught improved farming techniques and home management. Seaman Knapp, now 76, who started Boys Cotton and Corn Growing clubs in 1906, starts Girls Canning and Poultry Clubs; he will extend the work next year to include farm women and will be credited by some with having fathered the 4-H Club movement, but the name will come from Shambaugh's pin, which has the letter H on each of its three leaves to symbolize *head*, *hand*, and *heart*, with the county name *Page* in its center. A fourth H will be added, first to represent *home*, then to represent *health*, and 4-H will evolve into a national organization, sponsored by the U.S. Department of Agriculture.

4-H Clubs encouraged U.S. youngsters to improve the quality of agriculture and livestock.

Hydrox "biscuit bonbons" are introduced by the Loose-Wiles Biscuit Co. (*see* 1903; Oreo, 1912).

Aunt Jemima Pancake Flour is sold throughout the United States as pancakes become a year-round staple served at many meals rather than just at winter breakfasts (*see* 1893).

A manager of Delmonico's restaurant at New York complains that fine dining is being ruined through the practice of "beginning with cocktails and drinking Champagne pretty much all through the dinner" (*see* 1914).

The Budapest restaurant Gundel's opened by hotelier's son Károly Gundel opposite the park on Heroes' Square will for decades be one of the city's premier dining spots, large enough for banquets and balls. Restaurateur Gundel, whose specialties include palacsinta (pancakes stuffed with crushed walnuts and topped with hot chocolate and rum) will write the definitive *Short Hungarian Cookery Book* (*see* Lang, 1991).

The Los Angeles restaurant Little Joe's has its beginnings in the Italian-American Grocery Company, which will develop the city's first home-delivery grocery service, carrying food in open-sided trucks to the outlying farms of Azusa, Pasadena, and San Gabriel. It will grow into a full-service Italian restaurant, move in 1927 to 900 North Broadway, corner of College Avenue, and in the 1930s develop an Oriental cuisine when Chinese, displaced by the construction of Union Station, take up homes and businesses on nearby Hill Street, but continue to serve pastas and capuccino gelato as well as butterflied halibut.

New York's new Ritz-Carlton Hotel on Madison Avenue between 46th and 47th streets opens its Oval Room restaurant to the public December 15. The hotel will add a Crystal Room and a Ballroom in 1912, and by opening one wall of the Oval Room it will connect with the new rooms to create the city's most luxurious dining space. Chef Auguste Escoffier, who has come to New York to supervise the opening of the new hotel's kitchen, visits Pittsburgh for 2 weeks to organize the kitchens of that city's new Grand Hotel. Chef Louis Diat, 32, who 7 years ago became *potager* (soup chef) at the Paris Ritz and has worked under Escoffier for the past 4 years as *saucier* at the London Ritz, will run the kitchen of the new Ritz-Carlton for the next 30 years (*see* vichyssoise, 1917).

1911

A military coup establishes a new Honduras "banana republic" favorable to the interests of planter Samuel Zemurray, now 34, who for the past 6 years has been shipping bananas from lands that he has bought along the country's Cuyamel River (*see* 1899). He loans former Honduras president Gen. Manuel Bonilla enough money to buy the yacht *Hornet*, sends him out to the yacht in his own private launch at Biloxi, Miss., with a case of rifles, a machine gun, and ammunition, and provides him with the services of soldiers of fortune Guy "Machine Gun" Molony and Lee Christmas. When Bonilla and his cohorts oust the old Honduras government 6 months later, Zemurray gains valuable concessions (*see* United Fruit, 1929).

Famine reduces 30 million Russians to starvation (*see* 1907). Nearly one quarter of the peasantry is affected, but 13.7 million tons of Russian grain, mostly wheat, are shipped abroad (*see* 1947).

Riviana Foods, Inc., has its beginnings in the Southern Rice Sales Co., founded at New Orleans by local rice dealer Gordon S. Orne and New York salesman Julius S. Ross, who has been sent to New Orleans to sell a shipment of imported black-eyed peas. Southern's medium-grain rice will be promoted within a few years under the name River Brand Fluffy White Rice, and when production of long-grain rice increases the company will introduce it under the name Carolina Gold Rice. Southern will change its name to River Brand and in 1965 will become Riviana Foods.

Battle Creek, Mich., plants produce cornflakes under 108 brand names, but Kellogg's and Post Toasties lead the pack (*see* 1906; 1907). W. K. Kellogg buys out the last of his brother's holdings in the Battle Creek Toasted Corn Flake Co., going $330,000 into debt in order to gain virtually complete ownership of the company that will become Kellogg Corp. (*see* 40% Bran Flakes, 1915).

M. S. Hershey, Inc., has sales of $5 million (*see* 1903; 1918).

It took some years for the Hershey Bar to find its proper package design.

The Swiss chocolate firm Peter Cailler & Kohler Chocolates Suisses, S.A., is created as the Cailler Chocolate firm, founded in 1819, is acquired by Swiss General Chocolate Co., Peter and Kohler, in which Nestlé has a 29 percent interest (*see* 1904; 1920).

A sharp business recession enables Quaker Oats Co. to acquire the Mother's Oats brand, which has annual sales of $5 million (*see* 1901). Quaker's major competitor, the Great Western Cereal Co., is forced to abandon its Fort Dodge, Iowa, and Joliet, Ill., oat-milling facilities in order to save its profitable wheat flour business. It sells the oat mills and brand name to Quaker for $1 million in cash plus the market value of the mills' grain inventories, and Quaker will sell the same cereal under both the Quaker and Mother's labels (*see* Puffed Wheat, Puffed Rice, 1913).

The *De Luxe* goes into service for the Atchison, Topeka and Santa Fe Railroad between Chicago and Los Angeles, enabling just 60 passengers (who pay $25 each over and above regular rail-fare and Pullman charges) to enjoy Fred Harvey cuisine, vintage wines, and other amenities en route. It will continue until 1917, when wartime austerity will end it (*see Chief*, 1926).

U.S. inventor Benjamin Holt devises an improved combine that harvests, threshes, and cleans wheat (*see* 1904; 1905; Industrial Commission, 1901).

James D. Dole's Hawaiian Pineapple Co. packs more than 309,000 cases, up from fewer than 234,000 last year (*see* 1908). Dole hires Henry Ginaca, a young mechanical draftsman, to design a high-speed peeling and coring machine that will permit mass production of canned pineapple (*see* 1913).

Stainless steel, containing about 12 percent chromium, is patented in America. Resistant to rust and impervious to food acids, it will be used in cooking utensils beginning in about 1920.

Nonfiction: *The Gourmet's Guide to Europe* by Newnham Davis says, "An Italian gentleman never eats the salad when travelling in foreign countries, for his palate, used to the finest oils, revolts against the liquid fit only for the lubrication of machinery as so often is offered in Germany, England, and France."

Cookbook: *Mrs. Lincoln's Boston Cookbook* by Mary Johnson Lincoln, now 67.

Bombay's Taj Mahal Hotel opens on Apollo Bunder Pier to commemorate the visit of Britain's new king George V, 45, and his queen, Mary. Built by Sir J. N. Tata, it has electric lights and appliances that include electrically heated irons, dishwashing machines, a machine for sharpening knives, silver burnishers, an in-house soda water factory, and a main dining room that accommodates several hundred for mulligatawny soup, papad bread, and vegetarian and non-vegetarian specialties, the latter including minced beef pie, Madras curry, and pomfret curry.

China's Yangzi River floods its banks in early September, killing an estimated 100,000. Overpopulation has obliged many to live on marginal lands in hazardous areas of the floodplain (*see* politics, 1912).

Roosevelt Dam on the Salt River in the Arizona Territory is completed by the Bureau of Reclamation as part of the first large-scale U.S. irrigation project. The 284-foot-high rubble masonry arch has a crest length of 1,125 feet, creates a reservoir with a capacity of 1.64 million acre-feet, and will make the Phoenix area a rich source of fruits and vegetables.

The Columbia River salmon catch reaches a record 49 million pounds that will never be reached again (*see* 1866; 1938).

U.S. agricultural pioneer Seaman A. Knapp dies at Washington April 1 at age 77 (*see* 4-H Clubs, 1910). He has more than 700 instructors traveling through the southern states, working to make agriculture more profitable and conditions of rural life more attractive.

Polish biochemist Casimir Funk, 27, at London's Lister Institute introduces the word "vitamines." If the enzymes discovered by the late Wilhelm Kuhne in 1878 are to work properly, they sometimes require coenzymes, Funk discovers, and he calls these coenzymes "vitamines" in the mistaken belief that they all contain nitrogen and are all essential to life (*see* 1912; Drummond, 1920).

The Chemistry of Food and Nutrition by Columbia University chemist Henry Clapp Sherman, 35, reports research findings that adult protein requirements are 75 grams per day—somewhere between the 60 grams favored by W. O. Atwater (*see* 1895) and the 125 grams favored by Russell E. Chittenden (*see* 1904). Sherman has actually come to the conclusion that half a gram of protein per kilogram of body weight per day is sufficient for an adult but has doubled that amount to provide a margin of safety (he recommends two to three grams per kilogram of body weight for growing children and adolescents). His book becomes the new gospel of dieticians and home economists (*see* 1914).

Ellen Swallow Richards dies at Boston March 30 at age 68 (*see* 1908). She has given a lecture March 19 in which she has said that the high cost of living is due to the growing love of pleasurable sensations and the habit of speeding up life all along the line. Unless there is a high and noble purpose behind it all, she has said, it marks no social advance.

The Fasting Cure by novelist Upton Sinclair enjoys some popularity with faddists. Sinclair has moved to California.

Crisco, introduced in the spring by Cincinnati's Procter & Gamble, is the first solid hydrogenated vegetable shortening (see Normann, 1901) and P&G's first major food product. The company advertises Crisco as "a Scientific Discovery Which Will Affect Every Kitchen in America" but women who have been taught to cook with butter and lard are often reluctant to accept free one-and-a-half-

Hydrogenation of vegetable oils paved the way for new food products with longer shelf life. PHOTO COURTESY PROCTER & GAMBLE

pound cans of the product. The company issues a pamphlet in Yiddish after finding that its biggest users initially include Orthodox Jews, who are delighted to have a shortening which contains neither lard nor butter and can thus be used at any meal without violating kosher dietary laws. Crisco will have more widespread commercial success when wartime shortages of lard develop later in this decade (*see* Spry, 1936).

Mazola salad and cooking oil—the first corn oil available for home consumption—is introduced by E. T. Bedford's Corn Products Refining Co., which operates a corn oil refinery on the Illinois River at Pekin, Ill. (*see* 1906). Mazola will be distributed in Europe as Maizena.

Domino brand sugar is introduced by the American Sugar Refining Co. (*see* 1907; Jack Frost, 1913).

The first canned chili con carne and tamales are produced at San Antonio, Tex., by William Gebhardt, who will receive 37 patents for his mechanical innovations (*see* 1896).

A *Michelin Guide* to restaurants and hotels in Britain and Ireland is published for the first time and will continue until 1933 (*see* 1900). It will be revived in 1974 despite competition from the *Dunlop Guide*, put out by the British tire company of that name (*see* Kléber, 1952).

San Francisco's Swan Oyster Depot opens at 1517 Polk Street. Four Danish brothers have started the wholesale seafood shop and tiled-floor restaurant, which serves New England clam chowder, sand dabs, salmon steak, shrimp, squid, California spiny lobster (October to mid-March), crab "Louie," and Dungeness crabs (November to May or June) at a marble counter with stools.

1912

The Qing, or Manchu, dynasty, which has ruled China since 1644, ends January 1 as the nation becomes a republic with Gen. Sun Yat-sen, 45, as president. The final decades of the Qing dynasty have been marked by rebellions sparked not only by the disruptions of Western imperialism but also by rural unrest resulting from population pressures on finite resources of land and water.

The amount of China's cultivated land has fallen to three mu (one-half acre) per capita as population has increased, half what it was in 1729; starvation and malnutrition have become the most common causes of death. Peasants have resorted to infanticide, banditry, and other acts of violence in desperate efforts to keep their families alive (*see* agriculture, below).

U.S. food prices rise sharply, causing widespread distress. They will rise further next year (*see* 1916).

The U.S. Department of Justice orders dissolution of the 10-year-old International Harvester Trust (but *see* 1918).

Swiss bouillon cube king Jules Maggi (he has long since changed his first name from Julius) suffers a cerebral hemorrhage at Paris and dies a few months later at age 66 (*see* 1892; Nestlé merger, 1947).

The A&P begins an expansion program under John Hartford, a son of the founder (*see* 1880). From its present base of nearly 500 stores, the chain will open a new A&P store every 3 days for the next 3 years as it stops providing charge accounts and free delivery and bases its growth on one-man "economy" stores that operate on a cash-and-carry basis (*see* 1929).

The first self-service grocery stores open independently in California—the Alpha Beta Food Market at Pomona and Ward's Groceteria at Ocean Park. They are soon followed by Bay Cities Mercantile's Humpty Dumpty Stores (*see* Piggly-Wiggly, 1916).

Cleveland's West Side Market opens in the summer to bring farmers' produce directly to retail customers (*see* Arcade, 1895).

J. E. Brandenberger perfects the cellophane material he patented in 1908. He will found Société de Cellophane in 1915 and sell U.S. rights to E. I. du Pont (*see* Whitman's Sampler, below; Du Pont, 1926).

An actress arriving at New York poses for newspaper photographers at the ship's rail and exposes an unconventional expanse of leg; reporters call it "cheesecake."

Libby, McNeill & Libby buys an Alaskan salmon cannery. The company will operate an extensive fishing fleet with as many as 14 salmon canneries and will continue to market salmon under the Libby label even after it sells the fleet and canneries in 1959 (*see* 1909; tomato juice, 1923).

Chinese agriculture has developed through the Qing dynasty (above) with the introduction of new crops from the Western Hemisphere, but a peasant family may own an acre of land that is divided into 10 parcels, a few of them not much larger than a room. Dikes and boundary zones occupy considerable amounts of land, disputes over encroachment are common, and public roads narrow as peasants cultivate more and more of the dirt roadways until officials brutally repossess the right of way (*see* nutrition, below).

A new U.S. Homestead Act reduces from 5 years to 3 years the residence requirement of U.S. homesteaders (*see* 1909; 1916).

Louisiana rice planter Salmon L. Wright introduces a new rice variety that will be known as Blue Rose (*see* 1903). Now 60 and known as the "Burbank of rice," he will also develop the Lady Wright, Edith, and Early Prolific varieties but will make no effort to capitalize on his work, selling a 200-pound bag of seed at $25 when the standard price is $200. To stymie the ricebirds, blackbirds, and sparrows that deplete rice crops, Wright will develop a birdproof bearded, or barbed, rice whose seed has a sharp barb, between one-eighth and one-sixteenth of an inch long, which frustrates birds attempting to eat the rice.

Sun-Maid Growers of California has its beginnings in the California Associated Raisin Co., which will

California raisin producers joined forces to market their crop under the Sun-Maid label. LIBRARY OF CONGRESS

officially adopt the Sun-Maid Growers name in 1922 and within 70 years will be processing and marketing nearly 30 percent of the California raisin grape crop for a membership that will come to number 1,600 growers (*see* Thompson Seedless, 1876; Sun-Diamond Growers, 1980).

Diamond Walnut Growers has its beginnings in the California Walnut Growers Association. It will take the name Diamond in 1956, after having established the Diamond brand name, and by the 1990s will be handling more than 47 percent of California's annual walnut crop for 2,300 grower-members (*see* Sun-Diamond Growers, 1980).

Ocean Spray Cranberry Sauce is introduced by the Cape Cod Cannery Co., which buys berries from farmers who cultivate 26,000 acres (*see* Hall, 1816). President of the company is Boston lawyer Marcus L. Urann, who has been developing cranberry bogs in Plymouth County and has opened a new cannery at Hanson (*see* 1930).

Charles Seabrook goes into partnership with his father, Arthur, on the family's New Jersey truck farm (*see* 1893). An agricultural innovator, young Charles has installed overhead irrigation on the farm, whose size he will increase in the next few years to 273 acres. By 1914, Seabrook Farms will be selling 200 carloads of produce, mostly in the New York and Philadelphia markets, and by 1917 Seabrook will be cultivating more than 3,000 acres of owned and leased land (*see* cannery, 1920).

Chinese nutritional needs suffer as a result of population pressures on available farmland (above). One acre can be made through intensive cropping to yield 2,000 to 3,000 pounds of grain per year, but an individual needs 533 pounds a year to obtain 2,400 calories per day, which is scarcely enough to support the hard physical labor required for intensive agriculture.

Japanese biochemists J. Suzuki, T. Shimamura, and S. Ohdake extract an antiberiberi compound from rice hulls (*see* 1906; 1933).

U.S. biochemists Elmer Verner McCollum, 33, and Marguerite Davis discover in butter and egg yolks the fat-soluble nutrient that will later be called vitamin A. They establish that it was a lack of this nutrient that caused C. A. Pekelharing's Dutch mice to die prematurely in 1905 when given no milk. Yale biochemists Thomas B. Osborne, 53, and Lafayette B. Mendel, 40 (a onetime assistant to Russell E. Chittenden), make a similar discovery.

Die Vitaminen by Casimir Funk suggests that beriberi, rickets, pellagra, and sprue may all be caused by "vitamine" deficiencies (*see* 1911).

Morton's Table Salt is introduced in a blue and white asphalt-laminated paper canister with an aluminum pouring spout (*see* 1885). Beginning in 1914, the canister will bear the slogan "When It Rains It Pours" together with a trademark depicting a little girl holding an umbrella in the rain while holding a Morton's Salt canister upside down in her other hand with salt pouring from its open spout.

Hellmann's Blue Ribbon Mayonnaise is introduced by German-American New York delicatessen owner Richard Hellmann, 35, who has operated Hellmann's Delicatessen at 490 Columbus Avenue since

New York delicatessen owner Richard Hellmann went into business making mayonnaise.

1905, ladling out portions of mayonnaise from big glass jars into wooden boats for sale by weight. He begins packing the product in individual glass jars, and that meets with such success that he will build a three-story factory in Astoria, Queens, next year, and by 1915 will have given up the delicatessen to concentrate on manufacturing. He will build a larger Astoria plant in 1922 and by 1927 will have plants at Chicago, San Francisco, Atlanta, Dallas, and Tampa (*see* 1927).

Prince Macaroni Co. is founded on Prince Street in Boston's North End by three Italian Americans. The firm will outgrow its Prince Street quarters as it expands in the next 20 years and will move to Lowell, but it will remain Prince Macaroni (*see* Borden, 1987).

Oreo Biscuits are introduced by National Biscuit Company, whose two chocolate-flavored wafers with a cream filling compete with the Hydrox "biscuit bonbons" introduced in 1910. Nabisco will change the name of the English-style biscuit to Oreo Cream Sandwich in 1958, and William Turner, who has designed the product, will remain with Nabisco until his retirement in 1973.

Lorna Doone cookies are introduced by the National Biscuit Company (above). The shortcake cookies are named for the 1869 Richard Doddridge Blackmore novel, which is still required reading in many schools.

The Whitman Sampler, introduced by Philadelphia's Whitman Chocolate Co., is the first candy box to be wrapped in cellophane (*see* 1842; technology, above). Whitman's boxed chocolates gained national distribution in 1907 and began national advertising. Walter B. Sharp, the company's president, has an old embroidered sampler worked by his grandmother and uses its cross-stitched designs on a linenlike background as the illustration for the Sampler's cover.

The United States prohibits the sale of absinthe, a liqueur whose invention is credited to (or blamed on) a French physician, Pierre Ordinaire, who fled the Revolution in the 1790s and settled at Couvet, Switzerland, where wormwood (*Artemisia absinthium*) grew wild (two sisters in Couvet made absinthe before Ordinaire arrived, but it was he who bottled and promoted it as a medicinal cure-all) (*see* Pernod, 1805). Popular in Europe for a century but banned in Switzerland, the aromatic liqueur made from wormwood and other herbs produces gastrointestinal irritation, extreme nervousness, convulsions, hallucinations, blindness, loss of hearing, mania, stupor, and even death among habitual users (*see* France, 1915).

Royal Crown Ginger Ale and Chero-Cola are bottled by the Union Bottling Works at Columbus, Ga., which reorganizes under the name Chero-Cola Co. and issues franchises to bottle Chero-Cola to other Georgia bottlers (*see* 1914; Hatcher, 1905).

The Suvretta House opens outside St. Moritz, Switzerland, on Silvaplana Lake with views of the Corvatsch and the valley stretching south to Italy. It will grow to have 220 rooms, and its kitchen will rival those of the Palace (*see* 1896), the Kulm, and the Carlton.

The Paris bistro Benoît opens at 20, rue Saint Martin, near the Palais de Justice, serving mussel soup, marinated smoked salmon, bœuf à la mode, braised beef with carrots, poulet en croute with wild mushrooms, chocolate marquise, sponge cake with butter cream, vanilla or coffee-flavored crême anglaise, and frozen Grand Marnier with candied orange.

Rosa Lewis of London's Cavendish Hotel prepares a banquet for the British Admiralty (*see* 1909; 1914).

New York's Voisin restaurant opens in the new Montana apartment house at 375 Park Avenue, where it will serve the *beau monde* until the building is razed in 1955 to make room for a skyscraper (*see* 1959).

New York's Lafayette Restaurant introduces a $2 table d'hôte dinner that will still cost only $2 when manager Raymond Orteig dies in 1940 (*see* 1902). Served at half the price of comparable dinners elsewhere, the meal begins with cantaloupe, consommé, potage, or cherrystone clams, proceeds to a cassoulet of lobster, sautéed sweetbreads, spaghetti with a Menagère sauce, suprême of chicken, *pâté de la maison en gelée*, or steak, and mixed green salad, and ends with Camembert cheese or a selection of sweets, plus coffee (*see* 1949).

New York's Grand Central Oyster Bar opens at the new railroad terminal, whose lower level begins commuter train service in October (its upper level, for long-distance trains, will be inaugurated February 1 of next year). Union News Company, the concessionaire, will serve bluepoints, Cape Cods, Chincoteagues from Maryland's Eastern Shore, Gardiners Bays from eastern Long Island Sound, Lynnhavens, Mattitucks, Saddle Rocks, and other varieties, as well as fish and other seafood, for 62 years (*see* 1974).

New York entrepeneur Arnold Reuben opens a modest sandwich shop on upper Broadway and soon uses his magnetic personality to attract theatrical luminaries (who will persuade him to move closer to Times Square).

The first New York Horn & Hardart Automat opens at 1557 Broadway, between 46th and 47th streets (*see* Philadelphia, 1902). "For ordinary viands," says *Architecture and Building* magazine, "the proper coin is deposited in the slot and a turn of the knob throws open a little door and within the compartment, which is exposed, the food is found." The Automat has tiled floors, patrons sit at plain, circular tables, each with four chairs, the surrounding banks of food compartments are set in Victorian-style wooden frames surmounted by cut-glass mirrors. A second Automat will open in 1914 at 250 West 42nd Street, and by 1922 there will be 21 Horn & Hardart Automats, but they will not gain the height of their success until the 1920s, when steam tables are introduced to provide hot food (*see* 1991).

Mory's tavern opens at New Haven to serve Yale University students and professors.

1913

An aide to Germany's kaiser Wilhelm finds Auguste Escoffier preparing dinner for the emperor in the galley of the liner *Imperator*, recalls that Escoffier was taken prisoner during the Franco-Prussian War in 1870, and draws the matter to Wilhelm's attention, expressing fears that Escoffier may have some idea of poisoning the German emperor. Wilhelm summons the chef to his quarters, assures himself that Escoffier means him no harm, and says, "If you had been my prisoner I should never have let you go."

A South African Land Act that takes effect June 20 prevents Zulu, Mfengu, and other black tribesmen from owning any land outside a few arid, worthless parcels. The new law reserves about 90 percent of the country's land for whites only.

The California legislature passes a xenophobic Alien Land Act aimed primarily at Chinese and Japanese farmers such as Chin Lung (*see* 1898) and George Shima (*see* 1899). The act places a 3-year limit on leases of agricultural land and bans purchases of farmland by "aliens ineligible for citizenship"; the Issei (first-generation) Japanese circumvent the act by leasing and buying land in the names of their Nisei (second-generation) children, who are citizens by birthright, but the Native Sons of the Golden West and other nativist organizations will work to strengthen the act (*see* 1920; agriculture, below).

The Underwood-Simmons Tariff Act passed by Congress May 8 lowers import duties by an average of 30 percent, the first real break in tariff protection since the Civil War. Agricultural implements, raw wool, iron ore, pig iron, and steel rails are admitted duty free under the new law, and tariffs on raw materials and foodstuffs are substantially reduced. The new measure hurts many U.S. manufacturers; pressure mounts for restoration of tariff protection (*see* 1922).

Antitrust action brought by the U.S. Justice Department forces Corn Products Refining Co. to sell its half interest in Penick & Ford, a New Orleans firm that produces Brer Rabbit Molasses and Vermont Maid Syrup. E. T. Bedford's son Frederick Thomas Bedford acquires one-third of the company (*see* 1906; 1916; 1921).

Henry Ginaca perfects a pineapple-processing machine for James D. Dole's Hawaiian Pineapple Co. (*see* 1911). It can remove the shells from as many as 120 pineapples per minute, punching out the core, slicing off the ends, and scraping the pulp from the shell. By delivering the cylinders of fruit to the packing tables in a steady stream, it enables Dole to pack 600,000 cases, a figure that will climb by 1918 to more than a million (*see* 1922).

New Process Cork Co. is founded by New York inventor Charles E. McManus to compete with the Crown Cork & Seal Co. founded by William Painter in 1892. McManus patents a process for granulating natural cork and mixing it with a binder to form an economical substitute for pure, unadulterated cork. He will gain control of Crown Cork & Seal, and his Crown Cork International will grow to produce half the world's bottle caps.

The flavor enhancer 5´-inosinic acid, discovered by Tokyo University chemist Shintaro Kodoma, is 10 to 20 times more effective than the monosodium glutamate (MSG) discovered in 1908 and marketed under the name Ajinimoto.

Kansas City chemist C. J. (Curtis John) Patterson, 25, joins the newly established laboratory of the Ismert Hinke Co. His work in the next 6 years will lead to wheat being purchased on the basis of protein content rather than on the basis of dry gluten tests as in the past. The milling industry will adopt the new standard almost universally (*see* 1919).

Fiction: *Swann's Way* (*Du Côté de chez Swann*) by French novelist Marcel Proust, 42, whose memory of childhood (the remembrance of things past) has been awakened by the taste of a madeleine, the small, scallop-shaped butter cake (*see* Ranhofer's recipe, 1894): "Many years had elapsed during which nothing of Combray . . . had any existence for me, when one day in winter, as I came home, my mother, seeing that I was cold, offered me some tea, a thing I did not ordinarily take. I declined at first, and then, for no particular reason, changed my mind. She sent out for one of those short, plump little cakes called 'petites madeleines,' which look as though they had been moulded in the fluted scallop of a pilgrim's shell. And soon, mechanically, weary after a dull day with the prospect of a depressing morrow, I raised to my lips a spoonful of the tea in which I had soaked a morsel of the cake. No sooner had the warm liquid, and the crumbs with it, touched my palate than a shudder ran through my whole body, and I stopped, intent upon the extraordinary changes that were taking place. An exquisite pleasure had invaded my senses, but individual, detached, with no suggestion of its origin. And at once the vicissitudes of life had become indifferent to me, its disasters innocuous, its brevity illusory— this new sensation having had on me the effect which love has of filling me with precious essence; or rather this essence was not in me, it was myself. I had ceased now to feel mediocre, accidental, mortal. Whence could it have come to me, this all-powerful joy? I was conscious that it was connected with the taste of tea and cake, but that it infinitely transcended those savours, could not, indeed, be of the same nature as theirs. Whence did it come? What did it signify? How could I seize upon and define it? . . . And suddenly the memory returns. The taste was that of the little crumb of madeleine which on Sunday mornings at Combray (because on those mornings I did not go out before church-time), when I went to say good day to her in her bedroom, my aunt Léonie used to give me, dipping it first in her own cup of real or of lime-flower tea. The sight of the little madeleine had recalled nothing to my mind before I tasted it; perhaps because I had so often seen such things in the interval, without tasting them, on the trays in pastry-cooks' windows, that their image had dissociated itself from those Combray days to take its place among others more recent. . . . And once I had recognized the taste of the crumb of madeleine soaked in her decoction of lime-flowers which my aunt used to give me (although I did not yet know and must long postpone the discovery of why this memory made me so happy), immediately the old grey house upon the street, where her room was, rose up like the scenery of a theatre to attach itself to the little pavilion, opening on to the garden, which had been built out behind it for my parents."

U.S. dime store pioneer Frank W. Woolworth, 61, celebrates the opening of New York's 60-story Woolworth Building on Broadway near City Hall in April with a dinner to honor its architect Cass Gilbert, 53. Guests dine on caviar, oysters, turtle soup, turban of pompano with Austrian potatoes, breast of guinea hen with Nesselrode sauce, terrapin Baltimore style, royal punch, roast squab, walnut and grapefruit salad, frozen bombe, fancy cakes, coffee, and wines.

Ohio's Great Miami River floods its banks at Columbus March 25 after a 5-day rainfall that has dropped 10 inches of water. The flood kills 351, injures hundreds more, and creates property damage amounting to $100 million as germinating crops are destroyed.

California's Alien Land Act (above) motivates potato grower Chin Lung to buy 2,000 acres of land near Klamath Falls, Ore., where he will grow Oregon Gem potatoes. He bought 1,100 acres a few miles northwest of Stockton last year, naming it the Sing Kee Tract (Sing Kee is the rice-importing firm for which he worked when he first arrived in San Francisco in the early 1880s, and he has acquired the business), and for the next 10 years will grow potatoes in Oregon as well as in California (see 1920).

A severe freeze practically wipes out avocados on southern California ranches; out of more than 100 varieties, the only one that survives is the Fuerte (Spanish for strength), which will provide the basis of a revived commercial avocado industry. It was discovered 2 years ago by Carl Schmidt, then 21, of Altadena, Calif., who found it growing in the midst of coffee bushes in the Mexican garden of Alejandro Le Blanc at Atlixco. Assigned by the West India Nursery to find outstanding avocado specimens and locate the trees that bore them, Schmidt has shipped budwood from the trees home to Altadena by Wells, Fargo Express, and although many could not adapt to the climate and soil of California the tree from Le Blanc's garden has flourished. Members of the California Avocado Growers' Association will make pilgrimages to Atlixco in 1938 and again in 1948 to present budwood of the improved California version of the Fuerte avocado, invigorating Mexican stocks.

U.S. Department of Agriculture biologist Carl Frederic Kellerman, 33, undertakes the first campaign to result in the complete eradication of a plant disease. Ignoring Florida doomsayers who tell him that his cause is hopeless, he marshals a co-operative effort by growers against citrus canker and saves the state's valuable citrus industry from the highly contagious plant disease that will recur (see 1984).

Rabbits fed large amounts of cholesterol and animal fats are shown to develop hardening of the arteries (arteriosclerosis) by Russian pathologist Nikolai Anichkov (see Keys, 1953).

Pellagra kills 1,192 in Mississippi. The U.S. Public Health Service sends Hungarian-American physician Joseph Goldberger, 39, to study the disease, which is known to affect at least 100,000 in the Deep South (see 1907; 1915).

Congress amends the Pure Food and Drug Law of 1906 to make it more effective, as was done last year (see 1938).

Quaker's Puffed Rice and Quaker's Puffed Wheat are introduced by Quaker Oats Co., whose Chicago advertising agency, Lord & Thomas, is headed by Albert D. Lasker, 33. He has discovered that the factory making Quaker "Wheat Berries" and "Rice Berries" employs a mechanism resembling a blunt cannon to puff the grains up to eight times their normal size (see 1904). Lasker's chief copywriter, Claude Hopkins, comes up with the slogan "The Grains That Are Shot from Guns," and the advertising will puff sales 20- to 30-fold (see 1911; Aunt Jemima, 1926).

Peppermint Life Savers are introduced by Cleveland, Ohio, chocolate manufacturer Clarence Crane as a summer item to sell when chocolate sales decline. Crane uses a pharmaceutical company's pill-making machine to create the uniquely shaped peppermint with the hole in the middle which he advertises "for that stormy breath," and when New York streetcar advertising salesman Edward J. Noble, 31, tries to persuade him to use car cards for advertising Crane offers to sell the product for $5,000. Noble goes into partnership with his boyhood friend Roy Allen and buys Crane's trademark and remaining stocks of peppermints for $2,900, but he finds that the product's cardboard box absorbs the candy's volatile taste and aroma. Retailers have been stuck with hundreds of thousands of unsold Life Savers packages and will not reorder. Noble devises an easy-opening tinfoil package that keeps the mints fresh and permits a buyer to remove one mint at a time. He and Allen start producing hand-wrapped rolls of Life Savers in a New York loft under the name Mint Products, Inc. Since existing retail outlets are willing to accept replacements for the stale product on their shelves but will not pay for the new product, Allen opens new outlets, selling Life Savers to saloons, cigar stores, barbershops, restaurants, and pharmacies, and when retailers complain that the round packs roll off their counters, Noble supplies cartons designed to be set up as miniature display cases (see 1920).

Secretary of State William Jennings Bryan, 53, a Prohibitionist, serves Welch's grape juice in place of wine at a dinner given for the British ambassador. Cartoonists lampoon Bryan and make Welch's a household name (see 1897; Daniels, 1914).

St. Louis brewer Adolphus Busch dies at his hunting lodge near Langenschwalbach, Germany, October 10 at age 74.

New York's first Nedick's orange drink and frankfurter stand opens. Entrepreneurs Robert T. Neely and Orville Dickinson start an enterprise that will blossom into a $12 million chain.

The Paris restaurant De La Tour d'Argent, which claims to have begun in 1582, is acquired by André Terrail, son-in-law of Claudius Burdel, proprietor of the Café Anglais, which has been demolished to accommodate an extension of the Boulevard Haussmann (see pressed duck, 1890). Terrail will make the ground-floor dining room at 15, quai de la Tournelle famous for its boeuf soufflé and salmis de sarcelles (a ragout of migratory small wild ducks) as well as for its canard à presse. His son Claude, born in the building, will move the dining room in 1936 to a glass-enclosed penthouse on the sixth floor with a view of the Seine and Nôtre-Dame Cathedral (which will be lighted in the evening at his instigation) and will add to the menu such dishes as coustade de barbu Lagrené (brill surrounded by a soufflé and served with a mousseline sauce); lamb tornedos sautéed in clarified butter, glazed, and served on artichoke bottoms; and caneton Marco Polo (wild duck).

1914

A World War begins in Europe July 28—one month after the assassination of the heir to the Austrian throne in Bosnia. Germany declares war on Russia August 1 and on France August 3; German troops invade neutral Belgium August 4, and Britain declares war on Germany. Chef Auguste Escoffier of London's Carlton Hotel invents concentrated soups for the French Army, but his son Paul of the Alpine Chasseurs is killed in action.

The U.S. relief ship S.S. Massapequa reaches Belgium in November with a cargo of food sent by the Rockefeller Foundation to aid starving Belgians.

Berlin places German food supplies and allocations under government control December 26, and London thereupon declares all foodstuffs on the high seas to be contraband.

The world sugar market moves from Germany to New York, where the Coffee Exchange begins trading in sugar futures.

National Dairy Corp. has its beginnings as Chicago businessman Thomas H. McInnerney, 47, acquires ownership of Hydrox, a wholesaler of artificial ice, ginger ale, and ice cream. Formerly general manager of New York's Siegel Cooper department store, McInnerney will increase Hydrox sales in the next 9 years from $1 million to $4 million (*see* 1923).

Postum Cereal founder C. W. Post commits suicide May 9 at his Santa Barbara, Calif., home in a fit of depression at age 59. He was divorced 10 years ago, and his only child, Marjorie Merriweather Post, 27, inherits the company (*see* Post Toasties, 1906; incorporation, 1922; Jell-O, 1925).

James Ben Ali Haggin dies at Newport, R.I., September 12 at age 86, leaving an estate of about $15 million—some of it acquired through acquiring and irrigating vast expanses of agricultural land in California's Kern County and San Joaquin and Sacramento valleys (*see* 1877).

A Federal Trade Commission established by Congress September 26 to police U.S. industry is intended only to prevent unfair competition.

The Clayton Anti-Trust Act voted by Congress October 15 toughens the federal government's power against mergers and other combinations in restraint of trade.

Tasty Baking Co. is founded at Philadelphia by former Pittsburgh baker Philip J. Baur and Boston salesman Herbert C. Morris, whose firm has supplied dried eggs to the baking industry. Morris met Bauer in Pittsburgh and they discussed an idea which they thought might revolutionize bakery retailing: individual-size cakes which will be prewrapped at the bakery instead of cakes baked in slabs which storekeepers have to handle. Leaving Baur to develop recipes for the cakes, Morris has returned to Boston to wind up his affairs, has come down with appendicitis and nearly died from peritonitis, but while recovering in a Boston hospital has come up with the name Tastykake. Each man puts up $25,000 in borrowed capital, they take over a foundry building on Sedgley Avenue near 24th Street and install giant brick ovens, Morris orders a royal blue horse-drawn wagon, drives to Philadelphia's Germantown section, and with a wicker basket of 5¢ Tastykakes on his arm calls on grocers. The first day's receipts are $28.32, but gross sales by year's end exceed $300,000 and the company shows a profit, enabling it to hire more than the single employee with which it began (the entire U.S. baking industry employs only 11,400). Tasty will expand with more routes, and blue Tastykake wagons, drawn by grey horses 16 hands high, will become familiar in Philadelphia's Main Line communities, Baltimore, southern New Jersey, and central Pennsylvania. Baur and Morris make no deals, give no kickbacks, charge every store the same, and will decide how much a storekeeper can sell, supplying him only with that much product and no more; critics will call it high-handed, Baur and Morris will call it a policy of "selling less to sell more." By 1918, Tasty Baking will have sales of $1 million, and that figure will double in 1919 (*see* 1922).

Large-scale pasta production begins in the United States, which has imported almost all of its macaroni and spaghetti from Naples but which has been cut off from Italian sources by the outbreak of the European war (above) (*see* Carleton, 1899).

Italian-American pasta maker Vincent La Rosa and his five sons start a company at Brooklyn, N.Y., that will later move to Warminster, Pa. V. La Rosa & Sons will make macaroni, spaghetti, egg noodles, and prepared Italian-style foods in plants at Warminster and Milwaukee.

Thomas Lipton expands his retail grocery empire to include some 500 shops, a number that will grow to 600 at its peak (*see* 1909). He has acquired tea, cocoa, and coffee plantations, meatpacking plants, and factories, and has at least 20 British retail grocery rivals (*see* 1931).

French merchant Henri Androuët opens a Paris cheese shop at 41, rue d'Amsterdam near the Gare St. Lazare. Androuët's son Pierre will be born next year, grow to become *maître fromager*, and inherit the store, which he and his family will run for decades, providing customers for more than 80 years with Brie de Coulommiers (from fall through spring), Camembert, Emmenthal, Gorgonzola, Gouda, Livarot, Munster, Pont l'Eveque, Reblochon, Roquefort, Saint Nectare, and Stilton cheeses (among others) and Charente butter made from unpasteurized milk (*see* restaurant, below).

The Panama Canal opens to traffic August 3 just as Germany declares war on France (above). Built essentially on French plans at a total cost of 30,000 lives and some $367 million in U.S. money (on top of $287 million lost by the French in the 1880s), the canal uses a system of locks to carry ships 50.7 miles between deep water in the Atlantic and deep water in the Pacific (*see* 1906). It shortens the route between East and West Coast ports to 5,263 miles, enabling ships to carry California agricultural exports to Philadelphia, New York, or Boston in just 20 days.

The Houston Ship Canal opens to give Houston an outlet to Galveston Bay on the Gulf of Mexico. The 50-mile canal will make the Texas city a deepwater port and a major shipping point for U.S. grain.

The Cape Cod Ship Canal opens to link Buzzards Bay with Cape Cod Bay, Mass. The 17.4-mile canal enables coastal shipping to avoid the voyage round the cape.

Tank trucks are used for the first time to transport milk.

Cookbook: *Boston School Kitchen Textbook; Lessons in Cooking for the Use of Classes in Public and Industrial Schools* by Mary Johnson Lincoln.

Some U.S. margarine is now made entirely of vegetable oil compounds, but Americans still consume five pounds of butter for every pound of margarine (*see* 1890; 1919).

Average per capita U.S. candy consumption reaches 5.6 pounds, up from 2.2 pounds in 1880 (*see* 1919).

The passenger pigeon, which once dominated U.S. skies, becomes extinct September 1 as the last known bird of the species dies in the Cincinnati Zoo (*see* 1878).

Brooklyn-born fur trader Clarence "Bob" Birdseye, 28, pioneers fish freezing. An Amherst College dropout, he went to Labrador in 1912 and has noticed that fish caught through the ice there freeze stiff the instant they are exposed to the air and taste almost fresh when defrosted and cooked weeks later. Birdseye will return to the United States next year and marry Eleanor Gannett of Washington,

D.C., but will go back to Labrador in 1916 with his wife and weeks-old child (*see* 1917).

Van Camp Seafood is founded by Indianapolis packer Frank Van Camp, whose father, Gilbert, began packing pork and beans in 1861. His son Gilbert persuades him to sell the family's midwestern operation and enter the fast-growing California tunafish-packing business (*see* 1903). Father and son buy California Tunny Packing of San Pedro, contract with operators of 35 to 40 small Japanese-owned albacore boats to buy all the albacore the boats can catch, accept deliveries 7 days a week, and by October have developed a new method of purse seining to increase catches. The Van Camps will be building a new fleet of 15 modern 40-foot albacore boats within a year, they will turn the new boats over to the fishermen at no cost, and by finding new tuna banks off the Mexican Coast, rushing the catch back to the San Pedro cannery by tender, and lowering the price of canned tuna they will pioneer in making tunafish an American staple rather than a costly delicacy (*see* 1922).

U.S. ranchers herd cattle with Model T Fords.

British farmers produce less than one-fourth the nation's grain needs. Nearly 4 million acres of arable British lands have passed out of cultivation as Canada and India have emerged as major suppliers.

Irish aircraft designer Harry Ferguson, 29, receives a request from the government's Ministry of Agriculture to help in the effort to maximize farm production as German U-boats cut off imports of foodstuffs. Ferguson is dismayed to find vast acreages devoted to producing feed for "power-animals" and sets out to develop "integrating implements" that can be used with tractors (*see* 1918).

German scientists develop mercury fungicide seed dressings that will prevent losses to plant diseases. In years to come, the mercury will take severe tolls of wildlife and some human life.

U.S. farmhands begin annual migrations north from Texas, traveling in Model T Fords and harvesting crops up to the Canadian border as they ripen.

The Smith-Lever Act passed by Congress May 8 provides for agricultural extension services by Department of Agriculture county agents working through the land-grant colleges established under the 1890

Morrill Act. An outgrowth of work done by Seaman Knapp and Theodore Roosevelt, the act authorizes federal appropriations to support state and local funding of farm and home demonstration agents.

A national 4-H Club is founded 14 years after the first such club was organized in Macoupin County, Ill. Sponsored by the U.S. Department of Agriculture, the 4-H Clubs direct their activities toward youths in rural areas, trying to improve "head, heart, hands, and health," and will help end prejudice against "book farming" along scientific lines.

George Washington Carver reveals the results of experiments that show the value of peanuts and sweet potatoes in replenishing soil fertility (*see* Carver, 1896). Southern cotton planters have in many instances been ruined by the boll weevil and begun turning to peanut and sweet potato culture, especially when Carver shows the many peanut by-products he has produced in his laboratory—not only flour, molasses, and vinegar but also cheese, milk, and coffee substitutes, synthetic rubber, plastics, insulating board, linoleum, soap, ink, dyes, wood stains, metal polish, and shaving cream.

Some 200,000 British schoolchildren receive free meals under the School Meals Act of 1906 (*see* Milk in Schools Scheme, 1931, 1934).

Food Products by Columbia University's Henry C. Sherman is a textbook that analyzes various foods and recommends that Americans cut their meat consumption by 50 percent.

Mary Janes—individually wrapped penny candies that combine molasses with peanut butter—are introduced by Charles N. Miller, a 30-year-old Boston confectionery company that began operations in Paul Revere's old house.

Canadian troops go to France with survival kits containing chocolates made by Wm. Neilson Ltd., a Toronto company founded in 1893 to manufacture ice cream. Its founder turned to making chocolates in the wintertime, when few people bought ice cream, and is now producing more than 500,000 pounds of chocolate per year.

Secretary of the Navy Josephus Daniels orders that Welch's grape juice be served in place of the Navy's traditional rum grog (*see* 1923; Bryan, 1913).

The state of Washington bars beer sales. Seattle Brewing and Malting Co. president Louis Henrich moves operations to San Francisco and renames his company Rainier.

U.S. essayist-music critic James Huneker writes that "cocktails and the common consumption of spirits have banished all sense of taste values."

Chero-Cola has sales of more than $611,000. The company files an application to register the name Chero-Cola, Coca-Cola Co. institutes a lawsuit to bar use of the name, and litigation will continue for years (*see* 1912; 1918).

Mama Leone's has its beginnings in a restaurant opened in a New York brownstone at 239 West 48th Street. Leone's wine shop has been near the back of the Metropolitan Opera house since 1906, Leone's wife has run a little restaurant above the shop, and the 48th Street establishment will prosper with the help of Mama's sons Gene and Celestine, taking over two adjacent houses.

The Paris cheese shop Androuët (above) will open a second-floor restaurant that will be good enough to win a star in the Michelin Guide.

Rosa Lewis of London's Cavendish Hotel continues to be the city's most sought-after caterer (*see* 1912), but in the next few years she will see many of the sons and grandsons of her favorite clients go off to the war in France, never to return.

1915

Germany's War Grain Association confiscates all stocks of wheat, corn, and flour at fixed prices, suspends private transactions in grain, fixes a bread ration, and orders municipalities to lay up stores of preserved meat as the Great War intensifies and Britain blockades German ports.

A German cruiser sinks a U.S. vessel with a cargo of wheat for Britain, whose own annual wheat crop is large enough to feed the nation only for 8 weeks. British flour mills at Bristol, Hull, Liverpool, and other port cities have long depended on shiploads of wheat that arrived from Argentina in March, Australia in April, Africa and India in June, Russia and America in August, and Canada in November.

Grain merchant Léopold Louis-Dreyfus dies at Paris April 5 at age 81, leaving his vast trading empire to his surviving sons Charles and Louis (*see* 1904). Rivaled only by Bunge (*see* 1876), his company has grown to become Europe's major grain wholesaler, buying huge quantities of wheat, corn, barley, and other crops from Russia, Romania, other Balkan countries, Canada, Australia, and the United States for delivery to small customers at Antwerp, Berlin, Brussels, London, and Rome (*see* 1934).

Joseph Campbell Co. is incorporated as the Campbell Soup Co. under John T. Dorrance (*see* 1905; 1922; Franco-American, below).

Cuban sugar production is owned 40 percent by U.S., 20 percent by other foreign interests.

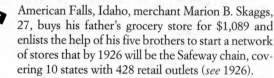

Franco-American is acquired by Campbell Soup Co. (above), which will market the company's canned spaghetti, canned soups, and other products. Started at Jersey City, N.J., in 1887 by émigré French soup maker Alphonse Biardot and his sons Ernest and Octave, Franco-American cans a wide variety of specialty items, including six kinds of truffled game pâté (*see* SpaghettiOs, 1965).

American Falls, Idaho, merchant Marion B. Skaggs, 27, buys his father's grocery store for $1,089 and enlists the help of his five brothers to start a network of stores that by 1926 will be the Safeway chain, covering 10 states with 428 retail outlets (*see* 1926).

Plans are completed for a double-hulled tanker that will carry California wines through the Panama Canal from dockside San Francisco to dockside Brooklyn, N.Y., at a cost of only 1¢/gal., with a cargo of steel rails to be carried on the return voyage, but U.S. entry into the Great War and Prohibition will abort construction of the vessel.

Corning Glass researchers Eugene C. Sullivan and William C. Taylor develop Pyrex glass, whose heat-resistant and shock-resistant borosilicate glass will be used in oven dishes and coffeemakers.

Cookbook: *The School Kitchen Textbook: Lessons in Cooking and Domestic Science for the Use of Elementary Schools* by Mary Johnson Lincoln. Fannie Merritt Farmer has died at Boston January 15 at age 57.

U.S. per capita consumption of white granulated sugar reaches a level twice what it was in 1880 as Americans give up molasses and brown sugar in favor of white sugar.

Cattleman Joseph G. McCoy dies at Kansas City October 19 at age 77 (*see* 1867).

The U.S. wheat crop totals 1 billion bushels for the first time as American farmers respond to high wartime wheat prices by plowing and planting millions of acres never before planted (*see* 1921; 1934). The Hessian fly introduced in 1776 causes $100 million worth of damage to the crop, which breaks all records nevertheless.

The Cortland apple is created in upstate New York by crossing a Ben Davis with a McIntosh.

The German warship *Kronprinz Wilhelm* puts into Newport News, Va., with 50 sailors suffering from beriberi (*see* Suzuki, 1912; Williams, 1933).

Pellagra is shown to be the product of southern diets based largely on corn and not a disease spread by any bacteria (*see* 1913). Joseph Goldberger of the U.S. Public Health Service has conducted tests using inmates of Mississippi's Rankin Prison, who have volunteered to go on corn products diets in return for sentence reductions (*see* Elvehjem, 1936).

U.S. dairy interests establish the National Dairy Council, partly at the suggestion of E. V. McCollum (*see* 1912). One purpose of the council is to fund nutrition research.

Mayo Foundation researcher Edward Calvin Kendall, 29, isolates the thyroid hormone thyroxine. Deficiencies produce goiters which Mayo Clinic co-founder Charles H. Mayo, now 50, has made a career of removing surgically (*see* Marine, 1905; Akron, 1916).

France outlaws the sale of absinthe March 16, and other countries quickly follow suit (*see* United States, 1912). The French government has used the excuse that alcohol is needed for gunpowder production to halt sale of the liqueur following 10 years of agitation triggered by the murder of his wife and two daughters by a delirious man who regularly consumed six quarts of wine, six brandies, and two absinthes each day.

Kraft processed cheese is introduced by Chicago's 5-year-old J. L. Kraft & Bros., which has developed a process that arrests the bacterial curing of cheese without subjecting it to such high temperatures as to cause oil separation (*see* 1909). James L. Kraft's four brothers have joined him as active partners in a business whose sales will jump from $5,000 this year to $150,000 next. Processed, or "American," cheese—ground bits of pasteurized cheddar or other natural cheese that is stirred with an emulsifier and water into a smooth, homogeneous fluid and packed initially in tins—will hereafter constitute a growing part of Kraft's cheese business (*see* 1917; Kraft-Phenix, 1928; National Dairy Corp., 1929).

Holsum bread is introduced by U.S. bakers affiliated with Chicago bakery service head W. E. (William Edgar) Long, 42, whose W. E. Long Co. encourages modern marketing practices such as wrapping each loaf of bread hygienically instead of delivering it unwrapped in open wagons, where it is exposed to flies and dirt.

Kellogg's 40% Bran Flakes are introduced by the Battle Creek Toasted Corn Flake Co. (*see* 1911; 1919).

Black tea still represents only about 30 percent of the tea consumed in America (*see* 1904).

The Singapore Sling is invented at Singapore's Raffles Hotel by barman Ngian Tong Doon, who mixes two ounces of gin, an ounce of cherry brandy, a few drops of Cointreau, an ounce of orange, lemon, or pineapple juice, and two or three dashes of Angostura bitters, adding a slice of pineapple or a cherry.

Van de Kamp's Saratoga Chips opens at Los Angeles January 6 in an eight-foot-wide storefront with a sign that reads "Made clean, kept clean, sold clean." Entrepreneur Lawrence Louis Frank, 27, has left his native Milwaukee, where his family has had a meat-packing company since before the Civil War, and in 1913 married Henrietta Van de Kamp in the Los Angeles home of his brother Ralph, who has had a small potato chip–manufacturing business in downtown L.A. Henrietta's brother Theodore J. Van de Kamp has loaned Frank $100 to open the potato chip shop, which soon begins carrying additional products (*see* Van de Kamp Bakers, 1918).

San Francisco's Clift Hotel opens in time to receive visitors to the city's Panama-Pacific International Exposition. Its dining room will be famous for its prime ribs, served with horseradish sauce and Yorkshire pudding, and its silver-domed trolleys of turkey and beef.

The first Kiwanis Club is organized, continuing the boom in U.S. men's luncheon clubs that began 10 years ago with the first Rotary Club (*see* Lions Club, 1917).

London's second J. Lyons & Co. Corner House, in the Strand, opens with 2,600 seats (*see* 1909). It will continue operating until 1976 (*see* 1928).

1916

Germany establishes a War Food Office as Britain's naval blockade forces strict rationing of food.

A German potato blight contributes to starvation that kills 700,000 civilians and weakens morale in the army.

France sets a maximum wheat price of 33 francs per quintal (220 pounds) to the farmer and sets controls on butter, cheese, and oil cakes. Parisians line up in milk queues.

A British Departmental Committee on Food Prices is established after a sharp rise in food prices by June has brought complaints of profiteering. On September 29 the government proposes one meat-less day each week September 29 in hopes of reducing prices. Two-thirds of Britain's sugar came from Austria-Hungary before the war, and sugar prices have risen steeply.

British bread prices begin moving up from 9½ d. per four-pound loaf, an Order in Council empowers the Board of Trade to regulate food supplies and fix prices, but the president of the Board of Trade tells the House of Commons in October that there is no need to establish a Ministry of Food or to appoint a food controller: "We want to avoid any rationing of our people in food."

British bakers face charges of profiteering in early November after raising the price of bread to 10 d. per four-pound loaf. Lower-class families say that costlier bread will deprive them of their staple diet, but bakers increase prices in the knowledge that prices will probably be frozen by law following a report by a commission on wheat imports. Thousands of trade unionists demonstrate in London's Hyde Park to protest the higher prices.

Port of London Authority chairman Hudson Ewbanke Kearley, 60, viscount Devenport, is appointed food controller in December, but the government is not prepared to ration food. Lord Devenport appeals to the public to make voluntary sacrifices; he decrees that bread is to be sold only in units or multiples of one pound, a regulation that will be followed until 1945 (*see* 1878; 1917).

$ U.S. food prices rise 19 percent as crop shortfalls, railcar shortages, and increased demand from Britain (above) combine to put pressure on prices of bread, potatoes, and cabbage. Prices continue to rise until they have nearly doubled (*see* riots, 1917).

A Federal Farm Loan Act passed by Congress July 17 provides for Farm Loan Banks throughout the United States and creates a Federal Farm Loan Board. The legislation makes it easier for U.S. farmers to obtain credit with which to buy land, acquire farm machinery, and generally improve their productivity (*see* Agricultural Credits Act, 1923).

The contest for control of Cargill ends in victory for the family of John MacMillan, now 55, who married the late Will Cargill's daughter Edna early in 1895 (*see* 1909). The MacMillans buy out Cargill's son William for $25,000 in cash plus some gold railroad bonds and notes with a value of $250,000 (*see* 1922).

Ohio farmer's son Dale W. McMillen, 36, buys a small Fort Wayne, Ind., grain elevator for $2,000 cash, assumes an $8,000 debt, and soon becomes a feed manufacturer, promoting under the name Wayne Feeds a concentrate feed, or supplement, which supplies ingredients not grown by the farmer who raises livestock. The supplement is designed to be mixed with the farmer's homegrown grain (*see* Allied Mills, 1929).

Wilson & Co. is founded at Chicago in a reorganization of the meatpacking firm Sulzberger & Sons, which started in 1853 as Swarzchild and Sulzberger, built a slaughterhouse at Cedar Rapids in 1871, bought a Kansas City plant in 1893, moved to Chicago in 1908, bought an Oklahoma City

plant in 1911, and in 1913 became the first U.S. meatpacker in Brazil. Thomas E. Wilson, head of the 2-year-old Wilson Sporting Goods Co., takes over as president of the reorganized company (*see* Ling-Temco-Vought, 1967).

U.S. courts break up the Corn Products Refining Co. "gluten trust" organized by E. T. Bedford in 1906, but Bedford retains control of a major share of U.S. corn-refining capacity (*see* 1913; 1923).

California Packing Co. is incorporated at San Francisco with a $16 million Wall Street underwriting promoted by George N. Armsby, son of Jacob (*see* 1865; Del Monte, 1891). Now the largest U.S. fruit and vegetable canner, Calpak operates 61 canneries, including some in Washington, Oregon, and Idaho (*see* 1895; 1917; seafood, below; Del Monte, 1967).

$ The Piggly-Wiggly opened at Memphis, Tenn., by food merchant Clarence Saunders begins the first supermarket chain (*see* California, 1912; San Francisco, 1923; King Kullen, 1930).

The Piggly Wiggly pioneered self-service grocery retailing.
LIBRARY OF CONGRESS

U.S. railroad trackage reaches its peak of 254,000 miles, up from 164,000 in 1890. The total will decline, but only marginally.

A mechanical home refrigerator is marketed for the first time in the United States, but its $900 price discourages buyers, who can buy a good motorcar for the same money (*see* 1925; Frigidaire, 1919; GE, 1927).

U.S. millers and bakers begin using potassium bromate (or, sometimes, calcium bromate) to mature their flour and improve its baking properties. Flour has heretofore had to be aged for some months to let oxygen condition it; the chemical ages the flour almost instantaneously, and the baking process converts its bromate into bromide, which is easily absorbed in digestion and perfectly safe. The chemical compound azodicarbonamide, which will come increasingly to replace bromate as a flour conditioner, will not bleach the flour but will oxidize its protein (gluten), making it more manageable and capable of producing lighter, more voluminous loaves of bread.

U.S. factories produce quantities of filled milk made with vegetable oil instead of butterfat to the consternation of dairymen (see 1923).

English physiologist Edward A. Sharpey-Schafer, 60, introduces the word "insuline" for the hormone produced by the islets of Langerhans in the human pancreas (see 1869; von Mering, 1889; Banting, 1922).

Cookbook: Mrs. Allen's Cook Book by U.S. author Ida Cogswell Allen (née Bailey), 32.

British fuel shortages motivate Parliament to pass a "summer time" act and most European governments do the same, advancing clocks one hour to make the most of available light. Britain moves her clocks ahead one hour May 21, but farmers protest that they must milk their cows in the dark and then wait idly until the sun has evaporated the dew before they can harvest hay (see Franklin, 1784; Congress, 1918).

Florida's Gulf Coast has a "red tide" caused by a proliferation of the dinoflagellate plankton Gymnodinium breve. The red tide kills millions of fish, whose nervous systems are immobilized by the expelled waste of G. breve (see 1932).

Calpak (above) owns a 70 percent interest in the Alaska Packers Association, whose Star Fleet continues as the last commercial sailing fleet to fly the American flag.

A Stockraising Homestead Act doubles the amount of land allowed under the Homestead Act of 1909, but even 640 acres—a full square mile—is too small in many areas (see 1862). Failed homesteaders will soon sell their land to stockmen bent on acquiring large ranches (see Taylor Grazing Act, 1934).

U.S. wheat farmers have another bumper crop despite an epidemic of black stem rust in the Dakotas. South Dakota State College student Edgar Sharp Mcfadden, 25, succeeds in cross-breeding Yaroslav emmer with several varieties of hard red spring wheat to create what will be known as the Yaroslav X Marquis cross. Mcfadden formed a Texas cattle-ranching partnership with his father at age 17 but has become more interested in plant epidemiology (see 1923).

The average U.S. corn farmer produces little more than 25 bushels per acre. Funk Brothers of Bloomington, Ill., ships the first hybrid seed corn to a Jacobsburg, Ohio, farmer. He pays $15 per bushel (see East and Shull, 1921; Golden Bantam, 1933).

The Japanese beetle Popillia japonica, whose grubs have arrived in the roots of imported nursery stock, appears for the first time in America at Riverton, N.J. The beetle will proliferate and damage millions of dollars worth of fruits and vegetables.

Russian-French bacteriologist Elie Metchnikoff dies of uremia July 15 at age 71, his arteries stiff with atherosclerosis (see 1907). It will turn out that Bulgarian peasants do not live so long as he believed, and his theory about the efficacy of yogurt to extend the lifespan will be substantially disproved (see Gayelord Hauser, 1950).

Vitamin B is isolated by E. V. McCollum, who believes it to be just one coenzyme (see 1912; Drummond, 1920; Smith, Hendrick, 1928).

The first large-scale study of iodine's effect on human goiter is conducted by U.S. physicians David Marine and E. C. Kendall (see 1905; Mayo Clinic, 1915). Girls in some Akron, Ohio, schools are given tablets containing 0.2 gram of sodium iodide, and the incidence of goiter in susceptible teenage girls given the tablets is found to drop markedly (see table salt, 1921).

Colorado Springs dentist Frederick S. Motley finds his patients' teeth are discolored but have few cavities. He begins to trace this to the fact that the city's drinking water contains fluoride salts in a concentration of two parts per million (see 1945).

Planters Nut and Chocolate introduces "Mr. Peanut" (see 1906). The company has conducted a contest among Suffolk, Va., high school students to find an appropriate trademark, the winner—Antonio Gentile, 14—has received a $5 prize for his sketch of an anthropomorphized peanut, and a commercial artist has added a monacle and a crooked leg (*see* Standard Brands, 1961).

Streit's matzohs are introduced by New York entrepreneur Aaron Streit, 41, who has gone into partnership with a Rabbi Weinberg and opened a matzoh bakery in Pitt Street on Manhattan's Lower East Side (*see* Manischewitz, 1888). Streit will incorporate the business in 1927, and when he dies 10 years later his son Jack, now 8, will take over, moving the plant to Rivington Street in 1933. Jack Streit will build the company into a manufacturer of 130 different kosher products, doing 65 percent its business before and during the Passover season.

Coca-Cola adopts the distinctive bottle shape that will identify it for years—a slimmer model of the waist-bulging bottle made at Terre Haute, Ind.,

Coca-Cola slimmed down its bottle and adopted the shape that would identify it for decades.

since 1913. The Supreme Court rules that if Coca-Cola is to claim a distinctive name it must contain some derivatives of cola beans and coca leaves but does not rule against the use of these substances in denatured form (*see* 1910; Woodruff, 1919).

Orange Crush Co. is incorporated at Chicago by entrepreneurs who employ a process developed by N. C. Ward using an orange concentrate obtained from the California Fruit Growers Exchange (*see* 1895). Made primarily of carbonated water and sugar, Orange Crush will be introduced into Canada and Latin America in the 1920s, and within 65 years it will be sold in more than 65 countries (*see* Hires, 1962).

The fortune cookie, created by Los Angeles noodle manufacturer David Jung, will soon be served at most Chinese restaurants. Chinese rebels in ancient times exchanged covert messages inside buns, and Jung has borrowed the idea, printing spurious Confucian adages and predictions on slips of paper which are concealed within thin folded cookies.

Nathan's Famous frankfurters have their beginning in a Coney Island, N.Y., hot dog stand at the corner of Stillwell and Surf avenues opened by Polish-American merchant Nathan Handwerker, 25, who sells his franks at 5¢ each—half the price charged by Feltman's German Gardens on Surf Avenue, where Handwerker has worked weekends as a counterman while making $4.50 per week as a delivery boy on the Lower East Side. Handwerker has invested his life savings of $300 in the hot dog stand and works 18 to 20 hours per day with his 19-year-old bride, Ida, who laces the franks with her secret spice recipe. Together, they prosper (*see* 1917).

Britain's Parliament enacts a licensing law that imposes opening and closing hours for public houses (pubs) and other places that serve alcoholic beverages: 11:30 in the morning until 3 in the afternoon and 5:30 to 10:30 (11 o'clock in London and a few other cities) from Monday to Saturday, noon until 2 o'clock and 7 to 10:30 on Sunday, Good Friday, and Christmas. When a publican announces, "Time, Gentlemen, please," all glasses must be cleared away. The law will stand until 1988.

1917

 The United States declares war on the Central Powers April 6 as Russian resistance ebbs. The hostilities have exhausted the resources of Britain and France, which have been fighting since 1914.

Allied troops on the Western Front sometimes ate under harrowing conditions but did not go hungry. LIBRARY OF CONGRESS

Riots have broken out in February in New York, Boston, and Philadelphia, where rising food prices have made it difficult for poor people to feed their families (*see* 1916). The New York rioters attack food shops and burn peddlers' pushcarts on the Lower East Side and in Brooklyn's Brownsville and Williamsburg sections, rejecting suggestions that they substitute rice for potatoes and milk for eggs and meat. Some 6,000 kosher poultry shops and 150 kosher poultry slaughterhouses close down just before Passover to protest wholesalers accused of cornering the market.

Beginning in February Britain's war bread is made from flour milled at an extraction rate of up to 81 percent with a compulsory admixture of 5 percent barley, oat, or rye flour to stretch available supplies. Food Controller Lord Devenport asks heads of families to limit their family bread consumption to four pounds per person each week, meat to 2.5 pounds, sugar to three-quarters of a pound.

Britain's House of Commons is stunned by news that 2 million tons of shipping have been lost to German U-boats and that the country has only 3 to 4 weeks' supply of food in stock.

200,000 Berlin factory workers strike for a week in April to protest a reduction in bread rations.

More than half the 875,000 tons of Allied shipping lost in April has been British. George V calls May 2 for national constraint on bread consumption.

European civilians often lacked food; admonishing U.S. civilians did little to help. LIBRARY OF CONGRESS

Prime Minister David Lloyd George, 54, prevails on the Admiralty to try convoying merchant vessels and convoys begin May 10 to safeguard shipments of U.S. foodstuffs, war matériel, and troops bound for Britain and Europe.

British retail food prices rise to 94 percent above July 1914 levels by the end of March. A four-pound loaf of bread fetches a shilling, and a Royal Commission reports that rising prices and faulty food distribution are creating industrial unrest.

Well-to-do Britons miss sugar, butter, and white bread, but price increases after July are at only one-fourth the rate earlier, and government subsidization of bread and other staples keeps food relatively cheap as compared with other commodities. Mostly because the war has virtually ended unemployment, British working-class diets actually improve, although potatoes are often in short supply, and long rows of women, many with children and some with infants in their arms, line up for margarine at London 2 weeks before Christmas.

An embargo proclamation issued by President Woodrow Wilson, 60, July 9 places exports of U.S. foodstuffs, fuel, iron, steel, and war matériel under government control. Congress passes a Food Control Act (Lever Act) August 10 and U.S. mining engineer Herbert C. Hoover, 43, who has served as chairman of the Commission for Relief in Belgium, is officially named food administrator (he has been unofficial administrator since March). Hoover encourages U.S. farmers with the slogan "Food Can Win the War."

Irish Republican Brotherhood leader Thomas Ashe dies September 25 at Mountjoy Prison while on a hunger strike following an attempt by prison authorities to feed him forcibly (he has led a campaign for prisoner-of-war status and, when this was refused, began the hunger strike with 29 others) (see 1920).

A Bolshevik Revolution begins at Petrograd (St. Petersburg) the night of November 6 (October 24 by the Julian calendar still used in Russia). Housewives waiting in endless bread shop lines have been demonstrating in protest, they are joined by soldiers from the Petrograd garrison, sailors from Kronstadt, and the factory workers' Red Guards, who seize government offices and storm the Winter Palace of the Romanovs. Russian peasants seize their landlords' fields.

U.S. wheat prices rise precipitously beginning in early spring as Allied governments, U.S. millers, and speculators bid up prices on the Chicago Board of Trade. Some 570 million bushels (92 percent) of the 620-million-bushel crop have left the farms by March and have been marketed before the price rise, so few farmers share in the bonanza. The Grain Corp. of Herbert Hoover's new Food Administration (above) buys, stores, transports, and sells wheat and fixes its price at $2.20 per bushel under terms of the Lever Act, which establishes control over fuel as well as food.

J. Lyons & Co. acquires W. H. and F. J. Horniman tea (see 1826) and Black & Green tea to supplement its Maharajah brand (see 1903; Greenford factory, 1923).

A&P founder George Huntington Hartford dies August 29 at Spring Lake, N.J. at age 83.

New York State's Erie Canal is replaced after 92 years by a modern barge canal 12 feet deep, 75 to 200 feet wide, 524 miles long. Steam power has made the old canal obsolete; the new barge canal makes use of an additional 382 miles of canalized lakes and rivers between Albany and lakes Ontario and Erie (see 1825; 1836).

Clarence Birdseye returns to his native New York to pursue the commercial exploitation of his food-freezing discoveries (see 1914). He has spent 3 years in Labrador, where obtaining fresh food for his young family has been an urgent problem. Birdseye has learned, after much experimentation, how to freeze cabbages in barrels of seawater, and he has found that frozen foods remain fresh when kept refrigerated at low temperatures (see 1923).

U.S. millers and bakers begin using benzoyl peroxide powder to age their flour and bleach it white (see nitrogen peroxide, 1903; potassium bromate, 1916).

Cookbook: Practical Food Economy by U.S. author Alice B. Kirk, published at Boston, says flatly, "Avoid fancy cooking."

Crème vichyssoise glacée is invented in the kitchen of New York's 7-year-old Ritz-Carlton Hotel. Chef Louis Diat has adapted his mother's hot soupe bonne femme to create a chilled cream soup of potatoes and leeks, using the white parts of the leeks and a half-and-half mixture of milk and cream, giving the mixture an extra screening, and adding a sprinkle of chives. He has named the soup vichyssoise after the spa located within 20 miles of his Bourbonnais home.

The Army Quartermaster Corps persuades chocolate companies to supply their product in 20-lb. blocks as a contribution to the war effort. Privates stationed at bases cut the blocks down into individual pieces, which they handwrap for distribution to the "doughboys."

StarKist Seafood has its beginnings in the French Sardine Co., opened at San Pedro, Calif., by Austrian-American entrepreneur Martin Bogdanovich, 35, and some partners who have invested $10,000 to start a cannery. Born on the Dalmatian isle of Vis, Bogdanovich came to San Pedro in 1908 with his bride, Antoinette; bought his first boat 2 years later; and has pioneered the idea of preserving fish on ice at sea (see 1944).

Sunsweet Growers has its beginnings in California Prune and Apricot Growers, which begins operations in March. The state's prune crop totals 224 million pounds, a new record (peaches, raisins, and other fruits also post record harvests), and the new growers' association is faced with the task of marketing three-fourths of the prunes at a time when the export market, which before the war took half the California prune crop and three-quarters of the dried apricot crop, has been closed by hostilities in Europe. The association selects Sunsweet as its trademark in August and, with the help of a national advertising campaign, succeeds in disposing of 105 million pounds of prunes and 13 million pounds of dried apricots at above-average prices (see prune juice, 1932).

Drought begins on the Western plains.

The Smith-Hughes Act passed by Congress provides funds to land-grant colleges for training home economics teachers, who will spread knowledge of new nutrition ideas based on economy and health rather than taste.

British military conscription finds that only three out of nine Britons of military age are fit and healthy. Poor nutrition is blamed.

Britain's Medical Council reports that at least half the children in industrial towns have rickets (see 1902).

Xerophthalmia is observed in Danish children whose diets are lacking in butterfats. Denmark has been exporting her butter to the warring powers even at the expense of her domestic needs, and dietary deficiency is endangering the children's eyesight (see Japan, 1904; McCollum, 1912).

The American Dietetic Association is founded at Cleveland.

U.S. bacteriologist Alice Evans, 36, begins work that will show the ability of the bacterium which causes contagious abortion (Bang's disease) in cattle to be passed to human beings, notably via raw milk, and produce undulant fever, or brucellosis (see Bruce, 1887; Bang, 1896). The dairy industry and medical profession will oppose Evans, but compulsory pasteurization of U.S. milk in the late 1920s will be achieved largely through her efforts in the next 9 years (see dairy practices, 1921).

The first national advertising for Del Monte brand canned fruits and vegetables appears April 21 in the *Saturday Evening Post* (see California Packing Corp., 1916). Calpak acquires the Hawaiian Preserving Corp., which owns pineapple fields and a cannery on Oahu, will acquire canneries in the next decade in Wisconsin, Minnesota, Illinois, and Florida, will start growing and packing pineapples in the Philippines, and will enter the sardine- and tuna-canning industries (see Del Monte, 1967).

The U.S. Army orders Kraft processed cheese from J. L. Kraft & Bros. (see 1915). By the end of next year the Army will have ordered 6 million tons (see 1921).

Stokely Brothers wins a U.S. Army contract for its canned vegetables (see 1898). Founder Anna R. Stokely and her son John were killed late last year, when their car stalled in the path of an oncoming train on a grade crossing at Newport, Tenn., and the company has been reorganized as Stokely Brothers (*see* 1921).

Clark Bars—honeycombed ground roasted peanuts covered with milk chocolate—are introduced by Pittsburgh candy maker David L. Clark, who started his business in 1886 and has done so well that 3 years ago he was able to buy a large factory built in 1892 by local cracker baker and confectioner James McClurg & Co.

New York's Hotel des Artistes opens at 1 West 67th Street. The cooperative apartment house has a communal kitchen for tenants (who will include dancer Isadora Duncan and screen idol Rudolf Valentino) and a restaurant, the Café des Artistes (*see* Christy murals, 1932).

The first Lions Club is organized as the boom in men's luncheon clubs continues (*see* Kiwanis, 1915).

Bon vivant financier James Buchanan "Diamond Jim" Brady dies in his $1,000-per-week ocean-view suite in Atlantic City's Shelburne Hotel April 13 at age 60, leaving a large bequest to the New York Hospital for research on urology. He barely survived gallstone surgery 5 years ago and has suffered for nearly 6 months from angina pectoris, diabetes, and severe kidney complications.

Nathan Handwerker counters rumors spread by his Coney Island rivals, who say that 5¢ hot dogs cannot be of the best quality (*see* 1916). He hires college students to stand at his counters wearing white jackets with stethoscopes hanging out of their pockets, and word spreads that doctors from Coney Island Hospital are eating Nathan's hot dogs.

1918

Hostilities in the Great War end in an armistice November 11 (*see* restaurant luncheon, below). "Hunger does not breed reform; it breeds madness," says President Wilson in an Armistice Day address to Congress. A dinner for 712 guests that evening at London's Carlton House begins with a potage à victoire and continues with other dishes prepared under the supervision of chef Auguste Escoffier.

Chef Auguste Escoffier supervised preparation of the London victory banquet following World War I.

British food rationing has begun with sugar January 1. The government has called January 22 for 2 meatless days per week a restaurants. Rationing of butter and margarine has begun February 25. By summer, all important foodstuffs are rationed except for bread and potatoes. Fresh meat is rationed by price, and consumers are required to buy from a particular butcher to avoid deception. Ration books are issued in July, and the bacon ration is raised from 8 ounces per week to 16 ounces. Other rationed commodities include eight ounces of sugar, five ounces of butter and/or margarine, four ounces of jam, and two ounces of tea (weekly).

Britain's flour-milling extraction rate is raised to 92 percent, up from 81 percent last year, with soy and potato flour mixed in to stretch Britain's short wheat supplies. The bread is dark and unattractive.

France rations bread and restricts consumption of butter, cream, and soft cheese. Manufacture and sale of all confectionery is banned.

U.S. Secretary of Agriculture David F. Houston issues a circular May 2 entitled, "Use Soy-Bean Flour to Save Wheat, Meat, and Fat." It gives recipes for "victory bread," soybean "meat loaf," and soybean mush croquettes, but few U.S. farmers produce soybeans, few facilities exist to process the beans, and few stores carry soy products (*see* agriculture, 1920).

U.S. sugar rationing begins July 1 with each citizen allowed eight ounces per week. U.S. Food Administrator Herbert Hoover asks for voluntary observance of wheatless Mondays and Wednesdays, meatless Tuesdays, porkless Thursdays and Saturdays, and the use of dark "Victory bread."

The U.S. Food Administration orders severe limitations on use of sugar in less essential food products, including soft drinks. As shortages of sugar continue, the Administration prepares to declare the entire soft drink industry nonessential and to order the industry closed down for the duration, but the threat fails to materialize and sugar prices begin to soar (*see* 1920; American Sugar Refining, 1919).

All food regulations are suspended in the United States in late December but remain in effect in Britain and Europe.

$ Britain's Hovis Bread-Flour Co. changes its name to Hovis Ltd. (*see* 1899). It began milling operations at Cape Town, South Africa, in 1905 and in New South Wales, Australia, a year later and in 1912 moved its London operation from the Imperial Mills, Westminster, to a new mill at the foot of Vauxhall Bridge. Having acquired Haverhill Mill in 1915, Hovis acquires Hedingham Mill and will make further acquisitions in the 1920s (*see* Canada, 1926).

Van de Kamp's Holland Dutch Bakers is incorporated at Los Angeles (*see* potato chips, 1915). Lawrence L. Frank will dress his saleswomen in blue-and-white costumes, hire a Hollywood art director to design a portable windmill store with a separate wooden cupola, body, and vanes, and build a chain of 36 such stores selling baked goods throughout southern California (*see* restaurant, 1922).

International Harvester's share of the U.S. harvesting machine industry falls to 65 percent, down from 85 percent in 1902. The Supreme Court dismisses a dissolution decree obtained by the Department of Justice from a district court (*see* 1912; 1927).

Italian-American pasta maker Emanuele Ronzoni, 48, acquires American-made macaroni machinery and incorporates under his own name. Production manager for the past 12 years of a Brooklyn, N.Y.,

macaroni factory, Ronzoni has seen the growing demand for U.S.–made pasta products. With the help, first, of his two daughter and, later, of his three sons, he will have so much success supplying the Italian-American market with macaroni, spaghetti, and egg noodles that he will build a large Long Island City, N.Y., factory in 1925 and will start selling under the Ronzoni name in 1932 (*see* Hershey, 1990).

New York's Breakstone Brothers moves to a larger building at 195 Franklin Street (*see* 1899). It has become a large producer of condensed milk for the armed forces and will soon begin manufacturing cream cheese at Downsville, N.Y. (*see* National Dairy, 1928).

Wartime demand has multiplied Nestlé sales (*see* 1905). Nestlé has 100 milk condenseries in the United States plus scores in other countries.

Cadbury's acquires Joseph Fry & Sons, pioneer producer of candy bars, in the first major British candy-company consolidation (*see* Cadbury Schweppes, 1969).

Harry Ferguson receives a British patent for a means of attaching a plow to a tractor (*see* 1914). Further patents will be issued to him from 1926 through 1929 as he develops hydraulic methods for ensuring automatic depth control in tillage (*see* 1920).

Hobart Manufacturing Co. inventor Herbert L. Johnston receives a patent April 23 for an electric mixing machine for stores and bakeries (*see* 1897). He will adapt it to kitchen use and will also invent electric food cutters, potato peelers, and potato slicers (thousands of young U.S. men are now peeling potatoes by hand for consumption by "doughboys").

U.S. inventor Charles Strite patents the first automatic pop-up toaster (*see* 1908). Designers in the next decade will invent bread-holding doors which pull down, out, or sideways so that slices of bread can be flipped over to toast the other side (*see* Toastmaster, 1926).

Milton S. Hershey hands over 500,000 of his 729,000 shares of Hershey Chocolate Co. stock to provide a $60 million endowment fund for the Milton Hershey School for Orphan Boys established in

Hershey Bar creator Milton S. Hershey used his fortune to endow an industrial school. PHOTO COURTESY HERSHEY FOODS

1909 (the gift will not be announced until 1923). The school will retain all of its Hershey stock until 1927, when some stock will be sold to the public to raise funds.

President Wilson orders a 1,700-piece service of Lenox china for the White House, the first U.S.-made porcelain to be used in the executive mansion (*see* 1889).

Average per capita British consumption of "butcher's meat" falls to 1.53 lb. per week, down from 2.36 in 1914. Average per capita sugar consumption falls to .93 lb., down from 1.49 in 1914 (*see* rationing, above), but calorie intake remains close to 1914 levels and the British eat far better than do their enemies.

U.S. candy sales escalate in the second half of the year as the Food Administration permits confectioners to use 80 percent of the amount of sugar they used before the war, up from 50 percent last year. Distribution of candy to soldiers in the field has increased men's demand for sweets; more significantly, perhaps, high wages have put more money into people's pockets and there is not that much to spend it on. Industry employs more women than ever before, and the chief candy buyers are women.

Americans call sauerkraut "liberty cabbage"; German toast becomes "French toast."

The North American lobster catch falls to a low point of 33 million pounds, down from its all-time high of 130 million in 1885.

Prime Minister David Lloyd George asks British women to help bring in the harvest.

Congress enacts a "summer time" daylight-saving law that follows the example of Britain and Europe. The new law angers U.S. farmers as it has angered the British (*see* 1916), and Congress will repeal the law next year, overriding President Wilson's veto.

More horses and mules are on U.S. farms than ever before, and enormous acreages are planted to oats for the animals, whose numbers will now decline.

Horse-drawn wheat combines used in the Pacific Northwest with 16- and 20-foot cuts are reduced in size to 12-foot cuts for use in Kansas and other prairie states. Machines with 8- and 10-foot cuts will be introduced in the 1920s.

U.S. Corn Belt acreage sells for two and three times 1915 prices.

The Dutch Staats-General appropriates money to drain the Zuider Zee for the creation of fertile dry land. The Dutch will build dams, dykes, sluiceways, watergates, canals, and locks to "impolder" more than 800,000 acres that will increase the territory of the Netherlands by 7 percent (*see* 1932).

English researcher Edward Mellanby shows that cod-liver oil contains an agent that cures rickets, giving recognition to a treatment used by North Sea mothers for generations (*see* McCollum, 1921).

Yale biochemists Lafayette Benedict Mendel and B. Cohen show that guinea pigs cannot develop vitamin C (ascorbic acid) and fall prey to scurvy even more easily than do humans (*see* Drummond, 1920; Szent-Györgyi, 1928).

Contadina canned tomato sauce is introduced by Hershel Fruit Products Co. of Hershel, Calif., which began processing and distributing tomato products 2 years ago (*see* Nestlé, 1963).

Old El Paso brand Mexican foods have their beginnings on a Deming, N.M., farm, where the Powell family starts canning vegetables. They will found the Mountain Pass Canning Co., which will develop a line of canned soups, refried beans, and sauces (*see* Pet Inc., 1968).

The nickel Hershey Bar, which weighed $\%_{16}$ oz. in 1908, now weighs $^{15}\!/_{16}$ oz. and the company's gross sales top $35 million, up from little more than $10 million in 1915.

Chero-Cola has sales of close to $1.5 million and establishes its own sugar refinery to maintain its supply (*see* 1914; 1920).

Jamaica's Red Stripe beer is introduced by Kingston brewers Desnoes and Geddes, whose dark, alelike brew will give way in 1934 to a light-tasting lager.

The Birmingham, Ala., cafeteria Britling's opened by restaurateur A. W. B. Johnson (he has taken the name from the 1916 H. G. Wells novel *Mr. Britling Sees It Through*) specializes in rice, chicken, fried fish, meat loaf, and other home-style foods served with hot vegetables and cool salads. It will be followed by many southern cafeterias, including Furr's (Lubbock, Texas); Luby's (San Antonio); Morrison's (a chain based in Mobile); Piccadilly (Baton Rouge); S&W (Asheville, N.C.); and Wyatt's (Dallas).

The New Orleans restaurant Arnaud's, opened at 813 Rue Bienville by Basque restaurateur Leon Bertrand Arnaud Cazenave, competes with Antoine's, Galatoire's, and the Commander Palace. Cazenave's daughter Germaine will take over upon his death in 1948 (*see* 1979).

The New York dairy restaurant Ratner's moves to larger premises at 138 Delancey Street near the Williamsburg Bridge (*see* 1905). Jacob Harmatz will buy out Morris Ratner's interest in the 1920 and will grow with help from Max and Louis Zankel (and crowds from the neighboring Loew's Delancey vaudeville theater) to serve onion rolls, bagels, challah, matzoh brie, chopped liver, lox, Nova Scotia salmon, vegetarian dishes, pastries, and blintzes, in addition to borscht, matzoh-ball soup, and gefilte fish.

The Paris restaurant Lucas at 9, place de la Madeleine plays host at lunch November 10 to Generals Foch, Joffre, and Pershing, who decide the hour for the armistice to be signed on the following day (*see* above; Lucas Carton, 1925).

The Dutch restaurant Royal opens at The Hague in a house built in 1534; its menu will feature Zeeland oysters, smoked eel, crabs thermidor, and ris de veau cardinale (with a lobster sauce containing claws).

1919

Belgian food prices drop by 50 percent, British by 25 percent, but prices remain high elsewhere in Europe in the wake of the Great War. German ports are blockaded until July 12. Eastern Europe has famine as a result of poor crops and the shortage of manpower. Vienna cuts bread rations to four ounces per week in late December.

French beef, mutton, pork, and veal prices have increased nearly sixfold since 1914, reports *Le Petit Journal*, and egg, cheese, and butter prices have increased fourfold. France removes restrictions on the sale of beans, peas, rice, eggs, and condensed milk, and then on bread, but while the wartime ban on sugar imports is lifted, the import duty on sugar is raised to almost prohibitive levels.

U.S. food prices remain far above 1914 levels. Milk is 15¢/qt., up from 9¢; sirloin steak 61¢/lb., up from 32¢; fresh eggs 62¢/doz., up from 34¢.

The Dairymen's League founded in 1907 is reincorporated at New York under the name Dairymen's League Cooperative Association. Members will pool their milk and sell it at different prices depending on how it will be used (*see* 1921).

Di Giorgio Farms is organized by Italian-American fruit merchant Giuseppe Di Giorgio, now 45, who started the Baltimore Fruit Exchange in 1904 and has begun buying acreage in California's San Joaquin Valley.

Barilla pasta production at Parma, Italy, reaches 300 quintals (30,000 kilograms) per day (*see* 1875). Riccardo Barilla, now 39, rented a building with a large warehouse in 1907–1908, has made frequent visits across the Alps to Germany since the war to increase his technical knowledge, and employs a workforce of 300. Barilla will diversify into egg-based pastas, and by the 1930s its pastas will be sold throughout Italy and her colonies (*see* 1948).

Henry J. Heinz dies at Pittsburgh May 14 at age 74 (*see* 1905). His company has grown to include seed farms, container factories, and more than a score of food-processing plants.

Nebraska Consolidated Mills is created September 29 by a merger of Henry Glade Milling Co. (*see* 1910), Ravenna Mills, Hastings Mills, and the Blackburn-Furry Mill of St. Edward, Nebr. Alva R. Kinney, 44, president of Ravenna Mills, heads the new company, which will double its milling capacity in 1922 by acquiring Omaha's Updike Mill and move its headquarters from Grand Island to Omaha (*see* Duncan Hines, 1951).

The Fleischmann Co. launches a national advertising campaign to urge housewives to buy bakery bread instead of baking at home. The company now sells most of its yeast to commercial bakers (*see* 1876; Standard Brands, 1929).

Red Star Yeast and Products Co. is adopted as the name of what began in 1882 as the Meadow Springs Distillery. Prohibition (below) does not hurt sales of yeast, and the Milwaukee concern now has more than 33 branches throughout the Midwest and East, including major outlets in Kansas City, Louisville, and Detroit. By 1921 it will have 50 branches, and that number will quickly grow to 80 as Red Star improves its yeast through an aeration process introduced last year.

American Sugar Refining enters production by acquiring Central Cunagua, a Cuban sugar plantation of 100,000 acres with a huge mill (central) a railroad, and a town of 1,000 (*see* 1911; 1920).

The Dutch margarine maker Van den Bergh accepts an invitation from Centra, a powerful rival to Schichte in the European margarine industry, and acquires a 50 percent interest in Centra in October (*see* 1871; 1895; 1905; 1908). Schichte tries to persuade Centra to work with it instead of with Van den Bergh and agrees November 20 to divide the European market with Jurgens, Van den Bergh, Centra, and other concerns in Austria, Hungary, and Czechoslovakia, with Schichte to receive half the profits and the other half to be divided among the others. The Dutch makers agree not to set up separate margarine factories in those countries or mount export drives there (*see* Margarine Union, 1920).

London's Crosse & Blackwell acquires local meat-sauce maker E. Lazenby & Sons (*see* 1776) and Dundee marmalade maker James Keiller & Sons (*see* 1797; Nestlé, 1960).

Paris *épicier* Pierre Legrand acquires a 39-year-old *épicerie* and *confiserie* at the corner of the Rue de la Banque and the Rue des Petits-Pères near the Bourse. He and his son will sell mustard, foie gras, and similar items but will concentrate mostly on wines, cognacs, and whiskies.

British and U.S. millers and bakers begin using Agene (nitrogen trichloride gas) to bleach their flour; their counterparts in many other countries follow suit (*see* benzoyl peroxide, 1917; Mellanby, 1946).

U.S. margarine production reaches a level of 1 pound to every 2.4 pounds of butter, up from 1 to every 5 pounds in 1914 (*see* 1881; 1921).

A Boston molasses tank explodes in the North End just before 1 o'clock on the afternoon of January 15, hurtling sharp-edged steel plates into the girders of the elevated railway (an El from the South Station is approaching along a trestle over the street en route to the North Station), killing at least 13, injuring 60, and sending a sticky flood of thick brown molasses down Atlantic Avenue. The United States Industrial Alcohol Company, whose Cambridge distillery produced alcohol for the manufacture of munitions beginning in 1914, had more than 2.3 million gallons of crude molasses in the tank, whose explosion is attributed to fermentation (experts dismiss rumors of foul play by temperance workers on the eve of Prohibition; *see* below).

The U.S. Food Administration allots candy makers 90 percent of their normal prewar consumption of sugar in the second half of the year, but they are still unable to meet the sharply increased demand for sweets (*see* 1918). Average per capita candy consumption is 13.5 pounds, up from 5.6 pounds in 1914.

Famine in eastern Europe (above) boosts demand for U.S. wheat. Prices soar to $3.50 per bushel and farmers are encouraged to plant wheat on land never before tilled (*see* 1915; 1921; dust bowl, 1934).

Nearly 500,000 acres of Jones Winter Fife wheat and 1 million acres of Red Wave, both developed by agronomist Albert N. Jones, now 76, are harvested in the United States with additional acreage in Canada (*see* 1886). Jones moved from Leroy, N.Y., to Newark, N.Y., in 1893 and to Batavia, N.Y., in 1905.

Wisconsin agricultural scientist John Charles Walker, 26, explores genetic resistance to plant disease in cabbages and joins the faculty of the University of Wisconsin, from which he received his doctorate and where he will pioneer in developing disease-resistant varieties of beans, beets, cucumbers, onions, and peas, as well as cabbages.

Diet evangelist Horace Fletcher dies of bronchitis at Copenhagen January 13 at age 68 (*see* 1903). He gave up his residence in New York's Waldorf Hotel before the war, took an apartment in 31st Street near First Avenue in order to spread his ideas where they would do the most good, and in 1912 lived on a diet of potatoes for 58 days. During the war he served as a food economist for the Commission for Relief in Belgium and demonstrated to 8 million starving Belgians his method for obtaining the optimum nutritive value from their food. Interest in "Fletcherism" (commonly called "Fletcherizing") has waned and will now disappear almost completely.

A team of scientists from Britain's year-old Accessory Food Factors Committee studies malnutrition in famine-stricken Vienna (above). Harriette Chick and her colleagues find scurvy common among infants, note a serious increase in rickets, and prove the success of good nutrition in curing rickets.

Edward Mellanby finds that rickets is not an infection as has been widely believed but rather the result of a dietary vitamin deficiency (*see* 1918; Drummond, McCollum, 1920; McCollum, 1922).

The U.S. Pure Food and Drug Law of 1906 is amended once again to eliminate loopholes (*see* 1912; 1913; but *see* Kallet, Schlink, 1932).

"Sunkist" is burned into the skin of a California orange with a heated flyswatter by California Fruit Growers Exchange executive Don Francisco, 27, who urges that citrus fruit marketed by the Exchange be stamped with the name. It will be the first trademark to identify a fresh fruit commodity (*see* 1895; Chiquita Banana, 1944).

Frigidaire is selected as the name of a new refrigerator produced by General Motors Corp., which has paid $56,000 to acquire Guardian Refrigerator Co., a one-man firm that was close to bankruptcy. The name has come out of a contest sponsored by GM, which will make Frigidaire almost a generic for refrigerator.

Kellogg's All-Bran is introduced by the Battle Creek Toasted Corn Flakes Co. (*see* 1915; 1922).

Malt-O-Meal hot cereal is introduced by Minneapolis miller John Campbell, whose family-owned company will make puffed rice and puffed wheat cold cereals at its Northfield, Minn., plant beginning in the 1960s and develop a business of duplicating other companies' breakfast foods and marketing them at lower prices without advertising.

The brand name Veryfine is introduced by the 54-year-old New England Vinegar Works, which began as the Standard Vinegar Co. at Somerville, Mass., was acquired in 1900 by its salesman Arthur E. Rowse, and was renamed in 1907 (*see* apple juice, 1944).

U.S. ice cream sales reach 150 million gallons, up from 30 million in 1909.

The Eskimo Pie has its beginnings in the "I-Scream-Bar," a chocolate-covered ice cream stick patented by Danish-born schoolteacher–candy store proprietor Christian Nelson of Onawa, Iowa (*see* 1921; Good Humor, 1920).

Peter Paul Manufacturing Co. is incorporated at New Haven, Conn., by candy maker Peter Paul Halajian and five Armenian-American friends named Kazanjian, Shamlian, Hagopian, and Choulijian (*see* 1899). Their first candy bar is a blend of coconut, fruits, nuts, and chocolate sold under the name Konabar (*see* Mounds, 1922).

Nestlé introduces the Nestlé Milk Chocolate Bar, with or without almonds, in U.S. markets. Nestle's sales have multiplied during the war and the company has 100 U.S. milk condenseries.

An 18th Amendment to the Constitution prohibiting the sale, transportation, importation, and exportation of intoxicating beverages is proclaimed January 16 to go into effect January 16, 1920; a War Prohibition Act passed last year goes into effect at the end of June to continue until demobilization. The Prohibition Enforcement Act (Volstead Act), drafted by

Minnesota congressman Andrew J. Volstead and passed over President Wilson's veto October 28, defines as "intoxicating" any beverage containing 0.5 percent alcohol or more but makes a few exceptions, such as wine for sacramental purposes (*see* 1920).

Thirsty Americans flock to Havana, where Sloppy Joe's is called the national American saloon.

Compania Ron Bacardí, S.A., is incorporated in Cuba by Facundo and José Bacardí and Henri Schueg, sons and son-in-law of the late Emilio Bacardí, who started the distillery in 1862. They have run the rum company as a partnership for some years following the death of the senior Bacardí. Bacardí Rum will grow to become the world's most popular brand of liquor, selling upward of 23 million cases per year by 1991.

Coca-Cola's Asa G. Candler turns 68 and sells out for $25 million to a group headed by Ernest Woodruff (*see* 1916; 1923).

Homogenized milk is sold successfully for the first time in the United States, at Torrington, Conn. (*see* 1904). Arthur G. Weigold of the Torrington Creamery has tried to sell the milk on his home-delivery routes, consumers accustomed to having a cream line at the top of their milk bottles have resisted the new product, but Weigold sells the milk to restaurateurs, many of whose patrons find it better tasting, more uniform in appearance, and more digestible than ordinary milk, although some object that it tastes sterilized (*see* 1932; Canada, 1927).

Louis Sherry's New York restaurant closes after 21 years on Fifth Avenue. It will reopen on Park Avenue, where it will continue for some years, and the Louis Sherry name will survive as a brand name for ice cream and chocolates.

New York's Algonquin Round Table gets under way in June with luncheons at the 17-year-old Algonquin Hotel (59 West 44th Street). Manager Frank Case, 49, will for years play host to journalists, literati, publishers, and actors (Franklin P. Adams, Robert Benchley, Heywood Broun, Marc Connelly, Frank Crowninshield, Edna Ferber, George S. Kaufman, Alfred Lunt, Dorothy Parker, Alexander Woollcott, and others) whose witty remarks ("I've got to get out of these wet clothes and into a dry martini") and malicious ripostes will be widely quoted, whether or not they originated over the luncheon table.

The New York restaurant L'Aiglon opens at 13 East 55th Street, opposite the St. Regis Hotel, where it will continue for more than 50 years. Named for Napoleon's only son, it will be popular for its French and Italian dishes, including crabmeat crêpes with Mornay sauce, *bisque d'homard*, spaghetti *ammiraglio* (linguine), Dover sole, brook trout *meunière*, sautéed pompano, and Napoléon maison filled with whipped cream that has been flavored with tangerine and orange liqueurs.

The New York restaurant The Lobster opens at 145 West 45th Street, where it will continue for more than 70 years. The sons of founders Max Fuchs and Simon Linz will carry on the business, wrapping lobsters in napkins and placing them in cold water, bringing the water to a boil, and letting it simmer for 15 to 20 minutes, depending on size, then plunging the lobster into cold water to stop the cooking at just the right moment (they will never plunge a lobster into boiling water, believing that this will cause the muscles to contract from shock and make the flesh tough). They also broil lobsters over charcoal, brushing them first with butter and then letting them broil, 8 minutes per side, shell side first.

The Los Angeles restaurant Vickman's opens to serve bacon and eggs, hotcakes, hamburgers, and sandwiches; it will move in 1930 to 1228 East 8th Street, where it will serve patrons at long tables in a large room decorated with pictures of Henry VIII, gaining a reputation for its baked goods, notably muffins, rum cake, strawberry pie, and chocolate chip cookies.

P. J. Tierney & Sons Dining Car Co. of New Rochelle, N.Y., begins producing well-lighted, fully equipped wagons for use as diners (*see* 1897). Booths will be added in the next decade to make them family eating places, dozens of manufacturers will be making them by the 1930s, mostly for New York, New Jersey, and New England, and efforts will be made to give them the glamour attached to railroad dining cars, but diners will attract undesirable elements and some cities, including Atlantic City, N.J., and Buffalo, will ban them.

1920

Russia suffers a disastrous drought in the wake of 7 years of war and civil war plus more than 2 years of

Bolshevik grain requisitioning. U.S. Secretary of Commerce Herbert C. Hoover organizes the American Relief Administration (ARA) and tries to negotiate Russian acceptance of Western food aid (*see* famine, 1921).

Two agitators for Irish independence die in Brixton Prison after fasting for 75 days in a protest demonstration (*see* Ashe, 1917). Cork Lord Mayor Terence James MacSwiney, 41 and a local Irish Republican Army chief, collapses on the fifteenth day, physicians are unable to save him, and his death October 25 produces widespread rioting.

California legislators enact a new Alien Land Act to prevent Asians from renewing their leases on farmland (*see* 1913; Oregon, 1923).

World economies struggle to revive in the wake of the Great War. Demobilized soldiers find few job openings. Britain orders unemployment insurance for all workers except domestic servants and farmworkers.

The Federal Trade Commission orders the separation of the Deering and McCormick harvesting machines manufactured by International Harvester Co. The FTC acts under terms of the Clayton Anti-Trust Act of 1914 (*see* 1918; 1927).

U.S. food prices will fall 72 percent in the next 2 years as farm prices plummet.

American Sugar Refining sells the sugar from its newly acquired Central Cunagua at an average price of 23.5¢ for the year (*see* 1919). The company nets $5.4 million, reinvests it in 200,000 additional acres of Cuban sugarfields, buys two small islands with a combined area of 350 square miles, and builds a new *central* (sugar mill).

The world sugar price drops from 30¢/lb. in August to 8¢ in December.

M. S. Hershey loses $2.5 million in the collapse of world sugar prices, and other large sugar consumers also take heavy losses.

Pepsi-Cola's Caleb Bradham has bought sugar at 22¢/lb., he loses $150,000, and Pepsi-Cola heads toward bankruptcy (*see* 1907; Guth, 1933).

Chero-Cola sales top $4 million, up more than 100 percent over 1918, but the company ends the year with debts of over $1 million that will not be entirely paid off until 1926 (*see* 1918; 1928).

European margarine makers Jurgens, Van den Bergh, the Schichte family, the Centra Group, and smaller companies join in a Margarine Union created November 22 in an effort to control prices (*see* 1919). A second pact, signed December 31 and covering Germany, Poland, Danzig, Switzerland, Romania, and Yugoslavia, provides that Schichte should receive half the shares, with the other half divided equally between Jurgens and Van den Bergh; under Article 10 of the agreement, no party is to come to terms with Lever Brothers without all parties agreeing (*see* Unilever, 1930).

New York's Vesuvio Bakery opens at 156 Sullivan Street. Italian-American baker Nunzio Dapolito will move in 1926 to 436 West Broadway and in 1933 to 160 Prince Street, where his son Anthony will still be baking and selling fresh Italian white and whole-wheat loaves, biscuits, braided breads, unusually shaped loaves, and—more notably—plain and peppered biscotti and sesame breadsticks—in the mid 1990s.

Kansas City chemist C. J. Patterson helps to develop Paniplus, trade name for a mixture of calcium peroxide and various buffering salts which, when added to bread, cake, and pastry doughs, increase their dryness and make them adaptable to high-speed manufacturing processes (*see* Patterson, 1913; 1925).

U.S. automaker Henry Ford, now 57, receives a visit in the autumn from Irish agricultural equipment designer Harry Ferguson, who brings with him a small plow and demonstrates the principles on which he is working (*see* 1918; Sherman-Ferguson, 1925).

"Winnie Winkle the Breadwinner" by cartoonist Martin Michael Branner, 31, begins in September in the 15-month-old New York *Daily News*. Wage earners are still called "breadwinners" despite diminishing U.S. consumption of bread and other baked goods (below).

Average per capita U.S. flour consumption drops to 179 pounds, down from 224 pounds in 1900, as Americans eat more meat, poultry, fish, and vegetables while reducing consumption of baked goods and pasta.

The ratio of domestic servants to the general U.S. population is half what it was in 1890, partly because immigration has ebbed, partly because of new and better-paying employment alternatives.

Middle-class women employ mostly day workers, who tend to be blacks rather than immigrants or native-born whites. Only relatively affluent households can afford live-in help.

 Overfishing of the Sacramento River forces the closing of San Francisco's last salmon cannery (*see* 1866).

Mac Fisheries Ltd., is founded by William Hesketh Lever of Lever Brothers (*see* 1886). He buys the Hebrides island of Harris and part of Lewis with a view to building a huge fishing and fish-processing industry, and, although he will withdraw in 1923 after crofters in Lewis object, his enterprise will become the world's largest chain of fish stores (*see* Angus Watson, 1922).

Perdue Farms is founded at Salisbury, Md., by former railroad worker Arthur Perdue, 34, who pays

Most U.S. poultry farmers specialized in eggs; chickens were a much riskier proposition. LIBRARY OF CONGRESS

$50 to buy 50 Leghorn chickens and builds a backyard chicken coop to produce table eggs. Perdue's son, Frank (Franklin Parsons), born May 9, will grow up to work with his father, taking time out to attend college for 2 years and, briefly, play semiprofessional baseball (*see* 1948).

Russian Bolshevik leader Vladimir Ilyich Lenin, 50, appeals to the U.S. Communist party for a report on American agricultural methods (*see* famine, 1921).

The American Farm Bureau Federation is founded. It will become the driving force behind mobilizing U.S. farmers' political efforts.

The U.S. soybean harvest reaches 1 million bushels, a figure that will increase more than 600 times in the next half century (*see* 1924; wartime circular, 1918).

The Persian lime begins to displace the West Indian, or key, lime on Florida plantations (year approximate). The key lime continues to predominate in most of the world and is generally considered more flavorful, but the Persian lime is more resistant to cold and insect pests.

The boysenberry, developed by U.S. breeder Rudolph Boysen, is a cross of blackberries, raspberries, and loganberries. Boysen does not capitalize on the new variety (*see* Knott, 1933).

Prohibition (below) will force California vineyard owners to diversify their production, to market as table grapes much of the fruit that has gone into wines and brandies, and to improve their methods of producing raisins, which will soon be marketed under the Sunmaid label.

"Vitamines" become "vitamins" through efforts by British nutritional biochemist J. C. "Jack" Drummond, who observes that not all coenzymes are amines (*see* Funk, 1911). Drummond labels the fat-soluble vitamin "A," the water-soluble vitamin "B," and the antiscorbutic vitamin "C" and with help from O. Rosenheim finds that the human liver can produce vitamin A from the provitamin carotene widely available in fruits and vegetables.

E. V. McCollum discovers a substance in cod-liver oil that can cure rickets and xerophthalmia. He has been at Johns Hopkins since 1917 (*see* 1917; Mellanby, 1918). Xerophthalmia is an abnormal dryness of the eye membranes and cornea that can lead to blindness (*see* 1921; vitamin D, 1922).

The Japanese government establishes a nutrition research center. A private research center also opens, along with the first school for nutrition education.

Botulism from commercially canned food strikes 36 Americans, 23 die, and the U.S. canning industry is motivated by failing sales to impose new production safety standards (*see* 1895; 1925).

La Choy Food Products has its beginnings in a fresh-grown bean sprout business developed by Detroit grocer Wallace Smith, who teams up with Ilhan New, a Korean he has known since both were students at the University of Michigan. Smith and New sell their bean sprouts in cans and glass jars (*see* 1922).

Seabrook Farms builds a modern cannery adjacent to the railroad tracks in the center of the New Jersey farmlands being cultivated by Charles Seabrook (*see* 1912; Birdseye, 1925).

Russian-American baker Adolph Levitt, 45, begins frying doughnuts in a New York bakery. Levitt was taken to Milwaukee at age 8 and dropped out of school 2 years later to help support his widowed mother and seven siblings. Having sold newspapers while he educated himself by reading encyclopedias, he came to New York 8 years ago to help run a bakery chain and has seen Red Cross workers dispensing doughnuts during the war. Fumes from his doughnut fryer disturb patrons of a nickelodeon next door, and Levitt sees an opportunity for an automatic doughnut-making machine whose buyers would provide a market for a standardized mix. He explains his idea to an engineer whom he meets on a train, and the two try to develop the kind of machine Levitt envisions (*see* 1921).

The Good Humor, created by Youngstown, Ohio, confectioner Harry Burt, is a chocolate-covered ice cream bar on a stick. Burt has read about the "I-Scream-Bar" patented last year by Christian Nelson and will obtain his own patent (*see* 1924).

A new Life Savers plant opens at Port Chester, N.Y., and Mint Products, Inc., is renamed Life Savers, Inc. (*see* 1913). Edward J. Noble and Roy Allen have patented the Life Savers design ("Nothing enclosed by a circle"), Allen has traveled the country seeking new salespeople, and Noble, who brings his mechanical engineer brother Bob into the firm as head of production, has increased sales by placing his nickel Life Savers next to the cash register at cigar stores and restaurants, instructing cashiers to include nickels in every customer's change. Americans buy 68 million rolls of Life Savers, up from 914,000 in 1914, 6.7 million in 1915, nearly 22.5 million in 1916, and 39 million in 1918 as Prohibition (below) proves a boon to the candy industry.

Baby Ruth is trademarked by Chicago's Curtiss Candy Co., founded 4 years ago in a back room over a North Halsted Street plumbing shop by candy maker Otto Young Schnering, now 28. Schnering has used his mother's maiden name for the company (German names are unpopular) and his lawyers will insist, disingenuously, that he has renamed his 5¢ chocolate-covered Kandy Kake roll of fudge, caramel, and peanuts not after the baby-faced baseball star George Herman "Babe" Ruth, 25 (who is acquired this year by the New York Yankees from the Boston Red Sox) but after the late daughter of the late President Cleveland (the trademark is patterned exactly after the engraved lettering of the name used on a medallion picturing the president, his wife, and their daughter that was struck for the World's Columbian Exposition of 1893 at Chicago). Schnering places 12-bar cartons of Baby Ruths in 89 stores in Kankakee, Ill., telling each merchant that he can keep the 60 cents on condition that he let Schnering put a sign in his window inviting patrons to "Try a Baby Ruth" (*see* Butterfinger, 1928).

The Oh Henry! candy bar is introduced by George Williamson, a onetime newspaper advertising copywriter who owns a small candy factory in downtown Chicago. A boy named Henry, he will later claim, would drop by every day to flirt with the girls making candy and the girls all said, "Oh, Henry!" Williamson promotes the bar by distributing a free Oh Henry! cookbook with recipes for dishes like Oh Henry! Surprise Pie and Oh Henry! Stuffed Tomatoes (ingredients: two Oh Henry!s, three tomatoes, mayonnaise, lettuce, and salt). Large-type advertisements in the *Saturday Evening Post*, *Collier's*, *Liberty*, and other leading magazines will prove more effective.

Goldenberg's Peanut Chews are introduced by Philadelphia's 30-year-old Goldenberg Candy Co.

Jujyfruits are introduced by Henry Heide Co., which has been making Jujubes for several years.

National Prohibition of sales of alcoholic beverages in the United States goes into effect January 16 (*see* 1919). A mock funeral for "John Barleycorn" is held January 15 at Norfolk, Va., by evangelist William Ashley "Billy" Sunday, 57, who has agitated for Prohibition but whose popularity now begins to fade.

Cartoonists had a field day caricaturing "puritanical" opponents of drinking. LIBRARY OF CONGRESS

Prohibition (above) will devastate the economy of the Madeira Islands, which for centuries have depended on the export of Madeira wines to America (*see* 1872). Sales of sherry and port will grow to surpass those of Madeira in later years, and Madeira, which costs more to produce but is priced to compete with sherry and port, will never regain its former dominance.

Consumption of alcoholic beverages will continue in the United States despite Prohibition (above) through illegal sales of bootleg beer and distilled spirits, legally permissible home-brewed wine, and homemade "bathtub gin," but fewer people will imbibe such beverages.

Australians defeat several attempts to pass Prohibition laws.

Defeat of a proposed Scottish Prohibition law December 5 cheers many Scotsmen. The "Wee Dram" supporters, backed by the distillery lobby (which has dropped "No Change" leaflets from airplanes), have used economic arguments to win out over churchmen, especially strict Sabbatarians, who deplore the high rate of drunkenness in Scotland, most notably in city slums.

Prohibition in the United States (above) booms sales of coffee, soft drinks, and ice cream sodas.

Soda jerks replaced bartenders at U.S. hotels when selling alcoholic beverages became illegal. LIBRARY OF CONGRESS

Howdy is introduced by St. Louis soft-drink maker Charles L. Rigg with backing from local coal merchant Edmund Ridgway. The new drink will have some success until citrus growers push through laws in some legislatures requiring that orange-flavored drinks contain real orange pulp and orange juice (*see* Orange Crush, 1916; 7-Up, 1929).

U.S. hotels begin in many instances to convert their bars into soda fountains and lunch counters, with soda jerks replacing bartenders, in order to comply with Prohibition rules.

The advent of Prohibition brings an end to the "free lunch" that has been a fixture at virtually every U.S. city bar and saloon (most did not give it away free but generally offered it at a nominal price of a nickel or so while charging 30¢ for a five-course businessman's lunch). The free luncheon buffet at Delmonico's in New York has included hard-cooked eggs with caviar, half a lobster, cold cuts, lobster aspic, pickled walnuts, hot roast beef, and Kentucky hams. Other fashionable restaurants have had similar spreads.

Prohibition will force the closing of such New York gastronomic palaces as Shanley's on the west side of Broadway (it will be replaced by the Paramount building).

The Baltimore restaurant Maison Marconi opens at 106 West Saratoga Street.

San Francisco's Far East Café opens at 631 Grant Avenue, serving wonton soup (dumplings in chicken broth with shrimp, mushrooms, and bamboo shoots) and other Cantonese-American dishes.

The Lyons restaurant Léon de Lyons opened by French chef Léon Jean will be acquired after his death by the Lacomb family.

The U.S. population reaches 105.7 million. Urban residents (54 million) for the first time exceed rural residents (51.5 million), but one in every three Americans still lives on a farm (*see* 1970).

1921

Famine kills 3 million Russians and threatens the existence of more than 20 million more as grain reserves run out (*see* 1920). Sailors have mutinied at Kronstadt in late February, and the country has few if any agricultural stockpiles. Frozen corpses are piled 20 feet high in the streets waiting for the ground to thaw so that burial pits can be dug. Herbert Hoover's American Relief Administration responds to an appeal from Russian writer Maksim Gorki, 53, raises more than $60 million in July, and enters Soviet Russia in August; the first meal of American relief food is served September 21, and

many are spared starvation (Gorki will credit American aid with having saved the lives of 3.5 million children, 5.5 million adults, 15,000 students, and at least 200 Russians of the learned professions).

A Russian Famine Relief Act signed into law by President Warren G. Harding, 56, December 22 authorizes the expenditure of $20 million for the purchase of U.S. corn, seed grain, and preserved milk to be sent to Russia. Supplemental government and private donations will eventually raise the total expenditure to $60 million, $12 million of it—at Hoover's urging—from the Russian government's gold reserve (*see* 1922).

A New Economic Policy (NEP) sponsored by V. I. Lenin is announced by Russia's Communist Party as industrial and agricultural production fall off and shortages become acute in food, fuel, and transportation.

The NEP (above) abolishes food levies to placate Russia's peasants and a limited grain tax is substituted. Some freedom of trade is restored to enable the peasants to dispose of what few surpluses they have, and some private commercial enterprises are permitted in the cities (*see* Armand Hammer, below).

Continental Grain receives a charter February 5 from the State of Illinois and begins operations at 332 South LaSalle Street, Chicago, with backing from Compagnie Continentale d'Importation, S.A., of Paris (CCI), headed by Jules Fribourg, now 44 (*see* 1904). The new company will become a major grain marketer and a powerful factor in world agribusiness (*see* 1933).

Columbia University medical school graduate Armand Hammer, 22, goes to Russia to help the Lenin government cope with its postwar disease plagues and collect $150,000 owed to his father's company for drugs shipped during the Allied blockade of Russian ports. Dr. Hammer, whose Russian-born father is in Sing Sing prison on an abortion conviction, travels to the Urals and barters a million tons of U.S. wheat for a fortune in furs, caviar, and precious stones.

The southeast Asian agribusiness colossus Charoen Pokphand Group has its beginnings in a Bangkok seed-importing shop opened by a Chinese émigré peasant farmer. He and his son Dhanin Cheara-vanont, born in 1939, will set up a chicken feed mill, and the son will take over the business in 1964, supplying Thai farmers with chicks and feed and buying their eggs and full-grown chickens at a guaranteed price (see 1981).

U.S. farmers overproduce on acreage planted during the war, and farm prices in July fall to levels 85 percent below 1919 highs. Nebraska farmers burn corn for fuel as the price of corn falls to 42¢ per bushel, down from $2. Wheat is $1, down from $3.50. The Harding administration tries to relieve the U.S. agricultural depression with an Emergency Tariff Act imposing high duties on imports of wheat, corn, meat, sugar, wool, and other farm products.

Molasses prices drop to 2¢/gal., down from 20¢ last year. Penick & Ford, which makes Brer Rabbit Molasses and Vermont Maid syrup, loses $9.5 million (see Corn Products Refining, 1913; sugar price drop, 1920; R. J. Reynolds, 1965).

Sioux Honey Association is founded at Sioux City, Iowa, by five men who pool $200 and 3,000 pounds of honey. Their product will be marketed under the trade name Sioux Bee Honey and the Association will grow to have more than 400 members in 26 states (plus one in Mexico and one in Canada), producing on average 40 million pounds of honey per year (20 percent of U.S. production). Within 25 years, Sioux Bee will be the only brand having national distribution in an industry dominated by regional companies.

World cacao prices collapse in the absence of any futures market mechanism. Speculative "hoarders" have used bank credits to buy up cacao beans produced from October through January in anticipation of the usual price advances, but when the banks suddenly begin calling the loans the cacao is thrown onto the market, prices break nearly 20¢ per pound, and cacao merchants sustain losses, as do importers and outside speculators, many of whom are ruined (see Cocoa Exchange, 1925).

Wholesale butter prices in the New York market fall to 29¢/lb., down from 76¢ during the war. Imports of Danish butter have increased, and Americans are using more margarine.

Donut Machine Corp. (later to be called Donut Corp. of America and, later still, DCA Industries) is founded by Arthur Levitt (see 1920). He and his engineer friend have built 11 machines before developing one that worked, and when he puts the 12th machine in the window of his Times Square bakery it stops traffic. The new company leases a factory at Ellicott City, Md., to produce a mix—the first fully prepared mix in America—for the new automatic machine. In the window of an antique shop, Levitt sees a plaque bearing the legend "As you ramble on through life, brother,/ Whatever be your goal,/ Keep your eye upon the doughnut,/ And not upon the hole." He will have the verse displayed in each of his Mayflower Donut Shops, and their success will lead to competitors such as Dunkin' Donuts (see 1950), Mr. Donut, and Winchell's.

Stokely Brothers suffers its first financial loss as the sharp postwar business recession brings hardship to many companies (see 1917; Van Camp, 1933).

The United States has 387,000 miles of surfaced road by year's end, up from 190,476 in 1909 (see 1930). More than a million trucks travel on U.S. roads and highways, up from 100,000 in 1909.

Cambridge, Mass., chemist Bradley Dewey, 34, discovers the first water-based latex sealing compound. The sealant will be used inside the crimped rims by which tops and bottoms are attached to cans, and Dewey's firm Dewey & Almy will be a major producer of the sealant and of the machines used to apply it.

Heart disease becomes the leading cause of death in America after 10 years of jockeying for the lead with tuberculosis. Coronary disease accounts for 14 percent of U.S. deaths, and the figure will increase to 39 percent in the next 50 years.

Half-hourly radio broadcasts begin March 6 to give quotations from the Chicago Board of Trade, but relatively few people have crystal sets to hear the prices, which are falling at a rate depressing to farmers.

The first stainless-steel flatware is introduced by the Silver Co. of Meriden, Conn., which initially markets only knives (no forks or spoons), mostly to hotels and restaurants that want to save on replating and on the labor costs of constant polishing. Most household flatware continues to be made from carbon steel that is shiny but quickly discolors. British scientists 8 years ago alloyed pure chromium with 35-point carbon steel, basing their work on the observation by a French metallurgist in 1820 that an alloy such as chrome, when added to carbon steel, made the steel resistant to rust. Stainless-steel flatware will come into wide use in U.S. and European homes beginning in the 1930s.

U.S. Communist Harold M. Ware persuades journalist Lincoln Steffens, 55, to donate more than $70,000 in lecture fees to buy tractors and other farm equipment for Russia. Ware has made a study of U.S. farming methods in response to last year's request by V. I. Lenin and notes that Russia has fewer than 1,500 tractors, many of them unrepairable wrecks (see 1922).

Botanist George Washington Carver of the Tuskegee Institute testifies before the House Ways and Means Committee on the value of peanuts, to which Georgia and South Carolina farmers are devoting more and more acreage (see Carver, 1914).

U.S. farmers average only 28.4 bushels of corn per acre and only 12.7 bushels of wheat. The U.S. soybean crop is little more than 1 million bushels.

President Harding appoints Henry C. Wallace secretary of agriculture (see Wallace's Farmer, 1895). Wallace, who has made enough money from the family farm journal to acquire five of the best stock and dairy farms in Iowa and adjoining states, will campaign for farm relief (see Agricultural Credits Act, 1923; Pioneer Hi-Bred, 1926).

Harvard biologist Edward Murray East, 42, of the Connecticut Agricultural Experiment Station, and Princeton botanist George Harrison Shull perfect a hybrid corn variety that will yield far more per acre than conventional corn (see 1905). Produced by removing the tassels of inbred corn so that it cannot seed itself, and then pollinating it from another inbred parent planted in the same field, it is based chiefly on germ plasm from Reid's Yellow Dent (see 1893). Hybrid seed permits growing plants of predictable size and quality that can be harvested mechanically, and by next year such seed will be available on a commercial basis to farmers who have never known anything but the flint corn (notably Tropical Flint) which has dominated world markets (see 1930; Pioneer Hi-Bred, 1926).

Vitamin pioneer E. V. McCollum finds that cod-liver oil is a preventive against rickets; he observes that rats fed large amounts of calcium develop bone deformities much like those seen in rickets but that the deformities are prevented if a little cod-liver oil is added to the rats' rations (see 1918; 1922).

U.S. embryologist Herbert McLean Evans, 39, at the University of California, Berkeley, shows with rat studies that mammals other than humans require an "antisterility" factor in their diets if they are to reproduce (see vitamin E, 1935).

U.S. table-salt makers introduce salt iodized with potassium iodide to prevent goiter, but iodization is not mandatory (see 1924; Akron study, 1916).

The Fundaments of Our Nutrition by Swiss physician M. O. Bircher-Bremer, 54, recommends ingestion of more uncooked foods.

Several states legislate sanitary dairy practices to improve the safety of U.S. milk, which often reaches consumers with a bacteria count of 500,000 or more per cubic centimeter (see 1900). Contaminated milk transmits undulant fever, brucellosis, bacillary dysentery, infectious hepatitis, typhoid fever, tuberculosis, and other diseases.

Pasteurization was essential unless milk was produced under the most sanitary conditions. LIBRARY OF CONGRESS

U.S. butter is "scored" on a point system that gives 45 points for top flavor, 25 points on the basis of composition, 15 on color, 10 on salt content, 5 on the wooden butter tub used for packaging. Butter that scores 92 out of a possible 100 is called extra grade or "New York extra," but out of 622 Minnesota creameries only 200 make butter good enough to command the premium price paid for 92-point "New York extra."

Land O' Lakes Butter, Inc., has its beginnings in the Minnesota Cooperative Creameries Association formed by Meeker County, Minn., creameries. The federation will burgeon into a Minneapolis-based empire of midwestern dairy farmers.

Trademarking butter gave a commercial advantage to midwestern dairy interests.

Bel Paese semisoft cheese is introduced by Italian cheese maker Egidio Galbani.

Kraft processed cheese is introduced in foil-wrapped five-pound loaves enclosed in rectangular wooden boxes instead of in tins (*see* 1917). Demand is so high that Kraft is soon making 15,000 boxes per day, and homemakers use the boxes as storage containers (*see* Kraft-Phenix, Velveeta, 1928; singles, 1947).

The name "Betty Crocker" is developed by Washburn, Crosby Co. of Minneapolis. The firm runs a picture puzzle contest in a national magazine, offering as a prize a pincushion in the shape of a Gold Medal Flour bag; more than 30,000 entries pour in, many with questions about baking; men and women employees join forces to handle all the mail, company advertising man Samuel C. Gale suggests that the replies will carry more authority if they are signed by a woman, he makes up the name Betty Crocker (a company director named Crocker has recently retired) and runs an in-house handwriting contest, secretary Florence Lindebergan wins, and the signature "Betty Crocker" in Lindebergan's hand is added to the notes that go out in reply to contestants' questions (*see* 1905; 1924).

Wise Potato Chips are introduced by Berwick, Pa., grocer Earl V. Wise, who finds himself overstocked with old potatoes. He peels them, slices them with an old-fashioned cabbage cutter, follows his mother's recipe for making potato chips, packages the chips in brown paper bags, and sells them in his grocery store (*see* George Crum, 1853; peeling machines, 1925). Wise will package his chips in cellophane beginning in the early 1930s (*see* Borden Co., 1964).

The Eskimo Pie replaces the "I-Scream-Bar" of 1919 as Omaha, Nebr., candymaker Russell William Stover, 32, teams up with Christian Nelson to sell franchises for the manufacture and sale of the chocolate-covered ice cream bars (*see* 1922; Good Humor, 1920).

Chuckles—hand-wrapped jelly candies—are introduced by Chicago candy industry veteran Fred W. Amend, 62, who has been in the business since 1875. He has perfected a formula for producing a jelly candy that does not break into a sweat as other jelly candies do, and his wife has suggested the name Chuckles.

The first White Castle hamburger stand opens in March with five counter stools in a plain 10-by-15-foot cement-block building at Wichita, Kans. Local insurance and real estate agent Edgar Waldo "Billy" Ingram, 40, last year met professional cook Walter Anderson, who in 1916 rented a remodeled streetcar, procured a griddle plate and icebox, and went into business. He had developed a new method of cooking hamburger sandwiches: instead of placing a thick beef patty on a griddle or skillet, allowing it to cook over a slow fire for an indefinite period, and serving it on a cold bun, Anderson has placed government-inspected beef on the griddle, flattened it with a spatula, mashed some shredded onions into it, turned the patty over, placed both halves of a bun over it to catch the heat, juices, and aroma, and cooked it for a short time over a hot fire. Ingram has sold Anderson a house, helped him obtain financing for a third hamburger stand, and solved a problem that arose over leasing a fourth location by putting his own name onto the lease agreement and going into business with Anderson. The partners have borrowed $700 to start the enterprise, repay the loan in 90 days, and will never borrow again, financing their growth from profits. When they find that pancake turners do not stand up under the pressure of flattening hamburger patties, they have two-inch-square wedges cut out of handsaw blades and create spatulas by having handles brazed to each wedge (a manufacturer will later produce proper spatulas for them). Ingram and Anderson will incorporate in 1924 as the White Castle System of Eating Houses, and Ingram will buy out Anderson's interest in 1933 (*see* 1925).

The Bickford's Cafeteria chain has its beginnings in a New York restaurant opened by Samuel L. Bickford, who has worked for New England's Waldorf System restaurant chain. In 1923 he will absorb his brother Harold's Travelers' Lunch, started at Paterson, N.J., 4 years ago, take over the White Castle System on the West Coast, acquire Boston's Hayes Lunch System, and grow to have 85 outlets, serving breakfast, lunch, and dinner with an emphasis on cleanliness, quick service, and hot coffee.

Lindy's Restaurant opens at 1626 Broadway in New York under the management of German-American restaurateur Leo "Lindy" Lindemann, 33, whose crullers, cheesecake, and coffee will be favored by newspapermen, politicians, and theater people for half a century.

Sardi's Restaurant opens in West 44th Street, New York, under the direction of Italian-American restaurateur Vincent Sardi, 35, and his wife, Eugenia, whose cannelloni and other dishes will attract the Broadway theater world for more than 70 years. Sardi's will move to 234 West 44th Street in 1927 when the first building is razed to make way for construction of the St. James Theater; Vincent Jr. will take over in 1946, and he will build a following with his oysters and clams on the half shell, smoked trout, smoked salmon, sautéed large shrimps, escargots de Bourgogne, vegetable minestrone, scrambled eggs with chicken livers and mushrooms that have been sautéed in butter and Madeira, Welsh rabbit, chicken pot pie à la John Golden (includes oysters stewed in cream), chicken à la king, osso buco, prime ribs, double lamb chops, prime sirloin, filet mignon, Yankee pot roast, roast beef hash, steak tartare, striped bass, rainbow trout, apple pie, zabaglione, and *boccone dolce*.

Louis Sherry's reopens under the direction of August Weisbrod on the ground floor of a new apartment house at 300 Park Avenue, where it will continue until the 1950s, but the glory days it knew as a restaurant for New York's conservative *haut monde* at Fifth Avenue and 24th Street are over.

The Los Angeles steak house Pacific Dining Car opens in West 7th Street (it will move in 1923 to West 6th and Witmer Streets). Operatic tenor Fred Cook and his wife, Grace, have built the place and will soon have a curing box for aging their own beef, then a small bar, and later additional rooms as they attract patrons with their steak and apple pie.

California's Nut Tree restaurant has its beginnings in a fig stand opened July 23 under a black walnut tree near the town of Vacaville by entrepreneur Helen Allison Power. Her grandfather, a pioneer fruit rancher who settled on the land in 1855, planted the tree in 1861; her fig stand will evolve into a roadside restaurant serving Chinese and Mexican dishes (turkey tamale) with fresh western fruits and vegetables (including corn on the cob and asparagus), bread (rye, white, and whole wheat) baked twice a day from western wheat, chocolate cake, strawberry shortcake, angel cheesecake decorated with orange slices and strawberries, deep-dish fruit pies, pumpkin pies, and chess pie (raisins and walnuts in a butterscotch filling).

The Lyons restaurant La Mère Brazier opens in the silkmakers' quarter. Eugénie Brazier, 26, who learned to cook and keep house after her mother died while she was still a child, will be the first and only woman to be awarded three starts by the *Guide Michelin*. She serves her patrons artichoke heart topped by a slab of foie gras, gratin of quenelles de brochet (pike dumplings), and poularde demi-deuil (chicken in half wine, rice, and noodles cooked in a bouillon which requires at least two hens to make). Mme. Brazier's son Gaston will carry on after her death in 1977 at age 82, and his daughter Gacotte will continue the tradition established by her grandmother.

1922

The American Farm Bureau Federation donates 15 million bushels of corn in January to help Herbert Hoover's European Relief Committee, the American Committee for China Famine Fund, and the Near East Relief Committee. The American Relief

Administration feeds some 10.5 million hungry Russians per day in August as famine continues in what will soon be the Soviet Union (*see* 1921). Before it ends, at least 5 million will have died, but Russia harvests a new crop that eases hunger, and the worst of the famine is over by fall (*see* 1923).

$ U.S. farmers remain in deep depression with a few exceptions such as California citrus growers (below).

The Capper Volstead Act passed by Congress February 18 exempts agricultural marketing cooperatives from antitrust law restrictions. The co-ops are subject to supervision by the secretary of agriculture, who is to prevent them from raising prices "unduly."

The Fordney-McCumber Tariff Act passed by Congress September 19 returns tariffs to the levels of the 1909 Payne-Aldrich Act. The new law gives the president power to raise or lower duties by 50 percent in order to equalize production costs but presidents will use that authority in 32 of 37 cases to further increase duties in response to appeals for protection by U.S. business and labor. A U.S. business revival led by the automobile industry begins 7 years of prosperity, but agriculture remains depressed.

A Grain Futures Act (Capper-Tincher Bill) passed by Congress September 21 curbs speculation, thought to have contributed to the collapse of grain prices in 1920. The new act, which supersedes an August 1921 act that has been declared unconstitutional by the Supreme Court, limits price fluctuations within any given period on U.S. grain exchanges.

Cargill boss John MacMillan sets up a New York sales organization to counter a Buffalo, N.Y., broker who has been taking away his East Coast business by leasing space at Duluth, buying spring wheat from samples at the Minneapolis Grain Exchange, and selling it to export houses at New York and Montreal (*see* 1916; 1929).

Quality Bakers of America is created as a cooperative purchasing service by independent wholesale bakers, whose survival has been threatened by the giant competition emerging with the growth of chain stores and chain bakeries. The co-op will become the industry's largest such group, with nearly 100 U.S. members and more than 30 bakers in Canada, Mexico, and Australia, many of whom will buy advertising services from QBA (*see* Sunbeam bread, 1942).

Philadelphia's Tasty Baking Co. closes its Sedgley Avenue plant and moves into a new Hunting Park Avenue building which they will expand fivefold by 1930 as sales increase (*see* 1914). The company has replaced many of its horse-drawn wagons with Model T Ford trucks and electric trucks, but the last Tasty cart horse will not be retired until 1941 (*see* 1932).

James D. Dole's Hawaiian Pineapple Co. buys the uninhabited 90,000-acre Hawaiian island of Lanai, 60 miles from the company's Honolulu cannery, to give Dole 20,000 acres of land that can be planted in pineapples (*see* 1913). Maui ranchers Frank and Harry Baldwin have acquired the island to use for cattle ranching and as a game preserve, but Dole thinks it is more suitable for pineapple production and pays the Baldwins $1.1 million with which to buy the Ulupalakua Ranch on Maui. He will build a 14,000-acre plantation on Lanai, with a modern cannery, a model workers' town, and an artificial harbor that can accommodate freighters.

Dole's company (above) is by far the largest of the 15 Hawaiian pineapple packers, producing 1.5 million cases out of the 4.8 million industry total, and Hawaiian Pineapple shareholders receive a 23 percent dividend (*see* 1930; flying contest, 1927).

Canada Dry Ginger Ale opens its first U.S. bottling plant on New York's 38th Street to avoid the long, costly haul from Canada and the high tariff on imports (*see* 1907; Fordney-McCumber Act, above). Shipments from the new plant begin April 28, and a full-page advertisement in the *New York Times* rotogravure section, prepared by N. W. Ayer & Son of Philadelphia, carries the headline "Down from Canada Came Tales of a Wonderful Beverage." The ginger ale sells at 35¢ per 12-ounce bottle but meets with immediate success despite its high price; a U.S. subsidiary will be chartered in February of next year, it will acquire property at Hudson, N.Y., for a new bottling plant, and additional plants will be built or acquired in Chicago and Los Angeles (*see* 1936).

Eskimo Pies produce $30,000 per week in royalties (the chocolate-covered ice cream bar sells at the rate of 2 million per day), but legal defense against patent infringers is so costly that Russell Stover sells his share in the company to Christian Nelson for $30,000 (*see* 1921; 1923; Reynolds, 1924).

Postum Cereal Co. is incorporated (*see* Post, 1914; Jell-O, 1925).

Campbell Soup Co. is established by a renaming of Joseph Campbell Co. (*see* 1933; Franco-American, 1915).

Insulin permits diabetics to enjoy diets with fewer restrictions. Canadian medical medical researchers Frederick Grant Banting, 31, and Charles Herbert Best, 23, isolate the hormone (Banting calls it "isletin") from canine pancreatic juices, use it to save the life of Leonard Thompson, 14, who is dying in Toronto General Hospital, and will license Eli Lilly Co. to make the first commercial insulin—the first treatment for diabetes other than diet limitation (*see* 1924; Sharpey-Schafer, 1916).

Van Camp Sea Food merges with White Star Canning and two other nearly bankrupt San Pedro, Calif., tuna packers after being hurt by the 1921 economic deflation and collapse of wartime markets (*see* 1914). The new company increases production and sales but lacks the equipment needed to make extended cruises and overcome the circumstances that make tuna fishing a seasonal business limited to albacore (*see* 1924).

Lever Brothers acquires Angus Watson Co. to help market its fish (*see* 1903; Mac Fisheries, 1920). Lever will sell canned fish under brand names such as Sailor, Skipper, and Tea Time.

V. I. Lenin permits small private farms to help Russia produce more food (*see* Stalin, 1928).

Harold M. Ware arrives in Russia with 21 tractors, other farm machinery, seeds, supplies, and food (*see* 1921). Ware is assigned to lands in the Urals, where he and his volunteer associates seed most of 4,000 acres in winter wheat and encourage peasants to give up their holdings and join a collective (*see* 1925).

California becomes a year-round source of oranges as Valencia orange production catches up with navel orange production (*see* 1875; 1906; Hart, 1867; Sunkist, 1919).

U.S. mining engineer Henry Byron Slater, 72, perfects a hypochlorite process to prevent decay of citrus fruits while in transit to market. He will receive his first patent for the process July 2, 1929.

The first U.S. soybean refinery begins operations at Decatur, Ill. Corn processor A. E. Staley removes at least 96 percent of the oil and sells the residue, or cake, to the feed industry for use in commercial feeds or to farmers to mix with other ingredients as a protein supplement for livestock (*see* 1906; soybeans, 1923; Tate & Lyle, 1988).

E. V. McCollum isolates vitamin D and uses it in successful treatment of rickets. The newly found vitamin is found to play some role in raising the amount of calcium and phosphate deposited in bones, but the mechanism remains a mystery (*see* 1923).

Experimental dogs produce hemoglobin quickly and avoid anemia when fed liver in tests made by University of Rochester pathologist George Hoyt Whipple, 44 (*see* Minot and Murphy, 1924).

Europe has its last reported case of botulism traceable to a commercial canner (*see* United States, 1925).

Clapp's Vegetable Soup—the first commercially prepared U.S. baby food—is introduced by Rochester, N.Y., restaurant manager Harold H. Clapp and his wife, Anna Louise (*née* Alberger), 30, who has begun canning the soup for neighbors' children after her husband used it to help nurse their infant son, Jack, through an illness at the suggestion of their physician. The Clapps start selling through drugstores and will promote the idea into a nationwide business, which they will sell to Johnson & Johnson in 1931 (*see* 1953; Gerber, 1927).

La Choy Food Products is incorporated by Wallace Smith and Ilhan New, who begin canning bean sprouts in metal cans at Detroit (*see* 1920; 1937).

Pep breakfast food is introduced by the Battle Creek Toasted Corn Flake Co., which changes its name to Kellogg Co. (*see* 1919; 1928).

The Mounds bar introduced by Peter Paul is a coconut and dark (bittersweet) chocolate bar made from a formula devised by former chemist George Shamlian (*see* 1919). It is wrapped in aluminum foil, and its immediate success encourages Peter Paul to build a plant at Naugatuck, Conn. (*see* automatic production, 1932).

Charleston Chew is introduced by the 2-year-old Fox-Cross Candy Co. of Emeryville, Calif. Named for the new dance floor craze, it is a nut roll of vanilla-flavored nougat covered with milk chocolate.

Harvard Law School dropout Robert Henry Winborne Welch, Jr., 23, enters the candy business, selling fudge in the streets of Cambridge, Mass. Welch entered the University of North Carolina at age twelve, was graduated 4 years later, won appointment to the U.S. Naval Academy, quit 2 years following the end of the war in Europe, and has spent 2 years studying law. Fudge is a notoriously difficult product to make, but Welch's Oxford Candy Co. cranks out chocolate-covered fudge under the brand name Avalon, sells it at three pieces for a dime, and will prosper for a time until he falls into financial difficulties and sells out to Daggett Chocolate Co. (*see* 1926).

Chicago restaurateur John R. Thompson opens his 103rd cafeteria in a chain that extends over much of the Midwest, building a reputation for absolute cleanliness (a white enamel nameplate is on each window), modest prices, no frills, and fast turnover.

New York's Colony Restaurant opens in 63rd Street off Madison Avenue under the direction of restaurateur Gene Cavallero, who serves liquor in demitasse cups (he keeps his liquor bottles in an elevator that is sent up to the top floor and left there when Prohibition inspectors arrive). The Colony will develop a reputation for fine cuisine.

New York bootlegger Matt Winkle advertises his "Kinvara Café" at 381 Park Avenue, across from the Racquet and Tennis Club, in the *Yale Daily News* and the *Daily Princetonian* (the ads show the proprietor, wearing a raccoon coat, leaning against a Stutz Bearcat roadster and bear the caption "Matt Winkle himself"). Most of the speakeasy's "wet goods" are kept in the pockets of an enormous overcoat that is worn summer and winter by a man who stands on the customers' side of the bar and hands bottles across to the barman as demand requires. In the event of a raid, he simply walks out with the customers. After Winkle surrenders to the law, his collegiate trade will shift to Dan Moriarty's at 216 East 58th Street, to the Puncheon Club at 21 West 52nd Street (*see* "21," 1930), and other watering holes that pay off the police or in other ways evade Prohibition laws.

The Los Angeles restaurant Tam O'Shanter has its beginnings in The Inn, opened on a new two-lane highway between Pasadena and Hollywood. Bakery co-owner Lawrence L. Frank has had his Hollywood art director friend Harry Oliver design a reproduction of a quaint Norman inn and gone into partnership with his brother-in-law Walter Van de Kamp to start the dining spot, which will become popular with film stars and business people (*see* baking company, 1918; Lawry's The Prime Rib, 1938).

1923

Russian famine relief continues until it becomes clear that the nation is approaching prewar levels of agricultural industrial production, even though these levels are low by Western standards. Herbert Hoover's American Relief Administration leaves Russia in July.

Oregon legislators adopt an Alien Land Act patterned on the California laws of 1913 and 1920 and aimed at Asian farmers. Chinese potato king Chin Lung, whose sons have been raised in China but have emigrated to join his enterprises, will have to stop his California operations next year when his leases run out and cannot be renewed; he will farm only in Oregon until 1933, when he will return to farm on land in his native district in China, which he buys this year.

 The German mark falls to 7,260 to the U.S. dollar January 2; Berlin has food riots when 14 municipal markets close because of a strike against higher prices charged at the stalls and booths in the markets.

The mark fails to 160,000 to the dollar by July, and unemployment combines with inflation to create social unrest; 1.5 million are unemployed, 4.5 million employed only part time, yet prices continue to rise and by July 30 the mark has depreciated to 1 million to the dollar.

The mark falls to 13 million to the dollar in September, to 130 billion to the dollar by November 1, and to 4.2 trillion to the dollar by the end of November. Prices rise so fast that workers are paid daily—and then several times a day. Middle-class people and pensioners are wiped out, formerly affluent Germans dispose of their possessions in order to eat, German peasants refuse to part with their eggs, milk, butter, or potatoes except in exchange for articles of tangible value, and they fill their houses with pianos, sewing machines, Persian rugs, even Rembrandts (*see* 1924).

An Agricultural Credits Act, passed by Congress through the efforts of Secretary of Agriculture Henry C. Wallace, helps U.S. agricultural and livestock interests, which remain in deep depression (*see* 1921; 1922). The new law provides for 12 Federal Credit Banks where farmers can obtain personal and collateralized loans for periods intermediate between the usual short-term commercial loans and the long-term loans secured by their farmland.

J. Lyons & Co. begins ice cream production on a large scale at Cadby Hall, whose R Block will for some years be the world's largest ice cream plant.

J. Lyons & Co. (above) opens the world's largest tea factory on a 70-acre site at Greenford, about 10 miles west of its Cadby Hall plant (*see* Maharajah, 1903; Horniman, Black & Green, 1917). Barges of tea chests arrive from the London docks via the Grand Union Canal, the factory (which also blends coffee) will be producing 1 million tea packets per day by 1925, and Lyons that year will buy an 8,000-acre tea plantation in Nyasaland (later Malawi), which it will own until 1977 (*see* packaged cake, 1926).

Anheuser-Busch at St. Louis diversifies into corn syrup as Prohibition continues to prevent legal sale of beer (*see* Michelob, 1897; yeast, 1926).

Pet Milk Co. is created by a reorganization of the Helvetia Milk Condensing Co., which moved to St. Louis in 1921 and began advertising in the *Saturday Evening Post* (*see* "Our Pet," 1894; Pet Dairy Products, 1929).

Birdseye Seafoods opens on New York's White Street (*see* 1917). Although Clarence Birdseye did not invent quick-freezing, his company is the first of its kind; he has received patents on his process, which is unique in the fact that it freezes foods in packages by pressing them between refrigerated metal plates. Birdsye has only $7 to spend on equipment, including an electric fan, ice, and salt; a friend has loaned him the corner of an icehouse to carry on his experimentation, but without the means to gain public acceptance he is forced into bankruptcy (*see* General Seafoods, 1924).

Archer Daniels Midland (ADM) is created by a merger of Archer Daniels Linseed Co. with Midland Linseed Products Co. The Archer family of Dayton, Ohio, was in the linseed oil business as early as the 1830s; John W. Daniels began his linseed oil business with his father-in-law at Piqua, Ohio, in 1879, founded the Daniels Linseed Co. at Minneapolis in 1902, and joined with George A. Archer in 1904. ADM will soon enter grain merchandising and will give up the linseed oil business in the 1950s to concentrate on grain and milling (*see* 1930).

National Dairy Corp. is organized at New York by Thomas McInnerny, who says the dairy industry is bigger than the automobile or steel industry but needs some organization to control the quality and service of its many small, local companies (*see* 1914). McInnerny's giant holding company consolidates 168 firms and will acquire many others, including Breyer's ice cream (*see* 1928; Breyer's, 1866; 1993).

A supermarket of sorts opens in San Francisco where a large steel-frame building opens on the site of a former baseball field and circus ground with 68,000 square feet of selling space and room to park 4,350 automobiles (shoppers are offered free parking for one hour). The Crystal Palace sells drugs, cigarettes, cigars, and jewelry as well as food and has a barber shop, beauty parlor, and dry cleaner (*see* Piggly Wiggly, 1916; King Kullen, 1930).

Synthetic citric acid is produced for the first time by fermentation and becomes an important food and beverage additive (*see* Scheele, 1784).

Corn Products Refining Co. patents a "Method for Making Grape Sugar (Dextrose)." Company research chemist William B. Newkirk, 35, has obtained the first pure dextrose from corn by finding a way to expel the corn molasses that impairs quality and flavor. His method, which involves making coarse dextrose crystals from which the molasses can be removed, will consume millions of bushels of corn each year. It yields a pure, crystalline dextrose with important uses in bakery products, beverages, candy, preservatives, and processed foods (*see* 1916; Bosco, 1956).

Congress calls filled milk a menace to health. The Filled Milk Act, passed after pressure from dairy interests, forbids use of nondairy ingredients (including low-fat vegetable oil to replace butterfat) in anything that is called (or looks like) a milk product (*see* 1916). The courts will overturn the law in 1973.

Cookbook: *Simple French Cooking for English Homes* by French chef X.-M. Boulestin, a friend of the novelist Colette, who came to London last year to see a publisher about another friend's etchings and was commissioned to write the cookbook. Boulestin will open a London restaurant under his own name in 1925.

Paris holds its first annual Salon Internationale des Arts Ménagers. Organized by Jules-Louis Breton, 51, a member of the Académie des Sciences who served as minister of inventions in the Great War, it is an exhibition of the home arts with many displays of household appliances that include new kitchenware.

U.S. sugar consumption reaches 106.39 pounds per capita, up from 65.2 pounds in 1900. Some sugar goes into illegal "moonshine" whiskey.

U.S. wheat farmers try to persuade one another to plant less, but overproduction continues in the absence of any effective farm organization.

44—that will remain for some years the strains most effective in resisting black stem and leaf rust.

Grasshoppers plague Montana. Forming a cloud 300 miles long, 100 miles wide, and half a mile high, the locusts devour every green blade, leaf, and stalk, leaving holes in the ground where green plants grew.

Soybean cultivation increases in eastern states with encouragement from higher freight rates that make it costly to feed cows with cottonseed from the Cotton Belt or with bran from Minneapolis flour mills (see Staley, 1922; McMillen, 1934).

The Macoun apple is created in upstate New York by crossing a McIntosh with a Jersey Black.

Irradiating foods with ultraviolet light can make them rich sources of vitamin D, says University of Wisconsin biochemist Harry Steenbock, 37, and he

Harry Steenbock irradiated foods with ultraviolet light to make them good sources of vitamin D. LIBRARY OF CONGRESS

U.S. farmers threshed so much wheat that overproduction pushed down prices. LIBRARY OF CONGRESS

Black stem rust attacks wheat on the Great Plains, but some of the hybrid varieties developed by Edgar S. Mcfadden, now 32, on his Webster, S.D., farm resist the disease entirely (see 1916). Mcfadden will develop two new hybrids—Hope and H-files for a patent on his discovery. Researchers including Alfred Hess at Columbia University have found that ultraviolet light from the sun and from mercury-vapor lamps can cure rickets (*see* McCollum, 1922), Steenbock has followed up on their studies, and he has found that stimulating the provitamins in foods can enable the human liver to convert them into vitamin D (*see* 1927; Rosenheim and Webster, 1926).

The May issue of the *Women's Home Companion* carries an article entitled "The Old Order Changeth" by Ruth Wadsworth, who writes, "With the revolution in clothes has come a revolution in our attitude toward avoirdupois. Once weight was an asset: now it's a liability, both physical and esthetic" (*see* 1907).

Welch's grape jelly is introduced (see 1897; tomato juice, Welch-ade, 1927).

The Popsicle has its beginnings in New Jersey, where Oakland, Calif., lemonade-mix salesman Frank Epperson is demonstrating his product. He accidentally leaves a glass of lemonade on a windowsill overnight, wakes in the morning to find it frozen around a spoon in the glass, and applies for a patent on his "Epsicle" (*see* 1924).

The Milky Way candy bar, developed in the Midway district between Minneapolis and St. Paul by confectioner Frank C. Mars, 39, is a mixture of milk chocolate, corn syrup, sugar, milk, hydrogenated vegetable oil, cocoa, butter, salt, malt, egg whites, etc. Mars began making candy with his Minnesota-born second wife, Ethel (*née* Healey), in their kitchen at Tacoma, Wash., in 1911 but has had little success and moved with Ethel to Minneapolis 3 years ago. Technicians at Pendergast Candy Co. of Minneapolis have stumbled on a way to produce a chewy center for the company's Emma bar, an excess of egg white in the recipe has given them a nougat that is fluffy rather than chewy, they have renamed their bar Fat Emma, and Mars has adopted the fluffy "Minnesota" or "Minneapolis" nougat for his own product. Inspired perhaps by his own astronomical name, he names his creation after the distant star galaxy and will see Milky Way sales leap in 1 year from $72,800 to $792,000, but in order to fill mounting orders he will be obliged to buy raw materials on a cash basis from Pearson Candy Co., founded in 1909, and while competitors will wrap

their products in foil to keep them fresh, Frank Mars will never use anything more expensive than semitransparent glassine paper (*see* 1930).

Reese's Peanut Butter Cups are introduced by former York County, Penna., farmer H. B. (Harry) Reese, 44, who took a job operating one of Milton Hershey's dairy farms in 1917 and later, with Hershey's blessing, started a candy company of his own, first at nearby Hummelstown, then at Palmyra, making bars of caramellike molasses and coconut (*see* 1942).

Russell Stover uses the money he received last year from his share in Eskimo Pie to open the first Russell Stover candy shop with his wife, Clara, in their house at Denver. He also starts a factory there to produce Mrs. Stover's Bungalow Candies. Stover will open a second factory in 1925 at Kansas City, a third in 1942 at Lincoln, Nebr., and by the time he dies in 1954 at age 66 there will be 40 Russell Stover stores, and Russell Stover candies will be sold through some 2,000 pharmacies and department stores (*see* Whitman's Sampler, 1993).

Almond Rocha is introduced by Brown and Haley of Tacoma, Wash., founded 4 years before the Great War. A candy with a crisp center made of crunchy roasted almonds, sweet butter, sugar, and other ingredients coated over with milk chocolate and rolled in chopped nuts, its high butter content will make it susceptible to turning rancid; by 1928 Almond Rocha will be packed in hermetically sealed tins, the first candy to be thus packaged (*see* 1942).

California's Louis M. Martini winery is founded just north of St. Helena; vintner Martini, who has been making wine since 1906, owns or leases vineyards on 600 acres in the Mayacamas Mountains between Napa and Sonoma counties, but Prohibition limits his production to sacramental wines (the winery will eventually be acquired by the Mondavi brothers).

The first commercially canned tomato juice is introduced by Libby, McNeill & Libby, which has expanded with plants in Ontario and Washington State, put up additional plants in California, and acquired a Hawaiian pineapple plantation on Molokai. Libby's tomato juice is described as "haylike" in flavor and "brownish" in color (*see* 1929).

Yoo-Hoo chocolate drink is introduced by New Jersey bottler Natale Olivieri, who has been producing fruit drinks by squeezing fresh fruit and has acquired a rotating pressure retort for processing chocolate and milk into a uniform, stable drink (year approximate). To meet growing demand, Olivieri will build a plant at Garfield, N.J. His son Albert will obtain backing from fellow golfers at the White Beeches Country Club in northern New Jersey to obtain and install an English hydrostatic sterilizer, which will carry the noncarbonated product through agitating, high-temperature steam chambers that ensure thorough heat penetration and prevent spoilage. Yoo-Hoo will be packaged in 12-ounce bottles and 8-ounce cans in addition to its initial 7-ounce bottle. Five vitamins and three minerals will later be added, and new Yoo-Hoo plants will be built at Carlstadt, N.J., in Florida, and at Baltimore. Yoo-Hoo will be 99 percent caffeine free.

Sanka Coffee is introduced in the United States (*see* Roselius, 1903; Postum Co., 1928).

The Waldorf chain of eastern U.S. cafeterias has 112 branches; close to 60 percent of its patrons are women.

Chicago restaurateur Gus Mann opens a seafood house decorated with portholes, fishnet, and a fake wheelhouse. Waitresses dressed as sailors serve patrons fresh fish and shellfish delivered daily by train.

Boston's Locke-Obers restaurant survives Prohibition by selling off the Locke section, with its mahogany bar, and scaling down the menu and operations of what remains.

Delmonico's restaurant at New York serves its last dinner May 21 to a gathering of invited guests and closes after 96 years. It has been the city's foremost eating place, rivaled only by Sherry's (*see* 1921), but has been unprofitable since the Volstead Act prohibited sale of wines and liquors (*see* 1925).

The Restaurant de la Pyramide opened at Vienne by French restaurateur Fernand Point, 26, will become an international gastronomic mecca. It takes its name from a nearby Roman pyramid that marked the turn of a chariot racetrack (*see* 1955).

1924

Germany's ruinous inflation ends as Berlin issues a new Reichsmark, imposes strict new taxes, and makes a sharp cut in the availability of credit for business expansion. The Reichsmark is backed 30 percent by gold, and its value is set at 1 billion old marks, which cease to be legal tender and are withdrawn from circulation under terms of a plan devised by a commission headed by Chicago banker Charles Gates Dawes, 59.

Continental Baking Co. is incorporated with headquarters at Chicago to manage a sprawl of nearly 100 plants that produce bread and cake under dozens of different labels. Created by a merger of United Bakeries and other companies, Continental will become the leading U.S. bakery firm (*see* Patterson, 1925; Wonder Bread, Hostess Cakes, 1927).

Distillers Corp., Ltd., is founded by Canadian distiller-bootlegger Samuel Bronfman, 33, and his brother Allan, 28, who borrow the name of Britain's 47-year-old Distillers Co. Ltd. and build their first distillery at Ville La Salle outside Montreal (*see* Distillers Corp.–Seagram, 1928).

Standard Milling Co. of Kansas City acquires the H-O Company, which produces H-O Oats and Presto Flour along with the breakfast food Force, still made by H-O of Canada and still popular in the United Kingdom (*see* 1902).

Production of the first row-crop tractors begins, enabling farmers growing row crops to give up animal power in favor of mechanical power and thus lower their operating costs as well as shortening their workdays. Previously existing machines are adapted to the new tractors: a cultivator, instead of being supported on wheels, is hung directly on the front of the tractor so that the farmer can guide its operation; a corn planter is mounted on the side or rear. But most farmers continue to use horses or mules for traction power, and tractors still have steel wheels with lugs; farmers will be slow to accept rubber-tired tractors, but it is such tractors, which can be operated on modern, hard-surface roads as well as in the fields, that will finally convert farmers to using mechanized traction rather than animal power (*see* Ferguson, 1914).

The first effective chemical pesticides are introduced (*see* DDT, 1939).

Argentine physiologist Bernard Alberto Houssay, 37, demonstrates that the pituitary gland, not just the pancreas, is involved in human sugar breakdown (*see* 1937; Banting, 1922).

Cookbook: *Mrs. Allen on Cooking, Menus, Service: 2,500 Recipes* by Ida C. Bailey Allen.

The Caesar salad is created by some accounts at Tijuana, Mexico, where Italian Air Force veteran Alex Cardini has joined his brother, Caesar, in the hotel (or restaurant) owned by Caesar. When a party of Californians arrives to celebrate July 4, Alex finds little in the cupboard to feed them other than eggs, romaine lettuce, dry bread, Parmesan cheese, garlic, olive oil, lemon juice, and pepper. He makes croutons of the dry bread, mixes them with the other ingrdients, calls the result Aviator Salad, and will rename it after his brother (anchovies will later be added, and sometimes Worcestershire sauce).

Americans consume on average 17.8 pounds of butter, 6.8 pounds of ice cream, 4.5 pounds of cheese, and more than 350 pounds of fluid milk per year (nearly one pint per day).

30 percent of U.S. bread is baked at home, down from 70 percent in 1910.

General Seafoods Co. is founded at Gloucester, Mass., by Clarence Birdseye and three partners, who next year will begin marketing quick-frozen fish fillets (*see* 1925).

Van Camp Sea Food shuts down and goes into receivership after having its credit with American Can Co. canceled for not paying long overdue bills (it had diversified to pack summer citrus fruits and produce). A heavy run of sardines encourages Frank Van Camp to borrow money and go back into business; he makes enough profit to pay off much of the firm's debts and will regain control next year (*see* 1922; 1926).

New York's Fulton Market supplies an estimated 20 percent of all the fish consumed in the United States (*see* 1907; 1939).

Owens Valley, Calif., farmers armed with shotguns sit atop the Los Angeles water gates and blow up the city's aqueduct 17 times to prevent drainage of water from their lands (*see* 1913). State militia drive off the farmers, but the conflict will continue for decades as the Owens Valley dries up.

Boston physicians George Richards Minot, 39, and William Parry Murphy, 32, show that eating liver prevents and cures pernicious anemia. Having studied C. H. Whipple's 1922 discoveries, they show that liver feedings have at least limited value in treating the disease in humans (*see* Cohn, 1926; Lilly, 1928; Castle, 1929).

Botulism from canned California olives causes 16 deaths in the Midwest. All inventories of canned olives are destroyed on orders from Washington, and food brokers refuse to handle lesser-known brands of canned fruits and vegetables such as those of Van Camp (above).

Wheaties is introduced by Washburn, Crosby Co., which will soon advertise the wheat-flake cereal (4.7 percent sugar) as "the breakfast of champions" (*see* 1921; General Mills, 1929).

Harry Burt obtains a patent for the Good Humor (*see* 1920; Brimer, 1926).

Eskimo Pie Co. is acquired by U.S. Foil Co. head Richard S. Reynolds, who has been supplying the company with metal foil (*see* 1922).

The Episcle is patented by Frank Epperson, who will sell the patent to the Joe Lowe Corp., founded in 1902 by food processor Lowe, now 41. Lowe will market the item under the name Popsicle and rename his company Popsicle Corp. (*see* 1923).

Bit-O-Honey candy bars are introduced by Chicago's Schutter-Johnson Co.

Lower cocoa prices enable Hershey Chocolate to increase the weight of its standard nickel bar from 1 oz. to 1⅜ oz. (*see* 1930).

Fruit-flavored Life Savers—fruit drops (cooked candies) made from California oranges, Sicilian lemons, and West Indian limes—are introduced by Life Savers, Inc., which will produce them as solid disks for 6 years until it can perfect machines that can pull the cooked candy into a rope that flows into a mold which creates rings that can be chopped off at a rate of 2,800 per minute and wrapped automatically in rolls of 11 (fewer than the mints because they are thicker) (*see* 1920).

Beech-Nut Coffee is introduced by Beech-Nut Packing Co. (*see* 1899; baby foods, 1931).

Soviet Russia repeals a 10-year-old prohibition against drinking alcoholic beverages (the law has been widely flouted).

New York's Madison Hotel opens in September in East 58th Street with Paul de Moreau as *chef de cuisine* (the hotel, whose dining room will compare with the best in the city, will survive until 1965).

The Stouffer restaurant chain has its beginnings in the Stouffer Lunch opened by local entrepreneur Mahala Stouffer and her husband, Abraham, who 2 years ago invested $12,000 to open a stand-up counter on a busy Cleveland street corner serving baked beans, corned beef hash, lasagna, and home-baked Dutch apple pie. Wharton School of Business graduate Vernon Bigelow Stouffer, 23, joins his parents and will encourage them to open a restaurant in nearby Shaker Square and others at Detroit, Pittsburgh, and New York. The lunch counter will grow into a nationwide operation of restaurants, inns, food services, and food products (*see* 1954).

The Los Angeles restaurant Pantry Café opens at 877 South Figueroa Street, corner of West 9th, serving patrons 24 hours per day. Proprietor Dewey Logan, who will run the place until his death in 1972, will start baking his own cakes and pastries when he can't find acceptable baked products elsewhere. A bakery shop will open next door in 1988, serving all the Pantry's specialties plus sandwiches.

J. Lyons & Co. is sole caterer to the British Empire Exhibition, which opens at Wembley in Middlesex. The company builds 34 restaurants and cafés, puts up 18 snack bars and kiosks, supplies all the food and drink from its Cadby Hall kitchens, and serves up to 26,000 exhibition visitors per day.

The Paris restaurant Chez Marius opens at 5, rue de Bourgogne with specialties that will include loup de mer (Mediterranean sea bass), oursins in season, suprême de barbue (filets of brill poached in white wine with a sauce of creamed tomatoes), coulis de homard, turbotin baked in a sauce of chopped herbs, poulet de l'estragon (November through March), and sweetbreads on asparagus tips.

The Johnson-Reed Immigration Act passed by Congress May 26 limits the annual quota from any country to 2 percent of U.S. residents of that nationality in 1890. The act totally excludes Japanese despite a warning by the Japanese ambassador of grave consequences should the United States abandon the "gentlemen's agreement" of 1908, which permits entry of scholars and professionals (*see* 1965).

1925

Italy's Fascist dictator Benito Mussolini, 42, announces a "wheat battle" to make the country independent in food; by the early 1930s, the Italian wheat crop will be 60 percent larger than in 1922 and Italy will be Europe's third-largest wheat producer (Russia being first, France second).

Harold Ware returns to Russia with 26 volunteers and $150,000 worth of U.S. farm equipment, seeds, and supplies (*see* 1921; 1922). Ware demonstrates mechanized farming on 15,000 acres of land in the northern Caucasus, and he is selected by Moscow to oversee a program of organizing huge mechanized state farms for the improvement of agricultural efficiency throughout Russia, a post he will hold until 1932 (*see* Stalin, 1928).

C. J. Patterson is founded January 1 by Kansas City bakery executive Patterson, now 35, to serve as a general service organization for millers and bakers (*see* Paniplus, 1920). A chemist for United Bakeries before it became part of Continental Baking last year, Patterson will merge his company into the Win M. Campbell Co. early in 1927 and then help form Campbell-Taggart Co. (*see* 1927).

U.S. cocoa merchants, importers, and brokers establish the New York Cocoa Exchange to avoid repetition of the disastrous price break of 1921; they adopt rules modeled on those of the Cotton Exchange and Chicago Board of Trade, enabling confectioners and other users of cocoa to hedge their purchases with futures just as millers, large bakers, and textile converters hedge theirs (*see* 1979).

Life Savers, Inc., goes public, selling 20 percent of its stock in the open market. The company is marketing 170 million nickel rolls of Life Savers per year and netting $1 million; co-founder Roy Allen, now 43, whose initial investment was $1,500, retires with a fortune of $3.3 million.

English soap magnate William H. Lever, first viscount Leverhulme, dies May 7 at age 73 (*see* Mac Fisheries, 1920; Unilever, 1929).

Dean Foods Co. has its beginnings in the Dean Evaporated Milk Co. founded at Pecatonica, Ill., by Michigan-born entrepreneur Samuel E. Dean, 49, whose firm will pioneer in selling fluid milk in paper containers through stores at a time when most dairies sell only in bottles for home delivery. Dean Milk will expand geographically, acquiring smaller dairies, making them profitable, and becoming a major producer of private-label dairy products, supplying Kroger, Jewel Tea, and other grocery chains with milk and milk products to be sold under such brand names as Creamland and Gilt Edge Farms (*see* 1966).

Wesson Oil and Snowdrift Co. is created by a reorganization of the Southern Cotton Oil Co. (*see* Wesson Oil, 1900; Hunt Foods, 1960).

Wise Potato Chips become so popular that Earl Wise builds a 32- by 75-foot concrete-block plant at Berwick, Pa., to replace the remodeled garage in which he has been producing chips since 1921. By 1942 the plant will have expanded to embrace more than 40,000 square feet of floor space (*see* automatic potato-peeling machine, below).

 Jell-O is merged into the Postum Cereal Co. (*see* 1906; 1926).

U.S. refrigerator sales reach 75,000, up from 10,000 in 1920, as prices come down and consumer incomes rise (*see* 1929; GE, 1927).

Automatic potato-peeling machines are introduced that will permit wide-scale production of potato chips (*see* Wise, above).

Clarence Birdseye and Charles Seabrook develop a deep-freezing process for cooked foods (*see* 1924). Tightly packed into a small carton, the food is encased in a metal mold and several such molds are placed in a long metal tube that is immersed in a low-temperature brine solution to produce a quick-contact process which Birdseye patents (*see* 1926).

Sherman-Ferguson Corp. is founded in the United States to produce plows for use with the Fordson tractor (*see* 1920). Production will be discontinued in 1928 (*see* 1935).

Collier's editor William Ludlow Chenery sends three staff writers on a nationwide tour to report on Prohibition. They find a breakdown in law enforcement of all kinds, and *Collier's* becomes the first major magazine to call for a repeal of the 18th Amendment, which has been in effect since January 1920. The magazine loses 3,000 readers but gains 400,000 new ones (*see* 1919).

U.S. physiologists L. S. Fredericia and E. Holm find that rats do not see well in dim light if their diets are lacking in vitamin A (*see* McCollum, 1920; Wald, 1938).

Minnesota Valley Canning Co. begins canning a new, European pea variety—Prince of Wales—which is much larger than the company's Early June variety albeit oblong in shape and wrinkled. Its private-label customers refuse the new variety, so the company brings them out under its own name, adopting as its advertising symbol a giant wearing a bearskin and carrying a club, but customers are not inspired to buy (*see* 1907; jolly Green Giant, 1935).

Mr. Goodbar, introduced by Hershey Chocolate Co., is made of milk chocolate embedded with peanuts. (Hershey now has gross sales of $60 million.)

White Castle System builds a brick hamburger stand at St. Louis, covers it with white enamel, and gives it a white porcelain-enamel interior to suggest absolute cleanliness (*see* 1921). White enamel will hereafter be the mark of all White Castle outlets as Billy Ingram and Walter Anderson expand (*see* New York, 1930).

Some 50 onetime regulars gather August 19 for a farewell luncheon in the ruins of the old Delmonico's restaurant at Fifth Avenue and 44th Street (*see* 1923). E. H. Nies, who as a boy started in one of the downtown Delmonico restaurants at 112 Broadway and rose to be assistant manager of the place now being demolished, recites verses he has written for the occasion: "More of the grape with fire divine/ Shall light the torch of pleasure gay,/ And where the gourmand paused to dine/ Hot dog and fudge shops have their day." Chicken and lobster salad, chicken à la king, minute steak (by Edwin Gould) and Lobster Newberg were all created at Delmonico's, Nies claims, and it was here that french fried potatoes, russian dressing, and terrapin were first served in New York. While bricks and lumber crash a few yards away as workmen prepare the site for a 30-story office tower, patrons enjoy soup, chicken, ice cream, coffee, and sweetmeats—prepared by Brooklyn caterers once employed by the 26th Street Delmonico's—at tables ornamented as in former days with candies in the shape of flowers; fruit is served in dishes made of ice with ferns frozen in them.

The Paris restaurant Lucas-Carton at 9, place de la Madeleine, gets its name as François Carton of the Café Anglais takes over (*see* 1918).

Vienna has 1,250 coffeehouses, down from 15,000 in 1842. Opened, typically, at 6 or 7 o'clock in the morning, closed at midnight, decorated as a rule with dark or wood-paneled walls, crystal chandeliers, well-spaced marble tables, well-upholstered benches covered with dark plush or tan leather, comfortable chairs, and cozy wall niches, the coffeehouse has a hushed atmosphere that makes it a home away from home for many a Viennese, who uses it as an escape from wife, children, employer, creditors, or whatever, and finds it a pleasant place to read, gamble, discuss the day's events, and enjoy not only coffee but also pastry and sometimes heartier fare. A good coffeehouse offers at least 28 kinds of coffee, including mokka, kapuziner (capuchin); coffee with doppelschlag (especially heavy cream); einspänner ("one-horse carriage": black coffee with whipped cream); masacarin (black coffee with crushed ice and rum, served in summer); Turkish varieties; and coffee *verkehrt* ("upside down": four parts milk to one part coffee).

1926

Josef Stalin, 46, establishes himself as virtual dictator of the Soviet Union, beginning a 27-year rule that will deemphasize world revolution but bring new repression to Soviet citizens (especially farmers; *see* 1928) and terror to Russia's neighbors.

A British general strike cripples the nation from May 3 to May 12, the strikers try to prevent ships from off-loading food, but the Royal Navy trains its guns on the strikers, volunteers maintain essential services, and food shortages are minimized.

Hovis flour is milled for the first time in Canada (*see* 1918). Hovis advertising in Britain since 1924 has been using the slogan "Don't say Brown, say Hovis" (*see* 1954).

Anheuser-Busch begins selling yeast as Prohibition continues to prevent the legal sale of beer (*see* corn syrup, 1923). Yeast for bread is grown from strains quite different from those used in brewing, but the fermentation experts at St. Louis are able to produce the strains demanded by bakers (*see* 1933).

The Good Humor Corp. is formed by Cleveland businessmen following the death of Harry Burt (*see* 1924). Tennessee entrepreneur Thomas J. Brimer, 26, and two brothers buy franchises and patent rights (*see* 1929).

Quaker Oats Co. acquires Aunt Jemima Mills for $4 million (*see* 1910; 1913).

Postum Cereal Co. acquires Minute Tapioca (*see* Stavers, 1894) and Igleheart Brothers with its Swans Down cake flour (*see* 1895; Jell-O, 1925; Hellmann's, Log Cabin, Walter Baker, Franklin Baker, 1927).

Colman's Mustard acquires R. T. French's Cream Salad Mustard and becomes the largest mustard producer on both sides of the Atlantic (*see* 1866; French's, 1904; advertising, below).

Safeway Stores is created by a merger of U.S. grocery store chains. Marion Skaggs joins his 428 stores with those of the Sam Seelig Co. of southern California to form a chain of 466 stores that will grow to surpass the A&P in sales by 1973 (*see* 1915; 1931).

First National Stores is created by a merger of Boston's 31-year-old Ginter Co. with the O'Keefe and John T. Connor companies.

IGA (Independent Grocers' Alliance Distributing Co.) is launched at Poughkeepsie, N.Y., where 60 eastern and midwestern retail grocers meet in the fall to organize a defense against inroads on their sales by such corporate chain store giants as A&P and First National (above). IGA will develop its own brands of coffee and other products as it grows to include more than 3,600 stores in 46 states.

Standard Fruit and Steamship Co. is created at New Orleans by a reorganization of the banana importing firm Vaccaro Brothers (*see* 1898). Standard Fruit now has a fleet of refrigerated steamships and extensive banana lands in Honduras that challenge the United Fruit Co. and Samuel Zemurray (*see* 1964).

The *Chief* departs from Chicago's Dearborn Station November 14 to begin daily Santa Fe Railroad service between Chicago and Los Angeles, providing passengers on its seven sleeping cars with Fred Harvey dining car cuisine (*see De Luxe,* 1911; *Super Chief,* 1936).

Clarence Birdseye develops a belt freezer for his General Seafoods Co., a small freezing plant on Fort Wharf at Gloucester, Mass. (*see* 1925). Postum Cereal boss Marjorie Merriweather Post puts in at Gloucester to have her yacht provisioned, her chef obtains a frozen goose from General Seafoods, she eats goose and seeks out Birdseye, who is selling quantities of frozen fish (and reviving the Massachusetts fishing industry) but is on the verge of bankruptcy. His freezing process impresses Post, but her stockbroker husband, E. F. Hutton, and board of directors oppose paying $2 million to buy Birdseye's patents and business (*see* 1929).

Machine-made ice production in the United States reaches 56 million tons, up from 1.5 million in 1894 (*see* 1889). Much of it is used to chill illegal beer, highballs, and cocktails (below).

An improved waterproof cellophane developed by E. I. du Pont chemists William Hale Church and Karl Edwin Prindle will revolutionize packaging, especially of snack foods such as potato chips (*see* Brandenberger, 1912). Du Pont has been making cellophane at Buffalo, N.Y., since 1924.

The Toastmaster Model 1A1, introduced by Waters-Genter Co. at $12.50, is the first automatic pop-up toaster (*see* 1918). The chrome, one-slice appliance promises in its advertising to produce "perfect toast every time" (*see* 1930; Universal, 1929).

The Theory of the Gene by Columbia University zoologist Thomas Hunt Morgan, 60, proves a theory of hereditary transmission that will be the basis for all future genetic research. Morgan's book *The Physical Bases of Heredity* appeared in 1919, and he has conducted experiments with fruit flies to pinpoint the location of genes in the chromosomes of the cell nucleus (*see* Bateson, 1902; Watson and Crick, 1953).

U.S. biologist Herman Joseph Muller, 35, finds that X rays can produce mutations. His work will speed up the process of mutation for gene studies and makes him a leading advocate for limiting exposure to X rays and for sperm banks to conserve healthy genes.

"Plant wizard" Luther Burbank dies at Santa Rosa, Calif., April 11 at age 77 (*see* 1875). He has manipulated hereditary traits by hybridizations made with little regard to the actual useful characteristics of the crossed parents.

Trofim Denisovich Lysenko, 28, gains notice for the first time in the Soviet Union. The agronomist puts ideology ahead of science and will have enormous influence on Soviet farm policies (*see* 1935).

U.S. biochemist James Batchellor Sumner, 38, crystallizes an enzyme and proves that enzymes are proteins.

Ergotism from infected rye breaks out in the Soviet Union; in some places, half the population is affected (*see* 1862; 1951).

Illegal liquor traffic has spawned a gigantic underworld of criminal activity since 1919 and is now estimated to be a $3.6 billion business. Widespread defiance of the Prohibition laws is encouraging citizens to flout other laws, and the "Noble Experiment" is clearly a failure (*see* Wickersham, 1931).

California's tuna packing industry collapses as albacore disappear from offshore waters. San Pedro packs only 51,223 cases, down from 358,940 last year, and the San Diego pack drops to less than 14,600, down from 95,000.

Van Camp Sea Food sales manager Roy P. Harper, 33, decides to promote yellowfin tuna, which can be packed all year round, and by eliminating all flakes, packing the yellowfin in solid pieces, and calling it "Fancy" tuna he creates a demand for fish heretofore scorned because its flesh is not the white meat associated with albacore. Harper has introduced the brand names Chicken of the Sea and White Star (see 1924, 1962).

California potato king George Shima of Empire Delta Farms dies of a stroke in April at age 61, leaving an estate of between $15 and $17 million (see 1899).

Pioneer Hi-Bred International has its beginnings in a hybrid seed company founded at Des Moines by Iowa farmer-editor Henry Agard Wallace, 37, who initiated an Iowa Corn Yield Contest some years ago and won it himself in 1924 with a misshapen red-kerneled hybrid which he named Copper Cross (see Shull, 1921). Wallace's father, Henry C., died 2 years ago and Henry A. has gone into partnership with his brother James and corn breeder Raymond Baker. His idea, he will write in 1932, is to "improve corn by controlling its pollination. The best hybrids of the future will be so much better than the best hybrids of today that there will be no comparison." His company, started with $4,900 raised by selling 49 shares at $100 per share, will grow to have laboratories, greenhouses, fields, processing plants, and research stations operating in 90 countries and will sell 645 million pounds of seed corn per year.

Harvard physician Edwin Joseph Cohn, 33, develops an oral liver extract to treat pernicious anemia (see 1930; Minot and Murphy, 1924; Castle, 1929; blood plasma, 1940).

The B vitamin proves to be more than one vitamin (see McCollum, 1916). Joseph Goldberger shows that rats can be cured of pellagra on a diet from which the heat-labile part of vitamin B has been removed (see 1915; Smith and Hendrick, 1928).

British biochemists O. Rosenheim and T. A. Webster show that sunlight converts the sterol ergosterol into vitamin D in animals (see Steenbock, 1923). Their findings explain why children who do not get enough sunlight are vulnerable to rickets (see 1930).

J. Lyons & Co. introduces packaged cake, pioneering national distribution of such products (see tea, 1923). The 4½ d. Lyons Swiss Roll, available with a variety of fillings, will become a household name throughout the United Kingdom, with sales reaching 2½ million in some weeks, and Lyons Individual Fruit Pies will be just as popular (the Cadby Hall factory will produce 2 billion of them).

The London advertising agency S. H. Benson launches a campaign for Colman's Mustard (above) that will continue for 7 years (see Bovril, 1893). Posters on the sides of buses ask, "Has Father joined the Mustard Club?" An advertisement in the Daily Mirror October 29 asks, "What is this Mustard Club?" A prospectus is published, 2,000 applications per day pour in, Colman's opens a special department with 10 young women to handle them, five Mustard Club songs are published, and the club motto ("Mustard makyth Methusaleh") appears in advertisements (see store, 1973).

Hormel Flavor-Sealed Ham is the first U.S. canned ham. George A. Hormel & Co. has been slaughtering upwards of a million hogs per year since 1924, produces its canned ham by a process patented by German inventor Paul Jorn, and enjoys immediate success (see Spam, 1937).

Liederkranz cheese maker Monroe Cheese Co. moves to Van Wert, Ohio, to obtain a dependable supply of fresh milk (see 1892; Borden, 1929).

Hain Foods has its beginnings at Los Angeles, where suburban farmer Harold Hain introduces canned carrot juice. He will broaden his product line to include all-natural soups, which he will sell to his neighbors, and will go on to produce a corn oil to be used for fried products in place of lard, butter, and other animal fats. By expeller-pressing the oil without heat (other than that generated by friction) or petroleum-based solvents, he will be able to claim natural health benefits, permitting him to sell his cooking oil and other products to health food stores. Hain will sell his company in 1940 to Herman Jacobs, and by the late 1940s and early '50s his products will begin to be sold in supermarkets under the Hollywood brand name, which will also be used for a growing line that will include mayonnaises, salad dressings, and safflower-oil margarines and will have strong sales on the West Coast. Hain safflower oils and peanut oils will gain national distribution (see 1983).

Spanish yogurt maker Isaac Carasso introduces flavored yogurt to Paris. He moves from Barcelona and opens a large factory to serve the larger French market but finds that the French prefer plain yogurt (*see* 1941; Dannon, 1942).

Holloway's Milk Duds, introduced by Chicago candy maker Milton J. Holloway, are chewy caramels covered in milk chocolate (*see* Pom Poms, 1948).

Boston candy maker Robert Welch reenters the business in the summer (*see* 1922). Capitalizing on the popularity of lollipops, he manufactures and sells the Papa sucker, a rich caramel on a stick, and does well enough to open a plant in Chicago. Sales will languish, despite the booming postwar demand for candy, so he will close the Chicago plant in 1928 and open a new one in Brooklyn, N.Y., where he will continue for 3 years while working, also, as an executive with E. J. Brach & Sons of Chicago (*see* 1934).

The Paris hotel Lancaster opens at 7, rue de Berri off the Avenue des Champs-Elysées. Formerly a private residence (*hôtel particulier*) and then an exclusive apartment house, the building was acquired last year by Émile Wolf of Montreux, who rebuilt it, adding floors and a rear wing, and filled the rooms with good French antiques, paintings, and lamps. The Lancaster and its elegant dining room will soon attract a clientele that includes royalty, aristocrats, and the Hollywood film crowd. It will be sold in 1970 to London's Savoy Group.

The Brussels restaurant Comme Chez Soi opens in the heart of the city. Chef-proprietor George Cuvelier serves moules et frites (steamed mussels and french-fried potatoes) and will do so well that in 10 years he will purchase a fine town house at 23, place Rouppe with a long, narrow dining room with beveled mirrors and a seating capacity of 40 at 14 tables.

The Zurich restaurant Zeughauskeller opens off the Bahnhofstrasse in a building that began as an armory in 1469, became a granary in 1529, and has been a warehouse since 1867. Specialties include country ham, beef goulash, sliced beef dried in Alpine air, rippli mit sauerkraut (smoked ribs of pork with sauerkraut), saftiger schinken, and a wide variety of sausages such as bauernrachwurst (roast beef and pork sausage) and bierwurst strudel mit senf (a thick slice of veal and ham sausage spread with mustard and encased in pastry).

London's Quo Vadis restaurant opens at 26–29 Dean Street, Soho, under the direction of a chef named Leoni whose cuisine will attract many authors and artists.

The New York restaurant Christ Cella opens as a speakeasy on the ground floor of a brownstone boarding house in East 45th Street. Italian-born restaurateur Christopher Cella, 29, serves liquor in coffee cups, saying that any society which denies a man a glass of wine at the end of the day is not worthy of the name, and attracts patrons with French cuisine, which will give way in time to hearty portions of T-bone and sirloin steak, thick lamb chops, soft-shell crabs in season, rice pudding, and apple pie (*see* 1947).

The New York chop house The Palm opens at 837 Second Avenue, between 44th and 45th streets. Italian-American restaurateurs Pio Bozzi and John Ganzi intended to name their place Parma after the capital of their native province, Emilia, but have been frustrated by a city clerk who has licensed the name Palm. Marriott Corp. (*see* 1927) will acquire The Palm and operate other restaurants under that name in Chicago, Dallas, East Hampton, N.Y., Houston, Las Vegas, Los Angeles, Miami, and Washington, D.C.

The Baltimore restaurant Haussner's opened by William Haussner will grow to serve 1,000 customers daily with seafood from the Chesapeake Bay, meat dishes, and German and Hungarian specialties—sauerbraten, potato dumplings, paprika schnitzel with spätzle (egg noodles), goulash—and strawberry pie.

The Los Angeles restaurant The Brown Derby, owned by Robert Cobb, introduces Cobb salad, made to Cobb's specifications of ripe avocado, fresh tomato, and watercress (purchased by Cobb as he walks to work) combined by his chefs with chopped lettuce, crisp bacon, chicken, Roquefort cheese, and hard-boiled egg arranged in a striped pattern in a flat bowl and topped with French dressing.

California entrepreneur Julius Freed opens a fresh orange juice stand in downtown Los Angeles and soon has sales of $20 per day. Real estate broker Bill Hamlin, who found Freed his location, uses his chemistry background to devise a formula for an orange drink with a smooth, frothy texture, patrons like it and say, "Give me an orange, Julius," Freed's sales leap to $100 per day, Hamlin quits the real estate business to develop the Orange Julius business, and by 1929 he will have 100 Orange Julius stands nationwide, selling nothing but the 10¢ drink and grossing nearly $3 million (*see* Canada, 1962).

1927

"A Report of the Investigation of the Peasant Movement in Hunan" by Chinese Communist Mao Zedong, 34, reports that the Communist-led Peasants' Association has adopted rules forbidding sumptuous feasts. In one county, guests are to be served only three kinds of animal food—chicken, fish, and pork—and there is a ban on egg-cake feasts, "which are by no means sumptuous." People have refrained from eating expensive foods, Mao reports, and use only fruit when making ancestral sacrifices. In another county, it is forbidden to serve bamboo shoots, kelp, or lentil noodles, and while in some parts of the country eight dishes may be served at a banquet, the number in one district is limited to five, in another only meat and three vegetable dishes may be served, and in a third there is a total ban on New Year's feasts. In the Beijing dialect, to have a job is to have *chiao ku* (grains to chew) and to have lost one's job is to have *ta p'o le fan wan* (a broken rice bowl).

The Supreme Court denies a Federal Trade Commission request for further dissolution of the International Harvester trust, whose McCormick and Deering harvesting machines have been separated by the court order of 1920.

American Sugar Refining's share of the U.S. sugar market falls to 25 percent, down from nearly 100 percent in 1899, but its 16-year-old Domino brand remains the top-selling table sugar. National Sugar Refining with its 14-year-old Jack Frost brand controls 22 percent of the market, and while 13 other U.S. companies refine imported raw sugar, none has more than a 7 percent share.

Campbell-Taggart is chartered July 14 at Kansas City with $3 million in capital as Win M. Campbell and A. L. Taggart take over the Manor Baking Co., which began selling its products December 8, 1925, with home delivery by horse and wagon (*see* 1944).

United Biscuit Co. is incorporated to challenge National Biscuit and Loose-Wiles for a share of the U.S. biscuit, cracker, and cookie market. The new holding company operates 12 regional baking companies (*see* Keebler, 1966).

Hershey Chocolate Co. is incorporated.

Switzerland's Sprüngli family wins an 18-year-old lawsuit against members of the Lindt family (*see* 1875). The dispute arose over Sprüngli's merger with Lindt.

Postum Cereal Co. acquires Hellman's Mayonnaise and extends distribution nationwide (*see* 1912; 1932). It also acquires Log Cabin Products (whose maple syrup content it will reduce from its 1887 level of 45 percent to 3 percent as maple sugar prices rise), Walter Baker Chocolate Co. (*see* 1824; German Chocolate Cake, 1958), and Franklin Baker Co. (*see* coconut, 1895; Calumet, Cheek-Neal, Sanka, 1928).

The S.S. *Île de France* arrives at New York on her maiden voyage. The 43,000-ton French Line "Boulevard of the Atlantic" receives a lavish welcome from publisher William Randolph Hearst, 44, whose editor, Henry Sell, 37, has arranged for invited guests to be helped from their cars to rolling chairs rented from an Atlantic City concessionaire, bundled into steamer rugs, and served by waiters pouring magnums of Dom Perignon '21 champagne as they are pushed 100 yards to the gangplank (violinists accompany each chair). In the main dining salon, which is decorated with pink satin trees and expensive shrubs sprayed with silver paint, guests are served a dinner that begins with caviar aux blinis and ends with a 90-year-old cognac from the cellars of the Hôtel de Paris at Monte Carlo.

U.S. pilot Charles A. Lindbergh, 25, makes the first solo flight across the Atlantic May 21 (*see* candy bars, below).

Hawaiian pineapple king James D. Dole offers a prize of $25,000 with a second prize of $10,000 to the first aviators who fly from the U.S. West Coast to Hawaii. Two of the four planes that compete for the prizes fail to arrive, a fifth plane that sets out in search of the missing fliers also disappears, and altogether the stunt ends with seven persons vanishing; their remains will never be found.

General Electric introduces a refrigerator with a "monitor top" containing a hermetically sealed compressor. The 14-cubic-foot refrigerator sells for

$525, few can afford it, but it will make GE the industry leader by 1930 (*see* 1925; 1929).

England has an epidemic of ergot poisoning from contaminated flour.

 April flood waters in the lower Mississippi Valley cover 4 million acres and cause $300 million in property loss (*see* Flood Control Act, 1928).

A survey of two Mississippi cotton-growing areas reveals that 94 percent of the farmers have their own milk cows.

 Harry Steenbock patents his 1923 discovery of vitamin D irradiation and assigns the patent to the Wisconsin Alumni Research Foundation, rejecting all commercial offers (*see* Borden's vitamin D fortified milk, 1933; Pet evaporated milk, 1934; but *see also* 1946).

Wonder Bread is introduced in a balloon-decorated wrapper by Continental Baking Co. (*see* 1924). The company moves its headquarters to New York as Kansas City baking executive M. Lee Marshall becomes board chairman (*see* sliced bread, 1930).

Hostess Cakes are introduced by Continental Baking Co. (above; *see* Twinkies, 1930).

Lender's Bagel Bakery is founded at West Haven, Conn., to produce the hard glazed rolls that have been known since 1919 as beigels (*see* 1610; bagel, 1932). Polish baker Harry Lender, who has recently arrived from Lodz, starts the first bagel bakery outside New York City to produce bagels for sale through Jewish delicatessens and and bakeries in New Haven. Lender's sons Murray and Marvin will take over the business and introduce flash-frozen bagels that can be shipped anywhere, and Lender's will become the largest U.S. bagel baker (*see* Kraft, 1984).

Burnham & Morrill of Portland, Maine, introduces B&M Brick Oven Baked Beans (*see* 1875). George B. Morrill, whose father died in 1901, borrowed money in 1910 to buy out the interests of George Burnham, who died in 1909. By 1955, B&M will have a plant at East Deering, Maine, employing 500 people year round packing beans, pork and beans (using molasses from the Caribbean), brown bread, meat products, and fish stews, plus a country plant that operates on a seasonal basis with 1,500 men and women packing string beans, corn, squash, and

blueberries for sale from New England south to Norfolk, Va., on the West Coast, and from Florida to New Orleans, with Brick Oven Baked Beans their biggest seller.

Gerber Baby Foods has its beginnings at Fremont, Mich., where local food processor Daniel F. Gerber, 28, is told by doctors to feed his sick daughter Sally strained peas. Gerber finds that strained baby foods are commercially available but are expensive, sold only in a few parts of the country, and available only at pharmacies only by a doctor's prescription (*see* 1928).

Pez peppermint breath mints (for smokers) are introduced at Vienna, taking their name from the German word *pfefferminz*. A plastic dispenser will be introduced in 1948, U.S. manufacture will begin in 1952, and Pez will be repositioned as a children's candy in a variety of fruit flavors—grape, lemon, orange, and strawberry—with heads of cartoon characters on the dispensers.

U.S. candy makers introduce bars with names such as Lindy's Lunch, Lindy Bar, and Flying Lindy in an effort to capitalize on the feat of Lindbergh (above). Lindbergh took five sandwiches on his historic flight but no candy bars.

England Confectionery Company moves into a vast new Art Deco factory across from MIT in Cambridge, Mass. (*see* 1901). Freight cars carrying candy ingredients can move right into the plant to discharge their cargoes (*see* Bolster, 1930).

Mike & Ike—chewy fruit-flavored candies—are introduced by Brooklyn candy maker Samuel Born, who also introduces chewy, cinnamon-flavored candies under the name Hot Tamales. Both are artificially flavored.

Kool-Aid is introduced by Hastings, Nebr., inventor-entrepreneur Edwin E. Perkins, who has built a business selling his Nix-O-Tine tobacco-quitting kit, Onor-Maid flavorings, spices, and the like by direct mail and through door-to-door salesmen. His Fruit Smack soft drink concentrate, which comes in six flavors (including cherry and grape) and enables a family to make a pitcherful for pennies, has been his best-seller, but it comes in heavy bottles which often break, so he has engaged a chemist to reduce the concentrate to a dry powder and has renamed it. Within 2 years, Perkins will have his entire family weighing out crystals, pouring them into envelopes, pounding the envelopes flat with wooden mallets, and packing them into boxes. He will move the business to Chicago in 1930 and by 1936 will be racking up net sales of $1.5 million (*see* General Foods, 1953).

Homogenized milk is introduced successfully by Ottawa's Laurentian Dairy, which sells its first bottle April 8 (*see* 1919). An unsuccessful attempt was made at La Colle, Que., from 1910 to 1912, and the progress of the milk has been retarded in part by health claims that had no scientific basis, but it will soon be available in Toronto and other Canadian cities (*see* 1932).

Welch's tomato juice (bottled) and the carbonated grape drink Welch-ade are introduced (*see* 1923; 1945)

The French Parliament passes a law July 22 demarking the Champagne zone 90 miles northeast of Paris. Only wine bottled in the demarked region may be labeled "champagne."

The Paris restaurant La Coupole opens at 102, boulevard du Montparnasse with a terrace that opens in the summer and is enclosed in winter. Specialties will include omelette *norvégienne*, frankfurters garnished with potatoes, oysters (claires more than belons or marennes), *oursins*, scallops, sole, daurade, turbot, *escargots de Bourgogne*, civet, *lièvre à la française, choucroute alsacienne, cassoulet d'oie toulousain*, a whole truffle in a layer of foie gras enveloped in a puff paste, meats grilled over charcoal, curry of lamb, curry of chicken, hot apple pie, lemon tart, *crêpe flambé*, soufflés, Fontainebleau (white cheese eaten with sugar and fresh, heavy cream), draft beer, stout, pale ale, Creole punch, Swedish punch, and cider.

Marriott's Hot Shoppe opens at Washington, D.C., at the corner of 14th Street and Park Road N. W. Utah-born entrepreneur John Willard Marriott, 27, has invested his savings of $1,000 plus $1,500 in borrowed capital to obtain an exclusive franchise to sell A&W Root Beer in Washington, Baltimore, and Richmond using syrup obtained from two westerners named Allen and Wright; his business has fallen off in the fall, he has hired a barbecue cook and has borrowed some recipes from the chef of the nearby Mexican Embassy, and he puts his bride, Alice,

behind the stove to make hot tamales and chili con carne. The nine-seat root beer stand will grow into the Marriott Corp., a worldwide empire of Hot Shoppes, Big Boy Coffee Shops, Roy Rogers Family Restaurants (*see* Hardee's, 1990), Farrell's Ice Cream Parlours, Palm restaurants (*see* 1926), and numerous business, hospital, and other institutional food service operations plus hotels.

Boston's Ritz Hotel opens May 18 at the corner of Arlington and Newberry streets, opposite the Public Garden, with a dining room that will be famous for its scrod breakfast.

New York's Russian Tea Room opens at 150 West 57th Street, serving tea, homemade pastries, and ice cream (it will not serve vodka until after Repeal in 1933, when its soda fountain will give way to a bar stocked with 20 varieties). Members of the Russian Imperial Ballet who fled the Revolution of 1917 have started the tea room as a meeting place for other Russian émigrés (*see* 1945).

The Los Angeles restaurant Les Frères Taix opens at 321 Commercial Street, charging 40¢ for lunch, 50¢ for dinner. Marius Taix, who came to California from his native France in the 1880s, baked French sourdough bread, left his bakery in the hands of a cousin in 1912 to build a hotel, or pension, on the site, and died last year; his son, Marius, Jr., a druggist who is able to obtain medicinal wines, takes over the place and is soon serving escargots, roast chicken, and trout amandine to city officials, who sit in a back room and order wine with their meals. Taix will build a larger, more formal restaurant in 1962 at 1911 Sunset Boulevard, between Silver Lake and Echo Park.

Los Angeles's Mayflower Hotel opens December 26 with a ground-floor restaurant, Ye Bull Pen, designed as a cattle shed. Diners walk across a straw-strewn concrete floor to reach their "stalls," which are lighted by coal-oil lamps, and eat $1.50 steaks on a plank. The 12-story hotel across from the Biltmore Hotel on Grand Avenue will be renamed Checkers in 1990.

1928

Former Secretary of Commerce Herbert C. Hoover, now 54, wins the U.S. presidential election after a campaign in which he has been quoted as promising a chicken in every pot and a car in every garage (a paraphrase of a remark reportedly made by France's Henri IV to the king of Savoy in 1606).

Josef Stalin orders collectivization of Soviet agriculture in the first Five-Year Plan (*see* 1926). Peasants burn crops, slaughter livestock, and hide grain from state collectors (but *see* 1931).

President Calvin Coolidge, 56, sets a protective tariff of 50 percent on genuine imported Swiss cheese. Wisconsin cheese makers present the president with a 147-pound wheel of Green County Swiss cheese to show their appreciation.

Progresso Foods has its beginnings in a firm started at New Orleans by an Italian immigrant named Taormina to import virgin Sicilian olive oil. His company will grow to become a major producer of ready-to-eat soups, bread crumbs, tomato sauces, marinated artichoke hearts, and pignoli nuts, as well as olive oil (*see* 1969).

Distillers Corp.–Seagram is founded in March by Samuel and Allan Bronfman, who last year bought out the Joseph E. Seagram & Sons company founded in 1870 and own a 40 percent interest in the new company (*see* 1924). Despite U.S. Prohibition laws, the Bronfmans are shipping hundreds of thousands of gallons of liquor that winds up in the United States, and they will make Seagram the world's largest producer of alcoholic beverages (*see* 1933).

Nehi Corp. is created by a reorganization of Chero-Cola Co., whose nearly 500 bottling plants are mostly in the South (*see* 1920; Royal Crown Cola, 1934).

Court rulings invalidate the 1919 Eskimo Pie patent, but the old "I-Scream-Bar" has such a large share of the chocolate-covered ice cream market that little is changed (*see* 1924).

Borden Co. acquires J. M. Horton Ice Cream Co. (*see* 1851) and Reid Ice Cream Corp., which holds the patents on Mel-O-Rol, a popular form of ice cream cone. Borden has expanded geographically by acquisition since the turn of the century, constructing condenseries in Tennessee and buying the U.S. and Canadian holdings of its chief competitor, Anglo-Swiss Condensed Milk Co.

Borden Co. (above) acquires the Merrell-Soule Co., originator of Klim (milk spelled backwards) whole milk powder, which has worldwide distribution. Merrell-Soule is also the manufacturer of None Such mincemeat, which becomes Borden's first non-milk-based food product and, along with condensed and evaporated milk, will be the start of a major line of grocery products. Borden is acquiring hundreds of other companies to maintain its lead over National Dairy Corp. (below; *see* 1929).

J. L. Kraft & Co. buys out its leading competitor, Phenix Cheese, which has been making processed cheese under license from Kraft, and creates the largest U.S. cheese company under the name Kraft-Phenix (*see* 1900; 1915; Velveeta, below; National Dairy Corp., 1929).

National Dairy Corp. acquires Breakstone Brothers and General Ice Cream (*see* 1923). Breakstone has pioneered in producing whipped salt-free butter and makes cottage cheese as well as cream cheese, which beginning in the 1930s will be sold in paper containers (*see* 1918; 1943).

Beatrice Creamery Co. acquires Pioneer Creamery of Galesburg, Ill., for $1.5 million with help from Clinton Howard Haskell, a nephew of Beatrice's late founder (*see* 1905). Pioneer's salty Holland brand butter is popular in New England markets and by the fall of next year Beatrice will be operating 50 subsidiary companies, 30 creameries, 33 milk plants, 54 ice cream plants, and dozens of cold-storage warehouses, ice plants, and the like from Ohio to Montana.

National Biscuit Co. acquires Shredded Wheat Co. for $35 million. Shredded Wheat's basic patent expired more than 16 years ago, and the Supreme Court will declare its name common property in 1938 (*see* 1900; Kraft General Foods, 1993).

Postum Cereal Co. acquires the Cheek-Neal Coffee Co., which markets Maxwell House coffee, rights to distribute Sanka coffee (*see* 1903; 1933), and Calumet Baking Powder (*see* Wright, 1889; General Foods, 1929).

Glidden Food Products Co. acquires Portland Vegetable Oil Co. and Wisconsin Food Producers Co. It will add Chicago's Troco Margarine Co. and additional margarine makers to gain a captive market for its refinery operations (*see* 1929).

Battle Creek, Mich., inventor Otto Frederick Rohwedder perfects the commercial bread slicer in January after 15 years of work (he made his first model in 1917, but it was destroyed in a fire), and it is used for the first time in a commercial bakery at Chillicothe, Mo., in May. Unlike machines used at delicatessens to cut off one slice of meat at a time, Rohwedder's reciprocating knife-frame slicing machine can slice an entire loaf in one operation. After a loaf is sliced it must be wrapped at once to keep the slices together, and many bakers, reluctant to invest in new equipment and labor, will wait to see whether sliced bread is more than a passing fad. Consumers are suspicious at first (sliced bread does grow stale faster) but will soon accept the product enthusiastically (*see* Wonder Bread, 1930).

U.S. companies use glyceride emulsifiers for the first time in baked goods, shortenings, margarines, ice creams, and other foods.

Radio: *The National Farm and Home Hour* debuts to attract rural U.S. family audiences.

"I say it's spinach and I say the hell with it," reads E. B. White's caption to Carl Rose's *New Yorker*

Broccoli, a form of cauliflower, was familiar to Europeans but new to American tables.

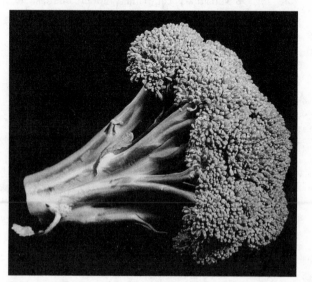

magazine cartoon December 8 showing a child refusing to eat broccoli. The vegetable has only recently been introduced into the United States from Italy by D'Arrigo Brothers, an enterprising grower in northern California's Santa Clara Valley (*see* Popeye, 1929).

At least 1,565 Americans die from drinking bad liquor, hundreds are blinded, many are killed in bootlegger wars. Federal agents and coast guardsmen are making 75,000 arrests per year, and enforcement of Prohibition laws costs U.S. taxpayers millions of dollars, but the laws are openly flouted.

A statue is unveiled at Vimoutiers, France, to honor Marie Harel, even though many question whether it was really she who reinvented Camembert cheese in 1791 (*see* 1859; 1890). Former French President Alexandre Millerand officiates at the ceremony, which has been arranged by an American cheese importer.

The first Feria Internationale del Tartuffo opens at Alba in Italy's Piedmont section. Giacomo Morra, head of Turtuffe More, the Piedmont's largest exporter of white truffles, has organized the fair.

A great meat pie, the largest ever, is carried through the streets of Denby Dale, Yorkshire, England, on a 10-ton lorry August 4. Created for an Infirmary Carnival, it is preceded by a band and followed by a procession, pursuant to a custom recorded as early as 1788. It weighs nearly six tons, measures 16 feet by 5, is 15 inches deep, contains 600 pounds of beef, five bullocks, 1,500 pounds of potatoes, 1,120 pounds of flour, 28 pounds of baking powder, and 224 pounds of lard—enough for 20,000 good-sized portions, which are served on souvenir plates.

A Flood Control Act passed by Congress May 15 provides an estimated $325 million to be spent over the course of 10 years for levee work on the lower Mississippi (*see* 1927).

Soviet scientists lead the world in plant breeding and genetic livestock development, largely as a result of biological research programs developed by Nikolai Ivanovich Vavilov to benefit socialist agriculture (but *see* 1940).

Vitamin C (ascorbic acid) is isolated from capsicums (peppers) at the Cambridge, England, laboratory of

Frederick Gowland Hopkins by Hungarian-born biochemist Albert Szent-Györgyi von Nagyrapolt, 35, who finds the capsicums nearly four times as rich in the antiscurvy vitamin as lemons are (*see* 1918; Lind, 1747; Hopkins, 1906; King, 1932).

U.S. biochemists M. I. Smith and E. G. Hendrick show that vitamin B is at least two vitamins and name the heat-resistant vitamin G, or B_2 (*see* 1926; McCollum, 1916; Warburg, 1932).

Eli Lilly introduces Liver Extract No. 43 to treat pernicious anemia (*see* Cohn, 1926; Castle, 1929).

Velveeta cheese is introduced by Kraft (above). A cooking cheese loaf with a taste all its own, Velveeta was originally developed in 1915 by Phenix Cheese Co. chemist Elmer E. Eldredge, who was employed to duplicate Swiss Gruyère processed cheese, separated the whey protein from the waste product whey produced in cheese making, mixed the protein with cheese (American, Swiss, and/or Camembert) and the antioxidant sodium citrate, and called it Phen-ett. Kraft scientists developed a similar product and called it NuKraft; the two companies agreed to share patent rights. Velveeta is sold as a unique product that children will like (*see* Miracle Whip salad dressing, 1933; Cheez Whiz, 1953).

Sliced bread (above) will increase use of butter and other spreads. A housewife who slices her own bread may cut only a few slices in order to avoid waste, and her family may eat only what has been sliced. They are more likely to eat extra slices if the bread is already sliced. Bread slices from O. F. Rohwedder's bread slicer, moreover, tend to be thinner than slices cut at home, and as the loaves have more slices this will result in greater use of butter, margarine, peanut butter, cheese, jams, and jellies.

Peter Pan Peanut Butter is introduced by Swift Packing Co.'s E. K. Pond division and is the first hydrogenated, homogenized peanut butter and the first to have national advertising (*see* 1904; Normann, 1901). E. K. Pond has been licensed to use a process invented in 1923 by Alameda, Calif., food processor J. L. Rosefield to stabilize peanut butter by replacing a significant part of its natural peanut oil with hydrogenated peanut oil. The new brand, which will soon be marketed by Swift's Derby Foods division, takes its name from the 24-year-old

James M. Barrie character (*see* Skippy, 1932; Jif, 1958).

National Biscuit Co. (above) introduces peanut butter cracker sandwich packets under the name NAB, selling the 5¢ packets through newsstands, drugstores, candy counters, and other such retail outlets (*see* Ritz, 1931).

Rice Krispies, introduced by Kellogg, will be advertised in 1932 as being "So crisp, it crackles in cream." A gnome wearing a baker's hat will appear on the cereal box's side panel in 1933, two other such gnomes will be added in print ads a year or two later, but the "Snap! Crackle! Pop!" trio will not be on the box until about 1937.

Daniel Gerber improves baby foods with improved methods for straining peas and finds by a market survey that a large market exists for such foods if they can be sold cheaply through grocery stores (*see* 1927). Gerber advertises in *Child's Life* magazine and offers six cans for a dollar (less than half the price of baby foods sold at pharmacies) to customers who will send in coupons filled out with the names and addresses of their grocers (*see* 1929).

The Butterfinger candy bar introduced by Chicago's Curtiss Candy Co. is a chocolate-covered honeycomb peanut butter confection which Otto Schnering sends to the South Pole with Admiral Richard E. Byrd, 39 (*see* Baby Ruth, 1920). Schnering has promoted Baby Ruth by chartering an airplane and parachuting candy bars down over Pittsburgh, causing a massive traffic jam as people rushed into the streets to scramble for the free candy. He will have Butterfingers dropped along with Baby Ruths on cities in 40 states, and the stunt will help make Curtiss brands national favorites (*see* Standard Brands, 1964).

Schrafft's Candy Co. moves into a large new Boston plant at 529 Main Street (*see* 1897; 1929).

Barricini Candy Co. is founded at New York.

California's Ahwahnee Hotel opens in Yosemite Park with a dining room 140 feet long. Guests take meals under a 40-foot-high ceiling as they admire the view of Yosemite Falls.

London's Oxford Corner House, the third such J. Lyons & Co. establishment, opens on the corner of

Oxford Street and Tottenham Court Road with seating for 2,500 (*see* 1915; 1933).

The Peninsula Hotel opens in Hong Kong December 11 with its own bakery, a delicatessen, and restaurants that include Gaddi's, which has five waiters for each table and will develop a reputation as the finest dining spot in East Asia.

1929

💲 Britain's Chancellor of the Exchequer Winston Churchill, 54, abolishes the 325-year-old tea duty April 15, knocking 4 d. off the price of a pound of tea.

Seventy-one percent of U.S. families have incomes below $2,500, which is generally considered the minimum necessary for a decent standard of living. The average weekly wage is $28, and the nation's economy worsens after Wall Street's Dow Jones Industrial Average plummets in October (*see* 1932).

Half of all U.S. farm families produce less than $1,000 worth of food, fiber, or tobacco each per year; 750,000 farm families produce less than $400 each.

The Agricultural Marketing Act passed by Congress June 15 encourages farmers' cooperatives and provides for an advisory Federal Farm Board with $500 million in revolving funds to buy up surpluses in order to maintain prices. The funds are inadequate, and since farmers cannot be persuaded to produce less, farm prices continue to drop.

British unemployment tops 12.2 percent, with more miners and workmen idle than during the general strike of 1926. Most working-class families in the Welsh coalfields exist on a dole of about $7 per week, and corner pubs close down for lack of trade.

Cargill opens an office in Argentina in order to have timely and accurate information on South American wheat prices (*see* 1922). Under pressure from its creditors' committee following the stock market crash (above), the company hires John Peterson, a Chase National Bank vice president, as chief executive (*see* 1931).

Eight of Good Humor franchiser Tom Brimer's refrigerated trucks are blown up after he refuses to pay protection money to Chicago racketeers, but the trucks are insured (*see* 1926). The resulting publicity is so good for sales that Brimer is able to pay stockholders a 25 percent dividend; one stockholder acquires a 75 percent interest in the company for $500,000.

Daniel Gerber begins selling strained baby foods through grocery stores (*see* 1928). Using leads supplied by mail-order customers, Gerber salesmen drive cars whose horns play "Rock-a-Bye, Baby," they sell 590,000 cans in 1 year, and other food processors are inspired to enter the baby food market.

Universal Foods has its beginnings in a Chicago company founded under the name Universal Cocoa Products. It will be a major producer and marketer of yeast under the Red Star label.

🤝 Unilever—the first multinational company in the consumer products industry—is created March 2 by a merger of Lever Brothers, the British soap colossus, with Europe's 10-year-old Margarine Union. Unilever is involved in enterprises as far ranging as growing coconuts and hunting whales. It will become a food giant second only to Nestlé in Europe and a rival to Procter & Gamble in the United States.

Peter Cailler Kohler merges with Nestlé (above) and Anglo-Swiss Condensed Milk Co.

Allied Mills is created by a merger of Dale W. McMillen's Wayne Feeds (*see* 1916) with a Peoria, Ill., company that has pioneered in processing soybeans (*see* McMillen, 1931; Continental Grain, 1965).

General Mills is created by a merger of the 63-year-old Minneapolis milling firm Washburn, Crosby Co. with 26 other U.S. flour millers; it is the world's largest miller (*see* Bisquick, 1931).

Postum Co. and Wall Street's Goldman Sachs Trading Co. pay $22 million to acquire Clarence Birdseye's General Seafoods Co. and its quick-freezing patents (*see* 1926). Goldman Sachs has put up $20 million but soon sells its interest to the 34-year-old Postum Co., headed by Marjorie Merriweather Post.

General Foods Corp. is created by a merger of Postum Co. (above) with Clarence Birdseye's firm. Postum has acquired Jell-O, Minute Tapioca, Swans Down cake flour (Igleheart Bros.), Hellmann's Mayonnaise, Log Cabin Syrup, Walter Baker Chocolate, Franklin Baker Coconut, Calumet Baking Powder, Maxwell House coffee (Cheek-Neal), and rights to distribute Sanka coffee (*see* 1928).

General Foods (above) acquires Diamond Crystal Salt for cash plus 100,000 shares of stock in the new General Foods Corp. (*see* 1886), but by the time the stock transfers have been completed the value of the stock has fallen from between 70 and 75 down to 42 in the general market collapse. Under General Foods management, Diamond Crystal will overproduce its slow-selling grades and be forced to dump thousands of tons of unsold salt into the St. Clair River; by 1935, it will be losing nearly $500,000 per year (*see* 1953).

General Foods (above) contracts with Seabrook Farms to develop machines for packaging frozen produce in order to market frozen lima beans under the Birds Eye label (*see* 1925; 1931).

Standard Brands is created through a merger engineered by J. P. Morgan Co. that combines Chase and Sanborn (*see* 1878), Fleischmann (*see* 1876), and Royal Baking Powder (*see* 1865), which has recently introduced Royal Gelatin desserts to compete with Jell-O (*see* Planter's, 1961).

The New York holding company National Dairy Corp. acquires Kraft-Phenix Cheese, which sells well over 200 million pounds of product—close to 40 percent of all the cheese consumed in the United States (*see* 1923; 1928). Kraft-Phenix has sales of more than $86 million, with net profits of more than $4.6 million (*see* Kraft Foods, 1955).

Borden Co. acquires Monroe Cheese Co. and begins to market Liederkranz on a nationwide basis (*see* 1892; 1928; Kraft, 1985). Borden also acquires Château Cheese Co., maker of the nation's second-leading brand of process cheese (*see* vitamin D milk, 1933; Elsie the Cow, 1936).

Glidden Food Products Co. acquires E. R. Durkee & Co.; it will sell all its food products under the name Durkee Famous Foods (*see* 1857; 1928; 1962).

United Fruit Company acquires Samuel Zemurray's Cuaymel Fruit after having acquired 22 other competitors since 1899 (*see* politics, 1911). Now 52, Zemurray receives 300,000 shares of United Fruit stock with a value in November of $31.5 million and is by far the largest stockholder (*see* 1932).

The English brewing giant Whitbread acquires the Mackeson brewery at Hythe, in Kent, and its Mackeson Milk Stout (*see* 1907).

Peter Paul Candies acquires J. N. Collins Co. of Chicago, makers of Walnettos, Honey Scotch, and Butter Scotch Caramels. The company needs goods to sell in hot-weather months when chocolate sales fall off.

W. F. Schrafft Co. of Boston merges with the Frank Shattuck Co., operator of Schrafft's restaurants (*see* 1906; 1928; 1967).

A&P stores grow to number 15,709; the chain has sales of more than $1 billion (*see* 1912; 1937).

Grand Union operates 685 stores, has 1,100 salesmen traveling some 120 home-delivery routes, and enjoys sales of $37 million (*see* 1872).

New York grocer Barney Greengrass opens a shop at 541 Amsterdam Avenue, near 79th Street, that will continue for more than 65 years with sawdust on its floor and groceries on its shelves. Greengrass, who will become known as the "sturgeon king," opened a shop in 1908 at 1403 Fifth Avenue, near 115th Street, specializing in lox and whitefish; he moved soon after to the corner of 113th Street and St. Nicholas Avenue and has followed his largely Jewish clientele out of Harlem to the Upper West Side, where such notables as Franklin D. Roosevelt, Irving Berlin, and the Marx brothers will come to buy his borscht, bagels, sable, whitefish, kippered salmon, smoked salmon, and—above all—smoked lake sturgeon. As Groucho Marx will say after Greengrass dies in 1956, he "may not have ruled any kingdoms or written any great symphonies, but he did a monumental job with sturgeon."

Sheffield Farms division of National Dairy Corp. (above) introduces milk packaged in paraffin-lined paper cartons into the New York City market in January. Says the *New York Times* January 9, "The carton is used once and then thrown away. It is opened quite simply by cutting off the narrow end of the cone. This should be a decided improvement over the old method of digging out with a fork the paper top of a bottle, with the constant risk of a spurting fountain of cream, even when the fork is in the hands of an experienced bottle opener. The new container should prove not only more sanitary but cheaper. The annual bill for lost, stolen and broken milk bottles in New York City is said to be around $2,500,000. The saving on this huge item should eventually be passed on to the consumers if they show a liking for the new package. Another economy, not to be computed in cold cash, would be the saving of wear and tear on the nerves of light sleepers, who would no longer be awakened by the early morning rattling of glass in the hands of the milkman." Health authorities have for years called glass milk bottles a source of contagious disease, and a few smaller dairies have experimented with nonreturnable paraffin-coated cardboard containers, but most consumers prefer glass-bottled milk to that in the cone-shaped "Seal-cone" containers manufactured by Sealed Container Corp. (*see* 1940; 1934).

U.S. electric refrigerator sales top 800,000, up from 75,000 in 1925, as the average price of a refrigerator falls to $292, down from $600 in 1920. The average price will be $169 by 1939, and the new refrigerators will use less electricity (*see* GE, 1927).

The Universal electric toaster, introduced by Landers, Frary & Clark, has a door that opens at the touch of a button; inside the door is the slice of bread, and the door pivots to permit toasting the second side of the bread (*see* Toastmaster, 1926; 1930).

Popeye the Sailor makes his debut January 17 in the 10-year-old syndicated U.S. comic strip "Thimble Theater" by E. C. (Elzie Crisler) Segar, 34. The somewhat cowardly sailor will soon prove to be a fighter whose prodigious strength is derived mainly from spinach, which he swallows by the canful. U.S. spinach consumption will increase by 33 percent in the next few years as children come to rate it third only to turkey and ice cream as their favorite food, and Popeye ("I'm strong to the finish 'cause I eats me spinach") will be credited with the increase (*see New Yorker* cartoon, 1927; agriculture, 1937).

Nonfiction: *The Englishman's Food* by J. C. Drummond and Anne Wilbraham (his second wife) is a pioneering 500-page study of English diet since the Middle Ages.

The Po' Boy sandwich gets its name by some accounts in a New Orleans streetcar strike (*see* 1895). New Orleans Public Service, Inc., has announced plans to convert streetcars to buses (which require no conductors and are easier to maintain), streetcar workers have struck in protest, some 10,000 strikers and sympathizers surround a streetcar operated by a strikebreaker at the foot of Canal Street July 5, police shoot two union pickets outside the Canal Street carbarn, several people are killed and hundreds injured in the ensuing violence, and former streetcar employees Bennie and Clovis Martin offer to provide food free of charge to any "poor boy," or union member, who enters their French Market coffee stand and restaurant. "We are with you till hell freezes, and when it does, we will furnish blankets to keep you warm," the brothers write to the strikers. Martin Brothers will later have signs on its St. Claude location proclaiming "Originators of 'Poor Boy Sandwiches.'" The sandwich has its counterparts in the "grinder," "hero," "hoagy," and "submarine" sold elsewhere in the country.

One heath hen survives in America, down from 2,000 in 1916, and the male of the species seen on Martha's Vineyard has no mate. It will be extinct after 1931.

Signs of drought begin to appear in the U.S. Southwest and upper Great Plains (*see* 1930).

Texas cattleman Charles Goodnight dies December 12 at age 93.

Soviet biologist Nikolai Vavilov endorses the government's push toward collectivized farms as a shortcut to scientific agriculture (*see* 1928; 1930).

The ruby variety of grapefruit with red flesh is discovered as a "bud sport," or mutation, on a McAllen, Tex., farm.

U.S. nutrition pioneer Joseph Goldberger dies of cancer at Washington, D.C., January 17 at age 54, having done work which will lead to the virtual elimination of pellagra in America. Despite his efforts, pellagra will be described in the 1932 *Encyclopaedia Britannica* as a "condition . . . believed to be diabetic in origin, possibly due to a vitamin deficiency" (*see* niacin, 1936).

Danish biochemist Carl Peter Henrik Dam, 34, finds that he can produce severe internal bleeding in chickens if he puts them on a fat-free diet (*see* vitamin K, 1935).

Harvard physician William B. Castle finds that pernicious anemia can be prevented only if the gastric juices contain an "intrinsic" factor necessary for the absorption of an "extrinsic" factor in foods (*see* 1928; Minot and Murphy, 1924; Cohn, 1926; vitamin B$_{12}$, 1948).

A survey in Baltimore shows that 30 percent of children have rickets. A similar study in London's East End shows that 90 percent of children are rachitic (*see* Steenbock, 1923; 1927).

Health via Food by U.S. physician William Howard Hay claims that the fermentation of undigested starch causes poisoning from within (*see* Salisbury, 1888). Dr. Hay, who recommends taking an enema or strong cathartic every day, agrees with J. H. Kellogg that meat is not a desirable food and says, "Ideal health cannot be attained with any other line of foods than those outlined by God to Adam and Eve in the Garden of Eden." Digestion of starch requires "alkaline conditions throughout the digestive tract," he writes, extrapolating from the fact that human saliva, which contains a starch-digesting enzyme, is alkaline. "Acid at any stage [of starch digestion] will permanently arrest this." "Arresting digestion means the onset of fermentation with disease not far behind." "Don't eat starchy foods with anything else and you'll have no need for medicine of any kind," says Dr. Hay, and his injunction against mixing starch and protein at the same meal (he warns that "alkalines," meaning fruits and vegetables, should also be consumed separately) will be echoed by other self-styled "nutritionists."

Colombo Yogurt has its beginnings at Andover, Mass., where Rose and Sarkis Colombosian, immigrants from Armenia, start making yogurt in their farm kitchen for family and friends. Yogurt will be slow to gain popular acceptance in America (*see* 1970; Dannon, 1942; Hauser, 1951).

Pet Milk establishes Pet Dairy Products Co. and enters the fresh dairy products business (*see* 1923; irradiation, 1934).

Oscar Mayer trademarks its wieners with a yellow paper ring on every fourth wiener to break the tradition of anonymity in meat sales (*see* 1883). Oscar G. Mayer, the Harvard-educated founder's son, joined the firm in 1909 and will buy a packing plant at Madison, Wis., as he leads the company toward national distribution (*see* 1944).

Casper, Wyo., popcorn-shop owner Bill O'Sullivan creates Karmelkorn, a caramel-coated popcorn that will be sold beginning next year by franchised stores in downtown locations near movie theaters (which do not yet have concession stands) and by franchised mom-and-pop Karmelkorn Shoppes. By 1993 there will be more than 190 Karmelkorn Shoppes nationwide plus six in Singapore (*see* Dairy Queen, 1986).

Libby, McNeill & Libby adopts a new method of pressing tomatoes for a juice that will make Libby's tomato juice the world's top-selling brand (*see* 1923). Libby packs 100,000 cases of tomato juice, a figure that will jump to 739,000 next year and to 4.5 million in 1931. It also begins packing pumpkin and squash (*see* pineapple juice, 1933).

Former Coca-Cola president Asa G. Candler dies at Atlanta March 12 at age 77. Coca-Cola has gross sales of $39 million and adopts the slogan "The Pause That Refreshes."

Seven-Up is introduced under the name Lithiated Lemon by St. Louis bottler Charles Grigg of 1920 Howdy fame. He markets the highly carbonated lemon-lime soft drink in seven-ounce bottles and sells 10,500 cases (*see* 1933).

French wines enjoy an exceptional year; the '29 vintage in all parts of the country will be remembered fondly for decades.

The New York restaurant Giovanni's has its beginnings in a speakeasy opened November 2 by Italian-American entrepreneur Giovanni Pramaggiore in East 55th Street. It will reopen a few doors away at 66 East 55th Street after repeal of Prohibition and will build a reputation with its clams; aspics; vegetable minestrone; blended vichyssoise; sorrel soup; lobster bisque; and cooked-to-order dishes such as pigeon-stuffed pheasant, pigeon stuffed with pâté de foie gras and wild rice and served with a Périgordine sauce, veal kidneys sautéed and served in a Marsala sauce, gnocchi à la romana, linguine carbonara, cannelloni made with homemade spinach-colored pasta, fresh stewed fruit, and zabaglione.

1930

British authorities in India release agitator Mohandas K. Gandhi, 60, from prison April 5 and allow him to recuperate just outside Bombay. Ashramites have left the Sarbamanti ashram outside Ahmedabad March 12 in a civil disobedience campaign and march 240 miles to the beach at Dandi, on the Gujerat Coast of the Arabian Sea, where Gandhi breaks the law by picking up a handful of salt crystallized by the evaporation of seawater. It is illegal to manufacture or sell salt except under license from the British, and Gandhi exhorts his fellow Indians to follow his example and break the monopoly. British forces are unable to deal with a protest on such a large scale.

The Smoot-Hawley Tariff Bill signed into law by President Hoover June 17 raises U.S. tariffs to their highest levels in history—higher even than under the Payne-Aldrich Act of 1909—and embraces a Most-Favored-Nation policy first introduced in 1923. Certain nations are granted large tariff concessions under an arrangement that will continue for more than 45 years. Congress has approved the measure in a special session called by President Hoover despite a petition signed by 1,028 economists.

Other countries raise tariffs in response to the Smoot-Hawley Tariff Act (above).

A general world economic depression sets in as world trade declines, production drops, and unemployment increases.

U.S unemployment passes 4 million, and national income falls from $81 billion to less than $68 billion.

The International Apple Shippers Association offers its fruit on credit to jobless men who will peddle apples on street corners and help the associ-

The onset of the Great Depression found onetime executives selling apples in U.S. city streets.

ation dispose of its vast surplus. By November, some 6,000 men are selling apples on New York sidewalks and more thousands are selling apples in other cities, but by the spring of next year the apple sellers will be called a nuisance and City Hall will order them off the streets of New York.

New York has 82 breadlines by year's end, Philadelphia 80. Small towns in Arkansas and Oklahoma have food riots with hungry crowds shouting, "We want food!" "We will not let our children starve!"

The U.S. Department of Agriculture establishes a Grain Stabilization Corp. to buy up surpluses that are depressing farm prices, but the $500 million appropriated to fund its activities is not nearly sufficient (*see* Commodity Credit Corp., 1933).

Prices of agricultural commodities, especially wheat, are weak all summer and fall as farmers continue to increase their planted acreage. The Grain Stabilization Corp. (above) does not begin buying on the Chicago Board of Trade until November 15.

Washington tried to stabilize farm prices by buying futures on the Chicago Board of Trade.

The mortgage debt of U.S. farms is $9.2 billion, up from $3.2 billion in 1910. Farmers have borrowed heavily to buy the machines they need to remain competitive.

The W. K. Kellogg Foundation is established at Battle Creek, Mich., by breakfast food pioneer William Keith Kellogg, now 70, who retired last year from the presidency of the W. K. Kellogg Co. (*see* 1906; 1951).

Campbell Soup president John T. Dorrance dies of heart disease September 21 at age 56, leaving his wife and five children $128 million.

Hawaiian pineapple canners pack 4.5 million cases, up 40 percent over last year. Next year they will pack 4.8 million cases, but most of the canned fruit will go unsold and James D. Dole's Hawaiian Pineapple Co. will lose $3,875,000 (*see* 1932).

Ocean Spray Preserving Co. merges with Cranberry Products Co. of New Egypt, N.J., and A. D. Makepeace Co. of Wareham, Mass., to create Cranberry Canners, a growers' cooperative (*see* 1912). The co-op will be joined in 1940 by the Wisconsin Sales Co. and in 1941 by Washington and Oregon growers; it will change its name in 1946 to National Cranberry Association (*see* 1959).

Archer Daniels Midland acquires control of Commander Larabee Corp. and becomes a major factor in flour milling (*see* 1923).

International Salt Co. acquires Sterling Salt Co. It will adopt Sterling as the trademark for all its salt products and will introduce Sterling table salt in 1934.

The first true supermarket opens in August at Jamaica, Long Island, where former Kroger Grocery and Baking Co. store manager Michael S. Cullen, 46, opens the King Kullen Market in an abandoned garage and meets with instant success (*see* 1923). Cullen has written Kroger president William H. Albers suggesting a plan for "monstrous stores . . . away from the high-rent districts" that will attract customers with aggressive price cutting. "I could afford to sell a can of milk at cost if I could sell a can of peas and make two cents," Cullen has written, but another Kroger executive has intercepted his letter. His advertising says, "King Kullen, the world's greatest price wrecker—how does he do it?" (*see* Big Bear, 1932).

Publix Super Markets have their beginnings at Lakeland, Fla., where former Piggly Wiggly grocery store manager George Washington Jenkins, 23, opens a store next door to the Piggly Wiggly. He hitchhiked from Georgia to Florida 5 years ago in hopes of making a fortune in real estate, found work cleaning toilets at the Piggly Wiggly, was running the store 6 weeks later, but has failed to impress its new owner. Jenkins names his place after a movie theater chain and will have 21 Florida supermarkets by 1950, 392 by 1992.

The United States has 694,000 miles of paved road, up from 387,000 in 1921, plus 2.31 million miles of dirt road (*see* 1940).

The comic strip "Blondie" debuts September 8 featuring playboy Dagwood Bumstead and his wife. More than 1,600 U.S. newspapers and some foreign papers will carry the strip, and the huge sandwiches created by Bumstead on evening forays to the refrigerator will become widely known as "dagwoods."

Cookbooks: *The Better Homes and Gardens Cookbook* is a U.S. best-seller. It will have sales of some 15 million copies in the next 45 years and be the all-time best-selling U.S. recipe collection. *Sushi tsu* by Japanese author Ganosuke Nagase.

Painting: *American Gothic* by Iowa genre painter Grant De Volsen Wood, 38, captures the spirit of the Midwestern farm couple depressed by low prices.

Birds Eye Frosted Foods go on sale for the first time March 6 at Springfield, Mass. General Foods introduces frozen June peas and frozen spinach, following them with frozen raspberries, cherries, loganberries, fish, and various meats, but the packets, kept in ice cream cabinets, are not readily visible and sell at relatively high prices (35¢ for a package of peas) (*see* 1929; 1931).

Dry ice (solid carbon dioxide) is introduced commercially in the United States for purposes such as keeping ice cream cold.

Sliced bread is introduced under the Wonder Bread label by Continental Baking (*see* 1927; Rohwedder, 1928).

The Toastmaster automatic toaster is introduced by McGraw-Electric of Elgin, Ill. (*see* first automatic pop-up toaster, 1926). Sliced bread (above) has increased consumption of toast at breakfast.

The *Star of Alaska* makes her final trip north from San Francisco to the Alaskan salmon canneries, ending the era of the great Star square-riggers (*see* 1893; California Packing, 1916).

Colorado-Utah rancher James Monaghan, 38, opens northwest Colorado cattle ranges to sheep grazing. He started working as a cowhand in summer roundups at age 16 and now heads the Rio Branco Wool Growers' Association.

Monfort of Colorado has its beginnings in a feedlot started by rancher Warren H. Monfort on a farm he has inherited outside Greeley. He will have cattle on feed all year round by 1934, and by 1968 the company will have 100,000 head of cattle fattening on alfalfa, grain, and sugar beets (*see* 1960).

Poultry farmers on the Delmarva (Delaware-Maryland-Virginia) Peninsula begin raising the broiler chicken, developed by the Department of Agriculture at Beltsville, Md., and USDA stations in other southern locations. Vulnerability to epidemics of coccidiosis, Marek's disease, Newcastle disease, and other poultry ills will restrict the size of flocks until after the mid-1950s, keeping poultry a seasonal food and limiting consumption of chicken, which will remain costlier than red meat for the next 30 years, but the battery-raised chicken will eventually replace the spring chicken (*see* Merck anticoccidials, 1956).

Tyson Foods has its beginnings at Springdale, Ark., where Kansas produce hauler John Tyson runs out of gas and decides to stay, using his truck to haul fruit for local orchardmen in the Ozark Mountain town. He soon branches out to trucking chickens and is presently delivering poultry to destinations throughout the Southeast and Middle West. Finding that growers do not always have enough birds to keep him busy, Tyson will acquire a hatchery to produce chicks for the growers, and by the late 1940s he will have added a farm, a feed mill, and growing houses to pioneer the concept of vertical integration in the poultry industry (*see* Rock Cornish game hen, 1965).

25 percent of Americans live on or from the farm, many of them on subsistence farms that operate outside the money economy. The total number of U.S. farms is roughly 6.3 million (*see* 1931).

Major U.S. crops produce barely $8 per acre, and the average annual farm income is $400 per family.

Tenant farmers work 4 out of 10 U.S. farms as compared with 9 out of 10 British farms, one-third of farms in western Europe, 78 percent of Australian farms, and 40 percent of Argentine farms.

"With the introduction of agriculture mankind entered upon a long period of meanness, misery, and madness, from which they are only being freed by the beneficent operation of the machine," writes English philosopher Bertrand Russell, 58, in his book *The Conquest of Happiness*.

55 percent of agricultural workers on Soviet farms are employed on collective farms (*see* Stalin's Five-Year Plan, 1928).

20 percent of the North American workforce is employed in agriculture as compared with 7 percent in Britain, 25 percent in France, and 40 percent in Japan.

The U.S. wheat crop comes in at 857 million bushels, despite crop failures due to drought in some areas (*see* below), and the world harvest is 3.8 billion bushels, not counting the Soviet Union, whose crop is sold in great quantities on world markets.

Farmers in the Corn Belt begin to drop their resistance to hybrid corn as test plantings demonstrate dramatically how the new corn can increase yields (*see* 1921; Bantam, 1933).

Unprecedented drought parches the U.S. South and Midwest. Arkansas is the worst hit, but the lack of rain reduces the Mississippi to a comparative trickle and much of the Ohio River Valley is also deeply affected. President Hoover summons a conference of governors, freight rates are reduced for the counties that have suffered most, but Hoover wants to minimize the role of the federal government and instead encourages efforts by the Red Cross to feed the needy. Private resources are soon overwhelmed, and Hoover asks for a congressional appropriation for the Red Cross but specifies that none of the money may be used to feed the needy lest it appear that Congress has funded a dole. The money is used to feed rabbits, which critics call "Hoover's hogs," while people starve. Refusing to admit failure, Hoover argues that the Red Cross handouts do not represent charity. Congress votes a $45 million Drought Relief Act December 20.

The McNary-Mapes Amendment to the 1906 Food and Drug Act requires labeling of substandard canned goods. The National Canners Association has urged the move as a safety measure and to eliminate competition from shoddy goods.

Hostess Twinkies are introduced by Continental Baking (above). Continental bakery manager James A. Dewar, 33, at Chicago has been turning out little sponge cakes for shoppers to use as the basis of strawberry shortcakes; when the strawberry season ends, he hits on the idea of filling the cakes with sugary cream to keep his cake line in production year round. A St. Louis sign advertising "Twinkle Toes Shoes" inspires him to call the cakes Twinkies.

Jiffy brand biscuit mix is introduced by Chelsea Milling Co. of Chelsea, Mich. (*see* Bisquick, 1931).

The first biscuit mix came from a previously obscure Michigan milling company.

Soup kitchens kept many struggling Americans alive in the early years of the Great Depression. LIBRARY OF CONGRESS

Vitamin D is isolated in its crystalline form calciferol and is soon being used to fortify butter, margarine, and other foods (*see* Steenbock, 1927; Borden's milk, 1933).

Edwin J. Cohn at Harvard Medical School develops a concentrate 100 times as potent as liver for treating pernicious anemia (*see* 1926; 1929; 1948).

Pure-food reformer Harvey W. Wiley dies at Washington, D.C., June 30 at age 85.

French's Worcestershire Sauce is introduced in five-ounce, paper-wrapped bottles with glass and cork stoppers by R. T. French Co. of Rochester, N.Y. (*see* cream salad mustard, 1904). An English chemist brought in by the company has perfected a piquant mixture of soy sauce, garlic, anchovies, tamarinds, distilled vinegar, corn syrup, sugar, salt, spices, and flavoring; the package will be changed but not the wood-aged product (*see* Lea and Perrins, 1823; potatoes, 1940).

Mott's Apple Sauce is introduced by Duffy-Mott Co., which heretofore has produced almost nothing besides cider and vinegar (*see* 1900; Sunsweet Prune Juice, 1933; apple juice, 1938).

Snickers candy bars are introduced by Mars, Inc., which obtains national distribution (*see* 1923). Frank Mars suspended his business at Minneapolis a few years ago, and Schuler Candy Co. of Winona produced Milky Ways until last year, when Mars was able to buy back the rights from Schuler for $8,000 and resume production, this time at Chicago. The new peanut-butter-nougat and peanut bars, covered in milk chocolate, will grow to become the nation's largest-selling brand (*see* 1932).

Hershey Chocolate increases the size of its nickel Hershey Bar from 1⅜ oz. to 2 oz. (*see* 1924; 1933).

New England Confectionery Co. covers peanut crunch with milk chocolate and introduces it as the Bolster bar (*see* 1927; Sky Bar, 1937).

Portugal's Hotel Palácio, founded by Fausto Figueredo, opens at Estoril and welcomes the Japanese crown prince Akihito, who is on his wedding trip with the princess. The hotel's high-ceilinged salons, opulent writing rooms, elegant bars, and grand dining room will attract international guests for more than 65 years.

Jack & Charlie's "21" Club opens in January at 21 West 52nd Street, New York. Restaurateur John Karl "Jack" Kriendler, 31, and his accountant cousin Charles "Charlie" Berns, 28, have been operating speakeasy saloons, beginning with the Red Head in 1922 and most recently the Puncheon Club (or Puncheon Grotto), and have in effect been subsidized by the Rockefellers, who have purchased their lease at 42 West 49th Street in order to clear the block for construction of Rockefeller Center. Kriendler and Berns store their illicit liquor behind secret walls and devise an arrangement that permits the bartender to push a button at the first sign of a raid by federal Prohibition enforcement agents, tilting the shelves of the bar to send all bottles down a chute to smash in the cellar and thus destroy evidence the agents need for a conviction. They will prosper at the new location and acquire the building at 19 West 52nd Street in 1935 as they attract patrons with crème andalouse, green turtle, and petite marmite soups; deep-fried whitebait and oyster crabs; duckling à l'orange; prime ribs; and chicken hash; served in a clublike atmosphere.

Chef Auguste Escoffier presides over a dinner that inaugurates New York's new Hotel Pierre on Fifth Avenue between 60th and 61st streets.

New York's first White Castle hamburger stand opens with virtually no competition (*see* 1921). Some restaurants serve hamburger, and hamburger sandwiches are sold also at carnivals, fairs, and amusement parks, but housewives who want to serve hamburger to their families order top round or some other cut of beef and ask their butchers to grind it for them. White Castle will pioneer such innovations as grill plates of cast aluminum that are easy to remove and clean, under-the-counter electric dishwashers, coffee mugs with slots in their bottom rims that permit dishwater to drain out, and exhaust systems that draw out cooking fumes (*see* St. Louis, 1932).

New York's first Chock Full o' Nuts coffee shops open to begin a chain that will grow to have 110 units selling frankfurters, raisin-bread-and-cream-cheese sandwiches, and orange drink, as well as doughnuts and coffee. Founder William Black (originally Schwarz) began with a subway nut shop (hence the name); his coffee shops will continue until the mid-1980s.

The Tokyo tempura shop Tenichi opens in the Ginza, where it will gain popularity with government ministers. The shop will also cater to the Akasaka Geihinkan, a guest house for foreign dignitaries and other special guests of the government.

French restaurateur Alexandre Dumaine and his wife, Jean (who runs the kitchen), purchase the 26-room Hôtel de la Côte d'Or at Saulieu, where they serve chickens from Bresse, cold saddle of hare with gooseberry jelly, sole from Boulogne, lobsters and shellfish from Roscoff in Brittany, papillotes of salmon-trout from Lake Annecy (286 kilometers distant), and butter from milk produced by cows that graze on the salt marshes of the deux Sèvres, reviving the culinary traditions of Carême and Escoffier.

1931

China's Yangzi River bursts a dam during a typhoon August 3, flooding 40,000 square miles, killing hundreds, and causing widespread famine that will kill more.

U.S. unemployment tops 8 million. Men and women in New York's Harlem compete with dogs and cats for the contents of garbage cans. Hunger marchers petition the White House December 7 for a guarantee of employment at a minimum wage but are turned away. President Hoover, who was U.S. food administrator from 1917 to 1918, opposes suggestions that the federal government distribute food to the needy, insisting that charitable organizations will provide what is needed, but while American Red Cross dieticians offer advice on how to eat economically, the Red Cross refuses to use its funds to help the unemployed (*see* Lewis, 1932).

Some 75 percent of Soviet farms remain in private hands despite the Five-Year Plan begun by Josef Stalin in 1928 to encourage collective farms and state farms. Liquidation of *kulaks* (rich private farmers) intensifies (*see* 1932).

Britain receives a French-American loan August 1, but London and Glasgow have riots September 10 to protest government economy measures.

Brazil establishes a National Coffee Department. The collapse of the world coffee market has brought economic disaster and helped precipitate a revolt in the southern provinces. The Coffee Department will supervise the destruction of large quantities of Brazil's chief export item in order to maintain good prices in the world market (*see* Nescafé, 1938).

U.S. sales of glass jars for home canning hit an 11-year high as sales of store-bought bottled and canned foods decline.

U.S. motorcar sales collapse and Detroit lays off another 100,000 workers, reducing employment in auto plants to 250,000, down from 475,000 in 1929.

Many Kansas counties declare a moratorium on taxes to help farmers survive as the U.S. wheat crop breaks all records, driving down prices. Elsewhere, farmers are forced off the land as banks foreclose on mortgages (*see* Farm Mortgage Financing Act, 1934).

Feed manufacturer Dale W. McMillen leases two Michigan sugar beet refineries but finds that beet sugar is scorned by U.S. consumers; grocers handle the product only at discount prices (*see* 1933; Allied Mills, 1929).

Safeway Stores reach their peak of 3,527 outlets (*see* 1926). The company will close many of its smaller grocery stores and open huge supermarkets.

U.S. mechanical refrigerator production tops 1 million units, up from 5,000 in 1921. By 1937 the industry will be producing refrigerators at the rate of nearly 3 million per year (*see* 1929).

Frigidaire division of General Motors adopts Freon 12 (dichlorodifluoromethane) refrigerant gas, invented by Thomas Midgley, 42, of Ethyl Corp. and C. F. Kettering, 55, of GM and produced by a Du Pont–GM subsidiary. Most other refrigerator makers follow suit, replacing ammonia and other more dangerous gases.

Prohibition is not working, reports President Hoover's Wickersham Committee, headed by former Attorney General George Woodward Wickersham, 73. Statistics will show that Americans are drinking less alcohol, but crime has increased significantly and efforts to control illegal sales of beer and whiskey are only marginally effective.

The United States has 7.2 million operating farms, up from some 6.3 million last year, with more than a billion acres of farmland in production and with the world's highest rate of cultivated food-crop acreage per capita. By 1935 the number of farms will be down to 6.84 million and by 1969, 3.45 million.

University of Wisconsin agronomist Ruebesch George Shams, 27, succeeds in transferring noncultivated wheat's resistance to stem rust caused by *Puccinia graminis* into the bread-wheat types, making a major contribution to wheat improvement. Shams will also develop varieties of bread and durum wheat which are genetically resistant to the Hessian fly and will develop new varieties, including the Henry, Russell, and Lathrop spring wheats, the Blackhawk and Tim Win winter wheats, and the Moore barley, to increase Wisconsin crop production.

Texas Panhandle wheat farmer Hickman Price, 45, harvests 600,000 bushels of wheat from 23,000 of his 30,000 acres—the largest single wheat crop ever raised by an individual—at a cost of 25¢ per bushel. A onetime publisher, Price dropped all his other activities 2 years ago to join his brother Andrew on the family farm. He has developed equipment that can plant and harvest 1,000 acres per day to industrialize large-scale wheat production, pioneering such low-cost methods as hitching two and three combine harvesters, or 60 feet of wheat drills, behind a single tractor and using floodlights for nighttime operations. Price has advanced scientific agriculture, using multiple seeders and harrows and systematizing wheat combining with delivery of grain to strategically located central loading stations, but he will sell most of his Texas wheatlands in 1936 after dust storms reduce their value.

A British Advisory Committee on Nutrition is organized to address the problem of poor nutrition among the poor. It devises new marketing schemes for farmers to put food within reach of more Britons, and a Milk in Schools Scheme subsidizes milk so that children may have it at cheap prices (*see* 1906; 1934).

British medical researcher Lucy Wills at Bombay discovers that pregnant women with nutritional megaloblastic anemia respond to diets containing autolyzed yeast (*see* Mitchell and Snell, 1944).

Swiss chemist Paul Karrer, 42, isolates vitamin A (*see* 1920; 1925; 1937).

The Supreme Court upholds a company that has been sued by the Federal Trade Commission for false advertising (*FTC v. Raladam*). The company has advertised its thyroid extract product, Marmola, as "a scientific remedy for obesity," and while the Court agrees with the American Medical Association that the ads are dangerously misleading it rules that such advertising is not unfair to competition (*see* 1914; Food, Drug and Cosmetic Act, 1938).

Daniel Gerber's Fremont Packing Co. adds salt to its baby foods (*see* 1929). Infants' taste buds are not sufficiently developed to discern any difference, but sales resistance has come from mothers who taste their babies' food (*see* 1941; MSG, 1951).

Mothers resisted buying Gerber's baby food until salt was added. Babies didn't notice the difference.

Researchers find that taste perception is largely an inherited trait: many more non-Europeans than Europeans (or white Americans) are capable of tasting the chemical phenylthiocarbamide (PTC), according to the research.

Beech-Nut Packing Co. introduces Beech-Nut Baby Foods, a line of 13 strained baby and junior foods in glass jars (*see* 1924). The foods will be sold on a national basis within the next year and impel other baby-food makers to market their products in jars.

Birds Eye Frosted Foods go on sale across the United States as General Foods expands distribution, but only a few retail grocers have freezer cases for displaying frozen foods (*see* 1930; 1940).

Bisquick, introduced by General Mills, is a prepared mix for biscuits containing sesame-seed oil to keep its flour and shortening from turning rancid. General Mills acquired Sperry Flour Co. last year and used it as the basis of a new western regional division whose salesman, Carl Smith, boarded a Southern Pacific train for San Francisco late one evening. Not having eaten since noon, he went to the dining car and was astonished that it was still serving dinner. The freshly made biscuits served with his meal were so good that he sought out the chef, who explained that he kept a blended mixture of lard, flour, baking powder, and salt in his icebox to be prepared for late orders. Smith suggested to General Mills chemist Charles Kress that the idea might have commercial possibilities, and Kress, noting that lard would turn rancid, has solved the problem by using sesame-seed oil as a shortening (it will later be replaced by soybean and/or cottonseed oil). Bisquick, which can be used to make pancakes as well as biscuits, will lead to the development of cake and muffin mixes.

Bisquick (above) has sales of more than 500,000 cases within 7 months and within a year has 95 imitators. It competes with Jiffy brand biscuit mix, introduced last year by Chelsea Milling Co., but by 1933 all but six competitors will have been eliminated.

Ballard & Ballard of Louisville, Ky., introduces Ballard Biscuits, made from refrigerated dough and packaged under pressure in cylindrical containers. Local baker Lively Willoughby has come up with the idea of saving time for housewives by preparing uncooked biscuits which can be stored in iceboxes for as long as 24 hours and then baked. He has hired boys with bicycles to deliver pans of the uncooked biscuits door to door and has finally devised a method of wrapping the biscuit dough in tinfoil and enclosing it under pressure in heavy paper tubes with metal lids to produce a product that stays fresh in the icebox for a week (see Pillsbury, 1951).

Wyler's Bouillon Cubes are introduced by Chicago entrepreneur Silvain S. Wyler, who imports the cubes, made to his own formula in Holland and Switzerland. Wyler's product line will grow to include four kinds of bouillon cubes, beef and chicken gravy mixes, dehydrated oregano and mint leaves, a meat tenderizer, dehydrated mixed vegetable flakes, and dried soup greens (see Borden Co., 1961).

Hotel Bar butter is introduced at New York with a package showing a silhouette of the city's skyline with hotels that include the new Waldorf-Astoria (below).

Reed's Butterscotch candy roll is introduced by a Chicago company that has been making hard candies since 1893.

Cryst-O-Mint Life Savers are introduced: ingredients are cooked until clear, not pressed cold like other Life Savers mints.

Parducci Wine Cellars is founded just north of Ukiah in California's Mendocino County by vintner Adolph Parducci, who started his first winery 15 years ago at Cloverdale in Sonoma County. He uses large redwood tanks for aging his varietal wines.

The Los Angeles restaurant El Cholo opens at 1121 South Western Avenue in a courtyard with a mission-style fountain. Proprietress Rosa Borquez serves enchiladas, chiles relleños, sonoran-style chimichangas, burritos, tacos, and green-corn and cheddar tamales (in season) and in a few years will be serving Margaritas.

New York's Waldorf-Astoria hotel opens October 1 on Park Avenue with its own butcher shop, bakery, and ice plant (it will soon have a fifth-floor wine cellar large enough to cradle 37,000 gallons of wine). The new hotel employs the old Waldorf's maître d'hôtel Oscar Tschirsky, now 65, who is paid $30,000 per year at a time when doctors and lawyers are lucky to make $5,000. He has been so heavily promoted as Oscar of the Waldorf that his calling cards are so inscribed (see Men's Bar, Palm Bar, 1934).

Physical culturist Bernarr Macfadden serves 1¢ meals at his New York and Boston restaurants.

Maxim's in Paris comes under new management as restaurateur Octave Vaudable buys the run-down establishment started in 1893 and makes Albert Blaser his maître d'hôtel (see 1907). Sole Albert (dipped in butter and fresh bread crumbs, then baked in vermouth) will be Maxim's most popular dish for decades, and the invention of Billi-bi (or

Billi Bi or Billy-By) will be credited to Maxim's chef Barthe, who will be said to have created the cream of mussel soup early in the century in honor either of U.S. bon vivant William B. Beebe (his friends called him Billy B.), U.S. tin magnate William B. Leeds, or Leeds's playboy-philanthropist son and namesake (*see* 1942).

Harry's Bar opens May 13 at the end of Venice's Grand Canal, where it intersects with the Calle Vallaresso. Former Hotel Europa bartender Giuseppe Cipriani, 31, from Verona names his establishment after Harry Pickering, a frail young Bostonian who used to drink at the Hotel Europa owned by Giuseppe's father. When Giuseppe discovered that Harry had lost all his money, he loaned him enough to survive; Harry spent much of the money on drinks and returned to Boston, Giuseppe never heard from him, but the young man returned to Venice in February and not only repaid the $5,000 loan but offered to invest another $5,000 if Cipriani would open a bar. Cipriani takes a long-term lease on the ground floor of a building near a vaporetto station, and although he struggles at first (the net for some days is only 60 or 100 lire), he begins to serve small homemade noodles, broiled scampi, cheese sandwiches, hamburgers, and the like from a tiny kitchen in the rear (*see* 1939).

Italian coffee roaster Antonio Padrocchi at Padua transforms his shop in June into a large café with Greek, Etruscan, Gothic, Pompeiian, Egyptian, and imperial salons.

The Paris bistro Allard, opened by Marcel Allard and his wife, Marthe, at 41, rue Saint-André-des-Arts, at the corner of the Rue de l'Éperon, occupies part of a building that dates at least to the early 18th century, and features home-style cooking. It will expand in 1964 by acquiring a boutique next door, enabling it to expand its kitchen slightly and allow 15 more guests to enjoy its *coquilles Saint-Jacques*; *matelote d'anguille* (eel stew in red burgundy wine); *bécasse* (in November); *canard au navets* (duck with turnips); veal *à la berrichonne*; *entrecôte marchand de vin*; *coq au vin*; leg of lamb *petit sallé* (with red beans); *bœuf à la mode*; *bœuf navarin*; fish (sea bass, pike, salmon, etc.) *au beurre blanc*; and terrines of hare, duck, and chicken livers.

The Lyons restaurant Chez La Mère Charles is acquired by the Chapel family, whose son Alain, a

veteran of de la Pyramide at Vienne, will win a third Michelin star at age 35 in 1973. His specialties will include *pâté chaud d'anguille et deux beurres*, mousse of chicken livers with sauce *écrevisse*, *caneton nantais grillé* (grilled duckling), *volaille de Bresse sautée en vinaigre*, soufflés, and *crème anglais* (custard sauce).

1932

Famine in the Ukraine and in the Caucasus begins taking a heavy toll. Not caused by nature, it is a deliberate, man-made famine created by dictator Josef Stalin, partly to raise capital for Soviet industrialization by selling grain abroad but also to force independent farmers into collectives, where they will work like serfs. Stalin has his troops seize livestock, seeds, and food stocks and keeps relief trains carrying food from entering the affected areas in order to force compliance of farmers with his collectivization efforts. Protesters are shot down with machine guns; some 7 million people—one-quarter of the population in the areas—will die of hunger and related causes in the next few years.

United Mine Workers boss John L. Lewis, 51, is quoted in the *New York Times* January 25 as saying, "The only thing that apparently inspires the Red Cross to extend assistance is a conflagration, flood, pestilence, or war. It doesn't make any difference to them how many people die of starvation, how many children suffer from malnutrition, or how many women are weakened" (*see* 1931).

More Americans are hungry or ill fed than ever before in the nation's history. The usual weekly relief check for a family of five in New York City is $6 in May, and the average weekly grant in Philadelphia that month is reduced to $4.39 (Philadelphia's relief funds will soon give out completely, leaving 57,000 families with no means of support). Nearly a million Americans go back to the land.

Congress votes March 7 to authorize giving needy Americans 40 million bushels of wheat held by the Federal Farm Bureau, which has bought the wheat in order to maintain prices. Distribution is to be handled by the Red Cross, which agrees reluctantly to take on the job, and another 45 million bushels of wheat are added July 5. By February of next year, the Red Cross will have distributed more than 8.5 million barrels of flour to 5,140,855 families in almost every county in America.

Britain abandons free trade for the first time since 1849. She imposes a 10 percent tariff on most imported goods but agrees at the Imperial Economic Conference at Ottawa to exempt Canada, Australia, New Zealand, and other Commonwealth nations, which in turn will provide markets for Britain's otherwise uncompetitive textiles, steel, motorcars, and telecommunications equipment, discouraging innovation in many industries (*see* agriculture, below).

Britain imposes tariffs and quantitative restrictions on many farm imports while subsidizing British farmers to help them survive the Depression. Imperial preferences are introduced to favor imports from colonial and Commonwealth countries, with special preferences given to dairy products, meat, and wheat from Australia, Canada, and New Zealand at the expense of Denmark and Argentina. Canadian wheat is given preference, but only on condition that it be offered at no more than 6¢ per bushel above grain from other sources, and only if it originates in Canadian ports.

Cargill Commission Co. takes over the lease of the 1.5 million–bushel Canadian Pool elevator at Buffalo and will soon expand its capacity at Buffalo to 11 million bushels (*see* 1929; 1933).

U.S. farm prices fall to 40 percent of 1929 levels. Wheat drops to below 25¢/bushel, oats to 10¢, sugar to 3¢/lb. Canadian farmers, who have few grain crops other than wheat, are hit even harder than those in the United States.

Iowa Farmers' Union militants start a 30-day strike August 9 to protest low farm prices. "Stay at home! Sell nothing!" say union members, who smash the windshields and headlights of farm trucks they catch going to market and block highways with chains and logs to enforce their strike.

The average U.S. weekly wage falls to $17, down from $28 in 1929, and 28 percent of households have no employed worker. Breadlines form in more cities (*see* 1930). U.S. unemployment reaches between 15 and 17 million by year's end, 34 million Americans have no income of any kind, and Americans who do work average little more than $16 per week.

Ralston Purina begins a sharp upward course under the direction of Donald Danforth, 33, who takes over from his father (*see* 1902). Danforth will move Ralston Purina into new consumer food areas in the next 24 years and increase sales from $19 million to more than $400 million.

United Fruit Co. profits drop, and the company's stock falls in value by midyear to $10.25 per share, down from $105 in November 1929 (and $158 in January 1929). Samuel Zemurray, who has gone into retirement at his lodge in the pine woods near New Orleans, sees his holdings decline in value to $4.5 million, down from $31.5 million, and persuades United Fruit's other directors to make him chief of operations; the stock climbs back to $26 within a few weeks on the strength of Zemurray's prestige alone, he calls office-bound executives "dead wood" and sacks them, regains control of the company's properties in the mosquito-infested lowlands of Honduras and Nicaragua, fights Louisiana's Gov. Huey P. Long, 39, operates under the philosophy of "What's best for the countries we operate in is best for the company," and will be president of United Fruit from 1938 to 1948 (*see* 1929; Chiquita Banana, 1944).

James D. Dole's Hawaiian Pineapple Co. verges on bankruptcy in late summer after losing nearly $8.5 million for the year (*see* 1930). A new company is organized under the same name with majority ownership vested in sugar interests, which have always been hostile to Dole's pineapple ventures; the Waialua Agricultural Co. and Castle & Cook Ltd. own 56 percent of the new Hawaiian Pineapple Co., which will later be reduced to slightly less than 50 percent. A Pineapple Growers' Cooperative Association is formed, marketing and production agreements are established to control the business on a quota basis, and a $1.5 million advertising campaign is launched to promote use of Hawaiian pineapple (*see* pineapple juice, 1933).

Norton Simon, Inc. has its beginnings in the Val Vita Foods Co. started by Chicago entrepreneur Norton Simon, 25, who has bought a bankrupt Fullerton, Calif., orange juice–bottling company for $7,000. He creates a line of canned fruits and vegetables, sales the first year are $43,000, they will grow in 2 years to more than $500,000, and in 10 years will be nearly $9 million (*see* 1942).

Sacramento Tomato Juice has its beginnings in the Bercut-Richards Packing Co. founded by Wheatland, Calif., machinist Thomas Richards, who was called in last year by a small fruit-canning cooperative to solve some production problems. He has been helped by Peter and Henri Bercut to buy the Sacramento facility, which he will turn from packing fruit to canning tomato juice under the Sacramento label.

Bridgford Foods Corp. has its beginnings at Anaheim, Calif., where local butcher Hugh Bridgford, 24, starts a firm that will become a major producer of snack foods (*see* 1962).

 Best Foods acquires Hellmann's Mayonnaise from General Foods (*see* 1903; 1927). It will market the product as Hellmann's Real Mayonnaise in eastern markets and as Best Foods Mayonnaise in western markets (*see* Corn Products Refining Co., 1958).

John Mackintosh & Sons Ltd. acquires Hailey Chocolate Co., founded in 1860 at Norwich, England. Mackintosh's founder died in 1920, and the company is now headed by his son Harold (*see* 1904; Rolo, 1937).

Big Bear Super Market opens at Elizabeth, N.J., and is the first large cut-rate self-service grocery store (*see* King Kullen, 1930). Local entrepreneurs

Supermarkets revolutionized U.S. food retailing, offering values that small grocers could not match.

Robert M. Otis and Roy O. Dawson have put up a total of $1,000 to take over an empty car factory on the outskirts of town, their Big Bear the Price Crusher store has 50,000 square feet of pine tables displaying meats, fruit, vegetables, packaged foods, radios, automobile accessories, and paints, and after 1 year they have made a profit of $166,000 selling Quaker Oats oatmeal at 3¢/box, pork chops at 10¢/lb. Traditional grocers persuade local newspapers to refuse Big Bear advertising and push through a state law against selling at or below cost, but Big Bear is quickly imitated by Great Tiger, Bull Market, Great Leopard, and others as the supermarket revolution gathers force.

Sales of Ford passenger cars to farmers fall to 55,000, down from 650,000 in 1929.

U.S. Route 66 opens to link Chicago and Los Angeles with a 2,200-mile continuous highway that will be called the "Main Street of America." It carries truckers and motorists west via St. Louis, Joplin, Oklahoma City, Amarillo, Gallup, Flagstaff, Winona, Kingman, Barstow, and San Bernardino and carries California farm products east.

The Welland Sea Canal, built in 1829, reopens to connect Lake Erie and Lake Huron after having been rebuilt to accommodate vessels up to 600 feet in length with a 22-foot draft.

"Betty Crocker" devotes two of her weekly General Mills radio shows to recipes and menus for families on relief.

Cookbook: *Modern Cook Book* by Ida Bailey Allen gives a recipe for escalloped tuna fish using canned tuna (*see* Van Camp, 1914) and instructions much like those given by Mrs. Beeton in 1865 for cod à la béchamel.

The word "bagel" is used for the first time by some accounts—a variation on the Yiddish word *beygl*, which has been spelled *beigel* since 1919 (*see* Lender's, 1927). The hard glazed roll will grow to outsell doughnuts in the United States.

Florida's gulf coast has its worst red tide since 1916. Millions of fish are killed (*see* 1946).

A dike closed May 28 after 9 years of work reclaims the Zuider Zee (Ijsselmeer) to create new Dutch farmland (*see* 1918).

Nobel laureate Otto H. Warburg, 49, and his colleagues at Germany's Kaiser Wilhelm Institute for Biology find a yellow coenzyme that catalyzes the transfer of hydrogen atoms (*see* vitamin B₂—riboflavin, 1935).

University of Pittsburgh biochemist Charles Glen King, 36, and his colleagues isolate vitamin C (ascorbic acid) (*see* 1933; Szent-Györgyi, 1928).

Frito corn chips are introduced by San Antonio, Tex., candy maker C. Elmer Doolin, who goes into a local café for a sandwich, is served a 5¢ side dish of corn chips created by Mexican cartoonist–café owner Gustave Olguin, pays Olguin $100 for his old potato ricer and the recipe for his tortillas fritas, and goes into business with his mother, Daisy (*née* Dean), and his brother Earl, using Olguin's converted potato ricer to cut tortilla dough into strips and producing 10 pounds per day. Brother Earl develops a machine to force the dough out under pressure, the Doolins will do well enough to move to Dallas, and they will license local companies to make Fritos, using machinery purchased at cost with Doolin-trained personnel, taking a royalty on each package sold (*see* Frito-Lay, 1961).

Philadelphia's Tasty Baking Co. changes its packaging to put three chocolate cupcakes into a 5¢ package instead of two (*see* 1922). Sales reached $6 million in 1928, will reach $16 million by 1951, and by 1964 the company will have 1,300 employees and be selling 800 million cakes and pies per year through more than 30,000 dealers serving the 12 mid-Atlantic states.

Skippy Peanut Butter is introduced by Rosefield Packing Co. of California, whose J. L. Rosefield cancels his exclusive licensing agreement with the makers of Peter Pan Peanut Butter (*see* 1928). Rosefield markets his own brand—possibly named after the comic strip started the same year he invented his process (1923)—and he also introduces the first smooth-base peanut butter containing chunks of roasted peanuts. Rosefield will patent a new type of cold-processed hydrogenated peanut oil in 1950, and by 1954 Rosefield Packing will have nearly 25 percent of the U.S. peanut butter market (*see* Best Foods, 1955).

Mounds candy bars are sold in packages of twin bars at the same nickel price formerly charged for one bar as Peter Paul converts a soap-wrapping machine to handle candy bars and uses machinery to replace hand wrapping while switching from a foil wrap to cellophane (*see* 1921; Almond Joy, 1947).

3 Musketeers—three candy bars in one—is introduced at a nickel by Mars, Inc. (*see* 1930). Included are a fluffy vanilla nougat, a fluffy chocolate nougat, and a fluffy strawberry nougat, each covered in milk chocolate (the product will later be changed to make it one chocolate-covered chocolate nougat). Frank Mars has a row with his only son, Forrest E., 28, who has a degree in industrial engineering from Yale and thinks he knows more than his father about how to run the company; Frank grants Forrest foreign rights to manufacture Milky Way, and the son goes to England, where he will manufacture Milky Way in a factory at Slough, outside London, and market it as the Mars Bar and Snickers under the name Marathon (*see* 1934; U.S. Mars bar, 1936; M&M's, 1941).

The Heath Bar introduced by retired downstate Illinois schoolteacher L. S. Heath is a 5¢ English toffee covered with milk chocolate and weighing only one ounce at a time when other companies are selling two-, three- and four-ounce bars for a nickel. The Heath Bar will survive despite this handicap.

Campbell Soup Co. introduces Campbell's tomato juice (*see* 1923; Libby's, 1929, 1933).

Prune juice is introduced by California's Sunsweet Growers, which lacks the distribution network needed to market the product (*see* 1917; Duffy-Mott, 1933).

The McDonald Dairy of Flint, Mich., introduces homogenized milk, promoting its soft curd and easy digestibility to gain consumer acceptance (*see* Canada, 1927). The University of Illinois introduces homogenized milk on its delivery routes. Consumers remain skeptical (*see* 1940).

Instant coffee is sold in Britain for the first time (*see* Nescafé, 1938).

Tea magnate Sir Thomas Lipton dies at London October 2 at age 81 (*see* 1914). His picture will appear on the red-and-yellow packages that identify

Lipton products beginning in 1934 (*see* Unilever, 1946).

White Castle runs an advertisement in St. Louis evening newspapers June 3 announcing that on the following day (a Saturday) the coupon in the ad plus 10¢ will buy five hamburgers (carry-out only) at any of the city's White Castle hamburger stands from 2 o'clock in the afternoon until midnight (*see* 1930). The regular price of a hamburger is 5¢; management has been assured by advertising experts that few customers, if any, will respond to the offer; but most of the stands have people lined up before 2 o'clock the next day awaiting the deadline, and by 3 o'clock most are running out of buns and meat. Supply houses call men back to work to bake buns and grind meat. White Castle later in this decade will begin using stainless steel (initially called "Allegheny metal"), even though a stainless-steel pan used to boil water for coffee costs $8 instead of 80¢ and a stainless-steel pail for freshly sliced onions costs $8 or $9 instead of 95¢ (*see* 1964).

New York's Algonquin Hotel has labor troubles; when waiters walk off the job at 1 o'clock as the three dining rooms are filling up with luncheon patrons, men at the Algonquin's Round Table, including playwright George S. Kaufman, don waiters' white jackets, the women (including actress Ina Claire) put on frilly aprons, and they all go to work serving lunch to the other patrons.

New York's Café des Artistes at 1 West 72nd Street commissions, Hotel des Artistes resident Howard Chandler Christy, 59, to decorate the walls with murals (*see* 1917). A prominent illustrator and notorious womanizer, Christy will complete the work in 1934, whereupon it will be found that the "native women" in his depiction of the 16th-century conquistador Ponce de Léon include many blondes wearing rouge and lipstick who bear more than a passing resemblance to some of Christy's chorus-girl companions (*see* 1975).

The Los Angeles restaurant Perino's opened at 4101 Wilshire Boulevard by Italian-American Alexander Perino charges the highest prices in town and will gain a reputation as the best dining spot west of the Mississippi (even, according to some, west of the Hudson). Perino, who arrived in America at age 15, will sell the place in 1968. It will be revived in the late 1970s.

San Francisco's Ritz French Restaurant opens on Post Street under the management of Bordeaux-born chef Calixte Lalanne, formerly a co-owner of the Old Poodle Dog, which closed 10 years ago during Prohibition (*see* 1849). Lalanne's son Louis will turn the Ritz into the Ritz Old Poodle Dog.

The French *boulangerie* (bakery) Poilane opened at 8, rue du Cherche-Midi in Paris's sixth arondissement by baker Pierre Poilane will grow to have five bakers working in shifts round the clock to supply some of the city's best restaurants with pain Poilane. Located in what was once the cellar of an 18th-century convent, it has an oven whose chimney rises eight stories high and uses dark flour from a mill that grinds wheat expressly for Poilane, turning out 8,000 loaves per week that will be delivered by nine trucks.

1933

✗ Adolf Hitler, 43, comes to power as chancellor of Germany January 30, capitalizing on economic distress and appeals to nationalism. Switzerland prepares for a possible war: a federal decree reduces the size of cattle herds to make the nation independent of foreign grain imports. Further decrees will forbid the sale of hard cheese, including Emmenthaler (the oldest, most important Swiss cheese, generally exported in giant wheels weighing from 150 to 220 pounds each) until it is at least 1 year old and, later, 2 years, in order to build a large stock of cheese as an emergency source of protein.

President Franklin D. Roosevelt, 51, enters the White House March 4 with more than 15 million Americans out of work and says, "The only thing we have to fear is fear itself." Even Americans with jobs have had their wages and hours reduced; wage earners' incomes are 40 percent below 1929 levels.

$ The world wheat price falls to an historic low of £4 per hundredweight, where it will remain through 1934. An International Wheat Agreement approved at London in August establishes country-by-country export quotas for the 1933 and 1934 harvests and provides for a 15 percent worldwide reduction in wheat acreages for next year; representatives of Argentina, Australia, Canada, and the United States sign the agreement, but Argentina exceeds her quota by 1 million tons, enforcing the acreage limitations will prove impossible, and the IWA will soon collapse.

Jules Fribourg of Continental Grain at Paris travels to America and buys 1 million tons of wheat from the Federal Farm Board, reselling it in Europe (*see* 1921; 1944).

At least a million destitute U.S. farm families receive direct government relief. While farm prices begin to inch up, a farmer must pay the equivalent of 9 bushels of wheat for a pair of work shoes, up from 2 bushels in 1909.

The average U.S. family income falls 40 percent below its 1929 level. A hired hand on a U.S. farm typically earns $216 per year ($18 per month) as compared to $260 for a sleep-in domestic servant ($21.60 per month), $4,218 for a lawyer, $3,382 for a physician, $3,111 for a college teacher, $2,250 for an engineer, $1,227 for a public school teacher, $907 for a construction worker (*see* typical food prices, below). Roughly 25 percent of U.S. workers are engaged in agriculture, down from nearly 50 percent in 1853 (*see* 1950).

U.S. farm prices drop 63 percent below 1929 levels as compared with 15 percent for industrial prices, since industrialists can control production more effectively than farmers can. Wheat sells in February for 32.3¢ per bushel, down from a 1909–1914 average of 88.4¢.

An Agricultural Adjustment Act voted by Congress May 12 authorizes establishment of an Agricultural Adjustment Administration (AAA) within the Department of Agriculture.

An Emergency Farm Bill becomes law in June, and the AAA (above) sets out to restore farm income by reviving 1909–1914 average prices for wheat, dairy products, cotton, tobacco, corn, rice, sugar, hogs, and peanuts.

A Farm Credit Act passed by Congress June 16 consolidates rural credit agencies under a Farm Credit Administration.

Secretary of Agriculture Henry Agard Wallace, now 44, orders limitation procedures to compensate for the fact that the AAA (above) was established after most crops were planted and pigs were farrowed. He has some 400,000 farrowed pigs destroyed and 330,000 acres of cotton plowed under.

Congress creates the Commodity Credit Corp. in the U.S. Department of Agriculture to buy surpluses and handle any subsidies payable to farmers for reducing their crop acreage (*see* 1930; 1935).

Chase National Bank vice president John G. Peterson resigns in August and goes to work for Cargill Elevator Co., which is in deep financial trouble (*see* 1929; 1931).

Midwestern farmers strike in October to force up prices by withholding products from market. They complain that the AAA has no real power (*see* 1932).

Sugar prices fall to 3¢/lb. in New York, and Puerto Rico has widespread hunger as wages are reduced (*see* 1920).

Feed manufacturer Dale W. McMillen gives up the leases he has held on two Michigan sugar beet refineries, buys an abandoned sugar beet refinery at Decatur, Ind., and launches an intensive advertising campaign to gain consumer acceptance for beet sugar (*see* 1931; Central Soya, 1934).

Grape production in the Chautauqua-Erie grape belt of New York State declines precipitously as the repeal of Prohibition (below) reduces consumer demand for grapes to be used for home wine making. The New York growers use little or no fertilizer or insect spray, average little more than one ton per acre, receive only $20 per ton, and have lost the table grape market to California growers.

New York entrepreneur Jacob M. Kaplan, 40, acquires a small winery at Brocton, N.Y., and establishes a floor price of $50/ton for grapes, guaranteeing the price before the grapes are picked. Kaplan, who has prospered in West Indian sugar and rum ventures during Prohibition, hires chemists and mechanical engineers to produce a uniform beverage efficiently and economically and encourages growers to improve their vineyards, concentrating on Concord grapes (*see* 1945).

Candy maker Otto Schnering introduces a 1 oz., 1¢ wrapped Baby Ruth bar and runs a help-wanted ad in the *Chicago Tribune* August 21, seeking women and girls to wrap his Curtiss Candy Co. products and people to help market them in time for Halloween trick-or-treat doorbell ringers (a relatively new tradition); by September he has a payroll of more than 7,500, up from 1,119 in May 1932 (his factory has four 6-hour shifts in order to give work to more people; women employees on straight wages earn a minimum of 31½¢ hourly, men 45¢; the minimum for men is nearly 30 percent higher than that approved by the National Recovery Administration for the candy-manufacturing industry).

Life Savers, Inc., employs about 150 young women on a piecework basis at $24 to $25 per 5-day week.

Typical U.S. food prices: butter 28¢/lb., margarine 13¢/lb., eggs 29¢/doz., oranges 27¢/doz., milk 10¢/qt., bread 5¢ per 20-oz. loaf, sirloin steak 29¢/lb., round steak 26¢, rib roast 22¢, ham 31¢, bacon 22¢, leg of lamb 22¢, chicken 22¢, pork chops 20¢, cheese 24¢, coffee 26¢, rice 6¢, potatoes 2¢, sugar 6¢ (but *see* earnings, above).

Harry & David of Medford, Ore., begin a mail-order fruit business that will develop by the early 1940s into the Fruit-of-the-Month Club. Harry and David Holmes inherited their father's pear orchard upon his death in 1914, Harry has made a trip to New York and obtained 467 Christmas orders, by 1936 they will have 37,000 orders, they will add candies and baked goods to their line of fresh fruit, the Holmes family will sell out in 1984, and by 1993 the company will be sending out catalogs offering 315 items, including a $290 deluxe Fruit-of-the-Month basket, and grossing $135 million (plus $10 million from nine retail shops), mostly from corporate accounts whose 1 million holiday orders require 5,000 seasonal employees (on top of the 700 who handle year-round orders).

Stokely–Van Camp is created by a merger of Stokely Bros. and Van Camp (*see* Frank Van Camp, 1914; Stokely, 1917). Stokely Bros. has grown by acquiring other canning companies, Van Camp has added to its pork-and-beans and ketchup line by canning New Orleans–style kidney beans, hominy, Vienna sausage, and other items (*see* 1939).

New England Confectionery Co. acquires Lovell & Covel, a small New England boxed-chocolate company.

More than 11 percent of U.S. grocery store sales are made through 18,000 A&P stores (*see* 1929; 1930; 1937).

Food Fair has its beginnings at Harrisburg, Pa., where Samuel and George Friedland, 36 and 31 respectively, pay $150 per month to rent a garage with 10,000 square feet of floor space and open the Giant Quality Food Price Cutter supermarket. Starting with a kosher butcher shop at Middletown, N.Y., in 1919, the Friedlands moved to Harrisburg in 1920. They sell butter at 19½¢/lb., eggs at 12¢/doz., and oranges at 7¢/lb., their first week's sales amount to $15,000, they open a second store at Reading, will open a third and fourth next year at York and Baltimore, and by 1950 Food Fair will be the nation's seventh-largest food chain, with 112 supermarkets.

The Tennessee Valley Authority Act passed by Congress May 18 creates a new federal authority, initially to maintain and operate a power plant at Muscle Shoals, Ala.

The *Brighton Belle* express goes into service on the 55-mile London-to-Brighton rail line with a restaurant car that can serve breakfast, lunch, dinner, or supper to 192 passengers in 55 minutes (*see* 1841). The menu offers soup of the day, kippers, fried filet of halibut, grilled sirloin steak, Welsh rabbit, ham, cheese, fruit juice, mineral water, beer, cider, sherry, and wines that include champagne, claret, burgundy, liebfraumilch, and a wide choice of other wines.

The Ford Motor Company's Industrialized American Barn at the Chicago World's Fair (below) demonstrates margarine made from soybeans. Ford chemical engineer Robert Boyer, 34, works on ways to substitute soybean forms for conventional foods (*see* 1937).

Nonfiction: *Down and Out in Paris and London* by English writer George Orwell (Eric Blair), 30, who writes of his experiences as a *plongeur* (dishwasher) at posh hotels and restaurants: "The customers of the Hôtel X. were especially easy to swindle, for they were mostly Americans with a sprinkling of English—no French—and seemed to know nothing whatever about good food. They would stuff themselves with disgusting American 'cereals,' and eat marmalade at tea, and drink vermouth after dinner, and order a *poulet à la reine* at 100 francs and then souse it in Worcestershire sauce. One customer, from Pittsburgh, dined every night in his bedroom on grape-nuts, scrambled eggs, and cocoa. Perhaps it hardly matters whether such people are swindled or not."

A Soil Erosion Service started by the U.S. Department of Agriculture helps farmers learn tilling methods that will minimize erosion. The seriousness of the problem gains recognition when a great dust storm November 11 to 13 sweeps South Dakota topsoil as far east as Albany, N.Y. (*see* 1909; 1935).

The TVA (above) will make Alabama's backwoods Sands Mountain region the nation's most profitable small-farming area, with the emphasis on raising corn and feeding it to chickens for production of poultry and eggs.

Golden Cross Bantam corn is introduced (*see* East, Shull, 1921; Pioneer Hi-Bred, 1926). The first commercial hybrid grain to be planted on a large scale, it permits farmers to increase their yields, which still average only 22.8 bushels per acre of land, but farmers accustomed to open-pollinated corn resist switching to hybrid seed, which they have to buy and whose plants require far more work (they have to detassel every other row, and that can mean 5,000 to 8,000 tassels per acre). Those who do plant hybrid seeds increase their yields dramatically (*see* Pfister, 1935).

Anaheim, Calif., grower Walter Knott, 43, rediscovers the boysenberry, developed in 1920, and makes it the basis of Knott's Berry Farms. He harvests five tons of the long, reddish black berries per acre.

U.S. biochemist Robert R. Williams, 47, isolates an antiberiberi vitamin substance from rice husks. Williams was born in India and began his professional career in Manila, where beriberi is a major health problem. It takes a ton of rice husks to produce less than 0.2 ounce of the substance (*see* Suzuki, 1912; vitamin B_1—thiamine, 1936).

Austrian chemist Richard Kuhn, 33, at Berlin's Kaiser Wilhelm Institute isolates a heat-stable B vitamin (*see* 1932; vitamin B_2—riboflavin, 1935).

Swiss chemist Tadeus Reichstein and his colleagues synthesize vitamin C (ascorbic acid) (*see* King, 1932).

Borden Co. introduces the first vitamin D–fortified milk (*see* 1930). Children are the chief victims of vitamin D deficiency and the chief consumers of milk (*see* Pet Milk, 1934).

H. Trendley Dean of the U.S. Public Health Service undertakes epidemiological studies that will relate a lack of fluoride intake to tooth decay (*see* 1916; 1939).

George Orwell (above) writes about the lack of hygiene in steamy Paris restaurant kitchens: "It is not a figure of speech, it is a mere statement of fact to say that a French cook will spit in the soup—that is, if he is not going to drink it himself. He is an artist, but his art is not cleanliness. To a certain extent he is even dirty because he is an artist, for food, to look smart, needs dirty treatment. When a steak for instance is brought up for the head cook's inspection, he does not handle it with a fork. He picks it up in his fingers and slaps it down, runs his thumb round the dish and licks it to taste the gravy, runs it round and licks it again, then steps back and contemplates the piece of meat like an artist judging a picture, then presses it lovingly into place with his fat, pink fingers, every one of which he has licked a hundred times that morning. When he is satisfied, he takes a cloth and wipes his fingerprints from the dish, and hands it to the waiter. And the waiter, of course, dips *his* fingers into the gravy—his nasty, greasy fingers which he is for ever running through his brilliantined hair. Whenever one pays more than, say, ten francs for a dish of meat in Paris, one may be certain that it has been fingered in this manner. In very cheap restaurants it is different; there, the same trouble is not taken over the food, and it is just forked out of the pan and flung on to a plate, without handling. Roughly speaking, the more one pays for foods, the more sweat and spittle one is obliged to eat with it."

Columbia University economics professor Rexford Guy Tugwell, 42, is named assistant secretary of agriculture and made head of the Food and Drug Administration. A self-proclaimed socialist, he vows to give "human rights" priority over "property and financial rights" and begins campaigning for a new pure food and drug law (*see* 1938).

"Reg. Penna. Dept. Agr." appears on packages of crackers, pasta, snack foods, and similar foods following adoption of a Pennsylvania state law ordering that bakeries and other premises producing such foods be licensed and inspected periodically for minimum cleanliness and worker health. Any company producing such foods must have its production facilites inspected, wherever they may be, if the foods are to be sold in Pennsylvania.

Ritz Crackers, introduced by National Biscuit Co., will be the world's largest selling crackers within 3 years. Crisper and less fluffy than soda crackers, they are butter crackers made with more shortening and no yeast, spread with a thin coating of coconut oil, and sprinkled with salt after baking. Nabisco bakes 5 million of the crackers; by 1936 production will be at the rate of 29 million per day.

Chocolate chip Toll House cookies are created at Whitman, Mass., by innkeeper Ruth Wakefield (*née* Graves), who figures that semisweet chocolate-bar pieces dropped into cookie batter will melt in the oven and thus save her the time and trouble of melting them separately beforehand. The chocolate stays firm, and the cookies turn out to be delicious. Wakefield and her husband, Kenneth, bought the Toll House Inn, built in 1709, 3 years ago, and opened a restaurant. Nestlé Corp. will start distributing chocolate "morsels" for inclusion in Toll House cookies beginning in 1939 and will acquire rights to the Toll House name.

Campbell's Chicken Noodle and Cream of Mushroom soups are introduced (*see* 1922; tomato juice, 1932; can production, 1936).

Kraft Miracle Whip Salad Dressing is introduced by National Dairy Products (*see* 1929). A spoonable product with a unique taste, it combines the best features of two existing products, boiled salad dressing, which is usually homemade, and mayonnaise, creating a new product category. Fancy cooks have for years gone to great labor to make boiled dressing for use on coleslaw, fruit salads, and the like; Miracle Whip, which will come to be used on sandwiches, tomatoes, etc., will grow to outsell mayonnaise in the United States.

Hershey Chocolate reduces the size of its nickel Hershey Bar from 2 oz. to 1⅞ oz. (*see* 1930; 1936).

Canned pineapple juice is introduced to Americans at the Chicago World's Fair. Dole has experimented with pineapple juice as early as 1910, but without a process to rupture pineapple cells and release their flavor and aroma the product was poor. Two Dole engineers, Symes Hoyt and Richard Botley, developed such a process last year, increasing recovery of juice from the fruit and opening up new horizons for pineapple growers and canners (*see* Dole,

1932). Pineapple juice gives Hawaiian Pineapple Co. a new lease on life, and it will soon be marketing industrial by-products such as liquid sugars, ascorbic acid, citric acid, and cattle feed made from pineapple rinds (*see* 1934).

Libby, McNeill & Libby has 17 booths at the Chicago World's Fair to sell Libby's juices, including the tomato juice introduced in 1929 and the new canned pineapple juice (above) (*see* Florida Citrus, 1954).

Tree-Sweet canned orange juice is introduced by Tree-Sweet Products of California. Los Angeles investment banker W. K. McCracken has put up less than $12,000 to back an inventor who has developed a new method for canning juice that retains more flavor and nutrients than other methods do. McCracken calls the process Instovac (*see* 1948).

Sunsweet prune juice—the first commercial prune juice—is introduced by the Duffy-Mott Co. under an agreement with Sunsweet Growers (*see* 1932; applesauce, 1930; apple juice, 1938).

Congress legalizes sale of 3.2 percent beer April 7, and the first team of Clydesdale horses to promote Budweiser beer appears a day later (the eight bay-colored Clydesdales used to pull the Budweiser Wagon are the idea of Augustus Busch, Jr., whose Anheuser-Busch has survived Prohibition by producing commercial yeast and sarsaparilla).

Repeal of Prohibition evoked cheers from many, including brewers, distillers, and bartenders. PHOTO COURTESY ANHEUSER-BUSCH

Brewing Corp. of America is founded by Cleveland entrepreneurs who take over an abandoned auto plant with money received in the liquidation of Peerless Motor Co. They will introduce Carling's and Black Label beers next year (*see* 1943).

The prohibition against sale of alcoholic beverages in the United States, which began early in 1920, ends December 5 as Utah becomes the 36th state to ratify the 21st Amendment, repealing the 18th Amendment after 13 years, 10 months, 19 days, 17 hours, and 32½ minutes, during which time an estimated 1.4 billion gallons of hard liquor have been sold illegally, making a mockery of the "Noble Experiment." Twenty-two states and hundreds of counties remain dry by statute or local option, and some states permit sale only in stores controlled by a state monopoly.

Repeal finds roughly half the whiskey aging in U.S. rack warehouses owned by National Distillers (Old Grand Dad, Old Taylor, Old Crow, Old Overholt, Mount Vernon).

Schenley Distillers is founded at New York by entrepreneur Lewis S. Rosenstiel, 42, who takes the name from the Schenley, Pa., location of Joseph S. Finch Co., a rye distillery that forms part of the new corporation that will be the leading U.S. distiller until 1937 and lead again from 1944 to 1947. Including Old Quaker distillery at Lawrenceburg, Ind., and the Kentucky distilleries of George T. Stagg at Frankfort, James E. Pepper at Lexington, and New England Distillers at Covington, Schenley owns 25 percent of the whiskey in U.S. rack warehouses.

Most of the remaining whiskey in U.S. rack warehouses is owned by Frankfort Distilleries (Four Roses) and Glenmore (Kentucky Tavern) which will both be acquired by Distillers Corp.–Seagram (*see* 1928). Seagram will build a large distillery at Lawrenceburg, Ind., to produce 5 Crown, 7 Crown, Kessler, and other whiskey brands that will dominate the market (*see* 1934).

Hiram Walker will build a large distillery at Peoria, Ill., to produce Imperial, Ten High, Walker's Deluxe, and other brands that will supplement Walker's Canadian Club brand. The company is now owned by Harry C. Hatch, who bought it in 1926 for $114 million, including $9 million for the goodwill attached to Canadian Club.

De Kuyper begins distilling cordials in America, producing Cherry, Apricot, and Blackberry Liqueur, Triple Sec, Crème de Cacao, and Crème de Menthe identical to those it has made in Holland since the 17th century.

7-Up is promoted as a mixer for alcoholic beverages by Charles Grigg of St. Louis, who renames his Lithiated Lemon and sells 681,000 cases of the soft drink (*see* 1929).

Repeal (above) dampens the boom in most soft drinks and in ice cream sodas.

Coca-Cola sales tumble to 20 million gallons of syrup (2.5 billion drinks), down from a 1930 peak of 27.7 million gallons (3.5 billion drinks).

A new automatic fountain mixer introduced by Coca-Cola Co. at the Chicago World's Fair mixes exact amounts of syrup and carbonated water, eliminating the chance of error by a counterman.

Pepsi-Cola is acquired by Loft candy store chief Edward Guth, who begins to bottle the drink in 12-ounce bottles (*see* 1920; Mack, 1934).

The Confréries des Chevaliers du Tastevin (Burgundian Wine Brotherhood) is founded by French wine merchant Georges Faiveley and tourist office head Camille Rodier at the Château Clos de Vougeot (*see* 1934).

The E. and J. Gallo winery is founded at Modesto, Calif., by Ernest Gallo, 24, and his brother Julio, 23, whose father committed suicide 6 weeks earlier after killing their mother with a shotgun. The Gallo brothers, who have learned about wine making from a book in the public library, sink their savings of $5,900 into an operation that will become the largest U.S. wine maker.

Iron miner Cesare Mondavi, who came to Minnesota from his native Italy in 1906, has been shipping wine grapes from Lodi, Calif., in the northern San Joaquin Valley back to Minnesota during Prohibition (federal law has permitted a family to make 200 gallons of fruit juice per year for its own use, and this was easily fermented into wine) (*see* 1943).

Gallagher's Steak House opens in May at 228 West 52nd Street, New York, with steak, a baked potato, and salad for $1.75 but with nothing stronger than 3.2 beer until December. The proprietors are former *Ziegfeld Follies* girl Helen Gallagher, widow of vaudevillian Ed Gallagher of Gallagher and Shean fame, and her second husband, Jack Solomon, who has persuaded her to leave the stage and open the restaurant with him. It will be famous for its sawdust floor and for serving just five appetizers, two soups, five entrées (sirloin steak, broiled lobster, roast beef, hamburger, and chicken), a few cold meats, five vegetables, two salads, homemade pies, and four or five other desserts (including rice pudding) and cheeses.

San Francisco's Blue Fox restaurant has its beginnings in the Blue Fox Café opened across from the morgue in Merchant Street by an Italian entrepreneur from Viareggio. It will be acquired in 1948 by Piero Fassio, a Piedmontese from Asti who will turn the place into an elegant, worldly eating place (*see* 1988).

Barcelona's Boadas bar opens at Tallers, 1 off the Romblon de los Estudios serving tapas, caviar, smoked salmon, and pâté. Havana-born proprietor Miguel Boadas Parere learned the trade working in his Spanish-born father's taverna. His son-in-law José Luis will take over after his death.

A fourth Lyons Corner House, staffed to serve 2,000 patrons, opens October 23 at London as part of the new 900-bedroom Cumberland Hotel at Marble Arch (*see* 1928). "Nippies" (waitresses) at the Maison Lyons Marble Arch pick up orders at stations marked "Fried fish," "Soups," etc. designed to make service as quick as possible. The Coventry Street, Strand, and Oxford Corner Houses are open 24 hours a day, deliveries of baked goods are made 11 times per day to each Corner House to make sure that bread and rolls are never more than 1 hour old, and the Corner Houses serve nearly 1 million meals per week.

New York's first restaurant liquor license after Repeal of Prohibition in December (above) is awarded to Lüchow's in 14th Street (*see* 1882). Patrons resume their enjoyment of wienerschnitzel and hasenpfeffer at Bock beer festivals, May wine festivals, Sommerfests, and Oktoberfests.

1934

British Prime Minister Ramsay MacDonald, 67, refuses February 22 to see 500 hunger marchers who have trudged from Glasgow to London.

A Farm Mortgage Financing Act passed by Congress January 31 creates a Federal Farm Mortgage Corporation to help farmers whose mortgages are being foreclosed (*see* 1931). Dust storms (below) will soon bankrupt more farmers.

The Midwestern drought will oblige New York merchants to import from abroad the wheat needed to supply East Coast flour mills; Jules Fribourg and Louis Louis-Dreyfus at Paris, unable to obtain enough U.S. grain, will increase their orders for Argentinian wheat and corn and import soft wheat and corn from Romania plus barley from Iran and North Africa (*see* 1915; 1972).

A Civil Works Emergency Relief Act passed by Congress February 15 appropriates another $950 million for the continuation of civil works programs and direct relief aid. Relief Administrator Harry L. Hopkins, 44, reports April 13 that 4.7 million families are on relief.

A Crop Loan Act passed by Congress February 23 authorizes loans to U.S. farmers to tide them over until harvesttime.

The Frazier-Lemke Farm Bankruptcy Act passed June 28 allows mortgage foreclosures to be postponed for 5 years (but *see* 1935).

Demagogic welfare schemes proliferate. Sen. Huey P. Long (D. La.) presents his Share Our Wealth Program, an "every man a king" wealth redistribution scheme.

The Jones-Costigan Act (Sugar Act of 1934) signed into law by President Roosevelt protects beet growers without raising tariffs by requiring that at least half of all U.S. sugar needs be supplied by domestic producers and grants subsidies to those producers. Quotas are assigned to offshore producers, including Cuba, Puerto Rico, and the Philippines, and the Department of State will use those quotas over the years to reward or punish foreign nations depending on how cooperative they are with U.S. interests (*see* Cuba, 1960).

"You Can Thank Jim Dole for Canned Pineapples," say advertisements for the Hawaiian Pineapple Co., which begins early in the year to market its products under the Dole label (*see* 1933). Its canned pineapple has been sold up to now under such names as Diamond Head, Outrigger, Hawaiian Club, and Paradise Island; Dole, now 56, has not had a controlling voice in Hawaiian Pineapple Co. policy since 1932, but now the Dole name is embossed on the tops of company cans and displayed on its labels (*see* 1958; Castle & Cook, 1964).

Central Soya Co. is incorporated October 2 at Decatur, Ind., with a capitalization of $125,000, and builds a plant at Decatur that uses a new expeller process for extracting oil from soybeans (*see* below). Dale W. McMillen has seen the potential of soybeans as a livestock feed (*see* Staley, 1922), and Central Soya's divisions include McMillen Feed Mills (*see* Allied, 1929); Central Sugar Co. continues as a separate corporation.

Tillie Lewis Foods Co. has its beginnings in Flotill Products, started in California's San Joaquin Valley by Brooklyn divorcée Myrtle "Tillie" Ehrlich, 28, with a $10,000 loan from Italian tomato canner Florindo Del Gaizo. Advised by the U.S. Department of Agriculture that pomodoro canning tomatoes cannot be grown in the United States, Ehrlich took her savings and sailed for Italy, met Del Gaizo aboard ship, convinced him that the tomatoes could be grown in California, persuaded him to loan her pomodoro seed, and has persuaded the Pacific Can Co. of Stockton to build a plant that she can rent. When Del Gaizo dies in 1937, she will borrow $100,000 to buy his interests in Flotill; she will marry A.F. of L. western director Meyer Lewis in 1947 and will later sell her Tillie Lewis Food Co. to Ogden Corp. for $6 million.

The Los Angeles Farmers Market opens at 6333 West Third Street with stalls that rent for 50¢ a day on 30-day leases. Started by 17 farmers who have had trouble selling their produce, the market will grow to cover 3 acres of buildings with 18 acres of parking space and with 160 individually owned stalls selling such items as Monzano bananas, Texas mustard greens, snow peas, black radishes, fresh figs, Louisiana sugar cane, Minnesota white veal, racks of lamb, country-style apple and potato sausages, German pumpernickel bread, fresh angelica, loganberries, and loquats.

Central Soya's Decatur, Ind., plant (above) employs an expeller process for extracting oil from soybeans that improves on the traditional hydraulic process, which is not only costly in time and labor but removes only 75 percent of the available oil in the bean. The expeller process removes up to 80 percent and produces a product of more uniform quality (*see* 1936; agriculture, below).

The Castanca Dairy Co. at Trenton, N.J., has a trial run in November of preassembled square, flat-topped, paraffin-lined, plug-opening milk cartons produced by American Can Co. (*see* 1929; Pure-Pak, 1936).

A new chilling process for meat cargoes improves on the process used in 1880 on the S.S. *Strathleven*.

MSG (monosodium glutamate) is produced commercially for the first time in the United States, which has depended until now on the flavor enhancer Ajinimoto imported from Japan (*see* 1908; 1947).

L'Ecole de Cordon Bleu outgrows its 39-year-old Paris quarters in the Palais-Royal; Mme. Distel moves the cooking school to 129, rue du Faubourg St. Honoré. To gain the coveted Grand Diplôme requires 40 2-hour sessions, for which Mme. Distel charges 450 francs; a single lesson with the class costs 25 francs, a private lesson 35 plus the cost of materials (*see* 1945; Petit Cordon Bleu, 1942).

Cookbook: *The Mystery Chef's Own Cook Book* by British advertising executive John Macpherson, 47, who came to America in 1906 in search of business and stayed, adopting the stage name Mystery Chef. His chapter "Famous Foreign National Dishes" gives recipes for sauerbraten, crêpes Suzettes, and the like (*see* 1949).

U.S. food-buying patterns begin shifting to consumption of red meats (especially beef and pork), fruits, green vegetables, and dairy products as industrial earnings start to improve.

New Deal programs helped teach American women how to stretch their food dollars. LIBRARY OF CONGRESS

Dust storms in May blow some 300 million tons of Kansas, Texas, Colorado, and Oklahoma topsoil into the Atlantic. At least 50 million acres lose all their topsoil, another 50 million are almost ruined, and 200 million are seriously damaged (*see* grain exporters, above; Soil Conservation Act, 1935).

Reckless cultivation of U.S. land brought erosion—and demands for conservation. LIBRARY OF CONGRESS

The Taylor Grazing Act passed by Congress June 28 sets up a program to control grazing and prevent erosion of western grasslands. The new law effectively closes the public domain to homesteading (*see* Stockraising Homestead Act, 1916).

Western ranchers begin two decades of wholesale slaughter of wild horses to clear the disintegrating ranges. The horse meat fetches 5¢ to 6¢ per pound (it is sold for human food, dog food, and chicken feed), the government pays a bounty to encourage the horse hunters, and by 1952 the wild horse population will be 33,000—down from 2 million in 1900.

The Taylor Grazing Act (above) establishes grazing districts under the control of the Department of the Interior.

The western dust storms (above) are an aftermath of imprudent plowing during the Great War, when farmers planted virgin lands in wheat to cash in on high grain prices.

"Okies" and "Arkies" from the dust bowl begin a trek to California that will take 350,000 farmers west within the next 5 years.

Mexico's agrarian revolution advances under Gen. Lázaro Cárdenas, 39, who is elected president July 2 and will resume distribution of the land to the pueblos as he also works to build the power of organized labor.

Nazi Germany starts the *Erzeugungsschlacht* program to expand domestic food production. By 1937 the country will be producing 90 percent of the food it consumes.

U.S. federal grain supervision offices adopt the Tag-Heppenstall moisture meter for testing the moisture content of wheat, corn, and other grain. Based on studies conducted in the past 10 years by Department of Agriculture chemist David Augustus Coleman, 42, it applies the principle of electric conductivity.

Drought reduces the U.S. corn crop by nearly a billion bushels, and the average yield per acre falls to 15.7 bushels, down from 22.8 last year (wheat yields average 11.8 bushels per acre).

U.S. soybean acreage increases to 1 million (*see* 1923; 1944; Central Soya, above).

British potato farmers blame a "slimming" craze for a drop-off in sales.

A "Milk in Schools" scheme improves nutrition among British schoolchildren by supplying one-third pint of milk each day to nearly half of all elementary school pupils (who pay little or nothing) (*see* 1906; 1931).

Phenylketonuria (PKU) is described for the first time. The condition affects infants who lack enzymes needed to metabolize the amino acid phenylalanine and may cause mental retardation if not quickly diagnosed and remedied by putting the infant on a diet low in phenylalanine.

Hungarian biochemist Paul György, 40, at Cambridge University discovers pyridoxine (vitamin B_6)—a coenzyme which cures dermatitis in rats. It will be synthesized in 1939.

Pet Milk Co. introduces the first evaporated milk products fortified with vitamin D, using the irradiation process (*see* Steenbock, 1927; Borden, 1933). It is the first company to do so.

Chicago candy maker Frank C. Mars dies of a heart attack and kidney disease at Baltimore's Johns Hopkins Hospital April 8 at age 50, leaving Mars Candy Co. to his second wife, Ethel, his daughter by his second marriage, and his son Forrest, whom he banished to England 2 years ago (*see* 3 Musketeers, 1932; M&M's, 1941).

Candy maker Robert Welch returns to Boston and goes to work as one of four vice presidents for the James O. Welch Company, founded in 1927 by his brother James, who once worked for Robert's old Oxford Candy Co. (*see* 1926). James began with a one-room operation in Cambridge making chocolate-covered fudge and has expanded his line to include Welch's Frappe Bar (a chocolate-covered nougat; "frappe" was the Boston word for milk shake), Welch's Brazil Nut Fudge, Welch's Pecan Penuche, and Welch's Coconut. He adds his brother Robert's Sugar Daddy (originally called Papa sucker) and it will soon be the company's best-seller. Robert, who resigned from E. J. Brach 2 years ago and closed his Brooklyn plant, is put in charge of sales and advertising; in that capacity he will help his brother's company grow to have plants and offices in Los Angeles, Chicago, Houston, Seattle, Atlanta, and Pittsburgh. The company will move from marketing bars and suckers to specializing in nickel boxes of miniature candies. Welch's Sugar Babies, soft caramel tidbits, will appear next

year and ride to success on Sugar Daddy's coattails (*see* 1945).

Wild Cherry Life Savers are introduced.

Pepsi-Cola is acquired by entrepreneur Walter Mack, who will promote Pepsi's 12-ounce bottle to challenge Coca-Cola (*see* 1933; 1939).

Royal Crown Cola is introduced by Nehi Corp. (*see* 1928; 1959; Hatcher, 1905; Diet-Rite, 1962).

Seagram's 7 Crown, introduced by Distillers Corp.–Seagram, will become the top-selling U.S. whiskey (*see* 1933; 1947).

The Napa Valley Wine Co-operative, organized by eight California growers, will have more than 150 members within 25 years, receiving more than 12,000 tons of grapes per year and producing 2 million gallons of wine.

Monarch Wine Co. is founded at Brooklyn, N.Y., to produce sacramental wines for use on religious occasions in place of homemade wines. Monarch will lease the name Manischewitz to gain acceptance for the strong, aromatic wine it presses from native American *Vitis labrusca* grapes (*see* Manischewitz, 1888); it will bottle wines under 17 other labels as it grows to become the largest U.S. producer of fruit wines (including blackberry, cherry, elderberry, and loganberry). Producing more champagne than America imports from France, Monarch's winery will grow to cover four city blocks, and Manischewitz wines will become popular with gentiles as well as Jews.

The first *chapitre* (chapter) of the Confréries des Chevaliers du Tastevin holds its first meeting in an old cellar at Nuits-Saint-Georges, where Georges Faiveley and Camille Rodier have started the fraternal group to promote sales of Burgundy wines, which have been hurt by the ongoing world economic recession (*see* 1933). They have unearthed a copy of the 1812 manuscript recording the procedures and formalities of the Confréries des Francs Buveurs Bourgignons. Sous-Commanderies of the Confréries will be established in other countries (the New York Sous-Commandery in 1940).

Carvel's frozen custard stand opens at Hartsdale, N.Y. Greek-American entrepreneur Thomas A. Carvel (originally Carvelas), 27, will have 21 soft ice cream stores by 1950 and by 1976 will have 680 franchised stores in 14 states (*see* Dairy Queen, 1940).

Ernie's opens at 847 Montgomery Street, San Francisco, under the management of restaurateurs Ernie Carlesso and Ambrosio Gotti, who have taken over Il Trovatore, a former hotel and dance hall. They redecorate with furnishings that once graced the Flood and Spreckels mansions.

Don the Beachcomber opens on Hollywood Boulevard, Los Angeles. Restaurateur Don Beach employs a Hawaiian decor, substituting sophisticated Cantonese cooking for such island staples as raw fish and poi, and serves fancy rum drinks in place of fermented taro root and coconut milk. Beach, who will have many imitators (*see* Trader Vic's, 1937), will relocate to Honolulu's Waikiki district, build a larger establishment there, sell it, and move on to Hong Kong, where he will open a floating restaurant.

New York's 3-year-old Waldorf-Astoria Hotel on Park Avenue opens a Men's Bar with a stand-up bar 60 feet long and seating facilities for 200. A man ordering a whiskey has a bottle placed on his table. Women are not admitted. A dry martini costs 35¢, champagne $1 per glass, a bottle of Louis Roederer 1926 Brut champagne $8.50. The Palm Bar, opened in early summer on the 18th floor (which also accommodates the private Canadian Club), will be used in winter in connection with dinners and other functions held in the Starlight Roof ballroom.

New York's Rainbow Room opens October 2 on the 65th floor of the still unfinished RCA (later GE) Building in Rockefeller Center with backing from Standard Oil millionaire-philanthropist John D. Rockefeller, Jr., 60. Jolly Coburn's Orchestra provides dance music for women in evening gowns and men in white tie and tails (less formal attire is not permitted), French chanteuse Lucienne Boyer makes her U.S. debut that evening, and guests at the inaugural dance (a benefit for the Lenox Hill Neighborhood Association) include Hollywood star Miriam Hopkins, 32, along with socialites from some of the city's richest families (*see* 1942; Rainbow Grill, 1935).

Prunier's opens in London at 72 St. James's Street. Simone Barnagaud-Prunier, a granddaughter of Alfred Prunier, who founded the Paris Prunier's in 1872, not only serves good seafood and tournedos Boston (topped with oysters and covered with hollandaise sauce) but also delivers prepared dishes to be served in homes along with French wines by the bottle or case from her cellar. Her restaurant will continue until her retirement in the 1960s.

The *Guide Michelin* published since 1900 by the French tire firm to evaluate European restaurants is given an elongated format.

1935

Josef Stalin decrees that Soviet children above age 12 are subject to the same punitive laws that apply to adults—8 years in a labor camp for stealing corn or potatoes, for example, or 5 years for stealing cucumbers.

The National Industrial Recovery Act (NIRA) of 1933 is unconstitutional, the Supreme Court rules May 27 in *Schechter Poultry Corp. v. United States.* The "sick chicken" case involves some New York wholesale kosher slaughterhouse operators (called "market men") who have been found guilty of violating the NIRA's "live poultry code" (promulgated under Section 3 of the NIRA), fined $5,000, and given 3-month jail sentences. Manhattan's Terminal Market, the nation's largest live poultry market, receives birds from 35 states (only 4 percent from New York State), and it is easy for a diseased bird in the Washington Market to be sold unwittingly, especially when people in the trade have long workweeks and are sadly underpaid. The defense counsel explains that "straight killing means you have got to put your hand into the coop and take out whichever chicken comes to you. You hand the chicken to the rabbi, who slaughters it." The Court concedes that "extraordinary conditions may call for extraordinary remedies" but rules unanimously that the code, which sets maximum hours and minimum wages, violates not only the commerce clause of the Constitution but also the separation of powers clause, since Congress may not delegate legislative power to the president and give him "an unfettered discretion to make whatever laws he thinks may be needed or advisable for the rehabilitation and expansion of trade or industry." The ruling is a setback for organized labor, which has been pushing for a 30-hour week to ease unemployment.

The Frazier-Lemke Farm Bankruptcy Act of 1934 is unconstitutional, the Supreme Court rules unanimously May 27 in *Louisville Joint Stock Land Bank v. William R. Radford*. Kentucky farmer Radford mortgaged his land for $9,000 and redeemed it for $4,445. Because the law permitted Radford to buy his land back on deferred payments at an interest rate of 1 percent when the going rate was 6 percent, it takes property without compensation, the court rules. Little use has been made of the law, anyway, and the farm mortgage situation has improved without recourse to it.

U.S. farm prices begin to rise as the Commodity Credit Corp. purchases surplus farm commodities for distribution among the needy (*see* 1933; AAA, 1938).

One-third of U.S. farmers receive U.S. Treasury allotment checks for not growing food and other crops or are committed to receive such checks under terms of the Agricultural Adjustment Act of 1933, but drought holds down production more than New Deal planting restrictions do (*see* Supreme Court decision, 1936).

Canada's Parliament establishes a Wheat Board with headquarters at Winnipeg, Man., to handle barley, oat, and wheat exports and to tell farmers how much they can plant each year with a guarantee that will sell their crops.

Britain and Ireland conclude a cattle and coal agreement that enables the Irish to ship some of their meat surplus, but the disastrous Anglo-Irish tariff war will not end until February of next year, when Dublin agrees to pay land annuities (*see* 1938).

The Rural Electrification Administration established by President Roosevelt's executive order May 11 will underwrite rural electric cooperatives and provide loans for transmission lines. Only 10 percent of 30 million U.S. rural residents have electrical service, but with help from the REA 90 percent of U.S. farms will have electricity by 1950.

An estimated 6.5 million windmills have been produced in the United States in the past half century. Most have been used to pump water or run saw-mills, but some "wind generators" have produced small amounts of electricity.

The French Line passenger ship S.S. *Normandie* goes into service on the North Atlantic, arriving at New York June 3 after crossing from Southampton in a record 4 days, 11 hours, 42 minutes. The 79,280-ton luxury liner has a dining room modeled on the Hall of Mirrors at Versailles, and her kitchen is 60 feet long by 17 feet wide and is equipped with an electric range that has 30 hot plates and 32 ovens. She employs 187 cooks, 9 butchers, 6 wine stewards, 10 bakers, and 15 pastry cooks. For each crossing she will take on 60,000 eggs, 4,000 chickens, 20 tons of potatoes, 16 tons of meat, 6 tons of fish, 24,000 liters of wine, and 7,000 bottles of fine wine and champagne. Her pantry contains 28,000 plates and 30,000 glasses (*see* 1938).

Pan Am Clipper flights provide the first hot meals to be served in the air.

Polyethylene, developed by the Alkali Division of Britain's Imperial Chemical Industries, is the first true "plastic" ever made from the polymerization of ethylene. Company chemists 2 years ago found small specks of a white solid material when they opened their retort after an attempt to force a copolymerization between liquid ethylene and an aldehyde, using extremely high temperatures to link small molecules into long chains; their polyethylene will find wide use in food packaging (*see* 1953).

The antioxidant qualities of vitamin E (alpha-tocopherol) isolated at the University of California, Berkeley (*see* nutrition, below) will prove valuable in extending the shelf life of many packaged foods.

Harry Ferguson perfects a hydraulic control mechanism applicable to many farm implements (*see* Sherman-Ferguson, 1925). Easy to operate, it provides for automatic depth regulation of tillage and protection of implements against breakage from obstructions, but there are no tractors on the market to which the hydraulically controlled implements can be attached successfully. Existing tractors are too heavy, cumbersome, and costly, Ferguson says, so he designs a new, lightweight tractor, sets up a British company to manufacture it, and begins production at Manchester. The machine costs more than mass-

Rubber-tired tractors, which could travel on highways, encouraged farmers to replace their horses. LIBRARY OF CONGRESS

produced U.S. tractors but finds a ready market in Scandinavia (*see* 1938).

A new harvester introduced by Allis-Chalmers Co. of Milwaukee is smaller and lighter than a conventional combine but capable of harvesting almost any kind of crop. Allis has a 14.1 percent share of the U.S. harvester market as compared with 32 percent for International Harvester, but its new harvester will raise the company's share to 45.6 percent by next year, while International Harvester's will fall to less than 12 percent (*see* 1937).

Chicago advertising copywriter Leo Burnett, 43, turns the 1925 "giant" symbol of Minnesota Valley Canning Co. into the jolly "Ho Ho Ho" Green Giant; he colors the giant green, dresses him in leaves, and starts a new advertising agency under his own name (*see* 1936; 1950).

Americans consume 50 million chickens but pay more for poultry than for red meat (*see* 1965).

U.S. food packers ship 240 million cases of canned goods, up from 160 million in 1931.

U.S. candy consumption reaches 13.7 pounds per capita, its highest level since 1930. Some of the increase is credited to individual wrapping and transparent cellophane packaging of bulk and penny goods, which previously have not sold well in summer because they looked sticky and unappetizing.

President Roosevelt signs a Soil Conservation Act into law and names Hugh Hammond Bennett, 54, to head the new Soil Conservation Service (*see* Soil Erosion Service, 1933). Bennett estimates that soil erosion is costing the United States $400 million in diminished productivity alone each year; he works to make Americans soil conscious.

Dust storms in western states stop highway traffic, close schools, and turn day into night (*see* 1934).

U.S. fish cutters launch a boom with the discovery that the small white fillet of ocean perch from the Atlantic tastes much like freshwater perch.

A record 42-pound lobster is caught off Virginia.

Fertilized eggs removed from the uterus of a rabbit are stored alive for several hours in a special blood serum and transplanted into the uterus of a virgin rabbit, where they will mature to permit virgin birth (*see* calf, 1950).

Japan achieves self-sufficiency in wheat production for noodles, having increased domestic production by 60 percent in just 3 years.

Soviet agronomist T. D. Lysenko calls his more scientific critics "Trotskyite bandits" and enemies of the state. "Bravo, Comrade Lysenko, bravo," says Josef Stalin, and Lysenkoism becomes Soviet agricultural gospel (*see* 1926; Vavilov, 1940).

Pfister Hybrid Corn Co. has its beginnings as El Paso, Ill., corn breeder Lester Pfister, 38, creates a double-crossed hybrid with outstanding yield that will make him a millionaire (*see* Pioneer Hi-Bred, 1926; Golden Bantam, 1933). A tenant farmer's son who dropped out of school and worked as a hired hand after his father died, Pfister has worked for years to inbreed a high-yielding nonhybrid yellow corn, covering row upon row of corn tassels with paper bags to avoid open pollination, winnowing 388 ears down to just four, and experimenting for 5 years with these four, making multiple crosses while incurring debts and feeding his family on cornmeal mush. By 1938, he will be grossing $1 million per year and will have invented a detasseling machine, and although he will sell most of his business in 1941 he will retain the parent company and family farm, which his son Dan will carry on.

The United States has 6.81 million operating farms, down from 7.2 million in 1931.

Five Acres and Independence by U.S. author Maurice Grenville Kains, 67, is a practical guide to conducting a small farm. It becomes a best-seller as thousands of urban Americans go back to the land.

A Resettlement Administration created by executive order April 30 works to move people from poor lands to better lands under the direction of administrator Rexford Guy Tugwell (*see* 1933).

British Colonial Medical Service physician Cicely D. Williams, 42, finds that kwashiorkor is related to a maize diet. She described a deficiency disease 2 years ago that was common among infants at Accra on the Gold Coast and gives its African name in a report to the British medical journal *The Lancet,* saying it is the disease that "the deposed baby gets when the next one is born," indicating that it may be caused by a lack of mother's milk. Symptoms include edema, bloated stomach, cracked skin, red or dirty gray hair, and even dwarfism (*see* 1951).

German researchers synthesize vitamin B_2 (*see* 1932; 1933). The vitamin will be called riboflavin.

University of California, Berkeley, biochemists Herbert McLean Evans, 53, and Oliver and Gladys Emerson isolate vitamin E (alpha-tocopherol) from wheat germ oil.

Vitamin K—essential for blood "koagulation"—is isolated by C. P. H. Dam and by Edward A. Doisy at St. Louis University (*see* 1937; Dam, 1929).

Eat, Drink and Be Wary by U.S. consumer advocate F. J. (Frederick John) Schlink, 44, relates horror stories related to food contamination (*see* Sinclair, 1905). A mechanical engineer and physicist who since 1931 has headed the 6-year-old Consumer's Research company, Schlink was co-author 2 years ago of a book entitled *One Hundred Million Guinea Pigs.*

Adolph's Meat Tenderizer, devised by San Francisco chef Adolphe Alfred Rempp, 24, is a powdered product that is easier to use than conventional liquid tenderizers.

The Kit Kat candy bar has its beginnings in the Chocolate Crisp, introduced by Britain's Rowntree & Co., which has expanded since the death of Joseph Rowntree in 1925 under the leadership of Seebohm Rowntree, now 64 (*see* 1897). He has established subsidiaries in Australia, Canada, Ireland, and South Africa. The new chocolate-covered wafer bar will be renamed Kit Kat in 1937, taking its name from London's Kit Kat Club, founded in 1703 by fashionable Whigs devoted to the Hanoverian succession (*see* Smarties, 1937).

Five Flavors Life Savers are introduced; fruit drops will rival mint flavors by 1937.

ReaLemon Lemon Juice is introduced by Chicago entrepreneur Irvin Swartzberg, whose physicians have told him to start each day with lemon juice and water but who has grown tired of squeezing lemons. He starts the Puritan Co. to supply lemon juice to bars, hotels, restaurants, and industrial users, and will sell ReaLemon to consumers beginning in 1941 (*see* Borden, 1962).

Krueger Beer of Newton, N.J., introduces the first canned beer.

The U.S. government sues Canadian distillers for $60 million in taxes and duties evaded during Prohibition. The amount will be lowered to $3 million, and Distillers Corp.–Seagram will pay half of it (*see* 1933; 1943).

Alcoholics Anonymous is founded at New York June 10 by ex-alcoholic Bill Wilson, 40, and his former drinking companion Dr. Robert H. Smith, who takes his last drink and works with Wilson to share with other alcoholics the experience of shaking the disease. Philanthropist John D. Rockefeller, Jr., will refuse requests to fund AA, saying that money will spoil its spirit, and it will spread through church groups. "Bill W.," whose anonymity will be preserved until his death in 1971, will be called by English novelist Aldous Huxley "the greatest social architect of our time."

The National Institute of Controlled Appellations of Origin (Institut National des Appellations d'Origines Contrôlées) established by France's Parliament ends 50 years of passionate legal and physical conflicts over French wine names.

Chef Auguste Escoffier dies of uremia at his Monte Carlo home, Villa Fernand, February 12 at age 88. Asked at one time what he would have done in Vatel's place had the soles not arrived in time (*see* 1671), he replied, "I would have taken the white meat of very young chickens and made filet of sole with them. Nobody would have known the difference." Having cooked for Napoleon III, three

French presidents, Queen Victoria, Edward VII, George V, and Kaiser Wilhelm, he retired at age 74 to the Riviera, with a pension of £1 per day from the management of London's Carlton Hotel. Escoffier received only a small part of the fortunes that have been reaped from the manufactured sauces which he created and the hotels bearing his name but has lived on his savings and on fees paid for the magazine articles he has written. His wife, who cooked all his meals at home until she was stricken with paralysis in 1928, has died earlier in the year, but Escoffier himself has enjoyed good health, ascribing it to a drink which he invented and took every night before retiring: the yolk of one fresh egg, beaten, and several spoonfuls of sugar mixed with a pony of champagne in a glass of hot milk. His final book, *On Cuisine*, was published last year after his editors deleted some passages containing intimate details of some of his royal clients. "To know how to eat is to know how to live," Escoffier has said, and "No man should have less than 2 hours for the chief meal of the day." The ideal dinner, he has said, consists of soup, a roast, two vegetables, and a sweet, with a pony of marsala, a good bordeaux, and, finally, champagne. He has always advocated simple foods and frowned on overeating.

The Zurich hotel-restaurant Eden au Lac opens. Hotelier A. L. Thurnheer will make it one of the city's three or four top eating places.

Swiss-born English chef Rudolf Richard buys London's 38-year-old Hotel Connaught (the Coburg until 1915), increases the number of its bathrooms to have one for every bedroom, and takes steps to improve the hotel's cuisine. It has four cooks in its kitchen, but by the time Richard dies in 1973, the Connaught will have Britain's finest restaurant, employing 42 chefs working in two brigades to serve 250 people per day (*see* Grill Room, 1955).

New York's Rainbow Grill (initially The Patio) opens in June beside the Rainbow Room atop the RCA Building (*see* 1934). A Hawaiian string orchestra provides the music (later performers will include Duke Ellington, Benny Goodman, George Shearing, Dave Brubeck, and Sarah Vaughan), and patrons are soon doing the new dance The Big Apple (described in the *Daily News* August 14 as "a combination of truckin', the Susi-Q, the Charleston, and the Shag

with a touch of St. Vitus' Dance thrown in." Table d'hôte dinner is $2.

Le Chambord opens under the El on New York's Third Avenue at 49th Street under the direction of French-born restaurateur Roger Chauveron, 33, who arrived in New York in 1924 and has worked as a waiter and cook at the Plaza Hotel, the Ritz-Carlton, the Astor, and the Commodore. He specializes in French provincial cuisine, vows that he will have the lowest prices in town, serves 75¢ luncheons and $1.25 dinners, but starts raising prices when patrons line up each evening outside his door. He will stop raising prices only when he discovers that they are 15 percent higher than those anywhere else (*see* 1950).

The Friendly Ice Cream Co. restaurant chain founded by S. Priestley Blake and his brother Curtis will grow by 1979 to have 600 full-service restaurants, most of them in New England and other northeastern states (*see* 1979).

Chicago printing salesman Duncan Hines, 55, sends out a pamphlet listing his favorite eating places in lieu of a Christmas card and receives so many requests for copies that he goes into business leasing "Recommended by Duncan Hines" signs for as much as $20 per year. Guidebooks by Hines will be published under titles that include *Good Eating* and *Lodging for a Night* (*see* 1950).

1936

💲 The Bureau of Labor Statistics places the "poverty line" at $1,330, but 38 percent of U.S. families (11.7 million families) have incomes of less than $1,000 per year.

Goya Foods has its beginnings in a concern started at New York by Puerto Rican entrepreneur Provenzio Unanue Ortiz and his wife, Carolina (*née* Casa), to import olives and olive oil. Sponsoring floats at almost every Puerto Rican Day parade and giving support to Spanish dance and theater groups, their business will grow—despite occasional quality and delivery glitches—to distribute some 750 items of beans, rice, flour, spices, and frozen foods, with close to 80 percent of the market for Hispanic foods in the U.S. Northeast. After Unanue's death in 1976, his

Hispanics were not yet a prominent U.S. minority group when Goya Foods began operations.

sons Joseph (now 10), Francisco (now 3), Charles, and Anthony will take over (Anthony will also die in 1976), and they—along with *their* children—will work to increase sales among the nation's rapidly growing Puerto Rican, Cuban, Mexican, and other Hispanic populations.

Canada Dry profits fall below $200,000, down from $3.5 million in 1930, as the Depression continues to sap demand for luxury foods and beverages (*see* 1922). The company builds a bottling plant at Miami, Fla., and establishes warehouses in major Florida cities; by 1960 it will have 103 bottling plants worldwide and will be marketing club soda, Tom Collins mix, quinine water, and fruit flavors as well as ginger ale.

The first Giant Food Store supermarket opens at Washington, D.C. Entrepreneurs Jacob J. Lehrman, 25, and N. M. Cohen pioneer self-service food retailing in the nation's capital.

The S.S. *Queen Mary* goes into service on the North Atlantic for the Cunard–White Star Line. The 80,774-foot passenger liner offers first-class passengers the finest cuisine.

The *Super Chief* leaves Chicago's Dearborn Station May 12 with a diesel engine and nine Pullman cars, offering weekly luxury service with Fred Harvey cuisine (and, by making the run in just 39 hours, much faster travel between Chicago and Los Angeles than the *Chief* has provided since 1926).

Central Soya sends two men to Germany to investigate a solvent extraction process, a chemical process that is essentially automatic and has the capacity to extract 95 percent of the available oil in soybeans (*see* 1934). Two small plants using the solvent extraction process are now operating in the United States; the German Hansa-Muhli extractor is designed for much larger capacity than Central Soya anticipated, but the company imports the extractor and draws up plans to double the capacity of its 2-year-old Decatur, Ind., plant to 275 tons per day. By early 1938, a massive five-story structure—the first Hansa-Muhli extraction plant—will be in operation (*see* 1941).

The Pure-Pak milk carton, produced by Ex-Cello-Corp., comes only in pint sizes but comes off the line at the rate of 40 quarts per minute (*see* Canco, 1934). Equipment acquired by Ex-Cell-O last year from American Paper Bottle Co. of Toledo, Ohio, has been designed by John Van Wormser and some associates to form, wax, fill, and seal the gable-top cartons, whose tops must be cut off (in 1941 a perforated tab will be developed which can be lifted to expose a pouring hole). Glass companies try to block use of the new cartons: Justice Salvatore A. Cotillo of the New York State Supreme Court rules June 16 in favor of Dairy Sealed, a Borden subsidiary, which has obtained an injunction against enforcement of a Milk Control Board order to charge 12¢/qt. for milk in fiber containers when milk in glass bottles sells for 11¢ (*see* 1939; glass bottles, 1940).

Campbell Soup begins manufacturing its own cans; it has been buying them from Continental Can but will now become the world's third-largest producer of food cans simply by supplying its own needs (*see* 1933).

The Waring Blendor, financed by U.S. bandleader Fred M. Waring, 36, begins mechanizing kitchen chores. Patented 14 years ago by Polish-American inventor Stephen J. Poplawski of Racine, Wis., to make malted-milk shakes, the $29.95 mixer with its "high" and "low" speed buttons proves ideal for making Waring's daiquiris. It is redesigned and renamed, introduced in September at the National Restaurant Show in Chicago, and marketed initially to bartenders (see Cuisinart, 1973).

General Mills uses the name "Betty Crocker" as a signature for responses to consumer inquiries. The fictitious authority is portrayed as a gray-haired homemaker, an image that will see numerous revisions as Betty Crocker becomes a major brand name for various General Mills products (see 1929; Kix, 1937).

Borden Co. introduces the cartoon character Elsie the Cow to serve as a symbol of purity and wholesomeness (see World's Fair, 1939).

A food column by Kansas-born cooking authority Clementine (Haskin) Paddleford, 37, begins appearing in the New York Herald Tribune. The column will be syndicated for 30 years, and Time magazine in 1953 will call Paddleford the best-known food editor in the country with an estimated weekly readership of 12 million.

Cookbooks: The Joy of Cooking by St. Louis housewife Irma Rombauer (née von Starkloff), 60, gives recipes in the most minute detail, telling the cook exactly what to look for. Rombauer, whose lawyer husband taught her to cook after their marriage in 1899, had a private edition printed 5 years ago for her grown children; her daughter Marion Rombauer Becker, now 35, will co-author future editions. Plats du jour by French author Paul Reboux. Le Petit Cordon Bleu, An Array of Recipes from Le Petit Cordon Bleu by English cooking expert Dione Lucas (Narnona Margaris Wilson), 27, and Rosemary Hume, who studied at L'École de Cordon Bleu in Paris and in 1931 set up a restaurant, cooking school, and catering service in London's Sloane Street near Knightsbridge (see New York school, 1942).

Fiesta ironstone dinnerware is introduced by the 65-year-old Homer Laughlin China Co. of Newell, W.Va., after its owner visits southern California and "discovers" Mexican-style objects. In the late 1930s and early '40s the company will be shipping more

than 12 million pieces, and although the line will be discontinued in 1970 it will be revived in 1986 as fully vitrified porcelain (with colors more subtle than those in the original ware).

President Roosevelt signs an Omnibus Flood Control Act into law.

Boulder Dam (later to be called Hoover Dam) on the Colorado River creates a lake 115 miles long (Lake Mead), whose waters irrigate 250,000 acres.

The Agricultural Adjustment Act of 1933 is unconstitutional, the Supreme Court rules January 6 in United States v. Butler, but the New Deal uses soil conservation as the basis of a new effort to limit planting.

The Soil Conservation and Domestic Allotment Act passed by Congress February 29 pays farmers to plant alfalfa, clover, and lespedeza rather than soil-depleting crops such as corn, cotton, tobacco, and wheat.

Drought reduces U.S. crop harvests and brings new hardship to farmers and consumers.

T. D. Lysenko's sensationalist agricultural nostrums gain full sway over Soviet agriculture (see 1935; 1940).

Soviet geneticist Nikolai Vavilov shows that the white potato Solanum tuberosum could not possibly have originated in Virginia as is commonly believed (see 1530; 1597; Vavilov, 1929; 1940).

A 4-year program begins in Nazi Germany to produce synthetic (ersatz) replacements for raw materials such as fats and livestock fodder.

Robert R. Williams synthesizes vitamin B_1 and gives it the name thiamine (see 1933; 1937).

University of Wisconsin biochemist Conrad Arnold Elvehjem, 35, isolates vitamin B_3 (nicotinic acid, or niacin) from liver extract. It has an instant positive effect on a dog sick with a canine version of pellagra (see 1915; 1938).

New York entrepreneurs who include Hearst magazine editor Henry Sell, now 46, start a company to market Vitamins Plus, a dietary supplement that includes liver and iron. Introduced at booths set up in cosmetic departments at Marshall Field, Saks

Fifth Avenue, Gimbel's, and Lord & Taylor, it is soon being sold nationwide through mail-order advertising (*see* Sell's Liver Paté, 1941).

The butter yellow dye *p*-dimethylaminoazobenzene is dropped from use in foods following revelations by Japanese biochemist M. Yoshida that the dye produces liver tumors in test rats.

Spry is introduced by Unilever's Lever Brothers to compete with the hydrogenated vegetable shortening Crisco introduced by Procter & Gamble in 1911. Within a year, Spry will have sales of $12 million, versus $25 million for Crisco, but it will later be discontinued.

Pillsbury registers the name Hungry Jack as a trademark for pancake flour. The name will later be used for a pancake mix, refrigerated biscuits (*see* Ballard, 1951), frozen microwave pancakes, dehydrated potato products, and syrup.

Blum's of San Francisco, the candy company founded by Simon Blum in 1892, comes upon hard times. Blum has died, as has his son Jack, and the firm has dwindled to 18 employees with annual volume of only $72,000. Jack Blum's son-in-law, Fred Levy, 27, takes over the business, and within 10 years it will be the city's largest industrial user of cream, producing 750 varieties of candy, delivering them in air-conditioned trucks, shipping them by plane to New York, and doing an annual business of $4 million in candies, cakes, pies, and frozen desserts.

Eastman, Ga., entrepreneur William Sylvester Stuckey opens a roadside stand to sell pecans to motorists en route to and from Florida. His wife, Ethel, turns her kitchen over to making batches of fudge and other candy, some of it containing pecans, and Stuckey offers the candy for sale along with his pecans. He quickly outgrows that stand and opens a retail store, the first of some 250 that will flourish throughout the South, Southeast, and parts of the Midwest.

Hershey Chocolate reduces the size of its nickel Hershey Bar from 1⅞ oz. to 1½ oz. (*see* 1933; 1937).

The 2¢ Chunky chocolate bar introduced at New York by Delancey Street candy maker and confectionery wholesaler Philip Silverstein weighs 1¼ oz. unwrapped and contains Brazil nuts and raisins. He names it after his "chunky" little baby granddaughter, and although its ingredients will change in years to come, when Brazil nuts become too expensive, it will survive, despite the fact that it appears to offer less candy for the money than most of its competitors.

The Mars Almond Bar, introduced by Mars Candy Co., will later be renamed the Mars bar (*see* 1932).

The Fifth Avenue bar introduced by William H. Ludens of Reading, Pa., has a peanut butter center with two almonds enrobed in milk chocolate (*see* 1881).

Spear-O-Mint Life Savers are introduced.

Orangina is introduced at the Algiers Trade Fair by Algerian entrepreneur Léon Béton and a Spanish pharmacist named Trigo. Béton learned of the sparkling, pasteurized orange drink from Trito when the two met 2 years ago at a Marseilles trade fair, has gone into partnership with him, and has arranged to have the drink packaged in small round bottles. Beton's son Jean-Claude will take over the business in the early 1950s and expand distribution (*see* 1957).

Dom Pérignon Champagne is introduced by France's House of Moët (*see* 1743). Memorializing the pioneer of sparkling wine (*see* 1698), it will be Moët and Chandon's prestige *cuvée*.

The Paris restaurant Le Relais-Plaza has its beginnings in a bar opened in the Hôtel Plaza-Athénée at 25, avenue Montaigne. Lucien Diat, brother of New York's Ritz-Carlton chef Louis Diat, is the chef.

The Paris restaurant Châtagnier opened by Gustave Châtagnier in a former coal shop at 75, rue du Cherche-Midi specializes in seafood au beurre blanc as prepared at the owner's native Nantes (the recipe for beurre blanc calls for 300 grams of fine, fresh butter, 45 grams of alcohol vinegar, 2 grams of finely chopped shallots, 5 grams of salt, 2 grams of freshly ground pepper, 50 grams of fish-and-wine court bouillon, and parsley). Châtagnier will also make a specialty of belon oysters, pink shrimps, pâté de maison, Parma ham, fresh goose livers from Hungary, dindonneau (baby turkey breast), lamb chops, châteaubriand, sea bass, fresh salmon from the Loire (from January 25 until the end of April), turbot, brill, perch, pike, scallops, and lobster.

The London restaurant Mirabelle opens at 47 Curzon Street, Mayfair, serving traditional French dishes (*see* 1946).

Howard Johnson's restaurants have their beginnings at Orleans on Cape Cod, where Wollaston, Mass., restaurateur Johnson, 39, has persuaded young Reginald Sprague to open an eating place that Johnson will supply with ice cream, fried clams, and frankfurters (*see* 1937).

The Beverly Hills, Calif., restaurant Dave Chasen's has its beginnings in a chili parlor opened at 9039 Beverly Boulevard by Russian-American vaudeville straight man Chasen, 37, who uses a $3,000 loan from *New Yorker* magazine editor Harold Ross to start a place with seven tables and eight bar stools that will expand within a few years to become a spacious white-tablecloth eating place, attracting celebrities not only with chili (although that will remain Chasen's signature dish) but also with hearty specialities such as hobo steak (New York–cut steak broiled with a thick layer of rough salt, finished at tableside, and dipped in hot butter just before it is served to make it sizzle), carpetbagger steak (a large sirloin slit and stuffed with oysters), spare ribs, prime ribs, boiled beef Belmont, and banana shortcake (layers of génoise, sliced bananas, and whipped cream). Chasen's widow, Maude, and her daughter will continue to operate the restaurant after Chasen's death and it will not close until 1995.

1937

"I see one-third of a nation ill-housed, ill-clad, ill-nourished," President Roosevelt says in his second inaugural address January 20 as the Great Depression continues. Roosevelt sends Washington, D.C. lawyer Joseph E. Davies, who 2 years ago married Marjorie Merriweather Post, as his ambassador to Moscow. Post sends ahead 2,000 pints of pasteurized cream, frozen by the Birdseye process, to the U.S. Embassy, along with 25 refrigerators (Soviet Russia has plenty of cream, but little of it is pasteurized and there are few electric refrigerators).

A survey by English economist G. D. H. (George Douglas Howard) Cole, 48, notes that the average British family of five with an income £500 to £600 more than that living on the average industrial wage consumes nearly 36 percent more meat, more than twice as much fish and fresh milk, more eggs, 56 percent more butter, but only half as much margarine, 16 percent fewer potatoes, and 12 percent less bread.

Garnac Grain Co. is founded at New York by Swiss caterer's son Frederic Hediger, who has worked for André at Antwerp (*see* 1877), obtains financial backing from André, and begins importing flaxseed from Argentina, Uruguay, and India for Staten Island paint makers. Garnac will grow to become an important wheat exporter.

The A&P begins opening supermarkets, as do other major U.S. food chains. Three or four smaller stores are closed down for every A&P supermarket opened (*see* 1929; 1958; King Kullen, 1930; Big Bear, 1932).

The supermarket shopping cart introduced at Oklahoma City June 4 begins a revolution in food buying. Sylvan N. Goldman, 38, who owns Standard Food Markets and Humpty Dumpty Stores, has noticed that customers stop buying when their wicker baskets become too full or too heavy to carry. He has taken some folding chairs, put them onto wheels, raised the seats to accommodate a shallow wire shopping basket, placed a second such basket on the seat, and used the chair back as a handle to push the X-frame contraption. Four U.S. companies will develop Goldman's invention into a computer-designed chromed-steel cart that can be nested in a small area.

The *Train Bleu* running between Paris and Monte Carlo has a dinner menu for January 29 that offers passengers foie gras, hot jambon, sardines, saumon fumé, choux-fleurs minerva, œufs et champignons à la provençal, suprême de langouste à la marseillaise, poulet en cocotte à la parisienne, haricots verts, fonds d'artichaut, buffet froid, pâté de canard, glace, charlotte russe, and café, all for 35 francs. The dishes are prepared in a five-by-eight-foot galley.

Ford Motor Company scientists trying to develop a synthetic wool fiber produce soy protein "analogs" that will be used as substitutes for bacon and other animal protein foods. They spin a textile filament from soybean protein and create a vegetable protein that can be flavored to taste much like any animal protein food (*see* 1949; Boyer, 1933; Worthington Foods, 1939).

The artificial sweetener sodium cyclamate, discovered by University of Illinois chemist Michael Sveda, is 30 times sweeter than sugar and has none of the bitter aftertaste of the saccharin discovered in 1879 (*see* 1950).

Britain gets her first frozen foods as Wisbech Produce Canners Ltd. introduces frozen asparagus in May at 2 s., 3 d. per pack, strawberries in June at 1 s. 2 d. per eight-ounce pack, garden peas in July at 9 d. per six-ounce pack, and sliced green beans in August at 1 s., 2 d. per six-ounce pack. Wisbech's S. W. Smedley has developed his own freezing process after studying American techniques on a visit to the United States, but Britain has only 3,000 home refrigerators as compared with more than 2 million in the United States (*see* Birds Eye, 1938).

Home freezers become commercially important for the first time in the United States as frozen food sales increase, but relatively few Americans have anything more advanced than an icebox. Icemen continue regular deliveries, delivering blocks of ice which drip into pans beneath iceboxes as they melt.

Allis-Chalmers improves its rubber-tired tractor and sells a lightweight combination tractor and combine for $1,000 (the competition charges that much for a tractor or combine alone) (*see* 1935). Sales of the new equipment propel Allis to third place in the U.S. farm equipment industry.

Diabetics are treated successfully for the first time with zinc protamine insulin, which further reduces the need for diet therapy but still requires daily injections (*see* 1924; oral drugs, 1942).

Fiction: *The Road to Wigan Pier* by George Orwell, who writes, "In the highly mechanised countries, thanks to tinned food, cold storage, synthetic flavouring matters, etc., the palate is a dead organ. . . . Look at the factory-made foil-wrapped cheese and "blended" butter in any grocer's; look at the hideous rows of tins which usurp more and more of the space in any food-shop, even a dairy; look at a sixpenny Swiss roll or a twopenny ice cream."

Cookbook: *L'Art culinaire moderne* by Cordon Bleu chef-professeur Henri Paul Pellaprat, 68, says in its introduction, "As entertaining is one of the housewife's duties, to help her in this task I have added some more extravagant dishes to each

chapter. . . . I have tried every one of the recipes on the stove . . . and I believe I have fulfilled the aim I set myself when I started to write this book: to give the housewife the most all-round training possible" (the book runs to more than 700 pages with 207 pages of colored illustrations); *Serve It Forth* by Scots-Irish California gastronome and prose stylist M. F. K. (Mary Frances Kennedy) Fisher, 29.

Film: Frank Borzage's *History Is Made at Night* with Charles Boyer as a Parisian maître d'hôtel who falls in love with Jean Arthur.

Drought ends in the United States, but stem rust attacks the wheat crop as it did in 1935 (*see* 1941).

U.S. spinach growers erect a statue to the comic-strip sailor Popeye, who is credited with having boosted consumption of the vegetable since the strip debuted in 1929 (*see New Yorker* cartoon, 1928).

A cartoon character's power to increase spinach sales inspired U.S. growers to commission a statue. LIBRARY OF CONGRESS

U.S. biochemists A. N. Holmes and R. E. Corbet isolate vitamin A crystals from fish-liver oils (*see* Karrer, 1931).

Vitamin K is produced in crystalline form (*see* 1935).

German biochemists K. Lohmann and P. Schuster discover that a diphosphate ester of thiamine (vitamin B_1) functions as the coenzyme cocarboxylase, without which pyruvic acid accumulates in bodily tissues and produces the toxic effects which quickly bring on the symptoms of beriberi (*see* 1936; synthetic thiamine, below).

Synthetic thiamine (vitamin B_1) is manufactured in the United States and Switzerland at $450 per pound, but further research will soon reduce the price to a few cents per pound (*see* enrichment proposal, 1938).

Pepperidge Farm Bread is introduced by Connecticut entrepreneur Margaret "Maggie" Rudkin (*née* Fogarty), 40, who has never baked bread before (her mother never even boiled an egg) but whose physician has told her that the asthmatic condition of her youngest son, Mark, requires that he be sent to Arizona. An early believer in the importance of B vitamins, she has decided, instead, to build up the boy's health with good whole-wheat bread. Having taken out her *Boston Cookbook* and followed directions, she remembered how, when she was 6 years old, her Irish grandmother used to make bread. Her stockbroker husband Henry A. Rudkin suffered an accident in a polo match at the Fairfield County Hunt Club 6 years ago and no longer keeps horses, so she sets up an oven in what used to be his polo pony stable on the family's 120-acre Pepperidge Farm (named for the black gum trees on the property). Her whole-wheat bread, she will later claim, helped young Mark so much that her physician requested that she make extra loaves for his other patients. Rudkin has persuaded a neighbor, Mary Farence, to help her bake, has added a white loaf made from unbleached flour, and has begun selling the breads, first to neighbors, then to the local grocery, then to other stores in the Fairfield, Conn., area, and now through Charles & Co., a New York City fancy food retailer, where it finds a good market at 25¢ per one-pound loaf when ordinary commercial

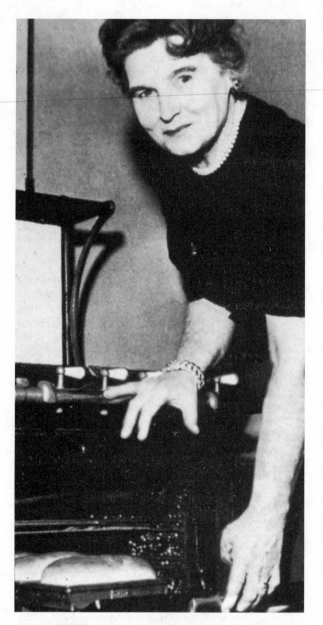

Margaret Rudkin baked the first loaves of Pepperidge Farm Bread in her Connecticut kitchen. PHOTO COURTESY CAMPBELL SOUP CO.

bread sells for 10¢. Mr. Rudkin, who takes the 7:38 brokers' special to New York each morning, brings along 24 loaves, hands them over to a porter at Grand Central Terminal for delivery to Charles &

Co., and continues by subway to Wall Street. The red-haired, green-eyed Mrs. Rudkin soon has to hire a truck to deliver her bread to New York, and by September of next year she will be baking 4,000 loaves per week to meet demand from steady customers in Maryland and Florida (*see* 1940).

General Mills introduces Kix corn puff cereal.

Spam is introduced by George A. Hormel Co., whose salty, fatty, ground pork-shoulder-and-ham product will become the world's largest-selling canned meat (*see* 1943). Jay C. Hormel, son of the founder, created the product to use up surplus pork shoulder, mixing it with ham, salt, sugar, and sodium nitrite and calling it spiced ham; competitors brought out similar products, Hormel saw that it needed a distinctive brand name, and actor Kenneth Daigneau, brother of a Hormel executive, won a contest last year (prize: $100) by coming up with the name.

Kraft Macaroni & Cheese Dinner is introduced nationally in yellow boxes (soon changed to blue) by National Dairy Products, which has adopted the idea of one of its St. Louis salesmen to combine grated American cheese with Tenderoni Macaroni. The product is advertised on the Kraft Music Hall radio show as "A meal for four in 9 minutes for an everyday price of 19 cents" (many stores sell it for as little as 10 cents).

Ragú Spaghetti Sauce has its beginnings in a spicy tomato-and-cheese sauce put up in mason jars at New York and distributed to friends and neighbors by Italian-American pasta, wine, and cheese importer Giovanni Cantisano and his wife, Assunta. They will soon sell the sauce to local stores under the name Ragú, Italian for "sauce" (*see* 1946).

A bolt of lightning kills La Choy Food Products founder Wallace Smith (*see* 1922). Ilhan New left the company in 1930, but its surviving management builds its first plant at Detroit (*see* 1942).

Hershey Chocolate raises the size of its nickel Hershey Bar from 1½ oz. to 1⅝ oz. (*see* 1936; 1938).

U.S. Army captain Paul B. Logan works out the formula for a heat-resistant high-energy chocolate ration consisting of three four-ounce bars made of chocolate, sugar, powdered skim milk, cocoa butter, vanillin, and oat flour, with added thiamine (vitamin B_1). Hershey Chocolate produces 90,000 test ration bars for the Army, which next year will rename the Logan Bar Ration D (for "daily") (*see* 1942).

Sky Bar, launched by New England Confectionery Co., is the first U.S. molded chocolate bar with four distinctly different centers—English toffee, honey nougat, nut butter toffee, and fudge parfait (*see* Bolster, 1930). A skywriting campaign announces the new bar.

Rolo, introduced by Britain's John Mackintosh & Sons, is a roll of chewy caramels enrobed in milk chocolate (*see* 1932; Rowntree Mackintosh, 1969).

Rowntree & Co. introduces Smarties—pellets of chocolate coated with a pastel-colored hard candy finish (*see* Kit Kat, 1935; Rowntree Mackintosh, 1969). Forrest Mars, who is making Milky Ways in a plant outside London, will copy the idea, using bolder colors for his hard candy shells (*see* 1934; M&M's, 1941).

Good 'n Plenty is introduced in a 5¢ box by Philadelphia confectioner Lester Gerstle Rosskam, whose German-born grandfather entered the distilling business in 1885, did so well making and selling Old Saratoga whiskey that he brought over his wife's three brothers from Germany, but started a confectionery business at the turn of the century when he found that none of his three sons wanted any part of the whiskey business. Rosskam's Good 'n Plenty consists of chewy licorice pellets encapsulated in a hard finish.

Root beer pioneer Charles E. Hires dies at Haverford, Pa., July 31 at age 83.

Howard Johnson's restaurants become a franchised operation as restaurateur Johnson hits upon the idea of franchising after having found it impossible to obtain bank financing for restaurants (*see* 1936). Johnson locates property which he leases to a Cambridge, Mass., widow who invests first $5,000 and then another $25,000; he constructs a building, hires employees, charges a small fee for the franchise but takes no part of the profits, retains exclusive rights to supply food including 28 flavors of ice cream, menus, table mats, and other items, and starts a chain of franchised orange-roofed restaurants, whose design and operation he will rigidly control (*see* 1952).

Oakland, Calif., entrepreneur Victor J. Bergeron enlarges his 3-year-old 25¢ lunch-and-beer parlor Hinky Dink's, decorates it with Polynesian fishnets and glass floats, and renames it Trader Vic's (*see* 1951; Don the Beachcomber, 1934).

The Winnetka, Ill., restaurant Indian Trail has its beginnings in a 30-seat tearoom opened by Harvey and Clara Klingeman, whose chicken fricassee, cherry pandowdy, apricot lattice pie, bread custard pudding, sour-cream apple pie, and raisin pie will be made for years without written recipes. Their teashop will grow into a restaurant seating 300.

The New York steak house Pen & Pencil opens at 205 East 45th Street. Restaurateur John Bruno's son, John, Jr., will take over in 1966 after graduation from Dartmouth Business School, buying short loins (containing the shell, tenderloin, and tail) from the Washington Street wholesale meat market.

The London restaurant A L'Écu (later A L'Écu de France) opens at 111 Jermyn Street with a kitchen staff headed by the French chef Herbodeau, last of the great London chefs to have worked for the late Auguste Escoffier. Its specialities include coquilles Saint-Jacques with sauce bonne femme or américain, filet de bœuf en croute périgordine, and rognons épicure (kidneys prepared in a port wine sauce with Dijon mustard and red currant jelly and served with a purée of brussels sprouts).

1938

💲 Britain and Ireland resume friendly relations after concluding a 3-year agreement to remove tariff barriers (*see* 1935). Britain turns over coast defense installations to Eire, and Dublin agrees to pay £10 million to satisfy land annuity claims.

Germany's trade balance shows a deficit of 432 million marks. The country has been bankrupt since 1931 by ordinary capitalist standards, and Reichsbank president Horace Greeley Hjalmar Schacht, 61, warns that the country's enormous armament program must be curtailed lest the catastrophic inflation of 15 years ago recur.

President Roosevelt asks Congress for help in stimulating the U.S. economy as business remains in recession with 5.8 million Americans still unemployed.

A revised Agricultural Adjustment Act eases restrictions on planting most U.S. crops, even providing for lime and mineral fertilizer supplies to farmer to increase yields. The new Agricultural Adjustment Administration (AAA) begins direct crop subsidy "parity" payments to farmers based on 1910–1914 farm prices.

The Commodity Credit Corp. established by the new AAA (above) supports U.S. farm prices by buying up surpluses for an "Ever-Normal Granary" designed to protect the nation against drought and plant diseases, distribute surpluses among the needy, and pay export subsidies that will encourage foreign sales by "equalizing" U.S. farm prices with lower world prices (*see* wheat exports, 1940; food stamps, 1939).

Birds Eye Frozen Foods Ltd. is established in England as a joint venture between General Foods and Unilever (*see* Wisbech, 1937). Lack of cold storage and refrigerated transport limit the marketing of frozen foods initially, but Birds Eye will grow to dominate the United Kingdom's frozen food business, British farmers will buy seeds from the company to permit uniformity of strain and quality, Unilever will own a majority interest by 1943, by 1946 there will be 100 shops stocking Birds Eye products produced in six plants (at Great Yarmouth, Lowestoft, Kirkby, Grimsby, Hull, and Eastbourne), and by 1948 there will be 900 such shops (*see* 1957).

The Girl Scouts of America, founded in 1912, contracts with Interbake Foods of Richmond, Va., to supply all its cookies. The Girl Scouts baked cookies beginning in the 1920s for fund-raising programs and have contracted with various commercial bakeries to pack cartons of cookies for spring drives (*see* 1975).

Gold Bond Trading Stamps are introduced by Minnesota entrepreneur Curtis LeRoy Carlson, 24, who has sold soap for Procter & Gamble at $150 per month before borrowing $50 to start a company that will make him a fortune (which he will parlay into a bigger fortune by acquiring Country Kitchen/TGI Friday restaurants and other enterprises).

The S.S. *Normandie* launched in 1935 entertains favored passengers at a Captain's Dinner July 28 with a menu that includes *caviar frais du Golfe de*

Riga de seigle-toast Melba, *consommé double doux, pommes d'amour, fillets de sole Miromesnil, suprême de Bresse Île de France, épinards de Lauris à la huile douce, selle de béhague, rôti à la broche, pomme à Lorette, terrine de foie gras de Strasbourg, salade Fauchon, boule de neige, corbeille de frivolités,* and *frais réfriches au marasquin.*

✽ Tractor builder Harry Ferguson returns to the United States, having proved his technical principles (*see* 1935). Henry Ford helps him arrange for mass production of his tractor and its hydraulically controlled attachments, decentralizing production by awarding contracts to numerous independently owned manufacturers, and production will begin in the fall of 1939 (*see* Massey-Ferguson, 1953).

Teflon (Fluon), discovered accidentally by Du Pont chemist Roy Joseph Plunkett, 28, is an excellent electrical insulation material, stable over a wide range of temperatures and resistant to most corrosive agents. Found while working on refrigerants, the polytetrafluoroethylene plastic will have many industrial uses; it will be marketed under the name Fluon by Britain's Imperial Chemical Industries, and its low coefficient of friction will make it popular as a coating for nonstick frying pans and other cooking utensils.

Dewey and Almy in Boston develop the Cryovac deep-freezing method of food preservation (*see* Birdseye, 1925).

⚕ The United States has her last reported case of "the milksick" as dairies virtually wipe out the often fatal disease by pooling their milk from a variety of herds. Also called the slows or the trembles, the disease is transmitted in the milk of cows that have eaten white snakeroot (*Eupatorium rugosum*).

⚱ Cookbooks: *Larousse gastronomique* by Prosper Montagné, now 73, who became head chef of the Grand Hotel at Paris soon after the turn of the century with 50 or more men under him, retired before 1912 because of his wife's ill health, and worked during the Great War to create dishes that could be prepared in division kitchens and transported to the front lines, where they had only to be heated. After the war, he opened a restaurant under the name Montagné—Traiteur (Montagné—Restaurant Keeper) at the corner of the Rue St. Honoré and the Rue de l'Échelle (the book will appear in an

English translation in 1961; *see* first U.S. edition, 1977). *French Cook Book* by French food critic André (Louis) Simon, 61.

⊕ Congress passes a Flood Control Act authorizing public works on U.S. rivers and harbors.

Arizona's 286-foot high Bartlett Dam is completed.

🐟 *Larousse gastronomique* (above) gives more than 50 ways to prepare Dover sole (*Solea vulgaris*) (*see* Kintner, 1877).

Efforts begin to help salmon and steelhead trout ascend the Columbia River via fish "ladders" as the river's fishing industry is threatened by power dams, such as the year-old Bonneville Dam, that have cut the fish off from spawning grounds.

Albacore tuna are found in large schools off the Oregon Coast, and salmon fishermen who have been supplying the Columbia River Packers Association since 1899 turn to tuna fishing (*see* Van Camp, 1926). The Association adopts the brand name Bumble Bee for its canned tuna after having used it for years on its canned salmon and builds the first tuna cannery in the Northwest, setting it up alongside its salmon cannery at Astoria, Ore.

🍎 Nicotinic acid (niacin) is found to prevent pellagra (*see* 1915; Elvehjem, 1936).

Enrichment of bread with the B_1 vitamin thiamine, synthesized by Robert R. Williams 2 years ago, is proposed at a scientific meeting in Toronto.

U.S. biochemist Roger J. Williams, 45, brother of the thiamine pioneer (above), synthesizes pantothenic acid, a minor B vitamin present in many foods.

Paul Karrer synthesizes vitamin E (alpha-tocopherol) and finds it to be an effective antioxidant (*see* Karrer, 1931; Evans and Emerson, 1935).

Studies of the chemistry of vision in poor light begun by Harvard biologist George Wald, 31, will show the importance of vitamin A in avoiding nyctalopia, or night blindness (*see* 1925).

☂ A new U.S. Food, Drug and Cosmetic Act signed into law June 27 updates the Pure Food and Drug Act of 1906 (*see* 1912; 1913; Tugwell, 1933). It establishes standards of identity for most food products, requiring that basic ingredients of about 400 such products be listed in the Code of Federal

Regulations, but only "optional" ingredients such as salt, sugar, and spices must be listed on labels. The new law is stricter than the old one, but critics say it is still not sufficiently protective of consumers' health (*see* Delaney, 1950).

The Wheeler-Lea Act gives the Federal Trade Commission jurisdiction over advertising that may be false or misleading even if it does not represent unfair competition (*see* 1931). The FTC, which receives special powers to regulate advertising of food, drugs, and cosmetics, enjoins Standard Brands from making claims that Fleischmann's Yeast is "rich in hormone-like substances" and will help prevent colds and cure constipation, indigestion, and related skin problems. Quaker Oats is enjoined from claiming that its cereal contains the "magical yeast vitamin," which curbs nervousness and prevents constipation while stimulating children's appetites and that one penny's worth contains as much of this B vitamin as three cakes of yeast.

The American Chamber of Horrors by Ruth De Forest Lamb details abuses in the U.S. food industry.

A can of meat put up in 1824 is discovered and its contents fed to test rats with no observable ill effects.

Lawry's Foods has its beginnings in a blended seasoning for salads and roast beef that will become known as Lawry's Seasoned Salt. Created by Lawrence L. Frank for his new Los Angeles restaurant Lawry's The Prime Rib (below), it combines 17 herbs and spices, has taken a year to perfect, is produced in a 25-by-15-foot room in the Mateo Street potato chip factory of Frank's brother Ralph, and will lead to an entire line of Lawry's food products (*see* 1950).

Nestlé introduces its Crunch bar and Hershey its Krackel bar, both made from crisped rice and milk chocolate.

Hershey Chocolate reduces the size of its nickel Hershey Bar from 1⅝ oz. to 1⅜ oz. (*see* 1947; 1939).

Mott's apple juice is introduced by the Duffy-Mott Co. (*see* Sunsweet prune juice, 1933). The company uses juice from Courtland, Golden Delicious, Ida Reds, McIntosh, Rhode Island Greening, Rome Beauty, 20 oz., York Imperial, and more than a dozen other varieties for its products (*see* Red Cheek, 1940; Clapp's, 1953).

Nescafé is introduced in Switzerland by Nestlé (above), which has been asked by the Brazilian government to help find a solution to Brazil's coffee surpluses. Nestlé has spent 8 years in research to develop the instant coffee product (*see* G. Washington, 1909; Instant Maxwell House, 1942).

Detroit's London Chop House opens across from the Penobscot Building with 75¢ steak dinners (a scotch and soda costs 25¢). Proprietor Lester Gruber, 33, is a University of Michigan dropout whose brother Samuel will join him next year; together, they will make the Chop House Detroit's leading bar and restaurant, and it will continue until 1991.

Chicago restaurateur Ernest Byfield, 48, of the College Inn opens the Pump Room at the Ambassador East Hotel in November, and it soon becomes a gastronomic meeting place for Broadway theater and Hollywood film industry people who must stop at Chicago en route from New York between the arrival of the *Twentieth Century Limited* and the departure of the *Super Chief*. Byfield's idea is to create a "celebrity palace" on Chicago's Gold Coast that will rival the Pump Room of 18th-century Bath, England. He sends limousines to Union Station to meet actors such as Ronald Reagan and Jane Wyman, and his waiters, dressed in knee breeches and tailcoats, serve patrons caviar at $8 per portion, double magnums of Krug's private *cuvée*, pheasant en plumage, and chicken curry in coconut shells. All food is placed on rolling tables containing open-hearth ovens for everything from soup to pastry, and waiters serve many items on flaming swords (Byfield will die of a heart ailment early in 1950 at age 60).

The Los Angeles restaurant Lawry's The Prime Rib opens June 15 in an undeveloped area at 116 North La Cienaga Boulevard between Santa Monica and downtown L.A. Van de Kamp baking executive Lawrence L. Frank, whose 16-year-old Tam O'Shanter continues to prosper, has designed 600-pound stainless-steel carts which can be rolled up to patrons' tables to permit carving of roasts as they watch. For $1.25, a patron can enjoy a generous-sized thick cut of roast prime rib of beef au jus (or, for slightly more, the "Diamond Jim Brady cut") with Yorkshire pudding, baked potato with butter and fresh chives (sour cream will not be offered until 1986), and a salad bowl (the tossed green salad is served before the main course—a new idea—from a bowl spinning on a bed of crushed ice). The "English cut," featuring three thin slices, will be added later, as will the scaled-down "California cut." Frank's seasoned salt (above) is offered with the beef and as part of the salad dressing. Started by Frank in partnership with his brothers Arthur and Harry and his brother-in-law Walter Van de Kamp, Lawry's The Prime Rib offers several other entrée choices, but they will be dropped within a year. The restaurant will pioneer in valet parking, and other Lawry's The Prime Rib restaurants will open in Beverly Hills, Chicago, and Dallas.

1939

✗ World War II begins one week after the August 23 signing of a mutual nonaggression pact between Nazi Germany and Soviet Russia. Russia is obligated under the agreement to supply Germany with 1 million tons of wheat per year and expedite delivery of Manchurian soybeans. Germany has stockpiles of 8.5 million tons of grain as her troops invade Poland September 1, and Berlin accuses London of having airlifted Colorado potato beetles onto German fields.

👤 Britain establishes a Ministry of Food with nutrition expert Professor J. C. (later Sir Jack) Drummond as scientific adviser. It draws up plans designed not only to maintain adequate supplies but also to improve the nation's nutrition, especially that of the poor. Shortages of sweets and sugar are reported at Christmas, but some areas have gluts of the same foodstuffs that in other parts of the country are hard to find, and some shopkeepers will serve only regular customers (*see* rationing, 1940).

Britain has reduced her dependence on imported food through subsidies to farmers and marketing schemes, but she remains the largest buyer of food in the world market, absorbing 40 percent of all food sold in international trade.

Soviet troops invade Finland November 30 (*see* 1940). Herbert Hoover organizes a drive for Finnish relief December 5, and Congress grants Finland $10 million in credit for agricultural supplies.

The U.S. Department of Agriculture introduces the first food stamp program in May to feed the needy of Rochester, N.Y. The program will continue until 1943 (*see* 1964).

Food stamps moved surplus farm products into the kitchens of needy Americans. LIBRARY OF CONGRESS

💲 17 percent of the U.S. workforce remains largely unemployed, but while the actual number of unemployed men and women has fallen from 15 million in 1933 to 9.5 million, even Americans with jobs have relatively low average incomes.

Nearly 25 percent of Americans are still on the land, but the average farm family has a cash income of only $1,000 per year.

Only 3 percent of Americans have enough income to pay any taxes, and 670,000 taxpayers account for 90 percent of all income taxes collected.

Thanksgiving Day is celebrated November 23—the fourth Thursday in the month rather than the last. Federated Department Stores chief Fred Lazarus, Jr., has persuaded President Roosevelt that a longer Christmas shopping season will help the economy, the president has issued a proclamation, and within a few years most states will pass laws making November's fourth Thursday Thanksgiving Day (*see* 1863). The holiday means big business for grocery stores and supermarkets.

Consolidated Foods has its beginnings as Chicago entrepreneur Nathan Cummings, 42, a onetime Montreal shoe wholesaler, takes an option to buy C. D. Kenny, a Baltimore sugar and coffee wholesaler for $1.2 million. He will exercise the option in 1941 and begin an amalgam of food retailers and processors under the name Consolidated Groceries (*see* 1951; 1954).

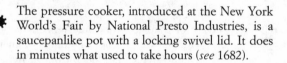 Borden Co. enters production of Swiss cheese by acquiring Carl Marty & Co. (*see* Elsie, 1936). The Depression has put a crimp in Borden's sales, but its profits have remained strong and it has acquired hundreds of small dairies (*see* Lady Borden ice cream, 1947).

G. F. Heublein & Bro. of Hartford, Conn., acquires rights to Smirnoff vodka for $14,000 (*see* 1892). Heublein boss John G. Martin, 33, an English-American grandson of Heublein founder Gilbert F. Heublein, has helped bring the company back into the liquor business in the past 6 years and employs Russian émigré Rudolph Kunett, whose Smirnoff Co. has been grossing $36,000 per year but is close to bankruptcy (*see* 1946).

The pressure cooker, introduced at the New York World's Fair by National Presto Industries, is a saucepanlike pot with a locking swivel lid. It does in minutes what used to take hours (*see* 1682).

Elsie the Cow appears at the New York World's Fair (above) (*see* 1936). The bovine trademark helps Borden Co. (above) to establish national awareness.

Cookbooks: *Streamlined Cooking* by Irma Rombauer gives a recipe for tunafish, mushroom soup (introduced by Campbell in 1933), and noodles; *The Common Sense Cook Book* by Ida Bailey Allen.

Parker Dam is completed across the Colorado River near Parker, Ariz., as part of the $220 million Colorado River Aqueduct System, which taps 1 billion gallons of water per day from the river, lifts it nearly one-quarter mile high, and transports it across 330 miles of desert and mountain to the 3,900-square-mile Metropolitan Water District of Los Angeles (*see* 1913). Located 155 miles below the 3-year-old Boulder Dam, the new $13 million project has been built up from 234 feet below the riverbed.

Fort Peck Dam is completed with WPA funds to control the Missouri River in Montana. The earth-filled dam rises 250 feet.

New York's Fulton Fish Market reopens in a new building put up to replace the 1907 structure, which fell into the East River 3 years ago. Fishmongers in the new market handle some 250 million pounds of seafood in the first year.

U.S. plant geneticists Paul Christoph Mangelsdorf, 40, and R. G. Reeves show that *Zea mays* originated from wild maize when winds blew the seeds north to the highlands of Mexico, where they mated with the wild grass *Tripsachum*, known to the Mexicans as *teosinte*, or "God's grass." The two flourished side by side for centuries before they mated, and from that cross came *Zea mays*, which is grown in many varieties—elf corn by the Mexicans for use in tortillas, northern flint corn for cornmeal, dent corn for southern spoon bread, sweet corn (*see* 1779), and various hybrids (*see* Mangelsdorf, 1941).

British farmers are urged by the government May 3 to plow up grazing land in order to increase domestic food production.

DDT is introduced in Switzerland and applied almost immediately and with great success against the Colorado potato beetle, which is threatening the Swiss potato crop. Swiss chemist Paul Müller, 40, of the Geigy Co. has developed the persistent, low-cost hydrocarbon pesticide (*see* 1943; Zeidler, 1873; Carson, 1962).

Japanese beetles menace crops in much of the United States (*see* 1916).

British bread, flour, and margarine are enriched and fortified with vitamins and minerals. Vitamins

A and D are added to margarine, calcium carbonate to flour.

The American Institute of Nutrition revives the idea of fortifying staple foods with vitamins and minerals (*see* 1936; 1941).

C. J. Cox of Pittsburgh's Mellon Institute urges fluoridation of U.S. drinking water in areas where it is not fluoridated by nature (*see* Dean, 1933; Grand Rapids, Newburgh, 1945).

British biochemists David Keilin and T. Mann demonstrate that zinc is an essential trace element, essential to the human enzyme carbonic anhydrase needed by the body to eliminate carbon dioxide waste.

General Foods introduces the first precooked frozen foods under the Birds Eye label, marketing a chicken fricassee and crisscross steak (*see* 1931). Competitors come out within the year with "frosted" creamed chicken, beef stew, and roast turkey (*see* Morton Packing, 1940).

Stokely–Van Camp enters the "frosted" food market in competition with General Foods (above) (*see* 1933; Pomona Products, 1955).

Worthington Foods is founded under the name Special Foods at Worthington, Ohio, by local psychiatrist George T. Harding III, 34, who heads the Seventh-Day Adventist sanitarium started by his father in 1919. The sanitarium has emphasized nutrition, encouraged vegetarianism in keeping with Adventist principles, produced whole-wheat bread in its kitchen, and bought "health foods"— including soy- and peanut-based meat substitutes, developed originally by John Harvey Kellogg— from Battle Creek Foods in Michigan and Madison Foods in Tennessee. Harding and his wife, Mary Virginia, have decided to make their own meat substitutes in order to save money, and they begin production in a burned-out two-story house, rinsing gluten with a garden hose, ladling gluten steaks out of kettles by hand, and packing them in cans whose labels they glue on by hand, one at a time. Former Battle Creek Foods salesman Bill Robinson is their only paid employee, peddling their "dark" meat Proast and "light" meat Numete to Seventh-Day Adventist institutions and to Catholic, Jewish, and Mormon communities. Sales will reach an annual

rate of $20,000 by the end of next year (*see* 1945; Loma Linda Foods, 1906; Ford's soy protein analogs, 1937).

A 5-minute Cream of Wheat is introduced to compete with quick-cooking Quaker Oats, which reduced its cooking time in 1922 from 15 minutes to 5 (*see* 1902).

Lay's Potato Chips are introduced by Atlanta's H. W. Lay Co., founded by Herman Warden Lay, 30; he has taken over Barrett Food Products, for which he was a route salesman in 1932 (*see* Frito-Lay, 1961).

Half-gallon paperboard milk containers are introduced on some U.S. home-delivery routes at a price 3¢ below that of two one-quart glass bottles, but most retail grocers charge a 1¢ premium for paperboard containers, knowing that customers will pay extra for the convenience of not having to return 3¢ deposit bottles to the store (*see* 1936; glass bottles, 1940).

Pepsi-Cola challenges Coca-Cola with a radio jingle written for $2,500 by Bradley Kent and Austen Herbert Croom to the old English hunting song "D'ye Ken John Peel": "Pepsi-Cola hits the spot/ Twelve full ounces, that's a lot/ Twice as much for a nickel, too/ Pepsi-Cola is the drink for you" (*see* 1934; 1949).

China consumes about 900 million pounds of tea, the United Kingdom about 469 million, India 111, the United States 97, Japan 75, Russia 63, Australia 51, Canada 43, the Netherlands 29, Eire 23, the Dutch East Indies 21.

Harry's Bar boss Giuseppi Cipriani pays 32,000 lire to buy a broken-down *osteria* on the Venetian island of Torcello, 50 minutes away by motor launch (*see* 1931). He installs a generator (the place has no electricity) and opens an inn which he names Locanda Cipriani, growing his own seasonal vegetables. Co-owner Harry Pickering will sell Cipriani his share in Harry's Bar next year and retire to Monte Carlo, where he will die in 1948, and Cipriani will expand the hotel-style bar, famous for its dry martinis, into a restaurant, with a kitchen headed by a chef hired from the nearby Hotel Europa (*see* 1960).

1940 ⎯⎯⎯⎯⎯⎯⎯⎯⎯⎯⎯⎯⎯⎯⎯⎯⎯⎯⎯⎯⎯⎯

Britain's Ministry of Food begins rationing January 8 with controls over butter, sugar, and bacon. Rationing follows thereafter of meat, cheese, preserves, and tea in fixed quantities per capita, allocating supplies equally and keeping prices at levels people can afford. Milk and eggs are allocated. A point system is instituted for canned meat, fish, fruit, and dried fruits, which can be purchased with special coupons; bread, flour, potatoes, and many other items remain unrationed. German U-boats sink 160,000 tons of British shipping in September. The fall of France (an armistice is signed June 22) has left Britain to carry on the fight against Germany and Italy with whatever help she can get from America and the Commonwealth nations.

Black markets flourish in occupied and unoccupied France. Bread and other food staples are rationed, and consumers pay premium prices to obtain more than their allotted rations. Britain has few instances of black markets; food subsidies operate to keep prices stable.

Berlin orders wholesale slaughter of Danish livestock to boost German morale with extra "victory rations" and to save on fodder, gambling that the war will be short. Cattle numbers are reduced by 10 percent, hogs by 30 percent, poultry by 60 percent, and by next year Danish output of animal products will fall to 40 percent below 1939 levels.

The extraction rate of British bread is raised to help compensate for shortages of other foods that provide the nutrients ordinarily lost from refined white bread. The Ministry of Food's Food Advice Division produces leaflets, films, and radio broadcasts in an effort to teach catering workers and the general public how to use unfamiliar foods, such as dried eggs and milk, how to make the best use of vegetables, and how to prepare dishes that require few rationed ingredients.

Britons increase their consumption of milk, thanks in large part to government schemes to provide cheap milk for expectant mothers and children under age 5, free milk to schoolchildren, and chocolate milk for adolescents. Consumption of cheese, potatoes, carrots, and green vegetables also increases.

Some 3 million tons of U.S. wheat are exported under the export subsidy program started in 1938. The subsidy averages 27.4¢ per bushel to equalize the higher U.S. price with the world price of wheat.

Argentina ships wheat and other foodstuffs to Europe. She will become the richest nation in South America in the next 5 years.

U.S. unemployment remains above 8 million, with 14.6 percent of the workforce idle.

Morton Packing Co. is founded at Louisville, Ky. The firm will enter the frozen food business in the late 1940s with a line of chicken, turkey, and beef pot pies to which it will later add fruit pies (see 1955).

The A&P sells cellophane-wrapped meat for the first time.

Nearly 15,000 U.S. retail stores are equipped to sell frozen foods, up from 516 in 1933.

The United States has 1.34 million miles of surfaced road, up from 694,000 in 1930, plus 1.65 million miles of dirt road (see 1950).

A freeze-drying process for food preservation is discovered (see Maxim, 1964).

Controlled atmosphere (CA) storage is used for the first time on McIntosh apples whose ripening is slowed by storage in gas-tight rooms from which the oxygen has been removed and replaced with natural gas. Cornell University professor Robert M. Smock has developed the process.

Owens-Illinois Glass introduces Duraglas for deposit bottles. The new bottle glass, which can stand up to repeated use by beer and soft drink bottlers, brings a boom to Owens-Illinois sales.

German-American biologist Max Delbruck, 34, Italian-American biologist Salvador Edward Luria, 28, and U.S. biologist Alfred Day Hershey, 31, pioneer molecular biology, making basic discoveries in bacterial and viral reproduction and mutation involving nucleic acid in cells (see Watson and Crick, 1953).

Celiac patients in Dutch hospitals improve after German occupation authorities requisition all wheat and rye flour. Hospital administrators discover that the disease (also called nontropical sprue) comes from an intolerance for gluten, the major protein in wheat and rye.

Cookbooks: *Hors d'Oeuvres and Canapes: With a Key to the Cocktail Party* by Oregon-born New York caterer James (Andrews) Beard, 37, co-owner of Hors d'Oeuvres Inc., who has until recently taught English and French at a New Jersey country day school after a career as actor and radio announcer. The book launches Beard on a career that will make his name a household word. *Ida Bailey Allen's Time-saving Cook Book* by Allen.

The fall of France (above) cuts off shipments of Roquefort and other French cheeses that have been popular in America, but U.S. technicians have learned how to control Roquefort spores scientifically and a number of companies will produce blue cheeses, aged for 6 months and given a quarter turn each day during the curing period, that will rival those from France.

U.S. red meat consumption reaches 142 pounds per capita on an average annual basis. The figure will increase to 184 pounds in the next 30 years.

The New York–New Jersey shad catch is 3,250,000 pounds, down from 13.5 million in 1890.

A shrimp trawler fishing in deep water off the Texas gulf coast returns to Port Isabel with a brown shrimp having a purple-tinged tail. Unlike the common white shrimp that is taken close to shore in shallow water, it is a nocturnal creature that has thus far escaped notice, but by the late 1950s it will have become the leading variety used in the shrimp industry (*see* 1949).

Santa Gertrudis cattle gain recognition from the U.S. Department of Agriculture as a new breed. Developed over the last 18 years by King Ranch boss Robert J. Kleberg, Jr., 44, the cattle have the cherry red coloring and beef quality of the English shorthorn first imported in 1834. The genetic stock of the new breed is five-eighths shorthorn, but the animals have the small hump, the heavy forequarters, and the hardiness of the Indian Brahma breed introduced in 1854. Steers reach a weight of 2,300 pounds and give up to 71.9 percent meat.

Kleberg's late father countered King Ranch's drought problems by digging deep artesian wells. He developed trench silos, brought in the first British breeds to run on the open range, persuaded the Missouri Pacific Railroad to run a line through the ranch, established the town of Kingsville, and cultivated citrus, palm, and olive trees (*see* 1885). King Ranch lands now cover nearly a million acres, an area roughly the size of Rhode Island. The ranch is the largest single beef cattle producer in America.

Shasta Dam is completed on the Sacramento River in northern California to help irrigate Sacramento Valley farms.

U.S. farmers have withdrawn from cultivation nearly one-third of the farmland tilled in 1930 —some 160 million acres—under programs instituted by the Soil Conservation Administration (*see* 1935).

Soviet geneticist Nikolai Vavilov is arrested and imprisoned in an underground cell for his opposition to T. D. Lysenko, who will dominate Soviet agriculture until 1964 with his unscientific ideas (*see* 1936; 1942).

An Agricultural Testament by British agronomist Sir Albert Howard, 67, favors use of natural fertilizers. Sir Albert was knighted upon his return to Britain after nearly 30 years in India, where his experience led him to subscribe to Mohandas K. Gandhi's statement that "the poor of the world cannot be helped by mass production, only by production by the masses." Having seen farmers in the state of Indore (who have learned early Chinese techniques of intensive agriculture and water management) use locally produced vegetable and animal manure for lack of more efficient fertilizers, he says that nations rich in labor but poor in capital must use their natural strengths rather than follow Western models, and that man must cooperate with nature rather than try to conquer natural forces: "Mother Nature never tries to farm without live stock; she always raises mixed crops; great pains are taken to preserve the soil and to prevent erosion; the mixed animal and vegetable wastes are converted into humus; there is no waste; the processes of growth and of decay balance one another; the greatest care is taken to store the rainfall; both plants and animals are left to protect themselves against disease" (*see* Rodale, 1942).

The U.S. soybean crop reaches 78 million bushels, up from 5 million in 1924 (*see* 1945).

The United States has more than 6 million farms, but while 100,000 farms have 1,000 acres or more, some 2.2 million have fewer than 50 acres (*see* 1959).

U.S. biochemist Vincent Du Vigneaud, 39, isolates the B vitamin biotin. He finds that a substance known as vitamin H is identical with the coenzyme R found in leguminous plants and is, in fact, a B vitamin. Du Vigneaud will elucidate the structure of biotin in the next 2 years, but while two kinds of dermatitis in infants will be found to respond to biotin therapy, no natural biotin deficiency will be observed in humans.

Vitasoy is introduced in Hong Kong by local entrepreneurs whose protein soft drink meets with little success until it is promoted with advertising that says, "Vitasoy will make you grow taller, stronger, prettier."

Boston businessman–diet reformer Edward W. Atkinson dies of a heart attack at Boston December 6 at age 81 (*see* 1889).

The U.S. Food and Drug Administration (FDA) established in 1906 is transferred from the Department of Agriculture to the Federal Security Agency, which will become the Department of Health, Education and Welfare in 1953 and the Department of Health and Human Services in 1980.

Arnold Bread has its beginnings at Stamford, Conn., where (Paul) Dean Arnold, 32, and his wife, Betty, have found an old Dhurkopf brick oven with a 16-square-foot hearth lined with English tile and put it into their backyard. A descendant of the Revolutionary War general (and traitor) Benedict Arnold, Dean has worked for Nabisco but quit after discovering that he was allergic to flour. He and Betty bake a bread loaf with a distinctive taste, Betty wraps each loaf by hand with an electric iron, and after working all night she sends Dean off in his old Pierce-Arrow sedan to see if anyone will buy the bread at 15¢ per loaf when the going price for commercial bread is 10¢. Betty's sister Emily gives up her job as a dietician at Stamford Hospital to help, and on the last night before a wrapping machine is delivered the two women wrap 1,500 loaves (*see* 1942).

Demand for Pepperidge Farm bread obliges Margaret Rudkin to rent an abandoned service station at Norwalk, Conn., and expand her baking facilities (*see* 1937). She buys her own spring wheat from the Northwest to ensure quality and expands her line to include melba toast and pound cake (*see* 1947).

The fall of France (above) increases demand for California wines among oenophiles cut off from supplies of Chambertin and Château Haut-Brion. Without proper pesticides, the French vineyards will sustain further damage from grape phylloxerae, whereas California vineyards—especially those of Almadén, Beaulieu, Berringer, Buena Vista, Christian Brothers, Concannon, Cresta Blanca, Inglenook, Korbel, Krug, Louis M. Martin, Paul Masson, Mayacamas, Martin Rey, Sebastiani, Souverain, Weibel, and Wente in the eight counties surrounding San Francisco Bay—will be trying by the end of the decade to produce wines of a quality that can match those of the French.

Red Cheek apple juice is introduced by the 4-year-old Berks–Lehigh Mountain Fruit Growers Association, an eastern Pennsylvania fruit-processing cooperative formed originally to promote and market fresh fruit, not only in eastern U.S. markets but also in Continental Europe and the United Kingdom. Instead of being made from by-products of slicing and peeling operations, Red Cheek is pressed from whole apples and its producers claim that it has more natural sweetness and flavor than competing apple juices, such as Mott's (*see* 1938). The organization will relocate from rented buildings at Boyertown, Pa., to larger quarters at Fleetwood, Pa., in 1942 (*see* Cadbury Schweppes, 1987).

A single-service valve system for homogenizing milk is demonstrated at the U.S. Dairies Exposition (*see* 1932). Produced by the Creamery Package Manufacturing Co. (later Crepaco), it consists of stainless-steel wires folded and pressed into a cone shape; milk is forced through the cone against a surface, and the system will soon displace older homogenizers, whose many piston rings make them difficult to keep clean. Close to 33 percent of the fluid milk sold in the United States is now homogenized, and by 1946 about half of it will be homogenized (*see* 1949).

An Illinois district court judge enjoins the city of Chicago to stop its 2-year efforts to prevent Dean Food Co. from marketing milk in paperboard cartons rather than bottles (*see* 1939). The city's Board of Health has claimed that the cartons harbored bacteria and were unsafe, unsanitary, and did not meet health department standards. Within days of the October ruling, Dean Food is delivering milk cartons to groceries at the same price as bottled milk; Chicago's two biggest dairies, Bowman and Borden-Wieland, follow Dean Food's lead, but the Board of Health files an appeal (*see* 1941).

A square, narrow-mouthed milk bottle introduced by glassmakers weighs only 17.75 ounces, versus 22 ounces for the traditional round bottle (which weighed 26 ounces at the turn of the century). Many consumers remain nervous about buying milk in cartons, believing the charges by various city and state health officials, and bottlers have become more efficient and reliable about sterilizing their bottles. The average life of a bottle has climbed from fewer than 20 trips to more than 35, and use of lighter bottles will further reduce breakage.

The United States imports 70 percent of the world coffee crop, up from 50 percent in 1934.

McDonald's hamburger stands have their beginning in a drive-in opened near Pasadena, Calif., by movie theater co-owners Richard and Maurice McDonald of Glendora (*see* 1948).

The first Dairy Queen soft ice cream stand opens June 22 at Joliet, Ill., serving sundaes, ice cream cones in two sizes, and take-home pints and quarts (*see* Carvel, 1934). Founder J. F. McCullough, who owns the Homemade Ice Cream Co. in Green River, Ill., suggested to Kankakee, Ill., ice cream shop proprietor Sherb Noble 2 years ago that Noble stage an "All the Ice Cream You Can Eat for Only 10 Cents" sale to introduce soft ice cream fresh from the freezer, more than 1,600 people lined up for the event August 4, 1938, a second sale 2 weeks later met with similar success, and McCullough last year acquired western U.S. rights to a continuous-type freezer patented by inventor Harry Ortiz. McCullough and Ortiz will pioneer in franchising the operation (Sherb Noble is the first franchisee), there will be 100 stores by 1947, and by

Depression-era Americans flocked to the Dairy Queen, giving the franchised chain a good start.

1950 Dairy Queen will be a nationwide system with 1,156 stores (*see* Canada, 1951).

Toots Shor's restaurant opens at 51 West 51st Street, New York. Philadelphia-born saloonkeeper Bernard "Toots" Shor, 35, is a onetime B.V.D. underwear salesman who stands 6 feet 2, weighs 250 pounds, and was a speakeasy bouncer for mobster Owney Madden during Prohibition. He will make his place popular among hard-drinking sports fans, sell his lease in 1958 for $1.5 million, open a new place at 33 West 52nd Street, and relocate thereafter to other locations.

New York's Quo Vadis restaurant has its beginnings in the Brussels, opened at 26 East 63rd Street. The Brussels will relocate in 1946 to East 54th Street, and Quo Vadis will continue under the management of Frino Robusti and Bruno Caravaggi, who will make it one of the city's top seven restaurants. They will retire in 1982, reassume control soon after when their successors fail, and continue for several years in partnership with executive chef Michael Bordeau, pastry chef Dietrich Schorner, and maître d'hôtel Giorgio Marigi.

1941

World War II explodes into a global conflict as more than 3 million German troops invade Soviet Russia June 22 in Operation Barbarossa and Japanese forces attack the U.S. naval base at Pearl

Harbor December 7. Newspaper reporters will talk about GIs fighting for Mom and "good old American apple pie," even though apple pie did not originate in America.

Britain receives her first U.S. Lend-Lease shipments of U.S. food April 16, just in time to avert a drastic food shortage. By December, 1 million tons of U.S. foodstuffs have arrived.

German troops surround Leningrad in September as Russia begins her most severe winter in 30 years. The city has no heat, no electricity, and little food. The Luftwaffe destroys food stocks stored in wooden buildings, and besieged Leningraders eat cats, dogs, birds, jelly made of cosmetics, and soup made from boiled leather wallets. Those able to work receive a bread ration of half a pound per day, others get only two slices, and the bread is often made of cheap rye flour mixed with sawdust, cellulose residues, and cottonseed cake. Thousands die of starvation; before the siege is lifted in 1944, 20 to 40 percent of Leningrad's 3 million people will have died in 900 days of hunger and related disease (see Stalingrad, 1942).

Soviet citizens outside Leningrad receive an estimated 1,800 calories per day, but people in occupied Finland, Norway, Belgium, and the Netherlands receive fewer than 1,800, and those in the Baltic states, Poland, France, Italy, Greece, and other Balkan countries are lucky to get 1,500.

Dutch bakers stretch their supplies of rye flour with peas and barley, giving their bread a sour taste. The Dutch brew tea from rose hips and the leaves of various wild plants in lieu of coffee or real tea, which is rarely obtainable, and the only milk available is usually skim milk (taptemelk) or buttermilk. Meat and cheese are in short supply, as are butter and margarine, and chocolate and anise-flavored products are almost never seen. Rapeseed oil (raapolie) is usually the only available vegetable oil (see nutrition, below).

Germany is the best fed of Europe's combatant nations. A rationing plan provides Germans with at least 95 percent of the calories received in peacetime—2,000 calories per day.

Japan begins rice rationing as demands of the military place a strain on supplies for the home front (see 1943). Sugar is almost impossible to obtain, but saccharin is plentiful.

The Office of Price Administration and Civilian Supply (OPA), created by President Roosevelt April 11, has New Deal economist Leon Henderson, 45, as its head, but wartime inflation increases the general price level by 10 percent for the year.

Paris yogurt maker Isaac Carasso returns to Barcelona, winds up his European affairs, and emigrates to New York (see 1926). An order from dictator Francisco Franco, 48, shielding Sephardic Jews from persecution has protected Carasso from Nazi seizure (see Dannon, 1942).

Basic U.S. food prices by December are 61 percent above prewar prices.

The United States imports 53 million bunches of bananas, mostly from the Caribbean and Central America.

Central Soya patents a new process for extracting oil from soybeans (see 1936). It will be the basis for the development of soybean meal for livestock feed, and Central Soya will employ it in the processing plants it builds at Gibson City, Ill.; Marion, Ohio; and elsewhere (see 1958).

The Chemex Coffee Maker designed by Peter Schlumbohn is introduced by Chemex Corp. of New York.

Gourmet magazine begins publication in January at New York under the direction of former National Parent-Teachers magazine publisher Earle Rutherford MacAusland, 51, who will attract not only such eminent food writers James Beard (below), Clementine Paddleford, M. F. K. Fisher, and Waverley Root, but also non–food writers such as Ray Bradbury, Leslie Charteris, Richard Condon, Ogden Nash, and Kenneth Roberts. Gourmet's editorial chef and food columnist is French-born cook Louis B. De Gouy, whose father was esquire of cuisine to the imperial court of Austria and who has himself studied under the late Auguste Escoffier. By the end of 1945, the magazine will have grown from 48 pages to 112 and will be headquartered in luxurious penthouse offices atop the Plaza Hotel. Nonfiction: "In Defence of English Cooking" by George Orwell, whose piece will be reprinted in the 1944 book *Britain in Pictures*. He singles out kippers, red sauce, horseradish sauce, red-currant jelly with mutton or hare, Yorkshire pudding, apples that include orange pippins, Devonshire cream, English pudding, treacle tart, apple dumplings, tart plum cake, Oxford marmalade, marrow jam, English bread (especially the soft part of the crust from a cottage loaf), and crisper and better biscuits than anywhere else. "Then, there are the English cheeses. . . . I fancy that Stilton is the best cheese of its type in the world with Wensleydale not far behind."

Cookbooks: *Casserole Cookery* by Baltimore author Marian Tracy is published in its first edition. It will be the vademecum of war brides and of young housewives for years to come. *Cooking Outdoors* by James Beard, who makes it acceptable for suburban men to don aprons and wield cooking implements.

Mexico's wheat harvest falls by half as stem rust devastates crops in the nation's breadbasket— Querétaro, Guanajuato, Michoacán, and Jalisco. Mexico is obliged to spend $30 million (100 million pesos) each year to import corn and wheat, leaving less for desperately needed power generators, machinery, and chemicals from abroad.

The Rockefeller Foundation begins a program to improve Mexican agriculture at the urging of Secretary of Agriculture Henry A. Wallace. It sends University of Minnesota rust specialist Elvin C. Stakman, 56, Cornell soil expert Richard Bradford, 46, and Harvard plant geneticist Paul Mangelsdorf to Mexico, and together they come up with a blueprint for redeveloping the country's rural economy (*see* 1942).

Europeans in German-occupied countries are advised to eat vegetables raw or with as little cooking as possible in order to retain as many of their nutrients as possible, and to eat potatoes unpeeled in order to preserve their vitamin content (*see* scarcities, above). Few housewives follow these directions.

A National Nutritional Conference for Defense convened by President Roosevelt examines causes of the physical defects found in so many young men called up by the draft. Mayo Clinic nutrition and diabetes expert Russell M. Wilder, 58, heads a group of experts in a study of the eating habits of 2,000 representative U.S. families (*see* 1943).

All too many young Americans called up in the draft were found to have nutritional deficiencies.

Only 30 percent of U.S. white bread is enriched with vitamins and iron. South Carolina becomes the first state to require enrichment.

The average fat content of U.S. frankfurters is 19 percent, up from 18 in 1935 (*see* 1969).

Buitoni Foods is founded at New York by Italian pasta maker Giovanni Buitoni, who has sung at Carnegie Hall to publicize his products (*see* 1883). Isolated in the United States since the outbreak of war in Europe late in 1939, he will make his new U.S. company a major producer of pasta and related canned and frozen foods (*see* Nestlé, 1988).

Spice Island Co. has its beginnings in an herb farm started by San Francisco stockbroker Frederick Johnson, whose company will be a major producer of vinegar, spices, and other food products.

The House of McCormick adopts a big "Mc" trademark (*see* 1921). It will build a potato dehydration plant in Maine next year at the request of the U.S. Army and work on developing DDT.

Sell's Liver Paté has its beginnings in a pâté made from pork livers, pork fat, onions, defatted wheat germ, milk powder, and yeast developed by publisher-promoter Henry Sell, who last year sold his Vitamins *Plus* to Vick Chemical Co. (*see* 1936). A Waldorf-Astoria chef has helped Sell by adding seasonings to the product, which will be sent in Red Cross parcels to U.S. prisoners of war held in Axis prison camps (*see* 1945).

Daniel Gerber's Fremont Canning Co. sells 1 million cans of baby food per week (*see* 1929; 1948).

Cheerios breakfast food, introduced by General Mills, is 2.2 percent sugar.

M&M's Plain Chocolate Candies are introduced by M&M Ltd., a company founded by Forrest E. Mars, who returned to the United States last year and opened a Newark, N.J., confectionery plant in partnership with R. Bruce Murrie, son of Hershey's chief executive officer William F. R. "Bill" Murrie (Mars will buy out Bruce Murrie's 20 percent interest in 1949) (*see* 1937). Their hard shells enable M&M's to withstand heat, which will soon win them popularity among U.S. servicemen and will lead to the slogan "The Milk Chocolate That Melts in Your Mouth—Not in Your Hand" (*see* Mars, Inc., 1943).

A U.S. Circuit Court of Appeals at Chicago confirms the safety of milk cartons in a ruling handed down August 4 upholding last year's district court decision.

California's Almaden Vineyards introduce Grenach varietal wines pressed from lightly colored red grapes used in Europe to make rosé wines (Spanish vintners in Rioja and Catalonia use them for their red wines).

The Los Angeles restaurant Romanoff's opens. Restaurateur Mike Romanoff, who is unrelated to Russia's royal Romanov family, will attract celebrities for decades with his food and personality.

New York's Fifth Avenue Hotel runs advertisements April 10 offering a "Sunday strollers' brunch, $1 per person, served from 11 A.M. to 3 P.M."

The New York restaurant Le Pavillon opens October 15 at 5 East 55th Street under the direction of Henri Soulé, 38, a Basque from Biarritz who managed the Café de Paris before coming to New York in March 1939 with 30 kitchen workers and 33 maîtres d'hôtel, captains, waiters, and wine stewards to run the restaurant at the World's Fair's French Pavilion. Soulé will later say that he learned to cook from his mother: "Maman would cut the cod into small pieces and poach them for about 10 minutes. Then, after removing the skin, she would mix in slices of potatoes she had boiled in their skins and add vinegar, oil, garlic, and chopped parsley. She always served [it] neither hot nor cold, but just tepid. What a dish! What a dish! Sometimes when I went home for a holiday, I would eat it morning, noon, and night." At age 14, Soulé became a busboy at the Continental Hotel in Biarritz. At 23 he was the youngest captain of waiters in Paris. His new eating place has a staff of 40, some of whom worked with Soulé at the fair, and charges $1.75 for a table d'hôte luncheon of hors d'oeuvres, plat du jour, dessert, and coffee (*see* 1957).

1942

Millions of Europeans live in semistarvation as German troops cut off areas in the Ukraine and north Caucasus that have produced half of Soviet wheat and pork production. Food supplies fall to starvation levels in German-occupied Greece, Poland, and parts of Yugoslavia.

U-boat activity off the U.S. Atlantic Coast takes a heavy toll of merchant ships bound for British and Russian ports with war matériel, men, and foodstuffs.

Famine kills some 1.6 million Bengalese as fungus disease ruins the rice crop near Bombay.

Oxfam is founded by Oxford University classical scholar Gilbert Murray, 76, to fight world famine.

U.S. sugar rationing begins in May after consumers have created scarcities by hoarding 100-pound bags and commercial users have filled their warehouses. One-sixth of U.S. sugar supplies have come from the Philippines, which are in Japanese hands. U.S. householders are asked by ration boards to state how much sugar they have stockpiled, and ration stamps are deducted to compensate; the weekly ration averages 8 ounces per person but will rise to 12 ounces.

A General Maximum Price Regulation Act voted by Congress April 28 freezes 60 percent of U.S. food items at store-by-store March price levels. Food prices have shot up by 53 percent since Pearl Harbor: apples sell for 10¢ each, a head of lettuce for 28¢, a watermelon for $2.50, oranges for $1/doz.

Idaho potato processor John Richard "Jack" Simplot, 33, wins a government contract to supply dehydrated potatoes to the armed forces. Simplot dropped out of school at age 14, sorted potatoes, rented 40 acres of land near Declo, raised hogs to supplement the income he derived from growing potatoes, plowed back his profits, and soon became the nation's largest shipper of fresh potatoes. A millionaire by age 30, he built a dehydrator last year and by 1945 will have supplied about 33 million pounds of dehydrated potatoes to the military (*see* frozen french fries, 1953).

Norton Simon liquidates his 10-year-old Val Vita Foods Corp., takes a personal profit of $2 million, and organizes Hunt Foods, changing the name of the 52-year-old Hunt Brothers Fruit Packing Co. of Hayward, Calif., which he has acquired. Joseph and William Hunt have built a reputation for quality, and Simon begins marketing under the Hunt name the various canned foods which Hunt Brothers has produced to be sold under private labels. He will buy other private-label canneries and will take advantage of wartime food and tin shortages to give the Hunt label national recognition (*see* 1945).

La Choy Food Products sells its Detroit plant to the government and moves to a 25-acre site at Archbold, Ohio (*see* 1937). La Choy will be the largest single customer for Michigan celery, which it will use along with mushrooms from Pennsylvania, bamboo shoots and water chestnuts from postwar Taiwan, mung beans from Oklahoma, Texas, Thailand, and South America, and domestic flour and soybeans as it becomes the world's leading producer of canned Chinese food.

Nationwide gasoline rationing is ordered in September, chiefly to reduce rubber consumption. Rationing has begun in May on the East Coast, where U-boat sinkings have reduced tanker shipments, but farmers are generally able to obtain all the gasoline they need for their tractors, trucks, and other machines. Milk deliveries are reduced to

Food helped U.S. fighting men win World War II. Civilians on the home front did their part. LIBRARY OF CONGRESS

Britain begins rationing sweets July 26.

U.S. hoarding of coffee leads to coffee rationing, which begins in November with consumers limited to one pound every 5 weeks.

Executive Order 9066, issued by President Roosevelt February 19, authorizes detention of some 120,000 Japanese Americans on the West Coast (but not in the Hawaiian Islands) and their relocation to virtual concentration camps in bleak areas of California, Idaho, Utah, Oregon, Washington, Colorado, Arizona, Wyoming, and Arkansas. Nearly two-thirds of the internees are native-born U.S. citizens (*see* agriculture, below).

More than 3.6 million American men remain unemployed, but the number has fallen from 9.5 million men and women in 1939.

An Emergency Price Control Act voted by Congress January 30 gives the Office of Price Administration (OPA) power to control prices (*see* 1941; 1946).

alternate days by government order to conserve rubber, gasoline, trucks, and manpower; in some cities, horse-drawn milk wagons reappear.

French medical researcher André Loubatière pioneers oral drugs for diabetics with his finding that sulfa drugs, developed in Germany 7 years ago, are closely related chemically to para-aminobenzoic acid (PABA) and produce a lowering of blood sugar levels without restriction of dietary sugar intake (see 1937).

Le Petit Cordon Bleu cooking school and restaurant opens at New York late in the year under the direction of English cooking experts Dione Lucas, now 33, and Rosemary Hume (see 1934; cookbook, 1936). They have been endorsed by Henri Pellaprat, chef and co-director of the Paris school, and authorized to award pupils the French diplôme. Charging $21 for six lessons, $144 for 48 lessons (96 hours), they will have more than 4,000 pupils in the next 8 years and will award perhaps 25 diplomas per year.

Cookbook: *How to Cook a Wolf* by M. F. K. Fisher helps Americans cope with wartime food (and servant) shortages. Sample chapter titles: "How to Be Sage Without Hemlock," "How Not to Boil an Egg," "How to Keep Alive," "How to Be Cheerful Though Starving," and "How to Practice True Economy" (see nutrition, below).

British and U.S. families change their eating habits as domestic servants leave to take jobs in war plants, shipyards, hospitals, and the like; many housewives take such jobs themselves, and sales of convenience foods increase as women have less time to spend in the kitchen.

U.S. munitions plants issue candy to workers in the same way as salt tablets. Candy carts circulate constantly through many factories, and efficency experts say candy is a quick and handy bracer against fatigue, which is a frequent cause of accidents. One U.S. rolling mill feeds 500 pounds of gumdrops to its steelworkers in July.

The U.S. Army buys candy in quantities that will reach 25 million pounds by early next year, believing that candy will make men more effective in combat. (In emphasizing the food value of candy, the Army is not only the best customer for candy but also its most effective publicist.)

The U.S. Navy orders supplies of Almond Rocha, which can survive heat better than most candy because it is packed in sealed tins (see 1923). Honey is too expensive for most candy makers to use as a substitute for sugar, and although corn syrup is plentiful, only so much of it can be used in place of sugar without having a noticeable effect on texture and taste; since it is cheaper than sugar, confectioners were using about as much of it as they could even before the war. Dextrose (corn sugar) has more urgent uses in the war effort. The candy industry, which employed 60,000 workers before the war, keeps losing good people to war factories: labor skilled in eye-hand coordination, essential to making miniature chocolates, is exactly the sort of labor welcomed in factories where trained fingers are needed to make and assemble the myriad small parts of intricate armaments.

Many U.S. candy items are discontinued when supplies of almonds, cassia, cinnamon, cloves, coconut, figs, filberts, ginger, gum arabic, mace, nutmeg, and walnuts run short. Most spices came from the East Indies before the war; gum arabic from the Egyptian Sudan; figs from Persia, Turkey, Arabia, and the Mediterranean; almonds, walnuts, and filberts from Italy, Spain, and France. Now these products sit rotting in warehouses overseas. Philippine coconut is no longer to be had and would be requisitioned for glycerine if it were. Deprived of coconut oil, candy makers must rely on domestic fats, which do not keep as well and shorten the shelf life of their products (but with demand for candy bars far outpacing demand, shelf life is no longer a major concern). Mexico has had a short vanilla crop; cargoes of vanilla are tied up at Réunion Island off Africa because shipowners would rather wait out the war than risk having their ships fall victim to U-boat attacks. But many popular flavors—such as peppermint, wintergreen, lemon, and orange—are in plentiful supply: oil of peppermint is a major crop in parts of Indiana and Michigan, factory-made methyl salicylate is identical in every way with natural oil of wintergreen, and Florida and California have no shortage of orange and lemon flavorings (see 1943).

K rations, packed for U.S. troops by Chicago's Wrigley Co., contain "defense" biscuits and compressed Graham biscuits, canned meat or substitute, three tablets of sugar, four cigarettes, and a stick of chewing gum in each combat ration. The breakfast ration includes also a fruit bar and soluble coffee (*see* below), the dinner ration flavored and plain dextrose tablets and a packet of lemon juice powder, the supper ration bouillon powder and a bar of concentrated chocolate called "Ration D." Hershey Chocolate has developed the new four-ounce chocolate ration, made without cocoa butter to keep it from spoiling (*see* 1937); a soldier can carry it in his pocket without having it melt, it contains nourishing ingredients in addition to chocolate, and it can sustain a man for a day when he has nothing else to eat. GIs call the new 600-calorie Ration D the Iron Ration. Wrapper instructions say the bar should be eaten slowly over the course of about a half hour, noting that it can also be "dissolved by crumbling into a cup of boiling water, if desired as a beverage."

U.S. Army K rations included Graham biscuits, canned meat, sugar, soluble coffee, and chocolate.

Japanese-American farmers interned under Executive Order 9066 (above) have tilled only 3.9 percent of California's farmland but have controlled 42 percent of the state's commercial truck crops—22 percent of the U.S. total—including as much as 90 percent of California's artichokes, cauliflower, celery, peppers, spinach, strawberries, and tomatoes. Rumors have circulated about "Jap" flower and vegetable fields planted "arrowlike," pointing to nearby military installations. The Native Sons of the Golden West and like-minded "patriots" have coveted the truck gardens, fruit stands, grocery stores, restaurants, and other property of the now dispossessed Japanese Americans, many of whom work as volunteers in the sugar beet fields of Utah, Idaho,

Montana, and Wyoming and are credited with saving the crop.

Americans cultivate "Victory Gardens" in backyards and communal plots as vegetables become scarce, especially in California, where two-thirds of the vegetable crop has been grown by Japanese Americans now being relocated to internment camps. Forty percent of all U.S. vegetables are produced in nearly 20 million Victory Gardens, but the number will fall as interest flags.

Britons "Dig for Victory" and raise vegetables in backyard gardens.

Soviet geneticist Nikolai Vavilov dies of malnutrition in the prison where he has been confined since 1940. Vavilov's anti-intellectual rival T. D. Lysenko advises Josef Stalin to switch from traditional grain crops to millet, which requires less moisture.

Elvin C. Stakman of the Rockefeller Foundation persuades Washington State plant pathologist J. George Harrar, 36, to leave his new post as head of the state university's plant pathology department at the end of the school year and lead the program to redevelop Mexico's rural economy (*see* 1941; 1943).

Organic Gardening and Farming begins publication at Emmaus, Pa., where electrical equipment manufacturer and dramatist manqué J. I. (Jerome Irving) Rodale, 43, bought an old farm 2 years ago. One of eight children of a grocer on New York's Lower East Side, Rodale was a sickly boy who built up his strength with body building and self-improvement courses. He has read the work of English agronomist Sir Albert Howard (*see* 1940) and convinced himself that organic farming (a term he invented) has been held back by a conspiracy of money-grubbing chemical fertilizer and pesticide manufacturers who make large grants to the agricultural colleges. Department of Agriculture experts say that highly mechanized modern farming would be impossible if it were dependent on bulky organic fertilizers, which are prohibitively inefficient to ship and handle, and would require far more manual labor, but Rodale discounts such objections. He sent out 10,000 flyers to farmers 2 years ago in an effort to get subscribers for a magazine that he called *Organic Farming*, failed to sell even one subscription, has changed the magazine's name, and finds some modest success among elderly gardeners (*see* 1948; Walnut Acres, 1946).

Florida becomes the leading U.S. producer of oranges, passing California. By the 1960s, Florida will be producing at least 75 percent of all the oranges in world trade.

Forty-two percent of U.S. white bread is enriched with B vitamins and iron, up from 30 percent last year. Louisiana and South Carolina enact laws requiring that corn staples be enriched.

The British flour extraction rates rise to 85 percent to stretch wheat supplies. The higher extraction rate raises levels of vitamins and minerals in British bread (which remains unrationed; see 1917).

Dublin has an epidemic of rickets, caused by eating whole-grain bread (the phytic acid in wheat bran blocks absorption of calcium, and this, combined with the fact that so many Dubliners get little calcium to begin with, results in fully half the city's children suffering from the deficiency disease).

"Almost any good dietician will tell you that a normal 'rounded' food plan includes all the necessary vitamins without recourse to pills and elixirs," writes M. F. K. Fisher (above) in How to Cook a Wolf. "Canned vegetables are usually good, and often have more of the all-necessary vitamins and minerals in them than do the same vegetables cooked at home. This is mostly because they are cooked within the can, and therefore lose none of their attributes. Also, the wily packers, anxious to build up the weight of each tin, use as much water as they dare, which by the time it gets to you is beautifully rich and full of flavor. Frozen vegetables are very good. The directions on the package should be followed carefully, except that usually even less time is needed than they say, to cook the peas or beans or corn to perfection."

Metropolitan Life Insurance Company of New York issues tables of "ideal" weights, giving figures for men and women of different "frame size" classes at different heights. Actuaries have said for at least 20 years that an applicant is a much better risk if he weighs 20 pounds below average and a much worse risk if he weighs even 10 pounds above average. The Met Life tables have an age scale which goes up to 30, the assumption being that weight gain is inevitable in middle age, and the "ideal" weights will be found to be far too high (see 1959).

U.S. troops stationed in Britain are forbidden to drink local milk, which is not pasteurized. Many diseases that affect Britons are ascribed to unpasteurized milk (see 1900).

Stamford, Conn., bread bakers Dean and Betty Arnold obtain a $1,500 loan from a local bank and move their operation to Port Chester, N.Y., where they take over a bakery whose three big Dhurkopf ovens have not been fired up since 1939 (see 1940). They will incorporate their business in 1947 and will expand their line to include Raisin Tea Loaf, Buttermilk Rye, Buttermilk Biscuits, Soya Nut Loaf, Hearthstone White, a two-pound Sandwich Loaf, Butter Rolls (possibly the first cellophane-bagged bakeshop-quality roll item to be offered by grocers), and Toasting Muffins, the first muffin sized to fit conveniently into an electric toaster. The Arnolds will obtain a 26-acre site in Greenwich, Conn., in the mid-1960s and build the world's largest bread and roll bakery under one roof.

Sunbeam Bread is introduced by some members of the 20-year-old Quality Bakers of America, who adopt the "Miss Sunbeam" trademark.

Dannon yogurt is introduced in New York by Swiss-born Spanish émigré Joe Metzger, who goes into business with Isaac Carasso (see 1941; Colombo, 1929). Metzger employs his son Juan, 23, at the company's Bronx factory, which initially turns out 200 eight-ounce jars per day for sale at 11¢ each, mostly to the ethnic local yogurt market, but Dannon will relocate to Long Island City next year and increase production (see 1950).

Kellogg's Raisin Bran is introduced by the Kellogg Co. (see 1928). The new breakfast food is 10.6 percent sugar (see 1950).

H. B. Reese discontinues his other lines to concentrate on just one item, the peanut butter cup, which he sells in quantity to the military (see 1923). His nickel package of peanut butter cups will lead to a single larger cup, marketed in an orange, yellow, and brown wrapper, which will become the company's sole product.

U.S. soft drink companies are allowed enough sugar to meet quotas of 50 to 80 percent of production attained in the base year 1941 but with no limit on sugar for beverages sold to the armed forces.

Instant Maxwell House coffee has its beginnings in the soluble coffee for K rations (above) that has been developed for the armed forces by General Foods at its Hoboken, N.J., Maxwell House coffee factory. The coffee will be introduced to the public after the war as Instant Maxwell House (*see* Nescafé, 1938).

The U.S. Army announces that it will offer a $750,000 contract to anyone able to supply it in quantity with a cheap, soluble orange juice powder (*see* 1945; Minute Maid, 1947).

New York's Rainbow Room closes to the public in January as blackout regulations are enforced to protect ships on the Atlantic from German U-boat attacks (*see* 1934; 1950).

New York's Le Veau d'Or opens at 129 East 60th Street, near Lexington Avenue (and Bloomingdale's department store) (date approximate). Specialties include soupe à l'oignon gratinée, céléri rémoulade, rognon de veau, coquilles Saint-Jacques, chocolate mousse, floating island, pèche Melba, and fruit tarts. Luncheons start at 65¢, dinners at $1.25. Restaurateurs Georges Baratin and Henri Guiguit will run the place until their retirement in the 1970s.

Paris restaurateur Octave Vaudable dies, leaving Maxim's to his son Louis (*see* 1931). He managed to remove 30,000 bottles of wine to a hideout in Burgundy before the Germans entered Paris in 1940, and German officers and high-ranking Nazis such as Hermann Göring and Joseph Goebbels now dine at Maxim's, which also attracts secret service operatives from other combatant powers. The restaurant will close in 1944 and not reopen until 1946; in later years there will be Maxim's restaurants in Chicago, Mexico City, and Tokyo (*see* 1948).

1943

The tide of war turns against the Axis in North Africa, the Pacific, and Italy and on the Russian front.

Soviet troops relieve Leningrad's 17-month siege in February, but the Germans will blockade the narrow corridor to the city more than 1,200 times in the next year and starvation will continue.

Japan has her worst rice crop in 50 years. The daily 1,500-calorie subsistence level cannot always be met.

Rinderpest kills most of Burma's livestock. Since animals provide most of the country's power for irrigation and cultivation, the Burmese rice crop declines, and little is left for export to Bengal (*see* 1944).

U.S. meat rationing begins March 29, but the ration is 28 ounces per week, and meat production rises by 50 percent. Meat consumption actually rises to 128.9 pounds per capita on an annual basis as the wartime economic boom puts more money into working people's pockets and meat prices are rolled back to September 1942 levels. GI's are served 4.5 pounds of meat per week (Navy men get 7 pounds), and creamed chipped beef is a staple of service chow lines as Washington takes 60 percent of prime and choice beef and 80 percent of utility-grade beef.

Cheese is rationed at the rate of four pounds per week per capita but requires red stamps that may also be used for meat. Americans ate cheese at an average per capita rate of 2.5 pounds per week before the war, but home economists estimate that the country's most affluent one-third ate cheese at the rate of 5 pounds per week, while the poor ate scarcely 1 pound.

U.S. butter consumption falls to 11 pounds per capita, down from 17 pounds in the 1930s, as Americans forgo some of their four-ounces-per-week ration in order to save red stamps for meat. Butter is often unavailable, since most butterfat is employed to make cheese for Lend-Lease aid, but many consumers churn their own.

First Lady Eleanor Roosevelt campaigns for a repeal of the 10 percent federal tax on artificially colored margarine (the tax is only ¼¢ per pound if colored by the consumer or used uncolored). As more consumers turn to margarine, millions of householders use vegetable dye to color their white margarine yellow (*see* 1950).

Flour, fish, and canned goods join the list of rationed foods, but coffee is derationed in July. Americans eat far better than do citizens of the other belligerent nations (Britons enjoy only about two-thirds of what Americans are allowed under rationing programs).

Mars, Inc., suffers a setback in May when a U.S. Circuit Court of Appeals reverses the decision of a lower court and orders an injunction restraining Mars from reducing the weight of Milky Way and other bars without reducing prices. Some nickel bars weigh only seven-eighths of an ounce; a Milky Way still weighs 2½ ounces. Mars has reduced this by 11 percent without lowering the price, the OPA has made the Mars action a test case, it is sustained in December when the U.S. Supreme Court denies Mars a review of the lower-court decision, and OPA crows that "Gen. Max." is enforceable, an "effective weapon for controlling price increases . . . before they get out of hand." (With the military buying most name-brand candy bars, the Court's ruling is almost academic. Small-time competitors have continued to violate regulations almost with impunity.)

Home-front U.S. candy lovers, unable to find Milky Ways or Hershey bars, make do with caramels (until dairy product shortages cut production of those), panwork and fudge, lozenges, gumdrops, marshmallows, creams, peanut and popcorn candies, glacéed fruits, miscellaneous confectionery, hard candies imported from Latin America, and salted peanuts (there is no price ceiling on peanuts; a shortage of fats has created a need for peanut oil, so the government supports a "floor" on peanuts to encourage production, and although wholesale prices of pecans, filberts, and Brazil nuts doubled last year and pistachio prices tripled, a bumper crop of California almonds actually makes almonds cheaper than they were in 1941, albeit not as cheap as peanuts).

💲 Presient Roosevelt issues a "hold-the-line" anti-inflation order in April. The wholesale price index published monthly by the Labor Department's Bureau of Statistics since 1913 stands at 103.1; by August 1945 it will have risen only to 105.8, thanks to price controls.

Agriculture Secretary Claude Wickard bans the sale of sliced bread in a move to hold down prices.

Breakstone Bros. acquires the Youngsville, N.Y., plant of Fairmont Creamery Co. (*see* 1928). It will introduce the first consumer-size, half-pound containers of cottage cheese in 1946 and in 1948 will acquire a Syracuse, N.Y., plant from Standard Brands for cream cheese production as it opens a Miami branch to extend distribution in the South.

Distillers Corp.–Seagram acquires Frankfort Distillers and its well-known Four Roses and Paul Jones brands (*see* 1933).

Brewing Corp. of America reaches a capacity of 1 million barrels per year by acquiring Cleveland's Tip Top and Forest City breweries (*see* 1933).

The Ecole de la Société Suisse des Hôtelières at Lausanne reopens on its 50th anniversary October 15 with help from former students, who have contributed more than $25,000 (*see* 1893). Sponsored by the Swiss Hotel Keepers Association, it will move in 1975 to Châlet-à-Gobet, a parklike site at an altitude of 2,700 feet six miles outside Lausanne, and by 1983 will have graduated more than 20,000 students from 70 countries. Emphasis is on hotel administration, and while the school's 3½-year course includes 395 hours of practical instruction in basic food preparation, it does not begin to meet the educational requirements of a professional chef.

Nonfiction: *The Gastronomical Me* by M. F. K. Fisher.

Cookbook: *Double-Quick Cooking for Part-Time Homemakers* by Ida Bailey Allen is aimed at U.S. women with jobs in war plants, shipyards, hospitals, and the like.

Spam, introduced 6 years ago by George A. Hormel Co., becomes all too familiar to GIs on every war front but is eagerly adopted by residents of Hawaii, where being able to afford canned goods is a mark of status. British troops (and civilians) consider the luncheon meat a delicacy, and quantities of it are shipped to Murmansk for Soviet troops on the eastern front.

The U.S. armed forces receive one quarter of the nation's output of canned fruits and juices; food consumption on the home front declines by 4 percent, consumption of fresh vegetables drops 11 percent.

U.S. housewives wash and flatten tins for recycling: one less tin can per week per family will save enough tin and steel to build 5,000 tanks or 38 Liberty Ships. They save kitchen fats to be exchanged for red ration points at the butcher's: one jar of kitchen fat contains enough glycerine to make a pound of black powder—enough to fill 6 75-mm. shells or 50 32-caliber bullets.

An estimated 20 percent of U.S. beef goes into black-market channels, bacon virtually disappears from stores, western cattle rustlers kill and dress beef in mobile slaughterhouses and sell the meat to packinghouses, and wholesalers force butchers to buy hearts, kidneys, lungs, and tripe in order to get good cuts of meat.

Butchers upgrade meat, selling low grades at ceiling prices and at the ration point levels of top grade.

Agronomist and agricultural chemist George Washington Carver dies at Tuskegee, Ala., January 5 at age 78.

A United Nations Conference on Food and Agriculture at Hot Springs, Ark., from May 19 to June 3 provides for a U.N. Food and Agricultural Organization (FAO; *see* 1945).

DDT is introduced to fight insect pests that destroy U.S. crops (*see* Muller, 1939; Rachel Carson book, 1961).

Mexican wheat production is spurred by research undertaken with support from the Rockefeller Foundation (*see* 1941). Mexican agricultural output will increase by 300 percent in the next 25 years, while the country's population increases by 70 percent (*see* Borlaug, 1944).

Plowman's Folly by Kentucky soil and crop expert Edward H. Faulkner says that plowing interferes with the natural capillary action of soil. Faulkner recommends disk harrowing, which works green vegetation into the soil and, he says, will mean less erosion, require less fertilizer, and produce better crops.

Less than one-fourth of Americans have "good" diets, according to a nutrition study undertaken in 1941.

"Recommended Daily Allowances" (RDAs) for various nutrients are published for the first time by the Food and Nutrition Board, National Academy of Sciences–National Research Council, whose recommendations—based on the needs of fast-growing teenage boys, many of them suffering from malnutrition after years of economic depression and service in the armed forces—are weighted on the high side: 70 grams of protein and 3,300 calories per day for a 70-kilo man, and high levels of vitamins and minerals. The recommendations will be modified in 1944 and several times later in future years, but always at relatively high levels (*see* School Lunch Act, 1946).

Texas and Alabama adopt bread enrichment laws. Seventy-five percent of U.S. white bread is enriched with iron and some B vitamins, up from 30 percent in 1941.

"Converted" rice is developed by Texas produce broker Gordon Harwell with English food chemist Eric Huzenlaub by pressure-cooking rough, unhulled rice in a way that diffuses the outer bran layers into the kernels' starchy protein and then steaming the rice in a way that partially gelatinizes the starch to seal in vitamins. Vacuum dried and then air dried to restore its original moisture content, the rice is subsequently hulled and its bran removed, yielding a product that retains 80 percent of the natural B vitamins found in rough rice, or paddy.

Japan acts to prevent beriberi, which is disabling many civilians. The Tokyo government distributes no white rice and orders citizens to eat *haigamai* (brown rice) or *hichibuzuki mai* (70 percent polished rice), but many, if not most, Japanese laboriously hull their *hichibuzuki mai* to obtain the white, glutinous, nutritionally deficient rice they prefer.

Uncle Ben's Converted Rice will be marketed after the war by Gordon Harwell (above) and will later be enriched with added B vitamins.

The Science of Nutrition by Henry C. Sherman reflects changes in thinking since his 1911 work.

Former Yale chemistry professor and nutrition pioneer Russell Chittenden dies at New Haven December 26 at age 87 (*see* 1904).

The price of bulk wine is frozen by the federal government at 28¢/gal.; the Charles Krug winery at St. Helena, Calif., is offered for sale at $87,000, and Cesare Mondavi of Lodi buys the winery with a $25,000 down payment (*see* Mondavi, 1934). Mondavi and his sons Robert and Peter will operate the winery after the war, tearing down the old vines and replanting them with Cabernet Sauvignon, Chardonnet, Riesling, and Sauvignon Blanc grapes, buying bulk grapes, fermenting the juice, putting the wine into gallon- and half-gallon jugs labeled

C. K. Mondavi, and shipping it east while selling their better wines under the Krug label (*see* 1946).

U.S. distillers produce alcohol for synthetic rubber production (*see* 1933). Liquor is generally scarce.

1944

Soviet troops recapture Novgorod January 20, relieve Leningrad completely a week later, and press on to more victories as Allied troops landed in Italy and Normandy draw German forces from the eastern front.

Dutch civilians are in many cases reduced to eating sugar beets and sometimes flower bulbs in order to survive. A poster put up by the Underground shows a prisoner in a German uniform with a ball and chain attached to one foot as he sits at a wooden table eating with a spoon from a bowl labeled "Pulp." The legend says, "Don't shoot a single Jerry. Let them eat pulp for 20 years."

An armored German column drives off with nine tons of Roquefort wheels; the French Underground (the Maquis) recovers the unaged cheeses and distributes them to the local population, which lacks bread to eat with the cheese but enjoys it nonetheless.

French troops liberate Paris August 25 after more than 4 years of German occupation and are soon joined by U.S. forces (*see* restaurants, below).

Britain cuts her food imports to half their prewar levels. Domestic wheat production has increased by 90 percent over prewar levels, barley and oat production by 100 percent, potato by 80 percent, vegetable by 45, and sugar beet by 19 despite the manpower shortage. "Land girls" and others have worked to achieve the agricultural production gains, and the Ministry of Food has economized on shipping space by importing dried eggs and milk, dehydrated vegetables, and boneless and compressed meat, recommending which foods may be produced at home and what deficiencies can best be met by imports. Far more cheese, dried milk, canned fish, and legumes such as peas, beans, and lentils are imported than before the war, while imports of nuts and fruits other than oranges have been sharply reduced.

British per capita calorie consumption is actually slightly higher than it was in 1939, and intake of vitamins and minerals is substantially higher, thanks to higher wages and efforts by the Food Ministry to maintain stable prices.

Bread, flour, oatmeal, potatoes, fish, fresh vegetables, and fruit other than oranges remain unrationed in Britain. Prices are controlled so that the average householder has about half the food budget available for unrationed foods after buying rationed foods plus foods whose distribution is controlled or allocated on a "points" basis.

U.S. meat consumption rises to 140 pounds per capita, up from 128.9 last year, as national income rises to $181 billion, up from $72.5 billion in 1939. A large proportion of the meat is sold through black-market channels organized by criminal elements.

Continental Grain president Jules Fribourg dies at New York July 16 at age 67 after more than half a century in the grain business (*see* 1933). He and his family escaped from Paris just before the arrival of German troops in 1940 and have taken refuge in the United States. Fribourg's painfully shy son Michel, 30, a private in the U.S. Army Intelligence Corps at Camp Richie, Md., will take command of the company next August. It has grown to have 2,000 employees, and Michel Fribourg will increase that number to 50,000 as Continental Grain grows to become an international food-handling and -processing concern with annual sales in the neighborhood of $15 billion (*see* 1963).

General Foods acquires Yuban coffee. The brand was developed before 1920 by the late sugar and coffee merchant John Arbuckle as a *"yuletide banquet"* for his friends and customers.

Only 10 U.S. grocers have completely self-service meat markets. The figure will increase to 5,600 by 1951, 11,500 by 1956, and 24,100 by 1960, when 35 percent of all meat sold at retail will be from self-service cases.

Ohio State University tests prepackaged foods in cooperation with companies looking beyond the war to explore ways to reduce losses in food distribution. By 1961, 88 percent of U.S. supermarkets will be prepackaging all or some of their produce, and 90 percent will be prepackaging all fish, smoked meats, and table-ready meats in transparent film (*see* polyethylene, 1935).

Oscar Mayer technicians develop a machine that encircles each wiener with the yellow band bearing the Oscar Mayer name (*see* 1929; General Foods, 1981).

Cookbook: *Gastronomisk Haandbog, kulinariske Studier med en grundig Gennemgang af alle franske vines Historie, Fremstilling, Aargange og Behandling* by Ali-Bab (French gastronome Henri Babinsky, 89).

U.S. consumption of candy reaches 20 pounds per capita, lower than the British rate but a U.S. record which will stand until the 1990s. Military procurement, high employment, and the dearth of other ways to spend money are responsible, but candy is not readily available in drugstores, cigar stores, restaurants, newsstands, movie theaters, or in the nation's 400,000 food stores, 241,878 filling stations, and 48,015 candy stores. Neighborhood candy stores go out of business by the thousand, leaving city youngsters without the soda fountains and public telephones that have made the candy store their date bureau and recreation center.

StarKist Seafood founder Martin Bogdanovich dies suddenly at age 62 while leading a war bond rally and is succeeded by his son Joseph, who will make StarKist the world's largest tuna processor (*see* 1917). The younger Bogdanovich will establish a research and quality control laboratory and construct canning facilities worldwide, first at Terminal Island, Calif., and later at Mayaguez, Puerto Rico, and Pago Pago, American Samoa (*see* Heinz, 1963).

A "Green Revolution" moves forward outside Mexico City as former E. I. du Pont plant pathologist Norman Borlaug, 30, joins the Rockefeller Foundation effort to improve Mexican agricultural production (*see* 1943; 1949; Salmon, 1945).

The average yield per acre in U.S. cornfields reaches 33.2 bushels, up from 22.8 in 1933 (*see* 1968).

U.S. soybean acreage reaches 12 million as new uses for the beans are found in livestock feed, sausage filler, breakfast foods, enamel, solvent, printing ink, plastics, insecticides, steel hardening, and beer (*see* McMillen, 1934).

U.S. farm acreage will decline by 7.3 percent in the next 20 years, dropping by 1.3 million acres per year. Some 27 million acres of noncroplands will be converted to farm use (mostly in Florida, California, Washington, Montana, and Texas), but 53 million acres of croplands will go out of production and be used for home and factory sites, highways, and the like.

All U.S. yeast-raised commercial bakery products—including coffee cakes, sweet buns, plain rolls, doughnuts, and crullers—are fortified with the same B vitamins and iron found in enriched white bread beginning January 16 by order of the War Food Administration.

Kentucky and Mississippi enact bread enrichment laws. Enrichment of flour is not mandatory, but the American Institute of Baking says that at least 75 percent of the flour sold at retail is fortified. Enrichment has its detractors, many of whom criticize it on political grounds, but restoring most of the B vitamins and iron lost in milling refined white flour is having the desired effect of reducing the U.S. incidence of diseases related to malnutrition.

U.S. biochemists H. Mitchell and E. Snell isolate folic acid (folacin). The B vitamin is thought at first to be effective against pernicious anemia, and while that claim will be disproven the vitamin does cure macrocytic anemia by stimulating the regeneration of both red blood cells and hemoglobin (*see* vitamin B_{12}, 1948).

Britain's rich do not eat as well as they did before the war, but the poorer third of the population enjoys better nutrition than it has in decades. British bakers are required to make the "national loaf," made up about 85 percent of whole-wheat flour, partly as a means of providing the nutrients found in enriched U.S. white bread; U.S. authorities find it more reasonable to restore certain food factors to the refined bread and cereal products that people want.

Chiquita Banana is introduced by the United Fruit Company in a move to make bananas a name-brand item rather than a generic commodity (*see* Sunkist,

1919; Zemurray, 1932). The bananas are advertised on radio with a tune composed by Len MacKenzie and performed by Ray Bloch's orchestra with vocalist Patti Clayton singing Garth Montgomery's lyrics: "I'm Chiquita Banana/ And I've come to say,/ Bananas have to ripen in a certain way:/ When they are fleck'd with brown and have a golden hue/ Bananas taste the best and are the best for you. / You can put them in a salad/ You can put them in a pie-aye/ Any way you want to eat them/ It's impossible to beat them/ But bananas love the climate of the very, very tropical equator/ So you should never put bananas in the refrigerator" (copyright 1945 Maxwell-Wirges Publications, Inc.). (The skins of refrigerated bananas do turn brown, which disturbs consumers, but the fruit keeps longer if refrigerated.) The son of United Fruit's president, Samuel Zemurray, now 66, will die in the wartime crash of an Army Air Force plane, and Zemurray will step down for a year in 1948 to handle business affairs in Louisiana, but he will serve as United Fruit's president again from 1949 to 1951 (*see* United Brands, 1968).

Seabrook Farms establishes its own brand after 13 years of packaging frozen foods for General Foods to sell under the Birds Eye label and for other companies to sell under their own labels. Seabrook sales will grow in the next 12 years to more than $27 million (*see* Snow Crop, 1957).

Campbell-Taggart Co. moves its headquarters from Kansas City to Dallas (*see* 1927). It will grow in 45 years to have 80 plants in North and South America and Europe (*see* Patterson, 1945).

Stokely–Van Camp moves into Hawaiian pineapple canning (*see* 1933; 1956).

Hershey Chocolate increases the size of its nickel Hershey Bar from 1¼ oz. to 1⅜ oz. (*see* 1941; 1946). GIs in Europe hand out Hershey Bars to children and use them as a medium of exchange.

Veryfine Apple Juice production tops that of vinegar and becomes the best-selling item made by New England Vinegar Works, which moved in 1930 to Littleton, Mass. (*see* 1919). Prune juice will be added to the product line in 1946, joining cider vinegar, white vinegar, canned and bottled apple juice, and apple jelly. The company name will be changed in 1958 to New England Apple Products (*see* 1975).

The 64-year-old New Orleans restaurant Commander's Palace is acquired by Frank and Elinor Moran, who refurbish the place and expand its menu. Its reputation for good food has been eclipsed somewhat by the notoriety of its upstairs rooms, and it has closed briefly after a fire early in the year forced some prominent men (allegedly including the mayor) to jump out of second-floor windows attired only in their underwear, but the Morans will restore its respectibility (*see* Brennan's, 1974).

The Paris restaurant Chez Michel opens at 10, rue de Belzunce near the Church of St. Vincent de Paul with 40 seats. Restaurateur Jean Chauvet employs as chef Michel Tounissoun, who will gain a following for such specialties as moules farcies en cocottes and coquilles Saint-Jacques (served from September to May).

The Paris restaurant Le Boule d'Or opens in the Place d'Aligre. It will move in 1967 to 13, boulevarde de La Tour-Maubourg after its original location is taken over to make room for a low-cost housing project. Its specialties will include *petits saucisses au vin blanc, chipolatas* from Brittany, *quenelles ambassades,* quiche Lorraine (some will say it's the best in Paris), crab soup, *potage germiny* (made from *avétrilles de Bretagne*), apple tarts, and lemon soufflé.

1945

World War II ends in Europe May 8 and in the Pacific August 14, but only after major new military and naval activity and the deaths of three of the world's five leading heads of state—Franklin D. Roosevelt, Benito Mussolini, and Adolf Hitler.

Japan mobilizes schoolchildren to gather more than a million metric tons of acorns for use in flour making to supplement scarce wheat and rice stocks.

CARE (Cooperative for American Remittances to Europe) is founded as a private relief organization to help deal with the misery widespread on the Continent. It ships ready-assembled U.S. food packages of good quality to European families and friends of people in America for $10 per package, including transportation, with delivery guaranteed at a time when packages sent through normal channels are highly susceptible to loss, theft, or damage.

Italians only reluctantly accept pea soup powder sent to relieve hunger because it is so unfamiliar, but powdered eggs gain universal acceptance.

The Food and Agriculture Organization (FAO) of the United Nations establishes headquarters at Rome, with Scottish biologist John Boyd Orr, 65, as director. He issues gloomy prognostications on the world food situation.

The Food and Agriculture Organization of the United Nations aimed to alleviate world hunger.

U.S. food rationing on all items except sugar ends November 23, but food remains scarce in most of the world. Black markets exist throughout Europe.

Britain introduces family allowances.

A U.S. tariff act empowers the president to encourage reciprocal trade by reducing tariffs to 25 percent of original schedule rates (*see* 1934; GATT, 1947).

Former Campbell-Taggart Co. baking executive C. J. Patterson reestablishes his own Kansas City company to serve the milling and baking industry (*see* 1925).

National Dairy Corp. changes its name to Kraft Foods Co. (*see* 1929).

Special Foods Co. changes its name to Worthington Foods, Inc. (*see* 1939). Wartime shortages have created a demand for meat analogs, the company has introduced new products such as Choplets, and sales are now at the rate of nearly $300,000 per year (*see* 1948).

Hunt Foods has sales of $19 million with after-tax profits of $530,000 (*see* 1942). Norton Simon buys United Can & Glass Co. to give Hunt its own container production facility and buys Ohio Match Co. to give it millions of match covers on which to print the slogan "Hunt for the Best," plugging Hunt Tomato Sauce and other Hunt products (*see* 1946).

U.S. gasoline and fuel oil rationing ends August 19.

U.S. food processors pioneer frozen orange juice, using knowledge gained in wartime production of powdered orange juice. They develop an easily frozen sludge of concentrated juice that can be reconstituted to taste far more like fresh-squeezed juice than ordinary canned juice does (*see* 1946).

Tupperware Corp. is founded by former E. I. du Pont chemist Earl W. Tupper, who has designed plastic bowls and canisters with a patented seal which permits them to be stored on their sides or upside down without leaking, a feature that will be demonstrated at Tupperware Home Parties.

L'Ecole de Cordon Bleu reopens at 129, rue du Faubourg Saint-Honoré in Paris under the direction of Belgian entrepreneur Mme. Élisabeth Brassard from Bruges (*see* 1934). Brassard, whose brother-in-law owns the building, will revive the prestige of the school, which declined under the management of Les Orphelins d'Auteil (a religious community) after the death of Mlle. Distel, gives early-morning courses for GIs as she enrolls young women of good families, most of them French, and *femmes du monde* who can no longer afford good cooks. She will run the school for more than 30 years, attracting students who will include Belgian-born film actress Audrey Hepburn and U.S. cook Julia Child (*see* 1964; cookbook, 1961).

Cookbook: *Fowl and Game Cookery* by James Beard, who served as a cryptographer with the U.S. Army from 1942 to 1943.

Returning GIs tell their wives, mothers, sisters, and girlfriends that they never want to see another can of Spam (*see* 1943), but the luncheon meat will continue to enjoy some popularity.

Some 85 percent of U.S. bread is commercially baked, up from 66 percent in 1939.

Wakefield Seafoods has its beginnings in Wakefield Deep Sea Trawlers, the first company to develop modern techniques for processing and freezing Alaska king crab. Entrepreneur Lowell Wakefield was piloting a herring seiner off Alaska's Kodiak Island in 1939 when he came upon a mountain of live king crabs left by an exceptionally low tide after a severe storm. When the U.S. Fish and Wildlife Service made a survey of Alaskan waters in 1940, Wakefield followed the government boat, and when the $100,000 appropriated for the survey ran out in 1941 he borrowed the boat's gear. He and his wife, Jessie, have evolved a method for cooking crabmeat and then freezing it; he has mortgaged his house and sold stock to buy a 143-foot trawler, and by the time she makes her second voyage she will be hauling in 800 crabs per hour, processing and freezing the big crabs as they are caught (*see* 1968).

Columbia River Packers Association executive Thomas E. Sandoz travels to Japan and contracts with Japanese fishermen to supply CRPA's Astoria albacore cannery with foreign tuna (*see* 1938; 1950).

U.S. Department of Agriculture agronomist Samuel C. Salmon, 60, discovers the semidwarf wheat variety Norin 10, whose two-foot stems respond quickly to water and fertilizer and do not fall over (lodge) from the weight of their grain heads. Salmon is a cereal improvement expert helping Japanese reconstruction as a member of Gen. Douglas MacArthur's occupation force. He finds Norin 10 on a visit to the Morioka experimental station in northern Honshu, returns home with some seeds which he grows in quarantine, Norin 10 proves to be extremely susceptible to leaf stripe and powdery mildew, but Salmon's colleague Orville Vogel crosses the Japanese wheat with resistant strains of U.S. wheat. Grains developed from Norin 10 will increase wheat harvests in India and Pakistan by more than 60 percent.

The U.S. soybean crop reaches 193 million bushels, up from 78 million in 1940.

The chemical 2,4-D (2,4-dichlorophenoxyacetic acid), developed as a war weapon and patented by E. I. du Pont as a plant growth regulator in 1943, is patented as a general weed killer by American Chemical Paint Co. The first selective plant killer, 2,4-D will be found to destroy broad-leafed plants such as bull thistle, cocklebur, ragweed, and wild mustard while leaving food crops such as corn and wheat unharmed, thus increasing crop yields by destroying moisture- and nutrient-consuming weeds without laborious cultivation.

The University strawberry developed by the University of California agriculture station will make strawberries a long-season, widely grown commodity.

A fluoridation program at Grand Rapids, Mich., is the first attempt to fluoridate community water supplies to reduce the incidence of dental caries in children. Newburgh, N.Y., follows suit, but the moves arouse widespread political opposition to government interference in people's lives; right-wing groups in some parts of the country mount ideological fear campaigns against fluoridation (*see* Dean, 1933; Cox, 1939; Britain, 1955).

Alabama, Georgia, Hawaii, Indiana, Maine, New Hampshire, New York, North Carolina, North Dakota, South Dakota, Washington, West Virginia, and Wyoming enact bread enrichment laws.

Nutrition researchers find that the amino acid tryptophan, abundant in milk, is a provitamin which triggers production of niacin (vitamin B$_3$) by the human liver. The discovery explains resistance to pellagra among infants who receive enough milk (*see* 1900; 1906; Elvehjem, 1936).

Self-styled nutritionist Carlton Fredericks, 37, is convicted of practicing medicine without a license and fined $500. The New York radio broadcaster, who has a doctorate in communications, will serve as a paid consultant to diet-supplement makers as he continues making dubious health claims for such products in books and on the air while criticizing fluoridation and the enrichment of flour and bread.

Sell's Liver Paté is introduced commercially (*see* 1941). The product will be joined in the next few years by Sell's Specialties such as canned braised beef, beefsteak-and-kidney pie, and corned beef hash.

C. A. Swanson & Sons at Omaha begins to develop a line of canned and frozen chicken and turkey products under the Swanson label, using experience gained in World War II, when nearly all of the firm's poultry was shipped to the armed forces. Called the Jerpe Commission Co. until now, the 45-year-old company has been owned since 1928 by Carl A. Swanson (*see* "TV Dinners," 1953).

Welch's Junior Mints—miniature chocolate-covered mint patties in a cardboard box—are introduced by the James O. Welch Co. of Cambridge, Mass. (*see* 1934). The Broadway play *Junior Miss* opened at New York's Lyceum Theater in November 1941, James Welch attended one of the 710 performances, and he has kept the title in mind (*see* Pom Poms, 1948).

Chocolate pioneer Milton S. Hershey dies at Hershey, Pa., October 13 at age 88.

The U.S. Army awards a contract for orange juice powder to the National Research Corp., which has adapted an evaporation technique, developed originally for penicillin by a Cambridge, Mass., firm, to concentrate citrus juice, hold it in cold storage, and dry it (*see* 1942). NRC president John M. Fox, 32, obtains plant financing from investors August 6, just before an atomic bomb is dropped on Hiroshima. While trying to eliminate problems involved in drying his product, he sets out to find consumer markets for frozen orange juice concentrate (*see* Minute Maid, 1947).

California wine-grape prices rise to $50, up from $15 before the war. Growers in the Napa Valley and elsewhere in the state plant more acreage to take advantage of the higher prices, paying field hands 40¢ per hour when they can find them; before the war they could pay as little as $1.75 for a 9-hour day.

Welch Grape Juice Co. is acquired by wine maker J. M. Kaplan, who has built his upstate New York winery into National Grape Corp. (*see* 1933; Welch's, 1927). Kaplan has encouraged the six small farmers' cooperatives that supply him with grapes to form a new, stronger cooperative and has arranged with the new National Grape Cooperative Association to set aside part of the sale price of each case of goods and accumulate funds for eventual purchase of National Grape by the cooperative. Welch's grape juice is a household name, but the company's $9-million-per-year business is declining and the farmers have persuaded Kaplan to buy it. He scraps the hundreds of thousands of five-gallon glass carboys used to store juice at the Welch plants, replaces them with refrigerated stainless steel tanks, and installs modern equipment (*see* 1956).

Coca-Cola Company registers the name "Coke" as a trademark (*see* 1942; 1955).

Constant Comment Tea is introduced by New York entrepreneur Ruth Bigelow (*née* Campbell), 50, an interior decorator who has gone into partnership with Bertha Nealey (*née* West), another decorator, to produce a tea blended of several different black Ceylon teas. Bigelow and her husband, David, a retiree, began blending the teas in their kitchen, packed it in canisters with hand-painted labels, and went out each afternoon in the family car to make deliveries to small Madison Avenue gourmet and gift shops and some department stores. She established a laboratory to continue her experiments, blends each one-pound batch separately in a glass jar, advises customers that one-half teaspoon of the tea is enough for three cups, and recommends serving it with orange or lemon peel and a little honey but no milk or sugar. Constant Comment will become the top-selling specialty tea in America, and the Bigelow family business will grow to have a factory at Norwalk, Conn., and another in Idaho, producing a line of more than 30 different teas, including decaffeinated teas, caffeine-free herbal teas, and one that includes natural orange flavoring and spices. Bigelow teas and gourmet products will gain nationwide distribution and find customers in many foreign countries.

The Alsatian Auberge L'Ill reopens on the Ill River at Illhaeusern between Sélestat and Colmar. Chef Paul Haeberlin, 21, and his brother Jean-Pierre, 19, take over the auberge founded by their grandfather in 1870 but bombed during the war along with the rest of the village. Paul has worked with Édouard Weber, who was once employed by Czar Nicholas II at St. Petersburg and, later, by the king of Greece

1945

and other royal families; his mother, 49, helps with the coffee machine, and the auberge's good fish (*filet de sole aux nouilles braisé au Riesling aux Armes de France*), butter, cream, *brioche de foie gras frais, cuisses de grenouille,* game, *poule suprême de pintadeau strasbourgeois* (breast of guinea fowl), *noisette de chevreuil Saint-Hubert, timbale de homard Prince Vladimir,* poached peach in pistachio ice cream, *sabayon au champagne,* and other specialities will gain it first one, then two, and (in the late 1960s) three Michelin stars.

The Paris restaurant Lasserre opens in a century-old private house at 17, avenue Victor-Emmanuel III (later avenue Franklin D. Roosevelt) near the Grand-Palais. Started by war orphan René Lasserre, 33, whose family's small restaurant at Bayonne failed during the war, it has a staff of 85, 30 tables, Saint Louis crystal, Limoges porcelain plates rimmed with gold, a cellar that will grow to have 150,000 bottles, and a sliding roof. Lasserre will gain a worldwide reputation for its canard de Challans à l'orange; pigeon André Malraux (boned pigeon stuffed with chicken livers); poussin Viroflay (chicken, completely boned and stuffed with fresh spinach leaves that have been lightly sprinkled with Provençal herbs, mixed with a few chopped chicken livers, roasted in the oven, deglazed with sherry, and served with a sauce containing bits of black truffle); mesclagne landes Mère Irma (hot foie gras in puff pastry); its wine list; and desserts that include pêche et poire frangipani, sucre filé brulé, and timbale Elysées (a ball of ice cream in a free-form crust of thin pie crust topped by strawberries or a peach covered with red currant sauce, surmounted by threads of spun sugar).

London's Brompton Grill opens in May at 243 Brompton Road under the direction of Cypriot Greek Nikolaus Karonias, a former waiter at the Café Anglais in Leicester Square, who has been joined by his father-in-law and brother in taking over a former patisserie opposite the Brompton Oratory, a fashionable church beyond Harrod's. House specialties will, after the end of food rationing, include *suprême de volaille de Kiev, suprême de volaille sous cloche, suprême de volaille Maryland, caneton à l'orange, tournedos Rossini, entrecôte bordelaise, escalope de veau Cordon Bleu, escalope de veau Holstein, jambon braisé florentine, ris de veau jardinière, ris de veau maréchale, veau marsala, rognon de veau Turbito, mignonette de bœuf Diane flambé,* liver and bacon kebab Spelos, Dover sole, lobster, and scampi.

New York's 65-year-old P. J. Clarke's saloon on Third Avenue at 55th Street gets a boost from *The Lost Weekend,* a Hollywood film starring Ray Milland as an alcoholic. Except for its hamburger grill, the place is a drinking establishment, not a restaurant (although it does serve beef-and-barley soup and eggs Benedict), but Clarke will retire in a few years and his landlord, the Lavezzo family, will take over, expanding in the late 1950s with a dining room that, beginning in the 1970s, will serve food prepared by French chef Raymond Richez, late of the Café Chauveron, and will gain a reputation for its chicken liver omelette, steak tartar, boiled brisket of beef, walnut-topped apple pie, lemon mousse, deep-dish blueberry and peach pies, Irish coffee (*see* 1953), and hot chocolate.

New York's Russian Tea Room, which has been serving blinis, shashlik, and such since the 1930s, is acquired by former high school chemistry teacher Sidney Kaye and other investors (*see* 1927). Kaye will buy out his partners in 1955 to become sole owner and will leave the restaurant's Christmas decorations up all year round to save labor and because "it looks so Russian." After Kaye's death in 1967, his second wife, Faith, a Broadway and TV actress, will take over, add glitz, and attract celebrities; the RTR will appear in such Hollywood films as *The Turning Point* (1977), *Manhattan* (1979), and *Tootsie* (1982).

1946

Britain announces February 7 that food rations will be cut in response to world shortages, but London's Covent Garden fruit merchants offer bananas March 8 for the first time since the war. A world wheat shortage forces rationing of bread, which was never rationed during the war. The government reduces the unit weight of a one-pound loaf of bread to 14 ounces, the two-pound loaf is reduced to 28 ounces, the four-pound loaf to 3½ pounds, and the measure effectively ends traditional measures of bread weight (*see* 1916). Restrictions on most other staple foods ensue, and by August there are reports of a black market in chocolate.

Britain announces March 28 that it will launch a program of free school milk and dinners.

Congress passes a National School Lunch Act as food prices soar (*see* Britain, 1906). Participating schools are entitled to funds and surplus foods which assist them in offering meals designed to meet one-third the Recommended Daily Allowance (RDA) of calories, vitamins, and minerals (*see* 1943; nutrition, below).

\$ President Harry S. Truman, 61, reestablishes the Office of Economic Stabilization February 21 to control inflation. The Office of Price Administration (OPA) expires June 29, when the president vetoes a Compromise Price Control act; Congress revives the OPA July 25 with a new Price Control act.

High meat prices bring demands that President Truman resign, but prices soften when the government withdraws from the market in the summer and prices break when the OPA (above) removes price ceilings in the fall.

U.S. meat price controls end October 15, and President Truman issues an executive order November 9 lifting all wage and price controls except those on rents, sugar, and rice.

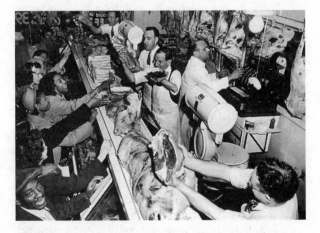

Decontrol of meat prices meant land-office business for America's butchers. LIBRARY OF CONGRESS

Hunt Foods has made "price at time of shipment" contracts with its customers and holds most of them to those contracts when prices break in the fall.

Hunt has 9-month sales of \$48 with after-tax profits of \$5 million (*see* 1945; Snider Catsup, 1952).

Sunshine Biscuits is created by a renaming of Loose-Wiles Biscuit Co. (*see* Hydrox, 1910). Now a major marketer of pretzels, potato chips, popcorn, peanuts, and other snack foods in addition to its saltines, Hi-Ho crackers, Cheez-It crackers, and other brands, Sunshine is second only to National Biscuit (Nabisco) as a biscuit, cookie, and cracker baker.

The U.S. inflation that will continue for more than 4 decades begins December 14 as President Truman removes curbs on housing priorities and prices by executive order. President Roosevelt's inflation control order of April 1943 kept prices from climbing more than 29 percent from 1939 to 1945 as compared with a 63 percent jump in the 1914–1918 period, but Truman is more worried about a possible postwar depression than about inflation.

🤝 Unilever completes its acquisition of Thomas J. Lipton Co.'s U.S. operations in September (*see* 1931). It has been increasing its ownership of the business since 1939, and although Lipton acquired a Chicago dehydrated-soup manufacturer in 1941 the business has been declining rapidly and will revive only when new products are introduced.

The Houston specialty food shop Jim Jamail & Sons has its beginnings in a small grocery store opened by Jamail and his sons Joe, Albert, and Harry, who have returned from military service. It will grow into a River Oaks establishment with its own Los Angeles produce broker and a staff of 150 providing customers (many of whom will arrive in Rolls-Royces) with 24 kinds of mustard, 22 brands of imported beer, 200 kinds of cheese, more than 200 kinds of preserves (including hot pineapple jam and jalapeño jelly), sourdough bread from San Francisco, English muffins from Chicago, superpremium ice cream from New York, and prepared dishes such as chicken-and-corn soup; Finnish carrot soup; cream of red snapper soup from Philadelphia; shrimp gumbo; paella Valencia; baked pompano; lemon sole; smoked rainbow trout; saltimbocca Florentine; Danish ham with eggs, potatoes, bacon, and Havarti cheese; chicken tetrazzini; calf's liver in Madeira sauce; veal, ham, and spinach pie; kibbee with pine nuts; 24 kinds of salad; and creamed Grand Marnier with strawberries. The store will stop opening charge accounts when the total reaches 3,500; some of its customers will fly to Houston every month or two from adjoining states and Mexico to buy provisions at Jim Jamail & Sons.

The Munich specialty food shop Käfer opens in the residential Bogenhaus district. Dallmayr, founded in 1671, has been bombed out, and Käfer is able to meet the needs of the city's best restaurants (*see* 1958).

 An electric rice saucepan introduced by Japanese entrepreneur Konoskuke Matsushita, 55, is the first low-priced Japanese electrical cooking appliance; it revolutionizes Japanese cooking.

An automatic espresso coffeemaker patented by Italian inventor Achille Gaggia will be introduced into England in the early 1950s, enabling Britons to enjoy good coffee in public places for the first time since the old coffeehouses that flourished in the 17th and 18th centuries, but machines in British espresso bars will seize up with their own sludge, few people will know how to maintain or repair them, and Britons will be left to suffer weak, unpalatable coffee.

Self-rising cornmeal is marketed for the first time.

The Culinary Institute of America has its beginnings in the New Haven Restaurant Institute, a storefront school founded at New Haven, Conn., by local lawyer Frances Roth and Katharine Angell, wife of a former Yale University president. They start with 50 students, who are quickly placed in jobs, and will move next year to a small estate outside New Haven, renaming their school The Culinary Institute of Connecticut, which will be changed in 1952 to The Culinary Institute of America as the school grows to attract students from all over the country (*see* 1972).

Nonfiction: *Here Let Us Feast* by M. F. K. Fisher.

Cookbook: *The Gentleman's Companion, An Exotic Cookery Book, and an Exotic Drinking Book* (two volumes) by Florida author Charles H. Baker, Jr., 51, who has worked as a purser on ocean liners and written a novel. His book, whose first volume appeared in 1930, will become a culinary guide to amateurs seeking excitement in the kitchen (*see* 1951).

Frozen french fries go on sale February 16 at the New York department store R. H. Macy. U.S. potato consumption has declined steadily since 1910, Maxson Food Systems of Long Island City has introduced the frozen fries, but the company will fail and potato consumption will not reverse its decline until 1962.

U.S. bread consumption drops as wheat and flour are exported to starving Europe. Domestic shortages lead to a compulsory long-extraction program, and demand for flour whiteners jumps as Americans are put off by bread that is not as white as usual.

The worst red tide in U.S. history begins in November on Florida's west coast, killing fish and shellfish by the millions and spurring efforts by the Fish and Wildlife Service to seek ways to the control *G. breve* (*see* 1916; 1932).

Mrs. Paul's Kitchens markets frozen deviled crabs in six-ounce packages at 59¢ retail and finds ready acceptance. Philadelphia entrepreneur Edward J. Piszek, 29, has spent 5 years learning the food business with Campbell Soup Co. and earning a degree in business adminstration at the University of Pennsylvania night school, a strike at General Electric has jeopardized his job there, he has gone into partnership with short-order cook John Paul, and each has invested $450 to start the new company, which will have distribution west to the Pacific by 1960 with a Mrs. Paul's line that will include frozen onion rings in addition to frozen fried scallops, precooked fish cakes, and fish sticks.

A Japanese land reform act drafted by U.S. occupation authorities dispossesses absentee landlords and sharply limits the amount of cultivable land an individual may own. Tenant farmers decline from nearly one-half the total to one-tenth.

Blizzards destroy wheat crops throughout Europe. Freak storms sweep over much of Britain at harvest time, wrecking crops in Suffolk after a wet summer has ruined hay crops in the North, in the mountains of Wales, and on the southern moors.

Walnut Acres Organic Farms has its beginnings in a 200-acre farm at Penn's Creek in central Pennsylvania. Paul and Betty Keene acquire the place, which has been in the same family for the past century, and takes advantage of the fact that the previous owners maintained a large dairy herd, whose droppings supplied natural fertilizer for the soil. The Keenes determine to operate the farm organically (*see* Rodale, 1942); their daughter Ruth will marry Robert Anderson, and the Andersons, helped by their daughter Malina and son Nate, will develop a mail-order line of organically produced or imported dry soup mixes, canned soups, cereals, pastas, canned pasta sauces, baked goods, rice, canned beef, canned beef hash, canned chilies, canned vegetables, pancake and muffin mixes, maple syrup, honey, vinegars, olive oil, ketchup, mayonnaise, peanut butter, fruit preserves, vegetable oils, olives, coffee, cocoa mixes, green tea, powdered dairy products, bottled fruit and vegetable juices, canned fruits, dried fruits, and nuts.

Court rulings invalidate vitamin D irradiation patents granted to Harry Steenbock in 1927. Steenbock's finding was a "discovery" rather than a patentable invention, say the courts. Even a farmer who lets his alfalfa be exposed to the ultraviolet rays of the sun would technically be infringing on the patents which have produced $9 million in royalties for the Wisconsin Alumni Foundation and funded research programs and professors' salaries.

The U.S. Department of Agriculture "formula menu" offered under the federal school lunch program (above) calls for 2 ounces of meat or meat substitute, ¼ cup of fruit or vegetables, and 8 ounces of milk (Congress has earlier established a free milk program) (*see* 1993).

Not by Bread Alone by Canadian-born Arctic explorer Vihjalmur Stefansson, 67, claims that a high-fat diet is far superior in every respect to a so-called "balanced" diet. Stefansson and his erstwhile companion of Arctic days, Karsten Anderson, participated in the late 1920s in a year-long supervised experiment at New York's Bellevue Hospital in which each man averaged between 2,620 and 2,650 calories per day of which at least 2,100 was derived from animal fat and the balance from animal protein (no eggs or dairy products were included), they thrived, and their "Eskimo diet" will be the basis of many best-sellers (*see* Keys, Pennington, 1953).

English biochemist and vitamin pioneer Edward Mellanby finds that the flour bleach Agene, used since 1919, combines with the amino acid methionine in wheat flour to form methionine sulfoximine, a compound which sends dogs into fits. Between 80 and 90 percent of British and U.S. millers and bakers use Agene, but it will turn out that it can also produce psychosis in humans and it will be banned beginning in 1949. Most millers and bakers will have turned by that time to chlorine dioxide gas, a safe, effective, and economical alternative, normally used in concentrations of 14 parts per million, that works by releasing oxygen which causes changes in the protein fraction of the flour and also bleaches yellow pigments.

Bakers have for some years been using calcium propionate in their bread to inhibit the growth of molds and bacteria which cause softening and discoloration. The molds and bacteria may not be destroyed in the oven if the interior of a loaf of bread does not reach 100° C., or 212° F., in the baking process, or they may contaminate the loaf after it is removed from the oven. Propionic acid is an innocuous substance which occurs in many foods, including Swiss cheeses, and acts as a natural preservative. Calcium propionate in bread serves as a dietary source of calcium, but, since calcium can interfere with some leavening agents, bakers use sodium propionate in pies and cakes.

French's Instant Potato is introduced by R. T. French Co. (*see* Worcestershire Sauce, 1930). French will move the operation from Rochester, N.Y., to Shelley, Idaho, in 1951 and use only Russet potatoes for the precooked mashed potato product.

Libby, McNeill & Libby enters the frozen food business, marketing its first frozen products at Milwaukee in November (*see* baby foods, 1934; Nestlé, 1970).

Ragú Sauce creators Giovanni and Assunta Cantisano open their first plant, at Rochester, N.Y., and begin to broaden distribution of the product throughout the northeastern United States, using a label showing a gondolier which their son Ralph has seen on the wall of a Philadelphia restaurant (*see* 1937; 1969).

Hershey Chocolate reduces the size of its nickel Hershey Bar from 1⅝ oz. to 1¼ oz. (*see* 1944; 1947).

U.S. frozen orange juice sales reach 4.8 million 6-ounce cans, but most consumers find the product

1946

unacceptable. A "cutback" technique developed by Louis Gardner MacDowell overconcentrates the juice and then adds fresh juice to the concentrate. C. D. Atkins and E. L. Moore help him refine the process to produce a concentrate whose sweetness, flavor, and acidity are more uniform after dilution than fresh-squeezed orange juice. The new frozen concentrate will find wide acceptance and boom demand for oranges, which are now in such oversupply that Florida growers have been cutting down trees and replacing them with avocado trees (*see* 1945; 1947).

Nearly 90 percent of the tea consumed in America is now black tea, up from about 30 percent in 1915. The cutoff of green tea from China and Japan at the end of 1941 has increased the percentage of black tea consumed. India and Ceylon continued production through the war, and India now supplies about 39 percent of total world tea exports, Ceylon about 26 percent, Java and Sumatra about 18 percent, China about 9 percent, Japan and Taiwan 8 percent.

A bumper California wine crop lowers prices of bulk wine to 50¢/gal.; Robert Mondavi, 32, insists on paying growers full price, and the firm loses nearly $500,000 (*see* 1943; 1966).

The Moscow Mule, created by Los Angeles restaurateur Jack Morgan of the Cock 'n Bull Restaurant on Sunset Boulevard and Heublein boss John G. Martin, consists of Smirnoff vodka and ginger beer served in a copper mug (*see* 1939). The new cocktail will help boom vodka sales in America (*see* 1948).

Brennan's French & Creole Restaurant opens in July in Bourbon Street, New Orleans. Local restaurateur Owen Edward Brennan, 36, who purchased the Old Absinthe House in 1943, has leased the Vieux Carré Restaurant across the street and renamed it (it will soon be known as Owen Brennan's Vieux Carré); he begins to develop a reputation for his marchand du vin sauce Brennan's, eggs hussard, eggs Sardou, quail in burgundy sauce with wild rice, milk punch, cream cheese Evangeline served with strawberries and cream, and bananas Foster sautéed in butter and brown sugar and flambéed with rum and banana liqueur, and then served over vanilla ice cream. Inspired by the 1948 Frances Parkinson Keyes novel *Dinner at Antoine's*,

Brennan will soon be promoting the idea of Breakfast at Brennan's (*see* 1954).

The New Orleans diner Camellia Grill opens at 626 South Carrollton Avenue. Patrons sit at the counter, receive white linen napkins, and enjoy pecan waffles, omelettes, hamburgers, other short-order dishes, and pecan pie served by experienced waiters.

Arthur Bryant's Bar-B-Cue is started at Kansas City by local cook Bryant, 44, who takes over a place started by his brother in the city's black section, lightens the hot sauce his brother uses, and soon has patrons (who sometimes include President Truman) waiting in line to be served barbecued beef, slices of ham, sausages, baked beans in a sweet sauce with chunks of meat, and french-fried potatoes—all on white bread wrapped in butcher's paper. There is no table service, patrons in three-piece suits will sit down at Formica-topped tables alongside men in work boots, take-out orders will be shipped by air to New York and Hollywood, and Bryant will remain the barbecue chef until his death late in 1982.

The first Runza restaurant opens at Lincoln, Nebr. Proprietor Sally Everett trademarks the name given to a picnic bun of yeast dough filled with ground meat, cabbage, and onions; her son Don will expand the business into a chain of Runza drive-ins in the 1960s.

The 10-year-old London restaurant Mirabelle is taken over by Polish restaurateur Erwin Schleyen and begins to flourish, competing with L'Écu de France (whose chef-manager Herbodau worked with Escoffier), the Coq d'Or, run by Sartori, and the Caprice, run by Mario Galatti. The Hungaria still basks in the afterglow of its prewar days, chef Toulemon is at the Connaught, Beaufort at the Trocadero. Scott's, Hatchett's, and L'Apéritif all keep up a standard that will later be forgotten. Schleyen moves the Mirabelle's restaurant into what was the courtyard, installs a roof with electrically operated windows that can be opened in warm weather, and turns one wall into glass doors that open onto a tinkling fountain, creating the ambience of a *fête champêtre* with parasols over the tables. He changes the menu three times per year, offering Whitstable oysters, smoked Scotch salmon, potted shrimps, *langoustine au whisky*, *homard en brioche*, spit roasts, charcoal-grilled meats, *brioche à la moelle*, beef Stroganoff Pojanski *à la crème*, and such traditional French dishes as *ris de veau maréchale*, *foies de volaille aux raisins*, *suprême de poulet*, and *poulet Grisons* (*see* 1988).

The Paris restaurant Taillevent opens at 15, rue Lamennais (a 19th-century mansion that was formerly the Paraguayan embassy) near the Étoile serving dishes that include *escargots Talleyrand*, *suprême de turbot* presented on *duxelles*, *poularde champagnoise*, *carré d'agneau* with *herbes de Provence*, *rognons Chambertin*, *soufflé au fromage* made with Comté cheese, *pommes d'amandine*, and *soufflés glacé au Cointreau*. Offering luxury without ostentation, it will gain its third Michelin star in 1972.

The Paris restaurant La Quetsch opens in December at 6, rue des Capucines near the Hôtel Ritz but will do almost no business until February. Heating is practically nonexistent, electricity goes off half a dozen times day and night, rationing is still in effect, and to obtain supplies a restaurateur must have friends in the country and at the seashore. La Quetsch attracts guests from the Ritz with its morning croissants, brioches, *petit pain au chocolate*, and *schnecken*, and it will grow to seat 100 diners (with quick turnover enabling it to serve close to 1,000 per day with truffled omelette; roast guinea hen *maréchal*; cassoulet of Toulouse; sweetbreads à la Bresse; matelote of eel; sautéed scallops Basque style; terrine of rabbit; and almond soufflé), with a delicatessen counter for take-out specialties, offering 150 varieties of sausage, salamis, liverwurst, and charcuterie; hams from Parma, Bayonne, Westphalia, Denmark, Prague, Hungary, and Savoy; dried beef of Grisons; 19 kinds of bread; 49 varieties of cheese (including Camembert soaked in cognac and studded with walnuts, cream of Gruyère perfumed with kirsch, etc.); artichoke hearts; Russian-style pickles; pearl onions; olives stuffed with pimiento or anchovy; stuffed green peppers; dolma (stuffed vine leaves) from Istanbul; hearts of palm; Greek-style marinated mushrooms; celery rémoulade; shredded carrots; roasts of veal, beef, and pork; Burgundian snails (to be reheated at home); long loaves of coulibiac (sold by the slice or by weight); puff-paste rolls filled with salmon, hard-cooked eggs, and mushrooms (to be reheated and served with melted butter); crocks with individual portions of duck *à l'orange*; tiny quiches Lorraines; tiny Neapolitan pizzas; eggs in aspic; smoked salmon; smoked trout; smoked sturgeon; smoked eel; caviar; pökelfleisch (corned beef); Alsatian kugelhupf; more than 20 kinds of petits fours; fruit tarts; pots de crème; and every brand of liquor and liqueur, by the glass at the bar or by the bottle to take out.

1947

Britain reduces meat rations again January 22 as worldwide food shortages continue in the wake of World War II. The coldest winter since 1880–1881 brings January and February blizzards that pile up 20-foot drifts, block movement of food on roads and railways, and keep fishing fleets from putting out to sea. Crop failures later in the year exacerbate the situation, and potatoes are rationed near year's end.

U.S. sugar rationing ends June 11, but President Truman urges meatless and eggless days October 5 to conserve grain for hungry Europe, and a Friendship Train leaves Los Angeles November 8 for a cross-country tour to collect food for European relief.

The Soviet Union continues food rationing until December but exports grain despite widespread hunger at home, just as the czarist government did in 1911.

The Marshall Plan proposed at Harvard commencement exercises June 5 by Secretary of State George C. Marshall, 66, would give financial aid to European countries "willing to assist in the task of recovery."

President Truman asks Congress November 17 to appropriate $597 million for immediate aid to France, Italy, and Austria. Congress authorizes $540 million December 23 for interim aid to France, Italy, Austria, and China and in the next 40 months will authorize $12.5 billion in Marshall Plan aid to restore the economic health of free Europe (and halt the spread of communism).

The General Agreement on Tariffs and Trade (GATT) signed by the major world powers will lead to a significant lowering of tariff barriers, end some tariff discrimination, and help revitalize world trade.

Chun King Corp. is founded by Hibbing, Minn., food salesman Jeno Paulucci, 29, who borrows $2,500, rents a quonset hut at nearby Grand Rapids that has been used as a rutabaga cannery, sets up a hydroponic garden to grow bean sprouts, and starts packing chicken chow mein in cans. Within a few weeks he is giving demonstrations of his product at supermarkets and selling 300 cases per day as he looks for larger production facilities at Duluth (see 1951).

Pace Foods has its beginnings in a bottled picante sauce introduced by San Antonio, Tex., entrepreneur David E. Pace, 33, who has been cooking and selling jams, jellies, and syrups in the back room of a local liquor store and distributing them in the afternoon from the back of a truck. Pace has experimented with jalapeño peppers, onions, garlic, and tomatoes, come up with a successful formula, and within a few years will have a line of "Tex-Mex" products that include chili con queso, chili paste, and Tampico hot sauce (see Campbell Soup, 1994).

Pet-Ritz Foods is founded by Beulah, Mich., entrepreneurs George and Althea Petritz (see Pet Milk, 1955).

Margaret Rudkin builds a modern bakery—the first Pepperidge Farm commercial bakery—at Norwalk, Conn., to keep up with growing demand for her breads, melba toast, and pound cake (see 1940; cookies, 1953).

Nestlé, S.A., becomes Nestlé Alimentana, S.A., following acquisition of Fabrique de Produits Maggi, S.A. (which now has 11 plants, including some in Czechoslovakia and Poland, plus 800 shops in Paris), and the Maggi holding company Alimentana, S.A., of Kempttal, Switzerland (see 1884; Maggi, 1912; Nescafé, 1938; Quik, 1948).

McCormick & Co. gains national distribution for its spices by merging with A. Schilling & Co., a San Francisco coffee, spice, and extract house founded in 1881 (see 1941). McCormick begins expanding into Latin America.

Reddi-Wip, introduced by Reddi-Wip, Inc., is the first major U.S. aerosol food product. Founder Marcus Lipsky advertises aerated "real" whipped cream in pressurized cans (see 1945; Abplanalp, 1953).

Kraft Singles are tested at Detroit, Mich., supermarkets by Kraft Foods Co., which has developed machinery that will slice and wrap processed cheese (see 1921). The packaged slices do not appear to be sliced, and customers are dubious, but Singles will gradually gain favor (see 1965).

MSG (monosodium glutamate) is marketed for the first time under the Ac'cent label (see 1908; 1934; "Chinese Restaurant Syndrome," 1968).

The synthetic antioxidant BHA (butylated hydroxyanisole) is introduced commercially in the United States to retard spoilage in foods and give them slightly longer shelf life. The additive prevents polyunsaturated oils from oxidizing and becoming rancid (see BHT, 1954).

The first commercial microwave oven is introduced by the Raytheon Co. of Waltham, Mass., whose Percy LeBaron Spencer, now 53, discovered in 1942 that microwaves used for signal transmission would cook food (they agitated molecules of a chocolate bar in his pocket, melting it). Raytheon's $3,000 Radarange restaurant oven employs an electronic tube (magnetron) developed in 1940 by John Randall and J. A. H. Boot of Birmingham University for British radar. It cooks quickly, but the results are unappetizing (see Amana, 1967).

A moisture meter developed by C. J. Patterson is an electronic device that permits direct reading of the moisture content of a wide variety of grains (see Patterson, 1945; Verv, 1961).

The finding that sexual reproduction occurs in bacteria will open up a whole new world of study and lay the groundwork for future work in bacterial genetics. Columbia University graduate student Joshua Lederberg, 22, and Yale geneticist Edward Lawrie Tatum, 37, make the discovery.

British agriculture sustains £20 million in losses March 16 as a gale blows across England's Fens, knocking down trees and creating floods that destroy potatoes, root crops, and poultry flocks. Homes and farm buildings are ruined, and floods make planting impossible.

Snowstorms isolate hundreds of British farms, killing more than a quarter of the sheep and lamb flock; 30,000 head of cattle die or have to be shot.

Britain's Labour government puts through an Agricultural Act designed to spare farmers the insecurities that existed before the war. Further legislation will give farmers capital grants, tax concessions, and price supports that amount to a generous subsidy which will have its counterpart in France, West Germany, other Western countries, and Japan.

The rat poison Warfarin discovered by University of Wisconsin biochemist Karl Paul Link, 46, is introduced to fight the rodent, which consumes a large portion of the world's grain production each year. The anticoagulant is based on the chemical coumarin, which occurs in spoiled sweet clover and causes animals to bleed to death by interfering with vitamin K, which enables the liver to produce the blood-clotting chemical prothrombin.

Reports begin to come in of fly and mosquito strains that have developed resistance to DDT and the British-developed benzene hexachloride.

U.S. agricultural chemical production reaches nearly 2 billion pounds, up from 100 million in 1934.

A rice-farming boom begins in the lower Mississippi valley.

Cookbooks: *Meta Given's Modern Encyclopedia of Cookery* by Chicago home economist Given is a two-volume work of 2,238 pages which will have sold more than 538,000 copies by 1955; *The Cordon Bleu Cookbook* by Dione Lucas (*see* school, 1942); *Food for Two* and *Pressure Cooking* by Ida Bailey Allen.

Philippine health authorities begin the "Bataan experiment" in an effort to solve the problem of beriberi (*see* thiamine, 1936; 1937). The study will show that beriberi incidence is reduced by nearly 90 percent in an area where people are given rice fortified with thiamine, niacin, and iron, while a control population has no reduction.

Borden Co. introduces Lady Borden Ice Cream, the first premium ice cream to have national distribution (*see* Swiss cheese, Elsie, 1939; Wyler, 1961).

Almond Joy is introduced to augment the popular Mounds bar. Peter Paul has survived the war by importing coconuts via small schooners from Honduras, El Salvador, Nicaragua, and other Caribbean countries (*see* 1932).

Hershey Chocolate reduces the size of its nickel Hershey Bar from 1½ oz. to 1 oz. (*see* 1946; 1954).

U.S. frozen orange juice concentrate sales reach 7 million cans, up from 4.8 million last year, but a glut of fresh oranges that has dropped prices from $4 per box to 50¢ and an oversupply of canned single-strength juice brings the fledgling concentrate industry to the brink of ruin.

Minute Maid Corp. has its beginnings in Vacuum Foods Co., headed by former National Research Corp. head John M. Fox, whose pioneer orange concentrate producing firm has lost $371,000 in the past year (*see* 1945). With more than $500,000 tied up in retail packages bearing the Snow Crop label, Fox goes door to door at Hingham, Mass., handing out free cans of concentrate and the names of local grocery stores where the product may be purchased; when stocks are cleaned out, he is convinced that he has a desirable product. Fox obtains a $50,000 loan from William A. Coolidge, whose Cambridge, Mass., firm initiated the development of citrus concentrates for the U.S. Army in 1942, and Coolidge gets venture capitalist John Hay (Jock) Whitney interested in Vacuum Foods (*see* 1949).

Snow Crop, the major marketer of orange juice concentrate, sells out to Clinton Foods after its distributors have gone broke by the dozens.

Seagram's 7 Crown becomes the world's largest selling brand of whiskey (*see* 1934). By 1971, Seagram will be selling 7.5 million cases of 7 Crown per year, half a fifth for every American man, woman, and child.

The New York restaurant Gian Marino opens at 221 East 58th Street. Originally from Abruzzi, Marino will operate the place for the next 40 years, attracting patrons with *lumache alla tirolese* (land snails dipped in beaten egg, rolled in breadcrumbs, walnuts, parsley, and garlic, and sautéed); *lumache con polenta*; *mozzarella in carrozza* (an egg-dipped Neapolitan fried cheese sandwich); pastas that include *paglie e fieno* (green and white noodles with mushrooms, peas, and cream sauce), *orecchiette alla barese* (with *broccoli di rape* and crushed red pepper), and *mezzenini alla siciliana* (macaroni baked with mozzarella, tomato, and eggplant); *calamari al nero* (squid sautéed in their own ink with lemon juice and olive oil); *triglie alla triestina* (red mullet with onion, tomato, and balsam vinegar sauce); striped bass alla pescatore; *pollo alla pastorella* (shepherdess style); *rostina annegati* (veal loin soaked in kidney fat with chopped rosemary); zabaglione with champagne in place of the usual marsala; cheeses; and wines.

New York restaurateur Arnold Reuben opens a new $1 million restaurant at 212 West 57th Street in February (*see* 1912). The "Reuben sandwich" has gained a worldwide reputation.

New York restaurateur Christopher Cella dies in a Princeton, N.J., hospital November 10 at age 54 (*see* 1926); his son Richard T., an Air Force Reserve brigadier general and MIT graduate, takes over Christ Cella's, which he will move to 160 East 46th Street when the original brownstone in East 45th Street is torn down and will gain a following not only for his sirloin steak, prime ribs, pot roast, and London broil, but also for his broiled Canadian lobsters, lobster Newberg, red snapper, striped bass, sea bass, pompano, sole, trout from the Fulton Market, bouillabaisse (Fridays), hashed brown potatoes, broccoli, asparagus with Hollandaise sauce, cheesecake, Napoléons, and ice cream.

The San Francisco restaurant India House opens at 350 Jackson Street, serving Pimm's Cup, Maharajah's Burra Peg (a split of champagne with Cointreau and brandy), mild chicken, shrimp, prawn, egg, and vegetable curry; warm lamb curry; and hot beef curry.

The 18-year-old London restaurant Wheeler's reopens above an oyster shop at 19 Old Compton Street. Entrepreneur Bernard Walsh has purchased the property, is soon selling 3,000 oysters per day (from 9 o'clock in the morning until midnight), will expand over four narrow floors, and within 20 years will have nine London restaurants (the original Wheeler's, the Brickhouse at 56 Frith Street, Little Wheeler's at 12a Duke of York Street, the Sovereign at 17 Hertford Street, Antoine's at 43 Charlotte Street, the Vendôme at 20 Dover Street,

the Ocean Dragon at 256 Brompton Road, the Carafe at 15 Lowndes Street, and the Alcove at 17 Kensington High Street), plus two at Brighton, serving 1 million oysters per year. Whereas initially he closes from May until the end of August, he will soon be open year round, serving Dublin prawns, mussels in season, 23 preparations of Dover sole (including sole Capri, with sliced bananas and chutney sauce), a dozen Scotch lobster preparations, scampi, plaice, scallops, skate, salmon-trout, and salmon.

The Paris restaurant La Coquille opens at 6, rue de Débarcadère specializing in *coquilles Saint-Jacques* (from November to mid-May), *boudin grillé flambé* (blood sausages, poached and grilled and served with potatoes and apples), *homard à l'américaine*, *estoffade de caneton aux truffes* (duckling braised in a red wine sauce with truffles), fricassee of chicken in a cream sauce with morels, stuffed pigeon, frogs' legs, and soufflé with noisettes.

1948

✗ Soviet occupation forces in Germany set up a blockade July 24 to cut off rail and highway traffic between West Germany and Berlin. An airlift begins July 25 with U.S. and British aircraft flying in food and supplies for the more than 2 million people of West Berlin, the airlift is carrying 4,500 tons per day by September, and it will continue until September of next year.

Britain ends bread rationing in July as wheat flour becomes more plentiful.

Italy ends food rationing and permits production of higher-quality pasta after years of restrictions, during which wartime black-market activities have doubled the nation's pasta factories from about 1,000 to 2,000. Parma's Barilla bakery was requisitioned by the Germans from 1943 to 1945 (*see* 1919), Riccardo Barilla's son Pietro returned from service on the Russian front to find his father ill, and Pietro has taken over management of the bakery along with his brother Gianni (*see* 1952).

A Foreign Assistance Act passed by Congress April 3 implements the 1947 Marshall Plan. The act authorizes spending $5.3 billion in the first year for economic aid to 16 European countries, creating the European Recovery Program (ERP) and Economic Cooperation Administration (ECA).

U.S. production, employment, and national income reach new highs, but renewed strikes bring a third round of inflationary wage boosts.

The U.S. cost-of-living index reaches an all-time high in August, and Congress passes an Anti-Inflationary Act to "protect the Nation's economy against inflationary pressures."

Frank Perdue, now 28, takes over management of his father's Perdue Farms, which now has 40 employees and is one of the largest egg producers on Maryland's Eastern Shore (*see* 1920; chickens, 1968).

Worthington Foods founder George Harding III accepts the presidency of Loma Linda University, part of a California Seventh-Day Adventist complex whose divisions include a manufacturer of meat analogs which compete with those of Worthington Foods (*see* 1906; 1945). Worthington has added the Meatless Wiener and Vega-Links to its product line (*see* 1960).

Gerber Products Co. sells 2 million cans and jars of baby food per week (*see* 1941; MSG, 1951).

 The first full-sized British supermarket opens January 12 at Manor Park, London, under the aegis of the London Co-Operative Society (*see* 1951).

The German supermarket chain Aldi, founded by Theodore Albrecht, 26, and his brother Karl, 28, will grow to have more than 2,200 stores, none of them stocking much in the way of meat or dairy products but each carrying 500 to 600 basic items, mostly canned and dry goods. By mid-1992 it will have 300 such stores in the U.S. Midwest and 40 in Britain.

The New York specialty food shop Balducci's opens as a 24-hour produce market at 1–5 Greenwich Avenue near the Avenue of the Americas. Grocer Louis Balducci, now 48, is an immigrant from Bari, Italy, who since 1917 has run a similar shop in Brooklyn with his wife, Maria. Their Greenwich Village store will grow to carry caviar, foie gras, smoked fish, cheeses (including the Androuet line from France, Italian Fontina, Val d'Aosta, and Parmi-

giano Reggiano, and English Cheddars), coffees (including Jamaican Blue Mountain, Hawaiian Kona, Swiss Le Semeus, and Italian Illy and Kimbo), fresh seafood (including triglie, Portuguese sardines, Puerto Rican sweetwater prawns, Florida oysters, New Zealand green-lipped mussels, and Idaho rainbow trout, with live lobster and trout tanks that will sometimes be used also for abalone and Dungeness crabs), meats (including Wagyu beef from Japan, buffalo, rattlesnake, and wild boar, available by special order, in addition to beef, veal, farm-raised venison, game birds, and free-range chicken and turkey), Polish kielbasa, Spanish chorizo, Cajun andouille, and German knackwurst (*see* 1972).

U.S. bon vivant Lucius Beebe, 45, reports in *Gourmet* magazine in May that food on Santa Fe Railroad dining cars is still prepared by the Fred Harvey organization and is still good (*see* 1876). The railroad has its own trout farms in Colorado, buys the pick of heavy beef at Denver and Kansas City, obtains fresh eggs and strawberries out of season, grapefruit in all seasons, and artichokes, asparagus, and avocados for its cars and restaurant, which feature California wines and Sierra cheese.

The Salton Hotray introduced by Polish-American engineer Lewis Salton, 37, keeps food warm but has little initial success as consumers rush to buy toasters and coffeemakers while showing little interest in new products. Employed by RCA since his arrival as a refugee by way of Lithuania, Siberia, Japan, and Panama, Salton quits his $8,000-per-year job and goes into business with three employees in a 1,000-square-foot New York loft in Reade Street.

Nonfiction: *The Unprejudiced Palate* by Italian-American writer Angelo M. Pellegrini, 44.

U.S. sales of oregano will increase by 5,200 percent in the next 8 years as demand is boosted by the growing popularity of pizza pies and other Italian specialties discovered by servicemen in Europe (*see* 1953).

General Mills introduces chiffon cake on its Betty Crocker radio show, calling it the "cake discovery of the century." Los Angeles insurance man Harry Baker created the cake in 1927 by beating salad oil (instead of butter, lard, or other solid shortening) into his batter. He has sold his cakes through the Los Angeles Women's Club, Hollywood's Brown Derby restaurant, and other outlets, but when he offered his recipe to General Mills during the war it was rejected. Baker came to Minneapolis after the war, baked cakes for Mills executives, and when they tasted his chiffon cake they bought the recipe, which will never be formulated into a mix. Bags of Gold Medal flour will contain recipe folders, and General Mills print advertising will help spread the word about chiffon cake.

Our Plundered Planet by U.S. zoologist Fairfield Osborne, 51, expresses concern about the growing use of DDT (*see* 1943; Carson, 1962).

Maine's Atlantic Sea-Run Salmon Commission begins a program to remove old dams that bar fish from migrating upstream to spawning grounds (*see* Columbia River, 1938). The commission starts to re-stock the Aroostook, Dennys, Machias, East Machias, Narraguagus, Penobscot, Pleasant, Sheep-scot, Union, and other rivers (*see* 1950; Anadro-mous Fish Act, 1965).

Lysenkoites opposed to hybridization take over the USSR's last remaining centers of pure biological research (*see* Lysenko, 1940). The centers were organized at the Lenin Academy of Agricultural Science and at the Institute of Genetics by the late Nikolai Vavilov (*see* 1954).

U.S. corn is now 75 percent hybrid (*see* Golden Cross Bantam, 1933).

Vitamin B_{12} (cyanocobalamin) is isolated from ani-mal livers as a red crystalline substance, making it possible to contain pernicious anemia with monthly injections (*see* Castle, 1929; folic acid, 1944). English biochemist E. L. Smith and Merck Laboratories bio-chemist Karl A. Volkers, 41, in the United States have used bacterial response and chromatography to isolate the vitamin, which will be synthesized in 1955. British biochemist Dorothy (Mary) Hodgkin (*née* Crowfoot), 38, begins using X-ray crystallogra-phy to analyze the complex structure of vitamin B_{12} in a project that will take 8 years (*see* 1955).

All 13 vitamins considered essential to human health have now been isolated and some synthesized.

The Organic Front by J. I. Rodale, now 50, makes extravagant health claims for the benefits of eating vegetables and fruits grown without chemical fertil-izers, herbicides, or pesticides (*see* 1942; *Prevention* magazine, 1950).

Aunt Fanny's Bakery is founded at Atlanta, where it will produce Pecan Twirls and other baked goods (*see* Pet Milk, 1966).

Welch's Pom Poms—caramel balls covered in milk chocolate—are introduced by James O. Welch Co. (*see* 1945). They will take some sales away from Milk Duds (*see* 1926) but will never have the popu-larity of Junior Mints.

U.S. sales of frozen orange juice concentrate leap to more than 12 million 6-ounce cans (*see* 1947; Minute Maid, 1949).

TreeSweet Products leases a processing plant at Ft. Pierce, Fla., in the heart of the citrus-growing Indian River country and adds canned Florida cit-rus juices to its California line (*see* 1933; 1956).

Nestlé's Quik chocolate milk additive is introduced in the United States to compete with Ovaltine, which dominates the market (*see* 1905). By 1976 Quik will have 64 percent of what will then be a $110 million market.

V-8 Cocktail Vegetable Juice, introduced by Camp-bell Soup Co., is a mixture of tomato, carrot, celery, beet, parsley, lettuce, watercress, and spinach juices (*see* Swanson, 1955).

G. F. Heublein & Bro. promotes its Smirnoff Vodka by using the newly introduced Polaroid camera. Company executives tour the country showing bartenders how to make the Moscow Mule, created 2 years ago, and take Polaroid pic-tures of them drinking the cocktail. A fad develops that helps to popularize the liquor that will soon be sold with the double-entendre advertising slogan "It Leaves You Breathless." Heublein will develop a series of vodka drinks, including the vodka mar-tini, the screwdriver (vodka and orange juice), and the Bloody Mary (vodka, tomato juice, lemon juice, and Worcestershire Sauce), and by the mid-1970s vodka will be outselling whiskey in the United States.

Vodka began its rise to popularity in America with promises not to leave "whiskey breath."

California wineries crush 1,281,495 tons of grapes (one ton yields between 150 and 160 gallons of table wine or between 90 and 100 gallons of fortified wine), but less than 35 percent of the total are wine grapes and only a fraction of these are of superior quality. Of the wine produced in California's northern coastal counties, including Napa and Sonoma, 85 percent are from wine grapes.

The McDonald's hamburger stand that opened in 1940 at Pasadena, Calif., is turned into a self-service restaurant by the McDonald brothers, who begin to franchise their name to other fast-food entrepreneurs. The McDonalds install infrared heat lamps to keep french fries warm (*see* Kroc, 1954).

The Baskin-Robbins ice cream chain begins its growth as California entrepreneurs Burton "Butch" Baskin and his brother-in-law Irvine Robbins, now 30, merges the small chains begun 3 years ago with Burton's, opened at Pasadena, and the Snowbird Ice Cream stand opened by Robbins December 7, 1945, at Adams and Palmer streets in Glendale. Baskin has run a retail clothing store in Chicago; Robbins has helped his father operate a dairy products business at Tacoma, Wash., and learned that there was more profit to be made from selling ice cream in the family's own small store in a local alley than in supplying products to grocers and druggists. They soon had eight stores, and sales were increasing, but they were not making money until they got the idea of selling the stores to their managers. They will choose the locations and supply the ice cream, which they will soon begin manufacturing themselves. Impressed by their marketing skills, the co-owner of a Phoenix ice-cream manufacturer will obtain a license to manufacture and sell product under the Baskin-Robbins name, and Baskin-Robbins will eventually have more than a dozen regional subcontractors making ice cream and handling local franchisees (*see* United Fruit, 1967).

The 160-year-old Paris restaurant Le Grand Véfours is taken over by Maxim's owner Louis Vaudable (*see* 1942), whose legendary establishment has been closed by the authorities on charges that Vaudable collaborated with the Germans in World War II. Vaudable has associated himself with Raymond Olivier, son of a Bordelaise caterer, and the two work to revive the fortunes of Le Grand Véfours, which within 3 years will have gained three stars in the Michelin guide. Chef Olivier will demonstrate cooking techniques on television worldwide, continuing for the next 35 years to oversee the kitchen of Le Grand Véfours (*see* 1984).

Former chef and cookbook author Prosper Montagne dies April 23 at age 83 in his house at Sèvres.

The New York restaurant Café Nicholson, opened before Christmas by John Nicholson at 323 East 58th Street (formerly the studio of sculptor Jo Davidson), has a kitchen staff headed by Virginia-born chef Edna Lewis, 31, whose menu features chicken and chocolate soufflé. Nicholson has found Spanish tiles more than a century old in a Puerto Rican warehouse and put them up on the walls himself; he has also acquired chairs, settees, mirrors, urns, and vases from the old Grand Union Hotel in Saratoga Springs, N.Y., to give his place a Victorian look that many patrons admire.

1948

The Food and Agriculture Organization (FAO) of the United Nations predicts that the world will have 2.25 billion mouths to feed by 1960 (*see* 1960).

1949

The Geneva Conventions adopted April 12 revise the conventions of 1864, 1907, and 1929. They provide for "free passage of all consignments of essential foodstuffs, clothing, and tonics intended for children under 15, expectant mothers, and maternity cases" in event of war but do not specifically outlaw sieges, blockades, or "resource denial" operations and do not address conflicts that are partly internal and partly international.

Soviet authorities officially lift the Berlin blockade May 12, but the airlift continues until September 30, when it ends after having completed 277,264 flights (*see* 1948).

The People's Republic of China is proclaimed October 1 at Beijing, with Mao Zedong as chairman of the Central People's Administrative Council.

Famine ravages the new People's Republic of China (above). The nation's cereal grain production falls to 110 million tons, down from 150 million before the war, when the population was smaller (*see* 1952).

Meat, dairy products, and sugar remain in short supply in Britain and sales are restricted, but rationing of chocolate and sweets ends April 24.

The Nobel Peace Prize is awarded to the U.N.'s FAO chairman John Boyd Orr, who is elevated to the peerage as Lord Boyd Orr of Brechin (*see* 1945). He observes that "hunger, which is the worst manifestation of poverty, is also the fundamental cause of the rebellion of the Asians against the economic domination of the European powers, a rebellion that cannot be put down with bombs and guns as long as these peoples remain convinced that their hunger and their poverty are sufferings to which they are not condemned by necessity."

The average American steel worker has $3,000 per year to spend after taxes, the average social worker $3,500, a high school teacher $4,700, a car salesman $8,000, a dentist $10,000. Typical food prices: pork 57¢/lb., lamb chops $1.15/lb., Coca-Cola 5¢ per 7-oz. bottle, milk 21¢/qt., bread 15¢/lb., eggs 80¢/doz.

The first edible vegetable-protein fiber made from spun soy isolate is introduced (*see* 1937). Chemical engineer Robert Boyer files for patents on a process for dehulling soybeans, turning them into oil flakes, milling the flakes into a flour that is more than 50 percent protein, and further processing the flour to make it 90 percent protein (*see* 1957).

General Mills and Pillsbury introduce prepared cake mixes, initially in chocolate, gold, and white varieties. Angel food cake and dozens of other flavors will later be added (*see* chiffon cake, 1948; Duncan Hines, 1951).

"Les Plaisirs du Table" ("The Pleasures of the Table") begins appearing in the Paris newspaper *Le Monde* under the byline La Reynière. Gastronome Robert J. Courtine, 39, will continue writing the column for more than 25 years.

Nonfiction: *Alphabet for Gourmets* by M. F. K. Fisher. An English translation by Fisher of the classic 1825 Brillat-Savarin book *Physiologie du Goût*, also published this year, will survive as the standard English version. *The History and Social Influence of the Potato* by English author Redcliffe Nathan Salaman, 75.

Cookbooks: *The Fireside Cookbook: The Complete Guide to Fine Cooking for Beginner and Expert* by James Beard; *With a Jug of Wine* by *Chicago Tribune* food writer Morrison Wood, who credits his wife with testing the recipes he uses and handling other details; *The Mystery Chef's Never Fail Cookbook* by John Macpherson, now 69 (*see* 1934); *The Practical Cook* by English author Fanny Craddock (*née* Phyllis Primrose-Pechey), 39, whose readers have lost their servants in World War II and are still short of meat, dairy products, and sugar (above).

A shrimp trawler off the Dry Tortugas brings in a sweet, pink deepwater shrimp whose habitat and nocturnal habits resemble those of the brown shrimp first caught on the Texas gulf coast in 1940.

The People's Republic of China (above) undertakes large-scale irrigation projects in Manchuria to permit rice cultivation in a region where sorghum is the staple food for most people, with rice eaten only at birthdays, weddings, funerals, and New Year celebrations. (Sorghum is prepared in the same ways as rice but has been much cheaper. Cornmeal bread is widely eaten by the poor.)

The Brannan Plan advanced by U.S. Secretary of Agriculture Charles F. Brannan, 45, proposes to increase U.S. food production without taking the profit out of farming. The plan employs a formula used by sugar beet and wool producers and would pay farmers directly the difference between the market price of a commodity and the price needed to give the farmer a fair profit; it gives the consumer the benefit of lower prices produced by greater supply but provides no payment for the 2 percent of farm operators who earn more than $20,000 per year and sell 25 percent of U.S. farm products. Brannan Plan supporters compare it to the minimum wage law of 1938 and Social Security law of 1935, but opponents call it socialism and Congress votes it down. The Price Parity Act passed October 31 supports wheat, corn, cotton, rice, and peanut prices at 90 percent of 1910–1914 levels through 1950, 80 to 90 percent through 1951, 75 to 90 percent on a sliding scale thereafter.

Latin America becomes a net grain importer after years as a net exporter, but some places begin to feel the effects of a "green revolution" (*see* Borlaug, 1944).

University of Illinois nutritionist William Cumming Rose, 62, shows that eight amino acids are "essential" to human health, a smaller number than is needed by rats. By feeding students and rats diets completely lacking in protein but containing pure amino acids, he demonstrates that the body can create the additional amino acids it needs if supplied with isoleucine, leucine, lysine, methionine, phenylalanine, threonine, tryptophan, and valine.

Threonine has not been considered an essential amino acid, but Rose (above) demonstrates its importance. Since rice is deficient in tryptophan, rice eaters suffer will suffer protein deficiencies unless their diets include a source of threonine (which is abundant in beans).

Sara Lee Cheese Cake is introduced by Chicago baker Charles Lubin, 44, whose refrigerated cream cheese product will make his Kitchens of Sara Lee (named after his 9-year-old daughter) one of the

world's largest bakeries. Lubin has owned and operated a chain of retail bakeries since 1935 and has decided to expand distribution to supermarkets (*see* 1953).

Pillsbury (above) inaugurates "Bake-Offs," designed to develop recipes using its flour. Beginning in 1968, contestants will be permitted to use Pillsbury mixes or refrigerated products as well as Pillsbury flour.

Frozen orange juice concentrate sales continue to soar (*see* 1948). A story in the June issue of *Reader's Digest* accelerates the boom. Minute Maid Orange Juice is promoted by crooner Bing Crosby, 46, who acquires 20,000 shares of stock in Vacuum Foods Co. on the advice of John Hay Whitney in exchange for a daily 15-minute radio show that pushes concentrate sales. Vacuum Foods renames itself Minute Maid Corp. (*see* 1947; 1953).

About 70 percent of fluid milk sold in the United States is now homogenized, up from 33 percent in 1940. Within a decade it will be almost impossible to obtain nonhomogenized milk, which does not keep as well and is more likely to pick up foreign odors. Homogenization will increase consumption of milk and milk products.

Pepsi-Cola reduces its sugar content and standardizes its recipe. Former Coca-Cola executive Alfred N. Steele, 48, replaces Walter Mack as head of Pepsi and sells the drink as "the light refreshment" (*see* 1934; 1939). Pepsi bottlers add their own sugar, while Coca-Cola supplies bottlers with syrup containing sugar.

New York's Hotel Lafayette and its restaurant close, ending an era in which the hotel was the equivalent of San Francisco's Palace and its restaurant competed with such eating places as Bustanoby's, Churchill's, Delmonico's, the Hoffman House, the Holland House, Martin's, Rector's, Shanley's, and Sherry's.

China's restaurants abolish tipping as the People's Republic adopts Communist principles.

1950 ————————————————————

Communist North Korean forces invade the Republic of South Korea June 25, beginning a 3-year Korean War that will involve 16 nations against the Communists. President Truman sends U.S. air and sea forces to help the South Koreans June 27; many of them will fall ill from eating *kim-chee*, the pickled vegetable mixture that Koreans keep in dark cellars or on roofs in less-than-sanitary conditions, and GIs will be forbidden to eat the staple that carries Koreans through their cold winters.

Moscow claims that the United States has released Colorado potato beetles on fields in East Germany as cold war tensions mount.

"Not in a quarter century have the food markets of Paris been fuller or more tempting," writes Genêt (Janet Flanner, 53) in the *New Yorker* magazine. "In the Rue du Faubourg Saint-Denis, there is a two-hundred-yard stretch of food shops and street barrows. The hucksters shout their prices and the shop apprentices have become barkers, standing at the shop doors and bawling about the luscious wares inside. . . . The street barrows are filled with hairy leeks and potential salads. The Rue du Faubourg Saint-Denis is not a rich district of the city, but these days it offers a Lucullan supply. Food is still what Parisians buy if they can. It is a nervous means of getting satisfaction, a holdover from the lean days of the Occupation."

U.S. farm prices will rise 28 percent in the next year as the Korean conflict fuels inflation and boosts food prices. The U.S. Consumer Price Index for all goods and services will rise by 10 percent in the next decade.

A federal tax of 10¢ per pound on U.S. margarine is removed, as are all federal restrictions on coloring margarine yellow. Butter is in such short supply that retail prices often top $1/lb. and U.S. consumers turn increasingly to margarine, whose average retail price is 33¢/lb. versus an average of 73¢ for butter, but butter will continue to outsell margarine until 1957.

Park-Hines Foods is founded by Ithaca, N.Y., advertising–public relations man Roy Hampton Park, 40, and restaurant critic Duncan Hines, now 70, to license products for sale under the Duncan Hines label (*see* restaurant guide, 1935). Hines has refused to endorse any products, but Park has persuaded him to allow products to bear his name (*see* cake mix, 1951).

Green Giant Co. is adopted as the name of the Minnesota Valley Canning Co., whose Green Giant symbol has helped make it the largest U.S. canner of peas and corn (*see* 1936; beans, 1958).

Cudahy Packing Co. moves from Chicago back to Omaha (*see* 1910). Headquarters will move to Phoenix, Ariz., in 1965.

Britain's first self-service grocery store opens July 31 at London. J. Sainsbury's store is the first in a chain that will grow to be the nation's largest (*see* 1869).

More than 75 percent of U.S. farms are electrified, up from 33 percent in 1940.

Cookbooks: *A Book of Mediterranean Food* by English food writer Elizabeth David (*née* Gwynne), 37. *The Ambitious Cook* by Fanny Craddock, who writes a newspaper column with her monocled husband, Maj. John Craddock, and will soon appear with him in formal dress on British television, demonstrating recipes and disputing French chef Raymond Olivier's contention that men are better cooks than women. "The British housewife's greatest handicap," she will say, "is the British husband—who just wants what Mum used to make." *Betty Crocker's Picture Cookbook* is a U.S. best-seller (*see* General Mills, 1936).

The Good Food Club founded by London gastronome Raymond Postgate, 54, with help from local journalist-humorist Stephen Potter, 50, aims to elevate the standard of British cooking and to keep prices reasonable, encourage the drinking of good wine, improve the quality of beer, earn foreign currency by raising the standards of British hospitality, reward enterprise and courtesy, and "to do all ourselves a bit of good, in due course, by publishing an annual which will make our holidays, travels, and evenings out enjoyable" (*see* 1951).

World fisheries' production regains its prewar level of 20 million tons per year (*see* 1960).

Only 82 Atlantic salmon are landed on the Maine coast, less than a thousand pounds as compared with 150,000 in 1889. Dams and pollution have reduced spawning (*see* 1948; Danish fishermen, 1964).

The Columbia River Packers Association joins with Pacific American Fisheries to form the Excursion Inlet Packing Co. and build a plant 60 miles west of

Juneau, Alaska (*see* 1945). CRPA built a cannery west of Bellingham, Wash., in 1946 to process fish from Puget Sound and the Fraser River, and it will acquire the Hawaiian Tuna Packers Association tuna cannery at Honolulu in 1956 to can the skipjack tuna known in the islands as aku (*see* 1959).

Oyster production from the Connecticut coast south to New Jersey reaches 3.3 million bushels (*see* 1966).

The first calf born of a virgin mother is delivered at the University of Wisconsin (*see* rabbit, 1935). Transplanting of fertilized ova will permit new developments in animal breeding.

Chinese party leader Liu Shao-chi promulgates an agrarian reform law, saying, "The industrialization of China should be based on the vast market of rural China." But while Mao Zedong says that China's future lies in mobilizing the peasantry, Liu follows Marxist orthodoxy, insisting that large farms depend on chemical fertilizers, electrification, tractors and other farm machinery, agronomists, and engineers. Most of the nation's budget goes to industrialization, but China's agricultural output nevertheless begins a rapid rise (*see* 1949; 1952).

The percentage of the U.S. available workforce employed on the land falls to 11.6 percent, down from 25 percent in 1933, and 20 percent of U.S. farmers will quit the land in the next 12 years (*see* 1960).

Insects damage $4 billion worth of U.S. crops, consuming more food than is grown in New England, New York, New Jersey, and Pennsylvania combined.

Composition of Foods—Raw, Processed, Prepared (Handbook No. 8), issued by the U.S. Department of Agriculture, lists the nutritional contents of 751 items, including some frozen foods (*see* 1895; 1963).

Prevention magazine begins publication at Emmaus, Pa. Publisher J. I. Rodale, now 52, who has published *Organic Gardening and Farming* since 1942, makes extravagant health claims for dietary supplements (Rodale and his wife will each take 70 vitamin and mineral pills per day to guard against pollution and replace nutrients lost in food processing). The magazine warns against the "evils" of fluoridation, DDT, mercury, phosphates, monosodium glutamate, and cyclamates (*see* below), and it will criticize wheat (saying that it can make people overly aggressive or

deaf), sugar (even worse), and milk (good only for infants). Initial subscribers—mostly elderly people who distrust "newfangled" methods and yearn for a simpler past—will soon find the magazine's pages filled with ads for dietary supplements (*see* 1971).

Look Younger, Live Longer by German-American food faddist Gayelord Hauser, 51, promises miracles to those who will eat the "wonder foods" yogurt, wheat germ, brewer's yeast, blackstrap molasses, and powdered skim milk. A condensation appears in the *Reader's Digest* and boosts demands for the "wonder foods" as the book becomes a best-seller (*see* below).

A House Select Committee on Foods and Cosmetics begins 3 years of hearings at Washington, D.C., under the chairmanship of Brooklyn, N.Y., Democrat James J. Delaney (*see* Swanson, 1956).

Dannon Yogurt sales spurt as a result of the Gayelord Hauser claims (above) (*see* Metzger, 1942). The company added a strawberry-flavored yogurt in 1947 and a vanilla-flavored yogurt in 1948 to augment its plain yogurt, but while Dannon will move to a larger plant in Long Island City, N.Y., next year, its sales will slump in 1952 as the Hauser-inspired fad for yogurt fades (sales will nevertheless remain at higher levels and will grow with the introduction of other flavors).

Kretschmer Wheat Germ sales double to $1.5 million as Saginaw, Mich., wheat germ producer Charles H. Kretschmer, Jr., cashes in on the boom started by Gayelord Hauser (above).

Sales of wheat germ, brewers' yeast, and yogurt got a boost from food faddist Gayelord Hauser.

Cyclamates are introduced commercially for use as artificial sweeteners (*see* Sveda, 1937). Sucaryl, introduced by Abbott Laboratories, is a cyclamate-based artificial sweetener (*see* No-Cal, 1952).

Sugar Pops breakfast food is introduced by Kellogg (*see* 1942; 1952).

U.S. foods use 19 synthetic colors; the number will decline to 11 by 1967.

General Foods introduces Minute Rice, developed by inventor Ataullah K. Ozai Durrani. He obtained an interview with a company executive 9 years ago, produced a hot plate, cooked up a pot of his rice in 10 minutes, and was given a laboratory in which to refine his precooked, quick-dried rice, which was distributed to GIs in K ration packages. General Foods scientists have learned that long-grain rice is better suited to precooking than short- or medium-grain and that rice shrinks less if it is cooked only partially. The new product is launched with the first consumer advertising ever put behind rice.

Lawry's Seasoned Salt is marketed for the first time in glass jars (the old metal container rusts), using a removable plastic shaker top which produces an airtight seal and will become standard in the industry (*see* 1938). Paste-on foil labels display the product name on one side and, when requested, a restaurant's name on the other. In the next 10 years, more than 2,000 restaurants will place Lawry's Seasoned Salt on their tables.

Coca-Cola's share of the U.S. cola beverage market is 69 percent, Pepsi-Cola's 15 percent. Coke's share will drop in the next 10 years to 52 percent, while Pepsi's will rise to 31 percent (*see* 1949).

The Boston restaurant chain Legal Seafoods has its beginnings in a fish market opened by Cambridge entrepreneur George Berkowitz next to Legal Cash Market grocery store opened in 1904 by his father, Harry, in Inman Square. Legal Cash trading stamps were a forerunner of S&H Green Stamps (*see* 1896), and the grocer has used that as the basis of his store's name (*see* 1968).

New York's Coach House restaurant at 110 Waverley Place in Greenwich Village (a former carriage house of retail merchant John Wanamaker) is purchased by Greek-American engineer Leon Lianides, who has studied at Paris, worked in every capacity from bus boy to *saucier* to chef, and will make the Coach House one of the city's top dining spots, famous for its black bean soup, broiled striped bass, cornsticks, and other American culinary classics.

New York restaurateur Roger Chauveron sells Chambord and retires after inheriting a 1,000-acre estate in France (*see* 1935). The estate, which has been in his family for 400 years, boasts a castle; a 30-acre pond; streams full of salmon, trout, pike, and bass; and forests with deer, partridge, pheasants, and wild geese; but Chauveron, whose grandfather owned a chain of auberges in the Dordogne, will grow bored, sell the estate for $200,000, and return in 1957 to open another New York restaurant under his own name at 139 East 53rd Street (*see* 1973).

New York's Rainbow Room reopens as a dining spot in October (*see* 1942), but music will not be revived for another 25 years (*see* 1975).

The Diners Club is founded to give credit card privileges at a group of 27 New York area restaurants. Lawyer Frank X. McNamara starts with 200 cardholders who pay an annual membership fee for the card, which will be accepted within a few years at hotels, motels, car rental agencies, airline ticket counters, and retail shops as well as at restaurants in most of the United States and in many foreign countries (*see* 1965).

Dunkin' Donuts has its beginnings in The Open Kettle, a coffee-and-doughnut shop opened in a converted awning shop at Quincy, Mass. Cornell graduate Robert M. Rosenberg, 36, who worked in a shipyard at Hingham during World War II, saw the need for a new kind of food service business, and invested $5,000 in 1946 to start Industrial Luncheon Services, a catering business. Rosenberg serves top-quality coffee at 10¢ per cup (others charge a nickel), and when he hears that another restaurateur may open a competitive shop he changes the name of his place to Dunkin' Donuts. By 1955 he will have six Dunkin' Donuts shops and will sign his first franchise agreement, starting a chain that will grow to have 100 shops by 1963 and 1,000 by 1979 (*see* Japan, 1971).

The British meat ration is reduced January 27 to its lowest level ever—the equivalent of four ounces of rump steak per week. A beef shortage leads to the consumption of 53,000 horses for food, but Britain produces enough food to supply half her domestic needs, up from 42 percent in 1914, when the population was 35 million as compared with 50 million today.

Congress votes June 15 to loan India $190 million to buy U.S. grain (see P.L. 480, 1954). A huge demonstration at New Delhi, organized by the Socialist party, has protested the Indian government's food policies.

The United States agrees to supply Yugoslavia with $38 million in food aid.

Food becomes more plentiful in the Soviet Union after years of scarcity, but deliveries of many, if not most, items are so irregular that long lines form outside shops when news spreads that the items are in stock. Shelves are full at shops that accept only hard (foreign) currency.

U.S. food prices climb steeply in the Korean War inflation. The nation suffers a beef shortage as affluent consumers increase their demand.

Ore-Ida Foods has its beginnings in a frozen-food factory purchased outside Ontario, Ore., by produce farmers who have pooled their resources. The group will buy a second factory at Burley, Idaho, in 1960 and merge with some other small companies in 1961 to form Ore-Ida Foods (see Heinz, 1965).

Jeno Paulucci's Chun King Corp. moves into a new plant with 2 million cubic feet of production and storage space (see 1947). Paulucci has outgrown his earlier Duluth plant and is spending 10 percent of his sales receipts on advertising as he expands operations to grow his own celery and mushrooms (see 1967).

Parks Sausage is introduced by Baltimore sausage maker Henry G. Parks, 34, whose firm will grow to become the seventh largest black-owned enterprise in America.

The W. K. Kellogg Foundation established in 1930 becomes a major philanthropic organization following the death of breakfast food pioneer William Keith Kellogg at Battle Creek, Mich., October 6 at age 91 (his brother John Harvey Kellogg died at the same age in 1943 after making a futile effort to reconcile the family's long-standing feud). Kellogg's will leaves the bulk of his fortune to the foundation, whose assets for more than 20 years will be surpassed only by those of the Rockefeller and Ford foundations and the Carnegie Corporation.

Duncan Hines Cake Mix, introduced at Omaha in June by Nebraska Consolidated Mills, comes in just one flavor—Three Star Special—which can be used to make a white cake (by adding water and egg white), a yellow cake (by adding water and a whole egg), or a chocolate devil's food cake (by adding water, an egg, and cocoa). The Omaha milling company has obtained a franchise from Park-Hines (see 1950) to use the Duncan Hines name on a mix created by company chemist Arlee Andre. Made initially under contract by Omaha's Omar Bakery, the new product captures 48 percent of the new prepared cake mix market within 3 weeks of its introduction (see Nebraska Consolidated Mills, 1919; General Mills, Pillsbury, 1949). Sales after 6 months are six times what was projected for a whole year; NCM hires 60 new employees for its new Cake Mix Division and buys a building in which it will begin next year to turn out 36,000 boxes per day for distribution in 12 states, including most of Iowa, Nebraska, Wyoming, Colorado, Utah, and Idaho (see 1955).

Pillsbury Co. acquires Ballard and Ballard of Louisville and its 20-year-old refrigerated, oven-ready biscuit package. Pillsbury will redesign Lively Willoughby's container, introduce a new container in 1976 that is easier to open, and make refrigerated biscuits an important part of its line (see 1949).

Nathan Cummings acquires two California companies to expand the food company he began with the acquisition of a Baltimore sugar and coffee wholesaler in 1941 and of the Chicago food wholesaler Sprague Warner in 1942 (see 1939). Gentry Foods is a major producer of dehydrated onions, garlic, and pepper products; Union Sugar a major beet-sugar refiner (see Consolidated Foods, 1954).

Trading stamps are revived by the small Denver grocery chain King Sooper, which begins offering S&H Green Stamps in June (see Sperry and Hutchinson, 1896).

Russian-born Manhattan food store owner Louis Zabar dies of cancer, leaving his business to his sons Saul, 22; Stanley, 18; and Eli, 7. Saul cancels his plans to enter medical school and will keep the business going while Stanley goes through college and law school, keeping the store on the west side of Broadway between 80th and 81st streets but selling four other self-service Broadway food stores (at 91st, 92nd, 96th, and 110th streets). Russian refugee Murray Klein, who arrived last year without a dime and worked briefly as a bottle sorter at Louis Zabar's 110th Street store, has been assistant manager of the 96th Street store and will eventually be brought in to manage the main store, which he will save from bankruptcy and turn into an emporium for gourmet foods and kitchen tools, selling not only smoked fish, pickled herring, coffee beans, and a few cheeses but also caviar and a vast array of other delicacies not be found elsewhere (except at much higher prices), including a panoply of ready-to-eat dishes (*see* E.A.T. restaurant, 1973).

Britain's first supermarket chain begins operations in September. Premier Supermarkets opens its first store in London's Earl's Court (*see* 1948).

Ergotism breaks out August 12 in the south of France, where people in the town of Pont-Saint-Esprit near Avignon have eaten bread containing illegal amounts of rye flour. Some 300 people are affected by August 20; 31 go mad, some believe that they can fly and plunge off rooftops, and 5 die in the largest epidemic since the Russian outbreak of 1926. French wage levels only now regain their Depression levels of 1938, and the ergotism episode is in part a consequence of heavy dietary reliance on cheap rye bread.

L'École des Trois Gourmandes opens at Paris. The French cooking school for Americans is conducted by Boston cook Julia Child (*née* McWilliams), 39, with French cooks Simone Beck (Simone-Suzanne-Renée-Madeleine Beck-Fischbacher), 47, and Louisette Bertholle (*see* 1961).

Cookbooks: *French Country Cooking* by Elizabeth David; *The South American Gentleman's Companion, An Exotic Cook Book and an Exotic Drinking Book* by Charles H. Baker, Jr. (*see* 1946).

U.S. candy consumption falls to 17.6 pounds per capita while Britons consume 30.1 pounds.

Sears, Roebuck, the largest U.S. retailer, moves to improve the quality of the candy it sells. It works with the National Confectioners Association and with manufacturers of scientific apparatus to come up with recommendations, the trade association helps candy manufacturers set up laboratories and obtain chemists to run them, and Sears then tells confectioners that in 3 years it will specify quality controls just as it specifies ingredient percentages.

The worst floods thus far in U.S. history inundate Kansas and Missouri; 41 die between July 2 and 19, 200,000 are left homeless, property damage reaches $1 billion.

A 2-year drought begins in Australia that will kill off millions of head of livestock and force rationing of butter.

Australian sheep raisers introduce the virus disease myxomatosis, which is endemic in South America, in an effort to kill off the rabbits which are consuming enough grass to feed 40 million sheep (*see* Austin, 1859). The introduction of hawks, weasels, snakes, and other predators has not appreciably reduced the rabbits' numbers, hundreds of thousands of miles of costly rabbit-proof fencing has not stopped them, but rabbits infected with the virus are released, the disease is communicated by mosquitoes and other insects, and in some areas 99 percent of the rabbits are eliminated before natural resistance to myxomatosis becomes dominant (*see* France, 1952).

U.S. Department of Agriculture entomologist Edward F. Knipling, 42, finds a new way to control insect populations biologically rather than chemically; he develops an irradiation method for sterilizing male insects and releases them to mate with females who will die without reproducing (*see* 1954).

British farms have 300,000 tractors, up from 55,000 in 1949.

Kwashiorkor is found to be a worldwide disease among children whose diets were protein deficient in infancy (*see* 1935). It goes by different names in different countries.

The Supreme Court rules in the case of *62 Cases of Jam v. The United States* that "within the understanding of ordinary English speech, a product should be deemed misbranded if it imitates another food, unless its label bear the word 'imitation.' "

Gerber Products starts using MSG (monosodium glutamate) in its baby foods to make them taste better to mothers (*see* MSG, 1934; 1969).

Tropicana Products is founded at Bradentown, Fla., to produce chilled, pasteurized orange and grapefruit juice. Italian-American entrepreneur Anthony T. Rossi, 51, established a business in the late 1940s to pack chilled fruit sections in glass jars and will develop ways to extract juice by varying degrees depending on the quality of the fruit (*see* 1955).

Orangina Co. is incorporated at Boufarik, Algeria (*see* 1936). French artist-designer Bernard Villemot will create his first Orangina poster in 1953, introducing the orange peel as a graphic symbol, and some 50 million bottles of the drink will be sold by 1957 (*see* 1962).

Totino's Italian Kitchen opens in northeast Minneapolis with a $1,500 bank loan obtained by Rose Totino, 37, and her husband, James, to start a pizza parlor, one of the first in the Middle West. They have used their car as collateral, baked a pizza pie for the bank's loan officer, and will pioneer in marketing frozen pizzas (*see* 1962).

Canada's first Dairy Queen opens (*see* 1940). There will be 438 Canadian Dairy Queens by 1993, many of them offering sandwiches and hot food as well as ice cream specialties (*see* Japan, 1972).

Trader Vic's moves from Oakland to San Francisco (*see* 1937). Chef Victor Bergeron, who claims to have invented the Mai Tai cocktail with some Tahitian friends in 1944, continues to work in the kitchen, creating *pupu* platters (appetizers which include spare ribs, fried prawns, crab balls, and sliced pork), Hawaiian luau–style dishes, and other treats that, together with exotic rum drinks, attract enough of the city's social and business elite to keep his tables filled at luncheon and dinner (*see* Los Angeles, 1955).

The Grill Room of London's Café Royal closes (*see* 1897). Italian-born entrepreneur Charles Forte will acquire the restaurant complex in 1954 (*see* Le Relais, 1971).

The London restaurant Mon Plaisir opens in September at 21 Monmouth Street (in the theater district) with a bistro menu: Jean and Georgette Viala offer patrons *soup à l'oignon*, *poireaux vinaigrette*, *baveuse* omelettes, grills with watercress and *frites*, *bœuf bourguignonne*, *côte de veau à l'estragon*, *tête de veau gribiche*, *poulet vinaigre*, *canard au petit pois*, cassoulet, *civet de lièvre* and other game in season, *fromage blanc*, fresh *framboises* in season, and a cheese board. It has no license but will later be licensed to serve wine and beer.

The Good Food Guide by Raymond Postgate is based on restaurant recommendations from readers of the *Leader* (whose editor is Stephen Potter; *see* 1950). It lists more than 500 eating places from Aberdeen to Wembley and will grow to have an annual circulation of 50,000 copies.

The U.S. population reaches 153 million, the USSR has 172 million, China 583 million, India 357, Pakistan 76, Japan 85, Indonesia 78, Britain 50, West Germany 50, Italy 47, France 42, Brazil 52.

1952

War-inflated U.S. food prices are so high that Gen. Dwight D. Eisenhower, 62, uses them as a campaign issue in his successful presidential campaign, but farm prices will fall 22 percent in the next 2 years and food prices will fall as a consequence.

Parma's Barilla brothers suspend bread baking to concentrate entirely on producing durum wheat and egg-based pastas (*see* 1948). At a time when Italy's pastas are still an unbranded commodity, the Barillas pioneer in packaging their products in standard cartons and—using the slogan "Barilla Pasta Makes Every Day a Sunday"—will create a trademarked image that will make Barilla the best-known pasta brand in Italy (*see* 1962).

Hunt Foods buys the Snider Catsup (ketchup) brand name and Snider ketchup plants from General Foods. Norton Simon broadens distribution of the brand (*see* 1946; Wesson Oil and Snowdrift, 1960).

The typical U.S. grocery store now carries about 4,000 different items, up from about 870 in 1928.

1952

By the mid-1960s the grocery will be a supermarket carrying some 8,000 items.

The Volga-Don Ship Canal opens between the Volga and Don Rivers in the Soviet Union. The 62-mile waterway provides a link for the Baltic–Black Sea route.

Nonfiction: *The Concise Encyclopedia of Gastronomy* by André L. Simon; *Townsmen's Food* by English chemist Magnus Pyke, 43.

Cookbooks: *Paris Cuisine* by James Beard (with Alexander Watt); *Solving the High Cost of Eating: A Cookbook to Live By* by Ida Bailey Allen.

New York State repeals its law against selling yellow-colored margarine; other dairy states continue to prohibit its sale (*see* 1943; 1967).

Rabbits infected with myxomatosis are released in France and the disease brings a sharp decrease in the French wild rabbit population (*see* 1951; 1953).

A giant Soviet tree-planting program undertaken by T. D. Lysenko is a fiasco, but Lysenkoism continues to dominate Soviet agriculture (*see* 1948; 1954).

The Declaration of Santiago extends the maritime and fisheries jurisdictions of Chile, Ecuador, and Peru to 200 miles from their coastlines, but the United States maintains her 3-mile limit and most other nations limit their jurisdictions to 12 miles (*see* 1966).

China's cereal grain production rises to 163 million tons, up from 110 million in 1949, but Asia's rice crop falls below the level of prewar harvests while populations have increased by roughly 10 percent from prewar levels (*see* 1956).

Drought reduces U.S. grain harvests. Farmers in Alabama, Georgia, Kentucky, Maine, Massachusetts, South Carolina, and Tennessee are declared eligible for disaster loans August 1, but while the drought will last for 5 years and be even more intense than the one in the 1930s, its effects will be tempered by tree stands planted in the Depression years and by contour plowing and new tilling methods, which combine to conserve available moisture and prevent creation of a new dust bowl (*see* 1953).

Nearly half of U.S. farms have tractors, up from one-quarter in 1940.

Reduce and Stay Reduced by New York City Department of Health physician Norman Jolliffe, 51, gives sound advice on weight maintenance (*see* Weight Watchers, 1963).

No-Cal Ginger Ale, introduced by Kirsch Beverages of Brooklyn, N.Y., uses cyclamates in place of sugar, is the first palatable sugar-free soft drink, and begins a revolution in the beverage industry (*see* cyclamates, 1950). Russian-American Hyman Kirsch, now 75, started a soft drink business in 1904 with a 14-by-30-foot store in Brooklyn's Williamsburg section. Physicians at the Kingsbrook Medical Center he founded asked Kirsch in 1949 to develop a sugar-free, salt-free soft drink for obese, diabetic, and hypertensive patients (*see* Diet-Rite Cola, 1962).

Kellogg's Sugar Frosted Flakes, 29 percent sugar, are introduced by Kellogg Co. (*see* 1950; 1953).

Oh Henry! bars switch from chocolate covering to confectioner's coating (cocoa combined with palm-kernel, coconut, or soybean oil or other vegetable fat in place of, or in addition to, cocoa butter) as its makers try to cut costs.

Pream powdered nondairy creamer for coffee is introduced by M. and R. Dietetic Laboratories, Inc., of Columbus, Ohio. Made of water, hydrogenated palm-kernel oil, sodium caseinate, sugar, dipotassium phosphate, propylenglycol monostearate, polysorbate 60, sterolyle-lactilate, salt, and artificial color and flavor, Pream keeps longer than real cream and costs less (*see* Coffee Rich, 1960; Coffee-Mate, 1961).

Nearly 40 percent of U.S. milk is now sold in waxed paperboard cartons rather than glass bottles (*see* 1936; 1967).

The first Holiday Inn opens on U.S. Route 70 at Memphis with a restaurant on the premises serving meals at reasonable prices.

Howard Johnson opens his 351st restaurant, making his Maine-to-Miami chain the world's largest (*see* 1937). Johnson has added a chain of higher-priced Red Coach Grills, has had 12 years' experience operating 24 eating places on the Pennsylvania Turnpike, wins a franchise to operate 10 restaurants on the new 118-mile New Jersey Turnpike, hires Pavillon restaurant chef Pierre Franey to upgrade

Motorists looked for the orange roof that meant fried clams and twenty-eight flavors of ice cream.

the quality of Howard Johnson dishes, and sells frozen Howard Johnson's specialties through supermarkets (*see* 1960).

The *Guide Kléber* begins publication at Paris under the direction of Reims-born editor Jean Didier, 28, who will compete with the *Guide Michelin*, using a Gallic crowned red rooster in place of Michelin's three stars for restaurants "worth a special trip," a crowned black rooster in place of two stars, a crowned marmite in place of one star, and crossed keys instead of Michelin's crossed spoons and forks for worthy hotels. French tire maker Kléber-Colombes has backed Didier, whose guide has a vermilion cover instead of Michelin's bright red. Their choices will often, but not always, coincide.

1953

✗ Sick and disabled Korean War prisoners are exchanged following the funeral of Soviet premier Josef Stalin, who has died March 5 at age 73. Many U.S. prisoners have died of malnutrition-related diseases because they were unwilling or unable to change their diets and eat the military rations of their captors. Turkish and U.S. prisoners who consume all the food they are issued have much higher survival rates.

$ Former Cargill salesman Dwayne Orville Andreas, 35, of Mankato, Minn., makes a deal to sell Moscow 150 million pounds of butter and the same amount of cottonseed oil. On his first visit to the Soviet Union in April of last year, Andreas was told that the Russians were short of vegetable oils and would be interested in buying from the United States. President Eisenhower favors the deal, Sen. Joseph R. McCarthy, 44 (R. Wis.), approves because it would help his constituents, but the deal comes under attack from U.S. anti-Communists; they note that Russian housewives, who have been paying 13 rubles ($3.25)/lb. for butter, would be able to buy it for 50¢/lb. while Americans pay 80¢ (they ignore the fact that storing surplus butter is costing U.S. taxpayers 67¢/lb. per year). Secretary of Commerce Sinclair Weeks refuses to issue an export license, and Andreas orders his Rotterdam traders to supply the Russians with cottonseed and linseed oil from other sources (much of the stored U.S. butter will turn rancid and be used to make soap) (*see* Andreas, 1966).

Some 63.4 million Americans are gainfully employed by September; unemployment falls to its lowest point since the close of World War II.

Minute Maid Corp. pays its first common stock dividend as orange concentrate sales top $36 million. Minute Maid's profits exceed $1 million (*see* 1949; 1954).

Royal Navy veteran Commander Edward Whitehead, 45, becomes president of Schweppes (USA) and, with Schweppes chairman Sir Frederick Hooper, negotiates a franchise with Pepsi-Cola Co. to bottle Schweppes in America (*see* 1858). Commander Whitehead drops the price 75 percent, despite warnings that he will lose the luxury market if he bottles the drink domestically and reduces its price; advertisements featuring his red-bearded face will help gain a large share of the market for Schweppes Quinine Water (a name used to comply with an FDA order based on the allegation that "Tonic Water" implies therapeutic qualities) (*see* acquisition, 1968).

Processed cheese pioneer James L. Kraft dies at Chicago February 16 at age 78 (*see* 1947). His brother John, who succeeded him as chairman of Kraft Foods in 1951, will be forced out of management and will start a company specializing in vegetarian products such as sesame seeds, which will be sold to the McDonald's chain for use on hamburger buns.

U.S. meatpackers begin moving out of Chicago to plants closer to western feedlots (*see* 1865; 1960; Cudahy, 1950).

Massey-Harris-Ferguson Ltd. is created in August by a merger of the Canadian farm implement company Massey-Harris with Harry Ferguson Co. (*see* 1890; Ferguson, 1938). The company will soon be renamed Massey-Ferguson, although the Massey family sold most of its interest in the company in 1926 and although it now ranks seventh among North American farm equipment makers. Former Kansas farm boy Albert A. Thornbrough, now 40, will become executive vice president in 1956, merge the two companies' distribution systems (which initially will often compete with each other), produce earnings of more than $13 million in 1958 (after losing nearly $5 million in 1957), acquire F. Perkins Ltd. of Peterborough, England, from which it has been buying 160,000 diesel engines per year, double its ownership to 50 percent in France's Standard-Hotchkiss Tractor Co., and make Massey-Ferguson the leading farm equipment company in Britain, France, Scandinavia, Ghana, Kenya, and Sri Lanka by 1962, and third only to John Deere and International Harvester in North America.

Duffy-Mott Co. acquires the Clapp's Baby Foods division of American Home Products, which acquired it from Johnson & Johnson (*see* 1921). Duffy-Mott will increase the Clapp's product line from 37 items to nearly 100 before discontinuing it (*see* Cadbury-Schweppes, 1982).

General Foods acquires Kool-Aid (*see* 1927), which has gained great popularity among children aged 4 to 12. Product envelopes have featured a glass of Kool-Aid and a dish of Kool-Aid-flavored sherbet, but beginning in 1956 they will show a frosted pitcher with a smiling face as General Foods expands the flavor selection to include lemonade and tropical punch, in both presweetened and unsweetened versions.

General Foods (above) sells its Diamond Crystal Salt Co. to Charles F. Moore, a grandson of Diamond Salt's founder, who has headed the GF division since last year (*see* 1886; 1929). Members of his family help Moore buy the assets and return it to private ownership; it will earn more money in its first 3 years under Moore's management than it did in 24 as a General Foods division.

The first underground freezer storage room is opened at Kansas City by local mine operator Leonard Strauss, who sees potential for food storage in the city's mined-out limestone quarries. Strauss employs the constant 45° to 54° F. temperature of the caves to reduce cooling costs, and his room will grow in the next 14 years into the world's largest refrigerated warehouse, handling 8 million pounds per day.

U.S. dairy scientist David D. Peebles develops a process that converts nonfat dry milk into crystals that retain all the protein, mineral, and vitamin content of fresh skim milk (*see* Carnation, 1954).

A plastic valve mechanism for aerosol cans developed by U.S. inventor Robert H. Abplanalp, 30, sharply lowers production costs. The Abplanalp valve will lead to the marketing of countless consumer products propelled by Freon gas from low-cost containers (*see* 1945).

Lawry's Products Co. introduces Lawry's Original Spaghetti Sauce Mix, the first dry seasoning mix to be marketed in a flexible pouch (*see* 1938; 1956).

"We wish to suggest a structure for the salt of deoxyribose nucleic acid (DNA)," begins a one-page article in the April 25 *Nature*. U.S. genetic researcher James Dewey Watson, 25, and English geneticist Francis H. C. Crick, 37, of Cambridge University write, "This structure has novel features that are of considerable biological interest," and in the following (May 30) issue they develop some of the implications of their model, which has the basic structure of a double helix and shows how the genetic material in animal and human cells can duplicate itself. Watson and Crick show that chromosomes consist of long, helical strands of the substance DNA, research studies conducted throughout the world confirm their experiments, and breaking the genetic code that determines the inheritance of all physical characteristics opens possibilities for creating new plant strains that resist disease, discourage pest infestation, and produce foods and vegetables with longer shelf life and better taste (*see* 1926; Ochos, 1955).

Winter storms on the North Sea wreak havoc; Dutch dikes burst February 1, drowning 1,800, leaving 100,000 homeless, and flooding large areas.

French rabbits infected with myxomatosis are released in Britain. The disease will wipe out most of the country's wild rabbits (*see* 1952; 1954).

 Soviet party leader Nikita Khrushchev, 59, defies warnings by agronomists that rainfall in the Kazakhstan Soviet Republic is undependable. He orders virgin lands in Kazakhstan to be plowed and planted with grain that will increase Soviet food production (*see* 1963).

Drought worsens in the U.S. Midwest; sections of 13 states are declared disaster areas (*see* 1952). Southern Missouri has an even dryer season than in 1936, pastures are dead to the grass roots, and farmers dump cattle on the market at sacrifice prices.

University of Minnesota physiologist Ancel Keys, 49, points out a correlation between coronary heart disease and diets high in animal fats, observing that the incidence of heart disease tends to be higher in communities where animal fats constitute a large part of people's diets (*see* 1957; Anichkov, 1913).

The Du Pont (Pennington) weight-loss diet issued by U.S. physician Alfred W. Pennington is one of many variations on the low-carbohydrate, high-fat "Eskimo" diet. Pennington has helped portly E. I. du Pont de Nemours executives lose weight (*see* Stefansson, 1946; Taller, 1961; Stillman, 1967).

Researchers at Basel, Switzerland, synthesize carotene, the provitamin of vitamin A, from acetone and acetylene (*see* 1920; Khorana, 1959).

The U.S. Food and Drug Administration (FDA) is placed in the new Department of Health, Education and Welfare.

Some 93 Japanese will be fatally poisoned in the next 7 years as a result of eating fish and shellfish contaminated with mercury wastes discharged into rivers at Minamata Bay in Kyushu and at Niigata in Honshu. Many more will go blind, lose the use of limbs, or suffer brain damage from mercury poisoning (*see* Huckleby family, 1969).

Sugar Smacks breakfast food, introduced by Kellogg, is 56 percent sugar (*see* 1952; 1955).

Sara Lee Kitchens proves that properly frozen baked goods can be marketed successfully. Sara Lee Cheese Cake has been selling at 79 cents since 1949, and sales have mushroomed (*see* 1956).

Cheez Whiz, introduced by Kraft nationwide July 1, is a stable processed cheese sauce (cheese, water, whey, sodium phosphate, milk fat, skim milk, salt, Worcestershire Sauce, mustard flour, lactic and sorbic acid, and coloring) in a jar designed by technicians originally to simplify making Welsh rabbit (which Americans insist on calling "Welsh rarebit") (*see* Velveeta, 1928). A survey of housewives has turned up more than 1,304 possible uses for the product, including macaroni and cheese, crackers and cheese, vegetables covered with cheese, cheeseburgers, and cheese dogs (hot dogs with cheese sauce), but the chief market will be in Puerto Rico, where Cheez Whiz will be combined with mayonnaise and Spam to create La Mexda.

A 98¢ frozen "TV Dinner"—turkey, cornbread dressing, gravy, peas topped with butter, whipped sweet potatoes flavored with orange juice and butter—on a three-section aluminum tray is introduced in December by C. A. Swanson & Sons of Omaha, which is now run by Carl Swanson's sons Gilbert and Charles and which 2 years ago began selling frozen chicken, beef, and turkey pot pies (*see* 1945). Swanson's food technologist Betty Cronin will be credited with having created TV Dinners, but the sweet potatoes in her turkey dinner turn watery and are quickly replaced with regular potatoes. Turkey, which will remain the most popular, is soon followed by fried chicken (which comes with a brownie but also has initial problems) and Salisbury steak. The products will presently sell for as little as 69¢ and suit the needs of working mothers burdened with baby-boom offspring, but Cronin's innovation will be blamed for dooming the family dinner as various family members opt for various TV Dinner choices (*see* Campbell, 1955).

J. R. Simplot introduces frozen french-fried potatoes on a commercial basis (*see* 1942). Simplot has built a canning and dehydration quick-freeze plant and will soon be supplying fries to McDonald's and other fast-food restaurants (*see* 1983).

Margaret Rudkin introduces a line of Pepperidge Farm butter cookies, withdraws them from the market within a few months, will find better cookies on a trip to Europe, and will enter in an agreement with the Belgian firm Delacre Cie. (*see* 1947; 1955).

White Rose Redi-Tea, introduced by New York's Seeman Brothers, is the world's first instant iced tea (*see* 1901; Lipton, 1958).

"Irish Coffee" is introduced at San Francisco's Buena Vista Café at the foot of Hyde Street Hill on the Beach Street cable line. *Chronicle* columnist Stanton Delaplane, 45, discovered the mixture of coffee, cream, sugar, and Irish whiskey in Ireland; he has given the recipe to proprietors Jack Koeppler and George Freedberg, and the drink soon accounts for 40 percent of Buena Vista's business.

U.S. pizzerias grow to number at least 15,000, and there are at least 100,000 stores where ready-made refrigerated or frozen pizzas may be purchased (*see* oregano, 1948). The Americanized pizza pies are thin, round layers of bread dough laden with tomato paste, mozzarella cheese, olive oil, pepper, and oregano; optional extras may include anchovies, eggs, mushrooms, onions, or sausages; the pizzas are baked on bricks or in metal ovens; and a few pizzerias offer the Sicilian pizza (baked in a pan and slightly thicker and more breadlike).

The Denny's fast-food restaurant chain has its beginnings in Danny's Donuts, opened at Lakewood, Calif., by entrepreneur Harold Butler, who tells his investors, "We're going to serve the best cup of coffee; make the best doughnuts; give the best service; keep everything spotless; offer the best value; and stay open 24 hours a day." By year's end the shop has earned $120,000, more Danny's Donuts have opened, the menu has grown to include sandwiches, the name will be changed next year to Danny's Coffee Shops, and in 1959 it will become Denny's Restaurants. Nearly 80 Denny's will be operating by the end of 1963, and none will serve doughnuts (*see* 1967).

The Newarker restaurant opens at Newark (N.J.) Airport under the direction of Restaurant Associates, headed by Jerome Brody, 25. Brody's father-in-law, Abraham Wechsler of the Wechsler Coffee Co., which supplies hotels and restaurants, acquired half ownership of a cafeteria chain in lieu of payment of overdue bills, and Brody has hired Joseph Baum, 33, to run the Newarker. Its kitchen is tiny, but Baum has retained Swiss chef Albert Stockli and dazzles patrons with oversize portions (e.g., seven oysters instead of the usual six and "three-clawed" lobsters); huge Absecon oysters (from an island off Atlantic City); flambéed dishes such as shashlik and steak chunks prepared tableside; and brandied coffee. The Newarker loses $25,000 its first year as three plane crashes force closings of the airport but attracts a following of suburban New Jersey residents and launches Restaurant Associates on the path to success (*see* Forum of the Twelve Caesars, 1957).

New Orleans's Bon Ton Café, opened at 401 Magazine Street by Alvin and Alzina Pierce of Bayou Lafource, pioneers Cajun cooking in the Crescent City (*see* 1784). The Pierces use recipes for crawfish, bread pudding, and other dishes passed on through their families (*see* 1979).

The suburban Paris restaurant Camelia at 7, quai Georges Clemenceau in Bougival is acquired by chef-*pâtissier* Jean Delaveyne. An auberge since 1820, it is where Alexandre Dumas *fils* met Marie ("Alfonsine") Duplessix, who became "La Dame aux camélias" in the 1848 novel and Violetta in the 1853 Verdi opera *La Traviata*. Delaveyne is an *ouvrier de France* who pioneers "la nouvelle cuisine française," steaming fish and meat and cooking vegetables briefly with a minimum of liquid. His brigade of 14 cooks serves 50 patrons at luncheon and dinner, preparing woodcock, *pigeonne* (squab), *salade d'écrevisse à pimprenelle* (crayfish), filet of turbot *au savayon l'oseille* (with sorrel), filet of John Dory with lobster mousse and sauce américaine, *tarte des mademoiselles Tatin*, and *rabelotte de poire en sorbet* (pear sherbet with caramel sauce).

The management of London's Gore Hotel at 189 Queen's Gate celebrates the coronation of Elizabeth II by opening an Elizabethan Room serving a meal from the time of Elizabeth I, with patrons sitting on wooden benches at huge oaken refectory tables and eating with pewter utensils from wooden trenchers a feast of two "removes" featuring boar's heads, stuffed peacock breast, lampreys, wild spinach, artichoke pies, and salmagundian syllabub. Rushes are strewn on the floor of the candlelit room, troubadours in costume sing with stringed instruments, and low-bodiced serving wenches wait on the tables, serving guests mead, ale, and claret in mugs. The hotel, which also has a formal dining room serving French dishes, will continue its Eliza-bethan Room for years.

1954

The U.S. Department of Agriculture fires its attaché at Tokyo because he does not meet "security requirements." Russian-American agricultural economist Wolf Isaac Ladejinsky, 55, had charge of Japanese land reform under Gen. Douglas MacArthur, his only interest in revolution is in a green one, and he will have reservations about that (*see* 1970). The government will admit its error, and Ladejinsky will work on land reform in south Vietnam at the urging of President Eisenhower.

French Radical-Socialist party leader Pierre Mendès-France, 47, becomes prime minister June 12 but will serve only until February of next year before his government falls. Frenchmen will remember him as the premier who urged his countrymen to drink more milk (his native province of Normandy is dairy country) and less wine.

Boston candy maker Robert Welch put his brother's company chemists and technicians to work finding a less expensive but satisfactory replacement for cocoa as prices of that commodity soared, and the company turns out 1,250,000 bars (and boxes) per day at Cambridge plus another 200,000 at Los Angeles, but Welch, who failed to gain the Republican gubernatorial nomination in Massachusetts 4 year ago, has turned his attention to writing a book, which is published under the title *The Life of John Birch* (Birch was a World War II intelligence officer who was shot and bayoneted to death at age 27 by Chinese Communists on August 25, 1945, while on a reconnaisance mission with some Nationalist Chinese) (*see* John Birch Society, 1958).

Britain finally ends all food rationing after 5 years of gradual decontrol. Meat is the last item to come off rationing.

Congress acts to relieve world hunger and put a prop under U.S. farm prices. The Agricultural Trade and Development Act (Public Law 480) signed into law by President Eisenhower July 10 empowers the Department of Agriculture to buy surplus wheat, butter, cheese, dry skim milk, vegetable oils, and other surplus foods for donation abroad, for barter, or to sell for native currency. P.L. 480 protects U.S. farmers from world market collapse (*see* agriculture, below).

U.S. October food prices: round steak 92¢/lb, up from 45¢ in 1944; sugar 52¢ per five-pound bag, up from 34¢; bread 17¢ per one-pound loaf, up from 9¢; coffee $1.10/lb, up from 30¢; eggs 60¢/doz., down from 64¢; milk 45¢ per half gallon, up from 29¢; butter 72¢/lb., up from 50¢; lettuce 19¢/head, up from 12¢ (*see* 1964).

Consolidated Foods Corp. is founded by Nathan Cummings, whose Consolidated Grocers Co. has acquired a number of minor food producers (*see* 1951). Consolidated Foods will grow by the mid-1960s into a manufacturing, marketing, and retailing business embracing some 43 companies with 14 processing units, 46 plants, 4 wholesale distribution units, 23 supply centers, 4 retail chains containing about 610 stores, and combined sales worldwide of $634 million (*see* Ocoma, 1955).

Minute Maid Corp. attains a sales volume of $100 million by paying $40 million to acquire the Snow Crop division of Clinton Foods (*see* 1947; 1953). The acquisition gives Minute Maid a complete line of frozen fruits, vegetables, fish, poultry, and various prepared foods in addition to Snow Crop's citrus concentrates, but Minute Maid will start losing money on Snow Crop in a year as private-label competition becomes stronger in the growing frozen food industry (*see* Seabrook, 1957).

Libby, McNeill & Libby acquires Florida Citrus Growers Corp. to expand its operations into canned and frozen citrus juices (*see* 1933; 1958).

California's Korbel winery is acquired by Adolph, Paul, and Ben Heck, whose ancestors were Alsatian wine growers (*see* 1862).

The Food and Drug Administration approves use of the synthetic antioxidant BHT (butylated hydroxytoluene) in U.S. foods. The additive will be widely employed to avoid rancidity and the breakdown of fatty acids and ascorbic acid (vitamin C) in many food products. It is just as effective as BHA, introduced in 1947, but is much cheaper.

A breakthrough in wheat genetics achieved by University of Missouri plant geneticist Ernest Robert Sears, 44, does for wheat genetics what Russia's Dmitri Mendeleev did for chemistry in 1870. Sears shows that specific chromosomes in wheat can be substituted to achieve desired changes, and he raises hopes for new hybrid wheat strains that will raise yields and will increase resistance to disease and drought.

Tiny cobs of corn dating to 5000 B.C. are found in the valley of Tehuacan southeast of Mexico City—the first wild corn ever discovered that can seed itself.

Cornell University agriculture professor emeritus Liberty Hyde Bailey dies at Ithaca, N.Y., December 25 at age 96 (*see* 1905). He has worked to establish extension courses in agriculture for farm men and women.

Cookbooks: *Italian Food* by Elizabeth David; *Famous Florida Recipes* by *Miami Herald* food editor Jeanne Voltz (*née* Appleton), 33; *The Complete Book of Barbecue and Rotisserie Cooking*, *Fish Cookery*, *The Complete Book for Entertaining*, and *How to Eat Better for Less Money* by James Beard; *Serve at Once: The Soufflé Cook Book* by New York author Myra Waldo.

Duncan Hines makes his first trip to Europe and asserts upon his return that American food is better than European (*see* 1950; 1957).

Congress passes a Watershed and Flood Prevention Act to protect farmers from water erosion.

Britain's wild rabbits near extinction, with the myxomatosis virus affecting some 90 percent of burrows in southern England alone (*see* 1953). Farmers say that rabbits have been destroying £50 million worth of food crops each year and that the virus is of vital importance for pest control, but scientists warn that the epidemic, if left unchecked, will badly damage the balance of nature.

Lake Erie produces 75 million pounds of commercial fish and remains relatively unpolluted.

President Eisenhower speaks out against agricultural price supports January 11, blaming them for overproduction and resultant surplus problems. He urges that the current carryover be set aside as an emergency reserve, that a modern parity system be instituted beginning in 1956, and that acreage and marketing quotas be continued (*see* P.L. 480, above).

A United Nations Food and Agriculture Organization (FAO) conference at Washington, D.C., ends March 21 with a statement that the long-range answer to farm surpluses lies in increased consumption, not production cuts. "Free-market prices might not be an adequate instrument for regulating supply and demand, particularly for those commodities which do not respond much to price changes. Serious hardships to all sections of the economy and social problems could be caused if farm incomes were left solely to the free play of market forces."

Nikita Khrushchev orders large-scale planting of new hybrid grain varieties in the Soviet Union, overriding Lysenkoite objections (*see* 1952; 1959).

A test program using sterilized males wipes out screwworm flies on the Caribbean island of Curaçao in 4 months (*see* Knipling, 1951).

Molybdenum is identified as an important nutritional trace element. The mineral is contained in the human enzyme xanthine oxidase, needed to convert purines into uric acid.

Let's Eat Right to Keep Fit by California nutrition evangelist (Daisy) Adelle Davis, 50, declares that fertile eggs are superior to infertile ones, opposes pasteurization of milk, and recommends dangerously high daily doses of vitamins A, D, and E (her fellow students at Purdue University in 1922 called her "Vitamin Davis" because of her obsession with the subject). By no means a qualified nutritionist (her 1927 bachelor's degree from the University of California at Berkeley was in household science, although she did later obtain a master's degree in biochemistry at the University of Southern California), Davis is the author of *Let's Cook It Right* (1947) and *Let's Have Healthy Children* (1951), and although her books are full of factual errors (many of the sources she cites will prove to have been misquoted or taken out of context) they will sell in the millions of copies (mostly in paperback), contributing to the phenomenal growth of the health food movement, which thrives on stories of pesticide residues and food additives, and the diet supplement industry, which thrives on the fallibility of physicians and the fact that so many Americans, being unable to afford proper medical advice, turn to self-help books of dubious merit. Davis will claim (falsely) that magnesium alone offers a useful treatment for epilepsy, that nephrosis patients should take potassium chloride, and that fluoridation of community drinking water poses a serious health risk.

Congress passes a pesticides amendment to the 1938 Food, Drug and Cosmetics Act requiring that pesticide makers show their data to the Food and Drug Administration as well as to the Department of Agriculture (*see* 1947).

A British group established by the minister of agriculture and the Ministries of Fisheries, Health, and Food reports no direct evidence of human illness arising from pesticide residues in foods but recommends appointment of an advisory committee to keep the situation under scrutiny in light of the fact that new and possibly dangerous compounds are being introduced at a growing rate.

Britain permits antibiotic feed supplements after tests confirm their value and show no undesirable effects. U.S. livestock producers use $50 million worth of the supplements per year.

British bakers introduce the first wrapped and sliced Hovis bread (*see* 1918; Hovis-McDougall, 1957).

Trix breakfast food, introduced by General Mills, is 46.6 percent sugar (*see* 1941; 1958).

Butterball turkeys are introduced by Swift-Eckrich Co., which has developed a device called a bar strap to obviate the need for skewers or trussing.

Cleveland's Stouffer family opens a frozen-food-processing plant on Woodland Avenue to produce frozen dinners for sale at supermarkets (*see* restaurant, 1924). Manager Wally Blankinship of the chain's Shaker Square restaurant has seen an upsurge in take-out orders and decided to freeze some of his most popular meals for sale at an adjoining retail store (*see* Swanson, 1945; Nestlé, 1973).

Mars, Inc. introduces M&M Peanut Chocolate Candies.

Hershey Chocolate reduces the size of its nickel Hershey Bar in March to ⅞ oz. but restores it to 1 oz. in June (*see* 1947; 1958).

Carnation Co. introduces instant nonfat dry milk, using a revolutionary process (*see* 1906; Peebles, 1953; Contadina, 1963).

The Philadelphia restaurant Coventry Forge Inn opens May 30 at Pottstown on Route 7, one mile west of Routes 100 and 23. Proprietor Wallis Callahan, 27, has a kitchen hand, Peter von Stark, formerly of Le Beau Manière in the south of France, who will go on to open La Panatière at 1523 Walnut Street (between 15th and 16th streets), bringing in as his chef Georges Perrier, who has worked under Fernand Point at La Pyramide (*see* Le Bec-Fin, 1969).

The New York restaurant–ice cream parlor Serendipity opens in a $550-per-month East 58th Street storefront (it will move in September 1959 to 225 East 60th Street) with six tables and 15 seats. Partners Preston "Patch" Caradine, 29 (who has come up with the name, taken from the crossword puzzle in the *Times* of London, and introduced southern family recipes from his native Arkansas), Stephen Bruce, and Calvin L. Holt, 29, have pooled $500 to start the place, which serves Aunt Buba's sand tarts, pecan cookies, and other treats that will attract celebrities, tourists, and local residents, especially those with children. It will be best known for its frozen hot chocolate blend.

New Orleans restaurateur Owen Brennan refuses his landlord's demand that he be given 50 percent of the business as a condition of renewing his lease and leases a building at 417 Royal Street (*see* 1946; 1955).

McDonald's begins the proliferation that will make it the world's largest food service company (*see* 1948). Milk shake machine salesman Ray A. Kroc, 52, receives such a large order from the California hamburger chain that he flies out to investigate, persuades Richard and Maurice MacDonald to sell him franchise rights, and will soon have hamburger stands with golden arches opening everywhere. Son

Ray Kroc saw a golden future in golden arches and made his vision come to fruition.

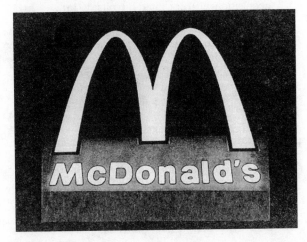

of an unsuccessful real estate man whose family came from Bohemia, Kroc spent 17 years with the Lily Tulip Co. and became sales manager for the Middle West before becoming a salesman for milk shake machines (*see* 1955).

The first Burger King hamburger stand opens at 3090 NW 36th Street, Miami, Fla., selling burgers and milkshakes at 18¢ each (the Whopper sandwich, introduced in 1957, will initially sell for 37¢). Founders James McLamore and David Edgerton have had extensive restaurant experience and decided, jointly, to offer reasonably priced food, clean and attractive surroundings, and fast service. McLamore tells his people, "There are only two things our customers have, time and money—and they don't like spending either of them, so we better sell them their hamburgers quickly." Franchisees will build Burger King into a worldwide chain with more outlets than any competitor except McDonald's (above; *see* 1967).

J. Lyons & Co. unveils Britain's first Wimpy hamburger bar at the Ideal Home Exhibition in London (its name is derived from a cartoon character in the 29-year-old comic strip "Popeye" who gets his strength from hamburgers the way Popeye gets his from spinach). The U.S. owner of a small Wimpy chain has sold Lyons on the possibilities of the idea in London, it meets with such success at the exhibition that Lyons opens one in its Oxford Corner House, Lyons and the U.S. owner agree to franchise additional outlets, and by 1972 there will be 573 Wimpy Bars in the United Kingdom, plus 321 more in 29 European and African countries (*see* Lyons acquisitions, 1972; United Biscuits, 1976).

The Shakey's pizza parlor chain has its beginnings in a Sacramento, Calif., pizzeria opened by local entrepreneur Sherwood "Shakey" Johnson and his wartime buddy Edward Plummer, who invest $850 each to start the place. Franchised pizza parlors will make Johnson and Plummer millionaires (*see* 1953; 1958).

1955

✊ Mao Zedong proposes rapid collectivization of Chinese agriculture (*see* 1950). Other leaders fear a repetition of the Soviet Union's experience in the late 1920s and early '30s, but Mao prevails and peasants who resist will be liquidated (*see* 1956).

💲 The National Farmers Organization (NFO), founded by farmers from northwest Missouri and southwest Iowa, will engage in collective bargaining in livestock, grain, and milk nationwide. The farmers have been disgruntled by livestock prices that are lower than their production costs.

A contract signed with American Can and Continental Can August 13 wins the United Steel Workers the first 52-week guaranteed annual wage in any major U.S. industry.

Duncan Hines cake mix sales (180 million packages) constitute two-thirds of total sales for Nebraska Consolidated Mills (*see* 1951), but freight costs squeeze profits, annual advertising costs approach the company's total net worth (nearly $4 million), and the quality of competitors' cake mixes now rivals that of the Duncan Hines mix (*see* Procter & Gamble, 1956).

🤝 Continental Baking acquires Morton Packing Co. and will make it the largest U.S. producer of pot pies, fruit pies, cream pies, and frozen bread dough (*see* Continental, 1930; Morton, 1940). Morton will also produce TV dinners, casseroles, cakes, sweet goods, English muffins, and other products (*see* ITT, 1968).

Campbell Soup Co. enters the frozen food business by acquiring control of C. A. Swanson & Sons, originator of the "TV Dinner" (*see* 1954). Campbell will expand the Swanson line of 11 prepared frozen items to 65 items in the next 17 years.

Campbell Soup Co. acquired Swanson's to capitalize on the growing market for TV dinners. PHOTO COURTESY CAMPBELL SOUP CO.

Consolidated Foods acquires Ocoma Foods of Omaha, Nebr., to enter the frozen poultry parts, frozen prepared foods, and butter businesses (*see* 1954). By year's end Consolidated's 15 wholesalers and processors have combined assets of $78 million and annual sales of $225 million, figures that will soon be dwarfed as Nathan Cummings continues to expand (*see* Sara Lee, 1956).

Pet Milk acquires Pet-Ritz Foods (*see* 1947; frozen pie crusts, 1962).

Corn Products Refining Co. acquires the chocolate-flavored milk supplement Bosco and Kasco dog food to supplement its Argo starch, Mazola corn oil, and Karo syrup (*see* 1923; Knorr, 1957).

Best Foods acquires Rosefield Packing Co. and its Skippy Peanut Butter brand (*see* 1932; Corn Products Refining Co., 1958).

Beatrice Foods acquires D. L. Clark Co. of Pittsburgh, maker of the popular Clark candy bar.

President Eisenhower submits a 10-year, $101 billion highway program to Congress (*see* 1956).

Tropicana's Anthony Rossi builds a port at Cape Canaveral, Fla. (*see* 1951). Unable to expand his fleet of trucks for shipping chilled orange juice to northern markets, Rossi buys an 8,000-ton ship with stainless steel tanks, builds a bottling plant at Whitestone, Queens, and begins sending juice north by ship, a practice which he will later abandon in favor of rail and truck shipment (*see* Seagram, 1988).

Spanish-born New York University biochemist Severo Ochoa, 49, announces the synthesis of ribonucleic acid (RNA), a basic constituent of all living tissues. It is a giant step toward the creation of life in the laboratory out of inert materials (*see* Watson and Crick, 1953).

Cookbooks: *Summer Cooking* by Elizabeth David; *The Casserole Cookbook* and *The Complete Book of Outdoor Cookery* (with Helen Evans Brown) by James Beard.

Gorton's of Gloucester moves into a new $1.5 million freezing plant it has leased at Gloucester, Mass. The 200-year-old firm begins producing frozen fish sticks and frozen fish dinners to supplement its traditional codfish cake business (*see* General Mills, 1968).

Dwarf Indica rice, introduced into Taiwan (Formosa), is higher yielding than most varieties but requires lots of fertilizer and insecticides.

Hurricane Janet hits Grenada in the British West Indies, destroying 75 percent of the island's nutmeg trees (*see* 1858). Grenada's trees have long supplied 40 percent of world nutmeg and mace production, the only other major source is the tiny island of Siaoe north of the Celebes, whose shipments are delayed by troubles in Indonesia, and since it takes 2 months for the nutmeg to reach Singapore and another 2 to reach New York, the price of nutmeg rises from 35¢/lb. to over $2.

Clove trees in Zanzibar suffer from fungus disease carried by ants, which may find opportunity in the wounds inflicted on the trees in harvesting. Unskilled natives strip off hard-to-reach branches, and it often takes years for the trees to recover.

Annual world consumption of vanilla beans reaches about 700 tons. The finest vanilla comes from Mexico's Mazatlán Valley, where it is cultivated by descendants of the Aztecs, but the islands of Madagascar, Réunion, and Comoro supply about 80 percent of U.S. imports, with some beans coming also from Tahiti, Java, and South America (*see* 1836).

A USDA survey finds that one-tenth of U.S. families live on nutritionally "poor" diets, a healthy improvement over 1943 findings.

British biochemist Dorothy Hodgkin discovers the composition of vitamin B_{12} (cyanocobalamin), raising hopes that the vitamin can be synthesized for low-cost treatment of pernicious anemia and other deficiency diseases (*see* 1948).

Health food advocate–publisher Bernarr MacFadden dies at Jersey City, N.J., October 12 at age 87.

Britain's first fluoridation of community drinking water begins November 17 in Anglesey (*see* 1945).

Special K breakfast food, introduced by Kellogg, is 4.4 percent sugar (*see* 1953; 1958).

Margaret Rudkin introduces a new line of Pepperidge Farm cookies under names such as Bordeaux, Lido, Milano, and Orléans (*see* 1953). The line will be expanded to include variations such as Hazelnut, Mint Milano, Double Chocolate Milano,

Hazelnut Milano, Oatmeal-Raisin, and Shortbread (*see* Campbell, 1961).

Coca-Cola Company uses the name "Coke" officially for the first time (*see* 1945; Minute Maid, 1960; Tab, 1963).

Ray Kroc opens his first McDonald's hamburger stand April 15 at Des Plaines, Ill., northwest of Chicago, selling hamburgers for 15¢, french fries for 10¢, and milkshakes for 20¢; he opens two more, both in California, and by 1959 he will have 100 such outlets as he seeks out managers skilled at personal relations (*see* 1954; 1961).

Colonel Sanders' Kentucky Fried Chicken has its beginnings as Corbin, Ky., restaurateur Harland Sanders, 65, travels the country in an old car loaded with pots and pans and a "secret blend of herbs and

Colonel Sanders called his Kentucky Fried Chicken "finger-lickin' good" and franchised the name.

spices" looking for prospective licensees. The roadside restaurant he ran for 25 years has been ruined by a new highway that diverted traffic from his location, his only income is a $105 monthly Social Security check, but Sanders will franchise hundreds of "finger-lickin' good" fast-food operators in the next 9 years and receive 3 percent of their gross sales in return for use of his name, spices, milk and egg dip, gravy mix, and paper supplies (*see* 1964).

Lum's has its beginnings in a Miami Beach frankfurter stand that will grow into a chain of more than 390 restaurants in the United States, the Caribbean, Spain, and West Germany. Local attorney Clifford Perlman, 29, will buy the 41st Street stand, which specializes in steamed frankfurters in beer, and by 1961 he will have four Lum's stands in Miami Beach.

Fernand Point of the Restaurant de la Pyramide at Vienne dies at his gastronomic mecca March 4 at age 58 (*see* 1923). His widow, Dominique ("Mado"), will continue until her death in 1986 to operate the ultimate expression of France's *haute cuisine* (*see* 1987).

London's Connaught Hotel opens a Grill Room with 44 seats May 2 (*see* 1935).

New York's Fifth Avenue Hotel advertises luncheon at $1, dinner up to $2.75, Sunday brunch $1.65. The Hampshire House on Central Park South advertises a prix fixe luncheon at $3.50.

Trader Vic's opens a Los Angeles restaurant at the Beverly Hilton, 9876 Wilshire Boulevard, Beverly Hills, with executive chef Ping Lee presiding over the Chinese oven, which cooks squabs, steaks, lamb chops (filled with Chinese black bean paste), and racks of Indonesian-style lamb (marinated for 24 hours in a honey-and-lemon-juice mixture and filled with peach chutney), saté of lamb chunks skewered with pineapple, suspended by hooks over the fire (*see* 1951). The French-Chinese-Polynesian cuisine also includes New York–cut steaks with Malagasy peppercorn butter; barbecued suckling pig (for parties of 15 or more on 1 week's notice); barbecued pork marinated in pineapple juice and served with chutney inside a slice of pineapple; barbecued salmon with a creamy caper sauce; grilled mahimahi with a lemon-and-macadamia-nut sauce; oysters on the half shell topped with crabmeat; Cosmo salad with sliced mushrooms and artichokes on limestone lettuce; rum ice cream with a praline sauce; banana fritters; and Chinese gooseberries with sour cream and brown sugar for dipping. Victor Bergeron's success will lead him to open Trader Vic restaurants in Bangkok, Singapore, Tokyo, London, and Hamburg as well as in New York (where it will replace the Plaza Hotel's Rendez-Vous for about 25 years), Chicago, and other major U.S. cities.

New Orleans restaurateur Owen Brennan invites favored patrons to join him in November for the official opening of his bar in the carriageway of the building he is redecorating for his restaurant, scheduled to reopen next spring. Brennan dies of a heart attack November 4 at age 45, leaving his sister Ella, now 30 and supervisor of his kitchen, to carry on the management. Specializing in luxurious breakfasts and brunches, she will continue for decades to make Brennan's a New Orleans landmark (*see* Commander Palace, 1974).

1956

✕ British paratroops land at Port Said November 5 to recover control of the Suez Canal that Prime Minister Anthony Eden, 59, says is vital if his country is not to starve. U.N. forces arrive November 15, the last Anglo-French forces leave Port Said December 22, and a U.N. fleet begins clearing the canal of scuttled ships December 27.

✊ Chinese authorities force some 100 million peasant families into large collective farms called Agricultural Producers' Cooperatives (*see* 1955). Millions of Chinese will be killed in the next few years for resisting collectivization.

Poland ends efforts to collectivize agriculture after a decade marked by little success. Communist party leader Władysław Gomułka, 51, reverses collectivization policies.

💲 President Eisenhower proposes a soil bank plan to ease the problem of declining U.S. farm income in a special January 9 message to Congress. Congress votes May 28 to authorize a program to pay farmers for withdrawing land from production (*see* AAA, 1938).

India receives a $300 million food loan August 29 to buy surplus U.S. farm products that are depressing domestic American prices (*see* P.L. 480, 1954).

Welch's grape juice has sales of $40 million for the year (*see* 1945). Jacob Kaplan sells it to the National Grape Co-Operative Association, whose 4,500 grape grower members become the first farmers in history to own an international business.

🤝 Procter & Gamble acquires the Duncan Hines Cake Mix division of Nebraska Consolidated Mills, giving that company an after-tax profit of nearly $1 million (*see* 1955). P&G makes its first entry into the prepared cake mix business; NCM, having established a new national brand in the food business, will later become a major player in the business of consumer food labels but meanwhile will build a business in poultry processing and livestock and poultry feed while expanding its milling business (*see* ConAgra, 1971).

General Baking Co. (later General Host Corp.) acquires Van de Kamp Baking Co. in August (*see* 1918). Lawrence L. Frank, now 69, remains with Van de Kamp, whose annual sales have risen to $36 million, and will continue as chairman of the board of Lawry's Products Co., headed by his son Richard N., until his death in 1970 (*see* 1953; 1958).

Procter & Gamble (above) acquires W. T. Young Co., manufacturer of Big Top Peanut Butter (*see* Jif, 1958).

Consolidated Foods acquires Sara Lee Kitchens and will expand Sara Lee's line of frozen foods to include fruit pies, Bavarian cream pies, dinner rolls in transparent oven baking bags, ravioli, lasagna, beef stroganoff, chicken and noodles au gratin, beef-and-pepper stew, etc. (*see* Lubin, 1949; Consolidated, 1955; Lawson, 1959).

Beech-Nut Packing Co. merges with Life Savers to create Beech-Nut Life Savers. Beech-Nut has sold chewing gum since 1910 and candy-coated Beechies chewing gum since 1933 (*see* 1920; 1928; 1931).

Stokely–Van Camp acquires Pomona Products Co. of Griffin, Ga., which packs Sunshine brand pimento peppers and other foods (*see* 1939; 1962).

Brown-Forman pays $18.5 million in cash to acquire Jack Daniel's whiskey from owners who include the heirs of Lem Motlow, whose Uncle Jack first made the Tennessee whiskey in 1866. Lynchburg, Tenn., has been dry since 1909, but the product enjoys wide popularity elsewhere.

 The Federal Aid Highway Act passed by Congress June 29 authorizes construction of a 42,500-mile network of roads to link major U.S. urban centers. Some 38,000 miles of the Interstate Highway System will be open by 1976, enabling trucks to carry foodstuff shipments once reserved for rail and barge carriers.

 U.S. canners ship 700 million cases of food, up from 400 million in 1940.

Frozen food pioneer Clarence Birdseye dies in his Gramercy Park Hotel suite at New York October 7 at age 69 (see 1929). He has developed an anhydrous method of taking the water out of food (four servings of dehydrated food can be carried in a container no larger than a cigarette package) as well as infrared heat lamps that are widely used in industry.

Rock paintings found 900 miles southeast of Algiers establish that the Sahara was once fertile land. A French archaeologist dates the paintings in the Tibesti Mountains to 3500 B.C.

Cookbook: *The Constance Spry Cookery Book* by English cooking school owner Spry with Rosemary Hume.

La Leche League International, Inc., has its beginnings in the Chicago suburb of Franklin Park, Ill., where Marian (Mrs. Clement R.) Tompson and Mary (Mrs. Gregory) White have mastered the technique of breast-feeding. Mrs. Tompson, the wife of a research engineer, ran into problems trying to breast-feed her first three children and was told each time by a physician to put the baby on the bottle. Mrs. White's husband, a physician, was taught nothing about breast-feeding in medical school. The two women determined to learn everything they could about breast-feeding, which was once an almost universal practice but is now used by only about 22 percent of U.S. mothers, down from 38 percent 10 years ago, partly because more mothers are in the workforce and find it difficult to accommodate breast-feeding on demand in their schedules. When Tompson and White nurse their babies in public at a fashionable North Side picnic, other women gather around admiringly. Atmospheric testing of nuclear weapons has produced radioactive fallout which has fallen on the grass and been consumed by cows, whose milk may contain six times as much strontium-90 as human milk, but mother's milk has numerous other advantages over milk from cows, goats, ewes, and mares. Tompkins and White have organized a meeting to discuss ways and means to encourage other mothers to breast-feed and instruct them in that "womanly art." They have enlisted the support of pediatricians, obstetricians, allergists, and other medical specialists who share their belief in the value of breast-feeding. Since the Virgin Mary's Spanish title is *Nuestra Señora de la Leche y Buen Parto* ("Our Lady of the Milk and Good Delivery") and Spanish wet nurses are called *madres de la leche*, the women call their information-dispensing organization La Leche League, but women in lower socioeconomic classes will continue to consider bottle-feeding more "modern" and convenient (the incidence of breast-feeding in the United States will decline to 18 percent in the next 10 years before recovering) (see La Leche League International, 1976).

A British survey shows that 6 of 10 Englishmen still eat their midday meals at home. Two out of three families eat potatoes at midday, and more than half the population enjoys roast beef or roast lamb at Sunday dinner, with fewer than 6 percent having pork or poultry. Milk pot pudding is the most popular sweet (dessert). Those who drink anything with their meals drink tea; only 10 percent drink coffee at midday and only 5 percent in the evening, and 3 percent at most have wine or beer with their meals.

Britain discontinues "National" flour under terms of the new Flour (Composition) Regulation.

Poultry raisers get their first effective coccidiostat to fight the disease that has prevented large concentrations of chickens and turkeys, which are prone to flock-destroying epidemics of coccidiosis. Farmers or their wives have raised backyard flocks of 20 to 50 chickens, and the cost of chicken has been higher than the cost of beef, since beef cattle can be raised more efficiently. The animal health products division of Merck Pharmaceutical Co. introduces Nicarb 25% (nicarbazin), which kills the deadly intercellular parasites that infect epithelial cells of the intestines and associated glands. In combination with higher-protein feeds, coccidiostats will permit companies to build three-story poultry houses with 30,000 birds per floor and have mature birds ready for market in just 42 days (*see* Tyson's Rock Cornish game hen, 1965).

Banana production shifts to Ecuador, which was not a major exporter before the war but rarely has high winds, provides good growing conditions, and will become the world's leading exporter within a decade, accounting for half the bananas shipped to the United States. The disease-prone Gros Michel banana grown in Central America and the Caribbean islands since 1820 gives way in many areas to the Cavendish (Valéry) variety, which is less vulnerable to disease and less likely to be blown down in hurricanes since it grows on a shorter plant. The banana will be America's most popular fruit, outselling apples.

Standard Fruit Co. begins banana operations in Costa Rica (*see* 1926; 1959).

Agenais prunes constitute 90 percent of the California crop (*see* 1856). By 1970, the state will be producing some 340 million pounds of prunes per year, mostly in the Santa Clara Valley, where Agenais growers will average 11,250,000 pounds per year.

Hollywood star and health food enthusiast Gloria Swanson, 57, lectures congressmen's wives on the hazards in American foods. The women will persuade their husbands to support a Food Additives Amendment to the 1938 Food, Drug and Cosmetic Act, which James J. Delaney (D. N.Y.) has been pushing without success (*see* 1950; 1958).

Parliament passes a new Food and Drugs Act to regulate the labeling of products sold in Britain (*see* 1860).

Catherine Clark's Country Baked Brownberry Ovens is founded in July at Oconomowoc, Wis., 30 miles west of Milwaukee, by local entrepreneur Clark, who uses freshly ground wheat flour to produce a dark loaf that will gain enough popularity to give the company sales of $6 million by 1972 (*see* Peavey, 1972).

Unilever's Van den Bergh division introduces Blue Band margarine, a new, higher-quality product designed to reverse a British trend away from margarine and back to butter (the government last year lifted its controls on edible fats). Blue Band spreads more easily than butter at low temperatures after being removed from the refrigerator, and by 1961 the decline in overall British margarine sales will have been arrested.

Lever Brothers introduces Imperial margarine, "the first margarine unconditionally guaranteed to bring you the tantalizing flavor formerly found only in the expensive table spread." Imperial is soon among the top four U.S. margarine brands, competing with Kraft's Parkay, Best Foods' Blue Bonnet, and Lever's own Good Luck brands.

TreeSweet Products switches from canning juices to producing frozen concentrates at a new $5 million plant at Ft. Pierce, Fla. (*see* 1947).

Busch Bavarian beer, introduced by Anheuser-Busch, augments its 80-year-old Budweiser and 60-year-old Michelob brands.

French chef Paul Bocuse, 30, quits de La Pyramide at Vienne to join his father, Georges, in the restaurant at Collonges-au-Mont-d'Or just north of Lyons. Bocuse was born in the building that houses the restaurant, which had its beginnings in 1765 when his great-great-great-great-great-grandfather Michel Bocuse, a miller, opened a tavern, serving fried fish from the Saône, goat cheese from neighboring farms, and Mont d'Or wine. He has trained with La Mère Brazier at Lyons (*see* 1921), Fernand Point at Vienne, and the Paris restaurant Lucas-Carton. Georges Bocuse will die next year, Paul will win his first Michelin star in 1958, he will be adjudged the *meilleur ouvrier de France* in 1961, and in 1965 his little nine-table bistro will win Michelin's coveted three-star rating as he attracts admirers with his *soupe d'homard*; *soupe de moules* Paul Bocuse; *terrine de grives au baies de Genèvre*; stuffed bass in pastry; potato *gratin dauphinois*; *mousse de truite à la Constant*; *dardine de colvert* (mallard gallantine); *filet de canard* (duck filets); *guillot*; *daube au maître Philéas Gilbert* (beef braised in red wine); *quasi de veau bourgeois* (round of veal); *andouilles de Fleury* (chitterlings from Fleury); *carré d'agneau aux herbes de Provence*; *carré d'agneau à la broche* (spitted rack of lamb); and other specialities, most of which must be ordered in advance.

London's Quality Chop House at 94 Varington Road, which dates to the 1860s, is acquired by Italian restaurateur Enrico Edo, who will run it for 29 years. Helped by his wife at the cash register and his daughter as waitress, he will make the Chop House London's most popular "caff," opening at 6 o'clock in the morning to serve breakfast (porridge, kippers, bacon and eggs, and bread and butter), followed by roasts, joints, stew, steak-and-kidney pie, toad-in-the-hole, and pudding, and closing at 4 in the afternoon. Edo will sell the place to a Spanish chef in 1985, but the new owner will fail (see 1990).

The Los Angeles restaurant La Scala opens at 9455 Santa Monica Boulevard, Beverly Hills. Proprietor Jean Leon will identify nearly every dish on his Italian menu with a Hollywood film star's name.

1957

A Great Leap Forward launched by Mao Zedong in the People's Republic of China puts more than half a billion peasants into 24,000 "people's communes" (see 1956). The people are guaranteed food, clothing, shelter, and child care but deprived of all private property.

Sputnik I, launched by the Soviet Union October 4, is the world's first man-made Earth satellite. The 184-pound sphere orbits the Earth once every 90 minutes in an elliptical orbit and is followed in November by Sputnik II, which weighs more than 1,000 pounds and carries a live dog, but *New York Times* correspondent Harrison E. Salisbury, 48, in Moscow hears a Russian say, "Better to learn to feed your people at home before starting to explore the moon."

The Treaty of Rome signed March 25 establishes a European (Economic) Community (the Common Market). Belgium, France, West Germany, Italy, Luxembourg, and the Netherlands remove mutual tariff barriers to promote the economy of Europe and make it a viable competitor with Britain and the United States (see 1972).

Kikkoman International is founded with headquarters at San Francisco as U.S. demand for soy sauce increases (see 1630; 1973).

Hawaii's pineapple industry packs more than 30 million cases of canned fruit, supplying 84 percent of U.S. demand and 72 percent of world demand. Hawaiian Pineapple Co.'s Honolulu fruit cannery is the world's largest, capable of converting 2.5 million pineapples into nearly 5 million cans of fruit and juice in one 24-hour period.

Britain's Hovis Ltd. and McDougall Trust Ltd. merge to create Hovis-McDougall Ltd. (see McDougall, 1864; Hovis, 1954). Hovis is the leading British miller of baker's flour, and, although it has virtually no bakery interests of its own, its Hovis brown bread remains the best-selling brand of its kind in the market; McDougall holds a strong position in the domestic flour business, selling directly to grocers, but the three largest British millers—Joseph Rank Ltd., Associated British Foods, and Spillers Ltd. have begun to acquire bakeries and are making it hard for other millers to compete (see Rank Hovis McDougall, 1962).

Britain's Birds Eye Ltd. becomes a wholly owned subsidiary of Unilever after 15 years of co-ownership with General Foods. Despite increased competition, Birds Eye will continue to enjoy a two-thirds share of the growing British frozen foods market 4 years hence.

Sen. Estes Kefauver, 54 (D. Ky.), investigates the effect on consumers of increasing mergers by U.S. bread bakers and other companies.

Seabrook Farms acquires Minute Maid's Snow Crop frozen vegetable and fruit division but not its citrus concentrates (see 1944; 1954).

Corn Products Refining Co. diversifies by acquiring C. H. Knorr, Europe's largest producer of dehydrated soups (see 1955; Best Foods, 1958).

A new process mixes high-protein soy flour with an alkaline liquid to create a spinning solution which is fed under pressure into spinning machines (see 1949). Food company engineers will develop improvements on this spinning technique, others will adapt extrusion methods from the plastics industry to develop new meat analogs from soy protein isolate (see Bac*Os, 1966).

U.S. per capita margarine consumption overtakes butter consumption for the first time. The average

American uses 8.6 pounds of margarine per year versus 8.3 pounds of butter (*see* 1960).

 African bees imported into Brazil escape from a breeding experiment and begin heading north at a rate of about 200 miles per year. Stings of aggressive "killer" bees will kill hundreds of people in the next 33 years.

Huge irrigation projects add 100 million acres of irrigated cropland to China's agricultural resource and give the nation 60 times as much irrigated cropland as Europe. The Chinese work to bring under control the Huanghe River, which has for centuries overrun its banks 2 years out of 3 to create floods that have produced havoc, famine, and desolation.

Chinese cereal grain production rises to 200 million tons after having increased in the past 7 years at an annual rate of 8 percent while the rest of the world has never exceeded a rate of 3 percent.

Hawaii has upward of 73,000 acres planted to pineapples, more than 30,000 of them by the Hawaiian Pineapple Co. (*see* above).

Diets high in saturated fats are related to atherosclerotic heart disease, says Ancel Keys in a paper published in the *Journal of the American Medical Association* (*see* 1953). Keys shows that male Japanese have low rates of heart disease but that rates rise when they adopt Western diets (*see* 1963).

Nitrite poisoning creates a scandal in Germany, where butchers are found to be using sodium nitrite to make meat look fresh and red, exposing consumers to the hazards of methemoglobinemia, which can produce dizziness, fatigue, nausea, and even death. An excess of nitrite can turn blood hemoglobin into methemoglobin, which cannot provide oxygen to the cells, and gross excesses can be perilous, especially to children, whose total blood volume is relatively low and whose stomachs are much less acid than those of adults. Lack of acidity makes it easier for intestinal bacteria to turn nitrates into nitrites.

A British Consumers' Association is founded to campaign for more informative labeling on a wide range of goods, including food products (*see* legislation, 1955).

Seabrook Farms (above) introduces Miracle Pack Prepared Foods (*see* 1944). Entrées such as beef goulash and chicken cacciatore are quick-frozen in individual portions and sealed in transparent polyester-polyethylene bags that are ready to be dropped into boiling water. In 14 minutes the food is cooked, the bag is snipped open at one end, and the contents are emptied onto a plate. Seabrook will add frozen vegetables for "waterless cooking" to the line next year.

Orangina has sales of 50 million bottles (*see* 1934). Now made from orange concentrate, the natural soft drink will have sales of about 500 million bottles by 1994 (*see* Pernod Ricard Group, 1984).

The Gino's fast-food stand opened by Baltimore Colts defensive end Gino Marchetti will grow in the next 17 years into an empire of 340 franchised hamburger-chicken stands in the mid-Atlantic states. Gino's will be merged into Marriott Corp.'s Roy Rogers chain in the late 1960s.

The Aware Inn opens in Los Angeles at 8828 Sunset Boulevard. Jim and Elaine Baker offer beef stroganoff; veal Teresa (with ham and mozzarella cheese); a superhamburger called the "Swinger" (with chopped onion, green pepper, tomato, olives, and grated Cheddar cheese); filet of sole amandine; and quiche Lorraine. By the 1970s the Aware Inn will be preparing food with filtered water (regular Los Angeles water is highly chlorinated) and emphasizing organically grown "natural" foods, including beef that has not been artifically fattened, farm-raised chicken, hard rolls made from stone-ground whole-wheat flour, and sweet butter and milk from the city's best dairy.

New York's Pavillon restaurant moves to the Ritz Tower at 111 East 57th Street following a dispute with Columbia Pictures boss Harry Cohn, whose company owns the building at Fifth Avenue and 55th Street (*see* 1941; Côte Basque, 1958).

New York's Forum of the Twelve Caesars restaurant opens December 12 at 57 West 48th Street with a decor by designer William Pahlman, who for $6,000 has acquired 17th-century paintings by Camillo Procaccini of the 12 Caesars from Julius to Domitian. Operated by Restaurant Associates of 1953 Newarker fame, it has tableware made in

Milan, its waiters are given a course on wine by James Beard, its chef Albert Stockli has read Apicius, its manager Alan Lewis was Joseph Baum's classmate at the Cornell Restaurant School, its wines are cooled in centurion helmets, and its four-page menu, bound with gold and a wax seal with a purple faille ribbon, quotes Catullus and offers "Provocatives," "Gustatories," "Roman Ramikins called Minutels, Favorites of the Augustan Courts," "A Harvest from the Seas and Rivers," "Sumptuous Dishes from All the Empire," "Birds—Wild and Otherwise—Baked in Clay under the Fiery Ashes," and "Epicurean Trophies of the Hunt." Specialties include flaming "Mad Nero Crepes" filled with honeyed nuts; pâté of wild boar with a piquant sauce of Damascus plums; rack of pork glazed in amber sugar with ginger apple slices; venison; pheasant *en plumage*; the "wild fowl of Samos"; chestnut-and-sausage-stuffed chicken on tonato risotto; frogs' legs sautéed in hazelnut butter; mussels Romulus with rémoulade sauce; sole with figs and toasted almonds; stuffed trout; mountain trout Tiberius "in herbs and Etruscan wine"; heather-smoked salmon; and hearts of leeks cooked whole "in the Roman tradition" (*see* Four Seasons, 1959).

1958

✗ *The Politician* by former Boston candy maker Robert Welch is an 80,000-word book that expands on a long letter which Welch wrote late in 1954. Together with 11 like-minded men, he meets at Indianapolis in early December and helps found the John Birch Society, which maintains that President Eisenhower was planted by Communists "for the purpose of throwing the game" and that George C. Marshall is also a Communist agent. Such views embarrass Robert's candy maker brother James, but thousands of Americans find them not unreasonable.

\$ U.S. unemployment reaches a postwar high of more than 5.1 million, and the Department of Labor reports that a record 3.1 million Americans are receiving unemployment insurance benefits. Economic recession grips the nation with nearly one-third of major industrial centers classified as having "substantial" unemployment.

The median U.S. family income is $5,087, up from $3,187 in 1948 (half of all families have incomes below the median, half above), but prices have climbed along with incomes. A pound of round steak that cost 90.5¢ in 1948 now costs $1.04, a Nathan's hot dog that cost 20¢ costs 25¢.

Some prices have fallen: a pound of chicken that cost 61.2¢ has come down to 46.5¢.

Former Malaysian commodities trader Robert Kuok, 35, returns to his homeland after 6 years in London and establishes Malayan Sugar Manufacturing Co. Kuok, whose father came to the country from China in 1911 and opened a grocery store, fled the country with his family in 1952 after his brother was killed in the jungle by government security forces. He will set up sugar plantations and sugar mills in Thailand as well as in Malaysia, will grow and refine sugar in Indonesia in partnership with ethnic Chinese businessman Liem Sioe Liong, now 42, and in 20 years will be known worldwide as the "sugar king," handling about 10 percent of the world's sugar trade.

Central Soya opens a fully automated feed mill—the most modern in the world—at Des Moines and in April of next year will incorporate its own barge line (*see* 1941). By 1967, the company will have a net worth of $93 million and annual sales of $520 million (*see* below).

Libby, McNeill & Libby builds a modern canned-meat factory in Illinois (*see* 1954; Nestlé, 1970).

United Fruit Co. agrees February 4 to establish a competitor in the banana industry. The agreement settles a 4-year antitrust suit brought by the U.S. government (*see* 1944).

Lawry's Products changes its name in April to Lawry's Foods (*see* 1956). Richard N. Frank hires Los Angeles designer Saul Bass to create a new logotype for the company, and Bass's bull's-eye "L" will appear on Seasoned Salt bottles and Spaghetti Sauce Mix beginning in 1960 as the Lawry's line expands (*see* Taco Seasoning Mix, 1967).

Hawaiian pineapple pioneer James D. Dole dies at his Honolulu home May 14 at age 80 (*see* 1934). The company that he founded in 1902 and from which he retired 10 years ago now employs 3,300 people year round plus 7,800 in the packing season and produces 30 million cases of canned fruit and juice per year (*see* Castle & Cook, 1964).

Beech-Nut Life Savers board chairman Edward J. Noble dies at his home on Round Hill Road, Greenwich, Conn., December 28 at age 76, leaving $3 million to his wife. He has established a $2 million trust fund for his daughter and left the residue of his large estate to the Edward John Noble Foundation, which makes substantial contributions to the furtherance of education.

Corn Products Refining Co. acquires Best Foods along with its Skippy Peanut Butter, Hellmann's Mayonnaise, and other brands as it continues to expand and diversify (*see* 1955; Hellmann's, 1912; Knorr, 1957; CPC International, 1959).

Central Soya (above) acquires the Chemurgy division of Glidden Co., thereby adding two large soybean-processing plants and new product lines, including soy lecithin (used an emulsifier in many foods) and soy flours.

Gerd and Helmut Käfer of the Munich specialty-food shop Käfer's start a modest business that will grow to occupy several buildings and become Germany's largest catering service, with nearly 400 full-time employees (*see* 1946). Sons of the store's founder, Gerd is 23, Helmut 21. They will cater a reception for the Bavarian government and become the government's official caterers.

Williams-Sonoma opens in San Francisco, specializing in imported cookware. Florida-born merchant Chuck Williams worked as an aircraft mechanic during World War II, acquired a Sonoma, Calif., hardware store 4 years ago, added housewares such as madeleine pans which he found in Europe, and will soon be selling charlotte bowls, soufflé dishes, tart molds, and other traditional French kitchen equipment—by mail order as well as in his shop. Williams will sell his operation in 1978 to investors Howard Lester and Jay McMahan, who will expand it by 1993 into a retail chain of 113 stores (including Williams-Sonoma, Pottery Barn, and Hold Everything stores), a mail-order division that prints nearly 100 million catalogues per year, and a cookbook division.

A&P stockholders agree December 12 to make voting shares in the food store chain available to the public after 99 years of private ownership, but the John A. Hartford Foundation, set up by the founder's son to fund medical research, remains by far the largest stockholder (*see* 1937; 1963).

Cookbooks: *The Food of France* by émigré U.S. journalist Waverley Lewis Root, 55, who weighed 135 pounds when he went abroad in 1927 to work for the Paris edition of the *Chicago Tribune* but whose interest in culinary matters will play a role in increasing his weight to 230 pounds; *New Barbecue Cookbook* and *House and Garden Cookbook* by James Beard.

General Foods prints a recipe for German Chocolate Cake on the label of its Baker's Sweet Chocolate (*see* 1927). Texas and Oklahoma women have for at least 10 years been passing round the recipe for the two-layer chocolate cake with caramel, coconut, and nut frosting (its unique flavor and texture come from the sweet chocolate).

Iceland extends her fishery limits to 12 miles offshore. The move will produce conflicts with British fishing vessels (*see* 1961).

Whalers kill 6,908 blue whales, the largest creatures ever to inhabit the earth. When hunting ceases in 1965, only one blue whale will be found, and it will be estimated that fewer than 1,000 remain in the seas.

China's wheat crop reaches 40 million tons, 2 million more than the U.S. crop, and cereal grain production jumps 35 percent above last year's levels despite a poor rice crop, but total food production falls far short of estimates. The dearth of food encourages peasants to neglect the grain crops of the collectives and raise vegetables and livestock which they can sell privately, if illegally (in some communes half the land is privately cultivated) (*see* 1957; 1959).

Congress mandates enrichment of U.S. rice, but the law does not apply to short-grain rice in the northern states, where that rice is a dietary staple among some ethnic groups.

Folk Medicine by Vermont physician D. C. (DeForest Clinton) Jarvis, 77, blames many ills on a lack of dietary potassium and extolls the alleged health virtues of apple cider vinegar (which he calls an all-purpose bactericide and a safeguard against all harmful intestinal tract bacteria) and honey. Potassium is abundant in meat, milk, vegetables (especially tomatoes), and fruit (notably bananas and oranges); most people consume well in excess of minimum daily requirements, and deficiencies are actually quite uncommon except among alcoholics with diseased livers (whose hyperaldosteronism causes them to excrete too much of the mineral) and people who have not eaten for a long time, have diabetic acidosis or tumors of the adrenal glands, take diuretics, have received excessive therapy with cortisonelike drugs, or have suffered considerable tissue destruction, as from burns. Henry Holt and Co. has published the food-fad book at the insistence of Texas oilman Clinton W. Murchison, 63, a major Holt stockholder, who has become a disciple of the Jarvis notions; the first printing is 5,000 copies, and by the end of next year more than 200,000 copies will have been sold.

A food additives amendment to the Food, Drug and Cosmetic Act of 1938 passed by Congress permits no food additives other than those used widely for many years and "generally recognized as safe" (GRAS) unless the FDA agrees after a thorough review of test data that the new additive is safe at the intended level of use (*see* Gloria Swanson, 1956).

The Delaney "cancer clause," inserted in the new amendment (above) by Congressman James J. Delaney, states that if *any* amount of any additive can be shown to produce cancer when ingested by humans or test animals, *no* amount of that additive may be used in foods for human consumption (*see* cyclamates, 1969).

Sweet 'n Low sugarless sweetener, introduced by Cumberland Packing Co. of Brooklyn, N.Y., uses saccharin in place of sugar.

Cocoa Puffs breakfast food, introduced by General Mills, is 43 percent sugar (*see* 1954; 1959).

Cocoa Krispies breakfast food, introduced by Kellogg, is 45.9 percent sugar (*see* 1955; 1959).

Jif Peanut Butter is introduced nationwide in August by Procter & Gamble (*see* 1956), which continues to produce Big Top Peanut Butter but will use its marketing skills to make Jif the top-selling brand, ahead of Skippy and Peter Pan.

Chicken Ramen—the world's first instant ramen (Chinese noodle) product—is introduced by Nissin Food Products of Japan, founded at Osaka August 25 by entrepreneur Momofuku Ando, 48. Ando traveled about his ravaged country after World War II, found few noodle shops where working-class people could buy quick, cheap meals, and saw a need for an easily transportable noodle package that could be prepared quickly and cheaply. He started a food-trading and -wholesaling company 10 years ago, has developed Chicken Ramen during a lull in business, and renames the company Nissin Foods. A bag (or pillow pack, or brick/block) type product, Chicken Ramen consists of quick-fried noodles which are placed in a bowl along with a packet of soup seasoning; boiling water is added, the bowl is covered, and in 3 minutes the dish is ready to eat. The product meets with immediate success, despite the fact that it sells for six times the price of fresh ramen noodles at any Japanese "ramen house" restaurant, and more than 10 other companies soon have competitive products on the market (*see* Yakisoba, 1963).

Rice-A-Roni is introduced by San Francisco pasta maker Vincent DeDomenico, whose father, Domenico, started out selling vegetables in 1912, built a macaroni factory, and got his four sons to sell the family's Golden Grain pasta to grocers from Sausalito to Eureka in the 1930s. Vincent watched his sister-in-law mix a can of Swanson's chicken broth with vermicelli and rice to produce a kind of pilaf, experimented by substituting dried soup for canned, and added the seasoned rice-and-pasta recipe to the side of one of his pasta packages. National distribution of Rice-A-Roni will begin in 1961, the product will gross $100 million its first year, DeDomenico will build another factory in Chicago, he will introduce Noodle-Roni, bread stuffing mixes, soups, etc., and will build a Seattle plant and another at San Leandro, across the bay from San Francisco (*see* Quaker Oats, 1987).

Green Giant canned beans are introduced (*see* 1950; 1961).

Hershey Chocolate reduces the size of its nickel Hershey Bar in January from 1 oz. to ⅞ oz. (*see* 1954; 1960).

Unilever's Thomas J. Lipton division introduces Instant Tea, but the powder, designed to be mixed with ice water, is slow to gain acceptance despite the general popularity of iced tea (*see* 1946; White Rose Redi-Tea, 1953; Snapple, 1987).

Pizza Hut opens at Wichita, Kans., to begin a fast-food franchise chain that will grow into the largest group of U.S. pizzerias. Frank Carney, 18, has read a story in the *Saturday Evening Post* about the popularity of pizza with teenagers and college students, borrowed $600 from his mother, found someone to teach him how to make pizzas, and gone into business. Within 16 years, Pizza Hut will have gross sales of $114 million, followed closely by Shakey's with annual sales of $100 million (*see* 1953; Little Caesar's, 1959; PepsiCo, 1977).

International House of Pancakes has its beginnings at Toluca Lake, Calif., where entrepreneur Al Lapin, Jr., opens a family restaurant offering pancakes in flavors and varieties that patrons are not likely to have at home. The chain will grow by mid-1994 to have 490 outlets in the United States, Canada, and Japan.

The Harlem restaurant La Famille opens at 2017 Fifth Avenue near 125th Street with an upstairs dining room that boasts white linen tablecloths. Benjamin James and his sister Willette Crane Murray, both from South Carolina, have run a catering business and now offer specialties that include mushroom soup, corn bread, braised short ribs of beef, veal parmesan, fried chicken, black-eyed peas, and string beans.

The New York restaurant La Côte Basque opens in October on the former site of Le Pavillon (*see* 1957). Bernard Lamotte has painted mural views of Saint-Jean-de-Luz, which are framed with actual shutters, awnings, and balustrades to create an illusion of being in France, and the cuisine rivals that of Le Pavillon. Henri Soulé runs both restaurants, the new place will change hands in 1962, it will fail under its new management, and it will be taken over once again by Soulé in July 1965 (*see* 1966; Rachou, 1979).

The American Express Card, introduced by American Express Co., requires an annual fee from "members" who use the card to charge restaurant meals and other expenses. American Express sets out to overtake Diners Club, which started the travel and entertainment card business in 1950.

Boston's Locke-Obers restaurant switches to frozen vegetables; few people notice.

Le Drugstore opens near the Arc de Triomphe at Paris serving American-style hamburgers, sandwiches, and elaborate desserts topped with whipped cream from aerosol cans (*see* Reddi-Wip, 1947). Created by Publicis director Marcel Blaustein-Blanchet and dripping with chrome and plastic, Le Drugstore will inspire dozens of imitations in Paris and scores in France's provincial cities.

1959

Soviet Premier Nikita Khrushchev and Vice President Richard M. Nixon, 46, have a confrontation at a Moscow trade fair but wind up drinking several bottles of Pepsi-Cola together. Pepsi receives exclusive rights to sell cola in the USSR, Coca-Cola instigates a Senate investigation, and it comes to light that Nixon was once offered the presidency of a foreign division of Pepsi and handled the Pepsi account for a New York law firm (*see* Khrushchev's Iowa visit, below).

President Eisenhower speaks out February 18 against continued emergency aid to the unemployed. He says the nation's economy is on a "curve of rising prosperity." A University of Michigan study shows that 10 percent of U.S. families live on the "poverty line" and 20 percent live below it (*see* 1957).

Congress approves a 2-year extension of a program for foreign disposal of surplus U.S. farm commodities. Some $250 million worth of surplus food is to go to needy Americans through food stamps (*see* 1939; 1964).

CPC International is incorporated to combine Corn Products Refining Co. and Best Foods (*see* 1958).

Royal Crown Cola Co. is created by a reorganization of Nehi Corp. (*see* 1928; 1934; Diet-Rite, 1962).

Consolidated Foods renews its acquisition drive in January by taking over Ohio's Lawson Milk Co. and its 170 stores retailing dairy and bakery products (*see* Sara Lee, 1956). Within 6 years Lawson will have 500 outlets, most of them 22 by 80 feet, selling milk in gallon containers (*see* Shasta, 1961).

Supermarkets account for 69 percent of all U.S. food store sales even though they represent only 11 percent of food stores.

Trading stamps given out by food stores increase prices by only 0.6 percent, says a U.S. Department of Agriculture Study (*see* 1951). Some 200,000 U.S. retailers offer trading stamps, with S&H Green Stamps accounting for 35 to 40 percent of the market. By year's end, Sperry & Hutchinson (which advertises the USDA findings) has over $80 million in cash and securities plus large interests in real estate, department stores, and other retail outlets, some of which it has financed.

Swiss pastry maker Gaston-Albert-Célestin Lenôtre, 39, moves from a town near Deauville and opens a *petite pâtisserie* at 44, rue d'Auteuil, Paris, with help and encouragement from his wife, Collette. He will expand into catering and become a *pâtissier-glacier-chocolatier-traiteur*. By 1974 he will have 300 employees and several factories (*laboratoires*).

The St. Lawrence & Great Lakes Waterway dedicated by Queen Elizabeth June 26 gives oceangoing vessels access to Great Lakes ports as far west as Duluth, some 2,342 miles from the Atlantic. The Seaway can accommodate vessels of up to 25-foot, 9-inch draught—80 percent of the world's saltwater fleet—but will prove costly to maintain.

The flavor enhancer 5'-nucleotides, marketed in Japan, is 10 to 20 times stronger than monosodium glutamate (MSG) (*see* 1947). U.S. marketing will begin in 1962.

Cookbook: *The James Beard Cookbook* (with Isabel E. Callvert).

China suffers catastrophic crop failures (*see* 1958, 1960).

Soviet Premier Nikita Khrushchev (above) visits Coon Rapids, Iowa, corn and hog farmer Roswell Garst and shows interest in hybrid corn, which has been scorned for decades by Lysenkoites (*see* 1954). Khrushchev wants to shift the Russian diet away from potatoes, bread, cereals, and turnips toward increased consumption of meat, milk, and eggs; he knows he will need more feed grains to support the switch (*see* 1963).

A corn farmer must have at least 1,000 acres to be a viable producer, says the U.S. Department of Agri-culture, but 1 million U.S. farms contain fewer than 50 acres. The country has 3.7 million farms, down from more than 6 million in 1940, when 2.2 million farms had fewer than 50 acres, and 136,000 farms have 1,000 acres or more, up from 100,000 in 1940.

Metropolitan Life Insurance Company of New York replaces its "ideal" weight tables of 1942 with two new tables based on findings which show that the old "ideal" weights were not ideal: one table shows "average" weights for men and women according to height and age, the other shows "desirable" weights for men and women according to height and frame size. The desirable weights are much lower than the average weight and are also somewhat lower than the ideal weights given in 1942. A small-framed woman of 5 feet, 6 inches, aged 25 or older, should desirably weigh from 114 pounds to 123, says the company; but the average woman of 5 feet, 6 inches, aged 25 to 29, actually weighs 133—10 to 19 pounds above her desirable weight. Averages for men show an even greater discrepancy to their desirable weights.

The Food and Drug Administration seizes 0.25 percent of the U.S. cranberry crop and orders cranberries from Washington and Oregon off the market. Residues of the weed killer aminotriazole have contaminated a tiny fraction of the crop, but the headlines alarm consumers and all cranberry sauce sales drop sharply.

The FDA bans use of diethylstilbestrol (DES) for emasculating cocks and promoting the growth of capons. University of Iowa researchers have developed DES in the past few years for poultry raisers, but feminizing effects have been observed in a restaurant worker who has eaten chicken necks containing residues from pellet implants (cattle raisers will continue to use DES in feed).

Frosty O's sugar-coated breakfast food is introduced by General Mills (*see* 1958; 1961).

Kellogg introduces Concentrate breakfast food—9.9 percent sugar (*see* 1958; 1961).

The National Cranberry Association changes its name to Ocean Spray, expands production and distribution of Cranberry Juice Cocktail, and introduces Dietetic Cranberries to overcome consumer resistance to cranberry sauce (above; *see* 1930). The association, which harvested its first million-barrel crop in 1953, adopts new promotion ideas that will boost consumption in years to come (*see* Cranapple, 1965).

Häagen-Dazs Ice Cream is introduced by Polish-born Bronx, N.Y., entrepreneur Reuben Mattus, 47, who since age 17 has been peddling his family's homemade ice cream to small candy stores and neighborhood restaurants, initially with a horse and wagon. Finding that most commercial ice cream has become cheaper, he puts more butterfat into his product than government standards require, uses less air filler, comes up with a Danish-sounding name (even though the umlaut does not exist in Danish), packs the ice cream in cartons adorned with maps of Scandinavia, creates a new category that will be called superpremium ice cream, and begins what will become a multimillion-dollar company (*see* 1983; Steve's, 1972; Ben & Jerry's, 1978).

Minute Maid Corp. proves to the Florida Citrus Commission that frost-damaged oranges can be used successfully in concentrates (*see* 1949). After several years of wild fluctuations in profit and loss, the company uses earth-moving machines to build 10-foot walls round 7,000 acres of marsh to reclaim savannah land that has been underwater 9 months of the year. It plants citrus trees from whose fruit it will make frozen juice concentrates and develops programs that permit growers to participate in the retail prices of concentrates, thus assuring a constant supply of fruit (*see* 1960).

Restaurant critic Duncan Hines dies at Bowling Green, Ky., March 15 at age 78.

Roger Viard, 40, takes over as maître d'hôtel at Maxim's in Paris, where he has worked since 1937. He succeeds Albert Blaser and, like his predecessor, will accept reservations and assign tables without regard to the fame or wealth of a patron.

The London restaurant La Terrazza opens at 19 Romilly Street. Two waiters, known as Mario and Franco, who have worked at Hatchett's and Mirabelle, will expand their little place into a large and elegant eating place featuring regional Italian dishes, chiefly from southern Italy, and will introduce new dishes such as *linguine à la vongole*, *pasta e fagiole* and *scampi à la certosine* (*see* Tiberio, 1962).

The London restaurant Le Toque Blanche opens in Kensington with 50 seats. Chef Fernand Fernez has worked in the kitchens of the casino at Monte Carlo and at Claridge's. He and his wife, Monique, who had their own restaurant last year on the Sussex coast, will open Le Coq Hardi nearby in 1965 (*see* 1970).

New York's Four Seasons restaurant opens in July at 99 East 52nd Street in the new Seagram Building at 375 Park Avenue under the management of Restaurant Associates (*see* Forum of the Twelve Caesars, 1957). Joseph Baum (who will claim to have been inspired by reading *haiku* poetry) has planned the new restaurant, it occupies 130,000 cubic feet of space, and its menu selections, plantings, flowers, banquette upholstery colors, table-linen colors, uniforms, graphics—even the colors of the typewriter ribbons—are changed four times per year. Seagram boss Samuel Bronfman's daughter, Phyllis Lambert, has acquired an original Picasso canvas, which hangs in the corridor leading to the restaurant's main dining room (the pool room). Metal sculptures by Richard Lippold hang over the bar in the grill room, anodized aluminum chains grace the huge windows, carpeting is hand loomed, a tank holds live trout for *truite bleu*, and the food prepared by Albert Stockli (with advice from James Beard) anticipates the nouvelle cuisine that will flourish beginning a decade hence, with emphasis on quality ingredients—the season's first raspberries; the rarest oysters; the first grouse from the queen's hunt; wild mushrooms collected by composer John Cage (an amateur mycologist); nubbin carrots grown by an Oregon farmer—and on simplicity rather than rich, heavy sauces (*see* 1973).

The Brasserie, opened on the north side of the Seagram Building (above), is a 24-hour French-style restaurant. Total cost of The Four Seasons and the Brasserie is $12.5 million—$2 million over budget—and The Four Seasons will never show a profit, but Restaurant Associates acquires Mama Leone's and will make more than enough money from that to defray its losses at The Four Seasons (*see* La Fonda del Sol, 1960).

The Seagram Building (above) has replaced the old Montana apartment house and its restaurant Voisin, which opened in 1912 and will be at 575 Park before moving in May 1963 to 30 East 65th Street, where it will survive briefly.

The first Little Caesar's pizza parlor opens at Garden City, Mich. (*see* Pizza Hut, 1958). Founder Michael Ilitch, 30, the son of poor Macedonian immigrants, joins with his wife to start the pizza parlor, will add a second store in 1961, and—with the help of an advertising campaign ("Pizza! Pizza! Two great pizzas! One low price")—will build an enterprise that will grow by 1993 to have nearly 4,500 franchised take-out stores, 1,125 of them owned by Ilitch (*see* Domino's, 1960).

1960

China's grain production falls below 1952 levels as the Great Leap Forward program begun in 1957 reduces harvests and produces starvation in the country that now has 100 million more mouths to feed than in 1952, but strict rationing avoids the famine tolls of pre-Mao times (*see* 1961; 1963).

The CBS television documentary *Harvest of Shame* awakens Americans to the hardships of the migrant workers who pick much of the nation's fruits and vegetables (*see* Chavez, 1962).

Cuba's President Fidel Castro, 33, signs an agreement at Havana February 13 with Soviet First Deputy Premier Anastas I. Mikoyan providing $100 million in credit and the Soviet purchase of 5 million tons of Cuban sugar. Castro, whose father had 10,000 acres of Cuban sugarfields (his mother was the cook at his father's mansion), threatens June 23 to seize all American-owned property and business interests to counter U.S. "economic aggression," Eisenhower cuts Cuba's sugar quota by 95 percent July 6 and declares that the United States will never permit a regime "dominated by international communism" to exist in the Western Hemisphere, Havana nationalizes all large commercial and industrial enterprises October 14, and Washington imposes an embargo October 19 on all exports to Cuba except medical supplies and most foodstuffs.

Cuba (above) and the Philippines have been supplying 97 percent of U.S. sugar imports. Cuba's quota of 2.9 million short tons under the 1934 Jones-Costigan Act is divided up among more than 30 other nations, all of which are eager to obtain 6¢/lb. for their sugar at a time when the world price is 2¢.

(U.S. sugar interests insist that no country can produce sugar at 2¢/lb., much less sell it at that price; they maintain that only 15 percent of the sugar grown worldwide is traded on the world market [the actual figure is more like 25 percent], and that this is excess sugar that is being "dumped" either by foreign governments or by producers whose governments subsidize sugar production, generally because unions resist mechanization and politicians are obliged to subsidize uneconomic sugar production at enormous cost.) In 2 years, the Philippines will be supplying 1.21 million tons of U.S. sugar imports, the Dominican Republic 870,000 tons, Peru 530,000 tons, and Brazil 400,000 tons, with smaller amounts coming from other Caribbean islands, Mexico, India, Taiwan, South Africa, Australia, Ecuador, Colombia, Turkey, Nicaragua, Guatemala, Costa Rica, El Salvador, Fiji, Mauritius, Argentina, and Venezuela. (Ireland has been granted a quota of 5,351 tons as a political favor to Speaker of the House John W. McCormack [D. Mass.], and buys sugar from Poland, paying 2¢/lb. and reselling it to the United States at 6¢/lb.)

Grain worth $6 billion piles up in U.S. government-owned storage facilities, congressmen file vigorous complaints about storage costs, but the reserves will drop sharply in the decade ahead as U.S. grain relieves world hunger (*see* India, 1966).

Arrowhead Mills is founded at Hereford, Tex., by Deaf Smith County wheat farmer Frank Ford with an old railcar, a small mill, and a few used grain bins for storage. Avoiding use of synthetic fertilizers, herbicides, and pesticides on his wheat, Ford will use a 30-inch stone grinder to produce flour, and although he will lose money for 7 years his company will grow into a multimillion-dollar business with a 20-acre milling, processing, packaging, and distributing complex that turns out some 250 natural whole-grain, bean, and seed products for sale mostly at health food stores.

Iowa Beef Processors (IBP) is founded at Denison, Iowa, by former Sioux City cattle buyers who include Currier J. Holman, 46. IBP will grow from a single slaughterhouse to become the world's largest meatpacker (larger than Swift, Armour, Wilson, Morrell, and Cudahy combined), but Holman will be convicted of having ties with a distributor who bribed supermarket executives and butchers' union officials.

Chicago's last packinghouse closes as meatpackers shift their activities to the West (*see* 1953).

Dole Corp. is created by a renaming of the 58-year-old Hawaiian Pineapple Co. started by the late James D. Dole (*see* 1922; Castle & Cooke, 1964).

Nestlé Alimentana, S.A., acquires Britain's 254-year-old Crosse & Blackwell, which in 1919 acquired E. Lazenby & Sons and James Keillor & Sons and has since acquired other firms.

Coca-Cola Company acquires Minute Maid Corp. (*see* 1959).

Hunt Foods merges with Wesson Oil and Snowdrift (*see* 1925; 1952; Wakefield, 1968; Norton Simon, 1969).

Seeman Brothers acquires Seabrook Farms (*see* 1957).

William Underwood Co. acquires Sell's Specialties (*see* liver paté, 1945; Pet Inc., 1982).

Worthington Foods acquires Battle Creek Foods (*see* 1948). Sales reach $1 million, partly through this and other acquisitions (*see* Miles, 1970).

Beatrice Foods acquires Holloway's Milk Duds and merges it with its D. L. Clark subsidiary, acquired 5 years ago.

Coffee Rich nondairy creamer is introduced by Buffalo, N.Y., dairyman Robert Edward Rich, 47, who has earlier developed a soybean-based whipping cream (*see* Pream, 1952). Rich bought his own milk company at age 21 after learning the family business, served as milk administrator during World War II, and will acquire small frozen food companies and a bakery as he builds a Rich Products empire. His cheap, nonspoiling creamer and other foods will give him a net worth of about $500 million by the 1990s (*see* Coffee-Mate, 1961).

Aluminum cans are used commercially for the first time for food and beverages (*see* below). They will come to represent the single largest use of aluminum, but many consumers will insist that foods and beverages taste better when packed in glass.

Cookbooks: *French Provincial Cooking* by Elizabeth David establishes the author as Britain's most inspirational food writer; *Mario of the Caprice* by London chef Mario Gallati; *How America Eats* by Clementine Paddleford; *Treasury of Outdoor Cooking* by James Beard.

U.S. margarine consumption reaches 9.4 pounds per capita, up from 8.6 pounds in 1957; butter consumption falls to 7.5 pounds, down from 8.3 (*see* 1963).

Aluminum cans (above) are not biodegradable (tin-plated steel cans rust in time) and present environmental problems of litter.

Large Soviet fishing fleets move south from Newfoundland's Grand Banks to pursue the herring which is plentiful off the U.S. Atlantic Coast. Using equipment far superior to that employed by U.S. fishermen and followed by well-equipped Canadian and Eastern European fleets, the Soviet trawlers and purse seiners will reduce herring populations by 90 percent, virtually wiping out the haddock that has been the lifeblood of Boston fishermen.

The world fisheries catch reaches 40 million tons, up from half that amount in 1950.

Fish in the Mississippi begin to die by the millions as pollution lowers oxygen levels in the water.

Monfort of Colorado, now headed by Kenneth Monfort, 35, opens the company's first meat-processing plant, handling 500 head per day (*see* 1930; 1968).

It takes 8 to 10 weeks and just seven pounds of feed to produce a meaty broiler chicken in the United States, down from 12 to 15 weeks and 12 pounds of feed for a scrawnier (but tastier) broiler in 1940. Soy protein now supplements corn in the feed (*see* coccidiostats, 1956).

U.S. corn yields per acre are up 75 percent over 1940, wheat yields are up 63 percent, livestock productivity is up 45 percent, milk production per cow up 30 percent, egg production per hen up 65 percent.

Ten percent of the U.S. workforce is on the farm, down from 18 percent in 1940, 11.6 percent in 1950.

1960

Granny Smith apples are sold for the first time in the United States. Imported initially from New Zealand to fill in during the summer months when few U.S.-grown apples are available, the bright green fruit—firm, tart, and juicy—gets its name from an Australian woman who found the first tree growing in her yard. Australian apples have been embargoed because of a fruit fly infestation, hence the New Zealand origin, but Granny Smiths will soon be coming to U.S. ports from South Africa and France before being grown in California.

Red No. 2 food dye receives provisional acceptance from the U.S. Food and Drug Admistration, which will renew such acceptance periodically for years despite mounting evidence that the amaranth sodium salt, which containins sulfur and naphtha, produces defects in some animals and thus may be hazardous to humans (see 1976).

Annual U.S. beef consumption reaches 99 pounds per capita.

Hershey Chocolate increases the size of its nickel Hershey Bar in August from ⅞ oz. to 1 oz. (see 1958; 1963).

Aluminum cans (above) will be used increasingly for beer and soft drinks. Ninety-five percent of U.S. soft drinks and 50 percent of beer is sold in returnable bottles typically used 40 to 50 times each (see 1962).

The U.S. soft drink industry markets more than 1.5 billion cases of 24 bottles each, up from 168 million cases in 1934.

The Four Seasons hotel chain started by Canadian entrepreneur Isadore Sharp, 28, will grow in 34 years to operate 45 luxury hotels worldwide, some of them with outstanding chefs and restaurants (see Philadelphia's The Fountain, 1983).

Harry's Bar at Venice gains a second floor as Giuseppe Cipriani, now 60, expands with a larger kitchen (see 1931). Cipriani opened the Hotel Cipriani in 1955 on the island of Giudecca, with financing from Guinness brewery head Lord Iveagh of Dublin. His restaurant, which closed toward the end of World War II but reopened, now makes its own pasta, bakes its own bread, employs 41 people (including Giuseppe's son Harry [Arrigo], 28, and 21 waiters) and serves more than 200 patrons per day (44 can sit at the bar, 60 upstairs) with dishes that include antipasto; risotto di seppie; fish risotto; fillets of John Dory; club sandwiches; hamburgers made with sirloin steak; and dolce that include chocolate cake.

La Fonda del Sol opens with 120 seats in New York's Time-Life Building at 123 West 50th Street serving Latin American and Caribbean islands dishes: pisco sours; bocaditos (guacamole, ceviche, empanadas, anticuchos, mejillón, relleno quesadilla, and escabache); Mexican foam soup; Aztec broth; cold pumpkin cream bisque; chilis rellenos; frijoles refritos; main dishes that include escabache chilleno; tortillas; Guayama shrimp; ají de gallena; and parrillade carbonada (the emphasis is on beef, chicken, lamb, and pork broiled on open grills). Alexander Girard has designed the place and brightened it with museum-piece folk art, Rudi Gernreich has designed the uniforms, and restaurateur Joseph Baum of 1959 Four Seasons fame serves complete dinners for $5.95 to $7.95, charging $3.25 for a pitcher of sangria, but the novelty will wear off and La Fonda del Sol, which cost more than $2 million, will close in September 1970 (Braniff Airways will acquire most of its Hispanic folk-art collection).

La Caravelle opens at 33 West 55th Street, New York, in December with 35 tables and a table d'hôte dinner priced at $7.50 to $9.50 (with chateaubriand it is $11) and a $5.50 luncheon (extra if it includes food from the broiler). Proprietors Fred Decré and Robert Meyzen, formerly of the Pavillon, have as their chef Roger Fessaguet, who will later become Meyzen's partner and whose specialties will include mousse de brochette caladoise; shrimp with champagne sauce capped with mushrooms; terrine Saint-Hubert (made with kid lardons, pheasant, or duckling); smoked trout en gelée; pigeon grand-mère en cocotte (with mushrooms, onions, baby potatoes, and bits of salt pork); poularde favorite; bread-and-butter pudding with custard and raisins (served with a creamy vanilla sauce); and crêpe ma pomme (prepared with sliced apples at tableside like crêpes Suzettes but with Calvados and brown sugar, and topped with vanilla sauce and whipped cream).

Boston's Pier Four restaurant opens over a landfill at the harbor and is soon the world's largest eating place. Albanian-American restaurateur Anthony Athanas, 49, started with the Hawthorne Restaurant at Lynn, Mass., in 1938 and has built up a chain of five Boston-area operations.

The Los Angeles restaurant Knoll's Black Forest Inn opens in February with 18 covers at 124 Santa Monica Boulevard. Norbert Knoll, from Stuttgart, and his wife, Hildegarde, offer German specialties—purée of Savoy cabbage flavored with mace; *schwabischer rostbrat* (grilled steak with sautéed onions, *spätzle*, sauerkraut, caraway seed, and red cabbage); veal from Wisconsin; *schweinebraten* (roast pork with gravy); fresh ham with bread dumplings; roast goose; *blut-und-leberwurst* (blood and pork liver sausage); potato pancakes; *schwarzwalder kirchtorte*; and *haselnusstorte*—in a *gemütlich* atmosphere. The Knolls will expand as they gain popularity.

The New Orleans Royal Orleans hotel in Royal Street opens a Rib Room whose beef dishes will attract patrons for decades.

Howard Johnson has 607 independently owned restaurants in his franchise, making it the third largest U.S. food distributor, surpassed only by the U.S. Army and Navy (*see* 1937). Now 63, Johnson heads a family-owned enterprise that operates 296 restaurants (*see* 1979).

Domino's Pizza begins operations at Detroit. Local entrepreneur Thomas Stephen Monaghan, 23, and his younger brother, Jim, were placed by their mother in a Catholic orphanage after their father died when Thomas was 4; Thomas studied for the priesthood, was expelled from seminary, joined the Marines, and attended the University of Michigan before dropping out. He borrows $500 to join brother Jim in buying a pizza parlor that competes with Little Caesar's (*see* 1959), will soon trade his Volkswagen to buy out Jim's interest, and will pioneer in delivering phone orders within 30 minutes. By 1993, Domino's will have some 5,200 outlets, 400 of them company owned.

The world population tops 3 billion, up from 2 billion in 1930.

1961

The Peace Corps, an organization of volunteers for overseas service, created March 1 by President John F. Kennedy, 43, will work to improve agriculture, education, and living standards in Third World countries.

President Kennedy dines with Soviet Premier Khrushchev and the president of Austria June 2 at Vienna's 221-year-old Schönbrunn Palace. Some 200 guests enjoy a dinner, served on Hapsburg china and silver and prepared by Demel's (*see* 1857): consommé printainier, asparagus tips and tartelettes, perch in white wine, small steaks and mushrooms, stuffed peppers, crème Vindobona, and mocha. Two Austrian wines—a white Loibner Kaiserwein and a red Oggauer Blaufränkisch—are served and the Vienna Philharmonic provides musical entertainment.

President Kennedy and the First Lady entertain Pakistan's President Ayub Khan July 11 with a dinner and concert at Mount Vernon—possibly the first time Mount Vernon has been opened for a state dinner since George Washington's era. Tables are set up on the lawn overlooking the Potomac River, and the menu consists of avocado and crab mimosa (topped with mashed hard-boiled egg yolk), poulet chasseur (chicken with a white wine sauce containing mushrooms, shallots, parsley, and butter) served with rice molded into a ring, framboises à la crème chantilly (raspberries with whipped cream), and petits fours.

China suffers further crop failures, creating a famine that kills millions throughout the country (*see* 1960; 1963).

An Alliance for Progress formed at Punta del Este, Uruguay, and announced by President Kennedy in March will spur economic and social development of Latin American countries which cooperate with the United States. Agrarian reform and tax reform are major objectives of the new *alianza*, created in August by an agreement signed with 19 Latin American countries, which are promised $10 billion in U.S. aid over a 10-year period.

A Latin American free trade association comes into force June 2.

U.S. ambassador to the United Nations Adlai E. Stevenson, 61, urges that the developed countries of the world each contribute 1 percent of their gross national product to the development of the emerging nations.

The Italian dairy company Parmalat S.p.A., founded at Parma, will grow to have divisions elsewhere in Europe and in the Americas, manufacturing tomato products, vegetable soups, fruit juices, baked goods, and pasta products in addition to dairy products (*see* shelf-stable milk, 1993).

Curtice-Burns Foods, Inc., is founded by 700 members of the Pro-Fac Cooperative in Rochester, N.Y., to process produce from local fields and farms, mostly in midwestern states, and sell the canned goods under private labels and brand names. It will grow to have 13 plants (owned by Pro-Fac and leased back to Curtice-Burns) with annual sales of close to $1 billion by 1993.

Banana king Samuel Zemurray dies of Parkinson's disease at New Orleans November 30 at age 84.

Campbell Soup Co. acquires Pepperidge Farms, Inc., January 9 for $28.2 million in stock (*see* 1955). Margaret Rudkin remains chairman of the board and will continue to be active in the business until September 1966.

Standard Brands acquires Planters Nut and Chocolate Co. (*see* 1916; 1929; Curtiss, 1964).

Borden Co. acquires Wyler & Co., now a leading maker of dehydrated soups and powdered drink mixes (*see* 1931; Lady Borden, 1947). It also acquires Greenwood Foods, the nation's largest packer of red cabbage and pickled beets (*see* ReaLemon, Comstock, 1962).

Frito-Lay, Inc., is created by a merger of Atlanta's H. W. Lay Co. and the Frito Co. of Dallas (*see* 1932; 1939). By 1994 the company will have captured 40 percent of the $10 billion U.S. salted snack food market (no one else will have more than 6 or 7 percent) (*see* PepsiCo, 1965).

R. J. Reynolds acquires Pacific Hawaiian Products Co. and its Hawaiian Punch as the giant tobacco company begins to diversify. Developed in the late 1930s and distributed nationally since 1950, Hawaiian Punch contains some pineapple, papaya, guava, passion fruit, and other juices but is nearly 90 percent water and sugar (*see* Penick and Ford, 1965; Procter & Gamble, 1989).

Consolidated Foods acquires Shasta Beverages, a West Coast bottler and distributor of soft drinks (*see* Lawson, 1959; Booth Fisheries, 1964).

Verv, introduced for the first time commercially, permits greater tolerance in the dough processing required by modern, high-speed baking methods (*see* moisture meter, 1947). Developed by C. J. Patterson, now 72, the product ensures greater uniformity in baked goods and gives them better keeping qualities. Patterson has also developed a new baking process that employs vertical mixing equipment and portable dough bowls that replace horizontal mixers and stationary mixing chambers.

Cookbooks: *Mastering the Art of French Cooking* by Julia Child, Simone "Simca" Beck, and Louisette Bertholle demystifies good French cuisine (*see* 1951). The authors have learned to cook from Henri-Paul Pellaprat of the Cordon Bleu (*see* Child, 1963) and their book will have sales of more than 1.25 million copies by 1974. *The New York Times Cookbook* by Mississippi-born food expert Craig Claiborne, 41, who has been the paper's food editor since 1957 and will remain in that job until 1971. *Summer Cooking* by Elizabeth David. *The James Beard Cookbook* by Beard (with Isabel E. Callvert). *The Natural Foods Cookbook* by U.S. author Beatrice Hunter (*née* Trum), 42.

Canned pet foods are among the three top-selling categories in U.S. grocery stores. Americans feed an estimated 25 million pet dogs, 20 million pet cats.

Britain and Iceland settle a fisheries dispute but controversy over fishing rights in the North Atlantic will continue with "cod wars" between the two.

The United States has a wheat carryover of 1.4 billion bushels in July, depressing farm prices, and the corn carryover in October exceeds 2 billion bushels, a record that will stand for more than 20 years. The Kennedy administration (above) will introduce an emergency feed grain program to reduce acreage planted to such grain (*see* 1963).

Widespread mechanical harvesting of processing tomatoes for use in canning, ketchup, paste, sauces, tomato juice, and tomato soup begins in California as farmers plant the tough-skinned VF 145-B7879 variety developed by researchers at the Davis campus of the University of California. Rising labor costs have threatened the industry in California, which produces much of the world's processing tomatoes. By 1975 California will be producing more than 7 million tons of processing tomatoes per year, up from 1.3 million in 1954 (table tomatoes will continue to be hand picked, partly because machine-harvested tomatoes must be in rows separated by wide spaces to permit passage of machines).

Calories Don't Count by Brooklyn, N.Y., physician Herman Taller, 52, is a U.S. best-seller. The book urges overweight people to cut out carbohydrates and increase consumption of fats (*see* 1967; Stefansson, 1946; Du Pont diet, 1953; Stillman, 1967).

Total breakfast food, introduced by General Mills, will be promoted for its nutritional qualities. General Mills also introduces Country Corn Flakes (*see* Lucky Charms, 1964).

Unilever introduces Mrs. Butterworth's Syrup, a product containing corn syrups, sugar syrups, butter (.4 percent), algin derivative, natural flavor, artificial flavor, salt, sodium benzoate and sorbic acid as preservatives, citric acid, and caramel color, to compete with Log Cabin (*see* pancake mix, 1982).

Green Giant enters the frozen foods business with frozen June peas, Niblets corn, green beans, and baby lima beans frozen in a pouch with butter sauce (*see* 1958; Pillsbury, 1979).

Sprite, introduced by Coca-Cola Co., is a lemon-lime drink that competes with 7-Up (*see* 1933; Tab, 1963).

Coffee-Mate nondairy creamer is introduced by Carnation Co. (*see* Pream, 1952; Coffee Rich, 1960). The powder is made of corn syrup solids, vegetable fat, sodium caseinate, and various additives (*see* "contented cows," 1906; Borden's Cremora, 1963).

New York's Lutèce restaurant opens February 16 at 249 East 50th Street with two beautifully appointed rooms on the second floor that sparkle with flat silver by Christofle and Baccarat crystal. Local Francophile André Surmain (originally Andrew Sussman) has engaged Paris chef André Soltner, 28, of Chez Hansi to prepare the meals at the 29-table restaurant, which takes its name from the original name for Paris. It offers a prix fixe lunch at $8.50 but will soon lower the price to $6.50 (dinner is entirely à la carte—soup, $2.25; first course, $4; main courses, $8.25; desserts, $2.75; wines $8.50 to $14; and a $1 cover charge). Lutèce, whose prices are generally considered outrageous, will struggle for 2 years before gaining a reputation as the city's temple of traditional French cuisine (*soufflé aux fruits de mer*; *mousseline de brochette Nantua*; *mignon de bœuf en croute*; *tournedos La Fontaine*; *canard aux pêchois*; *sole de la Manche belle meunière*; *poulet en croute*; and *poulet rôti basquaise*). The kitchen is too small for grilling or frying. Soltner, who begins work the day after stepping off a plane, will acquire full ownership in December 1972, and, with his Norman wife, Simone (*née* Gomez) (they will live upstairs), make the restaurant a favored haunt of celebrities.

The Harlem restaurant Sylvia's opens with four booths and a counter that seats 10. Former South Carolina hairdresser Sylvia Wood and her husband, Herbert, serve patrons fried chicken, barbecued ribs, grits, black-eyed peas, collard greens, sweet potatoes, fresh corn bread, and sweet potato pie. The Woods will move in the late 1960s to a larger place two doors away at 328 Lenox Avenue—a long, narrow, dinerlike room with a larger counter and tables along one wall—but demand will force them to add a large new dining room with wood paneling on one side and an exposed brick wall on the other, expanding their capacity to more than 100 (*see* Sylvia's Foods, 1993).

The London restaurant Cranks opens June 21 at 22 Carnaby Street with 50 seats and a vegetarian menu consisting mainly of salads, whole-grain rolls, soups, savories, and puddings served on hand-thrown stoneware. David Canter and his wife, Kay, have been inspired by the 1951 Gayelord Hauser book *Look Younger, Live Longer*, they have gone into partnership with Daphne Swann, and they use only fresh fruit and dairy products, 100 percent wholegrain flour, eggs from free-range hens, and raw Barbados sugar to prepare their dishes, which are made fresh each day from these basic ingredients. Cranks branches will open in the 1970s and '80s in Covent Garden and elsewhere in London and in the West Country, making Cranks the first and only vegetarian restaurant chain in Britain.

The Paris restaurant Chez Garin opens at 9, rue Lagrange with specialties that include *truite soufflé Camille Rodier*; it will have three stars in the *Guide Michelin* by 1963.

The Paris restaurant Chez Castel opens with 45 seats at 15, rue Princesse in the heart of Saint-Germain-des-Prés. Breton chef Marcel Le Fau makes foie gras marinated in champagne; *tarte à l'oignon* with a crust made from *pâté à foncer*; *œufs poché à murette*; corn on the cob; salad of corn kernels with cooked green pepper; steak *au poivre vert* with green peppercorns; onglet (a long-fibered cut of beef from under the ribs); *noisette de chevreuil*; and *hachis Parmentier* (served every Tuesday).

The Paris restaurant Le Soufflé opens at 636, rue du Mont-Thabor under the direction of André Faure, who offers not only cheese, seafood, raspberry (in season), noisette (hazelnut), and chocolate soufflés, but also *fond d' artichaut gourmand "farandole" de crudités*; *pipérade*; *ratatouille Niçoise*; Channel sole; turbot (Fridays); *entrecôte*; chateaubriand; lamb chops; côte de bœuf with fresh foie gras (in winter); bœuf à la mode; farm-bred chickens; gratin de volaille; poulet sauté estragon; and feuille follet (a kind of baked Alaska).

The San Francisco restaurant La Bourgogne opens at 320 Mason Street. Jean Lapuyade features Senegalese soup; Maine lobster; quenelles de brochet Nantua with Dover sole or European pike in a lobster sauce; Dover sole meunière Dunantes (poached in white wine and served with cream sauce and sliced artichoke hearts); Dover sole Chambertin (poached in red wine and served with a beurre rouge); saumon poché à la Dierstein in season; caneton au navettes; caneton à l'orange; carré d'agneau chevreuil Nesselrode; soufflés; and fraises maison.

The first Hardee's fast-food restaurant opens May 5 at Rocky Mount, N.C., serving charcoal-broiled hamburgers at 15¢, cheeseburgers at 20¢, french fries at 10¢, milk shakes at 20¢, soft drinks at 10¢, milk at 12¢, and coffee at 10¢. Wilbur Hardee, 42, opened a hamburger stand at Greenville, N.C., in the fall of last year, was soon averaging $1,000 per week in net profit, and attracted the attention of Rocky Mount businessmen Leonard Rawls, Jr., and Jim Gardner, who have persuaded him to go into partnership with them. Their charcoal broiler, one of only three of its kind in America, features a water-purifying system that floats away grease and keeps the charcoal free of impurities, and their success attracts former Baltimore Colts wide receiver Jerome J. "Jerry" Richardson, 25, and his college football teammate Charles Bradshaw, who with two other investors raise $20,000 to open the first Hardee's

franchised restaurant October 19 on Kennedy Street at Spartanburg, S.C. (*see* 1962; Denny's, 1987).

McDonald's hamburger stands begin a vast proliferation as Ray Kroc buys out the MacDonald brothers and acquires all rights to the MacDonald name for $14 million, including interest costs (*see* 1955). Kroc has established nearly 230 stands, borrowed $2.7 million to make his deal with the MacDonalds, will have 700 outlets by 1965, and will build McDonald's (the "a" in "Mac" was later dropped) into a worldwide chain (*see* 1967).

1962

The National Farm Workers Association (NFWA), founded by community leader César Estrado Chávez, 32, represents stoop labor in California's Coachella, Imperial, and San Joaquin valleys (*see* 1965; television documentary, 1960).

President Kennedy embargoes nearly all trade with Cuba February 3 but he reduces tariff duties on some 1,000 items March 7 to increase foreign trade.

African ministers meeting at Casablanca in April agree not only to establish a common market but also to set up an African payments union and an African development bank.

Compagnie Française des Produits Orangina (CFPO) is incorporated at Marseilles under the direction of Jean-Claude Béton, who establishes the first Orangina branches in French-speaking Africa and in the French overseas departments and territories (*see* 1951; 1984).

Stokely–Van Camp has grown to have 67 plants from New Jersey and Delaware in the East to California, Oregon, and Washington in the West, Florida in the South, and Michigan, Minnesota, and Wisconsin in the North packing more than 100 varieties of food (*see* 1939). Its subsidiaries operate pineapple canneries in Hawaii and Puerto Rico, and other subsidiaries operate close to 300,000 acres of orchards and groves to supply its plants, which sell canned and frozen foods in more than 80 world markets (*see* Sea Food Division, below; Quaker Oats, 1983).

Rose and James Totino of Minneapolis take the $50,000 they have saved for retirement after 10 years in the pizza parlor business and use it to start a frozen Italian entrée business (*see* 1951). By the end of their first year they will be $150,000 in debt, but, hearing about a company that can supply them with prebaked pizza crusts, they will obtain a $50,000 Small Business Administration loan and in 6 months will be out of debt. Sales of their frozen pizzas will increase by 35 percent per year (*see* Pillsbury, 1975).

Parma's Barilla brothers resume baking bread (*see* 1952). They now use 240,000 eggs per day for their egg-based pastas, they will be supplying 100,000 Italian retailers by 1965, a law passed 2 years later will give Italians a pasta made exclusively of durum wheat in a package that is sealed and guaranteed, and Barilla breadsticks and rusks will also be hugely popular (*see* Mulino Bianco, 1975).

 Rank Hovis McDougall Ltd. is created by a merger of the British flour-milling giant Joseph Rank Ltd. with Hovis McDougall Ltd. (*see* 1957).

Ralston Purina acquires Stokely–Van Camp's Van Camp Sea Food Division (above), whose Chicken of the Sea and White Star brands have made it the world's largest tuna packer (*see* 1926; Heinz's Star-Kist, 1963).

Borden Co. acquires ReaLemon-Puritan Co., the largest U.S. producer of reconstituted juices (*see* 1935), and Comstock Foods, the largest processor of sliced apples (*see* Wyler, 1961; Aunt Jane's, 1963).

Crush International acquires Hires Root Beer, which is now sold mostly in bottles although Hires extract will continue to be sold for homemade root beer until 1983 (*see* 1886; Orange Crush, 1916).

The Los Angeles specialty produce company Frieda's Finest (later simply Frieda's) founded by local entrepreneur Frieda Caplan, 39, will introduce and popularize fresh brown mushrooms grown in Orange County, Calif., field-ripened papaya and pineapple from Hawaii, passion fruit, doughnut peaches, blood oranges, kiwi fruit (Chinese gooseberries) from New Zealand (she will have kiwi tarts made by a restaurant chef to entice food editors and produce buyers), jicama, "sunchokes" (Jerusalem artichokes), chayote (mirliton, or vegetable pear), radicchio, black radishes, sugar snap peas, pearl onions, spaghetti squash, and cactus pears, marketing them all with brand names and recipe tags. Caplan and her two daughters, Karen Caplan and Jackie Caplan Wiggins, will build an all-woman sales force in the next 30 years to handle more than 500 items whose annual gross sales will total $23 million.

The S.S. *France* of the Compagnie Générale Transatlantique (French Line) leaves Le Havre for New York on her maiden voyage February 2. The last of the great transatlantic liners, she has a kitchen–dining room staff of 180, including 18 chefs; her on-board *boulangerie* turns out seven different kinds of bread (including 4,000 to 5,000 rolls per day), her *potagers* cook up 175 gallons of soup per day, her chefs create dozens of different dishes for every meal, and her *patissiers* produce nine different kinds of petits fours, plus endless varieties of other cookies and pastries. The ship takes on 15 tons of meat, 5.5 tons of poultry (including Bresse chickens), 5.5 tons of seafood (Dover sole, Scotch salmon, turbot, sturgeon, whiting, fluke, sea bass, ling, pollock, red mullet, mackerel, eels, oysters, crabs, clams, mussels, scallops, and lobsters), 30 tons of vegetables, 70,000 eggs, 330 pounds of Russian and Iranian caviar (60 pounds are served per night at no extra charge), plus cheese (Brie, Camembert, Duc de Bourgogne, Pont l'Évêque, Port-Salut, Roquefort, and Velençay), truffles, foie gras, fruit, and other delicacies for every round trip. Passengers consume 4,500 bottles of vintage wines (including 74 kinds of champagne, 50 of Bordeaux, 49 of Burgundy) in addition to 18,000 bottles of *vin ordinaire* on every round trip, to say nothing of vodka, rum, whiskey, and cognac.

The New York Central's *Twentieth Century Limited* between Chicago and New York charges $7.50 for a complete filet mignon dinner, but the luxury train has had coaches as well as Pullman cars since 1957 and its days are numbered (*see* 1902).

The first frozen bread dough is introduced by Bridgford Foods Corp. of Anaheim, Calif. (*see* 1932). A Bridgford baker has accidentally stored some already mixed dough overnight in a freezer, has thawed it out and found that it baked up well, and has experimented with the yeast to create a product that will rise after being frozen for months.

Nonfiction: *The Other America: Poverty in the United States* by former St. Louis welfare worker Michael Harrington, 34, says America has a huge "underclass" of employed people living below the poverty line and gives evidence of persisting hunger and malnutrition in the world's richest nation. His book revives interest in school lunch programs to combat malnutrition, distribution of farm surpluses to the poor, and a food stamp program that will expand the choices of free foods available to the poor. *Stalking the Wild Asparagus* by U.S. food forager–writer Euell (Theophilus) Gibbons, 51, introduces readers to the possibilities of wild foods. Born in Texas, Gibbons left home at age 15 and worked as a harvest hand, cowboy, carpenter, and trapper before hopping a freight car for California. He entered the University of Hawaii as a freshman at age 36 while working for the *Honolulu Advertiser* and has known since childhood how to live off the land. *The Great Hunger* by Irish author Cecily Blanche Woodham Smith (*née* FitzGerald), 66, is about the famine of the mid-1840s.

Cookbooks: *Contemporary French Cooking* by Waverley Root (with Richard de Rochemont); *Gastronomique: A Cookbook for Gourmets* by Ida Bailey Allen, now 77. *The Joyce Chen Cookbook* by Chinese-born Boston chef Chen, 44, who fled China's new Communist regime in 1949, taught cooking at home and at adult education centers in Cambridge, Mass., opened New England's first Mandarin restaurant in 1958 at Cambridge, and introduced such dishes as hot-and-sour soup, moo shu pork, and Peking duck to patrons who included Julia Child. Publishers have been reluctant to underwrite the expense of printing a book containing so many color pictures, but Chen has taken orders for 6,000 copies of the book, which is initially published privately. *Let's Cook It Right* by Adelle Davis.

Sculpture: *Two Cheeseburgers, with Everything* by Swedish-American sculptor Claes Oldenburg, 33.

The average Asian eats more than 300 pounds of rice per year as compared with 6 pounds in the West, and many rice-consuming nations, including the Philippines, do not produce enough for domestic needs. IRRI (below) will advance the "Green Revolution," but while per capita food production in the developing countries has increased in the past decade at an annual rate of 0.7 percent it will increase at an annual rate of only 0.2 percent in the decade ahead.

Frozen, dehydrated, and canned potatoes account for 25 percent of U.S. potato consumption.

Alaskan Eskimos are found to have high concentrations of cesium-137 in their bodies as a result of eating caribou meat, their staple food. The caribou have grazed on lichens and have absorbed fallout dust from atmospheric nuclear tests.

Silent Spring by U.S. biologist Rachel Louise Carson, 55, warns of dangers to wildlife in the indiscriminate use of persistent pesticides such as DDT (*see* salmon, 1969).

Florida loses nearly 8 million citrus trees as temperatures fall to 24° F. and remain below freezing.

An International Rice Research Institute (IRRI) is established in the Philippines at Los Baños with support from both the Ford and Rockefeller foundations and the Philippine government (*see* IR-5 and IR-8, 1964). Rockefeller Foundation experts Paul Mangelsdorf, J. George Harrar, Warren Weaver, Edwin J. Wellhausen, Robert F. Chandler, and others have toured Asian hunger areas and recommended creation of the institute.

Pet-Ritz Frozen Pie Crusts are introduced by Pet Milk, which has created an entirely new product category (*see* 1955).

Diet-Rite Cola, introduced by Royal Crown Cola, is the first sugar-free soft drink to be sold nationwide to the general public. The cyclamate-sweetened cola will soon have powerful competitors (*see* No-Cal, 1952; Tab, 1963).

Tab-opening aluminum-end cans for soft drinks and beer developed with backing from Aluminum Corp. of America make their first appearance (*see* 1960). Pittsburgh's Iron City beer in tab-opening cans is test-marketed in Virginia, many brewers question whether the cans are worth their extra cost, consumers cut their fingers opening the cans, but designers improve the tabs. Schlitz will introduce beer in the self-opening cans on a national scale in February of next year, more than 40 brands will be sold in the cans by July, more than 65 by August, and more than 90 percent of beer cans will be self-opening by 1970. Discarded tabs will be a hazard for bare feet until designs are further improved (*see* 1963).

The second franchised Hardee's fast-food restaurant opens January 20 at Fayetteville, N.C. (*see* 1961). Spartan Investment Co. of Spartanburg, S.C. (later Spartan Food Systems) will have more than a dozen franchised Hardee's by 1966. Hardee's Drive-Ins (the name will be changed to Hardee's Food Systems) starts its own distribution company, which will grow to have three plants and 10 distribution facilities across the country (*see* 1965).

The first Taco Bell fast-food restaurant opens at Downey, Calif. Entrepreneur Glenn Bell, 36, began on a shoestring 10 years ago with a one-man hamburger and hot dog stand at San Bernardino, immediately found himself in competition with the McDonald brothers, experimented with fast preparation of tacos, and by 1956 had three Taco Tía restaurants (in San Bernardino, Barstow, and Redlands), each making $50,000 per year. He began to franchise the Taco Tia name, formed a partnership to launch a chain of El Tacos restaurants, has sold his interest in El Tacos, and will soon have eight Taco Bell units in and about Long Beach, Paramount, and Los Angeles (*see* PepsiCo, 1978).

Canadian entrepreneurs Michael and Gladys Kronhaus acquire franchising rights to Orange Julius, form a company, open a freestanding Orange Julius stand at Burnaby, B.C., and gain rights to sell the drink at the Seattle World's Fair (*see* 1926). By 1993 there will be 104 Orange Julius stands in Canada, eight in Singapore, seven in the Philippines, three in Indonesia, one in Guam, and five in Puerto Rico (*see* Dairy Queen, 1987).

The London restaurant The Hunting Lodge opens at 16 Lower Regent Street (formerly the Hungaria) under the direction of Charles Forte with a menu that features Colchester, Whitstable, and Helford (in Cornwall) oysters; smoked salmon; lobster cocktail; cold potted Morecambe Bay shrimps; eels jellied in white wine; quail's eggs; Cheddar and Julien bacon flan (the British version of quiche); potted liver and bacon; potted duck; potted lobster; soused herring from Loch Fyne and Yarmouth; bloaters (small whole herrings, lightly smoked, split, and grilled); eel soup; stock soup;

fish pie (made with mullet, sea bass, plaice, or sole); lobster; turbot; halibut; hake (the fish may be ordered poached or grilled); roast saddle of hare with cherry sauce; Cumberland ring (a spicy sausage from the Lake District, curled up like the shell of a snail with Wiltshire shirred bacon); steak-and-kidney pudding; roast meats such as sirloin of Angus beef from a trolley; saddle of lamb; charcoal-grilled steak and lamb cutlets; grouse in season; pork chops with baked apple; cottage pie; treacle tart; strawberry syllabub in season; London syllabub year round; and trifle.

The London restaurant Tiberio opens at 22 Queen Street. Restaurateurs Mario and Franco have been so successful since 1959 with their Terrazzo that they are able to expand their operations, serving *ostriche à la veneziana* (oysters in their shells, covered with a light, cheese-flavored sabayon sauce); 10 soups; 15 pastas; sea bass stuffed with almonds and flavored with basil; Appian lamb roasted and served with a sauce of red currants; baby lamb Villa Cesari (lamb ribs with potatoes mixed with black truffles); *trippa Petronius*; *animelli di vitello à la crema* (sweetbreads and lobster in a creamy sauce); chicken stuffed with grapes and truffled rice cooked in Muscat wine and cream; and duckling braised in honey with a sauce of Curaçao, almonds, and oranges.

The Paris restaurant Relais Louis XIII opens at 8, rue des Grands-Augustins at the corner of the rue de Pont-de-Lodi under the direction of Odette Delanoy with chef André Marfeuille preparing filet of lamb, *rouget sauté à l'épicurienne*, *brochette de veau de Villeverneix*, and other specialties.

Ledoyen reopens September 24 in the Carré des Champs-Élysées, Paris, under the direction of Gilbert Lejeune, who has been with Laserre on the Avenue Franklin-Roosevelt for 20 years. Located in the gardens of the lower Champs-Élysées, framed by chestnut trees, weeping willows, flowering shrubs, lawns, and fountains, the restaurant opened originally in 1792 near the Place de Révolution (later the Place de la Concorde) as a *guinguette*.

The New York restaurant The Sign of the Dove opens in a renovated brick tenement at 1110 Third Avenue (northwest corner of 65th Street). Owner Joseph Santo, whose decor is initially more remarkable than the food he serves, will expand by acquiring adjacent buildings and will improve his kitchen (his brother Berge and Berge's wife, Henny, will take over daily management in years to come).

The New York restaurant La Grenouille opens in December at 3 East 52nd Street. Proprietor Charles Masson, who came to New York in 1939 to work with Henri Soulé at the French Pavilion at the World's Fair, has worked as headwaiter on the S.S. *Independence*, traveling between New York, Cannes, Capri, and Naples. His wife, Giselle (his nickname for her is "Grenouille," meaning "frog"), has signed a lease for the ground floor of the house and cabled Masson aboard the *Independence*. When he dies unexpectedly in 1975, his son and namesake will drop out of Carnegie-Mellon University to help his mother, filling the place with fresh flowers every day as his father did (the restaurant will continue until 1993).

1963

Famine continues in the People's Republic of China, where by some estimates 20 to 40 million people will have died by next year in what critics of Maoist agricultural policies will call the worst famine in history (*see* 1961). Beijing is forced to seek grain from the West, and Canada makes a major sale of wheat to the P.R.C. in August.

Soviet crops fail both in Kazakhstan and in Ukraine (*see* 1953). Fully one-third of U.S. grain exports in the next 3 years will go to drought-stricken India, but substantial quantities will also go to the Communist countries.

Canada completes a $500 million wheat sale to the USSR in September. "Comrade Khrushchev has performed a miracle," Muscovites joke; "He has sown wheat in Kazakhstan and harvested it in Canada."

Khrushchev declares the Kazakhstan virgin lands experiment a failure and seeks nearly 2 million tons of U.S. wheat. President Kennedy approves the sale, former Vice President Nixon and most other Republicans oppose it on grounds that it would help the enemy, but it goes through at year's end with support from President Lyndon B. Johnson, 55, who has taken office following the assassination of President Kennedy November 22. When the contracts are finally sold early next year, Continental Grain will handle the largest portion of the Soviet wheat sales, with Cargill, Inc.—headed since 1961 by Erwin E. Kelm, 52, who is the company's first chief executive not a Cargill or MacMillan—accounting for 500,000 tons of hard wheat and 200,000 tons of durum wheat (*see* 1964).

Typhoons destroy nearly half of Japan's standing crops. The resulting food shortages boost Japanese demand for imported foodstuffs.

The European Economic Community vetoes British entry after President Charles de Gaulle, 72, raises objections.

U.S. factory workers average more than $100 per week for the first time in history but unemployment reaches 6.1 percent by February.

The price of sugar on the New York Coffee and Sugar Exchange soars from 3¢/lb. to nearly 13¢ in 5 months as the lack of Cuban sugar (*see* 1960) and other factors make themselves felt (*see* 1973).

Sicilian-born Chicago pecan sheller John Sanfilippo dies, leaving his 41-year-old business to his son Jasper, 32. An uneducated laborer who went to work as a sheller at age 9, the elder Sanfilippo shelled 45 pounds of pecans per day, using primitive equipment, and saved enough on $6 per day to start the business, which has sold its product to nut shops and to a few large food processors for use in products such as candy bars. Jasper Sanfilippo will diversify beyond pecans and make deals with shellers of almonds, peanuts, and walnuts to distribute their products, arranging with food brokers to sell nuts to bakeries, candy bar companies, and other industrial customers (*see* 1974).

Procter & Gamble acquires J. A. Folger and Co. August 29 and enters the coffee business (*see* 1908). P&G will uses its marketing techniques to make Folger's the top-selling brand in the nation, surpassing sales of Maxwell House.

H. J. Heinz acquires StarKist Seafood, retaining Joseph Bogdanovich (*see* 1944). He renamed the company's giant Puerto Rican cannery StarKist Caribe in 1960, renames its Pacific cannery StarKist Samoa, and next year will introduce Charlie the

Tuna, an advertising character created by the Chicago advertising agency Leo Burnett (with help from Bogdanovich's actress sister Geraldine), who will give the name StarKist wide currency (*see* Charlie's Lunch Kit, 1992; Ore-Ida, 1965).

Carnation Co. acquires Contadina Foods, the northern California processor and distributor of tomato products founded in 1916 (*see* 1918).

Borden Co. acquires Aunt Jane's Foods, a leading packer of fresh and processed pickles (*see* ReaLemon, 1962; Wise Foods, 1964; Cremora, below).

Pet Milk acquires Downyflake Foods, makers of frozen waffles and other breakfast items.

Hershey Chocolate acquires the brands of H. B. Reese, who died in 1956 (*see* 1923).

New England Confectionery Co., close to bankruptcy, is acquired for just under $4 million by a New York holding company that will revive its fortunes.

Warner-Lambert Co. acquires Fox-Cross Candy Co., makers of Charleston Chew!, from Nabisco Confections, a division of National Biscuit Co.

Nabisco acquires James O. Welch Co., whose 10,000-square-foot factory at Cambridge, Mass., produces Sugar Daddy, Sugar Babies, Junior Mints, and Pom Poms.

The Great Atlantic & Pacific Tea Co. (A&P), still the leading U.S. grocery chain, completes a 1.5-million-square-foot food-processing facility—largest in the world—in upstate New York, anticipating sales volume of $17 billion to $18 billion by the early 1970s, but unlike its major competitors the A&P has failed to follow its customers as they moved to the suburbs and has stuck with smaller city groceries instead of building large supermarkets in the shopping malls (*see* 1958; 1975).

The dining car of the Illinois Central all-Pullman *Panama Limited* on its overnight run between Chicago and New Orleans serves a $9.95 "King's Dinner" that includes a Manhattan or martini, hors-d'oeuvres, fresh Gulf shrimp cocktail or crab morsels with a special sauce, imported vin rosé, fresh Gulf fish according to season, charcoal-broiled boneless sirloin steak with mushrooms, hot bread, choice of potato and vegetable, imported cheese and apple wedges with toasted crackers, and Illinois Central blended coffee with a choice of liqueurs—Crème de Cacao, Crème de Menthe, or blackberry.

Julia Child prepares *bœuf bourguignon* on television February 11 as she begins a series of cooking demonstrations on Boston's educational television station.

New York Daily Mirror Sunday feature writer Hyman Goldberg, 55, takes over the paper's cooking column and writes with tongue in cheek under the name "Prudence Penny." Son of a Bronx restaurateur who at age 16 became a copyboy on the *New York Sun*, he starts each column with a joke or anecdote. His recipe for making rum pie with a zwieback crust will say, "Break up zwieback. Keep rum bottle handy. If smashing of zwieback exhausts you, take a swig of the rum and resume zwieback breaking when strength returns." His recipe for baked apples will conclude, "Keep basting the apples until they are glazed. If you would like to get a little glazed yourself, pour a shot of rum or brandy into the apple before serving." Goldberg will be the author of two cookbooks, *Man in the Kitchen* and *Beginner's Cookbook*.

Cookbooks: *The Margaret Rudkin Pepperidge Farm Cookbook* by Rudkin; *An Herb and Spice Cook Book* by Craig Claiborne.

British sales of frozen foods reach £75 million, up from £7.5 million in 1955, but frozen vegetables, fish, meat, cake, and other items still account for only 1.5 percent of total food expenditures.

Average U.S. per capita meat consumption reaches 170.6 pounds, but veal consumption drops to 5 pounds, down from 9.7 in 1949. Average chicken consumption is 37.8 pounds per capita, up from 23.5 in 1945, when chicken was more costly than beef.

Average U.S. per capita butter consumption falls to 6.7 pounds, down from 18.3 in 1934 and 7.5 in 1960; margarine consumption rises to 9.3 pounds, up from 8.6 in 1957; cheese to 9.4 pounds, up from seven in 1949.

Bayonne, N.J., salad oil king Anthony De Angelis, 47, is indicted for fraud. His Allied Crude Vegetable

Oil & Refining Corp. has rigged its tanks, using seawater in place of salad oil which was to serve as collateral for warehouse receipts. The deficiency runs to 827,000 tons of oil valued at $175 million. De Angelis goes bankrupt, and some investors are ruined.

Fallout of radioactive strontium-90, strontium-89, cesium-137, barium-140, and iodine-131 in world rainfall reaches its peak after 2 years of atmospheric testing of nuclear weapons by the Soviet Union and the United States. Milk is particularly affected, since cows eat grass which has been contaminated by fallout (although mother's milk can have as much strontium-90 as cow's milk). The Food and Drug Administration, Public Health Service, Atomic Energy Commission, and state agriculture departments all take samples and issue monthly bulletins on radiation levels, which hereafter will decline (except in 1968, following test explosions by the Chinese and French); by 1970, rainfall will be depositing less than 5 percent as much strontium-90 as it does this year.

Thermal pollution kills millions of striped bass at a new Consolidated Edison nuclear generating plant on the Hudson before a mesh screen is erected to fence out the anadromous fish, letting them swim upriver to spawn.

Long Island, N.Y., oysterman H. Butler Flowers starts a Bayville hatchery to produce cultured bluepoints (*Crassostrea virginica*) as pollution and commercial dredging deplete supplies of the androgynous mollusks. Flowers is the last surviving Long Island oysterman (there were more than 1,000 when he started in the 1920s); his operation will grow to harvest about 20 million oysters per year and box them for sale at New York's Fulton Fish Market, where they will be sold for consumption at restaurants all over the country.

Mexican farmers plant high-yielding semidwarf wheat developed by Rockefeller Foundation scientists and introduced for the first time on a commercial basis (*see* 1945; Borlaug, 1944; 1966).

Congress shifts policy with regard to farm supports: instead of giving farmers high support loans, it inaugurates a deficiency payment system under which farmers are paid only when actual prices do not reach target prices. The new system allows prices to

decline beginning with this year's crop and will lead to greatly increased domestic use of feed grains.

The U.S. corn crop tops 5 billion bushels for the first time, up from 3 billion in 1906.

The number of U.S. farmers falls to 13.7 million—7.1 percent of the population. The number of man-hours employed in U.S. agriculture falls below 9 million, down from 20 million in 1940. The average farmworker produces enough food and fiber for 31 people, up from 15.5 in 1950 (*see* 1973).

Two U.S. botulism fatalities are traced to some canned tunafish. They are the first botulism deaths produced by commercially packed food in the United States since 1941 (*see* 1971).

Vitamin E is shown to be useful in treating severe cases of kwashiorkor, macrocytic anemia, and creatinuria (*see* 1938; Williams, 1931).

The U.S. National Research Council revises its "Recommended Daily Allowances" of nutrients (*see* 1943); the USDA revises its Handbook No. 8 to give data on 2,483 food items with vitamin and mineral content plus other information (*see* 1950).

Weight Watchers is founded by Queens, N.Y., housewife Jean Neditch, 39, who has reduced her own weight from 213 pounds to 142 with the help of a high-protein diet developed by Dr. Norman Jolliffe, now 62, of the New York City Department of Health. The Barbie Doll, introduced 4 years ago by the U.S. toy company Mattel, Inc., is helping to give young women an unrealizable ideal of slim beauty (*see Ziegfeld Follies*, 1907); some adopt drastic diet regimens, many have become anorexic in a pathological quest for weight loss. Weight Watchers represents a healthier approach. Using a form of group therapy, it completely proscribes some foods, permits others without restriction, and accustoms people to a diet on which they can stay without constant "yo-yo" gains and losses. Weight Watchers will grow into a worldwide operation with average weekly attendance of half a million and a line of frozen foods designed to help maintain proper weight (*see* cookbook, 1966; Nutri/System, 1971; Heinz, 1979).

The *Denominazione d'Origine Controllata* signed into law July 12 by Italy's president Antonio Segni aims to establish quality standards for wines (*see* France, 1935). It establishes rules for areas of production, type of soil, location of vineyards, variety of grape grown, pruning, cultivation, allowable yields per acre, allowable yield of juice per ton of grapes, minimum sugar levels, minimum acid and extract levels, methods of vinification, and minimum aging requirements but fails to distinguish between good wines and bad. Some wines—Brunello, di Montalcino, Chianti vino Nobile, di Montebulciano, Carmignano Rosso, Barolo Gattinara, Giorgiano Rosso, and Albana di Romagna—are held to even stricter guidelines, but the DOC laws quickly prove unworkable: classic old wine names are lumped with obscure and often far less deserving ones. The quality of Italian wines will hereafter decline as a result of the DOC laws, which encourage impossibly high yields and lower standards (*see* consumption figures, 1985).

Yakisoba, introduced by Japan's Nissin Foods, is a bag type fried ramen (chow mein style) that comes with a package of seasoning (*see* Chicken Ramen, 1958; Nissin Foods USA, 1970).

General Mills introduces Wundra "instantized" flour, which is granular in texture and pours like salt. So uniform that it needs no sifting, the new flour can be measured more accurately than other flour, says General Mills, never forms lumps, can be used in any recipe that calls for an all-purpose flour, and gives more consistent results in baking.

Hershey Chocolate lowers the weight of its nickel Hershey Bar in September from 1 oz. to ⅞ oz. (*see* 1960; 1965).

Tab, introduced by Coca-Cola, is a cyclamate-sweetened cola drink that competes with Royal Crown's Diet-Rite (*see* 1962; Diet Pepsi, 1965).

Dayton, Ohio, engineer Ermal Cleon Fraze, 50, obtains a patent for a pull-tab opener that will revolutionize the way people open soda and beer cans (*see* 1962). Having forgotten to bring a can opener to a family picnic 4 years ago, he used an auto bumper to open a beer can, stayed up all night figuring out an easier way, came up with a pull tab that attaches to can lids, and will later invent a version with a ring and prepuncturing tab. Fraze will assign patent rights to Aluminum Co. of America, and

within 25 years his tabs will be used on about 150 billion cans annually.

Borden Co. (above) introduces Cremora nondairy creamer (*see* Pream, 1952; Coffee-Rich, 1960; Coffee-Mate, 1961).

The Los Angeles restaurant The Bistro opens at 246 North Canon Drive, Beverly Hills. Restaurateur Kurt Niklas has for 13 years been a captain and—later—maître d'hôtel at Mike Romanoff's and has obtained backing from members of the business and film communities. His menu, chalked on a blackboard, offers frogs' legs Provençale, Hungarian goulash with spätzle, wiener schnitzel à la Holstein, chicken potpie, cassoulet with duck, *pot-au-feu* of boiled beef and chicken, herb-stuffed roast chicken, chicken casserole *grand-mère*, cappellini, and fresh fish.

The New York restaurant Victor's Cafe opens at 240 Columbus Avenue (71st Street). Emigré Cuban restaurateur Victor del Corral has started the place with $4,000 and runs it with his wife and daughters. The menu will grow to include 15 soups (many are as thick as stews); 14 rice dishes; seafood dishes (*paella* with lobster, shrimps, clams, scallops, and curry sauce; *camarones enchilados*); meat dishes (including stewed oxtail in wine sauce); 15 Cuban specialities (including curried *tocino*, *ajiaco criollo*, pork *tasajo*, *boniato*, *platano*, and—on weekends—*lechón asado con morros*); 17 desserts (including guava preserves with cream cheese, papaya with cream cheese, and *manzana à la reina*); beer; wine; and sangría.

The New York restaurant Elaine's, opened in April at 1703 Second Avenue by Elaine Kauffman, will attract celebrities, especially from the literary world, for more than 30 years.

New York's Restaurant Nippon opens at 145 East 52nd Street—the first restaurant in the city to serve rigorously authentic Japanese fare not geared to American tastes. Head chef Eigiro Tanaka has been chef to the Japanese prime minister Shigeru Yoshida and will head Nippon's kitchen staff until his death in 1978; proprietor Nobuyoshi Kuraoka, whose father owns restaurants in Tokyo and Yokohama, first came to America on a student visa in 1955. Nippon introduces the *sushi* bar to New York and will originate *negimayaki* (scallion-filled beef roll). Its initial menu offers *shiro miso wan*; *suytashi wan*; *torisashi* (thinly sliced raw chicken breast); *oshitashi* (spinach flavored with flecks of dried bonito); *totamago-yaki* (an egg dish made with fish, stock, and seaweed); *shioyaki* (fileted fish—striped bass or salmon); *uni-yaki* (broiled chopped squid); *shabu shabu*; *mizutaki* (a chicken and vegetable ragout); and *hamanabe* (a clam casserole); as well as the usual *sashimi*, *sushi*, *sukiyaki*, *tempura*, *teriyaki*, *tonkatsu* (deep-fried pork filet), and *yakitori*.

The Paris restaurant La Marée opens in November at 1, rue Daru under the management of Marcel Trompier, whose 50-seat place (with a staff of 25) specializes in Belon oysters (hot on the half shell with a champagne sauce), fois gras from the Landes in a *gelée de Muscat*, butter from the Charente, *filet de turbot à la moutarde*, and *demoiselle de Cherbourg* (small lobster from the Brittany coast); but while La Marée serves duck, quail, partridge, and ortolan, it does not offer chicken because, Trompier explains, he cannot obtain wheat-fed *poulet* and no other kind is acceptable.

The London nightclub Annabel's opens in the cellar of 44 Berkeley Square (the gambling club Clermont's is upstairs but unconnected). Proprietor Mark Birley, 32, is the 6-foot, 5-inch son of a portrait painter who lived at Vienna's Hotel Sacher as a British officer during the postwar occupation. He does not initially make cuisine a priority, having been told that he will lose money if he serves good food, but Annabel's will grow to have a membership of 4,000 and, under chef Howell Smith and his brigade of 12, will be one of the city's three or four best restaurants, serving, typically, seven soups (including beef tea, bisque de homard, vichyssoise, cold Senegalese, gazpacho, and thick pea); smoked salmon and beef from Scotland; roast grouse from Scotland (August 12 to November 1) with brussels sprouts, chestnuts, and bread sauce; butter from Normandy; filets of sole stuffed with a mousse of lobster; foie gras from Louis Henry in Strasbourg; San Daniele prosciutto and white truffles from Italy; hickory-smoked bacon from New York; asparagus flown in from places as far distant as Kenya and New Zealand depending on the season; good clarets; and chocolate ice made with English military chocolate.

Soviet Premier Nikita Khrushchev says in September, "If you feed people just with revolutionary slogans they will listen today, they will listen tomorrow, they will listen the day after tomorrow, but on the fourth day they will say, 'To hell with you.' " He is stripped of power in a coup d'état September 13 and replaced as party leader in October by Leonid Ilyich Brezhnev, 57 (*see* 1965; grain shipments, below).

The U.S. food stamp program conducted at Rochester, N.Y., from 1939 to 1943 is reactivated on a broad scale by the U.S. Department of Agriculture to help feed needy Americans (*see* 1959; 1967).

Atlanta restaurateur Lester G. Maddox, 48, closes his Pickwick Restaurant rather than submit to federal government orders that he serve blacks as well as whites. He has passed out pickax handles on the street in front of his restaurant to partisans who will cudgel any blacks who try to enter.

Continental Grain begins shipment of wheat to the Soviet Union January 28 despite a longshoreman's boycott against such shipments unless U.S. merchant ships are allotted the same amount of cargo assigned to foreign vessels (*see* 1963). Moscow has bought 400 million bushels; only 65.5 million have come from the United States because of the steep premium on freight charges for grain sent in U.S. bottoms, but Continental and Cargill, Inc., nevertheless profit handsomely from their $134 million in grain sales to the Soviet Union (*see* 1972; Allied Mills, 1965).

The U.S. baking industry employs 325,000 workers, up from 11,400 in 1914.

Forrest Mars, now 59, buys out his half sister (she is dying of cancer) to become sole owner of Mars, Inc. (*see* M&M's, 1941). He recruits executives from companies such as Procter & Gamble and will diversify by acquiring Uncle Ben's Rice and Kal-Kan Foods, a leading maker of canned dog food (*see* 1973).

U.S. October food prices: round steak $1.07/lb., up from 92¢ in 1954; sugar 59¢ per five-pound bag, up from 52¢; coffee 82¢/lb., down from $1.10; bread 21¢/lb. loaf, up from 17¢; eggs 57¢/doz., down from

60¢; milk 48¢ per half gallon, up from 45¢; butter 76¢/lb., up from 72¢; lettuce 25¢/head, up from 19¢.

Negotiations begin at Geneva November 16 to reduce world trade tariffs in the so-called first Kennedy Round of discussions (*see* 1963).

Dole Corp. is acquired by Honolulu's 113-year-old Castle & Cooke, which not only markets pineapple and pineapple juice but for the first time also markets fresh pineapple under the Dole Royal Hawaiian label, using jet planes to rush the fruit to East Coast U.S. markets, although most still goes by ship to West Coast ports (*see* 1934).

Castle & Cooke (above) also acquires most of Standard Fruit & Steamship Co., taking over the Vaccaro family's majority interest. It will operate Standard Fruit as a wholly owned subsidiary (*see* bananas, 1966).

Consolidated Foods acquires Booth Fisheries, the largest U.S. processor and distributor of frozen seafood products (*see* Shasta, 1961; Popsicle, 1965).

California's Inglenook Winery is acquired by United Vintners, a giant firm (better known as Petri) specializing in bulk wines (*see* 1879).

Pepsi-Cola Company acquires a company that controls the rights to Mountain Dew, a lemon-lime drink (*see* below; PepsiCo, 1965).

Standard Brands acquires Curtiss Candy Co. (*see* 1920; 1923; Planters, 1961; Nabisco Brands, 1981).

Borden Co. acquires Cracker Jack Co. (*see* 1893) and Wise Foods, which has become the largest potato-chip manufacturer in the eastern United States (*see* 1921; Aunt Jane's, 1963; pasta, 1973).

London's Fortnum & Mason in Picadilly installs a clock with chiming figures (*see* 1707); its works can be viewed by customers from the store's second floor.

The Paris building at 129, rue du Faubourg Saint-Honoré that houses L'École de Cordon Bleu is sold and the school moves to 24, rue du Champs de Mars near Les Invalides (*see* 1945). Students now are mostly Americans, and to gain the coveted *grand diplôme* a student must prepare a complete *déjeuner*, typically a gelée dish such as truite en gelée, vol-au-vent à la reine, chaud-froid de volaille,

bécasse au Chambertin, canard à l'orange cooked with Grand Marnier, and either Paris-Brest (a round pastry filled with praline butter cream) or a soufflé—all in 3 hours (the preliminary work takes 2 or 3 days).

Nonfiction: *Delights and Prejudices* by James Beard, now 61, is an autobiographical reminiscence; *Stalking the Blue-Eyed Scallop* by Euell Gibbons.

Cookbooks: *The Gourmet Cooking School Cookbook* by Dione Lucas with Darleen Gies; *First Slice Your Cookbook* by Scottish–U.S. author Lady Arabella Boxer, 33, who has started writing about food at the prompting of her cartoonist-editor husband, Mark; *The Delectable Past* by Trenton, N.J., author-bibliophile Esther Aresty, whose recipes are taken from cookbooks published between the early 15th century and 1901; *The American Heritage Cookbook* by the editors of *American Heritage* magazine.

Film: Sean Connery as British agent James Bond (007) in Guy Hamilton's *Goldfinger* popularizes the vodka martini ("shaken, not stirred").

Danish fishermen discover the major feeding grounds of the Atlantic salmon off the southwest coast of Greenland. They begin to take large catches of the fish, which average only seven pounds each, sharply reducing spawning runs up the rivers of Canada, England, France, Iceland, Ireland, Norway, Russia, Scotland, Wales, and the U.S. state of Maine (*see* 1950; 1969).

The International Rice Research Institute at Los Baños in the Philippines introduces high-yielding dwarf strains of Indica rice on an experimental basis under the names IR-5 and IR-8. The new "miracle" rice for tropical cultivation has been developed by crossing ordinary Indica rice with Japan's high-yielding Japonica variety (*see* 1962; 1965).

Unilever resurrects the name John West (*see* 1857; 1864) as the label for an array of imported foods, including sardines from Portugal, brisling (a sardine-like herring) from Norway, salmon from Canada and Alaska, salmon, tuna, shrimps, crabs, and prawns from Japan, salmon, shrimp, and prawns from the United States, tuna from Peru, and pilchards from South Africa, as well as peaches, mandarin oranges, dried fruit from Australia, asparagus from New Zealand, apples and pineapples from Malaysia, fruit from South Africa, currants from Greece, and tomato juice from Italy.

Kellogg introduces Pop-Tarts toaster pastries.

Lucky Charms breakfast food, introduced by General Mills, is 50.4 percent sugar (*see* 1961; 1966).

General Mills enters the fast-growing snack food market in May with the introduction of Bugles, Whistles, and Daisy*s—three shaped corn-based snacks made possible by new food technology; Bugles and Daisy*s will reach national distribution by June 1967, but only the horn-shaped Bugles will survive beyond February 1973. They will have sales of 2.4 million pounds per year by 1975 and more than 10 million pounds by 1990.

Chiffon Margarine and Seven Seas Salad Dressings are introduced nationwide by Anderson, Clayton & Co. of Houston, Texas (*see* 1904; Kraft, 1987).

Yoplait Yogurt is introduced by the French union of dairy cooperatives SODIAAL, whose technicians have invented a special process that makes their yogurt distinctive. Yoplait will be France's leading brand of yogurt within 5 years (*see* U.S., 1974).

Lotte, a 16-year-old Japanese chewing-gum maker, enters the chocolate business in competition with the industry leader Meiji Seika, founded in 1916; Fujiya, founded in 1910; and Exaki Glico, founded in 1919.

Awake is introduced by General Foods, which promotes the synthetic orange juice with a budget of $5 million—more than is spent to promote pure orange juice, whether frozen, chilled, or fresh.

Maxim is introduced by General Foods, which has spent huge sums to develop the freeze-dried instant coffee (*see* 1940; Instant Maxwell House, 1942; Taster's Choice, 1966).

Carnation Co. introduces Carnation Instant Breakfast in West Coast markets (*see* 1963; FTC, 1970; Nestlé, 1985).

Mountain Dew (above) was created about 19 years ago in Marion, Va., Knoxville, Tenn., or Johnson City, Tenn. (accounts vary). Each 12 oz. serving contains 54 milligrams of caffeine (as compared to 38.5 in Pepsi and 240 in a cup of coffee) and 170 calories (as compared to 150 in Pepsi). Pepsi-Cola will give the brand national distribution, and by

1995 the "heavy citrus" beverage will be America's sixth most popular soft drink, with $2.7 billion in sales (mostly to youths aged 12 to 24).

The U.S. government defines bourbon as whiskey that contains at least 51 percent corn liquor and is aged in new charred-oak barrels (*see* Bottled-in-Bond Act, 1897). Kentucky's Bourbon County has long since become "dry" by local option and has no legal distilleries.

French restaurateur Alexandre Dumaine retires from the Hôtel de Côte-d'Or, which promptly loses its three stars in the *Guide Michelin* (*see* 1930). Chef Françoise Minot succeeds Dumaine, and his restaurant will be awarded two stars by Michelin next year.

The West Berlin restaurant Maître opens at 10 Meinekestrasse. Paris-born restaurateur Henry Levy, 30, flies all his produce in from France, buys butter from the Charente, fleurette cream from Paris, foie gras from Landes, olive oil from Provence, and *loup de mer* from the Mediterranean. His menu includes *gâteau de foies blonds aux écrivisses* (duck- and chicken-liver mousse with crayfish); *pot-au-feu de lièvre* (hare stew); *ragout des huitres et Saint-Jacques au poireaux* (oyster and scallop ragout with leeks); lemon soufflé; and three dozen French cheeses.

The New York restaurant Le Périgord opens at 405 East 52nd Street. French-born owner Georges Briguet will attract not only East Side neighbors but also gastronomes from all over New York and other cities as well.

The Ginger Man (one of the restaurant's owners, Patrick O'Neal, has recently starred in a Broadway play of that name) opens in June in what was earlier a garage across from New York's Lincoln Center at 51 West 64th Street, offering an à la carte menu that features omelettes at $2 and $2.50, hors d'oeuvres at 75¢ (with coquilles $1.25), soups at 70¢, luncheon entrées at $2.75, dinner entrées at $4.25 (filet mignon is $4.50 at lunch or dinner), desserts mostly 75¢.

Benihana of Tokyo opens in New York at 61 West 56th Street. The *teppinyaki-hibachi*-style steak-shrimp-and-mushroom-bean-sprouts restaurant operated by Japanese-American Hiroaki "Rocky"

Aoki, 25, meets with instant success and will be followed by Benihana (Red Flower) restaurants in other U.S. cities (*see* Benihana Palace, 1970). Aoki stopped in New York en route to Rome 4 years ago as a member of Japan's Olympic wrestling team, ate at short-order hamburger grills, was struck with the idea that tabletop cooking as practiced in Tokyo's sukiyaki restaurants might appeal to Americans, obtained a degree in restaurant management at one of the city's community colleges, and has earned part of his initial investment by driving an ice cream truck.

The first Arby's fast-food restaurant opens July 23 at Boardman, Ohio, south of Youngstown, serving 69¢ roast beef sandwiches, potato chips, and Texas-sized iced tea. Founder Forrest Raffel and his brother Leroy are graduates of Cornell's School of Hotel and Restaurant Admnistration and the University of Pennsylvania's Wharton School of Finance, respectively, who in the 1950s bought an uncle's restaurant equipment business and started Raffel Brothers (R.B.). It became a leading food service consulting firm, designing and installing food service facilities for clients that included the Pittsburgh International Aiport, six Ohio Turnpike restaurants, and Standard Oil of Ohio's Hospitality Inn motel chain. They will franchise their operation (the first franchise restaurant will open next year at Akron), come close to bankruptcy a few years later during a shakeout in the fast-food industry, and by 1975 will have a chain of 500 outlets (*see* 1978).

The White Castle System started in 1921 has 100 outlets in 11 U.S. metropolitan areas, three bakeries, and two manufacturing plants, employs 3,000 people on an average workday, sells 120 million hamburger sandwiches at 12¢ each (five for 25¢ on takeout orders) plus 47 million cups of coffee, and has gross revenues of $30 million. A typical White Castle outlet is 45 feet square with a full basement and three grills, each capable of cooking at least 600 hamburgers per hour.

Colonel Sanders has more than 600 licensees offering his "finger-lickin' good" Kentucky Fried Chicken (*see* 1955). Now 74, Sanders sells the franchise business for $2 million, plus a guaranteed salary of $40,000 per year for life to act as a goodwill ambassador (*see* 1976).

1965

Pakistan and much of India suffer widespread starvation as monsoon rains fail and crops wither in a drought of unprecedented proportions.

"There is a global food catastrophe building up on the horizon which threatens to engulf the free world and the Communist world alike," says Thomas Ware of the Freedom from Hunger Foundation.

Soviet Russia suffers another crop failure as it did in 1963 and is forced to pay in gold for wheat from Australia and Canada. Canada has made a sale to the Russians in January at prices below the prevailing world level, triggering a price war between Ottawa and Washington in world markets. Moscow is discouraged from buying U.S. wheat by a presidential requirement that half of all shipments be made in U.S. vessels (at high cost) and by a longshoremen's threat not to load any grain for shipment to Communist Russia.

President Johnson outlines programs for a "Great Society" that will eliminate poverty in America January 4 in his State of the Union message; he signs a $1.4 billion program of federal-state economic aid to Appalachia into law March 9, but U.S. military involvement in Southeast Asia escalates, draining the U.S. economy.

Americans on average pay 18.5 percent of their total income for food, down from 24.4 percent in 1955. It is the lowest percentage in history and lower than any other country in the world.

The Diners Club of America, founded in 1950, reaches a membership of 1.3 million, American Express has 1.2 million after just 7 years, and major U.S. banks prepare to issue credit cards of their own. Not only restaurants but also hotels, motels, airlines, travel agencies, car rental agencies, and many retail stores now honor the credit cards.

Cavenham Foods is founded by British entrepreneur James Goldsmith, 32, who will soon acquire Bovril as he builds his candy and diet food producer into Europe's third-largest food processor after Unilever and Nestlé Alimentana, S.A.

Unilever (above) now has 500 businesses operating in more than 60 countries, up from 402 businesses in 40 countries in 1948. Its food businesses include canned goods, dehydrated foods, sausages, fish, cheese, ice cream, and fruit drinks; sales of its frozen foods reach £45 million, up from £2.5 million in 1953.

Unilever's Wall division has sales of £40 million, up from £3 million in 1951 (*see* 1840). Financing its research out of profits, Wall during World War II developed ways to produce heavy pigs efficiently. Its factories concentrate on bacon curing and sausage making.

Continental Grain acquires a 51.28 percent interest in Allied Mills, a major U.S. flour company, through a tender offer of stock (*see* 1964; 1970).

Pepsi-Cola president Donald M. Kendall, 44, engineers a merger with Frito-Lay to create PepsiCo, Inc. (*see* 1959; 1961).

R. J. Reynolds Co. acquires Penick and Ford as it continues to diversify (*see* Hawaiian Punch, 1961). The company's products include Brer Rabbit Molasses, Vermont Maid Syrup, My*T*Fine Puddings and Pie Fillings, College Inn Chicken à la King, and other College Inn prepared foods (*see* Chun King, 1966).

H. J. Heinz acquires Ore-Ida Foods (*see* 1951).

Consolidated Foods Corp. acquires Popsicle Industries (*see* Epperson, 1924; Booth Fisheries, 1964). A court order requires Consolidated to divest itself of 100 supermarkets and 26 drugstores with combined sales of more than $200 million (*see* Sara Lee Corp., 1985).

Kraft technicians develop machines that will wrap each of the company's Kraft Singles individually (*see* 1947).

General Foods introduces Shake 'n Bake in parts of New York and Ohio in February (it will go into national distribution early next year). The first complete seasoned coating mix, it comes in two versions, one for preparing chicken, the other for preparing fish. Each box contains an envelope of mix—enough for a 2½-pound chicken—and a plastic shaker bag: the mix (shortening lightly seasoned with herbs and spices) is emptied into the bag, pieces of chicken or fish moistened with milk or water are inserted, and the bag is shaken until the

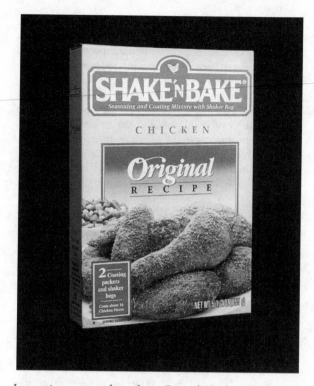

Innovative new products from General Foods proliferated in American supermarkets.

pieces are evenly coated. Advertisements say, "Now make crispy golden chicken without frying! If you love fried chicken but worry about fried foods, now you can give chicken a crisp, crunchy crust *in your oven*." "No batter to mix, no mess to clean up. Chicken's ready for the oven in 5 minutes!" An Italian Flavor version for chicken will be introduced in 1968 containing Parmesan cheese, oregano, and other spices and herbs; a Shake 'n Bake mix for pork will be introduced in 1969; and a Shake 'n Bake mix for hamburgers will go into national distribution in 1970.

Cool Whip is introduced by General Foods (above), whose scientists have come up with a whipped-cream-like product that costs less than whipped cream, comes in a resealable white plastic storage container, keeps longer (2 weeks in a refrigerator, up to 1 year in a freezer), does not have to be whipped, and has fewer calories. Within 3 months, Cool Whip is the best-selling processed topping in its test markets (Seattle and Buffalo), and will soon be available nationwide for use in layered Jell-O desserts, fruit salads, and imitation mousses, as well as for pie and Jell-O toppings.

Tang is introduced on a national basis in March by General Foods (above), whose scientists have spent a decade perfecting the fruit-flavored breakfast drink. It will eventually contain some orange juice solids but initially consists only of sugar, citric acid (for tartness), gum arabic, natural orange flavor, sodim carboxymethylcellulose, calcium phospate (to prevent caking), vitamin C, hydrogenated vegetable oil, vitamin A, artificial color, and the preservative BHA. The National Aeronautics and Space Administration (NASA) selects Tang for the galley of Gemini astronauts in space, and it will be in the galley of the Apollo mission that lands on the moon in July 1969.

Cookbooks: *Michael Field's Cooking School: A Selection of Great Recipes Demonstrating the Pleasures and Principles of Fine Cooking* by former concert pianist Field, 50, who studied at New York's Juilliard School of Music, cooked from an early age to make ends meet, made his concert debut in 1943, began a cooking school in his Scarsdale home and gave up his concert career 2 years ago, moved the school to a New York apartment, and never takes more than about 10 students at a time; *James Beard's Menus for Entertaining* and *James Beard's Party Book.*

Congress enacts a 5-year, $25-million anadromous fish program to conserve alewives, river sturgeon, salmon, shad, and striped bass, which swim upriver to spawn (*see* Maine, 1948).

Calico scallops come into use as a seafood with promising commercial possibilities as equipment is developed to process the deepwater mollusks, discovered off North Carolina and Florida in the 1950s. Fishing for calico scallops will become a major industry at Cape Canaveral, Fla., off the North Carolina coast, and in the Gulf of Mexico, with catches averaging 12 million pounds per year between 1984 and 1994.

The Arkansas catfish industry has its beginnings as a few farmers raise the fish to supplement income from field crops. By 1970 they will be harvesting 5.7 million pounds, and as farmers in other states get

into catfish raising the harvest will increase to 46.5 million pounds by 1975, 360.4 million by 1990, and 459 million by 1993. Whereas wild catfish will be scorned as food for the poor, commercially grown catfish will be given scientifically devised feed and raised in water whose quality is monitored to avoid muddy flavors. Refrigeration will ensure delivery of firm-fleshed fresh fish to markets all over the country.

The Rock Cornish game hen is created by Arkansas chicken processor Donald John Tyson, 35, who dropped out of the University of Arkansas to join the family firm in 1952 as a feed mill manager (*see* 1930). His father acquired a small northeastern poultry company 2 years ago to gain access to New England markets, and John has crossed the White Rock and Cornish breeds in an effort to create a specialty item which will command a higher price than commodity chickens in an industry notorious for its boom-and-bust cycles. The game hens come to market in 28 to 30 days (versus 42 or more for regular chickens), Tyson will have one Arkansas plant dedicated solely to processing them, and two-thirds of all Cornish game hens sold in the United States will come from Tyson (*see* 1967).

Dwarf Indica rice with higher per acre yields is introduced in India, the Philippines, and other Asian nations (*see* 1964; 1968; Taiwan, 1955).

U.S. farms fall in number to 3.5 million, down from 6.84 million in 1935, 3.7 million in 1959.

Former U.S. Secretary of Agriculture (and Vice President) Henry Agard Wallace dies November 18 at age 77. Some U.S. corn farmers now get 120 bushels of corn per acre (the average is over 85, up from 22.8 in 1933) and produce 9 billion bushels per year, of which 85 percent goes to feeding hogs, chickens, and cattle.

Dry milk sent abroad by the U.S. Department of Agriculture in aid programs is fortified with vitamins A and D at the insistence of the U.S. Public Health Service, but milk for domestic poverty programs (as in Appalachia, above) is not fortified. The Food and Drug Administration sets a mandatory limit of 400 International Units (IUs) of vitamin D per quart of irradiated milk sold in the United States, half the previous suggested daily dose.

British research has established that intakes above 400 IUs per day have no advantage, and intakes above 2,000 can have detrimental effects in some individuals. The FDA this year limits to 1,000 IUs the amount of vitamin D which can be contained in a single capsule; some capsules have contained as much as 50,000 IUs—125 times the Recommended Daily Allowance for a growing child. Some mothers, in addition to exposing them to plenty of sunshine, give their children concentrated doses of vitamin D, which in dosages of more than 20,000 IUs per day over a long term can produce nausea, vomiting, weight loss, constipation (or diarrhea), excessive urination because of kidney damage from calcium deposits, loss of muscle tone, hypercalcification at the ends of the long bones that interferes with normal bone growth, a numb, tingling feeling in the fingertips, and in a few rare cases even heart defects and mental retardation.

Half of all Americans enjoy "good" diets, up from less than one quarter in 1943, according to a new study.

Clifton, N.J., food faddist Beth Ann Simon dies in the autumn at age 24 after having dwindled away to just over 70 pounds on a "macrobotic" diet consisting solely of brown rice sprinkled with Gomashio (four parts sesame seeds to one part sea salt) eaten slowly with a little green tea. Disclaimed by Zen Buddhists, the diet is promoted by writer George Ohsawa, whose foundation is raided by Food and Drug Administration agents. They seize literature and illegally labeled foods, but cultists in the youth underground extol Ohsawa's diets and open "macrobiotic" diets. Convinced that the diet removed "poisons" from her body and soul, Mrs. Simon lost 20 pounds in her first month, persisted, developed scurvy, and died after 9 months from emaciation due to starvation. A Japanese-born Parisian, Ohsawa (originally Sakurazawa Nyoti) will himself die next year at age 73, and his followers will raise doubts as to whether Mrs. Simon really died or just came close to death, whether she lived in New Jersey or in New York's Greenwich Village, and whether she followed a "correct" macrobiotic diet.

Apple Jacks breakfast food, introduced by Kellogg, is 55 percent sugar (see 1964; 1966).

Campbell Soup Co. introduces Franco-American SpaghettiOs, created for children who have trouble spooning or forking up strands of canned pasta (see Franco-American, 1915).

Hershey Chocolate raises the weight of its 10¢ Hershey Bar in August from 1¼ oz. to 2 oz. (see 1963; 1966) and of its nickel Hershey Bar in September from ⅞ oz. to 1 oz. (see 1963; 1966).

Cranapple Fruit Juice is introduced by Ocean Spray Cranberries (see 1959).

Gatorade has its beginnings in a lemon-lime drink created by University of Florida kidney specialist Robert Cade, who has analyzed the body liquids lost in perspiration by football players, specifically the "Gators" of the University of Florida. By 1967, the National Football League will be using Gatorade, and it will be given also to racehorses and to children suffering from severe dehydration due to diarrhea or vomiting, but independent tests will fail to prove that it has significant advantages over plain water. Stokely–Van Camp will acquire Gatorade (see Quaker Oats, 1983).

Diet Pepsi is introduced by PepsiCo, Inc. (above; see Tab, 1963).

Home-delivered milk accounts for 25 percent of U.S. milk sales, down from more than 50 percent before World War II. The figure will be 15 percent by 1975.

The first international unit of Hardee's opens October 21 at Heidelberg, West Germany (see 1962). Frankfurters will be added to Hardee's menus next year, and by 1970 some 200 restaurants will be operating under the Hardee's name (see 1972).

Oxfam decides to support family planning projects as well as the programs for famine relief and food production which it has backed since its founding in 1942.

A new U.S. immigration act signed into law by President Johnson October 3 at the Statue of Liberty in New York Harbor permits entry by any alien who meets qualifications of education and skill, provided that such entry will not jeopardize the job of an American. Only 102 Chinese have entered the country legally since 1943; hereafter, at least 5,000 will enter each month, increasing the number of Chinese restaurants and Chinese kitchen help as Hunan and Szechuan cuisines gain popularity to augment the traditional Cantonese dishes that have been corrupted into "Chinese-American" food (Chaozhou, Fujian, Hakka, Hangzhou, Shandong, and Zhejiang cuisines will arrive by the 1990s).

1966

India suffers her worst famine in more than 20 years and imports more than 8 million tons of U.S. wheat and other foodstuffs, but rice eaters in Karala State riot in protest against eating wheat flour (see 1944).

The world food crisis reaches new intensity as total food production falls 2 percent below last year's output. Food production in Africa, Latin America, and the Far East falls well below prewar levels.

Drought begins in the Sahel—the 2,600-mile semidesert strip south of Africa's Sahara Desert. The Sahel embraces Mauritania, Senegal, Mali, Upper Volta, Niger, Chad, northern Nigeria, Cameroon, and parts of Ethiopia, the drought will kill thousands of head of cattle by 1975, and it will bring famine.

Dwayne Andreas, now 48, becomes head of Archer Daniels Midland (ADM), whose annual sales he will increase in the next 24 years from about $200 million to more than $8 billion (see HFCS, 1973).

California wine grower Robert Mondavi, now 52, quits the family's Charles Krug Winery to start his own Robert Mondavi Winery with two partners and an investment of $200,000 (see 1946); his brother Peter lets him use the Krug facilities while his own winery is being built, Robert will buy out the partners in 1969, and in the following few years he will invest $7 million in the business (see 1971).

The President's Commission on Food Marketing estimates that U.S. consumers pay up to 20 percent more buying nationally advertised brands rather than high-quality local brands.

Consumers boycott supermarkets at Denver and other cities, protesting high prices. A food chain in New York puts up signs claiming that "Grand Union Earns Less Than 1½ Pennies on Each Dollar of Sales . . . Not Much, Is It?" but the National Commission on Food Marketing concludes that food store profits are generally higher than for comparable industries and that in 20 years the grocery chains' returns on investment have averaged 12.5 percent and have never been lower than for other industries.

Food prices are higher in poor neighborhoods of U.S. cities than in better neighborhoods according to a study. Ghetto food merchants charge more to compensate for "shrinkage" (meaning theft).

Keebler Co. is created by a renaming of United Biscuit Co., which is now second only to Nabisco as a U.S. cookie and cracker producer (see 1927).

R. J. Reynolds Co. acquires Jeno Paulucci's Chun King Corp. for $63 million and makes Paulucci chairman of the board of R. J. Reynolds Foods (see 1951; Penick and Ford, 1965; RJR Nabisco, 1985).

Pet Milk changes its name to Pet Inc. and acquires Aunt Fanny's Bakery (see 1948; Mountain Pass Canning, 1968).

The Federal Trade Commission orders Beatrice, Borden, Kraft Foods, and Dean Foods to desist for 10 years from acquiring smaller dairy companies. Most will diversify into other areas. Dean has adopted a policy of not acquiring dairies in smaller cities, where the Teamsters Union has made it difficult to close down unprofitable operations.

Warner-Lambert acquires Williamson Candy, makers of Oh Henry!, but will sell it in 1970 to Ward Foods, which next year will acquire Chunky and Bit-O-Honey and in 1969 will acquire Blumenthal Brothers, makers of Goobers, Sno-Cups, and Raisinets.

Peter Paul pays $3 million to acquire Chicago's Walter H. Johnson Candy Co. and its PowerHouse bar.

Source Perrier acquires Le Compagnie de Vichy, which sells various Vichy waters (the leading one is Vichy Célestins) as well as operating Vichy's medical installations, band concerts, and gambling casinos (see mineral water consumption, below).

The Vatican rescinds the rule forbidding U.S. Catholics to eat meat on Friday, but fish sales drop only briefly.

Nonfiction: Stalking the Healthful Herbs by Euell Gibbons.

Cookbooks: Feasts for All Seasons by London-born journalist–film writer–director Roy Andries de Groot, 54, who came to America in 1941 after sustaining eye injuries in the London Blitz and lost his vision in 1961. When he came out of the hospital he told his wife, "Buy a leg of lamb. I want to find out if I can bone it with my eyes shut." He found that he could do it even better than before and decided, since he had a gift for describing how foods taste, to become a professional food writer. *A Second Slice* by Lady Arabella Boxer. *The New York Times Menu Cook Book* by Craig Claiborne. *Weight Watchers Cookbook* by Jean Niedetch.

U.S. per capita consumption of processed potatoes reaches 44.2 pounds per year, up from 6.3 pounds in 1950.

Washington yields to pressure from commercial fishermen and extends jurisdiction over territorial waters to 12 miles (*see* Declaration of Santiago, 1952). The United States has been the last major nation to maintain the three-mile limit.

The Hudson River shad catch falls to 116,000 pounds; the Bureau of Commercial Fisheries in the Department of the Interior stops keeping records of Hudson River shad, which are in any case generally tainted with oil and other pollutants.

Kazakhstan in the Soviet Union harvests a record 25.5 million tons of grain (*see* 1963).

The Rockefeller Foundation and Mexican government establish the International Maize and Wheat Improvement Center (CIMMYT) under the direction of Norman Borlaug (*see* 1944; 1970).

Castle & Cooke begins developing banana properties on the Philippine island of Mindanao for shipment to Japanese markets (*see* 1970; Standard Fruit, 1964).

An 8-year-old North Miami schoolboy introduces the giant African snail *Achatina fulica* into Florida. The snail reaches eight inches in length and a weight of one pound, it has 80,000 teeth, it can devour a head of lettuce overnight, and by 1969 it will be menacing the state's food crops.

The Good Sense Family Cook Book by U.S. author Gaynor Maddox quotes biochemist Charles Glen King, now 70 and associate director of Columbia University's Institute of Nutritional Sciences (later Institute of Human Nutrition) as saying that relying on dietary supplements is dangerous for most people. Supplements may make sense for alcoholics who ingest too many carbohydrates in what they drink without getting other nutrients, or for "physiologically peculiar types, who because of some obstruction or for some genetic reason cannot get all the nutrients they need" from what they eat, but "a vitamin deficiency can be identified only by a competent physician, not by a drug store clerk or a door-to-door salesman." The Food and Drug Administration says that vitamin and vitamin-mineral products on the market "contain as many as 75 ingredients. Only a few of these ingredients have any real value as food supplements," but as University of Chicago scientist Anton "Ajax" Carlson has said about dietary supplements, "Those who can afford to buy them don't need them; and those who need them can't afford to buy them."

Congress passes a Fair Packaging and Labeling Act. The new "Truth in Packaging" law calls for clear labeling of the net weight of every package, bans phony "cents off" labels and phony "economy size" packages, and imposes controls over the confusing proliferation of package sizes, but food will continue to be sold in packages that make it hard for supermarket customers to know how much they are paying per pound.

U.S. cola drink bottlers and canners receive FDA dispensation not to list caffeine as an ingredient. Cola drinks generally have 4 milligrams of caffeine per fluid ounce, coffee 12 to 16 milligrams.

Bac*Os, introduced by General Mills, are bits of soy protein isolate flavored to taste like bacon (*see* 1957; Boyer, 1949).

Kellogg introduces Product 19 breakfast food (*see* 1965; 1969).

Hershey Chocolate lowers the weight of its 10¢ Hershey Bar in June from 2 oz. to 1¼ oz. and of its nickel Hershey Bar in September from 1 oz. to ⅞ oz. (*see* 1965; 1968).

Nestlé introduces the $100,000 Bar, a combination of chewy caramel and crisped rice enrobed in milk chocolate.

Peter Paul (above) introduces Caravelle, a candy bar made of soft caramel, crisped rice, milk chocolate, and Brazil nuts, to supplement its Mounds and Almond Joy brands.

French consumers drink nearly 2 billion bottles of *eau minerale* per year (Badoit, Contrexéville, Evian, Perrier, Vichy Celéstins, and Vittel all have their devotees), thinking it good for their livers. Italians drink San Pellegrino (among other brands); Germans Apollinaris, Faschinger, and Überking; Austrians Gasteiner, Geussinger, Petersquelle, Preblauer, and Römerquelle; Swiss Eptinger, Hennic, and Passugger.

The Robert Mondavi Winery crushes its first grapes at Oakdale in California's Napa Valley. Mondavi will produce Chenin Blanc, Johannisberg Riesling, Chardonnay, and Fumé Blanc (a dryer version of Sauvignon Blanc) along with a Gamay Rosé and such red wines as Cabernet Sauvignon, Pinot Noir, and Zinfandel (*see* 1971).

Taster's Choice freeze-dried instant coffee is introduced by Nestlé to compete with the Maxim coffee introduced by General Foods in 1964. It will soon overtake Maxim in sales.

Freeze-dried coffees pushed ahead of earlier instants to gain dominance in the marketplace.

Restaurateur Henri Soulé of the Pavillon dies of a heart attack at La Côte Basque January 27 at age 62. *New York Times* food critic Craig Claiborne says of the 5-foot, 5-inch Soulé that he was "the Michelangelo, the Mozart, and the Leonardo of the French restaurant in America. He was a man of towering standards with cool disdain for the commonplace and the sham and keen appreciation for those who dined in his company on vintage champagne (almost always Dom Pérignon and in recent years, 1959); mousse of sole tout Paris; pilaff of mussels; pheasant with truffled sauce; and the dessert that was almost a trademark of Mr. Soulé, the fantasy of meringue, custard, and caramel called l'oeufs a la neige. Mr. Soulé's influence on the restaurant world, not only in New York, is beyond measure. His like may never be known in this country again."

The Ground Floor restaurant opens in February in the new CBS Building at 51 West 42nd Street. CBS chairman William Paley's wife Barbara ("Babe") (*née* Cushing) is credited with having said, "Nobody can be too rich or too thin" (also credited to the duchess of Windsor), but the Ground Floor's menu features offers scallops stuffed with shrimps *en brochette*; grilled Dover sole with langouste *au cognac*; fillet of brook trout sautéed with white grapes; veal chops with marjoram; sautéed sweetbreads with lobster and herb cream; steak *au poivre*; grilled venison chops; roast baby pheasant; whole roast duckling glazed with cassis; roast partridge; broccoli soufflé; braised celery; half pineapple in rum cream; Swiss kirsch torte; nougat Charlotte; œufs à la neige; chocolate bonbon cake; marzipan apple pie; *tarte à l'orange*; baked pear in red wine; hazelnut crêpe flambé Savarin with cherries Jubilee; crêpes with bananas flambé; and chocolate mousse made in a loaf with a glaze of bitter chocolate. The Ground Floor will be replaced in 1987 by the China Grill.

The London restaurant Le Français opens in March at 259 Fulham Road, supplanting the Provençal. Chef Jean-Jacques Figéac and mâitre d'hôtel Bernard Caen will expand by taking over an adjoining place to accommodate 78 patrons, who will enjoy *saumon en croûte* from the Loire; *jambon persillé* of Burgundy; *crêpe de sarrasin aux moules* of Brittany with stuffed eggplants and tomatoes; *tripes à la catalane Roussillon*; and *tarte au poireaux*.

The Paris restaurant Concameau opens with 14 round tables at 14, rue Pascal, near the Rue Mouffetard, with a Catalan-style party to which 100 guests are invited (the last do not leave until 8 o'clock the next morning). Catalan chef Jean-François Coll, whose father runs a cooking school at Bordeaux, offers a moderately priced five-course *menu* featuring *pâté de foie gras* from Toulouse; herring; omelettes; sausages; olives; raw vegetables; hard-boiled eggs; slightly salted Brittany butter in a crock; charcoal-grilled beef or lamb; grilled fish (turbot with herbs or fresh tuna Catalan style with wine, garlic, tomatoes, and green peppers); quail or hare with wild mushrooms; curry of lamb; *tripe à l'Armagnac*; half a truffled guinea hen; country sausage *en croûte*; *champignons*; *pommes frites*; green beans; white beans *paysanne*; celery hearts cooked with goose fat; salads with olive, walnut, or peanut oil; yeasty bread; profiterolle with ice cream and covered with chocolate sauce; and torte Catalan (open-faced apple pie). Portions are large, patrons may order extra helpings at no extra charge, and the prix fixe meal includes a carafe of wine.

The Paris restaurant Le Vivarois opens in October at 92, avenue Victor-Hugo under the proprietorship of restaurateur Claude Peyrot, 33, who began his career working in his family's pension hotel at Saint-Félicien in the Ardèche and has worked also for Fernand Point at Vienne, Raymond Thuylier at Les Baux, and Jean Druand and Francis Carton in Paris. Peyrot and his wife, Jacqueline (formerly a ski instructress), have tables designed by Eero Saarinen for Knoll and hang their white plaster walls with modern paintings and tapestries. Specialties include grilled *rouget* flown up each morning from the Mediterranean; thrush pâté; *escargots de Bourgogne*; truffled *dindon de Cannes à la Fernand Point*; *paupiettes* of chicken stuffed with foie gras; *paupiettes* accompanied by fresh morels and cream; roast quarter of lamb; side of beef *poêlé aux échalotes*; and *baba au marrons de l'Ardèche*.

1967

✘ The Republic of Biafra is proclaimed May 30 by Nigerian general Odumegwu Ojukwu, who leads the Ibo tribespeople out of the 13-year-old Nigerian Federation. The Lagos government calls the secession a rebellion, the Ibos buy arms and supplies from France, and hostilities will continue until 1970 between the Ibos and the Muslim Hausa Fulani conservatives to the north and the Yorubas to the west (*see* starvation, 1968).

Iran, South Africa, and Turkey have record grain crops, but hunger remains widespread in India.

More than 6 million tons of U.S. wheat are shipped to India under terms of the P.L. 480 legislation of 1954. Reserves of wheat stored in U.S. grain elevators fall sharply as more than one-fourth the export crop goes to India.

The World Food Problem, issued by the President's Science Advisory Committee, is a three-volume, 1,231-page report citing the pressures on food supplies of growing populations and increased affluence.

Famine—1975! by U.S. agronomist William Paddock and his brother Paul (a retired Foreign Service officer) observes that by 1975 today's infants and young children will be adolescents and young adults with appetites too great for world food production to satisfy. Famine is inevitable, say the Paddocks, and the United States must decide which countries can be saved and which cannot.

Sen. Robert F. Kennedy (Dem. N.Y.), 41, and former Sen. Joseph Clark visit backward areas of the South in the spring and "discover" hunger. Widespread hunger and malnutrition in the Mississippi Delta is reported to the Senate Select Subcommittee on Hunger and Human Needs by a medical team that has surveyed the region.

The Department of Agriculture returns $200 million of unused food aid funds to the Treasury. Some 2.7 million Americans receive food stamp assistance as of Thanksgiving (*see* 1964; 1969).

💲 The United States contributes one-seventh of 1 percent of her gross national product (GNP) to foreign aid, down from a full 1 percent in 1965 (*see* 1961).

European nations destroy fruit and vegetable surpluses in order to maintain prices.

U.S. farm prices fall as huge crops are harvested, and Agriculture Secretary Orville H. Freeman comes under attack from farmers. He had urged heavy planting in case India and Pakistan should need more U.S. grain.

Nearly 10,000 U.S. farmers receive more than $20,000 each in subsidies, more than 6,500 receive more than $25,000 each, 15 receive between $500,000 and $1 million each, 5 receive more than $1 million each, and 1 receives more than $4 million.

U.S. bread sells at 22¢ to 25¢ per one-pound loaf.

Del Monte Corp. is created by a reorganization of California Packing Corp. (*see* 1917). Del Monte has become an integrated international company controlling vast acreages of U.S. farmland and directly or indirectly employing thousands of farmworkers. It will be acquired by R. J. Reynolds (*see* 1986; 1993).

New York's Hunt's Point Market opens in the Bronx March 21 with a wholesale produce facility to serve the city's retail grocers and restaurants. Agitation has persisted since the 1930s for a relocation of the Washington Market, which has survived from the early 19th century.

Springdale, Ark., poultry processor Donald Tyson takes over management of his family's business following the death of his father and stepmother in a car-train wreck (*see* 1965; 1969).

Ling-Temco-Vought acquires Wilson & Co., third-largest U.S. meatpacker, and will soon sell off its Wilson Sporting Goods division to concentrate on meatpacking.

John Morrell & Co. is merged into AMK Corp., a small company organized by former rabbi Eli M. Black, 46, who has built up American Seal-Kap Corp. from a producer of paper caps for milk bottles into a diversified industrial company. Morrell is the fourth-largest U.S. meat packer and its acquisition makes AMK a major conglomerate (*see* Morrell, 1877; United Brands, 1968).

Campbell Soup Co. acquires Godiva Chocolates, a Belgian firm whose U.S. production will hereafter come out of a factory at Reading, Pa. (Connoisseurs will prefer to buy their Godiva chocolates in Brussels or Antwerp, where the bonbons are less sweet.)

The *Super-Marché de Poche* that opens in Paris is an automated supermarket in which shelves are automatically restocked.

A 6-day war between Israel and her Arab neighbors closes down Egypt's Suez Canal with scuttled ships and mines.

High-fructose corn syrup (HFCS) development is pioneered by Clinton Corn Processing Co. of Clinton, Iowa. Archer Daniels Midland (ADM), Standard Brands, and A. E. Staley Manufacturing Co. will build HFCS facilities, and by 1972 it will be possible to make HFCS that is sweeter than sucrose. Dextrose and other corn sugars control nearly 20 percent of the industrial sweetener market (which accounts for about two-thirds of the U.S. market for sugar), but these semisweet products lack any potential for replacing sugar (*see* 1974; ADM, 1973).

The first compact microwave oven for U.S. home use is introduced by Amana Refrigeration, a subsidiary of Raytheon with facilities at Amana, Iowa, which applies its consumer marketing experience to Raytheon's microwave technology (*see* 1947). Engineer Keishi Ogura of Japan Radio developed an improved electron tube 3 years ago, making possible a compact microwave oven that retails at $495.

Japanese microwave oven production reaches 50,000 up from 15,000 last year. Many Japanese households move directly from hibachi grills to microwave ovens.

Nonfiction: *Euell Gibbons' Beachcomber's Handbook* by Gibbons.

Cookbooks: *Charcuterie and French Pork Cookery* by English author Jane Grigson (*née* McIntire), 39. *The Best of Italian Cooking* by Rome-born author-translator Nika Stanton Hazelton (*née* Dittman), who came to New York in the early 1930s after several years as a journalist at Geneva and other European capitals, worked as a researcher for *Fortune* magazine, returned to Europe, but came back to New York in 1939 with her husband and young son. After her marriage failed, she took a job as an advertising copywriter at Macy's and remarried, this time to Harold Hazelton. *The International Encyclopedia of Cooking* by Myra Waldo. *James Beard's Barbecue Cookbook: Over 200 Recipes for Every Taste, from Appetizers to Desserts.*

Popular songs: "Alice's Restaurant" by U.S. folksinger Arlo (David) Guthrie, 20, who originally wrote the song to promote a Stockbridge, Mass., eating establishment/commune run by Alice and Ray Brock, two of his former schoolteachers, in an abandoned church. Its lyrics chronicle the events of Thanksgiving, 1965, when Guthrie (with some friends) loaded the dinner refuse into a Volkswagen van, carted it to the local dump, found the dump closed, left the garbage on a mound of trash outside the dump, and was later arrested for littering and jailed when he refused to pay a fine. Guthrie has incorporated other events, including his confrontation with his draft board, to create a song of social protest that is first entitled "Alice's Restaurant Massacre."

Annual U.S. beef consumption reaches 105.6 pounds per capita, up from 99 pounds in 1960, and the average American eats 71 pounds of other red meat.

Wisconsin permits sale of yellow margarine, becoming the last state to repeal laws against it, but like some other states it continues to impose special taxes on margarine at the behest of dairy interests (see New York, 1952),

The First Annual World Championship Chili Cook-off draws crowds to Terlingua, Tex. Other towns and cities will stage chili festivals to select chili cooks who will represent them in the national contest, which will be held in California's Antelope Valley and elsewhere.

A Fisherman's Protective Act passed by Congress appropriates funds to reimburse U.S. commercial fishermen for fines, lost time, and fish spoilage incurred through apprehension by foreign powers in waters the United States considers international (see Declaration of Santiago, 1952).

Britain has an outbreak of foot-and-mouth disease, forcing the slaughter of more than 100,000 animals.

Mao Zedong brings Chinese agriculture into the Great Proletarian Cultural Revolution, but the country is embroiled in virtual civil war. Peasants abandon collective grainfields to cultivate private gardens and sell in the black market. China continues to import from 4 to 7 million tons of wheat, mostly from Australia and Canada, as she has done since 1962 (but see 1986; 1993).

Herman Taller is convicted in federal court of conspiracy, mail fraud, and food and drug law violations in connection with his 1964 book Calories Don't Count.

The Doctor's Quick Weight Loss Diet by Brooklyn, N.Y., physician Irwin Maxwell Stillman recommends low carbohydrate intake, as did the Taller book (above). Stillman urges readers to drink eight 10-ounce glasses of water per day and claims that his program will remove from 7 to 15 pounds per week.

A U.S. Federal Meat Inspection Act takes effect after a campaign by consumer advocate Ralph Nader, 33, has persuaded Congress to strengthen the law of 1906.

Lawry's Taco Seasoning Mix is introduced by Lawry's Foods (see 1958). It will grow in the next 20 years to account for more than one-third of Lawry's seasoning mix sales, becoming the biggest-selling taco seasoning mix in America, and its success will lead Lawry's to introduce a leading brand of taco shells (see 1979; restaurants, 1971).

Margaret Rudkin of Pepperidge Farm fame dies at New Haven (Conn.) Hospital June 1 at age 69 (see Campbell, 1961). Her husband died in April of last year at age 81. The company which she started now has nationwide distribution and sells 70 million loaves of bread per year plus rolls, cookies, and other food products made in bakeries at Downingtown, Pa., and Downer's Grove, Ill., as well as at Norwalk. Rudkin's son William, 41, will serve as chairman until his retirement in 1991.

Imitation milk appears in Arizona supermarkets. Made from corn syrup solids, vegetable fat, sugar, salt, artificial thickeners, colors, and flavors, sodium caseinate, and water; the "milk" will be sold under such brand names as Moo, Farmer's Daughter, and Country Cousin.

About 70 percent of U.S. milk is sold in waxed paperboard cartons rather than glass bottles by November, up from less than 40 percent in 1952.

Pillsbury Co. acquires Burger King Corp. for $18 million to move into the fast-food business (see 1954). The Burger King chain now has 274 restaurants with 8,000 employees, but McDonald's has far more, and the founders of Burger King have sold the chains to Pillsbury in hopes of obtaining capital needed to catch up. The chain will grow in 10 years to have 2,000 restaurants, with locations in all 50 states plus some in Puerto Rico and Spain, but McDonald's will grow much faster (*see* 1986; McDonald's below).

The battle between franchised hamburger outlets was just heating up when Pillsbury entered it.

McDonald's test-markets the "Big Mac," borrowing the concept from Bob Wien, founder of the Big Boy drive-in chain, and offering two beef patties for 45¢ (*see* 1961). The Big Mac will be in all McDonald's outlets by the end of 1968, as will a 59¢ roast beef sandwich introduced this year by a Cleveland franchisee (*see* 1969).

Denny's opens its first foreign restaurant, at Acapulco, Mexico (*see* 1953; 1968).

United Fruit Co. pays an estimated $12 million to acquire the Baskin-Robbins ice cream chain, whose co-founder Burton Baskin dies suddenly and unexpectedly 6 months later but which soon will be selling product in more than 100 flavors, including Blueberries 'N Cream, Pralines 'N Cream, Huckleberry Finn, Baseball Nut, New England Maple, Chocolate Divinity, and Nuts to You (*see* 1948; United Brands, 1968; J. Lyons, 1973).

The Paris restaurant L'Orangerie opened in January on the Île Saint-Louis at 28, rue Saint-Louis-en-l'Île by stage and screen actor Jean-Claude Brialy with restaurateur Gérard Ferry serves Parma ham, fresh raw vegetables, pot-au-feu, roast lamb, grilled côtes de bœuf, sea bass, raie au beurre noir, médaillon de veau with mushrooms and cream, navarin of lamb, roast veal with leeks au gratin, sherbet, chocolate mousse, lemon tarte, fresh pineapple, and just three wines (*see* Los Angeles, 1977).

The Paris bistro Au Pactole opens with 40 to 45 seats at 44, boulevard Saint-Germain under the direction of owner-chef Jacques Maniere, who joined the Free French in his youth, served in various parts of Africa, was sent to Saint-Cyr after the war to be trained as an officer, and, after Saint-Cyr threw him out, established a truffle-canning factory in his native Périgueux before going to work in the kitchens of La Pérouse and, later, of Chez Max (where Max Puy taught him what he had to know). He offers a prix fixe meal of 25 francs, not including wine and service, and serves crayfish bisque; homemade pâté; crab salad or mushrooms *à la grecque*; poached egg Henri IV; sautéed chicken garnished with lobster; crayfish and rice; gigot of lamb; fricassée of veal with lemon; *côte de bœuf* with a pinch of basil; cheese; and dessert (cassis sorbet or homemade chocolate cake).

The London restaurant Le Gavroche opens in April at 61 Lower Sloane Street under the direction of Swiss chef-proprietors Albert and Michel Roux, 31 and 26, respectively, whose father, grandfather, and great-grandfather were all *charcutiers*. Each was apprenticed to a *pâtissier* at age 14, Albert has worked as chef for the French Embassy at London and for property developer Charles Clore, Michel has been chef at the the British Embassy at Paris and for Cécile de Rothschild. Specialties at their 52-seat trattoria include *soufflés Suissesses* (made with Gruyère cheese and a creamy sauce), rillettes grilled over fennel twigs and flamed with brandy at the table, crabs in a special green sauce with fresh herbs, *poussin Paulinette* (stuffed with a *mirepoix* of carrots, mushrooms, and green beans mixed with a mousseline of chicken and poached in chicken broth), and finely chopped filet of veal and fresh pineapple in a white curry sauce enriched with a little Hollandaise. By 1973, the Roux brothers will also be running the Poulbot in the City, the Waterside Inn at Bray, and the Brasserie Benoît at 32 Old Bailey (lunch only, Monday through Friday) (*see* 1982).

The London restaurant Locket's opens in the spring at Marsham Court, taking its name from that of the city's most expensive eating house at the end of the 17th century. Its "Fore-Dishes" include smoked Scotch salmon and potted shrimps, duck pâté with garlic, pheasant pâté with brandy, potted beef, smoked haddock, fish pie with mussels and scallops, whitebait, Scottish herring (rolled in oatmeal and fried in butter and bacon fat and served with a mustard sauce), and creamy white herring roes baked with bacon; diners go on to enjoy bisque of Cornish crabs with brandy; pheasant consommé with sherry; oxtail soup; lamb à la Shrewsbury; ox tongue with Cumberland sauce; lemon chicken with tarragon; lamb steak steeped in wine and fresh herbs; veal chops with butter, sage, and chervil; fresh red cabbage; braised celery; brussels sprouts; everlasting syllabub; lemon mousse; Athol brose (whisky, oatmeal, and honey); summer pudding in season (buttered bread filled with raspberries and currants, gooseberries, Alpine strawberries, or cherries, which are left overnight on the bread so that it soaks up the juices and is then sliced like a cake and served with cream); English cheeses; and English country wines made from apples, red currants, gooseberries, and elderberries.

The London restaurant Île de France opens in the Londonderry Hotel at 19 Old Park Lane. Chef Gerhart Reisenpaltt makes specialties of sole Westminister (cooked in sherry and garnished with tomatoes, asparagus, and lobster), filet of sole Île de France (with a cream sauce containing mushrooms and pernod), *quenelles de saumon en champagne*, and *feuilleté de homard*.

The London restaurant Hiroko opens in the West End with tatami rooms to serve the city's growing population of Japanese businessmen.

The New York restaurant Le Biarritz opens at 225 West 57th Street. Breton proprietor Ambroise Vaillant has worked at Le Pavillon and has specialties that include crabmeat crêpe, quiche; champignons del Montebeyan, and roast chicken in a champagne sauce. His wife, Marie-Louise, who is from the French Pyrénées, makes the pastries in her apart-

ment, using 75 pounds of *feuilleté* per week for the quiche, *millefeuilles*, strawberry tartlets, *crème patissière*, and gâteau Saint-Honoré.

1968

Thousands die of starvation in Biafra, whose Ibo tribespeople have seceded from Nigeria (*see* 1967).

Hunger in America, telecast by CBS May 21, documents conditions of deficiency diseases in the world's most affluent nation. Infants on Navajo reservations are shown to be suffering from marasmus, a wasting away of flesh that may cause them to lose the fat pads in their cheeks to a point where they can no longer suck. Some infants shown weigh only five pounds at age 1—less than they weighed at birth—and the CBS report observes that if they survive infancy they may well turn fat, even though malnourished, because their diets will be mostly starch.

A Poor People's March on Washington focuses its protest on U.S. hunger conditions. Originally planned by the late civil rights leader Dr. Martin Luther King, Jr., who has been shot dead April 4 at Memphis, the demonstration proceeds from May 3 to June 23 under the leadership of Ralph D. Abernathy, Jr.

The Citizens Board of Inquiry into Hunger and Malnutrition in the United States observes that federal food aid programs reach only 18 percent of the nation's poor.

A Senate Select Committee on Nutrition and Human Needs (McGovern Committee) is established by Sen. George Stanley McGovern (D. S.D.), 46, who served as director of the Food for Peace Program from 1960 to 1962 after serving a term in Congress. The new committee focuses on hunger and malnutrition (*see* nutrition, 1974).

The Department of Agriculture liberalizes its food stamp program (*see* 1967). It expands from two to 42 the number of counties where federal authorities will handle the program, which in some areas is resisted by local authorities (*see* 1969).

A nationwide boycott of table grapes organized by César Chávez of the United Farm Workers Organizing Committee gains support from much of the

Exploited farm workers received support from consumers who boycotted grapes and lettuce. CHIE NISHIO

public (*see* 1962). Chavez dramatizes "La Causa" ("The Cause") with long fasts.

💲 Farm labor represents only 7 percent of the U.S. workforce, down from 10 percent in 1960, although another 32 percent of the workforce is engaged in supplying the farmer or handling his produce.

The average U.S. farm subsidy is nearly $1,000, up from $175 in 1960, as the number of U.S. farms continues to drop off substantially. Many farmers receive far in excess of the average subsidy (*see* 1967).

Monfort of Colorado creates the world's first 100,000-head feedlot and is one of the first companies to produce boxed beef at its packing plants, portioning beef carcasses into primal—e.g., chuck, loin, rib, and round—or subprimal—e.g., chuck roll—cuts at the plant and boxing similar cuts together into 40-pound parcels instead of shipping out whole carcasses (*see* 1960; ConAgra, 1987).

🤝 Tenneco Corp. acquires Kern County Land Co., which will make it a major U.S. producer of lettuce and other field crops.

ITT (International Telephone and Telegraph) acquires Continental Baking for $280 in securities (*see* Wonder Bread, 1927; Morton Packing, 1955). ITT-Continental has 40 bread bakeries, 22 bakeries that produce both bread and cake, 6 or 7 cake bakeries, and more than a dozen plants that pack Morton Frozen Foods, snack items, and other foods (*see* Ralston Purina, 1984).

General Mills acquires Gorton's of Gloucester for $30 million to enter the frozen seafood business (*see* 1755; 1955).

Hunt-Wesson Foods acquires Wakefield Seafoods (*see* 1945; 1960; Norton Simon, Inc., 1969).

Pet Inc. acquires Mountain Pass Canning Co., whose products it will market under the brand name Old El Paso (*see* 1918; Schrafft's, below; Underwood, 1982).

Eli Black takes over United Fruit Co., adds it to the John Morrell and American Seal-Kap interests he merged into AMK Corp. last year, and creates United Brands (*see* Chiquita Banana, 1944; Baskin-Robbins, 1967). United Brands begins an effort to establish the Chiquita brand trademark for fresh lettuce (*see* crime, 1975).

Hershey Chocolate changes its name to Hershey Foods Corp. after acquiring some pasta companies, but the Chocolate Company remains its largest division (*see* 1969).

Continental Grain acquires a 51 percent interest in Agrocom, an Argentinian company whose consumer products include Taragui, a combination of tea and maté that is Argentina's leading brand of tea. Agrocom will later gain South American rights to market the General Foods brands Tang and Sanka.

Schweppes acquires Ty-Phoo Tea in a move to broaden its base (*see* 1953). It has previously acquired Rose's Lime Juice, Appolinaris of Malvern natural spring waters, Dubonnet, Harvey's canned foods, and a jam and preserves company (*see* Cadbury Schweppes, 1969).

London's Brooke Bond Tea Ltd. merges with Liebig's Extract of Meat Co. Ltd. to create the world's largest tea company, with nearly 40,000 acres of plantations in India, Sri Lanka (Ceylon), and East Africa, plus ranches in Argentina, Paraguay, and Rhodesia that cover more than 2.6 million acres, and more than 80,000 employees. Unilever will acquire Brooke Bond and turn it into Brooke Bond Foods Ltd.

⚡ The S.S. *Queen Elizabeth II* goes into service for the Cunard line, replacing the *Queen Elizabeth* launched in 1940. The new passenger liner carries 1,815 passengers, 1,000 in crew, and has four restaurants, including the Britannia (later to be called Tables of the World), which seats 834 transatlantic-class passengers. The three first-class restaurants include the Princess Grill, the Queen's Grill (for passengers in middle-priced first-class cabins, who pay a cover charge), and the Columbia (for passengers in lower-priced first-class cabins). For the round-trip transatlantic voyage the *QE2* carries 100 pounds of foie gras, 1,500 pounds of lobsters, 800 pounds of crabs, 25,000 pounds of beef, 3,000 pounds of veal, 6,500 pounds of lamb, 4,000 pounds of pork, 2,500 pounds of bacon, 5,000 pounds of chicken, 3,000 pounds of duck, 27,000 pounds of fresh vegetables, 300 hundredweight of potatoes, 1,000 bottles of pickles and sauces, 500 pounds of butter, 3,000 pounds of cheeses, 3,000 quarts of cream, 2,500 gallons of milk, 50,000 tea bags, 2,000 pounds of coffee, 5,000 pounds of sugar, 22,000 pounds of fresh fruit, 5,000 pounds of ice cream, 600 jars of baby food, 1,000 bottles of champagne, 1,200 bottles of wine, 1,000 bottles of whiskey, 600 bottles of gin, 6,000 bottles of beer, and 12,000 gallons of draft beer.

Nonfiction: *Food and Society* by Magnus Pyke; *Visions of Sugarplums* by New York writer Mimi Sheraton (*née* Solomon), 42, whose *Seducer's Cookbook* appeared in 1962. She will be food critic for the *New York Times* beginning next year and continue until 1975.

Cookbooks: *A Book of Middle Eastern Food* by Cairo-born English author Claudia Roden, whose great-grandfather was chief rabbi to the Ottoman Empire at Aleppo but whose family was wiped out after the 1956 Suez crisis and forced to leave Egypt; *The Cooking of Provincial France* by M. F. K. Fisher and the editors of Time-Life Books (*New York Times* food editor Craig Claiborne says, "At best, this book is a most dubious sample of the regional cooking of France" and suggests that because of it Franco-American relations are "more than likely to get worse"); *The Cooking of Italy* by Waverley Root and the editors of Time-Life Books; *The Cooking of China* by U.S. writer Emily Hahn, 63, and the editors of Time-Life Books; *Latin American Cooking* by former *Time* magazine Latin American editor Jonathan Norton Leonard, 65, and the editors of Time-Life Books; *American Cooking* by former *Holiday* magazine editor Dale Brown and the editors of Time-Life Books.

The U.S. Department of the Interior estimates that 15 million fish are killed by pollution each year, two-thirds of them commercial varieties.

58 percent of U.S. fish is imported, up from 41.4 percent in 1966.

The average American eats 11 pounds of fish per year, the highest since the mid-1950s.

Average output per U.S. breeding animal is roughly twice what it was in 1920.

Some 6,000 Utah sheep die when VX nerve gas from the U.S. Army's Dugway Proving Ground blows across the range.

Frank Perdue's Perdue Farms opens its first processing plant, introduces Perdue brand poultry, and launches it with the company's first advertising campaign, airing commercials on New York City radio stations (*see* 1948). Building on research done by poultry scientists at the U.S. Department of Agriculture experimental station in nearby Beltsville, Md., which has produced fryers/broilers that mature in 7 to 8 weeks year round, the Perdues have added hatcheries and a feed mill to their operations and done some crossbreeding in their flocks to create fatter chickens, which are fed marigolds to give their skins a yellowish tinge. Perdue contracts with farmers to grow his chickens, selective breeding continues, and Perdue will become his company's TV spokesman beginning in 1971 (*see* 1974).

Improved IR-8 rice strains from the IRRI in the Philippines produce record yields in Asia (*see* 1964). But the "miracle" rice requires more fertilizer and water than do such traditional strains as Bengawan, Intam, Peta, and Sigadio, IR-8 has little innate resistance to a virus carried by green leaf hoppers, and Filipinos do not like the cooking and eating qualities of the sticky new rice milled from IR-8.

India's wheat production is 50 percent above last year's level as a result of intensive aid by Ford Foundation workers, who have introduced new Pitic 62 and Penjamo 62 wheat strains from Mexico.

Desert locusts devastate crops in Saudi Arabia and other countries along the Red Sea in the first major locust plague since 1944.

U.S. farms have 5 million tractors, 900,000 grain combines, 780,000 hay balers, 660,000 corn pickers and shellers. Major crops are all harvested by machine, but Florida sugar growers use West Indian harvest labor on canefields too wet to support heavy machinery.

The average U.S. farm acre can produce 70 bushels of corn, up from 25 in 1916, and some farmers get 200 bushels (*see* 1973).

U.S. crop acreage produces yields 80 percent above those in 1920.

The Ruby Seedless table grape introduced by the University of California at Davis has been developed by Davis botanist Harold P. Olmo, 57, from a cross made in 1939 between Emperor and Pirovano 75 varieties (*see* Thompson Seedless, 1876). The reddish black to dark red grape ripens in the latter part of midseason and stores well. Europeans have enjoyed seedless red grapes for some years, but they will remain uncommon in America until the 1980s (*see* Flame Seedless, 1973).

Seedless red grapes were a novelty for Americans whose only seedless grapes had been green.

India's food minister Chidambara Subramaniam relates malnutrition to brain damage: "On the basis of studies in my own state of Madras, where I was Minister of Education, it has been estimated that between 35 and 40 percent of the children of India have suffered permanent brain damage by the time they reach school age because of protein deficiency. This means that we are, in effect, producing subhuman beings at the rate of 35 million per year. By the time they reach school age they are unable to concentrate sufficiently to absorb and retain knowledge."

Malnutrition in some parts of the United States is as grim as any he has seen in India or any other country, reports U.S. nutrition investigator Arnold E. Schaefer, 51, who at one school has found vitamin A deficiencies worse than those in children who have gone blind from keratomalacia. These Head Start Program children could go blind at any time, "five minutes from now or a year from now," says Schaefer. His 10-state survey of children's nutrient status embarrasses officials, who have claimed that the U.S. diet is the best in the world (*see* Nixon, 1969).

The average U.S. diet provides an estimated 3,200 calories per day, with 98 grams of protein, but millions of U.S. diets do not approach the average.

The Society for Nutrition Education is founded at San Francisco. It will work to counter misinformation about nutrition and disseminate accurate information.

Fundamentals of Normal Nutrition by former Drexel University nutritionist Corinne Robinson (*née* Hogden), 59, belittles the "charlatan" who distrusts commercial additives and, without evidence, berates American agriculture and food processors for a deficient food supply. The book receives relatively little attention, the lack of universal health insurance in the United States plays a role in encouraging trust in the promises of dietary supplements (and the books which promote them) at health food stores (rarely found in countries such as Britain, which do have universal health insurance), and the growing distrust of Americans in their government's Vietnam policy rubs off in many cases on their attitudes toward agribusiness and the food industry.

The Great Vitamin Hoax by U.S. author Daniel Takton raises an outcry among many Americans, who give anecdotal testimony to the effectiveness of dietary supplements (or apple cider vinegar) in curing them of various maladies or keeping them healthy (even though double-blind tests have in many cases shown placebos to be equally effective). Takton quotes a Food and Drug Administration official as saying that a teenage girl can satisfy one-third to one-half her daily nutrition requirements, including vitamins, by eating for lunch one hamburger on a roll, together with onion, ketchup, and a piece of cheese, a chocolate bar, and a glass of fruit juice. The lunch does not provide significant amounts of vitamin A or iron, but even a poor diet by U.S. standards is a good diet when compared with what most of the world has to eat.

U.S. physicians study "Chinese Restaurant Syndrome" (Kwok's disease) and trace it to an overuse of monosodium glutamate (MSG) by Chinese chefs (*see* Ikeda, 1908; Ac'cent, 1947). Symptoms include burning sensations, chest pain, dizziness, facial pressure, headache, and numbness (*see* baby foods, 1969).

Britain's Ministry of Health rules that the newsprint used by fish-and-chips shops is not a hygienic container for foods and makes such use illegal (*see* 1902). Many shopkeepers continue to use newsprint, because it retains heat, soaks up excess vinegar, and provides a sort of napkin on which to wipe fingers, but they put the fish and chips in a white wrapper inside the newsprint or use unprinted paper stock. The National Union of Journalists continues to telegraph an annual greeting to the Federation of Fish Friers, saying, "Your trade is wrapped up in ours."

Hershey Chocolate reduces the size of its 10¢ Hershey Bar in February from 1¼ oz. to 1½ oz. (*see* 1966; 1970) and of its nickel Hershey Bar from ⅞ oz. to ¾ oz. in May (*see* 1966; 1969).

Congress rules that the only wine sold in the United States as "Porto" is the fortified wine from Portugal's Douro region, whose production is strictly controlled by the Instituto do Vinho do Porto; California's portlike wines may not be labeled "Porto."

Italy enacts legislation tripling the area of vineyards outside Verona that may be said to produce Soave, a white wine whose low price will help it gain wide popularity in the United States. Hillside growers may call their country Soave Classico, but they must compete with growers on 15,000 acres of the flat Adige River plains, who have increasingly been replacing their grainfields with vineyards. The lowland growers are more intent on quantity than on quality.

California's Fetzer Vineyards are founded in Mendocino County's Redwood Valley by lumberman Bernard Fetzer, who will augment the grapes from his 120 acres along two miles of canyonland with some other grapes and use small French oak casks to age his Semillon, Sauvignon Blanc, Chardonnay, and other white wines, plus Cabernet Sauvignon, Pinot Noir, Zinfandel, and a red wine called Carmine Carignane.

Pet Incorporated (above) acquires the Schrafft's restaurant chain in January for about $25 million (*see* 1906; Riese brothers, 1973).

The first Michelin guide to New York appears, with ratings of restaurants (*see* Zagat, 1979).

Restaurateur Stewart Levin of Restaurant Associates takes over New York's Le Pavillon, making almost no change in its menu but relaxing somewhat the dress code maintained by the late Henri Soulé (*see* 1966; 1972).

Boston's first Legal Seafoods restaurant opens in Inman Square, Cambridge (*see* 1950). George Berkowitz and his son Roger begin by selling fish and chips in paper boats, accept no credit cards or reservations, are soon offering a vast variety of fresh seafood without frills, and will grow in the next 25 years to have 10 restaurants (serving smoked bluefish pâté, crab cakes, lobster milanese, Key lime pie, and strawberry shortcake), six retail markets, and a mail-order division capable of shipping fresh seafood (including all the makings of a clambake) to any destination in the United States (plus many foreign locations) (*see* Marco Solo, 1993).

The Red Lobster seafood restaurant chain has its beginnings in a place of that name opened at Lakeland, Fla., by veteran restaurateur William Darden, 55, who started his career at age 19 as manager, night cook, waiter, and counter server at a small lunch counter called The Green Frog at Waycross, Ga. He saved his money, acquired other restaurants in Georgia, South Carolina, and Florida, and 5 years ago joined with some partners to buy the landmark Orlando seafood house Gary's Duck Inn. His no-frills Red Lobster (an advertising agency has come up with the name) employs 30 to 40 people from the outset, its low prices quickly attract hordes of customers, the partners have to remodel it within a month to accommodate the crowds, and by 1970 there will be five Red Lobster restaurants in Florida (*see* General Mills, 1970).

Denny's Restaurants merges with Sandy's Restaurants, acquires Pioneer Restaurants, and opens the first Mother Butler Pie Shop (*see* 1967). It will be the first major restaurant chain to offer no-smoking sections in every one of its outlets (*see* 1977).

The San Francisco restaurant La Mirabelle opens at 1326 Powell Street. Fritz Frankel, Alfred Bermayr, and Gilbert Burossi offer bluepoint oysters, sea bass, salmon in season, quenelle of scallops with lobster sauce, mussels poulette, filet of sole mirabelle (poached in a fumet) and served with mussels or clams on the half shell, scampis à la façon du chef, Icelandic lobster tails on rice with garlic sauce, cervelle au beurre noire, crème de cresson, médaillon de veau burante, médaillon de bœuf marchand du vin; chocolate mousse, crème caramel; strawberries with sabayon sauce, raspberry and strawberry tarts, and caramelized apple tarts.

San Francisco's The Mandarin opens in the Woolen Building on Ghiardelli Square. Proprietress Cecilia Chang (*née* Syun Sun) left China in 1949, settled in Tokyo, ran a restaurant there called Forbidden City with cooks from Hong Kong, visited a sister in San Francisco 7 years ago, got involved in a Polk Street restaurant, became its sole owner, and developed a menu of Beijing, Shanghai, and Szechuan dishes.

San Francisco's The Golden Eagle opens at 160 California Street. Cook Jon Hadley creates recipes for dishes that include beer soup thickened with sourdough bread, pumpkin soup with ham and celery; brisket of beef vinaigrette, thread potatoes; skewered chunks of lamb marinated with anchovies and served on rice; chicken Devine (served with broccoli with Mornay sauce), hunter's stew, fishermen's prawns (with a sauce of orange marmalade, white wine, lemon juice, and olive oil), vitello tonnato; salad Niçoise, Philadelphia-style ice cream (made on the premises), and cœur à la crème (made with heavy cream, cottage cheese, and cream cheese in a heart-shaped mold with slices of sweetened strawberries).

The Paris restaurant L'Archestrate opens with a name commemorating a 4th-century B.C. cook from Gela in Sicily who wrote a long poem on gastronomy, extolling the quality of ingredients and simple seasoning. Launched by Lucas-Carton veteran Alain Senderens, 29, L'Archestrate will move to 84, rue de Varenne, near the Musée Rodin, and serve dishes that will include terrine de sole, a mousse made of écrivisse, and navets farcis au cidre (stuffed turnips braised in cider). Senderens will receive his third Michelin star for L'Archestrate in 1978, will return to Lucas-Carton in 1985, and will later open other restaurants.

1969

A booming U.S. economy employs a record number of workers; unemployment falls to its lowest level in 15 years, more Americans eat better than they have in a long time, but many still remain ill fed or malnourished.

A White House Conference on Food, Nutrition and Health opens in December under the chairmanship of Harvard's French-born nutritionist Jean Mayer, 49. It considers problems of hunger, malnutrition, food safety, food quality, deception and misinformation (Adelle Davis of 1954 *Let's Eat Right to Keep Fit* fame is called the nation's most notorious purveyor of nutrition misinformation), nutrition education, food production, and food availability in America. Mayer, who has founded the National Council on Hunger and Malnutrition in the United States, was the first witness before the Senate Select Committee headed by Sen. George McGovern, but while few of the conference's recommendations will result in legislation, funding for food stamp programs will increase in the next 5 years from $400 million to more than $3 billion (*see* 1970).

21 million U.S. children participate in the National School Lunch Program (*see* 1946). About 3.8 million receive lunch free or at substantially reduced prices, and the figure soon will rise to 8 million.

Campbell Soup Co. introduces Chunky Soups and launches them on the West Coast before Heinz can place its 2-year-old Great American Soup line in West Coast markets. The Heinz soups were profitable and patently superior to Campbell's regular line, but Heinz cannot match Campbell's advertising dollars out west and is forced to settle for being a regional brand (Campbell will settle an antitrust case out of court, and Heinz management will vow never again to enter the branded soup business).

Norton Simon, Inc. is created by a reorganization of Hunt-Wesson Foods which has just acquired Reddi-Wip (*see* 1947; Wakefield Seafoods, 1968). Simon has acquired distribution rights to some brands of liquor plus some magazines, puts them all into the new corporation, and yields control in order to devote himself to other interests.

Hershey Chocolate discontinues its nickel Hershey Bar November 24 (most candy bars have been selling at 10¢ retail since the late 1950s). Hershey has shrunk the bar from 1⅛ oz. down to ¾ oz. and says that further size reductions are impractical. The 10¢ Hershey Bar weighs in at 1½ oz. (*see* 1968; 1970).

Cadbury Schweppes is created in January by an exchange of shares (*see* Cadbury, 1918; Schweppes, 1968; Duffy-Mott, 1982).

Chesebrough-Ponds acquires Ragú Sauce from Ralph Cantisano, paying $43.8 million for the brand, whose annual sales have reached $22 million (*see* 1946). Ragú distribution is still confined to the Northeast, but the brand accounts for 20 percent of U.S. spaghetti sauce sales through supermarkets (the market will grow within 25 years to $550 million, with Ragú's share about 60 percent).

Imasco Foods Ltd., a Canadian conglomerate, acquires Progresso Foods for $30 million (*see* 1928; Ogden, 1979).

Tyson Foods acquires Prospect Farms, which has a contract to supply the Sambo's restaurant chain with frozen chicken, and thus gains its first foothold in the restaurant supply business (*see* 1967; Holly Farms, 1989).

Miller Beer is acquired June 12 by Philip Morris, which pays W. R. Grace $150 million for Grace's 53 percent share and will buy the remainder next year for $97 million. By 1978, Miller will be second in sales only to Anheuser-Busch.

Rowntree & Co. rejects a £37 million offer from General Foods and merges with John Mackintosh & Sons to create Rowntree Mackintosh Ltd., which by next year will be exporting product to more than 120 countries and by 1971 will have 22 factories

employing 28,800 (*see* Smarties, 1937; Hershey, 1973; Rowntree plc, 1987).

Paris tears down its Les Halles market and moves it nine miles south of the city to Rungis near Orly Airport. Les Halles has been "the belly of France" (in novelist Emile Zola's phrase) since at least 1137 (*see* 1866), but traffic congestion has forced removal of the Marché d'Intérêt National to its new site.

Hershey Chocolate (above) announces at year's end that it will break with its long-standing tradition and start advertising to hold its own with growing competition.

Nonfiction: *With Bold Knife and Fork* by M. F. K. Fisher. *The Supper of the Lamb: A Culinary Reflection* by New York Episcopalian minister Robert Farrar Capon, an expert cook who begins with a chapter on preparing an onion and includes nearly 80 pages of recipes (pages 192 to 271). Critics call his book "witty," "profound," "moving," and "beautiful." *Food in Antiquity: A Survey of the Diet of Early Peoples* by British Museum anthropologist Don Brothwell and his wife, Patricia.

Cookbooks: *Ma Gastronomie* by the late Fernand Point; *Leith's All-Party Cook Book* by London caterer Prudence Margaret Leith, 29; *The Cooking of the British Isles* by English writer Adrian Bailey and the editors of Time-Life Books; *The Cooking of Germany* by Nika Standen Hazelton and the editors of Time-Life Books; *The Cooking of Spain and Portugal* by U.S. novelist-playwright Peter S. Feibleman, 39, and the editors of Time-Life Books; *Russian Cooking* by U.S. writer Helen Papashvily (*née* Waite), 63, her husband, George, an immigrant from Soviet Georgia in 1923 who once owned a Russian restaurant in California, and the editors of Time-Life Books; *Middle Eastern Cooking* by former *Holiday* magazine staff editor Harry G. Nickles and the editors of Time-Life Books; *The Cooking of Japan* by former *Newsweek* Tokyo bureau chief Rafael Steinberg, 42, and the editors of Time-Life Books; *Craig Claiborne's Kitchen Primer* by Claiborne; *Betty Crocker's Cookbook.*

The Northeast Atlantic Fisheries Commission urges a ban on salmon fishing outside national fishing boundaries as the salmon catch declines in rivers of Canada, Britain, Europe, and the United States.

Coho salmon in Michigan lakes and streams prove to have DDT concentrations of 20 parts per million (*see* Rachel Carson book, 1962). The Food and Drug Administration seizes 28,000 pounds of fish, and Michigan restricts spraying of crops with DDT.

The FDA (above) notes that 90 percent of fish sold in the United States contain less than one part per million of DDT. Some critics demand a zero level, but commercial fishermen in some areas demand a higher level and even critics cannot demonstrate any real evidence that DDT is harmful to humans.

The average Wisconsin dairy cow yields 10 quarts of milk per day, up from six in 1940, as a result of breed improvements.

The average U.S. farmworker produces enough food and fiber for 47 people, up from 40 last year, as agricultural productivity continues to climb.

Opaque-2 corn, which becomes available for commercial planting in the spring, has a protein content of nearly 12 percent (most hybrid corn has about 8 percent). Purdue University scientists Edwin T. Mertz and Oliver E. Nelson have developed Opaque-2, whose protein content is about one-third that of soybeans, which has great potential for helping to solve problems of malnutrition in Central America, East Africa, and other parts of the world where people have traditionally eaten corn and do not get milk, soybeans, or other good dietary sources of protein.

Dutch fishermen working off the Norwegian coast in January boat a halibut whose liver, fried in the galley, is large enough to provide a feast for 11 of the 12 men aboard (the 12th man dislikes liver). One man eats two-thirds of a pound, ingesting about 30 million units of vitamin A (the equivalent of 2,000 multivitamin tablets), and all 11 take in enough to make them nauseous with hypervitaminosis A (far less serious than hypervitaminosis D [*see* 1965] but unpleasant nevertheless). The fishermen's skin turns red and swollen, and by the next morning it is peeling off in sheets. Nutrition experts warn that vitamin A is fat soluble and that taking 50,000 International Units per day for 18 months or more can produce a jaundiced look, not to mention night blindness, day blindness, or even mild xerophthalmia in adults, while in children it can cause bone defects (*see* FDA order, 1973).

Data compiled at great expense to U.S. taxpayers by Dr. Arnold Schaefer in last year's 10-state survey of children's nutritional status is transferred by President Nixon's executive order from computers in the Washington area to the Centers for Disease Control at Atlanta, whose computers are not compatible. The data will never be tabulated, and Schaefer is by some accounts told to keep quiet about his findings or risk finding himself unemployable.

The Little Bread Co. opens next to a natural foods restaurant in Seattle's Pike Place Public Market, beginning a nationwide cooperative whole-grain baking movement that will widen in the next decade, especially in university communities, featuring seven-grain loaves and loaves containing such ingredients as wheat berries, barley malt, tofu, miller's brand, soy flour, flaxseed (some will be made with nuts, saturated oils, and high-fat seeds). The stores will in some cases carry wheat-free, egg-free, sugar-free, and dairy-free breads for customers with special intolerances or allergies.

Britain's Ministry of Agriculture forbids use of penicillin and tetracycline in livestock feed lest drug-resistant strains of bacteria pass on their resistant "R-factor" to other bacteria.

The U.S. Food and Drug Administration forbids injections of most antibiotics in livestock and gives a trade group of veterinary drug producers up to 2 years to prove that a residue of two parts per million in meat poses no human health hazard. U.S. feed producers use $72.5 million worth of antibiotics per year, but FDA rules forbid use of such feeds within 3 to 5 days of slaughter.

Use of any antibiotics in feed and of DDT and herbicides on crops should be banned, says Britain's Swann Commission, a group set up to study the hazards of such substances.

The Ernest Lee Huckleby family at Alamagordo, Tex., just north of El Paso, consumes pork from hogs fed millet seed treated with mercury fungicide. Some of the children go blind and suffer brain damage from mercury poisoning (*see* Minamata Bay, 1953).

Arizona orders a 1-year moratorium on use of DDT after milk in the state proves to have high levels of the pesticide.

Mother's milk contains four times the amount of DDT permitted in cow's milk, says Sierra Club executive vice president David Brower in testimony before the House Merchant Marine and Fisheries Committee. "Some wit suggested that if [mother's milk] were packaged in some other container we wouldn't allow it across state lines," says Brower.

U.S. frankfurters have an average fat content of 33 percent, up from 19 percent in 1941, and some franks are more than half fat. The U.S. Department of Agriculture has proposed a 33 percent maximum, but a 25 percent maximum is favored by the Consumer Federation of America, the National Consumers League, and New York City Commissioner of Consumer Affairs Bess Myerson, whose pressure on President Nixon's Special Assistant for Consumer Affairs Virginia E. Knauer leads Knauer to endorse a 30 percent maximum, which is announced in December.

U.S. baby-food makers Gerber, Heinz, and Beech-Nut halt use of monosodium glutamate (MSG) pending further study after tests at Washington University School of Medicine in St. Louis show that baby mice fed large amounts of the flavor enhancer suffer damage to the hypothalamus area of their brains (see 1951; "Chinese Restaurant Syndrome," 1968). MSG has been on the Food and Drug Administration's GRAS (generally recognized as safe) list, and negative findings about it raise questions about the entire list.

The Food and Drug Administration removes cyclamates from its GRAS list in October and reveals plans to remove cyclamate-sweetened products from stores. It cites bladder cancers in test rats fed excessive amounts of cyclamates, but serious doubts will be raised as to the validity of the tests (see Delaney clause, 1958). A total ban on cyclamates will come only after Congress orders the FDA to prevent their sale over the counter.

Cyclamates (above) are employed in U.S. foods to the tune of 20 million pounds per year as compared with 20 billion pounds of sugar; 70 percent of the cyclamates are used in sugar-free soft drinks.

Kaboom breakfast food, introduced by General Mills, is 43.8 percent sugar.

Frosted Mini-Wheats breakfast food, introduced by Kellogg, is 28 percent sugar.

General Mills introduces Chipos, Procter & Gamble introduces Pringles. Both are fabricated potato chips made not from sliced potato fried in oil but rather from potatoes that have been cooked, mashed, dehydrated, and reconstituted into a dough that has been cut to a uniform size and shape, then packaged in break-proof, oxygen-free containers designed to give them longer shelf life. The Potato Chip Institute files a lawsuit to prevent the new products from being sold as potato chips but will lose in court (see 1975).

Sterling Vineyards begins production southeast of Calistoga in California's Napa Valley. The enterprise's three partners have assembled the most modern equipment to produce their Chardonnay, Chenin Blanc, Cabernet Sauvignon, Gamay, Merlot, and Zinfandel wines and will expand into modern white buildings that resemble churches built by Crusaders in the Greek islands.

The Mirassou Vineyards of San Jose, Calif., pioneer use of mechanical harvesting, developed in the early 1950s by agricultural engineer Lloyd Lamouria of the University of California at Sacramento with viticulturist Albert Winkler. Mirassou introduces the idea of field crushing, sealing grapes in tanks containing carbon dioxide within moments of picking rather than waiting anywhere from 2 to 20 hours, during which time oxidation can cause loss of flavor.

San Francisco's Carnelian Room opens in January atop the 52-story Bank of America Center at 555 California Street. Its menu offers quenelles of lobster and turbot; mascotte sautéed in Zinfandel and garnished with artichoke bottoms, Icelandic baby lobster tails Véronique, double consommé with sherry and cheese straws, fruit soups, cream of asparagus soup, chicken breast stuffed with oysters, médaillon de chevreuil aux chanterelles, scampis chablisienne, double lamb chops, filet of beef, chateaubriand, tartes, cakes, raspberries, and vanilla ice cream with Armagnac and framboise.

The San Francisco restaurant Le Club opens at 1250 Jones Street. Formerly a private club for residents of the Clay-Jones apartment house, it has been turned into a public eating place by lawyer J. Edward Fleishell, who hires French chef Guy Grenier and English manager Brian Griffin. Their menu features cream of carrot soup; roasts, racks, and saddles of lamb (from a French meat purveyor) and beef; émincé of veal with chanterelles; sautéed shrimp and mushrooms in a crêpe with a curry sauce; sautéed prawns in a lobster bisque sauce; Petaluma duckling with Cointreau sauce; dessert soufflés; apple tart; French bread pudding with crème anglaise; and gâteau Saint-Honoré from a pâtisserie in the Marina district.

The Los Angeles Thai restaurant Tepparod opens at 46–49 Melbourne Avenue, Hollywood, but will soon open a second, larger place on Hollywood Boulevard. The Seeboonruangs have run a restaurant in Bangkok using family recipes to prepare the fish sauce called nam pla, the fish or shrimp paste called kapin, and dishes that are often hot and spicy (a sour shrimp soup, for example, containing scallion rings, corander leaves, and chilies) but include also barbecued beef, a yam yai salad, sugary ice coffee and iced jasmine tea, and coconut ice cream.

The Seattle restaurant Brasserie Pittsbourg opens in the basement of the Pioneer Building. François and Julia Kissel serve lettuce soup made with homemade stock, veal and pork paupiettes, chicken with Jerusalem artichoke, mushroom salad, crème caramel, crème au cognac, mousse au chocolate, fresh fruit, and cheeses.

The New York restaurant Le Cygne (a name resonant of La Maison du Cygne on the Grand' Place in Brussels) opens at 53 East 54th Street with Bernard Herman, who has worked in the kitchen of the Paris restaurant Drouant, as chef. Former La Caravelle captains Michel Croucillat and Gérard Gallian offer a prix fixe luncheon at $5.75 and dinner at $8.75 (which they soon increase to $9.75). Specialities include fresh pea soup; terrine maison; English sole poached in wine and served in a light cream and wine sauce with a brunoise of thinly sliced truffles and lobster coral; braised salmon with champagne sauce; sweetbreads Prince Orloff braised with a Madeira sauce; truffles in soufflé with Grand Marnier; the beef Wellington that every other New York restaurant has been serving in the late 1960s; filet de bœuf with sauce Pérignon;

squab with olives; and duck à l'orange smitanie with a sour cream sauce and wild rice.

The New York restaurant Lindy's closes after 48 years on Broadway. Other "Lindy's" restaurants will open to cash in on the name but will have no ties to the original place opened by Leo "Lindy" Lindeman in 1921.

The Philadelphia restaurant Le Bec-Fin, opened in October by Lyons-born chef Georges Perrier, now 26, at 1523 Walnut Street, occupies premises which formerly housed La Panatière (*see* Coventry Forge Inn, 1954). Peter von Stark has moved La Panatière to larger quarters, where it will not survive, whereas Le Bec-Fin, serving 140 diners per evening (two sittings of 70 each) with 420 dishes (120 per sitting), each made to order from scratch in 70 minutes, will come to be regarded by most people as Philadelphia's finest eating place and by many as the best in America (by 1992 the prix fixe dinner will be $92).

The Paris restaurant Roger Lamazère opens with 180 seats at 23, rue de Ponthieu. Former music-hall magician Lamazère, 40, specializes in black truffles; his menu features confit d'oie (goose preserved in goose fat and aged for 6 months in stoneware crocks), cassoulet (pieces of goose from the confit cooked with white beans, scallops, or fresh duck liver with white grapes, and Toulouse sausages), and sherbet flavored with Armagnac. Having run the small Hôtel Proust near the Place Pigalle, Lamazère has bought the elegant Florence restaurant, renamed it, and changed its cuisine to reflect that of his native Toulouse.

The Paris restaurant Les Belles Gourmandes, opened in August with 32 seats at 5, rue Paul-Louis-Courier by chef-owner Henri Faugeron and his wife, Colette, features terrine of sweetbreads; sole "Tante Marie" (split, boned, filled with duxelles of mushrooms, and then braised in red Burgundy); snails extracted from their shells and fricasseed with herbs but no garlic; duck *à l'orange*; *coq au vin* served with a buckwheat pancake; *nymph en meurette* (frogs' legs poached in wine sauce, glacéed onions, mushrooms, and bacon and served with garlic toast); pineapple tart; and homemade hazelnut ice cream topped with chocolate and served in a meringue.

The Paris restaurant Le Récamier opens at 4, rue Récamier and soon attracts a following of editors, authors, and journalists. Proprietor Martin Cantegris, 27 (nickname: Badule), is the son of a doctor in Aix-en-Provence who works closely with Michel Olivier of the Bistrot de Paris. His chef, formerly of La Bourgogne, is Claude Clescienne, and his menu features grilled rougets de roche; coquilles Saint-Jacques meunière; filet de poisson Saint-Pierre with sorrel; turbot; stuffed sea bass en croute; mousse of pike in a Nantua sauce; feuilleté Récamier (a puff paste stuffed with a combination of ham, chicken, sweetbreads, smoked bacon, domestic mushrooms, and morels); calves' liver à l'Auvergnat; côte de bœuf; entrecôte with fresh peppercorns; bœuf en meurette; carré of roast lamb marinated in chopped fresh herbs; coq au vin; truffled terrine of duck au fin champagne; game in season; chocolate marquise; profiterolles with hot chocolate sauce; strawberry tarts; homemade apple pies; and dessert soufflés with Chartreuse.

McDonald's opens 211 new outlets, all serving Big Macs (which account for 19 percent of sales, attracting adults who have not heretofore been big McDonald's customers), fries, milk shakes, and cola drinks, but the company discontinues its roast beef sandwich, having failed to make money on the item because it did not properly calculate shrinkage. A high school dropout whose employees are themselves in many cases high school dropouts, Ray Kroc has a favorite inspirational maxim which appears on scrolls in his executives' offices: "Nothing in the world can take the place of persistence. Talent will not; nothing is more common than unsuccessful men with talent. Genius will not; unrewarded genius is almost a proverb. Education will not; the world is full of educated derelicts. Persistence and determination alone are omnipotent." Kroc is a stickler for quality and has refused to permit fillers such as soy protein in his hamburgers (see 1967; 1970).

The first Wendy's restaurant opens at Columbus, Ohio, serving hamburgers and chili. Entrepreneur David R. Thomas, 37, who has made $1 million taking over Kentucky Fried Chicken restaurants that were losing money and making them profitable, names the place after his daughter. He will build a chain of franchised Wendy's restaurants and pio-neer in offering baked potatoes and salad bars nationwide (see 1993).

Long John Silver's Fish 'n Chips opens August 18 on Southland Drive at Lexington, Ky. Started by entrepreneur Jerome Lederer's Jerrico Inc., which has a chain of coffee shops operating under the name Jerry's and two small chains of Italian-style food, Long John Silver's serves batter-dipped fish and chicken "peg legs," it will expand its menu to include baked fish and chicken meals plus a line of salads, and it will grow by 1994 to have 1,450 units, with operations in 35 states, Canada, Mexico, Saudi Arabia, and Singapore, serving 4.6 million patrons per week, consuming 40 million pounds of fish and 10 million pounds of chicken per year, employing 26,000, and generating annual revenues of more than $870 million (see Arby's, 1994).

1970

✕ Nigeria's civil war ends January 12 with the capitulation of Biafran chief of staff Brig. Gen. Philip Effiong after more than 30 months of conflict in which some 2 million people have died, many of them from starvation (see 1967).

👤 *Let Them Eat Promises: The Politics of Hunger in America* by U.S. author Nick Kotz reveals White House minutes showing that President Richard Nixon told Secretary of Agriculture Clifford M. Hardin after taking office last year, "You can say that this administration will have the first complete, far-reaching attack on the problem of hunger in history. Use all the rhetoric, so long as it doesn't cost any money." The administration's record will be better than this quotation suggests, but some state and county officials, believing that people who are not hungry will not work, have illegally demanded birth certificates and statements of financial need before issuing food stamps or distributing surplus food commodities to women with hungry children (the federal government distributes some 24 different staple items—including beans, cheese, cornmeal, and flour—to the needy because it is cheaper than storing them, but not every county gives away every commodity, and many counties distribute only 14 or 15 of the 24 on the list).

Needy Americans received surplus commodities distributed by the Department of Agriculture.

At least 1.3 million Americans have no income whatever and cannot afford to pay for food stamps, but Congress has been unwilling to establish a free food stamp program, the Department of Agriculture balks at giving away food stamps, and in many U.S. counties and cities there are people who are unable to obtain enough food to sustain even minimal dietary needs. The Farm Bureau Federation opposes federal help to anyone, including farmers; milk industry lobbyists have led the farm lobby's opposition to food for the needy.

The Central Committee of the Soviet Union approves a report by Premier Leonid Brezhnev in July conceding that food supplies are inadequate. The nation has record crops, harvesting 186 million metric tons of grain, but lacks the corn needed to increase its livestock herds. Continental Grain receives an order from Moscow for 500,000 tons of corn and fills it with grain from Argentina, Brazil, Mexico, France, and Thailand because it cannot obtain a waiver of the rule that half of any U.S. grain must be shipped in U.S. bottoms.

Forty Soviet ships lie idle in Cuban ports, waiting to load 400,000 tons of sugar that Fidel Castro has sold for cash on the world market in order to obtain hard currency.

Poland has a wet spring on the heels of a severe winter, flood and drought ensue, and these factors combined with a wet harvest sharply reduce crop yields. The resulting high food prices trigger a December 14 riot of Gdańsk shipyard and factory workers that brings down the government December 20, raising alarms in Moscow that the Soviet government may face revolution if citizens are not better fed.

Norman Borlaug of the International Maize and Wheat Improvement Center (CIMMYT), now 56, is awarded the Nobel Peace Prize for his development of high-yield strains of wheat and rice but says that the "Green Revolution" has only delayed the world food crisis for another 30 years (*see* population, below). Agricultural economist Wolf Ladejinsky, now 71, warns that the introduction of high-yield grains requiring large inputs of chemicals and technology will incite landlords to evict tenants from the land and replace them with machines.

Castle & Cooke's Standard Fruit division drops its Cabaña brand banana in U.S. markets and sells its bananas under the Dole label (*see* 1966).

Nissin Foods USA is founded at Gardena, Calif., to introduce Nissin ramen brands in the United States (*see* Yakisoba, 1963). The instant noodle products find a ready market (*see* Top Ramen, 1972).

Health Valley Foods is founded by Yugoslavian-born San Pedro, Calif., entrepreneur George Mateljan, 36, who has been in the tuna fish business with his father and seen a market in health food stores for low-sodium and salt-free canned albacore, packed in spring water. Health food stores sell mostly dietary supplements and herbal preparations, few packaged foods; Mateljan will give them a line of convenience foods, buying salmon and frozen fish products from other companies for sale under the Health Valley name (the fish line will later be dropped), expanding into cereals, canned fruits, juices, fat-free chili, baked beans, bakery goods, and snack foods, and by 1980 will be manufacturing his own at a large facility in the Los Angeles suburb of Irwindale, eschewing refined sugar and animal fats and using natural, organically grown ingredients whenever possible. B. F. Kroger and other supermarket chains will begin carrying the line, fat-free cookies will be introduced in the late 1980s, and the product line will have close to 200 items by 1995, including about 40 different cookies, nearly a dozen crackers, and 16 to 18 cereals; sales will have topped $125 million.

Colombo Yogurt Co. builds a new plant at Methuen, Mass., and introduces modern technology to yogurt making (see 1929). The leader in plain yogurt, Colombo next year will introduce a full line of refrigerated fruited yogurt plus the first soft-serve frozen yogurt, but distribution remains limited to New England and the Northeast (see Bongrain, 1978).

Nestlé acquires a majority interest in Libby, McNeill & Libby, which now has annual sales in excess of $350 million, and gains a foothold in canned and frozen foods. It soon sells Libby's Hawaiian pineapple plantations and in 1986 will sell Libby's fruit and vegetable canning divisions.

Continental Grain's Allied Mills division buys the agricultural products division Quaker Oats, giving it soybean-processing facilities plus entries into the broiler, egg, and canned dog food industries (see 1965; 1974; Soviet grain sales, 1972).

Miles Laboratories, whose products include One-a-Day Multi-Vitamins, acquires Worthington Foods (see 1960), which has grown to have the world's largest assortment of canned, frozen, and dry meat analog products (see 1982).

Tobler merges with Jacobs Suchard (see Tobler, 1864; Monheim, 1986; E. J. Brach, 1987; Philip Morris, 1990).

London's municipal government announces that the city's fruit, vegetable, and flower market at Covent Garden will be moved to Nine Elms, a 68-acre site on the south side of the Thames (see 1886). The actual move will not be made until 1974.

The Supermarket Trap: The Consumer and the Food Industry by California housewife Jennifer Cross concedes that the U.S. industry (she calls it the "Jolly Green Giant") provides quality and variety unequaled anywhere else in the world, has held price increases below the general average, and has constantly upgraded its stores and packages but says it is fraught with waste, offers too many products that fail, uses too many promotions to lure customers, and confuses shoppers by such means as giving pedestrian cuts of meat glamorous new names (the truth in packaging law has brought little change, she says, because the industry has muddled the government's regulatory program). Cross advises readers to save money by making as few trips as possible to the supermarket, always taking a shopping list and sticking with it, minimizing exposure to impulse purchases, keeping a record of prices for items purchased, and buying house brands.

The *Indian-Pacific Express* begins service in March between Sydney and Perth on the Trans-Australian Railway. The twice-a-week train runs 2,400 miles through forest, desert, mountains, and wheatfields while 144 passengers enjoy showers, early-morning tea, and a 49-seat dining car. It carries 500 steaks, 700 cans of beer, 50 bottles of wine, and a galley whose six-man crew prepares all food on board, with a breakfast that includes pineapple or tomato juice; compote of dried fruit; rolled oats, corn flakes, or muesli; bacon and eggs—poached, boiled, or scrambled; pork sausages with mashed potatoes and onion gravy or sirloin steak and tomato; toast; marmalade or honey; and coffee, tea, or milk.

Retired U.S. physicist Carl G. Sontheimer, 56, and his wife, Shirley, attend a housewares show in France, see a demonstration of a restaurant food preparation machine, decide that it can be adapted for use as a home appliance, and meet with its inventor, Pierre Verdun, who advises them that a home version is already in the planning stage. Sontheimer arranges to buy three prototypes of the proposed home version and acquires U.S. distribution rights, but he notes that it lacks safety features and has other shortcomings. Intending it as a part-time activity, he starts a company, initially to import a line of quality stainless-steel cookware, but will spend much of the next 2 years making refinements in Verdun's machine (see Cuisinart, 1973).

The National Research Council warns expectant mothers in the United States not to restrict weight gain too severely. A Committee on Maternal Nutrition of the NRC says that at least half of infant mortalities are preventable through use of prenatal care, adequately trained personnel at delivery, correction of dietary deficiencies, proper hygiene, and health education, and it says that a weight gain of 20 to 25 pounds in pregnancy is permissible.

Vitamin C and the Common Cold by U.S. Nobel laureate–chemist Linus C. Pauling, 69, claims that megadoses (up to 15 grams per day) of ascorbic acid will prevent or alleviate colds. Adelle Davis and J. I. Rodale have made similar claims, but Pauling (who has coined the term "megadose") has taken his cue from Irwin Stone, a Staten Island, N.Y., biochemist who has suggested that the foraging ancestors of prehistoric man ate enough subtropical leaves, fruit, and organ meats to ingest two to four grams—2,000 to 4,000 milligrams—of ascorbic acid per day. The contention that vitamin C combats the common cold will not be supported by clinical studies but will earn Pauling a fortune and make him the darling of dietary supplement producers, despite the fact that he makes no distinction between "natural" vitamin C and synthetic and questions the value of so-called "bioflavonoids," although some people with conditions such as sore gums will respond to drinking lemon

Nobel chemist Linus Pauling lent his prestige to promoters of vitamin C dietary supplements. LIBRARY OF CONGRESS

juice or eating peppers, when they are not helped by synthetic ascorbic acid pills.

Nonfiction: *Récits des Châteaux de la Loire* by French writer Maguellone Toussaint-Samat, 44; *Spices, Salt and Aromatics in the English Kitchen* by Elizabeth David; *The Enriched, Fortified, Concentrated, Country-fresh, Lip-smacking, International, Unexpurgated Foodbook* by New York author James Trager, 45, is a history of food and eating habits.

Cookbooks: *All Manner of Food* by Michael Field (Craig Claiborne calls it "one of the best books of the season" and "cordially" recommends it); *The French Menu Cookbook* by U.S. author by Richard Olney, who lives in Paris and Provence; *Classic French Cooking* by Craig Claiborne, French-born former (1953–1960) Pavillon Restaurant executive chef Pierre S. Franey, 49, and the editors of Time-Life Books; *Mastering the Art of French Cooking, Volume II* by Julia Child and Simone Beck (*see* 1961); *Cooking with Herbs and Spices* by Craig Claiborne; *The Cooking of the Caribbean Islands* by U.S. author Linda Wolfe and the editors of Time-Life Books; *American Cooking: New England* by Jonathan Norton Leonard and the editors of Time-Life Books; *The California Cookbook* by Jeanne Voltz, now food editor for the *Los Angeles Times*; *Gourmet Cooking for Free* by U.S. food forager Bradford Angier.

Fishermen net 69.3 million metric tons of fish from the world's oceans, more than three times the catch before World War II. A world catch of 180 million tons is possible, some U.S. government scientists suggest, but others express fears that fishermen are exhausting the sea's bounty.

A regulation issued in the spring by the Department of Agriculture sets standard sizes for imported tomatoes that are identical with those for domestic tomatoes. Imports from Mexico now exceed domestic tomato production, up from only 8 percent in 1961, and Florida growers have sought protection. More than 90 percent of the Mexican crop consists of vine-ripened tomatoes, many of them under the new minimum size of $2^{17}/_{32}$ inches in diameter for vine-ripened tomatoes, whereas only 17 percent of Florida tomatoes are vine ripened, the rest being picked green and then reddened with ethylene gas. The permissible size for such gas-reddened tomatoes is a quarter inch smaller than that for vine-ripened tomatoes. Tomato prices have risen as much as 30 percent as a result of size restrictions before the new regulation, and Mexican tomato growers are obliged to let their fruit rot along highways or be eaten by cattle. Charging arbitrary action on the part of the Department of Agriculture, Arizona brokers handling Mexican tomatoes file suit in federal court for injunctive relief from the new order, which keeps out 30 to 40 percent of Mexican tomatoes and lowers the quality of tomatoes available to U.S. consumers (only half of Florida tomatoes sent to market meet U.S. Grade No. 1 standards, as compared with 80 to 85 percent of Mexican tomatoes). The United States Court of Appeals at Washington, D.C., orders the USDA to hold public hearings, which are conducted at the headquarters of the Florida Tomato Committee in Orlando, and although representatives of U.S. consumer groups protest the regulation the USDA proceeds with its double standard for green-picked and vine-ripened tomatoes (*see* 1972).

The U.S. corn harvest falls off as a result of a new strain of the fungus *Helminthosporium maydis.* Since most U.S. corn is now genetically similar in its lack of resistance to the blight, much of the crop is lost, raising meat and poultry prices and raising alarms that an increasing decline in biodiversity may produce repeated disasters such as the Irish potato famine of the mid-1840s. Critics warn that agribusiness has come to depend on only 20 plant varieties (out of an estimated 80,000) for 90 percent of the world's food, and that 27,000 plant species are becoming extinct each year.

Nebraska-born Beaufort County, S.C., physician Donald E. Gatch pleads guilty in August to having maintained improper records of drugs dispensed by his office and is fined $500. He was quoted in the press last year as saying that he had seen 150 to 200 cases of pellagra, along with rickets, scurvy, kwashiorkor, and other malnutrition diseases. An effort to have Dr. Gatch's license suspended is unsuccessful, and he claims that he has been persecuted for revealing hunger conditions in Beaufort County: "They think maybe if they can discredit me, they can somehow discredit the fact that there are 20 million malnourished people in this nation."

U.S. breakfast foods come under fire July 23 from former Nixon administration hunger consultant Robert Burnett Choate, Jr., 46, who testifies before a Senate subcommittee that 40 of the top 60 dry cereals have little nutritional content. "The worst cereals are huckstered to children" on television, says Choate, but within a year he will admit that 45 of the 60 cereals he analyzed have improved their nutritional content dramatically and that even brands with such names as Apple Jacks, Cocoa Krispies, Fruit Loops, Puffa Puffa Rice, Sugar Frosted Flakes, and Sugar Pops are nutritionally respectable; he will later concede that even the worst ones have been reformulated.

The Food and Drug Administration permits some food companies to enrich foods that have never been enriched before. National Biscuit Co. responds to an appeal from the U.S. Department of Agriculture and produces enriched saltines, used by many older people, especially in low-income groups, as bread substitutes.

The Federal Trade Commission announces October 31 that Carnation Co. has promised to stop making what the FTC has called "unwarranted nutritional claims" in advertising for its Instant Breakfast, introduced in 1964.

Consumer Beware! Your Food and What's Been Done to It by U.S. author Beatrice Trum Hunter raises alarms about the safety of foods; *The Chemical Feast* by James Turner reports the findings of a Ralph Nader summer project and raises similar alarms.

High levels of mercury are found in livers of Alaskan fur seals in the Pribilof Islands. Liver tissue samples show a mercury content of 58 parts per million, and iron supplement pills made from freeze-dried seal liver are withdrawn from the market.

The FDA orders the recall of all lots of canned tuna fish in which mercury levels above 0.5 parts per million have been discovered. The December recall order is said to affect nearly one quarter of all canned tuna in U.S. markets, but by spring of next year it will turn out that only 3 percent of the canned tuna pack (nearly 200,000 cases) exceeds the 0.5 ppm FDA guideline.

Hamburger Helper is introduced by General Mills, whose technicians have developed the pasta-and-

General Mills launched a product that helped housewives stretch the ground beef they bought.

seasoning product during a meat shortage to help the homemaker stretch a pound of hamburger into a satisfying meal for five. It will enjoy so much success that General Foods will add variations (*see* Chicken Helper, 1985).

Orville Redenbacher's Gourmet Popping Corn is introduced by U.S. entrepreneur Redenbacher and his partner Charles Bowman, who in 1952 bought an agricultural business and 5 years ago found a yellow corn that expanded nearly twice as much as other brands and left almost no unpopped kernels. They have marketed their premium-priced popcorn under the name Red Bow, but a Chicago marketing firm has persuaded them to put Redenbacher's picture on the package and change the product's name. It will be America's largest-selling brand of popcorn within 5 years (*see* 1976).

Hershey Chocolate reduces the size of its 10¢ Hershey Bar in March from 1½ oz. to 1⅜ oz. (*see* 1968; 1973).

Wisconsin cheese makers produce 13,217,000 pounds of blue cheese, which is also made in Illinois, Iowa, and Oregon.

More than 75 percent of the world's coffee supply now comes from the Western Hemisphere. Americans consume about half the world's coffee output; U.S. men, women, and children drink an average of 2.4 cups of the beverage per day, but per capita consumption is even higher in Sweden.

New York's Broadway theaters respond to growing fears of late-evening street crime by raising their curtains at 7:30 instead of 8:30 as of Monday, January 3, forcing restaurants to serve dinner beginning as early as 4:30 in the afternoon. Many restaurateurs protest the new curtain time; Sardi's offers a choice of seven pretheater minidinners: a main dish, such as chicken or cannelloni, vegetables, dessert, and coffee, and it begins serving its after-theater supper at 9:30 instead of 10:30 as curtains fall just before 10 instead of just before 11.

New York's Benihana Palace opens at 15 West 44th Street, New York (*see* 1964).

London's newest Wheeler's restaurant opens in Appletree Yard, just off Duke of York Street, with an oyster bar on the first floor and restaurant tables on three upper floors, just like the original Wheeler's in Old Compton Street (*see* 1947).

London sees the opening of more Indian and Pakistani restaurants with *tandoors* (clay ovens) for dry-roasting dishes such as yogurt-marinated and spiced chicken. Students and other English patrons of modest means as well as the city's growing Asian population are attracted to the places, but most of the British order rice dishes rather than *nan*, *chapati*, and *parathi*.

The London restaurant Le Gaulois opens in September at 119 Chancery Lane. Chef Jean Viala and his wife, Monique, of 1951 Le Toque Blanc fame offer their patrons artichokes, *charcuterie, côte de porc, foie de veau Bercy, blanquette de veau, coq au vin, sauté de bœuf dijonnaise* or *berrichonne*, salmon in season; *jarret de vichyssoise, rognon au madère carbonade flamande*, ratatouille, *maïs au beurre*, and framboises.

The Red Lion Pub opened June 25 at 73, avenue des Champs-Élysées across from the Lido in Paris has dark wooden beams, a dartboard, whisky bottles hanging upside down behind the bar, draft beer, Guinness Stout, Red Barrel Keg bottled beer, Douglas Scotch Ale, Watney's, Stingo, and Martin's Pale Ale. Its bilingual menu offers steak-mushroom-and-kidney pies, cold veal and ham pie, *pâté en croûte*, *sauté de bœuf*; *rognon aux champignons en croûte*, grilled steak and chips, round steak grillé pommes frites, Dorchester chicken pie, *poulet à la Dorchester*, Welsh rabbit, Chester *fondue sur toast*, cottage pie, *hachis Parmentier*, sausages, mashed potatoes, apple pie, and custard.

The Los Angeles restaurant Le Sanglier opens at 18760 Ventura Boulevard in July. Savoy-born, Lyons-educated chef Alain Cuny specializes in red snapper or sand dabs *grenobloise* with lemon juice and capers; poached salmon with chablis in Nantua sauce or truffled sauce *normande*; fresh turbot from Holland; steamed mussels *marinière* (unusual on the West Coast); bouillabaisse (on Fridays) with pieces of spiny lobster, lingcod, king crab legs, clams, and sometimes mussels; wild boar (from a ranch near Carmel, September through April); *médaillon de veau Juliana* with bay shrimps and Madeira sauce; domesticated quail; pheasant in Madeira and morel sauce; *canard martiniquaise* with bananas and a rum sauce; canard sultan with peaches, pears, pineapple, and Pernod; *coupe glacée maison* (cognac ice cream with strawberries or raspberries and Grand Marnier); and *vacheron savoyard* (ice cream on a meringue base covered with whipped cream and sprinkled with almond slivers).

The Los Angeles Mexican restaurant Antonio's opens at 7472 Melrose Avenue. Former waiter Antonio Gutiérrez, who has taken over the lease of a Chinese restaurant, has only $400 left after paying for permits and repairs, but soon draws patrons with menu offerings that include traditional Hispanic specialties.

San Francisco's North Beach Restaurant opens at 1512 Stockton Street and soon attracts a clientele that includes politicians from all over the state, local artists, intellectuals, and businessmen. Bruno Orsini (a Tuscan who has worked as a chef at Milan) and Lorenzo Patrone cure their own hams in a cold basement room and will expand to have their own trawler to be assured of fresh fish—petrale Porto

Fino (stuffed with shrimp, clams, and crabs in season and served with a suprême sauce); rex sole, rock cod, sun bass—which will supplement their offerings of Dover sole; trout alla fiorentino (with spinach and white wine baked in paper with lemon and butter sauce); homemade pastas; chicken al mattone (half a small capon, pounded flat, sprinkled with rosemary sprigs, and sautéed for about 12 minutes with a brick to weigh it down); and desserts that include semifreddo (chilled layers of pandoro—vanilla cake—and zabaglione sprinkled with grated chocolate, brandy, sherry, port, and maraschino liqueur).

The San Francisco restaurant Mike's Chinese Cuisine opens at 5145 Geary Boulevard. "Mike" is Guangzhou (Canton)-born chef Kee Lum Won, who has for 10 years been head cook at the Four Seas restaurant in Chinatown. He and his wife, Lily, serve crystal shrimp, whole rock cod with scallions and coriander leaves, fried wontons, stir-fried beef with Chinese pea pods, and barbecued chicken salad.

McDonald's opens 294 new outlets (*see* 1969; 1971).

General Mills acquires the 2-year-old Red Lobster restaurant chain and uses its financial resources to begin opening more units throughout the country (*see* 1974).

Norman Borlaug (above) says in his Nobel Prize acceptance speech at Stockholm December 10 that only population control can win the battle against world hunger.

Only 1 in 22 Americans lives on a farm, down from 1 in 3 50 years ago.

1971

The Shah of Iran gives a gala banquet to observe the 2,500th anniversary of Persia, hiring the Paris catering firm Potel & Chavot to serve his 600 guests. The firm hires a jet, flies in 150 maîtres d'hôtel to supervise the 1,000 Swiss and Italian waiters who serve food flown in by Maxim's.

U.S. imports top exports by $2.05 billion—the first trade deficit since 1888. President Nixon kills the 10 percent surcharge on imports December 20 and raises the official gold price, thus devaluating the dollar by 8.57 percent.

ConAgra, Inc. is adopted February 25 as the new name of Nebraska Consolidated Mills, which has diversified from flour milling and will further expand into pet foods, grain storage and merchandising, and other areas (*see* 1956; Banquet Foods, 1980).

Maine Coast Sea Vegetables is founded at Franklin, Maine, by local entrepreneur Shepard Erhart and his wife, Linette, who market seaweed for sale to Japanese restaurants and other buyers.

The Chicago Union Stock Yards, which opened Christmas Day 1865, close July 30 as meatpackers continue to move their slaughterhouses closer to their sources of supply. Operations at the Stock Yards peaked in 1924 and have been declining ever since.

California winegrower Robert Mondavi sues his brother Peter on charges of having mismanaged the Charles Krug Winery (*see* 1966). Peter countersues, charging that Robert is conspiring with Seattle's Rainier Brewing Co. to take over Krug. The family battle will land in court in April 1976, a judge will order that Krug be sold to the highest bidder by February 1978, and Robert will wind up buying Peter's interest in Krug.

California's Beringer Vineyards and trademark are acquired by Nestlé (*see* 1876; Stouffer, 1973).

C. J. van Houten & Zoon is acquired by Leonhard Monheim AG of Aachen, Germany, which has been selling its Trump line of chocolates since 1857 and has been making chocolates since 1931 under license from Lindt & Sprüngli.

Nonfiction: *Food, Glorious Food* by Magnus Pyke; *Stalking the Good Life: My Love Affair with Nature* by Euell Gibbons.

Cookbooks: *Diet for a Small Planet* by U.S. author Frances Lappé (*née* Moore), 27, gives recipes for Roman rice and beans, masala dosai (Indian filled pancakes), curried rice, sukiyaki, enchiladas, and Brazilian *feijoada*. Creative combinations of beans, nuts, grains, and dairy products provide all necessary protein, Lappé says, and she scolds Americans for living so high on the "food chain." She is not really a vegetarian, she insists, and would eat meat were it not so ecologically wasteful to produce. Chickens raised on the open range are acceptable to her but difficult to find in an age of feedlots and poultry factories. Of the 20 million tons of protein fed to U.S. livestock in 1968, she calculates, only 2 million were retrieved for human consumption and the remainder lost—a deficit sufficient to provide 12 grams of protein per day to every person on the planet. *The Anarchist Cookbook* by U.S. author William Powell, 21, has a section on cooking with illegal drugs, giving recipes for "hash brownies" (which contain powdered hashish) and "pot loaf" (made with 1 cup of marijuana). It also gives step-by-step directions for making bombs at home. *The Making of a Cook* by French-American cook-teacher Madeleine M. (Marguerite) Kamman (*née* Pin), 40, who came to America in 1960, started Madeleine Kamman's School of Traditional French Cuisine 4 years later, and last year opened the Modern Gourmet Cooking School and Restaurant at Newton Center, Mass. *Cent Merveilles de la cuisine française* (*The Hundred Glories of French Cooking*) by *Le Monde* food columnist R. J. Courtine, now 61. *The Food of Italy* by Waverley Root. *The New York Times International Cook Book* by Craig Claiborne. *The Cuisine of Hungary* by Hungarian-born restaurateur George Lang, 47, who came to the United States as a violinist in 1946, worked in various kitchens, has been maître d'hôtel at New York's Four Seasons restaurant since 1963, and will hereafter be a consultant (*see* Café des Artistes, 1975). A goulash, he explains, can be either a soup or a meat dish, the word being derived from *gulyás*—a shepherd's dish made with meat cooked with onions until the liquid is gone, then placed in a bag made of a sheep's stomach, placed in the sun to dry, and moistened with a little water to make a stew (*gulyás hus*) or a soup (*gulyás leves*). *Fried, Deep Fried and Sautéed Dishes* and *Pies, Tarts, and Chou Puffs* by the late Michael Field, who has died of a heart attack March 21 at age 56. *American Cooking: The Melting Pot* by Columbia University history professor James P. Shenton, 46; Angelo M. Pellegrino, now 67; Dale Brown; *New York Times* editor Israel Shenker; and the editors of Time-Life Books. *American Cooking: The Eastern Heartland* by U.S. writer José (pronounced Josie) Wilson and the editors of Time-Life Books. *The L.A. Gourmet: Favorite Recipes from Famous Los Angeles Restaurants* by Jeanne Voltz (with Burks Hamner). *How to Eat (and Drink) Your Way Through a French (or Ital-*

ian) Menu by James Beard. *The New York Times Natural Foods Cookbook* by English-born *Times* food writer Jean (Daphne) Hewitt, 46, whose recipes use only whole grains, legumes (pulses), and organically grown fruits and vegetables but who also includes recipes for such cholesterol-rich dishes as calves' brains with scrambled eggs and potato tower made with bacon and whole milk. *Good Things* by Jane Grigson. *How to Cheat at Cooking* by *London Daily Mirror* magazine food writer Delia Smith, who at age 21 began work in a small Paddington restaurant, learned to cook, wondered why English food was so bad, and began reading English cookery books in the Reading Room of the British Museum. She will start a cooking column for the *Evening Standard* next year.

Annual U.S. beef consumption reaches 113 pounds per capita, up from 85.1 pounds in 1960. Consumption will peak at 128.5 pounds in 1976 as Americans eat more than 50 billion hamburgers, paying more than $25 billion for beef in various forms.

The French caves of Combalou turn out 5,316,000 well-aged Roquefort cheeses, each wrapped in foil and stamped with a red sheep (*see* 1407).

Gov. Nelson A. Rockefeller, 62, of New York permits year-round consumption of oysters, sale of which has heretofore been limited to the "R" months from September to April. The European oyster (*Ostrea edulis*) tastes gritty in the summer months because it keeps its young within its mantle cavity at that time of year, but the American oyster (*Crassostrea virginica*) discharges its eggs directly into the water (Pacific Coast oysters have been sold the year round).

The National Bureau of Standards reports early in the year that U.S. women's body measurements have grown from the 34-25-36 of size 12 in 1939 to 35-26-37, based on data from the Department of Agriculture, the U.S. Air Force, and mail-order houses. The upper arm of a misses' size 10 measures 10.12, up from 9.6 in 1939, and the upper thigh measures 20.25, up from 19.5, "at maximum girth."

Nutri/System is founded by U.S. entrepreneur Harold Katz, 34, who will franchise weight-loss centers in competition with Weight Watchers (*see* 1963). By 1983 it will be in all 50 states, with a total of 680 centers, putting participants on 800- to 1,200-calorie-per-day diets and guaranteeing that if they do not reach their goal weights on schedule they may use Nutri/System facilities and services without charge until they do attain their goals. Katz will have a net worth (on paper) of $300 million when stock in Nutri/System reaches $48 per share on the New York Stock Exchange late in 1982, but his program is high priced, participants are not exposed to grocery store food during the weight-loss phase, the prepackaged food they must buy is expensive, and Nutri/System will run into legal challenges (*see* 1990; Jenny Craig, 1983).

Magazine publisher J. I. Rodale (*Prevention, Organic Gardening*) is stricken with a fatal heart attack June 7 at age 72 while participating in the taping of an ABC-TV talk show with host Dick Cavett at New York. He was the subject the day before of a *New York Times Magazine* cover story in which he was quoted as saying that he would live to be 100 unless he was run down by a "sugar-crazed taxi driver" (he has written a book entitled *Natural Food, Sugar, and the Criminal Mind*). Medical associations have included Rodale Press health books in their "quackery" exhibitions, but circulation of *Organic Gardening and Farming* magazine began skyrocketing in 1968, adding young readers, many of them in the hippie movement, to its traditional base of elderly gardeners, and is now close to 700,000 (it jumped by 40 percent last year alone); it is quoted at times by ecologist Barry Commoner, 53, of the Center for the Biology of Natural Systems at Washington University, St. Louis, who has linked nitrate pollution to agricultural fertilizers and called synthetic pesticides, fungicides, and other long-lived compounds a threat to the balance of nature. Rodale's bookish son Robert, 41, takes over the $9 million family empire, based in Emmaus, Pa., and will change the thrust of the organic food movement to emphasize environmental concerns rather than health claims, but *Prevention* will continue to depend on advertising from makers of vitamin supplements, which are now sold at thousands of "health food" stores coast to coast. (Operating under wholesome-sounding names such as Nature's Bounty and sometimes displaying blemished fruits and vegetables in bins and barrels, their main stock in trade is vitamin and mineral pills and elixirs.)

The June issue of *Organic Gardening and Farming* (above) carries an article by food forager Euell Gibbons, who says, "I know there are those who say that they want not even a tiny amount of any poisonous substance in their system, but that can't be avoided. Did you know that there are many substances which are poisonous in large quantities which your body can not only tolerate in small quantities but absolutely must have in order to keep functioning?"

☂ The Food and Drug Administration orders the removal from stores of vitamin C pills containing sodium ascorbate (instead of ascorbic acid) without mentioning the fact on their labels. Last year's Linus Pauling book on vitamin C has created such a demand that manufacturers have trouble obtaining enough ascorbic acid and even some so-called rose hip supplements contain undeclared amounts of sodium ascorbate.

The FDA advises Americans to stop eating swordfish. The advisory issued in early May follows a study of more than 853 swordfish samples of which 811 had an average mercury content of one part per million and 8 percent had levels above 1.5 parts per million. Swordfish caught between 1878 and 1909 turn out to have about the same mercury content, and few people can afford to eat enough swordfish to make the mercury content a real danger (average per capita consumption is two ounces per year).

Botulism kills New York banker Samuel Cochran, Jr., 61, who enjoys Bon Vivant brand vichyssoise soup the evening of June 29 at his Bedford Village home and dies late the following evening at Mount Kisco's Northern Westchester Hospital. The FDA shuts down the Bon Vivant plant at Newark, N.J., and the company is forced into bankruptcy after 108 years in business. Campbell Soup Co.'s Paris, Tex., plant recalls its chicken vegetable soup in mid-July after finding botulinum contamination.

Consumer Beware! Your Food and What's Been Done to It by Beatrice Trum Hunter warns against processed foods.

The Center for Science in the Public Interest is founded at Washington, D.C., by consumer activist Michael F. Jacobson, 28, and fellow scientists Albert Fritsch and James Sullivan. Jacobson, who has a doctorate in microbiology from MIT, joined Ralph Nader's Center for Study of Responsive Law last year but has resigned to start CSPI, which will concentrate on food safety and nutrition with support from foundations and some 240,000 dues-paying members; he will become executive director in 1977, riling the food industry by singling out specific products (e.g., Campbell's soups, movie-theater popcorn popped in coconut oil, Häagen-Dazs ice cream) that are high in saturated fats, sodium, sugar, or nitrites but raising public awareness that will have desirable effects in improving many products, sometimes through Food and Drug Administration rulings, sometimes through voluntary action, sometimes even through federal legislation (*see* 1972).

🥛 New German laws take effect establishing four broad *Tafelwein* (table wine) and 14 quality wine regions, all of them on the Rhine or its tributaries (notably the Mosel). Vineyards in the Rheinhessen and Rheinpfalz produce about half of all German wines, but most of the fine Rieslings come from the Rheingau and Mosel-Saar-Ruwer regions.

Italian vineyard manager Piero Antinori, 33, introduces a mixture of San Giovese and Cabernet Sauvignon called Tignanello. Antinori, who took over his family's 600-year-old vineyard Renzo Cotarella, southwest of Florence, 5 years ago, will be credited along with his wine maker Giacomo Tachis, 43, with producing Super-Tuscans, a new category of wine that will put Italy in contention with France as a producer of premium-priced fine wines.

Celestial Seasonings Herbal Tea is introduced at Boulder, Colo., by U.S. entrepreneur Morris J. "Mo" Siegel, 21, his wife, Peggy, and their friends Wyck Hay and Lucinda "Celestial" Ziesing, who use herbs picked in the Colorado mountains to create a new product category in teas. They have sold a used Volkswagen to finance their operation and sew their teas into muslin sacks for sale at local health food stores. They will introduce Red Zinger next year, and the brand will soon appear under names such as Morning Thunder, Sleepy Time, Cinnamon Rose, and Mandarin Orange as it is introduced in supermarkets and gourmet shops. Celestial Seasonings in 10 years will account for 10 percent of the $800 million U.S. tea market, pushing Lipton and other rivals to market their own brands of herb tea. The teas will be introduced in England in 1981, by

Herbal tea was a counterculture hit before becoming a mainstream rival to Lipton, Tetley, et al.

which time they will be available in 40 different varieties (including citrus-based iced teas) and be stocked in 35 percent of U.S. supermarkets, mostly in gourmet and health food sections.

London's Hotel Capital opens in May in Basil Street, Knightsbridge. Former Glasgow kitchen hand David Levin, 34, who runs the place, employs Richard Shepherd, 25, who has worked at the Savoy, the Dorchester, and La Réserve at Beaulieu-sur-Mer as his chef (Shepherd has married a Beaulieu woman), and the hotel's small dining room serves clear borscht, *bisque de homard*, mousse of *coquilles Saint-Jacques*, ten main dishes and grills (including *loup de mer*, filleted Cornish bass, sole *rôtie au vin de banyeux*, rack of lamb *persillé aux herbes de Provence*, and *poussin rôti marjolain*), and *sorbet de fine champagne* (see Greenhouse, 1977).

The London restaurant Le Relais du Café Royal opens in the old Café Royal at 68 Regent Street under the direction of Georges Mouilleron, formerly sous chef at Le Gavroche (see 1967). The restaurant takes advantage of what many regard as the world's best wine cellar, with more than 50,000 bottles, mostly red Bordeaux, occupying 7,000 square feet of floor space beneath Regent Street. Mouilleron specializes in *charcuterie*, including *rosettes de Lyons* and *rillettes de Tours*, *jambon persillé comme à Chablis*, *fromage de tête campagnard*, *pâté de campagne*, *saucissons chauds à la lyonnaise*, grilled *boudin noir* and *boudin blanc* (served together with apple slices and boiled potatoes or with a Périgueux sauce), *tourne-*

dos Mme. Saint Ange, *caneton d'arblay*, *torta semifredda*, and hokey pokey (Italian egg custard-based ice cream), the old Café Royal having always been famous for its ice cream.

Chez Panisse opens August 28 in a former plumbing supply store at 1517 Shattuck Avenue, Berkeley, Calif., with a three-course dinner—paté maison, duck with olives, and almond tart—for $3.95. University of California, Berkeley, French cultural studies major and Montessori schoolteacher Alice Waters, 27, has borrowed $10,000 from her parents in New Jersey to start the restaurant, whose philosophy is to use only the freshest, finest-quality ingredients and prepare them simply, without fancy sauces. Her partners are pastry maker Lindsay Shere, Sunday brunch chef and wine buyer Tom Gurnsey, and headwaiter Jerry Budrick. Waters will change the menu for her five-course dinner every day.

The Los Angeles restaurant Mon Grenier opens at 1040 Ventura Boulevard, Encino, with 14th-century Belgian tapestries and pewterlike water goblets. Owner Grey Lion, originally from Lyon, has employed Lyonnais chef Robert Pichot, whose specialties include duck pâté in a puff pastry; shrimp salad; scampi maison with rémoulade sauce; *saumon en croûte* with Bearnaise sauce; *truite Brevel* stuffed with mousseline of salmon; *veau normande* flamed with Calvados; chicken Martinique (with a dark rum sauce containing peanuts, sautéed pineapple, and banana); lamb with white wine, tomato, and tarragon; pear Belle Hélène with chocolate sauce; peach cardinal with raspberry sauce; strawberries Marie-José dipped in chocolate, covered with Grand Marnier, and served with almond-studded whipped cream; sauce sabayon with strawberries; chocolate mousse; and fruit tarts.

The first Japanese McDonald's opens at Tokyo July 20 in 500 square feet of ground-floor space (formerly the handbag department of the Mitsukoshi department store in the Ginza) with a compact kitchen and stand-up customer counters. McDonald's has formed a joint venture with importer Den Fujita, 55, who started his own business at age 25 and has a 25 percent interest in the franchise (Daiichiya Baking Co. also has 25 percent but will sell its share to Fujita). Fujita promotes the hamburger as a revolutionary product, telling reporters, "The reason Japanese people are so short and have yellow skins is that they have eaten nothing but fish and rice for 2,000 years. If we eat McDonald hamburgers and potatoes for 1,000 years, we will become taller, our skin will become white, and our hair will become blond." The store on the Ginza takes in $3,000 its first day, sets a McDonald's record of $6,000 in one day 6 months later, and within 15 years Japan will have 549 McDonald's as compared to 503 in Canada, 229 in Germany (which gets its first McDonald's this year, with a modified menu featuring chicken breasts and beer), 204 in Britain, and 174 in Australia (where a fried chicken product will outsell hamburgers and where the preferred hamburger will contain lettuce, tomato, and mayonnaise rather than the pickle, relish, ketchup, and mustard popular elsewhere). By 1994, there will be 1,055 Japanese McDonald's restaurants and Fujita will be a billionaire.

Japan's first Dunkin' Donuts shop opens in September (*see* Canada, 1961). The chain will grow by 1994 to have 88 Japanese outlets (*see* Philippines, Thailand, 1981).

Lawry's California Center opens at Los Angeles in an eight-acre complex containing shops and several outdoor restaurants serving luncheon and, in the 6 warmer months, dinner (*see* Lawry's Taco Seasoning Mix, 1967). The Center will grow to attract some 600,000 guests per year.

McDonald's (above) opens a total of 312 new stores, almost all of them in the continental United States (*see* 1970; 1972).

1972

President Nixon arrives at Moscow May 22 and confers with Party Secretary Brezhnev in the first visit of a U.S. president to the Soviet Union. Nixon wins reelection in November despite scandals that have raised questions about his integrity and despite charges that he accepted a campaign contribution of more than $200,000 from McDonald's chairman Ray Kroc and has reciprocated by opposing any increase in the minimum wage (McDonald's makes extensive use of teenage labor in its operations; *see* education, below).

The worst drought since 1963 withers Soviet and Chinese grain crops, forcing Moscow to buy American grain or risk the political consequences of meat shortages by reducing livestock herds (*see* Poland, 1970). U.S. Secretary of Agriculture Earl Lauer Butz, 62, has visited the Crimea in April and suggested to Soviet minister of agriculture Vladimir V. Matskevich that the Ukraine's rich black soil be irrigated, but the Soviet budget has allocated few rubles for agricultural progress.

Soviet grain buyers arrive in the United States in late June, find U.S. wheat for July delivery selling at $1.40 per bushel, and place large orders. Continental Grain receives assurance from an assistant U.S. secretary of agriculture that the USDA will pay export subsidies to maintain the export price of U.S. wheat at $1.63 per bushel ($60 per metric ton), Moscow's buyers begin signing contracts, first with Continental, then with Cargill, Cook Industries, Louis-Dreyfus Co., Bunge Corp., and Garnac Grain Co. In just 6 weeks they buy a million tons of soybeans, several million tons of corn, and 20 million tons of wheat—more than half of it U.S. wheat, one-quarter of the entire U.S. wheat crop.

U.S. grain exports helped pacify hungry Soviet citizens but raised world food prices. LIBRARY OF CONGRESS

The European Economic Community (Common Market) created in 1957 by the Treaty of Rome moves to accept Britain, Ireland, Denmark, and Norway (which never joined) to membership with the Treaty of Brussels signed January 22. The House of Commons acts July 14 to permit British participation, and the EEC begins an expansion that could eventually embrace as many as 20 nations with 257 million people in the world's most powerful trading block (but *see* 1974).

Peavey Co. acquires Catherine Clark's Country Baked Brownberry Ovens (*see* 1956). Peavey will sell the business in 1981 to a division of Continental Grain (above), which will resell it in the spring of 1984.

Dixie-Portland Flour Mills acquires the 89-year-old J. Allen Smith Co. of Knoxville, Tenn., controlled since 1963 by Colorado Milling & Elevator Co., and renames it White Lily Foods (*see* 1904). The company's flours, used for everything from biscuits to piecrusts, and its buttermilk corn bread mix have gained widespread popularity in six southeastern states.

J. Lyons & Co. begins an acquisition drive, committing more than $100 million to buy stakes in nine foreign food companies, including the Dutch meat processor Homburg, 80 percent of the French meat processor Le Rosemont, a Dutch bakery firm, the Italian bakery firm Industria Riunite del Panforte de Sienna, a controlling interest in the U.S. doughnut mix company DCA Industries, and—in a $55 million purchase—the tea and coffee business of Squibb's Beech-Nut, Inc. Lyons controls 12 percent of the $385 million British tea market and increases its share by acquiring Beech-Nut, whose brands have a 5 percent market share (*see* Wimpy's, 1954; Tetley, Baskin-Robbins, 1973).

Melbourne financier John D. Elliott, 30, acquires Henry Jones, a small Australian jelly and preserves maker, to begin a career that will lead to his becoming chief executive of Elders XIL Ltd., a multibillion-dollar food and beverage conglomerate (*see* 1983).

Tootsie Roll acquires the Bonomo and Mason brands.

Balducci's in New York's Greenwich Village moves into larger quarters diagonally across the street to 424 Avenue of the America (*see* 1948). Still owned by the Balducci family and still open 7 days a week, it ceases 24-hour operations but now offers—in addition to fresh fruits (including feijoa) and vegetables (such as cardone, red Japanese eggplant, and purple asparagus); cheeses; coffees; meats; seafood;

fresh pastas; and sauces—prepared *tavola calda* dishes such as stuffed peppers (filled with spinach, ricotta cheese, and pignoli nuts); penne with spring dandelion, white beans, and pancetta; broccoli di rapa with fresh veal sausage; roast breast of veal stuffed with asparagus; calzone Barese stuffed with leeks, sweet onions, raisins, anchovies, and black olives; and Mama Balducci's pasta e fagioli (made with fresh cranberry beans) (*see* Fairway, 1975).

The Culinary Institute of America founded in 1946 reopens in September at Hyde Park, N.Y., where it has purchased a building occupied from 1903 to 1968 by the New York Province of the Society of Jesus and used as a Jesuit seminary. Substantially renovated with the help of grants from the food service industry and from individuals and renamed Roth Hall in honor of co-founder Frances Roth, the school gains recognition from the New York State Board of Regents, which grants it the right to confer an associate degree of occupational studies (*see* 1993).

McDonald's chairman Ray Kroc (above) has established Hamburger University at Elk Grove, Ill. Students learn how to clean grills, how to flip hamburgers, and how to know when a hamburger is done (when it turns brown around the edges), and receive the Bachelor of Hamburgerology with a minor in french fries.

Nonfiction: *Technological Eating, or, Where Does the Fish-Finger Point?* by Magnus Pyke; *Bite: A New York Restaurant Strategy* by *New York* magazine food critic Gael Greene, 38.

Cookbooks: *James Beard's American Cookery* not only gives recipes for classic American dishes but provides some history of regional cookery; *Boiled, Poached and Steamed Foods* by the late Michael Field; *The Chinese Cook Book* by Craig Claiborne (with Virginia Lee); *Simca's Cuisine* by Simone "Simca" Beck with Pat Simon; *The Edna Lewis Cookbook* by Virginia-born chef Lewis (with Evangeline Peterson).

Cream cheese production in U.S. factories reaches 127,428,000 tons, twice the amount produced per year in 1953. Imports of European cheeses have also doubled, and domestic production of Neufchâtel now tops 5 million pounds as demand increases among turophiles.

Soft-frozen yogurt is introduced at Cambridge, Mass., where The Spa on Harvard Square has put yogurt through a machine previously used to make soft ice cream. The new product, which has 25 to 30 calories per ounce versus 50 for ice cream, quickly becomes a favorite among students and faculty (*see* Bloomingdale's, 1974).

El Niño—a warming of ocean currents off the west coast of South America—drives away the anchovies used for the fish meal that goes into animal feeds. The anchovy shortage drives up prices of alternative protein sources, notably soybeans and soybean meal.

Tropical storm Agnes strikes the eastern United States from June 10 to June 20, creating what the U.S. Army Corps of Engineers calls the worst natural disaster in U.S. history. Parts of Florida, Virginia, Maryland, Pennsylvania, and New York are declared disaster areas as rivers overflow their banks, crippling transportation, destroying crops, and killing 134.

The Susquehanna River breaks through its dikes June 23, flooding the Wyoming Valley and creating havoc in the Wilkes-Barre area.

William Ruckelshaus of the new U.S. Environmental Protection Agency announces an almost total ban on domestic use of DDT by December 31 after the insecticide has been shown to cause cancer in test animals. It is clearly being stored in fatty tissues, and although scientists disagree on DDT's long-term effects there is good evidence that it is reducing bird populations by causing females to lay eggs with thinner shells.

Secretary of Agriculture Earl L. Butz (above) and former Secretary Clifford M. Hardin have warned that restrictions on pesticides such as DDT (above) will have catastrophic results.

Black sigatoka fungus is found in Honduran banana fields and begins to spread throughout Central America, attacking leaves and preventing photosynthesis. By 1979 it will be in Africa, threatening famine.

The Big, Fertile, Rumbling, Cast-Iron, Growling, Aching, Unbuttoned Bellybook by James Trager deals with nutrition, digestion, overweight, and related matters.

The Consumers Union files suit in U.S. District Court at Washington, D.C., to block the U.S. Department of Agriculture's 1970 regulation discriminating against Mexican tomatoes. Noting that its 350,000 members are "purchasers of tomatoes," the organization labels the USDA's regulation capricious and arbitrary. The marketing order remains on the books, but the USDA does not issue specific seasonal restrictions under it (*see* 1975).

The U.S. Food and Drug Administration issues a warning in April against the "food supplement" L-tryptophan, bans sales of pills containing the isolated amino acid pending a long federal safety review but makes few efforts to enforce the ban, which is simply ignored by health food manufacturers. Used by many to treat insomnia and premenstrual syndrome, L-tryptophan has been on the GRAS (Generally Recognized as Safe) list for years, but recent studies have linked intake of isolated amino acids to growth retardation, degeneration of certain organs, and bladder cancer in laboratory rats. L-tryptophan is inadvertently allowed to remain on the GRAS list (*see* 1989).

Eater's Digest: The Consumer's Fact Book of Food Additives by Michael F. Jacobson of the Center for Science in the Public Interest raises more questions about food safety (*see* 1971; Quaker 100% Natural, below).

The Natural Foods Primer, The Whole-Grain Baking Sampler, Additives and Your Health, Yogurt, Kefir, and Other Milk Cultures, and *Fermented Foods and Beverages* by Beatrice Trum Hunter continue the author's campaign against processed foods.

Quaker Oats introduces Quaker 100% Natural cereal—the first mainstream granola breakfast food product (the Center for Science in the Public Interest will blast 100% Natural as having nearly four grams of saturated fat per half-cup serving, even more than a McDonald's hamburger). Heartland Natural Cereal is introduced by Pet Inc. (formerly Pet Milk Co.). Kellogg prepares to introduce Country Morning, and General Mills will follow suit with its own heavily sugared version of Granola, made by Lassen Foods of Chico, Calif. Seventh Day Adventist Wayne Schlottauer, 34, sells out his Lassen Foods to a New York conglomerate.

Nissin Foods (USA) introduces Top Ramen, a bag-type product containing fried noodles with a soup packet (*see* 1970). The company opens a production facility, one of the first major Japanese facilities in the United States (*see* Cup O'Noodles, 1973).

Steve's Homemade Ice Cream has its beginnings in a Somerville, Mass., scoop shop opened by entrepreneur Steven Herrell, who will sell his super-premium ice cream business in 1977 for $80,000 (*see* Häagen-Dazs, 1959; Ben & Jerry's, 1978).

"Light" whiskey goes on sale in the United States for the first time July 1. Whiskey produced at more than 160° F. on or after January 26, 1968, mixed with less than 20 percent straight whiskey on a proof-gallon basis, and stored in used or uncharred new oak containers may be called "light whiskey—a blend."

Snapple Fruit Juices are introduced at New York by Unadulterated Food Products (it will be renamed Snapple Beverage Co.), started by local entrepreneurs Hyman Golden and Leonard Marsh,

Bottled fruit drinks challenged soda pop and began to gain popularity as a wholesome alternative.

both 40, in partnership with Arnold Greenberg, 50, who has been operating a health food store in St. Mark's Place (Golden and Marsh, brothers-in-law, have had a window-washing business). The company will grow in the next 20 years to have 26 plants bottling nearly 60 all-natural Snapple varieties, carbonated and noncarbonated (including Lemonade, Pink Lemonade, Strawberry Lemonade, Orangeade, Grapeade, Cherry-Lime Rickey, Apple 'n Cherry, French Cherry Soda, Amazin' Grape, Raspberry Royale Soda, Strawberry Soda, Creme of Vanilla Soda, Root Beer, Ginger Beer, Vitamin Supreme, Fruit Punch, Cranberry Royale, Raspberry Royale, Strawberry Royale, Dixie Peach, Mango Madness, and Kiwi Strawberry Cocktail), many containing 100 percent real fruit juice, for distribution nationwide (*see* iced tea, 1987).

San Francisco's Stanford Court Hotel opens in California Street on Nob Hill with a separate entrance for its Fournou Ovens restaurant, whose seven ovens include a wood-fired Chinese-style oven modeled on the 18th-century ovens in Casa Botín at Madrid. The main oven, which measures 40 square feet, cooks meat suspended on hooks over the fires of evergreen oak (with help from gas jets). Founder James Nassikas, who will sell the hotel in 1989, has engaged Provençal *chef de cuisine* Marcel Dragon, who has trained at the Crillon in Paris, the Colony in New York, and San Francisco's L'Étoile. Dragon cooks to order such dishes as rack of lamb with a sauce of thyme, mint, and rosemary; fresh Petaluma ducklings with a green peppercorn and kumquat sauce; filet de bœuf with a truffle sauce Périgourdine; rosette of veal; petrale sole meunière; fresh Dungeness crab cooked in a court bouillon; Dungeness crab legs Bercy with a white wine and shallot sauce; and Olympia oysters cooked in a garlic and hazelnut butter and covered with a puff pastry. The hotel's in-house pastry chef Bruno Leucinger has specialities that include praline ice cream pie with Italian meringue, a pastry horn filled with crème Chantilly, strawberry and kiwi tarts, *vacquoise* (a hazelnut meringue of mocha and buttercream layers), and layers of raspberries in crème patissiere in a puff pastry shell with a sweet Johannisberg Riesling.

The San Francisco restaurant Le Trianon opens at 242 O'Farrell Street. René Virdon, who was chef at the White House during the Kennedy administration and the first part of the Johnson administration, heads the kitchen and prepares dishes that include *huitres au curry*; *potage germiny* (sorrel soup with egg yolk); *bisque d'homard*; *chausson d'homard* in Nantua sauce; fillet of sole *de Douvres d'Antin* (with a white wine sauce with shallots, mushrooms, and tomatoes); *estouffé de canard aux olives* marinated for 2 days in red wine, Armagnac, and herbs; *gobbi de volaille au poivre vert*; *noisettes Danielle à la niçoise*; *dodine de faisan Saint-Hubert*; dodine of chicken with morels; chocolate mousse topped with sponge cake; almond tart; tarte Tatin; strawberry cheesecake; and chocolate and rum soufflé.

The Boston restaurant Harvest opens at 44 Brattle Street near Harvard Square, Cambridge. Architects Dan and Jane Thompson have hired chef Bob Kincaid, who sets a high culinary standard and will be followed by chefs who will include Lydia Shire.

Philadelphia enjoys a restaurant renaissance beginning with places such as The Black Banana and Lickety Split on and just off South Street.

New York's Le Pavillon restaurant serves a table d'hôte luncheon for $9, up from $1.75 in 1941 (*see* 1968). Dinner for two runs to about $50, including cocktails, first course, entrée, vegetable, dessert, coffee, and wine.

The Paris seafood restaurant Le Bernardin opens with 35 seats on the Left Bank serving dishes prepared by chef Gilbert Le Coze, 27. Son of a Breton fisherman, Le Coze and his sister Maguy have pooled their money and borrowed from friends to open the place, which is located in what used to be a small antique shop and takes its name from the folk song "Les Moines de Saint-Bernardin." Le Bernardin will move in 1980 to larger space near the Étoile and the Arc de Triomphe (*see* New York, 1986).

McDonald's opens 368 new stores and introduces the Egg McMuffin, which will be served throughout the chain by 1976, making McDonald's the first major fast-food chain to offer breakfast items (*see* 1971; 1973).

Hardee's acquires the Sandy's fast-food restaurant chain, based in Kewanee, Ill., adding more than 200 restaurants to give it a total of 639 in 33 states (*see* 1965). By 1976, it will have more than 1,000 restaurants, and in 1978 it will begin attracting breakfast

business with its Made From Scratch Biscuits (*see* Imasco, 1980).

Japan's first Dairy Queen outlet opens (*see* Canada, 1951). The Japanese operation will grow to have 108 stores by 1993 (*see* Orange Julius, 1987).

1973

A cease-fire in Vietnam January 28 ends direct involvement of U.S. ground troops in Indochinese hostilities.

Food prices soar in the United States, Japan, and Europe in the wake of last year's Soviet wheat and soybean purchases, which have forced up the price of feed grains and consequently of meat, poultry, eggs, and dairy products as well as of baked goods. U.S. consumer groups organize boycotts to protest rising prices, but prices will continue to rise even without the excuse of a "Russian wheat deal."

The price of raw sugar approaches the 1963 record of 12.6¢/lb. in May; some Caribbean nations have failed to meet their U.S. quotas, which have been reassigned to other Western Hemisphere nations and to the Philippines; the People's Republic of China has made some large purchases, and labor costs have increased, but the price will fall to 7.4¢/lb. in October (*see* 1974).

President Nixon orders a freeze on all retail food prices June 13, saying that he will "not let foreign sales price meat and eggs off the American table."

The U.S. Department of Agriculture arbitrarily cancels half of all open soybean and soybean meal export contracts. The Chicago Board of Trade issues an unprecedented ruling that bars entry into futures contracts on old-crop soybean meal. Poultry and livestock feeders, speculators, and others who have bought soybean meal at rising levels are unable to hedge their purchases by selling old-crop futures, prices collapse, and many companies, including ConAgra, sustain heavy losses.

President Nixon announces a temporary embargo June 27 on exports of soybeans and cottonseeds, shocking Japan, Korea, and other traditional customers for U.S. oilseeds. At least 92 percent of the soybeans Japan uses for tofu (bean curd), soy sauce, and cooking oil comes from the United States, soybean prices jump by 40 percent in less than a week in Japan, the White House lifts the embargo after 5 days in response to State Department pressure, the Department of Commerce approves shipment of all orders received prior to June 13 but announces that special licenses will be required for all subsequent orders and says contracted amounts will be cut in half (by 40 percent for soybean oil, cake, and meal).

Foreign buyers redouble their purchases of U.S. grain and soybeans lest further controls be applied, more than 30 million tons of U.S. wheat are sold for export by the end of July, U.S. farmers hold back their crops as buyers bid up prices, other farmers and ranchers cull flocks and herds as poultry raising and cattle production become unprofitable.

Soaring grain prices combined with sharply higher oil prices precipitate a world monetary crisis and then a worldwide economic recession, the worst since the Great Depression of the 1930s.

Speculative selling of U.S. dollars on foreign exchanges forces the second devaluation of the dollar in 14 months. Secretary of the Treasury George P. Shultz announces February 12 that the dollar is to be devalued by 10 percent against nearly all other major world currencies in a move to make U.S. goods more competitive in foreign trade. The devaluation brings the price of the wheat bought by Moscow last year down to $1.48 per bushel, making it a bigger bargain than ever for the USSR (which has thus far paid only $330 to $400 million), and fast-rising gold prices in the London market enable the Russians to sell their bullion at much more favorable rates than they had expected.

Continental Grain opens Zaïre's first modern flour mill in May; Minoterie Nationale Congolaise S.C.R.L., located downstream on the Zaïre River (formerly the Congo) from Kinshasa can grind 350 tons of wheat per day and is expected to make bread more widely available in a country where the staple foods are derived from manioc (bitter cassava, or tapioca root). Zaïre's imports of U.S. wheat will be less than 50,000 tons next year but will reach 140,000 tons in 1977, and the capacity of the flour mill will be expanded several times.

General Foods co-founder Marjorie Merriweather Post dies at her Washington, D.C., Hillwood estate September 12 at age 86, leaving a fortune in excess of $200 million. She gave her 17-acre Mar-a-Lago estate with its 50-room house in Palm Beach, Fla., to the federal government last year, which will not be able to afford its maintenance and will sell it.

Cargill, Inc., runs an advertisement in the *Wall Street Journal* December 21 reporting that it had net sales in the previous fiscal year of $5.2 billion, a net worth of $352.4 million, and net income of $107.8 million—about 33⅓ percent of sales. Like Continental Grain (above), which has probably had similar results through massive overseas grain sales and has a comparable net worth, Cargill—still headed by Erwin Kelm—remains privately owned and has never revealed its finances, but it has had to disclose them in connection with a bid to take over a cement company.

Kikkoman International opens a plant at Walworth, Wis., June 16 to brew soy sauce for the fast-

Japanese food gained popularity in America even as Washington halted soybean exports to Japan.

growing U.S. market, using a carefully controlled fermentation process (*see* 1957). The plant will also produce other soy-based Oriental-style cooking sauces, including Teriyaki Marinade & Sauce, Teriyaki Baste & Glaze, Stir-Fry Sauce, and Sweet & Sour Sauce.

U.S. candy maker Forrest Mars, now 68, turns management of M&M/Mars over to his sons Forrest Jr. and John but continues to dominate the company (*see* 1964; Ethel M chocolates, 1987).

Cargill (above) will spend more than $300 million in the next few years to open new grain-handling facilities in Duluth, Minn., and Terre Haute, Ind., expand its foreign and domestic soybean-processing capabilities, build plants to process high-fructose corn syrup (*see* 1974), and acquire Texas- and Kansas-based flour companies with their own grain elevators, 137 Canadian grain elevators, and Ralston-Purina's nationwide turkey-processing and -marketing facilities (it will also buy two steel companies, form a partnership to use Kentucky coal reserves, acquire a Memphis cotton company, and purchase a Nevada life insurance firm).

Archer Daniels Midland (ADM) acquires Corn Sweeteners Co., a high-fructose corn syrup (HFCS) producer started 3 years ago by Albert Andreas, a brother of Dwayne Andreas, who has been ADM's CEO since 1966, and Albert's son Martin (*see* 1966; HFCS, 1965, 1974).

J. Lyons & Co. acquires Tetley Tea through the purchase of Tetley Inc. in the United States (*see* 1972; Tetley, 1888). It will make Tetley the world's second-largest tea business—the top-selling brand in Ireland, Canada, and Portugal, second in Australia, Sweden, Switzerland, and the United States, and fourth in France (Tetley tea bags will be the market leader in the United Kingdom) (*see* Baskin-Robbins, below; Allied-Lyons, 1978).

Nestlé acquires the three Stouffer food products and services divisions of Litton Industries in March for a reported $104.5 million. One of the divisions produces and markets frozen foods (*see* French Bread Pizza, 1974).

Pet Inc. sells its Schrafft's ice cream, candy, and other businesses early in the year (*see* restaurants, below).

A committee formed in 1970 by U.S. grocers and manufacturers to improve productivity issues a recommendation in April for a Universal Product Code (U.P.C.) design for all supermarket items. The package code is designed to permit electronic scanners at checkout counters to "read" the price of each item and trigger a computer that will record the price automatically, thus eliminating checker error and facilitating inventory control (*see* 1974).

The Universal Product Code paved the way for electronic scanners at supermarket checkout counters.

Colman's Mustard opens a retail Mustard Shop at Norwich, England, to celebrate the firm's 150th anniversary. The only other independent English mustard company surviving from the 19th century is Taylor's of Newport Pagnell, established in the reign of William IV.

The shah of Iran uses the high price of grain as an excuse to boost the price of his nation's oil exports; other oil-exporting nations follow suit, and oil prices more than quadruple, causing inflation in the United States to exceed 10 percent for the first extended period in peacetime history.

 The Cuisinart food processor is introduced in January at the National Housewares Exposition in Chicago. Carl Sontheimer has lengthened the feed tube of Pierre Verdun's food preparation machine (*see* 1970), changed the cover design, improved the cutting blades and discs, added safety features to meet U.S. standards, and persuaded Verdun to manufacture the machine to his specifications, incorporating features which Sontheimer has designed and patented. The machine's $140 price tag is a stumbling block when blenders which resemble it retail for about $35, but Sontheimer, undiscouraged, takes the food processor to James Beard, Julia Child, Craig Claiborne, and other cooking authorities, whose praises will soon persuade buyers that the Cuisinart is a worthwhile investment ("This machine has change my life," Beard will write in his nationally syndicated column, "and I could no longer live without it." Claiborne will call it "a miracle machine" in the *New York Times* and make reference to "the twentieth-century French revolution"). The Cuisinart, which furthers the automation of kitchens that began with the Waring Blendor in 1936, is soon on sale at U.S. speciality gourmet shops, enabling homemakers to knead dough, grind sirloin steak, reduce a brick of Parmesan cheese to a uniform powder, and perform other kitchen tasks that were once impossibly time consuming (*see* 1978).

Nonfiction: *Amber Waves of Grain: The Secret Russian Wheat Sales That Sent American Food Prices Soaring* by James Trager; *Stalking the Faraway Places* by Euell Gibbons, who will die in late December 1975 at age 64.

Cookbooks: *The International Wine & Food Society's Guide to Fish Cookery* by Jane Grigson; *Recipes from Country Inns and Restaurants* by Delia Smith, who begins a BBC 1 cooking series which will continue until 1975; *Dinner Against the Clock* by Madeleine Kamman; *Le Gibier* (game cookery) by Paul Bocuse and Louis Perrier; *Beard on Bread* by James Beard; *Culinary Classics and Improvisations* by the late Michael Field; *Great Recipes from the New York Times* by *Times* restaurant critic Raymond Sokolov, 32; *Weight Watchers Program Cookbook* by Jean Nieditch; *The Los Angeles Times Natural Food Cookbook* by Jeanne Voltz; *Couscous and Other Good Food from Morocco* by U.S. food writer Paula Wolfert, 35.

U.S. farmers plant 322 million acres to wheat, up from 293 million acres last year, in response to higher prices. Wheat production hits a record 1.71 billion bushels—nearly 50 million metric tons—but the increased planting raises fears that easily erodi-

ble land is being plowed to take advantage of higher prices and that overpumping for irrigation will draw down water tables.

U.S. corn yields average 96.9 bushels per acre, up from 70 in 1968.

The average U.S. farmworker produces enough food and fiber for 50 people, up from 31 in 1963.

Farm labor represents 5 percent of the U.S. workforce, down from 7 percent in 1968.

The Flame Seedless grape introduced in California is a red variety bred at the Fresno Horticultural Field Station by John Weinberger and N. F. Harmon from a 1961 cross involving the Cardinal, Thompson Seedless, Fred Malaga, Tifafhi Ahmer, and Muscat of Alexandria varieties (*see* Ruby Seedless, 1968). The new table-grape variety will gain wide popularity in the next 20 years.

An amendment to the School Lunch Act (P.L. 92433) signed into law by President Nixon September 26 establishes the Women, Infants and Children (WIC) program to improve diets in the nation's most nutritionally vulnerable population group.

Nutrition labeling regulations promulgated by the Food and Drug Administration standardize the type of information to be presented on U.S. food packages. Responding to demands by consumer-group coalitions for more information about the foods in the marketplace, the FDA selects package labels as the vehicle for educating consumers on the nutritive values of foods and suggests a format for providing information on content in terms of calories, grams of protein, carbohydrate, and fat per serving, and the percentage of U.S. Recommended Daily Allowances (RDAs) of protein, nine vitamins, and five minerals.

The FDA (above) publishes regulations August 2 requiring that vitamin A be classified as an over-the-counter drug beginning January 1, 1975, when packaged in dosages exceeding 200 percent of the Recommended Daily Allowance (*see* Dutch fishermen, 1969). Vitamin D is to be classified as an OTC drug in dosages above 100 percent of the RDA, and this will apply also to most other vitamins and minerals with potencies exceeding 150 percent of the RDA (which many scientists consider too high to begin with). Dietary supplement makers have bumper stickers printed up with messages such as "FDA stands for Fraud, Deception, and Arrogance" and "God Giveth Vitamins, the FDA Taketh Away," they orchestrate a campaign to put pressure on Congress to limit the FDA's regulatory powers, and by October 3 some 70 bills have been introduced to that end (*see* Proxmire Amendment, 1976).

How Sodium Nitrite Can Affect Your Health by Michael F. Jacobson of the Center for Science in the Public Interest raises alarms about frankfurters and other meat products containing the preservative.

Unilever introduces Promise brand margarine with health claims of lower cholesterol content (*see* Promise Ultra, 1993).

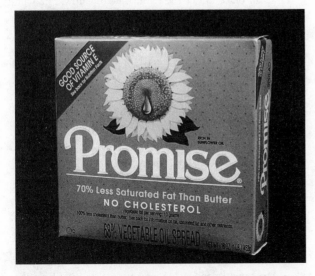

Margarine makers out-promised each other with health claims based on lower saturated-fat content.

General Foods introduces Stove Top Dressing in March in a bid to reach the growing market of Americans who rely on roast turkey and chicken as low-priced dinner entrées.

Nissin Foods (USA) introduces Cup O'Noodles, a cup-type ramen product containing seasoned and fried noodles with soup and garnish (*see* 1972; Oodles of Noodles, 1976).

Hershey Chocolate begins production of the Kit Kat wafer bar, which it has been importing from England since 1970 under an agreement with Rowntree Mackintosh (*see* 1935; 1969).

Hershey (above) has reduced the size of its 10¢ Hershey bar in January from 1⅜ oz. to 1.26 oz. (*see* 1970; 1974). It discontinues the line of chocolate coatings that it has produced for other confectioners but continues to use real chocolate for its own products.

General Foods (above) replaces the cocoa butter in its Walter Baker semisweet chocolate chips with palm-kernel oil after the price of cocoa has more than doubled in 6 months' time.

Peter Paul switches in September to confectioners' coatings for its Mounds and Almond Joy bars. The company says its research has shown that consumers cannot tell the difference or actually prefer the new coatings to chocolate, but many consumers say that confectioners' coatings do not have the same "mouth feel" as real chocolate and Peter Paul will soon return to chocolate coatings.

General Foods introduces Brim, a caffeine-free coffee that competes with its own Sanka brand.

Vodka outsells whiskey for the first time in the United States (*see* 1965).

Pet Inc. (above) announces an agreement June 20 to sell 22 of its 35 Schrafft's restaurants to veteran New York restaurateurs the Riese Brothers (Irving and Murray Riese), who operate some 200 eating places in the metropolitan area, including Lüchow's and several Longchamps, and will also acquire the Chock Full o' Nuts chain (*see* 1968). Riese Brothers will wind up closing Lüchow's and all of its Schrafft's, Longchamps, and Chock Full o' Nuts restaurants after running them into the ground (*see* 1974).

J. Lyons & Co. (above) pays United Brands $45 million to acquire an 83 percent interest in the Baskin-Robbins ice cream chain, which has grown to have 1,300 stands with another one opening every third day (*see* 1967). Lyons, which already has the largest-selling brand of ice cream in the United Kingdom, will begin opening Baskin-Robbins stands in Japan next year and by 1976 will have 1,600 stands operating in the United States, Canada, Japan, and Europe, many of them in department stores and shopping malls.

New York's Four Seasons is acquired by restaurateurs Paul Kovi (a graduate of the University of Transylvania) and Tom Margittai, who have worked at New York's Waldorf-Astoria and Sherry Netherland hotels and at Restaurant Associates; Seppi Ranggli, who has been with Restaurant Associates since 1966, is their executive chef and their initial efforts disappoint longtime patrons, but they will rejuvenate the lavish eating place, emphasizing regional American cookery (see 1959).

The New York food shop and restaurant E.A.T., opened by Eli Zabar and his wife, Abbie, at 867 Madison Avenue (corner of 72nd Street; it will move to 1084 Madison, near 80th Street), features bread and rolls baked to meet the owners' exacting standards (some of the city's best restaurants will buy their bread from E.A.T.). Zabar, now 29, is a younger brother of Saul and Stanley, who own the upper West Side food and cooking utensil shop along with Murray Klein. E.A.T.'s high-priced specialties include chicken salad with scallion cream cheese and meat loaf with hard-cooked eggs at the center.

The Philadelphia restaurant Frög opens at 264 South 16th Street under the management of Steve Pote, who has worked in the kitchen of Peter von Stark's second La Panatière (see 1963), and employs a Thai chef who has also worked at La Panatière and who will go on to open the Thai-French restaurant Alouette at 334 Bainbridge Street (corner of 4th Street). Frög, whose cuisine bears a strong Thai flavor, will move to a new location before closing in 1989 (see Commissary, 1977).

The Philadelphia restaurant Friday, Saturday, Sunday opens at 261 South 21st Street (between Locust and Spruce streets), near Rittenhouse Square. Commercial photographer Weaver Lilley, 30, and six friends in the advertising business have started the place with one partner, Tom Hunter, as chef. Hunter's simple, folksy dishes will give way in 1976 to a more Continental cuisine when Culinary Institute of America graduate Bill Weaver takes over and begins creating the restaurant's signature dish, cream of mushroom soup.

The Newport Beach, Calif., restaurant Ambrosia opens in May at 501 30th Street. *Chef de cuisine* Elimsa Nazman and his executive chef, Leif Pollis, specialize in caviar presented in an ice-carved sturgeon or swan; oysters Rockefeller; prosciutto and melon; sea bass quenelles; *saumon à la mousseline*; braised European turbot with salmon quenelles and shrimp sauce; *faisan de chef*; grills; roasts; *châteaubriand*, rack of lamb; *côte de bœuf à la moelle*; prime ribs with marrow and Bordelaise sauce; *noisettes Danielle en bassada*; salads of limestone lettuce and mushrooms; endives with Roquefort dressing; and chocolate-dipped strawberries injected with Grand Marnier and served with crème Chantilly flavored with strawberry purée (the menu will change four times each year).

Berkeley, Calif., restaurateur Ruth Reichl opens a small place under the name The Swallow. She will become food critic of the *Los Angeles Times* and, beginning in 1994, of the *New York Times*.

The Miami Beach restaurant Chauveron opens in December at 9561 East Bay Harbor Drive on Bar Harbor Island under the direction of Roger Chauveron, now 73 (see 1950). His specialities include pâté of game, oysters Chauveron, contrefilet of beef with sauce Périgourdine, and roast quail.

The Lyons restaurant La Tour Rose opens under the direction of chef Philippe Chavent, 23, who will continue in the Rue du Bœuf until June 1990, when he will move a few hundred yards up the street to large premises in a maze of three historic buildings, where, with chef Paul Brendlen, he will serve scallops with carrot "cake" in a parsley cream sauce, poached John Dory, and other delicacies.

McDonald's opens 445 new outlets (see 1972). H. J. Heinz has been supplying 90 percent of the chain's ketchup but cannot fill its orders due to a tomato shortage; by 1984, Heinz will be supplying less than 15 percent of McDonald's ketchup (see 1974).

The Quincy Family Steakhouse chain has its beginnings in the Western Family Steak House, founded at Greenville, S.C., by entrepreneur William Brittain and some partners. Brittain will persuade the others to change the restaurant's name in 1976 to Quincy (after one of his grandfathers), they will sell out in 1979 to TW Services (later Flagstar Companies), and by the end of 1984 there will be 198 Quincy Family Steakhouses (*see* Denny's, 1987).

1974

Ethiopia's army seizes Addis Ababa in late June after months of riots and mutinies to protest government handling of a famine that has killed at least 100,000 peasants (and possibly as many as 500,000 if surrounding areas are included), inundated the cities with refugees from drought-stricken areas, and produced food shortages and inflation. The death toll has been far greater than that in the more publicized famine in the sub-Saharan countries.

Bangladesh has famine; hundreds of thousands die.

A World Food Conference at Rome in November hears a U.S. refusal to make commitments for specific increases in food aid to needy countries. The impact on U.S. consumer prices in the face of tight supplies is a major reason, but there is also an emphasis on the importance of self-help in the needy countries, including material advances in population control.

Economic recession deepens in the world following last year's hike in oil prices by major petroleum producers. Inflation, meanwhile, raises prices in most of the free world. Double-digit (and even triple-digit) inflation is worst in Israel, India, Brazil, and Japan.

Ministers of the six European Common Market countries meet at Brussels in March but are unable to agree on joint agricultural policies or a common wine policy as member nations maintain programs designed to protect their farmers from competition with relatively high prices (*see* 1972). Negotiations with candidates for membership—Britain, Ireland, Denmark, and Norway—cannot be opened so long as enormous surpluses of butter, sugar, and cereal grains continue. Britons would pay more for food if Britain joined, the French and Belgians want no cuts in dairy product prices, the Germans will not accept lower grain prices, and Italians say there can be no cuts in production quotas for sugar and—as Europe's biggest wine producers—insist that there be no restrictions on cross-border sales of wine.

The U.S. House of Representatives votes 209 to 175 in early June to repeal the Jones-Costigan Sugar Act of 1934. A five-pound bag of sugar that sold for 79¢ last year and fetched $1.01 in May has risen to $1.59, congressmen have been criticized by consumers for burdening them with a "hidden tax," and they have also come under pressure from lobbyists representing both foreign exporters and domestic cane and beet-sugar farmers. Motions to bar sugar imports from South Africa because of its apartheid racial laws and from Venezuela because of its high oil prices are defeated. Opponents of the old Sugar Act say the market will now be free from import quotas for the first time in 40 years, but sugar prices keep rising, partly because worldwide sugar consumption has exceeded production since 1971 after years of gluts, partly because world sugar production is about 2 million tons short of the amount forecast as a result of poor beet crops in the Soviet Union (normally the largest producer), partly because of consumer hoarding in Britain and the United States (*see* below).

Traders in the London market bid up the world price of refined sugar to $950 per ton; ministers of the European Common Market agree to let Britain buy sugar at the much lower Community price in an effort to overcome opposition to British membership in the EC, but workers at Tate & Lyle, Britain's largest sugar refiner, block delivery of imports out of fears that rising imports from the EC will cost them their jobs.

Hurricane Carmen damages Louisiana's sugar crop in September, and raw-sugar prices move up on the New York exchange through October and November, with the March 1975 futures contract selling at 48.7¢/lb. by early November as the world spot price (sugar for immediate delivery) reaches a record 50.5¢/lb.

President Gerald R. Ford, 61 (who has come into office August 9 upon the resignation of President Nixon), effectively carries on the provisions of the expiring 1934 Sugar Act (above) November 18 when he announces a liberal quota for foreign sugar (but eliminates specific quotas for individual countries). He removes any quota for domestic production that existed under the old act, imposes no restrictions on increasing such production, and actually encourages greater production while urging consumers to limit their use of sugar.

The spot price of raw sugar on the New York market reaches 66¢/lb. November 21, up from 7.4¢ in October of last year. Secretary of Agriculture Earl Butz tells reporters that he would like to see the United States resume trading with Cuba (which produces 11 percent of the world crop), but domestic political pressures make such a resumption of trade impossible so long as Cuba remains a Communist nation. Sugar prices begin dropping the daily limit without any change in the anti-Cuba policy.

Use of high-fructose corn syrup (HFCS) soars as high sugar prices make it economical to substitute the corn sweetener, whose highest commercial grade is 93 to 94 percent as sweet as any cane or beet sugar (*see* 1967). Archer Daniels Midland (ADM) has built an HFCS plant at Decatur, Ill. (*see* 1973). Amstar, CPC International, Cargill, H. J. Heinz, and Anheuser-Busch have also built plants as HFCS comes into use by makers of canned goods, frozen foods, jams, jellies, preserves, pickles, ketchup, and some brands of ice cream. Average U.S. per capita consumption of HFCS will be nearly 10 pounds by 1977, up from 1 pound in 1972.

Companies that lost money in last year's collapse of the soybean market sell assets in order to reduce debts and pay interest on their loans. ConAgra, which lost between $17 and $18 million and came close to bankruptcy, sells 13 Montana grain elevators to Cargill for little more than $1 million, sells its North Kansas City corn mill to a midwestern grain elevator operator, and sells its Dixie Lily branded grocery product line for $5 million to Martha White, Inc., a southern miller. ConAgra hires 6-foot, 6-inch Charles "Mike" Harper, 46, a 20-year Pillsbury veteran, as chief executive officer; he will make further sales of assets next year but will then lead efforts to revive the company's fortunes through canny acquisitions (*see* Banquet Foods, 1980).

The U.S. Consumer Price Index rises by 12.2 percent following last year's 8.8 percent increase. Increases averaged less than 2.4 percent in the 25 years from 1948 to 1972, and the CPI actually declined in 1949 and 1954, but it will go up another 7 percent next year, 4.8 percent in 1976, and 6.8 percent in 1977.

Average U.S. food prices: white bread 34.5¢ per one-pound loaf (up from 27.6¢ last year); sugar 32.3¢/lb. (early in the year), up from 15.1¢; rice 44¢/lb., up from 26¢; potatoes 24.9¢/lb., up from 20.5¢; coffee $1.28/lb., up from $1.04.

The Federal Trade Commission overrules a judge who has said that United Brands acted illegally in acquiring six California and Arizona lettuce-farming operations. Commissioner Mayo Thompson demurs, saying that "making an expensive brand-name product out of something that has been previously sold in a low-cost commodity market is, in my view, a practice that is plainly incompatible with the maintenance of an effectively competitive market economy. The resources of this country's great corporations should be bent to the task of producing lower costs and prices for the consuming public, not higher ones as this respondent seems intent on doing," but the Commission rules that while United Brands, by virtue of being a big conglomerate, might be able to subsidize its lettuce-growing operations, the record does not indicate that this would have the effect of creating an uncompetitive situation.

The Union of Banana Exporting Countries, formed by Central and South American nations, pushes for higher fruit prices to offset climbing fuel costs. Honduras imposes a 50¢ tax on each 40-pound box of bananas in April; the tax is halved to 25¢ within 5 months after $2.5 million is deposited in the Swiss bank account of former finance minister Abraham Bennaton Ramos (*see* Black suicide, 1975).

Allied Mills becomes a wholly owned subsidiary of Continental Grain (above) March 30 (*see* 1970). In addition to its flour-milling and soybean-processing operations, Allied Mills has become a major producer and marketer of poultry, eggs, livestock feed, and pet foods. Allied enters the pork-processing industry August 8 by acquiring Loveland Packing Co. of Loveland, Colo., and will acquire a Georgia pork-processing plant in 1978 (*see* Coronado Feeders, 1975).

Continental Grain (above) acquires Pacific Seeds Australia Pty. Ltd. in August and becomes the largest Australian commercial developer of sunflower and grain sorghum seeds.

Chicago nut merchant Jasper Sanfilippo acquires Evon's, a midwestern brand whose owners have been unable to pay Sanfilippo's $90,000 bill (*see* 1963). He gains supermarket distribution for the first time (*see* 1987).

Yoplait Yogurt is introduced into the United States by Michigan Cottage Cheese, which has acquired U.S. rights to market the product (*see* 1964; General Mills, 1977).

Mrs. Fields Cookies is founded by California entrepreneur Debbi Fields, 21, who has persuaded Bank of America loan officer Edward Sullivan to back her in an enterprise that will grow in 17 years to have 800 stores worldwide selling fresh, soft, moist cookies made from Fields's recipes (*see* Famous Amos, 1975).

London's Covent Garden wholesale fruit, vegetable, and flower market moves after more than 300 years in the heart of town to a new site at Nine Elms in south London (*see* 1552; 1886; 1970).

The first supermarket checkout scanner goes into operation June 16 at Marsh Supermarket in Troy, Ohio—home of Hobart Manufacturing Co. (*see* Universal Product Code, 1973), but most retailers balk initially at installing the costly equipment needed, and consumers will protest elimination of individually marked prices.

The National Academy of Sciences urges a temporary worldwide ban on certain types of genetic manipulation, especially experiments involving the bacterium *Escherichia coli,* found in the human digestive tract, lest scientists create a virulent organism more deadly and more resistant than any found in nature (*see* 1976).

The "Heimlich maneuver" described in the June issue of *Emergency Medicine* by Cincinnati surgeon Henry Jay Heimlich, 54, will save thousands of people from choking to death on food: Place heel of hand on victim's abdomen slightly above the navel and well below the ribs; use other hand to press with sharp upward thrusts until obstructing food pops out. Heimlich says so-called "café coronaries" are easily distinguished from heart attacks—the victim

cannot speak, turns blue, and collapses. Mouth-to-mouth resuscitation will only push the food farther down, oxygen deprivation may cause permanent brain damage before an ambulance can get the victim to a hospital, hence the need for prompt use of the Heimlich maneuver.

Nonfiction: *American Fried: Adventures of a Happy Eater* by Kansas City–born author Calvin Trillin, 38, who has eschewed restaurants of "Continental cuisine" and explored back roads to eat at barbecue pits, chili parlors, and hamburger stands, enjoying crab cakes and sausage in Maryland, crawfish in Louisiana, chili in Cincinnati, delicatessen in New York City, and—most especially—barbecue at Arthur Bryant's Bar-B-Que ("the single best restaurant in the world") in his native Kansas City. Critic Raymond Sokolov of the *New York Times* supports Trillin's attack on "the insipid catastrophes of fastfood and deracinated 'gourmet' restaurants." *The American Food Scandal: Why You Can't Eat Well on What You Earn* by *New York Times* agriculture specialist William Robbins.

Cookbooks: *The Best of Italian Cookery* by Waverley Root; *Entertaining Menus* by English-born U.S. author Anne Willan, 36, who attended cooking schools in London and Paris after receiving her M.A. from Cambridge; *English Food* by Jane Grigson; *The Evening Standard Cookbook* by Delia Smith; *Beard on Food* and *The Best of Beard: Great Recipes from a Great Cook* by James Beard; *The Great Cooks Cookbook* by contributors who include Beard, John Clancy, George Lang, Leon Leanides, and Jacques Pépin; *The Store Cookbook* by Long Island storekeeper Bert Greene, 51, who 8 years ago co-founded The Store in Amagansett with Dennis Vaughan.

Average U.S. per capita candy consumption falls below 19 pounds, down from 20 pounds in 1944 (*see* 1978).

The Environmental Protection Agency bans use of the chlorinated hydrocarbon insecticides aldrin, dieldrin, and heptachlor, whose chemical structure is similar to that of DDT, after they have been shown to cause cancer in test animals (*see* 1972).

Hawaiian pineapples account for 33 percent of the world crop, down from 72 percent in 1950, as the industry shifts to the Philippines and Thailand.

Hawaiian pineapple growers continue to use heptachlor (above) to kill ants, they sell their plants to dairy farmers after they harvest the fruit, and heptachlor gets into the milk, butter, ice cream, and other dairy products consumed by Hawaiian children (*see* nutrition, below).

Nutrition evangelist Adelle Davis dies of bone marrow cancer at her Palos Verdes Estates, Calif., home May 31 at age 70 (*see* 1954). Her obituaries report that she considered herself a failure when she learned that she had bone cancer, since she had claimed that cancer was related to dietary inadequacies, but then she had realized that, although she had eaten well while growing up on an Indiana farm, her eating habits had changed for the worse in college and she had eaten what she called "junk food" until the 1950s. "I thought this was for people who drink soft drinks, who eat white bread, who eat refined sugar, and so on," she is quoted as having said. She advocated eating whole-wheat bread (she opposed enrichment of flour and packaged mixes, saying that when Germany defeated France in World War II it was because German black bread and beer were nutritionally superior to white bread and wine and warned that Russians ate much less of what she called "illness-producing" refined foods), milk (preferably unpasteurized), fresh fruit, an egg (preferably fertile) or two and some cheese every day, liver and fish several times each week. The notorious Manson clan that murdered some well-known people in Los Angeles 5 years ago lived mainly on candy bars, she said. She swallowed dozens of vitamin pills every day, carried brewer's yeast with her wherever she went, and although she has recently said about health food stores that it was "tragic the junk some of them sell and the misstatements they make," such stores continue to display her books and prosper by their association with her claims for dietary supplements. Davis has expressed the hope that her illness would not "dishearten" people who had followed her nutritional advice.

The U.S. Senate Select Committee on Nutrition and Human Needs (McGovern Committee) established in 1968 holds extensive hearings at which experts testify on shortcomings in the U.S. diet and in nutrition education (*see* 1975).

The use of heptachlor on Hawaiian pineapples (above) agitates proponents of organic farming,

Alarm over pesticide residues and additives spurred some consumers to buy "organic" produce. CHIE NISHIO

but some reputable biochemists will maintain that natural carcinogens in foods far outnumber the carcinogens in synthetic pesticides and are more potent, and that synthetic pesticides are, in fact, a boon to nutrition since they permit marketing of fruits and vegetables at lower prices that put them within the reach of more people. Many U.S. farmers use more chemical fertilizers, herbicides, and pesticides than necessary, however, and the runoffs of these chemicals pose environmental hazards that will bring increasing pressure to limit their use.

Eating May Be Hazardous to Your Health by U.S. author Jacqueline Verrett raises more alarms about food safety.

The Oven Stuffer roaster introduced by Perdue Farms after years of selective breeding is the first bird to be trademarked (*see* 1968). Frank Perdue has appeared in television commercials, saying, "It takes a tough man to make a tender chicken," and within 20 years Perdue Farms will have 13,500 employees in eight states processing 7 million chickens per week and 3.1 million pounds of turkey. It will be the largest integrated poultry producer in the Northeast (fourth largest in the United States), and its products, delivered fresh to supermarkets and smaller grocery and butcher shops, will be found from Maine to Florida and as far west as Chicago, with exports going to markets in South America, Eastern Europe, Japan, and China.

French Bread Pizza is introduced by Nestlé's Stouffer Frozen Food division to supplement its regular Stouffer frozen entrée line (*see* 1973; Lean Cuisine, 1981).

Soft-frozen yogurt is introduced at the New York department store Bloomingdale's and begins to attract national attention (*see* 1972). Dannon Foods will be the first to open a New York store, Dannyo, dedicated to selling the new product, and it will soon be on sale at licensed Dannyo stores in Atlanta, Washington, and other cities, Colombo and other makers will jump on the bandwagon, and sales of frozen yogurt next year will total nearly 415 million pounds ($300 million worth) (*see* 1990).

Hershey Chocolate discontinues its 1.26-oz., 10¢ Hershey Bar in January; it introduces a 15¢ bar weighing 1.4 oz. but reduces the size in May to 1.2 oz. and in September to 1.05 oz. as sugar and cocoa prices rise.

Life Savers enlarges the holes in its products to save sugar and raises prices from $1.15 per box to $1.72 in June, making the suggested retail price 15¢ per roll. New England Confectionery Co. reduces the diameter of its Necco Wafers from 1¼ inches to ¹⁵⁄₁₆ inch.

General Foods introduces Pop Rocks, a new candy that snaps and pops in the mouth. Company research chemist William Mitchell, who has created a tapioca substitute, imitation fruits, and carbonated ice, found a way to put carbon dioxide into a solid in 1956 while trying to make a carbonated beverage powder; the company has been trying ever since to find a way to market his invention, and in 5 years it will have sold 500 million packets of Pop Rocks.

Miller Lite beer is introduced by Philip Morris, which acquired the brewery in 1970. The low-calorie beer will lift Miller Brewing Co. from seventh place to second, just behind Anheuser-Busch.

The Schrafft's restaurant in New York's Chrysler Building closes March 29 after 44 years in business (*see* 1973).

The New York restaurant Le Cirque opens in late March at 58 East 65th Street with a three-course luncheon at $12.75. Chef Jean Vergnes has known owner-manager Sirio Maccioni since both worked at the Colony (he has more recently been chef at Maxwell's Plum), and the house specialities include seviche, petite marmite, consommé Célestine (made of chicken and tapioca and garnished with slices of chicken-filled pancake), Billy-bi, *potage Germiny*, pasta primavera, red snapper, lobster Marianne, *pipérade* (a Basque dish of sweet peppers, tomatoes, and eggs), duck terrine with *pâté de foie gras* and pistachios, roast baby pheasant *à la Souvarov* (stuffed with foie gras, truffled, and doused with brandy), chicken pot pie, Carpaccio toscane (top round of beef served in thin slices), steak-and-kidney pie, lamb curry, *choucroute garnie*, cassoulet with preserved goose, *bouilli* (boiled dinner with calf's head and brains included), *fettucine*, *risotto*, and kebabs. Dinner entrées average about $9, and the new eating place in the Mayfair Hotel will attract the fashion crowd and others (Oleg Cassini, Jacqueline Onassis, Beverly Sills, Barbara Walters) for more than 20 years as the prix fixe luncheon climbs to $29.95 (by 1994).

The New York restaurant Il Monello opens at 1460 Second Avenue (between 76th and 77th streets). Owner Adi Giovannetti, 30, worked as a scullion for Frank Giambelli after arriving at New York from his native Lucca 16 years ago; his Genoese chef Luigi Strazzuli, also a veteran of Giambelli's, prepares antipasto caldo, pallo dei sette colli, costoletta di vitello, bocconcini di vitello Il Monello (veal sautéed in butter tableside with Belgian mandarine, white wine, lemon juice), pollo Saint Elena (chicken sautéed with sweet sausage, black olives, and sliced onion—a Sardinian dish), pesta di pesce Fra Diavolo (sautéed sea scallops, mussels, clams, langoustine, striped bass, and/or red snapper with calamari rings, garlic, bay leaf, olive oil, and fish stock), osso bucco, rolled veal (at $6.20), Livornese fish stew (at $7, with other entrées at $5.50 to $9), and pastas of all sorts (at $4.40 to $5).

The Oyster Bar and Restaurant at New York's Grand Central Terminal closes July 31 after 62 years but reopens in September under the management of Restaurant Associates co-founder Jerome Brody, who is also proprietor of the Rainbow Room and Gallagher's Steak House. Brody leases the premises from the Metropolitan Transportation Authority and promises to restore the Oyster Bar's policy of serving only fresh fish and shellfish, cooked to order, with salmon and brook trout smoked on the premises.

Philadelphia restaurateur Kathleen Mulhern, 48, opens The Garden in a townhouse at 1617 Spruce Street. She will go to Paris twice a year and collect recipes for her chef, Maria Hennon, who will prepare asparagus feuilleté in a puff pastry; cold poached striped bass; Billy-bi (made from the essence of mussels and flamed with cognac); escargots; clams on the half shell; oysters stuffed with fennel and baked on seaweed; cold filet mignon served with rice salad and homemade apricot chutney; roast duckling with mango mousse; roast whole baby chicken; and cœur à la crème (cream cheese and whipped cream rippled with Armagnac on top of strawberries).

The 94-year-old New Orleans restaurant Commander's Palace is taken over by local restaurateurs Ella, Dottie, Dick, and John Brennan, who acquired the place 5 years ago (see 1944; Brennan's, 1955). They tear down plaster walls, replace them with glass, have handmade trellises created for the garden room, commission paintings for each room, and reorganize the kitchen to create new dishes while continuing to offer Creole and American favorites. Weekend jazz brunches will make the Garden District restaurant a rival to Brennan's in Royal Street.

The *Michelin Guide to Britain and Ireland* resumes publication in April after 4 years of work (see 1911). It sells for £2 (the 86-page section on London restaurants and hotels sells separately for 50 pence), gives no restaurant three or even two stars, and gives one star to only 25 (in France, Michelin gives three stars to 17 restaurants, two to 58, and one to 549, 73 of them in Paris). Egon Ronay, who edits the *Dunlop Guide*, is among those who ridicule Michelin's prejudice in awarding its single star to only two non-French London restaurants—Simpson's-in-the-Strand and the Chinese restaurant Lee Ho Fook in Gerrard Street, Soho. Rule's and Stone's Chop House receive three crossed spoons and forks but no stars.

General Mills opens its 100th Red Lobster seafood restaurant (at Omaha, Nebr.) (see 1970). It established an in-house department 3 years ago to purchase seafood, sends buyers to commercial fishing ports worldwide, and will open its 200th outlet in 1977 (at Falls Church, Va.) (see 1981).

McDonald's opens 515 new stores, giving it a total of more than 3,000 in the United States (Burger King has 2,000) (see 1973; 1980).

1975

The U.S. Senate Select Committee on Nutrition and Human Needs issues a report March 2 estimating that only 38 percent of eligible food stamp recipients receive the stamps and 20 million eligible Americans do not (see 1974). The number of recipients has risen to 17.9 million as of January 31, with 2 million new recipients joining in December and January as economic recession creates unemployment. A congressional Joint Economic Committee study shows that as of November 1973 the average food stamp recipient had a monthly income of only $364, of which 80 percent was drawn from federal and state programs for the poor. More than 70 percent of heads of participating families were not in the workforce. Both reports charge that the food stamp program is badly administered, distributing more stamps than it should in some instances and not reaching those most in need of help (see Dietary Goals, 1977).

New Delhi has massive demonstrations against the Indira Gandhi government March 6 as at least 100,000 people march through the city. Antigovernment violence breaks out at New Delhi June 30, and Gandhi announces steps to reduce prices, reduce peasants' debts, and achieve fairer distribution of land in an appeal for political support.

A U.S. agreement to sell the Soviet Union 6 to 8 million tons of wheat and corn per year is announced October 20, 10 days after President Ford has lifted an embargo on grain sales to Poland. Moscow agrees to buy a minimum of

6 million tons per year through 1981 (*see* 1980 embargo).

Famous Amos Chocolate Chip Cookies are introduced by former William Morris Agency talent agent Wally Amos, 39, who has borrowed $25,000 from celebrity friends to start a business (*see* Mrs. Fields, 1974). He markets his wares through department and specialty stores and through franchised outlets that attract customers with the smell of warm cookies. In 10 years, his company will have sales of more than $10 million, but it will be losing $300,000 and Amos will sell a majority interest for $1.1 million, annual sales under a series of other owners will decline to $6.3 million (and annual losses will climb to $2.3 million), but a San Francisco investment group will bring in former Nestlé marketer Keith Lively, Famous Amos sales will be up to $42 million by 1991, with operating income of $4.5 million, President Baking, the U.S. affiliate of Taiwan's largest food company, will buy the company in 1992 for $61 million (Lively will receive about $3 million), and sales for 1993 will reach close to $90 million, with earnings of $9.2 million.

Little Brownie Bakers of Louisville, Ky., wins a contract to supply some of the Girl Scout cookies that the Girl Scouts have been buying from Interbake Food since 1938 (*see* 1991).

Cargill, Inc., acquires Peavey Co.'s Canadian grain elevators, built in the early part of the century (*see* 1973). Peavey uses the proceeds to buy two chains of Nebraska-based retail farm stores and one West Coast chain (*see* ConAgra, 1982).

Continental Grain's Allied Mills division acquires Coronado Feeders in the Texas panhandle town of Dalhart to enter the cattle feedlot business (*see* 1974). It will expand its feedlot operations by acquiring Colorado and Kansas companies between 1978 and 1981, making it one of the nation's two or three largest cattle feeders, with a capacity of more than 25,000 head.

Pillsbury pays $22 million to acquire Totino's frozen pizza business (*see* 1962). Rose Totino becomes Pillsbury's first woman vice president, Pillsbury research-and-development people will improve the taste of her product, and by 1978

Totino's Crisp Crust Pizza will be the largest-selling brand of frozen pizza in America (*see* Jeno's, 1981).

The A&P announces March 13 that in the next 12 months it will close about 1,200 of its 3,500 stores along with warehouses and distribution points (*see* 1963). The food retailer is building 160 large new supermarkets and hemorrhaging money as competitors with more modern facilities and distribution systems undercut its prices and attract more upscale customers (*see* Tengelmann, 1979).

New York's Fairway Market opens at 2127 Broadway (between 74th and 75th streets) in competition with Balducci's (*see* 1972) and Korean greengrocers. Howard Glickberg, whose grandfather Nathan opened a grocery store on the site in the 1920s and turned it into a supermarket, goes into partnership with his brothers-in-law Harold Seybert and David Sneddon, sells fresh produce from the Hunt's Point Market, buys directly from three farmers in Long Island and Pennsylvania, undercuts the competition, and will soon be serving an estimated 30,000 customers per week from 3,700 square feet of space (it will expand to more than 5,000 square feet as demand grows for its bok choy (Chinese cabbage), daikon (Japanese white radish), shiitake (Japanese mushrooms), okra, collards, imported green beans, Jonathan and Northern Spy apples, French rolls, baguettes, Russian black bread, Lithuanian whole wheat bread, bagels, imported butters, 300 cheeses, cold cuts, smoked salmon, whitefish, chubs, smoked Scottish mackerel, local strawberries and sweet corn in season, coffees, and nuts.

Egypt's Suez Canal reopens June 5, just 8 years after the outbreak of the 6-day Arab-Israeli War.

Cookbooks: *Craig Claiborne's Favorites from the New York Times* (volume II will appear next year, volume III in 1977, volume IV in 1978); *Penny-Wise Perfect Dinners* by James Beard; *The Confident Cook: Basic Recipes and How to Build on Them* by London-born New York author Irena Chalmers, 30, who has studied at London's Cordon Bleu Cooking School after training originally to be a nurse; *To the King's Taste: Richard II's Book of Feasts and Recipes* by New York author Lorna J. (Janet) Sass, 29, who teaches writing at Queens College; *The Mushroom Feast: A Celebration of all*

Edible Fungi, Cultivated, Wild, and Dried Varieties, with More Than 100 Recipes to Choose From and *Cooking Carrots* by Jane Grigson; *Christmas Food & Drink* by Lady Arabella Boxer.

United Fruit Co. president Eli M. Black throws himself through the window of his office in New York's Pan Am Building February 3 and plummets 44 floors to his death (*see* United Brands, 1968). United Fruit has lost its leadership in the banana business to Castle & Cooke, earnings have declined, and company executives who have not quit have been fomenting an insurrection against Black. Improper payments by United Fruit to foreign governments will come to light to help explain Black's suicide.

Maine oystermen begin cultivating the European oyster *Ostrea edulis*, which grows faster than American varieties and fetches higher prices. York Harbor Export Co. will harvest its first crop in 1978 and be producing 500,000 oysters per year within a decade, by which time the *Ostrea edulis* will also be under cultivation in coastal waters of the Northwest, where aquaculturists in some places will be harvesting Olympia oysters (*Crassostrea lurida*) as well.

Eat Your Heart Out by *Texas Observer* editor and self-styled populist Jim Hightower, 32, is a critique of U.S. agribusiness and a defense of small-scale organic farming.

India's wheat crop is 24.1 million metric tons, up from 12.3 in 1965.

The U.S. Department of Agriculture agrees in September to take into account consumer interests with regard to tomatoes and to follow certain procedural safeguards before instituting any such orders as the one issued in 1970 (*see* 1972). The USDA has acted under a settlement approved by the District Court, importers of vine-ripened tomatoes gain a victory, imports of Mexican tomatoes increase, average U.S. per capita tomato consumption will rise by 1978 to 25.5 kilograms (including those used for processing), up from just 8.2 in 1920, but the taste and quality of commercial table tomatoes will remain a perennial source of complaint.

California produces about 86 percent of U.S. processing tomatoes and 76 percent of all tomatoes grown commercially.

A "black frost" decimates Brazil's coffee bushes, drastically reducing the output of the world's largest coffee producer and inflating retail coffee prices.

Nutrition Scoreboard by Michael F. Jacobson of the Center for Science in the Public Interest rates various food brands according to their nutritional value.

Japanese kabuki actor Mitsugoro Bando VIII dies of tetradotoxin poisoning after eating three or four portions of fugu liver (*see* Cook, 1774; Nippon restaurant, 1984).

The U.S. Food and Drug Administration issues a ruling that potato chip products not made from fresh potatoes must be labeled "potato chips made from dried potatoes" (*see* Chipos, Pringles, 1969). The ruling is to take effect in 1977, but the sales appeal of fabricated chips will have declined by that time and regular potato chips will be far more popular.

Mulino Bianco bread products are introduced by Parma's Barilla bakery, which was acquired in 1971 by the U.S. conglomerate W. R. Grace & Co. (*see* 1962; 1979).

U.S. consumption of soft drinks edges past coffee and will pass milk next year.

Apple & Eve is founded by New York entrepreneur Gordon Crane, 25, who has found that supermarkets carry filtered apple juices but no natural brands. Having started his business career 3 years ago as the first distributor for Celestial Seasonings teas (*see* 1971), Crane found that the business was labor intensive and profit margins small. He decided to go to law school but lacked money for tuition. He has taken $3,000 in savings, hired a New York artist to design graphics, contracted with an upstate cider mill to press apples for shipment to a Massachusetts bottling plant, and gone into business. Operating out of his parents' house in Bayside, Queens, he sells his first case of Apple & Eve in April; a food broker persuades supermarket chains, beginning with the 110-store Kroger chain, to stock the brand; Crane's mother, Ruth, handles order taking, bookkeeping, and customer relations; he begins law school at Hofstra University in September (he has a bachelor's degree from the University of Rhode Island); his brothers Cary, now 21, and Allan, now 29, will join the company next

Mott's and Red Cheek had to contend with a new rival in the world of apple juice.

year; and by the end of 1976 Apple & Eve will be on the shelves of several hundred New York supermarkets and selling at the rate of $400,000 per year. Supermarket customers have been clamoring for "natural" products, and sales will top $1 million by 1978, when Crane completes law school. He will expand his line to include apple-cranberry juice (sweetened only with unfiltered apple juice), and by 1992 his company will be racking up annual sales of $36 million in Northeastern and Florida markets.

New England Apple Products introduces 10-ounce Plasti-shield bottles for its Veryfine juices, revolutionizing the packaging of fruit juices and drinks (*see* 1944). The company set out to capitalize on the growing interest in health and fitness (*see* vending machines, 1981).

The Mexican and U.S. fast-food chain El Pollo Loco (The Crazy Chicken) has its beginnings in a small roadside restaurant opened at Guasave on the Pacific Coast by Mexican entrepreneur Francisco Ochoa, who will soon have 90 outlets in 20 Mexican cities (*see* 1980).

Craig Claiborne (above) puts in the winning bid of $300 for one of the prizes in a New York Public Television station June fund-raising auction. The prize, donated by American Express Co., consists of dinner for two at any price at any restaurant in the world that honors the American Express credit card. Claiborne, accompanied by Pierre Franey, jets to Paris in November, and sits down to a prearranged 31-course dinner (caviar, pheasant, lobster, nine costly French wines, etc.) at Chez Denis. The bill comes to $4,000, tips included, and Claiborne's front-page account of the meal in the *New York Times* (he says the lobster was "chewy," the pheasant lukewarm, and the dinner overall not the greatest meal he ever had) produces a torrent of mail from critics who deplore spending so much for a meal when millions of people throughout the world go hungry.

New York's Rainbow Room is taken over by restaurateurs Anthony May and Brian Daly, who revive the room's prewar tradition of dance music (*see* 1950). Sy Oliver's band will entertain patrons for the next 10 years.

The New York restaurant Café des Artistes at 1 West 67th Street closes after 58 years and its proprietor makes off with half the Howard Chandler Christy murals that have graced it since 1934. Restaurant consultant George Lang replaces the missing murals with mirrors that brighten up the place, brings in Breton chef André Guillou, and reopens with an innovative menu that will include rillettes; sautéed snails with prosciutto, onion, and toasted pumpernickel; seafood gazpacho; soup au poisson; bouillabaisse or *bourride*; cream of cucumber soup; consommé Bellevue; oysters on the half shell with sausages; clams on the half shell with a walnut-studded pork and veal pâté; *gravlaks* (salmon marinated with dill); sautéed bay scallops; striped bass; bluefish; halibut; roast duckling with tangerine sauce; *caneton à l'orange*; roast chicken with rosemary; charcuterie including Lyons-style sausage and headcheese (made with pigs' knuckles and veal sweetbreads); hot Lyonnais sausage en croute; hot chicken liver mousse with tarragon sauce; leg of lamb with flageolets; stuffed veal breast; steak *au poivre vert à la crème*; raw seasonal vegetables with spiced yogurt; carrot cake; orange savarin; macadamia nut pie; and Ilona torte (made of chocolate and nuts without flour).

The San Francisco restaurant La Pergole opens at 2060 Chestnut Street in the Marina district with chef Angelo Piccini, who has been hired by owner Luciano Maggiora to prepare pesto, fettucine, *tortellini alla panna*, shrimp Umberto, *scampi de la casa*, *vitello all'agrod di limone*, *piccata di vitello carciofi*, and *scallopine di vitello alla Pergole*.

The San Francisco restaurant La Potinière opens in September at 2305 Irving Street, near 24th Avenue, in the Sunset district. French-born owner Roger Necrosolas, originally from Quimperlé in the Finistère, employs Tyran as his chef and offers a menu that includes *bœuf bourguignon en criade Danielle à la provençal*, *feuillet au fromage*, *ris de veau au Oporto en croûte*, *canard à la pêche*, *gigot Danieaux* on a mirepoix of vegetables, poached red snapper fillets with Hollandaise and Bearnaise sauce, *pâté feuilleté*, *millefeuilles*, and chocolate mousse flavored with French vanilla. Dinner is $6.25 to $7.95.

The Los Angeles restaurant L'Ermitage opens at 730 North La Cienega Boulevard under the direction of patron-chef Jean Bertranou, a *pâtissier,* formerly of La Chaumière, who is helped by a former sous-chef at New York's Lutèce and a saucier from New York's La Caravelle. Designed to look like French country inn, it has a tankful of live trout for *truite au bleu* and serves also *côte de veau Prince Orloff*. A duck farm established by Bertranou outside Los Angeles breeds ducks for the restaurant's *aiguillettes de canard au Médoc*, made with mullard (a cross between the Pekin duck and Muscovy duck, with only 5 percent fat as compared to 45 percent in a Pekin duck); other specialties include *pâté feuilleté*, *pâté grisé*, *biscuit de Savoie*, fruit tarts, *gâteau de Pithiviers*, soufflés, and sherbets (including peach and cassis) (*see* 1980).

1976

Chairman Mao Zedong of the People's Republic of China dies September 10 at age 82, but Communist rule continues.

East Germany has a catastrophic grain harvest following a drought and suffers resulting food shortages.

Polish Prime Minister Piotr Jaroszewicz announces in March that food prices, frozen for the past 5 years, will be increased, he announces in late June that prices will rise as much as 100 percent to pay farmers for their produce, nationwide strikes and violence ensue, the price increases are promptly rescinded, but Communist party leader Edward Gierek, 63, announces in July that higher food prices are unavoidable. The party newspaper *Trybuna Ludu* cautions in August that Poland's small-plot farm structure has fallen 15 years behind other eastern European Communist countries, where collectivized farms dominate agricultural production, and 20 years behind the West but concedes that the strikes have arisen from "grave miscalculation" by Communist planners (*see* 1990; meat rationing, 1980; hyperinflation, 1989).

Hershey Chocolate increases the size of its 15¢ Hershey Bar in January from 1.05 oz. to 1.2 oz. as sugar and cocoa prices ease, and although it raises the price to 20¢ in December it also increases the size, this time to 1.35 oz. The world price of raw sugar falls back below 10¢/lb. by year's end, down from 66¢ in November 1974.

Hunt-Wesson Foods buys Orville Redenbacher's Gourmet Popping Corn, making Redenbacher and his partner, Charles Bowman, millionaires (*see* 1970).

Boston's Quincy Market reopens August 26, just 150 years after Josiah Quincy opened it, as Baltimore developer James Rouse, 62, restores the historic heart of the city.

New York City launches a Greenmarkets program that will grow to have 20 outdoor food markets selling direct from producer to consumer.

Conrail (Consolidated Rail Corp.) begins operations May 1 with 88,000 freight workers as the federal government attempts to maintain service on lines served by the now bankrupt Penn Central, Ann Arbor, Boston & Maine, Central of New Jersey, Erie Lackawanna, Lehigh and Hudson Valley, and Reading. Railroads carry less than 37 percent of U.S. freight.

Nonfiction: *Big Mac: The Unauthorized Story of McDonald's* by U.S. authors Max Boas and Steve Chain reports that the fast-food chain has exploited its workers by appropriating their tips and forcing them to take lie detector tests.

Fiction: *Blue Skies, No Candy* by *New York* magazine food critic Gael Greene, now 42, who has tried, she will tell a *Los Angeles Times* interviewer, "to describe female sexual response in a way that I thought I knew, in a fictional context. I decided I would do it in exactly the way that I would write restaurant reviews: let you know how it feels and smells and tastes and sounds." "I wake every day full of hope that I will discover some great new restaurant, or a glorious new dish, or even an enchanting new flavor," Greene will tell *Contemporary Authors*. "I have dedicated myself to the wanton indulgence of my senses. And I shall consider it fitting and divine if on my death bed my last words echo those of Pierette, the sister of Brillat-Savarin, who died at table shortly before her one hundredth birthday, 'Bring on the dessert. I think I'm about to die.' "

Cookbooks: *La Cuisine du marché: En hommage à Alfred Guérot* [born 1887] (in English, *Paul Bocuse's French Cooking*) by chef Bocuse, now 50; *The Saucier's Apprentice: A Modern Guide to Classic French Sauces for the Home* by Raymond Sokolov; *Eating in America* by Waverley Root (with Richard de Rochemont); *To the Queen's Taste: Elizabethan Feasts and Recipes Adapted for Modern Cooking* by Lorna J. Sass; *Cooking Spinach Compiled by Jane Grigson*; *Frugal Food* by Delia Smith; *Japanese Cookery* by English author Elisabeth Lambert Ortiz (with Mitsuo Endo).

A California drought forces compulsory water rationing February 1 in Marin County north of San Francisco. Water prices go up 40 percent March 1; critics complain that too much water is being used for irrigation, especially of ricefields (*see* 1977).

President Ford signs legislation April 13 extending U.S. jurisdiction over fishing rights to 200 miles offshore, effective March 1, 1977, and to ban fishing of 14 species unless they are shown to be in surpluses beyond the capacity of the U.S. fishing fleet. Japan's foreign ministry says that it regrets the unilateral U.S. action. Iceland has broken diplomatic relations with Britain over cod-fishing rights. Moscow imposes a 200-mile limit on foreign fishermen December 10.

La Leche League International Inc. has 2,868 groups in 42 countries working to "help mothers who wish to breast-feed their infants" and encourage breast-feeding (*see* 1956). By 1993, 56 percent of U.S. mothers will be breast-feeding their newborns, with encouragement from physicians and pediatricians as well as from La Leche, but as more and more U.S. mothers breast-feed their babies with unqualified, doctrinaire advice about giving "only the breast during baby's first month," and as hospitals increasingly discharge new mothers sooner after delivery and without supervision at home, more days-old babies will be returned to hospitals dehydrated and starved. Too weak to suck, they will be treated for "insufficient milk syndrome," sometimes with intravenous sustenance.

Dexatrim one-a-day diet pills are introduced by U.S. entrepreneur S. Daniel Abraham, 52, who has heretofore sold ointments to relieve itching and copied other pharmaceutical products (*see* Slim-Fast, 1977).

The Food and Drug Administration bans Red No. 2 dye in January, citing new concern that it may be carcinogenic, but does not order a recall of foods containing Red No. 2, which is the nation's most commonly used food coloring (*see* 1960). The maker of Red No. 2 challenges the ban, a U.S. appeals court blocks the FDA's action, the FDA gets permission from the court to ban Red No. 2 effective February 12, and Chief Justice Warren Berger refuses to postpone the ban. Many food manufacturers have been switching to Red No. 40, but Michael F. Jacobson of the Center for Science in the Public Interest urges the FDA and National Cancer Institute to persuade the FDA commissioner to ban Red No. 40 and recall products containing it.

The Proxmire Amendment to the Food, Drug, and Cosmetics Act limits the Food and Drug Administration's authority to regulate dietary supplements (*see* 1973). Sponsored by Sen. William Proxmire (D. Wisc.), 60, the amendment says that such supplements should be treated neither as drugs nor as food additives, that the public is entitled to be given information about health in conjunction with the sale of such supplements, but no regulatory action can be taken against manufacturers of supplements except in cases where a clear risk to public health exists (*see* 1992).

Fresh Horizons Bread is introduced with indigestible cellulose designed to provide fiber without calories; the Food and Drug Administration will force Continental Baking to withdraw health claims for the new product, and consumers will reject it.

Procter & Gamble introduces Puritan Oil, a salad and cooking oil that will be reformulated in the late 1980s to make its basic ingredient rapeseed (canola) oil (*see* FDA, 1985).

Oodles of Noodles, introduced by Nissin Foods (USA), is a bag-type ramen product containing fried noodles with a soup packet (*see* 1973). Nissin will open a second production facility in 1978 at Lancaster, Pa., and a third one in 1994 at Memphis, Tenn., as demand grows for its instant noodle products.

M&M/Mars introduces Starburst Fruit Chews, which contain actual fruit juices from concentrates.

Perrier Water is introduced in U.S. markets (*see* 1863). Although consumers prefer cheaper brands like Canada Dry Club Soda in blind taste tests, Perrier sales will reach $177 million in a decade as fitness-minded Americans switch from alcoholic beverages.

New York's Windows on the World restaurant opens on the top (107th) floor of the 3-year-old south tower of the World Trade Center with views of the Statue of Liberty, Staten Island Ferry, and other sights far below. Joseph Baum, who heads up the entire food service operation at the World Trade Center, offers drinks at the City Lights Bar, snacks at the Hors D'Oeuvrerie (which serves breakfast from 7:30 to 10:30 in the morning and reopens at 3 P.M. for tea and cocktails), wine at the Cellar in the Sky, and meals at the Restaurant. A Wall Street luncheon club during the week, Windows will be better known for its views than for its cuisine.

The New York restaurant Market Bar and Dining Rooms opens in the summer on the concourse of 5

World Trade Center (above), which occupies the site of the old Washington Market. Joseph Baum greets patrons with a bounteous display of each day's vegetables, arrayed at the entrance (as at the Washington Market) in crates and baskets, and has complimentary appetizers sent to each table along with good crusty breads. The bar features a whiskey sour made of bonded bourbon with honey and lemon juice; the Swiss-born chef Arnold Fanger offers baked clams; Cotuit oysters on the half shell; baked oysters with saffron and tomatoes; shrimp with daikon (Japanese radish); pâté of potatoes and spinach; gnocchi; homemade fettucine with creamed peas and broccoli; chicken soup with soup greens and dill; Provençal-style fish soup; mussel chowder with cabbage and bacon; French onion soup; baked tilefish in season; charcoal-broiled striped bass, bluefish, or scrod; striped bass baked with leeks and tomatoes; Hawaiian-style pan fry of shrimp, oysters, smoked sausage, and tomato; sauté of lobster and chicken; shellfish stew for two; skillet-fried sirloin; acorn squash with butter and honey; green beans; broccoli; kohlrabi gratiné; onion crisps with malt vinegar; hashed brown potatoes; snow peas; zucchini; double-chocolate layer cake; frozen chocolate soufflé; charlotte russe cake; and fresh pineapple with vanilla ice cream.

New York's Tavern on the Green reopens August 31 in Central Park under the management of Warner LeRoy, 42, son of Hollywood producer-director Mervyn LeRoy and a partner in the East Side restaurant Maxwell's Plum, who offers $2.85 hamburgers, chicken sandwich on potato bread for $2.50, rack of lamb or châteaubriand for $24.50. Opened originally in 1934 on the site of the park's former sheepfold, Tavern on the Green was run for a few years in the 1960s by Restaurant Associates (until executives called it Tavern in the Red), $2.5 million has been spent to refurbish it, and 600 invited guests, including James Beard, file past a buffet table, helping themselves to cold salmon, lamb stew, and turkey in aspic while others line up in the parking lot for samples of the world's largest ice cream sundae, created for LeRoy by Sealtest Foods with 1,500 gallons of ice cream, 150 pounds of chocolate topping, 50 pounds of strawberries, 50 pounds of almonds, and 25 pounds of maraschino cherries (three bikini-clad models serve the sundaes). Critics question the parks commissioner for permitting LeRoy to encroach on parkland, but the park stands to make $60,000 (5.5 percent of gross receipts) per year from the new Tavern on the Green where it received only $25,000 from the previous concessionaire. LeRoy will add more and more glitz to the place in the next 18 years as the Tavern on the Green becomes a major tourist attraction.

The New York restaurant Colombe d'Or (Golden Dove; it takes its name from a French restaurant outside Vence) opens September 10 at 134 East 26th Street, where Belgian-born proprietor Georges Studley, 45, and his wife, Helen, have paid $15,000 down to purchase a four-story building and its 30-seat restaurant (total price: $94,000), paid $6,500 to have it redecorated, and hired a young French-Italian woman as chef. Mimi Sheraton of the New York Times writes that all the prepared dishes "bordered on the dreadful," the Studleys hire Danish chef Kai Hanson, he will be murdered in October of next year, and a series of chefs will follow. But the Studleys will prosper, offering complimentary *tapenade* with provençal relish; soup de poisson (made with striped bass, cod, red snapper, sea trout, whiting, lobsters, garlic, and saffron); chilled purée of pea soup; gazpacho; cold dill and cucumber soup; cold tomato and basil soup; hot eggplant soup; cold octopus salad; *morue à la provençal* (cod with tomatoes); *paupiettes* of sole; *archiduc* (porgies) *provençal*; bouillabaisse; tuna steak braised in red wine with julienne peppers, onions, and tomatoes; *raie* (skate) *au gratin*; tilefish in a vol-au-vent with puréed asparagus and a white wine sauce; a terrine of pork and veal forcemeat inlaid with bits of calves' brains, rillettes of shredded pork, chilled duck fat, and chicken liver mousse with pistachio nuts; breast of goose marinated in brown sugar and molasses, smoked over applewood for 48 hours, and served in thin slices with melon; *matelote* of eel stewed in white wine with julian pimento and onion in a puffed pastry shell with wine sauce; fruit tarts; Paris-Brest; and homemade sherbets (*see* March restaurant, 1990).

The New York restaurant Pronto opens at 30 East 60th Street, replacing another Italian restaurant. Chef Polli Attillo specializes in veal scallopine alla Marsala, *bistecca alla pizzaiola* (a Neapolitan dish made with tomato, garlic, and marjoram), eggplant *alla parmagiana*, and baked artichoke bottoms.

New York's "21" Club hires its first waitress in November, becoming the first of eight city restaurants to settle a sex discrimination suit filed by the American Civil Liberties Union against La Caravelle, La Côte Basque, the Four Seasons, Lutèce, and others.

The Washington, D.C., restaurant Le Lyons d'Or opens at 2650 Virginia Avenue N.W. under the direction of French-born chef-owner Jean-Pierre Goyenvalle, 40, whose specialties will include crayfish with truffled butter; wild mushroom tureen with foie gras; pink lobster mousseline with red and yellow pepper coulis; Maryland crab cakes with basil and tomato slices; medallions of venison with pearl onions and red wine; saddle of venison with chestnut purée; chicken with lime sauce; pigeon with dates; duckling with fresh dates; free-range capon with cabbage; wild strawberry tart with pear coulis; lemon-curd tart with raspberries and strawberries; crème brûlée with raspberries or oranges; mousse of three chocolates (bittersweet, milk, and white); passion fruit and chestnut bavaroise; and rhubarb sorbet.

Obrycki's Olde Crab House in Baltimore is acquired from the Obrycki family by Rose and Richard Cernak, who will make the place at 1729 East Pratt Street (built as a tavern in 1765) a 100-seat restaurant famous not only for its fresh crab but also for blackfin crab cakes, deep-fried deviled crab cakes, blackfin imperial crabmeat in velouté sauce, and soft-shell crabs in season. Patrons wait in line, sometimes for more than an hour, to sit down at tables covered with stiff brown paper; supplied with extra napkins, crab knives, and wooden mallets, they dig into steaming heaps of blue crabs (cooked to a mottled red) that are heaped onto the paper by waitresses. The Cernaks will build a 250-seat Obrycki's across Register Street at 1727 East Pratt in 1986.

The Chicago restaurant Gordon's opens in July at 500 North Clark Street. Chef-proprietor Gordon Sinclair has specialties that include rack of lamb, organically grown vegetables (e.g., leaf lettuce, tomatoes, artichokes) from his downstate Illinois farm, and a flourless chocolate soufflé cake. He serves California and Washington wines plus a Piedmont grappa.

The suburban Chicago restaurant Le Français opens at 269 South Wheeling Avenue in Wheeling. Chef-proprietor Jean Banchet will run the place until 1989, giving midwesterners a taste of fine French cuisine, and Chef Roland Liccioni will carry on the tradition, serving fresh fish, venison with quince and rosemary, and desserts prepared by his pastry chef wife, Mary Beth.

The Palo Alto, Calif., restaurant La Terrasse opens at 3740 El Camino Real. Leon Sidella and his wife, Ingelor, employ as chef Raul Michel, who has worked at La Côte Basque in New York and whose specialties include crabmeat salad with dill, cucumbers, olives, and mayonnaise; roast loin of pork with orange sauce; and crème de menthe parfait.

Kentucky Fried Chicken founder Col. Sanders, now 86, eats at a New York City KFC outlet and calls it "the worst fried chicken I've ever seen" (see 1964). KFC owner Heublein, Inc., pays Sanders $200,000 per year to do advertising and public relations for the chain, which now operates 5,500 outlets with 10,000 cooks (see PepsiCo, 1985).

J. Lyons & Co. sells its Wimpy hamburger chain to United Biscuits (see 1954; Burger King, 1989).

The U.S. fast-food chain Au Bon Pain has its beginnings in a pastry shop company founded by the French oven manufacturer Paviallier (see 1978).

The Paris restaurant Chiverta opens in April at 3, rue Arsène-Houssaye off the northern side of the boulevard des Champs-Élysées. Proprietor Louis-Noël Richard has taken over a bar around the corner from the restaurant Taillevent and hired chef Jean-Michel Pedier. Their menu includes such dishes as foie gras de canard, parfait de foie gras, bavarois de saumon fumé, saumon fumé aux poireaux au vinaigre de Xérès (smoked salmon and leeks with sherry vinegar), escalope de saumon à l'oseille (with sorrel), macaron de lotte à citron verte (angler fish with lime), ragout de queues d'écrevisse (crayfish tail stew), salade de queues d'écrevisse, cassoulet de ménagère ou morilles, ris de veau mijoté au cidre, médaillon de veau au grande moutarde graines, aiguillettes de canard en salade, terrine de Saint-Jacques et de rascasse (scallop and hogfish ter-

rine), and sherbet flavored with griottes (sour cherries) or passion fruit.

London's 45-year-old Dorchester Hotel names Anton Mosimann, 29, as head chef. He received his *diplôme de cuisinier* before he was 18 (the youngest ever), headed the kitchen staff of the Swiss Pavilion at Expo '70 in Osaka when he was 23 (supervising the work of 30 Swiss and 90 Japanese), has worked at top hotels in Rome, Montreal, and elsewhere, and will revitalize the Dorchester's 85-seat Terrace Restaurant.

1977

President Jimmy Carter, 52, takes office January 20 and receives a report 2 days later from the National Research Council concluding that repeated widespread famine and malnutrition can be removed from the world within a generation if the United States and other countries mount a major research project on agriculture and nutrition. Food officials say in May that for the first time in 5 years the world is entering its primary growing season without fear that crop failures may generate food crises, but experts say that if the United States does not take steps to establish a grain reserve system that can hold surpluses against times of scarcity there will be boom-and-bust cycles which may bring mankind back to the brink of worldwide famine.

Food First: Beyond the Myth of Scarcity by Frances Moore Lappé and Joseph Collins, with Cary Fowler, reveals that Mali increased her exports of peanuts during the African famine of 1973 to 1974, that thousands of tons of donated rice rotted because poor people could not afford to buy it, and that underfed countries in Africa and Latin America are planting more and more of their best lands to cash crops for export to richer countries in North America and Europe. The authors argue that the world has enough food but that much of it is wasted or poorly distributed; that the plight of the poor has actually worsened in countries where the "green revolution" has improved yields; that small farms are more productive than large farms, with higher yields per acre; and that the solution is to help people use their own experience and capacities to help themselves.

$ Agitation to give domestic sugar growers more protection from imports leads the International Trade Commission to say in March that rising imports threaten the domestic industry. The Commerce Department recommends in May that domestic sugar be made eligibile for special aid, and when President Carter resists measures that would raise domestic sugar prices he is accused of having a bias in favor of Coca-Cola, the Atlanta-based company with which he has had a long-standing relationship. Sugar refiners, bakers, soft drink bottlers, confectioners, and consumer groups favor direct federal subsidies to growers rather than price support programs that would raise the price of sugar and products containing sugar, thus imposing a heavier burden on the poor than on the rich.

President Carter (above) winds up signing a farm bill that provides for generous loans to sugar growers, who forfeit their crops in lieu of repayment. By early 1979, the Department of Agriculture's Commodity Credit Corp. will have a stockpile of raw sugar for which taxpayers have, in effect, forked over nearly $500 million. The CCC will eventually accumulate about 300,000 tons of raw sugar, which it will sell at a substantial loss to ethanol manufacturers and to China.

Nearly half of all Chinese urban workers receive 5 to 10 percent wage increases late in the year. Deputy Premier Deng Xiaoping, 73, begins decommunizing the nation with capitalist programs that increase productivity.

H. J. Heinz closes its baby food plant at Chambersburg, Pa., because of declining consumption of processed baby food. Baker/Beech-Nut announces a new line of "natural" baby foods.

Colombo Yogurt Co. is acquired by Bongrain, a worldwide manufacturer of dairy products (*see* 1970). Colombo next year will introduce New England's first nonfat plain yogurt, and in 1988 it will add Nonfat Light Yogurt in a variety of fruit flavors (*see* 1991).

General Mills acquires the U.S. Yoplait Yogurt franchise in October, purchasing Michigan Cottage Cheese's two plants at Otswego and Reed City, Mich., and acquiring the U.S. license from Sodima to market Yoplait (*see* 1974). It establishes Yoplait USA as a new corporate subsidiary and continues to make the creamy yogurt using active yeast cultures shipped from France, Grade A whole milk, and the original French process, either plain or with the fruit (apple, blueberry, boysenberry, cherry, lemon, mixed berry, peach, piña colada in some markets, pineapple, raspberry, strawberry, or strawberry-banana) mixed evenly throughout. The yogurt is marketed with reference to its French heritage in six-ounce cups, but most consumers prefer Dannon or Colombo. Yoplait will not do well until it is reformulated for American tastes and repositioned as a low-fat American brand (*see* 1981).

Hershey Foods acquires Y&S Candies.

New York's Dean and DeLuca food emporium opens in August at 121 Prince Street in SoHo. Former publishing house employee Joel Dean has teamed up with former schoolteacher and cheese store owner Giorgio DeLuca to offer cheeses, smoked fish, quail eggs, 30 kinds of charcuterie, 15 types of pâté, bread loaves, fruit in and out of season, Italian honey, raspberry and blueberry vinegars, coffee beans, jams, preserves, and kitchen equipment. It will pride itself on having certain delicacies before anyone else and will grow to have several additional locations in the city.

New York's The Silver Palate opens at 274 Columbus Avenue. The tiny (165-square-foot) shop of entrepreneurs Sheila Lukins, 34, and Julee Rosso offer prepared dishes to meet the needs of working women, who have little time for elaborate entertaining and oftentimes little cooking experience, and will develop an international business. Within 10 years the concern will have more than 50 full-time employees, sell a line of products that will include sweet and rough mustard, plums preserved in brandy, caramel pecan sauce (all made with natural ingredients and without preservatives), have two shops in Tokyo, and serve customers that include Saks Fifth Avenue (the Silver Palate's first big account), Paris specialty shops, and Harrods food halls in London (*see* cookbooks, 1982, 1984).

Nonfiction: *Larousse Gastronomique* appears in its first U.S. edition (*see* 1938). Edited by an Amherst, Mass., writer-translator, the 1,063-page, four-pound dictionary of cookery will be a manual for U.S. chefs and food editors endeavoring to keep up with the growing American taste for European cuisine; *Food and Chinese Culture: Anthropological and Historical Perspectives* by Yale professor K. C. (Kwang-chih) Chang et al.; *English Bread and Yeast* by Elizabeth David; *The Taste of America* by veteran *New York Times* critic John L. Hess, 59, and his wife, Karen (*née* Loft), 58, who write, "One trouble is that Americans have forgotten how to be poor. Not that hard times were ever fun, but people coped better. In fact, the history of cookery is largely the triumph of housewives making do with what the gentry wouldn't touch. Eating high on the hog meant eating the fancy marketable cuts; the poor would get the jowl, the chitterlings, the feet, the tail and with them would make fine food. All the great tripe, snail, and sausage dishes are their inventions and all the chowders. What is *bouillabaisse* but a chowder that Marseilles women made of the trash fish that their husbands couldn't sell?"

Cookbooks: *Cuisiniers à Roanne* by Jean and Pierre Troisgros. *When French Women Cook* by Madeleine Kamman, who challenges Paul Bocuse's statement that there is no place for women in professional kitchens. She will tell an interviewer, "My interest in Cuisine des Femmes (food prepared by women) is almost as old as I am. I have been trained by an extremely gifted woman cook and raised by another one. I have studied the food of French and Italian women all over the map of France and Italy in great depth and I insist that creativity in the kitchen comes not only in the masculine, but also in the feminine. Let women get the formal technical kitchen education that has been reserved for men for those three centuries that classic cuisine lasted and one will see their creativity develop. They have not done so badly after all with natural instinct. Anyone who knows the wealth of ideas of French provincial cooking will vouch for that." *Mediterranean Cooking* by Paula Wolfert. *The Flavor of the South: Delicacies and Staples of Southern Cuisine* by Jeanne Voltz. *James Beard's Theory and Practice of Good Cooking. Dinner with Tom Jones* by Lorna Sass. *Delia Smith's Book of Cakes.*

U.S. and Soviet control of the sea is extended to 200 miles offshore March 1, matching the limit set by Chile, Ecuador, and Peru in their 1952 Declaration of Santiago (*see* 1966). Japan does not recognize Soviet claims to the waters surrounding Soviet-occupied islands claimed by the Japanese.

California has its worst drought year thus far in history (*see* 1976).

Dietary Goals for the United States, a report prepared by the staff of the Senate Select Committee on Nutrition and Human Needs (McGovern Committee), is released in its first draft (*see* 1974). The report, whose final version will be published in 1980, is based on the proposition not that people should eat more of what is good for them but less of what is bad for them. "Our diets have changed radically within the past 50 years," it says, "with great and often harmful effects on our health. . . . Too much fat, too much sugar and salt, can be and are directly linked to heart disease, cancer, obesity, and stroke, among other killer diseases." The report compares the average U.S. diet in 1976 with the average diet in 1909 and questions whether Americans are indeed the best-fed people in history: protein levels have held relatively constant, but Americans now get more of their proteins from fatty meats, eggs, and dairy products and fewer from whole grains which contain fiber and micronutrients. Although they now require fewer calories, they actually consume more, and where in 1909 they derived 40 percent of their calories from fruit, vegetables, and grains, in 1976 those foods contributed only 20 percent, with the rest coming from fats and refined sugars. Americans were consuming unprecedented quantities of sodium and more untested additives. The report linked these dietary changes to specific health problems, suggesting that 6 of the 10 leading causes of death—heart attacks, strokes, arteriosclerosis, cancer, cirrhosis of the liver, and diabetes—were related to diet, and, since these accounted for about half of all deaths, eating could be as life threatening as smoking (*see* 1980).

Slim-Fast meal replacement powder, intended for use as a liquid protein, is introduced by S. Daniel Abraham, who last year introduced Dexatrim diet pills. His products will make him a fortune (*but see* 1978).

A Canadian study linking saccharin intake with bladder cancer in rats leads the U.S. Food and Drug Administration to announce March 9 that it will ban use of saccharin in foods, soft drinks, chewing gum, and toothpaste (*see* 1907; cyclamate ban, 1969). Diabetics and dieters panic, Congress votes to delay the ban for 18 months, the British medical journal *Lancet* raises doubts that saccharin causes bladder cancer in humans, the FDA proposes label warnings and store signs pointing out the danger. Future studies will show that saccharin is at worst a weak animal carcinogen but may tend to enhance cancer-causing properties of other chemicals, especially to heavy smokers.

The powerful carcinogen aflatoxin, produced by the fungus *Aspergillus flavus*, contaminates corn crops in Georgia, North Carolina, and other southeastern states. Thousands of turkeys and hogs die, calves are born dead or stunted, slaughterhouses find liver tumors in cattle, and milk supplies are contaminated because cows have been fed tainted corn. Demand for southeastern corn plummets (acreage planted to corn in Georgia will shrink by 75 percent in the next 10 years), and the states stiffen inspection procedures and controls to prevent a recurrence. Peanut butter sales drop, and peanut-butter makers press the Department of Agriculture to test every truckload of peanuts, which are grown primarily in the Southeast; shelling plants will soon be required to send a sample from each lot to a federal or state laboratory for analysis (*see* 1984).

The U.S. Department of Agriculture begins efforts to reduce the amount of nitrites used by meat processors to color bacon following reports that crisply fried bacon contains nitrosamines—powerful carcinogens formed when the nitrites combine with amines produced naturally in the body. Some critics insist that no nitrites at all should be permitted, others point out that most human nitrite and nitrate intake is from leafy green vegetables. The meat industry says nitrates are needed to prevent development of botulinum toxins but will agree to use smaller amounts (*see* 1982).

Hershey Chocolate reduces the size of its 20¢ Hershey Bar in April from 1.35 oz. to 1.2 oz. and reduces it in July to 1.05 oz. (*see* 1976; 1978).

M&M/Mars introduces Twix Cookie Bars but devotes most of its efforts to increasing sales of its Snickers, M&M's, Milky Way, and 3 Musketeers.

PepsiCo pays $320 million to acquire the 19-year-old Pizza Hut fast-food chain from Frank Carney (whose 12 percent interest nets him $38 million and who will stay on to run the enterprise until 1980). The chain has grown to have 2,000 outlets; PepsiCo starts a campaign to Americanize the international chain's image, replacing the pizza-tossing Italian chef logo with the outline of a roof, and by 1993 there will be 7,600 Pizza Huts (*see* Taco Bell, 1978).

PepsiCo bought the Pizza Hut chain and used graphic design to give it a new image.

Denny's Restaurants introduce the Grand Slam breakfast (*see* 1967; 1981).

The French diet cuisine restaurant Des Prés et les Sources d'Eugénie operated by chef Michel Guérard, 44, and his wife, Christine, 35, at Eugénie-des-Bains southeast of Bordeaux gains its third Michelin star, making it one of only 18 in all of France (Paris now boasts only 6) to have that distinction. Guerard, who built up the modest Pot-au-Feu in the Paris suburb of Asnières into one of the city's nine three-star restaurants in the 1960s, has run the restaurant at Des Prés et Les Sources since 1972 as part of the thermal cure and weight-reduction spa owned by his wife. He went on a diet himself the following year but found ordinary diet food "disgusting." Eschewing butter, other animal fats, and salt, he uses defatted meats, vegetables, spices, herbs, and saccharin (legal in France) to create dishes such as tomato pie with pistou; grilled dumpling with green peppers; and bitter chocolate sherbet.

The suburban Hamburg restaurant Landhaus Dill opens at 404 Elbchaussee in Nienstedten. Austrian restaurateur Volkmar Preis, 26, who also runs Zimmer's Weinstube in town (where an Austrian cook prepares wiener schnitzel, *palatschinka*, and other Austrian specialties), offers his 50 patrons a French-style menu: *mousse de ris de veau*; terrine of pheasant; pike quenelles; sweetbreads with champagne cream sauce; *escalope de saumon au Chablis* with leeks; and the like.

The London restaurant The Greenhouse opens in the summer on the first floor of an apartment house at 27a Hay's Mews, Mayfair, near Berkeley Square. Hotelkeeper David Levin, who opened the Capital in 1971, presents a menu that offers pâté, egg mousse, dressed crab, fresh lobster soup, smoked salmon, plaice on the bone, smoked turkey with green figs, casserole of guinea fowl *bonne femme*, roast duck with orange sauce, rack of lamb, charcoal-broiled steaks, charcoal-grilled lamb kidneys, steak-and-kidney pie, roast beef, and veal cutlet in Madeira sauce. A meal for two costs about £15, including wine.

London's Caviar Bar-Restaurant opens at 22 Brompton Road. Financed and started by Viscount Richard Newport, 29, it serves 500 pounds of beluga, sevruga, and pressed caviar (mostly beluga) its first year and will serve 1,000 pounds its second (it also serves lobster bisque, smoked salmon, sturgeon, freshly caught lobster, dressed crab, salmon, turbot, sole, bass, *coquilles Saint-Jacques*, Brie, and strawberries).

The Los Angeles restaurant L'Orangerie opened at 903 North La Cienega Boulevard is an offshoot of the restaurant opened on the Île-St.-Louis by Gérard Ferry and actor Jean-Claude Brialy in 1967. Ferry and his wife, Virginie, operate the new place, which occupies rooms designed by French architect-designer Valerian S. Rybar. They import their fish (loup, rouget, lotte) directly from Brittany and their produce directly from various parts of France but will soon bring in northwestern salmon, Louisiana crayfish, Santa Barbara prawns, Atlantic swordfish, oysters cultivated in West Coast waters, and goose liver from New York State. Deserts include chocolate hazelnut mousse, apple tart, crêpe filled with lemon and orange custard sauces, almond and hazelnut praline mousse glacée with mango sherbet.

The Los Angeles restaurant Le Bagatelle opens in November at 8690 Wilshire Boulevard, Beverly Hills. André and Lucia Pister, who have established a reputation with charcuterie and French delicatessen, employ Burgundian chef Jean-Pierre Pelleet, whose dishes include soupe des pêcheurs provençal, bouillabaisse broth, fillet of sole Murat, truite sauce Murette (whole trout stuffed with duxelles, poached in red wine, and served with crayfish); pantin chaud à la mode de Saulieu (forcemeat of pork, veal, and rabbit livers in a pastry with Périgourdine sauce); sausage-stuffed birds; hot pâtés en croûte; squab stuffed with wild rice, truffles, and forcemeat of chicken breasts, pork, and veal marinated in brandy with a morel sauce; pork rillettes; fromage de tête (headcheese); terrine de volaille (country pâté of chicken or goose liver with pistachio nuts); rabbit pâté; lapin à la Piron (sauté of rabbit with mustard sauce and crêpes macerated with brandy); jambon persillé; céleri-rave remoulade; côte de veau Val Sucon (veal chop topped with goose liver and a sauce poivrade); foie de veau lyonnais; omelette morvandelle with mushrooms, potatoes, and artichokes; fruit tarts; and millefeuilles turinois (filled with a blend of chestnut chocolate purée with crème Chantilly and sauce anglaise).

The San Francisco restaurant La Colombe Bleue opens at 2633 Bridgeway. Proprietor George Lebugle was a Paris interior designer before coming to the area in 1966; his chef, Maurice Pinace, from Aix-les-Bains offers a menu that changes with the seasons and includes several first courses (vichyssoise, chilled cream of green bean—never onion soup—pâté of rabbit or duck), and 9 or 10 entrées (sea bass, swordfish, grouper, Pacific red snapper, *coquilles Saint-Jacques, lapin sauté chasseur rouchée Cardinal*—puffed pastry shell filled with Dungeness crab—penny-shrimp clams, mussels, scallops, poached salmon with beurre de Nantes, *navarin Danieaux, maigret de canard au poivre vert, canard Montmorency*, lamb chops stuffed with forcemeat baked en croûte, and grenadin of veal with tarragon sauce grenadine), with pastry desserts made by Lebugle himself: *diplomate* (chocolate mousse with small homemade sponge cakes in Bavarian cream infused with Grand Marnier and served with crème Chantilly), fruit tarts, rum babas, strawberry mousse or charlotte, and gâteau Colombe Bleue (a variation on Saint-Honoré). Table d'hôte dinners are $9.50.

The San Francisco restaurant La Mère Duquesne opens at the Del Cortez Hotel, 101 Shannon Alley off Geary Street. Normandy-born restaurateur Yvonne Duquesne, whose son Gilbert runs the Camembert in Mill Valley, has hired chef Claude Melchiori, also from Normandy, who has worked for 2 years at Maxim's and a year at London's Connaught. His menu offers poached salmon with hollandaise sauce; salmon mousse; *coquilles de fruit de mer* (scallops and large and small shrimp with mushrooms glazed with hollandaise sauce); *filets de sole Bréval*; *truite grenoblois*; *tripe à la mode de Caen*; *pot-au-feu*; calves' liver with onions in a meunière sauce served with rice, zucchini, and carrots; tournedos Masséna with artichokes, poached marrow, and sauce Périgourdine; tournedos with Armagnac and green peppercorns; *bœuf bourguignon*; *lapin chasseur*; boned squab stuffed with pâté de foie gras in a puff pastry with a morel sauce; *canard Montmorency*; roast pheasant with a potato in a nest of liver canapés; meringues; chocolate cake; buttercream éclairs; millesfeuilles; soufflés; and raspberries with poufs of whipped cream mixed with sour cream and a dash of kirsch.

Philadelphia restaurateur Steve Pote of 1973 Frög fame opens The Commissary, which will continue until 1994.

The New York steakhouse Smith and Wollensky opens on the northeast corner of Third Avenue and 49th Street, where The Restaurant Group headed by Alan L. Stillman has acquired the premises of another steakhouse, Manny Wolf's (Stillman has taken the names Smith and Wollensky at random from the telephone directory). Patrons lunch and dine on lump crabmeat, lobster cocktail, stone crabs, filet mignon, filet au poivre, sliced steak, sirloin steak, chopped steak, prime ribs, calf's liver, triple lamb chops, veal chops, cottage fried and hash brown potatoes, fried zucchinis, strawberry tart, deep-dish apple pie, and chocolate cake.

New York's River Café opens in July on a Brooklyn barge in the East River with a spectacular view of the Manhattan skyline. Proprietor Michael O'Keeffe has run several restaurants, including Puddings on Lexington Avenue at 90th Street, and

his first cook, Jean Deli-Pizzi, will be succeeded by such outstanding chefs as Larry Forgione (who will refuse to cook anything not French until O'Keeffe insists that he cook American), Charles Palmer, Rick Stefan, and George Morone, all of whom will go on in the next decade to have fine restaurants of their own, either in New York or in other cities.

1978

India has record agricultural production, but millions of farmers and their families face starvation because they cannot afford to eat what they grow. Health officials in Indonesia say half of that nation's population is malnourished.

Unemployment rises throughout the world with a U.S. rate of 6 percent, up from 4.9 in 1973. Britain's rate is 6.1 percent, up from 2.9; France's 5.5, up from 2.7; West Germany's 3.4, up from 0.8.

The price of raw sugar falls to 6¼¢/lb., but other prices rise and U.S. inflationary pressures force President Carter to act. He announces a program of voluntary wage-price guidelines October 24, resisting demands that he impose mandatory controls and raising fears that inflation will worsen.

Coca-Cola signs an exclusive agreement to bottle its drinks in the People's Republic of China. Pepsi-Cola has exclusive rights in the U.S.S.R.

Britain's Allied Breweries acquires J. Lyons & Co. in September and will change its name in 1981 to Allied-Lyons (*see* Tetley, 1973).

Philip Morris acquires 7-Up for $520 million. It will break up the soft drink company in 1986 and sell the parts after taking a big loss.

Campbell Soup Co. pays $33 million to acquire Vlasic Co. pending a Federal Trade Commission investigation into possible antitrust violations. Vlasic is a major manufacturer of pickles, relishes, peppers, and related food items.

Leonhard Monheim AG of Aachen, Germany, acquires General Chocolate of Belgium along with its German subsidiary, Novesia (*see* 1971).

The Canadian supermarket chain Loblaw's (owned largely by the 96-year-old Toronto food industry giant George Weston Ltd.) introduces No Name products that are equivalent in quality to heavily promoted national brand-name foods (Heinz, Kellogg's, etc.) and nonfood items but are priced 20 to 30 percent lower. Loblaw's head David Nichol, 38, who was recruited by George Weston's grandson W. Galen Weston, has upgraded the quality of the chain's house brands, he will expand the No Name line to include 2,000 products (sold only in Canada and mostly through Loblaw's No Frills chain), and, by introducing a line of President's Choice products (notably cereals, bottled juices, cookies, microwave popcorn, and pet foods, sold through such U.S. chains as Jewel, Lucky Stores, Acme, D'Agostino, and Wal-Mart), he will increase Loblaw's North American sales to $9 billion (Canadian) by 1993. Kroger will retaliate by upgrading its own house brands (sold under the Kroger label), Safeway will offer Safeway Select, and A&P Master's Choice (*see* Wal-Mart, 1993).

Cuisinart, Inc. of Greenwich, Conn., introduces the DLC series food processors, which incorporate improvements made in previous models (*see* 1973). The success of the original Cuisinart food processor has inspired competitors to produce models selling at prices as low as $30 and as high as $400. Featuring motors that are considerably stronger and more efficient, a unique new kneading blade, and greatly improved slicing and shredding discs, the DLC series has been designed by Cuisinart's research and development people and is manufactured in Japan.

Nonfiction: *Alice, Let's Eat: Further Adventures of a Happy Eater* by Calvin Trillin (*see* 1974). Critic Christopher Lehmann-Haupt of the *New York Times* writes that Trillin is not "just very funny; beneath the clown and self-deprecator lies a serious crusader for the virtues of regional American cuisines and against the pretentiousness and downright badness of American Continental restaurants that are modeled on the continent of Antarctica, where everything starts out frozen." *Food for Thought: Resurrecting the Art of Eating* by clergyman Robert Farrar Capon.

Cookbooks: *Cuisine Gourmande* by French chef-restaurateur Michel Guérard, who has spent some years in Tokyo and will become known as the apos-

tle of *cuisine minceur*; *Veal Cookery* by Craig Claiborne with Pierre Franey; *Jane Grigson's Vegetable Book*; *Cooking for Friends* by Prudence Leith; *Delia Smith's Cookery Course*, Part One (based on her new televised cooking lessons).

Michigan and Maine voters approve a ban on no-deposit, no-return bottles—a victory for environmentalists. The Glass Packaging Institute and other lobby groups work to prevent passage of "bottle bills" against nonreturnables. Oregon, Vermont, Iowa, and Connecticut have banned such bottles. Industry groups claim that litter-recycling laws are more effective than outright bans.

France harvests her first crop of commercially cultivated truffles in the spring after centuries of failed attempts. Scientists have sprinkled spores onto the roots of a greenhouse seedling, transplanted the seedling outdoors, and let nature take its course in the development of the mycorrhiza's symbiotic structure. In nature, truffles never break above the ground and must be smelled out by pigs, goats, or trained dogs. France's Périgord section is noted for its black truffles, northern Italy for its white truffles, but loss of forest lands and overharvesting have reduced production to less than a tenth of its level in the late 19th century.

A second edition of last year's McGovern Committee report, published in January, stands by its original contention that Americans can increase their protection against "killer diseases" by eating fewer animal fats and increasing their consumption of fruits, vegetables, and whole-grain cereals but modifies its recommendation that people eat less meat and more poultry and fish following attacks by the meat industry and criticism by the American Medical Association.

Columbia University College of Physicans and Surgeons nutritionists Ernest Wynder, John Weisburger, and Philippe Shubik announce in June that research into the nutritional causes of cancer indicates that American ways of cooking and eating may contribute to 40 percent of cancer deaths. Harvard Medical School physician George Blackburn says that 1 out of 10 deaths in cancer patients is caused by malnutrition, yet fewer than 1 percent of cancer patients receive nutritional therapy as part of their treatment.

The U.S. Public Health Service attributes 17 deaths to an over-the-counter liquid protein powder (*see* Slim-Fast, 1977); the Food and Drug Administration issues a warning against use of such products for losing weight, those who use them almost invariably regain any weight they lose, but liquid-diet products will proliferate, and Americans—especially women bent on achieving unrealistic body shapes dictated by fashion—will continue to buy them.

Hershey Chocolate introduces Reese's Pieces—peanut butter candies in multicolored glazed shells that make them resemble M&M's. Hershey also introduces the Whatchamacallit bar—caramel and peanut-flavor crisp covered in milk chocolate. In December the company introduces a 1.2 oz. Hershey Bar at 25¢.

Standard Brands introduces the Reggie Bar, a chocolate bar named for baseball star Reggie Jackson; 33 million are sold in less than 7 months; average per capita U.S. candy consumption falls to about 15 pounds (*see* 1974; 1984).

All remaining New York Automats except one at 200 East 42nd Street are converted to Burger King outlets (*see* 1912). Labor problems have been squeezing Automat profits; the chain's blue-collar clientele has gone to the suburbs; and unemployed and homeless people, nursing cups of coffee for hours, have discouraged other patrons, as did the declining quality of the chicken pot pie and creamed spinach and the disappearance of such favorites as warm apple pie with vanilla sauce. The 20-year-old Automat that remains will survive until 1991, mostly as a venue for parties.

Ben & Jerry's Homemade Ice Cream and Crepes opens May 5 in a converted Burlington, Vt., gas station. Hippie entrepreneurs Ben Cohen and Jerry Greenfield, both 27, who are well acquainted with Steve's in Somerville, Mass. (*see* 1972), have invested $12,000 to start a superpremium ice cream business that will grow to rival Häagen-Dazs (*see* 1959; 1985).

Au Bon Pain is acquired by Boston investment banker Louis Kane, 47, and some associates, who will expand the pastry shop concept into a chain of company-owned fast-food stores (*see* 1976). Kane

has been a director of Colombo, the yogurt-making company (*see* 1981).

Arby's introduces the Beef 'n Cheddar Sandwich and changes its logo from an old 10-gallon hat to a stylized cowboy hat (*see* 1964). The company was acquired 2 years ago by Royal Crown Companies and will open its 1,000th restaurant in 1980 (*see* Japan, 1981).

Taco Bell founder Glen Bell, now 52, sells his franchised Mexican-style food chain's 868 units to PepsiCo (*see* 1962), which will replace the chain's symbol (a Mexican sleeping under a sombrero) with a bell; Taco Bell will grow under PepsiCo's management in the next 16 years to have nearly 4,000 units, and it will contribute to PepsiCo's becoming the largest operator of fast-food restaurants (*see* Pizza Hut, 1977; Kentucky Fried Chicken, 1985).

Legislation signed by New York Governor Hugh L. Carey, 59, May 11 ends the ban on using the word "saloon" for an establishment selling alcoholic beverages, a holdover from Prohibition days.

The New York restaurant Le Chantilly opens at 106 East 57th Street. Roland Chenus (who has worked at Le Pavillon and as executive chef at La Côte Basque) and Paul Dessibourg (who has worked at La Côte Basque, Le Grenouille, and Le Périgord) offer dishes that include cream of mussel soup; lobster bisque; mushroom bisque; petite marmite, vichyssoise; onion soup gratiné; jellied madrilene; chicken consomme; potage parmentier; filleted lotte in a paillard stuffed with salmon mousse and chopped mint, poached in white wine and served with champagne sauce; poached baby salmon (raised in upstate New York), stuffed with a mousse of pike and sorrel; *marmite Saint-Tropez*—a boneless bouillabaisse of red snapper, striped bass, lotte, mussels, scallops, and saffron; ragout of lobster; *cervelas de volaille* (white sausages filled with a mousse of chicken, port, cream, eggs, and truffles, served on a *brunoise* of shredded vegetables); *noisettes d'agneau au poivre vert*; tarragon chicken; roast pheasant Périgourdine; *pâtissier* Tieter Schorner prepares black currant and cream cake, chocolate cake, and raspberry and blueberry tarts. The prix fixe dinner is $24.50 (luncheon is $10 less), but dinner for two with cocktails, wine, taxes, and tips costs about $100.

The New York restaurant La Gauloise opens at 502 Avenue of the Americas (Sixth Avenue) with authentic, classic, bourgeois French bistro classics such as lobster bisque, cassoulet, charcuterie, *choucroute garnie*, *céleri rémoulade*, *pâté de campagne*, *moules ravigote*, *artichaut vinaigrette*, *saucisson chaud*, gray sole, soft-shell crabs in season, *raie au beurre noir*, *barbue* (brill), and *rouget* (red mullet), *entrecôte au poivre*, *entrecôte Béarnaise*, steak tartare, grilled saddle of lamb, cold roast veal with tuna sauce, *crème caramel*, *crème brûlée*, *bavaroise*, mousse of white and dark chocolate, sorbets, and fruit tarts.

The Louisiana restaurant Patout's opened at New Iberia by chef Alex Patout and his sister Gigi features Cajun food, which will win awards at the 1984 World's Fair in New Orleans. The restaurant will close when falling petroleum prices depress the state's oil-based economy, but two Patout's will open in the French Quarter of New Orleans, another will open in Houston, and Patout's daughter Gigi will open a Patout's in Los Angeles.

The Los Angeles restaurant Le Dame opens at 8720 Wilshire Boulevard. Paris-born chefs Jean-Claude Bourlier, Eddie Karkhofs, and Michel Yhuelo offer a menu that includes cold veal tongue with sauce gribiche, watercress purée, *charcuterie garnie*, cassoulet, Danish-style salmon, pike quenelles, Hawaiian tuna steak, sea bass *en croûte*, halibut wrapped in spinach leaves, *barbue* (brill) poached and served with tarragon butter, *raie* (skate) with brown butter sauce in paper, *lotte de mer* with mustard sauce, lamb chops *provençal*, *médaillons* of veal with strawberry vinegar, roast loin of veal with sauce Soubise, chicken steamed with marjoram, *volaille au citron vert*, and poule-au-pot. Pastry chef Craig Borsoff has specialties that include peach tart, lemon meringue tart, flourless chocolate almond cake filled with chocolate mousse, Paris-Brest, and almond charlotte with a raspberry sauce.

Los Angeles's Orlando-Orsini Ristorante opens at 95-75 West Pico Boulevard. It will later become the Osteria Romana Orsini.

The Los Angeles restaurant Jimmy's opens at 201 South Marino Drive, between Beverly Hills and Century City. Irish-born restaurateur James Murphy, who has been maître d'hôtel at the Bistrot, offers chowders; mahimahi with toasted coconut shreds, sliced mango, and pineapple; sand dabs sautéed meunière; Vatrouchkis blini; double lamb chops; New York steak with Béarnaise sauce; calf's liver with sautéed apples, onion rings, and a whiskey sauce; and Scottish pheasant with wild rice and preserved plums.

The San Francisco restaurant L'Olivier opens at 465 Davis Court, off Jackson St. Christian and Guy Francoz, who have opened the place in the Golden Gateway, offer patrons sautéed prawns served with a Thai red curry paste over tagliarini, frogs' legs soup with tomato concassé, onion soup; lobster bisque, green salads including romaine hearts with crumpled Roquefort vinaigrette, grilled 'ahi with olive oil and black olives, sea bass baked with a brunoise of vegetables and finished with triple citrus butter, boned chicken breast stuffed with red bell peppers and shiitake mushrooms, venison wiener schnitzel, a thin steak covered with French truffles and chives and served with chanterelles and apple sautéed with cranberries, roast squab with apple vinegar sauce and julienned shiitake mushrooms, crème brûlée, coffee mousse, bittersweet chocolate cake with layers of génoise, and brandied cherries with a raspberry coulis.

Dublin's The Grey Door opens in July at 29 Pembroke Road off Fitzwilliam Street and competes with the venerable Bailey at 2 Duke Street, Snaffles at 47 Lower Leason Street, Le Coq Hardi in the Lansdowne Hotel at 29 Peprock Road, Ballsbridge, and other better-established restaurants by offering Russian and Finnish specialties in an intimate setting. Maître d'hôtel Karl O'Brien offers blini, pickled herring, caviar, pelmeni (Russian dumplings), repin salmon (cooked in a sauce of creamed dills, onions, and mushrooms), filet Novgorod (sauerkraut surrounded by kasha and garnished with sour cream, garlic butter, and caviar), chicken Kiev (stuffed with vodka-saturated butter and served on curried rice), and crêpes Suzettes.

The Lyons restaurant Le Fédora opens under the direction of Daniel Jeudéaux, who has worked at Maxim's in Paris and under Paul Bocuse. His classic Lyons specialties include *œufs pochés en meurette* (poached eggs in red wine sauce) and *fricassée de volaille au vinaigre de Xérès* (stewed vinegared chicken).

The Munich restaurant Aubergine opens October 2 at 8 Josephstrasse under the direction of chef-owner Eckart Witzigmann, 40. His specialties include *terrine de chevreuil* (venison terrine), truffled soup *à la façon de* Paul Bocuse, *mousse de brochet au coulis d'écrevisses* (pike mousse with crayfish purée), pike mousse with frogs' legs, salmon stuffed with celery root, fricassee of carp, poached pears and almond tulips, and fresh figs with almond ice cream and melba sauce.

The Michelin guide to London is published in English and is quite different from a French-language guide issued by Michelin 2 years ago.

1979

✗ Ghana has a political coup in June. Her cacao exports have fallen to the point where they account for less than 25 percent of the world market, down from 47 percent in the early 1960s. Rebels install Flight Lt. Jerry Rawlings, 32, as head of state; the head of the Ghana Cocoa Board flees the country (he has allegedly siphoned off milions of dollars into personal bank accounts abroad), and a new man heads efforts to resurrect the nation's cacao industry (*see* below).

💲 Double- and even triple-digit inflation plagues much of the world. U.S. prices increase 13.3 percent for the year, the largest jump in 33 years, and the Federal Reserve Board's move in October to tighten the money supply sparks a jump in loan rates that will continue for 6 months. Banks raise their prime loan rate to 14.5 percent October 9.

The New York Cocoa Exchange merges with the Coffee and Sugar Exchange.

Ghana's cacao production falls to a 20-year low, dropping the nation to third place behind the Ivory Coast (Côte d'Ivoire) and Brazil as a cacao exporter. The old and unproductive Amelonado Forastero cacao trees on Ghana's plantations yield only 300 pounds of cacao beans per acre on average (versus 800 pounds in the Ivory Coast and 1,400 pounds in Brazil), agriculture is inefficient, and farmers have little incentive to improve their methods. The government Cocoa Board has operated for years without rules and with no system of accounting, farmers typically work plantations of only two to five acres, and inflation far outpaces what a farmer can hope to receive for his crop. Farmers near the border smuggle an estimated 50,000 tons of cacao beans per year into the Ivory Coast, where prices are higher and the currency is freely convertible.

🤝 Pillsbury pays $148 million in January to acquire Green Giant, becoming a major factor in the frozen foods and canned goods industries (*see* 1961; *see* Grand Metropolitan, 1988).

Hershey Foods pays $8 million in January to acquire Skinner Macaroni Co., the sixth largest U.S. pasta producer. Founded in 1912 and based on Omaha, Skinner had sales last year of $20 million. Hershey owns another pasta company and will expand its presence in the business (*see* American Beauty, 1984; Friendly, below).

Borden Co. enters the U.S. pasta business by acquiring Creamette Co. (*see* Cracker Jack, Wise, 1964). Borden entered the Brazilian pasta business in 1973 when it acquired Adria, based in São Paulo and Brazil's largest pasta company. Further acquisitions will follow, and by the end of 1989 Borden will have subsidiaries marketing pasta throughout the United States, Canada, and Italy, making it the world leader in pasta sales (*see* Prince, 1987).

Pietro Barilla buys back his pasta and bread products company from W. R. Grace July 29, acquiring 25 percent of its stock with an option giving him until the summer of 1987 to buy the rest (*see* Mulino Bianco, 1975). A 1973 Italian law has fixed pasta prices, and Grace has given up its idea of creating a U.S.-style food conglomerate in Europe. After Pietro's death in September 1993, his sons Guido, Luca, and Paolo will assume management (*see* 1994).

H. J. Heinz pays $71 million to acquire Weight Watchers International, whose frozen dinners are produced under a licensing agreement by Foodway, Inc., which Heinz acquires for another $50 million (*see* 1963; Jean Neditch receives roughly $7 million; co-founders Albert Lippert and his wife, Felice, receive $7.6 million and $6.8 million, respectively). Weight Watchers now has weight-control classes in every state except Alaska. Its executive chef, Frank

Palumbo, took off 105 pounds using the program nearly 10 years ago and is called "the chef who lost his pot." Weight Watchers will grow in the next 15 years to have gross revenues of $1.6 billion.

Lawry's Foods is acquired by Unilever's Thomas J. Lipton subsidiary, but Lawry's Restaurants remain in the hands of the Frank and Van de Kamp families (*see* Taco Seasoning Mix, 1967; restaurants, 1971).

Ogden Corp. acquires Progresso Foods from Imasco, paying $40 million (*see* 1969). Progresso and allied items will be a $240 million business by 1984, accounting for 70 percent of Ogden Food Products Corp. sales and more than 70 percent of its earnings. Progresso will have two 75-ton clam dredgers operating off Cape May to supply its processing plant at Vineland, N.J., with fresh clams for spaghetti sauce, and it will be selling its products in 36 markets, mostly on the East and West coasts (*see* Pet Inc., 1986).

Rokeach acquires Mother's Soup Co., a Newark, N.J., firm that supplies soups and other products to the ethnic Jewish market.

The family-owned German food retailer Tengelmann Group pays $79 million to acquire a 42 percent interest in the Great Atlantic & Pacific Tea Co. (A&P) from the John A. Hartford Foundation, which has held its shares in A&P through a precipitous decline in their value (*see* 1975). Controlled by multimillionaire Erivan Haub, 46, Tengelmann will increase its stake to 51.3 percent by 1981, but A&P—until 1973 the largest U.S. grocery chain—has closed about half of its 3,468 stores, most of which have been poorly located, and will continue to lose money despite the introduction of European concepts calling for small outlets, low prices, and no frills (customers will even pay for their own paper bags). Stores in Tengelmann's successful Plus chain in Germany and Austria carry limited offerings—about 1,000 items each at discount prices, with no meat, dairy products, or fresh produce (*see* Aldi, 1948), but Americans accustomed to one-stop shopping prefer large supermarkets, which can afford to slash prices selectively on the very products that the A&P's new Plus stores will carry (*see* 1982).

The number of horses working on British farms falls to 3,575, down from 300,000 in 1950.

Judith Wurtman's book *Eating Your Way Through Life* (below) explains the functions of food additives, defining them to mean anything not naturally present in a food, including the vitamin A added to margarine. Their major function is to preserve foods from the destructive effects of the food's own enzymes, which cause them to discolor or become overripe too quickly; or from bacteria and fungi, which cause food to spoil and become dangerous to eat; or from oxygen, which causes foods to become dry, soggy, or rancid (or lose their vitamin C content). Antioxidants (most often BHA—butylated hydroxyanisole) delay oxidation. Sequestrants bind metals to prevent discoloration and inhibit reactions which cause rancidity; leavening agents (e.g., yeast, baking powder, phosphates) are added to make baked goods rise; mold inhibitors (e.g., calcium propionate, sodium diacetate) help keep baked goods from getting moldy; emulsifiers (e.g., lecithin, mono- and diglycerides, polysorbates) keep oil- or fat-containing ingredients mixed with the water base to give baked goods a light texture; humectants prevent foods such as marshmallows and shredded coconut from absorbing water; stabilizers and thickeners (gum arabic, gum tragacanth, guar gum, sodium carboxymethylcellulose, gelatin, carrageenan), give foods a smooth, thick texture and prevent ice crystal formation in frozen foods such as ice cream; firming agents maintain the firmness of fruits and vegetables during canning; artificial colorings and flavors make food more attractive or palatable (e.g., yellow vegetable coloring is added to margarine to make it look like butter); imitation ingredients replace natural ones to reduce calorie or cholesterol content or to lower cost.

Nonfiction: *Merchants of Grain* by Washington Post agriculture reporter Dan Morgan, 42, is a global look at the grain trade; *Compendium of Culinary Nonsense and Trivia* by restaurant consultant George Lang.

Cookbooks: *Craig Claiborne's New New York Times Cook Book* by Claiborne with Pierre Franey; *From My Mother's Kitchen* by Mimi Sheraton, now 53, who has been *Time* magazine's food critic since 1975 and will continue in that position until 1983; *Bert Greene's Kitchen Bouquets* by storekeeper Greene; *Food with the Famous* by Jane Grigson; *The Best of Prue Leith*; *Delia Smith's Cookery Course*, Part Two (*see* 1978; 1980).

Accidental release of dry anthrax spores in early April at the Microbiology and Virology Institute, a Soviet biological warfare facility in Sverdlovsk, contaminates an area with a radius of at least 3 kilometers and by some estimates kills several hundred persons. Tight censorship is imposed, but hundreds, perhaps thousands, of residents and military personnel reportedly die after inhaling the spores and contracting pulmonary anthrax. Soviet authorities say only that illegal sales of anthrax-contaminated meat have caused a public health problem. Critics charge Moscow with violating the 1975 Helsinki ban on developing biological weapons.

A Mexican offshore oil well blowout June 3 in the Gulf of Mexico contaminates Gulf fisheries with millions of gallons of oil in the largest spill ever recorded. After 3 months of uncontrolled spillage, the oil has traveled 600 miles from the hole drilled by Pemex explorers, shaking confidence in the ability of so-called blowout "preventers" and backup systems to protect the environment, straining U.S.-Mexican relations as the State Department conducts delicate negotiations over U.S. purchases of Mexican oil and natural gas. Ixtoc 1 continues to run out of control, defying efforts by the most experienced well cappers. An estimated 3.5 million barrels will have spilled into the sea by the time the flow is stopped in late March of next year.

Sardines return to California waters after an absence of some 40 years.

Hershey Foods acquires an experimental cacao plantation—Humming Bird Farm—in the Central American nation of Belize and begins efforts to improve the yields and quality of cacao trees.

The February issue of *The Physician and Sports-medicine* reports a survey of Big Ten conference football coaches' ideas of nutrition: most still emphasize protein and carbohydrate "supplements," despite lack of sound scientific support for carbohydrate "loading" except for endurance activities, such as marathon running, where it can be useful if undertaken several days before the event. "There are no magical secrets or mysteries about proper nutrition for athletes," says the publication's editor in chief. "Let us not be beguiled by the Pied Pipers of nutrition. . . . Let us stop acting like Simple Simons about something as straightforward as, if you will excuse the expression, meat and potatoes." (Most nutritionists recommend that athletes simply increase their caloric intake—eat more rather than eat differently.)

Eating Your Way Through Life by MIT research nutritionist Judith Wurtman notes that a varied, balanced diet ordinarily provides a full complement of vitamins and minerals; that a good diet should contain dark green vegetables (spinach, romaine lettuce, broccoli), yellow vegetables (carrots, squash, sweet potatoes) or fruits (peaches, cantaloupe), whole grains or cereals (whole wheat bread), and a source of vitamin C (citrus fruits, baked potatoes, strawberries, green peppers, parsley), dairy products for calcium, red meat (or eggs, lentils, beans such as kidney beans, brown rice, or peanuts) for iron, and shellfish or meat for zinc; that the body cannot tell the difference between "natural" vitamins and synthetic ones; that foods contain many nutrients which have not been incorporated into supplements; and that people who restrict their diets for any reason (e.g., religious, ideological, or extreme weight reduction) risk deficiencies, more often of minerals than of vitamins (*see* dexfenfluramine, 1982).

The Pritikin Program for Diet and Exercise by U.S. inventor Nathan Pritikin, 63, recommends a regimen of low-fat, low-cholesterol food combined with exercise. Pritikin, a college dropout who developed a heart problem (he calls it a "coronary insufficiency") in his early 40s, put himself on the same kind of diet and claims to have cured himself completely. He opened a Longevity Center at Santa Barbara, Calif., 3 years ago to conduct a 26-day, supervised program (cost: $3,000 plus $1,200 in medical expenses) and will open another one in Florida.

The Food and Drug Administration cracks down in July on misuse of amphetamines as appetite suppressants. Some 3.3 million prescriptions for amphetamines were written in the United States last year, the pills are also made in home laboratories, and many people have become addicted to Dexedrine, Desoxyn ("Dex," or "dexies"), Benzedrine ("bennies"), Biphetamine, or Methedrine ("speed"); a Philadelphia physician is sentenced in September to 2 years in prison and fined $250,000 for distributing 4 million amphetamine pills to patients at his weight-control clinic.

Paris police drop Breathalyzer tests for drivers after a public outcry and protests by restaurant owners that the spot checks are hurting business. Wine is sold legally at highway service stations, and some 5 million of France's 53.5 million people are heavy drinkers, 2 million alcoholics. Per capita consumption of pure alcohol is almost 17 quarts per year, the highest in the world, and alcoholism costs the nation some $4.5 billion per year in medical and social service costs.

The New Orleans restaurant K-Paul Louisiana Kitchen opens in Chartres Street with Cajun dishes prepared by chef Paul Prudhomme, 39, formerly of the Commander Palace (*see* 1953). Assisted in the front of the house by his wife, K. L. Henrichs, Prudhomme works in the kitchen to prepare jambalaya (with oysters, crabs, and sausages as well as the usual shrimp, rice, green peppers, tomatoes, and spices); crawfish *étoufée*; grilled crawfish and redfish; and bread pudding with lemon sauce and crème Chantilly. Prudhomme will claim that one of his cooks scorched a fish over a too-hot fire, creating "blackened" redfish: others will rush to copy K-Paul's success with the result that Gulf stocks of redfish will be depleted, causing the Louisiana regulators to declare a moratorium on catching the species (*see* cookbook, 1984).

The New Orleans restaurant Arnaud's, opened in 1918, brings in Egyptian-born Armenian chef R. C. Casbarian, who retains the Rock Cornish Game Hen Twelfth Night (a Creole version of coq au vin) and Watercress Salad Germaine, introduced by the late Arnaud Cazenave's daughter Germaine, but has a menu that includes also oysters Rockefeller; oysters Bienville; oysters O'Hanlon (with eggplant and onions); oysters Suzette (with lean bacon and pimiento); oysters Cathryn (with artichoke); artichoke soup; escargots with pastis; crabmeat; redfish; and crème brûlée.

The Los Angeles restaurant Michael's opens at 1147 Third Street, Santa Monica, with nouvelle cuisine dishes. Michael McCarty, 26, attended the Cornell School of Hotel Management, has spent 3 years at L'École Hôtelier at Paris and 2 at the Cordon Bleu, has studied at the Académie du Vin, and has worked at a restaurant outside Denver. His dinner chef Thomas O. Waxman, a onetime jazz trombonist who has worked at Chez Panisse in Berkeley, and his luncheon chef is Bill Pflug, an alumnus of the Culinary Institute of America at Hyde Park, N.Y. Mark Peel, who has apprenticed with Wolfgang Puck at Ma Maison (*see* Spago, 1982) and worked at De La Tour d'Argent, prepares terrines and ballottines. Menu listings include mache (corn salad), arugula, green beans, asparagus grown in Mexico for luxury restaurants, broiled seafood dishes (scallops from France, *rouget, daurade, bar*, shrimp from New Zealand, steamed oysters), mullard, and broiled meats. Desserts include fruits from New Zealand, raspberry and grapefruit sorbets, and chocolate soufflé. *Pâtissier* James Brinkley prepares shortbreads, macaroons, walnut and hazelnut sablés, Belgian chocolate cake (layers of génoise, melted chocolate, chocolate mousse, and chocolate curls), pithiviers filled with a mixture of almond meal and pastry cream, lemon tart, and other gâteaux and tarts.

San Francisco's Hayes Street Grill opens at 320 Hayes Street. Proprietors Robert Flaherty and Richard Sander have suspended Victorian globe lights from their high ceilings and installed a mesquite grill (such grills will soon be found in many Bay Area restaurants); they employ chefs Anne Powning Haskell (half French and French trained) and Patricia Unterman, whose specialties include lemon fish; grilled breast of mullard; free-range chicken; smoked poussin (baby chicken or rabbit); fresh local greens; wild mushrooms; chocolate, almond and apricot torte; blueberry tart; and bourbon pecan cake with caramel sauce and vanilla ice cream. Flaherty and Sander will open a pizzeria at 201 Ivy Street behind the Grill's kitchen.

The Washington, D.C., restaurant Jean-Louis at Watergate opens under the direction of French chef-restaurateur Jean-Louis Palladin, who began at age 12 as an apprentice at La Table des Cordeliers in Condom, France, and at age 28, working at the same restaurant after a year at the Hôtel de Paris in Monte Carlo, became the youngest chef ever to receive two stars in the Michelin guide. His boss and mentor at La Table des Cordeliers died in 1976, he did not get along with the man's widow, and he has come to the United States at the behest of Nicolas Salgo, the Hungarian-born real estate developer and part owner of the Watergate apartment complex. Palladin has 55 covers (14 tables) and his specialties include Belon oysters; Maine oysters and lobsters; Maryland oysters, crabs, and scallops; a soup made of corn purée, cream, and lobster; a noodle tureen with truffles and foie gras served on a tomato-basil coulis; zucchini flower stuffed with chicken, veal, or lobster mousse; and sautéed foie gras with peach slices and a caramelized peach sauce served with black ravioli made from squid ink.

New York's The Quilted Giraffe opens in the summer at 955 Second Avenue (between 50th and 51st streets). Chef Barry Wine, a onetime lawyer, and his wife, Susan, who is maîtresse d'hôtel, started originally at New Paltz, N.Y., and have a nouvelle cuisine menu that incorporates many oriental ingredients and ideas: chopped raw salmon topped with a raw quail's egg; fish mousse served with crème fraîche; hot crêpe of crabmeat and scallop strudel made of phyllo dough and garnished with asparagus; casserole of Burgundy snails with tomato and cream-laced pistou; creamed herring with sliced cucumbers; cream of mushroom soup made of enoki-daki, cèpes, and chanterelles; three pieces of lobster meat wrapped individually in cabbage leaves with sevruga roe and red and sweet peppers; fillet of grey sole; Mediterranean bécasse de mer (rouget, or sea woodcock); steamed salmon steak with sea salt and tomatoes; red mullet Saint-Pierre; John Dory; bay scallops with endives and nori (Japanese seaweed); striped bass garnished with snow peas and a sauce of veal and fish stock, buttercream, and grated ginger root; rack of lamb with Chinese mustard; ravioli filled with veal sweetbreads in a Madeira sauce topped with slivers of cooked tongue; roast veal with rosemary sauce; veal kidneys and pasta; chocolate-filled ravioli; white chocolate mousse topped with crushed praline; dark fudge cake; coconut-crusted chocolate buttercream cake flavored with coffee and cognac; and homemade caramel ice cream and blueberry-maple sherbet.

New York's La Côte Basque at 5 East 55th Street is acquired by Jean-Jacques Rachou, who revitalizes its kitchen and (in 1983) will enlarge its premises.

The New York restaurant Le Chanterelle opens at 89 Grand Street, corner Green Street in Soho. Proprietress Karen Waltuck has brought in Hollywood set designer Bill Katz to design the place; her husband, David, is the chef; and the specialties include terrine of smoked salmon with black caviar, beef consommé, cold lobster consommé in late summer, tuna steak, scallop mousseline, red snapper, shad roe with sorrel butter, salmon with rhubarb and leeks, lamb noisettes, squab in a game stock, filet of pork with braised fennel, fresh morels with sweetbreads or chicken, figs in red wine with whipped cream, homemade ice creams, cheeses from the nearby Dean and DeLuca shop, chocolate truffles, and butter cookies with orange peel (*see* 1989).

The *Zagat New York City Restaurant Survey* is introduced by local corporate lawyer Timothy Zagat, 40, and his lawyer wife, Nina, who like to eat out and have rated restaurants according to "customer satisfaction" as determined by 150 friends and acquaintances (*see* Duncan Hines, 1935). The burgundy-covered, pocket-sized Zagat Surveys will grow to cover more than 30 major U.S. and foreign cities with some 75,000 unpaid survey participants, most of them amateur critics who fill out extensive questionnaires, and by 1994 the Zagats will be grossing $7 million, of which they will net about $1.5 million after paying 25 full-time employees and covering other costs.

The British conglomerate Imperial Group Ltd. pays $620 million to acquire the Howard Johnson's restaurant-motel chain (1,040 restaurants—about one-quarter of them locally franchised—plus 520 motels) from founder's son Howard B. Johnson (*see* 1937). Gasoline shortages have hurt roadside restaurants, competition from fast-food chains has hurt Howard Johnson's most particularly, and most Howard Johnson's no longer serve 28 flavors of ice cream (*see* Marriott, 1985).

Hershey Foods (above) pays $164 million to acquire the Friendly Ice Cream Co. restaurant chain started in 1935. The chain will grow under Hershey's management from 600 outlets to about 850 in 15 states, with most of them in New England (*see* Tennessee Restaurant Co., 1988).

1980 ————————————————

💲 President Carter orders a partial embargo of U.S. grain sales to the USSR January 4 in response to the

December 1979 Soviet invasion of Afghanistan. Argentina ships grain to Russia, which has her second bad harvest in a row. Normal customers for Argentine grain receive shipments from other countries, and critics say the embargo of 17 million metric tons of grain hurts U.S. farmers more than it hurts Moscow. Grain shipments guaranteed by the 1975 agreement are not affected.

Poland imposes meat rationing in December for the first time since World War II, partly to meet a demand by striking workers. Meat shortages stem from the need to export meat for Western currency used to pay off Poland's huge foreign debt.

U.S. banks raise their prime rate (the rate on loans granted to favored customers) to 20 percent April 2 as the Federal Reserve tightens money. The rate falls to 12 percent by October but peaks at 21.5 percent in mid-December.

Double-digit inflation continues in the United States with prices rising 12.4 percent by year's end as compared to 13.3 percent last year, fueling opposition to President Carter. Some countries have triple-digit inflation. A U.S. recession in the second quarter cuts real output by 9.9 percent; the economy is on the rise again by fall.

British unemployment rises above 2 million for the first time since 1935 (when the workforce was one-third smaller) as recession depresses the economies of many countries. By year's end, unemployment reaches nearly 2.5 million, up from 800,000 early in 1975, and industrial production falls 5 percent as the government's monetarist policies try to stem a new burst of inflation, which again climbs above 20 percent, double the rate when Prime Minister Margaret Thatcher, 54, took office last year.

World sugar prices rise to 24¢/lb. by midyear, up 60 percent from 1979. Coca-Cola Co. is the world's largest user of sugar and leads in a switch to high-fructose corn syrup (HFCS) (below), which are about 25 percent cheaper than sugar. Many foods containing sugar, notably Jell-O, simply rise in price.

ConAgra acquires Banquet Foods, a major frozen foods company (*see* 1974; Peavey, 1982).

Dean Foods pays $34.4 million to acquire the $135 million (annual sales) MacArthur Dairy of Miami, Fla., as it expands into the South and Southwest through purchases of smaller companies (*see* 1925; FTC order, 1966). Still 25 percent owned by the founding Dean family and headed by a grandson of founder Samuel Dean, Dean Foods continues to grow by acquisition (*see* Larsen, 1986).

Perrier Group of America acquires Poland Spring (*see* 1904).

The Motor Carrier Act signed by President Carter July 1 curbs federal controls over interstate trucking, which carries most produce to market and foodstuffs of all kinds to retailers.

The Staggers Rail Act signed October 14 gives railroads more flexibility in setting rates and more authority to enter into long-term contracts with freight shippers, lets railroads drop unprofitable routes more easily, and deregulates in other ways.

CSX Corp., created in November by a merger of the Chessie System and Seaboard Coast Line Industries, becomes the largest U.S. railroad company, with 27,000 miles of track. The Chessie System embraces the Chesapeake & Ohio, Baltimore & Ohio, and Western Maryland railroads; Seaboard Coast Line embraces the old Seaboard Airline, Atlantic Coast Line, Louisville & Nashville, and other railroads.

The Burlington Northern becomes a 30,000-mile system November 21. Merger with the St. Louis–San Francisco Railway (Frisco Line) gives it track from Florida to the Northwest.

Cook's magazine begins publication in May at Westport, Conn. Publisher Christopher Kimball, 30, has started the magazine, which is dedicated to American cooking; former *Harper's Bazaar* production editor Mary Goodbody, 31, takes over as editor beginning with the second issue, and *Cook's* will take a fairly scientific approach to cooking, teaching basic and more advanced techniques while showcasing American chefs, recipes, regional foods, wines, and writers. It will continue until 1989, with circulation rising from 20,000 to 160,000, and Kimball will follow it with *Cook's Illustrated*, published out of Brookline, Mass.

Gourmet magazine editor-publisher Earle McAusland dies on Nantucket Island June 4 at 89. Condé

Nast will acquire his magazine, increasing its circulation and advertising.

Nonfiction: *Food* by Waverley Root, now 77, who has spent nearly a decade on the work, selections from which have been published in the *International Herald Tribune*. *Unmentionable Cuisine* by University of California, Davis, epidemiologist and preventive medicine professor Calvin W. Schwabe, who urges that we "expand our palates, . . . diversify our diets more, and . . . use our available overall food resources, particularly our protein resources, more efficiently and wisely." With the world's population projected to reach 6 million by the year 2000, up from 4.4 billion 2 years ago, reliance on beef amounts to a dietary imbalance that is unconscionably harmful to the world economy. Ideally, says Schwabe, every family would raise small meat animals such as pigs, sheep, goats, rabbits, poultry, or even guinea pigs (which still provide half the animal protein consumed in Peru). He also recommends greater use of beef hearts, tripe (intestines), sweetbreads (thymus gland), pork testicles, eel, shark, locusts, grasshoppers, and earthworms (which can be salted to taste like beef jerky). Much of the world, including the French and Chinese, make wide use of proteins that Anglo-Saxons scorn, Schwabe says.

Cookbooks: *Craig Claiborne's Gourmet Diet* by Claiborne with Pierre Franey; *Classic Indian Cooking* by U.S. author Julie Sahni; *Vogue Summer & Winter Cookbook* by Lady Arabella Boxer, who is food editor of the British edition of *Vogue* magazine; *Leith's Cookery Course* by Prudence Leith (with Caroline Waldegrave, principal and managing director of Leith's School of Food and Wine); *Delia Smith's Cookery Course*, Part Three (*see* 1979; 1982); *La Cuisine de nos grand-mères juives polonaises* by Laurence Kersz is published at Monaco.

World cocoa consumption rises to three times its 1950 level as a result of growing affluence in many countries. Switzerland is the largest consumer (although tourist purchases account for much of this), with Austria, Belgium, and Germany ranking next, the order varying from year to year. Norway is fifth, Britain sixth, the United States seventh, France eighth, Canada ninth, and Australia tenth.

Surimi fish paste gains growing acceptance as an alternative to costly seafood. The Japanese have been making surimi since about 1100 A.D., using fresh fish that has been minced, washed, and flavored; they developed technology in the 1960s for freezing the raw product at sea and have begun selling surimi worldwide, but a Food and Drug Administration ruling requires that U.S. manufacturers using surimi label the seafood imitation crab, lobster, shrimp, or whatever else it represents (the word "imitation" will be in small print by 1990). Made mostly from Alaskan pollock, surimi will have U.S. sales of 18 million pounds per year by 1983 and 150 million pounds by 1993 (the Japanese by then will be consuming more than 2 billion pounds of it) (but *see* Arctic Alaska, 1992).

Mexico unilaterally abrogates all fishing treaties with the United States December 29 after 15 meetings since 1977 have failed to settle disputes over tuna fishing rights.

World grain production: wheat, 445 million metric tons; rice, 400 million; maize, 392; barley, 162; millet/sorghum, 87; oats, 43; rye, 27; buckwheat, 2.

Britain has 133,000 full-time farmworkers, down from 563,000 in 1945.

Drought reaches into western Iowa, most of Illinois, all of Indiana, and much of Ohio, shortening some crops, especially peanuts. Conditions in the Corn Belt and Cotton Belt rival those of 1934, 1936, and 1953, and endless weeks of high temperatures and cloudless skies exhaust subsurface moisture in much of the Southeast, Southwest, and plains states. The Dakotas and Minnesota have their second dry year in a row. Winter wheat, harvested before the drought, is up 16 percent to a record 1.9 billion bushels, but feed grains are badly hurt, with the corn crop dropping 14 percent to 6.6 billion bushels.

U.S. corn yields average 90 bushels per acre, up from 43 in 1960, 25 in 1940, although Nebraska loses 75 percent of its corn crop. Wheat yields average 30.5 bushels per acre, up from 20.5 in 1960, 13 in 1940. Sorghum yields average 53 bushels, up from 24 in 1960, 12.5 in 1940. Soybean yields average 28 bushels, up from 22 in 1960, 16.2 in 1940. High yields and large reserves (1.7 billion bushels of corn, 901 million bushels of wheat) from past years keep prices down, but prices for corn and soybeans rise above the level before the embargo (above) and wheat nears the pre-embargo price of $3.80 per bushel by August. Farm income falls sharply from the 1979 peak of $33 billion as interest costs (above), higher diesel fuel prices, and other factors squeeze the capital-intensive U.S. farm economy.

U.S. farmland averages $609 per acre for the year, up from $525 last year. Acreage prices climb 20 percent or more in 13 states despite falling farm incomes.

The Supreme Court rules unanimously June 16 in *Bryant v. Yellen* that farmers in California's Imperial Valley may continue to receive Colorado River water regardless of the size of their farms and despite a 1926 law limiting to 160 acres the size of farms eligible for water from federal irrigation projects.

Dietary Goals for the United States, a report prepared by the staff of the Senate Select Committee on Nutrition and Human Needs (McGovern Committee), appears in its final version (*see* 1977) and recommends that sugar and salt consumption be reduced sharply. It targets meat, butterfat, eggs, and other foods high in saturated fats and cholesterol, recommending that people eat more poultry, fish, fruit, vegetables, and whole grains, with nonfat milk replacing whole milk. More specifically, it recommends that Americans cut their egg consumption by 50 percent, sugar and sweets by 50 percent, and animal fats by 16 percent while, at the same time, increasing consumption of whole-grain products by 66 percent, fresh fruit and vegetables by 25 percent, and skim milk by 12 percent. The American Medical Association opposes any such drastic change in dietary habits, saying that there is not enough scientific evidence to support the McGovern Committee's dietary goals and citing the "potential for harmful effects" (*see* 1980). The Food and Nutrition Board of the National Research Council also takes issue, saying that evidence of dietary fats being a cause of heart disease or cancer is inconclusive and contradictory; the Board concedes that high levels of serum cholesterol and low-density lipids are risk factors for heart disease but warns that there is no evidence to sup-

port claims that dietary intervention "will consistently affect the rate of new coronary events" and that the benefits of lowering fat intake to the levels recommended by *Dietary Goals* have "not been established." But the Board does suggest that the percentage of daily calories derived from fats be reduced to 35 percent (*Dietary Goals* suggested 30 percent), down from the national average of 40, and proposes a maximum upper limit for sodium intake.

The October 30 issue of the *New England Journal of Medicine* confirms the suspicion that some obese persons may be more "fuel efficient" than thin people and thus wind up with more pounds of body weight per 10,000 calories than those who are less fuel efficient: Boston researchers report a study of 21 severely obese people showing that their red blood cells use 22 percent less energy than the red blood cells of normal-weight control subjects. The results support a concept of "metabolic obesity," but nutritionists caution that reduced energy use remains to be shown in other body tissues and that the whole metabolic story is more complicated than simply decreased energy use.

Herbalife International is founded by California high school dropout Mark Hughes, 24, whose pills and liquids, allegedly made from exotic herbs and oils, promise weight loss, nutritional benefits, good health, and vitality. A pyramid of door-to-door salespeople will be producing annual gross sales of $437 million by 1985, when California authorities prosecute the company for fraud. The Food and Drug Administration will investigate Herbalife, as will a U.S. Senate subcommittee, sales will fall to $42 million by 1991, but Hughes will build an overseas sales force, promising cures for diabetes, eczema, lupus, and varicose veins, and by 1992 Herbalife will be generating $20 million in profits from sales of $405, enabling Hughes to buy a $20 million Beverly Hills estate.

European Community countries ban the use of hormones in cattle feed October 1 in response to a French boycott on veal that Britain and Belgium have echoed. The ban goes beyond a U.S. ban on using diethylstilbestrol (DES) issued early in the year. Its effect will be to make meat costlier while making veal taste better.

General Mills introduces Fruit Roll-Ups in test markets (they will reach national distribution in 1983). Traditionally called "fruit leather," the chewy fruit snack is made from real fruit that has been pressed into a thin, flat sheet and then rolled round a special plastic wrapper and encased in a plastic pouch. Available in four flavors (apple, apricot, cherry, and strawberry), it is unrolled and peeled from the plastic to be eaten (*see* Berry Bears, Shark Bites, 1989).

Coca-Cola announces in late January that it will substitute high-fructose corn syrup (HFCS) for half the sucrose used in Coke (*see* sugar prices, above). The company's decision has been based in part on lower corn prices resulting from President Carter's decision (above) to halt grain sales to Moscow.

Rum outsells vodka in the United States and outsells whiskey for the first time since the early 19th century (*see* vodka, 1973). All whiskeys except Canadian brands have declined in the 1970s while vodka, rum, and tequila have gained in popularity.

McDonald's test-markets Chicken McNuggets in March at Knoxville, Tenn., and gets such an enthusiastic response that its regular supplier, Keystone Foods, cannot meet its demands and it has to find a second supplier. Tyson Foods will produce a special chicken, nearly twice as large as the standard supermarket broiler (the new bird will be called "Mr. McDonald's"), which reduces the deboning problem by increasing the meat yield from each cut. The head of another fast-food chain said 2 years ago that consumers were "so preconditioned by McDonald's advertising blanket that the hamburger would taste good even if they left the meat out" (*see* 1984).

Hardee's is acquired by Imasco Ltd., a Canadian company that has been buying stock in Hardee's since 1975 and now buys the remaining 56 percent of shares outstanding (*see* 1972; 1982).

The first U.S. El Pollo Loco restaurant opens in December on Alvarado Street, Los Angeles (*see* 1975). It gains popularity with a policy of serving only fresh chickens, never frozen, preparing them with a butterfly cut, marinating them in a combination of herbs, spices, and fruit juices, cooking them over an open flame, and serving them with either corn or flour tortillas and fresh salsa (*see* Denny's, 1983).

Jean Bertranou of the Los Angeles restaurant L'Ermitage dies, and his widow, Lilliane, takes over with help from his nephew Patrick (*see* 1975). They elevate Michel Blanchet to the position of *chef de cuisine* and he introduces Los Angeles to the nouvelle cuisine ideas of Paul Bocuse, Michel Guérard, and others, preparing dishes that include terrines, ballottines, duck-liver mousse, and veal normande.

The Los Angeles restaurant La Toque opens at 8171 Sunset Boulevard. Chef Ken Frank, 25, offers patrons Japanese-style *oshiburi* (hot towels) before meals and a menu that includes some modified Japanese-style dishes (raw fish; enoki-dake mushrooms; and bean sprouts, mushrooms, watercress, and Roquefort cheese with a sherry, vinegar, and olive oil dressing). Other dishes, which change according to the season, include hot prawns; crevettes with a mustard sauce; terrine de bouillabaisse with saffron, New Zealand John Dory, scallops, and shrimp; saumon au Sauternes et l'endive; terrine [de coquilles] Saint-Jacques aux langoustines; selle d'agneau rôtie à la crème d'ail; poulet au miel et vinaigre Xérès; cheeses (but never Brie, Camembert, or Gruyère); desserts (by Lori Tannenbaum) that include chocolate mousse; tarts with champagne grapes; blueberries and raspberries on lemon cream. A five-course prix fixe dinner is about $35, with main dishes priced à la carte at between $16 to $22.

The Chicago restaurant Ambria opens in July at 2300 North Lincoln Park West. Spanish proprietor Gabino Sotelino offers French cuisine which by the 1990s will be prepared by a Japanese chef, Tashi Yagihashi. Specialties will include hamachi (yellowtail) in a soy-butter-ginger sauce and medallion of roast venison with a beef vegetable tart (beet or turnip root puréed, spread in a potato shell, and covered with potato strands in a blackberry sauce).

New York's Post House opens as a steak restaurant at 28 East 63rd Street, replacing La Passy, which went out of business in the mid-1970s after serving several generations of New Yorkers. The Post House will expand its menu to include not only filet au poivre, prime ribs, sliced steak, sirloin, filet mignon, filet of veal, triple lamb chops, and seven-chop rack of baby lamb, but also smoked salmon (from Petrossian); halibut steak; Norwegian salmon with dilled Chardonnay butter sauce; charred tuna steak; swordfish steak; 4- to 13-pound lobsters; lemon pepper chicken; flourless truffled torte; baum torte (an almond cake with apricot crème anglaise); and lemon-curd tart.

New York's The Odeon opens October 14 at 145 West Broadway, corner of Thomas Street, in TriBeCa (Triangle Below Canal). London-born brothers Keith and Brian McNally have started the place with Lynn Wagenknecht (who will later marry Keith) and Brooklyn-born chef Patrick Clark (who has worked at Michel Guérard's restaurant in France). Clark and Brian McNally will move on to work at other restaurants, leaving Lynn and and Keith to run The Odeon with Tony Sheck, a protégé of Clark's, in charge of the kitchen.

1981

Poland's grain crop increases by 11 percent to 20 million tons but is still short of demand. The government presses farmers in January to sell grain to the state to relieve drastic shortages of bread and other grain-related products; farmers will be permitted to purchase seed only if they replenish government granaries, says Warsaw.

President Ronald Reagan, 69, takes office January 20 with a commitment to favor free trade and oppose federal aid to agriculture, but his administration's farm bill has a "no-net-cost" provision that foreshadows increased protectionism for sugar, peanuts, and other farm commodities. The government will no longer take forfeitures of sugar in lieu of loan repayment, but it will support sugar prices at a level above the loan rate.

Congress votes 213 to 190 in mid-October to reject a revived sugar price support program favored by the House Agriculture Committee that would raise raw sugar prices by 20 percent, but Congress votes increased price support levels in December, effectively subsidizing Florida's Cuban-American Fanjol family, which controls about a third of the state's canefields, plus a second company, which controls another third (both employ seasonal West Indian labor to harvest cane on marshy land that cannot support heavy machines), a few large Hawaiian producers, and fewer than a thousand smaller Florida, Hawaii, Louisiana, and Texas cane growers plus beet-sugar producers in Minnesota, Idaho, and a dozen other states (*see* below).

The U.S. prime interest rate reaches 21.5 percent, highest since the Civil War, as double-digit inflation and high unemployment plague the economy.

Continental Grain and the Bangkok-based Charoen Pokphand Group form a joint venture to open China's first foreign-owned feed mill and chicken farm in the newly established Shenzhen economic zone created by Chinese party leader Deng Xiaoping (*see* Charoen Pokphand, 1921). By 1994, CP will be operating more than 75 animal feed mills across China and breeding 5 million chicks per day there in an enterprise that will stretch to Hong Kong and Jakarta.

Newman's Own Oil-and-Vinegar Salad Dressing is introduced by Hollywood film actor Paul Newman, 56, and his Westport, Conn., neighbor A. E. (Aaron Edward) Hotchner (a writer), 61, who have each invested $40,000 to start a company whose after-tax profits (about 18 percent of the retail price of its products) are to be donated to charity. Newman has always insisted on mixing his own salad dressing at restaurants, he has mixed the dressing in old wine bottles as Christmas gifts for friends, he and Hotchner have retained Ken's Foods of Framingham, Mass., to manufacture the dressing on a commercial scale, and they persuade their friend Stew Leonard, Sr., 51, who has built a Norwalk, Conn., food stand into a large store, to buy 10,000 cases. Newman's portrait appears on the label, he will follow the salad dressing with Industrial Strength Spaghetti Sauce, Lemonade (made from the recipe of his wife, actress Joanne Woodward, 51), regular and microwave popcorn, more salad dressings (including some for the Burger King chain), and Bandito Diabolo Spicy Sauce and Salsas (the portrait on the labels will show Newman with a handlebar moustache). The firm's letterhead bears the slogan "Shameless Exploitation in the Pursuit of the Common Good," and within 10 years Newman and Hotchner will have contributed an estimated $36 million to charities and hospitals.

Movie actor Paul Newman charitably lent his name—and his recipes—to a new line of food products.

Soybean curd was an alternative to dairy products, so why not make it taste like ice cream?

Tofu Time is founded in September by Brooklyn, N.Y., restaurateur David Mintz, 50, who has created Tofutti—a frozen dessert based on soybean curd rather than dairy products. He began experimenting with soybean curd 5 years ago, invented kosher beef stroganoff by substituting blended tofu for sour cream, developed a tofu cheese, a tofu rugelach, and other kosher tofu recipes for his Orthodox Jewish patrons, was told by experts that a tofu-based alternative to ice cream was "impossible," but refused to be discouraged. He has given up his restaurant, sold his catering business, and will now concentrate on developing new flavors—banana pecan, maple walnut, peanut butter, wild berry and well as chocolate and vanilla—of his cholestorol-free, lactose-free (but also calcium-deficient), honey-sweetened dessert product, which has half as many calories per serving as ice cream and can be enjoyed by people unable to eat ice cream. Tofutti will be sold through Häagen-Dazs and in less than 3 years will be available at 1,000 shops nationwide.

Nabisco Brands is created by a merger of Nabisco (National Biscuit Co.) and Standard Brands (*see* RJR Nabisco, 1985).

General Foods pays $464 million to acquire Oscar Mayer, now the leading U.S. marketer of sausage products (*see* 1944; Kraft General Foods, 1988).

Pillsbury acquires Jeno's Pizza from Jeno Paulucci and markets its product as a snack-time treat, differentiating it from Totino's Crisp Crust Pizza (*see* 1975).

Flying Foods International is founded at New York by entrepreneur Walter F. Martin II, who starts by working out of his apartment to fly in small quantities of fresh Dover sole by cargo jet from the Netherlands for sale to New York restaurants. Martin takes advantage of the fact that New York's John F. Kennedy Airport is the world's largest air cargo port. Paul Morates and Andrew Udelson soon join him, they acquire a riverfront warehouse in Long Island City, and André Soltner of Lutèce is one of their first customers, providing useful advice as the firm expands to import French *chicorée rouge* and fresh black truffles; *verdicchio*, bulb fennel, fresh white truffles, and baby artichokes from Italy; bell peppers from the Netherlands; *Cavaillon* melons from France; *haricots verts* from the Alps and high Pyrenees; *pleurotes*, black and white trumpets, *shiitake*, and *enoki daki* mushrooms; Mediterranean rockfish; Norway salmon; French *langoustine*; roe-bearing scallops from the Isle of Man; Maine scallops; California crayfish; live Louisiana crayfish; Hawaiian blue prawns; gilthead bream; John Dory, smoked eel, Wellington oysters, and green-shelled mussels from New Zealand; and fresh mozzarella di bufalo from southern Italy. Flying Foods will supply seed to Venezuelan melon growers, it will open its doors to consumers on weekends beginning in 1984, and by late 1985 it will have branches in Boston, Philadelphia, and Los Angeles as it grows to handle 20,000 tons of edibles per week and more than 280 separate items per day from Europe, South America, Africa, the Caribbean, and the Pacific to serve more than 750 restaurants nationwide (New York will account for about half the business). The partners will sell out in 1987 (*see* Gourmet Garage, 1992).

Aspartame gains FDA approval for tabletop use October 22. U.S. chemist James M. Schlatter discovered in 1955 while trying to develop an anti-ulcer drug that a mixture of the amino acids aspartic acid and phenylalanine had a sweet taste. Two teaspoons of sugar contain 32 calories; aspartame provides the same sweetening with four calories. Marketed by G. D. Searle under the brand name NutraSweet, the artificial sweetener is far costlier than saccharin but does not have saccharin's bitter aftertaste. Other countries have permitted the sale of aspartame, which is also made by Ajinimoto in Japan (*see* 1983).

Nonfiction: *Food and Drink in America: A History* by U.S. author Richard J. Hooker, 68; *Fading Feasts: A Compendium of Disappearing American Regional Foods* by *Natural History* magazine writer Raymond Sokolov, now 40; *Mushrooms* by English author Roger Phillips; *The Great American Waistline* by U.S. author Chris Chase.

Cookbooks: *French Regional Cooking* by Anne Willan, who since 1975 has been director of the École de Cuisine La Varenne cooking school in Paris; *The Cook's Handbook* by Prudence Leith; *Mediterranean Cookbook* by Lady Arabella Boxer; *Honest American Fare* by Bert Greene.

Beet sugar accounts for 34 percent of worldwide sugar consumption but 55 percent of U.S. consumption (*see* above).

38 cents of every U.S. food dollar is spent in a restaurant, fast-food outlet, or take-home store, up from 26 cents in 1960.

The U.S. Department of Agriculture responds to Reagan administration demands for cuts in the school lunch program by announcing in September that ketchup can be counted as a vegetable. The public outcry forces President Reagan to restore funds for school lunches, but his administration will try persistently to trim federal aid to many nutrition programs, despite evidence that poor nutrition contributes to significantly higher infant mortality rates, stunted growth, and learning disabilities in rural and urban America (*see* 1986).

The Beverly Hills Diet reaches the top of the best-seller lists. It is based on the dubious proposition that carbohydrates and proteins must never be eaten together (*see* Hay, 1929) because carbohydrates cannot be digested in acid conditions and undigested carbohydrates turn into fat.

Jane Brody's Nutrition Book by *New York Times* columnist Brody, 40 (her "Personal Health" column has been running since 1976), counters the nutrition quackery offered by less responsible writers.

Stouffer's Lean Cuisine frozen dinners are introduced by Nestlé's Stouffer division and gross $120 million their first year. By 1984 they will have nearly one-third of the $1.4 billion premium frozen dinner market, although Lean Cuisine Salisbury Steak has a lower calorie count, mostly because it comes in smaller portions and weighs less than Stouffer's regular frozen Salisbury Steak (*see* 1991; Healthy Choice, 1989).

Diet-conscious consumers eagerly accepted almost anything that might help them keep slim.

Adulterated rapeseed oil kills or maims 20,000 Spaniards in a scandal that receives little world attention (*see* 1985).

Nearly 120 nations vote in May to approve a voluntary international code that restricts marketing of infant formula to women, many of them illiterate, who have been encouraged to use infant formula rather than breast-feeding. The code has been drawn up under the auspices of the World Health Organization, which is concerned that formula in developing countries is often made from contaminated water or diluted to the point that infants are malnourished. The only dissenting vote is that of the United States, which has rejected the code as antagonistic to free trade and contrary to American antitrust laws and rights of free speech (*see* Nestlé, 1982).

Yoplait USA introduces Custard Style Yogurt in seven flavors (blueberry, coffee, lemon, plain with honey, raspberry, strawberry, and vanilla) beginning in June, using fruit purée and natural flavors (*see* 1977). Its rich, creamy texture finds more favor among U.S. consumers than the French-style yogurt sold by General Mills since 1977 (*see* 1982).

Hunt-Wesson increases the number of tomatoes in its Hunt Tomato Sauce from four to four and a half in response to consumer demand for a thicker sauce as Americans increase their average per capita pasta consumption to 13 pounds, up from 6.2 pounds in 1968.

Campbell Soup Co. introduces Prego Spaghetti Sauce, which contains visible herbs and spices. Developed by a Campbell chef who tried to duplicate the thick, seasoned sauce he made for his family back in Europe, Prego is advertised as tasting "so homemade you won't believe it came from a jar." It will have annual sales of more than $150 million by 1983 as it gains national distribution, and a No-Salt version will be added in 1985 (*see* 1987).

Kellogg introduces Nutri-Grain wheat cereal—vitamin-enriched flakes containing no sugar or preservatives—and follows it with other Nutri-Grain cereals.

Standard Brands (above) has lost the original recipes for its Curtiss Candy brands, and nobody at the old Curtiss factory outside Chicago remembers how to make the Baby Ruth and Butterfinger bars that once enjoyed such popularity. Nabisco Brands puts its research and development people to work developing and testing new formulations that will find favor with consumers.

President Reagan (above) is partial to jelly beans—especially Jelly Belly and Gummi Bear jelly beans, made by Herman Goelitz, Inc., of Fairfield, California and Goelitz Manufacturing of North Chicago.

New England Apple Products develops a pioneer vending program to make its Veryfine fruit juice products the leaders in single-serve juice products, basing its program on the new concept of dedicated vending machines (*see* 1975). By 1992 there will be 40,000 vending machines in U.S. offices, factories, schools, bus depots, train stations, and other locations, and Veryfine will be the top-selling brand both through machines and at convenience stores. The company will get out of the vinegar business in 1986, change its name in 1989 to Veryfine Products, and have $200 million in sales by 1990 (*see* iced tea, 1994).

Denny's opens its 1,000 restaurant (*see* Grand Slam Breakfast, 1977; El Pollo Loco, 1983).

Au Bon Pain owner Louis Kane takes Ronald Shaich, 27, into partnership and forms Au Bon Pain Co., Inc., which consists of three bakery shops and the Original Cookie Co., a 110-unit chain for which Shaich has been eastern regional director (*see* 1978). Each store bakes its own goods, but in order to ensure consistent quality Kane and Shaich set up a manufacturing plant to produce dough, which is frozen and then delivered to the stores for baking in special French ovens. Au Bon Pain will open its first bakery cart next year at Boston's Logan International Airport, establishing the concept of selling brand-name foods at airports. The idea will be so successful that in 1986 the company will give concessionaire rights to operate Au Bon Pain carts and kiosks in selected airports (*see* 1983).

Dunkin' Donuts opens its first shop in the Philippines in April (it will have 249 by 1994) and its first in Thailand in October (it will have 58 by 1994) (*see* Japan, 1971; Indonesia, 1985).

Arby's opens an outlet at Shibuya-ku, Japan—its first overseas restaurant (*see* 1978). It will open its first restaurant in Canada next year and its 1,500th outlet in 1985 at Slidell, La. (*see* 1991).

Dallas gastronomes hail the opening of The Mansion on Turtle Creek, a restaurant opened by oil heiress Caroline Rose Hunt, 54, in the former Shephard King mansion at 2821 Turtle Creek Boulevard. (The son of a Confederate Army general, King was a cotton broker whose living room—an exact replica of the salon of Bromley Castle in England, with cherubs and nymphs carved in its inlaid wooden ceilings—becomes the Mansion's main dining room. King imported antique Delft tiles for the floors and doors that once hung on a Spanish cathedral.) Hunt has purchased the place and decorated it with crystal, English silver, and French porcelain from her own personal collection. The Mansion's cuisine will hit its stride in 1985, when Dean Fearing, now 26, becomes its executive chef. Trained at the Culinary Institute of America, his specialties will include quail with fresh sweetbreads; smoked chilies; hot consommé with diced red bell peppers, black beans, and cilantro; pastas with jalapeño peppers; salads of jícama; seafood cocktail made with Gulf of Mexico crabmeat; smoked salmon with a sauce of red chili peppers; and lemon sole with black sesame seeds or a crust of crushed macadamia nuts and a sauce of basil and papaya.

John Clancy's Restaurant opens in the spring at 181 West 10th Street in New York's Greenwich Village. Clancy, who stands over 6 feet 6, learned about seafood working for his father's charter fishing boat on Long Island and has worked as a caterer, restaurant chef, test chef for cookbooks, television chef, and cooking instructor while writing three cookbooks. He is the first U.S. chef to have been invited to teach American cooking in Tokyo, and he specializes in grilling over mesquite (the southwestern shrub *Prosopis juliflora*), which he has shipped to him from Texas and whose smoke gives food an outdoorsy flavor. Clancy's dishes include sole bonne femme, lobster à l'armoricaine, littleneck clams and oysters on the half shell (sold by the piece at 80¢ and $1.25 each, respectively), shrimp cocktail slightly warmed to bring out the flavor, lobster bisque, New Orleans oyster soup, fishermen's stew (made of red snapper, striped bass, clams, mussels, scallops, and shrimp in a fish stock with crushed tomatoes, saffron, orange rind, leek, bayleaf, and thyme), and mesquite-grilled halibut, scallops, mako shark, and swordfish. Desserts: trifle, mocha tort, meringue pie, chocolate velvet, and apricot-glazed peach. (Clancy will lose control of his John Clancy restaurants and work as a chef first at Jake's Fish Market, Broadway and 89th Street, and, later, at Canard & Co., Madison Avenue at 92nd Street.)

General Mills opens its 300th Red Lobster restaurant (at Dallas, Tex.) (*see* 1974). By next year it will have Red Lobsters in 35 states, and it will open its 400th outlet in 1988 (at Union, N.J.) (*see* 1991).

The Paris restaurant Jamin, opened at 32, rue de Longchamp by chef Joël Robuchon, 36, will be awarded a third Michelin star in just 5 years, the shortest time ever. Robuchon bakes his own bread fresh each day for lunch and dinner and buys his fish, meats, and produce direct from suppliers instead of from wholesalers at Rungis. He will move at the end of 1993 to 55, avenue Raymond-Poincaré.

1982

Soviet food shortages in January produce widespread grumbling in Moscow. The government draws down grain reserves and increases imports to maintain livestock herds as crops fail for the fourth consecutive year. A C.I.A. analysis of the Russian diet finds that conditions have greatly improved, with greater reliance on meat and dairy products and less on bread and potatoes.

💲 President Reagan's budget address February 6 calls for much higher military appropriations and less spending on social programs.

Recession continues throughout most of the world, international trade declines, unemployment in the United States reaches 10.8 percent in November—the highest since 1940—and the number of Americans living below the poverty line is the highest in 17 years.

🤝 ConAgra acquires Peavey Co., which 7 years ago purchased ConAgra's Grand Island, Nebr., grain elevator and its adjoining mill for just $600,000 and razed the historic mill. Peavey not only is a major flour miller and grain merchandiser but has become a food processor and operates specialty retail stores (*see* Montfort, 1987).

General Foods acquires Entenmann's, the New York bakery chain, and will give national distribution to the company's chocolate chip cookies, crumb coffee cake, raspberry danish twist, chocolate frosted doughnuts, golden pound loaf, and other products (*see* 1898).

Campbell Soup Co. acquires Mrs. Paul's Kitchens to enter the frozen seafood and vegetable business (*see* 1946).

Procter & Gamble acquires Tender Leaf Tea.

Pet Incorporated acquires the 160-year-old William Underwood Co. and its Underwood, B&M, and Aćcent brands (*see* Sell's, 1960; Progresso, 1986).

Cadbury-Schweppes acquires Duffy-Mott Co. from American Brands, the tobacco-food conglomerate which bought it in 1967 (*see* Clapp's, 1953). The product line has been expanded to include Mott's Prune Juice and Mott's Clamato and Beefamato. It will be expanded further to include a shelf-stable concentrate product, various blended juices, Mott's Fruit Basket, and Grandma's Molasses (*see* Canada Dry, 1985).

Worthington Foods executives buy back their company October 15 from Bayer AG, which acquired Miles Laboratories 4 years ago (*see* 1970). Miles has introduced a Morningstar Farms line of cholesterol-free foods—including Breakfast Strips, Breakfast Patties, Grillers, Breakfast Links, and Luncheon Slices—but it is Morningstar Farms Scramblers—

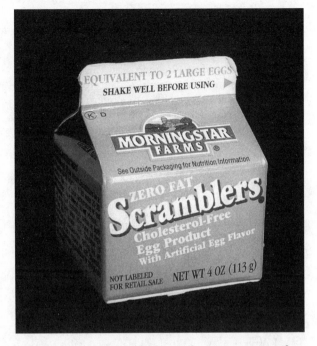

Substitutes for whole eggs found a market as worries grew about egg yolks and cholesterol.

scrambled eggs made with egg whites but no yolks—that will be Worthington's biggest-selling item (*see* Loma Linda, 1990).

💲 The Great Atlantic & Pacific Tea Co. (A&P) turns its first profit in years but continues to struggle (*see* 1979). The Tengelmann Group has brought in English food retailer James Wood, 52, to revive the grocery chain's fortunes; Wood, who became a grocer's apprentice at age 16 and worked his way up to become head of Cavenham Ltd., has closed all of the A&P's supermarkets in Chicago, Kansas City, and Louisville along with half the money-losing Plus discount stores, closed its Philadelphia stores and reopened them under the name Super Fresh, shut down almost all of the chain's food-processing facilities, and discharged 20,000 of the A&P's 60,000 employees. Only 1,055 stores remain, and the A&P is now the fifth-largest U.S. supermarket chain, trailing Safeway, Kroger, Lucky, and American Stores (Jewel Tea and others) in an industry that nets only .88 percent profit on sales.

London's Billingsgate Market closes after roughly 1,000 years of selling fish and other foods.

Nonfiction: *One Continuous Picnic: A History of Eating in Australia* by journalist Michael Symons, who describes his country's diet from the bush rations of the early settlers to modern once-a-week supermarket shoppers. A onetime restaurateur in Italy, Symons says that his countrymen have always relied on mass-produced convenience foods.

Cookbooks: *The Silver Palate Cookbook* by Sheila Lukins and Julee Rosso of the New York food specialty shop (*see* 1977) with chef Michael McLaughlin. A compendium of recipes for the shop and catering service's favorite dishes, it will have sales of more than 1 million copies. *The Chez Panisse Menu Cookbook* by Alice Waters. *Greene on Greens* by Bert Greene. *The Book of Bread* by U.S. authors Judith and Evan Jones, whose recipes include some for steamed Boston brown bread, Chinese steamed buns, biscuits, fried breads, and popovers. *Entertaining* by U.S. promoter Martha Stewart (*née* Kostyra), 33, with Elizabeth Hawes contains recipes that are mostly either derivative, overdifficult, or just plain don't work, but seductive illustrations (deep-dish pies inside woven baskets, poached pears with candied violets in a crystal bowl filled with wine, and the like) begin a multimillion-dollar empire of magazines, books, and videotapes. *Jane Grigson's Fruit Book* contains recipes for fruit with meat, fruit with fish, salads, jams, chutneys, candied fruit, fruit drinks, fruit liqueurs, and the like as well as dessert recipes; *Delia Smith's Complete Cookery Course* will have sales of nearly 2 million copies by 1994 (*see* 1980). *The Great British Cheese Book* by Berkshire shopkeeper Patrick Rance of Streatley-on-Thames, who specializes in rare British cheeses; *The Food and Cooking of Russia* by English author Lesley Chamberlain.

Waverley Root dies of a pulmonary ailment in his Paris apartment in the Rue du Cherche-Midi October 31 at age 79.

A U.S. patent for use of the French diet drug dexfenfluramine is issued to MIT brain researcher Richard Wurtman and his research nutritionist wife, Judith (*see* book, 1979). Dr. Wurtman has discovered that insulin raises brain levels of the amino acid tryptophan, which, in turn, is a raw material for production not only of niacin but of the brain chemical serotonin. Serotonin has been found to play a key role in regulating mood, and studies by Judith Wurtman have shown that the moods of obese subjects rise sharply after eating high-carbohydrate biscuits. Premenstrual women and smokers trying to quit tend to eat more carbohydrates, but overeaters seem to snack less and lose weight when given serotonin drugs such as dexfenfluramine (made by the French pharmaceutical firm Les Laboratoires Servier) (*see* Interneuron, 1988).

Nestlé Alimentana, S.A., issues guidelines March 16 for compliance with the voluntary international code that discourages unnecessary use of infant formula and encourages breast-feeding (*see* 1981). A 5-year boycott of Nestlé products has persuaded the world's largest supplier of infant formula to change its marketing practices, which have been blamed for contributing to countless infant deaths in developing countries (Nestlé distributes formula in 140 countries). Nestlé has been distributing free samples directly to mothers and promoting formula as a modern and superior alternative to mothers' milk. The company agrees to curtail distribution in hospitals and health care centers and says that it will provide samples only if they are requested by a physician or qualified medical professional (*see* 1984).

A U.S. Committee on Nitrate, Nitrite, and Alternative Curing Agents in Food reports in April that radiation and acid-producing chemicals may someday be used as substitutes for nitrates as preservatives for cured meats, but more research is needed to make them feasible (*see* 1977; radiation of produce, 1984). Nitrates and nitrites are used in foods primarily to prevent the growth of the deadly bacterium *Clostridium botulinum*, which multiplies in the absence of oxygen and produces botulism, but are also added to sausages and luncheon meats to impart a characteristic color and flavor. Concentrations of nitrates and nitrites in processed meats have been reduced since the discovery that ascorbate and erythrobate can also prevent the growth of the botulinum organism, and the committee recommends that vitamins C and E be added to bacon to prevent conversion of nitrite to potentially carcinogenic nitrosamines. (Whether nitrites are harmful when consumed as components of the foods in which they naturally occur—vegetables, dairy products, grains, and water—remains unknown, nor is it known whether nitrosamines formed in the stomach after the ingestion of nitrate and nitrite additives are carcinogenic; *see* fish, 1983.)

Unilever introduces Mrs. Butterworth's Pancake Mix (*see* syrup, 1961). The new product competes with the Quaker Oats Aunt Jemima brand.

Campbell Soup Co. (above) introduces Swanson Great Starts frozen breakfasts, a variation on a Swanson line launched in 1969.

Yoplait USA introduces Breakfast Style Yogurt in June (*see* 1981). Designed specifically to be eaten at breakfast and sold in five flavors (berries, orchard fruits, citrus fruits, apple cinnamon, and tropical fruits), it combines the creaminess of Original Style Yogurt with a chewy texture provided by wheat grains, walnuts, raisins, and chunks of fruit. The product will be reformulated in September 1984; orchard fruits and citrus fruits will be discontinued in November 1986) (*see* 1986).

Procter & Gamble introduces Citrus Hill Select orange juice, competing with Tropicana in the chilled, pasteurized juice business (*see* Tropicana, 1955). P&G will introduce Citrus Hill Plus Calcium in 1986 and Citrus Hill Lite Premium in 1987, both in grapefruit juice as well as orange juice versions.

Light (or Lite) beer had fewer calories than regular beer but just as much alcohol.

Bud Light, introduced by Anheuser-Busch, has fewer calories than the company's 106-year-old Budweiser beer and will soon be second in popularity only to Budweiser.

The Los Angeles restaurant Spago opens in February with picture windows overlooking Sunset Boulevard in West Hollywood, where it will be grossing $6 million per year by 1990. Started on a shoestring (*spago* is Italian for "string") by Austrian-born chef Wolfgang Puck, 31, the place has an airy, whitewashed dining room, designed by Puck's wife and partner, Barbara Lazaroff, and features gourmet pizzas (when some fine smoked salmon arrives, the bread runs out, and there is no time to bake more bread, he will create smoked salmon pizza) and fancy desserts. Puck, whose mother was a hotel chef but who ran away from home at age 14 to become a kitchen apprentice, worked at the Hôtel de Paris in Monte Carlo and at Maxim's in Paris before coming to America. He got a job as a cook at Indianapolis, met Patrick Terreil, and came to work as chef at Ma Maison in Los Angeles, where he has been chef since 1976. Puck will follow his success at Spago with Chinois on Main Street in Santa Monica, where he will create sautéed duck foie gras with pineapple when the market has no mangoes, and will go on to open Postrio in San Francisco (*see* Eureka, 1990).

The Los Angeles restaurant Siam Orchid opens in November on the top floor of the Beverly Center, 8500 Beverly Boulevard. Its owner is Thai entrepreneur Sasima Srivikorn, mother of four, whose investment company has started a large private school in Thailand, has built that country's first condominium, and owns two hotels, including Bangkok's The President. She is allowed an exemption to the Thai law forbidding export of raw teak, and she has used 17 tons of the hardwood in Siam Orchid. Its chef, Phenkae Amborist, has been head chef in the palace kitchens of Bhumibol Adulyadej, who has been Thailand's king since 1950. Specialties include *tom yum poh tack* (a seafood soup based on coconut milk with shrimps, scallops, mussels, and small pieces of rock cod); *hoh mok kanom krog* (a soufflé of shredded rock cod); *plo jah* (crab shells stuffed with a forcemeat of crabmeat, shrimp, pork, and chicken); *yum yai* salad (slivers of chicken and pork, tiny shrimp, coriander, and lace noodles); sliced galingale (a kind of ginger root) with lemon grass, coriander, lime, dried chili peppers, and red onions; and *plah rad prik* (wok-fried rock cod).

The Chicago restaurant AvanÏzare opens at 161 East Huron Street. Proprietors Dennis and Marvin Magid have hired Italian chef Dennis Terczak, whose specialties include panfried baby artichokes with mustard sauce; *carpaccio*; baked polenta with sausage, goat cheese, and tomato sauce; cream of arugula soup; tomato and basil soup; pastas that include *trenette di oca* with smoked goose, grilled *radicchio*, and pine nuts; grilled swordfish steak; marinated octopus; grilled veal chop; sautéed breast of chicken with *pancetta* (cured bacon); breast of duck with sautéed cabbage, *pancetta*, and raisins; *zuppa del contadino* (Amaretto-moistened pound cake layered with pastry cream and chocolate sauce and covered with *amaretti* [macaroons] and pistachio nuts); *cannoli*; cantaloupe granita; and risotto with cinnamon ice cream.

Miami's Grand Bay Hotel opens at 2669 South Bay Shore Drive, Coconut Grove, with 180 rooms and a Grand Café whose kitchen is headed by Jamaican-born chef Katsuo Sugiura. He has worked in France, Germany, and Scandinavia as well as in the United States, and his specialties include salmon, house-smoked or cured any of 10 ways; sautéed foie gras with ginger confit, served with asparagus, haricots verts, and a sauce made with passion fruit and grainy mustard; herbed seafood broth with scallops, squid, and shrimps; grilled *mahimahi* with ginger and tropical fruit; *mahimahi* with a tropical fruit sauce and sweet pickled bell peppers; steak with *tomatillo* and avocado; and loin of lamb smoked over oolong tea and hickory chips, served with grilled portobello mushrooms, yuca, and *calabaza* squash. Sugiura will continue until 1993, when he will be succeeded as chef by Pascal Oudin.

Lüchow's in New York moves in June to a building north of Times Square after 100 years in 14th Street (*see* 1933). It will survive for only a few years in its new location.

The New York restaurant The Water Club opens in November on a converted lumber barge in the East River at 30th Street and the Franklin D. Roosevelt Drive. Michael O'Keeffe of 1977 River Cafe fame has hired Toulouse chef Guy Peuch, whose offerings include chicken-liver mousse; Smithfield

ham with melon; clams and oysters (including Maine *belons*) on the half shell; Peconic Bay scallops with mustard sauce; smoked salmon and trout; homemade garlic sausage en croûte with lyonnaise potatoes; country-style pâté; lobster bisque; corn-and-crabmeat chowder; steamed or broiled red snapper stuffed with *duxelles*, tomato, and rosemary; Michigan lake perch; Dover sole *meunière*; turbot; poached striped bass; prime ribs with O'Brien potatoes; corned-beef hash; Yankee pot roast with potato pancakes; beef stew; roast half duckling with chestnut purée and a cinnamon-sprinkled pear poached in wine; *confit de canard*; *cassoulet*; corn fritters; baked or mashed sweet potatoes; mashed potatoes Colcannon; apple pie; pecan tart; fruit tarts; and chocolate cake.

The 15-year-old London restaurant Le Gavroche, now at 43 Upper Brook Street, receives its third Michelin star, serving French classics that include mussel soup, ravioli stuffed with skate, lobster with snails, tournedos with mushroom sauce; three-mustard veal kidneys, rabbit and risotto, pheasant, tarte Tatin, chocolate and spice soufflé, and other delicacies to well-heeled patrons who reserve tables at least 2 weeks in advance.

McDonald's efforts to build a chain of French fast-food restaurants end in failure as the company takes its Paris franchisee, Raymond Payan, to court and closes all its Paris restaurants, but by 1988 it will have reestablished itself as one of France's most popular fast-food chains.

Hardee's acquires the 650-unit Burger Chef chain from General Foods (*see* Imasco, 1980). It will open its 2,000th restaurant in October of next year (at Hampton, Va.) and in 1987 will open its 3,000th (at Augusta, Ga.) as it passes Wendy's to become the third-largest burger chain (*see* 1988).

General Mills opens its first Olive Garden restaurants to capitalize on the popularity of pasta and other Italian food; by 1994 there will be more than 370 Olive Garden restaurants nationwide along with nearly 650 Red Lobster restaurants serving swordfish steaks, red snapper, and Caesar salad in addition to lobster.

Kansas City Bar-B-Cue chef Arthur Bryant collapses at his restaurant and dies December 28 at age

80 (*see* 1946). Semiretired, he has always said, "I don't hire me no barbecue cook. I'm my own barbecue cook," but while some wonder how long the place can continue without him it will still be going strong in 1995.

1983

Soviet harvests are good for the first time since 1978, but food shortages persist in much of the country as they do in Poland, Romania, and other Iron Curtain countries (but *see* Hungary, below).

A new U.S.-Soviet grain agreement formally signed at Moscow August 25 pledges the USSR to buy at least 9 million metric tons of U.S. grain per year for the next 5 years and pledges the United States to supply up to 12 million tons. The figures are 50 percent higher than in the 1975 agreement, and there is no escape clause, as in 1975, suspending shipments in the event of shortages that would raise domestic food prices.

Economic recovery begins in the United States, inflation remains low, unemployment begins to drop, but the Census Bureau reports that 35.3 million Americans live in poverty—the highest rate in 19 years.

President Reagan tells a news conference in June of his boyhood poverty, vehemently denies that his programs favor the rich over the poor, but insists that 800,000 Americans who have lost their food stamps deserved to lose them because their incomes were 150 percent above the poverty level. The maximum food stamp allotment for a family of four enables that family to buy $58 worth of food per week; Reagan's Secretary of Agriculture John R. Block and his wife, Sue, try to live for a week on that much food with their daughter and the daughter's friend; Block says they were well fed but concedes that it is "impossible to really appreciate the plight of the poor."

A Economic Summit of Industrialized Nations at Williamsburg, Va., features a banquet of all-American foods at the Williamsburg Inn May 30. President Reagan and his wife, Nancy, have asked former *New York Times* food critic Craig Claiborne to assemble the best of American cooking for heads of state who include Britain's Margaret Thatcher, Canada's Pierre Elliot Trudeau, France's François Mitterrand, Japan's Yasuhiro Nakasone, and West Germany's Helmut Kohl. Claiborne has asked Wolfgang Puck from Los Angeles, Paul Prudhomme from New Orleans, Maida Heatter from Miami Beach, and Zerela Martinez from El Paso, Tex., to cook meals in their distinctive styles for other events at the summit meeting, but the menu for the May 30 dinner begins with American caviar on Sally Lunn melba toast and roast rack of lamb salad; boneless quail with wild rice stuffing is served with fresh asparagus; this is followed by California goat cheese with native olive oil; and the dessert is Florida citrus sherbets. The wines, all from California, include St. Clement Chardonnay, Freemark Abbey Cabernet Sauvignon, and a Schramsberg sparkling wine.

J. R. Simplot Co. enters the frozen vegetable and fruit business (*see* frozen french fries, 1953). It will soon be a leading supplier, with processing plants in Washington State, California, and Mexico. By 1995 the company will be processing nearly 2 billion pounds of frozen french fries, hash browns, and other potato products at plants in Oregon, North Dakota, and the People's Republic of China as well as at three in Idaho. It will be supplying half the fries used in the vast McDonald's fast-food chain. Its Agriculture Group, headquartered at Grand View, Idaho, will operate ranches and irrigated farms in six western states and fatten beef cattle with potato skins in four feedlots having a combined capacity of 200,000 head, making it the largest producer of beef cattle in the western United States.

Quaker Oats acquires Stokely–Van Camp for $208 million, outbidding Pillsbury by offering $77 per share (Pillsbury has offered $62). Both suitors have coveted Stokely's profitable Gatorade division (*see* 1965).

Pillsbury Co. has acquired Häagen-Dazs Co. in June for a reported $80 million. Häagen-Dazs has grown since 1959 to have annual sales of $115 million, with hundreds of franchised ice cream stores from coast to coast to supplement distribution of its products in supermarkets (*see* Ben & Jerry's, 1985; Sedutto, 1988).

Pet Inc. buys Hain Pure Foods from Ogden Corp., which acquired it from Herman Jacobs (*see* 1926; 1994).

Companies making "natural" foods became takeover targets for mainstream marketers.

Elders XIL Ltd. acquires Australia's Carlton and United Breweries Ltd. late in the year (*see* Elliott, 1972). Australia's largest brewing concern, with brands that include Skoal and Double Diamond, Carlton and United has been exporting to Britain and now controls 8 percent of the lager market in Britain, where beer consumption has been declining (*see* 1985).

Nestlé (Société des Produits Nestlé, S.A.) takes over Ward-Johnston Co.'s confectionery line of candy bars, including Oh Henry!, Chunky, Bit-O-Honey, Goobers, Sno-Caps, and Raisinets. Nestlé will upgrade the quality of chocolate in Oh Henry!, Chunky, and Goobers (*see* 1985; Baby Ruth, Butterfinger, 1990).

 Budapest's Central Market, opened in 1895, has bounteous displays in the autumn of grapes, plums, figs, beans, cabbages, eggplants, kohlrabis, and squashes; morels, chanterelles, and other fungi; apples and pears from Szeged; and sweet green grapes, Muscat grapes, and quinces to be served with wild game. Legs of mutton, hams, winter salamis, summer salamis, paprika salamis, sausages from Szeged and from Bercen, blood-and-liver sausages, and paprika-dusted slabs of bacon are suspended above long butcher counters along with the crisp chunks of fried bacon called *töpörtyü*; bunches of bright red peppers hang above vendors' stalls along with braids of garlic and bouquets of rosemary. There is no dearth of chickens, ducks, wild ducks, goose livers, woodcocks, smoked pork ribs, and pork loins. Much of France's foie gras, snails, woodcocks, pheasants, frogs' legs, and venison comes from Hungary (*see* agriculture, below).

Tyson Foods and other Arkansas poultry processors receive a boost from Governor Bill Clinton, 37, who has been elected to a second term (after losing an election) and gets a law through the legislature raising from 73,000 to 80,000 pounds the weight limit on trucks. The 73,000-pound limit, designed to protect the state's highways, put Arkansas poultry and trucking companies at a disadvantage and cost them millions of dollars in business lost to out-of-state competitors (*see* Holly Farms, 1989; Clinton, 1992).

Nonfiction: *Savoring the Past: the French Kitchen and Table from 1300 to 1789* by U.S. writer Barbara Ketcham Wheaton; *The British at Table, 1940–1980* by English author Christopher Driver, who has lived in various parts of the British Isles.

Cookbooks: *Il Talismano della felicità* by Italian-American cook Ada Boni; *Capon on Cooking* by Robert Farrar Capon; *The California Seafood Cookbook* by Isaac Cronin, Jay Harlow, and Paul Johnson; *The Observer Guide to European Cookery* by Jane Grigson; *The Sunday Times Complete Cookbook* and *The Wind in the Willows Cookbook* by Lady Arabella Boxer; *Wild Food* by Roger Phillips, who gives recipes for wild plants, mushrooms, and seaweed.

El Niño (a body of warm water) off the coasts of Ecuador and Peru upsets weather patterns worldwide by acting as a catalyst for prevailing conditions.

Maine and Puget Sound aquaculturists produce more than 350 metric tons of mussels.

Soviet fisherman stop hauling nets on the Aral Sea, which 10 years ago supplied 10 to 15 percent of the nation's freshwater catch. The 800-mile Kara Kum Canal, completed in the 1970s as part of an ill-conceived plan to turn the surrounding deserts into cotton- and rice-growing farmland, has siphoned water from the inland sea's two source rivers, creating flood control problems in some areas while lowering the Aral Sea's water level by 40 feet, shrinking it by one-third, doubling its salinity, killing most aquatic life, and creating an ecological disaster as winds blow dust and salt from the sea bottom, contaminated with pesticide residues, onto surrounding fields, poisoning water supplies and even mothers' milk (*see* 1985).

Hungary harvests abundant crops (*see* market, above); while other Eastern European countries import foodstuffs, Hungary's 150 state farms and 1,360 cooperatives, ranging in size from 50 to more than 60,000 acres, produce wheat and meat that constitute nearly 25 percent of the nation's exports. The big farms and co-ops occupy more than 70 percent of Hungary's arable land, but a farmworker is entitled to a private plot of just over an acre, and these private plots produce much of the country's pork and poultry.

The worst drought since 1936 combines with the largest acreage diversion in history to reduce the U.S. corn harvest by some 2 billion bushels (*see* 1988).

A payment-in-kind (PIK) program rewards U.S. farmers for not planting. This and other farm support programs cost taxpayers an unprecedented $21.5 billion and encourage marginally efficient farmers to continue.

A paper published in the February issue of *Annals of Internal Medicine* describes two patients who have developed symptoms of vitamin E deficiency—poor coordination and diminished reflexes—more than 20 years after undergoing surgical removal of much of their small intestines (*see* 1935). The patients have been unable to absorb dietary fat, and this has been true also of some prematurely born infants, but although most physicians emphasize the rarity of any deficiencies and warn that excess intake may pro-

duce headache, nausea, blurred vision, and gastrointestinal upsets, vitamin E supplements will gain popularity in this decade as an antioxidant with the same benefits as vitamin C and perhaps even more.

Jenny Craig, Inc. is founded by San Diego entrepreneur Sid Craig, 51, and his wife, Jenny, whose weight-loss program is similar to that of Nutri/System (*see* 1971) but reduces weight on average by one and a half to two pounds per week versus two to two and a quarter for Nutri/System. Like Nutri/System, it uses prepacked foods to eliminate supermarket temptations and limits daily calorie intake to 1,000 (and like Nutri/System, its claims will be challenged in court). When dieters lose half the weight intended, they may gradually introduce their own food choices into the diet regimen. Strenuous exercise is discouraged during weight loss.

Fallacies about weight loss abound; common erroneous beliefs include the notions that hard-cooked eggs, grapefruit, or some other food "burns up" calories, that a crash diet is a good way to begin a weight-loss program, that exercise is relatively unimportant since it takes so much energy expenditure to offset just 100 calories, that calories don't count, that eating more in the morning than in the evening will make it harder to gain weight.

Average U.S. per capita consumption of dairy products falls by 20 percent (of whole milk by more than 50 percent) from 1950 levels and of eggs by one-third due to mounting concerns that dietary cholesterol levels are related to heart disease, although nutritionists note that skim milk and egg whites do not raise cholesterol levels. More Americans choose fish and poultry in preference to roast beef and sirloin steak.

Studies published in the *Proceedings of the National Academy of Sciences, USA*, for May and in *Seminars in Oncology* for September suggest that the high rate of stomach cancer in Japan may be due to the fact that Japanese diets are periodically low in sources of vitamins C and E but constantly high in fish species prone to forming nitrosamines after being preserved with nitrate-containing crude salt or saltpeter. The high rate has been blamed on such things as high pickle consumption, soy sauce, and the talc on white rice, but the new studies identify several types of fish that produce nitrosamines and cause bacterial mutations after being treated with nitrite under conditions simulating those in the human stomach. The Japanese varieties sanma, aji, and iwashi are associated with the highest rates of genetic change; flounder and catfish show none at all; cod, haddock, bluegill, and canned sardines show low to moderate activity (*see* 1987).

Campbell Soup Co. introduces a line of Campbell's Home Cookin' soups.

Campbell Soup Co. (above) introduces Le Menu frozen dinners.

General Mills introduces Nacho Cheese Flavor Snacks (*see* 1964).

Häagen-Dazs creator Reuben Mattus, now 71, who has sold his brand to Pillsbury (above), will launch a new low-fat brand of ice cream under his own name (*see* 1959).

U.S. soft-drink makers begin using NutraSweet, initially in combination with saccharin, to sweeten diet beverages (*see* 1981).

The New York restaurant Carolina, opened in January at 355 West 46th Street by Eileen Weinberg and Martin Yerdon, specializes in corn chowder, fresh-baked corn bread and biscuits, Boston baked beans, barbecued smoked ribs, smoked beef brisket, smoked pork fillet, smoked pork shoulder, sliced braised duck with red pepper, broiled seafoods, crabcakes, strawberry shortcake with a biscuit crust, and mud pie.

The New York restaurant La Réserve opens February 11 at 4 West 49th Street. Managing owner Jean-Louis Missud's chef, André Gaillard, will die young in 1990 and be succeeded by French chef Dominique Payradeau.

The New York restaurant Hubert's opens at 105 East 22nd Street, just off Park Avenue South near Gramercy Park. Karen Hubert, a writer specializing in education, and Len Allison, who worked in video and films, lived together in Brooklyn in the mid-1970s, shared the cooking in their small house, served meals 3 nights each week at home to raise money to produce a television documentary, and went on to run a landmarked tavern with 22-foot ceilings in the Boerum Hill section near Brooklyn Heights. Allison works in the kitchen, Hubert in the front of the house, and they build up a following for their imaginative dishes (*see* 1988).

The New York restaurant Parioli Romanissimo, which opened in 1972 on First Avenue at 76th Street, moves into the ground floor of a neo-Renaissance town house at 24 East 81st Street. Proprietor Rubrio Rossi's specialties include broccoli purée; pastas; 3-week-old chicken with black truffles, rosemary, and wine; veal piccata *al limone*; *costoletto alla valdostone*; roast rack of veal; *bistecca alla pizzaiola*; Dover sole; red snapper; *branzino* (Mediterranean rockfish); ricotta cheesecake with a raspberry sauce; flourless chocolate cake with whipped cream; zabaglione; and French and Italian cheeses.

The New York restaurant An American Place (the name comes from that of Alfred Stieglitz's art gallery early in the century) opens in October with 50 seats at 969 Lexington Avenue between 70th and 71st streets (formerly the premises of Le Plaisir). Former River Café chef Lawrence P. Forgione, 31, offers dishes such as Willapa Bay oysters from Washington State; game-bird sausage; barbecued mallard; foie gras made from New York State ducks; pasta with Maine bay shrimp and Olympia oysters; Key West shrimp with mustard sauce; terrine of salmon, sturgeon, and whitefish; Albemarle Sound fish soup flavored not with the traditional pine bark but rather with "taste-alike" marjoram and smoked bacon; soft-shelled crayfish from Louisiana; sautéed lake perch; Long Island eels; New England cod cheeks; buffalo steak; ribs of baby beef; lamb in various forms; persimmon pudding; apple pandowdy; and shortcake with berries. Its prix fixe dinner is $45 per person plus cocktails, wine, tips, and taxes (*see* 1989).

The New York restaurant Il Cantinori opens at 32 East 10th Street serving Tuscan dishes. Florence-born restaurateur Pino Luongo, 30, arrived in New York 3 years ago to pursue a career as an actor (and escape Italy's military draft), found work as a busboy at the Greenwich Village Tuscan restaurant Don Sylvano, worked his way up to become manager, and has gone into partnership with Steve Tzolis and Nicola Kotsoni to start Il Cantinori, which serves peasant bread, pappa al pomodoro soups, and other basic fare (*see* Sapporo di Mare, 1988).

The Philadelphia restaurant The Fountain opens July 31 with 95 seats in the Four Seasons Hotel at 1 Logan Square with French chef Jean-Marie Lacroix, 39, as its chef. Lacroix, who has worked at the Four Seasons in Montreal, changes his menu daily, specializing in East Coast fish, venison, organic vegetables, and a brunch that is served all day (*see* Four Seasons hotels, 1960).

The Boston restaurant Jasper's opens in October at 240 Commercial Street, across from Lewis Wharf near Atlantic Avenue. Chef Jasper White, 29, and his wife, Nancy, have taken over an old molasses warehouse built in 1802 and can seat about 100. White and his longtime cooking partner Lydia Shire have managed the kitchens of the Parker House, Copley Plaza, and Bostonian hotels, and he has done extensive research into New England foods. He offers specialties that include fresh raw oysters (Belons, Pemaquids, and Spinney Creeks from Maine, Wellfleets from Cape Cod); raw scallops; littleneck clams; an appetizer salad of grilled duck with spiced pecans and papaya; Portuguese mussels with *chourico*; pumpkin-and-leek bisque with lobster; pan-roasted lobster; lobster and corn chowder (summer); finnan haddie and haddock chowder (winter); corn, pumpkin, and leek bisque with lobster; *bouillabaisse* with saffron and orange; pork fillets with littleneck clams and garlic sauce; New England boiled dinner; pot roast; rabbit and shellfish potpies; grilled bluefish; roast Atlantic salmon with a salmon roe sabayon and a ragout of wild rice and vegetables; apple crunch; apples poached in hard cider, topped with a caramel sauce, and served with spice cookies; burnt-sugar walnut tart with maple ice cream; peach and berry shortcake; Vermont-style spiced-chocolate tweed cake (made with mashed potato); and deep-dish blueberry pie.

Au Bon Pain acquires a centralized production facility in South Boston and changes from a croissant and bread bakery to a French bakery-café, adding coffee and installing seats (*see* 1981; New York, 1984).

Denny's Restaurants pays $11.3 million to acquire the U.S. operations of El Pollo Loco, which now has 17 charbroiled chicken restaurants north of the border (*see* 1980; Denny's, 1981). The U.S.

chain will grow in the next 10 years to have more than 200 outlets throughout California, Arizona, Nevada, and Texas, with overseas outlets in Japan, Guam, and the Philippines (*see* TW Services, 1987).

Pudgie's Chicken is founded at Bethpage, Long Island, by entrepreneur George Sanders, whose fresh (never frozen) skinless chicken attracts patrons who line up outside his take-out store each morning. He soon provides home delivery, will have two more stores by 1985, and by 1993 more than 100 franchisers will have opened Pudgie's Chicken stores in Connecticut, Massachusetts, New Jersey, Pennsylvania, Maryland, Ohio, North Carolina, Florida, and Texas as well as New York, where Long Island alone will have nearly 50 stores.

1984

Famine kills 300,000 Ethiopians as drought worsens in sub-Saharan Africa. Civil war and poor roads prevent aid from reaching the hungry, and 800,000 will die before foreign grain comes to the rescue next year.

U.S. economic growth rises at a rate of 6.8 percent, highest since 1951, while the Soviet economy, with grain harvests below target, grows by only 2.6 percent, lowest since World War II. U.S. consumer prices rise 3.9 percent, up only slightly from 1982 and 1983, and the inflation rate, 3.7 percent, is the lowest since 1967.

U.S. agriculture remains in distress as world markets shrink, partly because the dollar is so high. Costly federal farm programs come under fire.

International Harvester avoids bankruptcy by selling its farm equipment division to Tenneco. It confines itself to making trucks and will change its name in 1986 to Navistar.

Budweiser beer is introduced into Britain by Anheuser-Busch through a licensed brewing agreement with Grand Metropolitan Brewing; it will soon be the second-largest-selling premium packaged lager in the United Kingdom, with U.K. sales exceeding 1 million barrels by 1993.

Unilever acquires Shedd's Country Crock Spread.

Ralston Purina acquires Continental Baking in October, paying $475 million in cash to ITT, which has owned it since 1968. Continental's Wonder Bread is the the largest-selling brand in America (*see* 1995; Beech-Nut, 1989).

Ralston Purina (above) arranges to sell virtually all its soybean-processing operations to Cargill.

Kraft acquires Lender's Bagels, which has grown from a family business employing six to have a payroll of 600 (*see* 1927). Murray Lender does occasional commercials for Kraft while working with Marvin to serve fresh bagels to customers at H. Lender and Sons restaurants in suburban Connecticut.

Hershey Foods acquires Pillsbury's American Beauty Macaroni division, which has plants in Fresno, Denver, and Kansas City (*see* Skinner, 1979; Ronzoni, 1990).

Pernod Ricard Group acquires Orangina (*see* 1962). Pernod Ricard has owned the brand outside France since 1980 and launches it for the first time in Switzerland. It will be introduced in Britain in 1987, and dstribution of the natural soft drink will be expanded to Montreal, New York, Boston, Philadelphia, Washington, D.C., and San Francisco.

The U.S. Food and Drug Administration proposes February 14 to allow irradiation of fruits and vegetables with doses of up to 100,000 rads, to inhibit maturation, retard spoilage, and kill certain insects which infest produce. The controversial process has been known since the 1940s and subjected to years of testing by the U.S. Army but has not been considered economically viable despite widespread concern about pesticide residues on fruits and vegetables (it could replace use of pesticides after harvesting). Radiation-sterilized food has been used at British cancer centers for patients whose treatment has left them extremely vulnerable to infection, and food preserved by irradiation is sold in more than two dozen foreign countries. Opposition to irradiation in the United States has been based on worries about possible exposure of workers to radiation burns and about the resistance of botulinum bacteria to irradiation.

Nonfiction: *An Omelette and a Glass of Wine* (essays and articles) by Elizabeth David; *On Food and Cooking—The Science and Lore of the Kitchen* by California writer Harold McGee; *Square Meals* by U.S. writer Jane Stern (*née* Grossman), 37, and her husband, Michael (forward by M. F. K. Fisher).

Cookbooks: *Chef Paul Prudhomme's Louisiana Kitchen* by New Orleans Cajun chef Prudhomme, now 44, of K-Paul's Kitchen (*see* 1979; 1993); *Dishes from the Mediterranean* by Jane Grigson; *Foods of Italy* by Florentine-born chef-teacher Giuliano Bugialli, who in 1971 opened Italy's first cooking school with instruction in English (in the refectory of a convent at Florence); *Chez Panisse Pasta, Pizza and Calzone* by Alice Waters, Patricia Curtan, and Martine Labro; *Food for Friends* by U.S. food writer Barbara Kafka (*née* Poses), 52.

Average per capita U.S. candy consumption rises to 18.9 pounds, up from 17 pounds last year (*see* 1974, 1992).

Florida orders citrus growers in September not to harvest fruit even from fields certified by state agents to be free of citrus canker (*see* 1913). Florida has some 800,000 acres of commercial citrus groves, the bulk of its orange and grapefruit crop will not be ripe for picking until January, it can safely remain on the trees for months thereafter, but the highly contagious plant disease threatens the state's entire $2.5 billion citrus industry.

Nearly 20 percent of the $290 billion spent on retail foods by U.S. consumers goes for special "light" and "diet" foods. This does not include expenditures for cottage cheese, fruits, vegetables, skim milk, and other items purchased by weight-conscious Americans.

The Infant Formula Action Coalition announces January 29 that it is ending a 7-year boycott of Nestlé products pending an agreement to be ratified at Mexico City February 2 (*see* 1982).

Georgia state inspectors remove a brand of cornmeal from store shelves in February after finding that the five-pound bags contain more than 1,000 parts per billion of aflatoxin—50 times the level deemed safe for human consumption by the Food and Drug Administration (*see* 1977; 1988).

New York's 21-year-old Restaurant Nippon stages a fugu (blowfish) tasting despite federal Food and

Drug Administration rules against serving the fish for fear of tetrodotoxin, the potentially deadly poison found in the livers, entrails, and ovaries of the fish (*see* 1975). Nippon's proprietor, Nobuyoshi Kuraoka, will spend $100,000 in the next 4½ years in an effort to convince the FDA, the Japanese Ministry of Health and Welfare, and another Japanese agency that fugu shipped from Shimonoseki in Yamaguchi Prefecture can be consumed in New York without ill effects (*see* 1989).

Japan has a candy scare as extortionists announce that confectionery in retail outlets has been poisoned.

A Union Carbide pesticide plant operated entirely by Indians at Bhopal, India, leaks the lethal gas methyl isocyanate December 3, killing more than 2,000 outright and injuring 200,000. The death toll will rise to 3,500. India's Supreme Court in February 1989 will order Union Carbide to pay $470 million in damages.

Bottled Hidden Valley "ranch" dressings are introduced by a subsidiary of Clorox Co., which paid over $8 million to acquire Hidden Valley in October 1972. Alaskan plumbing contractor Kenneth "Steve" Henson used a family recipe to create the dressing in the 1950s, fed his crew with it, later opened a 95-acre guest ranch in the Santa Ynez Mountains overlooking Santa Barbara, Calif., built up a family-run mail-order business selling packaged seasonings for salad dressing, and in 1967 converted the ranch into a factory producing foil-packaged dressing mixes for sale in grocery stores.

Coca-Cola and Pepsi move in November to replace the remaining 50 percent sucrose in their soft drinks with high-fructose corn syrup (HFCS); by 1992, HFCS will be supplying bottlers with the equivalent of 8 million tons of sugar.

McDonald's chairman Ray Kroc dies at San Diego January 14 at age 81 (he suffered a stroke in December 1979 and soon afterwards entered an Orange, Calif., alcoholism treatment center). He has built up a family fortune of more than $500 million and his fast-food chain has grown to be the largest U.S. food-service organization, with 7,500 outlets in the United States and 31 other countries, three-quarters of them operated by franchisees (who have included a member of the House of Representatives from Virginia, a former under secretary of Labor, lawyers, dentists, advertising men, a chemist, and a golf professional); total systemwide sales last year were more than $8 billion (*see* 1985; Chicken McNuggets, 1980).

Au Bon Pain moves outside the Boston area for the first time and opens a shop in New York's Rockefeller Center (*see* 1983). Muffins and sandwiches will be added to the stores' menus in 1986, and in 1987 the company will begin repurchasing the handful of franchises that have been sold to operators in Washington, D.C., and Philadelphia (*see* 1991).

The Paris restaurant Le Grand Véfours loses one of its three Michelin stars following the retirement of chef Raymond Olivier (*see* 1948), but the Taittinger family, which owns the Hotel Crillon as well as making champagne, takes over the historic eating place and installs chef André Signoret, 33, of the Crillon's two-star kitchen. He will revive Le Grand Véfours's reputation.

The London restaurant Clarke's opens at 124 Kensington Church Street. English chef Sally Clarke, who has studied at the Cordon Bleu in Paris and worked at Michael's in Santa Monica, Calif., offers salads of thinly sliced beef filets with roasted bell peppers, Scottish scallops wrapped in prosciutto, broiled, house-made pastas, and desserts that include house-made ice creams, coffee granita and vanilla ice cream with lemon shortbread, house-made pastries, and chocolate truffles. Clarke will open a shop to carry breads, British cheeses, California wines, and other delicacies.

The New York restaurant Le Régence opens in April in the new Hotel Plaza Athénée at 37 East 64th Street, taking the name of its counterpart in Paris. Resident chef Jean-Robert de Cavel, who consults regularly with J.-O. Rostang (of La Bonne Auberge at Antibes) and his sons Michel and Philippe in Paris, has specialties that include *chartreuse de canard confit en demi-gelée, tomates acidulées; galette* of loosely bound lump crabmeat; lobster "ravioli"; lobster salad; sautéed lobster with asparagus and a sauce of pounded lobster roe; black sea bass with port wine applesauce; roasted squab in honey sauce with garlic flan; breast of duck with red berry sauce, duck foie gras, and artichokes in a hazelnut-oil dressing; raw tuna diced and served between thin wafers of pastry; lamb *carpaccio* with an olive purée; and rack of lamb chops with softened shallots in a timbale of black olive custard. Desserts, to be ordered at the start of the meal, include *imperiale au chocolat et à l'orange, sauce citron; crème brûlée; galette croustillante* (apple turnover with an apricot sauce); and lemon soufflé.

New York's Budapest Café opens in May at 1373 First Avenue (between 73rd and 74th streets). Owner Piroshka Savany is an architect who designed Le Cygne and remodeled the St. Regis Hotel's King Cole Bar. His Budapest-born chef Gábor Arbai features not only gulyás and paprikás but also dishes from all over Europe: cold cherry soup, cognac-spiked black bean soup, goose liver, calf's brains with scrambled eggs, galantine of pheasant with Cumberland sauce, smoked trout with creamed horseradish sauce, wiener schnitzel, *Rigó Jancsi, russwurm palacsinta* (chestnut purée–filled crêpe), and Hungarian chocolate torte.

New York's Manhattan Ocean Club opens at 57 West 58th Street. The New York Restaurant Group headed by Alan N. Stillman soon employs New Jersey–born chef Steve Mellina, who has studied at the Cordon Bleu in Paris and under Michel Guérard in the south of France. His specialties include fingerling trout appetizers, oysters on the half shell, stone crab claws in season, and seafood of all kinds. Dessert chef Kurt Kettmann, 27, is a onetime classical pianist who bakes fruit tarts to order and also prepares chocolate, white chocolate, and mocha mousses, pot au crème, raspberry mint bitter chocolate *crème brûlée*, flourless bitter chocolate macadamia-nut cake, orange coconut cake, Baum torte, and other sweets.

The New York restaurant Amsterdam's Bar & Rotisserie opens at 428 Amsterdam Avenue (between 80th and 81st streets) (a satellite will open under the same name late next year at 454 Broadway, near Grand Street; both will have white brick walls, bare wood floors, tables covered in gingham cloth, and gas-fired rotisseries). Executive chef Karen Fohrhaltz offers gravlaks made with Norwegian salmon, duck-liver mousse, roast pheasant salad with green beans, pork-filled wontons with gingered soy sauce, lentil soup, cream of butternut squash soup, shrimp, brook trout, salmon, rabbit, roast chicken, duck, pheasant, leg of lamb, loin of pork, shell steak, lingonberries, other fresh berries with mascarpone- or frangelica-laced custard sauce, shortcake with seasonal fruits, and a cheese and fruit plate.

New York's Petrossian opens in September at 182 West 58th Street (in the 75-year-old Alwyn Court apartment house). An offshoot of the Paris Petrossian, it features caviar (the sturgeon roes beluga, osetra, and sevruga plus salmon roe and smoked cod roe), Périgord goose and duck foie gras, champagne, and vodka by the glass or bottle. Lyons-born chef Michel Atlai prepares dishes that include fillet of red snapper with Dijon mustard sauce, poached salmon stuffed with a scallop mousse, and filet mignon with green peppercorns. The dessert cart's offerings include mocha cream cakes. Prix fixe luncheon is $27; dinner, $42, $59, and $98.

The New York restaurant Arcadia, opened in December at 21 East 62nd Street by Ken Aretsky and chef Anne Rosenzweig, 27, offers a variety of imaginative dishes, many of them only seasonally, that will establish Rosenzweig's reputation. Originally an anthropologist, she learned about food in Africa, returned to New York in 1980, and apprenticed to be a chef. Arcadia's menu features corn cakes with crème fraîche and American caviars, raw salmon marinated in minted lemon juice, grilled leeks in puff pastry with onion marmalade, warm figs with Gorgonzola and walnuts on greens, foie gras in lamb's lettuce, cheese fritters, grilled duck sausage with chestnuts and sautéed apple, pasta with sweet potatoes, roast quail with fiddlehead ferns, roast quail with Savoy cabbage and kasha (buckwheat groats), "chimney-smoked" lobster on saffron pasta, soft-shelled crabs with fried Vidalia onions, sautéed calf's liver with shallots, roast chicken with morels and zucchini-potato pancakes, fresh berries in a lemon-curd tart, chocolate bread pudding with brandied custard sauce, bittersweet chocolate mousse, and macadamia-nut tart with coconut whipped cream. The prix fixe dinner is $45 with surcharges for a few dishes (such as the "chimney-smoked" lobster), luncheon service is à la carte.

San Francisco's Square One restaurant opens at 190 Pacific Avenue, corner of Front Street. Proprietor Joyce Goldstein has run Chez Panisse in Berkeley (*see* 1971), she goes beyond that restaurant's emphasis on the cuisine of southern France and Italy, starts each day as if it were a new beginning (hence the name Square One), even changes the menu completely from lunch to dinner, and employs her son Evan, 23, as *sommelier* (*see* 1987).

The San Francisco restaurant Stars opens in July at 150 Redwood Lane. Chef Jeremiah Tower worked in the 1970s for Chez Panisse in Berkeley and developed its regional menus, helping to give it a reputation for innovation. (Tower also worked with Richard Olney in preparing the Good Cook series for Time-Life Books.) Featured dishes include potted smoked salmon and trout; New York-cut steak with black pepper and hot salsa; bacon-lettuce-and-tomato sandwiches made with toasted slices of Boudin sourdough spread with homemade mayonnaise and accompanied by greaseless homemade potato chips; steamed Manila clams; dungeness crabs and avocado salad; paillard of "spearfish" (Hawaiian wahoo); brioche filled with slices of lobster, poached garlic cloves, and marrow; smoked duck breast; poached cuts of red meat; Stilton cheese with green apples and walnuts; sweet chocolate cake with coffee crème anglaise; mocha torte; tarte Tatin; pumpkin pie with rum whipped cream; and soufflés.

The Los Angeles restaurant 385, opened at 385 North Cienega Boulevard by chef Roy Yamaguchi, 28, with financial support from 70 backers, can serve 200 to 300 patrons per evening with seafood *gyoza* (rice flour dumplings), New Zealand green-lip mussels, grilled salmon, swordfish, tuna steaks, grilled leg of duck, and desserts (by Cheryl Feeney) that include caramel hazelnut tart, chocolate tart, and lemon and orange cheesecake.

The Los Angeles restaurant Scalora, opened at 421 North Rodeo Drive in Beverly Hills by former Boston optometrist John Scalora, employs Italian chef Eugenio Martingnago, whose specialties include marinated anchovies; mussels on the half shell, pastas, *risotto peperone e lattuga*, lobster risotto, grilled swordfish; sautéed shrimp, veal dishes, *bresaola, carpaccio* (a beef dish originated by

Giuseppe Cipriani at Harry's Bar in Venice), game in season, *zuccotto* (layers of orange-glazed sponge-cake, chocolate mousse, and fruit-studded pastry cream); zabaglione, *ganache torte*, homemade ice cream; and strawberry mousse with kiwi and papaya sauces.

The Los Angeles restaurant Bistango, opened at 133 North La Cienega Boulevard, features braised veal shanks, calf's liver, calf's kidneys, Chinese chicken salad, seafood aspic, grilled fish, mussel soup, Norwegian salmon, salmi of roast squab (slices of breast meat with separate legs and thighs), noisettes of lamb, pizzas, ice cream sundaes, fruit and ice cream coupes, and orange sponge cake with coffee and chocolate filling and icing. Claude Segal, formerly of Ma Maison, is chef-proprietor.

The Grill opens at 9560 Dayton Way off Rodeo Drive, Beverly Hills, under the management of Robert Spivak, Richard Shapiro, and Michael Weinstock. It features traditional dishes, including homemade gravlaks, sourdough bread, corned beef hash, chicken potpie, short ribs, eastern calf's liver, New York steak with eggs and hashed brown potatoes (broiled over oak charcoal, not mesquite), John Dory, grilled shrimp in the shell, O'Brien potatoes, and Cobb salad.

1985

Mikhail Sergeevich Gorbachev, 54, becomes general secretary of the Soviet Communist Party after Konstantin Chernenko dies of emphysema March 11 at age 73. Moscow and Washington have reached a compromise agreement January 8 to resume negotiations toward limiting and reducing nuclear weapons and preventing an arms race in space. An agricultural specialist with no experience in foreign affairs, Gorbachev calls for sweeping economic changes in June, indirectly criticizing his predecessors.

 U.S. makers of superpremium ice cream—Häagen-Dazs, Ben & Jerry's, Steve's Homemade, Frusen Glädjé, and others—battle for market share. Pillsbury Co., makers of Häagen-Dazs ice cream, and Ben & Jerry's agree March 6 to stop coercing distributors not to carry the other company's superpremium ice cream (*see* 1983; Grand Metropolitan, 1988).

Consolidated Foods Corp. becomes Sara Lee Corp. in March by a vote of the stockholders (*see* 1956).

International Harvester is acquired by J. I. Case as sales of farm equipment plummet.

R. J. Reynolds acquires Nabisco Brands for $4.9 billion and becomes RJR Nabisco (*see* 1981). It sells off some of its properties to finance the deal (*see* Canada Dry, Kentucky Fried Chicken, below; Hawaiian Punch, 1989).

Britain's Cadbury Schweppes acquires Canada Dry beverages from RJR Nabisco (above) (*see* Duffy-Mott, 1982; A&W root beer, 1993).

Elders XIL Ltd. chief executive officer John D. Elliott, now 43, offers $2.3 billion in a bid to acquire Allied-Lyons plc, the British brewing, distilling, and food giant (*see* Allied, 1978; Elders, 1983). Elders has grown into a $4.5 billion conglomerate but is dwarfed by Allied, whose properties include Teacher's Scotch, Harvey's sherries, Tetley Tea, Baskin-Robbins ice cream, hundreds of J. Lyons & Co. restaurants, and some 7,000 British pubs (its beer division contributes 43 percent of its pretax profits) (*see* Hiram Walker, 1986).

Philip Morris acquires General Foods for $5.7 billion and becomes the largest U.S. consumer products company (*see* Kraft, 1988).

Nestlé, S.A., acquires Carnation Co., which introduces an instant breakfast with no added sugar (*see* 1964). Its name will be changed to Diet Instant Breakfast in 1991 (*see* Good Start infant formula, 1989).

God's Love We Deliver (GLWD), founded by philanthropists at New York, serves two meals per day to victims of AIDS (AutoImmune Deficiency Disease), which was first identified in homosexual men 4 years ago and will soon be found to affect heterosexuals, and needle-sharing drug addicts. GLWD will be serving 750 men, women, and children per day by 1994.

Nonfiction: *The Staffs of Life* by *New Yorker* magazine editor E. J. Kahn, Jr., 69; *All Manners of Foods: Eating and Taste in England and France from the Middle Ages to the Present* by English author Stephen Mennell; *Craig Claiborne's New York Times Food Encyclopedia* by former *Times* food editor Claiborne; *Are Salami and Eggs Better than Sex?* by Mimi Sheraton, now 59 (with comedian Alan King); *The Great American Food Almanac* and *American Bistro* by Irena Chalmers.

Cookbook author James Beard dies at New York January 23 at age 81 and is hailed as the father of American gastronomy (he has written thousands of

Julia Child and James Beard inspired cooks to new heights of gastronomic achievement. AP/WIDE WORLD PHOTOS

syndicated newspaper columns and numerous magazine articles as well as cookbooks, and he hosted one of the first television cooking shows). At Julia Child's suggestion, his Greenwich Village home at 167 West 12th Street is turned into the home of the Beard Foundation and made the site of cooking classes and almost nightly events related to food and its preparation.

Cookbooks: *The Observer Guide to British Cookery* by Jane Grigson; *One Is Fun!* by Delia Smith, containing recipes for single persons, will be translated into German, Italian, and Swedish and by 1994 will have sold more than 500,000 copies; *A New Book of Middle Eastern Food* by Claudia Roden (*see* 1968); *Cooking with the New American Chefs* and *The Great Chefs of Chicago* by former *USA Today* food editor Ellen Brown; *Barbecued Ribs and Other Great Feeds* by Jeanne Voltz; *Transylvanian Cuisine* by Paul Kovi, co-owner of New York's Four Seasons restaurant.

A farm bill signed by President Reagan December 23 provides for subsidy payments estimated to cost $52 billion over 3 years but favors large producers as smaller growers continue to go under.

The Food and Drug Administration grants GRAS (generally recognized as safe) status in January to rapeseed products, including seed, oil, and meal, that contain low enough levels of crucic acid and glucosinolates (both potential health risks to humans). Japan's most widely used cooking oil, rapeseed oil (it is quickly renamed canola oil) has the lowest saturated-fat content of any major vegetable oil— 6 percent as compared to 9 percent for safflower oil, 11 percent for sunflower oil, 13 percent for corn oil, 14 percent for olive oil, 15 percent for soybean oil (which now accounts for close to 70 percent of U.S. oilseed production), 18 percent for peanut oil, 27 percent for cottonseed oil, and 51 percent for palm oil. It comes from the seed of a member of the mustard family, grown widely in Canada, Japan, and elsewhere, and can be used in salad oil, margarine, and baked goods as well as for frying. U.S. production of canola oilseeds will climb from 27 million pounds in 1987 to nearly 420 million in 1994, and imports (80 percent from Canada) will increase from 2 million pounds to more than 990 million as demand increases for products low in saturated fat.

General Mills introduces Chicken Helper (*see* Hamburger Helper, 1970). It will soon have a line of pasta- or rice-based products that include Tuna Helper Pot Pie (with top and bottom crusts and a cream sauce containing peas and carrots), Sloppy Joe Bake Dinner (with a crust mix flavored to taste like a hamburger bun), Hamburger Helper Pizzabake dinner, Hamburger Helper Rice Oriental Dinner mix, Hamburger Helper Tacobake dinner, Tuna Helper Tetrazzini, Hamburger Helper Creamy Mushroom with Noodles, and Hamburger Helper Cheeseburger Macaroni.

Kraft Foods ceases production of Liederkranz cheese (*see* 1892).

Nestlé introduces Alpine White, a white chocolate bar that will soon be second only to Crunch in the Nestlé candy product line.

Average Italian per capita wine consumption falls to 82 liters (109 bottles), down from 110 liters (147 bottles) in 1972 (*see* consumer protection, 1968).

Coca-Cola announces in April that it is replacing its famous 99-year-old formula with a sweeter Coca-Cola designed for younger tastes. Protests from long-

Coke Classic was the same Coca-Cola formulated in 1886. Consumers resisted any change.

time Coke drinkers force the company to reintroduce its traditional beverage under the name Classic.

Pillsbury's restaurant chain Bennigan's hires New Orleans chef Paul Prudhomme to add 8 new Cajun items to its 74-item menu.

Marriott Corp. acquires the Howard Johnson's restaurant and motel chain from its British owners (*see* 1979). It will resell most of the motels to Prime Motor Inns, keeping only some 400 company-owned Howard Johnson's restaurants (many of which it will convert into Bob's Big Boy restaurants) (*see* 1986).

The average U.S. woman aged 19 to 50 gets 38 percent more of her calories at cafeterias, 60 percent more at full-service restaurants, and 120 percent more at fast-food outlets than in 1978.

PepsiCo acquires Kentucky Fried Chicken from RJR Nabisco (above) for $850 million and becomes the largest U.S. restaurant concern (*see* Pizza Hut, 1977; Taco Bell, 1978).

The average McDonald's fast-food store generates sales of $1.3 million as compared with less than $1.1 million for Burger King, $848,000 for Wendy's.

Boston Chicken has its beginnings in a Newton, Mass., fast-food restaurant featuring rotisserie-cooked chicken (*see* 1991).

Dunkin' Donuts opens its first Indonesian shop in July (*see* Philippines, Thailand, 1981). It will have 54 outlets in Indonesia by 1994, with outlets in Bandung, Jakarta, and Surabaya (*see* Allied-Lyons, 1989).

The San Francisco restaurant Annabel's opens at the Orchard Hotel, 566 Sutter Street. Nobela Wisniewksi, whose husband manages the hotel, is manager and general partner works with chef Daniel Durand to offer patrons traditional French dishes that include artichoke velouté soup, sautéed Dover sole with grapes, Irish salmon smoked over applewood, Malaysian prawns; fish terrine; salmon, John Dory, mullard, leg of lamb, Sonoma loin of lamb, *entrecôte*, Petaluma chicken, breast of chicken with sauce *aigre-douce*, homemade sausage, cheesecake with strawberries, raspberry tart with peach ice cream, chocolate tart with mint leaves, and lemon sorbet with mint leaves. An outside supplier bakes walnut rye bread and a dense white loaf with rosemary, both to the restaurant's specifications.

The West Los Angeles restaurant Primi opens at 10543 West Pico Boulevard in premises formerly occupied by Mangia. Piero Selvagio, proprietor of Valentino, has started the place, whose menu consists entirely of antipasti, pastas, and desserts. He has gathered promising young chefs from restaurants in and about Bologna and Milan to work at Primi.

The North Miami, Fla., restaurant Max's Place opens at 2286 Northeast 123rd Street. Chef-owner Mark Militello serves grilled mozzarella wrapped in prosciutto; Caesar salad with Portobello mushrooms; pancakes of shredded salsify; a stew of Florida conch with avocado and lime; a salad of lamb slices with eggplant marmalade; black grouper sautéed with orange segments, mint, and pecans; crusted fillet of Norwegian salmon; shrimp fresh from the Keys; farmed calico scallops; crabmeat; Everglades frogs' legs from frogs caught by Seminole tribespeople; Icky Sticky Coconut Pudding with Rum Toffee Sauce; and Junky Monkey Ice Cream (the ice creams are made in house and may be ordered with guavalike *jaboticaba*, French mulberries, passion fruit, *wampee*, strawberry fruit [Jamaica cherry], or other exotic tropical fruit).

Baltimore's Conservatory restaurant opens atop the city's Peabody Court Hotel at 612 Cathedral Street. Specialties include warm lobster salad in a truffled vinaigrette sauce, timbale of Norwegian salmon garnished with crème fraîche, *millefeuilles* of wild mushrooms in a chambertin sauce, new potatoes stuffed with escargots in a garlicky hazelnut butter, roast veal in tarragon gravy, medallions of beef tenderloin with chorn and truffles, roast breast of wild pheasant stuffed with chanterelles, *rouget* wrapped in potatoes served with a carrot flan, *salmon roulade* with spinach and shallots in a light curry sauce, triple chocolate mousse (semisweet, milk, and white chocolate), soufflés, savarin with raspberries and crème Chantilly, raspberry tart, and almond *succès*.

The New York restaurant Montrachet opens at 239 West Broadway, between White and Water Streets in TriBeCa. Proprietor Drew Nieporent's Connecticut-born, French-trained chef, David Bouley, 33, will be succeeded next year by another man and then by Debra Ponzek, who will remain until 1994, building a reputation for spiced and seared sashimi-grade tuna; grilled quail salad; cured salmon with quinoa; arugula salad; endive salad with pears, walnuts, and Roquefort; ballotine of sea scallops; hot foie gras; truffle-crusted salmon; roast chicken with potato purée; duck with salsify and sweet-potato flan; roast squab; loin of veal; crème brûlée; and caramelized figs with fromage blanc ice cream (*see* Bouley, 1987).

New York's Union Square Café opens at 21 East 16th Street. Proprietor Danny Meyer, 27, has engaged chef Ali Barker, who prepares Italian, French, and American dishes. Barker will be succeeded late in 1988 by Michael Romano, and the restaurant will succeed by offering good food at affordable prices.

Chicago's Everest Room opens in November at 440 South La Salle Street. Chef-proprietor Jean Joho, who studied with Paul Haeberlin and was chef at the Auberge de Lille in Alsace, has specialties that include galantine of salmon and cabbage, roast squab with cabbage and truffles, and—his signature dish—Maine lobster prepared with the Alsatian wine Gewürztraminer and ginger.

1986

✗ Sugar heiress Corazón C. Aquino, 53, assumes the presidency of the Philippines February 26 after winning election amid charges of ballot tampering by Ferdinand Marcos.

President Reagan defends his administration's budget priorities May 21, telling reporters that America's hungry are not suffering because assistance is unavailable but only from lack of knowledge of where and how to get help, but the Physicians' Task Force on Hunger in America and other private groups dispute claims that hunger in America has largely been eradicated, citing problems of the "new poor"—the unemployed, underemployed, and homeless who are forced to depend on government aid or private charity.

Hands Across America brings out an estimated 6 million Americans May 25 to hold hands and sing across 4,150 miles of road in support of the hungry and homeless. Even Tennessee farmers who have fallen on hard times participate in the event, which has been organized by promoter Kenneth Allan Kragin, 49, and clears an estimated $15 million for distribution to private groups such as the Aid to Africa Program.

$ More than 60,000 U.S. farms are sold or foreclosed as depression continues in the rural West and Midwest. At least 100,000 jobs on farms and in industries closely allied to agriculture have been lost since 1979. Foreign grain exporters undersell U.S. exporters despite the falling dollar, and the $14.21 billion U.S. trade deficit in May includes the first agricultural deficit in 20 years.

Prices of poultry, eggs, and many vegetables and fruits climb in late July throughout much of the United States as drought in the southern states reduces crop yields.

U.S. sales of farm tractors bottom out at 47,000 units, down from a peak of 157,000 in 1973 when grain prices were high, and combine sales fall to below 10,000, down from 30,000 per year in the 1970s.

🤝 Ralston Purina sells its Purina Mills for an estimated $500 million to BBP Nutrition Ltd., a food-and-agriculture subsidiary of British Petroleum, but retains its international feed business. Purina Mills has had annual sales of close to $1 billion.

The New York investment bankers Kohlberg Kravis Roberts (KKR) take Beatrice Foods private in a $6.2 billion leveraged buyout. KKR will spend the next few years selling off parts of the giant food conglomerate (*see* ConAgra, 1990).

Borden Co. acquires Beatrice Dairy Products from KKR (above), renames it Meadow Gold Dairy Products, extends its distribution of such products to 38 states containing more than half the nation's population, and further widens its lead as the largest U.S. dairy company by acquiring Midwest Farms from Southland Corp. Borden makes 13 other acquisitions at a total cost of $556 million.

RJR Nabisco sells its Del Monte frozen food brands (Chun King, Morton, and others) to ConAgra (*see* 1985; Montfort, 1987).

Nestlé's Carnation Co. acquires Libby's pumpkin and canned meat products.

Hiram Walker–Gooderham & Worts, the liquor division of Hiram Walker Resources, Ltd., agrees in March to accept a $2.6 billion buyout offer from the $6.6 billion British brewing, distilling, and food giant Allied-Lyons. Algerian-born Canadian real estate moguls Paul and Albert Reichmann acquire

Hiram Walker Resources in late April for $3.3 billion and then attempt to block the previously arranged sale of its liquor division. Allied's director Sir Derrick Holden-Brown, who began his business career as a trainee in Hiram Walker's London office, has arranged to buy Hiram Walker as part of an effort to fight off a $3.7 billion takeover bid by Melbourne's Elders XIL Ltd., which will acquire Courage Brewing Co. (see 1983). Britain's second-largest brewer and the world's fourth-largest (but second-most-profitable) distiller, Allied files a $5 billion lawsuit against the Reichmanns. The Ontario Supreme Court rules unanimously that the previously arranged sale to Allied-Lyons is valid. Allied-Lyons and the Reichmanns come to an agreement in September that gives Allied a 51 percent share of the Hiram Walker distillery for $831 million, leaving the Reichmanns with 49 percent but giving Allied the right to market not only Hiram Walker brands such as Canadian Club (see 1891) but also Ballantine's Scotch (see 1827) and Courvoisier cognac.

Dean Foods pays $167 million in stock to acquire Larsen Co. of Green Bay, Wis., which created the canned mixed-vegetable category in the 1920s, adding canned and frozen vegetables to its dairy business (see MacArthur Dairy, 1980). It will soon be the second-largest U.S. dairy processor and will also be supplying its private-label customers with aseptic-pack sauces, pickles, and canned and frozen beets, carrots, corn, green beans, lima beans, peas, potatoes, spinach, and mixed vegetables from Larsen's eight Wisconsin plants (see Shaw, 1988).

Pet Inc. acquires Progresso Quality Foods from Ogden Corp., which hereafter will concentrate on catering to airlines, managing sports stadia, and other activities (see 1979; Hain, 1983). Pet, which last year sold off its fresh dairy products division, also acquires Las Palmas Mexican Foods and, in Canada, Primo Foods Ltd. Pet will be a major player in the ethnic foods market.

I. Rokeach & Sons of Newark, N.J., is acquired by Malibu Israel Co., an Israeli concern that will continue the Rokeach and Mother's brands in the U.S. ethnic foods market (see Mother's 1979). Rokeach has a 65 percent share of the U.S. gefilte fish market.

Jacobs Suchard acquires the Monheim Group, which owns C. J. van Houten & Zoon (see 1971) and General Chocolate (see 1978; E. J. Brach, 1987).

Hershey Foods pays $100 million in October to acquire the confectionery operations of Dietrich Corp., maker of Luden's cough drops, Mellomints peppermint patties, and Fifth Avenue candy bars.

International Dairy Queen acquires Karmelcorn Shoppes and makes them part of its franchise system (see Dairy Queen, 1972; Karmelcorn, 1929; Orange Julius, 1987).

The U.S. Department of Agriculture approves release of the first genetically altered virus and the first outdoor test of genetically altered plants. The virus is used to fight a form of swine herpes; the plants are high-yield tobacco plants.

Nonfiction: *Much Depends on Dinner: The Extraordinary History and Mythology, Allure and Obsessions, Perils and Taboos of an Ordinary Meal* by South African–born Canadian college professor and radio personality Margaret Visser (*née* Barclay-Lloyd), 46; *Perfection Salad: Women and Cooking at the Turn of the Century* by U.S. author Laura Shapiro; *Mimi Sheraton's Favorite New York Restaurants*; *Road Food and Good Food* by Jane and Michael Stern.

Cookbooks: *The Arcadia Seasonal Mural and Cookbook* by New York's Arcadia restaurant chef/co-owner Anne Rosenzweig (mural by Paul Davis); *New American Classics* by California restaurant chef Jeremiah Tower of Chez Panisse, who writes, "Not wanting to be a slave over a kitchen stove is nothing new. Just because one's grandmother or grandmother's cook started baking pies at five in the morning does not mean she enjoyed it"; *The Wolfgang Puck Cookbook* contains recipes from Spago, Au Chinois, and other restaurants; *Marcella's Italian Kitchen* by Marcella Hazan; *Jane and Michael Stern's Coast-to-Coast Cookbook* contains chapters with titles such as "Street Food," "Bar Food," "Eat in the Rough," and "Three Kinds of Diners"; *The New Laurel's Kitchen* by U.S. authors Laurel Robertson, Carol Flinders, and Brian Ruppenthal: "Long before institutionalized religions came along—and temples, and churches—there was an unquestioned recognition that what goes on in the kitchen is *holy*. Cooking involves an enormously rich coming-together of the fruits of the earth with the inventive genius of the human being. So many mysterious transformations are involved . . . . In times past there was no question but that higher powers were at work in such goings-on, and a feeling of reverence sprang up in response."

 Film: Juzo Itami's *Tampopo* with Ken Watanabe as a truck driver who helps widow Nobuko Miyamoto turn her noodle shop into a successful business.

The Chernobyl nuclear power plant near Kiev explodes April 26, sending clouds of radioactive fallout across much of Europe, contaminating field crops and milk, and leaving vast tracts of land in the Ukraine uninhabitable and unarable, a condition that is expected to continue for thousands of years.

Soviet engineers have drained the Aral Sea—the world's fourth-largest freshwater lake—to create more farmland, millions of rubles have been wasted on ill-conceived and irresponsible irrigation schemes, and more rubles have been poured into fertilizers and pesticides in an effort to increase output under a collective system that has proved to be notoriously unproductive (*see* 1983).

The People's Republic of China grows 65.5 million metric tons of corn, second only to the 210 million produced by U.S. farmers (*see* 1967; 1993).

Congress appropriates $18.3 billion for federal nutrition programs in the fiscal year despite continuing Reagan administration efforts to reduce the figure (*see* 1981).

A nutritional survey of U.S. food shoppers indicates that concern about chemical additives among those questioned has declined since 1980 from 27 percent to 16 percent and concern about preservatives from 22 percent to 15 percent. The number of people looking for "natural" foods and therefore avoiding processed foods has dropped from 12 percent to 3 percent, but the number concerned about avoiding fats (17 percent) and calories (11 percent) has almost doubled and the number wishing to avoid dietary cholesterol has risen from 5 percent to 13 percent.

Pop Secret Microwave Popcorn, introduced by General Mills in January, comes in natural or butter flavor, requires no refrigeration, and can be

"Microwavable" became the hot button for new products as ownership of microwave ovens soared.

popped in less than 5 minutes in a microwave oven. U.S. consumption of popcorn has reached nearly 11 billion quarts—46 per capita—and Pop Secret will soon be second only to Orville Redenbacher in the $240 million microwave popcorn market. Pop Secret Light in both flavors, with 50 percent less fat than the original, will be introduced in 1990 (*see* 1993).

Campbell Soup Co. replaces the aluminum trays in its Swanson frozen dinners with plastic trays that permit the products to be microwaved.

Campbell Soup Co. (above) introduces Swanson Great Starts breakfast sandwiches (*see* 1982).

Yoplait USA introduces YoCreme Yogurt, made with real cream for a mousselike texture (*see* 1982). Sold in six-ounce pedestal cups in five flavors (amaretto almond, cherries jubilee, chocolate bavarian, raspberries with cream, and strawberries Romanoff), it gains national distribution by September (*see* 1987).

McDonald's and Burger King stop frying most foods in beef fat and release ingredient information for the first time, partly in response to pressure from the 15-year-old Center for Science in the Public Interest (*see* Hardee's, 1988). McDonald's introduces fresh salads in its outlets and will reduce the fat content its Big Mac sauce, adopt a policy of using only 100 percent vegetable oil in frying, serve 1 percent low-fat milk, make all its milk shakes and frozen yogurt desserts from 1 percent milk, and serve cholesterol-free blueberry and apple-bran muffins (*see* McLean Deluxe, 1991).

Burger King opens a record 546 new outlets world-wide, giving it a total of 4,743 restaurants in operation, including 402 offshore restaurants in 25 countries (*see* 1967; 1988). Like McDonald's (above), the chain will respond to public pressure by offering low-calorie, low-fat meals, but, like McDonald's, many of its menu items will be high in sodium.

Franchise Associates is incorporated by former Howard Johnson's franchisees, many of whom obtained their franchises from the late Johnson himself (*see* 1985). They have been distressed about being sold from one conglomerate to another, former Attorney General Griffin Bell has taken their case, Marriott Corp. and Prime Motor Inns have each put up $500,000 to enable them to incorporate, 54 licensees will buy stock in the new company next year, and by 1989 there will be 137 individually owned Howard Johnson's restaurants in 26 states, each serving fried clams and at least 18 flavors of ice cream if not 28.

The New York restaurant Le Bernardin opens in the new Equitable Life Building at 155 West 51st Street with Parisian chef Gilbert Le Coze, now 41, preparing seafood dishes—sea urchins with truffle juice, black bass spiced with coriander and basil and covered with extra-virgin olive oil, sea scallops served in their shells—that quickly gain accolades (*see* 1972). Le Coze and his sister Maguy will go on to open the Brasserie Le Coze in Miami's Coconut Grove section and also in Atlanta, leaving the New York kitchen increasingly in the hands of chef Eric Ripert (*see* 1994).

The Lyons restaurant Le Vivarais opens under the direction of Robert Duffaut, 36, serving shellfish consommé, Bresse chicken, and Charolais beef. Duffaut has worked for 6 years for René Chapelle outside Lyons and managed Chapelle's restaurants at Oslo and Kobe.

1987

💲 Soviet Party Secretary Mikhail Gorbachev demands reforms January 27 and on June 25 announces plans for a new direction in economic policy. Moscow's vast central planning system is braking the economy rather than stimulating it, he says.

Rowntree Mackintosh Ltd. changes its name to Rowntree plc (*see* 1969). It has acquired some French, Dutch, Australian, and Canadian companies and is now the world's fourth-largest manufacturer of confectionery and candy, with sales exceeded only by those of Mars, Inc., Hershey Chocolate Co., and Cadbury's (*see* Nestlé, 1988).

Chicago nut merchant Jasper Sanfilippo, now 56, builds a 200,000-square-foot plant at Bainbridge, Ga., to shell, roast, and jar peanuts (*see* 1974). He will soon open a California walnut-shelling plant and a Texas almond-processing plant, achieving vertical integration that brings his costs below those of his competitors and will make his private-label business second only to RJR Nabisco's Planters Life Savers Co., with annual sales in excess of $200 million by 1993.

🤝 Monfort of Colorado is merged into ConAgra, which becomes the third-largest U.S. meat packer (Iowa Beef Processors is first, Excel Corp. second). Monfort (*see* 1968) is the nation's largest lamb processor and fourth-largest beef processor, handling 500,000 to 1 million lambs per year and about 2.5 million head of cattle (its two Colorado feedlots feed 180,000 steers per year, and it is building a third lot which will feed an additional 100,000) (*see* Beatrice, 1990).

Borden Co. acquires Prince Co. of Lowell, Mass., now the top pasta and sauce company in New England (*see* 1912), and broadens its pasta business worldwide by acquiring Brazil's Paty, S.A., and Italy's Albadoro S.p.A. (*see* 1988).

Quaker Oats pays $275 million to acquire Golden Grain, producers of Rice-A-Roni and other foods (*see* 1958).

Borden (above) also acquires Laura Scudder's, the second-largest snack producer in California (*see* Wise, 1964).

Kraft Foods acquires Anderson, Clayton Co., makers of Chiffon Margarine and Seven Seas Salad Dressings (*see* 1964; Kraft General Foods, 1988).

Unilever acquires Durkee Industrial Foods and Pennant Frozen Foods.

Cadbury Schweppes acquires Red Cheek Co. in December from Berks-Lehigh Cooperative Fruit Growers and will broaden distribution of Red Cheek Apple Juice (*see* 1940).

Seagram Co. acquires Martell Cognac, owned since its founding in 1715 by the family of Charles Martel.

Jacobs Suchard acquires control of E. J. Brach Candies of Chicago and Belgium's leading chocolate maker Côte d'Or, defeating Nestlé in a takeover battle.

Leaf, Inc., acquires Chuckles and Pine Bros. plus nearly half of L. S. Heath and Sons (it will acquire the rest in 1989 plus Hollywood Brands, both from Sara Lee Corp.).

U.S. microwave oven sales reach a record 12.6 million (*see* 1967). Sears, Roebuck's Kenmore is the largest-selling brand, followed by Sharp and General Electric. Food companies rush to develop microwavable food products (*see* 1988).

The noncaloric fat substitute Olestra is submitted by Procter & Gamble for approval by the Food and Drug Administration, which will study the product for at least 7 years. A large, sucrose-polyester-based molecule with fatty-acid chains forming ester bonds with the sugar's hydroxyl groups, it is intended as a partial replacement for the fats in cooking oils, deep-fried foods, shortening, and snack foods. P&G scientists discovered SPE while searching for an easily digestible fat for premature infants, but instead of being easily digestible it resists hydrolysis by pancreatic lipases and, at least theoretically, passes through the gut without being absorbed (*see* nutrition, below; Simplesse, 1988).

Gene-altered bacteria to aid agriculture are tested April 24 despite alarms by some that scientists have unloosed a monster.

Nonfiction: *Histoire naturelle & morale de la nourriture* (*A History of Food*) by Maguellone Toussaint-Samat, whose introduction concludes, "One part of the globe does not know what to do with its excess produce, but prices rise in proportion to surplus stocks, since so much has to be paid to a second part of the globe for the energy required to produce it. As for the remaining part of the globe, the Third World countries with neither abundant harvests

nor oil, there is no saying yet whether its people will die of famine caused by drought or because of bad luck or through sheer incompetence. They urgently need help. It would be sad if the history of food were to end with the word FAMINE"; *Diet for a New America* by U.S. author John Robbins, who echoes Frances Moore Lappé's 1971 book with up-to-date statistics on the waste of grain and the devastation of land, water, and human resources resulting from large-scale cattle operations.

Cookbooks: *Mediterranean Cookery* by BBC television personality Claudia Roden; *The Cooking of Normandy* by Jane Grigson; *Microwave Gourmet* by Barbara Kafka; *The Community Supper Cookbook* by Jeanne Voltz.

Film: Gabriel Axel's *Babette's Feast* with Stéphane Audran as a refugee Parisian chef who inherits some money and uses it to import delicacies from Paris to a small Danish village, where she prepares a dinner that includes turtle soup with Amontillado sherry, blinis demidoff, champagne (Veuve Clicquot, vintage 1860), calilles en sarcophage, white wine (Clos de Vougeot, vintage 1845, from Chez Philippe in the Rue Montorgeuil), salads, cheese, baba au rhum, fresh fruit that includes figs, grapes, and pineapple, coffee, and cognac (Vic Ax Marc fins Champagne).

Brazilian landowners burn 80,000 square miles of Amazon rain forest in 79 days (July 15 through October 2), heightening environmentalists' fears that loss of oxygen from the forest will create a "greenhouse effect," increasing global temperatures and raising sea levels. Tax incentives encourage turning jungle into ranch land (*see* 1989).

The Laguna Madre Shrimp Farm on the inner coast of South Padre Island between Brownsville and Corpus Christi, Tex., produces nearly 400,000 pounds of shrimp, up from 200,000 pounds last year; commercial shrimp trawlers bring in close to 250 million pounds, but rising consumer demand is depleting supplies of wild shrimps.

The Procter & Gamble fat substitute Olestra (above) not only resists absorption but evidently interferes with the absorption of other lipids, including cholesterol and some fat-soluble vitamins, especially vitamin E. To prevent possible vitamin E deficiencies, the Olestra formula is bonded to vitamin E in large enough quantities to compensate for any interference with its absorption.

A study published in the February 28 issue of the *British Medical Journal* confirms earlier studies suggesting that while bacteria can convert nitrates to nitrites, and while intestinal flora can convert dietary nitrites into nitrosamines, groups of people in Canada, England, Japan, and Louisiana with high rates of stomach cancer have not had higher exposure to nitrates than groups with lower rates of the disease have. Epidemiologists explain that the major sources of nitrates are fruits and vegetables, which also contain vitamin C, and vitamin C effectively inhibits formation of nitrosamines. But in parts of the world where food preservation is inadequate, or where intake of preserved fish (*see* 1983), certain types of soy sauce, or fava beans is high, exposure to nitrosamines may indeed play a role in causing cancer.

The U.S. Food and Drug Administration bans most uses of sulfites in fresh foods after a 5-year campaign by the Center for Science in the Public Interest.

Kellogg introduces Just Right, a premium-priced breakfast food containing raisins, nuts, and dates (*see* Healthy Choice, 1994).

Yoplait USA reformulates its Original Style yogurt in February to give it more viscosity and promotes it as being "Now Thicker & Creamier" (*see* 1986). The General Mills subsidiary also introduces Yoplait 150, a nonfat yogurt containing 150 calories per six-ounce serving; available nationwide by August, it comes in blueberry, cherry, peach, raspberry, strawberry, and strawberry-banana, each with its fruit at the bottom of the cup. By the early 1990s, Yoplait will be second only to Dannon in U.S. yogurt sales.

Campbell Soup Co. introduces Campbell's Special Request soups containing one-third less salt than soups in its regular line to meet the needs of people on low-sodium diets. It also introduces Campbell's Cup dry soups.

Campbell Soup Co. (above) expands its 6-year-old Prego Spaghetti Sauce line with "chunky" varieties that include mushroom and tomato, tomato and onion, mushroom and onion, mushroom and green pepper, and sausage and green pepper. Prego onion & garlic spaghetti sauce will be added in 1990 (*see* 1991).

Ethel M Chocolates are introduced in March at Las Vegas, Nev., by Forrest Mars, now 82, who names his new company after his mother—the woman his father, Frank, left to marry another woman named Ethel (*see* 1973). Forrest has said that he did not want to die with M&M's as his only monument, so he has recruited two trusted colleagues, men who have been with him for more than a quarter century, and gone back into business, this time to make boxed chocolates, especially liquor- and liqueur-filled chocolates. Only one state—Kentucky—has permitted the manufacture of candy containing alcohol, although eleven, including Massachusetts, permit the *sale* of such candy. Pennsylvania legislators last year rejected a measure permitting the manufacture and sale of chocolates with up to 6 percent alcohol by volume, Hershey Chocolate having opposed the measure on the grounds that liquor-laced chocolates were inconsistent with values emphasized by the religious and medical communities, but Mars has successfully petitioned the Nevada legislature to enact a law permitting the manufacture and sale of confections containing up to 4 percent alcohol—far less than the percentage found in some European bonbons but enough to make Ethel M chocolates—spiked with crème de menthe, brandy, scotch, and bourbon—ineligible for sale across state lines. (The creamy chocolates are also available without a hint of alcohol.) Mars prices his chocolates at a relatively modest $10 per pound, targets the 20 million tourists who visit Nevada every year, and soon has Ethel M Chocolates on sale at 15 hotels in Las Vegas, Reno, and Lake Tahoe and at the Las Vegas Airport.

Snapple ready-to-drink bottled iced tea is introduced by the 15-year-old Snapple Beverage Co., which virtually creates a new category of soft drink that will grow in 6 years to have 14 Snapple tea flavors, including lemon, mint, orange, peach, raspberry (and four diet varieties)—and some high-powered competitors (*see* 1992; Lipton, 1958).

TW Services, Inc. acquires Denny's Restaurants and its chain of El Pollo Loco charcoal-broiled chicken outlets (*see* 1983). TW Services, which acquired Quincy's Family Steakhouses in 1979, will be headed beginning in 1989 by Jerry Richardson, whose Spartan Food Systems is the largest Hardee's franchisee (*see* 1961), it will become Flagstar Companies in June 1993, and by 1994 there will be more than 1,500 company-owned or franchised Denny's Restaurants in the United States and seven foreign countries.

International Dairy Queen acquires Orange Julius and makes it part of its franchise system (*see* 1962; Karmelkorn, 1986). By 1993, there will be more than 700 Orange Julius stands in the United States, Canada, Hong Kong, the Philippines, Singapore, and Puerto Rico serving not only the orange drink but also a variety of other blended fruit-flavored drinks, hot dogs, hamburgers, and nachos. Dairy Queen itself will have 4,860 U.S. outlets (803 in Texas alone), plus 611 in foreign countries.

Brooklyn-born entrepreneur Howard Schultz, 33, buys Starbucks—originally a Seattle coffee bean business—and starts building an empire of coffee bars to supplement the Starbucks wholesale and mail-order operations. He will have 470 coffee bars by late 1994, with 8,000 employees and annual sales of nearly $300 million.

Paris real estate developer Dominique Boullion visits New York on business and reads in the *New York Times* that a Japanese group has offered to buy the French restaurant La Pyramide, founded by the late Fernand Point, who died in 1955 and whose widow died last year. Boullion submits a higher bid, looks for a chef, and in 1989 will engage Patrick Henri Roux, who has learned his craft all over France and will quickly attract a wide local following as he wins a second star in the *Guide Michelin*, serving monkfish smoked over Canadian maplewood with a curry marinade, St. Pierre (John Dory) stuffed with wild mushrooms and served with a parsley sauce, and other specialties.

London's River Café opens on Thames Wharf between the Putney and Hammersmith bridges. Chef-restaurateurs Ruth Elias Rogers (whose Italian husband, Richard, has been the architect for the Pompidou Center at Paris and London's Lloyds Building) and Rose Gray are licensed at first only to serve lunch but will soon be doing dinner as well,

offering country-style Italian dishes that include *pappa al pomodoro*; good Tuscan bread; *minestradi di spinace*; *torta verde*; grilled wild salmon; grilled scallops with *bruscetta*; pan-roasted quail with mushrooms and polenta; calves' liver with polenta, green beans, and *pancetta*; charcoal-grilled corn-fed chicken with sage and garlic, served with fava beans; *bollito misto* (boiled beef, chicken, tongue, and cotaccino sausage with salsa verde); Italian peaches with zabaglione ice cream; and bittersweet chocolate-truffled tart.

The San Francisco–area restaurant Butler's opens on Redwood Highway between the Golden Gate Bridge and San Rafael. Its proprietors have closed their 15-year-old Charles Bistro, joined forces with restaurateur Perry Butler, and hired chef Heidi Insalata Krahling, whose specialties include shell and rib-eye steaks from beef raised on the Niman-Schell Ranch at Bolinas in the Point Reyes National Seashore, lamb curry, Mexican dishes, and chicken breast with corn-studded pancakes. Pastry chef Linda Preciado prepares raspberry tart in a chocolate-lime shell with almonds, peach and berry cobbler, marble cake, and cinnamon and clove ice cream.

San Francisco *sommelier* Evan Goldstein of Square One takes the examination given in England for prospective master *sommeliers* and at age 26 becomes the youngest person ever to pass, identifying the grape, country of origin, producer, and vintage of various wines in blind taste tests. There are only 11 master *sommeliers* in the United States, 4 of them in the Bay Area.

The Boston restaurant Hamersley's Bistro opens July 7 at 578 Tremont Street (it will move to larger space at 553 Tremont), offering "country food" based on Provençal cuisine. Chef Gordon Hamersley, 36, who has a bachelor's degree in English literature from Boston University, apprenticed in Europe, worked under Wolfgang Puck at Ma Maison in Los Angeles, and, most recently, has been sous-chef for Lydia Shire at the Bostonian Hotel. His specialties include braised dishes; roast chicken with garlic, lemon, and parsley; duck confit; grilled mushrooms and garlic on mixed-grain, housebaked, French-style country bread; and souffléed lemon custard.

The New York restaurant Bouley, opened August 6 at 165 Duane Street, will soon be ranked as the city's finest. David Bouley, who trained under Gaston Lenôtre, Roger Verget, Paul Bocuse, Paul Haeberlin, Joël Robuchon, and Freddy Girardet before becoming chef at the nearby restaurant Montrachet (see 1985), offers a $65 *menu dégustation* of eight small courses, beginning with a terrine of roasted beets and goat cheese or a dish of smoked fish, sea scallops with parsnip purée, langoustine tail with a red Sancerre sauce (also served with Maine lobster as an entrée), *pot-au-feu* with slices of pheasant breast and bits of barely cooked foie gras, ham with thyme infused in port sauce, batons of roasted root vegetables, sorbet in any of 40 different flavors, and soufflé (raspberry and chocolate pear) in a pool of strawberry *coulis*. Dessert chef Bill Yosses also prepares, among other things, feuilles of fig, bitter chocolate sorbet, and opera cake with chocolate icing. First courses are $6 to $16, main courses $20 to $27, desserts about $7.

The Chicago restaurant Frontera opens in March at 445 North Clark Street with Mexican dishes prepared by chef-proprietor Rick Bayless: chicken, guinea hen, or pork with *mole* sauce; red snapper or marlin with pumpkin-seed *mole* (pumpkin seed, *cilantro*, *tomatillos*, and herbs); and pork marinated in orange juice and grilled slowly over a wood-stove fire with roasted sweet onions.

The Chicago restaurant Charlie Trotter's opens in August at 816 West Armitage Avenue. Trotter, who has been head chef at Gordon's (see 1976) and worked with Bradley Ogden in San Francisco, offers a menu that varies according to what is best and freshest in various parts of America (a Maine diver harvests scallops for him when they are perfect).

The Minneapolis restaurant Shelly's Wood Roast opens in November at 2120 Hennepin Avenue South. Local business executive Shelly Jacobs, 43, has given the place a decor evocative of an isolated North Woods hunting lodge, designed an oven that roasts and bastes meat, fowl, and fish over indirect heat from the fire of a blend of woods, and serves patrons wood-roasted trout, salmon, duck, game, pepper steak, beef brisket, short ribs, spare ribs, lamb shanks, pork chops, sausage, green-apple pie,

two-tiered chocolate cake, strawberry shortcake, draft beer, and root beer floats.

1988

Moscow agrees April 14 to withdraw Soviet forces from Afghanistan (the first group leaves May 17), promises to have all 115,000 out by mid-February 1989, and agrees to restore a nonaligned Afghan state.

U.S. unemployment falls in April to 5.4 percent, lowest since 1974.

Median weekly U.S. earnings: lawyer, $914; pharmacist, $718; engineer, $717; physician, $716; college teacher, $676; computer programmer, $588; high school teacher, $521; registered nurse, $516; accountant, $501; editor, reporter, $494; actor, director, $488; writer, artist, entertainer, athlete, $483; mechanic, $424; truck driver (heavy), $387; carpenter, $365; bus driver, $335; laborer, $308; secretary, $299; truck driver (light), $298; machine operator, $284; janitor, $258; hotel clerk, $214; cashier, $192; (source: Bureau of Labor Statistics).

Pillsbury acquires Sedutto, a $5 million New York–based producer of specialty ice cream (see Häagen-Dazs, 1984).

Grand Metropolitan plc, a British conglomerate, pays $5.79 billion to acquire Pillsbury (along with its Häagen-Dazs ice cream division and its pizza and Burger King restaurant chains; see below). It sells Pillsbury's grain merchandising division to ConAgra and concentrates on its GrandMet Foods brands, which include Absolut vodka, Smirnoff, Popov, Gilbey's gin, Bombay gin, Cinzano, Metaxa, Heublein Cocktails, Almaden wines, Beaulieu wines, Lancers, González Byass (Tío Pepe sherry), Grand Marnier liqueur, Christian Brothers brandy, Bailey's cream liqueur, Romana sambuca, J&B scotch, Wild Turkey, Jack Daniel's, Southern Comfort, and Jose Cuervo. GrandMet will give worldwide distribution to Pillsbury brands, including Green Giant, Häagen-Dazs, Hungry Jack, and Totino.

The British sugar colossus Tate & Lyle acquires A. E. Staley for $1.9 billion, sells off its food service division, and increases its research and development staff by 25 percent to 150 (*see* 1922; high-fructose corn syrup, 1967). By 1990, Staley will be milling more than 400,000 bushels of corn per day, producing revenues of $1.1 billion, and contributing nearly half of Tate & Lyle's profits (*see* Stellar fat substitute, 1990).

Philip Morris buys Kraft Foods for $13.1 billion and adds it to the tobacco company's General Foods division, which becomes Kraft General Foods, the world's largest food company (*see* Anderson, Clayton, 1987). By 1994, food will account for half of Philip Morris's sales, but only 38 percent of its profits; beer will account for 7 percent of its sales and 4 percent of its profits (56 percent of profits will come from tobacco).

Seagram Co. buys Tropicana Products from Kohlberg Kravis Roberts (KKR) for $1.2 billion— 12 times Tropicana's pretax earnings (*see* 1955). Seagram will spend another $300 million to improve Tropicana's manufacturing and distribution facilities, and by 1993 Tropicana will have sales of more than $1.3 billion as Seagram works to make it a world brand.

KKR (above) agrees in October after a bidding contest to pay $24.9 billion for RJR Nabisco in the largest leveraged buyout ever. RJR Nabisco had sales last year of $15.8 billion, KKR partner Henry Kravis says, "Oreos will still be in childen's lunchboxes," but RJR Nabisco now has such a heavy debt burden that it will have to lay off some of its 125,000 employees and sell off parts of its business (*see* BSN, 1989).

Borden Co. expands its pasta business by acquiring Raineri Foods of São Paulo, Brazil, and Monder Alimenti S.p.A. of Milan, Italy's second-largest producer of dry-filled pasta (*see* 1987). It also gains exclusive U.S. distribution rights to the Italian-made De Cecco pasta, and it introduces Creamette Pasta, the first and only nationally distributed U.S. pasta brand, and Classico Pasta Sauce.

Dean Foods acquires Richard A. Shaw Co. of Watsonville, Calif., in September as it expands from processing dairy products to processing vegetables (*see* Larsen, 1986; Bellingham, 1990).

The French food conglomerate BSN buys Britain's H-B Foods, maker of Lea & Perrins Worcestershire Sauce (*see* 1837; 1989).

Nestlé acquires Buitoni-Perugina to expand its presence in the pasta and chocolate businesses.

Nestlé (above) bids $3.5 billion in the spring to acquire Rowntree plc (*see* 1987); Rowntree rejects the unsolicited bid; Prime Minister Margaret Thatcher announces in May that her government will wait for a report from regulators before making any decision about Nestlé's bid; Jacobs Suchard offers $4.3 billion; Rowntree rejects the bid; the Lord Mayor of York mounts a "Hands Off Rowntree" campaign; but three leading trading unions agree conditionally in June to support a foreign takeover if it does not threaten jobs. Nestlé announces that it will not increase its $3.7 billion offer but quietly raises the bid to $4.5 billion, which Rowntree accepts June 23.

Hershey Foods pays Cadbury Schweppes $300 million in August to acquire the U.S. license for Peter Paul's and Cadbury's brands, which include Mounds, Almond Joy, and York Peppermint Patty.

Tootsie Roll Industries acquires Charms Co., America's leading lollipop maker.

The Edgewater, N.J., Japanese supermarket Yaohan opens in September at 595 River Road in a shopping plaza devoted entirely to stores and eating places that cater to the 60,000 Japanese in the New York City area. Backed by the department store Yaohan in Shizuoka, which has six stores in California, the big store overlooking the Hudson River carries foods such as bamboo shoots, tofu, nagaimo root, Tokyo *negi*, and tuna steaks plus prepared dishes such as miso soup, seasoned radish, and sushi.

The Arkansas-based discount retailer Wal-Mart opens its first Super Center November 17 at Wheeler, Okla., selling meats, produce, dairy products, and baked goods in addition to the packaged foods that it has offered along with dry goods at its regular discount stores. By 1995 Wal-Mart will have more than 100 Super Centers, most of them in the Midwest, and they will be undercutting supermarket chains as well as Main Street grocers.

The fat substitute Simplesse, introduced in January by the NutraSweet division of Monsanto Corp., contains only 1⅓ calories per gram as compared with 9 for fat (*see* Olestra, 1987). It is intended for use in ice cream, yogurt, margarine, processed cheese, salad dressings, and other foods that are not fried or baked. NutraSweet says the product does not need FDA approval since it is made from milk and egg-white proteins that have been made microscopic in size through "microparticulation." The company insists that it is "made entirely from safe, natural foods which have not been changed in any way other than by the common changes which occur in cooking," but it is asked to submit its data for FDA review nevertheless (*see* below; Stellar, 1990).

Nonfiction: *Revolution at the Table: The Transformation of the American Diet* by Canadian (McMaster University, Hamilton, Ont.) history professor Harvey A. Levenstein, 50, who deals with the period from 1880 to 1930, when the idea grew that Americans must be taught to eat what was good for them, not merely what they liked; *The Food of China* by U.S. historian E. N. (Eugene Newton) Anderson, 47.

Cookbooks: *Good Old Food: A Taste from the Past by Irena Chalmers and Friends.*

U.S. food processors introduce 962 new microwavable products, up from 278 in 1986, as microwave oven ownership soars (*see* 1987). Such products account for 10 percent of the year's new entries, but while millions of Americans have microwave ovens that have cost them upwards of $200 each, and 87 percent of households have at least one, most people use them primarily for reheating, usually coffee or tea, after finding that microwaves ruin good meats and cannot match conventional ovens for baking. Some cooks and home economists will continue to defend the microwave oven, but by the mid-1990s major food companies such as Campbell Soup and Kraft will have quit developing microwavable items.

Global warming threatens mankind, NASA climatologist James E. Hansen, 47, tells the Senate Committee on Energy and Natural Resources June 23. Increased atmospheric levels of carbon dioxide and other heat-trapping "greenhouse" gases are probably to blame, he says.

Chinese floods in early August kill thousands along the eastern coast and leave hundreds of thousands homeless.

Bangladesh has floods in early September that cover much of the country, the worst in 70 years, with 1,000 dead and millions homeless. Donor nations rush aid, and the government asks that international experts work on flood control projects.

Brazilian rubber tapper Francisco "Chico" Mendes Filho is shot dead December 22 at his home in Xapuri, raising a worldwide storm of protest against ranchers who are clearing the western Amazonian rain forest. Mendes has rallied families to stand up against the chain saws and bulldozers (*see* 1989).

Leaders of the seven largest industrial democracies meet for 3 days at Toronto in June but rebuff President Reagan's demand that high priority be given to ending government farm subsidies by the year 2000. U.S. farm subsidies are $26 billion, up from $3 billion in 1981.

Drought reduces North American crops, and the hot summer raises fears that "global warming" (above) poses a threat to human survival. The U.S. grain harvest is only about 190 million metric tons as compared with 300 million in a more typical year, and in some parts of Iowa the corn crop is only one-quarter what it was last year; the United States is obliged for the first time in history to import grain for domestic needs (*see* 1989; aflatoxin, below).

Kellogg introduces Common Sense Oat Bran cereal, other cereal companies offer similar products, but although studies show that oat bran lowers blood serum cholesterol, and many responsible physicians and nutritionists endorse its use, most oat bran cereals contain sodium and saturated fats, and the promise of oat bran as a heart disease preventive will prove to be overblown (*see* 1990).

Nestlé, S.A.'s, Carnation subsidiary introduces Good Start H.A. (hypoallergenic) infant formula in a bid to seize part of the $1.6 billion U.S. infant formula market from Abbott Laboratories (Similac), Bristol-Myers (Enfamil), and American Home Products (SMA). Pediatricians are quick to recommend Good Start for colicky babies, but mothers of milk-allergic infants begin to report serious reactions: some babies vomit violently after ingesting Good Start and then go limp. Carnation also introduces Follow-up formula. Despite efforts to encourage breast-feeding, some 80 percent of U.S. infants are still given formula at least some of the time.

Eli Lilly Co. introduces Prozac, a drug which increases serotonin levels in the brain and works as an antidepressant. Patients on Prozac have been found to lose weight without dieting, Lily consults with MIT researchers Richard and Judith Wurtman, the company concludes that serotonin controls the brain's "satiety center," and it applies for Food and Drug Administration approval to market Prozac as a treatment for obesity (*see* 1994).

Interneuron Pharmaceuticals is founded by Richard and Judith Wurtman (above), who work to develop the serotonin-boosting diet drug dexfelfluramine (*see* 1982; 1994).

Critics of fat substitutes such as Simplesse (above) question whether such products can ever make much of a dent in fat consumption. Noting that average U.S. per capita consumption of artificial sweeteners reached 17 pounds in 1985, up from 5.7 in 1965, they point out that average per capita sugar consumption in those 20 years rose from 113.9 pounds to 130 (including corn sugars).

Columbia University's Teachers College nutritionist Joan Gussow raises doubts about Simplesse (above), telling a *Medical Tribune* reporter, "Fats are so much more significant calorically than sugar that I'm not going to go out on a limb and say for sure that [a fat substitute] won't make any difference, but non-caloric sweeteners have not in any way affected the intake of caloric sweeteners. That should be a kind of warning. And I think the idea that [Simplesse] is natural is bizarre. I heard someone say it was completely natural because all they'd done was take the casein molecule and stomp on it and bend it into some shape. I couldn't help thinking of the differences between various kinds of oils. They differ only in minute structural ways, and yet olive oil seems to have very different effects from other oils. And saturated fat isn't that different except for a few hydrogen molecules. So the idea that this product, because it was made from something natural, is still perfectly natural after some drastic stomping process, and shouldn't have to come under FDA scrutiny, is ridiculous. Obviously, it needs extensive testing. The trouble is, our methods of testing are totally inadequate, so I'm not sure what we'll find."

The U.S. Department of Agriculture changes its grading system for beef late in the year from Prime, Choice, and Good to Prime, Choice, and Select in response to requests from consumer groups and the meat industry. The aim is to facilitate marketing of a leaner alternative to Prime and Choice grades, which have higher fat contents. By 1993, 4.87 billion pounds of Select-grade beef will be sold, up from 423 million pounds of Good-grade beef in 1983, while sales of Choice-grade beef will remain constant at roughly 10 to 11 billion pounds.

Congress enacts legislation requiring warning labels on all alcoholic beverages.

Aflatoxin contaminates some of the drought-ravaged U.S. corn harvested in Illinois, Indiana, and Iowa (above; *see* 1977). The Food and Drug Administration is responsible for restricting interstate shipments of corn containing even the slightest amount of aflatoxin, but Reagan administration budget cuts have reduced the number of FDA inspectors and those who remain can only make spotty surveillances. Regulators and industry officials argue that the contaminated corn will be diluted by billions of bushels of clean corn, meatpackers say that livestock would get sick before aflatoxin residues affected their meat, but testing by many food companies, dairy farmers, ranchers, livestock finishers, and meat packers in the Midwest (which produces 70 percent of the nation's corn) is haphazard at best (southeastern states are far more efficient). The big Quaker Oats cereal mill at Cedar Rapids, world's largest, finds aflatoxin in roughly 20 percent of the corn it receives—20 times as much as usual—and employs security guards to give truckers the news that their corn has been rejected. Corn destined for foreign buyers is tested only on request; the Federal Grain Inspection Service (FGIS) tests hundreds of samples sent to it by grain dealers and farmers, but it informs the FDA about aflatoxin only if it is found in samples collected by FGIS employees. Japan, the Soviet Union, and other countries with stricter limitations on aflatoxin content reject entire shiploads of corn, and since aflatoxin in improperly dried corn can increase tenfold in just 3 days there are fears that when the corn comes out of elevators next spring it will have aflatoxin concentrations of 1,200 to 1,500 parts per billion, far above permissible levels, and that some ranchers and merchants will use the corn in violation of FDA standards (300 parts per billion for cattle nearing slaughter, 200 for mature hogs, 100 for breeding livestock, and 20 for dairy cows).

British Junior Health Minister Edwina Curry resigns December 16 after 2 weeks of controversy over her charge that most British eggs are infected with salmonella. Egg sales have plummeted, and raisers have slaughtered flocks.

U.S. food processors introduce 962 new microwavable products, up from 278 in 1986, as microwave oven ownership soars.

Hershey Foods (above) test-markets Kisses with Almonds, designed by Dennis Eshleman, 34, of the company's product development team (*see* Kisses, 1907; Hugs, 1993).

The London restaurant Mirabelle closes after 52 years at 47 Curzon Street but will soon be acquired by the Japanese leisure group OTA Resources Development Co. (*see* 1946). OTA will invest £6 million to restore it, restock its wine cellar, and add private dining facilities, including two Japanese Teppanyaki grill rooms.

San Francisco's Blue Fox restaurant is acquired by Gianni Fassio (*see* 1933). The block in which it stands at 659 Merchant Street was largely torn down in 1969 to build a Holiday Inn and the restaurant has fallen out of favor, but Fassio hires Patrizio Sacchetto as chef and will revive its fortunes.

The Los Angeles restaurant Locanda Veneta opens near the Beverley Center under the direction of Antonio Tommasi and John Louis de Mori. Tommasi's father was executive chef at Venice's Cipriani Hotel, and Mori's family has operated restaurants at Florence (*see* Ca'Brea, 1991).

The Miami, Fla., restaurant Lucky's opens in the Park Central Hotel. Executive chef Stuart Littlefield's menu features "black-ink angel-hair pasta pie with asparagus, smoked capon breast, and Wisconsin sharp cheese"; "blackened fish of the day and crayfish fettucine tossed with an herbed cream and finished with red caviar"; salmon; grilled veal loin chops; roast chicken breast; and freshly made desserts that include chocolate truffle ice cream made with amaretto brittle, laced with liqueur, and studded with chunks of nougat; chocolate meringue with raspberries wrapped in a chocolate "gift box"; and other ice creams and sorbets made in house.

New York's City Council enacts a law in April requiring restaurants with 50 seats or more to provide separate sections for smokers and nonsmokers. Many restaurants predict a slump in business, but their dire outlook will prove unfounded.

The Wainscott, N.Y., restaurant Sapporo di Mare opens on Long Island's South Fork under the direction of restaurateur Pino Luongo of 1983 Il Cantinori fame (*see* Le Madri, 1989).

New York's 58-year-old "21" Club restaurant retains Anne Rosenzweig of the Arcadia Restaurant to help rejuvenate its menu and style.

The 5-year-old New York restaurant Hubert's moves from East 22nd Street to 575 Park Avenue (the Beekman) at 63rd Street, where it replaces the stuffy Perigord Park. Len Allison and Karen Hubert offer patrons gravlaks terrine; oxtail consommé; rémoulade spiked with wasabi (Japanese horseradish); grilled squid with black olives vinaigrette; grilled lobster with poblano sauce; pirogies filled with crabmeat; fettucine with sweetbreads and oysters; house-made rabbit sausage in Mexican mole sauce; roquefort soufflé with Granny Smith sauce; chicken with pineapple chutney; small sirloin with chili ancho mayonnaise and a relish of fresh corn kernels and pickled green pepper dice. Dessert chef John Dudek, who first joined the couple as a dishwasher in Brooklyn, prepares dishes that include macadamia-nut tart with pineapple ice cream; bittersweet chocolate-mint ice cream; bittersweet chocolate cookies; lemon soufflé tart; pot de crème laced with white port and garnished with melon and mint; and chestnut layer cake with espresso butter cream. A three-course prix fixe dinner costs $55, a four-course dinner $65, and a five-course dinner $75.

The New York restaurant San Domenico opens at 240 Central Park South, near Columbus Circle. Restaurateur Tony May has started the place with

Bolognese banker Gianluigi Morini, who about 18 years ago opened another San Domenico in his 15th-century house at the town of Imola, near Bologna, and lured Mino Berghese, former chef to Italy's late Victor Emmanuel III, out of retirement to organize its kitchen. Morini later brought in Valentino Marcattilii, who serves as chef, also, for the New York restaurant, overseeing Milwaukee-born chef *de cucina* Paul Bartolotta, 28. A full-time expert from Italy prepares fresh pasta daily, and specialties include (in addition to pasta dishes such as gargalenni and spaghetti alla chitarra) shrimp skewered on rosemary branches, *fricassea* of Maine lobster with artichoke hearts, foie gras with puréed onion rings, double rib steak, braised guinea hen with Savoy cabbage and porcini, raw vegetables served in a bowl of crushed ice, *cassata* (a molded gelato with pine nuts and candied fruit) in a strawberry sauce, chocolate semifreddo with chocolate sauce, and banana gelato.

The New York restaurant Aureole opens at 34 East 61st Street. Charles Palmer of the River Café, who has gained backing from Steve Tzolis and Nicola Kotsoni of Il Cantinori and Periyali, features salmon smoked over applewood, lobster cocktail, sea scallop "sandwiches" made with freshly shredded potato, charcuterie, terrine of fresh duckling foie gras with smoked chicken, cornmeal spoon bread, garlic roasted capon breast, medallions of veal grilled over applewood, and sirloin steak with brandy sauce and potato cake. Fish chef Bonnie Calabrese turns out tuna steak with ginger-soaked leeks, filets of sea bass with squashes and pomme soufflé surrounded by cold smoked shrimp that have been fricasseed with the fish, grouper with bits of fried calamari and ratatouille. Pastry chef Rich Leach prepares "double lemon" millefeuilles, bittersweet chocolate coupe, frozen banana soufflé studded with bits of caramel, and cookies baked in house. Prix fixe dinner is $50.

McDonald's announces April 29 that it will open 20 Moscow restaurants, staffed by Soviet workers and run by Soviet managers trained at McDonald's Hamburger Universities. Instead of Big Macs, the restaurants will serve the Bolshoi Mak at 2 rubles ($3.38—about 1 percent of a month's pay for the average Russian). In a joint venture with the Food Services Division of the Moscow City Council, the

company will also build a food-processing plant to service the restaurants.

Britain's Licensing Act receives royal assent May 20, permitting 65,000 pubs in England and Wales to remain open from 11 o'clock in the morning until 11 o'clock at night on weekdays with more restricted hours on Sundays (*see* 1916). Most publicans are unwilling to pay extra wages and will continue to say "Time, Gentlemen, please" well before 11 o'clock (*see* Monopolies and Mergers Commission report, 1989).

Grand Metropolitan plc (above) will continue Burger King's international expansion, with new restaurants opening in the next few years in Germany, Hungary (*see* 1991), Mexico, Poland, and Saudi Arabia (*see* 1986; 1989).

Hershey Foods (above) sells its Friendly Ice Cream restaurant chain for about $375 in cash to the 3-year-old, Chicago-based Tennessee Restaurant Co., which adds Friendly's 850 full-service restaurants in 15 states to the 330 Perkins family restaurants it operates in Minnesota, Ohio, New York, Pennsylvania, and Florida. Tennessee Restaurant's chief executive officer Alvin Smith, 47, joined Burger King as CEO in 1977 after 11 years at McDonald's, left in 1980 to head up PepsiCo's restaurant operations, and owns one-third of Tennessee Restaurant.

The British brewing giant Whitbread announces in September that it will sell its eight hamburger restaurants to Burger King (above). Whitbread has the British franchise for Pizza Hut.

Pizza Hut announces in September that it will open its first Beijing outlets by year's end (*see* Kentucky Fried Chicken, below). Pizza has been available only at hotels catering to foreign visitors.

Hardee's adds Chicken Stix and Chicken Biscuit to its menus and becomes what it claims is the first major fast-food restaurant chain to switch completely to all-vegetable oil for its fried products (*see* 1982; McDonald's, Burger King, 1986; Roy Rogers, 1900).

Kentucky Fried Chicken announces in mid-November that of its 7,700 restaurants worldwide the one that sells the most fried chicken is its year-old Beijing outlet, which has sold $3 million worth in 1 year. It says that two more Beijing KFC stores will be opened.

1989

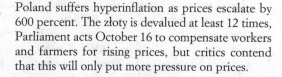

Soviet citizens gain rights and other Eastern Europeans overthrow despots in spontaneous uprisings after Beijing cracks down on dissidents with a bloody massacre.

Soviet troops complete their withdrawal from Afghanistan in February.

World grain reserves at the start of the year's harvest are equal to only 54 days of consumption, down from 101 days at the start of the 1987 season (*see* U.S. harvest, 1988).

Poland suffers hyperinflation as prices escalate by 600 percent. The złoty is devalued at least 12 times, Parliament acts October 16 to compensate workers and farmers for rising prices, but critics contend that this will only put more pressure on prices.

Yugoslavia suffers hyperinflation as prices increase at the rate of 10,000 percent annually.

Argentina suffers hyperinflation, with prices doubling and even tripling from month to month.

Moscow offers Soviet wheat growers hard currency incentives if they exceed certain production goal but continues to buy millions of tons of U.S. and other foreign grain.

Unilever renames its food division, which becomes Van den Bergh Foods Co., and markets margarines (Imperial and Promise brands), Thomas J. Lipton products, Mrs. Butterworth's syrups and pancake mix, Shedd's Country Crock Spread, and some smaller brands.

Tyson Foods acquires Holly Farms for $1.4 billion after a bidding contest with ConAgra (which receives $50 to halt its litigation in the matter). Tyson, which sells $250 million in assets to swing the deal, becomes far and away the world's largest chicken processor, with 47 plants in Arkansas and other states, all but two of them gained by acquiring other companies. Now a totally integrated food producer whose chickens have been going mostly

into institutional specialty cuts, chicken cutlets, and the like, Tyson has made 17 mergers in 28 years (*see* 1969) and its sales have grown in the 1980s from $390 million to $3.8 billion while profits have jumped tenfold as McDonald's, Kentucky Fried Chicken, and other fast-food chains joined its list of major customers. The Holly Farms acquisition moves Tyson into fresh frying and cut-up chickens for supermarkets. It will quickly expand Holly Farms's Quik-to-Fix chicken-fried steak line beyond its southern base, and its new beef products will enable Tyson to expand beyond the volatile poultry business.

BSN pays $2.5 billion to acquire RJR Nabisco's European cookie and cracker business, enabling it to sell Ritz Crackers, Fig Newtons, Planters nuts, and a host of other brands in addition to its Lu cookies, Danone and Gervaise yogurts, Maille mustard, Alora ketchup, H-B and Lea & Perrins sauces, Evian mineral water, Panzone pasta, and Kronenbourg beer (Strasbourg-based Kronenbourg is Europe's second-largest brewer). French entrepreneur Antoine Riboud, 70 (a brother of photographer Marc Riboud and of the late Schlumberger president Jean Riboud), has taken a $200 million container manufacturer and, through acquisitions over a 22-year period, created a $7 billion conglomerate—Europe's fourth-largest food company, topped only by Nestlé, Unilever, and Grand Metropolitan (BSN will rename itself Danone in 1994).

Ralston Purina acquires Beech-Nut Packing Co. (*see* Continental Baking, 1984; Ralcorp, 1994).

Pet Inc. acquires Van de Kamp's frozen seafood line.

Procter & Gamble acquires Fisher Nuts from Kohlberg Kravis Roberts' Beatrice-Hunt-Wesson in October (*see* 1986; ConAgra, 1990).

Procter & Gamble acquires Hawaiian Punch late in the year from RJR Nabisco's Del Monte division (*see* 1961).

Nonfiction: *Grande et petite histoire des cuisiniers: De l'antiquité à nos jours* by Maguellone Toussaint-Samat; *Appetite for Change: How the Counterculture Took on the Food Industry, 1966–1988* by Washington, D.C., historian Warren J. Belasco, who favors a strong alternative food network in communities to

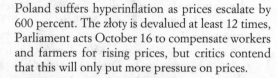

counteract fast food, frozen "gourmet" meals, and supermarket take-out counters.

Cookbooks: *La Varenne Pratique: The Complete Illustrated Cooking Course* by Anne Willan; *Delia Smith's Complete Illustrated Cookery Course*, which will have sales of nearly 500,000 copies by 1994; *Linda McCartney's Home Cooking* by U.S.-born English singer-author McCartney (*née* Eastman), 47, who has been married for 20 years to former Beatles musician Paul McCartney (both have been vegetarians for the past 15 years and have an organic farm 2 hours south of London) (the book will sell 250,000 copies worldwide by 1994); *The Way to Cook* by Julia Child; *Simple Fare* by California poet-restaurateur Ronald Johnson; *The Mediterranean Kitchen* by restaurateur Joyce Goldstein; *Pomp and Sustenance: Twenty-five Centuries of Sicilian Food* by U.S. author Mary Taylor Simeti, who is married to a Sicilian; *Madhur Jaffrey's Cookbook: Easy East/West Menus for Family and Friends* by Indian actress Jaffrey; *Fragrant Harbor Taste: The New Chinese Cooking of Hong Kong* by Ken Hom; *Jasper White's Cooking from New England* by the Boston restaurateur; *Microwave Gourmet Healthstyle Cookbook* by Barbara Kafka.

Film: Peter Greenaway's *The Cook, The Thief, His Wife & Her Lover* with Helen Mirren, Michael Gambon, Tim Roth, and Richard Bohringer is a parable set in a posh gourmet restaurant.

Brazil responds to world environmentalist opinion and suspends (but does not end) tax incentives that have favored land clearance in the Amazon jungle (*see* 1987). A low-interest World Bank loan of $8 million, plus $8 million appropriated by the Brazilian congress, provides funds to hire forestry agents, rent helicopters, and buy trucks, but a helicopter sent to investigate an illegal forest fire in Pará state is fired upon, and hired gunmen kill a forestry agent. Landowners who burn trees without permits are fined some $10 million by agents of the new Institute of Environment and Renewable Natural Resources. August rains put an early end to burning, but chain saws continue to fell trees, legally and illegally. Less than 88 percent of Brazil's forests remain by year's end, down from 99 percent in 1975.

Malaysia and the Philippines place advertisements in U.S. newspapers with claims that coconut and palm oils, used by food processors for flavor and to extend the shelf life of many products, have no effect on serum cholesterol levels and may sometimes actually lower cholesterol levels. Exports of palm oil account for 11 percent of Malaysia's gross domestic product, copra (dried coconut meat) and coconut oil represent a major industry in the Philippines, and the American Soybean Association has organized a letter-writing campaign to urge food processors to remove tropical oils from their products. Given the great preponderance of evidence that saturated fats such as these do raise cholesterol levels, Borden, General Mills, Keebler, RJR Nabisco, Pepperidge Farm, Pillsbury, Ralston Purina, and other major food processors have announced programs to reduce their use of tropical oils in baked goods such as bread, cookies, and crackers, but Nabisco's Triscuits continue to be made with palm oil and its Oreo cookies are still made with lard. Food technicians "hydrogenate" unsaturated oils to make them shelf stable but not to the levels of saturation found in tropical oils.

ConAgra CEO Charles M. Harper introduces 10 different low-calorie (310 or less per serving), low-fat, low-cholesterol, low-salt Healthy Choice frozen dinners to industry and media representatives at New York's Plaza Hotel in January. Harper suf-

Concerns about sodium, saturated fat, and cholesterol created a market for new food products.

fered a heart attack 2½ years ago and asked his company's food scientists to develop a line of good-tasting frozen food dinners that were healthier than any offered by the competition. By 1994, there will be 300 products in ConAgra's Healthy Choice line, including soups, frozen dinners, breakfast egg substitutes, and ice cream (*see* Beatrice, 1990; Kellogg, 1994).

Older people who do not get enough vitamins and minerals in their food may be able to bolster their immune systems and remain healthier if they supplement their diets with pills in modest doses, advises Canadian immunologist Ranjit Chandra, director of the World Health Organization's Center for Nutritional Immunology. A research professor at Memorial University of Newfoundland, he has studied 96 white, upper-middle-class men and women over age 65 who live in their own homes, giving half of them placebo pills and the other half pills containing 18 vitamins and minerals, mostly at levels near the U.S. recommended daily allowance (RDA). Those taking the supplements had significantly fewer infections, mostly respiratory infections, and were sick for only 23 days as compared to 48 for those not taking them. Responsible nutritionists generally discourage people from depending on dietary supplements, noting that foods contain substances which cannot be found in pills (broccoli, for example, not only is rich in beta carotene but also contains considerable quantities of suforaphane, which reportedly has strong anti-cancer properties); they concede, however, that little research has been done on the nutritional needs of older people, that such people, living alone, may lose the motivation to eat properly, and that supplements do make a certain amount of sense in such cases. An estimated 60 million Americans of all ages take dietary supplements on a daily basis, most of them "just to be on the safe side" but some in the hope that vitamins or minerals will somehow give them more energy, compensate for smoking or poor eating habits, alleviate arthritis pains, help some other condition, or extend their lives.

☂ The U.S. Environmental Protection Agency (EPA) reports in February that the chemical Alar (daninozide) poses a significant risk of cancer for humans but will not be banned for at least 18 months because tests thus far have not proved any

Apple sales dropped off as consumers fretted about orchard owners spraying trees with Alar.

imminent health hazard. Made by Uniroyal, the chemical has been used for 20 years to redden about 5 percent of the nation's apple crop, but several food chains stopped accepting Alar-treated apples in 1986. The International Apple Institute, representing about 90 percent of U.S. growers, announces in May that the growers, who have already suffered $50 million in losses from unsold apples, will voluntarily stop using Alar by fall. Uniroyal, while insisting that it is safe, halts domestic sales of Alar but continues to sell it abroad, raising criticism that imported apples and apple products may be affected. The Alar scare gives a boost to organically grown apples and other fruit, which are in some cases wormy or otherwise blemished, and some apple varieties are hard to find.

U.S., Canadian, and Japanese fruit consumption plummets in March following an alert by the U.S. Food and Drug Administration. The U.S. Embassy at Santiago has received an anonymous telephone call March 2, warning that Red Flame grapes en route from Chile have been injected with cyanide. The call is repeated March 9, the S.S. *Almería Star* out of Valparaiso arrives at Philadelphia March 11 and discharges its cargo of fruit at the Tioga Marine Terminal, Customs inspectors impound the cargo, and they proceed to impound 2 million crates of Chilean fruit—blackberries, blueberries, green apples, melons, peaches, pears, and plums as well as grapes—at airports and docks. The embargo continues for 11 days, but only three suspicious-looking grapes are found, and it will turn out that they were probably contaminated with cyanide in a Philadelphia testing laboratory. Some 20,000 Chilean food workers lose their jobs, hundreds of thousands feel the economic impact, Chilean growers will file a lawsuit against the U.S. government to recover more than $330 million in damages, and domestic grape producers also suffer severe financial losses as Americans, Canadians, and Japanese stop eating grapes of any kind for several weeks and also avoid almost any fruit at a time of year when most fruit other than bananas and citrus fruit is imported from Chile.

The first shipment of Japanese tora fugu (blowfish) to be approved by the Food and Drug Administration arrives at New York in March (see 1984). Restaurant Nippon owner Nobuyoshi Kuraoka has organized 24 other Japanese restaurant owners in New York to persuade the FDA to permit import of fugu and serve it under close FDA monitorship after their chefs have attended special seminars instructing them how to protect patrons from poisoning.

New Mexico physicians report three cases in women aged 37 to 43 of an unusual blood disorder—eosinophilia myalgia syndrome—marked by high white-cell count, body rash, muscle and joint pain, extreme weakness, and chewing difficulties. An *Albuquerque Journal* reporter discovers that all three women have been taking L-tryptophan, an amino acid sold as a food supplement, for insomnia and premenstrual syndrome (see 1972). Reports of eosinophilia begin to come in from physicians in Missouri, Arizona, Oregon, Mississippi, Texas, California, Virginia, and Minnesota. More than 50 such reports have come in by November 12, newspapers across the country carry front-page stories on L-tryptophan November 18, the FDA orders the recall of every product containing L-tryptophan as a major ingredient, but there are soon 287 cases of eosinophilia myalgia syndrome in 37 states and the District of Columbia; an Oregon woman has died. Within 5 months some 1,500 cases will have been reported, 63 will prove fatal, most victims being women who have taken the dietary supplement, but there will be protests that the FDA has been overzealous.

General Mills introduces Berry Bears and Shark Bites, both snack foods made with fruit (see Roll-Ups, 1980).

Hershey Chocolate reduces the size of its 40¢ Hershey bar slightly to 1.55 oz. in May and breaks ground in the summer for a new $100 million chocolate factory.

Hershey (above) introduces the Symphony bar—plain milk chocolate and a blend of creamy milk chocolate with almonds and toffee chips.

The Los Angeles restaurant Tulip opens at 8300 Melrose Avenue, a corner formerly occupied by Ma Maison Cooking School. Chef Maurice Peguet (he apprenticed in France under Alexandre Dumaine) has teamed up with Roland Gibert (formerly *chef de cuisine* at Bernard's in the Biltmore Hotel), and their specialties include braised veal shanks, roast chicken with morels, fricassee of fava beans with sorrel and wild mushrooms, ravioli with mullard duck and fresh snails in a green parsley *coulis*, French *rouget* (red mullet) with ratatouille, and *feuilleté* of salmon with mushrooms in a sabayon sauce. Pastry chef Patrick Compas produces chocolate *feuilleté* filled with chocolate mousse in a pistachio-studded chocolate terrine, apple tart in a Calvados sauce, hazelnut nougat *glacé*, a "sandwich" of hazelnut cream called a *craquelin*, anise-flavored *crème brûlée*, and *petits Pithiviers*.

The San Francisco restaurant 1001 Nob Hill opens across from the Mark Hopkins Hotel and the Pacific Union Club (earlier the James Flood mansion), replacing the windowless restaurant Alexis Mirable, opened in 1961 at the corner of California and Mason streets. Restaurateurs Leonce and Carolyn Picot have had windows put in to take advantage of the views and engaged Peter Morency of the Nikko Hotel as chef. He will leave late next year and be replaced by Émile Labrousse, originally from France's Périgord region but more recently of the Nikko, whose specialties will include caviar "pie," chowder, pan-fried oysters with a breadcrumb coating, a warm salad of sautéed escargots and diced potatoes, a warm terrine of wild mushrooms, walnut bread, tuna tartare seasoned with Japanese *tamari* and served with sweet potato chips and beets, cassoulet, medallions of pork served with buttermilk mashed potatoes and an onion marmalade, steak au poivre, and rack of lamb with ratatouille.

The San Francisco restaurant Monsoon opens in the Opera Plaza. Proprietor Bruce Cost was working for Xerox Corp. in New York in the 1970s when he began taking lessons in Chinese cookery with Virginia Lee; he taught Chinese cooking to Bard College students and residents of the Hudson Valley, moved to San Francisco in 1980, writes a popular column on Asian cooking for the Wednesday food edition of the *San Francisco Chronicle*, has written two cookbooks (*Ginger East to West* and *Bruce Cost's Asian Ingredients*), has given annual Chinese New Year's banquets at Chez Panisse, has hired that restaurant's pastry chef, David Lebovitz, to complement his chef Tony Gulisano, formerly of Chinois on Main Street in Santa Monica, and offers patrons Chinese, Thai, and Vietnamese dishes: *saté* of marinated grilled beef on bamboo skewers with peanut sauce; *jiaoci* (Chinese dumplings) with bacon, Chinese cabbage, and chives; Thai-style seafood salad containing squid, shrimp, poached lobster, scallions, cucumbers, and mint leaves; corn soup made with fresh white corn and Smithfield ham; Sichuan-style tea-smoked duck with house-made *hoisin* sauce and lotus rolls; steamed catfish; deep-fried spot prawns with pepper and coriander leaves cooked in a dry wok; ginger beef; beef fried with ginger and chilies; gingery pigs' feet with vinegar sauce; fresh bacon with black cured mustard greens; ginger cake; coconutty tapioca pudding with mangoes; and bitter almond ice cream with almond brittle and chocolate sauce and *litchis*.

The Boston restaurant Olives opens with 50 seats at 67 Main Street, Charlestown, but will become so popular that it will move in 1992 to an 85-seat space at 10 City Square. Chef Todd English, 29, and his wife, Olivia, also 29, are graduates of the Culinary Institute of America and have worked at the Boston restaurant Michela, they accept no reservations for parties of fewer than six, and they wow patrons with what many call the best food in town—bistro-style Italian, Greek, Spanish, and Portuguese dishes with portions large even by Boston standards.

The Boston restaurant Biba opens June 29 at 272 Boylston Street. Married when still in her teens, chef-owner Lydia Shire, 41, was left with young children in her early 20s and trained at the London Cordon Bleu before working at Harvest in Cambridge, Mass., and becoming chef at Boston's Bonhomme Richard. She went to work in 1982 as sous chef of the Seasons Restaurant in Boston, was promoted to executive chef, and in 1986 opened the restaurant of the Four Seasons Hotel in Beverly Hills.

The New York restaurant Alison on Dominick Street in TriBeCa (Triangle Below Canal) opens in an old brick house at No. 38 (Dominick is a two-block thoroughfare between Sixth Avenue and Hudson Street). Restaurateur Alison Price (*née* Becker), whose résumé includes a stint at the Gotham Bar and Grill, works with chef Thomas Valenti, who prepares cold poached mackerel, beet-root salad, smoked duck breast salad, ragout of mussels, braised lamb shanks, roast loin of rabbit with "double-smoked" bacon, sautéed skate with braised cabbage and brown butter; bavaroise with cantaloupe, apple bavaroise with a Calvados glaze, crème brûlée, chocolate hazelnut cake, and pastries. First courses are $5 to $12, main courses $17 to $26, desserts $5 to $9.

The 10-year-old New York restaurant Chanterelle moves to 2 Harrison Street, near Hudson Street, where it occupies what was once the lunchroom of the Mercantile Exchange, built in 1884 for traders who dealt originally in grain, butter and eggs, and Maine potatoes (operations were relocated to the World Trade Center in 1977).

The New York restaurant Le Madri opens at 168 West 18th Street, corner of 7th Avenue. Restaurateur Pino Luongo, who has opened a number of other places, has obtained backing from the Pressman family, which owns the building (and the clothing store Barney's one block to the south) (*see* Sapporo di Mare, 1988; Cocopazzo, 1990).

The New York restaurant An American Place moves late in the year into larger premises at 2 Park Avenue, with an entrance on East 32nd Street (*see* 1983).

Burger King opens a restaurant in Dresden, East Germany (*see* Budapest, 1991).

Grand Metropolitan PLC acquires Britain's UB (United Biscuits) restaurants in August and begins converting UB's Wimpy counter-service restaurants into Burger King restaurants (*see* 1976; 1988). Within 5 years there will be more than 7,100 Burger King restaurants in 50 countries worldwide.

Allied-Lyons acquires the 39-year-old Dunkin' Donuts chain, which has recorded increased revenues and earnings each year for the past 15 years (*see* Indonesia, 1985). The coffee-and-doughnut chain now has stores in the Bahamas, Puerto Rico, Brazil, Colombia, Venezuela, Saudi Arabia, Singapore, and Malaysia, as well as in the United States, Canada, Japan, the Philippines, Thailand, and Indonesia. It opened its first United Kingdom shops in September of last year, it will open its first shop in Ireland next March, it will acquire the Mr. Donut chain next year and open its 2,000th shop, and by 1994 it will have well over 3,000 outlets worldwide (including 2,426 in the United States and 218 in Canada plus shops in Mexico, Guatemala, El Salvador, Aruba, Argentina, and Hungary), with annual sales (more coffee than donuts) of $1.4 billion in the United States alone.

A report by Britain's Monopolies and Mergers Commission recommends that the brewing industry be separated from its "tied" houses (pubs that serve only one brand), eliminating the stranglehold of giant brewers such as Allied-Lyons, Bass, Courage, Watney, and Whitbread (*see* 1890). The brewers will manage to delay implementation of the "Supply of Beer Orders," issued in November, which limit the number of pubs that any one brewer can monopolize, but any brewer with more than 2,000 tied pubs will have to sell, or lease free of tie, half of its pubs above the 2,000 limit by November 1992. Bass is obliged to sell or "untie" more than 3,000 pubs; Whitbread, whose brands include Boddington's, Murphy's Irish Stout, Heineken, Stella Artois, and Stella Dry, has about 6,600 tied pubs and will have to reduce that number to about 4,300.

1990

✠ Germany reunites and the USSR crumbles as Iraqi aggression threatens to ignite a Mideast conflagration.

♟ Ethiopia avoids famine despite civil war as Western relief agencies find ways to deliver food and

supply monthly rations to some 3 million people in the northern part of the country, saving them from starvation.

The Soviet Union falls seriously behind on grain shipments to Cuba, forcing the Castro government to cut bread rations and hike some food prices. Cuba, in turn, fails to send as much citrus fruit as she has promised to the Soviet Union.

💲 Soviet President Gorbachev and his Cabinet approve a plan May 22 to double food prices as part of a gradual 5-year transition to a "regulated market economy." The plan calls for tripling the price of bread starting July 1, the first increase in 30 years, and raising other food prices beginning January 1 of next year. The government announces that it will continue to regulate prices of staples and subsidize low-income families, but the move toward a market economy sets off panic buying and hoarding. Authorities limit food sales to residents, frustrating millions of buyers who travel to cities in quest of foodstuffs that are scarcer elsewhere. Heavy subsidies to farmers end, and there are widespread protests in Ukraine and elsewhere.

President Gorbachev comes under increasing attack as Soviet citizens try to cope with shortages. The Parliament gives him virtually free rein September 25 to decontrol the economy, but trade among the old republics has broken down, a budget deficit forces the government to issue more rubles even though there is little to buy with them, prices escalate, Gorbachev moves cautiously, Moscow and Leningrad stores run out of bread, and state food stocks fall so low as to raise a threat of famine. Muscovites and Leningraders complain in November that food supply conditions are the worst since World War II (*see* 1991).

Roughly half of the states in the United States respond to unexpectedly higher prices for milk, orange juice, cereal, and infant formula by cutting allotments to poor women and children under the $2.1 billion federal Women, Infants and Children (WIC) program, but about a dozen states contribute their own money to maintain the allotments, recognizing that the program (which was spared by the Reagan administration) is effective in saving money (as well as lives) by improving health and thus cutting Medicaid costs. Congress acts in late

June to restore food allotments for poor women and children who have been cut from federal nutrition programs; the legislation permits borrowing of up to 3 percent of funds allocated for the fiscal 1991 program to make up for this year's shortfall; Bush administration officials say that they hope the bill will not set a precedent for such borrowing in future years.

Poland institutes free-market rules January 1, creating a glut of food and consumer goods, but at prices few can afford (*see* 1976). Warsaw University economist Leszek Balcerowicz, 43, and Harvard economics professor Jeffrey Sachs, 34, have been the leading architect of the "shock therapy," which Polish voters reject in the November elections and which some other Eastern bloc nations adopt late in the year as they struggle to change from decades of state-run economies with artificial prices and wages.

The Soviet Parliament approves a property law March 6, voting 350 to 3 to give private citizens the right to own the means of production—or at least small factories and other business enterprises—for the first time since the early 1920s.

America's record 8-year economic boom ends in July as the country goes into recession. Britain and France also slump, while Germany and Japan remain economically robust but will soon have economic downturns of their own.

GATT (General Agreement on Tariffs and Trade) talks at Brussels collapse December 11 over the issue of farm subsidies. Farm products account for 14 percent of world trade.

Americans spend at least $225 billion at grocery stores and supermarkets, an average of $46 per week per household.

Hershey Foods acquires Ronzoni Foods with all its dry pasta, pasta sauce, and cheese brands from Kraft General Foods (*see* 1918; Skinner, 1979; American Beauty, 1984). Hershey will introduce the brands into New England markets next year.

Worthington Foods acquires the LaLoma meat-substitute product line of Loma Linda Foods, which 2 years ago sold its Loma Linda brand name to the Dutch-based Nutricia Foods (*see* 1906; Worthington, 1982).

Dean Foods expands its frozen vegetable business by acquiring Bellingham Frozen Foods, which has plants at Bellingham, Wash., and Hartford, Mich. (*see* Shaw, 1988; Birds Eye, 1993).

ConAgra announces June 7 that it will buy Beatrice Co. for $1.34 billion, becoming the second-largest U.S. food company (only Phillip Morris's Kraft General Foods is larger). Kohlberg Kravis Roberts has hoped to get as much as $3 billion for what remains of Beatrice (*see* 1986) but settles for less than half that amount, acquiring 18 percent of ConAgra and becoming its largest shareholder. Other prospective buyers have been reluctant to take on such Beatrice brands as Hunt's Tomato Ketchup, Wesson oil, Swiss Miss puddings and cocoa mixes, Peter Pan peanut butter, and Orville Redenbacher's popcorn, all of which have relatively small market share, but ConAgra's Charles M. Harper has seen an opportunity. Having spent nearly $3 billion on more than 100 acquisitions in the past 16 years, he has had experts study Beatrice's plants, distribution network, and prospects and liked their findings. ConAgra has had sales of more than $15 billion in the fiscal year that ended May 27, with more than 60 percent of it coming from Country Pride Chicken, Banquet Frozen Foods, Healthy Choice, Chun King, Armour Bacon. It will now be in non refrigerated shelf-stable grocery store products as well.

Philip Morris pays more than $4 billion to acquire 80 percent of Jacobs Suchard, becoming the third leading player in Europe's food industry after Nestlé and Unilver and the world's third-largest producer of coffee and confections (the purchase includes Suchard's Tobler chocolate but does not include its Canadian operations or its E. J. Brach candy operation).

Nestlé acquires Curtiss Candy Co. (Baby Ruth and Butterfinger) from RJR Nabisco, raising its share of the U.S. candy bar market to 10 percent.

Tension increases between U.S. supermarkets and marketers as the latter introduce more and more new products (over 12,000 last year alone), clogging retail pipelines. More than 80 percent of the new items fail, and the added expense of introducing and then removing failed items cuts into the retailers' already razor-thin profit margins and forces them to raise other food prices.

The fat substitute Stellar introduced by Tate & Lyle's A. E. Staley division June 11 employs a process that restructures corn's starch molecules to make them attach more easily to water; the starch takes on a smooth, buttery consistency when whipped with water and can be used to make a mayonnaise that is 98 percent fat free and a cheesecake with 50 percent less fat. The Food and Drug Administration has agreed with Staley that Stellar, as a modified food starch, requires no prior approval for use in products such as baked goods, margarine, salad dressings, and ice cream. Monsanto's Simplesse (*see* 1988) can be used only in frozen dairy desserts such as ice creams, and Procter & Gamble continues to await FDA approval for its Olestra fat substitute (*see* 1987).

Cookbooks: *Cuisine de France* by Paul Bocuse; *All-Time Favorites: A Lifetime of Recipes for the First-Time Cook* by Irena Chalmers; *American Food: The Gastronomic Story* by Evan Jones (with more than 500 recipes produced in collaboration with Judith B. Jones); *Delia Smith's Christmas* by Smith, who has returned to television and whose new book will remain on the best-seller list until well after Easter of next year (by July 1994 it will have sold 800,000 copies). Jane Grigson has died in March at age 61.

Film: Henry Jaglom's *Eating* is about U.S. women's obsession with food, dieting, binging, bulimia, and sex.

A U.S. Census Bureau survey of 57,400 housing units, conducted in March, reveals that only one family in four is "traditional" in the sense of having two parents with children, but the decline in the number of such families has slowed since the 1970s, when it dropped sharply. The size of the average household is 2.63 people, down from 2.76 in 1980, 3.14 in 1976, and 3.57 in 1945. Size of family has important consequences for food-purchasing patterns and eating habits (*see* 1991).

U.S. tortilla sales reach 1.5 billion, up from 300 million in 1980, as the nation's Hispanic population swells and as non-Hispanic Americans turn increasingly to Mexican-style foods (*see* salsa sales, 1991).

U.S. sales of prepackaged frozen yogurt soar to $355 million, up from $160 million last year (*see* 1974). When first marketed in 1972, frozen yogurt had a tart flavor, but new technology has enabled processors to eliminate the tartness and Americans are quick to buy the new products, many of them under the impression that they are not only lower in calories than ice cream but also contain live, beneficial bacteria, although in fact most of them contain few of the bacteria (*Lactobacillus bulgaricus* and *Streptococcus thermophilus*) found in ordinary yogurt, which help to overcome lactose intolerance and combat intestinal infections (Häagen Dazs frozen yogurt has far and away the largest concentration of such beneficial bacteria—130 million per gram—as compared to as few as 6,200 in Elán, according to tests).

Maine fishermen trap 28 million pounds of lobster, topping the 1889 record of 24 million pounds.

Bumper wheat crops in America, China, and the USSR force prices down from $3.72 per bushel last year to $2.20.

A bumper Soviet potato crop rots in the fields amid economic wrangles (above) and political charges and countercharges.

U.S. plant breeder Dr. John S. Niederhauser, 74, wins the World Food Prize. His invention of disease-resistant potatoes is credited with having saved millions from starvation in Latin America, Africa, and Asia.

Economic Community ministers agree November 7 to reduce farm subsidies and other barriers to agricultural trade, but collapse of the GATT talks in December (above) threatens to reduce the subsidy cuts by nearly half.

An article in the *New England Journal of Medicine* questions the value of oat bran in reducing blood serum cholesterol. Sales of cereals such as Common Sense Oat Bran (*see* 1988) plummet as a result.

The $5 billion U.S. weight-loss industry comes under attack (*see* Nutri/System, 1971; Jenny Craig, 1983). Nutri/System, which now has 1,570 franchisees but no medical supervision, is sued in March by 19 women, who charge in the Dade County, Fla., circuit court that they suffered gallbladder damage on the company's diet and that the company's "counselors" or "specialists" are "essentially salespersons who receive minimal and inadequate training."

The Bush administration announces March 6 that it is proposing a plan for mandatory nutrition labeling on all packaged food—the first substantial change in 17 years. Calling the current system misleading, confusing, and lacking in vital information, administration officials say the new labels would have to give vital facts on amounts of fat, fiber, cholesterol, and calories that come from fat. Only 30 percent of labels are now required to have such information, and, although 30 percent of packaged food is labeled voluntarily, the remaining 40 percent is not labeled. The new labels would have to meet new definitions for phrases such as "low fat" and "high fiber," whose definitions are now decided on by manufacturers themselves. Agriculture Secretary Clayton Yeutter opposes the plan and calls for less labeling (*see* 1994).

Campbell Soup Co. turns out its 20 billionth can of tomato soup in January and introduces condensed cream of broccoli soup, which enjoys the biggest success of any new soup launched in 55 years.

The McDonald's hamburger chain introduces nonfat bran muffins and reduces the fat content of its milk, milk shakes, and frozen desserts.

Hardee's acquires the 648-unit Roy Rogers restaurant chain from Marriott Corp., giving it more outlets in Baltimore, Philadelphia, New York, Washington, D.C., and other major metropolitan markets (*see* 1988; Marriott, 1927). By 1994, Hardee's will be the world's fourth-largest restaurant chain, operating some 4,000 company-owned and franchise restaurants, about 530 of them under the Roy Rogers name, in 40 states and 11 foreign countries.

The New Orleans restaurant Bayona opens in April at 430 Delphine Street on the edge of the French quarter. Chef Susan Spicer, 38, who has run the kitchen at the Maison de Ville, dishes up a cuisine that is neither Cajun, Creole, nor traditional New Orleans but includes grilled shrimp with black bean cake and coriander sauce; wilted spinach and crabmeat salad with sherry vinaigrette; roasted black drum, snapper, or grouper over a bed of couscous wrapped in blanched and pickled grape leaves; seared bay scallops on a bed of vegetables; grilled quail on a bed of Japanese soba noodles with soy vinaigrette; corn fritters with a tarragon vegetable sauce; lemon buttermilk layer cake with raspberry sauce; rice pudding made with basmati rice (a long-grained, tubular rice, possessed of a special flavor and aroma, that is grown in the Himilayan foothills and aged before it is cooked) and mixed berries; and banana-rum gelato.

The New York restaurant March opens in March on the ground floor of a town house at 405 East 58th Street. Chef Wayne Nish, formerly of La Colombe d'Or (to which he will return in a few years), has teamed up with that restaurant's former general manager, Joseph Scalice, to start the new enterprise, which offers a prix fixe dinner at $45. Specialties include chunks of lobster on a bed of barley, cooked risotto style, with Japanese *shiso* leaves; braised *escargots* with chanterelle mushrooms and polenta, red sausage with "savory" bread pudding, salmon cured with coriander and chives and topped with caviar and crème fraîche, confit and grilled breast of duck, gnocchi made with fresh goat cheese, rack of lamb, walnut tart with hazelnut ice cream, grapefruit sorbet in gin with coriander seed, and vanilla custard with berries.

The New York restaurant Carmine's opens in August at 2450 Broadway, near 90th Street (formerly a Chinese restaurant). Proprietor Godfrey Polistina, who has gone into partnership with chef Michael Ronis and business manager Arthur Cutler, soon has customers lining up for 2 hours to get a table (reservations are accepted only for parties of six and more) and enjoy antipasti (fried zucchini, stuffed mushrooms, and roasted red bell peppers); soups (zuppa di mussels); any of at least 16 pastas (including linguine with calimari, shrimps, clams, mussels, and lobster); and main dishes that include swordfish and tuna steaks, *giambotto* (sausage with peppers, potatoes, and onions), and broiled porterhouse steak "pizzaiola"; braised escarole; gnocchi (made by Polistana's parents at Port Chester, N.Y.); *cannoli*; tortoni; spumoni; and Italian cheesecake.

The New York restaurant Mazzei opens at 1564 Second Avenue, near 81st Street, with a small library of books about the Italian agriculturist Philip Mazzei (1730–1816), who helped Thomas Jefferson (*see* 1773). Proprietors Giuseppe Guglielmi and Domenico Avelluto have engaged former Le Cirque pastry chef Frank DeCarlo as chef *di cucina* and offer patrons *seppie* (cuttlefish) from the Adriatic; clams; New Zealand mussels; wild mushrooms; *radicchio* with smoked mozzarella in a terrine; pastas that include gnocchi; grilled swordfish; tuna steak Livornese; *raie pepperoni* (white skate with slices of red, yellow, and green bell peppers); jumbo prawns baked in a wood-fired oven; roast chicken with hot Tuscan *peronzini*; and desserts that include ricotta cheesecake and fresh fruits (mostly from Europe), including green Italian grapes and, on occasion, blood oranges.

The New York restaurant Cocopazzo (Crazy Chef) opened by Pino Luongo at 23 East 74th Street has a kitchen staff headed by U.S. chef Mark Strausman (who will leave in May 1993) and will soon have a branch in Chicago as Luongo goes on to open Di Cola Cucina Café restaurants in Dallas, Houston, and Costa Mesa, Calif., with backing from the Pressman family (*see* 1989).

New York's Tom Cat Bakery opens in September in Long Island City to bake bread and rolls for the city's restaurant trade. Proprietor Noel Comess, 29, formerly a chef at the Quilted Giraffe, has bought an oven for $500 at auction, spent $20,000 to refurbish space in a 150-year-old building (originally a foundry), and produces white bread, baguettes, sourdough loaves, and rolls for restaurants such as Arcadia, Le Cirque, Lutèce, and the Union Square Café and stores such as Balducci's, Dean and DeLuca, and the Silver Palate. Comess will soon relocate to a larger room in the building (formerly an ice cream factory).

The Eureka Restaurant and Brewery opens in Los Angeles at 1845 South Bundy Drive, at Nebraska Street. Chef Wolfgang Puck and his wife, Barbara Lazaroff, have brought over a German chef to train the staff in the fundamentals of sausage making and offer fresh, hand-crafted beers; their executive chef, Jett Olen "Jody" Denton, a Texan, has specialties that include wild mushroom quesadilla, tomato and jícama salsa, pastas, roast salmon with a black bean sauce and goat cheese, Chinese-style roast duck, miyagi oysters, cheese ravioli, cumin-grilled lamb, rib-eye steak, and falafel. Desserts, made by Melinda Bugarin, include butterscotch pudding, buttermilk cake with fudge sauce, espresso ice cream, and maple crème brûlée (*see* Spago, 1982; Granita, 1991).

French restaurateur Charles Fontaine, formerly top chef at Le Caprice in Mayfair, reopens London's Quality Chop House (*see* 1956), which has closed. Fontaine has a kitchen brigade of five (at Le Caprice he had 22), including two porters, and will revive the fortunes of the Chop House.

The *Guide Michelin* awards a third star in March to the Restaurant Louis XV in the Hôtel de Paris at Monte Carlo, where Alain Ducasse, 33, becomes the youngest chef ever to be so honored. Ducasse, whose parents owned a farm that produced foie gras in the southwest of France, learned to cook from his grandmother, began his apprenticeship at age 16 in nearby Soissons, and has worked under Michel Guérard, Gaston Lenôtre, Roger Verget, and Alain Chapel.

French restaurateur René Chapelle dies suddenly at Millonay, 20 kilometers northeast of Lyons. His widow asks his first assistant, Philippe Jousse, 30, to take over the kitchen of the restaurant, but Michelin immediately removes one of its three stars. Jousse was chosen last year to run Chapelle's restaurant in Kobe, Japan, and carries on his master's tradition of serving gelées and a consommé made from lobster and crayfish shells, and he creates a new soup (crème de primeurs à l'estragon en gelées au crustacés—a pale green velouté of puréed spring vegetables flavored with tarragon and topped with crème fraîche).

1991

✗ Ukraine proclaims independence from the Soviet Union August 24, threatening to strip Russia of her most productive agricultural territories, but joins with Belarus, Russia, and eight other former Soviet republics December 21 in a Commonwealth of Independent States.

💲 Soviet food prices rise on schedule January 1 (*see* 1990), but citizens panic January 29 when the evening news reports that savings accounts have been frozen and 50- and 100-ruble banknotes will be withdrawn from circulation. Many have their savings in such notes, but the government decrees that large bills may be exchanged for their equivalent only up to a maximum of 1,000 rubles (about one month's salary), or 200 in the case of pensioners. The move is designed to halt inflation and quash black-market currency traders.

Inflation moderates in the United States, but food prices are 34 percent above the 1982–1984 average. Average U.S. food prices in January: white bread 70.5¢ per one-pound loaf, French bread $1.28, eggs (grade A, large) $1.10/doz., milk $1.38 per half gallon, chicken 89¢/lb., ground beef $1.65/lb. (all figures higher in the Northeast, lower in the South).

Borden Co. completes a $50 million St. Louis pasta factory with annual capacity of 250 million pounds, the largest such facility in North America, as it continues to expand its presence in the pasta business (*see* 1988; 1994).

The Girl Scouts of America raises about $290 million by selling 165 million boxes of Girl Scout cookies (*see* 1975).

Hershey Foods hikes the retail price of its standard Hershey Bar to 45¢ and pays about $40 million to acquire Gubor Schokoladen GmbH, a German producer of pralines and seasonal chocolates.

A Tokyo branch of the 96-year-old Paris cooking school L'École de Cordon Bleu opens in May with classes every day, including Sunday (the Paris, London, and Ottawa schools are all closed Sundays). Tuition is the equivalent of $4,000 to $5,000 per semester, but 20 percent of students at the Paris Cordon Bleu have been Japanese and it is much cheaper for them to study at Tokyo, where the school is a joint venture with Seibu Saison, the Japanese hotel–railroad–department store conglomerate.

Nonfiction: *Why We Eat What We Eat* by Raymond Sokolov, whose emphasis is on the foods introduced to Europe from the New World and vice versa; *Supermarketer to the World: The Story of Dwayne Andreas, CEO of Archer Daniels Midland* by E. J. Kahn, Jr.

Cookbooks: *Adventures in the Kitchen* by Los Angeles chef Wolfgang Puck; *Meatloaf* by U.S. author Sharon Moore includes more than 40 recipes for dishes that include wild game meat loaf (made from pheasant, rabbit, or venison), ethnic meat loaves (e.g., meat loaf stroganoff with mushrooms and sour cream; sushi loaf made with crabmeat rather than red meat); regional meat loaves (e.g., Tex-Mex meat loaf with chili powder and kidney beans, Corn Belt meat loaf with ground beef, pork, sausage, and crumbled corn bread) (Moore grew up in Pennsylvania Dutch country and only one third of her recipes call for ground beef); *Arabella Boxer's Book of English Food* and *A Visual Feast* by Lady Arabella Boxer.

A *New York Times*–CBS poll released in early December shows that the vast majority of U.S. families with children eat dinner together on a typical night despite pressures on single-parent families and those in which both parents work outside the home (*see* 1990).

U.S. sales of salsa outstrip those of ketchup by $40 million as Americans turn increasingly to hot, spicy, Hispanic-style foods (*see* tortilla sales, 1990). The food industry uses more and more ethnic spices to flavor products whose fat and salt content has been lowered.

California has its fifth straight year of drought. Farmers control 83 percent of the water delivered by vast federal, state, and City of Los Angeles dams, aqueducts, and reservoirs; they pay as little as $2.50 per acre-foot to irrigate their crops while cutbacks are imposed on angry residents of the booming cities, who resent use of precious Sierra Nevada and Colorado River water to grow crops such as rice.

Je mange, donc je maigris! (*I Eat, Therefore I Slim*) by French promoter Michel Montignac, 47, will have sales of 1.1 million in the next 2 years. Low-calorie diets are a great swindle, says the onetime pharmaceutical company executive; foods should be measured by their "glycemic index"—the blood sugar level they induce—rather than by calorie. He contends that sugar stimulates overproduction of insulin, which leads the body to store fat, so foods such as potatoes and white bread, which have a high glycemic index, should not be eaten with fats such as butter. Montignac, who has shed 35 pounds from his 5-foot, 8-inch frame (down to 165 pounds), started a chain of food boutiques, acquired a Bordeaux vineyard, and sells Montignac foie gras and Montignac chocolate by mail order. He will open a

240-seat Paris restaurant in October 1993, and chef Paul Bocuse will claim to have lost 40 pounds on the Montignac "diet," but while many nutritionists and cardiologists approve his recommendation that foods be cooked in olive oil and polyunsaturated fats, some caution that anyone will lose weight temporarily when deprived of sugar and starch and that obtaining 70 percent of one's calories from fats, as Montignac favors, increases the risk of heart disease.

Nestlé's Stouffer division reformulates its 10-year-old Lean Cuisine frozen food line to reflect consumer concerns about fat, cholesterol, and sodium (*see* 1994).

Colombo Yogurt Co. reintroduces its whole-milk yogurt under the name Colombo Classic, calling it a low-fat yogurt (*see* 1977). Next year it will introduce Colombo Slender Spoonfuls, a 100-calorie nonfat yogurt (*see* General Mills, 1993).

The Food and Drug Administration's new commissioner David A. Kessler announces in May that the FDA will stop major food companies from using the word "fresh" on labels of pasta sauce jars and cartons of processed orange juice. Without mentioning Kellogg's Heartwise cereal or other such brands, he says that the FDA will crack down also on the hundreds of products whose labels claim "low" or "no" cholesterol, use a heart symbol or the word "heart" in their brand names, or otherwise claim to have value in preventing heart disease. He notes that products such as potato chips may not contain cholesterol but are high in animal fats, which spur bodily production of cholesterol and lead to heart disease.

Stouffer's (above) introduces Homestyle entrées, which come in larger portions than its regular line of frozen foods.

Campbell Soup Co. expands its 10-year-old Prego Spaghetti Sauce line with Prego Tomato & Basil, Prego Extra Chunky Mushroom with Extra Spice, and Prego Extra Chunky Garden Combination (*see* 1987). It will introduce Prego Pizza Sauce next year and Prego Extra Chunky with "bigger, tender-crisp vegetables" in 1993 (*see* 1994).

Life Savers introduces Holes, marketed in plastic containers in a bid to compete with the Tic-Tacs produced by Italy's Ferrero S.p.A.

M&M/Mars introduces 12 new candy bar brands and raises its advertising budget.

Only 51 percent of Americans over age 10 drink coffee, down from 75 percent in 1971.

The last Automat closes April 9 at 200 East 42nd Street, New York, a location that did not open until 1958 and that has been charging high prices for what were once bargains (*see* 1978). Former Parks Commissioner Henry J. Stern, who used to stop at other Automats for lemon meringue pie between deliveries when he was young Western Union bicycle messenger, says of the Automat, "It was equivalent to the Woolworth Building and Macy's windows. It was the most public place in town." Kent L. Barwick, president of the Municipal Art Society, says, "Automats were right up there with the Statue of Liberty."

General Mills opens its 500th Red Lobster seafood restaurant (at Portland, Ore.) (*see* 1988). By 1994 there will be more than 630 outlets in 49 states, Canada, and Japan serving upwards of 86 million pounds of seafood (from the Atlantic, Pacific, Gulf of Mexico, and foreign waters) and freshwater fish (plus steak and chicken) to more than 130 million patrons.

Au Bon Pain opens its 100th store (*see* 1984). It will add 22 stores next year by reacquiring Au Bon Pain West, a midwestern operation which it franchised in the 1970s, and will execute franchise agreements with operators in Japan and Chile (*see* 1993).

McDonald's introduces the McLean Deluxe, a hamburger that is 91 percent fat free with just 10 grams of fat (*see* 1986). Carrageenan, an extract of Irish moss and other red algae used for years as a stabilizer and thickener in foods, has been substituted for much of the fat, but unless eaten immediately after cooking the McLean is tasteless and McDonald's patrons reject it. The Center for Science in the Public Interest has analyzed McDonald's Quarter Pounder and found that it weighs in at 420 calories, with 20 grams of fat and 8 grams of saturated fat—40 percent of the recommended daily limit—even without cheese or french fries.

The world's largest Burger King opens in August at Budapest as Grand Metropolitan vies with McDonald's for dominance in the Eastern European market (*see* Moscow, 1989). Burger King has advertised in the United States with the slogan "Have it your way," but this means only that the patron may choose any of various toppings: the Whopper and all other Burger King burgers are cooked well done. Grand Metropolitan's Burger King chain has grown to have 7,120 outlets in 50 countries with systemwide sales of $6.7 billion; its Budapest franchise is a joint venture by British and American investors with Hungary's state-owned Pannonia hotel chain.

Arby's opens its 2,500th restaurant, at Mexico City (*see* 1981). It becomes the first fast-food chain to introduce a complete light menu, with three sandwiches and four salads that are 94 percent fat free and contain fewer than 300 calories each (*see* 1994).

Boston Chicken is acquired by investors who move the company to the Chicago suburb of Naperville, Ill., and begin franchising operations (*see* 1985). Former Blockbuster Video franchiser Scott Beck, 32, whose father was a co-founder of Waste Management and who sold his Blockbuster stake back to the parent company for $120 million 2 years ago, heads a management team that uses computers to maximize efficiency and relies on just 23 large franchisees to expand. By year's end, there are 34 Boston Chicken restaurants and/or take-out locations, some of them company owned, and by mid-1994 there will be 330, with a new one opening every business day, all selling generous portions of fresh (never frozen) rotisserie chicken with mashed potatoes made from scratch at affordable prices.

Dublin's Commons Restaurant opens April 9 (50th anniversary of novelist James Joyce's death) in the basement of University College's Newman House (where Joyce once studied) on St. Stephen's Green. Proprietor Michael Fitzgerald, 38, and his chef, Gerard Kirwan, offer patrons French cooking with some Irish touches: warm foie gras; turbot baked in Irish bacon; guinea fowl stuffed with chicken; pheasant; veal sweetbreads, liver, and medallions of beef with three sauces; several kinds of pototoes; Cashel blue cheese, and Cooleeney camembert.

Boston's first Cambodian restaurant, Elephant Walk, opens in August in a onetime police headquarters at 70 Union Square, Somerville. Former Cambodian ambassador to Taiwan Kenthao de Monteiro, 66, could not return to his country after its takeover by the Khmer Rouge in 1975 and had to find a new life for himself, his wife, Longteine, now 53, and their two daughters. Longteine, who had learned to cook both French and Chinese food, opened a Cambodian restaurant at Béziers, west of Marseilles, under the name Amrita in 1980 and prospered, but the De Monteiros found the French to be racist and have moved to Boston with the help of their daughter Nadsa, who has married Robert Perry (with whom she attended school in Taiwan). Patrons of Elephant Walk can choose from a French menu (steak au poivre, coq au vin, canard à l'orange, salmon with sorrel sauce) or a Cambodian menu (a Khmer noodle soup with fried garlic and pork, marinated cubed beef with lime sauce, ground pork in coconut milk with peanuts and rice cakes, vegetable curry, mussels sautéed with basil, sliced and scented catfish steamed with coconut milk and served in banana-leaf cup, and *sangkhia*—a dessert of steamed butternut squash custard), all prepared by Longteine de Monteiro, who works in the kitchen 7 days a week.

The New York restaurant TriBeCa Grill opens at 375 Greenwich Street, near Franklin Street, in a onetime coffee warehouse that has been turned into the TriBeCa Film Center by screen actor Robert De Niro, Jr., and others. De Niro has engaged Drew Nieporent of the nearby Restaurant Montrachet to manage the place, which has a long bar, formerly used at Maxwell's Plum on Second Avenue and purchased at an auction of that restaurant's fixtures. Paintings, prints, and drawings on the wall are by Robert De Niro, Sr. Chef Don Pintabona, formerly of La Régence at the Plaza-Athénée and Aureole, prepares scallop chowder (with chunks of lobster at dinner), Thai-style fried oysters, pasta, salmon, red snapper, swordfish (grilled, sautéed, or roasted), duck sautéed in orange sauce with Szechwan chili peppers, steaks, veal chops, loin of pork with corn bread, and desserts that include citrus-flavored custard in a hollowed orange with a poppy-seed crust, cinnamon-scented applesauce cake with vanilla ice cream, chocolate torte, and cut fruit.

The New York restaurant Lespinasse opens in September at 2 East 55th Street in the 87-year-old St. Regis Hotel, which has been refurbished at a cost of more than $100 million. Named for Julie de Lespinasse, one of the great Parisian salon leaders in the reign of Louis XV, the restaurant has a kitchen headed by Swiss-born chef Grey Kunz. His specialties include cold poached chicken with foie gras over shreds of spaghetti squash with a dressing of green mango, ginger, and lime; fricassee of wild mushrooms and artichoke hearts; minted soup of braised cucumbers with couscous salad in the center; steamed black sea bass served in a bowl with a Thai-inspired kaffir lime-leaf "emulsion"; veal chops with tangerine-enhanced *sambal* (a peppery Indonesian sauce); ragout of venison in a brandied pepper sauce, short ribs of beef with a port glaze; dessert soups; apricot tart with a sauce of almond ice cream; and yogurt mousseline with slightly stewed berries. The prix fixe lunch is $38, dinner $50, and a five-course dinner with a sampling of desserts $64.

The Los Angeles restaurant Granita, opened in Malibu by Wolfgang Puck and Barbara Lazaroff, is a Mediterranean-style place specializing in seafood (*see* Eureka, 1990). Joseph Manzare is chef, Rochelle Huppen pastry chef.

The Los Angeles restaurant Ca'Brea, opened at 346 South La Brea Avenue by Antonio Tommasi and John Louis de Mori of 1988 Locanda Veneto fame, has twice as many seats as their earlier place and a chef, Mark Peel, whose specialties include *antipasti,* baked Manila clams with breadcrumbs and porcini, *tortelloni, bigoletti* (a Venetian paella) with "wild" herbs from Tommasi's garden, *risotto tortino,* veal chops, lamb chops, air-dried roast duck, and fresh fish. Pastry chef Michael Richard's desserts include *tiramisù* (vanilla cream custard), warm apple tart with balsamic vinegar sauce, pan-fried Venetian cream, and *dolce Maria* (a warm, round chocolate cake served with an espresso sauce).

The Los Angeles restaurant Drago opens at 2628 Wilshire Boulevard, Santa Monica. Sicilian-born proprietor Celestino Drago, 34, who opened Celestino in Beverley Hills 6 years ago, offers dishes that include *bresaola*, prosciutto, *carpaccio, valtellina* with pink grapefruit and arugula, *tortina di baccalà* (salt cod cake with a compote of onions and a warm vinaigrette sauce), spaghetti al cartoccio and other pasta dishes, pumpkin-filled spinach tortelloni with spinach tagliatelli and beef ragù, fresh New Zealand lamb, roast chicken, artichoke-stuffed quail with sausage forcemeat, roast rabbit with black olive sauce and bell peppers, grilled swordfish steak, cannoli, passion fruit crème brûlée, and ricotta cheesecake.

The Los Angeles seafood restaurant Water Grill opens in the Pacific Mutual Building at 544 South Grand Street, offering up to 40 varieties of fish and shellfish. The proprietors are the owners of Santa Monica's Ocean Avenue Restaurant, and the executive chef is Matthew Stein, a graduate of the Culinary Institute of America who has been a *saucier* at New York's Le Cirque. Specialties include oysters from many sources; mussels from Prince Edward Island; halibut cheeks, lobsters, monkfish, and scallops from Maine; spot prawns from Santa Barbara and Canada; sardines and sometimes anchovies from Santa Monica; black sea urchins from central California waters; dungeness crabs; Florida stone crab claws; amberjack, grouper, red snapper, and tilefish from the Gulf of Mexico; trolled salmon from Seattle; cockles on occasion from New Zealand; and roasted deline cod with artichokes and shiitake mushrooms. Pastry chef David James prepares chocolate nut torte with chocolate and caramel sauces and preserves, bluegrass pie, and a baked tart with a chocolate chip cookie–like filling served with fudge and vanilla sauces and vanilla ice cream.

The San Francisco restaurant Etrusca opens at 101 Spear Street in the Rincon Center. Executive chef Ruggero Galdi, a native of Bergamo, offers specialties that change every day but may include *riscaldata* (reheated) slices of bread sautéed in olive oil; white bean and vegetable soup cooked with thyme and rosemary; prosciutto and cheese baked in a wood-burning oven; *bresaola* (air-dried beef) with Tuscan olive oil; *pizzocheri di teglia* (whole-wheat fettucine with sautéed potatoes, braised green cabbage, and Fontina cheese); *maiale agrodolce* (braised pork loin with vinaigrette and chutneylike mustard); rack of veal with roasted porcini, grilled fennel, and potato gratin; oven-roasted rabbit with mushrooms and peppers; polenta with melted Fontina; grilled sturgeon; layers of chocolate genevoise with chocolate mousse and raspberry sauce; white chocolate semifreddo studded with raisins, chocolate chips, and nougat; and almond shortbread filled with lemon curd.

San Francisco's Cypress Club opens at 500 Jackson Street; it is named after the place in the 1939 Raymond Chandler detective novel *The Big Sleep*. Proprietor John Cunin, formerly manager and maître d'hôtel at Masa's, has engaged chef Cory Schreiber, 30, who prepares dishes that include tomato soup with a streak of yogurt and corn fritter, steamed mussels, celery Victor (a salad of poached celery hearts created nearly a century ago by Victor Hirtzler of the St. Francis Hotel), and Hangtown fry (a salad made with oysters and bacon). A *tandura* handles skewered veal tenderloins, California lamb loins, chicken, rabbit, quail, and whole fish (striped bass, pompano, or—more often—tai or sea bream from the South Pacific). Patrons enjoy also whole sautéed sand dabs laid across corn and green olives with potato cake on the side, spiced salmon, and *naan* (Indian teardrop-shaped bread). Desserts include chocolate chip ice cream sandwich, pear cake with hazelnut ice cream, crème brûlée with a frozen banana covered with chocolate and nuts, and passion fruit parfait.

The San Francisco restaurant Sol y Luna opens at 475 Sacramento Street serving tapas; gazpacho made with fennel; green-lipped mussels steamed in beer with thyme and lime; raisin-studded meatballs with hot tomato sauce; salt cod; Argentine churrasco (peppered rib-eye steak with bacon, marrow bones, and fried onions); paella; spicy chicken steamed in banana leaves with potatoes, red bananas, and guajillo chilies; and—inevitably—sangría. The proprietors are Ember Martin, who has Brazilian roots, and Fernando Moreno, whose family came originally from Ecuador; their chef, Amaryll Schwertner, leaves in a few months, along with the bread maker and pastry maker, but chef James Moffat, who has worked with Schwertner at the Santa Fe Bar and Grill, takes over with ideas picked up on his travels in Spain and Portugal before the restaurant opened.

The 81-year-old Budapest restaurant Gundel's reopens under the direction of New York restaurateur George Lang, now 70, who revives its old elegance.

1992

President George Bush visits a National Grocers' Association convention while campaigning in Florida and expresses astonishment at a state-of-the-art electronic scanner. More ordinary scanners are now commonplace in U.S. supermarkets, and a *New York Times* report makes it look as though Bush has never seen one. Cartoonists, satirists, and late-night television comedians ridicule the president, who has denied that his programs favor the rich over the middle class, and he loses his bid for reelection to Arkansas governor Bill Clinton, whose backers include Arkansas poultry tycoon Don Tyson of Tyson Foods (*see* Arctic Alaska, pork production, below).

Civil war in Sudan starves hundreds of thousands; similiar conditions prevail in Angola and Mozambique. Mozambique's 16-year bush war is declared over in October, but people in drought-stricken rebel territory, waiting for Red Cross food, don't know that a cease-fire has been signed at Rome. At least 1 million have died, and survivors are at the mercy of bands of armed soldiers roving the countryside out of control. Fertile land has prevented mass starvation on the scale of Somalia (below). Television does not show the victims of starvation, and little food relief is forthcoming from the West.

Famine kills more than 300,000 in Somalia as the nation falls into anarchy and armed thugs prevent world food aid from relieving starvation. Scenes of starving people appear on world TV screens, the U.N. Security Council moves December 3 to aprove U.S.-led military intervention, and the first of some 28,000 troops arrive in Somalia December 9 to expedite food deliveries.

European trade barriers have come down as of January 1, permitting free passage of food and other goods from one country to another.

World cacao prices fall to an 18-year low of $860 per metric ton in the summer before rebounding in 6 weeks to $1,055. Russia and other Eastern European countries that once were significant importers have reduced their demand as a result of economic difficulties, and a stockpile of 1.4 million tons (a 7-month supply) has depressed prices, but speculators note that drought (above) has sharply reduced African cacao output, tree fungi are reducing Brazilian yields, the pod borer weevil is damaging Malaysian crops, and low prices are making it hard for planters to buy pesticides.

Hershey Foods pays $180 million for an 18.6 percent stake in Freia Marabou AS of Oslo, Scandinavia's largest confectionery company, whose Skør chocolate bar it has been distributing in America, but Philip Morris finances its Jacobs Suchard AG subsidiary in outbidding Hershey for a majority interest in Freia Marabou.

H. J. Heinz acquires Wattie's, a New Zealand food conglomerate with an entry to the Japanese market. By 1994, 45 percent of Heinz sales will be outside the United States.

New York's Gourmet Garage opens at 47 Wooster Street in SoHo. Founded by entrepreneurs who include former Flying Foods partner Andrew Arons (*see* 1981), it sells specialty foods wholesale from 2 o'clock in the morning until 9 and opens for retail customers at 10, offering exotic vegetables, free-range chickens, and other items not readily obtainable elsewhere.

Nonfiction: *The Opinionated Palate: Passions and Peeves on Eating and Food* by Barbara Kafka; *The Artful Eater: A Gourmet Investigates the Ingredients of Great Food* by Vermont author Edward Behr, 41. M. F. K. Fisher dies of Parkinson's disease at her home on the Bouverie Ranch in Glen Ellen, Calif., June 22 at age 83.

Cookbooks: *Great Cooks and Their Recipes: From Taillevent to Escoffier* by Anne Willan. *Party Food: Small and Savory* by Barbara Kafka. *Recipes from an Ecological Kitchen* by Lorna J. Sass, whose vegetarian recipes—inspired by Frances Moore Lappé's 1971 book and John Robbins's 1987 book—emphasize whole grains, fruits, and vegetables. She urges her readers to "buy organic food as much as possible" and to "favor regional, seasonal produce." While admitting that vegetarian cooking "has gotten a pretty bad rep—most of it well deserved—for being tasteless, uniformly brown, time-consuming to prepare, and heavy enough to sink an ocean liner." Her dishes, she vows, will be none of these things.

Average per capita Japanese rice consumption falls to 143 pounds, down from about 260 pounds in 1962 (*see* 1994).

Average U.S. per capita candy consumption hits 22 pounds, up from 18.9 pounds in 1984 (*see* 1944). Hershey, Mars, and Nestlé account for 90 percent of the U.S. chocolate bar business and control nearly 50 percent of the entire candy market.

Canada declares a moratorium on cod fishing in July. Overfishing by Canadians and encroachments by foreign trawlers have depleted stocks of northern cod, and colder water temperatures off Newfoundland have kept the fish away. The Ottawa government will spend $1.5 billion on a 5-year retraining program for 33,000 unemployed Atlantic fishermen and fish plant workers, with far more going to pay for assistance checks (*see* United States, 1993).

Tyson Foods (above) pays $212 million to acquire Arctic Alaska Fisheries, a Seattle-based company whose 36 fishing and fish-processing ships make it the world's largest at-sea fleet not government owned. But Arctic Alaska's chief product is surimi (*see* 1980), and prices of surimi will fall from $2/lb. to 50¢/lb. next year when the Japanese reduce their purchases of the artificial crabmeat and lobster meat. When Moscow makes matters worse by refusing to let Arctic Alaska ships fish in Russian waters, Tyson's investment will turn sour (*see* pork production, below).

Tyson Foods (above) buys a packing plant at Marshall, Mo., remodels it, and begins to apply its techniques of efficient poultry products production to pork products production. U.S. pork consumption has been rising at the expense of beef consumption, the $26 billion pork industry is still dominated by small family farmers who raise hogs as a sideline, but major corporations will now increase their share of the market, building giant, integrated complexes capable of feeding and handling as many as 80,000 artificially inseminated sows that produce about 3,000 pounds of pork per year each—pigs which in 5½ months go to automated slaughterhouses as lean, 245-pound hogs. Branded Tyson pork chops and specialties such as precooked, microwavable, breaded, stuffed, and spiced pork will be on the market by the end of next year.

U.S. dairy cows decline in number to 9.8 million, down from 10.8 million in 1980, but the average annual milk yield per cow climbs to 15,423 pounds, up from 11,891 in 1980 (Japanese cows average 17,464 pounds, Swedish cows 14,399, Dutch cows 13,892, Danish cows 13,605, cows in India only 2,095). Wisconsin remains the leading U.S. dairy state, but California is now close behind (*see* milk consumption, below).

Southern Africa has the worst drought in this century (*see* above). Crops fail on the eastern side of the continent from South Africa to Egypt. The lack of rainfall in the planting season is linked by meterologists to El Niño—the warm-water current in the Pacific which affects global atmospheric circulation. South Africa, Zimbabwe, and Kenya, which are all usually food exporters, are forced to import large quantities of grain.

Zimbabwe's sugarcane crop falls to 12,000 tons, down from 450,000 tons last year, and exports are halted.

The U.S. Department of Agriculture introduces the Food Pyramid to replace the four basic food groups, which have been touted for decades as the basis for a healthy diet: complex carbohydrates—bread, cereal, rice, and pasta dishes (6 to 11 servings per day)—represent the base of the pyramid; fruits and vegetables (5 servings) the second layer; milk, yogurt, and/or cheese (2 to 3 servings) and other protein (2 to 3 servings) the third; fats, oils, and sugars are to be used "sparingly."

An article in the May issue of *Clinical Pharmaceutical and Therapeutics* by University of Rochester clinical pharmacologist Michael Weintraub reports that overweight patients given obesity pills lost on average 16 percent of their weight in 8 months and kept most of it off for 3 years. Weintraub argues that the patients suffered from a shortage of serotonin—the powerful brain chemical that affects not only mood but also obsessive behavior and feelings of satiety (*see* Wurtmans, 1982). The drug Weintraub used on 121 subjects in a 4-year trial sponsored by the National Heart, Lung, and Blood Institute, was Pondimin, a variation on the drug Prozac introduced by Eli Lilly early in 1988. Unlike amphetamines, which have enormous potential for abuse, Pondimin raises serotinin levels, Weintraub says, and when used in combination with exercise and a healthy diet has few serious side effects, although it does occasionally produce dry mouth, diarrhea, unsteadiness, and memory problems. Enthusiasts insist that the drug quells food cravings, but critics warn that its long-term effects are uncertain and potentially serious (*see* 1994).

The U.S. Public Health Service recommends in September that women of childbearing age consume extra folic acid.

The Nutrition Labeling and Education Act, which goes into effect for most U.S. foods December 31, is designed to curb misleading health claims (*see* Proxmire Amendment, 1976). Sen. Orrin Grant Hatch, 58 (R. Utah), has obtained a 1-year moratorium for makers of dietary supplements (his state has a $900 million supplement industry), with the understanding that beginning December 20, 1993, such manufacturers will be allowed to make health claims for their products only if the claims are supported by "significant agreement" within the scientific community (but *see* 1993).

Charlie's Lunch Kit, introduced by H. J. Heinz's StarKist unit in September, is a do-it-yourself tuna salad product that includes tuna fish and packets of mayonnaise and relish (*see* 1963). StarKist has more than 44 percent of the huge U.S. canned tuna market (average U.S. per capita consumption has risen to 3.7 pounds) and is the fifth-largest U.S. dry grocery brand. Aimed at working women who carry their own lunch to work, Charlie's Lunch Kit competes with Oscar Mayer's Lunchables—a mix of cold cuts, cheeses, and crackers—and Lunch 'n Munch, a similar product marketed by Sara Lee's Hillshire Farms unit (*see* Stouffer's Lunch Express, 1994).

Glory Foods, Inc. of Columbus, Ohio, introduces a line of 17 soul food products. They will be available in New York and southern markets by mid-1993 (*see* Sylvia's, 1993).

Unilever introduces an ice cream that is virtually fat free: in Britain it is sold as Walt's "Too Good to Be True," in Denmark as Frisko "For godt til at være sandt," and it will be introduced next year in Australia. Demand increases in Europe for Unilever's superpremium ice cream, Ranieri, and for its ice cream gâteau Romantica.

Average per capita U.S. consumption of whole milk falls to 79.6 pounds, down from 168 in 1975, but consumption of low-fat milk reaches 99.3 pounds, up from 53.2, and of skim milk 25 pounds, up from 11.5, as Americans try to curb their butterfat intake.

Coca-Cola introduces a ready-to-drink bottled iced tea under the Nestea label in partnership with Nestlé, competing with Snapple (*see* 1987), whose overall sales reach $232 million—up from just $13 million in 1988; PepsiCo follows suit in partnership with Unilever's Lipton division, and Lipton will soon overtake both with a premium-priced Lipton Original in bottles and Lipton Brisk in cans and 64-ounce bottles (*see* Liptonice, 1994).

AriZona brand bottled iced tea is introduced in a 24-oz. "single-serve" can May 5 by the Brooklyn, N.Y., beer distributor Ferolito, Vultaggio & Sons, founded in 1971 by John Ferolito and Don Vultaggio, who 6 years ago introduced Midnight Dragon Malt Liquor and this year launch Crazy Horse Malt Liquor in a 40-oz. bottle. Their ready-to-drink iced tea will have sales of more than 10 million cases next year with a 12.6 percent market share that will make it fourth in the U.S. RTD tea business (behind Snapple, Lipton, and Nestea), about 80 percent of sales being in New York, New Jersey, south Florida, and Detroit. They will also market their iced tea in cartons, along with lemonade and strawberry punch, and fill 20-oz. AriZona bottles with fruit drinks.

U.S. imports of Chilean wine increase to nearly 2 million cases, up from 220,000 in 1987, with the lion's share coming from Viña Concha y Toro, headed by Eduardo Guilisasti Tagle, 72. Chile's land and labor costs are lower than California's, and her climate favors wine growing better than does France's.

The 120-year-old Paris restaurant Prunier's is taken over by Jean-Claude Goumard and becomes Goumard Prunier. Goumard, who has been operating a nearby restaurant, brings in his chef, Georges Landriot, from up the street, and restores Prunier's sagging reputation, serving not only good oysters (claires, spéciales, belons) but also clams (palourdes), served on traditional seaweed and accompanied by rye bread; salade de tourteau mousseline d'herbes (crab salad with herbs); friture de pistes with sauce rélevé (fried squid with spiced and herbed mayonnaise); *fricassée de moules de bouchot aux girolles* (fricasee of cultivated mussels with yellow trumpet-shaped mushrooms); *brochette de langoustine aux herbes Thaï* (skewered Norway lobster with Thai herbs); *Saint-Pierre rôti aux épices indiennes* (roasted John Dory with Indian spices, served with basmati rice); Channel sole with braised green herbs and spinach; *croquant au chocolat* (chocolate mousse sheets interleaved with layers

of crisp caramel); *"calisson" aux framboises* (lozenge-shaped, almond-flavored millefeuilles with raspberries); and good cheeses.

The Washington, D.C., restaurant Red Sage opens at 605 14th Street N.W. Chef-proprietor Mark Miller began making chili dishes at his Coyote Café in Santa Fe, N.M., and soon has a long waiting list for reservations at the Red Sage.

The Los Angeles restaurant Posto opens at 14928 Ventura Boulevard in Sherman Oaks. Proprietor Piero Selvagio, who opened Primi in 1985, has sent his chef Luciano Pellegrini to Italy for 6 months to apprentice with a sausage maker and work in a fish restaurant. Pellegrini's specialties include *frico* chips with a freshly grated Parmesan cheese, pancetta-wrapped snails with *polenta* wedges and spinach, salmon spiced with juniper berries and star anise, *risotto al Barolo* with *brasato*, roasted tuna steak with red and yellow peppers and capers, *piadina* (an unleavened, crackerlike bread), and *panna cotta* (custard with an almond praline crown).

The Los Angeles restaurant Kippan opens at 260 North Beverly Drive in Beverly Hills. Chef David Kanai apprenticed for more than 10 years with master chef Fujita Kippan at Kyoto and has started the place with his wife, June, to serve not only traditional Japanese sushi and sashimi but also such dishes as *paella* made with dungeness crab and green-lipped mussels; deviled chicken *nikomi* (made with grapes and red wine, spiced with soy sauce and ginger, and served over spinach noodles); chicken, beef, and seafood curries; *saikyo-yaki* (buttered black cod grilled with bell peppers); pan-fried *calamari*; and cheesecake with kabocha squash.

1993

More than 10 percent of Americans—26.6 million people—rely on food stamps in January to help them get enough to eat. It is the highest number since the program began in 1964 and an indication that while the nation may be emerging from recession the economy is not generating enough new jobs. A national study released in mid-November by the Urban Institute shows that 12 percent of older Americans sometimes go hungry or must choose between paying rent and eating, or between buying their prescribed medicine and eating.

Farmers in India storm Cargill headquarters there in January and in July destroy the company's $2.3 million seed-processing center. New patenting laws under the General Agreement on Tariffs and Trade (GATT; *see* 1994) have threatened to raise prices as much as 60-fold on seed, and Former President George Bush refused to sign a Biodiversity Treaty at a Rio de Janeiro environmental conference last year because of a clause that would block such patenting laws. "Cargill is one of the biggest seed producers in the world who use their clout to impoverish Third World farmers," says M. D. Nanjundswamy, a law professor who champions the farmers' cause; "Cargill and other multi-nationals have a philosophy that threatens the very sovereignty of the nation." Cargill responds that it will not patent its seeds. Says a company spokesman, "Most hybrid varieties remain novel for 3 years. Do you know how long it takes for a patent to come through? Nothing less than a year." The hybrids in question have in many cases been developed by modifying one or two genes out of 23,000 in seeds that are native to India.

Rains return to sub-Saharan Africa in April, reversing the effects of the century's worst drought and helping some countries recover from devastating famine. But civil war continues to disrupt agriculture in Angola, Mozambique, Somalia, and Sudan, where some 15 million tons of grain are needed to relieve hunger.

Flagstar Companies, owner of Denny's fast-food chain, reaches a "Fair Share" Agreement with the National Association of Colored People (NAACP), which has charged the chain with refusing service to black customers, forcing them to wait longer than white patrons, or asking them to pay in advance. Flagstar agrees to spend $1 billion in the next 7 years on jobs and contracts for minorities (*see* 1994).

Raw sugar prices jump when Cuba's harvest comes in at only 4.28 million metric tons, the smallest in 30 years. Heavy rains have turned fields to mud, slowing machines and workers trying to cut cane when its sugar content is highest, fuel is short because Russian oil imports have ended, and the lack of convertible currency obliges antiquated sugar mills to make their own replacement parts when anything breaks. Sugar represents more than 60 percent of Cuban export, and the small crop is a blow to the nation's economy.

Russian bread prices rise October 15 as government subsidies end. The new price varies from 90 to 190 rubles per kilo, depending on variety, up from 13 to 25 in September of last year, and reaches close to 300 by year's end. Instead of subsidizing inefficient collective farmers and making bread so cheap that it was fed to animals, the government now subsidizes people receiving the minimum pension (14,620 rubles, or $12.18, per month), children under age 16, and students under age 18. The average monthly pension is about 24,000 rubles, the average monthly wage about 60,000 ($50).

A Mexican investor group headed by billionaire financier Carlos Cabal Peniche, 36, pays $525 million to acquire Fresh Del Monte Produce NV from RJR Nabisco. Grupo Cabal controls 85 percent of Mexico's tomato exports, 20 percent of her mango exports, and 30 percent of her avocado exports as well as being a leading exporter of bananas and pineapples (*see* 1994).

Kraft General Foods acquires Shredded Wheat from RJR Nabisco and markets it as a Post cereal (*see* 1928).

Campbell Soup Co. forms a venture with Nakano Vinegar to create Campbell Nakano, which will market Campbell soups in Japan.

Campbell Soup Co. (above) acquires a majority interest in Arnott's Ltd., Australia's largest and oldest (founded in 1868) commercial bakery. Australian-born David W. Johnson has been Campbell's CEO since January 1990.

Nestlé Group Mexico and NutraSweet Co. form Ingredientes Nutrativos, S.A., a joint venture to market food products in Mexico.

ConAgra acquires Hebrew National Foods, which has been bought and sold by several companies since the 1940s (*see* 1905). The U.S. market for kosher foods has grown to almost $2 billion, up from $1.25 million, with nearly half of annual sales coming in the weeks before Passover (although only 1.75 million of the 6 million customers for kosher foods are Jewish, the rest being Muslims, Seventh-Day Adventists, and others who consider kosher food healthier and are often willing to pay a premium for it). Coca-Cola, Coors, General Mills, Hershey, Kraft General Foods, Nestlé, and many other mainstream food companies have obtained kosher certification from the Orthodox Union, an umbrella organization whose mark—an O with a U inside—is found on more than 80 percent of U.S. kosher foods.

Sara Lee acquires Bessin Corp., which has made kosher meats since the 19th century and whose brands include Sinai Hot Dogs, the second leading kosher frankfurters after those of Hebrew National (above).

Archer Daniels Midland and Pillsbury announce a joint venture in August to market ADM's Harvest Burger meat substitute patties on a nationwide basis under the Green Giant label.

General Mills acquires Colombo Yogurt Co., which it will market along with its Yoplait brand (*see* 1991; Yoplait, 1984). Beginning in January of next year it will add Lemon Cream, Mandarin Orange, and Coffee & Cream to the Colombo product line.

Unilever acquires Kraft General Foods's ice cream division in September. Now the largest U.S. producer of ice cream, with annual sales of more than $350 million in a $2.2 billion industry, Kraft has been promoting its Breyer's brand as an "all-natural" product (*see* 1866; National Dairy, 1926). Kraft retains the Breyer's and Sealtest names for non–ice cream products, such as frozen yogurt, and retains its line of Frusen Glädjé superpremium ice cream. Breyer's is the leading single brand of ice cream in sales (Häagen-Dazs is third, Ben & Jerry's sixth). Unilever, which has owned Good Humor since 1961, acquired Isaly Klondike Co., maker of the Klondike Bar, and Popsicle Industries in January.

Kraft General Foods sells its Birds Eye frozen fruit and vegetable business in December for $140 million to Dean Foods, which becomes second only to Pillsbury's Green Giant as a U.S. processor of canned and frozen fruits and vegetables (Del Monte drops to third; *see* Bellingham, 1990). In addition to being a major producer of private-label dairy products for such major supermarket chains as Kroger and Jewel, Dean has been supplying canned and frozen vegetables under the brand names Larsen, Shaw, Freshlike, and Veg-all, cheese under the brand name McCadam, and pickles under the brand name Whitfield. It has become second only to Campbell Soup's Vlasic division (and bigger than Heinz) in pickles and marinated cucumbers. It supplies the cream cheese for Sara Lee Cheesecake and the ice cream for hundreds of Baskin-Robbins stores; it has helped McDonald's reduce the fat content of its milk shakes, tartar sauce, and Big Mac sauce; and it produces the ingredients for brands marketed by General Foods, Kraft, Nabisco, Nestlé, and other food industry giants; but profit margins in good years are two to five times higher on vegetables than on milk products, and Dean has seized the opportunity to expand in that area.

Russell Stover Candy Co. pays $35 million to acquire the Whitman's Chocolate trademark and related assets from Pet Inc. (*see* Whitman's Sampler, 1912; Stover, 1923). Whitman had 1992 sales of $85 million, but Pet wants to concentrate on its Old El Paso and Progresso foods, which account for 45 percent of its profits.

Nestlé acquires Source Perrier, including Perrier's Poland Spring subsidiary.

Coca-Cola announces April 27 that it will pay $195 million to acquire a 30 percent stake in the soft drink operations of Fomento Económico Mexicano, S.A., the Monterey-based company which holds Coke's biggest foreign franchise.

Cadbury-Schweppes announces September 9 that it will acquire A&W Brands, including root beer, cream soda, and Country Time Lemonade, for $334 million, increasing its share of the U.S. soft drink business to 5.6 percent (*see* Canada Dry, 1985).

Canadian private-label food marketer David A. Nichol, now 53, resigns from Loblaw in December to advise other manufacturers and retailers, including the U.S. discount chain Wal-Mart (*see* 1978; Wal-Mart, 1988). Trying to duplicate in food retailing its success in dry goods, Wal-Mart uses the President's Choice private-label line as a model for its Sam's American Choice line, sold at Super Centers and Sam's Club warehouse stores.

The Italian dairy giant Parmalat S.p.A. purchases worldwide rights to the Dasi UHT (Ultra High Temperature) aseptic processing system for shelf-stable milk (*see* Parmalat, 1961). Invented in the early 1980s but never fully developed or implemented, the Dasi system heats milk to a temperature of more than 280° F. for about 3 seconds (as compared to about 170° F. for 15 to 20 seconds in the case of regular pasteurized milk), not letting it touch any hot surface, and then cools it quickly before its taste can be "bruised." Parmalat also buys a 49 percent interest in Dasi Products of Decatur, Ala., which has been used to co-pack extended-shelf-life milk in bag-in-box packs for institutitional use. Available for some years in Europe, South America, and parts of Asia, the aseptically packaged milk comes in a package unlike any milk carton, has a shelf life of about 6 months without refrigeration before it is opened, tastes like fresh milk, sells at a premium price, and will be available in whole milk, low-fat 2 percent, and low-fat 2 percent chocolate milk versions in almost every state east of the Mississippi by 1995.

The Food and Drug Administration gives approval November 5 to bovine somatotropin (BST), a genetically engineered synthetic hormone intended to increase the amount of milk produced by dairy cows. Developed at a cost of more than $300 million by Monsanto Company, whose scientists have inserted a bovine gene into the genetic code of a common strain of bacteria, the drug must be injected once every other week. It is said to increase production by 10 to 20 percent in well-managed herds, is almost identical to the natural growth hormone produced by a cow's pituitary gland, and makes no discernible difference in the cow's milk, but critics say it may increase udder infections, which will lead to increased use of antibiotics that will wind up in milk. Overproduction of milk has depressed prices, forcing many small family dairy farmers out of business, and agricultural economists say widespread use of BST will mean a further reduction in the number of cows and dairy farms.

The FDA (above) withholds approval of the Flavr Savr tomato—the first genetically altered food. Created by molecular biologists at Calgene, Inc.,

using recombinant DNA techniques, the new tomato, which resists spoilage, encounters opposition from fear mongers who encourage restaurateurs to insist on "natural" tomatoes (*see* 1994).

Sainsbury's The Magazine begins publication in May with food pages and recipes (40 percent of the glossy monthly's contents) prepared by Delia Smith, who has started the magazine with her husband, Michael Wynn Jones.

Nonfiction: *I Love Spam: America's Best-loved Foods* by U.S. syndicated columnist Carolyn Wyman, who reviews new supermarket foods for newspaper readers; *Can You Trust a Tomato in January? The Hidden Life of Groceries and Other Secrets of the Supermarket Revealed at Last* by U.S. writer Vince Staten, whose subject is the evolution of product marketing aimed at increasing supermarkets' share of the consumer food dollar.

Fiction: *The Road to Wellville* by U.S. novelist T. Coraghessan Boyle is based on the Kellogg brothers, spoofing the health food industry, vegetarianism, and self-improvement movements.

Cookbooks: *Great Good Food: Luscious Lower-Fat Cooking* by Julee Rosso of New York's Silver Palate. *Creative Appetizers* by Anne Willan. *Delia Smith's Summer Collection*, published in May to accompany a 10-part BBC 2 television series, will have sold 750,000 copies by July 1994. *The Taste of Country Cooking* by Edna Lewis. *Chef Paul Prudhomme's Fork in the Road* by Prudhomme, now 53, whose low-fat cookbook is based on his efforts to attain what he calls his "ideal" weight of 325 to 350 pounds (at 5 feet, 9 inches, Prudhomme generally weighs 40 to 70 pounds more than that; *see* 1984). He recommends using nonfat dairy products and cooked, puréed chickpeas and other legumes as thickeners in place of butter and oil. *The Mediterranean Kitchen* by restaurateur Joyce Goldstein of San Francisco's Square One. *The Florida Cookbook: From Gulf Coast Gumbo to Key Lime Pie* by Jeanne Voltz.

Nearly 1,000 new cookbooks are published every year, but a Chicago food consulting firm will report next year that Americans spend 29.4 percent of their food dollars on restaurant meals, up from 21.7 percent in 1978, and only 50.6 percent in food stores, down from 59.3 percent.

Average annual per capita U.S. beef consumption declines to 65.1 pounds, down from 80.7 in 1973, but average ground beef (hamburger) consumption rises to 26.6 pounds, up from 21.9 in 1973, as Americans eat 29 billion hamburger portions—nearly 120 per man, woman, and child. Pork consumption rises to 52.3 pounds per capita, up from 49. Lamb consumption falls to 1.3 pounds, down from 2.4; veal to .9 pound, down from 1.4.

Average annual per capita U.S. wheat flour consumption rises to 140 pounds, the highest level since 1947 (when it was about 144 pounds). Per capita flour consumption approached 200 pounds early in the century, when life required more physical effort and larger caloric intake; it peaked at 166 pounds in 1943 during World War II (when other foods were rationed), sank to an all-time low of 110 pounds in 1971 and 1972, but has increased 59 percent since 1970. Wholesale bakers account for about half the flour used, with pasta manufacturers using 11 percent.

Average annual per capita U.S. egg consumption falls to 232, down from 321 in 1960, as concerns about blood serum cholesterol levels continue to discourage egg eating, even though some studies show that cholesterol levels are related far more to dietary fats and saturated fats than to intake of dietary cholesterol.

The Mississippi and Missouri rivers rise along with their tributaries beginning in April and flood their banks in July and early August, breaching levees, halting barge traffic, killing 50, inundating vast areas of eight midwestern states, and causing an estimated $8 billion in crop damage in the worst such flooding ever seen. The southeastern United States meanwhile has a withering drought.

Monsoon rains in northern India, Bangladesh, and Nepal swell rivers, cause massive landslides, kill more than 2,000, and destroy millions of acres of wheat and rice crops in Punjab, Haryana, and elsewhere.

Russian officials halt pollack fishing June 15 in their 200-mile-wide territorial zone in the Sea of Okhotsk, but while Japan agrees to join in a 3-year moratorium on fishing in a 35- by 300-mile area of converging boundaries, Poland, South Korea, and China question whether pollack stocks are in peril.

They announce in late July that they will reduce their fishing activities in the area by 25 percent.

Alaska fishermen harvest a record 191 million salmon, including 40 million sockeye salmon from Bristol Bay, and—despite salmon mortality caused by dams on the Columbia River—deliver 854 million pounds of wild Pacific salmon to supplement the fish produced on salmon farms in Chile, Norway, and elsewhere.

The U.S. cod catch falls to 49 million pounds, down 19 percent from last year and the lowest figure since 1973. Cod fishing has been banned on Newfoundland's Grand Banks, and spawning stocks from the Grand Banks south to the Georges Bank off Massachusetts are at a historic low (see 1994; Canada, 1992).

U.S. seafood consumption reaches new heights, having climbed 25 percent in just 5 years.

The People's Republic of China exports 12 million metric tons of corn, 500,000 of sorghum, 1.4 million of rice, and 1 million of soybeans. Beijing imports 6 million metric tons of wheat, but only because it is often easier to supply coastal areas with imported wheat than to ship it vast differences from other parts of China. The People's Republic is the world's largest producer of wheat and rice, second largest of corn (see 1986), and fourth largest of soybeans. Chinese wheat stocks at year's end exceed 20 million metric tons for at least the 12th straight year, and total grain stockpiles are about 500 million metric tons.

Russia harvests 99.1 million metric tons of grain and imports another 11 million tons to prevent shortages (see 1994).

Japan has a poor rice crop and agrees in December to accept rice imports and gradually reduce tariffs, despite vehement political opposition from rice farmers (see 1994; consumption, 1992).

U.S. pear growers harvest 949,000 tons of fruit, up by one-third from 1983. Close to 95 percent of the crop grows in northern California, Oregon, and Washington, and more than half are Bartletts.

Nutritionist (and Tufts University chancellor) Jean Mayer dies of a heart attack at Sarasota, Fla., January 1 at age 72.

Megadoses of the antioxidant vitamin E as a preventive against coronary disease gain vindication in May when the prestigious *New England Journal of Medicine* publishes two studies involving more than 120,000 men and women. Researchers at the Harvard School of Public Health and at Boston's Brigham and Women's Hospital indicate that healthy people with the highest intakes of vitamin E develop coronary disease at a rate of about 40 percent lower than comparable people whose vitamin E intake is lowest, regardless of their blood cholesterol levels. The Recommended Daily Allowance for vitamin E is 15 international units, yet people who took about 100 units per day fared best in the studies. Although scientists caution that any formal health claim must await clinical tests that are more stringently designed and until the risks of vitamin E megadoses can be calculated, the studies in the medical journal elate the dietary supplement industry (but *see* 1994).

The Food and Drug Administration gains authority to regulate marketing claims by the $4 billion U.S. dietary supplement industry for its vitamins, minerals, and herbs (*see* 1992). The moratorium for application of the Nutrition Labeling and Education Act, granted by Congress last year, expires December 18, but the Senate has voted in November to delay further any implementation of the FDA's authority. The industry has gained support from libertarians and flooded Congress with mail, persuading Sen. Orrin Hatch, Rep. Bill Richardson (D. N.M.), and others that curbs on its claims will hamper discussion of vitamins' and minerals' potential health benefits; the FDA insists that it is not trying to interfere with consumers who want to buy dietary supplements but merely to keep the supplements from being sold with false or un-proven claims, and it has the support of the Center for Science in the Public Interest, many consumer groups, the food industry, Sen. Edward M. Kennedy, 61 (D. Mass.), and Rep. Henry A. Waxman (D. Calif.). Under its powers to pursue unsubstantiated claims on a case-by-case basis, the FDA has taken action against marketers of 188 dietary supplements in the past 3 years, sometimes seizing products and giving the industry and its customers an excuse for charging that they have been the victims of persecution.

The U.S. Department of Agriculture finds that the average school lunch served under the School Lunch Act of 1946 contains 25 percent more total fat and 50 percent more saturated fat than recommended in dietary guidelines (*see* 1994).

Riley Detweiler, 16 months old, of Bellingham, Wash., dies of food poisoning in January after eating hamburger at a Jack in the Box fast-food restaurant; at least 300 people, mostly children in the Seattle area, are stricken, as well as some in Idaho; 143 are hospitalized for as long as 25 weeks. *Escherichia coli* bacteria are found in the restaurant's hamburgers, which turn out not to have been cooked to the 155° F. temperature required by state law. (McDonald's says it has always required that its hamburgers be cooked to 157°, and federal officials consider boosting the national standard above the usual 140° level). The Jack in the Box episode raises questions about federal meat inspection practices. U.S. Department of Agriculture officials say that pathogens are normal in the food supply, given the unavoidable defects in inspection, and that it is up to consumers to cook foods properly, but criticism rises against the way meat and poultry are produced. The new Clinton administration proposes to overhaul the federal system of meat inspection, which now relies on looking for discoloration and feeling for disease, by using scientific techniques and monitoring equipment to discover hazardous microorganisms.

The USDA requires all raw meat and poultry to be labeled with cooking and handling instructions in response to the Jack in the Box tainted hamburger episode (above), it extends the October 15 deadline for such labeling to mid-April of next year on everything but ground and chopped meat, and a federal judge rules in mid-October that the department has not observed requirements of the Administrative Procedure Act with regard to public notice of its action and allowing time for comment. Many meatpackers say that they will comply anyway.

The Center for Science in the Public Interest issues a report showing high levels of sodium, fat, and cholesterol in 15 popular Chinese restaurant dishes. Many Chinese restaurants in Boston, Chicago, New York, and Washington, D.C., report that sales have dropped by as much as 35 percent; devotees of true Chinese food say that diets in rural China consist 70 percent of carbohydrates, only 10 percent of fat.

Pet Inc. introduces Progresso Healthy Classics ready-to-serve soups in January (*see* acquisition,

1986). The low-calorie soups—chicken noodle, chicken rice, lentil, minestrone, and vegetable—contain one-third less sodium, little cholesterol, and almost no fat (*see* Grand Metropolitan acquisition, 1995).

Lever Brothers introduces Promise Ultra, a nonfat margarine with only five calories per serving, in U.S. markets.

SnackWell's cookies and crackers, introduced in June by RJR Nabisco, are made without tropical oils and include Reduced Fat Cheese Crackers, Reduced Fat Classic Golden Crackers, Fat Free Cracked Pepper Crackers, Fat Free Wheat Crackers, Fat Free Devil's Food Cookie Cakes, Fat Free Cinnamon Graham Snacks, Reduced Fat Bite-Size Chocolate Chip Cookies, Reduced Fat Crunchy Oatmeal Raisin Cookies, Reduced Fat Chocolate Sandwich Cookies, and Reduced Fat Creme Sandwich Cookies—a product that will soon outsell Nabisco's Oreo cookies to become the favorite U.S. cookie.

Sylvia's Food Products introduces a line of canned soul food based on the menu of the famous Harlem, N.Y., restaurant, now headed by the founder's son, Van D. Woods (*see* restaurants, 1961; Glory Foods, 1992).

Hershey Chocolate introduces Hugs—white chocolate-covered almonds that meet with instant success as companions to the Hershey Kisses introduced in 1907.

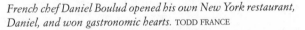

Wendy's opens 330 new outlets, bringing its total to 4,200 worldwide (two-thirds of them franchise restaurants), and adds 15,000 new employees (*see* 1969).

Au Bon Pain adds bagels, danish pastry, pecan rolls, scones, macaroons, and biscotti to its menus and acquires St. Louis Bread Co. with its 19 bakery cafés, which continue to operate under the St. Louis Bread name (*see* 1991; 1994)

The New York restaurant Daniel, opened in June at 20 East 76th Street, soon rivals Bouley as the city's

RJR Nabisco responded to consumer anxiety about the tropical oils in its crackers and cookies.

French chef Daniel Boulud opened his own New York restaurant, Daniel, and won gastronomic hearts. TODD FRANCE

finest. Chef-owner Daniel Boulod, 37, who has for 6 years been chef at Le Cirque, offers dishes that include foie gras, chilled lobster consommé, pumpkin-and-squash soup, linguine with white truffles, nine-herb ravioli, rib-eye chops, tripes gratinées, black sea bass, steamed skate, rillettes of squab, duck, game, rabbit, pork, quail salad, gratin de chocolat, fruit soup, wine-poached pear with verbena ice cream, baked red wine tart, and crème brûlée with macerated strawberries.

The Boston restaurant Marco Solo opens at 300 Boylston Street, Newton, at the Atrium. Marco Berkowitz, who operated Legal Seafood with his father, George, and brother Roger (*see* 1968) has had what many view as a falling-out with the family and ventured out on his own.

1994

U.N. forces lift the Serbian siege of Sarajevo, permitting food supplies to reach the Bosnian capital as the 2-year-old war continues, but the relief is short lived.

Japan's Imperial Palace announces in early March that "with the consent of their Majesties, the Emperor and Empress," royal meals will be served beginning the week of March 21 with rice grown in the United States, Thailand, and China. Pure Japanese rice has been scarce since last year's disastrous harvest, farmers have held back on deliveries, and the Cabinet orders that distributors must mix their rice to include at least 20 percent foreign rice, the price of at least one especially desirable type of Japanese rice soars to $7.75 per pound, black markets spring up to sell such rice, but a bumper crop of domestic rice depresses sales of imported rice, most of which winds up in warehouses.

Thousands of Rwandans die of hunger and related diseases as Hutu tribesmen slaughter Tutsis and then flee with their families into neighboring Zaïre to escape retribution from a new Tutsi government.

Cubans flee their island in makeshift rafts as food shortages worsen following the collapse of the former Soviet Union. A tightening of the U.S. embargo has blocked food imports and contributed to a lack of hard currency with which to pay for such imports; Cuba's climate is not conducive to producing wheat and many other staple food commodities. The individual food ration for July is 6 pounds of rice, 10 ounces of beans, half a pound of oil, 1 ounce of coffee, and 3 pounds of sugar; many Cubans barter other goods to obtain enough food.

Hunger among elderly Americans is surging, the *Wall Street Journal* reports in November, and decades-old programs such as Meals on Wheels cannot keep up. The *Journal* quotes a 1993 Urban Institute estimate that federal food-stamp programs and other food-assistance projects fail to reach at least two-thirds of needy older people, and "as many as 4.9 million elderly people—about 10 percent of the population aged 60 and older—are either hungry or malnourished to some degree, often because they are poor or too infirm to shop or cook." It quotes an assistant secretary for aging at the Department of Health and Human Services as saying, "For the first time, we have growing waiting lists. The level of malnutrition and real hunger is only increasing."

The Denny's fast-food chain agrees in May to pay more than $54 million to settle lawsuits filed by thousands of black customers (*see* 1993). It is the largest settlement ever made under U.S. public accommodation laws. Denny's has hired more black managers and announces November 8 that a black-owned Atlanta company will buy and operate as many as 47 Denny's restaurants in New York and New Jersey.

Canada agrees August 1 to restrict sharply her exports of wheat to the United States for 1 year following a dispute that arose in January at Shelby, Mont. Local farmer Hank Zell, 52, drove his truck to a grain elevator that ConAgra was using to import millions of bushels of Canadian grain, was told to get out of the way, and was soon joined by hundreds of other farmers in blockading the facility. This grassroots uprising threatened to precipitate a trade war, possibly involving California wine and Arkansas poultry; the U.S. International Trade Commission visited Shelby in April; and although the six commissioners split evenly on whether the grain imports were disrupting the overall U.S. wheat market, it was clear that the Canadian wheat was posing problems for Montana and North Dakota wheat farmers, as well as for U.S. taxpayers. Mostly because of poor U.S. wheat crops, Canadian wheat exports to the United States totaled about 100 million bushels in the fiscal year ending May 31, up from about 17 million in 1989 (a trifle compared to annual U.S. wheat exports of 1.2 billion bushels), and some of the commissioners concluded that the imported Canadian wheat had depressed the price of domestically grown wheat and cost U.S. taxpayers $170 million in additional farm payments over a 2-year period. U.S. trade representative Mickey Kantor says the reduction in Canadian imports will not have "any appreciable cost to consumers," but some consumer advocates disagree, noting that while only 6 percent of U.S. wheat imports come from Canada, that country accounts for 40 percent of imported durum wheat, used to make pasta. Semiprocessed durum wheat represents one-quarter of the cost of box of pasta and has nearly doubled in the past year because of poor U.S. harvests, say pasta makers, but wheat farmers note that the cost of raw wheat represents only 8¢ of a $1.50 box of pasta.

Russian farmers struggle to survive in a market economy as production of grain, meat, milk, and vegetables declines for a fifth straight year (*see* 1993). Fewer than 5 percent of the nation's 10 million farmworkers own even a small farm, the State Agriculture Ministry says that 68 percent of all farm machinery is more than 21 years old, tractor and fertilizer companies have gone out of business, fuel prices have soared, vegetables rot in the fields before they can be harvested, and Moscow imports Western surpluses.

U.S. hog prices fall 33 percent to their lowest levels in 20 years (*see* animal husbandry, below), but retail pork product prices in most places outside Iowa decline by only 2 or 3 percent, frustrating the hopes of the National Pork Council, farm state legislators, and farm groups that lower prices will increase consumption. The lower hog prices benefit meatpackers, grocers, and restaurants, but U.S. food prices generally increase by about 2 percent.

Subsidies to farmers cost consumers and taxpayers in the industrial countries more than $348 billion (about $394 per capita), down about 2 percent

from last year; many economists urge reform to reduce market distortions caused by direct subsidies and price supports, but some say that food prices would be higher without such supports.

Congress overwhelmingly approves a seventh General Agreement on Tariffs and Trade (GATT) (the Senate votes 76 to 24 December 1), Japan and other nations follow suit, and the resulting elimination of agricultural subsidies and lowering of tariff barriers promises to expand world trade, create jobs, and benefit everyone.

Stouffer Frozen Foods changes its name July 1 to Nestlé Frozen Foods (*see* Lean Cuisine, 1991). The company test-marketed Stouffer's Lunch Express and Stouffer's Lean Cuisine Lunch Express last year and introduces them nationally for the 11 percent of Americans who carry their lunch to work and, more specifically, for those who have microwave ovens at their places of work (76 percent of all workplaces, according to the Microwave Institute) (*see* Charlie's Lunch Kit, 1992). Light in calories and saturated fats, the eat-from-the-package products, which microwave in 5 minutes, come in 24 Lean Cuisine varieties, including Broccoli and Cheddar Cheese Potato, Cheese Lasagna Casserole with Vegetables, Fettucini with Chicken in Alfredo Sauce, Macaroni and Cheese with Broccoli, Mandarin Chicken, Pasta with Chicken in Herb Tomato Sauce, and Teriyaki Stir-Fry.

Barilla America is incorporated in July to help the Italian pasta and bread products company expand in the U.S. market (*see* 1979).

Allied-Lyons agrees in late March to acquire a controlling interest in Spain's Pedro Domecq Group (*see* 1730), a transaction valued at as much as £739 million ($1.11 billion) that makes Allied (now Allied-Domecq) second only to Grand Metropolitan plc (*see* 1988) as a producer and marketer of distilled spirits. Allied's Courvoisier cognac, Kahlua, Beefeater gin, and Hiram Walker brands have made it the world's fifth-largest distiller, Pedro Domecq's Presidente brandy and Sauza tequila make it the second largest, and it will divest itself of food companies to concentrate on spirits. Ramón Mora-Figueroa and his family retain a 27 percent interest in Pedro Domecq with a 6-year option to sell their stake to Allied for an additional £280 million.

Hain Pure Foods and its Hain and Hollywood brands is acquired from Pet Inc. April 13 by a U.S. investor group headed by former Häagen-Dazs executive Irwin Simon, 35 (*see* 1983). Simon has previously acquired Kineret, New York City's largest kosher frozen fish producer, and an all-natural frozen pizza company. Sales of Hain and Hollywood products—which now include rice cakes, canola oil, and 137 other food items—now exceed $80 million, and, counting sales of kosher frozen fish and all-natural frozen fish, Simon's companies gross close to $100 million.

Ralston Purina spins off its cereal division and Beech-Nut Packing Co. in April, creating a new company, Ralcorp, which will produce and market Beech-Nut baby foods and other products, Wheat Chex, Rice Chex, and other familiar Ralston brands (*see* 1989).

Swiss pharmaceutical giant Sandoz Ltd. acquires Gerber Products for $3.7 billion. Gerber has 73 percent of the U.S. baby food market but has had little success in penetrating overseas markets, even though France's per infant consumption of baby food jars is 55 dozen as compared with 50 dozen in the United States (the numbers for Eastern Europe and Asia are much lower).

Pillsbury announces in July that it will acquire Martha White, a 95-year-old, $165 million branded baking mix concern, based in Nashville, Tenn., that makes and markets fruit and corn muffin, cornbread, and dessert mixes in pouches plus packaged cornmeal, flour, grits, and corn bread mix.

Mexican financier Carlos Cabal Peniche agrees to buy Del Monte Foods Corp., the canned food company, from investors that include Citicorp and Merrill Lynch in a deal valued at more than $1 billion (*see* 1993), but Mexico's Finance Ministry accuses him September 5 of funneling between $200 million and $700 million to himself through illegal operations and issues a warrant for his arrest on criminal charges. Cabal is in Europe trying to raise capital from bankers there for the Del Monte purchase.

H. J. Heinz acquires Borden's $225 million food service business, which sells single-serving packages of condiments, sauces, and the like as well as bulk amounts of oil-based products such as mayonnaise.

Kohlberg Kravis Roberts agrees September 12 to acquire the rest of Borden Co. (including Borden and Meadow Gold dairy products, Creamette pasta, Wise snack foods, ReaLemon, and Cracker Jack) for $2 billion (*see* 1991). Borden was valued at $5.7 billion as recently as May 1991, but its management has failed to capitalize on the value of its brand names and move into products with higher profit margins. Former ConAgra boss Charles M. "Mike" Harper, now chairman of KKR's RJR Nabisco, will help try to make Borden more profitable.

H. J. Heinz outbids Campbell Soup Co. in October and agrees to pay nearly $200 million to acquire All American Gourmet Co., maker of Budget Gourmet frozen meals and side dishes, from Kraft General Foods. Budget Gourmet had 1993 sales of about $300 million, Heinz's Weight Watchers frozen foods had sales of about $350 million, and the acquisition puts Heinz into third place in frozen entrées, behind ConAgra (with its Banquet and Healthy Choice brands) and Nestlé (which owns Stouffer). Philip Morris, parent company of Kraft General Foods, sold its Birds Eye frozen vegetable and Breyer's ice cream businesses last year and has put its Kraft Food Services division up for sale in a continuing effort to divest itself of low-profit operations and concentrate on its high-profit cigarette business.

Canandaigua Wine Co. becomes the second-largest U.S. wine producer (Gallo remains the largest) by acquiring the Almaden and Inglenook wineries from Heublein, a subsidiary of Grand Metropolitan plc, for $130.5 million in cash. Canandaigua, which markets Paul Masson wines and Corona beer, also obtains Belaire Creek Cellars, Château La Salle, and Charles Le Franc table wines, Le Domaine champagne, Hartley and Jacques Bonet brandy, and wineries in Madeira and Escalon, Calif., in the deal.

The Canadian brewing giant John Labatt Ltd. spends $510 million to acquire a stake in Mexico's Femsa Cerveza, the 104-year-old division of Fomento Economico Mexicano, S.A., whose Carta Blanca, Dos Équis, Superior, Bohemia, and Tecate brands control 48 percent of the Mexican beer market. Labatt has outbid Molson Breweries of Canada Ltd., which is 20 percent owned by the Miller Brewing Co. subsidiary of Philip Morris (Femsa's major competitor, Grupo Modelo, which makes Corona, the nation's top-selling beer, is 17 percent owned by Anheuser-Busch.)

Quaker Oats agrees November 2 to acquire Snapple Beverage Co. for $1.7 billion, creating (with Quaker's Gatorade) the third-largest nonalcoholic beverage company in North America.

Campbell Soup Co. announces November 28 that it will pay $1.115 billion to acquire Pace Foods, the San Antonio company that has grown since 1947 to become the world's largest producer of salsas and other Mexican sauces.

Nestlé agrees December 16 to acquire Mexico's largest chocolate maker—La Azteca—from Quaker Oats (estimated price: about $160 million).

The genetically altered Flavr Savr tomato wins approval from the Food and Drug Administration May 18 (see 1993). Americans pay $4 billion per year to buy 4 billion pounds of tomatoes, but most store-bought tomatoes have little flavor as compared with home-grown varieties.

Nonfiction: *Consumed: Why Americans Love, Hate, and Fear Food* by New York writer Michelle Stacey, who deplores the obsession with avoiding dietary fats and says, "We must give up our hunger for certainty and for power over what remains the essential mystery of our lives and our deaths. The reward is large: a chance to live in harmony with our food rather than to struggle against it"; *The Hungry Soul: Eating and the Perfecting of Our Nature* by University of Chicago self-described humanist Leon R. Kass, who says people have become unconscious of what they eat; *The FDA Follies* by U.S. writer Herbert Burkholz, 60; *America's First Cuisines* by U.S. scholar Sophie Coe (née Dobzansky), 61, who writes about Aztec and Inca cookery; *Secret Formula: How Brilliant Marketing and Relentless Salesmanship Made Coca-Cola the Best-known Brand in the World* by Atlanta journalist Frederick Allen; *The Great Food Almanac* by Irena Chalmers.

Cookbooks: *Sheila Lukins All Around the World Cookbook* by New York's Silver Palate co-founder Lukins, now 51, whose book has a record initial printing of 350,000 copies; *In the Kitchen with Rosie: Oprah's Favorite Recipes* by U.S. television personality Oprah Winfrey's personal cook, Rosie Daley, 32, whose 50 recipes use a good deal of evaporated skim milk, nonfat cottage cheese, nonfat mayonnaise, and nonfat yogurt; *The Balti Cookbook* by Pakistani-born English cookery teacher Shehzad Husain, who gives recipes for breads, rice dishes, vegetables, and chutneys as well as for chicken, butter chicken, lamb tikka, spicy potatoes, and other stir-fry Balti dishes.

Films: Ang Lee's *Eat Drink Man Woman* with Sihung Lung is about a Chinese master chef in Taiwan and his grown daughters; Alan Parker's *The Road to Wellville* with Anthony Hopkins as breakfast food pioneer John Harvey Kellogg.

An international Convention on Desertification signed at Paris in October by some 100 nations establishes a "global mechanism" to prevent loss of agricultural lands, but some scientists insist that it is simply lack of rain—not overgrazing, overplanting, poor irrigation, and deforestation—that is creating problems in arid countries such as many in Africa. Rich nations pledge only modest amounts to fund the effort.

A flotilla of fishing boats chugs into Boston Harbor March 28 with signs protesting new federal rules restricting catches of cod, haddock, hake, and other bottom-feeding fishes, whose numbers have been sharply depleted (see Canada, 1992). In an effort to save the centuries-old Georges Bank fishery, Washington has imposed a moratorium on new fishing permits and cut by half the number of days that fishermen can spend at sea. Species formerly despised as "trash" fish—skate, ocean catfish (or wolffish), conger eel, and spiny dogfish—now attract purchasers unable, or unwilling, to pay as much as $9 per pound for fresh cod and even more for fresh haddock. President Clinton says March 21 that New England's fishing industry is in "virtual collapse" and offers $30 million in federal aid.

President Clinton calls the Washington State coastal area a disaster area as catches of pollack, salmon, and other Pacific species plummet, partly as a result of overfishing, partly because power projects have blocked spawning runs of anadromous fish (*see* Alaska, 1993).

U.S. hog farmers produce a record 17.5 billion pounds of pork as big corporations expand their operations, mostly in Missouri and North Carolina. Family farmers increase their herds and modernize to compete, but hog prices (above) fall far below break-even levels for many farmers.

The International Maize and Wheat Improvement Center (CIMMYT) in Texcoco, Mexico, announces in July that it has developed new strains of corn that can increase crop yields up to 40 percent in regions where drought and acidic soils present problems. Since half the 150 million acres of corn planted in the developing world are subject to drought, CIMMYT officials estimate that the new strains could feed 50 million more people per year.

Russia's grain harvest falls to about 90 million metric tons, down from 99.1 million last year, but the State Agriculture Ministry says in early September that it will import only 6 million tons. Imported grain cost on average 275,000 rubles ($170) per ton in the first half of the year, whereas grain procured locally cost only 72,000 rubles, but the ministry is quoted by the ITAR-Tass news agency as saying that it does not expect bread prices to increase substantially despite lower grain supplies.

The International Rice Research Institute (IRRI) at Los Baños in the Philippines announces in October that it has developed a new rice variety with the potential of increasing yields by 20 to 25 percent.

Florida's $8 billion orange, lemon, lime, and grapefruit industry comes under attack from the citrus leaf miner, a moth measuring only one-tenth of an inch long that disrupts photosynthesis by burrowing into the leaves of young trees. Entomologists suggest that the moth arrived from West Africa in 1992 with help from Hurricane Andrew but suggest that it may be controlled through biological means, as it has been in Australia and Southeast Asia, by using various species of wasps that lay eggs on the moth's larvae (newly hatched wasps eat the larvae). Florida's Citrus Commission has hired right-wing radio-TV commentator Rush Limbaugh as its spokesman, sparking calls for a national boycott, and the state's citrus industry

faces increasing competition from Mexico and Brazil (the Brazilian orange crop now exceeds that of Florida).

Brazil's coffee crop suffers the worst frost damage since 1975, causing a jump in U.S. coffee prices as roasters anticipate higher costs.

U.S. farmers harvest record crops of corn, rice, and soybeans and near-record crops of wheat; the number of farms drops to 1.9 million, the smallest number since 1850.

Provisions of the Nutrition Labeling and Education Act take effect May 2 and impose new U.S. labeling rules on makers of dietary supplements, who may no longer make therapeutic claims without providing the Food and Drug Administration with the same kind of proof required of food and pharmaceutical companies (*see* 1992; 1993). The $4 billion vitamin supplement industry spreads false fears that the FDA is planning to make their products available only by prescription, some Congressmen are deluged with letters of protest, often through campaigns orchestrated by the industry, and Congress gives the industry some relief.

The *Journal of the American Medical Association* (*JAMA*) has published a study in March saying that vitamin B$_3$ (niacin), used by many people to lower their cholesterol levels, is too toxic to be sold as a nonprescription drug. A team at the pharmacy school of the Medical College of Virginia did experiments with 46 patients taking high enough doses (2,000 to 3,000 milligrams per day) of the popular slow-release form of niacin to reduce cholesterol and found that it produced signs of liver toxicity in more than half of them, while older, less effective immediate-release forms produced only facial flushing, itching, rash, fatigue and other less serious side effects. Other experimental cholesterol-lowering drugs, while more expensive, produced fewer side effects. Dietary supplement makers counter that they do not sell niacin as an anticholesterol agent and make no claims on their packages that would instruct anyone to take three grams per day.

A major study published in the *New England Journal of Medicine* April 14 has suggested that supplements of vitamin A and E do not guard against heart disease or cancer and may actually have a negative effect (*see* 1993). Sponsored by the National Cancer Institute and Finland's National Public Health Institute, the study followed 29,000 male Finns, all of them long-term smokers aged 50 and over; one group took 20 milligrams per day of beta-carotene (vitamin A), another took 50 milligrams of vitamin E, a third group took both, and those in a fourth group were given placebos. After 5 to 8 years, the researchers could find no evidence that the supplements had helped; in fact, men taking beta carotene were more likely to die from lung cancer and heart disease, while those taking vitamin E were slightly more prone to have strokes from bleeding in the brain and slightly less chance of having prostate cancer, although the researchers said both effects could be due to chance. Dietary supplement industry sources insist that the subjects were not given large enough doses of the supplements and that the study means little since the subjects were such heavy smokers that they were not representative of the larger public.

A 4-year study published in the *New England Journal of Medicine* July 21 indicates that taking vitamin C, vitamin E, beta carotene, or all three does not prevent colon cancer. The study involved 864 people with records either of colorectal adenomas or precancerous polyps, but although there is good epidemiological evidence that people who consume fruits and vegetables containing vitamins C and E in large amounts have lower rates of colon cancer, those in the study who took dummy pills fared as well as those who took the vitamin supplements. Researchers theorize that fruits and vegetables may contain protective substances not found in vitamin supplements but urge that critics of vitamin supplements reserve judgment pending the outcome of further studies; the supplement industry's Council for Responsible Nutrition maintains that "generous intakes" of antioxidants "will help prevent a number of chronic diseases, including some cancers."

The Center for Science in the Public Interest reports in July that food at so-called Tex-Mex restaurants is higher in saturated fats and sodium than hamburgers or other traditionallly high-fat foods. An order of beef nachos has the fat content of 10 glazed Dunkin' Donuts; a typical taco salad with sour cream and guacamole has 1,009 calories, 58 percent of them from fat; and a cheese quesadilla has 900 calories, 59 percent of them from fat. Defenders of Mexican cuisine insist that real Mexican food contains far less fat, and "health-Mex" restaurant chains, which avoid lard in favor of such things as low-fat yogurt, capitalize on the CSPI findings.

The Clinton administration announces June 6 that new Department of Agriculture rules will set limits on the fat, cholesterol, and sodium content of school lunches—the biggest changes since the School Lunch Program was created in 1946 (it has grown to serve about 25 million students in 93,000 schools) (*see* 1993). Instead of setting "meal patterns" which require that schools offer minimum amounts of food in five broad categories (meat, bread, vegetables, fruits, and dairy products), the new rules will require schools to analyze all foods offered in a school week to ensure that meals meet federal guidelines for fat and sodium content and for specific nutrients such as protein, vitamin A, vitamin C, iron, and calcium, with only 30 percent of calories coming from fat (instead of the present 38 percent), only 10 percent from saturated fat (instead of the present 15 percent). Senate Agriculture Committee chairman Patrick J. Leahy (D. Vt.) has insisted that the Agriculture Department address concerns voiced last year by dieticians, stu-

Free school lunches may have been high in fat, but they kept many kids from going hungry. CHIE NISHIO

dents, and parents in four public hearings; he introduced a bill in April that would encourage schools to restrict or ban the sale of soft drinks and other items of "minimal nutritional value" in schools (dieticians say that children who fill up on soft drinks and snack foods are less likely to eat nutritious meals, which cost taxpayers $4.5 billion per year), but many schools are under pressure from fast-food chains to turn over their school lunch programs to McDonald's, Burger King, and the like.

A provision of the Nutrition Labeling and Education Act (above), which takes effect in August, requires that foods labeled "light" (or "lite") contain no more than half the fat content of the original product, and while some companies comply with

Forced to soft-pedal health claims, many food marketers modified product names.

the law by reducing fat content, others simply rename their products (Kraft Deliciously Light salad dressing becomes Kraft Deliciously Right, Kraft Light Singles become Kraft 1/3 Less Fat Singles, Fleischmann's Light Margarine becomes Fleischmann's Light Taste Margarine, Hebrew National's Lite Beef Franks become Reduced Fat Beef Franks, Procter & Gamble's Pringles Light Crisps become Pringles Right Crisps, Frito-Lay's Ruffles Light Choice become Ruffles Choice).

A critic of antifat and anticholesterol efforts notes that life expectancy in France is 74 for men, 82 for women, despite high intakes of animal fats, butter, cream, cheese, and red meat; in Switzerland, where diets are similar, life expectancy is 76 for men, 83 for women; and in Japan, where diets are low in animal fats, butter, cream, cheese, and red meat but high in rice, seafood, and soy products, life expectancy is 77 for men, 82 for women.

More Americans are overweight than ever, according to a study by the National Center for Health Statistics in the Centers for Disease Control and Prevention. One in three adults aged 20 to 74 were obese (meaning at least 20 percent overweight) in 1991, up from fewer than one in four in 1962 and just over one in four in 1980, according to the study, which is published in the *Journal of the American Medical Association* July 18. The percentage among black, non-Hispanic women was 49.6, up from 41.7 (among black men, 31.5 percent were obese, up from 22.2). Among Mexican-American women, 47.9 percent were obese, up from 41.4 percent in 1980 (among Mexican-American men, the percentage was 39.5, up from 31.0). A Norwegian study has shown that people who are somewhat overweight actually have *longer* life expectancies than those who meet "desirable" weight standards, but despite growing awareness that obesity has a negative impact on health, and despite a diet industry whose revenues total $40 to $50 billion per year, a professor of medicine at Columbia University says in a *JAMA* editorial that "The proportion of the population that is obese is incredible. If this was about tuberculosis, it would be called an epidemic. . . . The problem with obesity is that once you have it, it is very difficult to treat. What you want is to prevent it." With the federal government allotting each state a mere

$50,000 for nutrition education in schools, and the food industry spending $36 billion per year to tempt U.S. consumers with advertising, prevention is difficult.

Interneuron Pharmaceuticals has filed an FDA application in January for permission to market the antiobesity drug dexfenfluramine (*see* 1988). The Wurtman drug is half the molecule of Pondimin, which proved successful in the Weintraub study reported 2 years ago, and the Wurtmans claim that their drug omits the part responsible for Pondimin's occasional side effects. A Johns Hopkins study links dexfenfluramine with toxicity in monkeys' brains (a later study shows that the damage is easily reversible), and critics express doubts about using high-powered drugs to suppress appetite, but Michael Weintraub has become director of the FDA's office of over-the-counter drug evaluation, and, possibly through his influence, the FDA gives preliminary approval to Eli Lilly for use of Prozac in the treatment of bulimia (binge eating).

Kellogg introduces Healthy Choice breakfast foods under license from ConAgra (*see* 1989). Available in three versions (flakes, squares, and multigrain clusters), the cereals will be priced higher per ounce than Kellogg's premium-priced Just Right cereal and will be sweetened with either brown sugar (refined white sugar sprayed with molasses) or honey (neither is any "healthier" than ordinary refined white sugar, but both are widely perceived to be healthier). Kellogg's existing 45 brands hold a 37 percent share of the $8 billion breakfast food business.

General Mills reformulates its 53-year-old Cheerios and 68-year-old Wheaties cereals to meet competition from cheaper store-brand imitators.

Campbell Soup Co. introduces four new Prego Spaghetti Sauce varieties (*see* 1991): Zesty Garlic & Cheese, Zesty Basil, Zesty Oregano, and Mushrooms with Extra Spice.

Hain Pure Foods (above) introduces a line of water-based fat-free salad dressings.

Coca-Cola's Minute Maid division launches a Fruitopia line of fruit-based drinks in March, spending more than $30 million to introduce the products.

Coca-Cola's Minute Maid division launched a line of fruit drinks to compete with Snapple.

Veryfine Products introduces Chillers—an eight-product line of iced teas and lemonades—in mid-April (*see* 1981). U.S. sales of iced tea products jumped 91 percent last year, rising from 58 million cases to 111 million, and Veryfine goes into competition with Snapple, Coca-Cola (above), PepsiCo, Lipton (below), and others for a share of the rising market. The company, whose sales last year reached $220 million, moved in 1989 to Westford, Mass.

Liptonice, a carbonated iced tea, is introduced in Britain by PepsiCo in partnership with Unilever's Brooke Bond Foods Ltd. as an alternative to soft drinks (*see* 1992), but while Americans consume more than 332.7 million gallons of iced tea (not counting what they brew at home), Britons will be slow to accept tea that is not hot, preferring ginger ale, Coca-Cola, and citrus-flavored "squash" to other soft drinks.

New York's Gramercy Tavern restaurant opens in early July at 40 East 20th Street, where Union Square Café proprietor Danny Meyer, now 36, has joined forces with Tom Colicchio, chef at Mondrian, to lease the entire ground floor and basement of a building whose neighbors are now tenanted with advertising agencies, magazine publishers, and book publishers. Dishes include seared foie gras with honey-roasted onions and crushed potatoes; loin of baby lamb with basil and goat-cheese ravioli; roast sirloin of beef with chives, shallots, pearl onions, and Swiss chard; roast saddle of rabbit with mashed potatoes; roast squab with fava beans, salsify, onion rings, and sage; Provençal bass; lobster *americaine;* soft-shell crabs with tomato-onion *jus;* and shellfish stew with fingerling potatoes, which soon have the restaurant's 140 seats filled at both lunch and dinner.

New York chef-restaurateur Gilbert Le Coze dies of a heart attack at his health club July 28 at age 49. His executive chef, Eric Ripert, now 29, carries on the quality of Le Bernardin (see 1986).

Lutèce's chef-owner André Soltner, now 62, sells a majority interest in his 33-year-old New York restaurant October 11 to Ark, a company that owns or manages 30 restaurants, most of them in the Northeast, none of any gastronomic distinction. Eberhard Mueller, a chef at Le Bernardin (above), comes in as chef of Lutèce, and while Soltner and his staff of 42 remain, at least for the time being, longtime patrons fret that they may no longer count on enjoying such Alsatian dishes as onion tart; roasted duck with caramelized pears; braised baby lamb; and saddle of venison with chestnuts, red cabbage, and vinegar.

Au Bon Pain opens its 200th store, adds 20 new soups to its menus, and launches Choice from Au Bon Pain—self-service-style stores, each with a daily selection of about 10 different soups, a large salad-pasta-and-potato bar, and traditional Au Bon Pain sandwiches.

Burger King creates a furor at Berkeley, Calif., in May by telling the city's local franchisee, Beverly Tabb, that she must stop selling her $1.59 soy-based meatless hamburger alongside her Whoppers. A spokesperson for the Miami-based chain says that it test-marketed the Griller, a vegetarian patty, in 38 New York outlets last year and cannot permit sales of meatless hamburgers until it has evaluated the results of last year's test.

Arby's adds Chicken Fingers to its menu in July but continues to concentrate on roast beef (see 1991). It becomes the first global fast-food chain to institute a ban on smoking in all its company-owned restaurants—roughly 300 outlets out of a total that has grown to more than 2,700, including 106 in Canada, 15 in Mexico, and 31 in 15 overseas countries, including the Philippines (see 1991). Arby's parent company, Triarc (which also owns Royal Crown Cola), pays $525 million to acquire the 1,450-outlet Long John Silver's fast-food fish and seafood chain (see 1969).

Dunkin' Donuts introduces a second variety of coffee—a dark roast that represents the first change in the chain's coffee since its founding in 1950 (see 1989). It begins to install iced-coffee brewing machines and prepares to offer flavored coffees, including chocolate mint, French vanilla, and hazelnut.

Beijing's authoritarian government evicts McDonald's from its restaurant off Tiananmen Square—the world's biggest McDonald's—to make way for a commercial complex, abrogating the company's 20-year lease.

An Albuquerque, N.M., jury awards $2.9 million in August to Stella Liebeck, 81, who in 1992 ordered a 49¢ cup of coffee at a drive-in McDonald's window and received third-degree burns when she removed the lid to add cream and sugar and spilled the scalding hot coffee onto her lap, obliging her to spend 7 days in the hospital and have skin grafts. McDonald's, which sells 1 billion cups of coffee per year, says in its training manual that coffee should be brewed at 195° to 205° F. and held at 180° to 190°. A scientist testifying for McDonald's has told the jury that any coffee hotter than 130° could produce third-degree burns, but a physician testifying in behalf of the plaintiff has stated that 190° coffee takes only 3 seconds to produce such burns whereas 180° degree coffee takes 12 to 15 seconds and 160° coffee a full 20 seconds. The National Coffee Association says McDonald's coffee conforms to industry temperature standards, but a law student has found that no other Albuquerque restaurant serves coffee closer than about 20° to the 180° level at which McDonald's pours its coffee. The judge in the case reduces the jury award to $500,000; McDonald's appeals.

McDonald's and other fast-food restaurant chains impose no-smoking rules in company-owned outlets; many if not most franchisees follow suit. Red Lobster claims to have been the first national restaurant chain to provide no-smoking sections, and virtually all U.S. restaurants above a certain size now offer patrons the option of eating in a relatively smoke-free environment.

Maryland bans smoking in restaurants and bars beginning July 21. Other states—including Vermont, Utah, Washington, and California—have enacted legislation that forbids smoking in public places but have exempted bars and restaurants (although in some U.S. cities there are no such exemptions). Maryland's Secretary of Licensing William Fogle says, "We could not protect the health and safety of one employee and not another. Waitresses, for example, already have one of the heaviest burdens of cancer and respiratory disease among workers in the country." Philip Morris and R. J. Reynolds, which own a major part of the packaged food industry, try to raise fears that the government may also try to control alcohol, caffeine, or foods high in saturated fats or cholesterol, they mount legal challenges to restrictions on smoking, and they gain support from some restaurant owners, who fear that they will lose business, but other restaurant owners welcome the ban, recognizing that while 34 million Americans still smoke they represent only a dwindling minority of adults, that more affluent Americans tend to be nonsmokers who appreciate dining out in a smoke-free environment which permits them to smell and taste what they eat, that 80 to 90 percent of nonsmokers ask to be seated in the no-smoking section of a restaurant when one is available, and that even the best ventilation system cannot eliminate exposure to second-hand smoke.

1995

✗ "We must have both a political and strategic understanding of the importance of the food question,"

China's Communist Party president Jiang Zemin tells an emergency conference in February. China's 1994 grain output fell to 444.5 million metric tons last year, down from 456 million the year before, and the nation's population is growing at the rate of about 15 million per year.

Canada and Spain come close to severing relations in March after confrontations on the high seas of Newfoundland's Grand Banks (*see* below).

A House Agriculture Subcommittee votes March 7 to cut the U.S. food-stamp program by $16.5 billion over 5 years and require recipients of the stamps to meet strict new work standards. The program last year helped 27.8 million Americans at a cost of $24.5 billion, but the "Contract With America" manifesto that helped Republicans gain control of Congress in November proposed to eliminate the individual entitlement to food stamps, replacing it with a nutrition block grant to the states. Farm lobbyists and consumer groups try to thwart such moves and resist efforts to turn the 49-year-old federal school lunch program (which last year had 25.3 million participants and cost $4.9 billion) and the Special Supplemental Nutrition Program for Women, Infants and Children (6.5 million participants, $3.2 billion) over to the states, many of which would inevitably cut funding for the safety net that keeps millions of people from going hungry.

Farm lobbyists also work to stymie congressional efforts to reduce crop subsidies to farmers, which last year cost taxpayers about $10 billion (down from a peak of $25 billion in 1986), but although subsidies were established in the 1930s to protect farmers from wild price gyrations, and the subsidies are credited with helping to keep food costs low (Americans spend only about 12 percent of their budgets on food, far less than many foreigners) some U.S. farmers favor returning to a market-oriented economy.

Oregon and Washington State apples go on sale at Tokyo January 10 as Japan eases restrictions on fruit imports. Shoppers line up to pay the equivalent of 80¢ or more per apple (apples produced in Japan fetch about $1 each but can sell for more than seven times that much, and apple consumption is one-fifth to one-third less than in Europe or

America). Japan imports for the year total 12,000 to 15,000 tons—about 1 percent of the U.S. apple crop. Japan has been importing U.S. cherries for more than 15 years and the total Japanese market for cherries has tripled.

Grand Metropolitan PLC acquires Pet Incorporated for more than $2.6 billion in January, thus adding such brands as Progresso canned soups (*see* 1986) and Old El Paso Mexican foods (*see* 1968) to its existing line, which includes Green Giant, Häagen Dazs, and Smirnoff Vodka.

Seagram agrees to acquire Dole Food's juice unit for $285 million, expanding its Tropicana unit and reducing its dependence on liquor.

Dr. Pepper/Seven-Up Companies agrees January 16 to be acquired by Cadbury Schweppes for $1.7 billion. The deal gives Cadbury nearly half the $16.6 billion U.S. market for non-cola soft drinks and a 17 percent share of the $49 billion U.S. market for carbonated beverages.

Canandaigua Wine Co. announces March 23 that it will acquire some Guinness brands and world rights to eight United Distiller Glenmore spirit brands.

Interstate Bakeries of Kansas City announces April 12 that it will acquire Continental Baking from Ralston Purina for $461 million in stock. William P. Stiritz, 60, Ralston's chief executive officer since 1981, sold the company's tuna fleet and other operations in 1983, bought Continental Baking for $475 million in 1984, sold Jack-in-the-Box restaurant chain for $450 million in 1985, sold Purina Mills to British Petroleum for $545 million in 1986, paid Borden Co. $115 million that year for Drake Bakeries, sold it a year later for $176 million, sold its Van Camp seafood business for $260 million in 1988, bought Beech-Nut baby foods from Nestlé for $55 million in 1989, and has since concentrated on pet foods (and batteries).

A 14-year study by Harvard School of Public Health and Harvard Medical School researchers, published February 8 in the *Journal of the American Medical Association,* reports that women who gain 11 to 18 pounds after age 18 have a 25 percent greater chance of suffering, or dying of, a heart attack than women who gain less than 11 pounds, and men who gain weight are at even greater risk.

The average U.S. woman's height is 5 feet, 6 inches, and guidelines issued in 1990 by the U.S. Departments of Agriculture and Health and Human Services raised the acceptable weight for adults of that height at age 35 to between 130 and 167 pounds, up from 118 to 150 (for women) in 1985, but Dr. Walter C. Willett, the Harvard study's chief investigator, warns that gaining weight in middle age is not acceptable.

Results of a rigorous obesity study published in the *New England Journal of Medicine* March 9 by Rockefeller University researchers confirm that each human body naturally maintains a given weight equilibrium, adjusting its metabolism to burn calories more slowly after weight loss and more rapidly than normal after weight gain. Excessive dieting does not change this equilibrium, nor do obese people have slow metabolisms. From 65 to 70 percent of the calories consumed each day go simply to maintain heart, brain, kidney, and liver functions.

The FDA leans toward easing approval rules for a new generation of diet drugs, such as dexfenfluramine, which may boost levels of the brain chemical serotonin to reduce cravings for carbohydrate (*see* 1994).

No-smoking rules take effect April 10 in New York restaurants seating 35 or more; most restaurateurs and patrons obey the new city ordinance, which allows smoking only in some separate bar areas.

The Canadian Coast Guard seizes a Spanish trawler March 9 just outside Canada's territorial waters east of Newfoundland and late in the month cuts another Spanish trawler's nets, worth an estimated $76,000 plus the value of the fish—mostly Greenland halibut (erroneously called turbot) which the Spanish sell to buyers in Japan. Ottawa has unilaterally declared the area off limits to protect dwindling fish populations; the disappearance of cod and some other species has idled some 50,000 east coast Canadian fishermen, Spanish ships have long been notorious for using fine-meshed nets, and Canada says conservation measures must be backed up by tough international enforcement.

"Agriculture has become the weakest link in the national economy," says China's new agricultural czar (*see* above). The nation has 450 million farmers, but many are leaving the land for better paying jobs in cities, where they can double or even quadruple their annual income, and urbanization in Sichuan alone has consumed 10.6 million acres of arable land since 1978.

Ukrainian farmers barter pigs for gasoline as fuel shortages continue to cripple production. The Kiev government is unable to pay for Russian oil, which is no longer subsidized, and peasants rely on small, private plots to raise the food for their families.

Flooding of the Illinois, Mississippi, and Missouri rivers in May and early June prevent movement of barges loaded with corn for export markets, but the flooding is less severe than in 1993.

New studies question the cardiac protective benefits of diets high in fish and containing no more than 30 percent fat.

Mars Inc. terminates tan M&Ms in September after conducting a poll on color preferences. Introduced in 1949 to replace violet M&Ms, the tan candies are replaced by new blue M&Ms.

Pizza Hut announces March 25 that it will introduce Stuffed Crust Pizza—a pizza crust stuffed with an outer ring of string mozzarella cheese.

The U.S. Supreme Court rules unanimously in April that a brewer may list a beer's alcoholic content on its label, upsetting a 60-year-old ban on grounds that it violates the First Amendment. The victory by Adolph Coors Co. raises alarm among public health officials as brewers increase alcohol levels as a marketing ploy. U.S. beer generally contains about 3 to 5 percent alcohol, but new "ice" beers run 5 and 6 percent, malt liquors are as high as 7 percent, and some Canadian beers have raised their alcoholic content above 7 percent, although most brewers consider anything higher than 6 percent too harsh for U.S. tastes.

Index

Index

Index

Index

Index